Proceedings

of the

Society

for

Experimental Biology and Medicine

INCLUDING THE FOLLOWING SECTIONS

DISTRICT OF COLUMBIA NORTHWESTERN
SOUTHEASTERN SOUTHWESTERN

May–September

VOLUME 176

New York

CONTENTS

SCIENTIFIC PROCEEDINGS, VOLUME 176

Seven hundred-forty-eighth issue, May 1984 1

Seven hundred-forty-ninth issue, June 1984 95

Seven hundred-fiftieth issue, July 1984 223

Seven hundred-fifty-first issue, September 1984 337

Author Index 518

Proceedings of The Society for Experimental Biology and Medicine, Vol. 176, No. 4, September 1984. Published monthly except August by Academic Press, Inc., 111 Fifth Avenue, New York, N.Y. 10003. Second class postage paid at New York, N.Y. and at additional mailing offices. 1984: Subscription per year $80.00 U.S.A. and Canada; $106.00 outside U.S.A. and Canada. All prices include postage and handling. Send notices of change of address to the Office of the Publisher at least 6–8 weeks in advance. Please include both the old and new addresses. POSTMASTER: Send all changes of address to *Proceedings of the Society for Experimental Biology and Medicine*, 111 Fifth Avenue, New York, N.Y. 10003.

TABLE OF CONTENTS

Annual Report for 1983 512

Acknowledgment 514

MINIREVIEW

The Lupus Anticoagulant — N. Perico, F. Pusineri, G. Remuzzi .. 337

BIOCHEMISTRY/NUTRITION

Effect of Albumin on the *in Vitro* Conjugation of Bilirubin by Rat Liver Microsomes — N. Tavoloni, M. J. T. Jones, L. M. J. Isola, P. D. Berk 356

Strain Differences in Testes Degeneration, Myopathy, and the Lymphocyte Mitogen Response in Vitamin E-Deficient Rats — E. Gabriel, A. Bendich, L. J. Machlin 378

Radioimmunoassay of Bone Morphogenetic Protein in Serum: A Tissue-Specific Parameter of Bone Metabolism — M. R. Urist, R. T. Hudak 472

Effects of Dietary Salt, Fat, and Carbohydrate on Fluid and Salt Consumption of Rats — R. M. Threatte, M. R. Quinn 476

Cataract Formation following Limited Amino Acid Intake during Gestation and Lactation — G. E. Bunce, J. L. Hess, D. Davis 485

CELLULAR AND ORGAN PHYSIOLOGY

Mineralization in Rat Metaphyseal Bone Exhibits a Circadian Stage Dependency — J. E. Russell, B. Grazman, D. J. Simmons 342

Nonalgebraic Interaction between Pressor and Depressor Reflexes in Dogs: Evidence for a Central Site of Action — P. M. Lalley, J. E. Kendrick, G. L. Matson 384

On the Existence of Renal Vasodilator Nerves — H. Holdaas, G. F. DiBona 426

Hypotensive Response to Prostacyclin and 6-keto-PGE_1 following Hepatectomy in the Rat — J. Van Dam, R. B. Stinger, J. C. Penhos, P. W. Ramwell, P. A. Kot 438

Characterization of the Esterases of the Mitochondrial Fraction of Guinea Pig Cortical Renal Cells — G. Nicot, J.-P. Valette, J.-L. Dupuy, L. Merle, G. Lachatre, Y. Nouaille 467

DEVELOPMENT/GROWTH/AGING

Pulsed Electromagnetic Fields Increase the Rate of Rat Liver Regeneration after Partial Hepatectomy — V. Ottani, M. G. Monti, G. Piccinini, L. Pernecco, P. Zaniol, A. Ruggeri, B. Barbiroli 371

Analysis of Metopirone-Induced Hypertrophy of Adrenals in Fetal Rats Encephalectomized *in Utero* — M. Yamamoto, K. Arishima, Y. Eguchi, K. Mochizuki 403

Influence of the Major Histocompatibility Complex (*H-2*) on Glucocorticoid-Stimulated Pulmonary Surfactant Synthesis in Two Congenic Mouse Strains — L. S. Honig, B. T. Smith, H. C. Slavkin, H. G. Donahue 419

ENDOCRINOLOGY/METABOLISM

Intact and Carboxyterminal PTH Do Not Cross the Blood–Cerebrospinal Fluid Barrier — M. Akmal, S. Tuma, D. A. Goldstein, R. Pattabhiraman, L. Bernstein, S. G. Massry 434

HOST-PARASITE INTERACTION/IMMUNOLOGY/MICROBIOLOGY/VIROLOGY

Muramyl Dipeptide-Induced Enhancement of Phagocytosis of Antibiotic Pretreated *Escherichia coli* by Macrophages — H. Friedman, G. Warren 366

Interaction of *N*-Methyl-*N'*-nitro-*N*-nitrosoguanidine (MNNG) with Owl Monkey Kidney Cells in Enhancing the Yields of *Herpesvirus saimiri* (HVS) and Its Antigens — A. Faggioni, D. V. Ablashi, J. Dahlberg, G. Armstrong, S. K. Sundar 407

Effect of Temperature on Suppressor Cells in Chicken Spleen Cell Cultures — B. S. Bhogal, D. S. Chi, G. J. Thorbecke 414

ONCOLOGY/PATHOLOGY/RADIOBIOLOGY

Depression of *in Vivo* Clearance Function of Hepatic Macrophage Complement Receptors following Thermal Injury	B. G. CUDDY, D. J. LOEGERING, F. A. BLUMENSTOCK	443
Effects of Three Feeding Schedules on Tumor and Host of Lewis Lung Carcinoma-Bearing Mice	W. CHAN, S. MCELHANON, A. M. KAPLAN, W. L. BANKS, JR.	460
Early Nuclear Structural Changes of Transformed Human Amniotic Cells (WISH) in Presence of Type IV Collagen Detected by the Nuclear Refringency Assay	J. GERFAUX, B. MACÉ, F. CHANY-FOURNIER, A. POMPIDOU	490

PHARMACOLOGY/TOXICOLOGY

In Vitro Response of Hepatic Lysosomes to Endogenous and Exogenous Cationic Compounds	J. H. POWELL, M. M. REIDENBERG	346
Dopaminergic and Cholinergic Muscarinic Receptor Effects of L-Alphacetylmethadol (LAAM) and Its Metabolites	A. E. LANGLEY, S. G. SMITH, R. L. ZEID	350
The Tissue-Specific Accumulation of Hepatic Zinc Metallothionein following Parenteral Iron Loading	C. C. MCCORMICK	392
Effect of Nolinium Bromide on Vascular Smooth Muscle	R. R. BROOKS, S. M. JONES, A. F. MOORE	452

RAPID COMMUNICATIONS

Isolation and Culture of Human Intestinal Smooth Muscle Cells	M. F. GRAHAM, R. F. DIEGELMANN, C. O. ELSON, K. N. BITAR, H. P. EHRLICH	503
Ethanol Enhances *de Novo* Synthesis of High Density Lipoprotein Cholesterol	J. E. CLUETTE, J. J. MULLIGAN, R. NORING, K. DOYLE, J. HOJNACKI	508

AUTHOR INDEX FOR VOLUME 176 518

The Subject Index for Volume 176 will appear in the December 1984 issue as part of a cumulative index for the year 1984.

PROCEEDINGS OF THE SOCIETY FOR EXPERIMENTAL BIOLOGY AND MEDICINE **176,** 1–7 (1984)

MINIREVIEW

Release of Newly Synthesized Hormone from the Pancreatic Beta Cell[1] (41833)

R. W. DUDEK

Department of Anatomy, East Carolina University, School of Medicine, Greenville, North Carolina 27834

Work in the pancreatic beta cell and insulin secretion pioneered by Lacy (1, 2) and Orci (3–6) developed the concept of exocytotic release of hormone via secretory granules binding to the cell membrane. This work is well-known and has been adequately reviewed on a number of occasions. However, a number of pulse-labeling studies suggested that newly synthesized insulin (and insulin precursors) was secreted preferentially (7–12). Although little is known about the mechanism by which this occurs, it appears that islets store a portion of their total insulin in a labile compartment that contains newly synthesized hormone and is preferentially secreted in response to glucose. Recently, Halbane (13) and Gold *et al.* (14) concurrently demonstrated a number of conditions where newly synthesized hormone (proinsulin and insulin) is preferentially secreted from the beta cell, thereby providing some insight into the mechanism of preferential secretion. In addition, Gold *et al.* (14) showed that the percentage of radioactive proinsulin in secreted, newly synthesized hormone after 30 and 68 min of stimulation with 20 m*M* glucose was 71.3 and 62.6%, respectively. This means that a large proportion of the secreted, newly synthesized hormone is actually proinsulin and only about 30–40% is insulin. Interestingly, after 162 min of stimulation with 20 m*M* glucose the percentage of proinsulin in the secreted hormone decreased to 15.6%, implying that 85% of the secreted hormone was insulin. In light of this data, the cell biologist faces a dilemma of describing a morphological mechanism that accounts for the preferential release of newly synthesized hormone. A convincing explanation must address three strict requirements: (a) a description of the cellular compartment containing newly synthesized hormone (proinsulin and insulin), (b) a method for its secretion, and (c) a 1:1 quantitative accounting of the frequency of the event (release of newly synthesized hormone) and the suspected morphological correlate (unknown at this time). Such a 1:1 quantitative accounting has only been demonstrated for quantal neurotransmitter release and synaptic vesicle exocytosis in the frog neuromuscular junction (15).

Several possibilities exist for the compartment of newly synthesized hormone that is segregated from the remainder of older, stored insulin. Possible candidates for the compartment are: (i) islets from a particular region of the pancreas, (ii) islets of a particular size, (iii) a subpopulation of beta cell granules, or (iv) a subpopulation of beta cells within an islet. Islets from a particular pancreatic region or size as candidates for the compartment of newly synthesized hormone have been adequately dismissed (14). The possibility that the compartment is a subpopulation of beta cell granules remains viable at this time, but problematic. To conclude that the compartment of newly synthesized hormone is a subpopulation of beta cell granules may be justified based upon the experimental paradigm of the investigator, but this may prove untenable in the long run if the following points can not be adequately explained. First of all, synthesis occurs in the rough endoplasmic reticulum, transport and packaging occurs in the Golgi, and storage in secretory granules. Is not all the hormone that the Golgi packages newly synthesized at the time the Golgi sees it? The answer is yes. Consequently, all the hormone that the Golgi packages is newly synthesized hormone. At present, no evidence exists for two different packaging processes of insulin in the Golgi; one for newly synthesized hormone and another for older, synthesized hormone. If two different packaging processes in the Golgi can not be documented, then the possibility that alteration of the granules occurs within the cytoplasm (post-Golgi) remains

[1] Supported by Grant 81R319 from Juvenile Diabetes Foundation.

0037-9727/84 $1.50

open. To date, there is no evidence suggesting a cytoplasmic mechanism that segregates two granule populations. Although such a cytoplasmic mechanism may exist, I would suggest that it is difficult to imagine a sophisticated mechanism that could differentiate hormone within a membrane-bound granule based upon when, in time, it was synthesized. Secondly, the idea of two populations of granules, one containing newly synthesized hormone and the other containing older hormone may place an unreasonable capability upon the granule populations. Since 2.8 and 8.3 m*M* glucose preferentially stimulate the release of newly synthesized hormone, one would have to demonstrate that the granules containing newly synthesized hormone recognize the specific glucose level or signal. In contrast, 16.7 m*M* glucose causes the preferential release of older hormone from the beta cell. In this case, the granules containing older hormone would need to recognize the higher level of glucose or signal. In this scenario, we need to propose not simply that the beta cell recognizes glucose and secretes hormone in response to it, but that different beta cell secretory granules can recognize (directly or indirectly) different levels of glucose and respond to them.

The possibility that the compartment of newly synthesized hormone is a subpopulation of beta cells within an islet (perhaps exposed to a different intraislet environment) remains a viable candidate, especially in the light of recent evidence that cell heterogeneity is involved in the preferential release of newly synthesized prolactin from pituitary cells (16). As far as islet physiology if concerned, the question of whether all the beta cells or only a subset of beta cells respond to a particular secretagogue by secretion has never been adequately resolved. The reverse hemolytic plaque assay and the modifications reported by Neill and Frawley (17) may provide a powerful tool to gain insight into this question. However, even if a subpopulation of beta cells within an islet is responsible for the release of newly synthesized hormone, questions concerning the secretory mechanism of this subpopulation would still remain open.

In this review, I would like to raise and explore the possibility that two intracellular routes of secretion may exist within the beta cell, one route for release of newly synthesized hormone and the other route for release of older, stored hormone. In this regard, an alternate mechanism of secretion has been proposed by a number of investigators. Osamura *et al.* (18) reported that secretion of prolactin from cells in the anterior pituitary occurs via two pathways: (a) a long, regulated pathway and (b) a short, accelerated pathway. They suggested that the short, accelerated pathway is prolactin secretion occurring directly from the endoplasmic reticulum without passing through the other cellular compartments. A similar possibility has been suggested by Moriarty and Tobin (19) from their studies on the localization of TSH in pituitaries of thyroidectomized rats. They reported that TSH was primarily localized in the dilated rough endoplasmic reticulum (intracisternal) of hypertrophied TSH cells ("thyroidectomy cells"). They also found some extracisternal staining for TSH in the vicinity of rough endoplasmic reticulum and suggested that this might represent molecules of TSH in the process of secretion via a cytoplasmic route. Although these observations do not fit the classical concept of secretion, other interpretations of the data generated from the experiments of Palade (20) have been raised by Rothman (21). In addition, Farquhar (22) posed several possibilities to explain the increased secretion of TSH from thyroidectomy cells which contain few, if any, secretory granules. She noted that the ER membrane frequently approached the cell membrane in a manner similar to fibroblasts where discharge of glycoprotein occurs directly from the rough endoplasmic reticulum. Along these lines, Gold *et al.* reported that glucose "marks" beta cells thereby diverting newly synthesized hormone for immediate release before transiting the Golgi and packaging into granules (23). In addition, Dr. Boyne and I have reported that in islets stimulated with various levels of glucose followed by quick-freeze fixation and freeze-drying procedures, the endoplasmic reticulum binds orthogonally to the cell membrane of the beta cell and perforates the membrane, thereby forming pores leading to the extracellular space (24, 25). We concluded from this study that beta cells may secrete newly synthesized proinsulin and insulin directly from endoplasmic reticulum synthesis sites via the cortical endoplasmic reticulum and pores perforating the cell membrane. This mechanism eliminates the need for two populations of secretory granules and indicates that the compartment where newly synthesized hormone (proinsulin and insulin) resides is the lumen of the endoplasmic reticulum. That newly synthesized insulin may exist with the endoplasmic reticulum is compatible with current concepts of protein synthesis indicating that conversion of proinsulin to insulin *begins* in the endoplasmic reticulum and continues in the secretory granules (26, 27). We also observed granule discharge via exocytosis which would explain the release of older, stored hormone. Although the idea of beta cell secretion occurring directly from the endoplasmic reticulum needs substantiation by further critical tests and resurrects a controversy from long ago, I would like to suggest that this may be a viable possibility to explain the preferential release of newly synthesized hormone.

Since the beta cell secretes newly synthesized hormone and large amounts of proinsulin under certain circumstances and an adequate morphological explanation has been suggested, the question is whether this has any physiological significance. The routine use of 16.7 m*M* glucose as a stimulatory agent stems from the dose–response curve of insulin release indicating that at 16.7 m*M* glucose the insulin response is maximal and plateaus (28). However, the *in vivo* human situation indicates that the beta cell generally sees a range of glucose from 2.8 to 8.3 m*M*. At this range of glucose, newly synthesized hormone is preferentially secreted from rat islets. Therefore, if the data in the rat can be extrapolated to the human, the secretion of newly synthesized hormone with large amounts of proinsulin may be a common occurrence and one would assume has an important biological function in the human. In this regard, human portal blood values of proinsulin have been reported to range from a fasting level of 0.31 ± 0.11 to 2.12 ± 0.72 ng/ml during a glucose infusion of normal healthy subjects (29). We know the following about the half-life of insulin and proinsulin: (i) in an isolated perfused liver system, the clearance half-life for insulin is 17 min, whereas proinsulin is not cleared (30); (ii) the immunological half-life for insulin is 6–8 min and for proinsulin it is 18–20 min (31); (iii) the metabolic clearance half-life for insulin is 5 min, and for proinsulin it is 25 min (32); (iv) the half-disappearance time for insulin is 3–4 min, whereas for proinsulin it is 18–25 min (33). In all the above cases, the clearance half-life for proinsulin is significantly increased. Since the beta cell secretes newly synthesized hormone with significant amounts of proinsulin under certain circumstances and the proinsulin half-life is significantly elevated, proinsulin exists in the peripheral circulation. Human peripheral blood proinsulin values range from a fasting level of 0.19 ± 0.08 to 0.72 ± 0.04 ng/ml during a glucose infusion of normal, healthy subjects (29). In addition, other investigators have reported values of fasting peripheral proinsulin in normal healthy subjects of 0.16 ± 0.2 ng/ml (34) and a range of 0.05–0.4 ng/ml (35). This begs the question of whether proinsulin has any functional importance in the peripheral circulation. The evidence for biological activity of proinsulin has been reviewed by Rubenstein *et al.* (36) which indicates the proinsulin does indeed effect various metabolic parameters in fat cells and hemidiaphragm. More recently, Tompkins *et al.* (37) studied the mechanism of action of insulin and insulin analogues, including proinsulin, on hepatic and peripheral glucose turnover (rate of appearance and rate of disappearance) in dogs. They indicated that when comparisons between insulin and proinsulin are made at low levels of glucose, proinsulin behaves in a manner very similar to insulin. The problem concerning the biological activity of proinsulin centers around its possible conversion to insulin *in situ* at peripheral tissues. Although the available evidence is indirect and highly variable (36), Shaw and Chance (38) studied the *in vitro* effects of proinsulin on adipose tissue and diaphragm muscle. They concluded that proinsulin enhances the glucose metabolism of both tissues by being converted through enzymes present in these tissues (presumably at the cell membrane) to a molecule which is similar to or identical with insulin. Consequently, this study suggests that *in situ* conversion of proinsulin to insulin at peripheral tissues may occur. In addition, Rubenstein *et al.* (39) excluded the possibility of a large amount of conversion of proinsulin to insulin in the peripheral circulation, but their studies did not eliminate the possibility of *in situ* conversion at the peripheral tissue sites. I would like to emphasize that the *in situ* conversion of proinsulin to insulin is not the only available explanation for the biological activity of proinsulin. First of all, it is reasonable that proinsulin may have some affinity for the insulin receptor in the same way that proinsulin cross reacts with insulin antibodies. Secondly, proinsulin is structurally similar to a class of polypeptides called insulin-like growth factors (IGFs) or somatomedins (40). In addition to the insulin receptor (41), it is now well established that there are two distinct receptors for IGFs, Type 1 and Type 2 (42). The Type 1 receptor consists of three disulfide linked forms structurally similar to the insulin receptor and exhibits relative affinities for ligands in the following order: IGF-1 > IGF-2 > insulin. The Type 2 receptor consists of one single labeled species with the following relative affinities for ligands: IGF-2 > IGF-1, and no significant for insulin (43). With the growing body of evidence indicating a large number of heterogeneous receptor structures and the structural similarity of proinsulin to IGFs, it may be possible that proinsulin could exert its biological action by binding to one of the IGF receptors.

A theory based upon the presently available data as indicated in the above discussion is shown in Figs. 1 and 2. Figure 1 indicates the islet response to a mild glucose load in the range of 2.8–8.3 m*M* glucose. Under these conditions the beta cell secretes predominantly newly synthesized hormone, but the exact percentages of proinsulin and insulin released are not known. Since this data is not available, a critical assumption must be made that the percentage of proinsulin released under this condition is high. The values shown in Fig. 1 (70 and 30%) are taken from the work of Gold *et al.* (14) for the release of hormone during the *early* time point after stimulation with 20 m*M* glucose, namely, 30 min. All the secreted proinsulin passes through the liver unaltered into the peripheral circulation. Proinsulin is then delivered to the peripheral tissues where *in situ* conversion of proinsulin to insulin or receptor binding may occur to enhance glucose utilization. Consequently, secretion of proinsulin under certain conditions may be an interesting biological mechanism that allows passage of potentially active hormone through the liver without clearance for delivery to the peripheral tissues. It would seem that much more work is needed to document beta cell function during physiological levels of glucose (2.8–8.3 m*M*). Figure 2 indicates the islet response to intense stimulation which occurs with exposure to 16.7 m*M* glucose for a long duration as, for example, 162 min as shown by Gold *et al.* (14). This situation may occur *in vivo* immediately after a meal where the local concentration of glucose at the beta cell is high. In this case, the secreted hormone is older stored hormone containing approximately 70% insulin and 30% proinsulin (in this case, the exact percentages of proinsulin and insulin are known). Insulin delivered directly to the liver via the portal circulation activates the enzymes necessary for conversion of glucose to glycogen. This rapidly reduces the blood glucose level to a normal range. When the blood glucose level is lowered, the percentage of proinsulin secretion increases for delivery to the peripheral tissues.

Does this mechanism of hormonal release from the pancreatic beta cell offer any new clinical insight? If the mechanism as indicated in Figs. 1 and 2 adequately represents the human *in vivo* situation, then one wonders about some aspects of the insulin regime that insulin-dependent diabetics presently received. Between meals, that is mild glucose load, delivery of proinsulin into the portal circulation with subsequent conversion of proinsulin to "active" insulin by enzymes occurring on the peripheral tissues or binding of proinsulin to receptor sites would seem important. However, insulin-dependent diabetics are not treated with proinsulin. Is this why secondary complications of diabetes persist despite the regulation of blood glucose levels by subcutaneous injections of insulin? Perhaps, the nonphysiological insulin regime diabetics presently use keeps peripheral tissues in a insulinopenic state, thereby causing secondary complications. With recent and forthcoming developments in implantable insulin pumps and glucose sensors, perhaps both the form of hormone delivered (proinsulin or insulin) and timing of hormone delivery (pre- or post-prandial) should be taken into account. In addition, one of the major justifications for islet cell transplantation as a potential cure of insulin-dependent diabetes is that the trans-

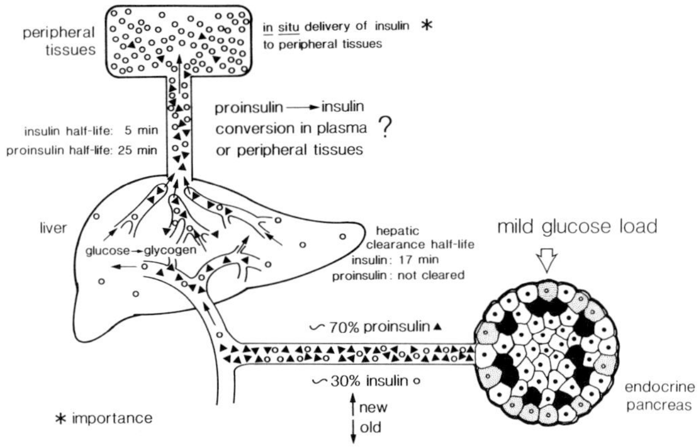

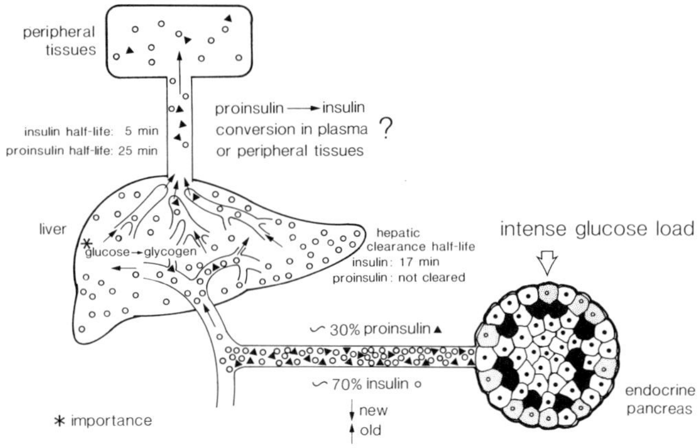

FIGS. 1 AND 2. These figures are diagrams of the events that may take place upon mild stimulation (Fig. 1) or intense stimulation (Fig. 2) of an islet. In Fig. 1, a low glucose load mildly stimulates the islet to secrete preferentially newly synthesized hormone containing a large percentage of proinsulin (we assume the percentage of proinsulin released is 70% as indicated in the text). Since proinsulin is not cleared by the liver it passes into the peripheral circulation unaltered for delivery to the insulin-dependent peripheral tissues. The critical step at this point is conversion of proinsulin into insulin. Although one could postulate that this conversion may occur in the plasma, evidence indicates that the conversion is *in situ* at the cell membrane of the peripheral tissue. During mild stimulation, the relative importance of events (as indicated by the asterisk) is to maintain the peripheral tissues in a normal functioning state by providing enough insulin for glucose metabolism to occur. The necessary amounts of insulin are provided by the secretion of proinsulin from the islet which is not cleared by the liver and which has a 25-min half-life for *in situ* conversion to insulin. Upon intense stimulation with a high glucose load as indicated in Fig. 2, the islet secretes predominantly older, stored hormone containing 70% insulin and 30% proinsulin. The secreted insulin is rapidly utilized by the liver to convert glucose into glycogen, thereby reducing blood glucose levels. The 30% of proinsulin released is delivered to the peripheral tissues for *in situ* conversion to insulin. Upon intense stimulation, the relative importance of events is the glucose to glycogen conversion in the liver (indicated by the asterisk) to reduce blood glucose levels.

plant exquisitely regulates the circulating blood glucose levels. Several laboratories have shown that normalization of glucose levels by transplantation of whole pancreas or islets minimizes or prevents the formation of diabetic lesions in the eye, kidney, and nerve (44–46). However, when blood glucose levels are strictly controlled in diabetic patients (47–49) by insulin infusion pumps or a strict regimen of insulin injections, the frequency of secondary complications does not decrease. This indicates that normalization of blood glucose levels may not be the only factor in ameliorating the secondary complications of diabetes. Interpreting these results with the latest information concerning insulin secretion, one could suggest that the observed beneficial effects of islet transplantation on the secondary complications of diabetes occur because the islet transplants are capable of secreting proinsulin for delivery to the peripheral tissues. Indeed, since the islet transplants more than likely secrete hormone in a physiological fashion as reported by Halban (13) and Gold *et al.* (14) the amounts of proinsulin and insulin secreted under various conditions (mild and intense stimulation), not only provide insulin for the liver to convert glucose to glycogen for the normalization of blood glucose levels, but also provide proinsulin for delivery to the peripheral tissues.

---

1. Lacy PE, Cardeza AF, Wilson WD. Electron microscopy of the rat pancreas: effects of glucagon administration. Diabetes **8**(1):36–44, 1959.
2. Lacy PE. Electron microscopy of the beta cell of the pancreas. Amer J Med **31**:851–859, 1961.
3. Orci L. A portrait of the pancreatic B-cell. Diabetologia **10**:163–187, 1974.
4. Orci L. Morphologic events underlying the secretion of peptide hormones. In: James VGT, ed., Endocrinology Proc V Int Congr Endocr Hamburg. Amsterdam, Excerpta Medica, p7, 1977.
5. Orci L, Like AA, Amherdt M, Blondel B, Kanazawa Y, Marliss EB, Lambert AE, Wolheim CB, Renold AE. Monolayer cell culture of neonatal rat pancreas: An ultrastructural and biochemical study of functioning endocrine cells. J Ultrastruct Res **43**:270–297, 1973.
6. Orci L. Macro- and micro-domains in the endocrine pancreas. Diabetes **31**:538–564, 1982.
7. Howell SL, Parry DG, Taylor KW. Secretion of newly synthesized insulin in vitro. Nature (London) **208**:487, 1965.
8. Sando H, Borg J, Steiner DF. Studies on the secretion of newly synthesized proinsulin and insulin from isolated rat islets of Langerhans. J Clin Invest **51**:1476–1485, 1972.
9. Sorenson RL, Steffes MW, Lindall AW. Subcellular localization of proinsulin to insulin conversion in isolated rat islets. Endocrinology **86**:88, 1970.
10. Gutman R, Fink G, Shapiro JR, Selawry H, Recant L. Proinsulin and insulin release with a human insulinoma and adjacent nonadenomatous pancreas. J Clin Endocrinol. Metab **36**:978–987, 1973.
11. Sando H, Grodsky GM. Dynamic synthesis and release of insulin and proinsulin from perifused islets. Diabetes **22**:354–360, 1973.
12. Schatz H, Nierle, C, Pfeiffer EF. (Pro-)insulin biosynthesis and release of newly synthesized (pro-)insulin from isolated islets of rat pancreas in the presence of amino acids and sulphonylureas. Eur J Clin Invest **5**:477–485, 1975.
13. Halban PA. Differential rates of release of newly synthesized and of stored insulin from pancreatic islets. Endocrinology **110**:1183–1188, 1982.
14. Gold G, Landahl HD, Gishizky ML, Grodsky GM. Heterogeneity and compartmental properties of insulin storage and secretion in rat islets. J Clin Invest **69**:554–563, 1982.
15. Heuser JE, Reese TS, Dennis MJ, Jan Y, Jan L, Evans L. Synaptic vesicle exocytosis captured by quick-freezing and correlated with quantal transmitter release. J Cell Biol **81**:275–300, 1979.
16. Neill JD, Smith PE. Pulse-labeled hormone release from single pituitary cells detected by surround immunoprecipitation and autoradioautography. J Cell Biol **97**(5):434a, 1983.
17. Neill JD, Frawley LS. Detection of hormone release from individual cells in mixed populations using a reverse hemolytic plaque assay. Endocrinology **112**(3):1123–1135, 1983.
18. Osamura RY, Komatsu N, Izumi S, Yoshimura S, Watanabe K. Ultrastructural localization of prolactin in rat anterior pituitary glands by preembedding peroxidase-labeled antibody method: Observations in normal, castrated, or estrogen-stimulated specimen. J Histochem Cytochem **30**:919–925, 1982.
19. Moriarty GC, Tobin RB. An immunocytochemical study of TSH storage in rat thyroidectomy cells with and without D or L thyroxine treatment. J Histochem Cytochem **24**:1140, 1976.
20. Palade GE. Intracellular aspects of the process of protein synthesis. Science **189**:347–358, 1975.
21. Rothman SS. Protein transport by the pancreas. Science **190**:747, 1975.
22. Farquhar MG. Processing of secretory granules by cells of the anterior pituitary gland. Mem Soc Endocrinol **19**:79, 1971.
23. Gold G, Gishizky ML, Grodsky GM. Evidence that glucose "marks" beta cells resulting in preferential release of newly synthesized insulin. Science **218**:56–58, 1982.
24. Dudek RW, Charles TM, Boyne AF. Preferential secretion of newly-synthesized insulin is predictable from the ultrastructure of stimulated, physically-fixed beta cells. J Histochem Cytochem **31**(8):1067, 1983.
25. Dudek RW, Boyne AF. Quick freezing suggests novel features associated with insulin secretion. J Cell Biol **97**(5):436a, 1983.
26. Noe BD, Baste CA, Bauer GE. Studies on proinsulin and proglucagon biosynthesis and conversion at the subcellular level II. Distribution of radioactive peptide

hormones and hormone precursors in subcellular fractions after pulse and pulse-chase incubation of islet tissue. J Cell Biol **74**:589–604, 1977.
27. Fletcher DJ, Quigley JP, Bauer GE, Noe BD. Characterization of proinsulin- and proglucagon-converting activities in isolated islet secretory granules. J Cell Biol **90**:312–322, 1981.
28. Lambert AE. The regulation of insulin secretion. Rev Physiol Biochem Pharmacol **75**:98–130, 1976.
29. Horwitz DL, Starr JI, Mako ME, Blackard WG, Rubenstein AH. Proinsulin, insulin, and C-peptide concentrations in human portal and peripheral blood. J Clin Invest **55**:1278–1283, 1975.
30. Stoll RW, Touber JL, Menahan LH, Williams RH. Clearance of porcine insulin, proinsulin and connecting peptide by the isolated rat liver. Proc Soc Exp Bio Med **3**:894, 1970.
31. Stoll RW, Touber JL, Winterschield LC, Ensinck JW, Williams RH. Hypoglycemic activity and immunological half-life of porcine insulin and proinsulin in baboons and swine. Endocrinology **88**:714, 1971.
32. Sonksen PH, Tompkins CV, Srivastava MC, Nabatto JD. A comparative study on the metabolism of human insulin and porcine proinsulin in man. Clin Sci Mol Med **45**:633, 1973.
33. Starr JL, Rubenstein AH. Metabolism of endogenous proinsulin and insulin in man. J Clin Endocrinol Metab **38**:305, 1974.
34. Mako M, Block M, Starr J, Nielsen E, Friedman E, Rubenstein AH. Proinsulin in chronic renal and hepatic failure: A reflection of the relative contribution of the liver and kidney to its metabolism. Clin Res **21**:631, 1973.
35. Melani F, Rubenstein AH, Steiner DF. Human serum proinsulin. J Clin Invest **49**:497–507, 1970.
36. Rubenstein AH, Melani F, Steiner DF. Circulating proinsulin immunology, measurement, and biological activity. In: DF Steiner and N. Freinkel, eds, Handbook of Physiology: Endocrinology. Waverly, Baltimore, Sect 7, Vol 1:pp515–525, 1972.
37. Tompkins CV, Brandenburg D, Jones RH, Sonksen PH. Mechanism of action of insulin and insulin analogues: A comparison of the hepatic and peripheral effects of glucose turnover of insulin, proinsulin and three insulin and analogues modified at positions A_1 and B_{29}. Diabetologia **20**:94–101, 1981.
38. Shaw WN, Chance RE. Effect of porcine proinsulin *in vitro* on adipose tissue and diaphragm of the normal rat. Diabetes **17**(12):737–745, 1968.
39. Rubenstein AH, Melani F, Pilkis S, Steiner DF. Proinsulin: Secretion, metabolism, immunological and biological properties. Postgrad Med J **45** (Suppl):476–485, 1969.
40. Blundell TL, Bedarkar S, Rinderknecht E, Humbel RE. Insulin-like growth factor: A model for tertiary structure accounting for immunoreactivity and receptor binding. Proc Natl Acad Sci USA **75**:180, 1978.
41. Pilch PF, Czech MP. The subunit structure of the high affinity insulin receptor. Evidence for a disulfide-linked receptor complex in fat cell and liver plasma membranes. J Biol Chem **225**(4):1722–1731, 1980.
42. Massague J, Czech MP. The subunit structures of two distinct receptors for insulin-like growth factors I and II and their relationship to the insulin receptor. J Biol Chem **257**(9):5038–5045, 1982.
43. Czech MP. Structural and functional homologies in the receptors for insulin and the insulin-like growth factors. Cell **31**:8–10, 1982.
44. Mauer SM, Sutherland DER, Steffes MW, Leonard RJ, Najarian JS, Michael AF, Brown DM. Pancreatic transplantation: Effects on the glomerular lesions of experimental diabetes in the rat. Diabetes **23**:748–753, 1974.
45. Sutherland DER, Steffes MW, Mauer SM, Brown DM, Najarian JS. Reversal of the secondary lesions of diabetes in rats by islet transplantation in the rat. Transplant Proc **7**(Suppl 1):747–749, 1975.
46. Gray BN, Watkins E. Prevention of vascular complications of diabetes by pancreatic islet transplantation. Arch Surg **111**:254–257, 1976.
47. Lauritzen T, Frost-Larsen K, Larsen HW, Deckert T, The Steno Study Group. Effect of 1 year of near normal blood glucose levels on retinopathy in insulin-dependent diabetics. Lancet **2**:200–203, 1983.
48. Lestradet H, Papoz L, Hellouin De Menibus CL, Levavasseur F, Besse J, Billaud BL, Battistelli F, Tric PH, Lestradet F. Long-term study of mortality and vascular complications in juvenile-onset (Type 1) diabetes. Diabetes **30**, 1981.
49. Tamborlane W, Sherwin R, Bergman M, Ebersole J, Puklin J, Felig P. Can treatment of diabetes with a portable insulin pump reverse diabetc complications? Diabetes **29**(Suppl 2A):18A, 1980.

PROCEEDINGS OF THE SOCIETY FOR EXPERIMENTAL BIOLOGY AND MEDICINE **176**, 8–13 (1984)

Magnesium Sulfate-Induced Water Secretion in Hamster Small Intestine[1] (41834)

MARK REICHELDERFER,[2] BARBARA PERO, VILJA LORENZSONN, AND WARD A. OLSEN

Gastroenterology Research Laboratory, William S. Middleton Memorial Veterans Hospital, 2500 Overlook Terrace, Madison, Wisconsin 53705, and Department of Medicine, Center for Health Sciences, University of Wisconsin, Madison, Wisconsin 53706

Abstract. We studied possible mechanisms of magnesium sulfate ($MgSO_4$)-induced diarrhea. *In vivo* perfusion of hamster small intestine with an isotonic electrolyte solution containing 50 m*M* $MgSO_4$ produced nearly three times as much fluid secretion as did a solution containing an equiosmotic amount of mannitol. We found that magnesium was absorbed at a faster rate than mannitol under these conditions, suggesting that differences in solute permeability do not explain the differences in secretory rates. Magnesium ion rather than sulfate appeared largely responsible for the effect as replacement of sulfate with chloride did not diminish the response. $MgSO_4$ perfusion of a proximal intestinal segment did not affect water transport in an isolated distal segment suggesting that release of cholecystokinin or alterations in serum levels of other hormones were not responsible. Intestinal permeability, morphology, and cyclic nucleotide levels were normal after $MgSO_4$ perfusion. Thus, $MgSO_4$-induced diarrhea cannot be explained by the usual mechanisms, and additional processes responsible for intestinal secretion must exist.

Magnesium salts have been widely used as cathartics since the early 17th century when the $MgSO_4$-rich water from a spring in Epsom, England was found to have a laxative effect (1). The mechanism of action of $MgSO_4$ is uncertain. Because magnesium is poorly absorbed, these compounds have been assumed to be osmotic cathartics (2, 3). Recent work, however, suggests that magnesium-induced intestinal secretion may not be accounted for solely by osmotic forces (4). In fact, decreased water and sodium absorption in rat jejunum has been reported as a consequence of elevated magnesium concentrations in blood (5). The purpose of our work, therefore, was to reexamine the role of osmotic forces in the effect and to also study some of the more recent suggestions that the secretory effect is mediated by release of cholecystokinin (CCK) (6), or changes in the serum levels of parathormone or calcitonin (5). We also examined other possible mechanisms including altered cyclic nucleotide metabolism and mucosal damage.

Methods. We studied male Syrian golden hamsters (Sprague–Dawley, Madison, Wisc.) weighing 100 to 150 g, using a modification of an *in vivo* perfusion technique (7). Nonfasting animals were anesthetized with 100 mg/kg of intraperitoneal pentobarbital sodium, and the abdomen opened in the midline. The small bowel was rinsed with warm saline and cannulated with polyethylene tubing distal to the hepaticopancreatic pedicle and proximal to the ileocecal junction. Solutions contained 20 μCi/l of [^{14}C]polyethylene glycol, (PEG, mol wt 4000, sp act 0.5 μCi/mg, New England, Boston, Mass.) as a nonabsorbable marker of net water flux (8), and were infused at 0.7 to 0.8 ml/min with a peristaltic perfusion pump (Polystaltic Model 2-6100, Buchler Instruments, Fort Lee, N.J.). The solutions were maintained at 38°C in a water bath and the animals kept warm with an overhead lamp. Experimental and control animals were perfused simultaneously.

The test solutions contained $MgSO_4$ at 12.5, 25, and 50 m*M* concentrations with corresponding control solutions containing mannitol at 15, 30, and 60 m*M* (11, 10, and 10 animals in each group at each comparison level, respectively). At each concentration level, $MgSO_4$ and mannitol contributed equal numbers of osmotic particles as measured by freezing point depression (osmometer model

[1] This study was supported by NIH grant AM 13927 and the Veterans Administration.

[2] To whom reprint requests should be addressed at William S. Middleton Memorial Veterans Hospital.

0037-9727/84 $1.50

3D, Advanced Instruments, Inc., Needham Heights, Mass.). Additional perfusions with 120 and 200 m*M* mannitol were also carried out (10 and 8 animals, respectively) to evaluate the effects of high concentrations of poorly absorbed solute. We also compared $MgSO_4$ with $MgCl_2$ at 50 m*M* concentrations to determine whether the magnesium or the sulfate ion was most important in eliciting secretion. In addition to $MgSO_4$ or mannitol, the solutions contained KCl and $NaHCO_3$ at 4 and 12 m*M* concentrations, respectively. Osmolality was adjusted to between 285 and 290 mOsm/kg by addition of NaCl. The pH of all solutions was adjusted to between 7.85 and 7.95 to allow us to compare our results with previous studies from our laboratory (7).

It should be emphasized that the design of these experiments allowed us to compare the effects of $MgSO_4$ with those of another relatively impermeant substance, mannitol, at concentrations chosen to provide similar osmotic loads of poorly absorbed solute. Measured total osmolality ($MgSO_4$ or mannitol plus the other solutes) was also similar between test and control solutions. In order to maintain a physiological osmolality we reduced the sodium concentration of our solutions as we increased the concentration of poorly absorbed solute (for example, the solutions containing the highest concentrations of $MgSO_4$ or mannitol had a sodium concentration of 107 m*M*). It is important to point out that the sodium concentrations of the mannitol and $MgSO_4$ solutions were identical for each comparison as shown in Table I.

Preliminary experiments indicated that a steady state of fluid movement was reached within the first 30 min of perfusion; consequently perfusates were collected from the distal cannula during each of the next two 20-min periods. Additional pentobarbital was given as needed through the perfusion period to maintain anesthesia. At the end of the perfusion, the animals were sacrificed, and the perfused segments removed and dried to constant weight at 100°C. Perfusion collections were centrifuged at 1000*g* for 10 min to remove debris. Two-hundred-microliter aliquots of supernatants and infusion solutions were then mixed with 15 ml of Aquasol (New England Nuclear), and radioactivity measured with a liquid scintillation spectrometer (Tri-Carb 3300, Packard Instruments, Downers Grove, Ill.) with an efficiency of 65–80%. Counts were converted to disintegrations per minute (dpm) by means of an automatic external standard and a card programmable calculator (Model 1266, Monroe Instruments, Orange, N.J.).

TABLE I. CONCENTRATIONS OF $MgSO_4$, MANNITOL, NaCl, AND TOTAL SOLUTE IN SOLUTIONS[a]

$MgSO_4$ solutions			Mannitol solutions		
$MgSO_4$ (m*M*)	NaCl (m*M*)	Osmolality (mOsm/K)	Mannitol (m*M*)	NaCl (m*M*)	Osmolality (mOsm/K)
12.5	129	289	15	129	292
25	122	289	30	122	289
50	107	288	60	107	291

[a] All solutions contained KCl 4 m*M* and $NaHCO_3$ 12 m*M*.

Water transport for each of the two 20-min collection periods was calculated, averaged, and expressed per gram of dry tissue weight. The following formula was used: Net flux = perfusion rate $(1 - [PEG]_i/[PEG]_o)$ where $[PEG]_i$ and $[PEG]_o$ are ^{14}C concentrations in the infusion solutions and perfusion collections, respectively. Positive values indicate absorption and negative values secretion.

Magnesium and mannitol absorption from 50 and 60 m*M* solutions, respectively, was measured in two 20- to 25-min collection periods as the ratio of amount infused to amount recovered. The two results were averaged and expressed as percentage recovered. Magnesium concentrations were measured by atomic absorption spectrometry (Model 372, Perkin–Elmer Corporation, Norwalk, Conn.) and mannitol as DPMs of ^{14}C with inclusion of 20 μCi [^{14}C]mannitol (sp act 45 mCi/mmole, New England Nuclear). The latter experiments did not include [^{14}C]PEG, and the isotope was counted as described above.

Split gut perfusions. $MgSO_4$-induced release of a gastrointestinal hormone such as CCK (6) which has secretory properties is an attractive possible mechanism of action of magnesium cathartics. Since in most species CCK cells are found in highest concentration in the proximal intestine (9, 10), we studied the effects of $MgSO_4$ perfusions of proximal intestine on the rates of fluid absorption in the distal bowel using a split gut preparation. We divided the entire small intestine into two segments which were perfused simultaneously at 0.7 to 0.9 ml/min. The first segment included the duodenum and proximal one-third of the rest of the small intestine and was perfused with either the 50 m*M* $MgSO_4$ solution or a control solution consisting of 137 m*M* NaCl, 4 m*M* KCl, and 12 m*M* $NaHCO_3$. Osmolality and pH of the solutions were adjusted as described above. The distal segment, consisting of the remaining small intestine, was perfused with the control solution containing 20 μCi/l of [^{14}C]PEG. After steady-state conditions were reached, 20-min collections of distal segment perfusate were treated as above and rates of net water transport calculated.

Intestinal permeability. Permeability was assessed by measuring intestinal clearance of intravenously administered inulin as previously described (7). We injected 25 μCi of [^{14}C]inulin (mol wt 6000, sp act 1.9 μCi/mg, New England Nuclear) into the inferior vena cava of hamsters with subsequent ligation of both renal pedicles. The small intestine was then perfused with the 50 m*M* $MgSO_4$ or 60 m*M* mannitol solutions (omitting [^{14}C]PEG). After a 30-min equilibration period, four 15-min collections were made since previous experiments had demonstrated constant plasma concentrations of the isotope from 20 to 90 min after injection. Twenty-microliter aliquots of plasma and 200-μl aliquots of collected samples were mixed with 150 μl of Soluene TM 100 (Packard Instruments Co., Inc.) and the isotope counted as above. Clearance was calculated as follows: Clearance = $(VC)/P$ where V is collection volume, C is ^{14}C concentration in collected sample and P is ^{14}C concentration in plasma. Mean clearance of the four collections was calculated and expressed per gram dry tissue weight.

Morphology. We used lanthanum permeability and binding as a means of assessing mucosal damage in previous studies of the effects of bile salts and fatty acids on hamster small intestine (7, 11). We therefore perfused the small intestine with lanthanum hydroxide after 60 min of perfusion with either 50 m*M* $MgSO_4$ or 60 m*M* mannitol and prepared the tissue for light and electron microscopy as described previously (7, 11).

Cyclic nucleotides. To measure the effect of $MgSO_4$ on mucosal cyclic AMP levels we perfused the animals for 60 min with either the 50 m*M* $MgSO_4$ or the 60 m*M* mannitol solution. The intestine was then quickly removed and rinsed in ice cold 0.05 *M* Tris buffer, pH 7.5, containing 8 m*M* theophylline. The gut was everted over a glass rod, rinsed again with buffer, and scraped with a glass slide over ice. The scrapings were weighed and deproteinized as follows. Boiling 0.05 *M* potassium phosphate buffer, pH 7.5, containing 8 m*M* theophylline was added to the scrapings (approximately 1 ml/150 mg) and the mixture boiled for 10 min, homogenized with a Polytron homogenizer (Brinkman Instruments, Inc., Westbury, N.Y.) at setting No. 4 for 10 sec and then 15 sec, and centrifuged at 2000*g* for 20 min at 4°C. The pellet was assayed for total protein content (12) and the supernatant stored at −20°C. The supernatant was subsequently thawed, centrifuged again at 2000*g* for 10 min, and assayed for cyclic AMP by a competitive binding method (13, 14) using an assay kit (Amersham, Arlington Heights, Ill.). The results were expressed as picomoles per milligram of mucosal protein. Total elapsed time between removal of intestine to addition of boiling buffer did not exceed 60 sec.

To determine effects on cyclic GMP levels, we perfused animals and prepared mucosal scrapings as described for the cyclic AMP studies. The scrapings were then frozen with liquid nitrogen and weighed. Total elapsed time to freezing was less than 60 sec. Ice-cold 6% trichloracetic acid was then added at 1 ml/100 mg of tissue, and the mixture homogenized at 4°C as above. The mixture was then divided into two aliquots. To the second aliquot we added 1.5 pmole of cGMP/0.3 ml of assay sample as an internal standard. Each aliquot was then centrifuged at 4°C at 2000*g* for 15 min. The pellet was assayed for total protein content (12). The supernatant was extracted with ether and evaporated to dryness under a stream of nitrogen at 70°C in a warm water bath. The residue was redissolved in 1.6 m*M* sodium acetate buffer and frozen at −20°C. The supernatant was subsequently thawed and centrifuged at 2000*g* for 10 min before measurement of cGMP by a competitive binding technique (15, 16) using a kit from Becton Dickinson, Orangeburg, New York. The percentage recovery was calculated by dividing the differences of the resulting amounts of cGMP by the known amount (1.5 pmole) added to the second aliquot. Mucosal cGMP was then determined by dividing by the percentage recovery and expressed as picomoles per milligram of mucosal protein.

Results. We found a dose related increase in water secretion with both $MgSO_4$ and mannitol as shown in Fig 1. At the lowest concentrations studied, mean net water fluxes were similar, approximating 0. Higher concentrations resulted in increasing fluid secretion, particularly with $MgSO_4$; a 50 m*M* $MgSO_4$ solution produced nearly three times the rate of secretion of the equivalent mannitol solution. These results confirm the observation that $MgSO_4$-induced secretion is not simply related to the presence of a poorly absorbed solute. In fact, as the figure shows, the secretion induced by very high concentrations of mannitol (120 and 200 m*M*) did not approach that seen with 50 m*M* $MgSO_4$. We also considered the possibility that the effective osmotic pressure of $MgSO_4$ might be greater than mannitol because the intestine might be less permeable to $MgSO_4$; thus, the effect of $MgSO_4$ would be greater even though measured osmolality was the same. Our results suggest, however, that permeability to $MgSO_4$ is less, not greater, than to mannitol: we found that 12.5 ± 1.4% (SEM) of Mg was absorbed as compared to 7.0 ± 1.0% of mannitol (eight perfusions each), $P < 0.01$.

The magnesium rather than the sulfate ion

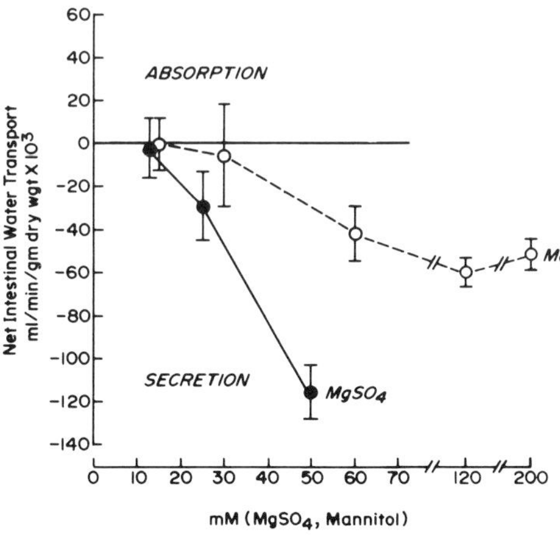

FIG. 1. Effects of $MgSO_4$ and mannitol on intestinal water transport. $MgSO_4$ resulted in a statistically significant increase in fluid secretion as compared to the mannitol control at the 50 m*M* concentration ($P < 0.001$), but the differences at the lower concentrations were not significantly different. Means ± SEM are shown.

TABLE II. EFFECT OF $MgSO_4$ ON MUCOSAL CYCLIC NUCLEOTIDE CONCENTRATIONS[a]

	Cyclic AMP[b]	Cyclic GMP[b]
50 m*M* $MgSO_4$	4.93 ± 0.62 (7)	4.43 ± 1.19 (11)
60 m*M* Mannitol	4.30 ± 0.29 (6)	2.80 ± 0.41 (10)

[a] Mean ± SEM are shown. Number of animals are given in parentheses.
[b] Expressed as picomoles/mg of mucosal protein.

appears largely responsible for the secretory effect. We found no significant difference in secretory rates between 50 m*M* $MgSO_4$ and 50 m*M* $MgCl_2$ (129 ± 17 (SEM) ml/min/g dry wt × 10^3 in eight perfusions compared to 212 ± 49 in nine experiments, respectively).

We found that fluid absorption from distal bowel was not affected by perfusion of the proximal segment with $MgSO_4$. Mean distal absorption was 30 ± 17 (SEM) ml/min/g dry wt × 10^3 for 12 proximal $MgSO_4$ perfusions and 44.1 ± 11 for 12 proximal electrolyte solution perfusions.

Fifty-millimolar $MgSO_4$ did not increase mucosal levels of either cAMP or cGMP in comparison to mannitol perfusion (Table II) and did not significantly alter inulin clearance (Table III). Previously reported effects of sodium ricinoleate on inulin clearance are shown for comparative purposes (7); we used an 8 m*M* concentration of fatty acid because it resulted in comparable rates of fluid secretion. Intestinal villi were morphologically intact on both light and electron microscopy, although intercellular spaces in the distal one-half of villi appeared more dilated after $MgSO_4$. Lanthanum binding was similar after $MgSO_4$ and mannitol perfusions and did not differ from our findings after saline perfusions (11).

Discussion. We chose concentrations of $MgSO_4$ that are likely to be found after therapeutic doses of the agent: for example, the relatively low dose of 5 g of $MgSO_4 \cdot 7H_2O$ in 200 ml of water is 101 m*M* in concentration. We found that concentrations much less than that produced significantly more water secretion than did equiosmotic mannitol, suggesting that the secretory effects of $MgSO_4$ are not explained by its osmotic activity alone. Furthermore, the differences between $MgSO_4$ and mannitol do not appear to be explainable by differences in intestinal permeability to the

TABLE III. EFFECT OF $MgSO_4$ ON CLEARANCE OF INULIN[a]

	50 m*M* $MgSO_4$	60 m*M* Mannitol	Saline[c]	8 m*M* Na ricinoleate[c]
Inulin clearance[b]	4.1 ± 1.5 (3)	2.0 ± 0.2 (4)	2.9 ± 0.5 (10)	35.9 ± 8.6 (5)

[a] Mean ± SEM are shown. Number of animals are given in parentheses.
[b] Expressed as μl/min/g dry weight.
[c] Data reported previously (7).

two substances. If the reflection coefficient for $MgSO_4$ were higher than for mannitol (i.e., $MgSO_4$ less permeable), more fluid would be secreted in response to $MgSO_4$ even if osmotic concentrations as measured by freezing-point depression were identical because the *effective* osmotic pressure of $MgSO_4$ would be higher (17). Our finding of minimal absorption of mannitol is consistent with previous reports that it is close to an impermeate solute with theoretical and effective osmotic pressures equal in human intestine, i.e., a reflection coefficient of 1.0 (17, 18). $MgSO_4$ is unlikely therefore to be less permeate than mannitol, and, in fact, our study demonstrates that it is more readily absorbed. Our perfusion results with high mannitol concentrations also support our belief that the osmotic pressure of $MgSO_4$ does not explain the secretory response. Even a 30-fold increase in mannitol concentration did not result in secretion at anywhere near the rate found with 50 m*M* $MgSO_4$. In fact, it did not significantly increase the rate over that found with 60 m*M* mannitol suggesting that maximal osmotic responses were achieved at the latter concentration.

Our studies also exclude the possibility that $MgSO_4$-induced secretion is the result of a sodium diffusion gradient as others have suggested (19). The suggestion was that the lower intraluminal sodium concentration, the result of replacement of NaCl by $MgSO_4$, might lead to movement of NaCl (and water) into the lumen. Since sodium concentrations were identical between each $MgSO_4$ solution and the corresponding mannitol solution, that suggestion is untenable.

Our study also demonstrates that the secretory effect of $MgSO_4$ is largely related to the magnesium ion rather than the poorly absorbed sulfate ion since $MgCl_2$ resulted in a response at least as great we found with $MgSO_4$. This finding is, of course, consistent with the notion that osmotic factors are unimportant in the effect, although it is at variance with a study in man where $MgSO_4$ was found to produce more secretion than $MgCl_2$ (19). We do not know the reason for the discrepancy between the two studies.

We explored several other possible mechanisms that might mediate magnesium-induced intestinal secretion. Our first thought was that intraluminal magnesium might release a duodenal hormone, especially CCK, into the circulation (20). Since CCK in pharmacologic doses, at least, affects intestinal fluid transport (21, 22), CCK or some other hormone might mediate the magnesium effect (6). A related hypothesis is that the fluid secretion is mediated by either an increase in serum calcitonin or a decrease in parathormone from magnesium absorption (6). We tested these hypotheses by dividing the small intestine into two isolated segments; if either were correct, proximal magnesium perfusion would have been expected to alter fluid transport in the isolated distal segment, but it did not. These results are consistent with those reported by others. Studies in man have shown that magnesium is a relatively weak stimulus to CCK release (19, 23) and studies in dogs have shown that stimulation of CCK release by a potent stimulant (sodium ricinoleate) does not affect fluid transport in a second isolated intestinal loop (24). It is conceivable, of course, that $MgSO_4$ stimulates release of a hormone from the ileum rather than from the proximal intestine or that a secretory effect of a hormone might be observable only in the jejunum. If either possibility were correct, we would not have detected it in our experiment, but both possibilities seem very unlikely.

We considered two other possibilities which might explain the $MgSO_4$ effect: intestinal mucosal damage (as appears related to the intestinal secretion found with fatty acids and bile salts (7, 11)) and altered levels of cyclic nucleotides (involved in the regulation of intestinal secretion (25–28)). We were unable to demonstrate significant changes by either light or electron microscopy, however, and mucosal levels of cyclic nucleotides did not change with $MgSO_4$. Thus our study has demonstrated that the mechanism of $MgSO_4$-induced secretion depends upon the presence of the magnesium but not the sulfate ion and is independent of both osmotic factors and the usual mediators of intestinal secretion.

1. Soper HW. The story of magnesium sulphate with special reference to its use in biliary drainage. Amer J Med Sci **169**:398–407, 1925.
2. Binder HJ, Donowitz M. A new look at laxative action. Gastroenterology **69**:1001–1005, 1975.
3. Donowitz M. Current concepts of laxative action: Mechanisms by which laxatives increase stool water. J Clin Gastroenterol **1**:77–84, 1979.
4. Wanitschke R, Ammon HV. Effects of magnesium sulfate on transit time and water transport in the human jejunum. Gastroenterology **70**:949, abstr, 1976.
5. DiBona GF, Swain LL. Effect of hypermagnesia on rat jejunal sodium and water transport. Amer J Physiol **231**:1771–1776, 1976.
6. Harvey RF, Read AE. Saline purgatives act by releasing cholecystokinin. Lancet **2**:185–187, 1973.
7. Cline WS, Lorenzsonn V, Benz L, Bass P, Olsen WA. The effects of sodium ricinoleate on small intestine function and structure. J Clin Invest **58**:380–390, 1976.
8. Miller DL, Schedl HP. Total recovery studies of nonabsorbable indicators in the rat small intestine. Gastroenterology **58**:40–46, 1970.
9. Polak JM, Bloom SR, Rayford PL, Pearse AGE, Buchan AMJ, Thompson JC. Identification of cholecystokinin-secreting cells. Lancet **2**:1016–1018, 1975.
10. Bryant MG, Bloom SR. Distribution of the gut hormones in the primate intestinal tract. Gut **20**:653–659, 1979.
11. Gullikson GW, Cline WS, Lorenzsonn V, Benz L, Olsen WA, Bass P. Effects of anionic surfactants on hamster small intestinal membrane structure and function: Relationship to surface activity. Gastroenterology **73**:501–511, 1977.
12. Lowry OH, Rosebrough NJ, Farr AL, Randall RJ. Protein measurement with the Folin phenol reagent. J Biol Chem **193**:26–275, 1951.
13. Gilman AG. A protein binding assay for adenosine 3′,5′-monophosphate. Proc Natl Acad Sci USA **67**:305–312, 1970.
14. Brown BL, Albano JDM, Elkins RP, Sgherzi AM. A simple and sensitive saturation assay method for the measurement of adenosine 3′,5′-cyclic monophosphate. Biochem J **121**:561–562, 1971.
15. Steiner AL, Parker CW, Kipnis DM. Radioimmunoassay for cyclic nucleotides. I. Preparation of antibodies and iodinated cyclic nucleotides. J Biol Chem **247**:1106–1113, 1972.
16. Steiner AL, Pagliara AS, Chase LR, Kipnis DM. Radioimmunoassay for cyclic nucleotides. II. Adenosine 3′,5′-monophosphate in mammalian tissues and body fluids. J Biol Chem **247**:1114–1120, 1972.
17. Fordtran JS, Rector FC Jr, Ewton MF, Soter N, Kinney J. Permeability characteristics of the human small intestine. J Clin Invest **44**:1935–1944, 1965.
18. Soergel KH, Whalen GE, Harris JA. Passive movement of water and sodium across the human small intestinal mucosa. J Applied Phys **24**(1):40–48, 1968.
19. Malagelada JR, Holtermuller KH, McCall JT, Go VLW. Pancreatic, gallbladder, and intestinal responses to intraluminal magnesium salts in man. Amer J Dig Dis **23**:481–485, 1978.
20. Harvey RF, Dowsett L, Hartog M, Read AE. A radioimmunoassay for cholecystokinin-pancreozymin. Lancet **2**:826–828, 1973.
21. Moritz M, Finkelstein G, Meshkinpour H, Fingerut J, Lorber SH. Effect of secretin and cholescystokinin on the transport of electrolyte and water in human jejunum. Gastroenterology **64**:76–80, 1973.
22. Matuchansky C, Huet PM, Mary JY. Effects of cholecystokinin and metoclopramide on jejunal movements of water and electrolytes and on transit time of luminal fluid in man. Eur J Clin Invest **2**:169–175, 1972.
23. Malagelada JR, DiMagno EP, Summerskill WHJ, Go VLW. Regulation of pancreatic and gallbladder functions by intraluminal fatty acids and bile acids in man. J Clin Invest **58**:493–499, 1976.
24. Gadacz TR, Gaginella TS, Phillips SF. Inhibition of water absorption by ricinoleic acid: Evidence against hormonal mediation of the effect. Amer J Dig Dis **21**:859–862, 1976.
25. Kimberg DV. Cyclic nucleotides and their role in gastrointestinal secretion. Gastroenterology **67**:1023–1064, 1974.
26. Turnberg LA. Intestinal transport of salt and water. Clin Sci Mol Med **54**:337–348, 1978.
27. Hughes JM, Murad F, Chang B, Guerrant RL. Role of cyclic GMP in the action of heat-stable enterotoxin of *Escherichia coli.* Nature (London) **271**:755–756, 1978.
28. Field M, Graf LH Jr, Laird WJ, Smith PL. Heat-stable enterotoxin of *Escherichia coli,* in vitro effects on guanylate cyclase activity, cyclic GMP concentration, and ion transport in small intestine. Proc Natl Acad Sci USA **75**:2800–2804, 1978.

Received December 21, 1981. P.S.E.B.M. 1984, Vol. 176.
Accepted January 20, 1984.

PROCEEDINGS OF THE SOCIETY FOR EXPERIMENTAL BIOLOGY AND MEDICINE **176**, 14–21 (1984)

Sensitivity to Corticosterone-Induced Cleft Palate Is Not Associated with H-2[1] (41835)

MARVIN L. TYAN

Medical and Research Services, Veterans Administration, Wadsworth VA Medical Center, Los Angeles, California 90073, and Department of Medicine, University of California School of Medicine, Los Angeles, California 90024

Abstract. The frequency of cleft palate (CP) and corticosterone levels in maternal plasma and amniotic fluid were determined in pregnant C57BL/10 (H-2^b) and congenic B10.A (H-2^a) mice after the ip injection of repository ACTH, corticosterone acetate, or desoxycorticosterone acetate (DOCA) on the 11th through 14th day of gestation. It was found that ACTH (a) induces CP in B10.A but not C57BL/10 mice, (b) induces CP in B10.A mice at about the same frequency noted when diluent alone is injected, and (c) produces an elevation in maternal plasma corticosterone levels 1.5- to 2.0-fold lower and amniotic fluid levels 3- to 5-fold lower than those found after the injection of 5 mg corticosterone acetate, a dose which induces a comparable frequency of CP in B10.A mice. The injection of 5 mg corticosterone acetate produced CP frequencies in C57BL/10 and B10.A mice of 4.9 and 3.3%, respectively, and increasing the dose to 9.2 mg resulted in significant increases in CP to 23.8 and 24.7%, respectively. DOCA at two dose levels induced CP in B10.A fetuses at about the frequency noted when diluent alone has been given. These findings show that susceptibility to corticosterone induced CP is not associated with the major histocompatibility complex of the mouse, H-2, as is the case with glucocorticoids (e.g., cortisone, dexamethasone), and they raise the possibility that factors other than or in addition to corticosterone may be involved in spontaneous or ACTH- or stress-induced CP.

Over 25 years ago an animal model for isolated cleft palate was developed in mice (1). It was shown that clefting of the developing secondary palate could be induced by the administration of cortisone to pregnant mice between the 11th and 14th days of gestation. Further, it was found that inbred strains of mice had different degrees of susceptibility to cortisone-induced cleft palate ((1,2); e.g., over 90% of the progeny of A/J and DBA/1 mice given 2.5 mg of cortisone developed cleft palate (CP), whereas only 20–25% of the offspring of similarly treated C57BL/6 or CBA/J mice had the defect). Subsequently, it has been shown that inbred strains of mice respond similarly when other glucocorticosteroids are given (3–5) and that several of the factors which determine susceptibility to glucocorticosteroid-induced CP are linked to the major histocompatibility complex of the mouse, H-2 (3, 4, 6).

Thus, cortisone, hydrocortisone, and a variety of their synthetic analogues induce CP in fetal mice, and to a great degree susceptibility is determined by the H-2 type of the mother and fetus, (3, 4). However, in the mouse corticosterone, a mineralocorticoid with weak gluconeogenic and anti-inflammatory properties, is the primary adrenal corticoid, and cortisol has not been detected in the plasma ((7, 8) and unpublished observations using HPLC, M. L. Tyan, J. J. Bonner, E. Canalis). The conventional wisdom has been that corticosterone is the agent responsible for "spontaneous" and stress-induced CP in the mouse. In support of this, it has been shown that corticosterone (9) and ACTH (10) can induce CP in A/J mice, and in the one published report where CP was induced in mice by the stress of transport the frequency varied significantly among the strains studied: A/J, 27%; DBA/2, 3%; CBA/J and C57BL/6, 0% (11). However, it has not been demonstrated that susceptibility to the teratogenic action of these agents is linked to the major histocompatibility complex as it has been with glucocorticoids.

To investigate this, pregnant congenic mice, C57BL/10 and B10.A, were injected with ACTH or corticosterone, corticosterone levels were measured in maternal plasma and amniotic fluid, and the incidence of CP was determined in the progeny. It was found that (a) plasma and amniotic fluid corticosterone

[1] This work was supported by USPHS Grant DE-05165 and VA Medical Research Funds.

0037-9727/84 $1.50

levels are similar in the two strains under basal conditions and after the injection of ACTH or corticosterone, (b) susceptibility to ACTH-induced CP appears to be associated with H-2, but (c) susceptibility to corticosterone-induced CP clearly is not. These findings suggest that corticosterone may not be the teratogenic agent in "spontaneous," or ACTH- or stress-induced CP.

Materials and Methods. Breeding pairs of C57BL/10Sn(H-2^b) and congenic C57BL/10.ASgSn(H-2^a) mice were purchased from Jackson Laboratory, Bar Harbor, Maine. Stock mice used in these experiments were bred in this Laboratory. The mice were fed Purina Laboratory Chow, and they were given acidified tap water.

In the experiments one male and two virgin 10- to 12-week-old females were placed in each cage. The day a vaginal plug was detected was considered Day 0 of pregnancy. On Days 11 through 14 the mice were injected ip with ACTH, corticosterone acetate, or desoxycorticosterone acetate (DOCA). The mice were killed on the 18th day of pregnancy, and the number of living fetuses and resorptions were recorded (dead fetuses, regardless of age were recorded as resorptions). Living fetuses were weighed and examined for gross external malformations. The oral cavity was inspected for the presence of CP, and the internal organs were examined for defects and to determine sex.

Repository corticotropin (HP Acthar Gel, 80 U.S.P. units/ml: diluent; 16% gelatin, 0.5% phenol, 0.1% cysteine) was obtained from Armour Pharmaceutical Company, Phoenix, Arizona. Corticosterone acetate was purchased from Sigma Chemical Company, St. Louis, Missouri and suspended (25 mg/ml) in an aqueous medium containing 0.45% NaCl, 0.2% polysorbate 80, 0.25% sodium carboxymethylcellulose, and 0.9% benzyl alcohol. DOCA (5 mg/ml; diluent; 0.08% methylparaben, 0.1% propylparaben in sesame oil) was obtained from Organon, Inc., West Orange, New Jersey. Control pregnancies were given ip punctures with a sterile needle on Days 11 through 14.

Corticosterone levels were determined in plasma and amniotic fluid by the microadaption of the acid fluorescence method described by Glick *et al.* (12). In the mouse which does not produce cortisol this method measures primarily corticosterone. Comparisons of means were made using Students' t test (13).

The sampling unit in the CP studies is the litter. The proportion of CP in each litter was transformed to an arcsine by using the table of Freeman–Tukey arcsine transformations for small sample sizes which was calculated by Mosteller and Youtz (14). This transformation has a weighting factor for litter size and for 0 and 100%. The proportion of CP per litter was transformed so that parametric analysis could be used. Means were compared using the Tukey–Kramer method (13).

Results. For comparative purposes, previously published data are presented in Table I showing the frequencies of CP obtained when C57BL/10 and B10.A mice were given 2.5 mg cortisone acetate on Days 11–14 or dexamethasone (80 mg/kg) or its diluent (creatinine 0.8%, sodium citrate 1%, methylparaben 0.15%, and propylparaben 0.02% in distilled water) on Day 12 (15, 16). It can be seen that B10.A mice are significantly more sensitive to the induction of CP by the glucocorticoids than are C57BL/10 mice. Further, B10.A mice appear to be more sensitive to CP induction by the specific or nonspecific effects of the diluent used with dexamethasone.

In the first experiments presented here C57BL/10 and B10.A pregnant dams were injected ip with 5 or 9.2 mg corticosterone acetate on Days 11 through 14 (Table II). It was found that the lower dose level produced resorption rates not significantly different from those noted when the same strains were injected with cortisone or dexamethasone as shown in Table I; however, the higher dose produced a twofold increase in the resorption rates. In neither case, was there a significant difference between the two strains. These results together with unpublished dexamethasone dose–response studies in C57BL/10, B10.A, B10.A(5R), B10.A(2R), B10.D2, B10.BR, and B10.A(18R) mice (J. J. Bonner and M. L. Tyan) suggest that the glucocorticoids, cortisone acetate and dexamethasone, have little effect on the normal resorption rate even at a relatively large dose (e.g., 400 mg (1.0 mM)/kg dexamethasone); however, corticosterone acetate at a dose of approximately 200 mg (0.6 mM)/kg doubles the rate in C57BL/10 and B10.A fetuses.

The injection of 5 mg corticosterone acetate

TABLE I. FREQUENCY OF ISOLATED CLEFT PALATE AMONG THE PROGENY OF CONGENIC C57BL/10 AND B10.A DAMS GIVEN ip INJECTIONS OF CORTISONE ACETATE ON DAYS 11 THROUGH 14 OR DEXAMETHASONE ON DAY 12

Strain	Corticosteroid (mg)	Number of litters	Total implants	Percentage resorption	Percentage cleft palate
C57BL/10	Cortisone acetate (2.5)[a]	14	98	12.5	36[c]
B10.A		18	147	13.0	92[c]
C57BL/10	Dexamethasone (80/kg)[b]	15	121	14.0	19.2[d]
B10.A		20	161	11.2	46.2[d]
C57BL/10	(220/kg)[b]	30	199	19.1	47.8[e]
B10.A		17	135	16.3	78.8[e]
C57BL/10	Diluent, Day 12[f]	13	100	26.0[g]	0.0[h]
B10.A		12	93	11.8[g]	2.4[h]

[a] Ref (15).
[b] Ref (16).
[c] C57BL/10 vs B10.A, $P < 0.01$.
[d] C57BL/10 vs B10.A, $P < 0.01$.
[e] C57BL/10 vs B10.A, $P < 0.01$.
[f] Ref (23).
[g] C57BL/10 vs B10.A, $P > 0.10$.
[h] C57BL/10 vs B10.A, $P < 0.05$.

produced comparably low frequencies of CP in the two strains studied (4.9 and 3.3%), and increasing the dose to 9.2 mg resulted in significant and equal increases in the rates (23.8 and 24.7%, Table II). These results suggest that barring complex differences in maternal–fetal metabolism and/or placental transport these two strains do not have genetic differences associated with H-2 which modulate susceptibility to corticosterone-induced CP. In the sham-injected controls the frequency of CP was significantly higher in B10.A mice (0.0% vs 3.6%), but the resorption rates were nearly identical.

DOCA is a mineralocorticoid with approximately seven times the sodium-retaining potency of corticosterone and essentially no anti-inflammatory activity. It has been reported that even at very high doses DOCA does not induce CP in susceptible strains of mice (5). To confirm this C57BL/10 and B10.A pregnant dams were injected ip with 1.0 or 2.5 mg DOCA on Days 11–14 (Table III). At the higher dose the mice received 0.5 ml of sesame oil ip; because of the absence of diluent controls it is not known if this contributed to the somewhat high resorption rates noted in these experiments. Two fetuses with CP were found

TABLE II. FREQUENCY OF ISOLATED CLEFT PALATE AMONG THE PROGENY OF CONGENIC C57BL/10 AND B10.A DAMS GIVEN ip INJECTIONS OF CORTICOSTERONE ON DAYS 11 THROUGH 14

Strain	Corticosterone (mg)	Number of litters	Total implants	Percentage resorption	Percentage cleft palate
C57BL/10	None[a]	15	109	27.5	0.0[b]
B10.A	None[a]	15	115	27.8	3.6[b]
C57BL/10	5	13	102	20.6[c]	4.9[e]
B10.A	5	13	113	19.5[d]	3.3[f]
C57BL/10	9.2	18	143	41.2[c]	23.8[e]
B10.A	9.2	21	176	49.4[d]	24.7[f]

[a] These mice were stuck in the lower abdomen with a sterile needle on Days 11 through 14.
[b] C57BL/10 vs B10.A, $P < 0.01$.
[c] C57BL/10, 5 mg vs C57BL/10, 9.2 mg, $P < 0.01$.
[d] B10.A, 5 mg vs B10.A, 9.2 mg, $P < 0.01$.
[e] C57BL/10, 5 mg vs C57BL/10, 9.2 mg, $P < 0.01$.
[f] B10.A, 5 mg vs B10.A, 9.2 mg, $P < 0.01$.

TABLE III. FREQUENCY OF ISOLATED CLEFT PALATE AMONG THE PROGENY OF C57BL/10 AND B10.A DAMS GIVEN ip INJECTIONS OF DESOXYCORTICOSTERONE (DOCA) ON DAYS 11 THROUGH 14

Strain	DOCA (mg)	Number of litters	Total implants	Percentage resorptions	Percentage cleft palate (No./total)
C57BL/10	1.0	8	57	10.4[b]	3.9 (2/51)[c]
B10.A[a]	1.0	11	83	27.7[b]	6.7 (4/60)[d]
C57BL/10	2.5	4	32	25.0	0.0 (0/24)
B10.A	2.5	9	66	30.3	2.2 (1/46)

[a] One litter was completely resorbed. If this pregnancy is not included, there were 74 implants of which 18.9% were resorbed.
[b] $P < 0.01$.
[c] Two affected fetuses were found in one pregnancy.
[d] Affected fetuses were found in three pregnancies.

in 1 of 12 C57BL/10 litters. The frequency of CP among B10.A litters was low and unrelated to dose (6.7 and 2.2%). These results suggest that DOCA has little or no ability to induce CP at pharmacological doses and that the CP induced in B10.A mice was most likely the result of the stress of injection as was noted in the dexamethasone diluent and sham injected controls (Tables I and II, respectively).

A major component of the response to stress in mice is the release of ACTH from the pituitary which results in adrenal stimulation and increased corticosterone secretion. If stress plays a role in the etiology of spontaneously occurring CP and if corticosterone the primary adrenal corticoid in the mouse is the agent through which the effect is mediated, then from the results reported above it would be expected that C57BL/10 and B10.A mice would be equally sensitive to CP induction by ACTH. It was found, however (Table IV), that (a) B10.A mice are significantly more sensitive to CP induction by ACTH than are C57BL/10 mice (5.2 and 7.7% vs 0%), (b) 8 and 16 units of ACTH induced essentially the same rate of clefting in B10.A mice, and (c) the rate of clefting was only slightly higher but not significantly different from that noted in the control groups (Tables I and II; no statistical comparison was made between the dexamethasone diluent controls and the ACTH group because of the differences in the diluents and the injection schedules). Therefore, it is not clear from these experiments whether the CP noted were induced by the physiological action of ACTH or if the effect was the result of the multiple injections or of a component of the diluent (not likely because again there was no dose effect). Whatever the case, B10.A mice are significantly more likely to develop CP under these conditions than are C57BL/10 fetuses.

Virgin C57BL/10 and B10.A mice were injected ip with diluent or 5.0 or 9.2 mg corticosterone acetate, and they were bled prior to and 2 and 6 hr after injection (Table V). It was found that the resting plasma corticosterone levels of the two strains were not

TABLE IV. FREQUENCY OF ISOLATED CLEFT PALATE AMONG THE PROGENY OF CONGENIC C57BL/10 AND B10.A DAMS GIVEN ip INJECTIONS OF REPOSITORY ACTH (HP ACTHAR GEL, ARMOUR) ON DAYS 11 THROUGH 14

Strain	ACTH (IU)	Number of litters	Total implants	Percentage resorptions[d]	Percentage cleft palate
C57BL/10	8	15	130	38.0	0[a]
B10.A	8	15	113	32.7	5.2[a,c]
C57BL/10	16	8	69	43.4	0[b]
B10.A	16	8	72	27.7	7.7[b,c]

[a] C57BL/10 vs B10.A, $P < 0.01$.
[b] C57BL/10 vs B10.A, $P < 0.05$.
[c] B10.A, 8 units ACTH vs 16 units, not significantly different.
[d] C57BL/10 vs B10.A, not significantly different at either dose level.

TABLE V. PLASMA CORTICOSTERONE LEVELS IN C57BL/10 AND B10.A VIRGIN MICE GIVEN CORTICOSTERONE ACETATE ip

Strain	Corticosterone (mg)	N	Plasma corticosterone (μg/100 ml) 0 hr	2 hr	6 hr
C57BL/10	None[a]	3	19.9 ± 18.4[b,c,d]	51.9 ± 19.8[c]	89.8 ± 12.0[d]
	5.0	3		959 ± 378	209 ± 87
	9.2	3		>2000	889 ± 89
B10.A	None[a]	3	36.1 ± 17.3[b,e,f]	58.4 ± 10[e]	66.5 ± 16.7[f]
	5.0	3		933 ± 52	178 ± 51
	9.2	3		>2000	991 ± 81

[a] These mice were bled at 0 time and 2 and 6 hr later.
[b] This value was derived from the nine samples obtained from this strain at 0 time. $P > 0.05$.
[c] $P < 0.05$.
[d] $P < 0.01$.
[e] $P < 0.05$.
[f] $P < 0.05$.

significantly different and that bleeding alone produced significant and comparable elevations of these levels. Plasma corticosterone levels were very similar in the two strains 2 and 6 hr after the injection of 5.0 and 9.2 mg corticosterone acetate.

Next pregnant C57BL/10 and B10.A mice were injected ip on the 11th or 13th day of gestation with 5 mg corticosterone acetate, and corticosterone levels were determined in maternal plasma and the amniotic fluid 2 hr later. It was found that the injection of corticosterone on the 13th day of gestation produced comparable maternal plasma and amniotic fluid levels in the two strains and that on the 11th and 13th days corticosterone levels in the amniotic fluid were approximately one-half those of the maternal plasma (Table VI).

In the last series of studies corticosterone levels were determined in the plasma of nonpregnant mice and in the maternal plasma and amniotic fluid of pregnant mice under basal conditions and 2 hr after the ip injection of 8 units of repository ACTH (Table VII). Again it was found that under basal conditions B10.A and C57BL/10 mice have comparable plasma corticosterone levels whether pregnant or not. Basal plasma corticosterone levels more than tripled between the 11th and 13th day of pregnancy and remained at this level to the 17th day as has been reported (17). The injection of ACTH produced a 2-fold increase in plasma corticosterone in nonpregnant mice, a 3-fold increase on the 11th day of gestation, and a 4-fold increase on the 13th day (the mice were injected on Days 11–13). The response of the two strains to ACTH were indistinguishable. Corticosterone levels in the amniotic fluid on the 13th day of pregnancy were approximately one-half maternal plasma levels and the injection of the mother with ACTH doubled fetal levels while increasing maternal plasma levels 4-fold. This suggests that a significant barrier exists to the equilibration of maternal plasma and amniotic fluid corticosterone levels. The injection of mice on the 13th day of gestation with 5 mg corticosterone produced maternal plasma corticosterone levels 1.5- to 2.0-fold greater and amniotic fluid levels 3- to 5-fold greater than those induced by 3 days of treatment with 8 units of repository ACTH.

TABLE VI. CORTICOSTERONE LEVELS IN MATERNAL PLASMA AND AMNIOTIC FLUID OF C57BL/10 AND B10.A MICE 2 hr AFTER THE ip INJECTION OF 5 mg CORTICOSTERONE ACETATE

Strain	Day of pregnancy	N	Corticosterone (μg/100 ml) Maternal blood	Amniotic fluid
B10.A	11	3	1475 ± 152[a]	791 ± 258[a]
C57BL/10	13	4	1052 ± 285[b]	535 ± 100[b]
B10.A	13	4	812 ± 328[c]	388 ± 212[c]

[a] $P < 0.01$.
[b] $P < 0.02$.
[c] $P > 0.05$.

Discussion. It has been demonstrated convincingly that the glucocorticoids, cortisone,

TABLE VII. PLASMA CORTICOSTERONE LEVELS IN PREGNANT AND NONPREGNANT C57BL/10 (B10) AND B10.A MICE UNDER BASAL CONDITIONS AND 2 hr AFTER THE ip INJECTION OF 8 UNITS OF REPOSITORY ACTH

Strain	Pregnant?	Day of gestation	ACTH?	*N*	Corticosterone (μg/100 ml) Plasma	*N*	Amniotic fluid
B10	No		No	16	47 ± 20[b]		
B10.A	No		No	10	48 ± 19[c]		
B10	No		Yes	9	110 ± 22[b]		
B10.A	No		Yes	8	105 ± 27[c]		
B10	Yes	11	No	3	35 ± 18[d]		
B10.A	Yes	11	No	6	40 ± 17[e]	2	36 ± 5
B10	Yes	11	Yes	9	97 ± 50[d]		
B10.A	Yes	11	Yes	8	133 ± 61[e]		
B10	Yes	13	No	6	133 ± 54[f,h]	4	48 ± 19[h]
B10.A	Yes	13	No	4	139 ± 24[g,i]	5	63 ± 26[i]
B10[a]	Yes	13	Yes	13	500 ± 115[f,j]	10	109 ± 52[j]
B10.A[a]	Yes	13	Yes	9	579 ± 122[g,k]	9	115 ± 55[k]
B10	Yes	16–17	No	3	134 ± 35		
B10.A	Yes	16–17	No	5	149 ± 40		

[a] These mice were given repository ACTH (8 units) ip on Days 11, 12, and 13.
[b–k] $P < 0.01$. Peak responses were obtained 2 hr after the injection of ACTH.

cortisol, dexamethasone, and others produce cleft palate in mice and that the degree of sensitivity to CP induction is determined to a great degree by genes linked to the major histocompatibility complex (1–6). However, these glucocorticoids do not exist naturally in the mouse, and, therefore, they can play no role in spontaneous or stress-induced disease.

Corticosterone is the major adrenal steroid found in the mouse, and it has been demonstrated here and previously that this agent can induce CP when administered in doses comparable to those used to induce CP with glucocorticoids (9, 18). However, unlike the glucocorticoids, sensitivity to corticosterone-induced CP has been shown here to be the same in C57BL/10 and B10.A mice, suggesting that H-2-associated genes may play little or no role in CP induced by this agent. Measurements of maternal plasma and amniotic fluid corticosterone levels at rest and after the administration of ACTH or corticosterone strongly suggest that there are no major differences between the two strains studied under basal conditions, in response to ACTH, in placental transport and/or in the metabolism of corticosterone, and from this, in tissue sensitivity. Although previous studies have shown that both resting and poststress plasma corticosterone levels are under genetic control and can vary significantly between strains, the reported results reveal no correlation with H-2 type and/or sensitivity to glucocorticoid induced CP (19, 20).

In addition, it has been reported that when maternal plasma corticosterone levels during restraint or food deprivation on the 14th day of gestation were compared with those following the injection of a dose of corticosterone (2.5 mg) sufficient to induce a comparable frequency of CP in the progeny (corticosterone 2.5%; restraint, 5%; food deprivation, 7%), it was found that (a) levels were slightly lower in the restrained and food-deprived mice and (b) although there was a significant correlation between high maternal corticosterone levels and the frequency of CP in the offspring of the restrained mice, there was no correlation in the food-deprived group (18). In the studies reported here a near identical dose–response relationship in the frequency of CP was noted when corticosterone was given to the two congenic strains; however, there is no correlation between plasma and amniotic fluid corticosterone levels and CP frequency when comparisons are made between (a) ACTH-treated C57BL/10 and B10.A mice or (b) the ACTH- and corticosterone-treated groups (Table VIII).

The stresses of restraint, food and/or water deprivation, and shipment clearly produce elevations of plasma corticosterone and low frequencies of CP (11, 18, 21, 22). However, as noted above, the elevation of plasma corticosterone produced by stress consistently has

TABLE VIII. COMPARISON OF MATERNAL PLASMA AND AMNIOTIC FLUID CORTICOSTERONE LEVELS (μg/dl) AND CP FREQUENCY IN C57BL/10 AND B10.A DAMS GIVEN CORTICOSTERONE ACETATE, 5 mg,OR ACTH, 8 UNITS ON DAYS 11 THROUGH 14[a]

	C57BL/10			B10.A		
	Maternal plasma	Amniotic fluid	Percentage CP	Maternal plasma	Amniotic fluid	Percentage CP
Corticosterone, 5 mg	1052 ± 285	535 ± 100	4.9	812 ± 328	388 ± 212	3.3
ACTH, 8 units	500 ± 115	109 ± 52	0.0	579 ± 122	115 ± 55	5.2
None	133 ± 54	48 ± 19	0.0	139 ± 24	63 ± 26	2.4

[a] Corticosterone levels were determined on Day 13.

been reported to be lower than that noted when corticosterone is given at a dose which induces the same frequency of clefting. Further, sensitivity to stress-induced CP appears to be strain dependent ((11), and sham-injected controls, Table 11), but the evidence presented here suggests that sensitivity to corticosterone-induced CP may not be.

Similarly, ACTH (a) causes elevations of plasma and amniotic fluid corticosterone levels which are significantly lower than those produced by a dose of corticosterone which produces a comparable CP frequency in H-2[a] mice (10), and (b) does not induce CP in a strain which is resistant to glucocorticoids (C57BL/10). Further, ACTH induces CP in susceptible strains at about the frequency noted in diluent, saline, or sham-injected groups, and no dose–response relationship could be demonstrated in the experiments reported here. This suggests that the effect may not be the result of the physiological action of ACTH but rather that of just another physiologically undefined stress.

When viewed together these and other observations raise the possibility that factors other than or in addition to corticosterone may be involved in spontaneous, ACTH-, or stress-induced CP. The evidence for this is summarized as follows: (a) at a given dose, corticosterone induces CP in C57BL/10 and B10.A mice at the same frequency, but B10.A mice are more susceptible to stress or ACTH induced CP; (b) basal, poststress, and post-ACTH maternal blood and amniotic fluid corticosterone levels are nearly identical in C57BL/10 and B10.A mice; (c) there is no consistent correlation between the level of plasma or amniotic fluid corticosterone levels and the frequency of CP (compare ACTH- vs corticosterone-treated groups, restraint vs food deprivation (18), and ACTH-treated C57BL/10 vs B10.A); (d) the frequency of CP induced in B10.A mice by ACTH is not significantly different from that induced by saline, diluent, or sham injection; (e) stress-induced suppression of lymphocyte stimulation by PHA but not stress-induced lymphopenia can be demonstrated in adrenalectomized rats indicating that stress-induced modulation of immunity is a complex phenomenon involving several mechanisms (24); (f) ACTH and β-endorphin are coreleased from the anterior pituitary in animal stress models (25); and (g) Plasma corticosterone levels are temporally related to immunological hyporeactivity but not to hyperactivity which may be modulated by any number of pituitary neurohumors (26). To sum stress-induced CP does not appear to be caused by the direct action of corticosterone, ACTH-induced CP is most likely caused by the stress of injections rather than the pharmacologic action of the agent, and recent reports raise the possibility that nonadrenal factors may play a role in stress-induced CP.

1. Fraser FC, Fainstat TD. Production of congenital defects in the offspring of pregnant mice treated with cortisone. Pediatrics **8**:527–533, 1951.
2. Kalter H. Interplay of intrinsic and extrinsic factors. In: Wilson JG, Warkany J, eds. Teratology: Principles and Techniques. University of Chicago Press, Chicago, Chapter 3, 1965.
3. Bonner JJ, Slavkin HC. Cleft palate susceptibility linked to histocompatibility-2 (H-2) in the mouse. Immunogenetics **2**:213–218, 1975.
4. Melnick M, Jaskoll T, Slavkin HC. Corticosteroid induced cleft palate in mice and H-2 haplotype: Maternal and embryonic effects. Immunogenetics **13**:443–449, 1981.
5. Pinsky L, DiGeorge AM. Cleft palate in the mouse: A teratogenic index of glucocorticoid potency. Science **147**:87–88, 1965.

6. Bonner JJ, Tyan ML. Backcross test demonstrates the linkage of glucocorticosteroid induced cleft palate susceptibility to H-2. Teratology **26**:213–216, 1982.
7. Badr FM, Spickett SG. Genetic variation in the biosynthesis of corticosteroids in *Mus musculus*. Nature **205**:1088–1090, 1965.
8. Spackman DH, Riley V. Corticosterone concentrations in the mouse. Science **200**:87, 1978.
9. Hackman RM, Brown KS. Corticosterone-induced isolated cleft palate in A/J mice. Teratology **6**:313–316, 1972.
10. Heiberg K, Kalter H, Fraser FC. Production of cleft palates in the offspring of mice treated with ACTH during pregnancy. Biol Neonat **1**:33–37, 1959.
11. Brown KS, Johnston MC, Niswander JD. Isolated cleft palate in mice after transportation during gestation. Teratology **5**:119–124, 1972.
12. Glick D, Von Redlich D, Levine S. Fluorometric determination of corticosterone and cortisol in 0.02–0.05 milliliters of plasma or submilligram samples of adrenal tissue. Endocrinology **74**:653–655, 1964.
13. Sokol RR, Rohlf FJ. Biometry. San Francisco, Freeman, 2nd ed, 1981.
14. Mostellar F, Youtz C. Tables of the Freeman–Tukey transformation for the binomial and poisson distributions. Biometrika **48**:433–440, 1961.
15. Tyan ML, Miller KK. Genetic and environmental factors in cortisone induced cleft palate. Proc Soc Exp Biol Med **158**:618–621, 1978.
16. Bonner JJ, Tyan ML. Glucocorticoid-induced cleft palate in the mouse: Two major histocompatibility complex, H-2, loci with different mechanisms. Genetics **103**:263–270, 1983.
17. Salomon DS, Gift VD, Pratt RM. Corticosterone levels during midgestation in the maternal plasma and fetus of cleft palate-sensitive and -resistant mice. Endocrinology **104**:154–156, 1979.
18. Barlow SM, McElhatton PR, Sullivan FM. The relation between maternal restraint and food deprivation, plasma corticosterone, and induction of cleft palate in the offspring of mice. Teratology **12**:97–104, 1976.
19. Eleftheriou BE, Bailey DW. Genetic analysis of plasma corticosterone levels in two inbred strains of mice. J Endocrinol **55**:415–420, 1972.
20. Levine S, Treiman DM. Differential plasma corticosterone response to stress in four inbred strains of mice. Endocrinology **75**:142–144, 1964.
21. Barlow SM, McElhatton PR, Morrison P, Sullivan FM. Effects of stress during pregnancy on plasma corticosterone levels and fetal development in the mouse. J Physiol Soc **239**:55P–56P, 1974.
22. Barlow SM, Quyyumi AA, Rajaratham DV, Sullivan FM. Effects of stress and adrenocorticotrophin administration on plasma corticosterone levels at different stages of pregnancy in the mouse. Experientia **32**:1480–1481, 1976.
23. Bonner JJ, Tyan ML. Cleft palate susceptibility maps in two H-2 subregion, H-2K to I-B and G to H-2D. J Immunogenet **9**:243–248, 1982.
24. Keller SE, Weiss JM, Schleifer SJ, Miller NE, Stein M. Stress-induced suppression of immunity in adrenalectomized rats. Science **221**:1301–1304, 1983.
25. Risch SC, Kalin NH, Janowsky DS, Cohen RM, Pickar D, Murphy DL. Co-release of ACTH and β-endorphin immunoreactivity in human subjects in response to central cholinergic stimulation. Science **222**:77, 1983.
26. Monjan AA, Collector MI. Stress-induced modulation of the immune response. Science **196**:307–308, 1977.

Received May 24, 1983. P.S.E.B.M. 1984, Vol. 176.
Accepted January 17, 1984.

PROCEEDINGS OF THE SOCIETY FOR EXPERIMENTAL BIOLOGY AND MEDICINE **176**, 22–26 (1984)

Effect of Perfusate pH on Coronary Flow and Adenosine Release in Isolated Rabbit Heart[1,2] (41836)

S. JAMAL MUSTAFA[3] AND M. MAHY MANSOUR[4]

Department of Pharmacology, School of Medicine, East Carolina University, Greenville, North Carolina 27834

Abstract. This study was undertaken in an attempt to further understand the relationship between adenosine and H^+ ion. Using Langendorff hearts from male rabbits, the perfusion fluid pH was lowered from 7.4 to 7.1 and 6.8 with CO_2. A 31 and 86% increase in coronary flow with a simultaneous increase in the release of adenosine by 61 and 128% was observed at pH 7.1 and 6.8, respectively. A direct relationship between adenosine release and coronary flow with a correlation coefficient of 0.99 was found at pH values of 7.4, 7.1, and 6.8. The degradation products of adenosine namely inosine and hypoxanthine were unchanged at 7.1 and 6.8 from 7.4. These data support a role for adenosine in the regulation of coronary flow and suggest a relationship between adenosine and H^+ ion.

Adenosine, a vasoactive metabolite plays an important role in the physiological regulation of coronary blood flow (1). Several investigators (2–4) support the view that cations such as hydrogen ion and potassium ion may influence the adenosine-induced increases in coronary flow. Additionally, adenosine antagonists (theophylline and aminophylline) have been reported (5–11) to partially attenuate the reactive hyperemia which occurs subsequent to the release of coronary inflow occlusion. However, similar concentrations of these adenosine antagonists have been reported (5) to abolish the increase in flow responses to exogenous adenosine. Further, a decrease in pH (12, 13) along with the release of adenosine (9–11, 14) have been observed during myocardial ischemia. These investigations suggest that the response to adenosine may be modified by other factors during ischemic insult and perhaps this is the reason why the concentration of adenosine antagonists which effectively inhibit the response to exogenous adenosine are unable to block reactive hyperemia completely.

Recently, we have reported (15) that the lowering of perfusion fluid pH from 7.4 to 6.8 can significantly inhibit the uptake of adenosine. Thus, this investigation was an attempt to test the hypothesis that lowering of the perfusion pH can inhibit the myocardial uptake of adenosine leading to an increased release of adenosine in the perfusate. Therefore, we measured the release of adenosine by altering the pH of the perfusion solution from 7.4 to 7.1 and 6.8 with a simultaneous measurement of coronary flow from rabbit heart using the Langendorff preparation.

Methods. Hearts from rabbits, 1–1.5 kg, of local strain were quickly excised and perfused through the cannulation of the aorta using a Krebs–Ringer bicarbonate buffer containing (in m*M*): glucose, 5.5; pyruvate, 2.0; NaCl, 127.5; KCl, 4.7; $CaCl_2$, 2.5; KH_2PO_4, 1.2; and $NaHCO_3$, 24.9. The perfusion fluid was maintained at 37°C and equilibrated with 95% O_2 + 5% CO_2 (pH 7.4). The perfusion pressure was maintained at a height of 65 cm of H_2O throughout the experiment. Changes in the pH of the perfusion solution were maintained by changing the proportions of O_2 and CO_2 to give the desired pH. The concentration of CO_2 required (<10%) to change the pH to 7.1 and 6.8 was not enough to induce hypoxia and therefore change the coronary flow and adenosine release.

The aortic inflow rate, which equals to the total coronary flow was monitored with an electromagnetic flow meter (Biotronex model BL-610), the flow probe was interposed in the perfusion line several centimeters above the heart. The flow transducer was connected to

[1] Supported by HL 27339.

[2] This work was conducted at the University of South Alabama Medical School, Mobile, Ala.

[3] To whom reprint requests should be addressed.

[4] Present address: Department of Physiology, Faculty of Medicine, Al-Azhar, University, Cairo, Egypt.

0037-9727/84 $1.50

a polygraph (Beckman model R411) for a continuous recording of the total mean coronary flow. The apex of the heart was connected by means of a thread to a force displacement transducer (Grass FT .03) and connected to a physiograph for continuous recording of the rate and force of contraction.

An initial 30-min period was allowed for the stabilization of the heart before actual experimentation. The control response for flow, heart rate, and contractions were recorded. A period of 10 min was allowed after each change in the pH of the perfusion fluid to achieve maximal effect before collecting the subsequent 10-min samples of the perfusate from the heart. Changes in coronary flow, heart rate, and force of contraction were recorded. The preparation was checked for its autoregulatory response. A 30-sec occlusion of inflow resulted in more than twofold increase in coronary flow at the release of occlusion. The samples were analyzed for adenosine, inosine, and hypoxanthine according to the method described by Watkinson *et al.* (16) using enzymatic analysis and recording the absorbance changes on dual-wave length, double-beam spectrophotometer (Aminco model DW-2). Student's *t* test was used for the level of significance and the results are expressed as the mean ± SE.

Results and Discussion. The results show an increased release of adenosine when the hydrogen ion concentration is raised in perfusion medium. Figure 1 shows the release of

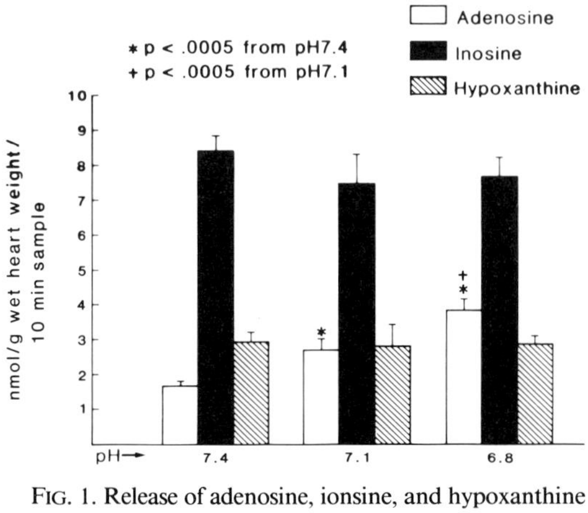

FIG. 1. Release of adenosine, ionsine, and hypoxanthine in the perfusates of isolated rabbit hearts at pH values of 7.4, 7.1, and 6.8. The values are represented as means ± SE from 10–17 different experiments.

adenosine, inosine, and hypoxanthine at pH values of 7.4, 7.1, and 6.8. The amount of adenosine released into the perfusate increased from a control value of 1.68 ± 0.17 nmole/g wet weight/10 min of collected sample at a pH of 7.4 to 2.7 ± 0.29 nmole/g wet weight/10 min at pH 7.1, a 60% rise. This value was raised to 128% (3.83 ± 0.36 nmole/g wet weight/10 min) from its control value by changing the pH to 6.8 using CO_2. On the other hand the concentrations of inosine and hypoxanthine in the coronary perfusates were unchanged. Further, the sum of adenosine, inosine, and hypoxanthine was unchanged at pH 7.1 but slightly higher (insignificant) at pH 6.8 from pH 7.4. It has been reported (1) that the dephosphorylation of adenosine-5′-monophosphate is the major pathway for the production of adenosine, therefore, the expected changes will take place in the intracellular adenine nucleotide pool if the activities of nucleoside phosphorylase and xanthine oxidase are unaltered at various pH values and not in the sum of perfusate adenosine, inosine, and hypoxanthine. Our data support this view. The values reported here for adenosine and its degradative products are similar to those reported by Fredholm *et al.* (17) using isolated rabbit hearts. The concentration of adenosine at pH 6.8 was significantly higher than the concentration at pH 7.1 and 7.4.

Figure 2 shows the relationship between adenosine release, coronary flow, and pH changes. Using adenosine release (nmole/g wet heart weight/10 min sample) or coronary flow (ml/min/g wet heart weight) as *y* axis, and pH changes as *x* axis, a positive correlation ($r = 0.99$) was found at pH values of 7.4, 7.1, and 6.8. Also, a positive correlation ($r = 0.99$) was found between adenosine release (*x* axis) and coronary flow (*y* axis) at all the pH values (not shown). This is similar to the observation of several investigators (1, 16, 18, 19) where a direct relationship between adenosine release, coronary flow, and oxygen consumption has been reported. In our experiments, the heart rate was not altered during the pH changes. The force of myocardial contraction was not affected by lowering the pH to 7.1 but was significantly lower at pH 6.8. It has been reported (20, 21) that changes in myocardial contraction can affect the coronary blood flow. However, in our studies the degree

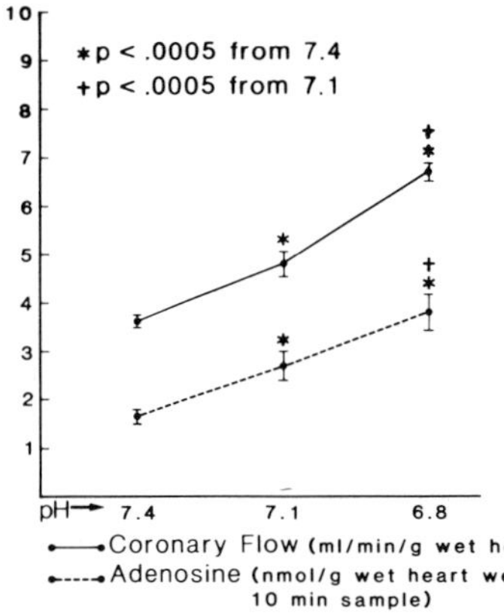

FIG. 2. Correlation between the release of adenosine or coronary flow from the rabbit hearts at pH values of 7.4, 7.1, and 6.8. The values are represented as means ± SE from 10–17 experiments. A correlation coefficient of 0.99 was found for adenosine release or coronary flow at different pH values.

of correlation between adenosine and coronary flow is 98% at all the pH values. It is unlikely that the changes in contractility caused the increase in coronary flow and adenosine release at pH 6.8. In fact, the decrease in myocardial contractility at pH 6.8 would be expected to lower the metabolic activity and therefore, decrease the release of adenosine. Further, the fact that the parallel increase in coronary flow and adenosine release at pH 7.1 was not accompanied by a change in contractility rules out its involvement in the observed increases in coronary flow.

Several investigators (2, 22–24) have studied the effect of H^+ ion concentration on the vascular response to adenosine but this is the first report where the actual release of adenosine has been measured at varying pH values. Degenring (23) using isolated guinea pig hearts studied the effect of acidosis and alkalosis in normoxic and hypoxic hearts with a simultaneous measurement of myocardial adenine nucleotides and nucleosides and coronary flow. He reported (23) a significant increase in coronary flow and myocardial adenosine both in normoxic and hypoxic hearts under acidosis (pH 7.0), whereas the reverse was true for alkalosis (pH 7.8). The pH in this case (23) was adjusted by using HCl or NaOH. Our data are in agreement with the studies of Degenring (23). However, on a quantitative basis, our data show an increase in coronary flow of 31% and an adenosine release of 61% at pH 7.1, whereas Degenring (23) found only an increase of 13% in coronary flow and an increase of 25% in tissue adenosine under normoxic conditions at pH 7.0. This is possibly due to the fact that the acidosis in our study was induced by increasing the CO_2 and in the study by Degenring (23) HCl was used to induce acidosis. It is likely that CO_2 has dual effects, indirectly by increasing the H^+ ion concentration and directly on the coronary vessels (25). However, it is quite possible that CO_2 has a better diffusibility due to the higher lipid solubility. In fact, this laboratory has reported (24) earlier that bovine large and small coronary vessels relaxed more when the pH of the media was adjusted by CO_2 rather than by adjusting the bicarbonate. In some of the experiments, where the acidosis was induced by HCl, the increase in coronary flow was less dramatic than with CO_2 (data not reported).

Degenring (23) in his studies measured the myocardial levels of adenosine during various experimental conditions. In the light of new information (26), more than 90% of adenosine in the tissue is intracellular and therefore, may not reflect the interstitial concentration of adenosine available at the resistance vessel site. In the present study, the amount of adenosine measured in perfusates is an appropriate reflection of interstitial concentration of adenosine available for vasodilation. There is a linear correlation between the amount of adenosine released into the perfusates and coronary flow at pH 7.4, 7.1, and 6.8. Our data, therefore, support a role for adenosine under varying H^+ ion concentrations. Similar results have recently been reported by Downing *et al.* (27), who showed an increased response in hypercapnic acidosis to exogenous adenosine both in normal and diabetic lambs and attributed these responses to changes in H^+ ion concentration.

This study supports our earlier observations (15) where we found an inhibition in the uptake of adenosine in cultured heart cells by increasing the H^+ ion concentration. In the earlier report (15), the pH changes were carried out using an acid or base. In this investigation the pH changes were carried out by altering the perfusate CO_2. This change in H^+ ion concentration would result in the inhibition in the uptake of adenosine (endogenous), thereby increasing its concentration in the extracellular fluid as reflected in perfusate adenosine concentrations and thus an increase in coronary flow. It is clear from these studies that increase in H^+ ion concentration whether induced by CO_2 or an acid (HCl) can inhibit the uptake of adenosine into the cardiac cells and thereby increase its extracellular concentration to which the resistance vessels are exposed. However, other possibilities such as the effect of increased CO_2 on the metabolism of adenosine in the heart, increased binding of adenosine to its receptor (28) or an interaction between H^+ ion and Ca^{2+} at the level of vascular smooth muscle cannot be ruled out from these studies.

In conclusion, the present study demonstrates that the lowering of the perfusate pH from 7.4 to 7.1 and 6.8 results in an increase in coronary flow with a simultaneous increase in the release of adenosine from the heart. These data provide an explanation as to why theophylline and aminophylline are unable to antagonize the reactive hyperemic response. This is due to the fact that in reactive hyperemia the added influence of acidosis leads to levels of adenosine higher than the blocking capacity of antagonist. However, adenosine antagonists at similar concentrations can inhibit the response to exogenous adenosine due to the absence of acidosis (5–8). The data further support a role for adenosine in the regulation of coronary flow and suggest a relationship between adenosine and H^+ ion. The exact nature of this relationship is not known and needs further investigation.

The authors express their appreciation to Mrs. Linda Pope for typing this manuscript.

1. Berne RM. The role of adenosine in the regulation of coronary blood flow. Circ Res **47**:807–813, 1980.
2. Merrill GF, Haddy FJ, Dabney JM. Adenosine, theophylline, and perfusate pH in the isolated, perfused guinea pig heart. Circ Res **42**:225–229, 1978.
3. Young MA, Merrill GF. Differential effects of adenosine and hypoxia on potassium-induced dilation in the isolated, perfused guinea pig heart. Blood Vessels **19**:292–300, 1982.
4. Merrill GF, Young MA, Tozzi CA, Grosso PC, Marcus KM. Adenosine coronary vasodilation and sympathetic adrenergic vasoconstriction during altered CO_2. Artery **10**:395–411, 1982.
5. Afonso S, Ansfield TJ, Berndt TB. Coronary vasodilatation responses to hypoxia before and after aminophylline. J Physiol (London) **221**:589–599, 1972.
6. Bittar N, Pauly TJ. Myocardial reactive hyperemia responses in the dog after aminophylline and lidoflazine. Amer J Physiol **220**:812–815, 1971.
7. Eiken E, Wilcken DEL. Myocardial reactive hyperemia in conscious dogs: Effect of dipyridamole and aminophylline on responses to four and eight seconds coronary artery occlusion. Aust J Exp Biol Med Sci **51**:617–630, 1973.
8. Eikens E, Wilcken DEL. The effect of dipyridamole and aminophylline on responses to sixty-second coronary artery occlusion in dogs. Aust J Exp Med Sci **51**:631–642, 1973.
9. Olsson RA. Changes in content of purine nucleosides in canine myocardium during coronary occlusion. Circ Res **26**:301–306, 1970.
10. Olsson RA, Snow JA, Gentry MK. Adenosine metabolism in canine myocardial reactive hyperemia. Circ Res **42**:358–362, 1978.
11. Rubio R, Berne RM, Katori M. Release of adenosine in reactive hyperemia of the dog heart. Amer J Physiol **216**:56–62, 1969.
12. Eichenhoff JE, Hafkenshiel JH, Landmesser CM. The coronary circulation in the dog. Amer J Physiol **148**:582–596, 1947.
13. Scott JB, Radawski D. Role of hyperosmolarity in the genesis of active and reactive hyperemia. Circ Res **28**(Suppl 1):26–32, 1971.
14. Raberger B, Schultz W, Kraupp O. Coronary reactive hyperemia and coronary dilator action of adenosine during normal respiration and hypercapnic acidosis in the dog. Clin Exp Pharmacol Physiol **2**:373–382, 1975.
15. Mustafa SJ. Effect of varying pH (H^+) on the metabolism of adenosine in isolated heart cells. J Mol Cell Cardiol **12**:335–346, 1980.
16. Watkinson WP, Foley DH, Rubio R, Berne RM. Myocardial adenosine formation with increased cardiac performance in the dog. Amer J Physiol **236**:H13–H21, 1979.
17. Fredholm BB, Hedquist P, Vernet L. Release of adenosine from the rabbit heart by sympathetic nerve stimulation. Acta Physiol Scand **106**:381–382, 1979.
18. Berne RM, Foley DH, Watkinson WP, Wayne L, Miller H, Winn R, Rubio R. Role of adenosine as a mediator of metabolic vasodilation in the heart and brain: A brief overview and update. In Baer HP, Drummond GI, ed. Physiological and Regulatory Functions of Adenosine and Adenine Nucleotides. New York, Raven Press, pp117–126, 1979.
19. Miller WL, Belardinelli L, Bacchus A, Foley DH, Rubio R, Berne RM. Canine myocardial adenosine and lactate production, oxygen consumption and coronary blood flow during stellate ganglia stimulation. Circ Res **45**:708–718, 1979.

20. Gregg DE. Coronary circulation in health and disease. Philadelphia, Pa., Lea & Febiger, 1950.
21. Sabiston DC Jr, Gregg DE. Effect of cardiac contraction on coronary blood flow. Circulation **15**:14–20, 1957.
22. Molnar JI, Scott JB, Frohlich ED, Haddy FJ. Local effects of various anions and H^+ on dog limb and coronary vascular resistances. Amer J Physiol **203**:125–132, 1962.
23. Degenring FH. The effect of acidosis and alkalosis on coronary flow and cardiac nucleotide metabolism. Basic Res Cardiol **71**:287–290, 1976.
24. Mustafa SJ, Ghai G. Effect of adenosine on the relaxation of coronary arteries at varying pH values. Basic Res Cardiol **76**:380–386, 1981.
25. Turnheim K, Pittner H, Kolassa N, Kraupp O. Relaxation of coronary artery strips by adenosine and acidosis. Eur J Pharmacol **41**:217–220, 1977.
26. Olsson RA, Saito D, Steinhart CR. Compartmentalization of the adenosine pool of dog and rat hearts. Circ Res **50**:617–626, 1982.
27. Downing SE, Lee JC, Weinstein EM. Coronary dilator actions of adenosine and CO_2 in experimental diabetes. Amer J Physiol **243**:H252–H258, 1982.
28. Dutta P, Mustafa SJ. Binding of adenosine to the crude plasma membrane fraction isolated from dog coronary and carotid arteries. J Pharmacol Exp Ther **214**:496–502, 1980.

Received July 5, 1983. P.S.E.B.M. 1984, Vol. 176.
Accepted January 24, 1984.

PROCEEDINGS OF THE SOCIETY FOR EXPERIMENTAL BIOLOGY AND MEDICINE **176**, 27–31 (1984)

Evidence for Increased Peroxidative Activity in Muscles from Streptozotocin–Diabetic Rats[1] (41837)

CAROL J. LAMMI-KEEFE,[2] P. B. SWAN, AND P. V. J. HEGARTY

Department of Food Science and Nutrition, University of Minnesota, St. Paul, Minnesota 55108

Abstract. The ability of cardiac and skeletal muscles from diabetic rats to metabolize superoxide and hydrogen peroxide was determined by the activities of superoxide dismutase (SOD) and catalase, respectively. Male and female Sprague–Dawley rats, 43 days old, were made diabetic with a single intravenous injection of streptozotocin (70 mg/kg body weight). On the 80th day after injection the blood glucose concentration of these rats was increased fourfold, and the plasma insulin concentration was decreased four- to fivefold compared to controls. Body weights of male diabetic rats were 61% and those of female diabetic rats were 66% of their *ad libitum*-fed controls. The seven different skeletal muscles examined weighed less in the diabetic rats than in controls of the same age and body weight. The hearts of the diabetic rats weighed more than those of controls of the same age and body weight. Comparison to the body weight controls allowed the distinction of specific effects due to lack of insulin from effects due to retardation in muscle growth. Increased catalase activity in all muscles examined from diabetic rats (plantaris, gastrocnemius, and heart) suggested a response in catalase activity similar to that of starved rats. SOD activity was not altered in the diabetic rat skeletal muscles and erythrocytes, but was somewhat decreased in the heart.

The importance of superoxide dismutase (SOD) and catalase in controlling tissue levels of potentially toxic superoxide radicals and hydrogen peroxide has been emphasized (1, 2). The presence of highly reactive forms of oxygen in cells can lead to disruption of cellular functions and damage to membranes. SOD and catalase have been studied extensively in red blood cells (3–5), lung (6), and liver (7–9). These enzymes appear to be central to the defense of the cell against oxidative damage. Their role in skeletal muscle is less well studied. However, both enzymes are present in muscle (10) and it is assumed that their role in this tissue is similar to that demonstrated in other tissues. Catalase is located primarily in peroxisomes in liver (11) and appears to be located in microperoxisomes in both cardiac (12) and skeletal muscles (13). SOD is located in mitochondria and in the cytosol in liver (14).

The metabolism and morphology of skeletal muscles in diabetic and starved animals is similar in many respects. Decreased utilization of glucose (15, 16), increased utilization of fatty acids and ketones (15, 17, 18), lighter muscle weights, or fewer muscle fibers (19–21) have been observed in both conditions. There is increased catalase activity in muscles from starved animals (10, 22), but catalase activity in muscles of diabetic animals has not been reported previously. In a short-term experiment, Horie *et al.* (23) have reported an increase in the peroxisomal β-oxidation of fatty acids in livers from alloxan-diabetic rats, but the catalase activity in these livers was unaltered 7 days after injection of alloxan. Certain tissues from streptozotocin-treated rats have been reported to have decreased SOD activity compared with *ad libitum*-fed controls (24, 25). This is in contrast to the unchanged SOD activity in muscles of starved rats (10).

The similarity in muscle metabolism during the starved and diabetic states coupled with the observation that muscle catalase activity increases during starvation suggested that catalase activity might be increased in diabetes. If so, this finding could add to an understanding of the changes occurring in muscles in response to a lack of insulin. The experiment

[1] Supported in part by the Science and Education Administration of the U.S. Department of Agriculture under Grant 5901-0410-8-0014-0 from the Competitive Grants Office.

[2] Present address: Department of Nutritional Sciences, University of Connecticut, Storrs, Conn. 06268.

0037-9727/84 $1.50

reported here was designed to test the hypothesis that catalase activity would be increased in the diabetic state and that this increase was specific to the lack of insulin and not simply due to the retardation in growth observed in the young diabetic rats.

Materials and Methods. Male and female Sprague–Dawley rats born in our laboratory were divided into four groups of six males and six females each. A baseline control group was killed at the beginning of the experiment when the rats were 43 days old, and muscles and organs were weighed. The other groups were: nondiabetic rats fed *ad libitum,* diabetic animals fed *ad libitum,* and weight-paired control animals whose food intake was restricted so that their body weights matched those of diabetic animals. All rats were housed individually and fed a commercial cereal based diet (Ralston Purina, St. Louis, Mo.). The room lighting cycle consisted of 12 hr of light and 12 hr of dark. Lights were on from 1900 hr until 0700 hr.

Rats were made diabetic at the start of the experiment (43 days of age, 188 g body weight) with a single intravenous injection of streptozotocin (70 mg/kg body weight) (Sigma Chemicals, St. Louis, Mo.). Polydypsia, polyuria, and polyphagia, as well as blood glucose and insulin levels (Table I), were diagnostic indicators of diabetes. Control animals were sham-injected with a solution of 5% dextrose in 0.9% saline. Eighty days after streptozotocin injections, blood was collected from nonfasted rats at 0800 to 1000 hr by heart puncture under ether anesthesia, and the animals were killed by carbon dioxide. Seven skeletal muscles (biceps brachii, sternomastoideus, soleus, plantaris, gastrocnemius, extensor digitorum longus, and tibialis anterior) and the heart were dissected, weighed, and stored in ice until dissections were completed. These seven skeletal muscles were chosen so that there was at least one muscle from the forelimb, hindlimb, and trunk. Thus, an indication of the effect of diabetes on muscles throughout the body was obtained. The gastrointestinal tracts were removed and weighed to determine empty body weights to correct for the substantial intestinal contents of polyphagic, diabetic animals. Blood glucose estimations were made from frozen plasma samples by the glucose 6-phosphate dehydrogenase method (26), and insulin levels were measured by the radioimmunoassay method of Hales and Randle (27).

Enzyme activities were determined im-

TABLE I. BODY AND ORGAN WEIGHTS, PLASMA GLUCOSE, AND INSULIN LEVELS IN CONTROL AND DIABETIC MALE AND FEMALE RATS

	Start	Weight control		Diabetic		*Ad libitum*-fed control
Males						
Body wt (g)						
Whole	188 ± 17	279 ± 10	NS	280 ± 18	<0.01	393 ± 8
Empty	169 ± 16	259 ± 10	NS	225 ± 20	<0.01	366 ± 8
Glucose (mg%)		143 ± 11	<0.01	595 ± 21	<0.01	171 ± 19
Insulin (U/ml)		64 ± 10	<0.01	17 ± 4	<0.01	93 ± 20
Heart (g)	0.65 ± 0.04	0.87 ± 0.04	<0.05	1.12 ± 0.10	NS	1.20 ± 0.03
Plantaris (mg)	178 ± 25	306 ± 16	<0.05	223 ± 23	<0.01	421 ± 12
Gastrocnemius (mg)	966 ± 125	1649 ± 56	<0.05	1164 ± 123	<0.01	2155 ± 52
Females						
Body wt (g)						
Whole	145 ± 5	203 ± 10	NS	195 ± 12	<0.01	245 ± 5
Empty	131 ± 5	183 ± 9	NS	155 ± 11	<0.01	234 ± 2
Glucose (mg%)		124 ± 4	<0.01	629 ± 30	<0.01	149 ± 8
Insulin (U/ml)		42 ± 11	NS	13 ± 2	<0.01	74 ± 12
Heart (g)	0.56 ± 0.02	0.67 ± 0.02	<0.05	0.80 ± 0.04	NS	0.84 ± 0.02
Plantaris (mg)	135 ± 4	245 ± 18	<0.05	177 ± 17	<0.01	295 ± 8
Gastrocnemius (mg)	720 ± 33	1266 ± 35	<0.01	867 ± 77	<0.01	1509 ± 37

Note. Data are expressed as means ± SEM. Each value represents the mean of six animals. Statistical comparisons are made between the diabetic group and the weight control and *ad libitum*-fed control groups using Student's *t* test (38).

mediately following tissue dissections. Methods for tissue preparations are described elsewhere (10). Assay procedures for catalase and SOD were those of Baudhuin *et al.* (28) and Misra and Fridovich (29), respectively. Blood samples for each group of rats were pooled and centrifuged at 4°C, 1000*g* for 10 min. The packed blood cells were washed once with an equal volume of cold 0.9% saline and recentrifuged. Three milliliters of cold water was added to 3 ml of packed blood cells and the blood cells were lysed in an ice bath for 2 h with gentle stirring. Catalase activity was determined in 300 μl of this lysate. To the remaining 5.7 ml was added 2.4 ml of a mixture of chloroform:ethanol (3:5) at 0°C to precipitate the hemoglobin, followed by 0.9 ml of cold water, with mixing. This mixture was centrifuged for 10 min at 1000*g* and the supernatant removed for SOD assay (30).

Results. Body weights of the diabetic male and female rats were significantly less than the *ad libitum*-fed control group (Table I). Glucose levels were elevated and insulin levels were low in the diabetic rats when compared with either control group (Table I), thus confirming their diabetic state.

Weight of the retroperitoneal fat pad was less in the diabetic rats when compared to either control group. Weight of the heart in the diabetic rats was the same as that in the *ad libitum*-fed controls, but larger than the weight-paired controls. Each of the seven skeletal muscles from the streptozotocin-induced diabetic rats weighed less than the corresponding muscle from the weight-paired control rats despite the similarity in body weight (unpublished data). The weights of the plantaris and gastrocnemius muscles are given in Table I. The weights of the liver and kidneys were significantly greater in the diabetic rats when compared to either control group (unpublished data).

Catalase activity in muscles from diabetic rats was significantly higher than in nondiabetic animals, *ad libitum*-fed (Table II). When the comparison is made with the nondiabetic body weight control group the elevation in catalase activity due to diabetes was significant in the plantaris muscle. Catalase activity in muscles from the weight control group was not different from that in muscles from the *ad libitum* control group. Catalase activity in erythrocytes was similar in all three groups (unpublished data). This observation is in agreement with a recent study on children with insulin-dependent diabetes mellitus which showed no change in erythrocyte catalase (31).

SOD activity remained unchanged in the plantaris and gastrocnemius muscles of the diabetic rat (Table II). There was a slight decrease in SOD activity in the hearts of diabetic rats. The downward trends in SOD activity

TABLE II. CATALASE AND SUPEROXIDE DISMUTASE ACTIVITIES IN THE MUSCLES AND ERYTHROCYTES OF STREPTOZOTOCIN-DIABETIC RATS AND CONTROL RATS

Tissue	Weight control		Diabetic		*Ad libitum*-fed control
			Catalase[a,b]		
Heart	47.1 ± 1.2	NS	88.4 ± 10.9	<0.05	39.7 ± 9.0
Plantaris	6.2 ± 0.8	<0.05	17.2 ± 1.8	<0.05	4.1 ± 0.6
Gastrocnemius	6.0 ± 1.5	NS	14.6 ± 0.2	<0.05	4.2 ± 0.6
			Superoxide Dismutase[a,c]		
Heart	179.6 ± 3.6	NS	125.7 ± 5.8	<0.05	202.3 ± 6.1
Plantaris	33.1 ± 4.3	NS	34.6 ± 9.2	NS	50.4 ± 4.7
Gastrocnemius	49.6 ± 7.3	NS	46.6 ± 6.6	NS	46.3 ± 6.9

Note. Data are expressed as means ± SEM.

[a] Each determination represents a pool of two to three muscles or pooled blood from two to three rats. There was one female group and one male group. Because enzyme activities did not differ between males and females, these were combined and the paired *t* test used to determine the statistical significance of the differences (38).

[b] μg eq/g wet tissue weight ($\times 10^{-1}$).

[c] μg eq/g wet tissue weight.

in the erythrocytes from the diabetic rats in the present study was similar to that observed in erythrocytes from children with insulin-dependent diabetes mellitus (31).

Discussion. It has been suggested that increased catalase activity in skeletal muscles reflects muscle wasting (22). However, the diabetic rats in the present study did not lose weight, they simply failed to gain at the usual rate. Yet, the catalase activity in their muscles was elevated, whereas, the catalase activity in muscles from rats similarly restricted in growth (due to food restriction) was not different from *ad libitum*-fed controls. Thus, the elevated catalase activity was not a response to muscle wasting (loss of muscle) but, as we have suggested previously (10), was more likely a reflection of altered energy metabolism in diabetic muscles (15, 16). Muscle catalase activity is elevated in response to feeding hypolipidemic drugs (32) and diets high in fat (33). Under these conditions, as well as during starvation and diabetes, relative utilization of fatty acids as a source of energy is increased in muscles.

Assuming that muscle catalase is located in microperoxisomes as has been suggested by others (12, 34), its increased activity may reflect increased activity of the hydrogen peroxide-generating fatty acyl CoA oxidase that initiates the β-oxidation of fatty acids in peroxisomes (35). Hence, our data suggest that microperoxisomes in muscle may play an important role in the adaptation of muscle to the lack of insulin.

Matkovics (24) has reported decreased SOD activity in heart, an undesignated skeletal muscle, and red blood cell hemolysates from streptozotocin-diabetic rats. In the present study there was no change in SOD activity in the gastrocnemius or the plantaris but a slight decrease in the cardiac muscle. Earlier studies indicated that muscle SOD was unchanged during short-term starvation (10). Thus, the effects of diabetes and starvation on SOD activity in muscles are less than the effects on catalase activity. However, the SOD activity in muscle should probably be investigated more thoroughly, including measurements of the total activity in mitochondria versus that in the sarcoplasm. For example, should there be an alteration in the activity of mitochondrial SOD, this may be difficult to observe unless the muscle is carefully fractionated to quantitatively recover the mitochondria in the fraction being assayed for enzyme activity and to separate this fraction from the sarcoplasmic fraction that also contains SOD (14).

Crouch *et al.* (36) reported a direct effect of streptozotocin on SOD activity. It is unlikely that the lack of response in SOD activity in this experiment was due to such a direct effect because streptozotocin has a short half-life in tissues (37). The tissues in the present experiment were assayed 80 days after the injection of streptozotocin. The lack of a change in SOD activity in skeletal muscles of diabetic rats is in keeping with the observations in starved rats. In 12-month-old rats, which were starved until they lost 39% of their body weight, SOD activity was unchanged in both heart and skeletal muscles (10).

We favor the idea that an increase in muscle catalase activity is reflecting a change in fatty acid metabolism due to a lack of insulin. This may be due to changes in the availability of fatty acids to muscles in the diabetic animal, or to alterations in the pathways for fatty acid oxidation.

1. Michelson AM, Puget K, Durosay P, Bonneau JC. Clinical aspects of the dosage of erythrocuprein. In: Michelson AM, McCord JM, Fridovich I, eds. Superoxide and Superoxide Dismutases. New York, Academic Press, pp467–499, 1977.
2. Del Maestro RF. An approach to free radicals in medicine and biology. Acta Physiol Scand Suppl **492:**153–168, 1980.
3. Nicholls P. Contributions of catalase and glutathione peroxidase to red cell peroxide removal. Biochim Biophys Acta **279:**306–309, 1972.
4. Bartosz G, Tannert Ch, Fried R, Leyko W. Superoxide dismutase activity decreases during erythrocyte aging. Experientia **34:**1464, 1978.
5. Das SK, Rajagopalan CN. Superoxide dismutase, glutathione peroxidase, catalase and lipid peroxidation of normal and sickled erythrocytes. Brit J Haematol **44:**87–92, 1980.
6. Crapo JD, Tierney DF. Superoxide dismutase and pulmonary oxygen toxicity. Amer J Physiol **226:**1041–1047, 1974.
7. Fahimi HD. Cytochemical localization of peroxidative activity of catalase in rat hepatic microbodies (peroxisomes). J Cell Biol **43:**278–288, 1969.
8. Lazarow PB, deDuve C. The synthesis and turnover of rat liver peroxisomes. V. Intracellular pathway of catalase synthesis. J Cell Biol **59:**507–524, 1973.
9. Reiss U, Gershon D. Rat-liver superoxide dismutase. Eur J Biochem **63:**617–623, 1976.
10. Lammi-Keefe CJ, Hegarty PVJ, Swan PB. Effect of

starvation and refeeding on catalase and superoxide dismutase activities in skeletal and cardiac muscles from 12-month-old rats. Experientia **37**:25–26, 1981.
11. deDuve C, Baudhuin P. Peroxisomes (microbodies and related particles). Physiol Rev **46**:323–357, 1966.
12. Herzog V, Fahimi MD. Microbodies (peroxisomes) containing catalase in myocardium: Morphological and biochemical evidence. Science **185**:271–273, 1974.
13. Hand AR. Peroxisomes (microbodies) in striated muscle cells. J Histochem Cytochem **22**:207–209, 1974.
14. Weisiger RA, Fridovich I. Superoxide dismutase: Organelle specificity. J Biol Chem **248**:3582–3592, 1973.
15. Randle PJ, Garland PB, Hales CN, Newsholme EA, Denton RM, Pogson CI. Interactions of metabolism and the physiological role in insulin. Rec Progr Horm Res **22**:1–44, 1966.
16. Ruderman NB, Goodman MN, Conover CA, Berger M. Substrate utilization in perfused skeletal muscle. Diabetes **28**(Suppl 1):13–17, 1979.
17. Hagenfeldt L, Wahren J. Human forearm metabolism during exercise. vi. Substrate utilization in prolonged fasting. Scand J Clin Lab Invest **27**:299–306, 1971.
18. Ruderman NB, Houghton CRS, Hems R. Evolution of the isolated perfused rat hindquarter for the study of muscle metabolism. Biochem J **124**:639–651, 1971.
19. Armstrong RB, Gollnick PD, Ianuzzo CD. Histochemical properties of skeletal muscle fibers in streptozotocin-diabetic rats. Cell Tissue Res **162**:387–394, 1975.
20. Layman DK, Swan PB, Hegarty PVJ. The effect of acute dietary restriction on muscle fibre number in weanling rats. Brit J Nutr **45**:475–481, 1981.
21. Hegarty PVJ, Rosholt MN. Effect of streptozotocin-induced diabetes on the number and diameter of fibers in different skeletal muscles of the rat. J Anat **133**:205–211, 1981.
22. Stauber WT, Bird JWC, Schottelius BA. Catalase: An enzymatic indicator of the degree of muscle wasting. Exp Neurol **55**:381–389, 1977.
23. Horie S, Ishii H, Suga T. Changes in peroxisomal fatty acid oxidation in the diabetic rat liver. J Biochem **90**:1691–1696, 1981.
24. Matkovics B. Effects of plant and animal tissue lesions on superoxide dismutase activities. In: Michelson AM, McCord JM, Fridovich I, eds. Superoxide and Superoxide Dismutases. New York, Academic Press, pp501–515, 1977.
25. Crouch R, Kimsey G, Priest DG, Sarda A, Buse MG. Effect of streptozotocin on erythrocyte and retinal superoxide dismutase. Diabetologia **15**:53–57, 1978.
26. Carroll JJ, Smith N, Babson AL. A colorimetric serum glucose determination using hexokinase and glucose-6-phosphate dehydrogenase. Biochem Med **4**:171–180, 1970.
27. Hales CN, Randle PJ. Immunoassay of insulin with insulin antibody precipitate. Biochem J **88**:137–146, 1963.
28. Baudhuin P, Beaufay H, Rahmen-Li Y, Sellinger OZ, Wattiaux R, Jacques P, deDuve C. Tissue fractionation studies: 17, Intracellular distribution of monoamine oxidase, aspartate aminotransferase, alanine aminotransferase, D-amino acid oxidase and catalase in rat liver tissue. Biochem J **92**:179–184, 1964.
29. Misra HP, Fridovich I. Superoxide dismutase: A photochemical augmentation assay. Arch Biochem Biophys **181**:308–312, 1977.
30. Michelson AM, Puget K, Durosay P, Bonneau JC. Clinical aspects of the dosage of erythrocuprein. In: Michelson AM, McCord JM, Fridovich, I, eds. Superoxide and Superoxide Dismutases. New York, Academic Press, pp467–499, 1977.
31. Hagglof B, Marklund SL, Holmgren G. CuZn superoxide dismutase, Mn superoxide dismutase, catalase and glutathione peroxidase in lymphocytes and erythrocytes in insulin dependent diabetic children. Acta Endocrinol (Copenhagen) **102**:235–239, 1983.
32. Behrens MI, Soza MA, Inestrosa NC. Increase of muscle peroxisomal enzymes and myotonia induced by sodium senopin, a hypolipidemic drug. Muscle Nerve **6**:154–159, 1983.
33. O'Brien NM, Hsu M-H, Park JHY, Hegarty PVJ, Swan PB. Differential response to meal feeding and subsequent starvation on catalase activity in muscles from rats fed fat-free, high saturated or high polyunsaturated fat diets. J Nutr **112,** xxx, Abstr, 1982.
34. Christie KN, Steward PJ. Catalase in skeletal muscle fibers. J Histochem Cytochem **27**:814–819, 1979.
35. Osumi T, Hashimoto T. Acyl-CoA oxidase of rat liver: A new enzyme for fatty acid oxidation. Biochem Biophys Res Commun **83**:479–485, 1978.
36. Crouch RK, Gandy SE, Kimsey G, Galbraith RA, Galbraith GMP, Buse MG. The inhibition of islet superoxide dismutase by diabetogenic drugs. Diabetes **30**:235–241, 1981.
37. Bhuyar BK, Kuentzel SL, Gray LG, Frazer TJ, Wallach D, Neil GL. Tissue distribution of streptozotocin. Cancer Chemother Rep **58**:157–165, 1974.
38. Daniel WW. Biostatistics: A Foundation for Analysis in the Health Sciences. New York, Wiley, 1978.

Received June 1, 1983. P.S.E.B.M. 1984, Vol. 176.
Accepted January 24, 1984.

PROCEEDINGS OF THE SOCIETY FOR EXPERIMENTAL BIOLOGY AND MEDICINE **176**, 32–37 (1984)

Attenuation of Psychosocial Stress-Induced Hypertension by Gamma-Linolenic Acid (GLA) Administration in Rats (41838)

D. E. MILLS AND R. WARD

Department of Health Studies, University of Waterloo, Waterloo, Ontario N2L 3G1, Canada

Abstract. This study investigated a model of psychosocial stress-induced hypertension in the rat, and examined effects of the prostaglandin E precursor, gamma-linolenic acid (GLA) on the development of hypertension during psychosocial stress. In the first study, male rats were housed four/cage for an acclimation period of 21 days, followed by a 14-day control period. An experimental group ($N = 12$) was then placed in isolation cages for 14 days, then regrouped for a 7-day recovery period. Controls ($N = 12$) remained group-housed. Eight animals per group were sacrificed after the experimental period, and four per group after recovery for organ weight analysis. Mean systolic blood pressure (BP) was similar between groups during the control period (126 ± 2 and 125 ± 2 mm Hg), but increased during isolation, reaching 140 ± 2 mm Hg ($P < 0.001$) by Day 14. During recovery BP returned to control levels. No changes in heart rate, heart weight/body weight or adrenal weight were seen. The second study utilized a protocol similar to that of the experimental group of the first study, minus the recovery period. On Day 1 of the control period 28-day osmotic pumps were implanted ip, releasing olive oil or GLA in olive oil. Four groups of rats (N = 8/group) received either (i) olive oil (controls), (ii) 0.018 mg GLA/hr, (iii) 0.040 mg GLA/hr, or (iv) 0.040 mg GLA/hr with no stress. Organ weights were obtained following stress in groups 1–3. Controls developed a sustained elevation in BP within 24 hr of isolation. Animals receiving 0.018 mg GLA/hr developed elevated BP upon isolation, but the BP was less than that of controls on Days 1 ($P < 0.05$) and 14 ($P < 0.001$) of isolation. Animals receiving 0.040 mg GLA/hr demonstrated a greatly attenuated rise in BP vs controls ($P < 0.001$) on all isolation days. GLA in unstressed rats had no effect on BP. Heart rate, heart weight/body weight, and adrenal weight were unchanged in all groups. These data suggest that (i) isolation is a useful tool for investigating reversible psychosocial stress-induced hypertension, and (ii) GLA, while not affecting BP in unstressed animals, produces a dose-dependent attenuation of the BP response to chronic stress.

Prostaglandin E (PGE) has been reported to decrease systemic blood pressure (BP) in both animals (1–4) and man (5–11). However, its clinical usefulness as an antihypertensive agent is limited by its rapid degradation *in vivo* (68–90% inactivated in one pass through the lungs) and side effects, such as dizziness, nausea, and abdominal cramping which result from its hypotensive action (8–11).

It has been suggested that administration of the polyunsaturated fatty acid precursors of the E series prostaglandins, gamma-linolenic acid (GLA) or dihomo-GLA, might elicit decreases in BP while eliminating both the side effects of acute PGE administration, and degradation problems. Studies in rats (12) and rabbits (13) have demonstrated that dietary supplementation with dihomo-GLA increases the dihomo-GLA content of plasma lipids, as well as excretion of the major prostaglandin E-series metabolite, 7 α-hydroxy-5,11-diketo-tetranorprostane-1, 16-dioic acid. Similarly, dihomo-GLA administration in man is associated with elevated platelet dihomo-GLA levels, as well as ability to synthesize PGE (14). These studies suggest that dietary PGE precursors can be used to increase endogenous prostaglandin E_1 (PGE1) and prostaglandin E_2 (PGE2) biosynthesis.

Preliminary studies have also examined the effects of GLA supplementation on BP regulation. Oil of the evening primrose (Efamol), a rich source of GLA and linoleic acid (2-series prostaglandin precursor) has been found to decrease BP in genetically hypertensive rats (15) and in women with pregnancy-induced hypertension (16). These findings suggest that GLA may be useful in controlling pathophysiologic elevations in BP via increasing PGE1 and/or PGE2 synthesis. However, it is not known whether or not PGE or its precursors are effective in modifying reversible

0037-9727/84 $1.50

elevations in BP, such as those which occur during stress, which are believed to contribute, in some instances, to the development of essential hypertension (17–19).

The present study sought to evaluate the effects of administration of the PGE1 and PGE2 precursor, GLA, on psychological stress-induced hypertension in rats. The model for psychological stress used was that of social isolation following group housing, which has been reported to produce a reversible hypertension in Wistar rats (20–22).

Materials and Methods. *Experimental animals.* Fifty-six adult male Sprague–Dawley rats weighing 125–150 g were purchased from Charles River, St. Constant, Quebec. Animals were maintained in a temperature (21 + 1°C)- and light-cycle-controlled room (lights on 0600–2000 hr) throughout the course of the study and were given rat chow and tap water *ad lib.* In addition, all animals were housed in groups (four/cage) for a 3-week acclimation period prior to the beginning of the study.

Agents administered. All exogenous agents used in the study were administered by means of 28 day, constant flow (2.29 μl/hr) osmotic minipumps (Alzet 2ML4) implanted ip under fluothane anesthesia on Day 1 of the study. Gas chromatograph analysis of the GLA (Sigma) demonstrated purity > 99%. The olive oil (OL) carrier for the GLA was shown by gas chromatograph to contain 0.4% alpha-linolenic acid and 9.6% linoleic acid.

Experiment 1. The effects of isolation on BP, heart rate (HR), and organ weight.

Following acclimation all animals remained housed four/cage for a 14-day control period. On Day 15, 12 animals (experimental) were removed from group cages and placed in individual (isolation) cages for a 14-day experimental period. During this time the control animals ($N = 12$) remained housed four/cage. Following the experimental period, isolated animals were regrouped for a 7-day recovery period, while control animals remained in original groups. During the study BP, HR, and body wt were determined on Days 7, 14, 16, 21, 28, and 35. The tail cuff method (23, 24), utilizing a doppler flow transducer was used to measure BP and HR on the conscious rats, which were heated in a 34°C incubator for 10 min prior to measurement. At the end of the experimental period (Day 28), 8 animals from each treatment group were sacrificed, and the heart and adrenal glands were removed and weighed after cleaning and rinsing in physiological saline. Similarly, at the end of the recovery period the remaining 4 animals per group were sacrificed for organ weight determination.

Experiment 2. The effects of GLA on the BP and HR responses to psychosocial stress.

Animals in this experiment underwent a similar protocol as the experimental (stressed) group in Experiment 1, with the following exceptions. Following acclimation, animals were divided into four treatment groups and had 28-day, osmotic minipumps implanted. Pumps released either (i) OL ($N = 8$), (ii) 0.018 mg GLA in OL/hr ($N = 8$), (iii) 0.040 mg GLA in OL/hr ($N = 8$), or (iv) 0.040 mg GLA in OL/hr ($N = 6$) with no stress exposure. Following a 14-day control period (four/cage) all animals, except those in group 4, were isolated for a 14-day experimental period. At the end of the experimental period (Day 28) groups 1–3 were sacrificed for organ weight determination, as previously described. Measurements of BP, HR, and body wt were made on Days 7, 14, 16, 21, and 28. The availability of reagents limited group 4 to six animals, but housing four/cage was permitted by the addition of two nonexperimental animals to one of the cages.

Data analysis. Analysis of BP, HR, and body wt were performed using a 2-way ANOVA on repeated measures. Organ weight data were analyzed using a 2-way ANOVA. Where a significance of $P < 0.05$ was achieved, a planned comparison test (25) was performed to determine which subgroups differed from the others.

Results. *Experiment 1.* The BP response to stress is shown in Fig. 1. Although there were no differences in BP between groups during the control period, isolation produced a significant increase in BP, from 125 ± 2 mm Hg ($\bar{x}$ ± SE) to 137 ± 2 mm Hg ($P < 0.05$ vs grouped), within 24 hr. The BP of stressed animals continued to rise on Days 21 and 28, reaching 140 ± 2 mm Hg ($P < 0.001$ vs grouped), while that of control animals did not change significantly from control period values. Following 7 days of recovery the BP of experimental animals decreased to control period levels (125 ± 2 mm Hg), which were

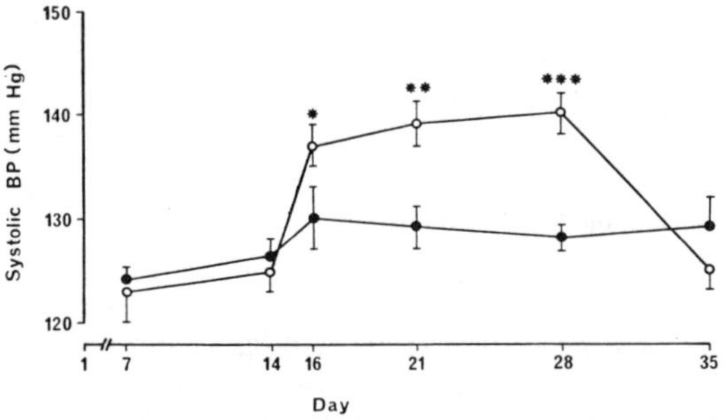

FIG. 1. Systolic blood pressure (BP) of adult male rats group-housed for 5 weeks (●) and of rats placed in isolation for 2 weeks (○) following 2 weeks in group housing. *$P < 0.05$ vs group-housed; **$P < 0.01$ vs group-housed; ***$P < 0.001$ vs group-housed.

not significantly different from control group values. There were no significant changes in HR during the study in either group (data not shown) in comparison to Day 7 means of 308 ± 8 bpm for controls and 347 ± 12 bpm for experimental groups. Similarly, there were no differences in body weight gain by either group during the study (data not shown). Heart and adrenal gland weight data are shown in Table I. On Day 28, mean heart weight of the stressed rats was significantly greater than that of the control rats ($P < 0.001$). However, this difference did not appear in the heart weight/BW ratio. There were no differences in either adrenal weight or adrenal weight/body wt ratio between groups on Day 28. On Day 35 there were no differences in heart or adrenal weights or weight ratios between groups of animals.

Experiment 2. The BP response to GLA treatment during stress is illustrated in Fig. 2. Olive oil-treated rats (controls) demonstrated a significant increase in BP from 128 ± 3 to 146 ± 2 mm Hg ($P < 0.001$) within 24 hr of isolation, which leveled off at 142 ± 2 mm Hg by Day 28. Administration of GLA at a rate of 0.018 mg/hr (1.1 mg/kg/day) had no effect on baseline BP, which was similar to that of OL-treated animals, but slightly attenuated the BP rise 24 hr after isolation (142 ± 2 mm Hg) on Day 16 ($P < 0.05$ vs OL). Furthermore, BP in this group failed to plateau during the isolation period, falling off on Day 28 to 132 ± 2 mm Hg ($P < 0.001$ vs OL). Administration of GLA at a rate of 0.040 mg/hr (2.4 mg/kg/day) also had no effect on baseline BP, but significantly attenuated the isolation-induced BP rise on Days 16 (133 ± 1 mm Hg, $P < 0.001$ vs OL), 21 (132 ± 1 mm Hg, $P < 0.001$ vs OL), and 28 (131 ± 2 mm Hg, $P < 0.001$ vs OL). The administration of 0.040 mg GLA/hr to unstressed rats had no

TABLE I. MEAN BODY (BW), HEART, AND ADRENAL WEIGHTS IN CONTROL AND SOCIALLY ISOLATED RATS FOLLOWING THE EXPERIMENTAL (DAY 28) AND RECOVERY (DAY 35) PERIODS (EXPERIMENT 1), AND IN SOCIALLY STRESSED RATS RECEIVING OLIVE OIL (OL) OR GAMMA-LINOLENIC ACID (GLA) BY OSMOTIC MINIPUMP (EXPERIMENT 2)

	Heart wt (g)	Heart wt/ 100 g body wt (g)	Adrenal wt (g)	Adrenal wt/ 100 g body wt (g)	Body wt (g)
Experiment 1					
Day 28					
Control (N = 8)	1.129 ± 0.048	0.268 ± 0.010	0.058 ± 0.003	0.015 ± 0.001	409.6 ± 11.2
Isolated (N = 8)	1.319 ± 0.043***	0.307 ± 0.009	0.058 ± 0.002	0.014 ± 0.001	433.4 ± 11.7
Day 35					
Control (N = 4)	1.028 ± 0.050	0.241 ± 0.012	0.063 ± 0.005	0.015 ± 0.001	428.7 ± 3.5
Isolated (N = 4)	1.098 ± 0.068	0.253 ± 0.006	0.063 ± 0.005	0.015 ± 0.001	435.2 ± 15.9
Experiment 2					
Day 28					
OL (N = 8)	1.186 ± 0.052	0.288 ± 0.006	0.060 ± 0.002	0.015 ± 0.001	410.5 ± 13.0
0.018 mg GLA/hr (N = 8)	1.175 ± 0.041	0.284 ± 0.011	0.060 ± 0.003	0.015 ± 0.001	413.9 ± 7.5
0.040 mg GLA/hr (N = 8)	1.034 ± 0.035*	0.295 ± 0.006	0.062 ± 0.002	0.019 ± 0.007	350.0 ± 5.9***

Note. Values are means ± SE.
* $P < 0.05$ vs controls.
*** $P < 0.001$ vs controls.

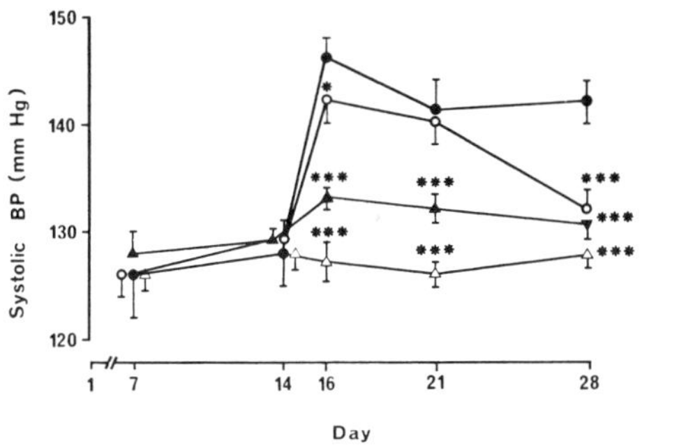

FIG. 2. Systolic BP before and during social isolation in adult male rats receiving olive oil (●, $N = 8$) or GLA at calculated rates of 0.018 mg/hr (○, $N = 8$) and 0.040 mg/hr (▲, $N = 8$) via osmotic minipump implanted ip on Day 1. An additional group receiving 0.040 mg GLA/hr (△, $N = 6$) was not placed in isolation. (Means + SE; $*P < 0.05$ vs olive oil group; $***P < 0.001$ vs olive oil group.

effect on BP over the 28-day treatment period. No significant changes in HR or BW gain were seen in any of the treatment groups over the course of the study, nor were there significant differences in control period HR between groups (data not shown). Similarly, there were no differences in heart weight, adrenal weight, heart weight ratio, or adrenal weight ratio between groups on Day 28 (Table I).

Discussion. In the present study, isolation of group acclimated, intact, male Sprague–Dawley rats for 14 days produced a persistent elevation in BP of 15–20 mm Hg. This hypertension was unaccompanied by an increase in HR over the same period, and was reversed following the cessation of isolation. Similar studies on male Wistar rats undergoing a 15-day isolation period have reported BP increases of 20–25 mm Hg., accompanied by initial elevations in HR which disappeared after 5 days of isolation (20). The variation in response to this psychosocial stress may be related to strain differences in stress sensitivity, or differences in experimental protocol which would cause isolation to be a more severe stressor in the earlier studies.

No changes in BW, heart weight/body weight, or adrenal weight/body weight were observed as a result of isolation in the present study. Similarly, a previous study using social interaction as a stressor has reported no change in body weight gain due to the stress (26), and BP elevations following 12 weeks of electric shock were found to have no effect on heart weight/body weight in normotensive rats (27). However, increases in relative heart weight and adrenal weight have been observed following long-term (months) isolation stress (28), and after electric shock stress (27), respectively. The absence of cardiac and adrenal hypertrophy in the present study may be due to either the shorter duration or different nature of the stressor.

The fact that isolation stress did not produce irreversible hypertension in any studies using normotensive animals (20–22) suggests that either a longer duration of stress than was used is required to produce irreversible changes in BP regulation, or that there are other, possibly genetic, factors that predispose an individual to develop irreversible hypertension from reversible stress-induced hypertension. This is supported by the observation that certain borderline hypertensive rats, related to the genetically hypertensive rat (SHR), develop irreversible hypertension following 12 weeks of electric shock (29).

Another finding of the present experiments is that chronic administration of the PGE precursor, GLA, attenuates the stress-induced BP rise, while not affecting basal (unstressed) BP levels. This effect of GLA on BP during stress occurs in the absence of significant changes in HR, suggesting that GLA is not mediating its effect through an alteration in sympathetic activity. However, the observation that an effect is seen only during presumed heightened sympathetic activity (30) suggests that GLA may be influencing the response to sympathetic stimulation. While there is ample evidence that PGE is able to modify the peripheral vascular response to catecholamines, there is disagreement as to whether the influence is that of potentiation, as demonstrated in certain isolated preparations (31–33, 36), or inhibition, as shown *in vivo* (34, 35). It has also been suggested that at low doses PGE potentiates catecholamine-induced vasoconstriction, and at high doses inhibits it (37).

A possible explanation of why GLA exerts a depressor effect on BP only during stress is that GLA administration might increase dihomo-GLA and/or arachidonic acid stores in the basal condition, so that under conditions of stimulated PGE biosynthesis, there is a greater production of PGE. An increase in sympathetic activity during stress might cause an increase in PGE1 or PGE2 production which would be augmented by elevated dihomo-GLA and/or arachidonic acid stores resulting from GLA treatment.

A second possibility is that GLA leads to increased PGE levels in the unstressed animal, but that this PGE only exerts its vasodepressor effects when in the presence of elevated catecholamine levels, as during stress. This explanation is unlikely, since PGE administration exerts potent hypotensive activity even under basal conditions (1–7).

The fact that GLA treatment attenuates stress-induced increases in BP, while having no effect on BP in unstressed animals, makes it an attractive prospect for use as an antihypertensive agent, particularly in cases of labile hypertension, such as can occur during periods of stress or other situations involving sympathetic stimulation.

This work was supported by a grant from the Ontario Heart Foundation. The authors thank J. Ward for conducting gas chromatographic analyses of agents used in the study, H. Kong for his technical assistance, and S. Hurlburt for her patient secretarial assistance.

1. Somova IL, Dochev DH. Studies on the mechanism of the diuretic action of prostaglandin E_1. Dokl Bolg Akad Nauk **26:**1277–1282, 1973.
2. Tyler T, Leffler C, Wallis R, Cassin S. The effects of prostaglandins of the E-series on pulmonary and systemic circulations of newborn goats during normoxia and hypoxia. Prostaglandins **10:**963–970, 1975.
3. McQueen D, Bell K. The effects of prostaglandin E_1 and sodium meclofenamate on blood pressure in renal hypertensive rats. Eur J Pharmacol **37:**223–235, 1976.
4. Cassin S, Tyler T, Leffler C, Wallis R. Pulmonary and systemic vascular responses of perinatal goats to prostaglandins E_1 and E_2. Amer J Physiol **236:**H838–H832, 1979.
5. Pipkin FB, O'Brien PMS, Sant-Cassia LJ. The effect of prostaglandin E_1 on the pressor response to angiotensin II in second trimester human pregnancy and in the non-pregnant subject. Clin Exp Hypertens **B1:**493–504, 1982.
6. Bergström S, Carlson LA, Ekelund LG, Oro L. Effects of prostaglandin E_1 on blood pressure, heart rate, and concentrations of free fatty acids of plasma in man. Proc Soc Exp Biol Med **118:**110–112, 1965.
7. Carlson LA, Eriksson I. Femoral artery infusion of prostaglandin E_1 in severe peripheral vascular disease. Lancet **1:**155–156, 1973.
8. Bergström S, Cuner H, von Euler US, Pernow V, Sjovall J. Observations on the effects of infusion of prostaglandin E in man. Acta Physiol Scand **45:**145–151, 1959.
9. Bergström S, Carlson LA, Ekelund LG, Oro L. Cardiovascular and metabolic response to infusions of prostaglandin E_1 and to simultaneous infusions of noradrenaline and prostaglandin E_1 in man. Acta Physiol Scand **69:**332–339, 1965.
10. Carlson LA, Ekelund LG, Oro L. Clinical and metabolic effects of different doses of prostaglandin E_1 in man. Acta Med Scand **183:**423–430, 1968.
11. Carlson LA, Ekelund LG, Orö L. Circulatory and respiratory effects of different doses of prostaglandin E_1 in man. Acta Physiol Scand **75:**161–169, 1969.
12. Willis AL, Comaik K, Kuhn DC, Paulsrud J. Dihomo-gamma linolenate suppresses platelet aggregation when administered *in vitro* or *in vivo.* Prostaglandins **8:**509–519, 1974.
13. Oelz O, Seyberth HW, Knapp HR, Sweatman BJ, Oates JA. Effects of feeding ethyl-dihomo-γ-linolenate on prostaglandin synthesis and platelet aggregation in the rabbit. Biochim Biophys Acta **431:**268–277, 1976.
14. Kernoff BA, Willis AL, Stone KJ, Davies JA, McNicoll GP. Antithrombotic potential of dihomo-γ-linolenic acid in man. Brit Med J **2:**1441–1444, 1977.
15. Hoffman P, Förster W. Effects of sunflowerseed oil, linseed oil, evening primrose oil, and hydrogenated palm kernel oil on hypertension development in spontaneously hypertensive rats. Prostaglandins Med **11:**43–44, 1983.
16. Moodley J, Norman R. Preliminary Studies on efamol in pregnancy-induced hypertension. Prostaglandins Med, in press.
17. Dembroski TM, McDougall JM, Shields JL. Physiologic reactions to social challenge in persons evidencing Type A coronary-prone behavior pattern. J Hum Stress **3:**2–9, 1977.
18. Levi L, Kagan A. Psychosocially-induced stress and disease—problems, research strategies and results. In: Selye H, ed. Selye's Guide to Stress Research. New York, Van Nostrand Reinhold, Vol 1:p118, 1980.
19. Martin RL. Hypertension and Stress. Sem Fam Med **2:**25–34, 1981.
20. Gardiner SM, Bennett T. The effects of short term isolation on systolic blood pressure and heart rate in rats. Med Biol **55:**325–329, 1977.
21. Gardiner SM. The effects of social contact on hypertension induced by short term isolation in the rat. J Physiol **269:**62–63P, 1977.
22. Gardiner SM, Milmer KE, Bennett T. Effect of adrenalectomy on the development of isolation-induced hypertension in rats. Clin Sci **61:**511–519, 1981.
23. Rowberg A, Franklin C, van Citters RL. Nontraumatic method for measurement of blood pressure in animals with tails. J Appl Physiol **27:**301–302, 1969.
24. Buñag RD. Validation in awake rats of a tail-cuff method for measuring systolic pressure. J Appl Physiol **34:**279–282, 1973.

25. Keppel G. Design and Analysis: A Researcher's Handbook. New Jersey, Prentice–Hall, p85, 1973.
26. Henry JP, Stephens PM, Santisteban GA. A model of psychosocial hypertension showing reversibility and progression of cardiovascular complications. Circ Res **36**:156–164, 1975.
27. Lauter JE, Barker GF, Hubbard JW, Schaub RG. Effects of stress on blood pressure and cardiac pathology in rats with borderline hypertension. Hypertension **3**:496–505, 1981.
28. Baer H. Long-term isolation stress and its effects on drug response in rodents. Lab Anim Sci **21**:341–349, 1971.
29. Lawler, JE, Barker GF, Hubbard JW, Schaub RG. Pathophysiological changes associated with stress-induced hypertension in the borderline hypertensive rat. Clin Sci **59**:3075–3105, 1980.
30. Moore KE. Studies with chronically isolated rats: Tissue levels and urinary excretion of catecholamines and plasma levels of corticosterone. Canad J Physiol Pharmacol **46**:553–558, 1968.
31. Greenberg S, Long JP. Enhancement of vascular smooth muscle responses to vasoactive stimuli by prostaglandin E_1 and E_2. Arch Int Pharmacodyn Ther **206**:94–104, 1973.
32. Horrobin DF, Manku MS, Karmali R, Nassar BA, Davies PA. Aspirin, indomethacin, catecholamine, and prostaglandin interactions on rat arterioles and rabbit hearts. Nature (London) **250**:425–426, 1974.
33. Coupar, IM, McLennan PL. The influence of prostaglandins on noradrenaline-induced vasoconstriction in isolated perfused mesenteric blood vessels of the rat. Brit J Pharmacol **62**:51–59, 1978.
34. Weiner R, Kaley G. Influence of prostaglandin E_1 on the terminal vascular bed. Amer J Physiol **217**:563–566, 1969.
35. Kadowitz PJ. Effects of prostaglandins E_1, E_2 and A_2 on vascular resistance and responses to noradrenaline, nerve stimulation, and angiotensin in dog hindlimb. Brit J Pharmacol **46**:495–500, 1972.
36. Malik KU, Ryan P, McGiff JC. Modification by prostaglandins E_1 and E_2, indomethacin, and arachidonic acid of the vasoconstrictor responses of the isolated perfused rabbit and rat mesenteric arteries to adrenergic stimuli. Circ Res **39**:163–168, 1976.
37. Manku MS, Horrobin DF, Karmazyn M, Cunnane SC. Prolactin and zinc effects on rat vascular reactivity: Possible relationships to dihomo-γ-linolenic acid and to prostaglandin synthesis. Endocrinology **104**:774–779, 1979.

Received September 15, 1983. P.S.E.B.M. 1984, Vol. 176.
Accepted January 25, 1984.

PROCEEDINGS OF THE SOCIETY FOR EXPERIMENTAL BIOLOGY AND MEDICINE **176**, 38–41 (1984)

Sodium Transport in *Rana pipiens* Gastric Mucosa (41839)

L. L. SHANBOUR, Y.-J. KUO, AND M. J. JACKSON

Department of Physiology and Cell Biology, University of Texas Medical School at Houston, Houston, Texas 77025, and Department of Physiology, George Washington University School of Medicine, Washington, D.C. 20037

Abstract. The transport properties of frog gastric mucosa *in vitro* have been reexamined in conditions analogous to those used in studies on mammalian systems in which net movements of sodium were observed. Net transport of sodium across frog gastric mucosa was not observed to occur when the mucosal surface was bathed with a well-buffered solution of near neutral pH, indicating that failure to demonstrate sodium transport across frog stomach in previous work could not be ascribed to the low pH value of the solution usually used as the mucosal fluid. Addition of 5×10^{-4} *M* amphotericin B to the mucosal solution elicited net transport of sodium and an increase in short-circuit current. These findings indicate that sodium transport may contribute to the electrolyte physiology of frog gastric mucosa in some experimental conditions, and may limit the utility of the three-variable model proposed by Hogben.

Studies on *in vitro* preparations of gastric mucosa from several mammalian species (1–5) have suggested that the mammalian stomach differs in an important respect from the extensively studied frog gastric mucosa (6–8). The mammalian tissues have generally been found to maintain net transport of sodium from the secretory, to nutrient surface in the absence of transmural gradients of electrochemical potentials, but sodium transport across frog gastric mucosa has previously been reported to occur only under hypoxic conditions (9, 10).

A survey of the literature suggested that this discrepancy may reflect a difference in the conditions used to study amphibian and mammalian tissues. In general, an unbuffered solution of pH less than 5 has been used as the mucosal medium in studies on frog stomach, but a well-buffered solution of pH greater than 7 has usually been employed in studies on mammalian systems. Because net sodium transport across rabbit gastric mucosa was inhibited when the pH of the secretory medium was decreased (11), and sodium transport was observed in a study on an amphibian species (*Necturus*) in which the pH of the secretory medium was maintained greater than 7 (12), the transport properties of the frog gastric mucosa were reexamined using conditions analogous to those employed in experiments on mammalian tissue.

Methods. The preparation of frog (*Rana pipiens*) gastric mucosa used in the present experiments was essentially similar to that described in several previous studies (7, 8, 13). The tissue was taken from the fundic region of the stomach, separated from the muscle coats by dissection, and mounted between lucite chambers with an exposed surface area of 1 cm^2.

For studies on the transport of sodium and chloride, both surfaces of the tissue were bathed by 10 ml of a well-buffered incubation solution with the following composition (m*M*): NaCl, 70; NaHepes, 20; $NaHCO_3$, 19; KCl, 3; KH_2PO_4, 2; $MgSO_4$, 1; glucose, 10. The solutions were equilibrated with 95% O_2/5% CO_2 before, and during the experiment, and maintained the pH value of both nutrient and secretory solutions at 7.2 throughout the study. The experiments were conducted at room temperature. Transmucosal potential difference (PD), resistance (R), and short-circuit current (I_{sc}) were evaluated using the automatic voltage clamp system described previously (14). For flux estimation, 3 μCi of ^{22}Na or ^{36}Cl were added to the solution on one side of the tissue, a 1-hr period allowed for equilibration, and the flux estimated from the appearance of tracer in the initially unlabeled solution during 20-min periods.

For studies on acid secretion, the solution bathing the mucosal surface of the tissue was replaced by an isoosmotic solution of NaCl. The pH of this solution was maintained con-

0037-9727/84 $1.50

stant by titration with 5 mN NaOH by means of a Radiometer pH stat.

Amphotericin B was obtained from the Sigma Chemical Company, and was applied as a concentrated stock solution in dimethylsulfoxide (DMSO). Results were expressed as means ± SM. Statistical significance was estimated by the t test for paired data, and the differences with a P value less than 0.05 were considered to be significant.

Results. Preliminary studies showed that, in control conditions, the *in vitro* preparation of frog gastric mucosa used in our experiments was stable for at least 3 hr of incubation. Figure 1 shows that addition of DMSO to the mucosal solution produced no change in the electrical variables (PD, R, I_{sc}), but addition of a DMSO solution of amphotericin B (to give a final concentration of 5×10^{-4} M in the bath) elicited a prompt increase in I_{sc} and a decrease in R. The changes in I_{sc} and R were of equivalent magnitudes with the result that PD did not change significantly.

Figure 2 shows that the opposed unidirectional fluxes of sodium did not differ significantly from each other in the control condition, indicating that a net movement of sodium did not occur in this situation. Addition of DMSO to the mucosal solution did not change the sodium fluxes, but exposure to 5×10^{-4} M amphotericin B increased both of the sodium fluxes. The increase in the mucosal-to-serosal flux was larger than that of the serosal-to-mucosal flux, indicating that a

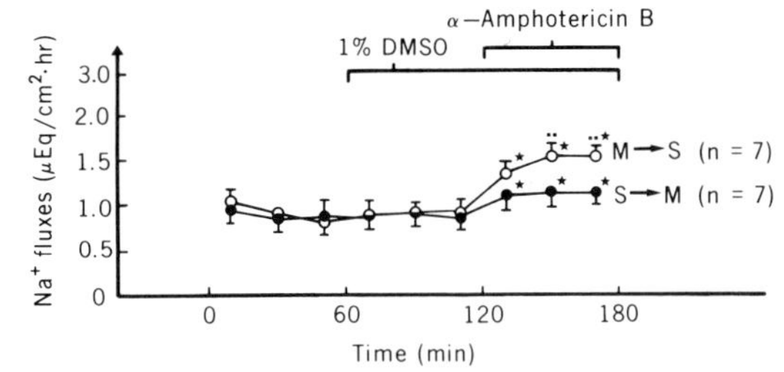

FIG. 2. Unidirectional fluxes of sodium during DMSO (1%) and α-amphotericin B conditions (5×10^{-4} M). N = 7. Single asterisk denotes significant difference at P < 0.05 from value at 120 min. Double asterisks denote significant difference at P < 0.05 between unidirectional fluxes.

net movement of sodium in the mucosal-to-serosal direction was maintained in the presence of amphotericin B.

The mean value of the net flux of sodium observed in the presence of amphotericin B was 0.35 ± 0.04 μeq cm^{-2} hr^{-1}, and the increase in I_{sc} associated with exposure to amphotericin B was 0.48 ± 0.04 μeq cm^{-2} hr^{-1}, suggesting that the transport of sodium was equivalent to more than 70% of the change in I_{sc}.

Figure 3 shows that the preparation maintained a net secretory movement of chloride

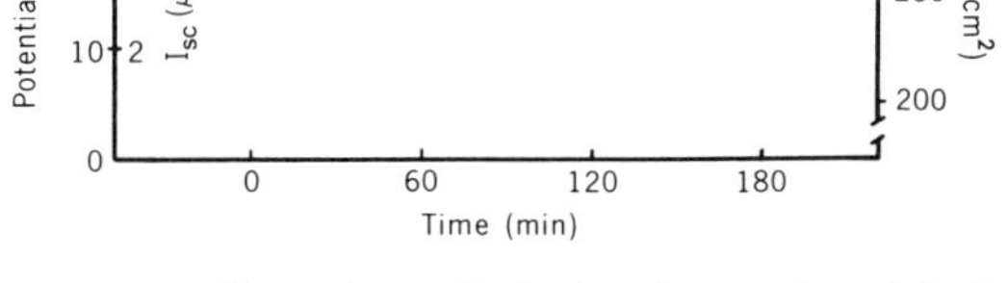

FIG. 1. Effects of DMSO (1%) and α-amphotericin B (5×10^{-4} M) on potential difference, short-circuit current and electrical resistance in isolated frog gastric mucosa. N = 14. Asterisk denotes significant difference at P < 0.05 from value at 120 min.

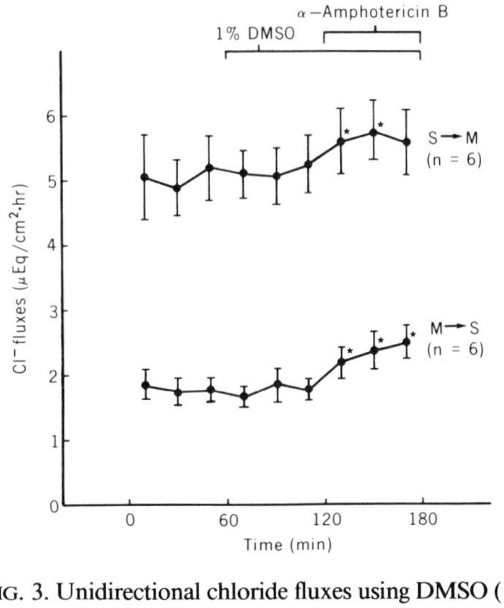

FIG. 3. Unidirectional chloride fluxes using DMSO (1%) and α-amphotericin B conditions (5×10^{-4} M). N = 6. Asterisk denotes significant difference at P < 0.05 from value at 120 min.

in the control condition, and after addition of DMSO to the mucosal fluid. Exposure to 5×10^{-4} *M* amphotericin B produced significant increases in both chloride fluxes, but the changes in the two fluxes were equivalent and the net movement of chloride did not change after addition of amphotericin B. Thus, in the control condition, the net movement of chloride was -3.3 ± 0.08 μeq cm^{-2} hr^{-1}, and after addition of amphotericin B this quantity was -3.2 ± 0.16 μeq cm^{-2} hr^{-1}.

Figure 4 shows that the basal secretion of acid remained constant during the control period of incubation, and after addition of DMSO to the mucosal fluid. Exposure to 5×10^{-4} *M* amphotericin B resulted in a prompt decrease in acid secretion, but the effect was transient and lasted for only one sampling period. Subsequently the basal secretion of acid returned to the level observed in the control period, and was maintained at this value during the remainder of the experiment.

Discussion. The primary objective of these experiments was to examine the transport of sodium across frog gastric mucosa *in vitro* when the mucosal surface of the tissue was bathed with a well-buffered solution of near neutral pH. The experiments showed that the tissue did not maintain a net movement of sodium in this condition. Several observations indicated that the failure to demonstrate net sodium transport in these studies could not be ascribed to a nonspecific depression of tissue function in the conditions used. Thus the rates of chloride transport and basal acid secretion, and the electrical variables were all of comparable magnitudes to values reported in previous studies. In addition, our experiments showed that net transport of sodium was maintained in tissue treated with amphotericin B, indicating that a sodium transport process was demonstrable when the properties of the tissue were modified. Accordingly, it was concluded that the frog gastric mucosa did not normally effect net transport of sodium when the mucosal surface was bathed with a well-buffered solution of pH greater than 7, and that the lack of sodium transport demonstrated in previous studies on the tissue could not be ascribed to the low pH of the solution used as the mucosal medium in most of the earlier work.

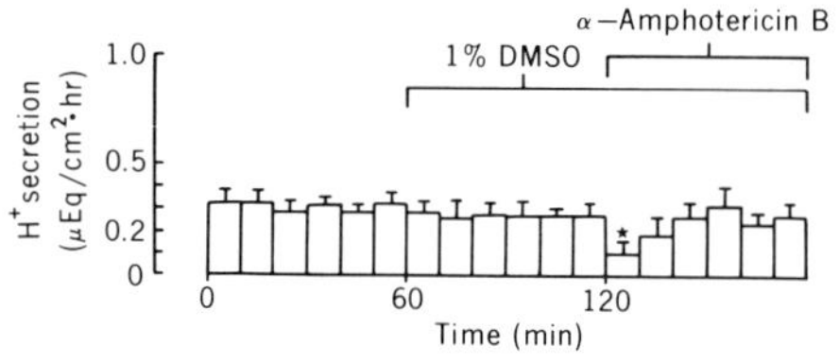

FIG. 4. Basal acid secretion during DMSO (1%) and α-amphotericin B conditions (5×10^{-4} *M*). $N = 6$. Asterisk denotes significant difference at $P < 0.05$ from value at 120 min.

The mechanism of action of amphotericin B in eliciting the sodium transport process in frog gastric mucosa *in vitro* was not investigated. In other systems it has been shown that the action of amphotericin B on sodium transport was associated with the introduction of cation selection channels into the apical membrane of epithelial cells (15, 16), and it may be that a similar mechanism contributed to the effects of amphotericin B observed in the present experiments. This suggestion carries the implication that the principal difference between the frog gastric mucosa and the mammalian systems, with respect to sodium transport, lies in the presence of sodium entry channels in the sodium transporting cells of mammalian stomach, and the absence of such channels in the frog tissue. However, the effects of amphotericin B on frog gastric mucosa were not restricted to sodium movements. The agent also increased permeability to chloride, and transiently modified the basal rate of acid secretion, and the possibility that the action of amphotericin B was associated with modification of cellular regulatory mechanisms of more general significance cannot be discounted at present. The latter proposal suggests that the frog gastric mucosa includes mechanisms controlling the sodium transport process that are not present, or depressed in the corresponding mammalian systems.

Previously, Flemström and Öbrink (9) and Flemström (10) have shown that net transport of sodium across frog gastric mucosa *in vitro* may be induced by decreasing the partial pressure of oxygen to which the tissue is exposed. In contrast to our findings, the hypoxia induced stimulation of sodium transport was not associated with a variation in I_{sc}, suggesting that the actions of amphotericin B and hypoxia may be mediated through the different mechanisms. Thus the present studies, together with those of Flemström and Öbrink (9) and Flemström (10), raise a question concerning the general validity of the simple three-component model proposed by Hogben (6) as a description of the transport properties of frog gastric mucosa *in vitro*. This model is summarized by the expression:

$$I_{sc} = J_{net}^{Cl} - J^{H^+}$$

in which J_{net}^{Cl} represents the rate of chloride transport, and J^{H^+} represents the rate of acid secretion. The earlier studies (9, 10) and those described here demonstrate that the assumption that only chloride and acid require consideration as transported species is not generally valid, and that net movements of sodium may be stimulated in some experimental conditions. In addition, the present work has suggested that in at least some situations the sodium transport process may contribute to the electrical characteristics of the tissue.

This study was supported by NIH Grants AA00196 and GM22369. We are indebted to Mr. J. Pastore for assistance in the preparation of the manuscript.

1. Kitahara S, Fox KR, Hogben CAM. Acid secretion, Na^+ absorption, and the origin of the potential difference across isolated mammalian stomachs. Amer J Dig Dis **14**:221–238, 1969.
2. Forte JG, Forte TM, Machen TE. Histamine-stimulated hydrogen ion secretion by *in vitro* piglet gastric mucosa. J Physiol **244**:15–31, 1975.
3. Fromm D, Schwartz JH, Quijano R. Transport of H^+ and other electrolytes across isolated gastric mucosa of the rabbit. Amer J Physiol **288**:166–171, 1975.
4. Mierson S, Kuo Y-J, Shanbour LL. Transport in mammalian gastric mucosa. In: Dinno, MA, and Callahan, AB, eds. Membrane Biophysics: Structure and Function in Epithelia. New York, Liss, pp205–228, 1981.
5. Bowen JC, Kuo Y-J, Pavlik W, Williams D, Shanbour LL, Jacobson ED. Electrophysiological effects of burinamide and 16,16-dimethyl prostaglandin E_2 on the canine gastric mucosa. Gastroenterology **68**:1480–1484, 1975.
6. Hogben CAM. Active transport of chloride by isolated frog gastric epithelia. Origin of the gastric mucosa potential. Amer J Physiol **180**:641–649, 1955.
7. Rehm WS. Acid secretion, resistance, short-circuit current and voltage-clamping in frog's stomach. Amer J Physiol **203**:63–72, 1962.
8. Forte JG, Davis RE. Oxygen consumption and active transport of ions by isolated frog gastric mucosa. Amer J Physiol **204**:812–816, 1963.
9. Flemstrom G, Obrink KJ. Active Na^+ transport in isolated frog gastric mucosa during hypoxia. Biochim Biophys Acta **203**:184–185, 1970.
10. Flemstrom G. Na^+ transport and impedance properties of the isolated frog gastric mucosa at different O_2 tensions. Biochim Biophys Acta **225**:35–45, 1971.
11. Machen TE, Silen W, Forte JG. Na^+ transport by mammalian stomach. Amer J Physiol **234**:E288–E235, 1978.
12. Flemstrom G, Sachs G. Ion transport by amphibian antrum *in vitro*. I. General characteristics. Amer J Physiol **228**:1188–1198, 1975.
13. Sanson SC, Kuo YJ, Shanbour LL, Weinman EJ. The transport of urate in frog gastric mucosa. Proc Soc Exp Biol Med **170**:363–366, 1982.
14. Shanbour LL. An automatic voltage-clamp system for *in vivo* or *in vitro* studies. Amer J Dig Dis **19**:367–371, 1974.
15. Bentley PJ. Action of amphotericin B on the toad bladder: Evidence for sodium transport along two pathways. J Physiol **196**:703–711, 1968.
16. Frizzell RA, Koch MJ, Schultz SG. Ion transport in rabbit colon. I. Active and passive components. J Membr Biol **27**:297–316, 1976.

Received July 29, 1983. P.S.E.B.M. 1984, Vol. 176.
Accepted February 6, 1984.

PROCEEDINGS OF THE SOCIETY FOR EXPERIMENTAL BIOLOGY AND MEDICINE **176**, 42–47 (1984)

Cholesterol Esterification by Mammary Gland Microsomes from the Lactating Rat (41840)

A. CATHARINE ROSS AND JANICE F. ROWE

Department of Physiology and Biochemistry and Department of Pediatrics, The Medical College of Pennsylvania, Philadelphia, Pennsylvania 19129

Abstract. Cholesterol esterification by fatty acyl-CoA:cholesterol acyltransferase (ACAT, EC 2.3.1.26) has been demonstrated in microsomes prepared from breast tissue of the lactating rat, employing the incorporation of [1-^{14}C]oleoyl coenzyme-A into cholesteryl[^{14}C]oleate. The regulation of this activity *in vitro* was studied by supplementing microsomes with unesterified cholesterol supplied either as a dispersion in acetone or by incubating microsomes with cholesterol-enriched serum lipoproteins prior to enzyme assay. ACAT activity was increased by more than 80% when the ratio of unesterified cholesterol to microsomal protein was increased from 29 to 48 μg/mg protein, indicating that the normal cholesterol content of mammary gland microsomes does not saturate this enzyme. Cholesterol esterification could be inhibited nearly completely *in vitro* by addition of the polar steroid progesterone (93% decrease in ACAT activity with 75 μM progesterone) and, to lesser extents, by estradiol and retinol. Enzyme assays were also performed after incubating microsomes with *N*-acylamides that inhibit cholesteryl ester synthesis in other systems. Under conditions where the mammary gland ACAT reaction was inhibited by more than 82%, the esterification of retinol was reduced by less than 30% and incorporation of [^{14}C]oleoyl-CoA into triglycerides was not inhibited at all. These studies indicate that the lactating mammary gland contains ACAT activity having properties similar to ACAT in other organs. The presence of ACAT activity in the lactating mammary gland provides a possible mechanism for the synthesis of cholesteryl esters found in milk. It can also be inferred that ACAT in mammary gland microsomes is likely to be distinct from the microsomal acyltransferases that catalyze the esterification of retinol and glycerides.

Among the many lipid constituents of milk are cholesterol and its esters. Considerable attention has been given to the determination of the cholesterol concentration in milks from various species and its relationship to diet (1–4). Of total milk cholesterol, about 10–15% is present in esterified form in bovine milk (5) and in rat's milk (6). Little is known of the origin of this esterified cholesterol; reasonable possibilities include uptake of esterified cholesterol from serum lipoproteins, and esterification of cholesterol within the lactating gland (7).

Most acyltransferases that catalyze lipid ester synthesis are membrane-bound, microsomal enzymes. As such, relatively little is known about the properties, specificities, and regulation of these enzymes. Recently, we described the esterification of vitamin A (retinol) by microsomal membranes prepared from the lactating mammary gland of the rat (8). During these studies we became interested in whether the lactating mammary gland can also esterify cholesterol and whether a unique enzyme catalyzes each esterification reaction. This report provides evidence for a microsomal fatty acyl-CoA:cholesterol acyl-transferase (ACAT) in this organ and examines the effects of membrane cholesterol content, hormones, and other lipids on this enzymic process.

Materials and Methods. *Materials.* [1-^{14}C]-Oleoyl-CoA from New England Nuclear or Amersham Radiochemicals was diluted with oleoyl-CoA from P-L Biochemicals to a specific activity of 14–24 dpm/pmole. Progesterone and other steroids were obtained from Steraloids, Inc., and retinol, dithiothreitol, and bovine serum albumin (BSA, essentially fatty acid free) were purchased from Sigma Chemical Company. Two *N*-acylamides, Sandoz drugs 58-035 and 57-118, were generously provided by Dr. John Heider of Sandoz, Inc., Hanover, New Jersey. Their chemical names, respectively, are 3-[decyldimethylsilyl]-*N*-[2-(4-methylphenyl)-1-phenylethyl] propanamide and *N*-(1-oxo-9-octadecenyl)-DL-trypto-

0037-9727/84 $1.50

phan(Z)ethyl ester. Each *N*-acylamide was dissolved in dimethylsulfoxide and appropriate amounts were added to microsomes so that the final concentration of dimethylsulfoxide was maintained constant at 1% (wt/vol).

Preparation of microsomes. Microsomes were prepared as described previously (8) from breast tissue of Sprague–Dawley rats lactating for 1–14 days and fed a standard laboratory diet (Wayne Lab-blox). Microsomes were suspended at 4–10 mg protein/ml in 0.15 *M* potassium phosphate buffer, pH 7.4, frozen in Dri-Ice/acetone, and stored at −65°C. Under these conditions, microsomal ACAT activity was stable for 6–8 weeks and essentially equal to that in fresh microsomal membranes. Cholesterol in microsomes was determined by gas–liquid chromatography (9) and protein was measured by the dye-binding method of Bradford (10).

Incubations. Microsomes in 0.15 *M* potassium phosphate buffer, pH 7.4, were pipetted into glass screw-cap tubes on ice and additions such as dithiothreitol and BSA were made in the same buffer so that the volume equalled 0.17 ml. To begin the esterification reaction, an appropriate amount of [1-^{14}C]oleoyl-CoA in 30 μl buffer was added and tubes were incubated at 37°C in a shaking waterbath for specified times. Each incubation condition was tested in duplicate or triplicate and a blank containing boiled microsomes was also incubated for each condition. Each incubation was stopped by addition of 1 ml ethanol and an internal recovery standard of cholesteryl[^{3}H]oleate (approximately 1500 cpm) was added along with 50 μg each of unlabeled cholesteryl oleate, methyl oleate, and triolein for detection after TLC. Neutral lipids were extracted by adding 4 ml hexanes and 1 ml water, with shaking after each addition. After a brief centrifugation, 3.5 ml of the hexane upper phase was taken to dryness under nitrogen and applied to plastic-backed thin-layer plates of silica gel (Baker-flex IB2) which were developed in hexane/diethylether/acetic acid, 85/15/1 by volume. Lipids were visualized by a brief exposure to iodine vapors and zones containing lipid esters were cut and placed in scintillation vials with 10 ml of ScintiLene (Fisher Scientific Co.) for determination of ^{3}H and ^{14}C in a Beckman 7500 scintillation spectrometer. After correction for isotope overlaps, counts per minute were converted to disintegrations per minute by reference to calibrated [^{3}H]- and [^{14}C]toluene standards. Value for blanks containing boiled microsomes have been subtracted in all cases.

Progesterone and other lipids (Table I) were added in 2 μl acetone to 0.17 ml of microsomes in the presence of dithiothreitol and BSA and were incubated at 37°C for 10 min before addition of [^{14}C]oleoyl-CoA.

For incubation with lipoproteins, 1-ml portions of microsomes (4 mg protein) were incubated for 1 hr at 30°C with either 0.2 ml phosphate buffer, pH 7.4, or with 0.2 ml of a lipoprotein solution of density < 1.06 g/cm^3 from a cholesterol-fed rabbit, added at 40 and 158 μg unesterified cholesterol/mg microsomal protein. After incubation, microsomes were reisolated by centrifugation (11) and suspended in phosphate buffer for measurements of cholesterol, protein content, and ACAT activity.

Results. *Demonstration of ACAT activity.* When mammary gland microsomes from normal lactating rats were incubated with [^{14}C]oleoyl-CoA, cholesteryl[^{14}C]oleate was detected after thin-layer chromatography. Incubation conditions were varied to determine how the esterification of microsomal cholesterol varied with the concentration of oleoyl-CoA, time of incubation, amount of microsomal protein, and presence or absence of a reducing agent (dithiothreitol) and of BSA. Figure 1A shows that cholesteryl ester synthesis reached a plateau with approximately 50 μ*M* [^{14}C]oleoyl-CoA; these incubations were conducted in the presence of 2 m*M* dithiothreitol and 80 μ*M* BSA. With a saturating

TABLE I. EFFECT OF LIPIDS ON MAMMARY GLAND ACAT ACTIVITY IN VITRO

Lipid addition	ACAT activity, percentage of control[a] ($\bar{x}$ ± SD, N = 3)	Significance (P)
Progesterone, 15 μ*M*	44.01 ± 1.21	<0.001
Progesterone, 75 μ*M*	7.33 ± 1.81	<0.001
17-β-Estradiol, 75 μ*M*	69.7 ± 2.55	<0.001
Retinol, 75 μ*M*	69.7 ± 7.11	<0.005
Cholesterol, 75 μ*M*	123.5 ± 6.08	<0.025

[a] Control incubations that included the acetone vehicle were run with each test substance or group. Control values equalled 15.9 ± 2.62 pmole/0.2 mg protein in an 8-min incubation period.

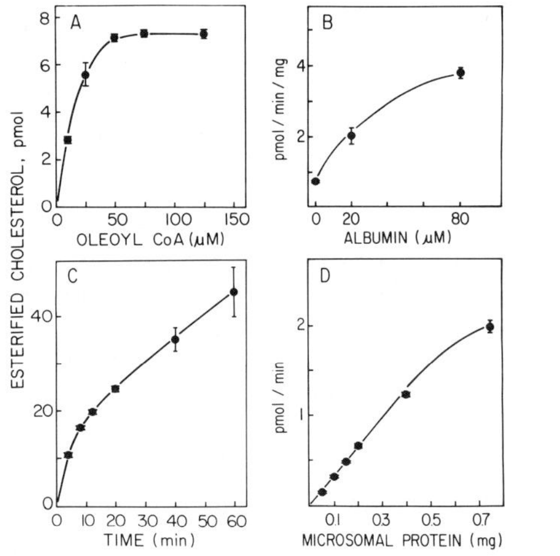

FIG. 1. Effects of concentration of oleoyl-CoA, time of incubation, microsomal protein, and concentration of BSA on yield of esterified cholesterol. (A) Incubation included mammary gland microsomes (0.2 mg protein), 2 m*M* dithiothreitol, 80 μ*M* BSA, and the indicated concentrations of [^{14}C]oleoyl-CoA in 0.2 ml of 0.15 *M* potassium phosphate buffer, pH 7.4. Incubation time was 8 min. (B) Incubations included 2 m*M* dithiothreitol, 62.5 μ*M* [^{14}C]oleoyl-CoA, 0.2 mg microsomal protein, and varying amounts of BSA. Incubation time was 30 min. (C) Conditions were the same as those for A, except that all incubations contained 100 μ*M* [^{14}C]oleoyl-CoA and incubation times varied from 4 to 60 min. (D) Incubations included 2 m*M* dithiothreitol, 80 μ*M* BSA, 100 μ*M* [^{14}C]oleoyl-CoA, and the indicated amounts of microsomal proteins. A different preparation of microsomes having consistently higher ACAT activity was used for the time course. Data are the means ± SD of triplicate incubations corrected in each case for a blank that contained boiled microsomes.

concentration of oleoyl-CoA, exclusion of BSA reduced cholesterol esterification to 19.6% of the value observed with 80 μM BSA (Fig. 1B). Exclusion of dithiothreitol had little effect on ACAT activity. Subsequent studies generally employed 50 or 100 μ*M* [^{14}C]oleoyl-CoA, 80 μ*M* albumin, and 2 m*M* dithiothreitol. A time course (Fig. 1C) indicated that esterification continued for at least 60 min, although the rate of esterification decreased somewhat after a short time. An incubation period of 8 min or less was chosen for most routine incubations. Under these conditions, esterification increased linearly with amount of microsomes up to approximately 0.4 mg of protein (Fig. 1D).

Modulation of ACAT activity in vitro. Since the acyltransferase reaction that is measured with [^{14}C]oleoyl-CoA utilizes endogenous microsomal cholesterol, it is possible that the rate of esterification is limited by membrane cholesterol content. Two experiments were conducted to determine whether addition of cholesterol to rat mammary gland microsomes could increase the yield of esterified cholesterol. Addition of cholesterol as a dispersion in acetone (25 μg cholesterol/0.2 mg microsomal protein) significantly increased the yield of esterified cholesterol as compared to control incubations to which only acetone was added (17.5 ± 0.6 vs 10.8 ± 0.5 pmole cholesteryl ester/30 min, $P < 0.001$). Since the amount of cholesterol incorporated into the microsomal membrane under these conditions was unknown, a second experiment was conducted in which mammary gland microsomes were incubated with serum lipoproteins as a source of free cholesterol, then reisolated by ultracentrifugation before incubation with [^{14}C]oleoyl-CoA to measure ACAT activity. Lipoproteins of $d \leq 1.063$ (very-low- and low-density lipoproteins) from a cholesterol-fed rabbit were utilized since these are enriched in both esterified and unesterified cholesterol and have been shown previously by Rothblat *et al.* (11) to be more efficient donors of cholesterol than are normal lipoproteins. Figure 2 shows that prior incubation with lipoproteins did enrich mammary gland microsomes with unesterified cholesterol, and that subsequent

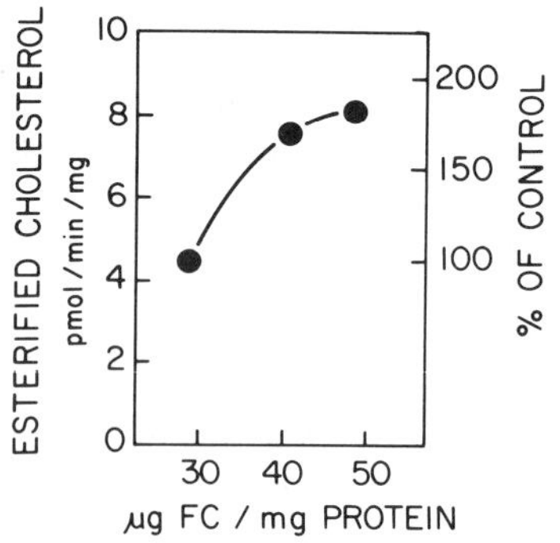

FIG. 2. Microsomal ACAT activity after enrichment of membranes with free cholesterol (FC) by exposure to serum lipoproteins. Points are the means of triplicates of 0.084–0.103 mg protein incubated for 8 min with 50 μ*M* [^{14}C]oleoyl-CoA, 2 m*M* dithiothreitol, and 80 μ*M* BSA.

synthesis of cholesteryl [^{14}C]oleate was also increased after this treatment. Enrichment from 29 to 41 μg cholesterol/mg microsomal protein resulted in 61% increase in ACAT activity, while further enrichment to 48 μg/mg protein resulted in an 81% increase. We may infer from these experiments that ACAT in normal rat mammary gland microsomes is not saturated with cholesterol since provision of extra cholesterol *in vitro* increased both microsomal cholesterol content and the rate of cholesteryl ester synthesis.

Experiments were also conducted to determine whether mammary gland ACAT activity can be modulated *in vitro* by polar steroids such as progesterone. Flint *et al.* (12) showed that progesterone can inhibit ACAT in ovarian extracts, a finding since confirmed in other microsomal systems (13–16). This inhibition by progesterone was reversed by removal of progesterone, but was not overcome by addition of exogenous cholesterol (14). It appears most likely that progesterone perturbs the microsomal membrane and, perhaps, limits the interaction of ACAT with cholesterol. Table I shows that addition of progesterone to rat mammary gland microsomes also inhibited cholesterol esterification: in the presence of 75 μ*M* progesterone, ACAT activity was reduced to only 7.3% of its control value whereas partial inhibition was obtained at a lower concentration of progesterone. Retinol (vitamin A_1), which has been shown to penetrate and expand phospholipid monolayers (17), also significantly reduced the esterification of microsomal cholesterol, as did 17-β-estradiol.

It has recently been found that various *N*-acylamides effectively reduce the esterification of cholesterol *in vitro* and in isolated microsomal membranes (18), as well as in cultured cells (19). We have asked whether these compounds also inhibit ACAT in mammary gland microsomes and, if so, whether the response of ACAT is similar to or different from that of other microsomal acyltransferases. Compound 58-035, a potent inhibitor of cellular cholesterol esterification, was added at concentrations from 2.5 ng to 1.28 μg per incubation (0.2 mg protein in 0.2 ml). At concentrations of 90 ng/incubation and greater, ACAT activity was reduced by at least 85% (Fig. 3). Compound 57-118 at 1.5 μg/incubation also inhibited ACAT by more than 92%

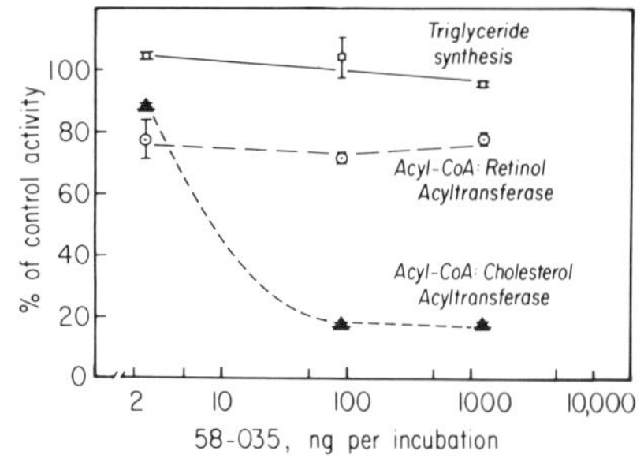

FIG. 3. Effect of compound 58-035 on mammary microsomal ACAT, acyl CoA:retinol acyltransferase, and triglyceride synthesis. Microsomes [0.2 mg protein having 7 μg free cholesterol per mg) from a rat on Day 4 of lactation were incubated for 15 min at 37°C with 58-035 (2.5 ng (5.5 pmole), 90 ng (197 pmole), or 1.28 μg (2.8 mmole)) prior to enzyme assay for 4 min. Control activities in microsomes to which only dimethylsulfoxide was added were: ACAT (▲), 36.5 pmole/min/mg protein; acyl CoA:retinol acyltransferase (⊙), 294 pmole/min/mg; and triglyceride synthesis (□), 75.4 pmole/min/mg. Points are the means (± range) of duplicate incubations.

(data not shown). Compound 58-035, at the same concentrations that inhibited ACAT activity, had no effect on the incorporation of oleate from oleoyl-CoA into triglycerides. When acyl-CoA:retinol acyltransferase was assayed under similar conditions, at least 70% of activity was retained at all concentration of 58-035 that were tested (Fig. 3). It appears, then, that these acylamides block ACAT nearly completely and selectively when added to isolated mammary gland membranes.

Discussion. Acyl-CoA:cholesterol acyltransferase, first described in rat liver membranes (20), has now been found in microsomes of numerous tissues and organs (21). However, ACAT has not been described previously in the lactating mammary gland. The presence of this enzyme suggests that esterified cholesterol in milk may indeed derive from the esterification of cholesterol within this tissue during milk fat biosynthesis.

The regulation of ACAT is still poorly understood. ACAT is an intrinsic membrane protein and most assays of its activity have utilized endogenous microsomal cholesterol as one substrate. Attention has been called to the availability of endogenous cholesterol as a potential factor limiting esterified cholesterol synthesis (11, 14, 21–26). Enrichment of cellular membranes with cholesterol *in vitro* has been found to enhance esterified cholesterol synthesis (11, 14, 23–25) providing evidence that the membrane environment around ACAT does not always provide a saturating concentration of cholesterol. Using a solubilized, partially purified, reconstituted preparation of pig liver ACAT, Doolittle and Chang (26) have recently demonstrated dependence of esterified cholesterol production on the amount of cholesterol in the liposomal membrane. The present study has shown that the normal cholesterol content of the mammary gland microsomal fraction does not support a maximal rate of esterified cholesterol synthesis and that enrichment with free cholesterol *in vitro* can enhance ACAT activity significantly. Enrichment of liver microsomes with cholesterol and increased ACAT activities also have been found after cholesterol feeding (15). However, our experience with the lactating rat has been that feeding animals a diet containing 1% cholesterol–10% olive oil from days 4 to 14 of lactation produced very little change in either the cholesterol content of mammary gland microsomes or in their ACAT activity.[1] Thus, the membrane environment around mammary gland ACAT is likely to provide less than saturating concentrations of cholesterol over a considerable range of dietary cholesterol intakes.

Effects of exogenous steroids on ACAT in microsomal fractions from various tissues have been reported in the past few years. Inhibition by progesterone appears to be a consistent property of ACAT in ovary (12), placenta (27), liver (14), fibroblasts (13), and mammary gland. Other steroids at comparable concentrations have had lesser effects *in vitro*. Simpson and Burkhart (27) found partial (52%) inhibition of placental ACAT by 17-β-estradiol (100 μM), and our results with mammary gland membranes are quite similar. It is not yet known whether steroid hormones regulate ACAT activity acutely *in vivo* under physiological conditions, or whether their effects *in vitro* are due to the surface-active properties of these lipids at relatively high concentrations. Retinol, which is also surface active (17), had similar inhibitory effects on mammary gland, and liver,[1] microsomal ACAT.

Recent studies by Heider *et al.* (18) have shown the ability of the *N*-acylamide 57-118 to block esterified cholesterol synthesis in rabbit intestine and isolated microsomal membranes. The question of whether ACAT is selectively inhibited, or whether other fatty acyltransferases are also blocked, has been explored very recently using cultured hepatoma cells as well as isolated hepatoma or liver membranes (19). These studies have demonstrated essentially complete inhibition of ACAT under conditions where the esterification of glycerides, phospholipids, and retinol was reduced little, if at all. Although the mechanism of this selectivity is not yet understood, our observations permit the conclusion that membrane-bound ACAT is likely to be a distinct acyltransferase whose activity can be modulated independently from that of other lipid acyltransferases. Our comparison in the present report of ACAT, acyl-CoA:retinol acyltransferase, and triglyceride synthesis in rat mammary gland microsomes substantiates our previous results and supports the independence of cholesteryl ester and retinyl ester synthesis in this tissue.

We thank Dr. John Heider of Sandoz, Inc., for generously supplying the *N*-acylamides used in this work and Dr. George Rothblat for his helpful suggestions. This work was supported in part by NIH Grants HL-25744 and HD-16484, and funds from the W. W. Smith Charitable Trust.

[1] A. C. Ross and J. F. Rowe, unpublished results.

1. Potter JM, Nestel PJ. The effects of dietary fatty acids and cholesterol on the milk lipids of lactating women and the plasma cholesterol of breast-fed infants. Amer J Clin Nutr **29**:54–60, 1976.
2. Mellies MJ, Ishikawa TT, Garside P, Burton K, MacGee J, Allen K, Steiner PM, Brady D, Gleuck CJ. Effects of varying maternal dietary cholesterol and phytosterol in lactating women and their infants. Amer J Clin Nutr **31**:1347–1354, 1978.
3. Green MH, Dohner ML, Green JB. Influence of dietary fat and cholesterol on milk lipids and on cholesterol metabolism in the rat. J Nutr **111**:276–286, 1981.
4. Whatley BJ, Green JB, Green MH. Effect of dietary fat and cholesterol on milk composition, milk intake and cholesterol metabolism in the rabbit. J Nutr **111**:432–441, 1981.
5. Jenness R. The Composition of Milk. In: Larson BL, Smith VR, eds. Lactation: A Comprehensive Treatise. New York, Academic Press, Vol 3:p21, 1974.

6. Raphael BC, Patton S, McCarthy RD. The serum lipoproteins as a source of milk cholesterol. FEBS Lett **58**:47–49, 1975.
7. Patton S. Origin of the milk fat globule. J Amer Oil Chem Soc **50**:178–185, 1973.
8. Ross AC. Retinol esterification by mammary gland microsomes from the lactating rat. J Lipid Res **23**:133–144, 1982.
9. Rothblat GH. Cholesteryl ester metabolism in tissue culture cells I. Accumulation in Fu5AH rat hepatoma cells. Lipids **9**:526–535, 1974.
10. Bradford MH. A rapid and sensitive method for the quantitation of protein utilizing the principles of protein–dye binding. Anal Biochem **72**:248–254, 1976.
11. Rothblat GH, Naftulin M, Arbogast LY. Stimulation of acyl CoA:cholesterol acyltransferase activity by hyperlipemic serum lipoproteins. Proc Soc Exp Biol Med **155**:501–506, 1977.
12. Flint APF, Grinwich DL, Armstrong DT. Control of ovarian cholesterol ester biosynthesis. Biochem J **132**:313, 1973.
13. Goldstein JL, Faust JR, Dygos JH, Chorvat RJ, Brown MS. Inhibition of cholesteryl ester formation in human fibroblasts by an analogue of 7-ketocholesterol and by progesterone. Proc Natl Acad Sci USA **75**:1877–1881, 1978.
14. Lichtenstein AH, Brecher P. Properties of acyl-CoA:cholesterol acyltransferase in rat liver microsomes. Topological localization and effects of detergents, albumin, and polar steroids. J Biol Chem **255**:9098–9104, 1980.
15. Erickson SK, Shrewsbury MA, Brooks C, Meyer DJ. Rat liver acyl-coenzyme A:cholesterol acyltransferase: its regulation in vivo and some of its properties in vitro. J Lipid Res **21**:930–941, 1980.
16. Brown MS, Ho YK, Goldstein JL. The cholesteryl ester cycle in macrophage foam cells. J Biol Chem **225**:9344–9352, 1980.
17. Bangham AD, Dingle JT, Lucy JA. Studies on the mode of action of excess of vitamin A. 9. Penetration of lipid monolayers by compounds of the vitamin A series. Biochem J **90**:133–140, 1964.
18. Heider JG, Pickens CE, Kelley LA. Role of acyl CoA:cholesterol acyltransferase in cholesterol absorption and its inhibition by 57-118 in the rabbit. J Lipid Res **24**:1127–1134, 1983.
19. Ross AC, Go KM, Heider JG, Rothblat GH. Selective inhibition of acyl-coenzyme A:cholesterol acyltransferase by compound 58-035. J Biol Chem **259**:815–819, 1984.
20. Goodman DS, Deykin D, Shiratori T. The formation of cholesterol esters with rat liver enzymes. J Biol Chem **239**:1335–1345, 1964.
21. Spector AA, Mathur SN, Kaduce TL. Role of acyl-coenzyme A:cholesterol *O*-acyltransferase in cholesterol metabolism. Progr Lipid Res **18**:31–53, 1979.
22. Nilsson A. Increased cholesterol-ester formation during forced cholesterol synthesis in rat hepatocytes. Eur J Biochem **51**:337–342, 1975.
23. Hashimoto S, Dayton S. Stimulation of cholesterol esterification in hepatic microsomes by lipoproteins from normal and hypercholesterolemic rabbit serum. Biochim Biophys Acta **573**:354–360, 1979.
24. Suckling KE, Stange EF, Dietschy JM. Modulation of hepatic and intestinal acyl-CoA:cholesterol acyltransferase by (de-) phosphorylation and substrate supply in vitro. FEBS Lett **151**:111–116, 1983.
25. Tavani DM, Tanaka T, Strauss JF, Billheimer JT. Regulation of acylcoenzyme A:cholesterol acyltransferase in the luteinized rat ovary: Observations with an improved enzymatic assay. Endocrinology **111**:794–800, 1982.
26. Doolittle GM, Chang TY. Solubilization, partial purification and reconstitution in phosphatidylcholine liposomes of acyl CoA:cholesterol acyltransferase. Biochemistry **21**:674–679, 1982.
27. Simpson ER, Burkhart MF. Acyl CoA:cholesterol acyltransferase activity in human placental microsomes: Inhibition of progesterone. Arch Biochem Biophys **200**:79–85, 1980.

Received October 31, 1983. P.S.E.B.M. 1984, Vol. 176.
Accepted February 3, 1984.

PROCEEDINGS OF THE SOCIETY FOR EXPERIMENTAL BIOLOGY AND MEDICINE **176**, 48–53 (1984)

In Vitro Covalent Binding of 3-[^{14}C]Methylindole Metabolites in Goat Tissues[1] (41841)

TAMMY M. BRAY,[2] JAMES R. CARLSON, AND MARK R. NOCERINI

Department of Animal Sciences, Washington State University, Pullman, Washington 99164

Abstract. Covalent binding of 3-[^{14}C]methylindole (3[^{14}C]MI) in crude microsomal preparations of goat lung, liver, and kidney was measured to determine if a reactive intermediate was formed during the *in vitro* metabolism of 3-methylindole (3MI). The bound radioactivity was highest in lung compared to liver and kidney. The amount of bound radioactivity per nanomole of cytochrome *P*-450 was approximately 10 times higher in the lung compared to liver. No detectable bound radioactivity was found when 3-[^{3}H]methyloxindole was used as the substrate. Cofactor requirements and the effects of inhibitors indicate that a mixed function oxidase (MFO) system is involved in formation of a reactive intermediate. Inhibitors and conjugating agents that are known to reduce the severity of 3MI-induced lung injury such as piperonyl butoxide (MFO inhibitor) and glutathione (conjugating agent) significantly decreased the *in vitro* binding of 3[^{14}C]MI. The results indicate that a reactive intermediate is produced during the metabolism of 3MI by the MFO system. The organ specificity in binding suggests that covalent binding by lung microsomes may be related to the mechanism of 3MI-induced lung injury.

3-Methylindole (3MI) is the main ruminal fermentation product of tryptophan which causes acute pulmonary edema and interstitial emphysema in cattle, sheep, and goats (1–3). 3MI is also a bacterial degradation product of dietary tryptophan in the large intestine of rats, pigs, and man (4). Cigarette smoke contains approximately 4 to 50 μg 3MI per cigarette formed by pyrolysis of tryptophan in tobacco leaves (5). The toxic effects of 3MI in ruminants are limited to the lung. The effects of 3MI administration are rapid and cell selective with the most severe effects on nonciliated bronchiolar epithelial (Clara) cells and alveolar Type I cells (6).

3MI is rapidly metabolized by the mixed function oxidases (MFO) and at least 10 metabolites are excreted in the urine, the majority of which are 3-methyloxindole (3MOI) and its derivatives (7). The parent compound (3MI) is not directly responsible for toxicity since MFO inducers and inhibitors can alter 3MI metabolism and the severity of lung injury (8). Also, infusion of 3MOI or indole-3-carbinol does not induce lung damage (9). These results suggest that a metabolic step prior to the formation of 3MOI is responsible for the toxicity.

There is ample evidence that MFO metabolism can result in activation of nontoxic parent compounds to reactive intermediates with potent mutagenic, carcinogenic, or cytotoxic effects. These effects may be mediated by the formation of reactive electrophilic compounds which covalently bind to cellular macromolecules and interfere with normal cellular function. Covalent binding of radioactive metabolites to macromolecules in *in vitro* microsomal preparations or *in vivo* systems has been widely used as an indication of the formation of reactive intermediates (10, 11). The objectives of this experiment were (a) to determine the extent of covalent binding of 3MI and 3MOI in an *in vitro* microsomal system, (b) to study the organ(s) specificity of covalent binding, and (c) to investigate the effect of MFO inhibitors and conjugating agents on the covalent binding.

Materials and Methods. *Materials.* Methyl-3-[^{14}C]methylindole was obtained by commercial synthesis, from New England Nuclear, Boston, Massachusetts. 3-[G-^{3}H]methyloxindole was obtained by synthesis of 3MOI (12), followed by custom tritium labeling using the tritium gas exposure method (New England Nuclear). Glucose-6-phosphate, glucose-6-

[1] Scientific paper No. 6567. College of Agriculture Research Center, Washington State University, Pullman. Project 1893. This work was supported in part by NIH Grant HL13645.

[2] Author to whom all correspondence should be sent. Present address: Department of Nutrition, University of Guelph, Guelph, Ontario N1G 2W1, Canada.

0037-9727/84 $1.50

phosphate dehydrogenase, NADP, nicotinamide, reduced glutathione (GSH), and UDP–glucuronic acid were obtained from Sigma Chemical Company, St. Louis, Missouri. Piperonyl butoxide was obtained from ICN Pharmaceuticals, Plainview, New York, and SKF-525A was a gift from Smith, Kline and French, Philadelphia, Pennsylvania. Liquid scintillation counting fluid (Bray's solution) and tissue solubilizer (Protosol) were obtained from New England Nuclear, Boston, Massachusetts.

Animals. Five crossbred yearling wether goats, weighing 20 to 30 kg were maintained on pelleted alfalfa and given access to trace mineralized salt and water. The goats were killed by an intravenous dose of sodium pentobarbital. The blood was drained immediately, and the lung, liver, and kidneys were removed and placed in ice for the determination of covalent binding and enzyme assays.

Determination of covalent binding. Freshly removed tissues (liver, lung, or kidney) were homogenized in 3 vol of 1.15% KCl–0.1 *M* phosphate buffer, pH 7.4, at 4°C using a Polytron (Brinkman Instruments, Inc., Westbury, N.Y.), and centrifuged at 10,000*g* for 25 min. To approximate equal amounts of protein in the incubation mixtures, 1 ml of liver supernatant or 2.0 ml of lung and kidney supernatant were used. The substrates (2 ml), 3[^{14}C]MI or 3[^{3}H]MOI, were added in an amount of 2 μmole which contained 0.26 μCi of radioactivity. A NADPH generating system consisting of 1.30 μmole NADP, 50 μmole nicotinamide, 20 μmole glucose-6-phosphate, and 25 μmole $MgCl_2$ in 2 ml of 0.1 *M*, pH 7.4, phosphate buffer was used. When crude microsomal preparation (10,000*g* supernatant) was used, no exogenous glucose-6-phosphate dehydrogenase was added. When microsomes (resuspension of 100,000*g* pellet) were used, 2 units of glucose-6-phosphate dehydrogenase was added in the system. In addition, one of the following MFO inhibitors or conjugating agents (0.5 ml) was added to the incubation mixtures, piperonyl butoxide, 1.5 μmole; SKF-525A, 5.7 μmole; GSH, 7.5 μmole, or UDP–glucuronic acid, 4.3 μmole. The incubation mixtures with a total volume of 6.5 ml was incubated at 37°C for 30 min. The reaction was stopped by the addition of 0.5 ml of 14% perchloric acid ($HClO_4$) followed by centrifugation at 10,000*g* for 10 min. The precipitate was extracted with acetone (7 × 20 ml) and methanol (3 × 20 ml). The precipitated protein was solubilized with 3 ml of Protosol and an aliquot of the covalently bound radioactivity was counted in 10 ml of Bray's solution. Preliminary experiments determined that covalent binding of 3[^{14}C]MI to $HClO_4$ precipitates increased linearly when using mixtures containing up to 3 μmole 3MI and with incubation times up to 1 hr. In order to measure the degree of nonspecific binding, a control tube for each animal was treated in an identical manner except that the 10,000*g* supernatant was boiled for 5 min to inactivate the MFO system. Other control tubes in which the NADPH generating system was omitted produced similar results. Counting efficiency was determined, using the channels-ratio method of quench correction for liquid scintillation counting.

Localization of covalent binding. The 10,000*g* supernatant (crude microsomes) was usually used as the source of MFO in this study. To determine if the covalent binding is catalyzed by the enzyme in microsomal fraction only, microsomal fraction (resuspension of 100,000*g* pellet) or soluble fraction (100,000*g* supernatant) was incubated individually with 3[^{14}C]MI and cofactors as described in previous section. The covalent binding of 3[^{14}C]MI metabolite in each fraction was determined. To investigate if the reactive 3[^{14}C]MI metabolite covalently binds microsomal protein preferentially, after 30 min of incubation with 3[^{14}C]MI, the crude microsomal preparations were further fractionated into 100,000*g* pellets and 100,000*g* supernatant by ultracentrifugation for 1 hr. The proteins in the microsomal and soluble fractions were precipitated with 1 ml of 14% $HClO_4$. The distributions of covalently bound radioactivity in the protein of subfractions from goat liver, lung, and kidney were determined as described in the aforementioned section.

MFO enzyme assays. Microsomes used for enzyme assays were from liver, lung, and kidney of each goat isolated by a differential centrifugation method (13). The protein content of the microsomal fraction was determined by the method of Lowry *et al.* (14). The cytochrome *P*-450 contents of the lung and liver

TABLE I. COVALENT BINDING OF RADIOACTIVE SUBSTRATES IN CRUDE MICROSOMAL PREPARATIONS FROM GOAT LIVER, LUNG, AND KIDNEY

	Covalently bound radioactivity[a] (nmole/10 mg protein/30 min)		
Substrates	Liver	Lung	Kidney
3-[^{14}C]Methylindole	9.0 ± 2.5[b]	32.1 ± 6.0[c]	2.0 ± 1.0[d]
3-[^{3}H]Methyloxindole	2.0 ± 1.0	ND[e]	ND

[a] Means ± SEM of five animals per group.
[b–d] Values in the same row with different superscripts are significantly different ($P < 0.05$; Duncan's multiple-range test).
[e] ND, not detectable.

were determined by difference spectrophotometry using the extinction coefficient of 91 mM^{-1} cm^{-1} (15). The activity of antipyrine *N*-demethylase was determined by quantifying the production of formaldehyde (16). Aniline hydroxylase activity was determined by the method of Imai *et al.* (17) in which *p*-aminophenol formation was measured.

Statistical analysis. Standard errors of the mean were determined for each data set, and either Student's *t* test or Duncan's multiple-range test was used to test for statistical differences (18).

Results and Discussion. Radioactivity expressed as nanomoles of 3[^{14}C]MI or 3[H^3]MOI covalently bound to crude microsomal protein of goat liver, lung or kidney is presented in Table I. When 3[^{14}C]MI was used as the substrate, significant covalent binding occurred in the lung, liver, and kidney, and the lung contained the highest binding. When 3[^{3}H]MOI was used as the substrate, covalent binding was not observed in lung and kidney tissues, and a trace amount was present in the liver. These results indicate that a reactive intermediate, capable of binding macromolecules, is formed during the metabolism of 3MI. The higher covalent binding of ^{14}C radioactivity in lung microsomal preparations compared to liver or kidney may be related to the tissue specificity of 3MI toxicity, suggesting that the MFO metabolism of 3MI in the lung may be responsible for organ specificity. The lack of binding by 3[^{3}H]MOI also may reflect the relative *in vivo* lung toxicity of these substrates. Preliminary experiments determined that binding of ^{14}C radioactivity was not observed when the NADPH generating system was deleted from the incubation media. Carbon monoxide treatment or boiling of the en-

TABLE II. THE EFFECT OF MFO INHIBITORS AND CONJUGATING AGENTS ON THE COVALENT BINDING OF 3-[^{14}C]MI METABOLITES IN CRUDE MICROSOMAL PREPARATIONS OF GOAT LIVER, LUNG, AND KIDNEY

	Covalently bound radioactivity[a] (nmole/10 mg protein/30 min)		
Treatment	Liver	Lung	Kidney
Control	9.0 ± 2.5	32.1 ± 6.0	2.0 ± 1.0
MFO inhibitors			
Piperonyl butoxide	3.0 ± 1.1[b]	3.5 ± 0.4[b]	ND[c]
SKF-525A	11.0 ± 3.4	40.5 ± 7.4	ND
Conjugating agents			
Glutathione	2.0 ± 1.0[b]	5.2 ± 1.5[b]	ND
UDP–glucuronic acid	10.5 ± 3.5	31.5 ± 2.3	ND

[a] Means ± SEM of five animals per treatment.
[b] Values are significantly different ($P < 0.05$) from the control in the same tissue by Student's *t* test.
[c] ND, not detectable.

TABLE III. COVALENTLY BOUND RADIOACTIVITY OF 3[^{14}C]MI METABOLITE IN MICROSOMES AND SOLUBLE FRACTIONS OF GOAT LIVER, LUNG, AND KIDNEY

	Covalently bound radioactivity[a] (nmoles/10 mg protein/30 min)		
Fraction	Liver	Lung	Kidney
Microsomes	48.0 ± 1.0[b]	131.0 ± 10.0[c]	10.0 ± 1.0[d]
Soluble	0.01 ± 0.00	0.05 ± 0.03	0.02 ± 0.01

[a] Means ± SEM of four incubations per group.
[b–d] Values in the same row with different superscripts are significantly different ($P < 0.01$; Duncan's multiple-range test).

zyme also inhibited covalent binding. Thus, an NADPH-dependent MFO is most likely the enzyme system in the 10,000*g* supernatant responsible for the activation of 3MI. This is also supported by *in vivo* experiments in which induction or inhibition of the MFO system with phenobarbital or piperonyl butoxide altered the metabolism of 3MI and the susceptibility to 3MI-induced lung disease in goats (8). Hanafy and Bogan (19) have also shown that 3[^{14}C]MI is covalently bound to microsomal protein when incubated with bovine lung microsomes and that the binding is cytochrome *P*-450 dependent.

Table II shows the effect of MFO inhibitors or conjugating agents on the covalent binding of 3[^{14}C]MI in the crude microsomal preparation from goat liver, lung, and kidney. The addition of piperonyl butoxide or GSH significantly inhibited covalent binding in the lung and liver, but SKF-525A or UDP–glucuronic acid had no effect at the concentration used. No binding of 3[^{14}C]MI occurred when kidney crude microsomal preparations were used. Piperonyl butoxide is often used as a synergist with insecticides because of its ability to covalently bind to the terminal oxidase of MFO system (20). SKF-525A is also a known MFO inhibitor, but it had no effect on the 3[^{14}C]MI binding in both liver and lung of goats. When bovine lung microsomes were used, SKF-525A inhibited 64% of the covalent binding of 3MI metabolites (19). The lack of inhibition of covalent binding by SKF-525A in goat tissues may reflect the species difference in the substrate specificity of the MFO system involved.

GSH is a nucleophilic tripeptide of ubiquitous tissue distribution (21). Tissue GSH concentration can influence the toxicity and organ specificity of xenobiotics (22). The reduction in covalent binding of 3[^{14}C]MI metabolite by GSH addition suggests that the 3MI metabolite may be electrophilic. The activated 3MI metabolite could be conjugated directly with GSH molecule *in vitro*. UDP–glucuronic acid is quantitatively an important conjugation agent using glucose as the precursor (23). However, addition of UDP–glucuronic acid in the microsomal incubation mixture did not affect the covalent binding of 3[^{14}C]MI suggesting that glucuronide conjugation to 3MI does not occur *in vitro*.

Two experiments were carried out to determine, first, if the activation of 3[^{14}C]MI to reactive intermediate is specific by the enzyme in the microsomal fraction, second, if the reactive intermediate will attack the macromolecules in microsomal fraction preferentially when the crude microsomes were used. Table III shows the covalently bound radio-

TABLE IV. COVALENTLY BOUND RADIOACTIVITY OF 3-[^{14}C]METHYLINDOLE IN SUBFRACTIONS OF CRUDE MICROSOMAL PREPARATIONS OF GOAT LIVER, LUNG, AND KIDNEY

	Covalently bound radioactivity[a] (nmole/10 mg protein/30 min)		
Subfractions	Liver	Lung	Kidney
100,000*g* Pellet	11.2 ± 1.4[b]	33.0 ± 2.3[c]	2.4 ± 1.1[d]
100,000*g* Supernatant	ND[e]	0.57 ± 0.06	0.17 ± 0.02

[a] Means ± SEM of three incubation samples per group.
[b–d] Values in the same row with different superscript letters are significantly different ($P < 0.05$) by Duncan's multiple-range test.
[e] ND, not detectable.

TABLE V. Cytochrome *P*-450 Content and MFO Activities in Goat Liver, Lung, and Kidney

	Liver	Lung	Kidney
Cytochrome *P*-450 (nmole/mg protein)	1.21 ± 0.32[a]	0.44 ± 0.10[b]	ND[c]
Aniline hydroxylase (nmole product formed/10 mg protein/min)	4.5 ± 1.2[a]	1.9 ± 0.6[b]	ND
Aminopyrine demethylase (nmole product formed/10 mg protein/min)	4.3 ± 0.8[a]	0.8 ± 0.2[b]	ND

[a,b] Means ± SEM of five animals per group. Values in same row with different superscripts are significantly different ($P < 0.05$; Student's *t* test).
[c] ND, not detectable.

activity of 3[^{14}C]MI in microsomal and soluble fractions when the incubation medium consists of either 100,000*g* pellet or 100,000*g* supernatant. The data clearly indicated that the microsomal fraction is mainly responsible for the activation of 3MI. The soluble fraction does not contain enzyme that could activate 3MI as indicated by the trace amount of radioactivity in soluble fractions of all three types of tissues. Again, the lung has the highest covalently bound radioactivity in the microsomal proteins compared to liver and kidney. Table IV depicts the distribution of covalently bound radioactivity in protein of microsomal and soluble fractions when 3[^{14}C]MI was incubated with crude microsomal mixtures. The result indicated that the microsomal fraction has high affinity for 3[^{14}C]MI metabolite or the binding is specific for microsomal protein. The higher covalent binding in the microsomal fractions may also suggest an electrophilic 3MI metabolite is produced which reacts with macromolecules adjacent to its site of formation. The lung microsomes have higher radioactivity than that of liver or kidney which is consistent with the results obtained when 3[^{14}C]MI was incubated with crude microsomal preparation (Table I) or 100,000*g* pellet (Table III).

The cytochrome *P*-450 content and the NADPH-dependent microsomal enzyme activities in liver, lung, and kidney are summarized in Table V. The pulmonary cytochrome *P*-450 content is one-third that of liver. The activity of aniline hydroxylase and aminopyrine demethylase in the lung is one-half or one-fifth that of the liver levels, respectively. Even though there was significantly more binding in lung microsomes compared to liver, the total cytochrome *P*-450 content and enzyme activities were significantly lower in lung than in liver. The ratio of nanomoles of covalently bound 3[^{14}C]MI of cytochrome *P*-450 was 7.4 in the liver and 72.7 in the lung. This suggests that a form of cytochrome *P*-450 with high affinity to 3MI as substrate may be present in lung. This form of cytochrome *P*-450 may be responsible for the production of the reactive intermediate. Alternatively, differences in the tissue concentrations of conjugating agents or enzymes (i.e., tissue GSH level and GSH-S-transferase activity) could also influence the detoxification of 3MI and the degree of covalent binding in these tissues.

1. Carlson JR, Dickinson EO, Yokoyama MT, Bradley B. Pulmonary edema and emphysema in cattle after intraruminal and intravenous administration of 3-methylindole. Amer J Vet Res **36**:1341–1347, 1975.
2. Carlson JR, Yokoyama MT, Dickinson EO. Induction of pulmonary edema and emphysema in cattle and goats with 3-methylindole. Science **176**:298–299, 1972.
3. Bradley B, Carlson JR, Dickinson EO. 3-Methylindole-induced pulmonary edema and emphysema in sheep. Amer J Vet Res **39**:1355–1358, 1978.
4. Yokoyama MT, Carlson JR. Microbial metabolites of tryptophan in the intestinal tract with special reference to skatole. Amer J Clin Nutr **32**:173–178, 1979.
5. Hoshika Y. Simultaneous gas chromatographic analysis of lower fatty acids, phenols, and indoles using a glass capillary column. J Chromatogr **144**:181–185, 1977.
6. Bradley BJ, Carlson JR. Ultrastructural pulmonary changes induced by intravenously administered 3-methylindole in goats. Amer J Pathol **99**:551–556, 1980.
7. Hammond AC, Carlson JR. The metabolism and disposition of 3-methylindole in goats. Life Sci **25**:1301–1306, 1979.
8. Bray TM, Carlson JR. Role of mixed function oxidase

in 3-methylindole-induced acute pulmonary edema in goats. Amer J Vet Res **40:**1268–1272, 1979.
9. Potchoiba MJ, Carlson HR, Breeze RG. Metabolism and pneumotoxicity of 3-methyloxindole, indole-3-carbinol and 3-methylindole in goats. Amer J Vet Res **43:**1418–1422, 1982.
10. Jollow DJ, Smith C. Biochemical aspects of toxic metabolite formation, detoxification, and covalent binding. In: Jollow DJ, Kocsis JJ, Snyder R, Vainio H, eds. Biological Reactive Intermediates. New York, Plenum, pp42–59, 1977.
11. Gillette JR. A perspective on the role of chemically reactive metabolites of foreign compounds in toxicity. 1. Correlation of changes in covalent binding of reactive intermediates with changes in the incidence of severity of toxicity. Biochem Pharmacol **23:**2785–2791, 1974.
12. Hinman RL, Bauman CP. Reactions of 3-bromooxindoles. The synthesis of 3-methyleneoxindole. J Org Chem **29:**2431–2437, 1964.
13. Mazel P. Experiment illustrating drug metabolism *in vitro.* In: LaDu BN, Mandel HG, Way EL, eds. Fundamentals of Drug Metabolism and Drug Deposition. Baltimore, Williams & Wilkins, p546, 1971.
14. Lowry OR, Rosebrough NJ, Farr AL, Randall RA. Protein measurements with the Folin phenol reagent. J Biol Chem **193:**265–275, 1951.
15. Omura T, Sato R. The carbon monoxide-binding pigment of liver microsomes. 1. Evidence for its hemoprotein nature. J Biol Chem **239:**2370–2378, 1964.
16. Parkinson A, Safe S. The detection of enzyme induction by rat liver microsomes prepared by isoelectric precipitation. J Pharm Pharmacol **31:**444–447, 1979.
17. Imai Y, Ito A, Sato R. Evidence for biochemically different types of vesicles in the hepatic microsomal fraction. J Biochem (Japan) **60:**417–428, 1966.
18. Steel RGO, Torrie JH. Principles and Procedures of Statistics. New York, McGraw–Hill, 1980.
19. Hanafy MSM, Bogan JA. The covalent binding of 3-methylindole metabolites to bovine tissue. Life Sci **27:**1225–1231, 1980.
20. Levine BS, Murphy SD. Effect of piperonyl butoxide on the metabolism of dimethyl and diethyl phosphorothionate insecticides. Toxicol Appl Pharmacol **40:**393–406, 1977.
21. Franklin MR. Inhibition of mixed function oxidators substrates forming reduced cytochrome P-450 metabolic-intermediate complexes. Pharmacol Ther **2:**227–245, 1977.
22. Boyd SC, Sasame HA, Boyd MR. Effects of cold-restraint stress on rat gastric and hepatic glutathione: A potential determinant of response to chemical carcinogens. Physiol Behav **27:**377–379.
23. Dutton GJ. Control of UDP-glucuronyltransferase activity. Biochem Pharmacol **24:**1835–1841, 1975.

Received November 30, 1983. P.S.E.B.M. 1984, Vol. 176.
Accepted February 6, 1984.

PROCEEDINGS OF THE SOCIETY FOR EXPERIMENTAL BIOLOGY AND MEDICINE **176,** 54–59 (1984)

Teratogenic Effect of AY 9944 in Rats: Importance of the Day of Administration and Maternal Plasma Cholesterol Level (41842)

VERONIQUE BARBU,† CHARLES ROUX,* ROLANDE DUPUIS,* JEAN GARDETTE,† AND JEAN-CLAUDE MAZIERE†

**Laboratoire d'Embryologie, Service du Pr. Ch. Roux, and †Laboratoire de Biochimie, Service du Pr. J. Polonovski, Faculté de Médecine Saint-Antoine, 27, rue Chaligny, 75571 Paris Cedex 12, France*

Abstract. An inhibitor of cholesterol synthesis, AY 9944 (*trans*-1,4-bis(2-chlorobenzylaminomethyl) cyclohexane dihydrochloride) is teratogenic. A single dose of AY 9944 (50 mg/kg or 75 mg/kg) given to Wistar pregnant rats on the second, fourth, sixth, seventh, or eighth day of gestation induced malformations such as holoprosencephaly. They were often limited to isolated pituitary agenesis. The highest percentage of holoprosencephalic fetuses was found when AY 9944 was given on the fourth day of gestation. Whatever the dose and the day of administration, the lower the maternal plasma cholesterol level, the more frequent were holoprosencephalic fetuses. Therefore, it is suggested that the decrease in maternal plasma cholesterol level is at least one of the factors provoking holoprosencephaly.

We have previously reported that AY 9944 (*trans*-1,4-bis(2-chlorobenzylaminomethyl) cyclohexane dihydrochloride), an inhibitor of cholesterol synthesis, given to pregnant Wistar rats on the second, third, and fourth days of gestation at a dose of 50 mg/kg/day induced fetal abnormalities such as holoprosencephaly (1, 2). Pituitary agenesis, which can be considered a minor form of holoprosencephaly, was the most frequently observed abnormality. These abnormalities are initiated around the 10th day of embryonic development. We have also shown that this early administration of AY 9944 produced a significant decrease of maternal plasma sterol level on the 10th day of gestation. Pituitary agenesis was found only when maternal plasma sterol level was below 0.30 g/liter (3).

The present studies were conducted to delineate the relationships between fetal abnormalities and the day of treatment with AY 9944 or maternal plasma sterol level during gestation. A single dose of AY 9944 was therefore given on the second, fourth, sixth, seventh, or eighth day of gestation and maternal plasma sterol level was measured on various days of gestation. The nature of the sterols was determined by thin-layer chromatography.

Materials and Methods. Female virgin Wistar rats weighing about 200 g (Lessieux Elevage) were mated with males of the same stock overnight. Vaginal smears were examined in the morning. The presence of spermatozoa designated the first day of gestation. The animals were fed a stock diet (Union de l'Alimentation Rationnelle 103) with the following composition: 3100 cal/kg, 12% water, 20% protein, 4% lipid (25% from animal origin, 75% from vegetable origin), 54.5% carbohydrates, 4% cellulose, and 5.5% salt mixture. The vitamin content of the diet was composed of the major vitamins A, B, D, K, E, and other vitamin cofactors.

The females were assigned to three groups (according to dosage given) and 11 subgroups (according to day of treatment).

Group 1. Wistar control rats given 5 ml/kg of distilled water by intubation.

Groups 2 to 6. Wistar rats given by intubation a single dose of 50 mg/kg of AY 9944 in 5 ml/kg of distilled water, respectively, on the second, fourth, sixth, seventh, or eighth day of gestation.

Groups 7 to 11. Wistar rats given by intubation a single dose of 75 mg/kg of AY 9944 in 5 ml/kg of distilled water, respectively, on the second, fourth, sixth, seventh, or eighth day of gestation.

On Day 0 (before mating) and on the 10th and 21st days, blood was taken from the orbital sinus for analysis of plasma cholesterol concentration. Plasma was kept frozen at −20°C until assayed by an enzymatic method (4, 5)

0037-9727/84 $1.50

TABLE I. EFFECT OF AY 9944 ON FETAL MORTALITY AND ABNORMALITIES

Rats	Day of administration of AY 9944	Number of litters	Number of implantations	Number of live fetuses	Fetal mortality (%)	Number of fetuses with holoprosencephaly	Percentage holoprosencephaly among live fetuses
A							
Control		10	106	88	17.0	0	0
Treated by	2nd	5	50	43	14.0[a]	5	11.6***
50 mg/kg	4th	13	105	75	28.6*	29	38.7†
AY 9944	6th	11	103	61	40.8†	22	36.1†
	7th	12	105	72	31.4**	4	5.6[a]
	8th	14	172	138	19.8[a]	8	5.8[a]
B							
Control		10	106	88	17.0	0	0
Treated by	2nd	7	63	46	27.0[a]	22	47.8†
75 mg/kg	4th	13	103	53	48.5†	41	77.3†
AY 9944	6th	14	174	82	52.9†	36	43.9†
	7th	7	81	34	58.9†	6	17.6†
	8th	13	133	81	39.1†	6	7.4*

Note. Treated female Wistar rats received either 50 or 75 mg/kg of AY 9944 in 5 ml/kg distilled water by intubation at various days of gestation. Control female Wistar rats received 5 ml/kg distilled water by intubation.

[a] N.S. compared to control rats.

* $P < 0.05$ compared to control rats.

** $P < 0.02$ compared to control rats.

*** $P < 0.01$ compared to control rats.

† $P < 0.001$ compared to control rats.

(Kit Biomérieux) which tests both 7-dehydrocholesterol and cholesterol. The maternal plasma lipids were extracted according to the Folch's method. Thin-layer chromatographs have been assayed. One-half of the plates were dipped in 10% aqueous $AgNO_3$. The plates were then chromatographed in two solvent systems: the first half of the plate in chloroform/methanol/water, 65/25/4 (v/v/v); then in chloroform/di-isobutylketone, 90/10 (v/v). The sterols were separated in the silver nitrate part and seen after sulfuric acid treatment of the plates and read under UV light.

Females were killed on the 21st day of gestation by cervical dislocation. Fetuses were weighed, examined under a dissecting microscope, and fixed in Bouin's fluid. They were dissected, and their heads were sectioned according to the technique of Wilson (6).

Results. Administration of a single dose of AY 9944 to pregnant rats on different days of gestation resulted in high fetal mortality and teratogenesis (Table I, Fig. 1). The main malformations observed were of the holoprosencephalic type.

In the 50 mg/kg group, fetal mortality was significantly higher than in controls after administration on the fourth, the sixth, or the seventh day of gestation. The highest incidence was observed in the subgroup given the drug on the sixth day. Holoprosencephaly was observed in all groups. It was particularly frequent when the drug was given on the fourth or sixth days (39 vs 36%).

In the rats given 75 mg/kg on the fourth, sixth, seventh, or eighth day of gestation, fetal mortality was significantly higher than in controls; the highest rate was found in the sixth or seventh day subgroups. After administration on the eighth day of gestation, fetal mortality decreased to a level close to that of rats given the drug on the second day. Holoprosencephaly was observed in all groups. As in the 50 mg/kg group, the maximum effect was

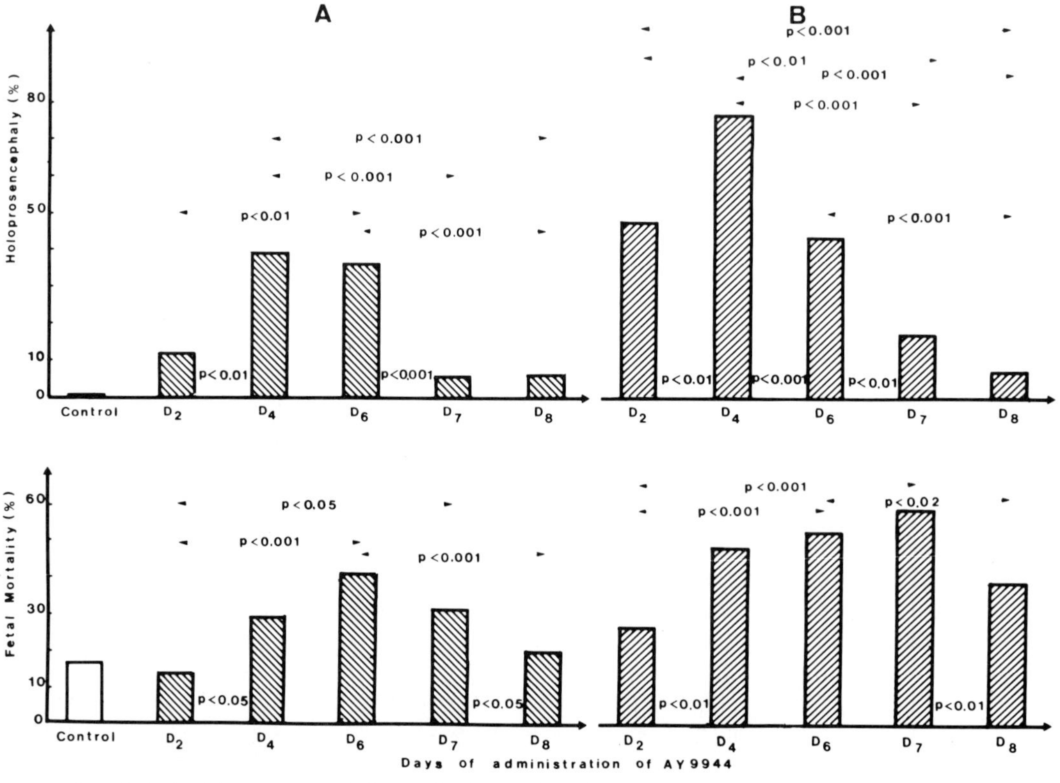

FIG. 1. Rate of holoprosencephaly and fetal mortality when a single dose of AY 9944 was given on the second, fourth, sixth, seventh, or eighth day of gestation. A, 50 mg/kg; B, 75 mg/kg.

found after administration on the fourth day of gestation: 77% of fetuses were holoprosencephalic.

Thus, the fetal mortality and the percentage of live fetuses with holoprosencephaly depended on the day of administration of AY 9944 for both doses. As a whole, 52% of the 73 rats treated with a single dose of AY 9944, at any of the doses tested, gave abnormal fetuses.

The variations in maternal plasma sterol level as a function of the number of days elapsed after administration of AY 9944 are presented in Fig. 2. As plasma sterol level was measured on the 10th and 21st days of gestation, the number of days that elapsed after administration of the drug varied according to the day it was given. The lowest values of maternal plasma sterol level on the 10th day of gestation were obtained 6 days after treatment in the 50 mg/kg group and 6 to 8 days after treatment in the 75 mg/kg group. After this time, plasma sterol level returned rapidly to normal values. (Assays repeated every 2 days in five animals given 75 mg/kg on the 4th day of gestation showed the same curve.) Moreover, the lower the maternal plasma sterol level on the 10th day, the more frequent was holoprosencephaly in fetuses. Figure 3 shows the relationship between the incidence of fetal holoprosencephaly and maternal sterol concentration. Figure 4 shows that the thin-layer chromatography allowed us to point out the following fact: 7-dehydrocholesterol was one major sterol present among the plasma sterols in treated rats. Therefore, the enzymatic assay giving the sum of both 7-dehydrocholesterol and cholesterol, the decrease of maternal plasma sterol level can be considered as a decrease of maternal plasma cholesterol level.

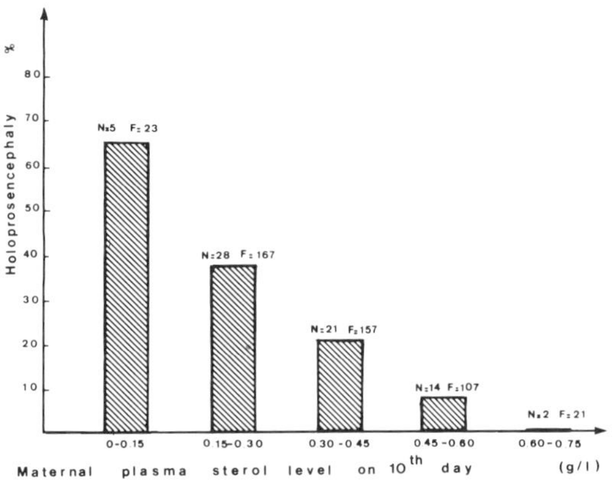

FIG. 3. ▨, Global rate of holoprosencephaly as related to maternal plasma sterol level measured on the 10th day of gestation ranged in classes of 0.15 g/liter. N, number of litters; F, number of live fetuses. Correlation coefficient $r = -0.971$ ($P < 0.01$).

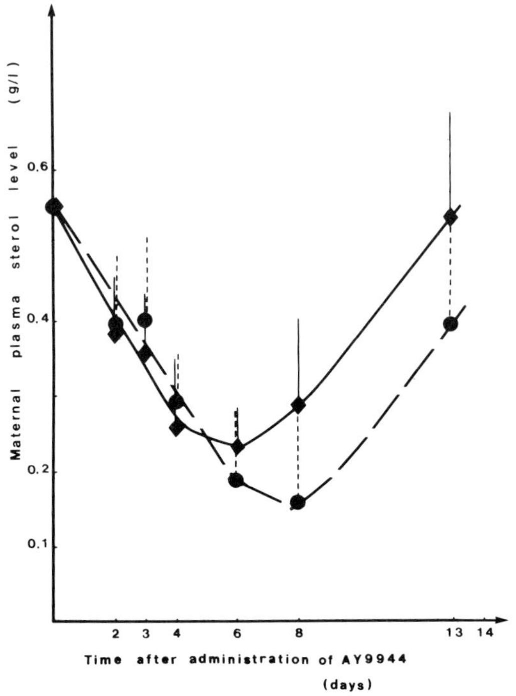

FIG. 2. Maternal plasma sterol level measured on various days after administration of a single dose of AY 9944. —♦—, 50 mg/kg; —●—, 75 mg/kg.

Thus, a strong inverse correlation was found between maternal plasma cholesterol level on the 10th day of gestation and the percentage of holoprosencephaly which occurred.

Discussion. As the mammalian embryo is entirely dependent on its mother, all modifications of the maternal milieu can affect its development. Numerous authors (7–9) have shown that maternal deficiencies can induce fetal malformations. Therefore, administration of drugs producing maternal deficiencies can result in fetal abnormalities. Currently, it is well known that early rat embryos have a limited capacity to synthesize cholesterol from acetate (10, 11) and most embryo cholesterol

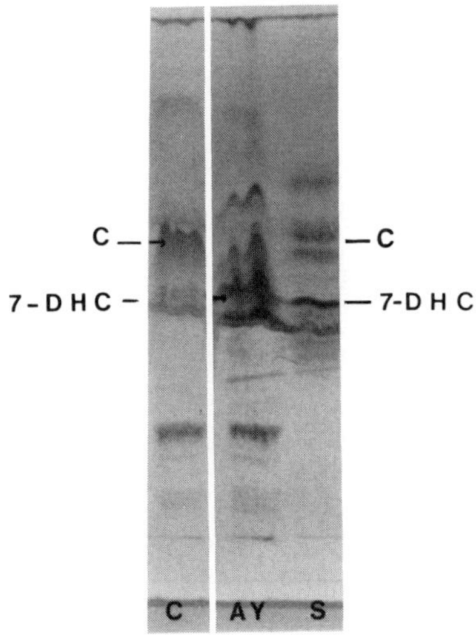

FIG. 4. Thin-layer chromatography of lipid extracts of maternal plasma on the 10th day of gestation. Bands: C, free cholesterol; 7-DHC, 7-dehydrocholesterol. Columns: C, control maternal plasma; AY, maternal plasma of Wistar rat treated by one single dose of AY 9944: 75 mg/kg on the 4th day of gestation; S, Standards of different sterols.

is of maternal origin until the 13th day of gestation. Thereafter, the ability to synthesize cholesterol increases progressively (11).

Consequently AY 9944, which inhibits cholesterol synthesis and induces a decrease of maternal plasma cholesterol level, is embryolethal and teratogenic, producing holoprosencephalic fetuses when given during the first few days of gestation. The results reported here demonstrate that the efficiency of a single dose of the drug depends on the concentration and day of administration.

The rates of malformation observed in 7th and 8th day subgroups were low and statistically nonsignificant when compared with controls, but they must be taken into account, since this kind of malformation is never observed spontaneously in rats.

The strong inverse correlation between the rate of holoprosencephaly and the concentration of maternal plasma sterol level on the 10th day of gestation suggests that decrease of maternal sterol level is at least one of the factors provoking holoprosencephaly. Chromatographic assay of the lipid extract from maternal plasma allowed us to confirm that the relative accumulation of 7-dehydrocholesterol implied a decrease of maternal plasma cholesterol.

Other previously reported results support this hypothesis. We have shown that AY 9944 teratogenesis and embryo lethality could be prevented by administration of hypercholesterolemia-provoking diet (12). In rats given AY 9944 on the 2nd, 3rd, and 4th days and fed a hypercholesterolemia-provoking diet before and during gestation, maternal plasma cholesterol level was higher than normal on the 10th day of gestation and fetuses were not malformed. These results led to the hypothesis that its teratogenic action is correlated with the decrease of maternal plasma cholesterol level.

These quantitative modifications are not the only ones to be considered. Concomitant qualitative modifications of sterols and lipids in mothers and fetuses must also play an important role. It is known that, after administration of AY 9944, the nature of synthesized sterols is modified. There is a clearcut decrease of cholesterol and an accumulation of 7-dehydrocholesterol (13–17). It can be hypothesized that the replacement of cholesterol by 7-dehydrocholesterol in cell membranes could play a role in the perturbation of differentiation where cell–cell interactions are known to be very important.

Furthermore, preliminary work has indicated the complex nature of the lipid modifications occurring after administration of AY 9944. In addition to sterols, phospholipids and sphingolipids were also found modified. Since they are essential constituents of the cell membrane, these changes could also modify its fluidity and, therefore, cell–cell interactions.

In addition, it can be hypothesized that a direct action of the drug could also play a role in provoking holoprosencephalic malformations. In fact, *in vitro* experiments have demonstrated a significant decrease in membrane viscosity, which was too rapid to be due to complex lipid modifications and must be attributed to a direct action of the drug on cell membranes (unpublished data).

In conclusion, in pregnant rats given a single dose of AY 9944, we observed a strong inverse correlation between the rate of fetal holoprosencephaly and the decrease of maternal plasma cholesterol level. It is suggested that the mechanisms of AY 9944 teratogenesis are complex.

In addition to a quantitative effect on cholesterol, modification of the nature of the sterols, as well as the phospholipids and sphingolipids in embryo cell membranes, could play a role in producing such abnormalities. A direct action of the drug itself may also be possible.

1. Roux C, Aubry M. Action tératogène chez le Rat d'un inhibiteur de la synthèse du cholestérol. C R Soc Biol **160:**1353–1357, 1966.
2. Roux C, Dupuis R, Horvath C, Giroud A. Interpretation of isolated agenesis of the pituitary. Teratology **19:**39–44, 1979.
3. Roux C, Dupuis R, Horvath C, Talbot JN. Teratogenic effect of an inhibitor of cholesterol synthesis AY 9944 in Rats = correlation with maternal sterolemia. J Nutr **110:**2310–2312, 1980.
4. Richmond W. Preparation and properties of a cholesterol oxidase from *Nocardia* sp. and its application to the enzymatic assay of total cholesterol in serum. Clin Chem **19:**1350–1356, 1973.
5. Richmond W. The automated enzymic assay of free and total cholesterol in serum. Z Klin Chem Klin Biochem **12:**226, 1974.
6. Wilson JG. Embryological considerations in teratology. In: Wilson JG, Warkany J, eds. Teratology Principles and Techniques. Chicago, Univ of Chicago Press, pp251–277, 1965.
7. Giroud A, Lefèbvres-Boisselot J, Dupuis R. Légèreté des déficiences B2 tératogènes. Arch Fr Pédiatr **10:**1–3, 1953.
8. Giroud A, Lefèbvres J, Dupuis R. Légèreté de la carence pantothénique au stade tératogène. C R Soc Biol **155:**974–975, 1961.
9. Hurley LS, Mutch PB. Prenatal and postnatal development after transitory gestational zinc deficiency in rats. J Nutr **103:**649–656, 1973.
10. Chevalier P. Transferts et synthèses du cholestérol chez le Rat au cours de sa croissance. Biochim Biophys Acta **84:**316–339, 1964.
11. Pratt HPM. Lipids and transitions in embryos. In: Johnson MH, ed. Development in Mammals. Amsterdam, North-Holland, pp83–129, 1979.
12. Roux C, Horvath C, Dupuis R. Teratogenic action and embryo lethality of AY 9944[R]: Prevention by a hypercholesterolemia provoking diet. Teratology **19:**35–38, 1979.
13. Dvornik D, Kraml M, Dubuc J, Givner M, Gaudry R. A novel mode of inhibition of cholesterol biosynthesis. J Amer Chem Soc **85:**3309, 1963.
14. Kraml M, Bagli JF, Dvornik D. Inhibition of the conversion of 7-dehydrocholesterol to cholesterol by AY 9944. Biochem Biophys Res Commun **15:**455–457, 1964.
15. Givner ML, Dvornik D. Agents affecting lipid metabolism. XV. Biochemical studies with the cholesterol biosynthesis inhibitor AY 9944 in young and mature rats. Biochem Pharmacol **14:**611–619, 1965.
16. Dvornik D, Hill P. Effect of long-term administration of AY 9944 an inhibitor of dehydrocholesterol reductase, on serum and tissue lipids in the rat. J Lipid Res **9:**587–595, 1968.
17. Chappel C, Dubuc J, Dvornik D, Givner M, Humber L, Kraml M, Voith K, Gaudry R. An inhibitor of cholesterol biosynthesis. Nature (London) **201:**497–498, 1964.

Received July 28, 1983. P.S.E.B.M. 1984, Vol. 176.
Accepted January 27, 1984.

PROCEEDINGS OF THE SOCIETY FOR EXPERIMENTAL BIOLOGY AND MEDICINE **176**, 60–69 (1984)

Characterization of Cells Isolated and Cultured from Human Bone (41843)

JON E. WERGEDAL AND DAVID J. BAYLINK

Department of Medicine, Loma Linda University, Loma Linda, California 92350, and Jerry L. Pettis Veterans Administration Hospital, Loma Linda, California 92357

Abstract. Cells isolated from samples of human iliac crest and human femoral heads by collagenase digestion have been successfully cultured in Fitton–Jackson modified BGJ_b culture medium supplemented with penicillin (100 units/ml), streptomycin (100 μg/ml), and fetal calf serum (10%). Although only a low proportion of the cells survived the initial plating (<1%), cells established in culture were readily passaged. Examination of cells obtained at intervals during the collagenase digestion showed that the percentage of cells that attached increased with time of digestion. Rapid sample preparation of rat bone did not substantially increase the number of cells attaching. Thus, it seems unlikely that the low survival was due to loss of viability during sample transportation and preparation. Of several media tested BGJ_b supplemented with 10% fetal calf serum supported the best growth. Population doubling time averaged 104 hr. Cultured human bone cells were assayed for alkaline phosphatase activity using the azo dye method with naphthol ASTR phosphate as the substrate. A portion of the cells (19%) demonstrated high activity in all cultures examined regardless of the passage number of the culture. Autoradiography of cells exposed to [^{3}H]thymidine showed incorporation of the label into both alkaline phosphate-positive and -negative cells. The stimulation of cell proliferation by growth factors was studied by determining the incorporation of [^{3}H]thymidine into DNA. The specific skeletal growth factor from human bone stimulated cell proliferation several-fold with a half-maximal effect at 5 μg/ml. Insulin, epidermal growth factor, and a crude preparation of somatomedin C also stimulated cell proliferation.

The study of bone diseases has been largely focused on systemic causes. Local bone cell defects are less well known and more difficult to study. One way to examine the bone cell activity is to isolate and culture the cells *in vitro.* Methods for isolating and culturing bone cells have been developed and applied to a number of species (1–6). Work on human bone cells has been largely confined to isolation of tumor cell lines. However, Singer and co-workers have grown human bone cells from explants of bone biopsies of normal subjects and from patients with Paget's disease (5, 6). They demonstrated that human bone cells could be maintained in long-term cultures.

An initial report from this laboratory demonstrated the successful isolation and culture of human bone cells from samples of iliac crest (7). These cells have the expected characteristics of bone cells including alkaline phosphatase activity and 1α-hydroxylase activity for 25-hydroxyvitamin D. The availability of a method of preparation and culture of human bone cells opens up the possibility of many different types of direct studies on the cells under carefully controlled conditions. For example the proliferation and response to mitogens can be compared in cells from normal and diseased subjects.

The present study examines the conditions for isolating and culturing human bone cells from samples of femoral heads and iliac crests. In addition the cultured cells have been characterized by examining their proliferation response to various systemic and local growth factors.

Materials and Methods. *Bone samples.* Human bone cells were obtained from needle biopsies of the iliac crest and from femoral heads removed during hip replacement operations. The entire iliac crest biopsy was used, but only the trabecular bone from the femoral head was used. The data in the tables and figures was obtained mainly from cells isolated from two femoral heads from female subjects and two iliac crest biopsies. Iliac 1 cells were from a female osteoporotic and Iliac 2 cells were from a male hyperparathyroid subject. Rat bone cells were isolated from bone samples obtained by dissection of the distal femoral metaphysis of 100-g rats. Chick bone cells were

0037-9727/84 $1.50

obtained from fetal chick calvariae as previously described (1).

Bone cell isolation. Bone samples were rinsed briefly in Fitton–Jackson modified BGJ_b culture medium (from Gibco), diced finely with a scalpel, and placed in a sterile tube with 5 ml of crude collagenase (2 mg/ml) in BGJ_b culture medium. The samples were incubated for 2 hr at 37°C with shaking. The cell suspension was drawn off and the residual bone chips rinsed three times with culture medium or Hank's buffered salt solution. The combined cell suspension and rinse solution were centrifuged at 150*g* for 12 min in a refrigerated centrifuge. The cell pellet was washed by resuspending in fresh medium and centrifuging again. The cell pellet was resuspended in culture medium containing 10% fetal calf serum and plated at a density of 10^3–10^4 cells/mm^2.

Cell culture. The culture medium was Fitton-Jackson modified BGJ_b culture medium and contained penicillin (100 units/ml), streptomycin (100 μg/ml) and 10% heat inactivated fetal calf serum unless otherwise noted. The culture medium was changed every 2–3 days. Cultured cells were freed for passaging by exposure to trypsin (0.05%)–EDTA (0.02%) for 5 to 15 min following a rinse with serum free medium.

Population doubling. To determine the population doubling time cells were plated in microwell plates. For most determinations 1.5×10^3 cells were plated in the 30 mm^2 wells. After cultures were established cell density measurements were made at the beginning and end of a 3–7 day period. To determine the cell density the medium was removed, the cells were rinsed once with serum free medium and 0.05% trypsin, 0.02% EDTA was added. When the cells had rounded up, but were still attached, they were counted in an inverted microscope using a calibrated grid eye piece and phase contrast optics. Five grid areas (0.3 mm^2) were counted in each well and 3 to 6 wells were analyzed per assay. Different wells were counted for initial and final values and the cells discarded after counting. Doubling time was calculated from the equation: doubling time = number of days/3.32 (log final cell count − log initial cell count).

Thymidine incorporation. The incorporation of [^{3}H]thymidine into DNA was determined using a method developed by Gospodarowicz *et al.* (8) and adapted for chick calvarial cells in our laboratory (1). The bone cells were plated in microwell (30 mm^2/well) or multiwell (200 mm^2/well) plates in BGJ_b culture medium containing 10% fetal calf serum at a density of 100 cells/mm^2. After several days, the cells were rinsed twice with serum-free medium and incubated for 4–24 hr in serum-free medium. The medium was drawn off and replaced with medium containing the test agents. After 16 hr [^{3}H]thymidine was added (2 μCi/ml for multiwell plates, 5 μCi/ml for microwell plates). The medium was drawn off 4 hr later. The cells were then rinsed twice with phosphate-buffered saline and frozen to kill the cells. The cells were removed from the plate with a Q-tip swab dipped in 12.5% trichloroacetic acid. The Q-tips were rinsed twice with trichloroacetic acid and once with 95% alcohol for 10 min each. The end of the Q-tip was clipped off, placed in a scintillation vial with 5 ml of aquasol (New England Nuclear), and the level of radioactivity determined in a scintillation counter. This Q-tip method has been previously shown to give comparable values to other methods for determining uptake of [^{3}H]thymidine into DNA (1).

Alkaline phosphatase. The histochemical localization of alkaline phosphatase in cells was determined by the azo dye method of Burstone (9). The substrate was naphthol ASTR phosphate (3-hydroxy-2-naphthoic acid 4-chloro-2-methylanilide, sodium salt) (80 mg/100 ml). The diazonium was red violet LB diazonium salt (5-chloro-4-benzamido-2-methylbenzene-diazonium chloride, hemizinc chloride salt) (60 mg/100 ml). The reagents were dissolved in Tris buffer (50 m*M*) containing NaCl (100 m*M*), KCl (5 m*M*), $CaCl_2$ (1 m*M*), and $MgCl_2$ (1 m*M*) and adjusted to pH 8.6. For the determination the medium was removed and the cell cultures rinsed once with buffer before incubating for 20 min at 37°C with the substrate.

Materials. Crude collagenase and the culture media were obtained from Gibco. Somatomedin was a crude preparation provided by Dr. M. Spencer, University of California, San Francisco. Epidermal growth factor, fibroblast growth factor, multiplication stimulatory factor, platelet-derived growth factor, and insulin were obtained from Collaborative Research. Transferrin was obtained from Sigma Chemical Company. Human skeletal growth factor was prepared as previously described (10).

Results. *Primary cultures.* Preparation of cells by a standard approach of freeing the cells by crude collagenase digestion and plating the cells in Fitton–Jackson modified BGJ_b culture medium supplemented with 10% heat-inactivated fetal calf serum resulted in cell cultures with a fibroblast-like morphology. Cells have been successfully isolated and established in culture from more than 10 different bone specimens including both iliac crest and femoral head specimens. Cells attaching to the culture dish were initially bipolar and then became more stellate similar to what has been reported for bone cells from human bone explants (5, 6) and from other species (1, 2). Some marrow cell types were evident initially but disappeared during continued culture. As the bone cells approached high density there was frequent cell to cell contact through cell processes. Cells did not form confluent epitheleoid-like monolayers but tended to remain separated and began to form multilayers before all areas of the dish were covered.

Although cells were successfully cultured from a number of samples, the percentage of isolated cells that attached and spread out on the bottom of the dish was very low (<1%). Initially some cultures of iliac crest needle biopsy specimens were unsuccessful probably because of the small sample size and low cell survival. In more recent work, cultures have been more consistently obtained (seven out of eight specimens).

Investigation of low survival. Several experiments were carried out to determine if the low cell survival was due to loss of viability during sample preparation. Cells from a human femoral head specimen were drawn off at different times during the collagenase digestion procedure. Aliquots of the cells were taken for counting and Giemsa staining of cell smears. Cell samples obtained by rinsing the bone samples contained mainly red blood cells but also contained some cells that attached (Table I). A high proportion of the cells isolated during the first 20 min of collagenase digestion could be identified as marrow cells.

TABLE I. EFFECT OF TIME OF TREATMENT WITH CRUDE COLLAGENASE (2 mg/ml) ON CELL RELEASE (NOT INCLUDING RED BLOOD CELLS) FROM SAMPLES OF HUMAN FEMORAL BONE (FEMUR 1) AND ON THE PERCENTAGE OF CELLS ATTACHING IN PRIMARY CULTURE

Treatment period (min)	Cells released[a] (% of total)	Cells surviving (% of cells)
Initial rinse	5	0.075
0–20	55	0.083
20–60	21	0.29
60–120	18	1.1

[a] Mean of two determinations except for only one value for cell survival at 60–120 min. The precision of the determination of cell survival (SD/mean × 100) estimated from the difference between duplicates was 56%.

A greater percentage of the cells released during the 20- to 60-min period and the 60- to 120-min period attached and spread in the culture dishes than those released earlier in the digestion. Thus, prolonged digestion with collagenase does not appear to be responsible for the low survival.

There was usually a significant and unavoidable lapse of time between the removal of the bone sample from the patient and the start of the collagenase digestion. To determine if this delay could be responsible for the low percentage of cells attaching in primary culture, cells were isolated from rat femoral metaphysis at different times after removal of the bone from the rat. A rapid sample preparation (less than 30 min between killing the rat and the start of digestion) was compared with a slow preparation (samples stood for 1 additional hr at room temperature in culture medium after removal from the rat). The rapid sample preparation did not substantially increase the percentage of isolated cells surviving (0.083% vs 0.051%, average of two samples). Of the cells isolated from rat femoral metaphysis, a relatively low percentage attached and spread out similar to the cell isolates from human trabecular bone. Isolation of rat bone cells using the protease inhibitor tosyl-lysine-chloromethyl ketone in the isolation medium also failed to increase the number of rat bone cells attaching (0.018% vs 0.028% for controls). From the above observations it seems unlikely that the low survival of the human bone cells is due to a rapid loss of viability during sample transportation and preparation.

In primary cultures of bone cells it was

noted that any large fragments of bone, i.e., those that contained several trabeculae, became covered by a layer or layers of cells after about a week in culture. No cells were evident on the surfaces of bone chips immediately following collagenase digestion, nor did small bone chips become covered by layers of cells in primary cultures until late in the cultures when cells also covered the bottom of the dish. Thus, the cells did not appear to preferentially colonize the bone surfaces. Cells were first evident in the large pores within the large bone chips. Thus, they probably arose from cells trapped within the pores of the large chips.

Passaging cells. Cultured human bone cells were readily passaged with either trypsin (0.05% trypsin, 0.02% EDTA in phosphate-buffered saline) or pancreatin (25%). Cultured cells were also passaged with crude collagenase (1 to 2 hr in 2 mg/ml crude collagenase in BGJ_b culture medium at 37°C). Collagenase treatment appeared to give slightly better cell dispersions than trypsin treatment when cultures with high cell densities were passaged. Passaged cells plated well (60–90%) even at relatively low plating densities (Fig. 4).

Human bone cells were successfully plated in primary culture in either BGJ_b or Ham's F12 containing 10% fetal calf serum. Of several media tested for their ability to support cell growth BGJ_b appeared to support the best growth. Cell density after 2 weeks of culture was 321 cells/mm^2 in BGJ_b but 87 and 159 for medium 199 and CMRL 1060, respectively (mean of two determinations). Little cell proliferation occurred in the absence of fetal calf serum. The optimum concentration appears to be 10% or above (Fig. 1).

Alkaline phosphatase activity. One of the characteristics of osteoblasts is the presence of high alkaline phosphatase activity. When assayed cytochemically for alkaline phosphatase activity between 10 and 40% (average 19%) of the cells in a given preparation (femur or ilium) demonstrated intense staining (Fig. 2, Table II). Staining was evident over the entire cell. This is consistent with the activity being located in the cell membrane. These results demonstrate that there are high alkaline phosphatase levels in the cell membranes of a significant portion of the cultured human bone cells. There was some gradation in the levels of staining intensity between cells. In cultures

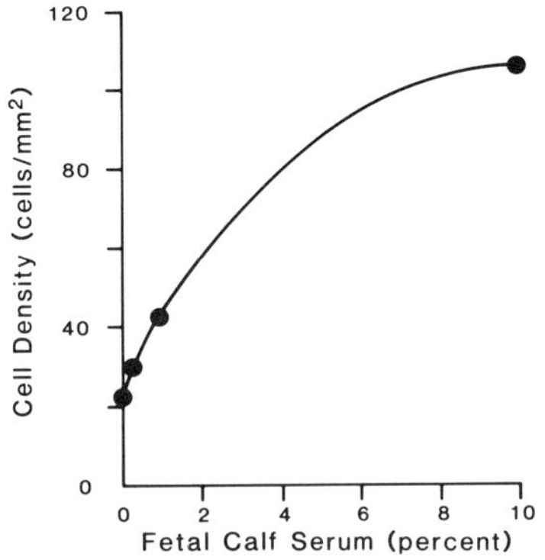

FIG. 1. Increase in cell density with increasing levels of fetal calf serum. Human bone cells (Femur 1) were incubated in BGJ_b culture medium containing varying levels of fetal calf serum for 8 days. Each point is the mean of three determinations.

of human foreskin cells few cells (<1%) were positive for alkaline phosphatase under the same staining conditions. The percentage of positive cells did not appear to decrease with age of the culture.

High alkaline phosphatase activity is a characteristic of osteoblasts or osteoblast precursors. The presence of substantial activity (cells clearly stained after 20 min at 37°C) in some of the cultured cells indicates their osteoblastic nature. The total number of alkaline phosphatase-positive cells increased with time in the bone cell cultures. Because mature osteoblasts do not divide *in vivo* the increase in alkaline phosphatase-positive cells in culture could be due to differentiation from inactive precursors rather than division of the alkaline phosphatase-positive cells. When cultures of human bone cells were exposed to [^{3}H]thymidine for 24 hr, uptake of thymidine was evident in both alkaline phosphatase-positive and -negative cells by autoradiography (Fig. 2). Thus the alkaline phosphatase-positive cells continue to synthesize DNA and presumably divide as well.

Cell proliferation assays. To determine the rate of population growth the change in cell density with time was determined (Fig. 3). Population growth closely approximated a logarithmic rate between cell densities of 50 to 400 cells/mm^2 and decreased at higher densities. For cells isolated from three different femoral heads the population growth rate in BGJ_b medium supplemented with 10% fetal

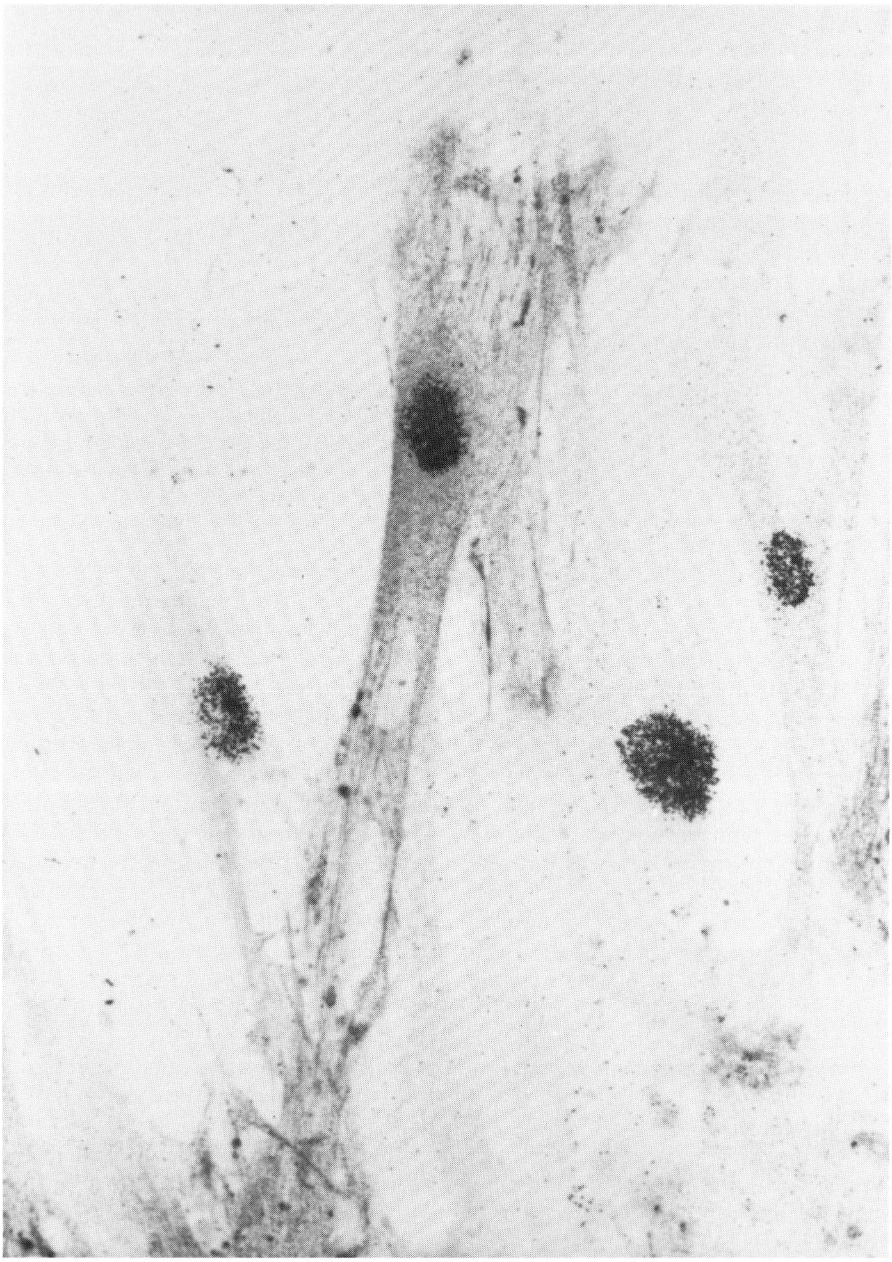

FIG. 2. Autoradiographs of human bone cells (Femur 1) exposed to [^{3}H]thymidine and stained for alkaline phosphatase. Round clusters of grains indicate nuclei which have incorporated [^{3}H]thymidine into DNA. Labeled nuclei are evident in some cells which stained because they contain alkaline phosphatase and in some which were unstained. Cells cultured in chamber slides were exposed to 2 μCi/ml [^{3}H]thymidine for 24 hr, rinsed twice with fresh medium, and stained for alkaline phosphatase activity. The chamber was removed and autoradiography performed as previously described (19) except that the scintillator was not used and the slides were exposed for 10 days.

calf serum averaged 0.23 doublings per day for a generation time of 104 hr. Cells isolated from the trabecular bone of the femoral head gave similar growth rates to those cells isolated from the iliac crest (Table III). The population growth rate was determined at several different

TABLE II. PERCENTAGE OF ALKALINE PHOSPHATASE-POSITIVE CELLS IN HUMAN, CHICK, OR RAT BONE CELL CULTURES

Bone sample[a]	Passage	Percentage of total
Human bone		
Femur 1	6	13
Femur 2	3	29
Iliac crest 1	4	10
Iliac crest 2	4	14
Chick calvaria[a]		10
Rat femur[a]		10

[a] Chick and rat bone cells were from primary cultures, Human bone cells were isolated from four different bone specimens and analyzed after several passages.

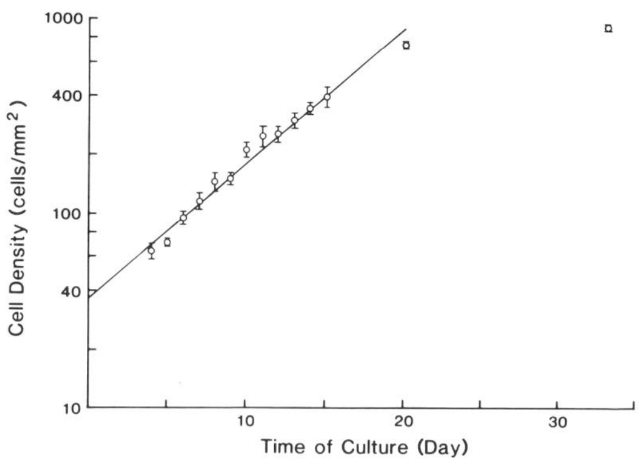

FIG. 3. Increase in cell density with time in culture. Human bone cells incubated in BGJ_b + 10% fetal calf serum. The line was drawn from the regression equation from the correlation (r = 0.990) between the log of the cell density and time of culture between 4 and 20 days. Each point is the mean ± SE of eight determinations.

passages for a few samples. Although a firm conclusion cannot be drawn because of the limited amount of data, an analysis of the data indicated that there was no effect of passage number on the population growth rate (Tables III, IV).

Cell proliferation was also assayed by determining the incorporation of [^{3}H]thymidine into DNA. Several parameters were investigated to determine the best conditions for cell proliferation assays. Passaged human bone cells plated well even at low cell concentrations (Fig. 4). The cell proliferation rate was highly dependent upon the density of the cell cultures. Figure 5 gives the results of two experiments in which passaged cells were plated over a range of different cell densities with the incorporation of [^{3}H]thymidine expressed as a function of cell density. The incorporation rate reached a maximum at a density of 100 cells/mm^2 and decreased at higher cell densities.

Effects of growth factors. A specific skeletal growth factor (SGF) has been isolated from human bone in our laboratory (10, 11). SGF stimulates the proliferation of cultured human bone cells (Fig. 6). The estimated concentration for half-maximal stimulation was 5 μg/ml of the human SGF. This is similar to the concentration required to stimulate cell proliferation by fetal chick calvarial cells (11).

Several agents known to increase growth of cultured cells were tested under serum-free conditions using the [^{3}H]thymidine incorporation assay. Insulin at 1 μg/ml consistently stimulated cell proliferation (Femur 1, 230, Iliac 1, 260, and Iliac 2, 304% of control, mean of four to six determinations). Cells isolated from femoral heads responded similarly to those isolated from the iliac crest. Transferrin has been shown to stimulate proliferation of cells from a number of tissues (12). However, neither purified human transferrin nor transferrin plus Fe were stimulatory to the bone cells (Table V). BGJ_b medium does not con-

TABLE III. POPULATION GROWTH RATE IN GENERATIONS (CELL DOUBLINGS) PER DAY OF HUMAN BONE CELLS FROM THREE DIFFERENT SAMPLES AT DIFFERENT PASSAGES

	Passage						
Bone sample[a]	1	2	3	4	5	6	7
Femur 1	0.195	0.160	—	—	—	0.141	0.153
Iliac crest 1	—	—	0.182	0.101	—	0.155	—
Iliac crest 2	—	—	—	0.248	—	0.191	—

[a] There were three to six wells counted per assay.

TABLE IV. ANALYSIS OF VARIANCE OF THE DETERMINATION OF POPULATION GROWTH RATE (GENERATIONS/DAY) OF HUMAN BONE CELLS[a]

Source of variance	Degrees of freedom	Variance	F	Significance
Between samples	2	0.01107	3.77	$P < 0.05$
Between passages	6	0.00326	1.11	ns
Within assay[b]	19	0.00293		

[a] The change in cell density with time was determined for samples from three different subjects assayed at two to four different passages with three to six wells counted per assay (see Table V).

[b] Within assay deviation, 0.054. Precision of assay (deviation/mean × 100) 32%.

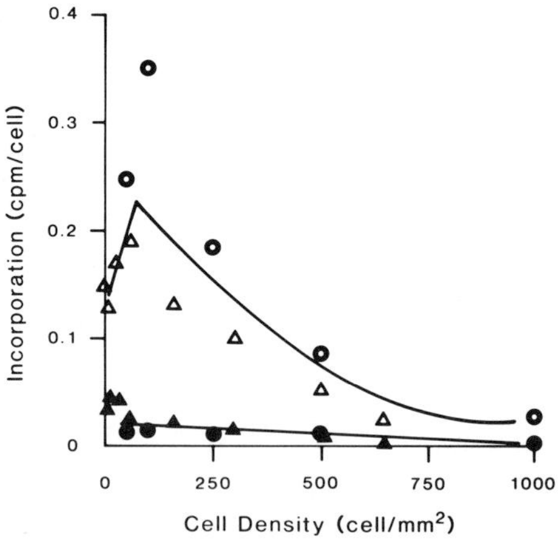

FIG. 5. Incorporation of [^{3}H]thymidine into DNA of human bone cells (Iliac 2) as a function of cell density in the presence (open symbols) or absence (closed symbols) of 10% fetal calf serum. Cells were exposed to fetal calf serum for 20 hr and to [^{3}H]thymidine for 4 hr. Triangles represent one experiment and circles represent a second. There were six determinations per point.

tain several of the trace metals. The addition of a mixture of Fe (1 μm), Cu (1 μm), Zn (2.5 μm), Mn (0.5 μm), and Co (2.5 μm) also failed to stimulate thymidine incorporation (84 ± 26% of control, mean ± SD).

In addition to insulin several other growth factors were tested for their effect on proliferation of cultured human bone cells (Table V). Epidermal growth factor and a crude preparation of somatomedin C stimulated cell proliferation. Platelet-derived growth factor was inhibitory in the presence of insulin. Cells isolated from fetal chick calvarial cells were also inhibited by platelet-derived growth factor

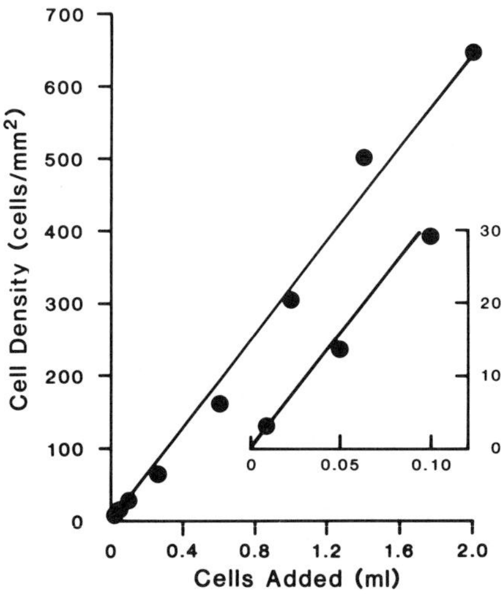

FIG. 4. Number of passaged human bone cells (Femur 1) attaching as a function of the amount of cell suspension added 24 hr after plating in BGJ_b culture medium containing 10% fetal calf serum. The inset shows a magnified portion of the graph at the smallest amounts of cell suspension added. Each point is the mean of two determinations.

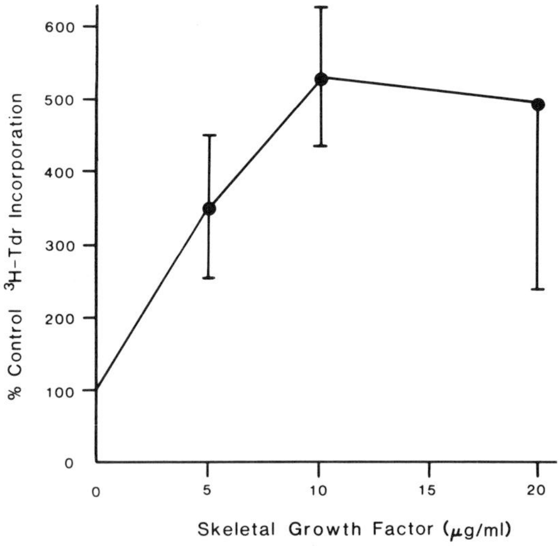

FIG. 6. Incorporation of [^{3}H]thymidine into DNA of human bone cells (Femur 1) as a function of the concentration of human skeletal growth factor. Cells were exposed to the factor for 20 hr and to the thymidine for 4 hr. Symbols represent the means and SD of six samples.

TABLE V. EFFECT OF MITOGENS ON [^{3}H]THYMIDINE INCORPORATION INTO HUMAN BONE CELLS AND FETAL CHICK CALVARIAL CELLS

Mitogens[a]	Concentration (μg/ml)	Uptake as percentage of control[b]	
		Human cells	Chick cells
Insulin	1	199 ± 76^c	313 ± 219^c
Somatomedin	1	161 ± 35^c	337 ± 75^d
Epidermal growth factor	0.5	153 ± 22^c	$207 \pm 16^{d,e}$
Fibroblast growth factor	0.5	127 ± 66	—
Multiplication stimulatory activity	5	78 ± 66	—
Platelet derived growth factor	1	—	157 ± 27^c
Platelet derived growth factor[f]	1	49 ± 29^c	45 ± 45^c
Transferrin + Fe (4 μM)	5	34 ± 18^d	—

[a] Factors were tested in separate experiments. Human cells were from passages three to six of Femur 1.
[b] Mean ± S.D., six samples per assay.
[c] $P < 0.05$.
[d] $P < 0.01$.
[e] Concentration of the factor was 1 μg/μl.
[f] Assayed in the presence of 1 μg/ml insulin.

in the presence of insulin but were stimulated by this factor in its absence.

Discussion. Our studies show that cells can be isolated and cultured from samples of human bone using the same collagenase digestion methods used for studying bone cells from other species. The cells obtained by these methods appear to have the same characteristics as those isolated from explants of normal or Pagetic human bone by Mills *et al.* (5, 6). The percentage of alkaline phosphatase-positive cells (19 vs 25%), the population doubling time (4.4 vs 4–10 days), and the general morphology of the cells in culture appear to be similar for cells obtained by collagenase digestion of the bone matrix in our studies or by culture of explants by Mills and co-workers. The ability to obtain cultures of human bone cells allows the study of those cells from individual patients under the controlled conditions of *in vitro* culture. This provides a different avenue of approach to the investigation of bone diseases in which the defect is suspected to reside within the bone cells themselves. In addition, the mechanisms of action of various factors controlling bone metabolism can be examined at the cellular level with normal human bone cells and can be compared with results obtained with bone cells from other species.

The low percentage of cells that survive the isolation procedure and attach and spread out on the bottom of the culture dish makes it difficult to carry out any studies on primary cultures. Additional passages are necessary to obtain sufficient cells to study. However, once established, cultures can be readily passaged and appear to retain their characteristics in later passages. The reason for the low survival in primary culture remains unclear. Cells released from the bone late in the collagenase digestion period (after most marrow and red blood cells have been released) still had a low percentage of attachment. Therefore, the high number of other cell types present was not responsible for the low survival values. No evidence could be found for a loss in viability during sample preparation. The low survival appears to be a characteristic of the bone cells themselves.

Cell cultures started from the iliac crest samples and femoral head samples had similar proliferation rates, similar levels of alkaline phosphatase-positive cells and similar proliferation responses to addition of insulin. The agreement in these responses indicates that similar cell populations were being isolated and cultured from the two types of bone samples. Therefore, the parameters of cell culture study established with the larger femoral head samples should be applicable to the iliac crest specimens.

In a number of other bone cell culture studies it has been found that the characteristics of the cultured bone cells changed with time (13–15). The levels of cell proliferation and alkaline phosphatase activity were maintained through a number of passages in our study. In addition the ability of the cultured human bone cells to convert 25-hydroxyvitamin D to 1α,25-dihydroxyvitamin D was previously shown to be maintained through at least five passages (7). Although a more detailed study may still show that some changes in the levels of these activities are occurring with time in culture, it is evident that these activities are not greatly changed with time in culture over 5 to 10 passages. Thus the cultured cells provide a reasonably stable population to carry out studies with appropriate controls for passage number.

The low percentage of cells that attach and grow in primary culture raises the question of how representative these cells are of bone cells *in vivo.* The measured characteristics of the cultured bone cells are those to be expected if the cells are truly bone cells. These characteristics include:

(i) A significant portion of the cells have high alkaline phosphatase activity, which is a characteristic of osteoblastic cells.

(ii) The presence of 1α-hydroxylase activity for 25-hydroxyvitamin D, which is found in only a few tissues including bone (16).

(iii) Responsiveness to the skeletal growth factor, which appears to be specific for skeletal tissue (11).

The cultured human bone cells also appear to be similar to cultured bone cells from other species with respect to the above characteristics, their appearance in culture and their response to growth factors. The responses of the human cells to various systemic and local growth factors, although not identical, were very similar to the responses of fetal chick bone cells (Table V). Some of the differences between the responses of the two species may be related to differences between fetal and adult tissue. Fetal chick bone cell preparations have a much higher percentage of cells that attach in primary culture (25%) than do the human cell preparations and are therefore less likely to be a selected subpopulation of the bone cell population. The fetal chick bone cell preparations are also essentially free of marrow cells in contrast to the initial human cell preparations. The similarities between the chick cell cultures and the human bone cultures lend some credence to the idea that these cultures will prove to be representative of bone cells *in vivo.*

The isolated bone cell preparations initially contain marrow cells as well as bone cells. Other workers have reported that marrow cells do not survive under the culture conditions used in this study (17), and differentiated marrow cells were not evident after several days in culture in our studies. The cultured bone cells thus do not appear to contain cells of the hemopoietic cell line although precursor cells may still be present. One cell line that ought to be present is the determined osteogenic precursor cells that Freidenstein and coworkers (17) as well as others (18) have shown to be present in low concentration (10^{-5}) in marrow from a number of species including man.

While the evidence indicates that the cell cultures contain "bone" cells, it is evident from the alkaline phosphatase cytochemistry that the cell population is not homogeneous. Bone cell cultures from other species have been shown to have considerable heterogeneity (4, 13, 15). Therefore it is not surprising to find heterogeneity in the human cell cultures. The low alkaline phosphatase-positive cells are presumably still osteogenic cells since the presence of alkaline phosphatase-positive cells is not necessary for the demonstration of osteogenic potential (18). We do not know to what extent the cell cultures may be contaminated with "non-bone" cells, except that it is clear that fibroblasts or other "non-bone" cells are not overrunning the culture.

Invaluable technical assistance was provided by Malcolm Ghazel and Kathleen King. Assistance in the preparation of the manuscript was provided by Penny Nasabal. This work was supported in part by NIH Grant AM 31062.

1. Puzas JE, Drivdahl RH, Howard GA, Baylink DJ. Endogenous inhibitor of bone cell proliferation. Proc Soc Exp Biol Med **166:**113–122, 1981.
2. Peck WA, Birge SJ Jr, Fedak SA. Bone cells: Biochemical and biological studies after enzymatic isolation. Science **146:**1476–1477, 1964.
3. Smith DM, Johnston CC Jr, Severson AR. Studies of the metabolism of separated bone cells. I. Tech-

niques of separation and identification. Calcif Tissue Res **11**:56–69, 1973.
4. Wong GL, Kent GN, Ku KY, Cohn DV. The interaction of parathormone and calcium on the hormone-regulated synthesis of hyaluronic acid and citrate decarboxylation in isolated bone cells. Endocrinology **103**:2274–2282, 1978.
5. Mills BG, Singer FR, Weiner LP, Holst PA. Long-term culture of cells from bone affected by Paget's disease. Calcif Tissue Int **29**:79–87, 1979.
6. Mills BG, Singer FR, Weiner LP, Holst PA. Cell cultures from bone affected by Paget's disease. Arthritis Rheum **23**:1115–1120, 1980.
7. Howard GA, Turner RT, Sherrard DJ, Baylink DJ. Human bone cells in culture metabolize 25 $(OH)D_3$ to $1,25(OH)_2D_3$ and $24,25(OH)_2D_3$. J Biol Chem **256**:7738–7740, 1981.
8. Gospodarowicz D, Bialecki H, Greenburg G. Purification of the fibroblast growth factor activity from bovine brain. J Biol Chem **253**:3736–3743, 1978.
9. Burstone MS. Hydrolytic enzymes in dentinogenesis and osteogenesis. In: Sognnaes RF, ed. Calcification in Biological Systems. Washington, DC, Amer Assoc Advan Sci, p217, 1960.
10. Farley JR, Baylink DJ. Isolation and partial purification of a putative coupling factor from human bone. Trans Assoc Amer Physicians **44**:80–87, 1981.
11. Farley JR, Baylink DJ. A putative coupling factor from human bone: Effects on bone cells *in vitro*. Calcif Tissue Int **33**:292, 1981.
12. Sato G, Reid L. Replacement of serum in cell culture by hormones. In: Biochemistry and Mode of Action of Hormones II, International Review of Biochemistry. Vol 20:pp219–251, 1978.
13. Nijweide PJ, Van der Plas A, Scherft JP. Biochemical and Histological studies on various bone cell preparations. Calcif Tissue Int **33**:529–540, 1981.
14. Burks JK, Peck W. Bone cell: A serum free medium supports proliferation in primary culture. Science **199**:542–544, 1978.
15. Peck WA, Burks JK, Wilkins J, Roda SD, Rodan GA. Evidence for preferential effects of parathyroid hormone, calcitonin and adenosine on bone and periosteum. Endocrinology **100**:1357–1364, 1977.
16. Turner RT, Puzas JE, Forte MD, Lester GF, Gray TK, Howard GA, Baylink DJ. *In vitro* synthesis of 1α,25-dihydroxycholecalciferol and 24,25-dihydroxycholecalciferol by isolated calvarial cells. Proc Natl Acad Sci USA **77**:5720–5724, 1980.
17. Friedenstein AJ. Determined and inducible osteogenic precursor cells. In: Hard Tissue Growth, Repair and Remineralization. Elliot K, Fitzsimmonds DW, eds. New York, Assoc Sci Pub, pp169–185, 1973.
18. Englesom CC, Ashton BH, Allen TD, Owen ME. The osteogenic capacity of bone marrow cells. Cell Biol Int Rep **4**:742, 1980.
19. Langager JM, Howard GA, Baylink DJ. An improved technique for rapid autoradiography of cells and tissue sections. Histochemistry **75**:523–531, 1982.

Received March 7, 1983. P.S.E.B.M. 1984, Vol. 176.
Accepted February 6, 1984.

PROCEEDINGS OF THE SOCIETY FOR EXPERIMENTAL BIOLOGY AND MEDICINE **176**, 70–76 (1984)

Essential Role of Sodium and Chloride for Theophylline-Induced Choleresis in the Isolated Perfused Rat Liver (41844)

M. SAWKAT ANWER,*,†,‡ DIETMAR HEGNER,*,[1] AND LARRY R. ENGELKING‡

**Institute of Pharmacology, Toxicology, and Pharmacy, College of Veterinary Medicine, University of Munich, Munich, West Germany; †Division of Gastroenterology, University of California School of Medicine, San Diego, California 92103; and ‡Department of Medicine, Tufts University School of Veterinary Medicine, Boston, Massachusetts 02111*[2]

Abstract. Active secretion of electrolytes by hepatocytes is believed to be responsible for bile acid-independent canalicular bile flow (BAICF). Theophylline, which enhances BAICF, has been shown to enhance electrogenic Cl^- secretion in a number of other epithelia. Such transport is dependent on Na^+ and Cl^-. Thus, the mechanism of theophylline choleresis may also involve stimulation of electrogenic Cl^- secretion of the liver. This hypothesis was tested by studying the effect of ion substitution on theophylline choleresis in isolated perfused rat livers. Addition of theophylline (0.1 mmole) and dibutyryl cAMP (0.05 mmole) to 100 ml perfusate, as a single dose, increased bile flow and biliary secretion of Na^+ and Cl^- reversibly. These effects of theophylline were virtually abolished when perfusate Na^+ (146 m*M*) was replaced by Li^+ (146 m*M*) or choline$^+$ (120 m*M*), and when Cl^- (127 m*M*) was replaced by 120 m*M* NO_3^-, acetate$^-$ or isethionate$^-$. Since even the permeable ions like Li^+ and NO_3^- could not substitute for Na^+ and Cl^-, these results show that the effect of theophylline on BAICF is specifically dependent on the presence of Na^+ and Cl^- in the perfusate. We propose, by analogy to other epithelia, that an electrogenic Cl^- secretion mechanism is present in the liver. Theophylline, acting via cAMP, stimulates this transport process, thereby enhancing BAICF.

A fraction of canalicular bile flow is independent of hepatic bile acid secretion and is stimulated by a number of drugs without changing the rate of bile acid secretion (1). This fraction is commonly known as the bile acid-independent canalicular bile flow (BAICF). Existing evidence suggests that active transport of inorganic electrolytes into the canaliculi is responsible for the BAICF (1–3). However, the mechanism of hepatic electrolyte transport and its relation to bile formation are not clearly understood. The major obstacle to the clarification of hepatic electrolyte transport is our inability to sample bile and conduct electrophysiological studies at the level of canaliculus. Nonetheless, the availability of pharmacological agents, which selectively alter one or more transport functions in other epithelia, should permit further insight into the mechanism of hepatic electrolyte and fluid transport.

Theophylline is a drug known to stimulate the BAICF of dogs (4, 5) and rats (6) *in vivo.* The mechanism of theophylline-induced choleresis is considered to be via cAMP, since theophylline is a potent inhibitor of phosphodiesterase. In unrelated studies using other epithelia, it has been shown that procedures which result in an elevated intracellular cAMP and/or cytosolic free Ca^{2+} level, also enhance electrogenic Cl^- secretion (7). Together, these experimental findings raise the possibility that electrogenic Cl^- secretion is involved in BAICF. Studies using other epithelia further showed that electrogenic Cl^- secretion is dependent on both Na^+ and Cl^- (7). If such a mechanism exists in liver, and if theophylline acts similarly as in other epithelia, then theophylline should stimulate BAICF by enhancing Cl^- transport across hepatocytes. If this condition is satisfied, the choleretic effect of theophylline should be associated with an increase in the biliary secretion of Na^+ and Cl^-, and should be dependent on both Na^+ and Cl^-.

In the present study, we examined the effect of theophylline on biliary secretion of Na^+

[1] Deceased, May 14, 1982.

[2] Present address of authors.

0037-9727/84 $1.50

and Cl^- using isolated perfused rat livers. Ion-substitution studies were performed to test whether Na^+ and Cl^- are required to exhibit the choleretic effect of theophylline.

Materials and Methods. *Materials.* Theophylline, lactate dehydrogenase, 3-hydroxysteroid dehydrogenase, NAD, and NADH were obtained from Sigma Chemical Company, Munich, West Germany. Taurocholate (TC) was purchased from Calbiochem, San Diego, California. [^{14}C]Erythritol was purchased from New England Nuclear, Boston, Massachusetts. All other chemicals were products of Merck, Darmstadt, West Germany. Inbred male Wistar rats (250–350 g) maintained on a standard laboratory diet (Altromin) served as liver donors in all experiments. Liver weights varied from 7 to 13 g.

Isolated perfused rat liver. Each liver was surgically prepared by methods previously described (8), connected to the perfusion apparatus, and maintained at 37°C (9). They were perfused with 100 ml of recirculating erythrocyte-free perfusate (pH 7.4) under a hydrostatic pressure of 15 cm. Erythrocyte-free perfusion medium was used to avoid any possible effect of ion replacement on erythrocytes. The perfusion rate through the liver was initially adjusted to 4–5 ml/min × g liver to ensure an adequate oxygen supply (10). The pH was maintained between 7.3 and 7.4 by addition of 0.15 *M* HCl, $NaHCO_3$, LiOH, HNO_3, or acetic acid, dependent upon the perfusate medium. The routine viability criteria included: (i) stable perfusion rate throughout the experiment, (ii) perfusate lactate/pyruvate ratio around 10, and (iii) relatively stable bile flow during the control period. Experiments which did not satisfy these criteria were not included.

The composition of the basic perfusion medium was as follows: 120 m*M* NaCl, 4.7 m*M* KCl, 26 m*M* $NaHCO_3$, 1.2 m*M* KH_2PO_4, 1.3 m*M* $CaCl_2$, 0.6 m*M* $MgSO_4$, and 5.5 m*M* glucose. In order to study the effect of Na^+ and Cl^- on bile formation, NaCl was replaced by an equimolar concentration of choline-Cl, $NaNO_3$, Na-acetate, or Na-isethionate. Complete replacement of Na^+ and Li^+ was obtained by substituting NaCl and $NaHCO_3$ with equimolar concentrations of LiCl and $LiHCO_3$, respectively. The perfusates were gassed with 95% O_2 and 5% CO_2. Viability criteria were not affected significantly by these ion substitutions (8).

Experimental design. The liver was perfused with the appropriate experimental perfusate from the start of each experiment. Theophylline (0.1 mmole; perfusion concentration 1 m*M*) was injected as a single dose after 60 min of perfusion. Bile was collected in a preweighed vial and the bile volume was determined gravimetrically assuming a density of 1.0. Perfusate samples were collected at the midpoints of the bile collection periods. Erythritol clearance was studied routinely by adding 2 μCi of [^{14}C]erythritol to the reservoir at the start of each experiment. The bile to plasma ratio of [^{14}C]erythritol was close to 1 in each experiment (1.06 ± 0.054; mean ± SD), indicating canalicular origin of bile.

Isolated plasma membranes from rat liver. Isolated plasma membranes were used to determine if theophylline affects the activity of sodium and potassium activated Mg^{2+}-ATPase (Na^+,K^+-ATPase). Plasma membranes were isolated under isotonic conditions according to the method of Coleman *et al.* (11). The purity of the plasma membranes was routinely followed by measuring the activities of marker enzymes for plasma membranes (5′-nucleotidase and Na^+, K^+-ATPase), endoplasmic reticulum (glucose-6-phosphatase) and mitochondria (succinate dehydrogenase). Specific activities of our marker enzymes have been previously published (8). Protein content of plasma membranes was determined by the method of Lowry *et al.* (12) using bovine serum albumin as standard. The activity of Na^+,K^+-ATPase was determined by the method of Emmelot *et al.* (13).

Analytical methods. The concentrations of Na^+, K^+, and Li^+ in perfusate and bile were determined using flame photometry. Chloride concentrations were determined by coulometric titration using a chloridometer (Corning, Model 920). Radioactivity was measured in a liquid scintillation counter with quench corrected by external standard ratios. Total bile acids were determined by an enzymatic method using 3-hydroxysteroid dehydrogenase (14). The perfusate lactate and pyruvate concentrations were determined enzymatically using lactate dehydrogenase. Osmolarity was measured by the freezing-point depression method using a microosmometer (Kanuer, West Germany). Bile was isosmotic to perfusate in all studies.

Statistical methods. The effect of drug on bile flow and biliary secretion of Na^+ and Cl^- was determined by comparing values after injection of drug at 60 min to the average value of 30- to 60-min collection periods (predrug controls). The paired *t* test was used to detect differences in experimental parameters with $P < 0.05$ considered significant.

Results. *1. Effect of sodium replacement on theophylline choleresis.* Preliminary studies showed that addition of 0.1 mmole theophylline to 100 ml perfusate produced consistent choleresis. Thus, a 0.1 mmole dose of theophylline was used in all studies. Addition of theophylline after 60 min of perfusion with a Na^+-containing perfusate resulted in a rapid increase in bile flow (Fig. 1) which remained significantly elevated through 120 min. When perfusate Na^+ was replaced by Li^+, theophylline caused an initial decline in bile flow followed by an increase with a peak value at 80 min, then a second decline back to basal level at 90 min (Fig. 1). Theophylline caused a slight increase in bile flow when perfusate Na^+ (145 m*M*) was partially replaced by choline$^+$ (120 m*M*) (Fig. 1). Complete replacement of Na^+ by choline$^+$ was not studied since this results in erratic perfusion flow (10). Theophylline did not significantly affect the viability of the perfused liver under our experimental conditions (Table I). These results indicate that neither Li^+ nor choline$^+$ can completely replace Na^+ in theophylline choleresis.

The biliary concentrations of Na^+ and Cl^- were similar to their perfusate concentrations and were not significantly affected by theophylline. Thus, the biliary secretion of these electrolytes paralleled bile flow. Theophylline increased biliary secretion of Na^+ and Cl^- when livers were perfused with NaCl-containing perfusate. Replacement of Na^+ by Li^+ or choline$^+$ reduced the theophylline-induced increase in biliary Cl^- secretion (Fig. 1). The low endogenous bile acid secretion was not affected by theophylline (1.61 ± 0.42 vs 1.48 ± 0.37 nmole/min $\times$ g liver, $N = 30$). These results indicate that theophylline-induced bile

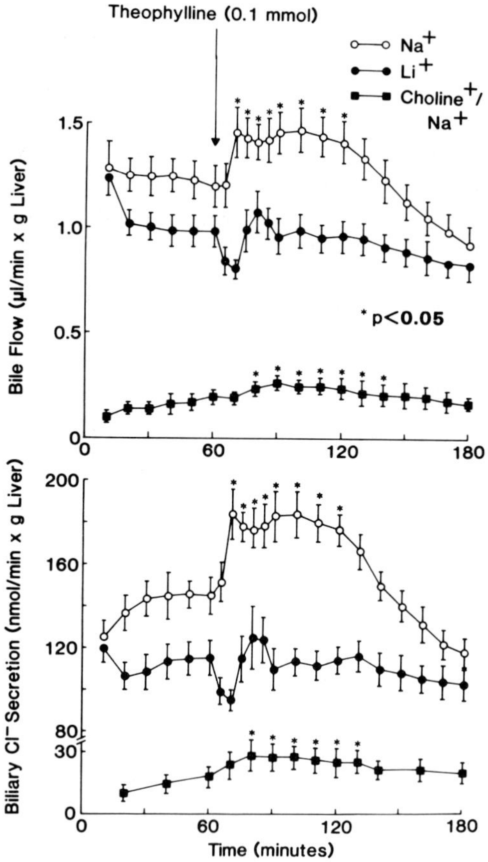

FIG. 1. Effect of Na^+ replacement on theophylline-induced bile flow and biliary Cl^- secretion. *Significantly higher than the 30- to 60-min control values. Means ± SE ($N = 5$).

flow and biliary Cl^- secretion is Na^+ dependent.

To determine if this Na^+ dependency is due to activation of Na^+,K^+-ATPase, the effect of theophylline on the activity of this enzyme in plasma membranes from isolated rat livers was determined. Theophylline up to a concentration of 10 m*M* failed to activate this enzyme (Table II). Thus, it seems unlikely that the effect of theophylline is directly mediated via Na^+,K^+-ATPase.

2. Effect of chloride replacement. Theophylline produced very little, if any, choleresis when the perfusate Cl^- (127 m*M*) was replaced by 120 m*M* NO_3^-, acetate$^-$, or isethionate$^-$. The biliary concentration of Cl^- under these

TABLE I. EFFECT OF THEOPHYLLINE AND DB cAMP ON VIABILITY OF ISOLATED PERFUSED RAT LIVERS[a]

Perfusate	Treatment	Perfusate flow (ml/min × g liver)		Lactate/pyruvate ratio		Perfusate K^+ concentration (mmole/ liter)	
		1st hr	2nd hr	1st hr	2nd hr	1st hr	2nd hr
$NaCl + NaHCO_3$	Control	4.7 ± 0.13	4.8 ± 0.12	11 ± 1.8	12 ± 2.1	5.6 ± 0.14	5.8 ± 0.16
	Theophylline	4.6 ± 0.11	4.6 ± 0.13	10 ± 1.3	12 ± 1.8	5.6 ± 0.15	5.7 ± 0.13
	DB cAMP	4.5 ± 0.12	4.6 ± 0.11	11 ± 1.4	11 ± 1.3	5.5 ± 0.12	5.8 ± 0.14
Choline-Cl + $NaHCO_3$	Control	4.7 ± 0.14	4.8 ± 0.13	10 ± 1.8	11 ± 1.7	5.9 ± 0.26	7.8 ± 0.48
	Theophylline	4.8 ± 0.15	4.7 ± 0.16	9 ± 1.6	11 ± 1.4	6.0 ± 0.23	7.7 ± 0.39
$LiCl + LiHCO_3$	Control	4.5 ± 0.13	4.6 ± 0.15	12 ± 1.7	12 ± 1.8	6.6 ± 0.34	8.4 ± 0.56
	Theophylline	4.5 ± 0.14	4.5 ± 0.17	10 ± 1.3	11 ± 1.4	6.5 ± 0.28	8.6 ± 0.61
$NaNO_3 + NaHCO_3$	Control	4.9 ± 0.13	4.8 ± 0.15	11 ± 1.4	10 ± 1.1	5.7 ± 0.18	5.9 ± 0.21
	Theophylline	4.6 ± 0.12	4.6 ± 0.13	12 ± 1.3	11 ± 1.4	5.6 ± 0.13	5.8 ± 0.19
Na-acetate + $NaHCO_3$	Control	4.5 ± 0.15	4.6 ± 0.17	11 ± 1.6	11 ± 1.5	5.7 ± 0.19	5.7 ± 0.15
	Theophylline	4.9 ± 0.17	4.8 ± 0.16	12 ± 1.3	13 ± 1.6	5.6 ± 0.20	5.9 ± 0.17
Na-isethionate + $NaHCO_3$	Control	4.7 ± 0.16	4.7 ± 0.20	10 ± 1.8	9 ± 0.7	5.8 ± 0.16	5.9 ± 0.20
	Theophylline	4.5 ± 0.18	4.6 ± 0.21	11 ± 1.3	11 ± 1.4	5.5 ± 0.13	5.7 ± 0.16

Note. Values are means ± SEM of 30 determinations (six determination for each hour and experiment).
[a] Theophylline also did not significantly affect these parameters during the 3rd hour of perfusion.

conditions was less than 10 m*M* and was not altered by theophylline. The theophylline-induced increase in biliary Na^+ secretion was also virtually abolished by Cl^- replacement (Fig. 2). The viability of the perfused liver was not affected significantly by theophylline under these conditions (Table I). Since even the permeable NO_3^- could not substitute for Cl^-, these results indicate that Cl^- is specifically required for theophylline-induced Na^+ secretion and bile flow.

3. Effect of dibutyryl cAMP (DB cAMP). If theophylline acts via cAMP, DB cAMP should also increase bile flow and biliary electrolyte secretion. Addition of 50 μmole of DB cAMP promptly increased bile flow and biliary secretion of Na^+ and Cl^- (Fig. 3). DB cAMP did not significantly affect the viability of the perfused liver (Table I) nor the biliary bile acid secretion (1.82 ± 0.52 vs 1.76 ± 0.42 nmole/min × g liver, $N = 30$).

TABLE II. EFFECT OF THEOPHYLLINE ON RAT LIVER PLASMA MEMBRANE Na^+, K^+-ATPase ACTIVITY

Theophylline concentration (m*M*)	Na^+,K^+-ATPase activity (μmole P_i/hr × mg protein)
0	14.0 ± 0.87
0.01	13.7 ± 0.90
0.1	13.8 ± 0.89
1.0	13.7 ± 0.91
10.0	13.9 ± 0.88

Note. Values are means ± SEM ($N = 8$).

Discussion. These studies were designed to determine if the choleretic effect of theophylline could be explained by the proposed mechanism of action of theophylline in other epithelia (7). Our results clearly indicate that theophylline stimulates canalicular bile formation in the isolated perfused rat liver. This choleresis is associated with an increase in biliary secretion of both Na^+ and Cl^-. Since endogenous bile acid secretion was not altered, this effect cannot be due to theophylline-induced secretion of bile acid.

Replacement of Na^+ and Cl^- by other ions virtually abolished the effect of theophylline on bile flow and biliary secretion of Na^+ and Cl^-. Since the viability of the perfused liver was not significantly affected (Table I), the failure of theophylline to increase bile flow and biliary electrolyte secretion when Na^+ and

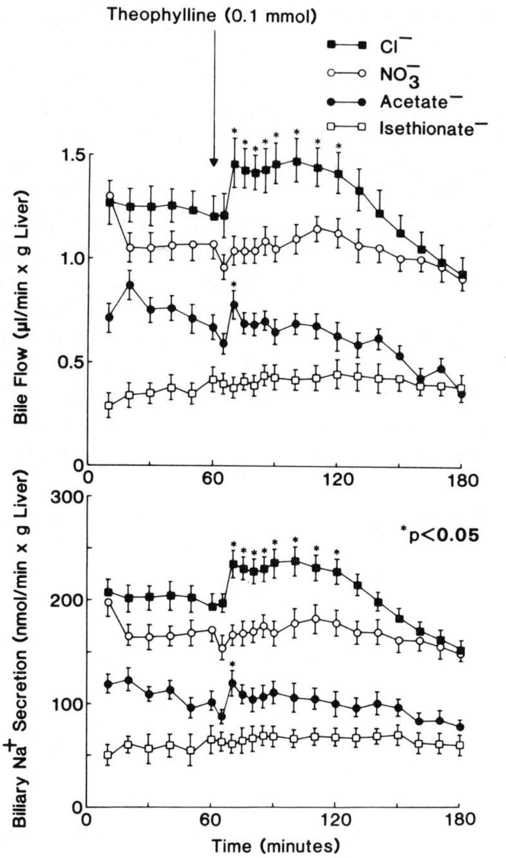

FIG. 2. Effect of Cl^- replacement on theophylline induced bile flow and biliary Na^+ secretion. *Significantly higher than the 30- to 60-min control values. Means ± SE ($N = 5$).

Cl^- were replaced by other ions is unlikely to be due to any toxic effect of theophylline. Thus, the effect of theophylline is dependent on both Na^+ and Cl^-. Since even the permeable ions, such as Li^+ and NO_3^-, could not substitute for Na^+ and Cl^-, it is unlikely that a passive mechanism is responsible for theophylline-induced biliary secretion of these ions. We previously showed that the choleretic effect of taurocholate, an osmotic choleretic, increased when Na^+ and Cl^- were replaced by Li^+ and NO_3^- (15). A similar effect would have been anticipated if theophylline had been acting as an osmotic choleretic. Since the choleretic effect of theophylline declined under these conditions, it is unlikely that the choleretic effect of theophylline is due to the osmotic effect of the secreted drug. Moreover, studies in dogs (16) indicated that the choleretic effect of theophylline cannot be explained by the osmotic effect of the secreted drug alone. Thus, it is more likely that there is a specific transport system for these ions and that theophylline acts by modifying this transport system. Possible modifications of Na^+,K^+-ATPase seem unlikely since theophylline up to a concentration of 10 m*M* does not affect the activity of this enzyme in liver plasma membranes (Table II).

The effects of theophylline observed in these studies are similar to effects in other epithelia (7). Thus, it is likely that theophylline acts via similar mechanisms in the liver. Theophylline

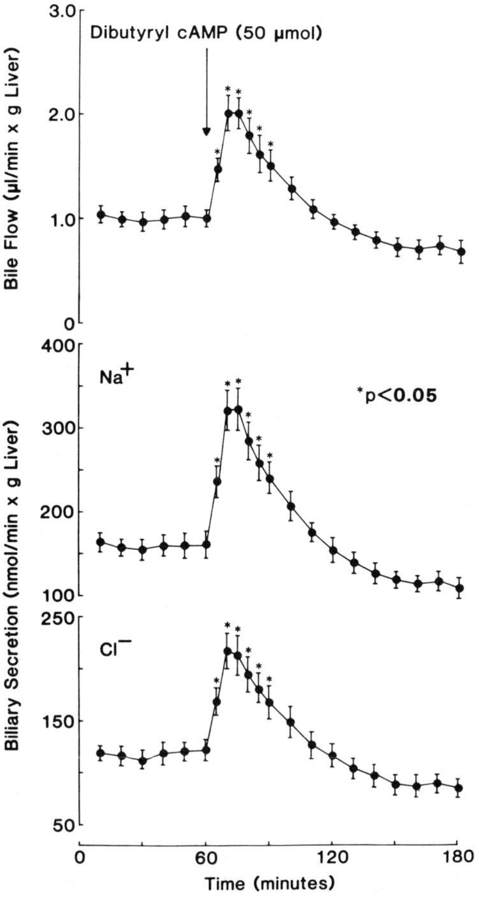

FIG. 3. Effect of dibutyryl cAMP on bile flow and biliary secretion of Na^+ and Cl^-. *Significantly higher than the 30- to 60-min control values. Means ± SE ($N = 5$).

is known to stimulate electrogenic Cl^- secretion and inhibit Na^+-coupled Cl^- reabsorption in different epithelia (7). Both processes are dependent on Na^+ and Cl^- (7). Since theophylline-induced effects in our studies are also dependent on both Na^+ and Cl^-, either or both mechanisms may be involved in the liver. Unfortunately, our studies cannot distinguish between these two possibilities. However, since there is no compelling evidence that indicates theophylline induces reabsorption of fluid from canaliculi, we propose that theophylline increases BAICF by stimulating electrogenic Cl^- secretion. In this case, the electrogenic Cl^- transport would involve secretion of Cl^- across the canalicular membrane followed by Na^+ through the paracellular pathway in order to maintain electroneutrality.

Frizzel *et al.* (7) proposed that electrogenic Cl^- secretion may involve Na^+-coupled Cl^- transport at the contraluminal membrane, i.e., sinusoidal membrane of liver cells. The present findings indicate that a major fraction of theophylline-induced Cl^- secretion is specifically dependent on Na^+ (Fig. 1) which support the hypothesis of Frizzel *et al.* A similar mechanism has been proposed in recent reviews (3, 13), and was supported by our previous ion-replacement studies in isolated perfused rat livers (8). However, attempts to obtain direct evidence for the presence of Na^+-coupled Cl^- transport were unsuccessful in cultured rat hepatocytes (17). Thus, biliary Cl^- secretion may not involve Na^+-coupled Cl^- transport at the sinusoidal membrane. Alternatively, this transport mechanism may be present in the liver, and may become quantitatively important only during theophylline choleresis.

The present study showed that although replacement of Na^+ by Li^+, and Cl^- by NO_3^- decreased basal bile flow only slightly, the choleretic effect of theophylline was virtually abolished in the presence of Li^+ and NO_3^-. These differences in the effect of Li^+ and NO_3^- indicate that more than one ion transport mechanism is involved in the formation of bile acid independent bile. One of those mechanisms seems to be specific for Na^+ and Cl^-, and is stimulated by theophylline.

This study also showed that DB cAMP stimulates bile flow and biliary secretions of Na^+ and Cl^- (Fig. 3). Thomsen and Larsen (18) also reported that DB cAMP is choleretic in rats and in the isolated perfused rat liver. Since theophylline is known to act via cAMP, these results are in agreement with the hypothesis that theophylline acting via cAMP stimulates BAICF. This mechanism has been questioned by others. Baker and Kaplan (19) reported that intraperitoneal injection of DB cAMP failed to stimulate bile flow in rats, and Poupon *et al.* (20) reported that an increase in hepatic cAMP levels induced by various drugs was not always associated with choleresis in rats. Since Baker and Kaplan (19) injected DB cAMP intraperitoneally, it is possible that an effective hepatocellular concentration was not achieved. The results (20) indicating that increases in cAMP levels were not always associated with choleresis are difficult to explain. It is, however, also possible that drugs used to increase hepatic cAMP levels may have other effects which in turn might have influenced bile flow. Other possibilities may include compartmentation of cAMP in liver cells. Since theophylline and DB cAMP are also choleretic in dog and man (4, 5, 16, 21), it seems probable that cAMP plays a role in BAICF and that theophylline acts via cAMP in liver cells.

In conclusion, the present study provides indirect evidence for the presence of an electrogenic Cl^- secretory mechanism in liver cells. Theophylline acting via cAMP, stimulates this transport system thereby enhancing bile acid-independent canalicular flow.

This study was supported in part by a grant from Deutsche Forschungsgemeinschaft and U.S. Public Health Grant AM 30799. The authors gratefully acknowledge the excellent technical assistance of Mrs. U. Rueberg and Mr. Haag, and are thankful to Dr. A. F. Hofmann, Dr. J. L. Barnhart, and Dr. W. G. M. Hardison of the University of California School of Medicine, San Diego, Calif. for critically reading the manuscript. The authors also acknowledge the excellent editorial assistance of Ms. Vicky Huebner. A portion of this study was published in abstract in *Hepatology* (**1**, 491, 1981).

1. Forker EL. Mechanism of hepatic bile formation. Annu Rev Physiol **39**:323–347, 1977.
2. Boyer JL. New concepts of mechanisms of hepatocyte bile formation. Physiol Rev **60**:303–326, 1980.
3. Erling S. Hepatocyte bile secretion: Current views and controversies. Hepatology **1**:352–359, 1981.

4. Barnhart JL, Combes B. Characteristics common to choleretic increments of bile induced by theophylline, glucagon and SQ-20009 in the dog. Proc Soc Exp Biol Med **150**:591–596, 1975.
5. Kaminski DL, Brown WH, Deshpande YG. Effect of glucagon on bile cAMP secretion. Amer J Physiol **238**:G119–G123, 1980.
6. Knodell RG. Alterations in bile flow and Na^+-K^+ biliary excretion induced by theophylline and ethacrynic acid (40043). Proc Soc Exp Biol Med **157**:306–311, 1978.
7. Frizzell RA, Field M, Schultz SG. Sodium-coupled chloride transport by epithelial tissues. Amer J Physiol **236**:F1–F8, 1979.
8. Anwer MS, Hegner D. Role of inorganic electrolytes in bile acid-independent canalicular bile formation. Amer J Physiol **244**:G116–G124, 1983.
9. Miller LL, Bly CG, Watson ML, Bale WF. The dominant role of the liver in plasma protein synthesis. J Exp Med **94**:431–445, 1951.
10. Sugano T, Suda K, Shimada M, Oshino N. Biochemical and ultrastructural evaluation of isolated rat liver systems perfused with a hemoglobin-free medium. J Biochem **83**:995–1007, 1978.
11. Coleman R, Mitchell RH, Finean JB, Hawthorne JN. A purified plasma membrane preparation from rat liver under isotonic conditions. Biochim Biophys Acta **135**:573–579, 1967.
12. Lowry DH, Rosenberg NJ, Farr AL, Randall RJ. Protein measurement with the folin phenol reagent. J Biol Chem **193**:265–275, 1951.
13. Emmelot P, Bos CJ, Bennediti EL, Rumke PH. Studies on plasma membranes. I. Chemical composition and enzyme content of plasma membrane isolated from rat liver. Biochim Biophys Acta **90**:126–145, 1964.
14. Anwer MS, Kroker R, Hegner D. Bile acid secretion and synthesis by isolated rat hepatocytes. Biochem Biophys Res Commun **64**:603–609, 1975.
15. Anwer MS, Henger D. Importance of solvent drag and diffusion in bile acid dependent bile formation: Ion substitution studies in isolated perfused rat liver. Hepatology **2**:580–586, 1982.
16. Barnhart JL, Combes B. Effect of theophylline on hepatic excretory function. Amer J Physiol **227**:194–199, 1974.
17. Scharschmidt BR, Van Dyke RV, Stephens JE. Chloride transport by intact rat liver and cultured rat hepatocytes. Amer J Physiol **242**:G628–633, 1982.
18. Thomsen OO, Larsen JA. The effect of glucagon, DB cAMP and insulin on bile production in the intact rat and the isolated perfused rat liver. Acta Physiol Scand **111**:23–30, 1980.
19. Baker AL, Kaplan MM. Effects of cholera enterotoxin, glucagon, and dibutyryl cyclic-AMP on rat liver alkaline phosphatase, bile flow, and bile composition. Gastroenterology **70**:577–581, 1976.
20. Poupon RE, Dol ML, Dumont M, Erlinger S. Evidence against a physiological role of cAMP in choleresis in dogs and rats. Biochem Pharmacol **27**:2413–2416, 1978.
21. Levine RA, Hall RC. Cyclic AMP in secretin choleresis. Evidence for a regulatory role in man and baboons but not in dogs. Gastroenterology **70**:537–544, 1976.

Received November 7, 1983. P.S.E.B.M. 1984, Vol. 176.
Accepted February 6, 1984.

PROCEEDINGS OF THE SOCIETY FOR EXPERIMENTAL BIOLOGY AND MEDICINE **176**, 77–83 (1984)

Effects of Folic Acid Malnutrition on Rotaviral Infection in Mice[1] (41845)

JOHN D. MORREY,* ROBERT W. SIDWELL,*,† ROGER L. NOBLE,*
BILL B. BARNETT,* AND ARTHUR W. MAHONEY‡

Department of Biology, †Department of Animal, Dairy, and Veterinary Science, and ‡Department of Nutrition and Food Science, Utah State University, Logan, Utah 84322

Abstract. A study was undertaken to determine if dietary deficiencies of folic acid would influence rotaviral diarrheal disease in infant mice. Female mice were fed diets containing essentially no folic acid, 25% of a normal quantity of folic acid, or a normally recommended quantity of folic acid, beginning at time of breeding and continuing through periods of gestation and lactation. Two-day-old infants from these dams were exposed to purified murine rotavirus or to sterile virus diluent and the severity of the rotaviral infection monitored. Infants from the low folic acid group had significantly lower folate levels in their livers, indicating a deficiency was achieved, and developed more severe disease manifestations than those infants from the dams receiving the normal folic acid levels in their diet. The infection enhancement was seen as increased incidences of diarrhea and a significantly greater number of mice exhibiting high intestinal rotaviral antigen titers. Serum rotavirus antibody titers were below detectable levels in a significant number of these same infants.

A close association exists between diarrhea and malnutrition, with malnourished children having a higher incidence of severe diarrhea resulting in increased mortality (1, 2). A substantial number of the total episodes of diarrhea have been attributed to rotavirus infection (1).

Noble *et al.* (3) demonstrated in infant mice that general malnutrition, as established by nutrient dilution, and protein deficiency dramatically enhanced the severity of the murine rotaviral disease. Conceptually, some specific nutrients may be responsible for the adverse effect of malnutrition on rotaviral diarrhea, since it is known that deficiencies of certain specific nutrients profoundly affect immunologic response (4, 5). Among such nutrients affecting host immune response is folic acid, which is one of the first limiting nutrients in human diets (6). Folate deficiencies in mice have been shown to reduce the number of plaque-forming units in the spleen and severely impair hemagglutinin antibody in response to red blood cell challenge. Cell-mediated immunity is also reduced as seen by reduction in dermal sensitivity response of phytohemagglutinin, and decreased T-cell population in peripheral blood and spleen (5). The present study investigated the combined pre- and postnatal effects of diets deficient in folic acid on rotaviral disease induced in infants born to these dams.

Materials and Methods. *Diet.* The amounts of folic acid in three different diets were determined using data of the National Academy of Sciences (7). Folic acid in concentrations of 0, 0.125, and 0.50 μg were added per gram of basal diet to make, respectively, deficient, marginal and normal folic acid diets as recommended for normal growth. The basal diet contained (g/kg diet): casein 150, corn oil 60, mineral mix (3) 11.6, vitamin mixture (3) prepared without folate 20, $CaCO_3$ 16.75, $NaHPO_4 \cdot H_2O$ 29.8, cellulose 50, corn syrup 50, and dextrose to make 1 kg. Diets were pelleted. Both food and distilled water were provided *ad libitum.*

Mice. Specific pathogen-free Swiss–Webster mice used in this study were designated Crl: CFW (SW) BR, (Charles River, Wilmington, Mass.), and had been previously found to be quite susceptible to murine rotavirus infection (3). Immediately upon arrival of the adult mice, precautions were taken to not inadvertently expose the mice to rotavirus by placing them in a limited-access, disinfected room. The mice were housed in disposable cages with

[1] Supported by the Thrasher Research Fund and the Utah Agricultural Experiment Station. Utah Agricultural Experiment Station Publication No. 2886.

0037-9727/84 $1.50

filter tops (Lab Products, Inc., Federalsburg, Md.); bedding was changed frequently to avoid coprophagy. Mice infected with rotavirus were kept in a building separate from the housing of the uninfected mice and personnel working with these infected animals were denied access to rotavirus-free areas.

Virus. Murine rotavirus (MRV) was obtained from Dr. M. Collins of Microbiological Associates Inc. (Bethesda, Md.). The virus had RNA band patterns similar to the bovine and human rotaviruses (8), verifying that it was a rotavirus. Stock virus was prepared by inoculating mice by oral gavage (po) with MRV, then harvesting the intestines 4 days later. These were homogenized to a 10% w/v suspension of 0.01 *M* phosphate-buffered saline (PBS), pH 7.2, which was then Freon-extracted and purified further by centrifugation in a cesium chloride density gradient. The virus was collected at a density of 1.3 to 1.4 g/ml and dialyzed against 0.01 *M* PBS, pH 7.2. The virus stock, from which no bacteria could be isolated, was titered in infant mice to determine the 50% infectious dose (ID_{50}); an approximate 100 ID_{50} viral inoculum was used in these studies.

Experimental design. Two sexually mature females were bred with one male. The mice were randomized to the diets by alternately assigning a diet to each mouse. At least 25 female mice were fed each diet group, beginning at the time of introduction of the male and continuing through 24 days after birth of their young. At 2 days of age, 50% of their infants were infected po with rotavirus and the remainder were sham-infected with PBS. Sham-infected mice were housed separately from the infected animals. The presence of diarrhea in the infant mice was measured on Days 1–5, 10, and 20 post-virus infection by slightly pressing the abdomen of the infant and observing for the presence or absence of a highly conspicuous, copious diarrhea. Each litter was weighed on Days 1–5, 10, and 20 post-virus infection.

Intestines from 25–30 infants from each diet group were collected to assay virus titer on Day 4 post-virus infection. The intestines were excised at the pyloric valve to the anus, diluted 1:10 in PBS, pH 7.2, homogenized, and assayed for rotavirus by ELISA. Portions of the duodenum, ileum, and jejunum were also collected and placed in Formalin at 20 days post-virus infection. The Formalin-fixed intestines were subsequently imbedded in paraffin, sectioned, and stained with hematoxylin–eosin stain for histological examination.

Stomachs from infants were removed on Day 4, and serum was collected on Day 20 post-virus infection. At least 20 stomachs from each diet group were processed for antibody assays by homogenizing the curdled milk contents in a 1:5 dilution of PBS. Livers were excised from infant mice at 1 and 4 days post-virus infection, homogenized in a tissue grinder, and assayed for folic acid.

Upon collection of the tissues, all specimens were stored at −20°C. The assays were done soon after the collection of the sample.

Folic acid assay. The liver folic acid levels were assayed by the method of Bennett *et al.* (9) by placing a portion of homogenized liver in media without folic acid to a standardized concentration of 10% (w/v). Commercially prepared Folic Acid Casei Medium was used (Difco Laboratories, Detroit, Mich.). *Lactobacillus casei* ATCC 7469, which depends on extraneous folic acid for growth, was seeded to the media. The degree of growth, as measured by absorbance at 670 nm, was proportionate to the amount of folic acid in the liver. A standard curve was calculated to quantitate the folic acid in the liver.

Titration of viral antigen. Viral antigen in intestinal homogenates was assayed by ELISA (10). The test was performed by first filling 96-well microtiter plates (Polyvinyl V-well, Dynatech, Alexandria, Va.) with ammonium sulfate precipitated guinea pig anti-simean rotavirus immunoglobulins, and then incubating for 18 hr at 4°C. The wells were washed nine times for 30 sec each with distilled water. All subsequent washings were the same. Serial dilutions of the samples in Brain Heart Infusion Broth (BHI, BBL Microbiology Systems, Cockeysville, Md.) were added to the wells and incubated overnight at 4°C. After washing the wells again, rabbit anti-human rotavirus peroxidase conjugate (DAKO, Accurate Chemicals, Westbury, N.Y.) containing 20% fetal bovine serum and 2% normal guinea pig serum was added to the wells and incubated 3 hr at 37°C. After washing, Rotazyme substrate (Abbott Laboratories, North Chicago, Ill.) was added and incubated 30 min at room temperature. After stopping the reaction with 1 *N* HCl, the absorbance at 490 nm was read on a Microelisa reader MR 590 (Dynatech Laboratories, Inc., Alexandria, Va.). Titers were expressed as the highest dilution giving a $P/N > 2.1$, where P is the absorbance at 490 nm of the sample and N is the average of six wells containing rotavirus-negative intestinal homogenate.

Titration of serum and stomach milk antibody. Milk and serum anti-rotavirus antibodies were assayed using blocking of bovine rotavirus (BRV) detection by ELISA (11). Equal volumes of Freon-extracted cell culture-propagated BRV and varying twofold dilutions of the mouse serum, or milk to be tested for anti-rotavirus antibody were incubated together at 37°C. After 1 hr incubation, titration of bovine rotavirus in these mixtures was carried out as described above for titration of viral antigen. A 50% reduction in absorbance at 490 nm between the mean of three positive controls containing no sera compared to the mean of three negative controls (BHI) was considered positive for rotaviral-specific antibody. This 50% reduction end point was as described by Yolken *et al.* (11). The end point of the sample being tested was the highest dilution that was positive for antibody.

Statistical analysis. The percentage weight gain data were analyzed by expressing the experimental design in the form of a model, $y = I_i + D_j + C_{(ij)k} + T_l + ID_{ij} + IT_{il} + DT_{jl} + IDT_{ijl} + E$, where I was infected or sham-infected, D was diet, C was cages and T was days after inoculation. The analysis of variance was computed by RUMMAGE program (Bryce, G. R. Data Analysis in Rummage—A User's Guide. Brigham Young University, Provo, Utah).

Means for antigen and antibody titers were calculated by obtaining the $\log_{10}$ of the inverse of each titer, averaging those values, obtaining the antilog of that mean, and obtaining the inverse to arrive at the mean for the antigen or antibody titers. The data for serum antibodies, intestinal antigen, and presence of diarrhea were analyzed by chi-square analysis using Yate's correction for small sample size.

Chi-square analysis for antibody data was performed by obtaining the mean of all the data, and using the mean value as a division line; those values above the mean were connoted (+) and those below were connoted (−) for use in the statistical analysis.

Results. The folic acid contents of livers from infant mice used in this study are summarized in Table I. Infants from mice receiving 0 μg folic acid/g diet had reduced quantities of folate in their livers, indicating the diet was sufficient to achieve a folic acid deficiency in the animal. Mice that received the higher dietary levels of folic acid exhibited no apparent decrease of folate in their livers.

The results of the diet/infection study are summarized in Table II. The sham-infected mice from dams receiving the lowest folic acid diet gained less weight ($P < 0.05$) than the sham-infected mice from the dams fed the two diets having higher levels of folic acid. The sham-infected mice fed the marginal folic acid diet appeared also to gain less weight than did the mice receiving the highest folic acid diet; the difference, however, was not statistically significant. More obvious in Table II is the substantially reduced weight gains of the rotaviral infected infants compared with those of the uninfected infants ($P < 0.001$, when compared to uninfected controls). Although infected infants from mice fed the 0 μg folic acid/g diet had the overall lowest weight gains, the differences as compared with the infected animals in the higher folic acid diet groups were not statistically significant.

The proportion of mice exhibiting profuse diarrhea on Days 2–5 post-virus inoculation are also seen in Table II. The diarrhea had totally subsided in all groups by Day 10. Mod-

TABLE I. FOLIC ACID CONTENT[a] OF LIVERS FROM UNINFECTED INFANT MICE OF EACH FOLIC ACID DIET

Age of mice	Diet[b] 0	0.125	0.50
3 Days	3.8 ± 1.5[c]	5.1 ± 1.5	5.3 ± 0.9
6 Days	3.7 ± 0.9	4.5 ± 1.0	6.2 ± 1.2

[a] Micrograms of folate per gram of liver.
[b] Micrograms of folate per gram of basal diet.
[c] Mean ± standard deviation. From left to right the number of samples per diet group assayed were 6, 3, 4, and 4, 13, 3.

TABLE II. EFFECT OF PRE- AND POSTNATAL DIETARY FOLIC ACID DEFICIENCIES ON ROTAVIRUS INFECTION IN INFANT MICE

	Folic acid concentration in diet[a] (μg/g)					
	0		0.125		0.5 (Control)	
	Infected	Uninfected	Infected	Uninfected	Infected	Uninfected
No. of mice	136	138	91	60	85	68
Av initial wt (g)	2.1	2.0	2.1	2.0	2.2	2.0
Mortality (%)	0	0	2	0	0	0
Day 20 wt gain (%)	400	520*	442	542	430	595
Total incidence of diarrhea[b] (%)	61**	0	48	0	50	0
Mean intestinal viral titer[c]	544 (180–1640)[e]	0	740 (266–2058)	0	386 (206–724)	0
Mean rotaviral antibody titer[d] (dams' sera)	10 (6.2–17.4)	0	9 (3.5–24.5)	0	13 (7.2–22.4)	0
Mean rotaviral antibody titer[d] (infants' sera)	2.4 (1.6–3.8)	0	3.7 (2.0–6.8)	0	3.2 (1.8–5.6)	0

[a] Diets of dams from which infants were taken.
[b] Days 2–5 post-virus exposure.
[c] Titers expressed as reciprocals. Intestines taken 4 days post-virus exposure.
[d] Titers expressed as reciprocals. Sera taken 20 days post-virus exposure.
[e] Standard error.
* $P < 0.05$, ** $P < 0.01$ (compared with controls).

erate ($P < 0.05$) increases in incidence of diarrhea were seen, particularly on Day 2 in the infants from the lowest folic acid dietary group (76% compared to 60% in the mice from the highest folic acid diet group). These differences were still seen on Day 3, but had appreciably declined in all groups by Day 4.

The individual rotaviral antigen titers in intestines from infected infants killed on Day 4 are indicated in Fig. 1. Mean antigen titers, seen in Table II, were increased in the mice from the folate-deprived groups. Although these increased titers were not statistically significant, it was quite apparent that all intestines from the control group had lower titers (none >640) than those from the folate deficient groups. By utilizing chi-square analysis where those titer values greater than or equal to 1280 were connoted (+) and those below 1280 were connoted (−), the number having high titers in the lowest and marginal folic acid diet groups were significantly increased ($P < 0.05$) compared with the control (0.5 μg/g) folic acid diet group, indicating the folate deficient diets may have enhanced the MRV infection in a significant number of the infants. No serum rotaviral antibody or intestinal rotavirus was found in uninfected dams and infants.

A small degree of cytoplasmic vacuolization in the epithelial cells at the tip of the villi was seen in infected mouse intestines from all three dietary groups. There was no difference in the severity of this degeneration between any of the three dietary groups.

Milk in the stomachs of infected infants at 4 days post-virus infection was assayed for rotaviral-specific antibody, but no antibodies were detected at the lowest dilution (1:5) tested. Serum rotaviral antibody titers of infected dams and infants from each dietary group killed on day 20 are summarized in Table II, and individual antibody titers for the infants' sera are seen in Fig. 2. Sera from infants in the lowest folic acid dietary group had

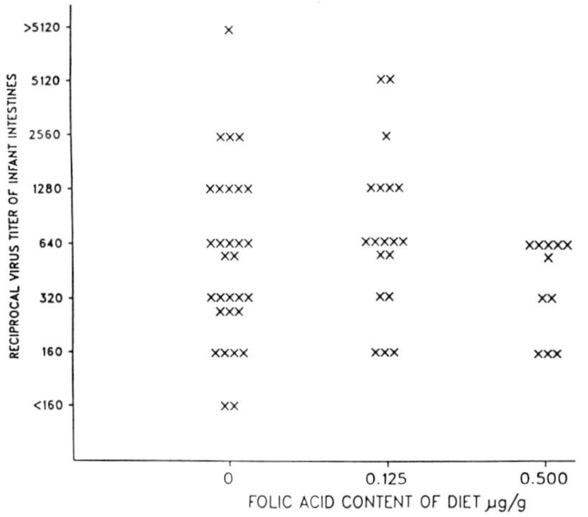

FIG. 1. Reciprocal virus titers in intestines from infected infant mice 4 days post-virus inoculation whose dams received pre- and postnatally 0, 0.125, and 0.5 μg/g folic acid diets.

overall lower titers than did those from either marginal or normal folic acid groups. A significant number ($P < 0.05$) had titers of <1:4. The rotaviral antibody titer of the dams' sera was not appreciably altered in any group. These animals were not directly infected with rotavirus, but were presumably exposed to the virus by being in close proximity to their experimentally infected infants.

Discussion. Varying levels of folic acid in a basal diet were fed to female mice to cause reduced or normal folic acid levels in their progeny. A folic acid deficiency was observed in the infant mice born to dams fed the most deficient diet as evidenced by the reduced concentrations of folic acid in the infants' livers. It is noteworthy to compare the values of the folic acid concentrations in the livers with the studies of Klipstein and Lipton (12). They observed the normal range of folic acid in mouse livers to be 6.0 to 13.4 μg/g (μg folic acid/g wet liver) and the range for deficient animals to be below 5.3 μg/g. We also observed similar values of 5.3 to 6.2 μg/g and 3.7 to 5.1 μg/g for the respective normal and deficient folic acid liver concentrations. The folic acid deficiency observed in our study was not believed to be severe, since slight weight retardation was the only clinical manifestation of the deficiency.

The rotaviral disease was moderately enhanced in infants from the deficient and marginal folic acid diet groups. This was apparent by the increased rotaviral titers of the infant mice in these folate deficient groups, and in an increased proportion of mice with diarrhea which was most pronounced early in the infection, i.e., Days 2 and 3 post-virus exposure. The diarrhea, when occurring, was readily apparent as a profuse yellow liquid. The increased incidence of diarrhea may have been a direct manifestation of the increased virus present in the intestine. It is surprising that despite this increased diarrheal incidence in the folate-deprived mice, the weight gain was not influenced to a greater degree than was observed (maximum of 30% reduction by Day 20). It was previously reported by Noble *et al.* (3) that general malnutrition or protein deprivation increased the severity of the rotaviral disease to the point of significant numbers of mice dying of the infection. Such deaths were not seen in the present study, and indeed are an unusual occurrence in experimentally induced rotaviral infections in mice. One change in protocol, however, between the study of Noble *et al.* and the present study was our use of a more purified virus, which may have been less capable of killing the mice.

As was also observed by Noble *et al.* (3), we found that lessened weight gain of the in-

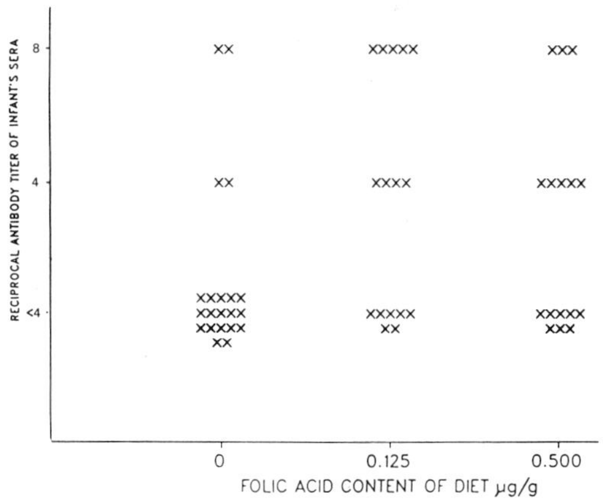

FIG. 2. Reciprocal rotaviral antibody titers in sera from infected infant mice 20 days post-virus inoculation whose dams received pre- and postnatally 0, 0.125, and 0.5 μg/g folic acid diets.

fant mouse is a good parameter to measure the severity of the rotaviral disease. Such failure to gain weight is probably due to diarrhea-induced dehydration. Using this weight gain parameter, it was determined that the infection was apparently of sufficient magnitude to inhibit weight gain in 20 days by over 150%.

Folic acid deficiencies have been reported to affect disease status in several studies involving microbial infections. Nelson *et al.* (13) observed that infant guinea pigs fed a folate-deficient diet for 2 weeks were highly sensitive to infection with *Shigella flexneri,* with 89% of the animals dying after challenged compared to no deaths occurring in similar animals fed a normal diet. Williams *et al.* (14) reported that rats deprived of folic acid post-weaning had a decreased resistance to infection with *Salmonella typhimurium.* Similarly folate-deprived rats have also been found to develop higher and more prolonged parasitemias when infected with *Trypanosoma lewisi* (15). Chicks from a Newcastle disease virus-vaccinated flock which were raised on a folate deficient diet were reportedly markedly more susceptible to later lethal infection with the virus (16). In all these studies, a considerable deranged immunocompetence was noted in the folate-deprived animals.

It was noted in the present study that serum rotaviral specific antibody titers in the folic acid deficient infant mice were lower than the titers of the control mice. This effect was likely due to the reduced folic acid levels and is not surprising when one considers the central role of folic acid in cellular DNA synthesis (17). Among the effects on humoral immunologic response brought about by folic acid deficiency reported by others are decrease in hemagglutination titers (18), decrease in number of antibody-forming cells (19) and decreased bacterial agglutinating antibody titers (16). We saw no significant effect in this study on the folic acid-deprived dams' serum rotaviral antibody titers, but all the titers were quite low and perhaps the time of serum collection was not ideal for achievement of maximal antibody levels. The dams were not directly infected, but presumably became infected from the diarrheic discharge of their infants. The failure to detect maternal antibody in the milk was probably because the sampling time (4 days) was so soon after virus exposure. Other studies being run in our laboratories (B. Barnett, personal communication) have demonstrated that immunized dams excrete high titers of rotaviral antibody in their milk which can be readily assayed by the method described in this report.

The results of this study provide additional insight into the role the water-soluble vitamin, folic acid, may play in the resistance of a host to virus infection.

---

1. World Health Organization. Control of diarrhoeal diseases: WHO's programme takes shape. WHO Chron **32**:369–372, 1978.
2. Wray JD. Direct nutrition intervention and the control of diarrheal diseases in preschool children. Amer J Clin Nutr **31**:2073–2082, 1978.
3. Noble RL, Sidwell RW, Mahoney AW, Barnett BB, Spendlove RS. Influence of malnutrition and alterations in dietary protein on murine rotaviral disease. Proc Soc Exp Biol Med **173**:417–426, 1983.
4. Nalder BN, Mahoney AW, Ramakrishnan R, Hendricks DG. Sensitivity of the immunological response to the nutritional status of rats. J Nutr **102**:535–542, 1972.
5. Gross RL, Newberne PM. Role of nutrition in immunologic function. Physiol Rev **60**:188–302, 1980.
6. Leevy CM, Cardi L, Frank O, Gellene R, Baker H. Incidence and significance of hypervitaminemia in a randomly selected municipal hospital population. Amer J Clin Nutr **17**:259–271, 1965.
7. National Academy of Sciences. Nutritional Requirements of Domestic Animals. Washington, DC, Nat Acad Sci, 2nd ed, No 10, 1972.
8. Smee DF, Sidwell RW, Clark SW, Barnett BB, Spendlove RS. Inhibition of rotaviruses by selected antiviral substances: Mechanisms of viral inhibition and in vivo activity. Antimicrob Agents Chemother **21**:66–73, 1982.
9. Bennett M, Berry V, Chanarim I, Ardeman S. The folic-acid activity of liver. J Clin Pathol **17**:27–30, 1964.
10. Yolken RH, Kim HW, Clem T, Wyatt RG, Kalica AR, Chanock RM, Kapikian AZ. Enzyme-linked immunosorbent assay (ELISA) for detection of human reo-like virus agent of gastroenteritis. Lancet **2**:263–266, 1977.
11. Yolken RH, Wyatt RG, Barbour BA, Kim HW, Kapikian AZ, Chanock RM. Measurement of rotavirus antibody by an enzyme-linked immunosorbent assay blocking assay. J Clin Microbiol **8**:283–287, 1978.

12. Klipstein FA, Lipton SD. Intestinal folate-deficient mice. Amer J Clin Nutr **23**:132–140, 1970.
13. Nelson JD, Haltalin KC. Effect of neonatal folic acid deprivation on later growth and susceptibility to Shigella infection in the guinea pig. Amer J Clin Nutr **25**:992–996, 1972.
14. Williams EAG, Gross RL, Newberne PM. Effect of folate deficiency on the cell-mediated immune response in rats. Nutr Rep Int **12**:137–144, 1975.
15. Aboko-Cole GF, Lee CM. Interaction of nutrition and infection: Effect of folic acid deficiency on resistance to *Trypanosoma lewisi* and *Trypanosoma rhodesiense.* Int J Biochem **5**:693–698, 1974.
16. Little PA, Oleson JJ, Roesch PK. The effect of pteroylglutamic acid on some immune responses in chicks. J Immunol **65**:491–498, 1950.
17. Naugs KM, Newberne PM. Effects of dietary folate, vitamin B_{12} and methionine/choline deficiency on immune function. Advan Exp Med Biol **135**:63–91, 1981.
18. Pruzansky J, Axelrod AE. Antibody production to diphtheria toxoid in vitamin deficiency status. Proc Soc Exp Biol Med **89**:233–238, 1958.

Received September 26, 1983. P.S.E.B.M. 1984. Vol. 176.
Accepted February 13, 1984.

PROCEEDINGS OF THE SOCIETY FOR EXPERIMENTAL BIOLOGY AND MEDICINE **176**, 84–87 (1984)

Progesterone Is Not Responsible for the Blood Pressure Fall in Late-Pregnant New Zealand Genetically Hypertensive Rats (41846)

REBECCA MORGAN BOYD AND PHILIP G. BAER

Department of Pharmacology, University of Tennessee Center for the Health Sciences, Memphis, Tennessee 38163

Abstract. In various models of experimental and genetic hypertension in rats, blood pressure is markedly reduced during late pregnancy. The period during which the blood pressure reduction occurs is also the period when plasma progesterone is maximally elevated, and administration of progesterone to renal hypertensive rats has been reported to reduce blood pressure (J. Armstrong, 1959, *Proc. Soc. Exp. Biol. Med.* **102**:452–455). To test the possibility that elevated plasma progesterone is responsible for the blood pressure reduction in late pregnancy, on Day 14 of pregnancy a group of New Zealand genetically hypertensive (NZGH) rats was ovariectomized and implanted with progesterone-filled capsules, to maintain plasma progesterone at low levels just sufficient to maintain pregnancy, and compared with intact, pregnant NZGH. Ovariectomy did not alter the characteristic course of blood pressure reduction seen in late-pregnant intact NZGH rats. In addition, daily administration of progesterone (15 mg/kg, sc) for 14 days did not alter blood pressure of either nonpregnant NZGH rats or New Zealand normotensive rats with chronic 1-kidney, 1-clip hypertension. It is concluded that blood pressure of NZGH rats is reduced to near normotensive levels in late pregnancy, as reported for other models of rat hypertension, but that elevated plasma progesterone levels are not requisite for that reduction and do not reduce blood pressure of renal hypertensive rats.

In genetically hypertensive rats of the Okamoto (SH) strain, and in rats with other forms of experimental hypertension, blood pressure falls progressively during the last week of pregnancy to nearly normotensive levels, remains reduced through parturition, and then returns rapidly to prepregnancy hypertensive levels by the first or second day postparturition (1–5). Also during the last week of pregnancy in the rat, plasma progesterone levels rise, reaching a sustained peak at a time coinciding with the reduction of blood pressure, and then fall rapidly, returning to prepregnancy levels at a time coinciding with the return of blood pressure to hypertensive levels (4, 6). In addition to these temporally coincident patterns of inverse changes in blood pressure and plasma progesterone levels, Armstrong (7) has reported that daily administration of progesterone, at a dose similar to the amount produced by late-pregnant rats (8), reduced blood pressure of 1-kidney, 1-clip hypertensive rats. From these various findings, investigation of the possibility that elevations in plasma progesterone levels contribute to the reduction of blood pressure in late-pregnant hypertensive rats appeared to be warranted.

The effect of pregnancy on blood pressure of the New Zealand strain of genetically hypertensive (NZGH) rat has not been reported. We noted in preliminary studies of pregnant NZGH rats that blood pressure was decreased just prior to parturition. The present studies were carried out to document fully the effect of pregnancy on blood pressure in NZGH rats, a model of genetic hypertension not previously studied in this regard, and to investigate the possibility of a causal relationship between changes in plasma progesterone levels and changes in blood pressure in late-pregnant genetically hypertensive rats.

Materials and Methods. Rats used in this study were from the colony of New Zealand normotensive (NZNR) and genetically hypertensive (NZGH) rats maintained at this institution. Rats were housed in group cages, with three to five rats per cage, in a room with controlled temperature (24°C) and humidity (50%), illuminated from 6:00 AM to 6:00 PM, and received tap water and standard rat chow (Purina No. 5001; sodium 174, potassium 282 meq/kg) *ad libitum.* Systolic blood pressure was measured by tail sphygmomanometry after warming the rats for 10 min at 37°C.

Studies in pregnant NZGH. Rats were mated overnight and Day 1 of pregnancy was

0037-9727/84 $1.50

determined from vaginal smears and/or the presence of a cervical plug. At two to five-day intervals before, during, and after pregnancy, blood pressure was determined and the rats were lightly anesthetized with halothane to permit sampling of blood (0.2 ml) from the tail for determination of plasma progesterone. On Day 14 of pregnancy, one group of rats was ovariectomized and implanted with progesterone-filled Silastic capsules (1.5 × 40 mm), to maintain low progesterone levels just sufficient to prevent spontaneous abortion.

Studies in nonpregnant NZGH. Systolic blood pressure of virgin female NZGH rats was measured before, during and after treatment with progesterone. Rats received daily subcutaneous injections of either progesterone (Sigma, 15 mg/kg/day) or peanut oil vehicle (1 ml/kg) for a period of 14 days.

Studies in 1-kidney, 1-clip hypertensive NZNR. Fourteen-week-old female NZNR were anesthetized with halothane; the right kidney was removed and a silver clip, 0.2 mm i.d., was placed on the left renal artery (9). Six weeks later, after the rats had developed stable hypertension, daily injections of progesterone (Progesterone injection, USP; Eli Lilly Co.; 15 mg/kg) or vehicle were given for a period of 14 days; blood pressure was measured two or three times a week.

Analytical and statistical methods. Progesterone in plasma was measured by radioimmunoassay using a commercially available kit (Coat-A-Count Progesterone, Diagnostics Products Corp., Los Angeles). Values are expressed in the text, figures, and tables and group means ± the standard error of the mean. Statistical significance was determined by Student's *t* test for unpaired values, or by analysis of variance followed by Neuman–Keuls test for multiple variables, as appropriate (10); a *P* value of less than 0.05 was taken to indicate statistical significance.

Results. As shown in Fig. 1, in intact pregnant NZGH rats plasma progesterone increased from prepregnancy levels of 20 ng/ml to 70 ng/ml on Days 17 and 20; systolic blood pressure remained constant at prepregnancy levels of 160–170 mm Hg until Day 14, then declined steadily to a minimum value of 135 mm Hg on the last day of pregnancy. After parturition, blood pressure rose rapidly, returning to prepregnancy levels by the second

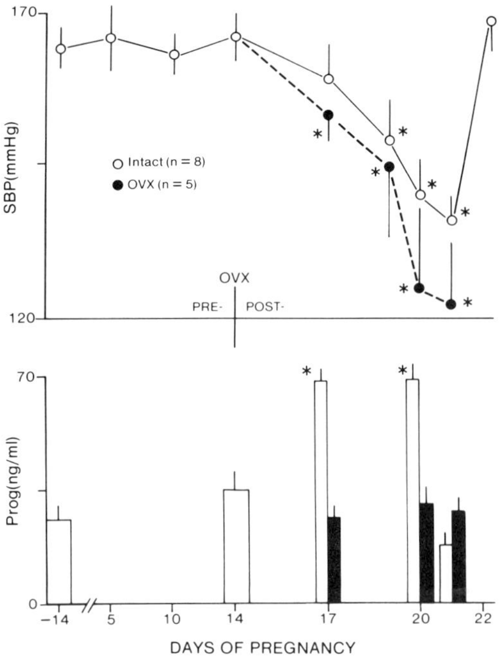

FIG. 1. Systolic blood pressure (SBP, upper panel) and plasma progesterone concentration (PROG, lower panel) in pregnant NZGH rats. Intact rats are indicated by open circles and bars; rats that were ovariectomized and implanted with progesterone capsules on Day 14 of pregnancy are indicated by solid circles and bars. * Indicates $P < 0.05$ compared with prepregnancy values.

day postparturition. In rats that were gonadectomized and implanted with progesterone-filled capsules on Day 14 of pregnancy, plasma progesterone did not exhibit the characteristic late-pregnancy increase, but remained instead at levels similar to those seen in nonpregnant rats. Despite prevention of the characteristic rise in plasma progesterone, blood pressure of the gonadectomized rats fell during late pregnancy as did that of intact rats, beginning about Day 14 and reaching a minimum value of 125 mm Hg on Day 21 of pregnancy. The gonadectomized rats were unable to deliver successfully and were sacrificed on Day 23 of pregnancy; blood pressure remained reduced until the rats were killed.

NZNR female rat blood pressures, shown in Fig. 2, rose progressively after renal artery constriction and contralateral uninephrectomy, from a control level of 125 mm Hg, to 220 mm Hg by the fourth week after clipping, and did not change thereafter. Daily injections

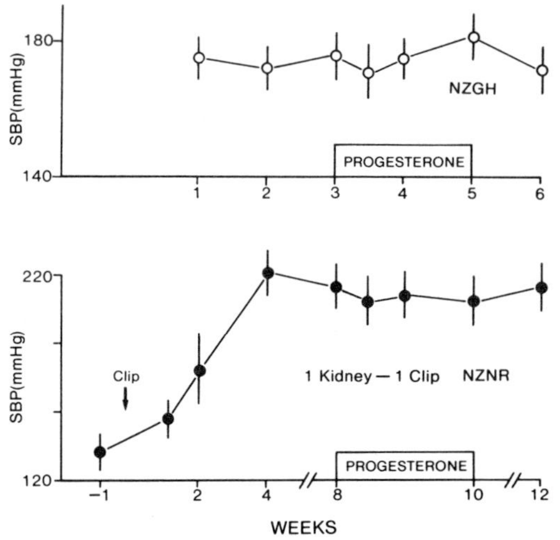

FIG. 2. Systolic blood pressure (SBP) of New Zealand genetically hypertensive rats (NZGH, upper panel) and of New Zealand normotensive strain rats with chronic 1-kidney, 1-clip hypertension (lower panel) before, during, and after daily administration of progesterone (15 mg/kg, sc) for 14 days.

of progesterone for 14 days had no effect on blood pressures of these renal hypertensive rats. Also shown in Fig. 2, blood pressures of NZGH rats were not altered during a 2-week course of daily progesterone treatment.

Discussion. First noted in renal hypertensive rats (1), reduction of blood pressure during late pregnancy has also been reported to occur in renal hypertensive rabbits and dogs (2). In other rat models of experimental hypertension the phenomenon appears to be less consistently demonstrable. For example, in rats made hypertensive by mineralocorticoid treatment and excess sodium chloride intake, blood pressure was reported to fall during late pregnancy by some investigators (3, 5), while others reported no such effect (11, 12). In the present study, we found that blood pressure of NZGH hypertensive rats fell during the last days of pregnancy to approximately normotensive levels; the timecourse and extent of the blood pressure reduction closely resembled those reported by other investigators to occur in another model of genetic hypertension, the Okamoto SH rat (3, 4). Despite extensive investigation, the mechanism underlying this rapid reduction of blood pressure, and the subsequent and even more rapid rise back to hypertensive levels, has not been defined. The possibility that the changes in blood pressure might be related to changes in progesterone levels has not, to our knowledge, been previously tested. Several pieces of information suggested that progesterone could be responsible. First, Armstrong reported that progesterone treatment reduced the blood pressure of 1-kidney, 1-clip hypertensive rats, renal hypertensive dogs, and human essential hypertensive patients to nearly normotensive levels, and that pressure returned rapidly to hypertensive levels when progesterone treatment was stopped (7). Second, in pregnant rats plasma progesterone rises to a maximum on Days 15–20, then falls back to prepregnancy values by Day 1 postparturition (6); blood pressure in pregnant hypertensive rats changes in a mirror-image fashion with respect to progesterone, falling from about Day 15 of pregnancy to a minimum level on Days 20–21, then rising rapidly back to prepregnancy values by the first or second day postparturition (4, 5). And, third, the dose of progesterone reported to reduce blood pressure of hypertensive rats was 15 mg/kg/day (7); this amount is quite similar to the calculated rate at which progesterone is produced, 4.55 mg/day, in Day 15 pregnant rats (8).

The findings of the present study, however, do not support the hypothesis that progesterone is responsible for blood pressure changes in late-pregnant hypertensive rats and, in addition, are in clear conflict with one of the published findings (7) that was basic to the formulation of that hypothesis. From our finding that blood pressure fell during the last days of pregnancy in ovariectomized rats as it did in intact rats, it is clear that the high levels of progesterone characteristic of this phase of pregnancy are not requisite for the blood pressure reduction. In addition, administration of progesterone to NZGH rats, at doses equal to or in excess of the rate of progesterone production in late pregnancy, had no effect on blood pressure. Finally, we were unable to confirm the previously reported (7) hypotensive effect of progesterone in hypertensive rats, although the model of hypertension (1-kidney, 1-clip), the progesterone formulation (Injection Progesterone USP; Eli Lilly and Co.), and the dosage schedule and experimental protocol were identical to those of the earlier study; we have no explanation for the disparity between the results of the two studies. In any case, the results of this study indicate that progesterone is not a factor in the blood pressure reduction of late pregnancy in NZGH rats, since the pressure reduction occurred even when the late rise in progesterone was prevented, and administration of progesterone did not affect blood pressure of nonpregnant NZGH.

The authors express their appreciation to Bill Warren for his expert technical assistance with these studies. This work was supported by USPHS Grants HL-23548 and HL-00806.

1. Page EW, Patton HS, Ogden E. The effect of pregnancy on experimental hypertension. Amer J Obstet Gynecol **41**:53-60, 1941.
2. Grollman A. Effects of pregnancy on the course of experimental hypertension. Amer J Physiol **151**:373–379, 1947.
3. Takeda T. Experimental study on the blood pressure of pregnant hypertensive rats. I. Effect of pregnancy on the course of experimentally and spontaneously hypertensive rats. Japan Circ J **28**:49–54, 1964.
4. Aoi W, Gable D, Cleary RE, Young PCM, Weinberger MH. The antihypertensive effect of pregnancy in spontaneously hypertensive rats. Proc Soc Exp Biol Med **153**:13–15, 1976.
5. Moore HC, Biliczki FP. Failure to maintain steroid hypertension during pregnancy in the rat. J Pathol Bacteriol **95**:281–287, 1968.
6. Pepe GJ, Rothchild I. A comparative study of serum progesterone levels in pregnancy and in various types of pseudopregnancy in the rat. Endocrinology **95**:275–279, 1974.
7. Armstrong JG. Hypotensive action of progesterone in experimental and human hypertension. Proc Soc Exp Biol Med **102**:452–455, 1959.
8. Pepe GJ, Rothchild I. Metabolic clearance rate of progesterone: Comparison between ovariectomized, pregnant, pseudopregnant and deciduoma-bearing pseudopregnant rats. Endocrinology **93**:1200–1205, 1973.
9. Brooks B, Brown GB, Muirhead EE. Rectangular renal artery clip for standardized hypertension in the rat. Arch Pathol **93**:116–117, 1972.
10. Kirk RE. Experimental Design: Procedures for the Behavioral Sciences. Belmont, Calif., Wadsworth, 1968.
11. Page EW, Glendening MB. Influence of pregnancy upon hypertension induced in rats by sodium chloride and desoxycorticosterone. Proc Soc Exp Biol Med **82**:466–468, 1953.
12. Douglas BH, Langford HG. Effect of DCA and post DCA hypertension upon the course of pregnancy in the rat. Proc Soc Exp Biol Med **120**:238–240, 1965.

Received December 15, 1983. P.S.E.B.M. 1984, Vol. 176.
Accepted February 10, 1984.

PROCEEDINGS OF THE SOCIETY FOR EXPERIMENTAL BIOLOGY AND MEDICINE **176**, 88–94 (1984)

Monocrotaline-Induced Pulmonary Endothelial Dysfunction in Rats (41847)

AGOSTINO MOLTENI,* WILLIAM F. WARD,† CHUNG-HSIN TS'AO,* CURTIS D. PORT,*[,1] AND NORMAN H. SOLLIDAY‡,§

*Departments of *Pathology, †Radiology, and Medicine, Northwestern University Medical School, Chicago, Illinois 60611, and §Christ Hospital, Oak Lawn, Illinois 60453*

Abstract. To study the role of endothelial damage in the pathogenesis of lung injury induced by the pyrrolizidine alkaloid monocrotaline, three functions (angiotensin converting enzyme (ACE) activity, plasminogen activator (PLA) activity, and prostacyclin (PGI_2) production) associated with the pulmonary endothelium were examined, and were correlated with pulmonary arterial perfusion and ultrastructure in rats receiving monocrotaline in their drinking water (20 mg/liter) for 1–12 weeks. Lung ACE activity increased after 1 week of monocrotaline, then decreased steadily from 1 to 6 weeks, before plateauing at approximately 55% of normal. PLA activity in monocrotaline-treated lungs did not change significantly for the first 2 weeks, then decreased to 59 and 79% of the control value after 6 and 12 weeks, respectively. In contrast, PGI_2 production increased progressively, reaching 140 and 270% of the control level after 6 and 12 weeks of monocrotaline treatment, respectively. These endothelial functional changes were not accompanied by significant changes in pulmonary arterial perfusion as visualized by ^{99m}Tc lung scans. Electron microscopy of monocrotaline-treated lungs revealed endothelial damage (perivascular and subendothelial edema, degeneration) starting at 1 week, and inflammatory and hemorrhagic reactions starting at 2 weeks. At 6 and 12 weeks, monocrotaline-treated rats also exhibited increased pulmonary arterial wall thickness, right heart enlargement, and cardio- and hepatomegaly. Thus, monocrotaline-induced pulmonary injury is accompanied, and in some cases preceded, by structural and functional abnormalities in the pulmonary endothelium.

The pyrrolizidine alkaloid monocrotaline induces pulmonary hypertension and hepatotoxicity in rats (1, 2). Consumption of the parent plant, *Crotalaria spectabilis,* is a veterinary problem in grazing animals, and may represent a potential hazard for herbal tea users (3). While the mechanism of monocrotaline toxicity is not clear, it is accompanied by well-documented histopathologic and ultrastructural changes in the pulmonary endothelium (4–9). In contrast, relatively little is known concerning endothelial *function* in monocrotaline-treated lungs. Monocrotaline has been reported to decrease both angiotensin converting enzyme activity (10–12) and 5-hydroxytryptamine clearance (13, 14) in rat lung, although single injections of large doses were employed in three of these studies (10, 11, 13). Oral administration of monocrotaline may require several weeks to produce pulmonary endothelial dysfunction (12, 14).

Angiotensin-I-converting enzyme (ACE) activity, plasminogen activator (PLA) activity, and prostacyclin (PGI_2) production are among the many metabolic activities of the pulmonary endothelium, and are known individually to respond to a variety of insults (15–18). As a group, these three metabolic activities have been found in this laboratory to be a convenient and fairly sensitive index of endothelial function in irradiated rat lung (19). Therefore in order to study the role of endothelial dysfunction in the pathogenesis of monocrotaline-induced lung injury, we measured pulmonary ACE and PLA activities and PGI_2 production, and correlated these with arterial perfusion and ultrastructure in rats receiving monocrotaline in their drinking water for up to 12 weeks.

Materials and Methods. *Experimental design.* Male Sprague–Dawley rats (Harlan Industries, Madison, Wisc.) weighing 325–350 g were housed in pairs at 23 ± 1°C and given standard lab chow (Ralston Purina Co., St. Louis, Mo.) *ad libitum.* Half of the animals were provided with tap water, and half were given water containing monocrotaline (S. B. Penick Co., Lyndhurst, N.J.) at a concentra-

[1] Present address: Searle Pharmaceutical Co., Research and Development, Skokie, Illinois 60677.

0037-9727/84 $1.50

tion of 20 mg/liter. Periodic measurements revealed relatively constant daily water consumption of 35 ml/rat, resulting in a drug dose of approximately 2.0 mg/kg/day at the start of the experiment. The monocrotaline concentration in the drinking water was not increased as the animals gained weight. Body weight was recorded weekly.

Lung perfusion scans. Pulmonary arterial perfusion scans were obtained from randomly selected animals in both treatment groups after 1, 2, 4, 6, or 12 weeks. Animals were anesthetized with intraperitoneal sodium pentobarbital (Diabutal, Diamond Industries, Des Moines, Iowa), 35 mg/kg, and were injected with approximately 300 μCi of ^{99m}Tc-labeled macroaggregated albumin in 0.3 ml of 0.9% NaCl in the femoral vein. Thoracic scintigrams were obtained from an Ohio Nuclear gamma camera with a pinhole collimater, as described previously (20).

Autopsy procedure. Groups of six to eight rats were autopsied after 1–12 weeks of treatment. Animals were anesthetized with pentobarbital, and a blood sample was obtained from the abdominal aorta. The blood was allowed to clot at room temperature for 30 min, and the serum was separated and stored at −20°C. The abdominal aorta was then transected to exsanguinate the animal. The left lung was cut into quarters, perpendicular to the spinal axis, and termed the cephalic, subcephalic, supracaudal, and caudal regions, respectively, from the cephalic end.

ACE activity. The subcephalic region of the left lung was weighed, frozen in liquid N_2 and stored at −20°C. ACE activity in homogenized lung and blood serum was determined within 72 hr of autopsy by the spectrophotometric method of Cushman and Cheung (21), using the synthetic substrate hippuryl-L-histidyl-L-leucine (Sigma Chemical Co., St. Louis, Mo.). Protein concentration in the lung homogenate and serum was determined by the biuret method. ACE activity was expressed in mU/mg protein, as described previously (22).

PLA activity. The cephalic and caudal regions of the left lung were frozen in liquid N_2 and stored at −20°C. PLA activity was determined by the fibrin plate lysis method of Astrup and Albrechtsen (23). The data were expressed in area (mm^2) of the fibrin plate lysed under standard *in vitro* conditions as described previously (24).

PGI_2 production. The supracaudal region of the left lung was minced, weighed, and incubated in 3.0 ml of Dulbecco's phosphate-buffered saline (Gibco, Grand Island, N.Y.) containing glucose (1 mg/ml) for 10 min at 37°C. Aliquots of the incubation medium were transferred to a tube containing aspirin (final concentration 1 m*M*) to prevent further production of PGI_2. The samples were frozen and stored at −70°C until radioimmunoassayed for 6-keto-$PGF_{1\alpha}$ the stable metabolite of PGI_2 (New England Nuclear, Boston, Mass.). The data were expressed as nanograms 6-keto-$PGF_{1\alpha}$ produced per milligram wet weight of lung during the 10-min incubation.

Electron microscopy. Two control and two monocrotaline-treated rats were sacrificed for electron microscopy at each treatment time. The animals were anesthetized with pentobarbital and exsanguinated. The thoracic organs were removed *en bloc,* and the lungs were perfused via the trachea with 4°C glutaraldehyde–paraformaldehyde fixative at a pressure of 22 cm of water, as described previously (25). Lung samples were postfixed in osmium tetroxide and embedded in epoxy resin. Thick sections were stained with toluidine blue, and areas of interest were thin-sectioned, stained with uranyl acetate and lead citrate, and examined on a Hitachi HU-12 transmission electron microscope.

Organ weights. The liver was weighed at autopsy, and the heart was weighed after fixation in 10% phosphate-buffered Formalin (pH = 7.4). Organ weight was expressed as a fraction of body weight. The heart was dissected, and the right ventricle (RV) and the left ventricle plus septum (LV + S) were weighed separately. Right ventricular hypertrophy was evaluated on the basis of RV/LV + S weight ratios.

Statistical analysis. The effect of time and monocrotaline administration on ACE and PLA activity and PGI_2 production was determined by two-way analysis of variance (26).

Results. *Pulmonary arterial perfusion.* Thoracic scintigrams indicated that neither control nor monocrotaline-treated rats developed pulmonary arterial perfusion defects at any time throughout the study.

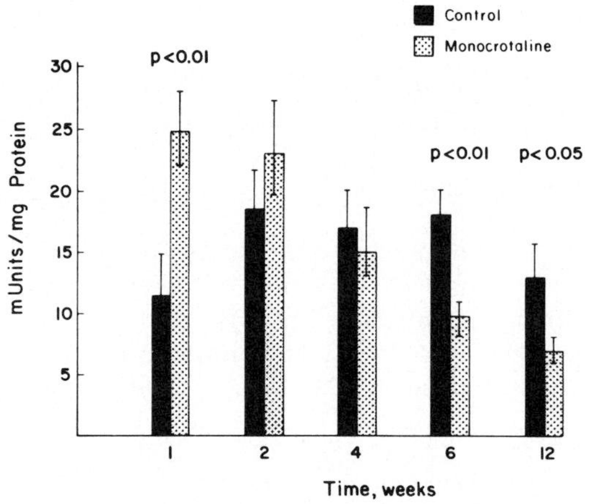

FIG. 1. Pulmonary angiotensin-I-converting enzyme activity (A-I-CE) (mU/mg protein) as a function of treatment time in control rats (solid bars) and animals receiving monocrotaline, 2.0 mg/kg body wt/day, po (stippled bars). Mean ± SEM; six to eight animals per group.

ACE activity. ACE activity in the lung of control animals ranged from 11.2 ± 3.8 to 18.8 ± 6.1 mU/mg protein, and did not change significantly with time (Fig. 1). In contrast, monocrotaline-treated rats exhibited a significant ($P < 0.01$) increase in ACE activity after 1 week, followed by a steady decrease in enzyme activity to approximately 55% of the corresponding control values at 6 and 12 weeks (Fig. 1). Changes in lung ACE activity were not accompanied by significant changes in serum activity of the enzyme (Table I), nor by significant changes in lung wet weight (unpublished data).

PLA activity. PLA activity in the lung of control animals increased steadily from a value of 141 ± 9 mm^2 of fibrin plate lysed to 193 ± 5 mm^2 lysed during the 12-week study (Fig. 2). In rats receiving monocrotaline, PLA activity was normal for the first 2 weeks, then decreased to 86, 59, and 79% of the corresponding control activity at 4, 6, and 12 weeks, respectively (Fig. 2).

PGI_2 production. Monocrotaline had no significant effect on the production of 6-keto-$PGF_{1\alpha}$ by the lung of rats sacrificed after 1, 2, or 4 weeks of treatment (Fig. 3). After 6 and 12 weeks, however, production of this prostaglandin increased to 140 and 270% of the corresponding control levels, respectively (Fig. 3).

Ultrastructural changes. Electron microscopic evaluation of monocrotaline-treated lungs revealed capillary subendothelial edema, and venous and arterial perivascular edema starting at 1 week. Interstitial inflammatory

TABLE I. THE EFFECT OF MONOCROTALINE ON BODY AND ORGAN WEIGHTS AND SERUM ACE ACTIVITY IN RATS

Endpoint	Group[a]	Weeks of treatment: 1	2	4	6	12
Body weight (g)	CON	353 ± 6[b]	379 ± 5	410 ± 10	443 ± 19	488 ± 9
	MONO	359 ± 16	387 ± 7	378 ± 7*	391 ± 8*	447 ± 14
Heart weight (mg/100 g body wt)	CON	340 ± 10	320 ± 10	331 ± 7	330 ± 21	310 ± 10
	MONO	320 ± 10	330 ± 10	325 ± 11	390 ± 20*	360 ± 20*
RV/LV + S[c]	CON	0.11 ± 0.01	0.12 ± 0.01	0.11 ± 0.01	0.11 ± 0.01	0.10 ± 0.01
	MONO	0.10 ± 0.01	0.09 ± 0.02	0.13 ± 0.01	0.16 ± 0.01*	0.15 ± 0.02*
Liver weight (g/100 g body wt)	CON	3.66 ± 0.10	4.06 ± 0.27	3.74 ± 0.11	3.83 ± 0.07	3.59 ± 0.12
	MONO	3.79 ± 0.13	3.83 ± 0.08	3.84 ± 0.09	4.11 ± 0.14*	3.92 ± 0.15*
Serum ACE (mU/mg protein)	CON	0.69 ± 0.05	0.68 ± 0.04	0.64 ± 0.07	0.80 ± 0.10	0.67 ± 0.10
	MONO	0.68 ± 0.07	0.59 ± 0.05	0.66 ± 0.05	0.51 ± 0.07	0.70 ± 0.11

[a] Control group (CON) or monocrotaline-treated, 2.0 mg/kg body wt/day, po (MONO).
[b] Mean ± SEM; six to eight animals/group.
[c] Right ventricle (RV) weight as a fraction of the weight of the left ventricle plus septum (LV + S) of the heart.
* Different from CON, $P < 0.05$.

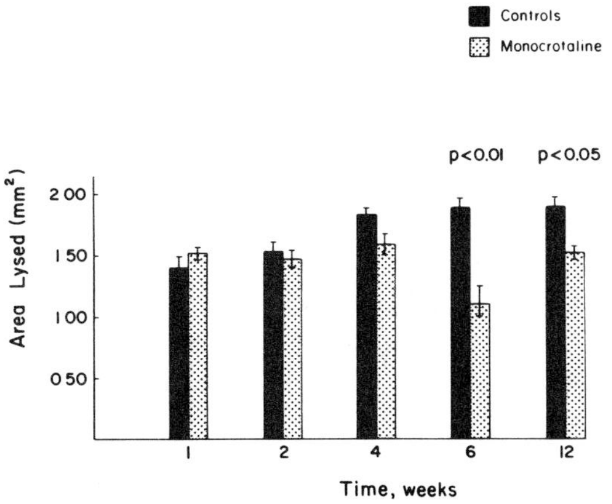

FIG. 2. Pulmonary plasminogen activator activity (mm^2 of fibrin plate lysed) as a function of treatment time in control rats (solid bars) and animals receiving monocrotaline, 2.0 mg/kg body wt/day, po (stippled bars). Mean ± SEM; six to eight animals per group.

cell infiltrates around small veins and arteries were observed at 2 weeks, as were interstitial red blood cells. While the edema tended to subside by 6 weeks, interstitial inflammatory cells and red blood cells accumulated through 12 weeks of treatment. Increased interstitial collagen was observed in the monocrotaline-treated lungs by six weeks. Capillary endothelial fragmentation and degeneration also were evident by 6 weeks (Fig. 4).

Starting at 4 weeks, there was a progressive increase in the thickness of the walls of pulmonary arteries and arterioles in the monocrotaline-treated animals. This increased wall thickness was the result of a combination of smooth muscle cell hypertrophy and hyperplasia, increased connective tissue and edema in the media, and multiple elastic laminae.

Body and organ weight. Animals treated with monocrotaline for 4 weeks or longer developed a slight but significant retardation of body weight gain (Table I). Monocrotaline-treated animals also exhibited significant cardio- and hepatomegaly at 6 and 12 weeks. The cardiomegaly was associated specifically with a progressive right ventricular hypertrophy from the 4th to the 12th weeks of monocrotaline administration (Table I).

Discussion. These data demonstrate that monocrotaline-induced lung injury is accompanied by structural and functional abnormalities in the pulmonary endothelium. Endothelial dysfunction in the lungs of rats receiving oral monocrotaline includes decreased ACE and PLA activity, and increased PGI_2 production observed in the present study, as well as decreased serotonin uptake reported previously (14). Pulmonary dysfunction in our monocrotaline-treated rats (2.0 mg/kg/day, po) requires 4–6 weeks to become significant, which may explain why Huxtable *et al.* (14) failed to detect changes in lung activity of ACE, 5′-nucleotidase, and monoamine oxidase in rats consuming monocrotaline (3.6 mg/kg/day, po) for 3 weeks. Large single injections of monocrotaline (60–105 mg/kg, sc), in contrast, suppress ACE activity and serotonin uptake within 10 days (10, 11, 13).

After 4–6 weeks of oral monocrotaline, rats also develop changes associated with pulmonary hypertension and cor pulmonale, i.e., increased pulmonary arterial wall thickness, right ventricular hypertrophy, cardiomegaly, and hepatomegaly. The development of these anatomic manifestations of monocrotaline induced pulmonary hypertension is preceded by a transient increase in lung ACE activity, and by ultrastructural evidence of endothelial injury (capillary subendothelial edema and

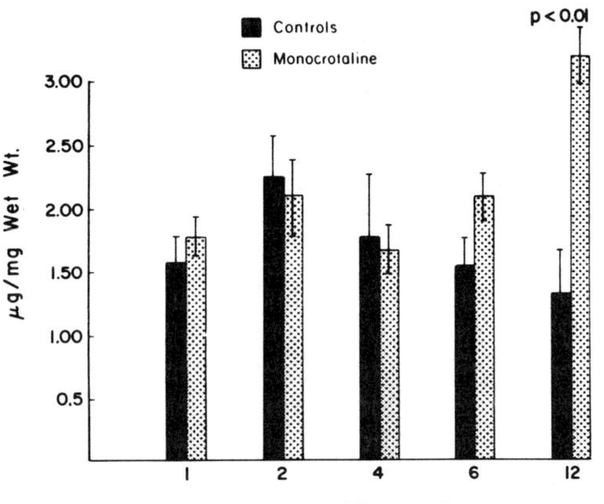

FIG. 3. Pulmonary prostacyclin (PGI_2) production (ng 6-keto-$PGF_{1\alpha}$/mg wet weight) during a 10-min *in vitro* incubation as a function of treatment time in control rats (solid bars) and animals receiving monocrotaline, 2.0 mg/kg body wt/day, po (stippled bars). Mean ± SEM; six to eight animals per group.

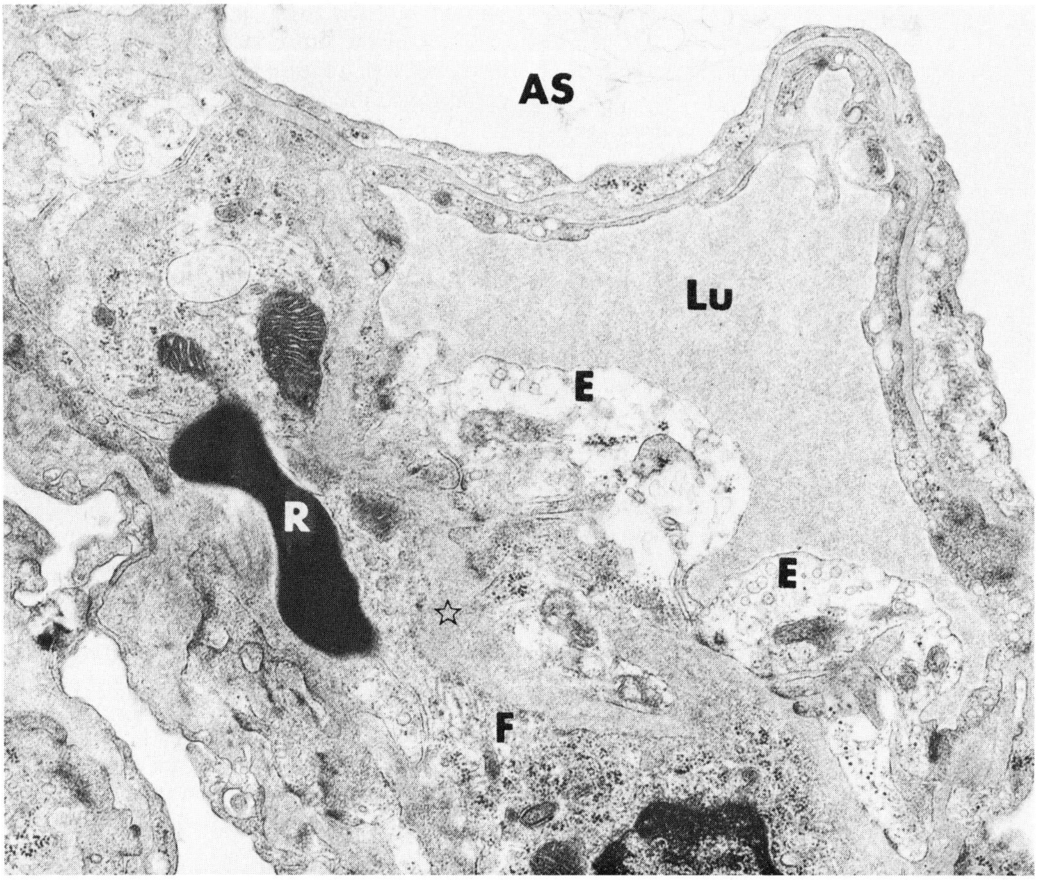

FIG. 4. Electron micrograph of the lung of a 6-week monocrotaline-treated rat. Two endothelial cells (E) of the capillary are electron lucent and apparently degenerated. The subendothelial space of these cells is swollen (*). A red blood cell (R) is present in the interstitium. Fibroblasts (F) contain numerous ribosomes and polysomes. As, airspace; Lu, lumen of capillary. ×14,740.

perivascular edema of small arteries and veins) after 1 week of drug treatment. After single injections of large doses of monocrotaline, however, lung ACE activity falls steadily, without exhibiting an initial increase in enzyme activity (10). Both decreased ACE activity, presumably resulting in reduced angiotensin II-mediated vasoconstriction, and increased PGI_2 production, presumably resulting in increased vasodilation, would appear to be appropriate compensatory responses to pulmonary hypertension in monocrotaline-treated lungs. That inappropriate ACE activity may play a role in the pathogenesis of experimental pulmonary hypertension is suggested by the observation that ACE inhibitors ameliorate the hypertensive response to both monocrotaline (12) and chronic hypoxia (27, 28). Despite significant changes in ACE activity in the lungs of monocrotaline-treated rats, blood serum levels of the enzyme do not fluctuate. Thus serum ACE activity is not a reliable index of lung status in this model. Kay *et al.* (10) found a similar disparity between lung and serum ACE activity following monocrotaline injections.

The monocrotaline-induced endothelial dysfunction observed in the present study is not accompanied by pulmonary arterial perfusion defects as determined on ^{99m}Tc lung scans of anesthetized animals. In contrast, Meyrick *et al.* (9) found that rats fed *Crotalaria* seeds exhibited narrowing of arterial lumens and reduced background haze in arteriograms performed on thawed frozen lungs injected intraarterially with Micropaque and gelatin (60°C) at a pressure of 100 cm H_2O. While the two techniques differ in many respects, together they may indicate normal regional distribution of perfusion through a partially occluded, overly muscularized (9, 10) arterial network in monocrotaline-treated lungs. This then might lead to increased pulmonary arterial pressure (14), and the development of right heart enlargement.

The changes in ACE and PLA activity and in PGI_2 production observed in the present study are not unique to monocrotaline-induced pulmonary injury. Identical responses occur in the lung following ionizing radiation (19, 22, 24, 25) and bleomycin (Ward *et al.*, unpublished data). This endothelial dysfunction implies perturbations in both the hemodynamic and fibrinolytic activity of the injured lung. While the time of onset of endothelial dysfunction differs among the several insults (and among routes of administration of the same insult), the pattern of response is qualitatively similar in the several models of lung injury. These metabolic abnormalities may reflect endothelial cell death, or dysfunction of surviving cells, or a combination of the two. Electron micrographs reveal endothelial degeneration and fragmentation coincident with the development of abnormal metabolic activity.

In conclusion, the present data indicate that endothelial injury is a prominent feature of the lung's response to the pyrrolizidine alkaloid monocrotaline. Monocrotaline-induced pulmonary damage is accompanied by, and in some cases preceded by both structural and functional abnormalities in the pulmonary endothelium.

This study was supported in part by PHS Grant HL25106, awarded by the National Heart, Lung and Blood Institute, DHHS, and by Christ Hospital, Oak Lawn, Illinois. Portions of these data were presented at the 67th Annual Meeting of the Federation of American Societies for Experimental Biology, Chicago, Illinois, April 10–15, 1983. The excellent technical assistance provided by Diane Gardner, Lisa Hahn, and Ann Shih-Hoellwarth is greatly appreciated.

1. Kay JM, Heath D. Observations on the pulmonary arteries and heart weight of rats fed on *Crotalaria spectabilis* seeds. J Pathol Bacteriol **92**:385–394, 1966.
2. Kay JM, Harris P, Heath D. Pulmonary hypertension produced in rats by ingestion of *Crotalaria spectabilis* seeds. Thorax **22**:176–179, 1967.
3. Kay JM, Heath D. *Crotalaria spectabilis:* the Pulmonary Hypertension Plant. Springfield, Ill, Thomas, 1969.
4. Kay JM, Smith P, Heath D. Electron microscopy of *Crotalaria* pulmonary hypertension. Thorax **24**:511–526, 1969.
5. Butler WH. An ultrastructural study of the pulmonary lesion induced by pyrrole derivatives of the pyrrolizidine alkaloids. J Pathol **102**:15–19, 1970.
6. McLean EK. The toxic actions of pyrrolizidine (*Senecio*) alkaloids. Pharmacol Rev **22**:429–483, 1970.
7. Smith P, Heath D. Evagination of vascular smooth muscle cells during the early stages of *Crotalaria* pulmonary hypertension. J Pathol **124**:177–183, 1977.
8. Meyrick B, Reid L. Development of pulmonary arterial changes in rats fed *Crotalaria spectabilis*. Amer J Pathol **94**:37–50, 1979.
9. Meyrick B, Gamble W, Reid L. Development of *Crotalaria* pulmonary hypertension: hemodynamic and structural study. Amer J Physiol **239**:H692–H702, 1980.
10. Kay JM, Keane PM, Suyama KL, Gauthier D. Angiotensin converting enzyme activity and evolution of pulmonary vascular disease in rats with monocrotaline pulmonary hypertension. Thorax **37**:88–96, 1982.
11. Keane PM, Kay JM, Suyama KL, Gauthier D, Andrew K. Lung angiotensin converting enzyme activity in rats with pulmonary hypertension. Thorax **37**:198–204, 1982.
12. Molteni A, Solliday N, Port C, Ward WF. Partial prevention of monocrotaline-induced pulmonary arterial changes by the angiotensin-1-converting enzyme (A-1-CE) inhibitor SQ14225. Fed Proc **41**:451, abstr, 1982.
13. Hilliker KS, Bell TG, Roth RA. Pneumotoxicity and thrombocytopenia after single injection of monocrotaline. Amer J Physiol **242**:H573–H579, 1982.
14. Huxtable R, Ciaramitaro D, Eisenstein D. The effect of a pyrrolizidine alkaloid, monocrotaline, and a pyrrole, dehydroretronecine, on the biochemical functions of the pulmonary endothelium. Mol Pharmacol **14**:1189–1203, 1978.
15. Molteni A, Zakheim RM, Mullis KB, Mattioli L. The effects of chronic alveolar hypoxia on lung and serum angiotensin-1-converting enzyme activity. Proc Soc Exp Biol Med **147**:263–265, 1974.
16. Gerber GB, Dancewicz AM, Bessemans B, Casale G. Biochemistry of late effects in rat lung after hemi-

thoracic irradiation. Acta Radiol Phys Biol **16**:447–455, 1977.
17. Goldsmith JC, Jafvert CT, Lollar P, Owen WG, Hoak JC. Prostacyclin release from cultured and *ex vivo* bovine vascular endothelium. Studies with thrombin, arachidonic acid, and ionophore A23187. Lab Invest **45**:191–197, 1981.
18. Lazo JS. Angiotensin converting enzyme activity in mice after subacute bleomycin administration. Toxicol Appl Pharmacol **59**:395–404, 1981.
19. Ward WF, Molteni A, Ts'ao C, Solliday NH. Radiation injury in rat lung. IV. Modification by D-penicillamine. Radiat Res, in press.
20. Ward WF. Radiation-induced pulmonary arterial perfusion defects: modification by D-penicillamine. Radiology **139**:201–204, 1981.
21. Cushman DW, Cheung HS. Spectrophotometric assay and properties of the angiotensin-converting enzyme of rabbit lung. Biochem Pharmacol **20**:1637–1648, 1971.
22. Ward WF, Molteni A, Solliday NH, Port CD. Radiation injury in rat lung. II. Angiotensin converting enzyme activity. Radiat Res **96**:294–300, 1983.
23. Astrup T, Albrechtsen OK. Estimation of the plasminogen activator and the trypsin inhibitor in animal and human tissues. Scand J Clin Lab Invest **9**:233–243, 1957.
24. Ts'ao C, Ward WF, Port CD. Radiation injury in rat lung. III. Plasminogen activator and fibrinolytic inhibitor activities. Radiat Res **96**:301–308, 1983.
25. Ts'ao C, Ward WF, Port CD. Radiation injury in rat lung. I. Prostacyclin (PGI_2) production, arterial perfusion, and ultrastructure. Radiat Res **96**:284–293, 1983.
26. Dixon WJ, Massey FJ Jr. Introduction to Statistical Analysis. New York, McGraw–Hill, 2nd ed, 1957.
27. Zakheim RM, Mattioli L, Molteni A, Mullis KB, Bartley J. Prevention of pulmonary vascular changes of chronic alveolar hypoxia by inhibition of angiotensin-1-converting enzyme in the rat. Lab Invest **33**:57–61, 1975.
28. Rabinovitch M, Gamble WJ, Williams G, Reid L. SQ14,225 converting enzyme inhibitor diminishes pulmonary artery hypertension secondary to chronic hypoxia in rat. Fed Proc **39**:765, abstr, 1980.

Received December 19, 1983. P.S.E.B.M. 1984, Vol. 176.
Accepted February 9, 1984.

PROCEEDINGS OF THE SOCIETY FOR EXPERIMENTAL BIOLOGY AND MEDICINE **176**, 95–104 (1984)

MINIREVIEW

Immunity to Type II Collagen in Rheumatoid Arthritis: A Current Appraisal[1] (41848)

DAVID E. TRENTHAM

Department of Medicine, Harvard Medical School, and the Department of Rheumatology and Immunology, The Brigham and Women's Hospital, Boston, Massachusetts 02115

". . . in this iconoclastic view, pannus is the result, rather than the cause, of cartilage injury" (1).

This review will briefly analyze current concepts regarding the pathogenesis of rheumatoid arthritis (RA) with major emphasis devoted to the hypothesis that anti-self reactivity specific for the cartilage type (native type II) of collagen is a major effector mechanism in the disease. The intent is to update more extensive reviews of immunity to collagen in the rheumatic diseases (2–7).

The Synovium in Health and Disease. The relatively few studies of the histology of the human synovium in various disease states suggest that this membrane has a limited capacity to react to immunologic, viral, bacterial, physical, or metabolic insults. Perhaps it is not too simplistic to envision two basic kinds of immunologically mediated synovitis in humans. The first type would consist of pannus formation and mononuclear inflammatory cell infiltration that culminates in articular cartilage and bone destruction. This situation is represented by the disease termed, nosologically, RA. The second type would be comprised, predominantly, of polymorphonuclear-leukocyte infiltration and subsynovial neovascularization in the absence of pannus formation and connective-tissue destruction. This process is exemplified by the diarthrodial-joint lesion in systemic lupus erythematosus. Proliferative synovitis will be the focus of this review.

The older morphologic studies of the normal human synovium have been supplemented by recent investigations of the synovium of the knee in healthy young-adult rats using light and transmission electron microscopy (8, 9). These pursuits have confirmed the existence of the dichotomous synovial cell types proposed by Barland *et al.* (10), i.e., the type A phagocytic appearing cell and the type B synoviocyte, the principal function of which is apparently the secretion of joint lubricants.

In addition to this reaffirmation, these animal analyses have prompted an awareness that the normal synovium is not, universally, a one- to two-cell-layer-thick lining. Areas in the rat knee contiguous to cartilage can attain a thickness of five to eight cell layers in the absence of inflammatory-cell infiltrates (8). Whether this occurrence is a premorbid event, is indicative of microtrauma-induced injury or merely delimits areas providing the bulk of hyaluronate synthesis is unknown. It is equally uncertain whether there is a counterpart of this regional synovial thickening in human diarthrodial joints.

A final insight afforded by these ultrastructural studies of the normal rat synovium is the frequent occurrence of pentalaminar inclusions, resembling viral particles, within the lysosomes of synoviocytes (8). The existence of inclusion bodies has been reported in human synoviocytes as well (1), but their potential role in health and disease is conjectural.

Current Concepts Regarding the Pathogenesis of RA. In this review, only notions regarding the pathogenesis of RA for which substantive supporting data exist will be mentioned. Although an exogenous-agent etiology continues to be an attractive conjecture (11), the absence of direct evidence of viral involvement in RA precludes its further discussion. RA was, historically, perhaps the first disease perceived as an expression of autoimmunity (due to the recognition of rheumatoid factor). In the past decade, RA has begun to be further appreciated as an autoimmune or, at least, an immunologically mediated disease.

Initial evidence favored RA representing an intraarticular immune complex induced process (1). The profound decreases in complement levels in the synovial fluid of patients with RA (12, 13) and the hints that antigen–antibody containing material had been isolated (14, 15) provided provocative indications of the validity of this theory.

[1] Supported in part by USPHS Grant AM-21490.

0037-9727/84 $1.50

But the majority of the work accomplished since that time has been consistent with the possibility that RA is a disease propagated by delayed-type hypersensitivity (16). Initial evidence for the concept was afforded by the recognition that immunocompetent cells could passively transfer disease in the model of inflammatory synovitis induced in rats with complete Freund's adjuvant (adjuvant arthritis) (17, 18). The rapid amelioration of joint inflammation in RA during thoracic-duct drainage (19), the recognition that the vast majority of lymphocytes within the rheumatoid synovium are, phenotypically, T cells (20, 21), the identification of lymphokine-like substances in the synovial fluid of patients with RA (22), and the suggestions that total-lymphoid irradiation can selectively suppress T-cell but not B-cell processes in concert with disease improvement (23–25) have fostered the theory that RA is a T-cell-produced disorder. Recently, immunohistochemical techniques have provided a compelling hint that the rheumatoid synovium is the site of antigen-presenting macrophages contiguous to activated T cells (26); the lesion in its entirety resembling a delayed-type hypersensitivity response to relevant-antigen challenge.

Thus, the intraarticular events of RA could prove to be subserved partially by T cells and their soluble mediators. However, it is equally probable that at least some of the extraarticular manifestations of RA, such as vasculitis, are B-cell and complement provoked. This global envisioning of the pathogenesis of RA would integrate the immunologically mediated features of the disease. If the evidence for immunologic mediation of RA is accepted, then the search for candidate autoantigens in the disease becomes a paramount issue.

History of the Theory that Type II Collagen Functions as an Autoantigen in RA. The hypothesis that collagen functions as an autoantigen in RA may have been at least partially formulated before the era of rheumatoid factor (27–31). Initial studies of the immunological properties of collagen used type I and found that it possessed antigenicity (29, 31, 32–39). The isolation of type II collagen from cartilage in 1969 (40) and type III collagen from several human tissues in 1974 (41) demonstrated that these three so-called interstitial collagens actually comprised a family of biochemically distinct macromolecules providing support for different tissues (42). This discovery prompted additional interest in the possible role of these collagens as type-specific autoantigens in rheumatoid arthritis (43–46). In attempting to raise reference antisera, it was found that native type II collagen is arthritogenic in the rat (47). Later, it was recognized that type II collagen-induced arthritis can also occur in mice (48). This review will now describe the histologic and immunologic features of collagen arthritis and relate them to those observed in adjuvant arthritis, since these two models continue to be the most frequently studied experimental counterparts of RA.

The Morphology of Experimentally Induced Synovitis in the Rat. Serial morphologic studies of the peripheral joint lesion in collagen (8) and adjuvant (49–52) arthritis of rats have failed to show any distinguishing feature. In both diseases, the initial lesion that can be discerned histologically occurs within the synovium and consists of two simultaneous events: (i) synoviocyte disruption and a change from a flattened to a rounded cellular appearance and, (ii) intrasynovial edema and fibrin deposition within and upon the surface of the synovium and articular cartilage (8). Shortly thereafter, evidence of synovial hyperplasia, intra- and subsynovial neovascularization, and pannus extending over the surface of the normally denuded cartilage is observed. Mitotic events in cells that appear to have originated within the synovium (as opposed to being macrophage-like elements carried to the synovium in the blood after arising in the bone marrow) are occasionally seen. Pannus formation continues for several days in the absence of inflammatory-cell infiltration, but by the time the lysosomes of synoviocytes become filled with debris, polymorphonuclear leukocytes and mononuclear-inflammatory cells appear in this granulation tissue. Coincident with the ingress of these inflammatory cells is the inception of cartilage and bone destruction. Microabscess-like areas comprised of either polymorphonuclear leukocytes or mononuclear-inflammatory cells are often juxtaposed with the erosive lesions in these models. A final inflammatory stage of experimentally induced synovitis in the rat is a persistent, hyperplastic synovium packed with dense infiltrates of mononuclear cells and granulomatous areas (8). Immunofluorescence techniques show a paucity of immunoglobulin and complement deposited in the arthritic synovium (8). As in the RA synovium (20, 21), T cells predominate in collagen arthritis.

Little is known concerning the truly inceptual event in RA, although the evidence of synovial hyperplasia, neovascularization (53), and T-cell infiltration (54) in the early stages of RA appears convincing. In established disease, there is a close histologic resemblance in the experimental models to the biopsy picture of RA. The occasional occurrence of auricular chondritis in collagen-immunized (4, 55–57) or irradiated (58) rats resembling the lesion in relapsing polychondritis (59) should also be noted, as well as the report that immunization with type II collagen can induce endolymphatic hydrops, a lesion resembling that occurring in Meniere's disease, in guinea pigs (60).

Immunologic Aspects of Experimental Arthritis. Readily detectable humoral and cellular responses to collagen develop around the inception of collagen arthritis in rats (52, 61–66). Paralleling the exceptional arthritogenicity of this protein, type II collagen-induced immunity in both rats (46, 61, 66) and mice (43, 68) is antigen specific. In one study, evidence favoring an antibody-mediated pathogenesis of collagen arthritis in mice was afforded by a peaking of antibody titers to collagen coincident with the onset of arthritis (68). Thymidine-incorporation assays indicated that there was a transient cellular sensitization to type II collagen that occurred prior to the beginning of arthritis (68), further implying that antibodies rather than T-cell immunity to collagen were critical to the inception of this disease. However, murine experiments in the reviewer's laboratory, using a radiometric ear assay to measure delayed-type hypersensitivity to collagen, have shown that *in vivo* evidence of cellular sensitivity to collagen develops later, around the time that arthritis emerges. These contrasting findings render it impossible to conclude, at present, from studies of afferent sensitization to collagen whether antibody- or cellular-mechanisms play a role in the pathogenesis of collagen arthritis in either rats or mice.

Investigations using cobra-venom factor to induce transient complement depletion (69, 70) and antigen-presenting cells to suppress collagen arthritis (71) or induce delayed-type hypersensitivity in the absence of antibody responses to collagen (72) have suggested that antibody responses to collagen are involved in the induction of collagen arthritis in rats. However, nonspecific effects of cobra venom (73) and the theoretical possibility that T suppressor cells influencing arthritis were primed by the antigen-presentation protocol (74) urge caution in the interpretation of these data. It should also be pointed out that environmental manipulation can affect the morphologic manifestations of collagen arthritis (75, 76) and could have influenced the results obtained in these studies. Finally, evidence suggesting that collagen arthritis in rats is more complex than simply an antibody-mediated disease has been obtained in studies using psychological stress (75, 76), passive transfer of the phenomenon of collagen-specific suppression of disease (77), and administration of eicosapentaenoic acid (78), dimethyl sulfoxide (79), and retinoic acid (80). The observation that T-cell-deficient (nude) rats are refractory to the induction of collagen arthritis (81) indicates that type II collagen is a T-cell-dependent immunogen. This finding also suggests a T-cell dependency for this disease. Nonetheless, it is possible that the resistance found in this nude-rat strain is conferred by non-T-cell-mediated genetic mechanisms that, at present, have not been elucidated. Thus, these studies have not provided definitive evidence regarding the role of B and T cells in the primary pathogenesis of collagen arthritis.

What is known about the possible role of collagen immunity in adjuvant arthritis? Cellular sensitivity to collagen in this model has been found in some (33, 52, 82) but not all (83) studies. Only extremely preliminary and indirect indications exist, at present, that collagen immunity is involved in any aspect of the primary pathogenesis of this disease (82–84), and evidence to the contrary has also been reported (85, 86).

Insights Afforded by Passive Transfer Experiments. Much more convincing data regarding the pathogenesis of collagen arthritis and adjuvant arthritis has been provided by passive transfer experiments (87–90). These studies have strongly implied that both collagen and adjuvant arthritis are immunologically mediated processes. However, transfer experiments in neither model have shown definitively the relative roles of T- and/or B-cell pathways in the primary disease.

Collagen arthritis was first transferred by intravenously injected spleen and lymph node cells from rats immunized with type II collagen (87). More recent work has demonstrated that synovitis can be induced in rats (88, 90) or mice (89) by intravenous injection of IgG antibodies specific for native type II collagen. Unanswered questions exist, at present, regarding the results of all of these experiments.

Cell transfer produced a lesion that resembled a milder form of the primary disease, i.e., substantial pannus formation, cartilage and bone erosion, and predominantly mononuclear inflammatory cell infiltration. Moreover, the disease persisted until the latest time of evaluation, 24 days after cell transfer. No antibodies to collagen were detected in the sera of the arthritic recipients (87), suggesting that antibody production by the recipient did not explain the induction of synovitis in this system. However, no evidence has been reported, at present, that collagen arthritis can be passively transferred by T cells, and subsequent attempts using T-cell-enriched fractions or thoracic-duct lymphocytes have been negative in the reviewer's laboratory. Therefore, cell transfer of collagen arthritis has not provided conclusive evidence of T-cell involvement in collagen arthritis.

Similarly, serum transfer experiments have failed to furnish irrefutable evidence that collagen arthritis is a B-cell-mediated disease. Several serum-transfer protocols have given negative results (72, 87). Subsequent work has shown that synovitis can be induced by this system, but disease in the recipient occurs only when large amounts of immunoglobulin-containing material is injected (88–90). Moreover, the lesion created by antibody has been extremely transient, resolving in, at most, a week or 10 days (88–90). Although cartilage destruction can occur (88–90), other morphologic aspects of the synovitis induced by antibody appear to differ from the primary disease. Although one group reported some pannus formation in rats (88) and mice (89), another laboratory has concluded that intravenous injection of affinity-purified IgG antibody to type II collagen induces polymorphonuclear-leukocyte infiltration but not pannus in rats (90). An articular disease characterized by polymorphonuclear-leukocyte dominance would not recapitulate the chronic proliferative synovitis observed after cell transfer (87), in primary collagen arthritis (8), or in RA. Additional work in this area is, therefore, required.

At present, the chief importance of cell and serum transfer of collagen arthritis is in showing that products of B cells, and perhaps T cells, reactive to heterologous type II collagen, can induce synovitis. The exact relationship of these data to collagen arthritis and RA is unknown.

Although there is no direct evidence that T-cell sensitization to collagen can induce arthritis, indications do exist that T cells can incite a proliferative synovitis in rats. Again, these data must be interpreted with restraint. Syngeneic T cells from rats with adjuvant arthritis stimulated with concanavalin A *in vitro* can induce synovitis following intravenous injection (91). However, it has not been demonstrated that the transferred disease represents the complete counterpart of adjuvant arthritis, since T cells not exposed to concanavalin A are ineffectual in disease transfer (91). Likewise, in vitro propagated T cells from rats with adjuvant arthritis, reactive to both mycobacterial and homologous type II collagen (82) or exclusively mycobacterial (92) antigenic stimulation, are capable of inducing inflammatory synovitis in irradiated recipients. These data also provide an indication that T cells can produce experimental synovitis. However, spontaneous arthritis can occur, on rare occasions, in rats, and total lymphoid irradiation can induce an inflammatory synovitis as well (58). For these reasons, the possibility exists that the irradiation regimen was involved in the induction of arthritis in these propagated T-cell transfers. Currently, the only immunologic moiety that is clearly capable of inducing joint inflammation would be IgG antibody to native type II collagen. Further work with T cells is required before this claim can be convincingly asserted.

Afferent Sensitization to Collagen in RA. It is evident that some patients with RA have antibodies to the interstitial collagens in their sera (32, 35, 93–105) and that a proportion exhibit cellular sensitivity to collagen (24, 26,

98, 102, 104–111). Antibodies to collagen are also reported to be present in the synovial fluid of some patients with this disease (36, 97). These humoral (96, 98, 103) and cellular (26, 98) reactivities appear to be specific for collagenous determinants. However, the titers of such serum antibodies are low (98, 102, 103), and they do not correlate with signs or symptoms of RA (98, 103). Moreover, collagen reactivity is not restricted to RA; being present in a variety of diseases characterized by inflammation of connective tissue (34, 37–39, 94, 99, 102–104, 108, 110–115), as well as on rare occasions in normal subjects (104, 110). These data tell the investigator little concerning possible collagen-induced effector mechanisms in RA.

Immunogenetic Regulation of Collagen Immunity in Rodents. The immune response to collagen in rats (55, 116) and mice (117, 118) appears to be, as is the case with most protein immunogens (117), regulated by immune-response (Ir) genes. In addition, susceptibility to collagen arthritis in rats (55, 116) and mice (118) and to adjuvant arthritis (119) is influenced by genetic mechanisms as well. But immunogenetic pathways that control collagen reactivity in humans have not been convincingly identified. Preliminary indications that HLA-DR4 governs one's ability to respond, cellularly, to collagen (110, 111) have failed to receive support from the findings in other studies (104, 107). *In vitro* assays of cellular immunity to protein antigens continue to be relatively imprecise, and this fact mandates additional work on this problem.

Speculations Regarding the Possible Role of Type II Collagen-Specific Autoantibodies and T-Cell Factors in the Pathogenesis of RA. Based on the available evidence, several theories regarding the possible role of collagen immunity in the pathogenesis of RA can be proposed. The morphologic features, mimicking those occurring in RA, that can be created by sensitization to a constituent of cartilage or by adjuvant injection argue that further studies of experimentally inducible synovitis are of potential merit.

The first speculation relates to epitope-specific collagen reactivities being critical to the pathogenesis of rodent and human disease. Lessons in human lupus and myasthenia gravis illustrate this reasoning. Autoimmune diseases represent states in which a panoply of autoantibodies and sensitized lymphocytes exist (120). Antibodies against denatured DNA are found in many diseases but increasing evidence suggests that exquisitely specific anti-native DNA responses are a major effector mechanism in lupus (120). In myasthenia gravis, a number of anti-self reactivities exist, but it now appears that anti-acetylcholine receptor reactivities are the process intimately involved in the pathogenesis of the disease (121). A few patients with RA that possess high titers of antibodies specific for native type II collagen have been identified (103). All of these data are consistent with the possibility that critical epitopes on type II collagen, a probably complex multideterminant protein antigen (4), may function in the primary pathogenesis of RA. If preliminary evidence from a leukapheresis trial suggesting that RA is a heterogeneous disorder (122) is correct, then certain patients with RA in which anti-collagen reactivity is a fundamental pathogenetic mechanism may exist.

The second speculation relates to collagen antibodies versus anti-collagen T-cell factors in the pathogenesis of RA. A variety of antigen-specific T-cell-derived inducer and suppressor factors have been identified in rodent systems (74). If RA is a T cell mediated disease, and if autoimmunity to collagen is involved, then a unifying pathway would be provided by a type II collagen-specific arthritogenic lymphokine functioning in the human disease. Evaluating the effect of collagen-sensitized T-lymphocyte products on cultured synovial cells is experimentally feasible and could lead to insights in this area.

Finally, the rigorous test of whether collagen immunity is involved in RA must await trials involving antigen-specific immunosuppression (4, 5). Protocols capable of achieving antigen-specific attenuation of experimental arthritis in the rat (71, 77, 123) have been identified. Adaptations of these techniques may someday be evaluated in the human disease.

Conclusion. Studies of the immunologic properties of native type II collagen in the past decade have delineated a new field in connective-tissue disease. The opinion that cartilage injury may not be merely the result of pannus but that the origin of synovial hyperplasia could, in some way, be related to cartilage is no longer iconoclastic. The recent advances in the field of collagen immunology have provided data which are clear cut, but the proper interpretation of the experimental results is, at present, only partially evident. In the near future, additional work may answer the questions posed in this review; out of controversy could come certainty.

---

1. Zvaifler NJ. The immunopathology of joint inflammation in rheumatoid arthritis. Advan Immunol **16**:265–336, 1973.
2. Furthmayr H, Timpl R. Immunochemistry of collagens and procollagens. Int Rev Connect Tissue Res **7**:61–99, 1976.
3. Beard HK, Faulk WP, Conochie LB, Glynn LE. Some immunological aspects of collagen. Progr Allergy **22**:45–106, 1977.
4. Trentham DE. Autoimmunity to collagen as a disease mechanism. In: Weissman G, ed. Advances in Inflammation Research. New York, Raven Press, Vol II:pp149–164, 1981.
5. Trentham DE. Collagen arthritis as a relevant model for rheumatoid arthritis: evidence pro and con. Arthritis Rheum **25**:911–916, 1982.
6. Stuart JM, Townes AS, Kang AH. The role of collagen autoimmunity in animal models and human diseases. J Invest Dermatol **79**(suppl):121S–127S, 1982.
7. Trentham DE. Immunity to collagen in rheumatoid and experimental arthritis. In: Franklin EC, ed. Clinical Immunology Update. New York, North-Holland/American Elsevier, pp37–55, 1983.
8. Caulfield JP, Hein A, Dynesius-Trentham R, Trentham DE. Morphologic demonstration of two stages in the development of type II collagen-induced arthritis. Lab Invest **46**:321–343, 1982.
9. Graabaek PM. Ultrastructural evidence for two distinct types of synoviocytes in rat synovial membrane. J Ultrastruct Res **78**:321–339, 1982.
10. Barland P, Novikoff AB, Hammerman D. Electron microscopy of the human synovial membrane. J Cell Biol **14**:207–220, 1962.
11. Person DA, Sharp JT. The etiology of rheumatoid arthritis. Bull Rheum Dis **27**:888–893, 1976.
12. Pekin TJ Jr, Zvaifler NJ. Hemolytic complement in synovial fluid. J Clin Invest **43**:1372–1382, 1964.
13. Townes AS, Marcus RL. Complement-fixing activity of rheumatoid synovial fluid. Ann Rheum Dis **31**:393–401, 1972.
14. Marcus RL, Townes AS. The occurrence of cryoproteins in synovial fluid; the association of a complement-fixing activity in rheumatoid synovial fluid with cold-precipitable protein. J Clin Invest **50**:282–293, 1971.
15. Zubler RH, Nydegger U, Perrin LH, Fehr K, McCormick J, Lambert PH, Miescher PA. Circulating and intraarticular immune complexes in patients with rheumatoid arthritis. J Clin Invest **57**:1308–1319, 1976.
16. Trentham DE. Strategies for medical treatment based on current understanding of the pathogenesis of rheumatoid arthritis. Clin Orthop Relat Res **182**:31–36, 1984.
17. Waksman BH, Wennersten C. Passive transfer of adjuvant arthritis in rats with living lymphoid cells of sensitized donors. Int Arch Allergy Appl Immunol **23**:129–139, 1963.
18. Pearson CM, Wood FD. Passive transfer of adjuvant arthritis by lymph node or spleen cells. J Exp Med **120**:547–560, 1964.
19. Paulus HE, Machleder HI, Levine S, Yu DTY, MacDonald NS. Lymphocyte involvement in rheumatoid arthritis: studies during thoracic duct drainage. Arthritis Rheum **20**:1249–1262, 1977.
20. Van Boxel JA, Paget SA. Predominantly T-cell infiltrate in rheumatoid synovial membranes. N Engl J Med **293**:517–520, 1975.
21. Abrahamsen TG, Froland SS, Natvig JB, Pahle J. Elution and characterization of lymphocytes from rheumatoid inflammatory tissue. Scand J Immunol **4**:823–830, 1975.
22. Stasny P, Rosenthal M, Andreis M, Cooke D, Ziff M. Lymphokines in rheumatoid synovitis. Ann NY Acad Sci **256**:117–131, 1975.
23. Kotzin BL, Strober S, Engleman EG, Calin A, Hoppe RT, Kansas GS, Terrell CP, Kaplan HS. Treatment of intractable rheumatoid arthritis with total lymphoid irradiation. N Engl J Med **305**:969–975, 1981.
24. Trentham DE, Belli JA, Anderson RJ, Buckley JA, Goetzl EJ, David JR, Austen KF. Clinical and immunologic effects of fractionated total lymphoid irradiation in refractory rheumatoid arthritis. N Engl J Med **305**:976–982, 1981.
25. Field EH, Strober S, Hoope RT, Calin A, Engleman EG, Kotzin BL, Tanay AS, Calin HJ, Terrell CP, Kaplan HS. Sustained improvement of intractable rheumatoid arthritis after total lymphoid irradiation. Arthritis Rheum **26**:937–946, 1983.
26. Klareskog L, Forsum U, Scheynius A, Kabelitz D, Wigzell H. Evidence in support of a self-perpetuating HLA-DR-dependent delayed-type cell reaction in rheumatoid arthritis. Proc Natl Acad Sci USA **79**:3632–3636, 1982.
27. Jarcho S: Lupus erythematosus associated with visceral vascular lesions: A series of autopsied cases. Bull J Hopkins Hosp **59**:262–273, 1936.
28. Klemperer P, Pollack AD, Baehr G. Diffuse collagen disease: acute disseminated lupus erythematosus and diffuse scleroderma. J Amer Med Assoc **119**:331–332, 1942.
29. Waksman BH, Mason HL. The antigenicity of collagen. J Immunol **63**:427–433, 1949.
30. Glynn LE. Aetiology of rheumatoid arthritis with

regard to its chronicity. Ann Rheum Dis **28**(suppl):3–4, 1969.
31. Steffen C. Consideration of the pathogenesis of rheumatoid arthritis as collagen autoimmunity. Z Immunitätsforsch **139**:219–227, 1970.
32. Steffen C, Timpl R. Antigenicity of collagen and its application in the serologic investigation of rheumatoid arthritis sera. Int Arch Allergy Appl Immunol **22**:333–349, 1963.
33. Steffen C, Wick G. Delayed hypersensitivity reactions to collagen in rats with adjuvant-induced arthritis. Z Immunitätsforsch **141**:169–180, 1971.
34. Michaeli D, Fudenberg HH. Antibodies to collagen in patients with emphysema. Clin Immunol Immunopathol **3**:187–192, 1974.
35. Michaeli D, Fudenberg HH. The incidence and antigenic specificity of antibodies against denatured human collagen in rheumatoid arthritis. Clin Immunol Immunopathol **2**:153–159, 1974.
36. Cracchiolo A, Michaeli D, Goldberg LS, Fudenberg HH. The occurrence of antibodies to collagen in synovial fluids. Clin Immunol Immunopathol **3**:567–574, 1975.
37. Stuart JM, Postlethwaite AE, Kang AH. Evidence for cell-mediated immunity to collagen in progressive systemic sclerosis. J Lab Clin Med **88**:601–607, 1976.
38. Kravis TC, Ahmed A, Brown TE, Fulmer JD, Crystal RG. Pathogenic mechanisms in pulmonary fibrosis: Collagen-induced migration inhibition factor production and cytotoxicity mediated by lymphocytes. J Clin Invest **58**:1223–1232, 1976.
39. McAdam KPWJ, Fudenberg HH, Michaeli D. Antibodies to collagen in patients with leprosy. Clin Immunol Immunopathol **9**:16–21, 1978.
40. Miller EJ, Matukas VJ. Chick cartilage collagen: a new type of $\alpha 1$ chain not present in bone or skin of the species. Proc Natl Acad Sci USA **64**:1264–1268, 1969.
41. Chung E, Miller EJ. Collagen polymorphism: Characterization of molecules with the chain composition $[\alpha 1(III)]_3$ in human tissues. Science **183**:1200–1201, 1974.
42. Miller EJ. Biochemical characteristics and biological significance of the genetically-distinct collagens. Mol Cell Biochem **13**:165–192, 1976.
43. Nowack H, Hahn E, Timpl R. Specificity of the antibody response in inbred mice to bovine type I and type II collagen. Immunology **29**:621–628, 1974.
44. Hahn E, Nowack D, Götze D, Timpl R. H-2-linked genetic control of antibody response to soluble calf skin collagen in mice. Eur J Immunol **5**:288–291, 1975.
45. Beard HK, Ueda M, Faulk WP, Glynn LE. Cell-mediated and humoral immunity to chick type II collagen and its cyanogen bromide peptides in guinea pigs. Immunology **34**:323–335, 1978.
46. Hahn E, Timpl R, Miller EJ. The production of specific antibodies to native collagens with the chain compositions, $[\alpha 1(I)]_3$, $[\alpha 1(II)]_3$ and $[\alpha 1(I)]_2\ \alpha 2$. J Immunol **13**:421–423, 1974.
47. Trentham DE, Townes AS, Kang AH. Autoimmunity to type II collagen: an experimental model of arthritis. J Exp Med **146**:857–868, 1977.
48. Courtenay JS, Dallman MJ, Dayan AD, Martin A, Mosedale B. Immunisation against heterologous type II collagen induces arthritis in mice. Nature (London) **283**:666–668, 1980.
49. Pearson CM, Wood FD. Studies of arthritis and other lesions induced in rats by the injection of mycobacterial adjuvant. VII. Pathologic details of the arthritis and spondylitis. Amer J Pathol **42**:73–86, 1963.
50. Burstein NA, Waksman BH. The pathogenesis of adjuvant disease in the rat. I. A histologic study of early lesions in the joints and skin. Yale J Biol Med **37**:177–194, 1964.
51. Mohr W, Wild A, Paulini K. Proliferation of synovial tissue cells in rats with adjuvant disease. Pathol Microbiol (Basel) **43**:1–9, 1975.
52. Trentham DE, McCune WJ, Susman P, David JR. Autoimmunity to collagen in adjuvant arthritis of rats. J Clin Invest **66**:1109–1117, 1980.
53. Schumacher HR, Kitridou RC. Synovitis of recent onset: A clinicopathologic study during the first month of disease. Arthritis Rheum **15**:465–485, 1972.
54. Lindblad S, Klareskog L, Hedfors E, Forsum U, Sundström C. Phenotypic characterization of synovial tissue cells in situ in different types of synovitis. Arthritis Rheum **26**:1321–1332, 1983.
55. Griffiths MM, Eichwald EJ, Martin JH, Smith CB, Dewitt CW. Immunogenetic control of experimental type II collagen-induced arthritis. I. Susceptibility and resistance among inbred strains of rats. Arthritis Rheum **24**:781–789, 1981.
56. Cremer MA, Pitcock JA, Stuart JM, Kang AH, Townes AS. Auricular chondritis in rats: An experimental model of relapsing polychondritis induced with type II collagen. J Exp Med **154**:535–540, 1981.
57. McCune WJ, Schiller AL, Dynesius-Trentham RA, Trentham DE. Type II collagen-induced auricular chondritis. Arthritis Rheum **25**:266–273, 1982.
58. Trentham DE, Brahn E, Williams W, McCune WJ, Belli JE. Connective tissue disease can develop in rats either spontaneously or after total lymphoid irradiation. J Rheumatol, in press.
59. Trentham DE. Case Records of the Massachusetts General Hospital. N Engl J Med **307**:1631–1639, 1982.
60. Yoo TJ, Yazawa Y, Tomoda K, Floyd R. Type II collagen-induced autoimmune endolymphatic hydrops in guinea pig. Science **222**:65–67, 1983.
61. Trentham DE, Townes AS, Kang AH, David JR. Humoral and cellular sensitivity to collagen in type

II collagen-induced arthritis in rats. J Clin Invest **61**:89–96, 1978.
62. Stuart JM, Cremer MA, Dixit SN, Kang AH, Townes AS. Collagen-induced arthritis in rats: Comparison of vitreous and cartilage derived collagens. Arthritis Rheum **22**:347–352, 1979.
63. Stuart JM, Cremer MA, Kang AH, Townes AS. Collagen-induced arthritis in rats: evaluation of early immunologic events. Arthritis Rheum **22**:1344–1351, 1979.
64. Morgan K, Clague RB, Shaw MJ, Holt PJL. Native type II collagen-induced arthritis in the rat. I. Incidence and humor response to collagen. Ann Rheum Dis **39**:285–290, 1980.
65. McCune WJ, Trentham DE, David JR. Gold does not alter the arthritic, humoral or cellular responses in rats with type II collagen-induced arthritis. Arthritis Rheum **23**:932–936, 1980.
66. Clague RB, Morgan K, Shaw MJ, Holt PJL. Native type II collagen-induced arthritis in the rat. II. Relationship between the humoral immune response to native type II collagen and arthritis. J Rheumatol **7**:775–782, 1980.
67. Dynesius-Trentham RA, Rowland D, LaRoche E, Trentham DE. Rat leukocyte inhibitory factor (LIF): similarities to human LIF and generation by cells from rats with collagen-induced arthritis. Cell Immunol **63**:362–373, 1981.
68. Stuart JM, Townes AS, Kang AH. Nature and specificity of the immune response to collagen in type II collagen-induced arthritis in mice. J Clin Invest **69**:673–683, 1982.
69. Morgan K, Clague RB, Shaw MJ, Firth SA, Twose TM, Lenox Holt PJ. Native type II collagen-induced arthritis in the rat: The effect of complement depletion by cobra venom factor. Arthritis Rheum **24**:1356–1362, 1981.
70. Kerwar SS, Bauman N, Oronsky AL, Sloboda AE. Studies on type II collagen-induced polyarthritis: Effect of complement depletion. J Immunopharmacol **3**:323–338, 1982.
71. Schoen RT, Greene MI, Trentham DE. Antigen-specific suppression of type II collagen-induced arthritis by collagen-coupled spleen cells. J Immunol **128**:717–719, 1982.
72. Schoen RT, Mehlman H, Trentham DE, Perry L, Greene MI, David JR. Autoimmunity induced by type II collagen-coupled spleen cells. J Immunol **127**:2275–2279, 1981.
73. Salant DJ, Belok S, Madaio MP, Couser WG. A new role for complement in experimental membranous nephropathy in rats. J Clin Invest **66**:1339–1350, 1980.
74. Greene MI, Benacerraf B. Studies on hapten specific T cell immunity and suppression. Immunol Rev **50**:163–186, 1980.
75. Rogers MP, Trentham DE, McCune WJ, Ginsberg BI, Rennke HG, Reich P, David JR. Effect of psychological stress on the induction of arthritis in rats. Arthritis Rheum **23**:1337–1342, 1980.
76. Rogers MP, Trentham DE, Dynesius-Trentham R, Daffner K, Reich P. Exacerbation of collagen arthritis by noise stress. J Rheumatol **10**:651–654, 1983.
77. Brahn E, Trentham DE. Antigen-specific suppression of collagen arthritis by adoptive transfer of spleen cells. Clin Immunol Immunopathol, in press.
78. Prickett JD, Trentham DE, Robinson DR. Dietary fish oil augments the induction of arthritis in rats immunized with type II collagen. J Immunol **132**:725–729, 1984.
79. Trentham DE, Rowland D. Dimethyl sulfoxide does not suppress the clinical manifestations of collagen arthritis. J Rheumatol **10**:114–116, 1983.
80. Trentham DE, Brinckerhoff CE. Augmentation of collagen arthritis by synthetic analogues of retinoic acid. J Immunol **129**:2668–2672, 1982.
81. Klareskog L, Holmdahl R, Larsson E, Wigzell H. Role of T lymphocytes in collagen II induced arthritis in rats. Clin Exp Immunol **51**:117–125, 1983.
82. Holoshitz J, Naparstek Y, Ben-Nun A, Cohen IR. Lines of T lymphocytes induce or vaccinate against autoimmune arthritis. Science **219**:56–58, 1983.
83. Trentham DE, Dynesius-Trentham RA. Attenuation of an adjuvant arthritis by type II collagen. J Immunol **130**:2689–2692, 1982.
84. Welles WL, Battisto JR. Suppression of adjuvant arthritis by antibodies specific for collagen type II. Immunol Commun **10**:673–685, 1981.
85. Cremer MA, Stuart JM, Townes AS, Kang AH. Collagen-induced polyarthritis in rats: a study of native type II collagen for adjuvant activity. J Immunol **124**:2912–2918, 1980.
86. Iizuka Y, Chang Y-H. Adjuvant polyarthritis. VII. The role of type II collagen in pathogenesis. Arthritis Rheum **25**:1325–1332, 1982.
87. Trentham DE, Dynesius RA, David JR. Passive transfer by cells of type II collagen-induced arthritis in rats. J Clin Invest **62**:359–366, 1978.
88. Stuart JM, Cremer MA, Townes AS, Kang AH. Type II collagen-induced arthritis in rats: Passive transfer with serum and evidence that IgG anticollagen antibodies can cause arthritis. J Exp Med **155**:1–16, 1982.
89. Stuart JM, Dixon FJ. Serum transfer of collagen-induced arthritis in mice. J Exp Med **158**:378–392, 1983.
90. Kerwar SS, Englert ME, McReynolds RA, Landes MJ, Lloyd JM, Oronsky AL, Wilson FJ. Type II collagen-induced arthritis: Studies with purified anticollagen immunoglobulin. Arthritis Rheum **26**:1120–1131, 1983.
91. Taurog JD, Sandberg GP, Mahowald ML. The cellular basis of adjuvant arthritis. II. Characterization of the cells mediating passive transfer. Cell Immunol **80**:198–204, 1983.

92. Holoshitz J, Matitiau A, Cohen IR. Arthritis induced in rats by cloned T lymphocytes responsive to mycobacteria but not to collagen type II. J Clin Invest **73**:211–215, 1984.
93. Michaeli D, Fudenberg HH. The incidence and antigenic specificity of antibodies against denatured human collagen in rheumatoid arthritis. Clin Immunol Immunopathol **2**:153–159, 1974.
94. Cracchiolo A, Michaeli D, Goldberg LS, Fudenberg HH. The occurrence of antibodies to collagen in synovial fluids. Clin Immunol Immunopathol **3**:567–574, 1975.
95. Andriopoulos NA, Mestecky J, Miller EJ, Bradley EL. Antibodies to native and denatured collagens in sera of patients with rheumatoid arthritis. Arthritis Rheum **19**:613–617, 1976.
96. Andriopoulos NA, Mestecky J, Wright GP, Miller EJ. Characterization of antibodies to the native human collagens and to their component α chains in the sera and the joint fluid of patients with rheumatoid arthritis. Immunochemistry **13**:709–712, 1976.
97. Menzel J, Steffen C, Kolarz G, Kojer M, Smolen J. Demonstration of anticollagen antibodies in rheumatoid arthritis synovial fluids by ^{14}C-radioimmunoassay. Arthritis Rheum **21**:243–248, 1978.
98. Trentham DE, Dynesius RA, Rocklin RE, David JR. Cellular sensitivity to collagen in rheumatoid arthritis. N Engl J Med **299**:327–332, 1978.
99. Foidart J-M, Abe S, Martin GR, Zizic TM, Barnett EV, Lawley TJ, Katz SI. Antibodies to type II collagen in relapsing polychondritis. N Engl J Med **299**:1203–1207, 1978.
100. Clague RB, Shaw MJ, Lennox Holt PJ. Incidence of serum antibodies to native type I and type II collagens in patients with inflammatory arthritis. Ann Rheum Dis **39**:201–206, 1980.
101. Beard HK, Ryvar R, Skingle J, Greenbury CL. Anticollagen antibodies in sera from rheumatoid arthritis patients. J Clin Pathol **33**:1077–1081, 1980.
102. Trentham DE, Kammer GM, McCune WJ, David JR. Autoimmunity to collagen: A shared feature of psoriatic and rheumatoid arthritis. Arthritis Rheum **24**:1363–1369, 1981.
103. Stuart JM, Huffstutter EH, Townes AS, Kang AH. Incidence and specificity of antibodies to types I, II, IV and V collagen in rheumatoid arthritis and other rheumatic diseases as measured by ^{125}I-radioimmunoassay. Arthritis Rheum **26**:832–840, 1983.
104. Kammer GM, Trentham DE. HLA-DR4 is not a requisite for autoimmunity to collagen in rheumatoid arthritis. Arthritis Rheum, in press.
105. Dyer PA, Clague RB, Klouda PT, Firth S, Harris R, Holt PJL. HLA antigens in patients with rheumatoid arthritis and antibodies to native type II collagen. Tissue Antigens **20**:394–396, 1982.
106. Endler AT, Zielinski C, Menzel EJ, Smolen JS, Schwägerl W, Endler M, Eberl R, Frank O, Steffen C. Leukocyte migration inhibition with collagen type I and collagen type III in rheumatoid arthritis and degenerative joint diseases. Z Rheumatol **37**:87–92, 1978.
107. Smolen JS, Menzel EJ, Scherak O, Kojer M, Kolarz G, Steffen C, Mayr WR. Lymphocyte transformation to denatured type I collagen and B lymphocyte alloantigens in rheumatoid arthritis. Arthritis Rheum **23**:424–432, 1980.
108. Stuart JM, Postlethwaite AE, Kang AH, Townes AS. Cell-mediated immunity to collagen in rheumatoid arthritis and other rheumatic diseases. Amer J Med **69**:13–18, 1980.
109. Dayer J-M, Trentham DE, David JR, Krane SM. Collagens stimulate the production of mononuclear cell factor (MCF) and prostaglandins (PGE_2) by human monocytes. Trans Assoc Amer Physicians **93**:326–335, 1981.
110. Solinger AM, Bhatnagar R, Stobo JD. Cellular, molecular, and genetic characteristics of T cell reactivity to collagen in man. Proc Natl Acad Sci USA **78**:3877–3881, 1981.
111. Solinger AM, Stobo JD. Immune response gene control of collagen reactivity in man: Collagen unresponsiveness in HLA-DR4 negative nonresponders is due to the presence of T-dependent suppressive influences. J Immunol **129**:1916–1920, 1982.
112. Meghlaoui A, Herbage D, Huc A, Monier JC. Mise au point d'une technique immunoenzymatique (ELISA) pour la détection des anticorps anti-collagène de type I et II: recherche de ces anticorps au cours de la polyarthrite rhumatoïde du lupus érythémateux disséminé et de la lèpre. Ann Immunol **132**:287–305, 1981.
113. Mackel AM, Delustro F, Harper FE, LeRoy EC. Antibodies to collagen in scleroderma. Arthritis Rheum **25**:522–531, 1982.
114. Suou T, Hirayama C. Antibodies to denatured bovine collagens in sera of patients with liver disease. Clin Exp Immunol **39**:119–124, 1980.
115. Adar R, Papa MZ, Halpern Z, Mozes M, Shoshan S, Sofer B, Zinger H, Dayan M, Mozes E. Cellular sensitivity to collagen in thromboangiitis obliterans. N Engl J Med **308**:1113–1116, 1983.
116. Griffiths MM, Dewitt CW. Immunogenetic control of experimental collagen-induced arthritis in rats. II. ECIA susceptibility and immune response to type II collagen (calf) are linked to RTI. J Immunogenet **8**:463–470, 1981.
117. Rosenwasser LJ, Bhatnagar RS, Stobo JD. Genetic control of the murine T lymphocyte proliferative response to collagen: Analysis of the molecular and cellular contributions to immunogenicity. J Immunol **124**:2854–2859, 1980.
118. Wooley PH, Luthra HS, Stuart JM, David CS. Type II collagen-induced arthritis in mice. I. Major his-

tocompatibility complex (I region) linkage and antibody correlates. J Exp Med **154**:688–700, 1981.

119. Battisto JR, Smith RN, Beckman K, Sternlicht M, Welles WL. Susceptibility to adjuvant arthritis in DA and F_{344} rats: A dominant trait controlled by an autosomal gene locus linked to the major histocompatibility complex. Arthritis Rheum **25**:1194–1200, 1982.
120. Schoen RT, Trentham DE. Drug-induced lupus: an adjuvant disease? Amer J Med **71**:5–8, 1981.
121. Drachman DB, Adams RN, Josifek LF, Self SG. Functional activities of autoantibodies to acetylcholine receptors and the clinical severity of myasthenia gravis. N Engl J Med **307**:769–775, 1982.
122. Wahl SM, Wilder RL, Katona IM, Wahl LM, Allen JB, Scher I, Decker JL. Leukapheresis in rheumatoid arthritis: Association of clinical improvement with reversal of anergy. Arthritis Rheum **26**:1076–1084, 1983.
123. Staines NA, Hardingham T, Smith M, Henderson B. Collagen-induced arthritis in the rat: Modification of immune and arthritic responses by free collagen and immune anti-collagen antiserum. Immunology **44**:737–744, 1981.

P.S.E.B.M. 1984, Vol. 176.

PROCEEDINGS OF THE SOCIETY FOR EXPERIMENTAL BIOLOGY AND MEDICINE **176**, 105–108 (1984)

RAPID COMMUNICATION

RADIOIMMUNOASSAY OF ATRIAL NATRIURETIC FACTOR (ANF) IN RAT ATRIA

J. GUTKOWSKA, G. THIBAULT, R.W. MILNE, P. JANUSZEWICZ,
P.W. SCHILLER, M. CANTIN AND J. GENEST

Clinical Research Institute of Montreal, 110 Pine Avenue West,
Montreal, Quebec, Canada H2W 1R7

Abstract. We describe a solid phase radioimmunoassay for atrial natriuretic factor (ANF) and its application for measurement of this peptide in homogenates of rat atria. The method uses a synthetic 26 amino-acid fragment (8-33 ANF) of the native peptide. Sample (or standard) are incubated with the rabbit anti-8-33 ANF antiserum in peptide (8-33 ANF)-coated wells. Then an excess of I^{125} goat anti-rabbit IgG is added. The radioactivity bound is directly proportional to the amount of ANF present. The concentration of immunoreactive ANF has been found to be about 4 times higher in the right atrium than in the left atrium of the rat.

Introduction. It is now well established that mammalian cardiac atria contain a biologically active peptide capable of producing natriuresis, diuresis (1-3), and vasorelaxation (4,5), which has been called atrial natriuretic factor (ANF). Recently, this peptide has been purified, sequenced and synthesized (3,6,7). A synthetic fragment (8-33 ANF), composed of the 26 amino acids from residues 8 to 33 of ANF, has been found to have the same biological activity as the native peptide. We now report a radioimmunoassay for ANF using the synthetic 8-33 ANF fragment and its application in the measurement of ANF in rat atria.

Materials and Methods. The synthetic 8-33 ANF peptide has been generously supplied by Dr. R.F. Nutt (Merck, Sharp and Dohme Lab., West Point, PA).

Sprague-Dawley rats weighing 200-250 g were decapitated and the hearts quickly removed. After washing in cold 0.1 M PBS buffer, pH 7.4, the atria were carefully dissected. The two atria from one rat or the right and left atrium separately were homogenized in 2 ml of 1 M acetic acid for 10 seconds, and centrifuged for 20 min at 30,000 rpm. The supernatant was lyophilized overnight. The lyophilized atria were dissolved in 500 µl 0.01 M ammonium acetate buffer, pH 5.0, and 100-µl aliquots were stored frozen at -20°C until assayed. Dilutions of 1:10 in 0.1 M PBS containing 1% ovalbumin were used for the assay.

Production of antisera to 8-33 ANF:

For immunization, 8-33 ANF was coupled to bovine thyroglobulin using carbodiimide (8). One hundred µg of this conjugate in 1 ml saline emulsified with 1 ml of complete Freund's adjuvant was injected intradermally at multiple sites on the shaved backs of New Zealand white rabbits (1.5 kg). The animals were reimmunized at monthly intervals with 100 µg 8-33 ANF-thyroglobulin conjugate in incomplete Freund's adjuvant and bled by ear artery 10 days after the injection. Two of three rabbits produced high titer antisera. For all our studies the fourth bleeding from one rabbit was used (17/4).

Preparation of labelled goat anti-rabbit:

Anti-rabbit γ-globulin were produced in goats. Goat anti-rabbit IgG was purified by affinity chromatography on Protein A-sepharose (Pharmacia Inc., Uppsala, Sweden) (9).

Fifty µg of anti-rabbit IgG was labelled with I^{125} using the Chloramine-T method (10). Purification of radiolabelled tracer was performed on an anion exchange resin (AG-1-X8, 100-200 mesh, Chloride form, Bio-Rad).

Preparation of the standard curve:

The synthetic 8-33 ANF peptide was used as a standard. A stock solution of 1 mg/ml in 0.01 M ammonium acetate buffer, pH 5.0, was fractionated in 10-

0037-9727/84 $1.50

μl aliquots and stored frozen at -20°C. The stock solution (10 μl) was diluted before use in 0.1 M PBS buffer, pH 7.4, 1% ovalbumin to a concentration of 1000 ng/ml, the most concentrated point of the standard curve. Serial two-fold dilutions were then prepared with the assay buffer to final concentrations ranging from 7.8 to 1000 ng/ml. One hundred μl of standards were used for preparing the standard curve.

Radioimmunoassay procedure:

The radioimmunoassay was performed in Removawells (Dynateck Laboratories Inc., Alexandra, VA). The wells were coated with 200 μl of 1 μg 8-33 ANF/ml in 0.005 M glycine buffer, pH 9.5, for 2 hr at room temperature. The peptide solution was then discarded and the wells were exposed for 30 min at room temperature to 400 μl of 0.1 M PBS buffer containing 1% ovalbumin to saturate the plastic in order to minimize the non-specific binding of radioactivity. The wells were then washed in 0.15 M NaCl containing 0.025% Tween 20. The standards or samples (100 μl) and the antibody against 8-33 ANF diluted 1:32,000 (100 μl) were added and the wells were incubated 2 hr at room temperature. The wells were next washed in 0.15 M NaCl 0.025% Tween 20 and 200 μl of I^{125} anti-rabbit IgG diluted in PBS buffer with 1% ovalbumin was added to the well. Non-specific binding was determined in the wells coated only with PBS buffer 1% ovalbumin or the wells coated with peptide 8-33 ANF. After an overnight incubation at 4°C the wells were washed in Tween 20 buffer and the bound radioactivity was determined in an LKB gamma counter. Results were expressed as B/B_o where B = cpm of bound radioactivity — cpm non-specifically bound. Bo = cpm bound in absence of standard — cpm non-specifically bound.

Results. To determine the optimal conditions for the assay, the effects of concentration, pH, time and temperature for coating the wells with 8-33 ANF and for the incubations with anti-ANF antibody and I^{125} goat anti-rabbit IgG were studied. To establish coating conditions, concentrations of 8-33 ANF from 0.01 to 2 μg/ml (200 μl/well) diluted in buffer from pH 6.0 to 10 were incubated at 4°C or room temperature. Binding was determined using excess anti-ANF antibody. The appropriate dilution of anti-ANF was then determined by incubating at either 4°C or room temperature doubling dilutions, from 1000-fold to 128,000-fold (in the assay buffer pH 7.4, 1% ovalbumin), with either the most concentrated ANF standard 100 ng/well or diluent. Based on these preliminary experiments, the coating conditions chosen consisted in a 2-hour incubation at room temperature with 8-33 ANF at a concentration of 1 μg/ml (200 μl/well). Prolonged incubation did not increase the binding. Varying the incubation time from 30 min to 8 hr at 4°C and room temperature for the first antibody before adding tracer demonstrated that 2 hr at room temperature is optimal. The second immunological reaction was slower and I^{125} anti-rabbit IgG had to be incubated for at least 16 hr at 4°C to achieve the maximum binding.

The standard curve obtained in these conditions is shown in Figure 1. The detection limit, defined as the lowest concentration of ANF that gives a binding which differs significantly from Bo at the 95% confidence interval, was 0.78 ng/well which corresponds to the lowest concentration of the standard. The working range extends from 0.78 to 100 ng/well.

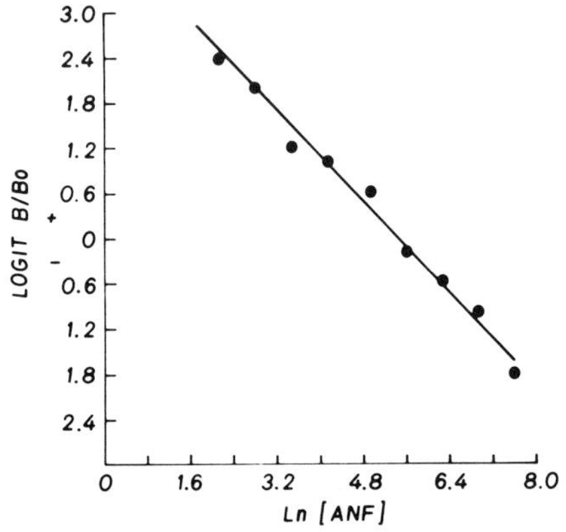

Fig. 1. Standard curve for radioimmunoassay of 8-33 ANF.

The anti-8-33 ANF used in this study showed cross-reactivity with different fragments of native ANF such as 3-33 ANF (95%), 10-33 ANF (99%) and propeptide, composed of 73 amino acids (23%). These peptides were isolated from rat atrial homogenates during the purification of ANF.

The within and between-run precision were assessed by measuring two rat atria homogenates with different concentrations of ANF. The mean values for 10 determinations in a single run were 151 ± 15.4 ng/ml and 20.5 ± 4.0 ng/ml. The between assay CV for the same samples assayed in duplicate in four different runs ranged from 9.5% to 15%.

The analytical recovery, as determined by addition of 1 µg/ml of 8-33 ANF peptide to 6 rat atria homogenates, was between 75% to 100% (mean ± SD 87 ± 14.2%).

The different dilutions of homogenates of rat atria showed parallelism with the standard curve.

This assay was applied for measurement of ANF in homogenates of rat atria. We have found under these conditions about 4 times higher concentrations of immunoreactive ANF in right rat atrium (means ± SD 0.74 ± 0.14 µg/atria) than in left atrium (0.17 ± 0.08 µg/atria). When both atria were extracted together from each rat (n = 10), the concentration of 2.2 µg/left and right atria of immunoreactive ANF was found.

Discussion. To our knowledge the present paper is the first report of a radioimmunoassay of atrial natriuretic factor. This method is sensitive enough to determine the content of immunoreactive ANF in rat atria. The range for measurement of ANF by the described method is 0.78 to 100 ng and is therefore broad enough to measure accurately a wide range of ANF concentrations in rat atria. The procedure requires only a 2-hour incubation of anti-ANF antibody and sample in previously prepared antigen-coated wells followed by an overnight incubation with the labelled second antibody. The wells in several plates can be coated simultaneously and the plates stored at 4°C for at least one week.

The determination of immunoreactive ANF by radioimmunoassay have shown much higher concentrations (about 4 times) in the right than in the left atrium. This potent atrial natriuretic factor has been found to be stored in the specific atrial granules, which are present in atrial muscle of mammals (11). These specific granules are of three different types A, B, and D, and have morphological and histochemical properties similar to the storage granules of polypeptide hormones (13). The number of these specific granules determined by quantitative ultrastructural and cytochemical methods is significantly greater in the right atrium of rat than in the left (12,13).

The difference in concentration of immunoreactive ANF between the rat atria may be related to the differences in left and right atrial pressure or to yet unidentified reflex mechanisms operating in the atria, including the described granules and stretch or osmoreceptors.

References

1. de Bold AJ, Borenstein HB, Veress AT, Sonnenberg H. A rapid and potent natriuretic response to intravenous injection of atrial myocardial extract in rats. Life Sci **28**:89-94, 1981.
2. Garcia R, Cantin M, Thibault G, Ong H, Genest J. Relationship of specific granules to the natriuretic and diuretic activity of rat atria. Experientia **38**:1071-1073, 1982.
3. Thibault G, Garcia R, Cantin M, Genest J. Atrial natriuretic factor. Characterization and partial purification. Hypertension **5** (Suppl I): I-75-I-80, 1983.
4. Garcia R, Thibault G, Cantin M, Genest J. Effect of a purified atrial natriuretic factor on rat and rabbit vascular strips and vascular beds. Am J Physiol: in press, 1984.
5. Currie MG, Geller DM, Cole BR, Boylan JG, YuSheng W, Holmberg SW, Needleman P. Bioactive cardiac substances: potent vasorelaxant activity in mammalian atria. Science **221**:71-73, 1983.
6. Thibault G, Garcia R, Seidah NG, Lazure C, Cantin M, Chrětien M, Genest J. Purification of three rat atrial natriuretic factors and their amino acid composition. FEBS Lett **164**:286-290, 1983.
7. Seidah NG, Lazure C, Chrětien M, Thibault G, Garcia R, Cantin M, Genest J, Nutt RF, Brady SF, Lyle TA, Paleveda WJ, Colton CD, Ciccerone TM, Veber DF. Amino acid sequence of homologous rat atrial peptides: natriuretic activity of native and synthetic forms. Proc Natl Acad Sci USA: in press, 1984.

8. Skowsky WR, Fisher DA. The use of thyroglobulin to induce antigenicity to small molecules. J Lab Clin Med **80**:134-144, 1972.
9. Delacroix DL, Vaerman JP. Simple purification of goat IgG1 and IgG2 subclasses by chromatography on Protein A-sepharose at various pH. Molec Immunol **16**:837-840, 1979.
10. Greenwood FC, Hunter WM. The preparation of ^{131}I labelled human growth hormone of high specific radioactivity. Biochem J **89**:114-123, 1963.
11. Cantin M, Gutkowska J, Thibault G, Milne RW, Ledoux S, MinLi S, Chapeau C, Garcia R, Genest J. Immunocytochemical localization of atrial natriuretic factors in the heart and salivary glands. Histochemistry **80**: in press, 1984.
12. de Bold AJ. Morphometric assessment of granulation in rat atrial cardiocytes. J Mol Cell Cardiol **10**:717-724, 1978.
13. Cantin M, Timm-Kennedy M, El-Khatib E, Huet M, Yunge L. Ultrastructural cytochemistry of atrial muscle cells. VI. Comparative study of specific granules in right and left atrium. Anat Rec **193**:55-69, 1979.

Received February 27, 1984.
P.S.E.B.M. 1984, Vol. 176.
Accepted April 11, 1984.

PROCEEDINGS OF THE SOCIETY FOR EXPERIMENTAL BIOLOGY AND MEDICINE **176,** 109–118 (1984)

Mechanism of the Stimulatory Effect of Phorbol 12-Myristate 13-Acetate on Cellular Production of Plasminogen Activator (41849)

HIROMI ASHINO-FUSE, GHISLAIN OPDENAKKER, AKIRA FUSE, AND ALFONS BILLIAU

Rega Institute for Medical Research, University of Leuven, B-3000 Leuven, Belgium

Abstract. The human Bowes melanoma cell line secretes a plasminogen activator identical to the extrinsic tissue plasminogen activator (EPA) and different from the urokinase-like plasminogen activators mostly found in human tumor lines. In the continuous presence of 100 ng/ml of phorbol 12-myristate 13-acetate (PMA) the 24-hr production of EPA was increased 5.3-fold (average). Preincubation of the cultures for a limited time period (optimally 3 to 6 hr) also resulted in an increase of the subsequent 24-hr production. EPA produced in the presence of PMA was serologically indistinguishable from that produced spontaneously and its molecular weight as defined by sodium dodecyl sulfate (SDS)–polyacrylamide gel electrophoresis and fibrin–agar zymography was the same as that of spontaneously produced EPA. Treatment of the cells with actinomycin D inhibited PMA-induced EPA production. Also, RNA extracted from PMA-treated cells became enriched in mRNA for EPA. It is concluded that PMA acts by enhancing the transcription of the EPA gene. Cell-associated EPA levels were increased, even when tested as early as 3 hr after initiation of the PMA treatment, thus failing to support the view that increased EPA synthesis occurred as a result of depletion of the cellular pool.

Phorbol esters such as phorbol 12-myristate 13-acetate (PMA) have strong inflammatory and tumor promoting activities (1). The mechanisms underlying these activities are not known. At the cellular level, PMA modulates formation of various proteins. Thus, in rat pituitary cells it stimulates prolactin synthesis and release (2). In certain cell systems it has been described to induce ornithine decarboxylase, an enzyme that is rate limiting in polyamine synthesis (3). In other systems it causes a decrease in production of fibronectin (4). Prostaglandin metabolism has also been reported to be affected (5, 6). Recently, PMA has been shown to stimulate the synthesis of immune interferon (7) and interleukin 2 (8) by lymphocytes.

PMA can also enhance or induce production of plasminogen activator(s) (PA(s)) by normal or transformed cells (9–16). PAs are cellular proteases which can only act by activation of plasminogen into plasmin. Many cell lines produce a PA with molecular weight ($\simeq$33,000 and 55,000), enzyme kinetic, and serological properties of urokinases. Other cell lines, in particular those derived from melanomas (e.g., the Bowes melanoma line) produce an activator of a higher molecular weight ($\sim$72,000) with properties indistinguishable from those of the so-called tissue or extrinsic plasminogen activator (EPA) that was previously isolated from fresh tissues such as uterus (17, 18).

Observations on the secretion of PA by specialized cells—granulosa cells (19), trophoblastic cells (20), macrophages (21), and neuroblastoma cells (22)—have led to the concept that the plasminogen-dependent proteolytic systems play an important role as space-creating agents in organogenesis, regeneration of damaged tissues, and various other remodeling processes of tissues. In addition, suggestive evidence has been presented for PA secretion to be associated with cellular transformation (23–32), and in particular with metastatic behavior of tumor cells (33).

It is not known whether modulation of PA formation by PMA has any significance in terms of the well-known cocarcinogenic potential of PMA. Neither is the molecular–biological basis of the effects of PMA fully understood. Following exposure of cells to PMA, the cellular content of EPA mRNA rapidly increases (34). Although this indicates that the process of transcription is affected, the possibility remains that PMA also, or even primarily, affects other stages of the protease formation and excretion.

0037-9727/84 $1.50

This kinetic study of the stimulation of PA production by PMA in Bowes melanoma cells gives evidence in favour of an effect on transcription and against an effect on excretion.

Materials and Methods. *Cell culture.* The human melanoma cell line, Bowes, was obtained from Dr. D. B. Rifkin (Rockefeller University, New York, N.Y.). The cells were grown in culture flasks (75-cm^2, Costar, Cambridge, Mass., No. 3075) using modified Eagle's minimum essential medium supplemented with 10% (final concentration) heat-inactivated newborn calf serum, 100 units/ml of penicillin, and 100 μg/ml of streptomycin. The cells were rendered mycoplasma-free by passage as a solid tumor in nude mice; attempts to subsequently clone the cell line were unsuccessful.

For experiments the cells were transferred by trypsinization, into 1.6-cm-diameter wells (24-Multiwell plate, Costar, No. 3524) at 1.5 to 4 $\times$ 10^5 cells per well. After culturing for 1 to 3 days, the medium was removed, the cells were washed twice with serum-free medium, and used for the experiments described in the Results section.

Stimulation of EPA production by PMA. PMA was added at indicated time intervals in serum-free medium, and the cultures were incubated at 37°C. At indicated times the culture fluids were removed, supplemented with 0.01% Tween 80 (final concentration) and frozen at −20°C for subsequent assay.

For determination of cell-associated EPA, the medium was removed, the cells were washed twice with phosphate-buffered saline (PBS) and 0.2 to 0.5 ml of PBS containing 0.2% Triton X-100 was added to each well. Lysates were stored at −20°C and were assayed within 1 week.

EPA determination. Assays for EPA in samples of serum-free culture medium or cell lysates were performed using microtiter plates (Falcon Plastics, Oxnard, Calif., cat. No. 3040F). The plates were coated with ^{125}I-labeled fibrin as described by Hoylaerts *et al.* (35). Purified human plasminogen (9 μg) was added to all wells. Subsequently dilutions of the samples to be assayed or of an urokinase standard preparation were added. The volume of the total reaction mixture was 200 μl. The plate was rotated at 37°C and at fixed time intervals aliquots were taken to measure released ^{125}I in a gamma scintillation counter (Packard, PGD, Auto-Gamma). Units of activity were expressed as international units per milliliter using urokinase as the standard.

Protein determination. Protein was determined fluorimetrically using bovine serum albumin as a standard (36).

Immunological characterization. Serum-free culture medium in which PA content had previously been determined was diluted to 10 to 20 units/ml with serum-free medium containing 0.01% Tween 80.

Equal volumes of increasing concentrations of antibody against the human EPA were added and the mixtures were incubated at 37°C for 1 hr. The reaction mixture was then diluted and the activity was determined.

Measurement of rapidly labeled cellular RNA. Cells were labeled with [^{3}H]uridine (New England Nuclear Corp, Boston, Mass; 27.4 Ci/mmole) at concentrations indicated in the text. After 1 hr incubation at 37°C, the cells were washed with ice-cooled PBS and lysed by adding an aliquot of a 1% solution of sodium dodecyl sulfate. An equal volume of 20% trichloroacetic acid was added to the lysates. The precipitates were caught on membrane filters which were counted in a liquid scintillation counter.

mRNA extraction and purification. Cells were harvested in PBS containing 0.01% EDTA and extracted as described by Opdenakker *et al.* (37). Briefly, the cells were washed twice with cold PBS and resuspended in 15 ml/10^9 cells of a hypotonic buffer containing 10 m*M* NaCl, 3 m*M* magnesium acetate, and 20 m*M* Tris–HCl, pH 7.4. Ribonucleosyl vanadyl complexes (10 m*M*) were added as a RNase inhibitor. After swelling for 10 min at 4°C, cells were lysed with 1/3 vol of hypotonic buffer supplemented with 5% sucrose and 1.2% Triton N-101. After homogenization nuclei were removed by centrifugation and RNA was extracted with the phenol method in the presence of 1% SDS. The total RNA was precipitated overnight at −20°C with 2 vol of ice-cold ethanol and 1/10 vol of 1 *M* NaCl.

The poly(A)-rich RNA fraction was isolated by affinity chromatography on oligo(dT)-cellulose (type 7) essentially as described by Aviv and Leder (38) except for the use of sodium instead of potassium salt. After chromatography RNA was precipitated with ethanol/

NaCl overnight. Before oocyte injection this precipitated RNA was washed twice with cold 75% ethanol, dried under vacuum, and dissolved in bidistilled water for 1 hr at 4°C.

Translation in oocytes and PA assay. Mature oocytes, stage V (39) were injected with 50 nl of RNA solutions and incubated in groups of 10 at 19°C for 48 hr, according to the procedures originally described by Gurdon *et al.* (40). The oocyte culture medium was harvested, supplemented with Tween 80 to a final concentration of 0.01%, and assayed for the presence of PA.

Electrophoresis and zymography of PA. A vertical slab-gel electrophoresis apparatus was used. The separation gel contained 9% acrylamide and 0.23% bisacrylamide in 0.375 *M* Tris–HCl buffer, pH 8.8, with 0.1% sodium dodecyl sulfate (SDS). Stacking gels were made of 4% acrylamide and 0.23% bisacrylamide in 0.138 *M* Tris–HCl buffer, pH 6.8, containing 0.1% SDS (41). Activator samples, containing 0.1 to 1 units, were applied in a volume of 20 μl. The samples contained 2% SDS. Zymography was carried out by the fibrin–agar overlay method (42). The gels were washed in 2.5% Triton X-100 to remove the SDS. After a brief rinse in distilled water, the gels were layered on indicator gel slabs containing 1.25% agar, purified human plasminogen (5 μg/ml), thrombin (0.06 units/ml), and fibrinogen (2 mg/ml). The polyacrylamide gel indicator slab assemblies were incubated at 37°C in a humid environment. After the reaction, the electrophoretic gel was removed and the fibrin layer was stained.

Reagents. Bovine fibrinogen (Poviet, Organon-Teknika, Oss, The Netherlands), thrombin (Leo Pharmaceuticals, Ballerup, Denmark), human urokinase, human plasminogen (NH_2-terminal glutamic acid-plasminogen), ^{125}I-labeled fibrinogen, antiserum against EPA, and purified EPA from Bowes melanoma cell cultures were kindly provided by Dr. D. Collen. The anti-EPA antiserum was purified by affinity chromatography on sepharose-bound EPA and had no neutralizing activity against urokinase, as previously shown (18). Phorbol 12-myristate 13-acetate (PMA) was obtained from Sigma Chemical Company, St. Louis, Missouri. Oligo(dT)-cellulose (type 7) was obtained from PL Biochemicals Inc., Milwaukee, Wisconsin.

Results. *Effect of PMA on cell viability.* Since determination of EPA in culture medium could only be done in the absence of serum, it was necessary to define conditions under which the combined cytotoxic effect of PMA and nutrient depletion were minimized. Figure 1 shows the results of an experiment in which the effect of replenishment of growing cultures with serum-free medium containing PMA was tested on further outgrowth of the cells. It can be seen that for a period of 48 hr after removing the serum the cells continued to divide. The effect of PMA on this further outgrowth of the cultures was dose- and time-dependent. With small doses (1 and 10 ng/ml) the cells continued to divide, although to a lesser degree than in the controls, for the whole 48-hr observation period. With higher doses (50 and 100 ng/ml) there was still some increase in cell number for 24 hr but then the cell number decreased indicating that, with time, PMA became cytotoxic. PMA at 500 ng/ml was cytotoxic from the beginning.

Kinetics of the enhancement of EPA release by PMA treatment. Incubation of melanoma cells in the presence of PMA resulted in enhanced production of extracellular EPA. The time and dose response relationships of this effect were investigated.

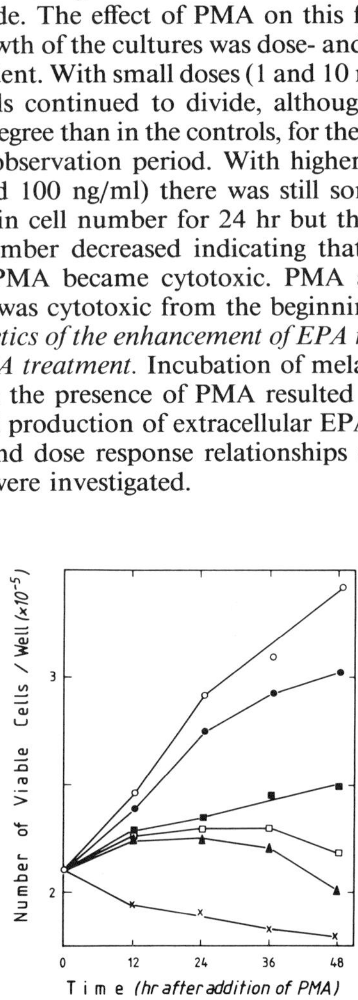

FIG. 1. Effect of PMA on multiplication of Bowes melanoma cells. Cultures were seeded at 1.6 × 10^5 cells/1.6-cm-diameter well in medium containing 10% serum. After 48 hr incubation the cultures were washed and refed with serum-free medium containing PMA in final concentrations of 0 (○), 1 (●), 10 (■), 50 (□), 100 (▲), or 500 (×) ng/ml.

In a first type of experiment confluent melanoma cell cultures were incubated for 48 hr in the presence of various concentrations of PMA; samples of the supernatant fluid were taken at several time intervals and their content of EPA was determined. The results were plotted in different ways. In Fig. 2a the yields of PA are given as units per milliliter of culture fluid; in Fig. 2b the same data are plotted as units per 10^5 viable cells. The dose–response curves in these different plots were very similar: increments in production with the very high doses of PMA (100 and 500 ng/ml) were somewhat less pronounced when the effects of PMA on cell viability were not taken into account. Expression of PA production per milligram of cellular protein also yielded a similar dose–response curve. Indeed, cellular protein content of the cultures varied very little with dose of PMA: only with 500 ng/ml was there a decrease of about 10%.

Over a total of 15 experiments a dose of 100 ng/ml of PMA caused an average 5.3-fold increase in 24 hr production of EPA (SE = 0.91). Between 24 and 48 hr, EPA production had a tendency to level off, especially in cultures treated with >50 ng/ml of PMA.

In the previous experiment PMA was left in the culture medium for the whole duration of the experiment. Under these conditions the drug may be cumulatively absorbed and disturb cell metabolism more than necessary for the study of the initial phases of induction. It therefore seemed advisable to design an experimental protocol in which short pulses of PMA treatment were given. Under these circumstances a fixed amount of PMA may be expected to adsorb to the cells; removal of excess PMA at a suitably chosen time may then avoid variability due to additional uptake of PMA from the medium.

To determine the minimum amount of time necessary for PMA to trigger maximal induction of EPA, cultures were refed with serum-free medium and incubated for 24 hr. PMA (100 ng/ml) was added to these cultures for time intervals of 3, 6, 12, and 24 hr preceding the end of this incubation period. Supernatant fluids were collected, and the cultures were washed, refed with fresh serum-free medium, incubated for another 24-hr period, and harvested again. The results of this experiment are shown in Fig. 3. Enhancement of total EPA production (i.e., production in the two harvests taken together) was as pronounced in cultures preexposed to PMA for 3 or 6 hr

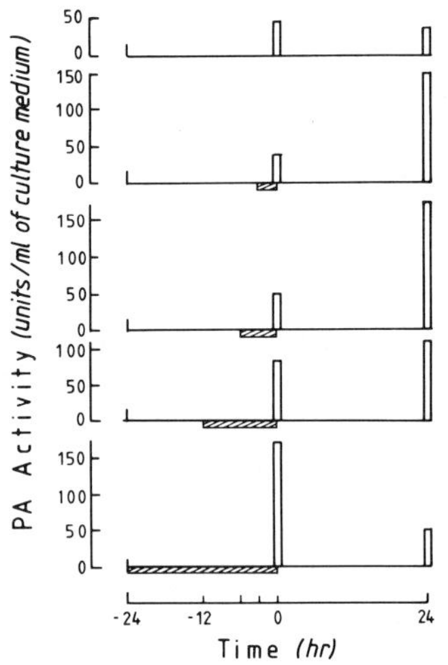

FIG. 3. Twenty-four-hour yields of EPA in Bowes melanoma cell cultures pretreated for various time intervals with 100 ng/ml of PMA. Confluent cultures were washed, refed with serum-free medium, and incubated for 24 hr. PMA was added to these cultures for time intervals of 3, 6, 12, and 24 hr (horizontal shaded bars) preceding the end of this incubation period. Supernatant fluids were harvested, and the cultures were washed, refed with fresh serum-free medium, reincubated for another 24-hr period, and harvested again.

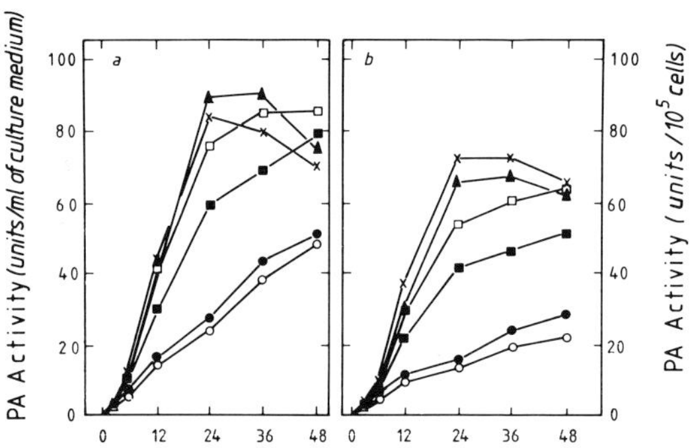

FIG. 2. Effect of increasing doses of PMA on production of EPA by Bowes melanoma cells. Confluent cultures were washed, refed with serum-free medium containing PMA in final concentrations of 0 (○), 1 (●), 10 (■), 50 (□), 100 (▲), or 500 (×) ng/ml, and incubated for various time intervals. Culture fluids were harvested for PA assay. The activity was expressed as units/ml of culture medium (a) and as units/10^5 viable cells (b).

as in cultures incubated for 12 or 24 hr. With short pulses the enhancement was seen in the second harvest, while with long treatment courses it was more apparent in the first harvest. This is what could be predicted from the results of Fig. 2 if the time course of EPA production is the same in the pulsed and in the continually treated cultures. Thus, a short pulse of PMA treatment of 3 to 6 hr appeared sufficient to obtain maximal stimulation of EPA production. Consequently, this experimental design was preferred for further kinetic studies.

Increased transcription of EPA-mRNA in PMA-treated melanoma cells. Two types of experiments were done to determine whether the increase in production of EPA might be due to increased transcription. In a first type of experiment the effect of actinomycin D on production of EPA was studied; in the second type of experiments the amount of EPA-specific mRNA was directly determined.

Table I shows the effects of PMA and of actinomycin D on overall RNA synthesis in the Bowes melanoma cells. Actinomycin D at 100 ng/ml inhibited the synthesis of rapidly labeled RNA by 86%, and this dose was used to evaluate the effect of such inhibition on EPA synthesis. PMA at 10 and 100 ng/ml caused a slight increase in [^{3}H]uridine incorporation when measured at 6 hr after labeling, and a slight decrease when measured after 22 hr.

In order to study the effect of inhibition of RNA synthesis on EPA production by control and PMA-treated cells, sets of cultures were refed with 0 or 100 ng/ml of actinomycin D. After 30 min, each set was divided in three subsets and 0, 50, or 100 ng/ml of PMA was added to the media of these subsets. The cultures were then incubated for 3 or 6 hr, washed, refed with serum-free medium, and reincubated. EPA was assayed on samples of the medium harvested after 24 hr. The results are represented in Fig. 4. It can be seen that actinomycin D inhibited spontaneous as well as PMA-induced EPA production. This inhibition occurred despite the fact that cell viability after 48 hr incubation was 90% in cultures pretreated with actinomycin D for 3 hr and 80% in cultures pretreated for 6 hr.

In a second type of experiment the amount of poly(A) RNA with specific EPA-mRNA activity was directly determined. Confluent cultures of melanoma cells (stationary 175-cm^2 flasks) were washed and refed with serum-free

TABLE I. EFFECT OF ACTINOMYCIN D AND PMA ON INCORPORATION OF [^{3}H]URIDINE INTO RNA OF BOWES MELANOMA CELLS

Dose of drugs[a] (ng/ml)		Acid-insoluble cellular radioactivity at:			
		6 hr		22 hr	
Actinomycin D	PMA	cpm/10^5 cells	% of control	cpm/10^5 cells	% of control
—	—	25,750	100	26,160	100
—	—	28,300			
20	—	11,170	41	—	
100	—	4,450	16	7,320	28
500	—	2,750	10	—	
—	10	29,420	109	24,010	91
—	10	29,660			
—	100	29,100	113	18,725	75
—	100	32,105			
100	10	4,840	19	7,020	27
100	10	5,600			
100	100	5,320	17	5,350	20
100	100	4,130			

[a] At time 0 hr cell monolayers were decanted, washed, and refed with medium containing the appropriate concentration of actinomycin D. PMA, at the appropriate concentration was added at time 30 min. At 6 and 22 hr sets of cultures were decanted, washed, and refed with 1 ml of medium containing 1 μCi of [^{3}H]uridine. After 1 hr absorption of the label the cells were washed with ice-cooled PBS and processed for measuring acid-insoluble radioactivity.

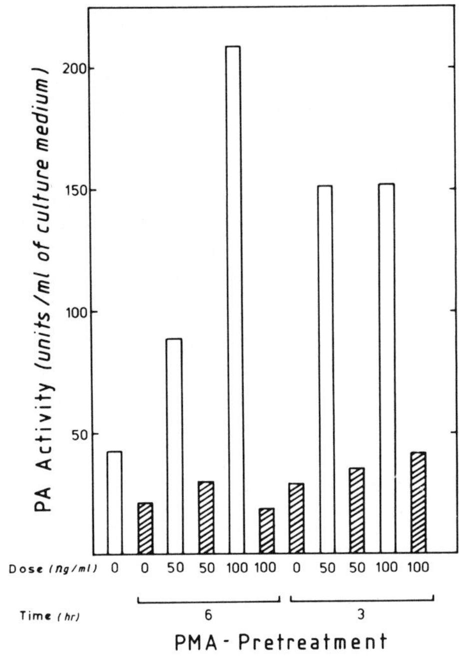

FIG. 4. Inhibitory effect of actinomycin D on production of PA by Bowes melanoma cells pretreated with PMA. Confluent cultures were preexposed to actinomycin D (0.1 μg/ml) for 30 min, then treated for 3 or 6 hr with PMA, washed, refed with serum-free medium, and incubated. After 24 hr culture fluids were harvested for PA assay. Empty bars: not treated with actinomycin D; filled bars: treated with actinomycin D.

medium containing 0, 1, 10, or 100 ng/ml of PMA. After 6 hr incubation at 37°C, the medium was decanted and the cells were detached by adding PBS with 0.01% EDTA. Cytoplasmic RNA was extracted with the phenol method, and the poly(A)-rich fraction was isolated by chromatography on oligo-dT cellulose. For each dose of PMA about 10^8 cells were available for extraction. The yields of poly(A) RNA were 27.3, 25.4, 40.6, and 81.3 μg per 10^8 cells in the case of cells treated with 0, 1, 10, and 100 ng of PMA, respectively. Thus, there was a clear-cut increase in amount of total cytoplasmic mRNA. In order to determine whether PMA caused a specific increase in the amount of EPA-specific RNA, xenopus oocytes were injected with 10 and 20 ng/oocyte of the poly(A)-RNA preparations, and PA was assayed on the medium harvested after 48 hr incubation. The results of this experiment are represented in Fig. 5. It can be seen that with increasing doses of PMA added to the melanoma cells, the poly-A RNA became indeed enriched in mRNA specific for EPA. From the lateral shift in the dose–response curves shown in the figure the increase in specificity induced by 100 ng/ml of PMA can be estimated to be about 6-fold. Taking into account the 3-fold increase in total poly(A) RNA per cell, one can estimate at 18-fold the increase in total EPA-specific mRNA content in cells treated for 6 hr with 100 ng/ml of PMA.

Serological characterization of activator produced in the presence of PMA. In order to verify that the PA produced after stimulation with PMA was of the same type as that produced by unstimulated cells (and not, e.g., of the urokinase type), aliquots of culture supernatants of both PMA-stimulated and unstimulated melanoma cells were incubated with increasing concentrations (0.1 to 1000 μg IgG/ml) of a highly specific, neutralizing antibody against EPA, and devoid of activity against urokinase. After incubation for 60 min at 37°C the mixture was assayed for enzymatic activity. For both supernatants the kinetics of neutralization were identical as shown in Fig. 6: 2.5 μg IgG/ml of the antibody reduced the enzymatic activity of 10 to 20 units/ml by 50% and 10 μg IgG/ml neutralized it completely.

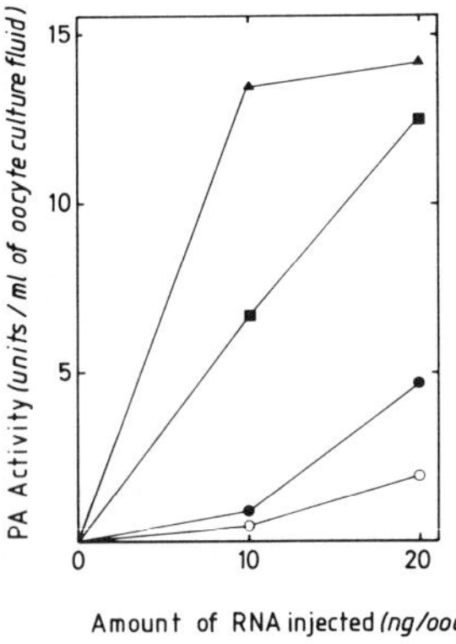

FIG. 5. Increased production of EPA-mRNA by Bowes melanoma cells after exposure to PMA. Confluent cultures were washed, refed with PMA at 0 (○), 1 (●), 10 (■), or 100 (▲) ng/ml in serum-free medium, incubated for 6 hr, and processed for mRNA extraction. Translation was tested by injection in oocytes. The oocyte culture fluid was harvested and assayed for EPA.

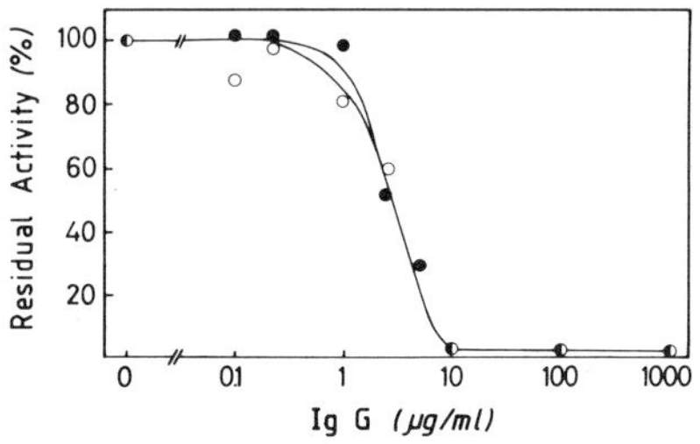

FIG. 6. Serological neutralization of EPA produced in Bowes melanoma cells. Diluted or undiluted aliquots of culture supernatants (10 to 200 units/ml) of both PMA-treated (●) and nontreated (○) cells were incubated with equal volumes of increasing concentrations (0.1 to 1000 µg IgG/ml) of a highly specific antibody against EPA. After incubation for 60 min at 37°C the mixture was assayed for enzymatic activity.

Additional evidence that no second type of protease, e.g., urokinase-like, was involved in the PMA-induced enhancement of plasminogen activator, came from analysis by electrophoresis and zymography of the product. As shown in Fig. 7 only a single band of enzyme activity was detectable in the culture supernatants and cell lysates from both control and PMA-treated cells. The activity migrated at a position that coincided with that of purified EPA and that differed from the position of urokinase.

Another control experiment consisted in adding PMA to the assay of EPA. This did not influence the assay results, indicating that the increases in EPA concentration noted in PMA-treated cultures was not due to a direct effect of PMA on the assay system.

Effect of PMA on cell-associated EPA. Increased EPA-mRNA levels and EPA release, as seen in the experiments described above, might be secondary to PMA-induced depletion of the preexisting cellular pool of EPA. Thus, if PMA would primarily act by enhancing externalization of cell-associated EPA, the cell could react with increased transcription and translation of EPA mRNA so as to replenish the EPA pool. In this case one would expect to see a decrease in the level of cell-associated EPA early after exposure of the cells to PMA. Figure 8 shows the results of an experiment done to test this possibility. Cell-associated EPA was measured before PMA treatment and after 3, 6, 15, 24, 36, and 48 hr of PMA treatment. At all time points the level of cell-associated EPA showed a dose-dependent increase.

Discussion. Many human tumor cell lines produce proteases which activate plasminogen. Most of these are of the urokinase type and various studies have shown that their production is increased by treatment with phorbol

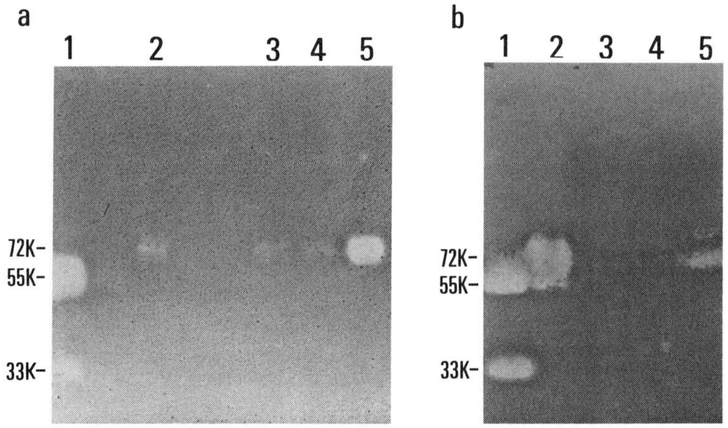

FIG. 7. Fibrin–plasminogen–agar zymogram of PA electrophoresed by SDS–polyacrylamide gel. After the appearance of the zones of fibrinolysis the indicator gel was stained and photographed. (a) Culture fluids: Lanes 1 and 2, human urokinase and purified EPA from Bowes melanoma cells as standards, respectively; Lanes 3, 4, and 5, nontreated, PMA-treated (10 ng/ml), and PMA-treated (100 ng/ml) for 24 hr, respectively. (b) Cell lysates: Lanes 1 and 2, human urokinase and purified EPA from Bowes melanoma cells as standards, respectively; Lanes 3, 4, and 5, nontreated, PMA-treated (10 ng/ml), and PMA-treated (100 ng/ml) for 24 hr, respectively.

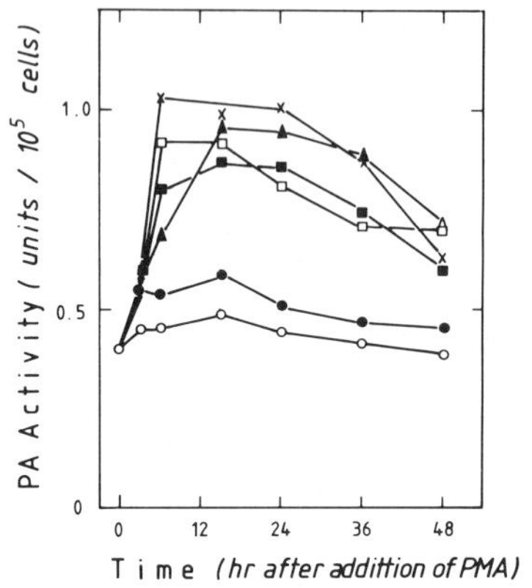

FIG. 8. Effect of increasing doses of PMA on the intracellular level of PA in Bowes melanoma cell cultures. Confluent cultures were washed, refed with serum-free medium containing PMA in final concentrations of 0 (○), 1 (●), 10 (■), 50 (□), 100 (▲), or 500 (×) ng/ml and incubated for various time intervals. After culture fluid was removed, cells were washed with PBS, and lysed by 0.2% solution of Triton X-100.

esters. The Bowes melanoma cell line studied here produces a different plasminogen activator called tissue type or extrinsic plasminogen activator (EPA) (18). We found that treatment with the phorbol ester PMA caused a distinct increase in the production of this EPA by Bowes melanoma cells. Under optimal conditions of dosage and time of exposure to PMA the production could be increased up to 13-fold.

The enhancing effect of PMA on production of extracellular EPA became apparent within 3 to 6 hr after its addition. Also, short incubation times (e.g., 3 hr) were sufficient to obtain full stimulation of EPA production similar to those seen in cultures exposed for 24 hr. This raises the possibility that continuous presence of PMA in or at the cells may not be required for full stimulation. However, PMA is known to firmly attach to the cells, and therefore extensive washing may still leave considerable quantities associated with the cells (43).

Spontaneous as well as PMA-enhanced production were blocked by pretreatment of the cells with a dose of 100 ng/ml of actinomycin D. The same dose also inhibited the synthesis of rapidly labeled RNA by 84%, suggesting that new mRNA synthesis is required for PMA to be able to enhance EPA synthesis. Additional evidence supporting an effect of PMA on transcription is that incubation of the cells for 6 hr with PMA at 100 ng/ml caused a 3-fold increase in total cellular poly(A^+) RNA and an 18-fold increase in EPA-specific mRNA. While this increase would amply explain the usual 6-fold increase in EPA production by the cells, it is not certain whether it is brought about by increase in synthesis of the mRNA or a decrease in breakdown. However, taken together with the results from the experiments with actinomycin D, our data are highly suggestive for an effect of PMA on the rate of transcription of EPA-specific mRNA. Direct measurements on EPA-mRNA synthesis will require the availability of specific DNA-probes (Opdenakker *et al.,* in preparation).

The question whether PMA acts primarily by enhancing externalization of preexisting intracellular enzyme was addressed by determining cell-associated enzyme at different times after exposure to PMA. At all times, cell-associated EPA was increased rather than decreased in PMA-treated cultures. Cell-associated EPA levels were increased, even when tested as early as 3 hr after initiation of the PMA-treatment, thus failing to support the view that increased EPA synthesis occurred as a result of depletion of the cellular pool. It remains possible, however, that a very early depletion, not detected by current techniques, preceded the increase in cell-associated EPA levels and served as the primary trigger for transcription enhancement.

In certain cell systems PMA has been shown to induce a plasminogen activator with a molecular weight (~50,000 Da) different from that of the plasminogen activator spontaneously produced (~75,000 Da) (9, 44). The two activators may be products of different genes or variants of the same gene product. In the latter case one would expect them to be serologically related. Christman *et al.* (9) have shown by immunoinhibition studies that in several hamster cell lines the two activators are serologically different, and that only one type was induced by PMA. EPA spontaneously produced by our Bowes melanoma cells has been purified to homogeneity and its molecular weight was estimated at 72,000 (16). Analysis by gel electrophoresis indicated that PMA did not induce plasminogen activator(s) with a different molecular weight. Also, the product released by PMA-treated cells was completely neutralizable by antibody specific for spontaneously produced EPA. Similarly the oocyte translation product of mRNA from PMA-treated melanoma cells was serologically characterizable as EPA (data not shown). Therefore, the possibility that enhanced production of EPA was due to induction of a second type of activator (e.g., an activator of the urokinase type) can be eliminated.

Various hypotheses have been formulated to explain the tumor-promoting effect of PMA. In particular, certain models for two-stage carcinogenesis are based on the assumption that the promotor modifies gene expression resulting in altered management of carcinogen (initiator)-induced lesions. Our studies provide supportive evidence that PMA can indeed affect transcription of certain genes. In the present study we have only studied expression of one gene, that of EPA. Work in progress in which mRNA from PMA-induced melanoma cells is being investigated by translation in cell-free systems, has already revealed that PMA induces production of several other mRNAs (34).

This work was supported by research contracts of the "Algemene Spaar en Lijfrentekas" and the "Geconcerteerde Onderzoeksacties." G.O. is supported by fellowship (Aspirant) of the Belgian Nationaal Fonds voor Wetenschappelijk Onderzoek. We thank Professor Dr. D. Collen (Center for Thrombosis and Vascular Research, Department of Medical Research, University of Leuven) for providing EPA-specific antibody and reagents for PA assay. The authors also thank Miss Christiane Callebaut for editorial help.

1. Diamond L, O'Brien TG, Baird WM. Tumor promoters and the mechanism of tumor promotion. Advan Cancer Res **32**:2–74, 1980.
2. Osborne R, Tashjian AH Jr. Tumor-promoting phorbol esters affect production of prolactin and growth hormone by rat pituitary cells. Endocrinology **108**:1164–1170, 1981.
3. Yuspa SH, Lichti U, Ben T, Patterson E, Hennings H, Slaga TJ, Colburn N, Kelsey W. Phorbol esters stimulate DNA synthesis and ornithine decarboxylase activity in mouse epidermal cell cultures. Nature (London) **262**:402–404, 1976.
4. Blumberg PM, Driedger PE, Rossow PW. Effect of a phorbol ester on a transformation-sensitive surface protein of chick fibroblasts. Nature (London) **264**:446–447, 1976.
5. Ohuchi K, Levine L. Stimulation of prostaglandin synthesis by tumor-promoting phorbol-12,13-diesters in canine kidney (MDCK) cells. J Biol Chem **253**:4783–4790, 1978.
6. Crutchley DJ, Conanan LB, Maynard JR. Induction of plasminogen activator and prostaglandin biosynthesis in HeLa cells by 12-*O*-tetradecanoylphorbol-13-acetate. Cancer Res **40**:849–852, 1980.
7. Yip YK, Pang RHL, Oppenheim JD, Nochbar MS, Henriksen D, Zerebeckyj-Eckhardt I, Vilcek J. Stimulation of human gamma (immune) interferon production by diterpene esters. Infect Immunol **34**:131–139, 1981.
8. Sando JJ, Hilfiker ML, Salomon DS, Farrar JJ. Specific receptors for phorbol esters in lymphoid cell populations: Role in enhanced production of T-cell growth factor. Proc Natl Acad Sci USA **78**:1189–1193, 1981.
9. Christman JK, Copp RP, Pedrinan L, Whalen CE. Specificity of response in hamster cells induced to produce plasminogen activator by the tumor promotor, 12-*O*-tetradecanoylphorbol-13-acetate. Cancer Res **38**:3854–3860, 1978.
10. Goldfarb RH, Quigley JP. Synergistic effect of tumor virus transformation and tumor promoter treatment on the production of plasminogen activator by chick embryo fibroblasts. Cancer Res **38**:4601–4609, 1978.
11. Goldfarb RH, Quigley JP. Purification of plasminogen activator from Rous sarcoma virus transformed chick embryo fibroblasts treated with the tumor promoter phorbol 12-myristate 13-acetate. Biochemistry **19**:5463–5471, 1980.
12. Jaken S, Gefen C, Black PH. Dexamethasone inhibition and phorbol myristate acetate stimulation of plasminogen activator in human embryonic lung cells. Biochem Biophys Res Commun **99**:379–384, 1981.
13. Jaken S, Black PH. Regulation of plasminogen activator in 3T3 cells: Effect of phorbol myristate acetate on subcellular distribution and molecular weight. J Cell Biol **90**:727–731, 1981.
14. Wigler M, Weinstein IB. Tumor promotor induces plasminogen activator. Nature (London) **259**:232–233, 1976.
15. Vassalli JD, Hamilton J, Reich E. Macrophage plasminogen activator: Induction by concanavalin A and phorbol myristate acetate. Cell **11**:695–705, 1977.
16. Wilson EL, Reich E. Modulation of plasminogen activator synthesis in chick embryo fibroblasts by cyclic nucleotides and phorbol myristate acetate. Cancer Res **39**:1579–1586, 1979.
17. Wilson EL, Becker MLB, Hoal EG, Dowdle EB. Molecular species of plasminogen activators secreted by normal and neoplasmic human cells. Cancer Res **40**:933–938, 1980.
18. Rijken DC, Collen D. Purification and characterization of the plasminogen activator secreted by human melanoma cells in culture. J Biol Chem **256**:7035–7041, 1981.

19. Beers WH, Strickland S, Reich E. Ovarian plasminogen activator: Relationship to ovulation and hormonal regulation. Cell **6**:387–394, 1975.
20. Strickland S, Reich E, Sherman MI. Plasminogen activator in early embryogenesis: Enzyme production by trophoblast and parietal endoderm. Cell **9**:231–240, 1976.
21. Unkeless JC, Gordon S, Reich E. Secretion of PA by stimulated macrophages. J Exp Med **139**:834–850, 1974.
22. Krystosek A, Seeds NW. Plasminogen activator release at the neuronal growth cone. Science **213**:1532–1534, 1981.
23. Ossowski L, Unkeless JC, Tobia A, Quigley JP, Rifkin DB, Reich E. An enzymatic function associated with transformation of fibroblasts by oncogenic viruses. J Exp Med **137**:112–126, 1973.
24. Rifkin DB, Loeb JN, Moore G, Reich E. Properties of plasminogen activators formed by neoplastic human cell cultures. J Exp Med **139**:1317–1328, 1974.
25. Unkeless J, Danø K, Kellerman GM, Reich E. Fibrinolysis associated with oncogenic transformation: Partial purification and characterization of the cell factor, a plasminogen activator. J Biol Chem. **249**:4295–4305, 1974.
26. Christman JK, Silagi S, Newcomb EW, Silverstein SC, Acs G. Correlated suppression by 5-bromodeoxyuridine of tumorigenicity and plasminogen activator in mouse melanoma cells. Proc Natl Acad Sci USA **72**:47–50, 1975.
27. Jones PA, Laug WE, Benedict WF. Fibrinolytic activity in a human fibrosarcoma cell line and evidence for the induction of plasminogen activator secretion during tumor formation. Cell **6**:245–252, 1975.
28. Laug WE, Jones PA, Benedict WF. Relationship between fibrinolysis of cultured cells and malignancy. J Natl Cancer Inst **54**:173–179, 1975.
29. Paranjpe MS, Eaton SA, Boone CW. Neoplasms produced from C3H/10T 1/2 cells attached to plastic plates; saturation density, anchorage dependence and serum requirement of in vitro lines correlated with growth aggressiveness in vivo. J Cell Physiol **96**:63–72, 1978.
30. Tucker WS, Kirsch WM, Martinez-Hernandez A, Fink LM. In vitro plasminogen activator activity in human brain tumors. Cancer Res **38**:297–302, 1978.
31. Markus G, Takita H, Camiolo SM, Corasanti JG, Evers JL, Hobika GH. Content and characterization of plasminogen activators in human lung tumors and normal lung tissue. Cancer Res **40**:841–848, 1980.
32. Adelman SF, Howett MK, Rapp F. Tumorigenicity of herpesvirus-transformed cells correlates with production of plasminogen activator. Mol Cell Biol **1**:408–417, 1981.
33. Wang BS, McLoughlin GA, Richie JP, Mannick JA. Correlation of the production of plasminogen activator with tumor metastasis in B16 mouse melanoma cell lines. Cancer Res **40**:288–292, 1980.
34. Opdenakker G, Ashino-Fuse H, Van Damme J, Billiau A, De Somer P. Effects of 12-*O*-tetradecanoyl-phorbol-13-acetate on the production of mRNAs for human tissue type plasminogen activator. Eur J Biochem **131**:481–487, 1983.
35. Hoylaerts M, Lijnen HR, Collen D. Studies on the mechanism of the antifibrinolytic action of tranexamic acid. Biochim Biophys Acta **673**:75–85, 1981.
36. Böhlen P, Stein S, Dairman W, Udenfriend S. Fluorometric assay of proteins in the nanogram range. Arch Biochem Biophys **155**:213–220, 1973.
37. Opdenakker G, Weening H, Collen D, Billiau A, De Somer P. Messenger RNA for human tissue plasminogen activator. Eur J Biochem **121**:269–274, 1982.
38. Aviv H, Leder P. Purification of biologically active globin messenger RNA by chromatography on oligothymidylic acid–cellulose. Proc Natl Acad Sci USA **69**:1408–1412, 1972.
39. Dumont JN. Oogenesis in *Xenopus laevis* (Daudin). I. Stages of oocyte development in laboratory maintained animals. J Morphol **136**:153–180, 1972.
40. Gurdon JB, Lane CD, Woodland HR, Marbaix G. Use of frog eggs and oocytes for the study of messenger RNA and its translation in living cells. Nature (London) **233**:177–182, 1971.
41. Evers JL, Patel J, Madeja JM, Schneider SL, Hobika GH, Camiolo SM, Markus G. Plasminogen activator activity and composition in human breast cancer. Cancer Res **42**:219–226, 1982.
42. Granelli-Piperno A, Reich E. A study of proteases and protease-inhibitory complexes in biological fluids. J Exp Med **148**:223–234, 1978.
43. Dicker P, Rozengurt E. Stimulation of DNA synthesis by transient exposure of cell cultures to TPA or polypeptide mitogens: Induction of competence or incomplete removal. J Cell Physiol **109**:99–109, 1981.
44. Jaken S, Black PH. Correlation between a specific molecular weight form of plasminogen activator and metabolic activity of 3T3 cells. J Cell Biol **90**:721–726, 1981.

Received October 31, 1983. P.S.E.B.M. 1984, Vol. 176.
Accepted February 22, 1984.

PROCEEDINGS OF THE SOCIETY FOR EXPERIMENTAL BIOLOGY AND MEDICINE **176**, 119–122 (1984)

Cooling Augments Platelet-Induced Contraction of Peripheral Arteries of the Dog (41850)

LARS ERIK LINDBLAD, JOHN T. SHEPHERD, AND PAUL M. VANHOUTTE

Department of Physiology and Biophysics, Mayo Clinic and Mayo Foundation, Rochester, Minnesota 55905

Abstract. The effect of cooling on platelet-induced contractions was studied. Rings of canine saphenous arteries were suspended for isometric tension recording in organ baths filled with aerated physiological salt solution. Norepinephrine, 5-hydroxytryptamine, and autologous aggregating platelets all caused contractions that were augmented by cooling the bath content from 37 to 24°C. These contractions were inhibited, in a concentration-dependent manner, by the serotonergic antagonist ketanserin. The $alpha_1$-adrenergic antagonist, prazosin, in concentrations causing progressive inhibition of contractions evoked by norepinephrine did not affect the response to either 5-hydroxytryptamine or platelets. Aggregating platelets were found to release 5-hydroxytryptamine in sufficient amounts to account for the observed contractions. Pretreatment of platelets with the cyclo-oxygenase inhibitor meclofenamate reduced the amount of thromboxane liberated by aggregating platelets but did not influence evoked contractions. These observations suggest that aggregating platelets cause contraction of the canine saphenous artery by releasing 5-hydroxytryptamine. They demonstrate that cooling markedly augments contractions of peripheral arterial smooth muscle caused by aggregating platelets.

Local cold enhances the constrictions of cutaneous vessels caused by norepinephrine released from adrenergic nerves or by circulating catecholamines; the action of other vasoactive agents, such as 5-hydroxytryptamine (serotonin) is also enhanced by cooling (1). Patients with Raynaud's phenomenon are characterized by prolonged constriction (spasm) of the digital arteries when exposed to a cold stimulation, particularly when they are emotionally upset. Platelets contain vasoconstrictor substances such as 5-hydroxytryptamine and thromboxane A_2. To judge from data obtained in isolated blood vessels, aggregating platelets can release these substances in amounts sufficient to cause sustained contraction of vascular smooth muscle (2, 3). Activation of platelets with subsequent release of vasoactive substances may be of pathogenic importance in patients with Raynaud's phenomenon (4–6). The present study was undertaken to determine the effect of local cold on platelet-induced contractions of peripheral arteries.

Materials and Methods. The experiments were performed on saphenous arteries taken from mongrel dogs of either sex (15–28 kg) anesthetized with sodium pentobarbital (30 mg/kg iv). The blood vessels were cut into rings (approximately 3 mm in length). The experiments were performed in organ chambers containing 25 ml of physiological salt solution (millimolar composition: NaCl, 118.3; KCl, 4.7; $MgSO_4$, 1.2; KH_2PO_4, 1.2; $CaCl_2$, 2.5; $NaHCO_3$, 25.0; calcium-EDTA, 0.026; glucose, 11.1) and aerated with a 95% O_2–5% CO_2 gas mixture. Each ring was suspended by two stainless-steel stirrups passed through the lumen. One stirrup was anchored inside the organ chamber and the other was connected to a force transducer for recording of isometric tension (7, 8). All preparations were progressively stretched to the optimal length for contraction by measuring the contractile response to electrical stimulation of the adrenergic nerves (9 V, 2 msec, 16 Hz, 10 sec) (7, 9, 10). For cooling experiments, the temperature of water flowing through a water jacket surrounding the chamber was altered, thereby lowering bath temperature from 37 to 24°C in approximately 1.5 min (11). Bath temperature was continuously monitored using a thermistor probe.

Platelet suspensions were prepared from autologous blood collected in modified acid-citrate–dextrose anticoagulant (12). Because of the combined presence of Ca^{2+} in the physiological salt solution and collagen in the arterial ring, spontaneous platelet aggregation occurred following addition of 375 μl of the

0037-9727/84 $1.50

suspension to the bath containing the arteries as evidenced by clearing of the initially turbid solution and the release of 5-hydroxytryptamine and thromboxane B_2. In some experiments, platelet suspensions were incubated with meclofenamate (1×10^{-5} *M*) for 30 min and washed once before addition to the organ chamber.

5-Hydroxytryptamine determinations. Samples of physiological salt solution containing aggregated platelets were withdrawn from the organ chamber following stabilization of the vessel response to aggregating platelets. To determine the amount of 5-hydroxytryptamine released, 2-ml aliquots of bath fluid were centrifuged (3000*g*, 10 min, 4°C) and the supernatant was frozen at −20°C until analysis. Aliquots of supernatant were adjusted to pH 6.1 and applied to columns of cation exchange resin (Amberlite CG 50, 200–400 mesh). The amine was eluted and then separated by reversed-phase high-pressure liquid chromatography (μ Bondapak C_{18} column) with electrochemical detection (13).

Thromboxane B_2 determinations. Two-milliliter aliquots of thawed supernatant, obtained as above, were brought to pH 3.5 with 1 *M* citric acid. Thromboxane B_2 was extracted twice with chloroform:methanol (2:1, 6 ml), and the organic solvents were evaporated to dryness in a 37°C water bath under a stream of nitrogen. One-hundred-microliter aliquots of standards and diluted samples were assayed by displacement of [^{3}H]thromboxane B_2 from thromboxane B_2-antiserum in a total incubation volume of 300 μl at 4°C. The reaction was stopped after 2 hr by addition of a 1 ml solution of dextran-coated charcoal. After centrifugation (3000*g*, 5 min, 4°C), the supernatant containing the antibody-bound [^{3}H]thromboxane B_2 fraction was counted in a scintillation counter, and the concentration of thromboxane B_2 was estimated by comparison with a standard curve (14).

Drugs. The following pharmacological agents were used: 5-hydroxytryptamine creatinine sulfate, norepinephrine bitartrate (Sigma), ketanserin bitartrate (Janssen), prazosin hydrochloride (Pfizer), sodium meclofenamate (Parke-Davis), [^{3}H]thromboxane B_2 (New England Nuclear), and thromboxane B_2-antiserum (Seragen).

Prazosin was dissolved in 100 μl of dimethyl sulfoxide before addition to distilled water to make the stock solution. All other drugs were dissolved in distilled water. Concentration of drugs are expressed as final molar (*M*) bath concentration. Antagonists were added to the bath at least 20 min before determining their effect.

Calculations and statistical analysis. In each experimental group the number of rings equals the number of dogs. In all experiments involving repeated exposures to an agonist, control preparations obtained from the same vessel were studied in parallel to correct for changes in sensitivity with time.

When exposed to the agonists many of the rings showed a biphasic response—an initial peak followed by a smaller stable response. For calculations only the stable responses were used. The data are expressed as means ± SEM. Statistical analysis was performed using Student's *t* test for paired observations (two-tailed). Differences were considered to be significant if *P* values were less than 0.05.

Results. Platelets were added to the bath solutions (1.1×10^7 to 3.3×10^7/ml). Contractions of similar magnitude were obtained with aggregating platelets, exogenous 5-hydroxytryptamine (1×10^{-7} to 1×10^{-6} *M*) and norepinephrine (1×10^{-6} to 1×10^{-5} *M*) in control solution. The experiments were then repeated in the presence of increasing concentrations of prazosin and ketanserin (1×10^{-8} to 1×10^{-6} *M*). The contractions to norepinephrine were depressed in a concentration dependent fashion by both ketanserin and prazosin. Ketanserin but not prazosin caused a concentration-dependent depression of contractions to both platelets and 5-hydroxytryptamine (Fig. 1).

Following addition of platelet suspension ($1.9 \pm 0.6 \times 10^7$/ml, $N = 6$) to the organ chambers, completion of the platelet aggregation and stabilization of the vessel response the concentration of 5-hydroxytryptamine in the solution was $1.9 \pm 0.4 \times 10^{-7}$ *M*. Pretreatment of platelets with meclofenamate (1×10^{-5} *M*) for 30 min did not significantly influence contractions to aggregating platelets (5.3 ± 1.3 and 5.6 ± 1.5 g, with untreated and treated platelets, respectively; $N = 6$). The concentration of thromboxane B_2 was less in bath fluid withdrawn from organ chambers with meclofenamate incubated platelets than

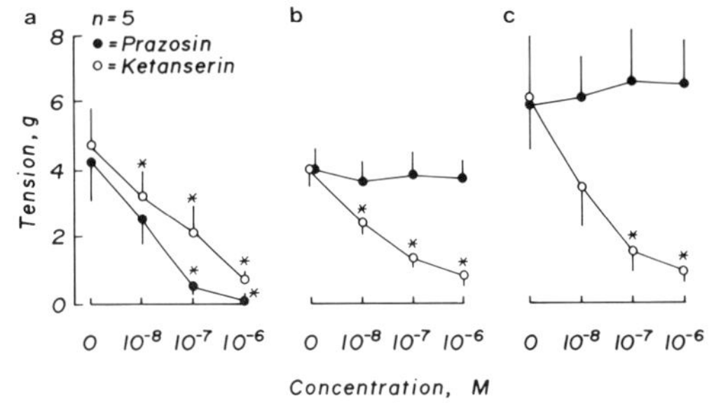

FIG. 1. Effect of increasing concentrations (1×10^{-8} to 1×10^{-6} *M*) of ketanserin and prazosin, respectively, on contractions evoked by (a) norepinephrine (1×10^{-6} to 1×10^{-5} *M*); (b) 5-hydroxytryptamine (1×10^{-7} to 1×10^{-6} *M*); and (c) aggregating platelets (1.1×10^7/ml to 3.3×10^7/ml). Asterisks denote a significant difference from control (*N* = 5).

in solution obtained from chambers where untreated platelets had been used ($4.5 \pm 1.3 \times 10^{-9}$ *M* and $1.2 \pm 0.3 \times 10^{-9}$ *M*, respectively; *N* = 4).

Cooling from 37 to 24°C had no significant effect on resting tension of the vessels (*N* = 6). Rings were contracted to comparable tension levels using exogenous norepinephrine (1×10^{-6} *M*), 5-hydroxytryptamine (1×10^{-7} to 3×10^{-7} *M*) and autologous aggregating platelets ($2.1 \pm 0.7 \times 10^7$/ml). After stabilization of the vessel response cooling from 37 to 24°C caused a similar augmentation of the contractions caused by norepinephrine, 5-hydroxytryptamine and aggregating platelets (Fig. 2). In rings (*N* = 6) contracted with 20 or 40 m*M* KCl, cooling caused significant decreases in tension (from 4.6 ± 0.8 to 1.7 ± 0.3 and 11.6 ± 1.8 to 5.3 ± 0.9 g, respectively).

Discussion. The present study confirms that when autologous platelets are added to physiological salt solution in organ chambers, the resulting aggregation causes the release of both 5-hydroxytryptamine and thromboxane (e.g., (2, 3)). The contraction of the canine saphenous artery to aggregating platelets is mediated mainly by 5-hydroxytryptamine. This conclusion is based on the observation that (a) inhibition of cyclo-oxygenase, causing a decreased release of thromboxane, did not affect the contractile response evoked by platelets; and (b) the serotonergic antagonist ketanserin, antagonized the platelet-induced contractions. Although the present study confirms that ketanserin also inhibits alpha$_1$-adrenoceptor activation (e.g., (15–18)), this is not likely to play a role in the antagonism of the platelet-evoked response, as the selective alpha$_1$-adrenergic antagonist prazosin was without effect.

As in other cutaneous vessels such as saphenous veins (see (1)) cooling greatly augmented the contractile response to exogenous norepinephrine and 5-hydroxytryptamine but reduces that to depolarizing solution (19, 20). Previous work in the saphenous vein of the dog has demonstrated that moderate cooling causes an instantaneous increase in the affinity of the postjunctional alpha-adrenoceptors for norepinephrine (11). The comparison between the effect of cooling on responses to norepinephrine and 5-hydroxytryptamine suggests that cooling affects the response to both monoamines in a comparable fashion in the saphenous artery. The present study demonstrates that, despite the possible inhibitory effect that cooling may have on the aggregation-release reaction (21), the increased responsiveness of the smooth muscle cells allows for a markedly augmented response to platelets at the lower temperature tested.

Activation of platelets has been reported in patients with peripheral vascular disease characterized by cold-induced vasospasm. These conditions include Raynaud's disease (4–6) as

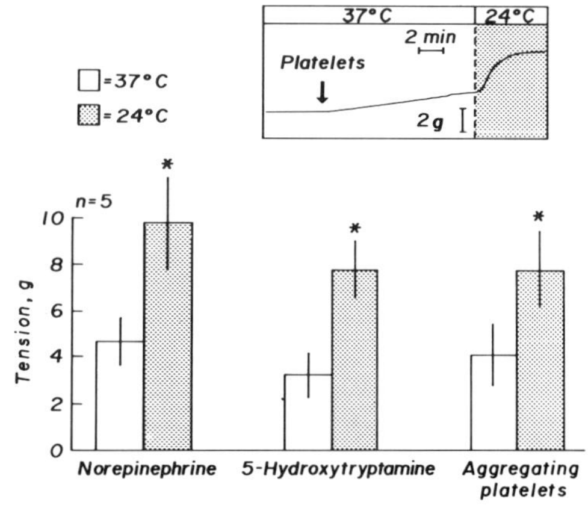

FIG. 2. Contractile tension at 37 and 24°C evoked by (a) norepinephrine (1×10^{-6} *M*); (b) 5-hydroxytryptamine (1×10^{-7} to 3×10^{-7} *M*); and (c) aggregating platelets ($2.1 \pm 0.7 \times 10^7$/ml). Asterisks denote significant difference between values and 37 and 24°C (*N* = 5).

well as Raynaud's phenomenon induced by use of vibrating tools (4). The present observations on canine cutaneous arteries suggest that the cold-induced augmentation of the contractile response to aggregating platelets, mediated by released 5-hydroxytryptamine may be of importance *in vivo.* This would help explain the favorable therapeutic effect of ketanserin in patients with Raynaud's phenomenon (22).

The authors thank Dr. G. M. Tyce for determination of 5-hydroxytryptamine and Dr. J. C. Romero for measurements of thromboxane. We also thank Mr. R. R. Lorenz for preparing the illustrations and Mrs. J. Beckman for excellent secretarial assistance. Supported in part by NIH Grant HL 05883 and the Swedish Work Environmental Fund.

---

1. Vanhoutte PM. Physical factors of regulation. In: Bohr DF, *et al,* eds. Handbook of Physiology. Baltimore, Williams & Wilkins, Sec 2, Vol 2:p447, 1980.
2. De Clerck F, Van Nueten JM. Platelet-mediated vascular contractions: Inhibition of the serotonergic component by ketanserin. Thromb Res **27**:713–727, 1982.
3. Cohen RA, Shepherd JT, Vanhoutte PM. Inhibitory role of the endothelium in the response of isolated coronary arteries to platelets. Science **221**:273–274, 1983.
4. Blunt RJ, George AJ, Hurlow RA, Strachan CJL, Stuart J. Hyperviscosity and thrombotic changes in idiopathic and secondary Raynaud's syndrome. Brit J Haematol **45**:651–658, 1980.
5. Zahavi J, Hamilton WAP, O'Reilly MJG, Leyton J, Cotton LT, Kakkar VV. Plasma exchange and platelet function in Raynaud's phenomenon. Thromb Res **19**:85–93, 1980.
6. Kallenberg CGM, Vellenga E, Wouda AA, Hauwthe T. Platelet activation, fibrinolytic activity and circulating immune complexes in Raynaud's phenomenon. J Rheumatol **9**:878–884, 1982.
7. De Mey J, Vanhoutte PM. Interaction between Na^+,K^+ exchanges and the direct inhibitory effect of acetylcholine on canine femoral arteries. Circ Res **46**:826–836, 1980.
8. De Mey J, Vanhoutte PM. Uneven distribution of postjunctional $alpha_1$ and $alpha_2$-like adrenoceptors in canine arterial and venous smooth muscle. Circ Res **48**:875–884, 1981.
9. Vanhoutte P, Clement D, Leusen I. The reactivity of isolated veins to electrical stimulation. Arch Int Physiol Biochem **75**:641–657, 1967.
10. Vanhoutte P, Leusen I. The reactivity of isolated venous preparations to electric stimulation. Pfluegers Arch **306**:341–353, 1969.
11. Janssens WJ, Vanhoutte PM. Instantaneous changes of alpha-adrenoceptor affinity caused by moderate cooling in canine cutaneous veins. Amer J Physiol **234**:H330–H337, 1978.
12. Dewanjee M, Rao SA, Didisheim P. Indium-111 tropolone, a new high-affinity platelet label: Preparation and evaluation of labelling parameters. J Nucl Med **22**:981–987, 1981.
13. Tyce GM, Yaksh TL. Monoamine release from cat spinal cord by somatic stimuli: an intrinsic modulatory system. J Physiol **314**:513–529, 1981.
14. Strand JC, Edwards BS, Anderson ME, Romero JC, Knox FG. Effect of imidazole on renal function in unilateral ureteral obstructed rat kidneys. Amer J Physiol **240**:F508–F514, 1981.
15. Van Nueten JM, Janssen PA, Van Beek J, Xhoneux R, Verbeuren TJ, Vanhoutte PM. Vascular effects of ketanserin (R 41 468), a novel antagonist of $5\text{-}HT_2$ serotonergic receptors. J Pharmacol Exp Ther **218**:217–230, 1981.
16. Van Nueten JM, Leysen JE, Schuurkes JAJ, Vanhoutte PM. Ketanserin: A selective antagonist of $5\text{-}HT_2$ serotoninergic receptors. Lancet Feb 5, 297–298, 1983.
17. Fozard JR. Mechanism of the hypotensive effect of ketanserin. J Cardiovasc Pharmacol **4**:829–838, 1982.
18. Kalkman HO, Timmermans PBWM, van Zwieten PA. Characterization of the antihypertensive properties of ketanserin (R41468) in rats. J Pharmacol Exp Ther **222**:227–231, 1982.
19. Vanhoutte PM, Shepherd JT. Effect of temperature on reactivity of isolated cutaneous veins of the dog. Amer J Physiol **218**:187–190, 1970.
20. Rusch NJ, Shepherd JT, Vanhoutte PM. The effect of profound cooling on adrenergic neurotransmission in canine cutaneous veins. J Physiol (London) **311**:57–65, 1981.
21. Sixma JJ. Methods for platelet aggregation. In: Triplett DA, ed. Platelet Function, Laboratory Evaluation and Clinical Application. Chicago, Amer Soc Clin Pathol, p87, 1978.
22. Stranden E, Roald OK, Krogh U. Treatment of Raynaud's phenomenon with the $5\text{-}HT_2$ receptor antagonist ketanserin. Brit Med J **285**:1069–1071, 1982.

Received October 4, 1983. P.S.E.B.M. 1984, Vol. 176.
Accepted February 21, 1984.

PROCEEDINGS OF THE SOCIETY FOR EXPERIMENTAL BIOLOGY AND MEDICINE **176**, 123–131 (1984)

Effects of Rat Atrial Extract on Sodium Transport and Blood Pressure in the Rat[1,2] (41851)

MOTILAL B. PAMNANI, DAVID L. CLOUGH, JING S. CHEN, WILLIAM T. LINK, AND FRANCIS J. HADDY

Department of Physiology, Uniformed Services University of the Health Sciences, 4301 Jones Bridge Road, Bethesda, Maryland 20814

Abstract. Atrial cardiocytes contain specific atrial granules (SAGs) which are the storage site of atrial natriuretic factor (ANF). The purpose of the present study was to determine whether ANF produces natriuresis by inhibiting Na^+-K^+ pump activity and whether this factor is similar to the humoral sodium transport inhibiting factor (HSTIF) previously demonstrated in acutely volume expanded animals and humans as well as in experimental and human essential hypertension. Our results indicate that, in contrast to the HSTIF, ANF does not inhibit membrane Na^+,K^+-ATPase, vascular smooth muscle cell Na^+-K^+ pump activity, or sodium transport in the toad bladder. Intravenous infusion of ANF in the bilaterally nephrectomized, hexamethonium-treated rat produces only a small transient pressor response, probably due to potentiation of endogenous norepinephrine. These findings strongly suggest that the ANF is not the same as the HSTIF detected on acute volume expansion and in some forms of hypertension. They also suggest that the diuretic and natriuretic effects of ANF are due to mechanism(s) other than blood pressure elevation and inhibition of Na^+-K^+ pump activity.

Mammalian atrial myocytes contain specific atrial granules (SAGs) (1–3) and the number of these SAGs is affected by water and electrolyte balance (4–6). SAGs are absent in ventricular myocytes and intravenous infusion of rat atrial, but not ventricular, extract into rats produces a rapid and potent diuretic and natriuretic response (7, 8). Tissue fractionation studies suggest that SAGs are the storage site of ANF (9, 10). Similar diuretic and natriuretic effects of atrial extracts from various other mammalian species have also been demonstrated (11, 12). The mechanism of action of ANF is unknown.

Plasma from either acutely volume expanded animals or animals with low-renin, volume-dependent hypertension has been shown to contain HSTIF which inhibits vascular Na^+-K^+ pump activity (13, 14), short circuit current in the toad bladder (15–17), and renal Na^+,K^+-ATPase activity (18–20). This factor(s) also has vasopressor activity and sensitizes small vessels to vasoactive agents (21, 22). It has, therefore, been proposed that inhibition of Na^+-K^+ pump activity by humoral sodium transport inhibiting factor (HSTIF) may play a role in the elevation of total peripheral resistance associated with hypertension (14, 23) and may also be responsible for the natriuresis and diuresis associated with acute volume expansion (24, 25). The chemical structure of HSTIF is unknown.

The question, therefore, arises as to whether the ANF is similar or identical to the HSTIF. If these factors are one and the same, then the ANF should have transport and hemodynamic effects similar to those of HSTIF. We, therefore, examined the effects of rat atrial extracts having natriuretic and diuretic activity on: (i) vascular Na^+-K^+ pump activity, (ii) renal and myocardial Na^+,K^+-ATPase activities, and (iii) Na transport in the toad bladder. We also examined the effect of these extracts on blood pressure in rats.

Methods. Atrial and ventricular extracts were used in four types of experiments to determine their effects on: (i) urine flow and sodium excretion in the rat, (ii) vascular Na^+-K^+ pump activity and renal and myocardial Na^+,K^+-ATPase activities, (iii) sodium

[1] Supported by U.S. Public Health Research Grant HL-21525 from the National Heart, Lung, and Blood Institute and Uniformed Services University Grants C07607, C07604, and C07662.

[2] Preliminary reports appeared in *Physiologist* **24**:59, 1981, and in *Physiologist* **25**:330, 1982.

0037-9727/84 $1.50

and water transport in the toad bladder, and (iv) blood pressure in the rat.

Preparation of atrial and ventricular extracts. Male Wistar rats weighing between 250 and 300 g with documented normotension were used in this study. Rats were maintained on normal rat chow (Agway, Inc., 0.42% sodium) and drank tap water *ad libitum* until sacrificed, for the study, by decapitation. Each atrial and each ventricular extract was prepared from pooled atria and pooled ventricles obtained from 5 to 10 rats (atrial tissue from each rat weighed 80–100 mg). The hearts were excised and immediately placed in cold phosphate-buffered saline (PBS, 10 m*M* sodium phosphate in 0.9% NaCl, pH 7.4). Atria (with atrial appendages) and ventricular apices were excised and pooled separately in PBS (100 mg myocardial tissue/ml of PBS). For ATPase studies the tissue extracts were prepared in distilled water (diuretic and natriuretic activities of atrial extracts prepared in PBS and distilled water were the same). The tissues were homogenized with a polytron homogenizer (PT-10 ST Probe, Brinkman Instruments) at the number 8 setting for 30 sec. The homogenates were boiled at 100°C for 5 min and then centrifuged at 36,000*g* (Sorval RC-5 Refrigerated Centrifuge) for 90 min and supernates of boiled atrial extract (SA) and supernates of boiled ventricular extract (SV) were removed and stored at −70°C until assayed.

I. Diuretic and natriuretic activity. Diuretic and natriuretic activities were assayed using the method of deBold *et al.* (7). Male Wistar rats (250–300 g) with documented normotension were used for the assay. The animal was anesthetized with sodium pentobarbital, 50 mg/kg. The external jugular vein was cannulated for intravenous infusions and the urinary bladder was cannulated for collection of urine. Normal saline at 37°C was infused iv at the rate of 0.15 to 0.21 ml/min for 20 min and then at the slower rate of 0.02 ml/min for 60 min. Control urine output was calculated from the urine collected during the last 30 min of the slow infusion period. At the end of the slow infusion period, SA was infused at the rate of 0.5 ml for 4 min. Saline infusion at the slow rate of 0.02 ml/min was then restarted. Urine was collected during SA infusion and for an additional 36 min following completion of SA infusion. A control Wistar rat similarly prepared underwent exactly the same assay procedure except that the animal was infused with SV rather than SA.

II. Effects on Na^+-K^+ pump and membrane Na^+,K^+-ATPase activities. (a) Effect on vascular Na^+-K^+ pump activity. We used our standard technique to study the effect of SA on ouabain-sensitive radioactive rubidium (^{86}Rb) uptake, a measure of Na^+-K^+ pump activity, by rat tail arteries (14). Briefly, tail arteries were excised from pentobarbital anesthetized normotensive rats. The arteries were quickly cleaned of adventitia and placed in Krebs–Henseleit solution. Each artery was divided in half. One-half was preincubated at room temperature in SA and the other half in SV. After 2 hr of preincubation, ouabain-sensitive and insensitive ^{86}Rb uptakes were measured as previously described for boiled plasma supernates, i.e., without sodium preloading in order to examine steady state pump activity (14).

(b) Effects on myocardial and renal Na^+, K^+-ATPase activities. Male Wistar rats weighing between 200 and 250 g were anesthetized with Na pentobarbital (75 mg/kg, ip) and their hearts and both kidneys were excised and rinsed in a cold solution (0°C on ice) containing 5 m*M* ethylenediaminetetraacetic acid (EDTA), 0.25 *M* sucrose, and 5 m*M* histidine-HCl (pH 7.4). The atria, right ventricles and large arteries and veins were removed from the heart and microsomes were prepared from the left ventricle including the septum. Renal arteries, veins, papillae, and capsules were removed from the kidneys, and after midsagittal bisection, the cortex was dissected from the medulla and microsomes were prepared from the cortex by the same method used for the left ventricles. The tissues were generally used immediately but were occasionally frozen in the rinsing solution (−40°C) for short periods of time (less than 1 week).

Microsomal fractions were prepared from the left ventricle (and kidney cortex) as described previously (26). Briefly, the left ventricle or both cortexes were homogenized (motor-driven Teflon pestle) in approximately 10 vol of a cold buffered solution containing 0.15% deoxycholate. The homogenate was centrifuged (Sorvall RC 5 centrifuge, SM-24 rotor) at 1100*g* for 10 min and 12,300*g* for 20 min to remove the nuclear and mitochondrial fractions and the supernate was centrifuged at 49,000g for 1 hr to obtain the microsomal fraction. The microsomal fraction was resuspended in a cold buffered solution containing 1 *M* NaI and was stirred repeatedly for 1 hr on ice. It was then recovered by a final centrifugation at 49,000g for 1 hr, resuspended in 10 m*M* imidazole-HCl (pH 7.4), and frozen until used (not more than 2 weeks).

Total ATPase activity was assayed in duplicate by measuring the amount of inorganic phosphate (P_i) liberated from ATP (Boehringer Mannheim Biochemicals) during incubation of microsomes for 1 hr at 37°C in 1 ml of a medium containing (m*M*): 120 NaCl, 10 KCl, 2.5 $MgCl_2$, 2 Na_2ATP, 0.5 ethylene glycol bis(aminoethyl ether) *N,N'*-tetraacetic acid (EGTA), 40 Tris–HCl (pH 7.5), and 0, 0.05, 0.15, or 0.35 ml SA or SV. Mg^{2+}-ATPase activity was assayed under similar conditions except that KCl was replaced by 1 m*M* ouabain. Na^+,K^+-ATPase activity was calculated, in the presence or absence of SA or SV by subtracting Mg^{2+}-ATPase from total ATPase activity. Any contaminant P_i contributed by the supernates was therefore subtracted along with Mg^{2+}-ATPase activity. In preliminary studies we verified that the supernates did not affect the linearity of the P_i assay. P_i was assayed by the method of Fiske and SubbaRow (27) and protein was assayed by the method of Lowry *et al.* (28). Na^+,K^+-ATPase activities were expressed as fractional activities (FA) and were obtained by dividing the activity in the presence of supernate by the control activity in the absence of supernate.

III. Effects on Na^+ and water transport in the toad bladder. Hemibladders of the toad were prepared and mounted as sacs by the methods previously described by Chen and Walser (29). In each experiment, both control and experimental bladders were bathed on both sides with phosphate buffered sulfate Ringer's solution (PR) containing (m*M*): 55 Na_2SO_4, 1 $CaSO_4$, 1 $MgSO_4$, 3 K_2SO_4, 2.4 Na_2HPO_4, 0.6 NaH_2PO_4. The initial fluid volumes in the mucosal and serosal baths were 15 and 50 ml, respectively. Both bathing media were vigorously stirred. All experiments were performed at room temperature (22–25°C).

After equilibration for 60–90 min under open circuit conditions, the bladders were continuously short-circuited throughout the experiment. When short circuit current (SCC) in both bladders became almost steady, electrical parameters in each bladder were measured as previously described (30). SA was then added to both sides of the experimental bladder, with a bath volume ratio of SA to PR equal to 0.045, and SV was added to both sides of the control bladder in the same manner. Electrical parameters in each bladder were again measured when a maximal change in SCC was observed approximately 5–10 min after the addition of either supernate. In order to assess the effect of SA or SV on passive membrane permeability of the toad bladder, SCC was eliminated by ouabain (2 m*M*).

In some experiments, the effects of SA and SV on unidirectional water fluxes across the toad bladder were also studied under short circuit conditions. The method for measuring unidirectional water flux using a tracer was slightly modified from one previously described for measuring nonelectrolyte flux (31). When SCC in the toad bladder became almost steady, about 0.1 μCi/ml of $[^3H]H_2O$ was added to either the mucosal or serosal bathing medium. Measurement of unidirectional water flux began after about 10 min of mixing. Because the bladder is highly permeable to water, three 1-ml samples were withdrawn simultaneously from both bathing media at 8- to 12-min intervals. SA or SV was then added to both sides of the bladder as described above. When the inhibitory action of the supernate was complete and a SCC was again observed, three 1-ml samples were again withdrawn from both bathing media. Each 1-ml sample was then counted in 10 ml of Aquasol-2 (New England Nuclear) using a liquid scintillation counter. The cumulative counts obtained at each interval were expressed as the ratio of the counts per minute of the sample obtained from the "cold bath" to that of the sample simultaneously withdrawn from the "hot bath" to which the isotope had been added. Unidirectional water flux was obtained with a computer program ("FLUX") which calculated linear regression of cumulative counts crossing the membrane (corrected for diminishing bath volume at each interval) against time. Flux was expressed as ml/hr/mg of wet weight. The wet weight of the toad bladder was obtained after blotting on filter paper at the conclusion of each experiment.

IV. Effect on blood pressure. Normal Wistar rats (250–350 g) with documented normotension were bilaterally nephrectomized (2NX) and then used for bioassay 24 hr later. Under pentobarbital anesthesia (50 mg/kg, ip), the common carotid artery was cannulated (PE 50) for the measurement of arterial pressure. The external jugular vein was cannulated for injection of drugs and infusion of SA or SV. After a stabilization period of 20 min, ganglion blockade was produced by injection of hexamethonium chloride (HEX); doses of 1 mg, usually three or four doses, were given until there was no further fall in the blood pressure. When the blood pressure was steady, the pressor effects of 4, 5, 10, and 50 ng of norepinephrine (NE) were recorded. SA or SV was then infused intravenously at the rate of 0.2 ml/min for 10 min (same volume of SA which produced a pronounced diuretic and natriuretic effect) and its effect on blood pressure recorded. At the end of the infusion period, the NE dose–response relationship was again determined.

In another series of experiments, 10 ng NE were mixed with 0.05, 0.1, and 0.15 ml of SA or SV. The mixtures were then injected intravenously in 2NX, HEX-treated rats.

Since the results of these experiments suggested that SA potentiates the pressor effect of NE, we repeated the infusions of SA and SV in autonomically blocked (phentolamine 1 mg in 50 μl saline, propranolol 2 mg in 50 μl saline, and atropine 1 mg in 50 μl saline given separately at 3-min intervals) (AB) rats.

Student's t test was used to compare the diuretic, natriuretic, and the pressor activities of SA and SV. The paired t test was used to compare the effects of SA and SV on ^{86}Rb uptakes, myocardial and renal Na^+,K^+-ATPase, SCC, and other parameters measured in the toad bladder. Analysis of variance and Duncan's multiple range test were used to determine the significance of differences in the dose–response studies. In all these comparisons, $P < 0.05$ was considered to be a significant difference.

Results. SA produced a prompt (within 2 to 4 min) and brisk diuresis and natriuresis (Fig. 1). Urine excretion increased 10-fold and sodium excretion increased 25-fold (from 0.28 to 7.17 μeq/min). The diuretic and natriuretic responses were complete in about 40 min. SV was essentially without effect.

Ouabain-sensitive ^{86}Rb uptake (which reflects Na^+-K^+ pump activity) by normal tail arteries incubated in SA was not different from that by arteries incubated in SV (Fig. 2). This was also the case for ouabain-insensitive ^{86}Rb uptake (which in part reflects passive penetration of ^{86}Rb into cells which depends upon permeability, surface area and concentration gradient).

Figure 3a shows cardiac Na^+,K^+-ATPase (FAs) as a function of the volume of SA and SV in 1 ml of assay medium. The values were not different at 0.05 or 0.15 ml. However, at 0.35 ml the FA with SV was significantly less than that with SA. Figure 3b shows that the renal Na^+,K^+-ATPase FAs observed in the presence of SA and SV were not significantly different at any of the three volumes tested.

Addition of SA or SV to the toad bladder produced an immediate decrease in SCC, reaching a minimum in about 6 min, but the changes were not significantly different (Fig. 4a). This was also the case for membrane potential (ψ_{sp}), measured under open circuit conditions, and total tissue conductance (g_t), calculated as SCC/ψ_{sp} (Figs. 4b, c). Passive

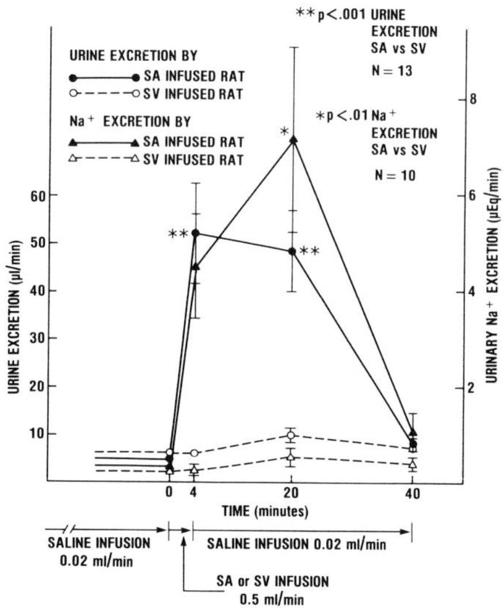

FIG. 1. Urine (circles) and urinary sodium (triangles) excretion rates by assay rats before, during and following intravenous infusion of atrial supernate (SA, closed symbols) and ventricular supernate (SV, open symbols).

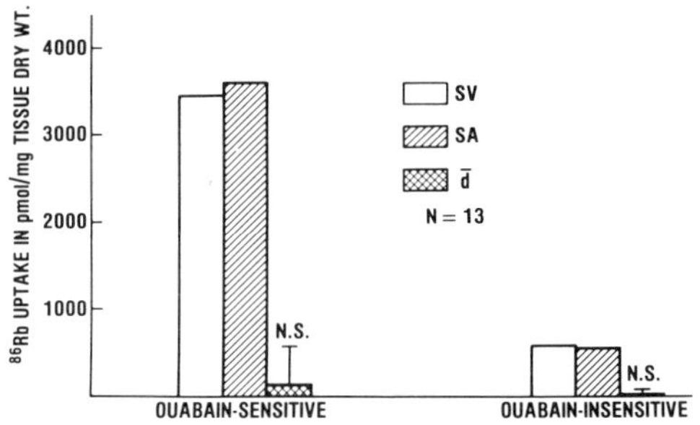

FIG. 2. Ouabain-sensitive and insensitive ^{86}Rb uptakes by tail arteries from normal untouched rats incubated in atrial supernate (SA) and ventricular supernate (SV). $\bar{d}$ Represents mean and SE of the differences.

membrane conductance (g_p), i.e., the ouabain-insensitive conductance measured after elimination of SCC with 2 m*M* ouabain, was not different in SA- and SV-treated bladders (not shown) and not different from the value previously found in bladders bathed in the same Ringer's solution. Ouabain-sensitive conductance (g_a), calculated as the difference between g_t and g_p, decreased on addition of SA or SV but again the changes were not different (Fig. 4d). The E_{Na} of the sodium pump, calculated as SCC/g_a, was essentially unaffected by treatment with SA or SV (Fig. 4e). Both SA and SV reduced serosal-to-mucosal water flux by about 32% and increased mucosal-to-serosal water flux by about 20 to 24% (Table I).

Relative to infusion of SV, infusion of SA into 2NX, HEX-treated rats increased mean arterial pressure by about 15% ($P < 0.005$) (Fig. 5). However, the effect was transient, disappearing by the fourth minute of infusion. Pressor responses to various doses of NE were essentially the same before and following SA or SV infusion (Fig. 6) except that 50 ng of NE following SV infusion produced significantly less pressor response than 50 ng of NE before SV infusion. However, when the NE–extract mixtures were injected, the mixtures containing SA produced greater responses than the mixtures containing SV (Fig. 7). The pressor responses to the SA–NE mixtures appeared to be dose dependent (Fig. 7). Infusion of SA into 2NX rats with AB (Fig. 5) failed to produce the transient pressor effect observed in 2NX rats treated with HEX (Fig. 5).

Discussion. These studies show that, although SA has potent natriuretic and diuretic activities and SV does not, the effects of SA on cardiac and renal Na^+,K^+-ATPase activities, rat tail artery Na^+-K^+ pump activity, and toad bladder sodium transport do not differ from those of SV. SA does not raise blood pressure even in animals whose buffering mechanisms have been blocked. These findings indicate that ANF is different from the HSTIF seen on acute volume expansion and in low-renin hypertension and that it probably causes natriuresis and diuresis by mechanisms other than pressure elevation and Na^+,K^+-ATPase inhibition.

deBold *et al.* (7) first reported the potent natriuretic and diuretic activities of atrial extract. Sonnenberg *et al.* (32) showed that administration of probenicid reduces but does not prevent the diuretic responses to atrial extract. Since probenicid blocks the organic acid transport system in the proximal tubule, the authors concluded that probenicid reduces the delivery of ANF to the distal tubules where ANF probably acts (8, 33). Its mechanism of action at this site is unknown.

In our experiments, SA relative to SV failed to inhibit Na^+,K^+-ATPase activity in microsomes prepared from myocardium and kidney cortex. Thibault *et al.* (34) also found that

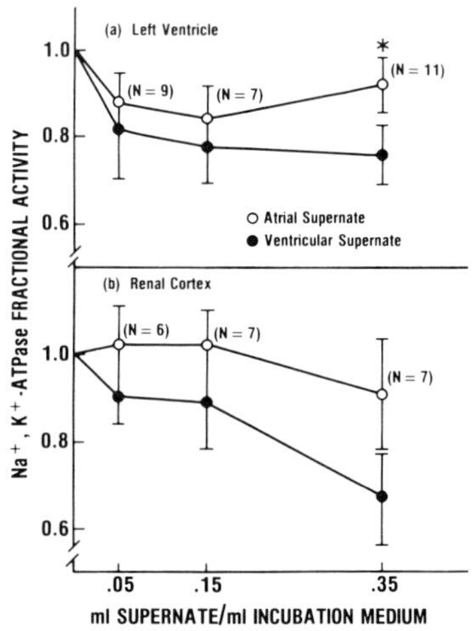

FIG. 3. Effects of atrial and ventricular supernates on Na^+,K^+-ATPase activities of microsomes from left ventricle (a) and renal cortex (b). Vertical bars represent SE. * Indicates significant difference ($P < 0.05$) between the effects of atrial (0.35 ml) and ventricular (0.35 ml) extracts.

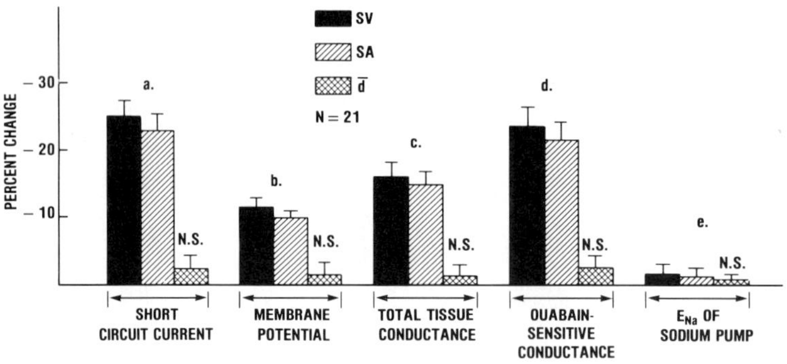

FIG. 4. Effects of atrial supernate (SA) and ventricular supernate (SV) on various parameters measured in the toad bladder. $\bar{d}$ Represents mean and SE of the differences.

atrial extract does not inhibit renal Na^+,K^+-ATPase activity. Furthermore, SA did not inhibit ouabain-sensitive ^{86}Rb uptake by rat tail arteries relative to SV and had no effect on the driving force of the sodium pump (E_{Na}) in toad bladder. Since these findings indicate that SA does not effect Na^+,K^+-ATPase and Na^+-K^+ pump activities, its potent natriuretic and diuretic activities must be due to some other mechanism(s). Possibilities include increased permeability of the tubular cell to water and/or sodium. Our data fail to support these possibilities since SA, relative to SV, had no effect on any of the relevant parameters measured in the toad bladder nor did it effect ouabain-insensitive ^{86}Rb uptake by the rat tail artery; the similar changes produced by SA and SV in the toad bladder must have resulted from nonspecific effects of the supernates. It should be pointed out, however, that the fluxes of water across the toad bladder were measured in the absence of an osmotic gradient. It is possible that SA and SV would produce different effects on water flux if they were measured in the presence of an osmotic gradient.

Another possible mechanism by which SA could induce potent diuresis is through an increase in the glomerular filtration rate (GFR). In our studies, infusion of SA in an amount sufficient to cause potent diuretic and natriuretic effects produced only a small transient increase in blood pressure in the 2NX, HEX-treated rats (possibly due to potentiation of endogenous NE). This pressor effect appears to be insufficient to produce the potent diuresis and natriuresis observed by increasing GFR. Additionally, deBold *et al.* (7) and Briggs *et al.* (8) have shown that atrial extract does not alter GFR except in high doses. Kleinert *et al.* (35) showed that, in the isolated rat kidney perfused at constant pressure, atrial extract significantly increases renal vascular resistance, GFR, filtration fraction, and sodium excretion. These authors also showed (36) that these effects were calcium dependent since they were abolished by perfusion with low

TABLE I. EFFECTS OF ATRIAL AND VENTRICULAR SUPERNATE ON UNIDIRECTIONAL WATER FLUXES IN THE SHORT-CIRCUITED TOAD BLADDER

Serosal-to-mucosal water flux (ml/hr-mg)				Mucosal-to-serosal water flux (ml/hr-mg)			
Experimental		Control		Experimental		Control	
PR	PR + SA	PR	PR + SV	PR	PR + SA	PR	PR + SV
0.060 ± 0.011 (7)	0.041 ± 0.006 (7)	0.061 ± 0.008 (7)	0.042 ± 0.006 (7)	0.064 ± 0.006 (7)	0.077 ± 0.008 (7)	0.054 ± 0.005 (7)	0.067 ± 0.006 (7)

Note. PR, phosphate-buffered sulfate Ringer's solution; SA, atrial supernate; SV, ventricular supernate. The ratio of added volume of SA or SV to initial bath fluid volume is 0.045.

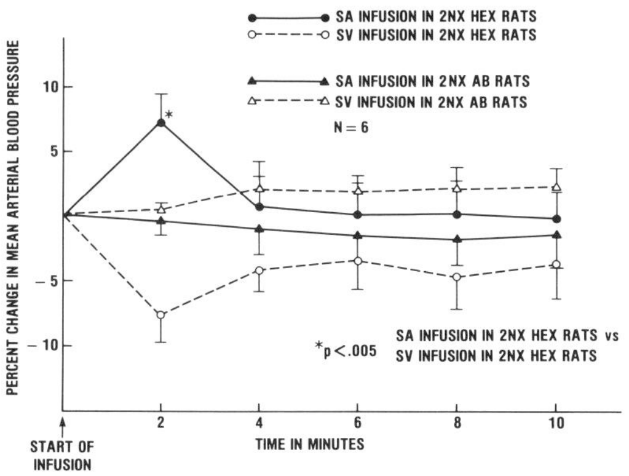

FIG. 5. Effects of 10-min intravenous infusions of atrial supernate (SA, closed symbols) and ventricular supernate (SV, open symbols) on mean arterial pressure in bilaterally nephrectomized (2NX), hexamethonium (HEX)-treated rats (circles) and in bilaterally nephrectomized (2NX), automically blocked (AB) rats (triangles). AB achieved with phentolamine, propanolol, and atropine. Vertical bars represent SE. * Indicates significant difference ($P < 0.005$) between the pressor effect of SA versus SV in 2NX, HEX-treated rats.

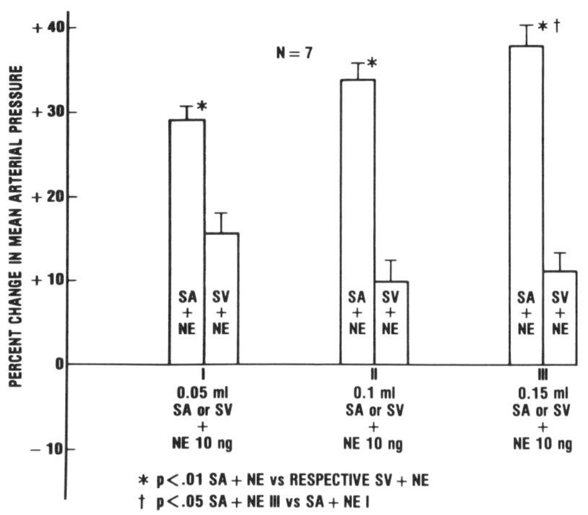

FIG. 7. Percentage change in mean arterial blood pressure on intravenous injection of mixtures of atrial supernates (SA) or ventricular supernate (SV) with norepinephrine (NE) in bilaterally nephrectomized (2NX), hexamethonium (HEX)-treated rats.

$[Ca^{2+}]$ and were decreased by verapamil. In intact animals, however, atrial extract decreased both peripheral and renal vascular resistance (36). More recently this laboratory reported (37) that atrial extract contains a factor which acts as a functional competitive inhibitor of angiotensin II in isolated blood vessels. This could explain diuresis and natriuresis if, through this action, ANF alters renal vascular hemodynamics. More studies are needed in this area.

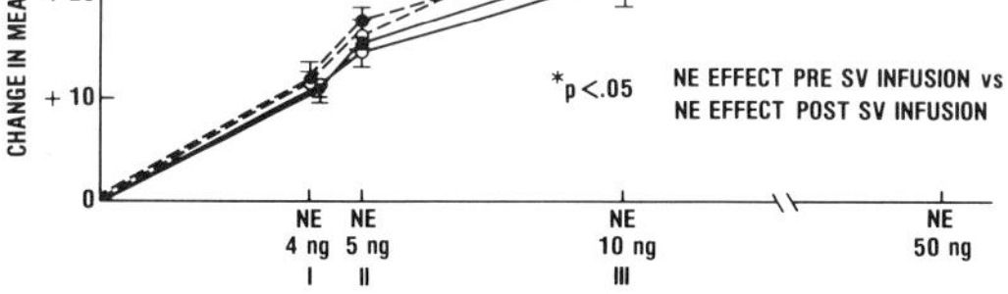

FIG. 6. Effects of intravenous bolus injection of norepinephrine (NE) before (dashed lines) and after (solid lines) infusion of atrial supernate (SA, closed circles) and ventricular supernate (SV, open circles) on mean arterial blood pressure in bilaterally nephrectomized (2NX), hexamethonium (HEX)-treated rats. Vertical bars represent SE. * Indicates significant differences ($P < 0.05$) between the pressor effects of 50 ng NE before and after SV infusion.

Our finding of a small transient pressor response to SA seems to differ from those of Camargo *et al.* (36) who reported decreases in peripheral and renal resistances and deBold *et al.* (38) who reported a fall in blood pressure lasting about 20 min following intravenous infusion of atrial extracts in rats. Trippodo *et al.* (12) also reported a transient fall in mean arterial pressure following intravenous infusion of crude atrial extract; partially purified extracts, however, had no effect on the blood pressure. The difference between our results and those of other investigators may be related to our use of 2NX, HEX-treated rats. We saw no effect on the blood pressure in 2NX, AB rats, suggesting that it does not have an overall direct effect on cardiovascular muscle.

Our findings strongly suggest that the ANF present in SA is different from the HSTIF present in acutely volume-expanded animals (13, 15, 16, 18, 19, 21, 24, 25, 39) and humans (40) as well as in some forms of low-renin experimental hypertension (13, 14, 17, 41, 45) and in human essential hypertension (20, 23, 43, 44). The HSTIF *in vitro* inhibits renal Na^+,K^+-ATPase (18–20, 24) and Na^+-K^+ pump activity in vascular smooth muscle cell (13, 14, 41, 42) and SCC in the toad bladder (17). It also depolarizes vascular smooth muscle cells (45) and causes increased vascular reactivity (21). It seems to come from or be influenced by the anteroventral third ventricular (AV3V) area of the brain (14). In contrast, the results of our present study indicate that the ANF *in vitro* does not inhibit renal or myocardial Na^+,K^+-ATPase. Furthermore, ANF does not inhibit vascular smooth muscle cell Na^+-K^+ pump activity or pump activity in the toad bladder. Finally, it has only negligible effects on blood pressure. These findings, indicate that the actions of ANF and the HSTIF are different and that the two factors probably are not the same. However, since ANF is harvested directly from atria and not from plasma, a note of caution is in order; it is possible, that, if released into the circulation, structural alterations due to the action of circulating hydrolytic enzymes may cause the factor to behave differently, possibly like a HSTIF.

We thank Karen Knoble, Thomas Martin, and Martin Jagusiak for excellent technical assistance and Patricia Prather for expert and patient editorial assistance.

---

1. Kich B. A significant electron microscopic difference between the atria and ventricles of the mammalian heart. Exp Med Surg **13**:404–428, 1955.
2. Huet M, Benchimol S, Castonguay Y, Cantin M. The chemical nature of human atrial specific granules. In: Roy PE, Harris P, eds. Recent Advances in Studies on Cardiac Structure and Metabolism. Vol 18:pp59–76. Baltimore, University Park Press, 1975.
3. deBold AJ. Morphometric assessment of granulation in rat atrial cardiocytes: Effect of age. J Mol Cell Cardiol **10**:717–724, 1978.
4. Marie JP, Guillemot H, Holt PY. Le degre' de granulation des cardiocylis auricularis. Elude planimé trique au cours des differents apports d'eau et du sodium chez le rat. Pathol Biol **24**:549–554, 1976.
5. deBold AJ. Heart atrial granularity effects of changes in water electrolyte balance. Proc Soc Exp Biol Med **161**:508–511, 1979.
6. Cantin M, Michelakis AM, Ong H, Ballak M, Beuzeron J, Benchimol S. Relationship of specific granules to renin activity in the myocardium. In: Chavoz E, Smirnov V, Dhalla HS, eds. Advances in Myocardiology. New York, Plenum, Vol:3:pp519–529, 1982.
7. deBold AJ, Borenstein HB, Veress AT, Sonnenberg H. A rapid and potent natriuretic response to intravenous injection of atrial myocardial extract in rats. Life Sci **28**:89–94, 1981.
8. Briggs JP, Steipe B, Shubert G, Schnermann J. Micropuncture studies of the renal effects of atrial natriuretic substance. Pflueger Arch **395**:271–276, 1982.
9. deBold AJ. Tissue fractionation studies on the relationship between an atrial natriuretic factor and specific atrial granules. Canad J Physiol Pharmacol **60**:324–330, 1982.
10. Garcia R, Cantin M, Thibault G, Ong H, Genest J. Relationship of specific granules to the natriuretic and diuretic activity of rat atria. Experientia **38**:1071–1073, 1982.
11. deBold AJ, Salerno TA. Natriuretic activity of extracts obtained from hearts of different species and from various rat tissues. Canad J Pharmacol **61**:127–130, 1983.
12. Trippodo NC, MacPhee AA, Cole FA. Partially purified human and rat atrial natriuretic factor. Hypertension **5**(Suppl I):I81–I88, 1983.
13. Pamnani MB, Clough DL, Huot SJ, Haddy FJ. Sodium-potassium pump activity in experimental hypertension. In: Vanhoutte PM, Leusen I, eds. Vasodilatation. New York, Raven Press, pp391–403, 1981.
14. Pamnani MB, Huot SJ, Buggy J, Clough DL, Haddy FJ. Demonstration of a humoral inhibitor of the Na^+-K^+ pump in some models of experimental hypertension. Hypertension **3**(Suppl II):II96–II101, 1981.
15. Gonick HC, Saldanha LF. A natriuretic principle from kidney tissue of volume expanded rats. J Clin Invest **45**:247–255, 1975.
16. Buckalew VM Jr, Martinez FJ, Green WE. The effect of dialysates and ultrafiltrates of plasma of saline-loaded dogs on toad bladder sodium transport. J Clin Invest **49**:926–935, 1970.
17. Chen JS, Pamnani MB, Huot SJ, Link WT, Clough DL, Haddy FJ. Effect of plasma supernate from dogs with one-kidney, one wrapped hypertension on short circuit current in the toad bladder. Physiologist **25**:280, 1982.
18. Hillyard SD, Lu F, Gonick HC. Further characterization of the natriuretic factor from kidney tissue of volume-expanded rats: Effects on short circuit current and sodium-potassium-adenosine triphosphatase activity. Circ Res **38**:250–255, 1976.
19. Gonick HC, Kramer HJ, Paul W, Lu R. Circulating inhibitor of sodium potassium activated adenosine triphosphatase after expansion of extracellular fluid volume in rats. Clin Sci Mol Med **53**:329–334, 1977.
20. Hamlyn JM, Ringel R, Schaeffer J, Levinson PD, Hamilton BP, Kowarski AA, Blaustein MP. A cir-

culating inhibitor of (Na^+ + K^+)ATPase associated with essential hypertension. Nature (London) **300:** 650–652, 1982.

21. Plunkett WC, Hutchins PM, Gruber KA, Buckalew VM Jr. Evidence for a vascular sensitizing factor in plasma of saline-loaded dogs. Hypertension **4:**581–589, 1982.
22. Michelakis AM, Mizukoshi H, Huang C, Murakami K, Imagami T. Further studies on the existence of a sensitizing factor to pressor agents in hypertension. J Clin Endocrinol **40:**90–96, 1975.
23. MacGregor G, de Wardner H. Is a circulating sodium transport inhibitor involved in the pathogenesis of essential hypertension? In: Fregly MJ, Kare MR, eds. The Role of Salt in Cardiovascular Hypertension. New York, Academic Press, pp331–343, 1982.
24. Gonick HC. Mechanism of action of natriuretic hormone: inhibitor of Na-K-ATPase. In: Kramer HJ, Krück F, eds. Natriuretic Hormone. Berlin/Heidleberg, Springer-Verlag, pp108–121, 1978.
25. Raghavan SRV, Gonick HC. Partial purification and characterization of natriuretic factor from rat kidney. Proc Soc Exp Biol Med **164:**101–104, 1980.
26. Clough DL, Pamnani MB, Haddy FJ. Decreased myocardial Na,K-ATPase activity in one-kidney, one clip hypertensive rats. Amer J Physiol **245:**H244–H251, 1983.
27. Fiske CH, SubbaRow Y. The colorimetric determination of phosphorus. J Biol Chem **66:**375–400, 1925.
28. Lowry OH, Rosebrough NJ, Farr AS, Randall RJ. Protein measurement with Folin phenol. J Biol Chem **193:**265–275, 1951.
29. Chen JS, Walser M. Passive ion fluxes across toad bladder. J Membr Biol **18:**365–378, 1974.
30. Chen JS, Walser M. Sodium fluxes through the active transport pathway in toad bladder. J Membr Biol **21:**87–98, 1975.
31. Chen JS, Walser M. Bicarbonate ions in active sodium transport across toad bladder. Amer J Physiol **1:**F210–F214, 1977.
32. Sonnenberg H, Chong CK, Veress AT. Cardiac atrial factor—an endogenous diuretic? Canad J Physiol Pharmacol **59:**1278–1279, 1983.
33. Pollock DM, Banks RO. Atrial natriuretic factor: Effects on renal function in volume contracted, in volume expanded, and in distally blocked rats. Fed Proc **41:**990, 1982.
34. Thibault G, Garcia R, Cantin M, Genest J. Atrial natriuretic factor. Characterization and partial purification. Hypertension **5**(Suppl I):I75–I80, 1983.
35. Kleinert HD, Camargo MJF, Sealey JE, Laragh FJ, Maack T. Hemodynamic and natriuretic effects of atrial extract on the isolated perfused rat kidney. Physiologist **25:**298a, 1982.
36. Camargo MJF, Kleinert HD, Sealey JE, Laragh JH, Maack T. Characterization of the renal vascular effects of atrial extract on the isolated perfused rat kidney. Proc Fifth Sci Meeting Inter Amer Soc Hypertension P-60, 1983.
37. Kleinert HD, Atlas SA, Sealey JE, Laragh JH, Maack T. Atrial extract (AE) inhibition of angiotensin II (A II) contractile response in the rabbit aortic ring. Abstracts of the Council for High Blood Pressure Research 37th Annual Fall Conference and Scientific Sessions, American Heart Assoc, Dallas, p40, 1983.
38. deBold AJ. Atrial natriuretic factor of the rat heart. Studies of isolation and properties. Proc Soc Exp Biol Med **170:**133–138, 1982.
39. Gruber KA, Whitaker JM, Buckalew VM Jr. Endogenous digitalis-like substance in plasma of volume expanded dogs. Nature (London) **287:**743–745, 1980.
40. Kramer HJ. Antinatriferic and natriuretic activities in human plasma following acute and chronic salt loading. In: Kramer HJ, Krück F, eds. Natriuretic Hormone. Berlin/Heidelberg, Springer-Verlag, pp24–33, 1978.
41. Huot SJ, Pamnani MB, Clough DL, Haddy FJ. The role of sodium intake, the Na^+-K^+ pump activity and a ouabain-like humoral agent in the genesis of reduced renal mass hypertension. Amer J Nephrol **3:**92–99, 1983.
42. Haddy FJ, Pamnani MB, Clough DL. Humoral factors and the sodium-potassium pump in volume expanded hypertension. In: Worcel M, ed. New Trends in Arterial Hypertension. INSERM Symposium, Vol 17:pp189–199, 1981.
43. Poston L, Sewell RB, Wilkinson SPA, Richardson JP, Williams R, Clarkson EM, MacGregor GA, deWardener HE. Evidence for a circulating sodium transport inhibiting factor in essential hypertension. Brit Med J **282:**847–849, 1981.
44. Burris JF, Pamnani MB, Huot SJ, Jemionek JF, Freis ED, Haddy FJ. Sodium-potassium (Na^+-K^+) pump activity in low renin essential hypertension. Clin Res **30:**733A, 1982.
45. Pamnani MB, Harder DR, Huot SJ, Bryant HJ, Kutyna FA, Haddy FJ. Vascular smooth muscle membrane potential and a ouabain-like humoral factor in one-kidney, one clip hypertension in rats. Clin Sci **63:**31s–33s, 1982.

Received October 3, 1983. P.S.E.B.M. 1984, Vol. 176.
Accepted February 22, 1984.

PROCEEDINGS OF THE SOCIETY FOR EXPERIMENTAL BIOLOGY AND MEDICINE **176**, 132–137 (1984)

Effect of 5-Thio-D-glucose on Hexose Transport and Metabolism in the Mouse Small Intestine[1] (41852)

MICHAEL J. KELLEY AND THERESA S. CHEN

Department of Pharmacology and Toxicology, University of Louisville, Health Sciences Center, Louisville, Kentucky 40292

Abstract. 5-Thio-D-glucose (5TG) elicits a time-dependent effect on net D-glucose transport and metabolism in the mouse small intestine. When incubation periods were less than 45 min, 5TG inhibited net D-glucose transport. As incubation periods were lengthened to 60 min or greater, net D-glucose transport was potentiated by 5TG, with a concomitant inhibition of lactate production from exogenous D-glucose. Furthermore, D-glucose inhibited 5TG transport at every time point studied. Initial velocity profiles done with 5TG and D-glucose, respectively, resulted in a K_T of 6.3 mM and a T_{max} of 18.5 μmole/g/30 min for 5TG; while for D-glucose the K_T was 11.7 mM and the T_{max} was 43.4 μmole/g/30 min. Competitive inhibition between 5TG and D-glucose was demonstrated. The apparent K_I's for 5TG and D-glucose were 3.0 mM and 9.3 mM, respectively. These findings indicated that 5TG has a lower affinity for the hexose-transport carrier than D-glucose. 5TG was also found to inhibit 3-*O*-methyl-D-glucose (3MG) and D-galactose transport in a dose-dependent manner. Basal levels of lactate production were not affected by 5TG nor did 5TG affect lactate levels in the presence of 3MG. These results suggest that 5TG decreases intestinal utilization of D-glucose via glycolysis to partially account for the observed increase in net transmural transport of D-glucose.

5-Thio-D-glucose (5TG), first synthesized by Feather and Whistler (1), is an analogue of D-glucose with sulfur substituted for oxygen in the pyranose ring. Rao *et al.* (2) found no evidence of important alteration in ring conformation of 5TG as compared to D-glucose. Using everted rings of hamster small intestine, Critchley *et al.* (3) and Barnett *et al.* (4) demonstrated that 5TG is accumulated against a concentration gradient. Little information is available concerning the transmural transport of 5TG and its effect on the transport and metabolism of D-glucose in the small intestine.

5TG was shown to inhibit several enzymes involved in D-glucose metabolism in rabbit skeletal muscle (5, 6) and to induce glycosuria and hyperglycemia when administered either orally or intraperitoneally to rats (7). Furthermore, we previously demonstrated that 5TG potentiates net D-glucose transport in the mouse small intestine (8). Since the small intestine is known to metabolize 50% of the D-glucose transported (9), 5TG may play an important role in the intestinal utilization of D-glucose and thus contribute to the diabetogenic effect of 5TG observed *in vivo* (7). Therefore the purpose of this investigation was to further characterize the transport process of 5TG and its effect on the transport and metabolism of hexoses in the small intestine *in vitro*.

Materials and Methods. *Materials.* 5-Thio-D-glucose, PGO enzymes, *o*-dianisidine diHCl, lactic acid, lactic acid dehydrogenase (LDH), NAD^+, Tris buffer, and meta-phosphoric acid were purchased from Sigma Chemical Company (St. Louis, Mo.). Radioisotopes were purchased from New England Nuclear Corporation (Boston, Mass.).

Animal treatment. Male Swiss–Webster mice purchased from Laboratory Supply Company (Indianapolis, Ind.) weighing 30 to 40 g were used in this study. The mice were maintained on stock diets and water *ad libitum* and a 12-hr light–dark cycle in quarters not sprayed with insecticides. Animals were sacrificed by cervical dislocation and decapitation. The abdomen was opened, then the jejunal section of the small intestine was removed and washed with Ringer's solution.

Intestinal transport of sugars. The everted intestinal sac technique (10) was employed to study the transmural transport of 5TG, D-glucose, 3-*O*-methyl-D-glucose (3MG), and D-ga-

[1] Portions of this work were presented at the annual meeting of FASEB, April 1983, Chicago, Ill.

0037-9727/84 $1.50

lactose. D-[^{14}C(U)]Glucose, 3-*O*-methyl-[D-^{14}C(U)]glucose, and D-[^{14}C(U)]galactose were the tracers used for analysis where specified. Both mucosal and serosal fluids were composed of mammalian Ringer solution, containing the same desired sugar(s) at identical specified concentrations. The sacs were incubated at 37°C in Dubnoff metabolic shaker, under 1 atm pressure of 95% O_2–5% CO_2 for desired intervals of time. At the end of the incubation, the sacs were removed, gently blotted on filter paper, and weighed. The serosal fluid was drained and centrifuged.

Analyses. When tracers were employed, a 50-μl serosal sample was pipetted into 10 ml of an aqueous scintillation fluid (11), prepared by combining 4 g of Omniflours (98% PPO and 2% Bis-MSB, New England Nuclear Corp.), 1 liter toluene, and 500 ml Triton X-100 (Rohm and Haas, Philadelphia, Pa.). Radioactivity was determined in an automatic liquid scintillation counter and concentrations were calculated from the specific activities of standard solutions.

D-Glucose was determined by a glucose oxidase method (Glucostat, Sigma Chemical Co.). 5TG was not found to be a substrate for this assay, in agreement with Hoffman and Whistler's finding (7). 5TG was estimated using the reducing sugar assay described by Nelson (12). L-Lactate was measured via an LDH assay (13).

Statistical analyses were performed by one-way analysis of variance with a Duncan's multiple-range test for significance. Regression lines were calculated by the least-squares method. The values are expressed as mean ± SE.

Results. *Transport studies.* The net transmural transport of D-glucose and 5TG across the mouse small intestine was linear as a function of time (Figs. 1A and B). Addition of D-glucose to 5TG caused an inhibition of 5TG transport. However, the transport of D-glucose in the presence of 5TG exhibited a biphasic effect. At time intervals less than 45 min, 5TG inhibited net D-glucose transport. If incubated for longer than 45 min, 5TG caused an enhanced rate of D-glucose transport.

Velocity profiles were done with 5TG and D-glucose, as substrates (Figs. 2A and B), respectively. The K_T for 5TG was found to be 6.3 mM and the T_{max} was 11.5 μmole/g/30 min; while D-glucose had a K_T of 11.7 mM and a T_{max} of 43.5 μmole/g/30 min. As indicated in Fig. 2, 5TG and D-glucose are competitive inhibitors of each other in terms of transport. Since the apparent T_{max} values for 5TG and D-glucose were so vastly different, we could not validly compare K_T values to estimate the relative affinity of either compound for the hexose-transport carrier. We, therefore, determined the apparent K_I values

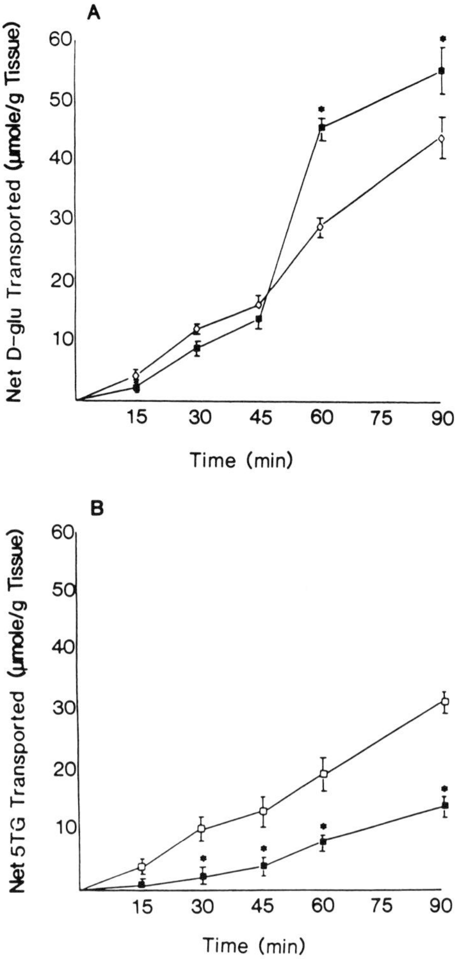

FIG. 1. Time profiles of D-glucose transport in the mouse small intestine. Values are the means ± SE of four experiments. (A) Net D-glucose transported at 5.5 mM alone (◇) and in the presence of 5.5 mM 5TG (■). *Denotes significantly different from D-glucose alone ($P < 0.01$). (B) Net 5TG transported at 5.5 mM alone (□) and in the presence of 5.5 mM D-glucose (■). *Denotes significantly different from 5TG alone ($P < 0.01$).

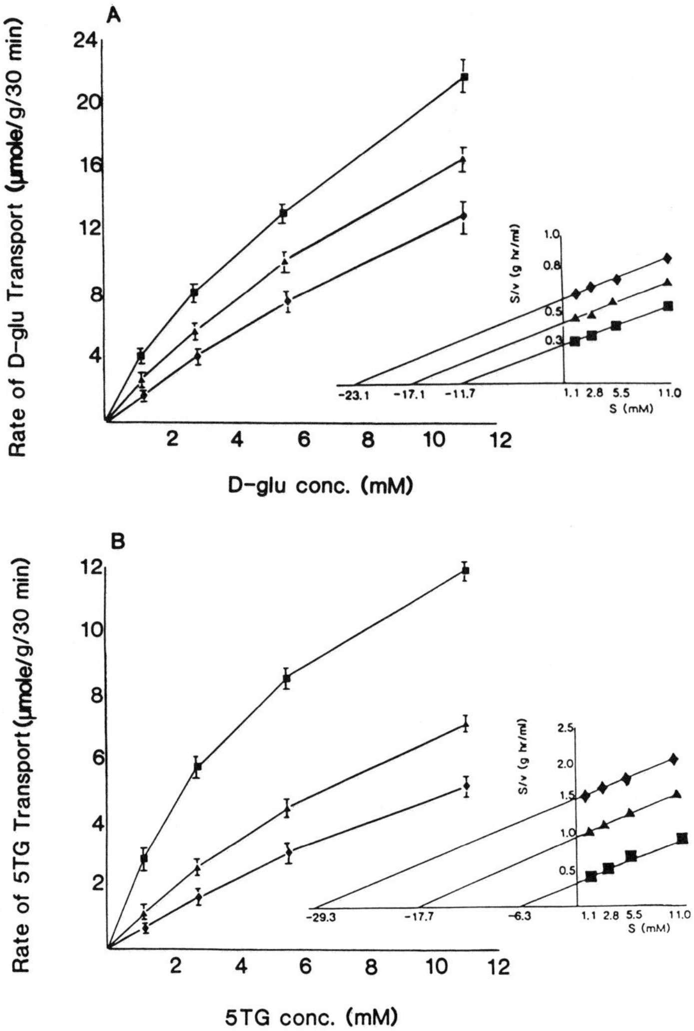

FIG. 2. Initial velocity profiles of D-glucose and 5TG in the mouse small intestine. Values are the means ± SE of four experiments. (A) Rate of D-glucose transport (■) and in the presence of 5.5 m*M* 5TG (▲) or 11.0 m*M* 5TG (◆). Insert: Hanes–Woolf plot of the above data. (B) Rate of 5TG transport (■) and in the presence of 5.5 m*M* D-glucose (▲) or 11.0 m*M* D-glucose (◆). Insert: Hanes–Woolf plot of the above data.

for both 5TG and D-glucose. Table I shows that 5TG has a K_I of 9.3 m*M*; while D-glucose has a K_I of 3.0 m*M*. This data demonstrated that D-glucose has a greater affinity for the hexose-transport carrier than 5TG.

Since 5TG enhanced the net transport of D-glucose after 45 min of incubation, the effect of 5TG on the transport of two other actively transported hexoses was investigated. As illustrated in Table II, 5TG inhibits the net transmural transport of both 3MG and D-galactose in a dose-dependent manner. The rates of 3MG transport were only 51 and 30% of control values in the presence of 5.5 and 11.0 m*M* 5TG. Likewise, the rates of D-galactose transport were 85 and 57% of control, respectively, in the presence of 5.5 and 11.0 m*M* 5TG. However, the apparent rates of D-glucose transport increased 85 and 114% over control values in the presence of 5.5 and 11.0 m*M* 5TG, respectively. This increase was dose-related although the effect of 5.5 and 11.0 m*M* 5TG was not significantly different from each other.

TABLE I. KINETIC-TRANSPORT PARAMETERS

Substrate	K_T (mM)	V_T (μmole/g/ 30 min)	K_I (mM)
5.5 mM D-glucose	11.7	43.5	—
5.5 mM D-glucose + 5.5 mM 5TG	17.1	41.7	9.3
5.5 mM D-glucose + 11.0 mM 5TG	23.1	40.0	9.3
5.5 mM 5TG	6.3	18.5	—
5.5 mM 5TG + 5.5 mM D-glucose	17.7	18.5	3.0
5.5 mM 5TG + 11.0 mM D-glucose	29.3	18.9	3.0

Metabolism. In the mouse small intestine, net lactate production from exogenous D-glucose was linear over time (Fig. 3). The addition of 5TG to D-glucose caused a significant inhibition of lactate production after 45 min of incubation (Fig. 3). As illustrated in Fig. 4, the rate of lactate production in the presence of 5TG (2.28 ± 0.61 μmole/g/hr) did not differ significantly from basal levels (6.55 ± 0.31 μmole/g/hr). Likewise, 5TG did not affect lactate production in the presence of 3MG (3.42 ± 0.42 μmole/g/hr), a nonmetabolizable sugar analogue. However, the rates of lactate production from exogenous D-glucose were inhibited 44 and 66% in the presence of 5.5 and 11.0 mM 5TG, respectively. Furthermore, we have found that 5TG is not converted to D-glucose, since D-glucose levels in the presence of 5TG did not differ from basal values (unpublished results).

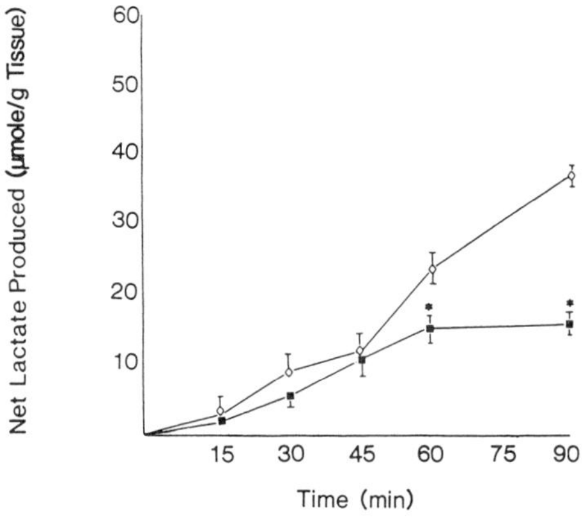

FIG. 3. Time profile of lactate production from exogenous D-glucose in the mouse small intestine. Values are the means ± SE of four experiments. In the presence of 5.5 mM D-glucose (◇) and 5.5 mM of both D-glucose and 5TG (■). *Indicates statistical significance of values compared to time-paired D-glucose alone ($P < 0.01$).

Discussion. 5TG is an analogue of D-glucose which shares many chemical and physical properties (1). We have previously demonstrated that 5TG is actively transported across the mouse small intestine by a Na^+- and energy-dependent, phloridzin- and ouabain-sensitive mechanism (8). Critchley *et al.* (3) have shown competitive inhibition between 6-deoxy-D-glucose and 5TG, but to our knowledge no one has shown a direct interaction between D-glucose and 5TG transport. We demonstrated that D-glucose and 5TG are competitive inhibitors of each other, in terms of transport. Furthermore, the affinity of 5TG

TABLE II. EFFECT OF 5TG ON THE TRANSPORT OF VARIOUS ^{14}C-HEXOSES ACROSS THE MOUSE SMALL INTESTINE

Treatment	3MG		D-Galactose		D-Glucose	
	Rate of transport (μmole/g/hr)	% of control	Rate of transport (μmole/g/hr)	% of control	Rate of transport (μmole/g/hr)	% of control
Control[a]	22.86 ± 4.04[b] (14)	100	27.02 ± 1.98 (9)	100	29.62 ± 5.52 (11)	100
+5.5 mM 5TG	11.66 ± 2.28[c] (14)	51	22.96 ± 2.70[c] (10)	85	54.67 ± 4.52[c] (19)	185
+11.0 mM 5TG	6.84 ± 1.74[c,d] (8)	30	15.36 ± 2.22[c,d] (10)	57	63.48 ± 7.12[c] (19)	214

[a] 5.5 mM of test sugar alone.
[b] Mean ± SE, number in parenthesis is the sample size.
[c] Significantly different from control ($P < 0.01$).
[d] Significantly different from 5.5 mM 5TG ($P < 0.01$).

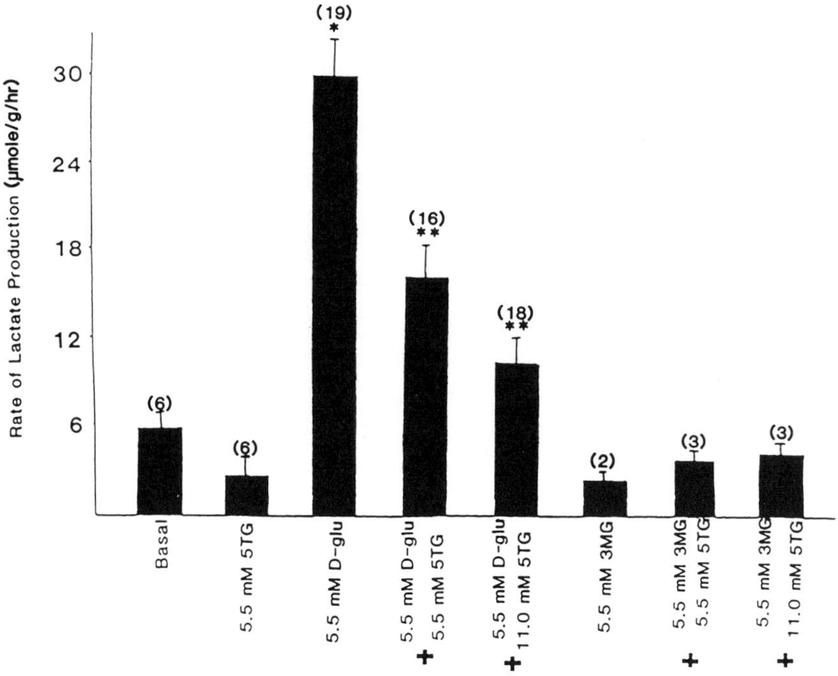

FIG. 4. Average rate of lactate production in the mouse small intestine under various conditions. Values are the means ± SE and the number in parenthesis is the sample size. *Denotes significantly different from basal levels ($P < 0.01$). **Denotes significantly different from basal levels and from 5.5 m*M* D-glucose ($P < 0.01$).

for the hexose-transport carrier was found to be lower than that of D-glucose in the mouse small intestine.

5TG elicited a biphasic effect on net D-glucose transport and a time-dependent inhibition of lactate production from exogenous D-glucose. The initial inhibition of D-glucose transport by 5TG is most likely due to competition at the hexose-transport carrier. The latter potentiation of net D-glucose transport by 5TG is presumably related to inhibition of D-glucose utilization in the intestine, since 5TG is not converted to D-glucose.

In addition, we demonstrated that 5TG inhibits 3MG and D-galactose transport, yet fails to affect lactate production in the presence of 3MG. The difference between potentiation and inhibition of net hexose transport by 5TG appears to relate to differences in hexose metabolism. Pritchard and Porteous (9) demonstrated that 50% of the D-glucose transported across the small intestine is metabolized, mainly to lactate (>90%). In contrast, it is well known that neither 3MG nor D-galactose is appreciably metabolized in the small intestine. Further evidence for a direct effect of 5TG on D-glucose metabolism by 5TG is obtained by Hellman *et al.* (14); where they demonstrated an 80% decrease in D-glucose metabolism by 5TG as measured by CO_2 production from pancreatic islets. Thus 5TG inhibited the intestinal utilization of D-glucose via glycolysis to partially account for the increase in net transmural transport of D-glucose.

It has been shown that 5TG is a potent inhibitor of phosphoglucomutase ($K_I = 16.2$ μM) as well as phosphorylase a and b, thereby blocking glycogen synthesis and degradation (5, 6). Pritchard and Porteous (9) demonstrated that intestinal glycogen stores were increased up to 130% of basal values in the presence of exogenous D-glucose. In addition, 10% or more of the glucose absorbed by the mucosal cells is oxidized via the hexosemonophosphate shunt (HMS) (15). 5TG-6-phosphate has been shown to be an inhibitor of glucose-6-phosphate dehydrogenase (5), which is the rate-limiting step of the HMS (16). Our data (Figs. 3 and 4) demonstrated that 5TG inhibits D-glucose metabolism via glycolysis. However, it is possible that the inhibitory effects of 5TG on glycogen turnover and the HMS may also contribute to the increase in net transmural transport of D-glucose.

Preliminary studies by Hoffman and Whistler (7) demonstrated that 5TG is capable of eliciting a diabetogenic effect when administered either orally or intraperitonelly to rats. They suggest that the diabetogenic effect may be partially due to inhibition of D-glucose uptake in various tissues. We demonstrated that 5TG interacts with D-glucose at both the transport carrier and the metabolic pathways in the mouse small intestine. The interaction between 5TG and D-glucose demonstrated *in vitro* may also be a contributing factor for the diabetogenic effect of 5TG observed *in vivo*.

The authors are grateful to Dr. K. C. Huang for providing valuable advice and discussion, and to Mrs. Sandi Bell for typing the manuscript.

1. Feather MS, Whistler RL. Derivatives of 5-deoxy-5-mercapto-D-glucose. Tetrahedron Lett **15**:667–668, 1962.
2. Rao VSR, Foster JF, Whistler RL. Ring conformation in methyl and β-D-xylothiopyranosides as demonstrated by nuclear magnetic resonance. J Org Chem **28**:1730–1731, 1963.
3. Critchley DR, Eichholz A, Crane RK. Transport of 5-thio-D-glucose in hamster small intestine. Biochim Biophys Acta **211**:244–254, 1970.
4. Barnett GEJ, Ralph A, Munday KA. Structural requirements for active intestinal transport "The nature of the carrier-sugar bonding at C-2 and the ring oxygen of the sugar." Biochem J **118**:843–850, 1970.
5. Chen M, Whistler RL. Action of 5-thio-D-glucose and its 1-phosphate with hexokinase and phosphoglucomutase. Arch Biochem Biophys **169**:392–396, 1975.
6. Chen M, Whistler RL. Action of 5-thio-D-glucose in the control of glycogen depolymerization. Biochem Biophys Res Commun **74**:1642–1646, 1977.
7. Hoffman DJ, Whistler RL. Diabetogenic action of 5-thio-D-glucopyranose in rats. Biochemistry **7**:4479–4483, 1968.
8. Kelley MJ, Chen TS. Effects of 5-thio-D-glucose on the transport of D-glucose, D-galactose and 3-*O*-methyl-D-glucose in the mouse small intestine: Potentiation vs. competition. Pharmacologist **24**:248, 1982.
9. Pritchard PJ, Porteous JW. Steady-state metabolism and transport of D-glucose by rat small intestine *in vitro*. Biochem J **164**:1–14, 1977.
10. Wilson TH, Wiseman G. The use of sacs of everted small intestine for the study of the transferance of substances from the mucosal to serosal surface. J Physiol **123**:116–125, 1954.
11. Kobayashi Y, Maudsley DV. Practical aspects of liquid scintillation counting. Methods Biochem Anal **1**:55–133, 1969.
12. Nelson N. A photometric adaptation of the Somogyi method for the determination of glucose. J Biol Chem **153**:375–380, 1944.
13. Tietz NW. Blood gases and electrolytes. In: Tietz NW, ed. Fundamentals of Clinical Chemistry. Philadelphia, Saunders, 2nd ed, p936, 1976.
14. Hellman B, Lernmark A, Sehlin J, Taljedal I, Whistler RL. The pancreatic β-cell recognition of insulin secretagogues III, "Effects of substituting sulfur for oxygen in the D-glucose molecule." Biochem Pharmacol **22**:29–35, 1973.
15. Davenport HW. Intestinal digestion and absorption of carbohydrate. In: Davenport HW, ed. Physiology of the Digestive Tract. Chicago, Year Book Med Publ, 5th ed, p195, 1982.
16. Cunningham EB. Carbohydrate Metabolism. In: Cunningham EB, ed. Biochemistry, Mechanisms of Metabolism. New York, McGraw–Hill, p392, 1978.

Received December 23, 1983. P.S.E.B.M. 1984, Vol. 176.
Accepted February 23, 1984.

PROCEEDINGS OF THE SOCIETY FOR EXPERIMENTAL BIOLOGY AND MEDICINE **176**, 138–142 (1984)

The Effects of $CdCl_2$ on the Maternal-to-Fetal Clearance of ^{67}Cu and Placental Blood Flow[1] (41853)

R. J. CHERTOK,[2] B. KULLGREN, AND D. BURBANK

Oak Ridge Associated Universities, Medical and Health Sciences Division, Oak Ridge, Tennessee 37831

Abstract. Copper is an essential element while Cd is an extremely toxic heavy metal of questionable biological usefulness. Cadmium has been reported to interfere with the metabolism of Cu, be teratogenic, and decrease blood flow in the fetal placenta. Because of these reported biological interactions of Cd and Cu, this investigation was conducted to determine the effects of Cd on placental transport of ^{67}Cu and placental blood flow in the guinea pig. All guinea pigs used were 60 ± 1 days pregnant. A placental perfusion technique was used to measure the maternal-to-fetal clearance of ^{67}Cu and $^{3}H_2O$ across the placenta. The clearance of $^{3}H_2O$ served as an indicator of placental blood flow on the maternal side of the circulation. The results indicated that an iv injection of 1 mg Cd/kg body weight resulted in an immediate increase in the clearance of ^{67}Cu which declined over the next 8 min to an elevated level compared to the extrapolated best-fit curve of control values. This iv injection of $CdCl_2$ concomitantly reduced the maternal-to-fetal clearance of $^{3}H_2O$ across the placenta. In conclusion, an acute exposure of the pregnant female to $CdCl_2$ results in an increased maternal-to-fetal clearance of ^{67}Cu and a reduced placental blood flow that can alter the supply of nutrients to the developing embryo or fetus, and therefore modify normal development.

Copper is an essential element, but is also potentially toxic. Because of this dual property, homeostatic mechanisms have evolved to compensate for excesses or deficiencies of copper by controlling intestinal absorption and excretion.

After copper is absorbed, it is transported bound to plasma protein (1) and perhaps to amino acids (2). Shortly thereafter, almost all of the copper is deposited in the liver (3) where approximately 80% is bound to hepatocuprein (4), copper chelatin (5), and metallothionein (6) in the cytosol. The remaining 20% is found in lysosomes (7) or incorporated into other specific copper proteins such as cytochrome C oxidase (8). Copper deficiency is a rare condition because most diets supply a relative abundance of the metal (9). Although the normal infant is born with a store of copper (10), deficiencies have been associated with anemia, neutropenia, and severe demineralization of the bone in premature and full-term infants (11, 12). Similarly, copper toxicosis is rare but does occur where a genetic defect in copper metabolism is present (Wilson's disease) (13).

Cadmium is an extremely toxic heavy metal of questionable biological usefulness (14). In addition to its presence in products such as fungicides, fertilizers, pigments, metal alloys, plastics, coal, and fuel oil, it is also a by-product of recovery processes for zinc, lead, and copper. Cadmium is a cumulative poison, and no apparent homeostatic mechanism operates to maintain body concentrations at an approximately constant level independent of intake (15).

The reported intestinal absorption of Cd is 1 to 8% of the dose (15–19). However, other studies have indicated that absorption can be influenced by dietary constituents such as the essential metallic ions zinc, iron, copper, and calcium (20).

Cadmium has been reported to interfere with the metabolism of copper by reducing its intestinal absorption and increasing its urinary excretion (21). Rats fed 1.5-μg Cd/g diet with a normal copper content (3-μg Cu/g diet) had a reduced ceruloplasmin activity, whereas rats on a diet of 6- or 18-μg Cd/g diet and a normal Cu content had a considerably reduced plasma and liver Cu concentration and serum

[1] This work was performed in conjunction with the Department of Energy under contract DE-AC05-76OR00033 and the Environmental Protection Agency under interagency agreement 79-X0533.

[2] To whom all correspondence should be addressed.

0037-9727/84 $1.50

ceruloplasmin activity (22). Bone malformations from simple Cu deficiency were also noted. Similar effects of Cu deficiency resulting from Cd intoxication have been observed in pregnant ewes and lambs (23).

Cadmium has been reported to be teratogenic in the golden hamster (24) and mice (25). Gerber *et al.* have reported that lead, another heavy metal, reduced placental blood flow but did not change fetal uptake of α-amino isobutyrate in mice (26). Levin and Miller have also reported that Cd decreased blood flow to the fetal placenta 12 to 16 hr and 18 to 24 hr after sc injection of $CdCl_2$ into rats (27).

Because of the reported biological interactions of Cd and Cu, this investigation was designed to determine the effects of Cd on the placental transport of ^{67}Cu and placental blood flow in the guinea pig.

Materials and Methods. Strain 13 guinea pigs from a closed colony maintained at Oak Ridge Associated Universities, Medical and Health Sciences Division, were used for these studies. The guinea pigs were bred, allowed to farrow, and bred again so that the gestational age was known within ±24 hr. All guinea pigs used were 60 ± 1 days pregnant.

The placental perfusion technique used was adapted from that described by Twardock (28) and modified by Kelman (29). The dams were anesthetized with sodium pentobarbital (28 mg/kg) injected ip and Innovar-Vet (Pitman-Moore, 0.44 ml/kg) injected im and secured to a plastic rack in a supine position. A jugular vein was cannulated, and a slow, continuous iv drip of Ringer's lactate solution was maintained throughout the experiment. A carotid artery was cannulated to obtain blood samples at 9- to 10-min intervals. Then the guinea pig was placed in a bath of Ringer's solution maintained at 37°C. A uterine horn was exteriorized by laparotomy and a fetus was exposed by an incision through the uterus and amniotic sac. The uterus, placenta, and fetus were immersed in the Ringer's solution. The umbilical vessels were stripped of connective tissue and ligated near the fetus. Then an umbilical artery was cannulated with a hubless needle fastened to tubing connected to a peristalic pump and a reservoir containing the perfusion fluid (guinea pig serum) maintained at 37°C. An umbilical vein was cannulated to collect the perfusion fluid at 4-min intervals. Perfusion rates were held steady at 0.7 ml/min. Preliminary experiments indicated that perfusion of the placenta at rates greater than 1 ml/min for extended periods (1 to 2 hr) allowed radiolabeled albumin to pass from the perfusing fluid into the maternal circulation. Also, perfusion at a rate of 0.7 ml/min could be maintained for periods as long as 2 hr without an abrupt change in the placental transport of ^3H_2O from dam to fetus. At the start of the perfusion, 100 μCi of ^3H_2O and 20 μCi of $^{67}CuCl_2$ were injected into the dam via the cannulated jugular vein. Perfusate sample collections were started 28 min later to allow time for equilibration of the ^{67}Cu in the animal. Twenty-four minutes after starting the perfusate collection, 1 mg Cd/kg body weight was injected into the cannulated jugular vein. Collection of perfusate samples continued for an additional 28 min.

The data are expressed as the clearance of tritiated water or ^{67}Cu from the maternal to fetal circulation. The formula used for the calculation was

$$\text{Clearance} = P/M \times R,$$

where clearance is milliliters of maternal plasma that contained the amount of ^3H or ^{67}Cu that entered the perfusate in 1 min (ml/min), P is the perfusate concentration of ^3H or ^{67}Cu, M is the maternal plasma concentration of ^3H or ^{67}Cu, and R is the perfusate rate. The M values for ^3H and ^{67}Cu are approximations based on extrapolations between the encompassing plasma concentration values to the mean time of each perfusate collection.

Results. The data from seven animals have been normalized to reduce the animal-to-animal variability associated with placental blood flow and placental transport mechanisms. The data for ^{67}Cu clearance from 4 to 24 min were fitted to the exponential equation $y = ae^{-bx}$ where a is the intercept, b is the slope, and x is time. The data were then normalized to the value at 4 min as determined from the equation. The data for ^3H_2O were normalized in the same manner except that the data were fit to the linear equation $y = a + bx$. It has been demonstrated that the clearance of ^3H_2O is a linear function of perfusate flow rate and has been suggested that variations in ^3H_2O

clearance are the result of variations in the placental blood flow from the maternal circulation (29).

The clearances of ^{67}Cu and ^3H_2O across the guinea pig placenta from dam to fetus and the effects of an iv dose of $CdCl_2$ (1 mg Cd/kg body weight) are illustrated in Figs. 1 and 2. The clearance of ^{67}Cu declined with time according to the equation $y = ae^{-bx}$ where $a = 0.1942$ and $b = 0.0207$ (Fig. 1). The r^2 value for goodness of fit was 0.965. Twenty-four minutes after the start of perfusate collection, $CdCl_2$ was injected and the clearance of ^{67}Cu increased dramatically. This increased clearance of ^{67}Cu declined for approximately the next 8 min and then assumed a parallel, but elevated, level compared to the best-fit curve extrapolated to 52 min. These data indicated an immediate effect of $CdCl_2$ on the transport properties for ^{67}Cu in the placenta.

The results of $CdCl_2$ injection on the clearance of ^3H_2O are illustrated in Fig. 2. For the 24 min prior to injection of $CdCl_2$, the clearance of ^3H_2O was a linear function with time, and the data were fitted to the equation $y = ax + b$, where $a = 0.6454$ and $b = 0.0024$. The r_2 value was 0.7201. Immediately following the injection of $CdCl_2$, there was a decline in clearance of ^3H_2O for 4 min, after which the clearance essentially followed the same pattern as before the injection of $CdCl_2$. However, the clearance of ^3H_2O was at a lower level, indicating a reduced maternal blood flow to the placenta.

Discussion. In the experiments reported here, the injection of $CdCl_2$ resulted in an immediate increase in the clearance of ^{67}Cu (Fig. 1) and an immediate decrease in the clearance of ^3H_2O (Fig. 2). Although the clearance of ^{67}Cu returned to a lower level, it remained elevated compared to the extrapolated values derived from data collected prior to the injection of $CdCl_2$. The increase in ^{67}Cu clearance is even more evident when the decreased load of ^{67}Cu delivered to the placenta as a result of the decreased blood flow is considered. These data indicate $CdCl_2$ has an immediate effect on the placental blood flow as well as an alteration of the transport properties of the placenta for ^{67}Cu.

By injecting Cd directly into the fetus, Levin and Miller (30) have shown that fetal death in the rat is not the result of direct effects of Cd on the fetus. They have also suggested that

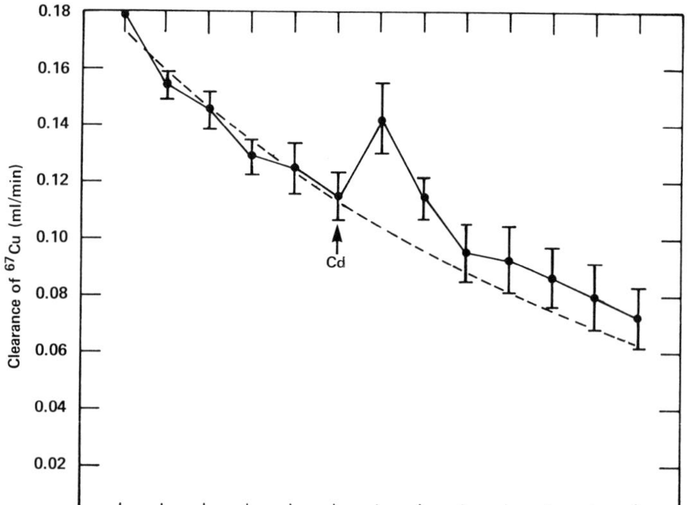

FIG. 1. Clearance of ^{67}Cu (±SEM) as a function of time. Arrow indicates time of iv injection of 1 mg Cd/kg body weight. The broken line represents the data for 0 to 24 min fitted to the equation $y = ae^{-bx}$, where $a = 0.1942$, $b = 0.0207$, and x = time. The value of $r^2 = 0.965$. Each point is the mean of 7 determinations.

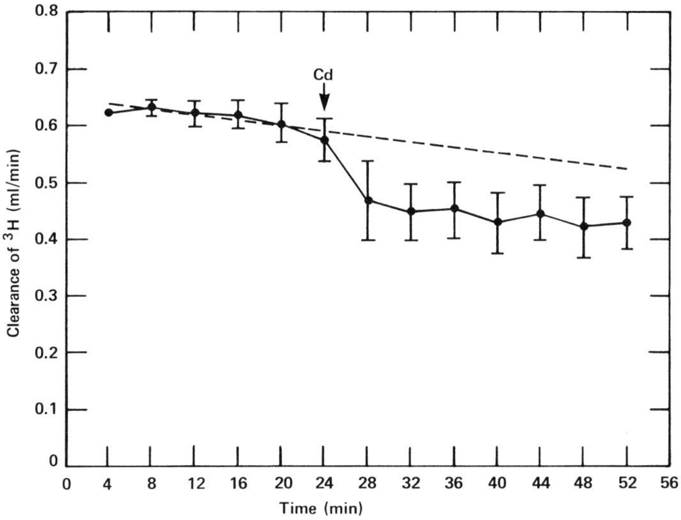

FIG. 2. Clearance of ^{3}H (±SEM) as a function of time. Arrow indicates time of iv injection of 1 mg Cd/kg body weight. The broken line represents the data for 0 to 24 min fitted to the equation $y = ax + b$, where $a = 0.6454$, $b = 0.0024$, and $x =$ time. The value of $r^2 = 0.7201$. Each point is the mean of 7 determinations.

fetal death does not result from renal toxicity of Cd (27).

Gerber *et al.* (26) investigated the effects of dietary lead on placental blood flow and the fetal uptake of α-amino isobutyrate in mice. A microsphere technique was used to measure placental blood flow. Their results indicated lead caused a reduced blood flow to the placenta but did not alter the fetal uptake of α-amino isobutyrate on a per-weight basis.

Levin and Miller (27), also using a microsphere technique, investigated the effects of Cd on the fetal placental blood flow in the rat. On day 18 of gestation, sc injection of 40 μmole of Cd/kg did not statistically reduce the placental blood flow 8 to 10 hr later. However, 12 to 16 hr and 18 to 24 hr after the Cd treatment, the rats experienced a reduced blood flow to the fetal placenta of 40 and 73%, respectively.

Levin and Miller (31) have reported that following sc injection, the placenta accumulated Cd more rapidly than all maternal organs except the liver. They further postulated that the high concentrations of Cd in the placenta might result in cellular damage to the trophoblastic tissue or to the fetal vascular endothelium. Since fetal development depends on a delicately balanced supply of nutrients, an interruption or alteration in this supply could cause a retardation, abnormal growth, or death of the developing embryo or fetus. These experiments indicate that an acute exposure of the pregnant female to $CdCl_2$ results in an increased maternal-to-fetal clearance of ^{67}Cu and a reduced blood flow to the placenta and thus alters the supply of nutrients to the developing embryo or fetus, which could alter the normal progress of development.

1. Bearn AG, Kunkel HG. Metabolic studies in Wilson's disease using Cu^{64}. J Lab Clin Med **45**:623–631, 1955.
2. Neumann PZ, Sass-Kortsak A. The state of copper in human serum: Evidence for an amino acid-bound fraction. J Clin Invest **46**:646–658, 1967.
3. O'Reilly S, Pollycove M, Tono M, Herradora L. Abnormalities of the physiology of copper in Wilson's disease. II. The internal kinetics of copper. Arch Neurol. **24**:481–488, 1971.
4. Mann T, Keilin D. Haemocuprein and hepatocuprein, copper-protein compounds of blood and liver in mammals. Proc R Soc London Ser B **126**:303–315, 1938.
5. Morell AG, Shapiro JR, Scheinberg IH. Copper binding protein of human liver. In: Walsh JM, Cummings JN, eds. Wilson's Disease. Some Current Concepts. Oxford, Blackwell, pp36–42, 1961.
6. Evans GW. Copper homeostasis in the mammalian system. Physiol Rev **53**:535–570, 1973.

7. Sternlieb I, van den Hamer CJA, Morell AG, Alpert G, Gregoriadis G, Scheinberg IH. Lysosomal defect of hepatic copper excretion in Wilson's disease (hepatolenticular degeneration). Gastroenterology **64**:99–105, 1973.
8. Dallman PR. Cytochrome oxidase repair during treatment of copper deficiency: Relation to mitochondrial turnover. J Clin Invest **46**:1819–1827, 1967.
9. Scheinberg IH, Sternlieb I. Copper metabolism. Pharmacol Rev **12**:355–381, 1960.
10. Wilson JE, Lakey ME. Failure to induce dietary deficiency of copper in premature infants. Pediatrics **25**:40–49, 1960.
11. Cordano A, Placko RP, Graham GG. Hypocupremia and neutropenia in copper deficiency. Blood **28**:280–283, 1966.
12. Ashkenazi A, Levin S, Djaldetti M, Fishel E, Benvenisti D. The syndrome of neonatal copper deficiency. Pediatrics **52**:525–533, 1973.
13. Sternlieb I. Evolution of the hepatic lesion in Wilson's disease (hepatolenticular degeneration). Progr Liver Dis **4**:511–525, 1972.
14. Schroeder HA, Nason AP, Tipton JH, Balassa JJ. Essential trace metals in man: Zinc-relation to environmental cadmium. J Chron Dis **20**:179–210, 1967.
15. Cotzias CG, Borg DC, Selleck B. Virtual absence of turnover in cadmium metabolism: ^{109}Cd studies in the mouse. Amer J Physiol **201**:927–930, 1961.
16. Decker CF, Byerrum RU, Happert CA. A study of the distribution and retention of cadmium-115 in the albino rat. Arch Biochem Biophys **66**:140–145, 1957.
17. Richmond CR, Findlay JS, London JF. Whole-body retention of cadmium-109 by mice following oral, intraperitoneal and intravenous administration. U.S. Atomic Energy Commission, University of California. Los Alamos Scientific Publication LA-3610-MS, Los Alamos, New Mexico, pp195–200, 1966.
18. Miller WJ, Blackmon DM, Martin WF. Cadmium absorption, excretion and tissue distribution following single tracer oral and intravenous doses in young goats. J Dairy Sci **51**:1836–1839, 1968.
19. Doyle JJ, Pfander WH, Grebing SE, Pierce JO. Effect of dietary cadmium on growth, cadmium absorption, and cadmium tissue levels in growing lambs. J Nutr **104**:160–166, 1974.
20. Bremner I. Heavy metal toxicities. Quart J Biophys **7**:75–124, 1974.
21. Anke M, Henning A, Schneider HJ, Ludke H, Von Cagern W, Schlegal H. The interrelations between cadmium, zinc, copper and iron in metabolisms of hens, ruminants and man. In: Mills CF, ed. Trace Element Metabolism in Animals. Edinburgh, Livingston Press, p317, 1970.
22. Campbell JK, Mills CF. Effects of dietary cadmium and zinc on rats maintained on diets low in copper. Proc Nutr Soc **33**:15A–17A, 1974.
23. Mills CF, Dalgarno AC. Copper and zinc status of ewes and lambs increased dietary concentrations of cadmium. Nature (London) **239**:171–173, 1972.
24. Holmberg RE, Ferm VH. Interrelationships of selenium, cadmium, and arsenic in mammalian teratogenesis. Arch Environ Health **18**:873–877, 1969.
25. Schroeder HA, Mitchener M. Toxic effects of trace elements on the reproduction of mice and rats. Arch Environ Health **23**:102–106, 1971.
26. Gerber G, Maes J, Deroo J. Effect of dietary lead on placental blood flow and on fetal uptake of α-amino isobutyrate. Arch Toxicol **41**:125–131, 1978.
27. Levin AA, Miller RK. Fetal toxicity of cadmium in the rat: Decreased utero-placental blood flow. Toxicol Appl Pharmacol **58**:297–306, 1981.
28. Twardock AR, Austin MK. Calcium transfer in perfused guinea pig placenta. Amer J Physiol **219**:540–545, 1970.
29. Kelman BJ, Walter BK. Use of perfusion in the study of placental transport of mercury and cadmium. In: Mahlum DD, Sikov MR, Hackett PL, Andrew FD, eds. Developmental Toxicology of Energy-Related Pollutants. Oak Ridge, Tennessee, U.S. DOE/TIC, Conf-771017, p555, 1978.
30. Levin AA, Miller RK. Fetal toxicity of cadmium in the rat: Maternal vs fetal injections. Teratology **22**:1–5, 1980.
31. Levin AA, Miller RK. Fetal toxicity of cadmium in the rat: Time course of placental uptake of Cd. Abstract, Society of Toxicology, 19th Annual Meeting, 1980.

Received July 25, 1983. P.S.E.B.M. 1984, Vol. 176.
Accepted February 23, 1984.

PROCEEDINGS OF THE SOCIETY FOR EXPERIMENTAL BIOLOGY AND MEDICINE **176**, 143–147 (1984)

Genetic Obesity and the Muscle Satellite Cell[1] (41854)

D. R. CAMPION,* R. W. PURCHAS,† R. A. MERKEL,‡,§ AND D. R. ROMSOS§

**USDA-ARS Richard B. Russell Agricultural Research Center, Athens, Georgia 30613; †Department of Animal Science, Massey University, Palmerston North, New Zealand; ‡Department of Animal Science, and §Department of Food Science and Human Nutrition, Michigan State University, East Lansing 48824*

Abstract. The nuclear content of skeletal muscles from lean and obese (ob/ob) male mice was investigated. Four lean and four ob/ob mice were examined at 2, 3, 5, 8, and 16 weeks of age. Differences in body weight between the two phenotypes were significant after 5 weeks of age. For all ages in the soleus and after 3 weeks of age in the gastrocnemius, muscle wet weight and length were less in ob/ob mice than in lean mice. Age did not influence the incidence of myonuclei in fiber cross sections for either muscle. Compared to lean mice the incidence of myonuclei per fiber cross section was significantly lower for ob/ob mice in the soleus muscle but not in the gastrocnemius muscle. The incidence of satellite cells in fiber cross sections and the percentage of nuclei within the basal lamina that were satellite cell nuclei decreased as age increased. Muscle fibers of ob/ob mice contained fewer myonuclei either because of shorter muscle length (gastrocnemius), or because of the combined effect of shorter muscle length and fewer myonuclei per unit length (soleus). The lower apparent number of myonuclei in the muscles of ob/ob mice was associated with a lower apparent number of satellite cells.

In postnatal skeletal muscle total muscle mass is directly related to total muscle DNA content (1). Since the amount of DNA per nucleus is constant within an animal, DNA content must be a direct reflection of nuclear content. The rate of myonuclear proliferation, then, will influence the rate of accretion of muscle mass. Addition of new myonuclei postnatally to growing myofibers is the result of mitosis in satellite cells and the subsequent incorporation of daughter nuclei into the myofiber (2). Therefore, the quantity and/or rate of mitotic activity of satellite cells are presumably important variables that orchestrate postnatal muscle growth.

In certain models of obesity, such as obese (ob/ob) mice and obese Zucker rats, the growth potential of the lean body mass is diminished (3, 4). This characteristic is expressed in the early postweaning period in the ob/ob mouse and has been suggested as a predisposing factor for obesity (3, 5). The role of satellite cells in the reduction of growth potential of lean body mass has not been previously described in this model or any other model of obesity. The relation between muscle nuclear content and other linear measurements of muscle growth were examined in this study in lean and ob/ob mice at various postnatal ages.

Materials and Methods. Four pairs of male lean (ob/+ or +/+) and obese (ob/ob) mice were obtained from the Michigan State University breeding colony of C57BL/6J-ob/+ mice at 2, 3, 5, 8, and 16 weeks of age. Mice were weaned at 3 weeks of age and fed a stock diet (Wayne Lab-Blox, Allied Mills, Chicago, Ill.) *ad libitum*. Mice were housed at 23–25°C in solid-bottomed cages with lights on from 0700 to 1900 hr each day.

At 2 weeks of age, preobese and nonobese mice were tentatively identified by oxygen consumption measurements (6). Preobese ob/ob mice consume less oxygen than nonobese (ob/+ or +/+) mice. Identification of preobese and nonobese mice was confirmed by measurement of body fat after removal of the gastrocnemius and soleus muscles and stomach contents. Carcasses with 10–15% fat were designated lean while those with 17–22% were designated ob/ob (6). Immediately after sacrifice with diethyl ether, hind limbs were fixed *in situ* by infusion of buffered (0.1 *N* phosphate, pH 7.2) 2% glutaraldehyde solution into the left ventricle after first flushing the system with a solution of 0.5% sodium citrate and 0.9% NaCl. The posterior vena cava was

[1] Michigan Agricultural Experiment Station Article No. 10960.

0037-9727/84 $1.50

cut prior to the infusion. After 30 min, blocks of tissue approximately 1 mm square and several millimeters in length, were taken from the white portion of the medial head of the gastrocnemius muscle and from the soleus muscle. The blocks were fixed for an additional hour with 2% glutaraldehyde in phosphate buffer. Then the blocks were washed with buffer containing 4.5% sucrose and stored at 0–3°C in sucrose buffer for up to 4 weeks before being shipped on ice to the Richard B. Russell Agricultural Research Center where the blocks were postfixed in osmium and finally embedded in Epon.[2] Sections, approximately 70 nm thick (silver interference) were put onto 250-μm-mesh copper grids and stained with lead citrate and uranyl acetate. Cross sections of 100 muscle fibers from each animal were examined for fiber diameter (minimum diameter) and for the presence of myonuclei and of satellite cell nuclei. From these data, the percentage of fibers in cross section that exhibited myonuclei and satellite cell nuclei and the percentage of nuclei within the basal lamina that were satellite cell nuclei were calculated (7). At 2, 5, and 16 weeks of age, nuclear lengths were determined on longitudinal muscle sections (1 μm thick) that were stained with methylene blue–azure II.

Analysis of variance was conducted according to the Statistical Analysis System of Barr *et al.* (8). An arcsine transformation was conducted on the percentage data prior to analysis.

Results. Morphologically, satellite cells of lean and obese mice were indistinguishable in their ultrastructural characteristics. At 2 weeks of age, relatively more of the satellite cells in both phenotypes exhibited an ultrastructure characteristic of an activated cell (9).

Obese mice were significantly heavier (Table I) than lean mice after 5 weeks of age. The gastrocnemius muscle of obese mice, when compared to lean mice, was lighter in weight and shorter in length after 3 weeks of age. After 5 weeks of age, fibers in the gastrocnemius muscle of obese mice had a smaller diameter than did the fibers of lean mice.

Wet weight and length of the soleus muscle of obese mice were significantly lower over all ages when compared to lean mice. Fiber diameter was initially smaller then larger at 3 and 5 weeks of age, before again becoming smaller at 8 and 16 weeks of age in soleus muscle of obese mice when compared to lean mice.

Results from measurement of muscle nuclear content are summarized in Table II. In the gastrocnemius muscle, the percentage fibers with myonuclei present did not vary significantly with phenotype or age. But, in the soleus muscle, the percentage fibers with myonuclei present was significantly lower across all ages in ob/ob mice than in lean mice. The percentage fibers with satellite cell nuclei present decreased with age in both muscles, as did the percentage nuclei within the basal lamina that were satellite cell nuclei. Nuclear length, determined in 5-week-old mice was similar between phenotypes. The overall mean nuclear length was 12.1 ± 0.1 μm for gastrocnemius muscle and 12.0 ± 0.1 μm for soleus muscle.

Discussion. Phenotypic expression of the obese condition in ob/ob mice normally occurs about 5 weeks postnatally (10). Bergen *et al.* (3) previously reported that by 5 to 6 weeks of age total fat-free residue and total protein were less in hind limbs of ob/ob mice than in lean mice. Our data, as well as that of others (11–14), also showed that the skeletal muscle mass was less in ob/ob mice than in lean mice. Furthermore, the temporal sequence that led to the expression of phenotypic differences in muscle weight, length and fiber diameter varied for the two muscles. Phenotypic differences in these traits were already evident at 2 weeks of age in the soleus muscle; no differences existed in the gastrocnemius muscle until 5 to 8 weeks of age. In many species, e.g., fowl (15) and pig (16), the incidence of myonuclei in fiber cross sections increases with age. On the other hand, mice of the C57BL/6J strain, as well as those of several other strains of mice (17, 18), exhibit little change after 2 weeks of age in the percentage fibers with myonuclei present. The reason for this species variation is not known.

The percentage fibers with satellite cell nu-

[2] Mention of a trade name, proprietary product, or specific equipment does not constitute a guarantee or warranty by the U.S. Department of Agriculture and does not imply its approval to the exclusion of other products which may be suitable.

TABLE I. EFFECT OF PHENOTYPE AND AGE ON BODY WEIGHT AND MUSCLE DIMENSIONS[a]

Trait	Phenotype	Age (weeks)					Standard error
		2	3	5	8	16	
Body weight[b] (g)	Lean	7.5	10.0	19.6	27.5	32.4	0.9
					**	**	
	Obese	7.1	11.0	18.8	40.6	55.6	0.9
Gastrocnemius							
Wet weight[b] (mg)	Lean	8.0	17.2	37.9	64.6	67.0	2.1
				**	**	**	
	Obese	6.4	17.3	28.5	48.3	46.4	2.1
Length[b] (mm)	Lean	51	66	81	94	96	2
				**	*d*	**	
	Obese	51	65	71	90	85	2
Fiber diameter[b] (μm)	Lean	18	24	25	43	46	1
					**	d	
	Obese	17	24	24	35	43	1
Soleus							
Wet weight[c] (mg)	Lean	1.6	2.4	5.2	8.4	9.4	0.4
	Obese	1.5	2.2	4.3	6.7	8.6	0.4
Length[c] (mm)	Lean	51	62	73	81	81	2
	Obese	49	62	65	80	73	2
Fiber diameter[b] (μm)	Lean	18	19	27	38	36	8
		*	**	*	**	**	
	Obese	15	23	30	31	33	8

[a] Each value is the least-squares mean from four animals.
[b] Phenotype × age interaction was significant, $P < 0.01$.
[c] Main effects of phenotype and of age were significant, $P < 0.01$. Interactions were not significant ($P > 0.05$).
[d] Within trait and age, effect of phenotype tended to be significant ($P < 0.10$).
* $P < 0.05$ for phenotypic comparison within trait and age.
** $P < 0.01$ for phenotypic comparison within trait and age.

clei present and the percentage nuclei within the basal lamina that are satellite cell nuclei normally decreases with age in the mouse (17–19). However, due to small sample size and very low satellite cell nuclear frequencies, statistical analyses were not conducted on satellite cell nuclear traits. Discussion of these limitations is presented in detail elsewhere (20–22). To obtain an estimate of phenotypic differences for nuclear traits, data for muscle length and nuclear traits were pooled within phenotype across ages (Table III). The apparent number of nuclei was calculated by the formula PL/d, where P equaled the percentage fibers in cross section with nuclei present, L equaled muscle length, and d equaled nuclear length. Considering only phenotypic differences, then, the gastrocnemius and soleus muscles were both about 8% shorter in ob/ob mice than in lean mice. Apparent myonuclear number was 14 and 23% less in the gastrocnemius and soleus muscles, respectively, of ob/ob mice when compared to the muscles of lean mice. The lower apparent number of myonuclei in the gastrocnemius muscle of ob/ob mice was primarily due to differences in muscle length (Table I) while the lower number in the soleus muscle was due to differences in muscle length and in the percentage fibers with myonuclei present (Table II).

Apparent satellite cell number was also lower in muscles of ob/ob mice than in muscles of lean mice. No appreciable difference was observed in the percentage of nuclei within the basal lamina that were satellite cell nuclei. Similarity in this latter trait between phenotypes, both across ages (Table III) and within the various ages (Table II), suggests that incorporation of satellite cell nuclei per se into myofibers was not influenced by phenotype. The fact that there are fewer myonuclei contained within the two muscles of the ob/ob

TABLE II. EFFECT OF PHENOTYPE AND AGE ON MUSCLE NUCLEAR CONTENT[a]

Trait	Phenotype	Age (weeks) 2	3	5	8	16
				%		
Gastrocnemius						
Fibers with myonuclei[b]	Lean	60.2 ± 3.4	57.5 ± 3.7	53.2 ± 4.3	61.5 ± 2.5	61.0 ± 11.2
	Obese	63.5 ± 1.4	61.0 ± 2.1	54.2 ± 2.2	54.2 ± 1.9	56.5 ± 2.6
Fibers with satellite cell nuclei	Lean	11.0 ± 1.1	3.5 ± 0.6	1.5 ± 0.5	1.8 ± 0.2	0.5 ± 0.3
	Obese	8.5 ± 1.8	3.8 ± 0.8	1.2 ± 0.2	1.5 ± 0.3	0.8 ± 0.5
Nuclei within basal lamina that were satellite cell nuclei	Lean	15.5 ± 1.5	5.7 ± 0.9	2.9 ± 1.0	2.4 ± 0.4	0.7 ± 0.4
	Obese	11.6 ± 2.1	5.8 ± 1.2	2.2 ± 0.4	2.7 ± 0.6	1.3 ± 0.9
Soleus						
Fibers with myonuclei[b,c]	Lean	61.5 ± 2.5	61.0 ± 2.1	58.5 ± 4.9	56.5 ± 4.4	68.8 ± 6.7
	Obese	58.0 ± 1.4	59.2 ± 4.9	54.0 ± 1.8	45.5 ± 6.1	51.5 ± 9.9
Fibers with satellite cell nuclei	Lean	11.8 ± 0.8	5.5 ± 2.0	2.2 ± 0.5	2.2 ± 0.5	0.5 ± 0.5
	Obese	9.2 ± 2.3	5.5 ± 1.0	3.0 ± 0.6	3.5 ± 0.3	0.5 ± 0.3
Nuclei within basal lamina that were satellite	Lean	16.2 ± 1.2	8.0 ± 2.6	3.6 ± 0.5	3.8 ± 0.8	1.0 ± 0.9
	Obese	13.5 ± 2.8	8.9 ± 2.3	5.3 ± 1.0	7.7 ± 1.6	1.3 ± 0.9

[a] Values are means ± SEM of four animals; observations were made on cross sections of fibers.
[b] For both muscles the percentage fibers with myonuclei present did not change significantly ($P > 0.05$) with age, and the phenotype × age interaction was also not significant ($P > 0.05$).
[c] The percentage fibers with myonuclei present was significantly lower ($P < 0.05$) in the soleus muscle of obese mice when compared to lean mice.

mice is associated with the finding that there are fewer satellite cells in ob/ob mouse muscle when compared to the muscle of lean mice. Purchas *et al.* (23) recently reported that the proportion of satellite cell nuclei in the gastrocnemius muscle of ob/ob mice which showed proliferative activity was lower than in the same muscle of lean mice at 2 and 3 weeks of age. Thus, the total myonuclear content of ob/ob mice is probably restricted by mitotic activity of the satellite cell as well as by the number of satellite cells.

TABLE III. PHENOTYPIC MEANS FOR SELECTED TRAITS[a]

Trait	Phenotype	Muscle: Gastrocnemius	Soleus
Muscle length (mm)	Lean	78	70
	Obese	72	65
Fibers with myonuclei (%)	Lean	60.7	61.2
	Obese	57.9	53.6
Apparent myonuclear number[b]	Lean	3910	3570
	Obese	3440	2900
Fibers with satellite cell nuclei (%)	Lean	3.6	4.5
	Obese	3.1	4.3
Apparent satellite cell number[b]	Lean	232	262
	Obese	184	233
Nuclei within basal lamina that were satellite cell nuclei (%)	Lean	5.6	6.5
	Obese	5.1	7.3

[a] Values were pooled across ages; $N = 24$.
[b] Calculated by formula $n = PL/d$, where P = percentage fibers in cross section with nuclei present, L = muscle length, and d = nuclear length.

1. Allen RE, Merkel RA, Young RB. Cellular aspects of muscle growth: Myogenic cell proliferation. J Anim Sci **49**:115–127, 1979.
2. Moss FP, Leblond CP. Satellite cells as the source of nuclei in muscles of growing rats. Anat Rec **170**:421–436, 1971.
3. Bergen WG, Kaplan ML, Merkel RA, Leveille GA. Growth of adipose and lean tissue mass in hind limbs of genetically obese mice during preobese and obese phases of development. Amer J Clin Nutr **28**:157, 1975.
4. Shapira JF, Kircher I, Martin RJ. Indices of skeletal muscle growth in lean and obese Zucker rats. J Nutr **110**:1313–1318, 1980.
5. Carnie JA, Smith DG. Diabetes, obesity and heat production—possible links. Fed Eur Biochem Soc Lett **110**:8–10, 1980.
6. Thurlby PL, Trayhurn P. The development of obesity in preweanling ob/ob mice. Brit J Nutr **39**:397–402, 1978.
7. Campion DR, Marks HL, Richardson RL. An analysis of satellite cell content in the semimembranosus muscle of Japanese quail (*Coturnix coturnix japonica*) selected for rapid growth. Acta Anat **112**:9–13, 1982.
8. Barr AJ, Goodnight JH, Sall JP, Helwig JT. A User's Guide to SAS 76 (SAS Institute, Inc., Raleigh, NC, 1976).
9. Campion DR. The muscle satellite cell. A review. Int Rev Cytol **87**:225–247, 1984.
10. Ingalls AM, Dickie MM, Snell GD. Obese, new mutation in the house mouse. J Hered **41**:317, 1950.
11. Thurlby PL, Trayhurn P. Regional blood flow in genetically obese (ob/ob) mice. Pflueger Arch **385**:193–201, 1980.
12. Cuendet GS, Loten EG, Jeanrenaud B, Renold AG. Decreased basal, noninsulin stimulated glucose uptake and metabolism by skeletal muscle isolated from obese-hyperglycemic (ob/ob) mice. J Clin Invest **58**:1078–1088, 1976.
13. Trostler N, Romsos DR, Bergen WG, Leveille GA. Skeletal muscle accretion and turnover in lean and obese (ob/ob) mice. Metabolism **28**:928–933, 1979.
14. Trostler N, Amin R, Shafrir E. Increased protease activity in muscles of obese (ob/ob) mice. Int J Obesity **6**:557–566, 1982.
15. Moss FP. The relationship between the dimensions of the fibers and the number of nuclei during normal growth of skeletal muscle in the domestic fowl. Amer J Anat **122**:555–564, 1968.
16. Campion DR, Richardson RL, Reagan JO, Kraeling RR. Changes in the satellite cell population during postnatal growth of pig skeletal muscle. J Anim Sci **52**:1014–1018, 1981.
17. Schultz E. A quantitative study of the satellite cell population in postnatal mouse lumbrical muscle. Anat Rec **180**:580–596, 1974.
18. Cardasis CA, Cooper GW. An analysis of nuclear numbers in individual muscle fibers during differentiation and growth: A satellite cell–muscle fiber growth unit. J Exp Zool **191**:347–358, 1975.
19. Allbrook DB, Han MF, Hellmuth AE. Population of muscle satellite cells in relation to age and mitotic activity. Pathology **3**:233–243, 1971.
20. Abercrombie M. Estimation of nuclear population from microtome sections. Anat Rec **94**:239–247, 1946.
21. Maruenda E, de, Franzini-Armstrong C. Satellite and invasive cells in frog sartorius muscle. Tissue Cell **10**:749–772, 1978.
22. Atherton GW, James NT. Stereological analysis of the number of nuclei in skeletal muscle fibers. Acta Anat **107**:236–240, 1980.
23. Purchas RW, Romsos DR, Allen RE, Merkel RA. Muscle growth and satellite cell proliferative activity in obese (ob/ob) mice. J Anim Sci, submitted, 1984.

Received September 13, 1983. P.S.E.B.M. 1984, Vol. 176.
Accepted February 24, 1984.

PROCEEDINGS OF THE SOCIETY FOR EXPERIMENTAL BIOLOGY AND MEDICINE **176**, 148–153 (1984)

Induction of Testicular Differentiation in the Fetal Mouse Ovary by Transplantation into Adult Male Mice (41855)

TERUKO TAKETO, HORACIO MERCHANT-LARIOS,* AND SAMUEL S. KOIDE

The Population Council, Center for Biomedical Research, 1230 York Avenue, New York, New York 10021, and
**Instituto de Investigaciones Biomedicas, Universidad Nacional Autonoma de Mexico, Apartado Postal 70228, Mexico 20 D.F., Mexico*

Abstract. Mouse ovarian primordia on the 12th or 13th day of gestation frequently developed testicular structures in addition to ovarian structures by the 14th day after transplantation into a site beneath the kidney capsules of adult male mice. Electron microscopic examination of the testicular portion of ovotestes revealed all types of testicular somatic cells, i.e., Sertoli, myoid, and Leydig cells, but not spermatogenic cells. On the other hand, after transplantation into adult female mice ovarian grafts developed only ovarian structures. We conclude that female gonadal somatic cells differentiate into testicular components in a male host environment.

Sexual differentiation in mammals involves a sequence of events. Genetic sex is determined at fertilization by the combination of sex chromosomes, which are in turn responsible for gonadal development. A gene(s) located on the Y chromosome, interacting with autosomal genes, induces testicular differentiation, and in its absence, gonadal primordia differentiate into ovaries (1). However, the mechanism by which the genes control gonadal differentiation is not clear. One way to elucidate the mechanism is to study the condition(s) under which gonadal sex can be reversed experimentally.

Gonadal sex reversal in mammals that is caused by mutation or translocation of genes involved in testis determination has been reported in the human, mouse, and goat. For example, sex-reversed (Sxr) female mice develop as phenotypic males with testes because a segment of the Y chromosome is translocated to the X chromosome (2). However, sex reversal of mammalian gonads with normal chromosomes is very rare. One example is the freemartin condition in cattle, sheep, and goats, where testicular components are formed in the ovary when the circulation of a female fetus is shared with that of a male (3, 4). The mechanism of this phenomenon remains unclear, primarily because of the difficulty in reproducing the freemartin condition experimentally. For studying the regulation of gonadal sex differentiation, it is important to establish an experimental system in which gonadal sex can be reversed frequently. It has been reported that fetal rat ovaries develop testis-cord-like structures when transplanted into a site beneath kidney capsules (5), into the omenta (6), or into a subcutaneous (7), intraocular (8), or scrotal (9) position of adult rats. However, the tubular structures developed in the transplanted ovaries were not considered "testicular" by some investigators (10).

We report here that when transplanted into adult male mice, mouse fetal ovaries frequently developed testicular structures which contained all types of testicular somatic cells. On the other hand, fetal ovaries transplanted into adult female hosts developed only ovarian components. The results show that gonadal somatic cells undergo testicular differentiation in a male host environment, regardless of the genetic sex of the gonads.

Materials and Methods. Ovarian primordia with the mesonephroi attached were isolated from mouse fetuses between the 12th and 16th day of gestation (dg). The day when copulation plugs were found was defined as Day 0. SJL/J strain and NCS strain (Rockefeller University) mice were used. On the 12th dg or later, fetal testes were distinguished from fetal ovaries by observing for striation of testis cords under a dissecting microscope. One of each pair of fetal gonads was transplanted into a site beneath the kidney capsules of an adult male mouse, and the other into the same site of an adult female mouse. On the 14th day after transplantation, the gonadal grafts were dissected out and processed for histological examinations. For light microscopic study,

0037-9727/84 $1.50

tissues were fixed in Bouin's solution, sectioned with paraffin, and stained with hematoxylin and eosin. For electron microscopic study, tissues were fixed in Karnovsky's solution (11) and embedded in Epon after OsO_4 fixation. Semithin sections (100-nm thickness) were stained with silver–methenamine solution and examined with a light microscope.

Results. Twenty-five fetal ovaries of NCS strain on the 12th or 13th dg were transplanted into male mice. As summarized in Table I, 20 ovarian primordia developed testicular structures. Of these masculinized ovaries, 17 also developed follicular structures (ovotestes) while 3 developed only testicular structures. The ratio of testicular to ovarian structures varied with each ovotestis. The other 5 ovarian primordia developed only follicular structures. In female hosts, on the other hand, all 12 ovarian primordia developed typical follicular structures. Since the NCS mouse is outbred, we repeated this experiment in SJL/J inbred strain mice; 6 of 13 ovarian primordia developed testicular structures when transplanted into male hosts, whereas all 14 ovarian primordia developed only ovarian structures when transplanted into female hosts. In contrast to ovarian primordia transplanted on the 12th or 13th dg, fetal ovaries transplanted on the 14th dg or later into male hosts did not develop testicular structures (except for one transplant in SJL/J), and formed well-advanced follicles containing oocytes of normal morphology.

We examined the seminiferous tubules that developed in ovarian transplants and identified well-differentiated testicular somatic cells. Light micrographs of a representative ovotestis are shown in Figs. 1 and 2. For comparison, a light micrograph of an ovary transplanted into a female host is shown in Fig. 3; the morphology, with follicular structures at various stages of development (Types 2–5b according to Peters' classification) (12), was comparable to that of 1-week-old mouse ovaries (13, 14). The ovarian portions of the ovotestes contained oocytes surrounded by follicular cells whose developmental stages (mainly Types 2–3b) were considerably retarded in comparison with those of ovaries transplanted into female hosts. Similar developmentally retarded follicles were seen in the ovaries that were transplanted into male hosts and did not develop any testicular structures, although these ovaries also contained more advanced follicles (Types 2–5b). The testicular portions of the ovotestes contained Sertoli cells and myoid cells (or interlamellar cells) (15) composing seminiferous tubules, and Leydig cells in the interstitial region. In the seminiferous tubules, oocytes were occasionally present, but spermatogenic cells were never observed. Electron micrographs of the Sertoli cells (Fig. 4) showed slightly advanced morphology, typical of that observed in testes of the 2-week-old mouse (16). Electron micrographs of myoid cells and Leydig cells in ovotestes are shown in Figs. 5 and 6. As in the normal testis, numerous microfilaments were seen in the myoid cells of the testicular portion of ovotestes, but not in the theca cells enclosing the follicles in the ovarian portion (and in the ovaries transplanted into female hosts). Furthermore, ultrastructures characteristic of steroidogenic (Leydig) cells were found only in the interstitial region of testicular portions, whereas in the ovarian portions, such steroidogenic cells were found only inside the follicles.

TABLE I. Development of Ovarian Primordia Transplanted into Adult Mice

Mouse strain	Developmental age of transplants[a]	Sex of hosts	Number of experiments	Development into: Testes	Ovotestes	Ovaries
NCS	12–13	Male	25	3	17	5
	12–13	Female	12	0	0	12
	14	Male	9	0	0	9
SJL/J	12	Male	13	2	4	7
	12	Female	14	0	0	14
	14–16	Male	9	0	1	8

[a] Day of gestation.

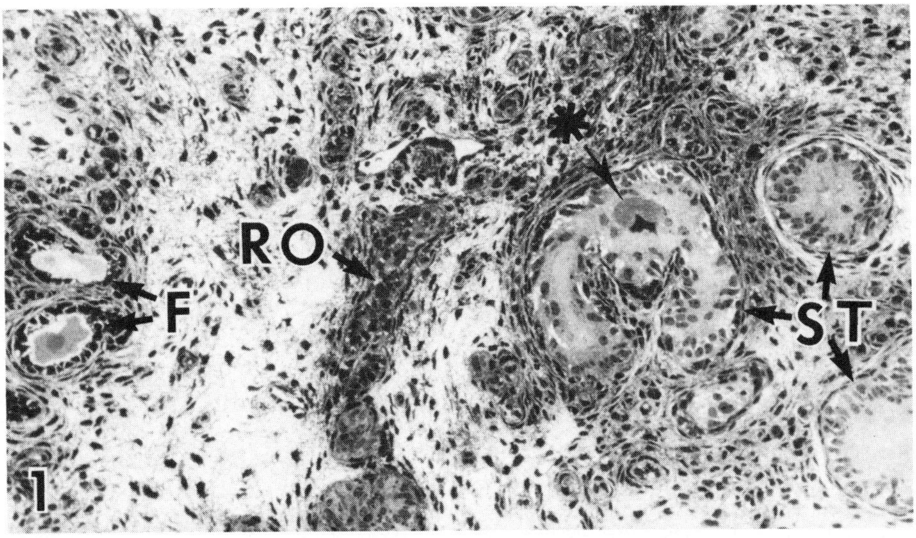

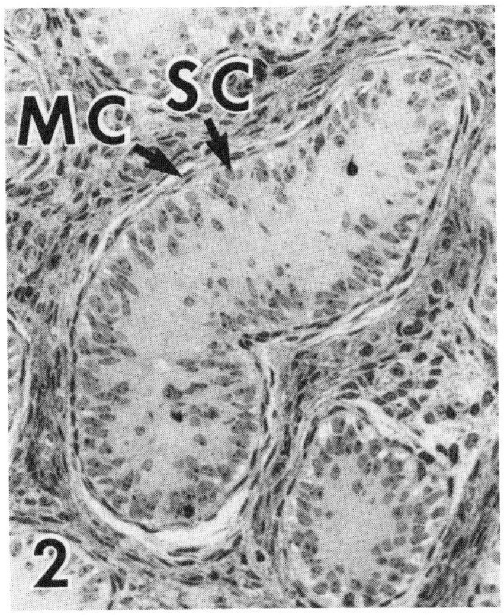

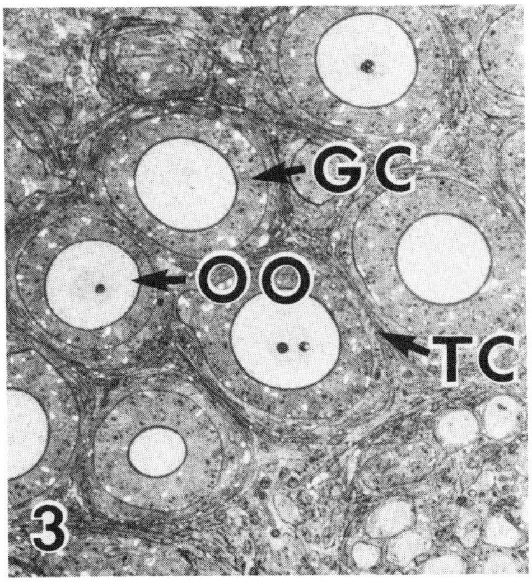

FIG. 1. An ovotestis developed in a male host. Note three types of epithelial structures surrounded by basal lamina and dense connective tissue; ovarian follicles (F), rete ovarii (RO), and seminiferous tubules (ST). A remnant of degenerating oocyte (*) is seen in a seminiferous tubule. ×60.

FIG. 2. Testicular part of the ovotestis shown in Fig. 1. The seminiferous tubule is surrounded by a layer of myoid cells (MC), whereas Sertoli cells (SC) are arranged around the inside of the basement membrane of the seminiferous cord. Note absence of germ cells. ×90.

FIG. 3. An ovary developed in a female host. Well-developed follicles contain multilayers of granulosa cells (GC) and large oocytes (OO). TC, thecal cells. ×90.

Discussion. We showed that testicular structures that developed in ovarian transplants did not merely represent the different arrangement of ovarian components, but involved the differentiation of ovarian precursor cells into testicular components. The capacity of ovarian primordia to form testicular structures was restricted to those transplanted at early stages of development (until the 13th dg) and it appeared to be lost during the course of ovarian differentiation. In NCS mice, testicular differentiation in male fetuses begins on the 12th dg, whereas fetal ovaries remain undifferentiated until the 13th dg, when pri-

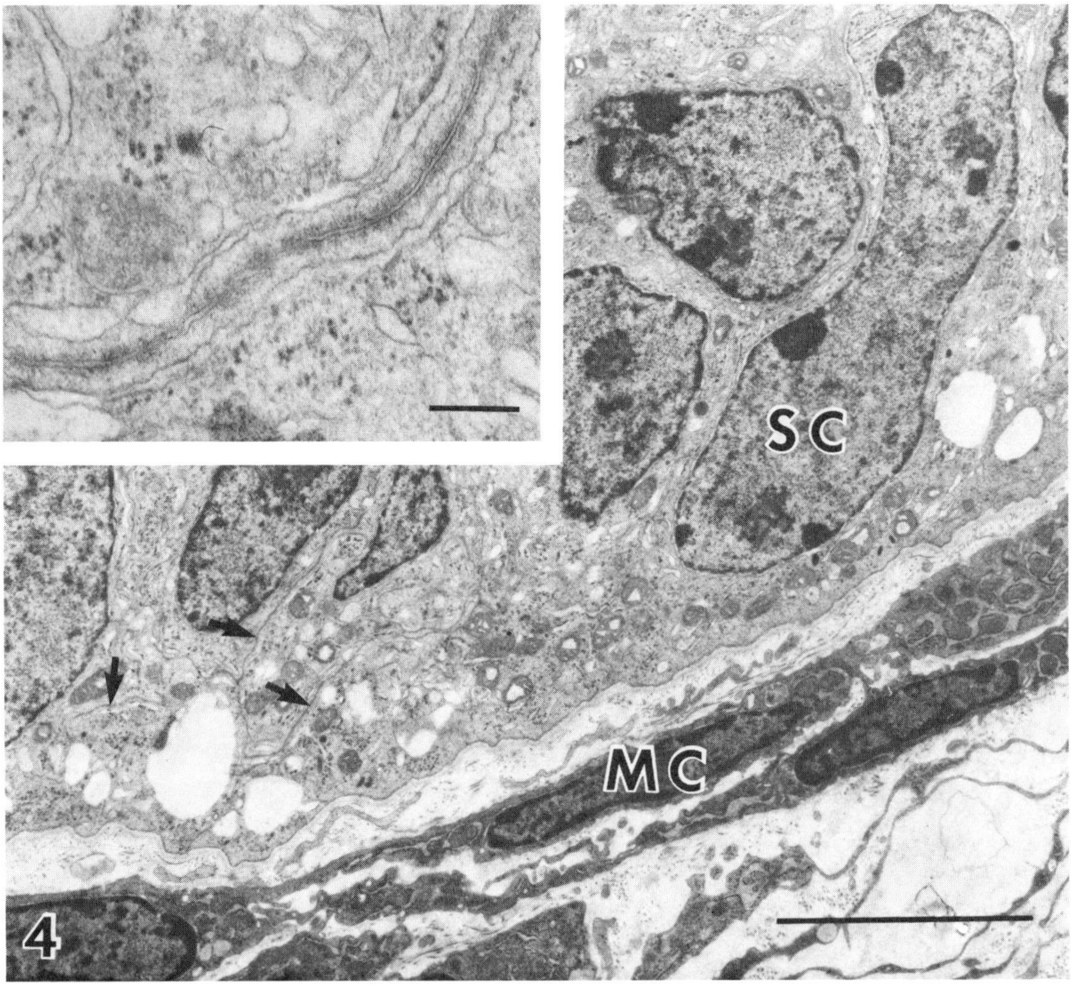

FIG. 4. Electron micrographs of a part of the seminiferous tubule of an ovotestis developed in a male host. Note typical "intersertoli contact specializations" (arrows) between Sertoli cells (SC). Myoid cells (MC) are seen outside the basal lamina. Scale bar indicates 5 μm. Inset: A part of an "intersertoli contact specialization," which is characterized by the presence of an intercellular space (about 7–9 nm) and a flat cisternum of endoplasmic reticulum running parallel to juxtaposed Sertoli cell plasma membranes with some ribosomes on the cytoplasmic side. Note the accumulation of a layer of electron-dense filamentous material between the plasma membrane and the associated cisterna of the endoplasmic reticulum. Scale bar indicates 0.2 μm.

mordial germ cells start premeiotic DNA synthesis without accompanying ovary-specific organization (17). On the 14th and 15th dg, germ cells enter meiotic prophase and are frequently surrounded by epithelial cells, which are probably precursors of granulosa cells. These aggregates of somatic cells and germ cells are enclosed by basement membranes and designated as "sex cords" (14). It is our contention that, when placed in the male environment, these sex cords develop into seminiferous tubules, and the pregranulosa cells differentiate into Sertoli cells; this hypothesis is consistent with the findings of occasional oocytes within the seminiferous tubules in ovotestes (Fig. 1) and of epithelial cords containing both Sertoli cells and pregranulosa cells (data not shown). It is noteworthy that the development of the Sertoli cells always coincided with the differentiation of surrounding

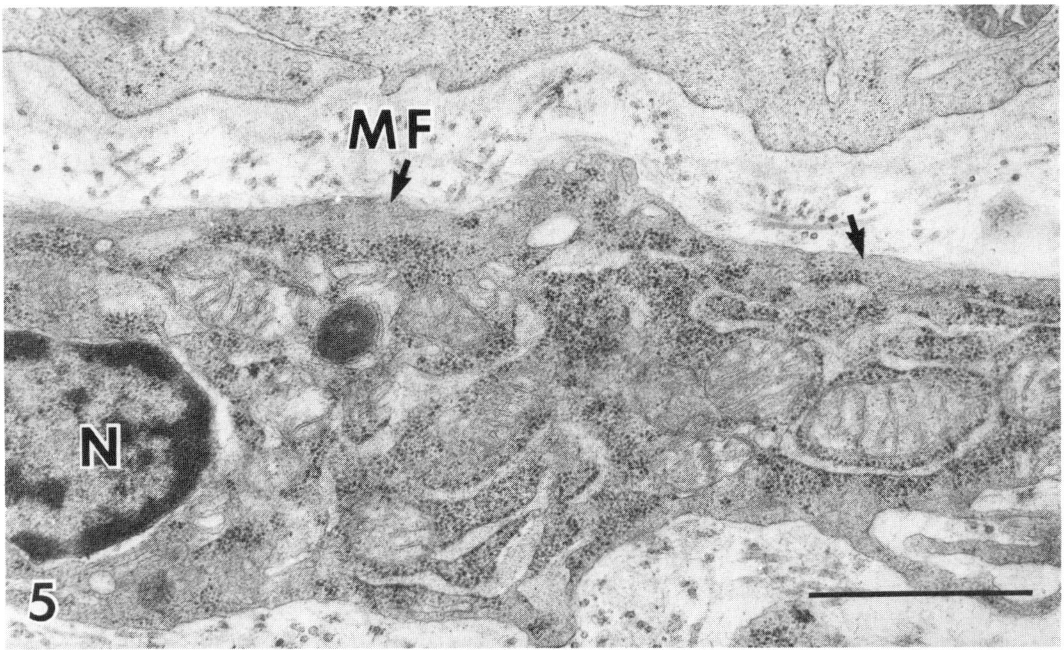

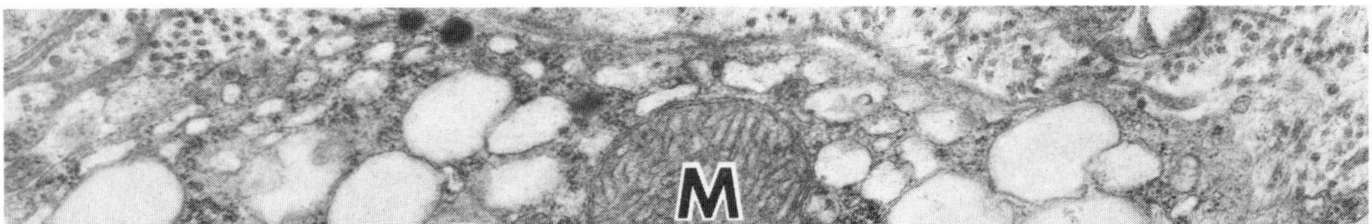

FIG. 5. A part of a myoid cell of an ovotestis with numerous microfilaments (MF) occupying the cytoplasmic matrix. N, nucleus. Scale bar indicates 1.0 μm.

FIG. 6. A part of a Leydig cell of an ovotestis with abundant lipid droplets (L), nucleus (N), and large mitochondria (M) with tubular cristae. Scale bar indicates 1.0 μm.

stromal tissue into testis-specific cells, i.e., myoid cells and Leydig cells. The same mechanism may be involved in the induction of these three types of testicular components, or, alternatively, the differentiation of one cell type may induce that of the other.

The testicular structures that developed in ovarian transplants were devoid of germ cells except for occasional oocytes, which often degenerated. This observation supports the finding by other investigators that XX germ cells do not transform into spermatogonia and cannot survive in the testicular environment (18). In contrast, it has been reported that XY germ cells survive and enter meiosis precociously in an ovarian environment (18) or even in a male environment outside the testis cord (19). Therefore, sex determination of somatic elements and that of germ cells appear to be under the control of different factors. The present study shows that gonadal sex reversal resulting from transplantation is restricted to the somatic elements.

The experimental model reported here has provided a useful system for studying the mechanism regulating sex differentiation of gonadal somatic components. The present results indicate that mouse ovarian primordia are bipotential for the direction of sex differentiation, and the direction can be controlled by factor(s) present in adult, and probably fetal, male mice. This male-specific factor induces differentiation of testicular cells and thereby formation of seminiferous tubules. However, the induction of testicular structures in ovarian primordia might be indirect. It is possible that a male host environment caused the disappearance of oocytes, which in turn prevented follicular development, and permitted the precursor cells to differentiate into testicular components; these three phenomena were coincident in the development of ovotestes.

We thank Braulio Centeno for technical assistance. This work was partially supported by Rockefeller Foundation Grant GA PS 8208 and NICHD Grant HD-13184 and HD-18669.

1. Simpson E. Sex reversal and sex determination. Nature (London) **300**:404–406, 1982.
2. Singh L, Jones KW. Sex reversal in the mouse (*Mus musculus*) is caused by a recurrent nonreciprocal crossover involving the X and an aberrant Y chromosome. Cell **28**:205–216, 1982.
3. Lillie FR. The free-martin: A study of the action of sex hormones in the foetal life of cattle. J Exp Zool **23**:371–451, 1917.
4. Jost A, Vigier B, Prepin J, Perchellet JP. Studies on sex differentiation in mammals. Recent Progr Horm Res **29**:1–35, 1973.
5. Buyse A. The differentiation of transplanted mammalian gonad primordia. J Exp Zool **70**:1–41, 1935.
6. Holyoke EA. The differentiation of embryonic gonads transplanted to the adult omentum in the albino rat. Anat Rec **103**:675–699, 1949.
7. Moore CR, Price D. Differentiation of embryonic reproductive tissues of the rat after transplantation into post-natal hosts. J Exp Zool **90**:229–265, 1942.
8. Torrey TW. Intraocular grafts of embryonic gonads of the rat. J Exp Zool **115**:37–38, 1950.
9. Mangoushi MA. Scrotal allografts of fetal ovaries. J Anat **120**:595–599, 1975.
10. Ozdzenski W, Rogulska T, Batakier H, Brzozowska M, Bembiszewska A, Stepinska V. Influence of embryonic and adult testis on the embryonic ovary in the mouse. Arch Anat Microsc **65**:285–294, 1976.
11. Karnovsky MJ. A formaldehyde–glutaraldehyde fixative of high osmolarity for use in electron microscopy. J Cell Biol **27**:137A, abstr, 1965.
12. Peters H. The development of the mouse ovary from birth to maturity. Acta Endocrinol **62**:98–116, 1969.
13. Merchant H, Zamboni L. Presence of connections between follicles in juvenile mouse ovaries. Amer J Anat **134**:127–132, 1972.
14. Merchant-Larios H. Germ and somatic cell interactions during gonadal morphogenesis. In: Van Blerkom J, Motta PM, eds. Ultrastructure of Reproduction. Boston/The Hague/Dordrecht/Lancaster, Nijhoff, pp19–30, 1984.
15. Fawcett DW, Heidger MP, Leak VL. Lymph vascular system of the interstitial tissue of the testis as revealed by electron microscopy. J Reprod Fertil **19**:109–119, 1969.
16. Flickinger JC. The postnatal development of the Sertoli cells of the mouse. Z Zellforsch **78**:92–113, 1967.
17. Taketo T, Koide SS. *In vitro* development of testis and ovary from indifferent fetal mouse gonads. Dev Biol **84**:61–66, 1981.
18. Short RV. Sex determination and differentiation. Brit Med Bull **35**:121–127, 1979.
19. Upadhyay S, Zamboni L. Ectopic germ cells: Natural model for the study of germ cell sexual differentiation. Proc Natl Acad Sci USA **79**:6584–6588, 1982.

Received December 8, 1983. P.S.E.B.M. 1984, Vol. 176.
Accepted March 6, 1984.

PROCEEDINGS OF THE SOCIETY FOR EXPERIMENTAL BIOLOGY AND MEDICINE **176**, 154–163 (1984)

The Effects of Trifluoperazine on Calcifying Tissues in the Immature Rat (41856)

ADELE L. BOSKEY,* DINA LEWINSON,** AND PETER G. BULLOUGH*

**Hospital for Special Surgery, Cornell University Medical College, New York, New York 10021, and **Technion, Faculty of Medicine, Haifa, Israel*

Abstract. When the antipsychotic drug trifluoperazine is given to immature rats during stages of rapid bone development, severe localized derangement in their growth plate architecture results. In addition, 3 weeks of treatment with doses of 3 mg/kg body wt/day had marked effects on the anatomic distribution of bone mineral, and on the quantitative chemical composition of the bone matrix. Specifically, ash contents and Ca/P ratios were decreased and mineral crystals appeared larger and/or more perfect in the treated animals. The finding of decreased hexosamine content and alterations in bone lipid composition could be interpreted as specific effects of the drug on calmodulin activity.

Calmodulin (CaM), the "calcium-binding regulatory protein" that has been found in all eukaryotic cells in which it has been sought (1–5), has recently been localized in several mineralizing tissues including the developing tooth germ (6) and immature bone (7). The antipsychotic drug, trifluoperazine (a phenothiazine), has been used *in vitro* as a competitive inhibitor of CaM (8–11). In order to gain some knowledge of the involvement of CaM in processes related to mineralization, trifluoperazine was given to immature rats during a period of maximal growth. Histological studies and several biochemical parameters of mineralization were analyzed as an index of the effect of this drug on the mineralization process.

Materials and Methods. Fifteen female Sprague–Dawley rats, 4 weeks of age, weighing 76–82 g, were divided into three groups. Six received daily intramuscular injections (3 mg/kg body wt) of trifluoperazine-HCl (Stelazine, Smith, Kline and French Laboratories, N.Y.) for 21 days. Five were treated similarly for periods of 1 (one animal), 3 (two animals), and 5 (two animals) days. The remaining 4 animals received no drug, and served as controls. At the indicated times, animals were weighed, anesthetized with Fluothane, and sacrificed by heart puncture. Individual plasma samples were used for analyses of calcium, phosphate, cholesterol, glucose, and creatinine concentrations, and alkaline phosphatase activity (Technicon, SMA-12; analyses performed by the Hospital for Special Surgery Clinical Laboratories). All long bones, ribs, and scapulae were removed immediately after sacrifice and microradiographed. The left legs (femur, fibula, and metatarsals) were fixed in phosphate-buffered Formalin. One tibia from each animal was fixed in phosphate-buffered Formalin, embedded in methyl methacrylate, and cut into 4-μm sections; the non-decalcified sections were stained with von Kossa and hematoxylin and eosin stains. The other Formalin-fixed bones were decalcified, embedded in paraffin, and sections were stained with hematoxylin and eosin, safranin O, and the van Geisen method.

The bones from each animal, other than those used for histology, were cleaned of soft tissues and visible marrow by scraping with a fine scalpel; they were then divided under a dissecting microscope into growth plates, metaphyseal cancellous, and diaphyseal cortical bone. Comparable tissue types (e.g., all cortical bone) from a single animal were pooled, and the pooled tissues quick-frozen in liquid nitrogen and lyophilized. Because the growth plates from a single animal did not provide sufficient material for all analyses, growth plates from all 21-day-treated animals were pooled and analyzed together. Growth plates from all the control animals were similarly pooled to provide sufficient material for analysis. Lyophilized tissues were ground in a liquid nitrogen-cooled colloid-mill. The cancellous bone, which had a high blood and marrow content, was washed in ammonium-bicarbonate buffer (pH 7.8), until the wash water was hemoglobin free (Ames, Hematest), and relyophilized. (Growth plates and cortical

0037-9727/84 $1.50

TABLE I. SERUM CHEMISTRY AFTER 21 DAYS[a]

	Calcium (mg/dl)	P_i (mg/dl)	CHL (mg%)	Creat. (mg%)	Alk. P. (IU)	Glucose (mg/ml)
C (*N* = 4)	10.13 ± 0.32	9.50 ± 0.13	81 ± 6	1.5 ± 1.0	3.4 ± 0.6	187
T (*N* = 6)	8.85 ± 0.65	7.95 ± 0.6	64 ± 7	0.45 ± 0.3	3.2 ± 0.9	234
P	0.001	0.0003	0.003	0.04	NS	*b*

Note. C, control; T, treated.

[a] Mean values for calcium, inorganic phosphate, cholesterol, creatinine, alkaline phosphatase, and glucose ± SD; compared based on *t* test.

[b] *N* = 2. Sufficient serum was not available from most animals to measure glucose.

bones, lacking significant amounts of blood and bone marrow, were not washed.)

Aliquots of lyophilized tissues were subjected to replicate X-ray diffraction analyses using Cu K-alpha radiation. Where measurable, the line width of the c-axis (002) reflection was used as an estimate of crystallite size and perfection (12). Weighed aliquots of the samples which had been used for X-ray diffraction were dried at 100°C, ashed at 600°C, and used for determination of mineral content. The ashed samples were then dissolved in 3 *N* HCl and the Ca (13) and P (14) content of the ash determined.

The remaining lyophilized tissue was used for determination of collagen hydroxyproline (15), hexosamine (16), total lipid, and Ca-acidic phospholipid-phosphate, Ca-PL-PO_4 (17), contents. The lipid class composition of the noncomplexed lipids was determined using thin-layer chromatography (18), followed by quantitative colorimetric analysis of cholesterol and cholesterol ester (19), free fatty acids (20), triglyceride (21), and phospholipid (22). In some cases, aliquots of the phospholipids were further separated into phosphatide classes by thin-layer chromatography (23) prior to measurement of organic phosphate content (22). Ca-PL-PO_4 complexes, dissociated in formic acid (17), were analyzed for phospholipid composition in a similar manner.

Results. Trifluoperazine treatment caused rats to become lethargic relative to the nontreated but similarly handled controls. Growth was impaired and treated animals had significantly ($P < 0.05$) less weight gain (80 ± 8 g in 21 days) than controls (93 ± 13 g in 21 days). Radiographically, there were no detectable differences between treated and control bones. Biochemical examination of the serum of the treated animals showed these animals were significantly hypocalcemic, hypophosphatemic, hypocholesterolemic, and hyperglycemic (Table I). Treated animals also had reduced serum creatinine levels. During the initial 1–5 days of treatment the serum chemistries were not significantly different from the control values suggesting that changes occurred after that time.

Microscopic examination of the growth plates of the animals treated for 21 days showed, in comparison with controls, cellular disorganization and matrix disorganization. With regard to the first of these abnormalities, it can be seen in Fig. 1 that the trifluoperazine-treated animal has fewer cells than the control, and that the normal columnar arrangement of the cells is lost in the treated animals. Matrix

FIG. 1. (A) Photomicrograph of the proximal tibial growth plate in a control animal, stained at the left with hematoxylin and eosin, and at the right stained with the von Kossa stain for phosphate. From these photographs, the thickness of the calcified zone of the cartilage can be appreciated. Note, too, the orderly cellular columns of chondrocytes. (B) Photomicrograph of the proximal tibial growth plate in an animal treated with trifluoperazine for 21 days. There is disorderly arrangement of the cell columns, as compared with the controls, and in addition there appear to be fewer cells. Just above the calcified zone, there is a dissolution of the cartilage matrix, with resultant cleft formation, which is filled with blood. (C) Photomicrograph of another field of the same growth plate shown in (B). From this photograph and from (B), it can be appreciated that there is, in addition to those changes noted in (B), a loss of the normal linear regularity of the calcified zone of the cartilage and the underlying metaphyseal bone, as compared with the control (A). All figures undecalcified sections; ×84.

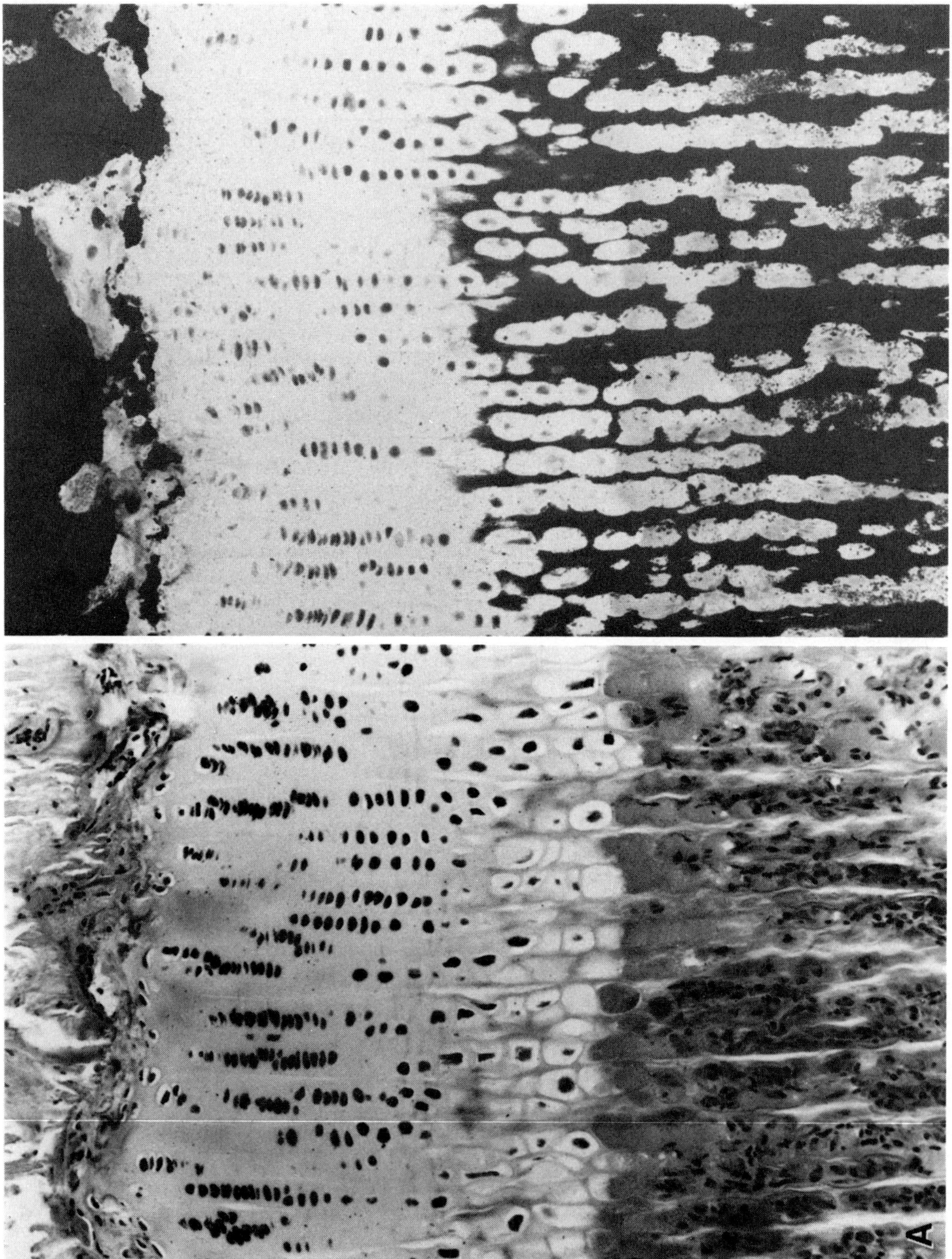

FIG. 1.

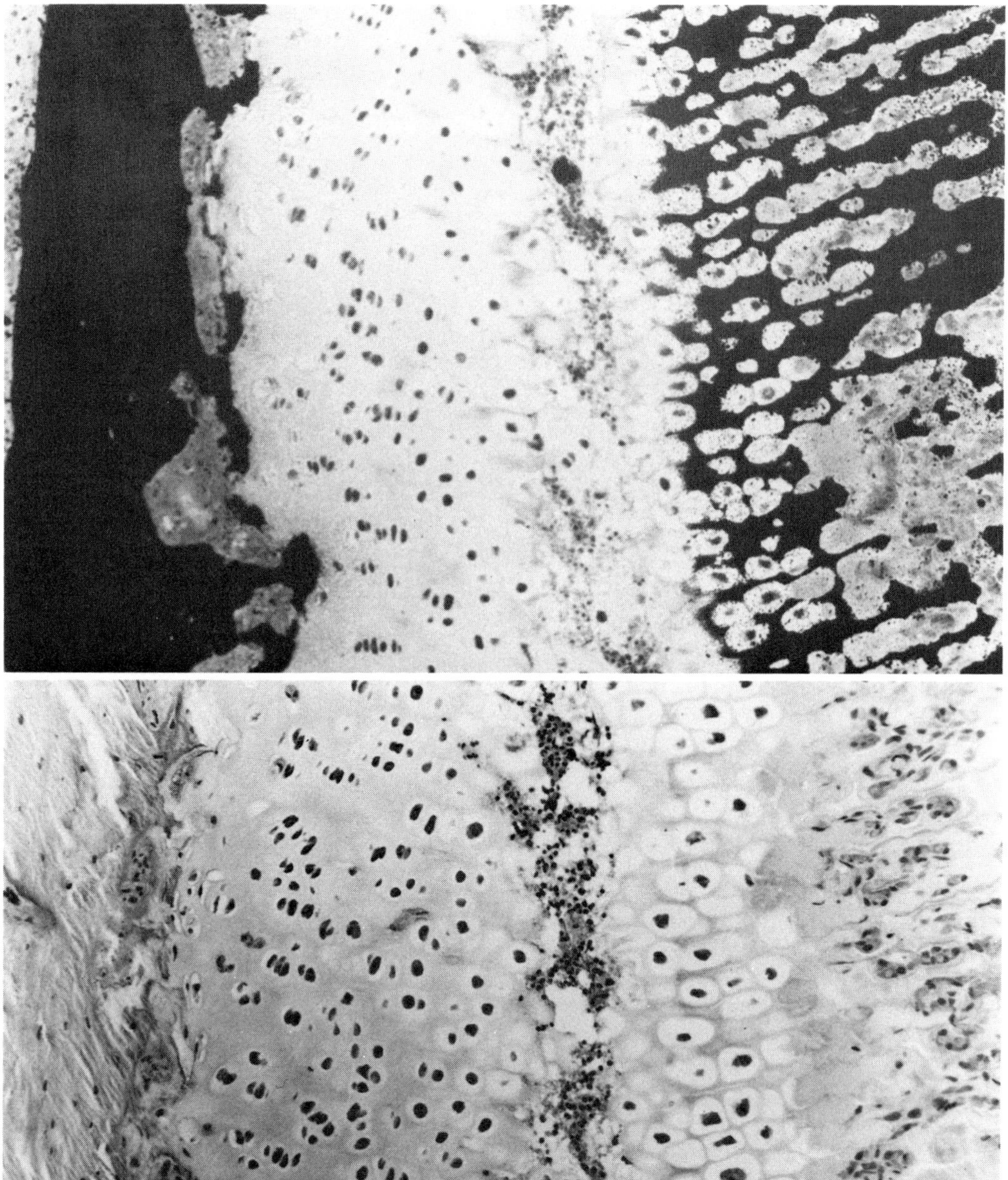

FIG. 1—*Continued.*

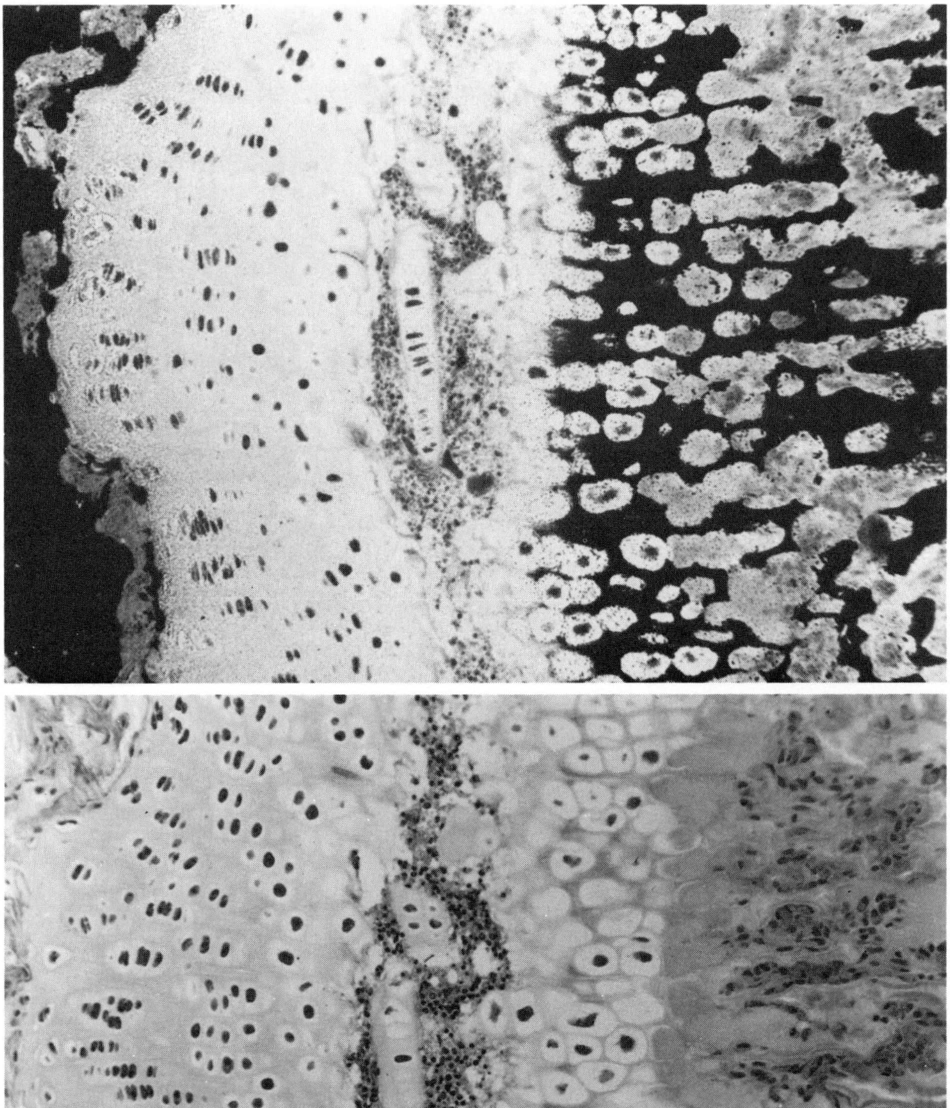

FIG. 1—*Continued.*

TABLE II. CHEMICAL COMPOSITION OF THE BONES OF TRIFLUOPERAZINE-TREATED (T) AND CONTROL (C) RATS

	Growth plates		Cancellous bone		Cortical bone	
	T	C	T	C	T	C
Mineral						
Ash (wt %)	46	49	60 ± 6*	70 ± 2	66 ± 4	70 ± 2
Ca/P (M)	1.61	2.58	1.53 ± 0.28*	2.18 ± 0.18	1.64 ± 0.1*	1.96 ± 0.13
β_{002}	ND	ND	ND	ND	0.54 ± 0.02*	0.56 ± 0.008
Matrix (% Demin. dry wt)						
Hydroxyproline	33 ± 5	34 ± 4	40 ± 4	43 ± 3	67 ± 9	76 ± 7
Hexosamine	10.6 ± 0.1*	12.5 ± 0.2	7.5 ± 1.9*	8.7 ± 0.5	3.8 ± 0.6	4.6 ± 1.1
Lipid	7.5 ± 0.2	7.6 ± 0.3	10.2 ± 0.2	10.4 ± 0.3	5.8 ± 1	6.4 ± 2
Ca-PL-PO_4	0.59 ± 0.2*	2.6 ± 0.2	0.65 ± 0.2	0.58 ± 0.11	0.90 ± 0.5	0.89 ± 0.2

Note. ND, Not determined. Bone data are means ± SD for six treated and four control animals.
* Significantly different from control, $P < 0.05$ based on t test. For growth plate means (and SD) based on replicate (three or four) determinations.

failure was seen to occur just above the calcified zone of the cartilage, and the resultant clefts were filled with blood and disorganized cartilage tissue. These changes were not apparent in the 1- to 5-day-treated animals. Safranin O and van Geison stains failed to show significant microscopic alterations in the proteoglycan and collagen of the matrix.

The chemical composition of the treated bones was not detectably altered by the 1- to 5-day treatment, but was significantly altered in animals treated for 21 days (Table II). Ash content and Ca/P molar ratios were decreased in all tissues from the treated animals. Further, the mineral crystals in the treated cortical bones, based on crystallographic analysis of the c-axis line width were either larger, and/or more perfect, than control bones. The collagen content of the treated bones was not altered, but hexosamine content was decreased in all three components of the treated bones, and calcium-acidic phospholipid phosphate content was significantly decreased in epiphyses of the treated animals. The phospholipid composition of the Ca-PL-PO_4 complexes throughout the treated and nontreated bones was constant, consisting of 33.8 ± 0.7 mole% phosphatidyl inositol and 33.2 ± 0.4 mole% phosphatidyl serine.

The lipid class composition of the growth plates and cancellous bones of TFP-treated animals was also different from that of controls, but there were no differences in cortical bone lipids (Table III). Triglyceride levels were decreased in growth plates of the treated animals, while cholesterol content decreased within the growth plates, and increased in the cancellous bone. Cholesterol ester contents were decreased in both the growth plates and the cancellous bone of the treated animals.

TABLE III. BONE LIPID COMPOSITION (wt% OF TOTAL LIPID)[a] IN TRIFLUOPERAZINE-TREATED (T) AND CONTROL (C) RATS

	Growth plates		Cancellous bone		Cortical bone	
	T	C	T	C	T	C
Triglyceride	18.9 ± 1.4*	25 ± 1.5	49 ± 2	56 ± 1	21.6 ± 0.6	20.2 ± 0.6
Free fatty acid	7.6 ± 1	7 ± 1	9.5 ± 2	7 ± 1	13 ± 3	13 ± 3
Cholesterol	2.4 ± 0.05*	5.2 ± 1	7.2 ± 1.4*	3.1 ± 0.8	2.6 ± 0.1	2.1 ± 0.07
Cholesterol ester	5.1 ± 0.2*	8.3 ± 1	9 ± 3*	16 ± 3	5.6 ± 0.5	6.1 ± 0.08
Phospholipid	16 ± 2	16 ± 3	15 ± 3	11 ± 6	14 ± 4	12 ± 4

[a] Assumes C16 free fatty acids, triolein, cholesterol palmitate, and dipalmitoyl phosphatidyl choline for calculation of weight percentage. All values are means ± SD.
* Differs from control, $P < 0.05$ based on t test.

Although the total phospholipid content of the bones (based on lipid phosphorus content) was not altered by the 21-day TFP treatment, the composition of the phospholipids was appreciably altered by this treatment. Thus the proportion of phospholipids (Table IV) consisting of lysophosphatides was significantly decreased in both the treated growth plates and the treated cancellous bone. Treated cortical bone similarly contained fewer lysophosphatides, although the differences between treated and control cortical ones were less pronounced (not shown).

Discussion. This preliminary study demonstrates that the antipsychotic drug, trifluoperazine, TFP, when given to immature rats, causes alteration of the normal structure of the epiphyseal growth plate, and the adjacent calcifying cartilage and cancellous bone. The cells that appeared most severely damaged were the hypertrophic chondrocytes i.e., those cells which are most intimately involved in preparation of a calcifiable matrix (24).

There has been a recent increase in interest in those factors which control the dynamic process of physiologic calcification in bone and cartilage. In this laboratory we have been particularly interested in the control systems dependent on the complexed acidic phospholipids and the proteoglycans. In this regard, the chemical composition of both the inorganic and organic matrix of the bones of the TFP-treated animals was significantly altered. Bones of treated animals had decreased mineral content, and the mineral present consisted of hydroxyapatite crystals that appeared more mature than those in control bones. The organic bone matrix in the treated animals had a normal collagen hydroxyproline content, but hexosamine content and lipid composition were significantly different from control. [With regard to the reported lipid composition, it is necessary to comment on the recovery of the total lipid pool. The composition of total lipids as shown in Table III was calculated based on several assumptions. To estimate the weight percent of total lipids belonging to each lipid class it was assumed that: all fatty acids were palmitic acid, all triglycerides were triolein, all phospholipids were dipalmitoyl phosphatidyl choline, and all cholesterol esters were cholesterol palmitate. The fact that the total lipids recovered (excluding the 15–20% (25) mono- and diglycerides whose content was not measured for the growth plate and cortical bone) was less than 60 wt% of the total lipid applied indicates these assumptions are not fully valid. However, it must be noted that these deficiencies should not affect the comparison of similar tissues. Previous experience (25) suggests that 8–12% of the total lipids applied to silica gel plates for thin-layer chromatography are lost in recovery. In the cancellous bone, where the major lipid present was triglyceride probably due to marrow and hematopoetic tissue contamination, the errors associated with these assumptions are less apparent. It should be noted that in general the overall lipid composition reported is in good agreement with the results reported for can-

TABLE IV. PHOSPHOLIPID COMPOSITION (PERCENTAGE OF TOTAL LIPID PHOSPHORUS) OF TFP-TREATED (T) AND CONTROL (C) GROWTH PLATES AND CANCELLOUS BONE

	Growth plate		Cancellous bone	
	C	T	C	T
Phosphatidyl choline	60 ± 5	60 ± 5	17 ± 2	24 ± 6*
Lysophosphatidyl choline	4 ± 1	2 ± 1	7.3 ± 0.2	6.1 ± 2
Phosphatidyl ethanolamine	14 ± 1	13 ± 5	20 ± 3	20 ± 3
Lysophosphatidyl ethanolamine	2.7 ± 0.3	1.7 ± 0.1	4.8 ± 0.7	2.8 ± 0.8*
Sphingomyelin	5 ± 1	4.5 ± 1	3.7 ± 1.8	3.1 ± 0.5
Phosphatidyl glycerol	0.6 (tr)	0 (tr)	8.4 ± 0.7	3.8 ± 0.7*
Diphosphatidyl glycerol	2.2 ± 0.3	2.4 ± 0.1	10.2 ± 0.6	11 ± 1
Phosphatidyl serine	7 ± 1	2 ± 1*	4 ± 3	4.7 ± 2
Lysophosphatidyl serine	1 ± 1	0.8 ± 0.2	6 ± 1	2.9 ± 1.1*
Phosphatidyl inositol	1.8 ± 0.1	1.9 ± 0.1	6.1 ± 0.1	5.6 ± 0.9
Phosphatidic acid	0.6 ± 1	2 ± 1	4.6 ± 1.7	5.5 ± 2
Lysophosphatidic acid	1.3 ± 0.1	1.1 ± 0.1	5.3 ± 2	2.9 ± 0.9*

Note. Values are means ± SD. tr, Not detected on all plates.
* Differs from control, $P < 0.05$ based on t test.

cellous, cortical, and epiphyseal bone by Sakai *et al.* (26). However, these investigators did find a higher fatty acid content than we report. The observed phospholipid composition for the control growth plate agrees well with that reported by Wuthier *et al.* (27); the cancellous bone phospholipids appear to be contaminated with marrow lipids, and should not be taken as indicative of cancellous bone lipid composition. However, despite the high concentration of lysophosphatides, the overall content (lysophosphatide + phosphatide) of each individual phosphatide class, with the exception of sphingomyelin, is in excellent agreement with the values reported for compact bone (28).]

There are many possible explanations for the observed matrix and mineral alterations. Some of the biochemical alterations in the bones of the TFP-treated animals may be due to the severe growth plate disruption, and the presence of blood elements from the hemorrhaging tissues. Most of the experimental observations in the TFP-treated animals can be explained in terms of calmodulin inhibition. Trifluoperazine, a phenothiazine derivative, is a competitive inhibitor of calmodulin (9–11, 29–31). It should be noted that TFP also may induce alterations in cell membrane properties, which are apparently independent of calmodulin inhibition (11, 31), due to the lipophilic (membrane-binding) character of the drug. Thus, a toxic effect of TFP on the cells, independent of calmodulin inhibition cannot be ruled out.

There are at least five calmodulin-regulated systems in bone which may be implicated in the observed biochemical and anatomic alterations:

(*1*). Calmodulin is required for cellular differentiation and mitosis (5, 32), processes required for the differentiation of cartilage cells during endochondral ossification (24, 33).

(*2*). Calmodulin stimulates the ATP-dependent transport of calcium out of the cell (30) and out of the mitochondria (10) in other tissues. It is reasonable that the same is true for cartilage cells, where such a Ca pump has been demonstrated (34), and where the flux of Ca out of the mitochondria and cell are crucial for mineralization (35). Any interference with the efficiency of this Ca pump could affect the ability of the chondrocyte to pump out calcium, and might lead to improper mineralization. The low serum Ca levels, and the decreased Ca/P ratios in the bones of treated animals could be a result of the inability of the cells to get rid of their Ca.

(*3*). Calmodulin is the Ca-dependent regulator of phospholipase A2 (36, 37), an enzyme whose activity peaks in the hypertrophic zone of the growth plate (38). Phospholipase A2 is thought to be involved in the production of extracellular matrix vesicles, which are the membrane-bound bodies believed to be the site of initial mineral deposition in cartilage (24). The decreased proportions of lysophosphatides throughout the treated growth plates and cancellous bones might be attributed to impaired activity of this enzyme. It has also been suggested that the formation, or release and formation of Ca-PL-PO_4 complexes, which are hydroxyapatite nucleators (39), is dependent on phospholipase A2 action: a hypothesis supported by decreased Ca-PL-PO_4 concentrations in the treated growth plates.

(*4*). Calmodulin is also required, perhaps associated with the activation of phospholipase A2, for exocytosis (5, 40). It is thus of interest to note that the concentration of noncollagenous proteins released into the medium by bone cells in tissue culture is decreased in the presence of TFP (41). Many of these noncollagenous proteins are involved in the regulation of hydroxyapatite deposition both *in vitro* and *in vivo* (42) and a decrease in their content in the extracellular matrix of the TFP-treated animals could contribute to the observed abnormal mineralization.

(*5*). Calmodulin is also involved in the regulation of carbohydrate metabolism (4, 5), and thus calmodulin inhibition could affect proteoglycan, and glycosaminoglycan synthesis and degradation. Decreased levels of hexosamine are indicative of such abnormalities. Since intact proteoglycans are essential for normal cartilage architecture and the control of mineral deposition (42), the observed matrix derangement, and abnormal mineralization could also be explained, in part, by proteoglycan abnormalities.

In addition, although calmodulin has not yet been shown to be required for the Ca-dependent "base exchange" enzyme (43) required for the synthesis of phosphatidyl serine, the observed decreased phosphatidyl serine concentrations might suggest such a requirement.

The observed loss of bone mineral in the TFP-treated animals might also be due to increased resorption, on the basis of hyperparathyroidism secondary to the observed TFP-induced hypocalcemia, or to disuse osteoporosis in the lethargic animals. The apparent increased hydroxyapatite particle size and decreased Ca/P ratios of the mineral in the treated animals are similar to that found in some osteoporotic bones (44), and also supports the contention that increased resorption and/or decreased formation might be taking place.

It should be noted, that TFP does not, at dosages of 1.0 or 10 mg/kg/day, even over extended periods, accumulate in bones (45). However, the effects of TFP on bone, may only be observable during periods of active endochondral ossification. Further, these effects are not likely to be dependent on the accumulation of the drug in bone, but rather should be related to the effect of the drug on metabolically active cells. It should be noted that the only other study of the effect of TFP on bone (46) examined only the fluoride content of ashed bones and not the nature of the bone itself. Additional morphological and chemical studies at the ultrastructural level, and in isolated, *in vitro* systems, will be needed to clarify the short- and long-term effects of TFP on mineralizing tissues, and to verify that this effect is due to calmodulin inhibition. Nonetheless, the clinical implications of this study should not be overlooked.

In conclusion, the finding of TFP-induced mineralization defects may have clinical significance, since the dosage of drug used is comparable to the recommended adult dose, although it is higher than the starting dosage (0.05 mg/kg body wt) that is recommended for the treatment of psychotic diseases in children. However, it should be noted that there are no specific reports of growth disturbances in TFP-treated children, although there are several reports of osteopenia in individuals treated with this and other neuroleptic drugs (46–49). The immature rats in this study were given TFP during a stage of maximal endochondral growth, 4–6 weeks after birth. This time period has been widely used in our laboratory (50), and in others (51, 52), to characterize the effect of vitamin D and its metabolites on mineralization. The apparent abnormalities in the bones of these rats after as short a period as 3 weeks suggests that TFP can markedly inhibit normal skeletal metabolism especially during periods of rapid growth.

Supported by NIH Grants DE-04141 and AM-19776. This is Publication Number 170 from the Laboratory of Ultrastructural Biochemistry.

---

1. Cheung WY. Calmodulin plays a pivotal role in cellular regulation. Science **207**:19–27, 1980.
2. Klee CB, Crouch TH, Richman PG. Calmodulin. Annu Rev Biochem **49**:489–515, 1980.
3. Means AR, Dedman JR. Calmodulin—an intracellular calcium receptor. Nature (London) **285**:73–77, 1980.
4. Oldham SB. Calmodulin. Its role in calcium-mediated cellular regulation. Miner Electrolyte Metab **8**:1–12, 1982.
5. Stoclet, JC. Calmodulin—an ubiquitous protein which regulates calcium-dependent cellular functions and calcium movements. Biochem Pharmacol **30**:1712–1779, 1981.
6. Hubbard MJ, Bradley MP, Kardos TB, Forrester IT. Calmodulin-like activity in a mineralizing tissue: The rat molar tooth germ. Calcif Tissue Int **33**:545–548, 1981.
7. Lewinson D, Boskey AL. Calmodulin localization in bone and cartilage. Cell Biol Int Rep **8**:11–18, 1984.
8. Weiss B, Levin RM. Mechanism for selectively inhibiting the activation of cyclic nucleotide phosphodiesterase and adenylate cyclase by antipsychotic agents. Advan Cyclic Nucleotide Res **9**:285–303, 1978.
9. Levin RM, Weiss B. Binding of trifluoperazine to the calcium-dependent activator of cyclic nucleotide phosphodiesterase. Mol Pharmacol **14**:690–697, 1977.
10. Prozialeck WC, Cimino M, Weiss B. Photoaffinity labeling of calmodulin by phenothiazine antipsychotics. Mol Pharmacol **19**:264–269, 1981.
11. Hirata M, Suematsu E, Koga KT. Calmodulin antagonists inhibit Ca^{2+} uptake of mitochondria of guinea pig peritoneal macrophages. Biochem Biophys Res Commun **105**:1176–1182, 1982.
12. Cullity BD. Elements of X-ray Diffraction. New York, Addison–Wesley, pp. 97–99, 1956.
13. Willis JB. The determination of metals in blood serum. I. Calcium. Spectrochim Acta **16**:259–272, 1960.
14. Crouch ST, Malmstadt HV. A mechanistic investigation of molybdenum blue method for determination of phosphate. Anal Chem **39**:1084–1089, 1967.
15. Hutterer F, Singer EJ. A modified method for hydroxyproline determination. Anal Chem **32**:556–558, 1970.
16. Blumenkrantz N, Asboe-Hansen G. An assay for total hexosamine and a differential assay for glucosamine and galactosamine. Clin Biochem **9**:269–274, 1976.
17. Boskey AL, Posner AS. Extraction of a calcium–phospholipid–phosphate complex from bone. Calcif Tissue Res **19**:273–283, 1976.
18. Freeman CP, West OD. Complete separation of lipid classes on a single thin-layer plate. J Lipid Res **7**:324–327, 1970.
19. Kates M. Techniques of lipidology. Isolation, analyses, and identification of lipids. Amsterdam, North-Holland, pp360–361, 1975.

20. Kates M. Techniques of lipidology, isolation, analyses, and identification of lipids. Amsterdam, North-Holland, pp361–364, 1975.
21. Fletcher MJ. A colorimetric method for estimating serum triglycerides. Clin Chim Acta **22**:393–397, 1968.
22. Fiske CV, Subbarow Y. The colorimetric determination of phosphorus. J Biol Chem **66**: 375–400, 1925.
23. Getz GS, Jakovic S, Heywood, J, Frank J, Rabinowitz M. A two-dimensional thin-layer chromatography for phospholipid separation. The analysis of yeast phospholipids. Biochim Biophys Acta **218**: 441–453, 1970.
24. Wuthier RE. A review of the primary mechanism of endochondral calcification with special emphasis on the role of cells, mitochondria and matrix vesicles. Clin Orthopaed **169**:219–242, 1982.
25. Boskey AL, Raggio CL, Bullough PG, Kinnett JG. Changes in the bone tissue lipids in persons with steroid- and alcohol-induced osteonecrosis. Clin Orthopaed Rel Res **172**:289–295, 1983.
26. Sakai T, Cruess RL, Yoshinari T, Iida K. Effect of estrogen upon the lipids of various regions of the long bones of the rat. Endocrinology **86**:167–171, 1970.
27. Wuthier RE, Majeska RJ, Collins GH. Biosynthesis of matrix vesicles in epiphyseal cartilage. I. In vivo incorporation of ^{32}P orthophosphate into phospholipid of chondrocyte, membrane and matrix vesicle fractions. Calcif Tissue Res **23**:135–139, 1977.
28. Dirksen KTR. Calcified tissues. In: Snyder F, ed. Lipid Metabolism in Mammals. New York, Plenum, Vol 2:pp237–289, 1977.
29. Thulin E, Forsen S, Drakenberg T, Anderson T, Seamon KB, Knebs J. The interaction between calcium binding proteins and trifluoperazine as studied by ^{113}Cd and ^{43}Ca NMR. In Siegel FL, Carafoli E, Kretsinger RH, MacLenna DHJ, Wasserman RH, eds. Calcium Binding Proteins, Structure and Function. Amsterdam, North-Holland, pp243–244, 1980.
30. Raess BU, Vincenzi FF. Calmodulin activation of red blood cell (Ca^{+2}-Mg^{+2})-ATPase and its antagonism by phenothiazines. Mol Pharmacol **18**:253–258, 1980.
31. Bereza UL, Brewer GJ, Mizukami I. Association of calmodulin inhibition, erythrocyte membrane stabilization and pharmacologic effects of drugs. Biochim Biophys Acta **692**:305–314, 1982.
32. Sasaki Y, Hidata H. Calmodulin and cell proliferation. Biochem Biophys Res Commun **104**:451–456, 1981.
33. Borg TK, Runyan R, Wuthier RE. A freeze-fracture study of avian epiphyseal cartilage differentiation. Anat Rec **199**:449–457, 1981.
34. Peck WA, Kohler KG, Barr S. Calcium-mediated enhancement of the cyclic AMP response of cultured bone cells. Calcif Tissue Int **33**:409–416, 1981.
35. Lee NH, Shapiro IM. Ca^{2+} Transport by chondrocyte mitochondria of the epiphyseal growth plate. J Membr Biol **41**:349–360, 1978.
36. Moskowitz N, Schook W, Puszkin S. Interaction of brain synaptic vesicles induced by endogenous Ca^{2+}-dependent phospholipase A2. Science **216**:305–307, 1982.
37. Wong PY-K, Cheung WY. Calmodulin-stimulated human platelet phospholipase A2. Biochem Biophys Res Commun **90**,473–480, 1979.
38. Wuthier RE. The role of phospholipids in biological calcificational distribution of phospholipase activity in calcifying epiphyseal cartilage. Clin Orthopaed **90**:191–200, 1973.
39. Boskey AL, Posner AS. The role of synthetic and bone extracted Ca–phospholipid–phosphate complexes in hydroxyapatite formation. Calcif Tissue Res **23**:251–258, 1977.
40. Steinhardt RA, Alderton JM. Calmodulin confers calcium sensitivity on secretory exocytosis. Nature (London) **295**:154–157, 1982.
41. DiMuzio MT, Bhown M, Butler WT. The biosynthesis of glycosylated and phosphorylated proteins in bone and dentin organ cultures. Abstracts Fifth Annual Scientific Meeting of the American Society for Bone and Mineral Research, A26, 1983.
42. Boskey AL. Current concepts of the biochemistry and physiology of calcification. Clin Orthopaed **157**:165–196, 1981.
43. Ansell GB, Spanner S. Phosphatidylserine, phosphatidylethanolamine, and phosphatidylcholine. In Neuberger A, van Deenen LLM, eds. Phospholipids. Amsterdam, Elsevier pp1–50, 1982.
44. Thompson DD, Posner AS, Laughlin WS, Blumenthal NC. Comparison of bone apatite in osteoporotic and normal Eskimos. Calcif Tissue Int **35**:392–393, 1983.
45. Horikawa EK, Steelman R, Flanagan TL, Van Loon EJ. Determination of fluoride ion in femurs of rats receiving organic fluoride. J Med Pharm Chem **2**:541–551, 1960.
46. Baastrup PC, Christiansen K, Transbol I. Calcium metabolism in schizophrenic patients on long-term neuroleptic therapy. Neuropsychobiology **6**:56–59, 1980.
47. Martin A, Moline J, Etienne T, Rigalleau J, Weill JD, Rougereaux A. Effets des psychotropes sur le metabolisme phosphocalcique. J Pharmacol Clin **2**:16–20, 1975.
48. Richens A, Rowe DJF. Disturbance of calcium metabolism by anticonvulsant drugs. Brit Med J **4**:73–76, 1970.
49. Christiansen K, Rodbro P, Lund M. Incidence of anticonvulsant osteomalacia and effect of vitamin D: Controlled therapeutic trial. Brit Med J **4**:695–701, 1973.
50. Boskey AL, Timchak DM. Phospholipid changes in the bones of the vitamin D deficient, phosphate-deficient, immature rat. Meta Bone Relat Res **5**:85–89, 1984.
51. Simon DR, Berman I, Howell DS. Relationship of extracellular matrix vesicles to calcification in normal and healing rachitic epiphyseal cartilage. Anat Rec **176**:167–180, 1973.
52. Anderson HC, Cecil R, Sajdera SW. Calcification of rachitic rat cartilage in vivo by extracellular matrix vesicles. Amer J Pathol **79**:237–254, 1975.

Received July 14, 1983. P.S.E.B.M. 1984, Vol. 176.
Accepted February 27, 1984.

PROCEEDINGS OF THE SOCIETY FOR EXPERIMENTAL BIOLOGY AND MEDICINE **176**, 164–167 (1984)

Altered Bile Acid Physiology during Lactation in the Rat[1] (41857)

MERRY J. G. BOLT, THERESA M. LEE, AND HOWARD MOLTZ[2]

Department of Medicine and Committee on Biopsychology, The University of Chicago, Chicago, Illinois 60637

Abstract. There is evidence that the rate of bile acid secretion increases significantly during lactation in the rat. We show that this increase in secretion rate is accompanied by an expanded bile acid pool and that occasioning the enhancement of both pool size and secretion is an increase in bile acid synthesis. The hypothesis is advanced that maternal prolactin, promoted by suckling young, amplifies cholesterol-7α-hydroxylase, the rate-limiting enzyme in bile acid biosynthesis, and perhaps HMG-CoA reductase, the rate-limiting enzyme in cholesterogenesis.

Lactation in the rat is accompanied by a marked elevation in bile acid secretion (1, 2). The functional value of such a change may derive from at least two events. First, the nursing female exhibits approximately a threefold increase in food intake to meet the metabolic demands of milk production (3, 4). This probably intensifies the need for bile acids, since bile acids are important for keeping biliary cholesterol in solution and for facilitating intestinal lipid absorption. Second, the nursing rat emits a maternal pheromone which can be experimentally induced in the nulliparous female by feeding cholic acid (5). This pheromone induces preweanling young to approach the feces of the mother. The ensuing consumption of these feces by the pups has been shown to be essential for their growth and survival (6).

Yet despite the suggested importance of an increased bile acid secretory rate during lactation in the rat, the phenomenon has received relatively little attention. Accordingly, several basic questions remain unanswered. For example, is the increased secretory rate achieved by an increase in hepatic synthesis, or by an increase in the rate at which bile acids cycle through the gut and return to the liver? The latter might be expected insofar as the gut undergoes extensive hypertrophy and hyperplasia during lactation (7, 8). On the other hand, if increased synthesis underlies increased secretion, is the elevated synthesis accompanied by an expansion of the bile acid pool? Herein we show that the bile acid pool is indeed expanded and that the expansion is achieved by a stimulation of bile acid synthesis.

Material and Methods. Bile was collected from mature female Wistar rats that were born and reared in the authors' laboratory. They were either pregnant for 18 days or lactating for 1, 5, 14, or 21 days, respectively. For purposes of comparison, bile was also collected from nulliparous females and from females 14 days postlactation. A total of 28 animals was used. Each had unlimited access to water and to Teklad diet containing 4% fat. (Teklad Standard Diets, P.O. Box 4220, Madison, Wisc. 53711.)

While the animal was anesthetized with ketamine HCl (8–10 mg/100 g body wt), the common bile duct was cannulated with PE 10 tubing, and the cannula was externalized dorsally. In each case the cannulation was begun between 1000 and 1400 hr to control for diurnal variations in bile acid synthesis. The tubing was secured by a specially designed rodent jacket and tether (Alice King Chatham Medical Arts, 5043 Onaknoll Avenue, Los Angeles, Calif. 90043) and then threaded through a swivel. The swivel allowed normal movement and, for those females that were lactating, free access to nursing young. Bile flowed continuously into tared vials contained in a fraction collector programmed at 2-hr intervals for 24 hr.

Total biliary bile acids were assayed in each 2-hr fraction by an enzymatic spectrophoto-

[1] We thank Diane Hinkens for expert technical assistance. Supported by Grant HD 06872 and Biomedical Research Support Grant PH5 S07RR07029 to H.M. and by the Clinical Nutrition Research Center, The University of Chicago.

[2] Requests for reprints should be sent to Howard Moltz, Committee on Biopsychology, The University of Chicago, Chicago, Ill. 60637.

0037-9727/84 $1.50

metric method employing hydroxysteroid dehydrogenase (Worthington STDHP). The method employed was an amalgam of those described by Talalay (9), Iwata and Yamasaki (10), and Javitt and Emerman (11). In brief, a 3-ml reaction volume was made to contain 0.058 *M* Na pyrophosphate buffer, pH 9.5; 0.172 *M* hydrazine hydrate; 0.417 m*M* NAD; 0.27 units hydroxysteroid dehydrogenase; and 0.01 ml rat bile. The standard curve was linear to 0.35 m*M* bile acids. We allowed the reaction 1 hr to ensure completion and computed bile acid molarity based on the extinction coefficient of NADH at 340 nm.

Results and Discussion. We constructed a "washout curve" (12) for each animal by plotting bile acid secretion (μmole/g liver/2 hr) *vs* time. Using the criteria of Mok *et al.* (12) we calculated: (a) *pool size* as the total amount of bile acids obtained from the time of cannulation until the time bile acid secretion reached a low point *minus* the amount due to basal synthesis; (b) *basal synthesis* rate as the mass of bile acids contained in the 2-hr fraction falling at the low point of the washout curve, the point, that is, at which all recycling bile acids have been removed; (c) *secretion rate* per 24 hr as micromoles of bile acids obtained in the first 2-hr fraction multiplied by 12; and, finally, (d) *circulation frequency* as the ratio of secretion rate to pool size.

These parameters are illustrated in Fig. 1 for nulliparous, 18-day pregnant, lactating, and postlactating rats, respectively. As seen in Panel A, basal synthesis rate was elevated significantly by Day 5 of lactation relative to that in both nulliparous and pregnant females. This heightened synthesis was also in evidence on Days 14 and 21 of lactation. Two weeks postlactation, synthesis was again at prelactational levels.

Panel B shows that bile acid secretion was also elevated during lactation, as previously reported (1, 2). However, the secretion rate, unlike the synthesis rate, was not heightened significantly until Day 14. Thereafter secretion followed the same course as synthesis, remaining high on Day 21 of lactation and then declining to nulliparous and pregnant levels 2 weeks after lactation.

As seen in Panel C, bile acid pool size was also elevated significantly, but not until Day 21 of lactation, that is not until after the ele-

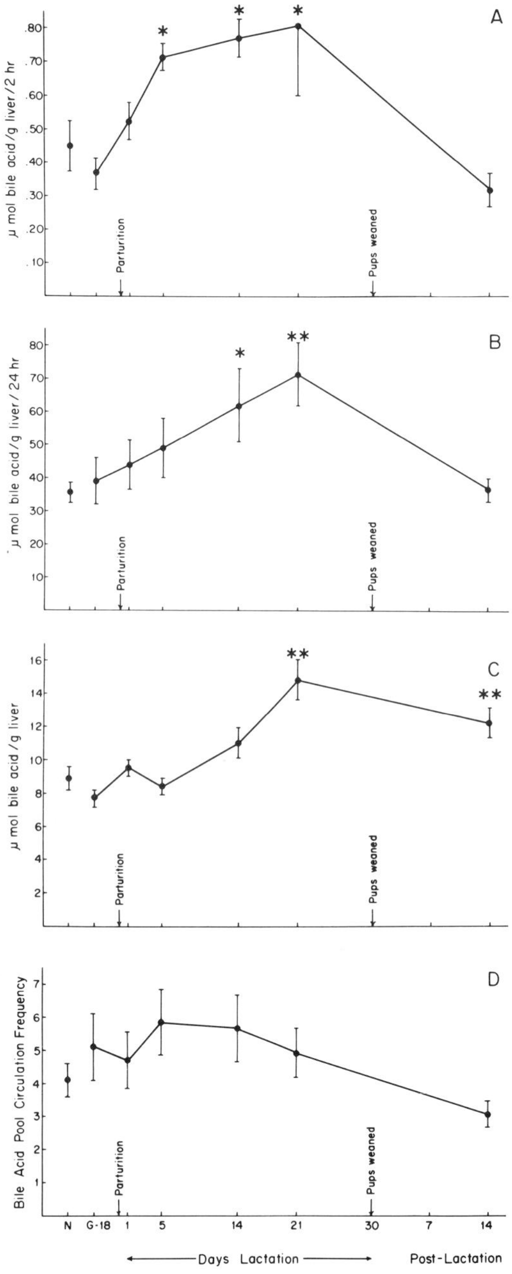

FIG. 1. Changes in basal bile acid hepatic synthesis rate (A), 24-hr bile acid secretion rate (B), bile acid pool size (C), and bile acid pool circulation frequency (D) over time for nulliparous (N), 18-day gestation (G-18), lactating, and postlactating rats. The bars represent the standard error of the mean with four animals per group. The data were analyzed using an SPSS program for one-way ANOVA (21) *a priori* comparison of all groups to nulliparous control, and the Student–Newman–Keuls post-hoc ranking (22). * $P \leqslant 0.05$; ** $P \leqslant 0.01$.

vation of synthesis and secretion rates. Pool size subsequently decreased, although at 2 weeks postlactation it was still above nulliparous and gestational levels. This may reflect the lag-time needed for pool size, once expanded, to return to baseline. It would be of interest to monitor pool size at points later than 2 weeks postlactation.

Finally, circulation frequency was not heightened during lactation, as illustrated in Panel D. The observed elevation in secretion rate, therefore, cannot be attributed to an increased rate of bile acid reabsorption.

Liver weight has been observed to increase in the lactating rat (13, 14). We also found liver weight as a fraction of body weight to be higher in each group of lactating females than in each group of nonlactating females—nulliparous, pregnant, and postlactational, respectively (see Table 1). Accordingly, the data presented in Fig. 1 are expressed as units per g liver rather than as units per 100 g body weight to eliminate the effects of liver size, as such, on bile acid physiology.

The results of the present experiment leave no doubt that profound changes occur in bile acid physiology during lactation in the rat. Pool size expands, and secretion and synthesis rates increase. Since the observed increase in synthesis rate preceded changes in pool size and secretion, it is reasonable to conclude that the elevation in bile acid synthesis was causal, occasioning the enhancement of both secretion rate and pool size. This conclusion, of course, raises the question of what stimulated bile acid synthesis.

Vonk *et al.* (15) presented data showing a positive correlation between biliary bile acid output and food intake during the circadian feeding cycle of the rat. However, they did not study the hyperphagic animal, nor did they study bile acid synthesis. We found that pregnancy did not enhance bile acid synthesis, even though pregnancy is associated with a 60% increase in food intake (3). It seems unlikely, therefore, that the heightened synthesis evinced by our lactating females was the result of the hyperphagia that typically accompanies lactation (3, 4).

We think that it is possible that the enhanced bile acid synthesis that we observed reflected an elevation in cholesterol-7α-hydroxylase. This hepatic enzyme is considered to be rate limiting in bile acid production, and it is enhanced by thyroxine and corticosterone, respectively (16, 17). Perhaps prolactin, which is increased in the lactating female by the suckling litter, also amplifies the enzyme. Such a hypothesis has not been tested.

It is also possible that prolactin amplifies 3-hydroxy-3-methyl glutaryl-CoA reductase (HMG-CoA reductase), the rate limiting enzyme in cholesterol biosynthesis. First, hepatic HMG-CoA reductase increases during lactation (18), as does the biliary output of cholesterol (1). And second, agents that stimulate cholesterol synthesis stimulate bile acid production as well (19, 20).

It would be of interest to study both cholesterol-7α-hydroxylase and HMG-CoA reductase to determine whether or not, in fact, their activity is affected by elevated blood levels of prolactin. It would also be of interest to determine whether or not lactation in other mammalian species, including the human, is accompanied by alterations in bile acid physiology similar to those that we observed in the rat.

TABLE I. RATIO OF LIVER WEIGHT TO BODY WEIGHT FOR NULLIPAROUS, 18-DAY GESTATION, LACTATING, AND POSTLACTATING RATS

Group	Liver weight[a] (g/100 g body wt)	Statistical[b] significance P
Nulliparous	3.13 ± 0.06	—
18-Day gestation	3.62 ± 0.18	NS
1 Day lactation	4.35 ± 0.34	<0.001
5 Days lactation	4.68 ± 0.20	<0.001
14 Days lactation	4.85 ± 0.26	<0.001
21 Days lactation	4.09 ± 0.20	<0.001
2 Weeks post-lactation	3.55 ± 0.15	NS

[a] Values are means ± standard errors.
[b] Statistical methods are described in Fig. 1.

1. Klassen CD, Strom SC. Comparison of biliary excretory function and bile composition in male, female, and lactating female rats. Drug Metab Dispos **6**:120–124, 1978.
2. Kilpatrick SJ, Bolt M, Moltz H. The maternal pheromone and bile acids in the lactating rat. Pharmacol Biochem Behav **12**:555–558, 1980.

3. Cripps AW, Williams VJ. The effect of pregnancy and lactation on food intake, gastrointestinal anatomy and the absorptive capacity of the small intestine in the albino rat. Brit J Nutr **33**:17–32, 1975.
4. Kilpatrick SJ, Moltz H. Hyperphagia is irrelevant for pheromonal emission in the rat. Physiol Behav **26**:1129–1131, 1981.
5. Kilpatrick SJ, Bolt M, Moltz H. Induction of the maternal pheromone by cholic acid in the virgin rat. Physiol Behav **25**:31–34, 1980.
6. Moltz H, Lee TM. The maternal pheromone of the rat: Identity and functional significance. Physiol Behav **26**:301–306, 1981.
7. Burdett K, Reek C. Adaptation of the small intestine during pregnancy and lactation in the rat. Biochem J **184**:245–251, 1979.
8. Jolicouer L, Asselin J, Morisset J. Trophic effects of gestation and lactation on rat duodenum. Biomed Res **2**:113–118, 1981.
9. Talalay P. Enzymic analysis of steroid hormones. Methods Biochem Anal **8**:119–143, 1960.
10. Iwata T, Yamaski K. Enzymatic determination and thin layer chromatography of bile acids in blood. J Biochem (Tokyo) **56**:424–431, 1964.
11. Javitt NB, Emerman S. Effect of sodium taurolithocholate on bile flow and bile acid excretion. J Clin Invest **47**:1002–1014, 1968.
12. Mok HYI, Perry PM, Dowling RH. The control of bile acid pool size: Effect of jejunal resection and phenobarbitone on bile acid metabolism in the rat. Gut **15**:247–253, 1974.
13. Kennedy GC, Pearce WM, Parrott DMV. Liver growth in the lactating rat. J Endocrinol **17**:158–160, 1958.
14. Flint DJ. Changes in the number of insulin receptors of isolated rat hepatocytes during pregnancy and lactation. Biochim Biophys Acta **628**:322–327, 1980.
15. Vonk RJ, VanDoorn ABD, Strubbe JH. Bile secretion and bile composition in the freely moving, unanesthetized rat with a permanent biliary drainage: Influence of food intake on bile flow. Clin Sci Mol Med **55**:253–259, 1978.
16. Myant NB, Mitropoulos KA. Cholesterol 7α-hydroxylase. J Lipid Res **18**:135–153, 1977.
17. Bekersky I, Mosbach EH. Effect of hormones on bile acid metabolism. In: Nair PP, Kritchevesky D, *et al.* eds. The Bile Acids. New York, Plenum, p249, 1973.
18. Walker BL, Hahn P. Hepatic microsomal 3-hydroxy-3-methyl glutaryl-CoA reductase activity in the lactating rat. Canad J Biochem **59**:889–892, 1981.
19. Takeuchi N, Ito M, Yamamura Y. Regulation of cholesterol 7α-hydroxylation by cholesterol synthesis in rat liver. Atherosclerosis **20**:481–494, 1974.
20. Mathé D, Chevallier F. Factors determining biotransformation of cholesterol to bile acids in the rat. Digestion **20**:121–136, 1980.
21. Hull CH, Nie NH. SPSS Update 7-9. New York, McGraw–Hill, 1981.
22. Winer BJ. Statistical Principles in Experimental Design. New York, McGraw–Hill, 2nd ed, 1973.

Received September 21, 1983. P.S.E.B.M. 1984, Vol. 176.
Accepted February 24, 1984.

PROCEEDINGS OF THE SOCIETY FOR EXPERIMENTAL BIOLOGY AND MEDICINE **176**, 168–174 (1984)

Differential Effects of Adrenergic Agents on Plasma Levels of Immunoreactive β-Endorphin and α-Melanotropin in Rats (41858)

DOUGLAS J. PETTIBONE AND GREGORY P. MUELLER

Department of Physiology, Uniformed Services University of the Health Sciences, 4301 Jones Bridge Road, Bethesda, Maryland 20814

Abstract. Parallel measurements of plasma α-melanotropin-like immunoreactivity (α-MSH-LI) and β-endorphin-like immunoreactivity (β-END-LI) were used to examine the differential adrenergic control of β-END secretion from the anterior lobe (AL) versus the intermediate lobe (IL) of the rat pituitary gland *in vivo*. Changes in plasma α-MSH-LI levels after treatment with various adrenergic agents served as an index of the secretion of the peptides by the IL. Secretion of β-END-LI from the AL *in vivo* was evaluated using the selective inhibitory effects of dexamethasone on AL release. Inhibition of glucocorticoid synthesis by metyrapone or activation of α-adrenoceptors by clonidine increased ($P < 0.05$) plasma levels of β-END-LI while plasma levels of α-MSH-LI were not affected by either treatment. By contrast, peripherally administered isoproterenol, norepinephrine or epinephrine, each increased plasma levels of α-MSH-LI together with β-END-LI in a dose-dependent manner. The synthetic glucocorticoid, dexamethasone, significantly attenuated the rise in plasma β-END-LI induced by norepinephrine and epinephrine but did not affect the rise in α-MSH-LI. The isoproterenol-induced rises in β-END-LI and α-MSH-LI were inhibited by the β-adrenergic blocker propranolol. By contrast, the α-adrenergic blockers, phentolamine or prazosin, reversed the effect of epinephrine on both peptides while propranolol had no significant effect. The effects of epinephrine, therefore, appear to be α-adrenergic, whereas those of isoproterenol are β-adrenergic. These studies extend earlier findings to indicate that clonidine is a selective activator of AL corticotroph secretion *in vivo*. On the other hand, other adrenergic agents such as norepinephrine, epinephrine, and isoproterenol appear to stimulate secretion from both corticotrophs as well as melanotrophs.

Recent *in vitro* studies from several laboratories have shown that in the rat, β-endorphin (β-END)-related peptides are synthesized, stored, and secreted by cells of both the anterior lobe (AL) and intermediate lobe (IL) of the pituitary gland (1–5). While it has become clear that specific hormones and neurotransmitters differentially affect the release of β-END-like immunoreactivity (β-END-LI) from the two lobes *in vitro* (6–9), the possible independent control of β-END-LI release from the AL versus the IL *in vivo* has been more difficult to study. Since recent studies indicate that in the rat only the AL releases appreciable amounts of opiate-active β-END$_{1\text{-}31}$, whereas the IL secretes primarily inactive forms (i.e., shorter and acetylated β-ENDs) (2, 5), it may be of considerable physiologic importance to recognize the origin of blood-borne β-END-LI released under different conditions.

Several approaches have been considered for evaluating the proportion of blood-borne β-END-LI which originates from the AL or IL. For example, since β-lipotropin (β-LPH), the immunoreactive precursor to β-END, is secreted by the AL, but not the IL *in vitro* (8–11), a stimulus which predominantly increases a form of plasma β-END-LI related to β-LPH (as determined by gel filtration) is thought to indicate largely an AL response (12–14). A second approach is to measure plasma α-melanotropin-like immunoreactivity (α-MSH-LI) which appears to be a specific marker for hormone released from IL melanotrophs. Since α-MSH and β-END peptides are cosynthesized and presumably coreleased from IL melanotrophs (1–5, 15, 16), parallel increases in plasma concentrations of α-MSH-LI and β-END-LI without an associated increase in β-LPH suggests *in vivo* release from the IL. The use of plasma β-LPH and α-MSH as indices of AL and IL secretion, respectively, is further strengthened by a third approach involving the use of a glucocorticoid. *In vitro* experiments demonstrate glucocorticoids, in small amounts, inhibit the release of AL β-END-LI without affecting IL secretion (8, 14). Thus, consistent with the physiologic function

0037-9727/84 $1.50

of glucocorticoids in regulating the pituitary–adrenal axis, dexamethasone may be used to selectively prevent the release of β-END-LI (and adrenocorticotropin) from AL corticotrophs but not β-END-LI (and α-MSH-LI) from IL melanotrophs.

We have previously shown *in vitro* that α- and β-adrenergic stimulation releases β-END-LI selectively from the AL and IL cells, respectively (6). To determine whether α- and β-adrenergic mechanisms exert similar differential control over the secretion of β-END-related peptides from these two lobes *in vivo,* we tested the effects of various adrenergic agents on plasma levels of β-END-LI and α-MSH-LI, the latter being a specific marker for IL secretion. AL secretory activity was determined using glucocorticoid (dexamethasone)-specific inhibition of stimulated plasma β-END-LI levels.

Materials and Methods. Male, Sprague–Dawley rats weighing 150–200 g (Taconic Farms, Inc., Germantown, Pa.) were housed under a 12:12-hr light:dark cycle, having free access to standard rat chow and tap water. The animals were handled once daily for at least 3 days prior to each experiment.

After decapitation, blood was collected into tubes containing 500 μl 10% ethylenediaminetetraacetic acid plus bacitracin (30 μg/ml) and kept on ice. The tubes were centrifuged and plasma was stored at −70°C until assayed.

Plasma β-END-LI was measured by a radioimmunoassay described previously (14, 17). The assay (antiserum C-55) detects β-END (i.e., $\beta\text{-END}_{1\text{-}31}$), purified human β-LPH (gifts of D. Orth, A. Parlow), and several modified forms of β-END (i.e., *N*-acetyl-$\beta\text{-END}_{1\text{-}31}$, *N*-acetyl-$\beta\text{-END}_{1\text{-}27}$, and $\beta\text{-END}_{1\text{-}27}$) on an equimolar basis. Peptides related to the *N*-terminal amino acid sequence of β-END (i.e., leu- and met-enkephalin), however, do not cross-react in the assay. Since the peptides which do cross-react in the present assay are all considered to be synthesized in, and released from, the same pituitary cells as β-END (2, 3, 5, 10), it is likely that changes in total β-END-LI in plasma reflect the secretory activity of these cells.

A new radioimmunoassay for plasma α-MSH was developed. α-MSH (4.5 mg) (Peninsula Labs, San Carlos, Calif.) was conjugated to bovine thyroglobulin (25 mg) (Sigma Chemical Co., St. Louis, Mo.) using 1-ethyl-3-(3-dimethylaminopropyl)carbodiimide HCl (Bio Rad Labs, Richmond, Calif.) (100 mg) (18) and injected intradermally in an emulsion of equal volumes of Freund's complete and incomplete adjuvants into adult male New Zealand white rabbits (~150 μg α-MSH bound to conjugate/ml/rabbit, Dutchland Laboratory Animals, Inc., Denver, Pa.). Boosting injections were similarly made every 4 weeks and the antiserum chosen (H50) for the assay was collected by ear vein after the fourth administration of conjugate. Radioiodinated α-MSH was prepared as described elsewhere (19) and purified by cation-exchange (SP Sephadex C-25) using slight modifications of Mroz *et al.* (20). Routinely, unextracted plasma was assayed at 100 and 200 μl in duplicate and plasma from hypophysectomized rats which was free of α-MSH-LI was included in the standard curve. The assay (500-μl total volume, 0.5 *M* phosphate buffer, pH 7.4, 0.05% bovine serum albumin, 0.02% sodium azide) of unextracted plasma (50–300 μl) and 1 *N* HCl extracts of rat intermediate lobe produced curves that were parallel to standard α-MSH. Used at a final dilution of 1:250,000 the antiserum specifically bound 35% of the iodinated α-MSH at equilibrium (3 days at 4°C). It should be noted that the inclusion of α-MSH-free plasma in the standard curve increased the effective antibody titer; without plasma a final dilution of 1:100,000 was needed to produce 35% maximum binding at equilibrium. This beneficial effect was due to the reduced nonspecific binding of radiolabeled α-MSH to the glass RIA tubes. Separation of free from bound radioactivity was done by charcoal adsorption and centrifugation (21). The assay, which detects 6–10 pg α-MSH, cross-reacts on an equal molar basis with des-acetyl-α-MSH (Peninsula) and diacetyl-α-MSH (Bachem). It does not, however, detect up to 30 ng/tube of any of the following: deamidated α-MSH, β-MSH, ACTH 1–10, 1–13, or 1–24 (Peninsula), β-END peptides, or β-LPH. Intra- and interassay variation for plasma were 5 and 15%, respectively, for 10 determinations.

The following drugs were used: *l*-epinephrine (Sigma, St. Louis, Mo.), *l*-norepinephrine (Sigma), *l*-isoproterenol (Sigma), clonidine

(Boehringer Ingelheim, Ltd., Ridgefield, Conn.), *d,l*-propranolol (Sigma), phentolamine (Ciba-Geigy, Summit, N.J.), prazosin (Pfizer, Groton, Conn.), dexamethasone (Carter-Glogan Labs, Glendale, Ariz.), metyrapone (Ciba-Geigy).

All values are group means ± SEM. Statistical differences between groups as determined by analysis of variance and Duncan's multiple-range comparison test were considered significant at the $P < 0.05$ level.

Results. *Effects of metyrapone.* Metyrapone (100 mg/kg ip), a glucocorticoid synthesis inhibitor, evoked a brisk rise in plasma β-END-LI, 20 to 60 min after injection (Fig. 1) without affecting plasma α-MSH-LI, suggesting that under conditions of AL stimulation (by removal of negative feedback by corticosterone) α-MSH-LI is not secreted. This supports the concept that plasma α-MSH-LI, which disappears after total hypophysectomy (data not shown), is originating solely from the IL.

Effects of adrenergic agonists and antagonists. Like their effects on plasma levels of β-END-LI (6) the administration of isoproterenol, epinephrine, or norepinephrine all significantly increased plasma levels of α-MSH-LI in a dose-related manner (Fig. 2). The epinephrine- and isoproterenol-induced rises in plasma α-MSH had parallel time courses to those of plasma β-END-LI (6) with peak effects occurring 30 min after injection (Fig. 3). By contrast, clonidine at doses (up to 1 mg/kg) which increase plasma β-END-LI three to fourfold (22), did not influence plasma α-MSH-LI up to 60 min after injection (Fig. 2, Table IV).

To further characterize adrenergic receptor mechanisms involved in the changes in plasma levels of β-END-LI and α-MSH-LI after the various agonists, the effects of several α- and β-adrenergic blockers were investigated. The administration of the β-adrenergic blocker, propranolol (5 mg/kg ip), 30 min after isoproterenol (300 μg/kg sc) significantly attenuated the drug-induced rise in plasma β-END-LI (Table I) and fully blocked the increase in plasma α-MSH-LI (Table I). In contrast, propranolol (5 mg/kg ip), did not significantly influence the epinephrine-induced rise in plasma β-END-LI or α-MSH-LI (Table II and III). Pretreatment with the α-adrenergic antagonist, phentolamine (5 mg/kg ip), however, significantly inhibited the epinephrine-induced rise in both peptides (Table II). Similar antagonism of the epinephrine effect on plasma α-MSH-LI and β-END-LI was obtained by prior administration of another α-adrenergic blocker, prazosin (600 μg/kg ip,

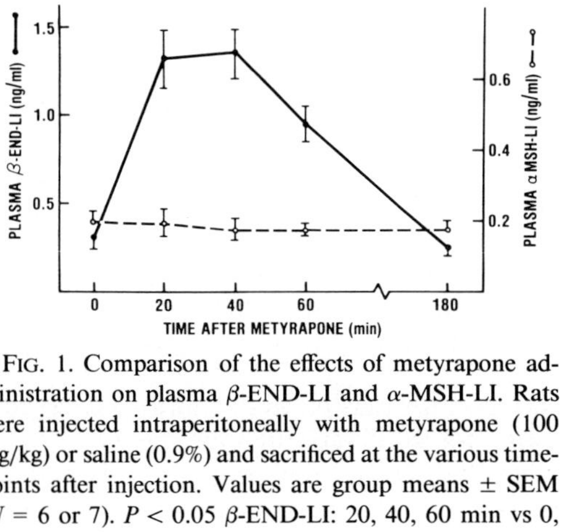

FIG. 1. Comparison of the effects of metyrapone administration on plasma β-END-LI and α-MSH-LI. Rats were injected intraperitoneally with metyrapone (100 mg/kg) or saline (0.9%) and sacrificed at the various timepoints after injection. Values are group means ± SEM ($N = 6$ or 7). $P < 0.05$ β-END-LI: 20, 40, 60 min vs 0, 180 min.

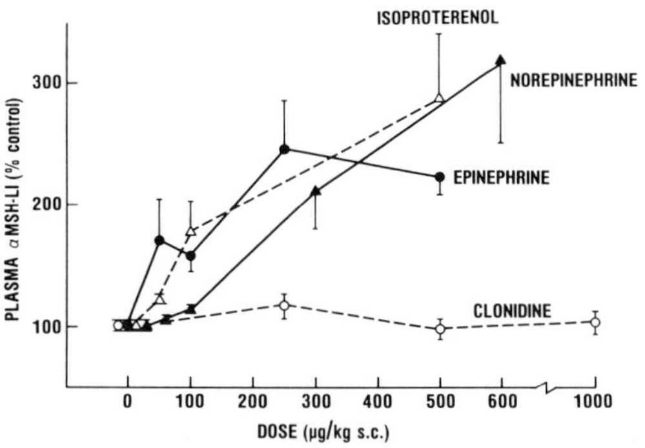

FIG. 2. Dose-related changes in plasma α-MSH-LI after various adrenergic agonists. Rats were injected with the indicated doses of the following drugs (or their vehicles) subcutaneously: isoproterenol, epinephrine, norepinephrine (0.9% saline plus 6 mg% ascorbic acid), clonidine (0.9% saline). The animals were sacrificed 30 min after isoproterenol and epinephrine or 15 min after clonidine. Data are plotted as percentage of control values and represent group means ± SEM ($N = 6$ or 7). Control plasma α-MSH-LI values for each experiment are: isoproterenol 0.22 ± 0.04 ng/ml; epinephrine 0.14 ± 0.02 ng/ml; norepinephrine 0.27 ± 0.02 ng/ml; clonidine 0.35 ± 0.03 ng/ml. $P < 0.05$ vs control: isoproterenol 100, 500 μg/kg; epinephrine 100, 250, 500 μg/kg; norepinephrine 300, 600 μg/kg.

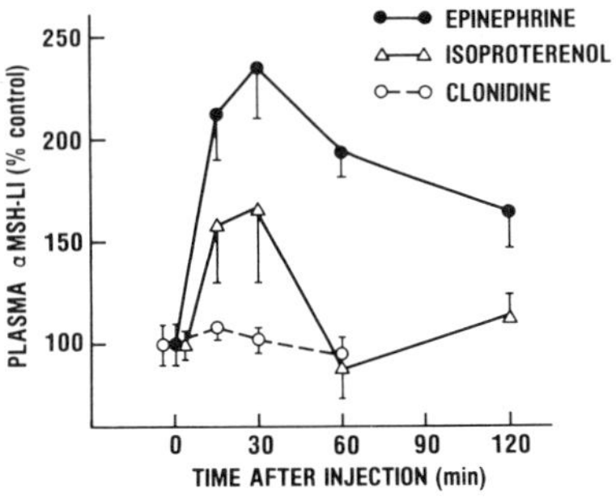

FIG. 3. Time-related changes in plasma α-MSH-LI after epinephrine, isoproterenol, or clonidine. Rats were administered either epinephrine (100 μg/kg), isoproterenol (200 μg/kg), or their vehicle (0.9% saline plus 6 mg% ascorbic acid) or clonidine (500 μg/kg) or its vehicle (0.9% saline), subcutaneously, and sacrificed at the indicated time points after injection. Data are plotted as percentage of control values and represent group means ± SEM. Control plasma α-MSH-LI values for each experiment are: epinephrine 0.21 ± 0.2 ng/ml; isoproterenol 0.21 ± 0.01 ng/ml, clonidine 0.28 ± 0.03 ng/ml. $P < 0.05$ vs control: epinephrine 15, 30, 60, 120 min; isoproterenol 15, 30 min.

TABLE II. EFFECTS OF PHENTOLAMINE AND PROPRANOLOL ON EPINEPHRINE-INDUCED RISE IN PLASMA β-END-LI AND α-MSH-LI

	Plasma immunoreactivity (ng/ml)	
Treatment	β-END-LI	α-MSH-LI
SAL + SAL	0.16 ± 0.01	0.21 ± 0.01
PHENTOL + SAL	0.27 ± 0.05	0.19 ± 0.02
PROP + SAL	0.17 ± 0.01	0.24 ± 0.02
SAL + EPI	1.42 ± 0.09[a]	0.83 ± 0.12[a]
PHENTOL + EPI	0.50 ± 0.08[b]	0.24 ± 0.02
PROP + EPI	1.32 ± 0.14[a]	1.18 ± 0.13[a]

Note. Rats were injected with either 0.9% saline (SAL), phentolamine (PHENTOL, 5 mg/kg ip), or propranolol (PROP, 5 mg/kg ip). Thirty minutes later they received either vehicle (0.9% saline containing 6 mg% ascorbic acid) or epinephrine (EPI, 200 μg/kg sc) and were sacrificed 30 min thereafter. Values represent group means ± SEM ($N = 6$ or 7).
[a] $P < 0.01$ vs all other groups.
[b] $P < 0.01$ vs SAL + SAL.

Table III). The clonidine-induced rise in plasma β-END-LI also appears to be α-adrenergic because pretreatment with prazosin blocked its effect as well (Table IV).

Effects of dexamethasone. The administration of dexamethasone (60 μg/kg ip, 4 hr) significantly attenuated the rise in plasma β-END-LI elicited by norepinephrine (400 μg/kg sc, 30 min) and epinephrine (250 μg/kg sc, 30 min) (Fig. 4). The two- to threefold rise in plasma α-MSH-LI induced by both agents was not significantly affected by dexamethasone.

Discussion. These studies demonstrate that various adrenergic agonists evoke the release of β-END-LI and related peptides differentially from cells of the AL (i.e., corticotrophs) versus cells of the IL (i.e., melanotrophs) *in vivo*. For

TABLE I. BLOCKADE BY PROPRANOLOL OF ISOPROTERENOL-INDUCED INCREASE IN PLASMA β-END-LI AND α-MSH-LI

	Plasma immunoreactivity (ng/ml)	
Treatment	β-END-LI	α-MSH-LI
SAL + SAL	0.22 ± 0.02	0.22 ± 0.02
PROP + SAL	0.25 ± 0.05	0.21 ± 0.03
SAL + ISOPROT	1.50 ± 0.11[a]	0.33 ± 0.02[a]
PROP + ISOPROT	0.88 ± 0.10[b]	0.24 ± 0.02

Note. Rats were injected with either 0.9% saline (SAL) or propranolol (PROP, 5 mg/kg) intraperitoneally. Thirty minutes later they received either vehicle (0.9% saline containing 6 mg% ascorbic acid) or isoproterenol (IsoPROT) (300 μg/kg sc) and were sacrified 30 min later. Values are group means ± SEM ($N = 6$ or 7).
[a] $P < 0.01$ vs all other groups.
[b] $P < 0.05$ vs SAL + SAL and PRO + SAL.

TABLE III. BLOCKADE BY PRAZOSIN OF EPINEPHRINE-INDUCED RISE IN PLASMA β-END-LI AND α-MSH-LI

	Plasma immunoreactivity (ng/ml)	
Treatment	β-END-LI	α-MSH-LI
SAL + SAL	0.27 ± 0.03	0.43 ± 0.05
PRAZ + SAL	0.34 ± 0.05	0.40 ± 0.03
PROP + SAL	0.22 ± 0.03	0.42 ± 0.07
SAL + EPI	2.29 ± 0.24[a]	0.79 ± 0.13[a]
PRAZ + EPI	0.50 ± 0.14	0.42 ± 0.03
PROP + EPI	1.60 ± 0.21[b]	0.91 ± 0.14[b]

Note. Rats received either 0.9% saline (SAL), prazosin (PRAZ, 600 μg/kg), or propranolol (PROP, 5 mg/kg) intraperitoneally 30 min before either vehicle (0.9% saline plus 6 mg% ascorbic acid) or epinephrine (EPI, 150 μg/kg) subcutaneously; the animals were sacrificed 30 min later. Values are group means ± SEM ($N = 6$ or 7).
[a] $P < 0.01$ vs all other groups.
[b] $P < 0.01$ vs all other groups except SAL + EPI.

TABLE IV. BLOCKADE BY PRAZOSIN OF CLONIDINE-INDUCED INCREASE IN PLASMA β-END-LI

Treatment	Plasma immunoreactivity (ng/ml)	
	β-END-LI	α-MSH-LI
SAL + SAL	0.47 ± 0.06	0.32 ± 0.01
PRAZ + SAL	0.47 ± 0.07	0.32 ± 0.03
SAL + CLON	1.16 ± 0.24[a]	0.30 ± 0.02
PRAZ + CLON	0.62 ± 0.04	0.31 ± 0.02

Note. Rats were injected with either saline (SAL, 0.9%) or prazosin (PRAZ, 600 μg/kg) intraperitoneally followed 30 min later by a second injection of saline (0.9%) or clonidine (CLON, 500 μg/kg) subcutaneously; the animals were sacrificed 30 min later. Values are group means ± SEM (N = 6 or 7).

[a] $P < 0.01$ vs all other groups.

example, the administration of clonidine, while increasing plasma levels of β-END-LI, has no effect on plasma α-MSH-LI indicating that IL melanotrophs probably do not contribute to the plasma β-END-LI response following clonidine. This interpretation is strengthened by previous studies in which clonidine was shown to stimulate β-END-LI release from AL cells but not IL cells *in vitro* (11). Further, the rise in plasma β-END-LI evoked by clonidine was fully inhibited a dose of dexamethasone which does not affect IL secretion ((14), Fig. 4). The failure of clonidine to alter plasma levels of α-MSH-LI in the present study, therefore, is consistent with α-MSH-LI being a specific marker of IL function. This approach which has recently been utilized elsewhere (15, 16) is further supported by the ineffectiveness of metyrapone or dexamethasone to alter plasma levels of α-MSH-LI (see Figs. 1, 4).

Among α-adrenergic agents, clonidine is unique in its ability to selectively stimulate β-END-LI release from the AL without altering IL secretion. This point is emphasized by both the present findings with norepinephrine and epinephrine, as well as by other findings (unpublished) with adrenergic agents such as α-methylnorepinephrine and phenylephrine (0.3–1 mg/kg, ip) all of which evoke dose-dependent, parallel increases in plasma β-END-LI and α-MSH-LI. Moreover, dexamethasone pretreatment completely prevents the plasma β-END-LI response to clonidine (14) but only partially inhibits β-END-LI release evoked by mixed AL and IL stimulating agents (e.g., norepinephrine and epinephrine, Fig. 4). Consistent with the view that glucocorticoids selectively inhibit AL secretion *in vivo,* under the present conditions dexamethasone fails to influence the rise in plasma α-MSH-LI following norepinephrine or epinephrine injection (Fig. 4).

Although the mechanisms by which clonidine increases pituitary β-END-LI release is mediated via an α-, but not β-adrenergic receptor, the specific α-adrenoceptor subtype involved is not readily defined *in vivo.* We have shown that the α_2-adrenergic antagonist, yohimbine, as well as other adrenergic blockers with mixed α_2/α_1 activity (i.e., phentolamine, phenoxybenzamine) blocked the effects of clonidine on β-END-LI (21), findings which are consistent with the predominant action of clonidine on α_2-adrenoceptors (22). Unexpectedly, however, in the present study we observed that the specific α_1-antagonist, prazosin, also fully blocked clonidine's effect on plasma β-END-LI. Although it is conceivable that at the doses used here (500 μg/kg ip) clon-

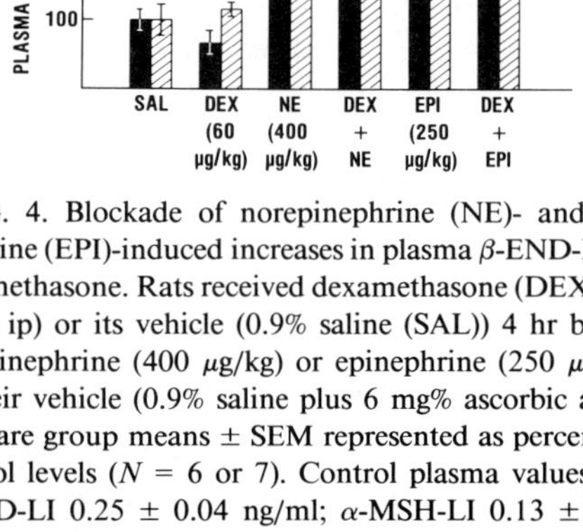

FIG. 4. Blockade of norepinephrine (NE)- and epinephrine (EPI)-induced increases in plasma β-END-LI by dexamethasone. Rats received dexamethasone (DEX) (60 μg/kg ip) or its vehicle (0.9% saline (SAL)) 4 hr before norepinephrine (400 μg/kg) or epinephrine (250 μg/kg) or their vehicle (0.9% saline plus 6 mg% ascorbic acid). Data are group means ± SEM represented as percentage control levels (N = 6 or 7). Control plasma values are: β-END-LI 0.25 ± 0.04 ng/ml; α-MSH-LI 0.13 ± 0.03 ng/ml. $P < 0.05$ β-END-LI: SAL vs NE, EPI, DEX + EPI; EPI, NE vs DEX + EPI, DEX + NE; α-MSH-LI: SAL vs NE, EPI, DEX + NE, DEX + EPI.

idine exhibits significant α_1 activity, this does not appear to be the case since clonidine failed to stimulate the release of α-MSH-LI in a manner similar to that observed for norepinephrine and epinephrine (Tables II and III, Figs. 2 and 4). One would anticipate that clonidine would have access to the same α-adrenergic sites which mediate α-MSH-LI release in response to the catecholamines. It is possible, however, that the adrenoceptor regulating the pituitary β-END-LI response to clonidine is also capable of interacting with prazosin. *In vitro* data indicate that this may be the case for the adrenoceptor located directly on the corticotroph cell (23). Alternatively, multiple counteractive actions of clonidine in the brain and/or periphery could result in a condition under which no net change in α-MSH-LI release occurs.

The present findings that the α-adrenergic antagonists phentolamine and prazosin inhibit the stimulatory effect of epinephrine on plasma β-END-LI are in agreement with our earlier observations using phenoxybenzamine (6). The inhibition of the epinephrine-induced rise in plasma α-MSH-LI by α-adrenergic blocking drugs but not by propranolol (Tables II, III), however, was unexpected because the bulk of evidence indicates that a β-adrenergic mechanism stimulates IL secretion *in vitro* and *in vivo* (9, 15, 25–27). Indeed, the attenuation by propranolol of the increase in plasma β-END-LI and α-MSH-LI observed after the β-adrenergic agonist, isoproterenol (Table I) reinforces this possibility. It is unlikely, that epinephrine is directly stimulating α-adrenergic mechanisms on melanotrophs after its intraperitoneal administration because *in vitro* findings indicate that epinephrine acts solely as β-adrenergic agonist on IL cells in culture (6). Therefore, under the present conditions it seems likely that peripheral administration of epinephrine evokes α-MSH-LI release through actions within the brain. The circumventricular organs do exhibit incomplete blood–brain barriers and thus provide sites at which even polar molecules like epinephrine can gain entry into the central nervous system. Accordingly, the α-adrenergic receptor which mediates α-MSH-LI release in response to injected epinephrine may reside within the brain although unknown peripheral mechanisms and/or a generalized sympathetic response may also mediate the increase in IL secretion. Similar consideration must be taken in interpreting the results obtained with the other centrally active agents administered peripherally.

In summary, α-adrenergic stimulation by peripherally administered epinephrine enhances release of peptides *in vivo* from both corticotrophs and melanotrophs of the rat pituitary. In addition, the release of peptides from melanotrophs is also activated by isoproterenol through β-adrenergic receptors. The present data, however, do not rule out that a portion of the plasma β-END-LI stimulated by isoproterenol arises also from corticotrophs of the AL; it has been reported recently (13) that dexamethasone pretreatment antagonizes isoproterenol-induced stimulation of plasma β-END-LI. The present results showing that clonidine administration does not influence plasma α-MSH-LI extends our previous findings suggesting that this agent is a specific stimulator of β-END-LI from the AL *in vivo* (14).

1. Bloom FE, Battenburg E, Rossier J, Ling N, Leppalroto J, Vargo JM, Guillemin R. Endorphins are located in the intermediate and anterior lobes of the pituitary gland, not the neurohypophysis. Life Sci **20**:43–48, 1977.
2. Eipper EA, Mains RE. Further analysis of post-translational processing of β-endorphin in rat intermediate pituitary. J Biol Chem **256**:5689–5695, 1981.
3. Herbert E, Roberts J, Phillips M, Allen R, Hinman M, Budarf M, Policastro P, Rosa P. Biosynthesis, processing and release of corticosterone, β-endorphin and melanocyte stimulating hormone in pituitary cells culture system. In: Martini L, Ganong WF, eds. Frontiers in Neuroendocrinology. New York, Raven Press, Vol 6:pp67–102, 1980.
4. Li CH, Chung D, Doneen BA. Isolation, characterization and opiate activity of β-endorphin from human pituitary glands. Biochem Biophys Res Commun **72**:1542–1547, 1976.
5. Mains RE, Eipper BA. Differences in the post-translational processing of β-endorphin in rat anterior and intermediate pituitary. J Biol Chem **256**:5683–5688, 1981.
6. Pettibone DJ, Mueller GP. Adrenergic control of immunoreactive β-endorphin release from the pituitary of the rat: *In vitro* and *in vivo* studies. J Pharmacol Exp Ther **222**:103–108, 1982.
7. Przewlocki R, Hollt V, Voight KH, Herz A. Modulation of *in vitro* release of β-endorphin from the separate lobes of the rat pituitary. Life Sci **24**:1601–1608, 1979.

8. Vale W, Rivier J, Guillemin R, Rivier C. Effects of purified CRF and other substances on the secretion of ACTH and β-endorphin-like immunoreactivities by cultured anterior or neurointermediate pituitary cells. In: Collu R, Barbeau A, Ducharme JR, Rochefort J-G, eds. Central Nervous System Effects of Hypothalamic Hormones and Other Peptides, New York, Raven Press, pp163–176, 1979.
9. Vermes I, Mulder GH, Smelik PG, Tilders FJH. Differential control of β-endorphin/β-lipotropin secretion from anterior and intermediate lobes of the rat pituitary gland *in vitro.* Life Sci **27**:1761–1768, 1978.
10. Eipper BA, Mains RE. Existence of a common precursor to ACTH and endorphin in the anterior and intermediate lobes of the rat pituitary. J Supramol Struct **8**:25–34, 1978.
11. Pettibone DJ, Mueller GP. Clonidine releases immunoreactive β-endorphin from rat pars distalis. Brain Res **221**:409–414, 1981.
12. Hollt V, Bergmann M. Effects of acute and chronic haloperidol treatment on the concentrations of immunoreactive β-endorphin in plasma, pituitary and brain of rats. Neuropharmacology **21**:147–154, 1982.
13. Knepel W, Anhut H, Nutto D, Hertting G. The effect of isoprenaline on plasma concentrations of immunoreactive β-endorphin and lipotropin in the conscious rat. Naunyn-Schmiedeberg's Arch Pharmacol **317**:154–158, 1981.
14. Pettibone DJ, Mueller GP. Evidence for independent secretion of β-endorphin immunoreactivity from rat pars distalis *in vivo.* Endocrinology **110**:469–473, 1982.
15. Berkenbosch F, Vermes I, Binnekade R, Tilders FJH. β-Adrenergic stimulation induces an increase of the plasma levels of immunoreactive α-MSH, β-endorphin, ACTH and of corticosterone. Life Sci **29**:2249–2256, 1981.
16. Vermes I, Berkenbosch F, Tilders FJH, Smelik PG. Hypothalamic deafferentation in the rat appears to discriminate between the anterior lobe and intermediate lobe response to stress. Neurosci Lett **27**:89–93, 1981.
17. Mueller GP. Attenuated pituitary beta-endorphin release in estrogen-treated rats. Proc Soc Exp Biol Med **165**:75–81, 1980.
18. Goodfriend TL, Levine L, Fasman GD. Antibodies to bradykinin and angiotensin: A use of carbodiimides in immunology. Science **144**:1344–1346, 1964.
19. Greenwood FC, Hunter WM, Glover JS. The preparation of ^{131}I-labelled human growth hormone of high specific radioactivity. Biochem J **89**:114–123, 1963.
20. Mroz EA, Leeman SE. Substance P. In: Jaffe BM, Behram HP, eds. Methods in Radioimmunoassay. New York, Academic Press, Vol 2:pp121–139, 1978.
21. Gottlieb CW, Lau KS, Wasserman LR, Herbert V. Rapid charcoal assay for intrinsic factor (IF), gastric juice unsaturated B_{12} binding capacity, antibody to IF, and serum unsaturated B_{12} binding capacity. Blood J Hematol **25**:875–884, 1965.
22. Pettibone DJ, Mueller GP. α-Adrenergic stimulation by clonidine increases plasma concentrations of immunoreactive β-endorphin in rats. Endocrinology **109**:798–802, 1981.
23. Guyenet DG, Cabot JB. Inhibition of sympathetic preganglionic neurons by catecholamines and clonidine: Mediation by an α-adrenergic receptor. J Neurosci **8**:908–917, 1981.
24. Giguere V, Cote J, Labrie F. Characteristics of the α-adrenergic stimulation of adrenocorticotropin secretion in rat anterior pituitary cells. Endocrinology **109**:757–762, 1981.
25. Berkenbosch F, Vermes I, Tilders FJH. Epinephrine as a potent releaser of immunoreactive β-endorphin in rats. Eur J Pharmacol **72**:97–100, 1981.
26. Bower A, Hadley ME, Hruby VJ. Biogenic amines and control of melanophore stimulating hormone release. Science **184**:70–72, 1974.
27. Munemura M, Eskay RL, Kebabian JW. Release of melanocyte-stimulating hormone from dispersed cells of the intermediate lobe of the rat pituitary gland: Involvement of catecholamines and adenosine 3′,5′monophosphate. Endocrinology **106**:1795–1803, 1980.

Received September 26, 1983. P.S.E.B.M. 1984, Vol. 176.
Accepted February 24, 1984.

PROCEEDINGS OF THE SOCIETY FOR EXPERIMENTAL BIOLOGY AND MEDICINE **176,** 175–182 (1984)

Evidence that Reverse Transcriptase Is a Component of Murine Epididymal Fluid (41859)

ANN A. KIESSLING

Department of Anatomy, School of Medicine, Oregon Health Sciences University, Portland, Oregon 97201

Abstract. The sperm-free fluid fraction of epididymal semen obtained from males of four mouse strains contained a DNA polymerase activity with properties of murine retrovirus reverse transcriptase (RT). Epididymal fluids from two of the strains of mice, NIH Swiss and New Zealand Black (NZB), had an order of magnitude more enzyme activity per microgram of protein than did the fluids of C57Bl/6 and Balb/c males. Most of the enzyme activity in the Swiss and NZB males, but not in the C57Bl/6 and Balb/c males, banded in isopycnic sucrose gradients at the buoyant density of retrovirus particles. The males were fertile and free of tumor or other detectable disease up to 17 months of age. The evidence suggests RT activity is ubiquitous in the male reproductive tract of mice and may or may not be associated with virus particles.

DNA polymerases β and γ have been isolated from mammalian spermatozoa by several investigators, but not DNA polymerase α, the most abundant DNA polymerase in mammalian somatic cells (1–5). Consistent with the presence of mitochondria in the midpiece of sperm tails, mitochondrial DNA polymerase (DNA polymerase γ (6)) has been isolated from bull sperm tails. The DNA polymerase γ class of enzymes effectively utilizes the synthetic RNA polymer, Poly(A), as a template for DNA synthesis in the presence of oligo(dT) primer. The ability to utilize poly(A)·oligo(dT) as a template-primer for DNA synthesis *in vitro* is a property that DNA polymerase γ has in common with reverse transcriptase (RT), the DNA polymerase in retroviruses that reverse transcribes virus RNA genomes into DNA copies.

During the purification of mouse sperm DNA polymerase γ in this laboratory, it became apparent that epididymal semen from Swiss males contained additional poly(A)·oligo(dT)-stimulated DNA polymerase activity that was not associated with the sperm. DNA polymerase activities in murine epididymal fluids have not been previously reported. The enzyme activity was characterized and the work extended to other mouse strains. The results of these studies, reported here, provide evidence that the enzyme activity was RT, it was present in epididymal secretions *in vivo,* and it may be a ubiquitous component of murine epididymal fluids that is independent of the presence of virus particles.

Materials and Methods. *Epididymal fluid collection and separation from sperm.* Epididymides from mature males were dissected free of adnexa, and the luminal contents (15–30 μl/epididymis) were extruded by gently milking each epididymis and a portion of the ductus deferens with dissecting forceps into 50–100 μl of buffer A (0.01 M Tris–HCl, pH 7.4; 0.1 M KCl; 1 mg/ml bovine serum albumin) plus 0.67 M sucrose. Sperm suspensions obtained in this manner were contaminated with fewer than 1% extraneous cells as determined by direct count in a hemocytometer. The suspensions were centrifuged at 8000g for 3 min to obtain a supernatant fraction and a sperm pellet which was resuspended in one original volume of fresh buffer A plus 0.67 M sucrose. Less than 0.1% of the sperm remained in the supernatant fraction under these fractionation conditions. Enzyme to be stored was adjusted to 0.25% Nonidet-P40 (NP-40, Shell), 5 mM dithiothreitol (DTT), and 40% ethylene glycol and stored at −20°C. Enzyme preparations were stable under these storage conditions for at least 9 months.

Fluorescence determinations. Fluorochromasia of the sperm was assessed as previously described (7). Briefly, a 10 mM stock solution of dicarboxyfluorescein diacetate (DCFA) in dimethylsulfoxide, a generous gift of Dr. Donner Babcock, was diluted to 5 μM in buffer A immediately prior to the addition of 5 to 10 μl of epididymal sperm suspension yielding a final sperm count of approximately 1×10^7/ml. Wet mount preparations of the sperm were

0037-9727/84 $1.50

viewed at a magnification of 1000× with a Zeiss Photomicroscope III set initially on dark-field illumination. Fluorescence was viewed and photographed by switching to an Osram HBO-200 ultraviolet light source using primary filter BG12 and secondary filter "50."

Sucrose density gradient centrifugation. Epididymal fluid enzyme fractions were diluted with one equal volume of Buffer A and layered atop a 10–70% linear gradient of sucrose in TKE (0.01 *M* Tris–HCl, 0.1 *M* KCl, 0.001 *M* EDTA). Isopycnic centrifugation was carried out at 40,000 rpm in a SW 50 rotor for 16 hr and the gradients fractionated as previously described (8). Aliquots of each gradient fraction were adjusted to 0.25% NP-40, 5 m*M* DTT, and assayed for DNA polymerase activity in the presence of DNA and poly(A) · oligo(dT) as described below.

DEAE-cellulose chromatography. A 1-ml column of DEAE-52 cellulose (Whatman) was equilibrated in PB (0.015 *M* potassium phosphate, pH 8.0; 35% ethylene glycol; 1 m*M* DTT). Enzyme activity in supernatant and pellet fractions was solubilized by exposure to 1% NP-40, 20 m*M* DTT, 0.5 *M* KCl, and 40% ethylene glycol for 20 min at 4°C. The enzyme samples were diluted 1:5 with the equilibration buffer, applied to the column, and the column washed with 1 vol of equilibration buffer. Enzyme activity was eluted by the stepwise addition of 0.1, 0.2, and 0.4 *M* potassium phosphate in PB.

Gel filtration. Molecular size estimates were made by chromatography on a 100-ml column of Sephadex G-150 equilibrated with 0.05 *M* potassium phosphate in PB. Aldolase (mol wt = 160,000), bovine serum albumin (mol wt = 64,000), and ovalbumin (mol wt = 43,000) were used as molecular size standards.

Protein measurements. A modification of the amido schwarz dye binding assay for protein (11) was used to estimate protein concentrations. Protein aliquots were adjusted to 2% sodium dodecyl sulfate (SDS) and spotted directly onto nitrocellulose filters (Millipore HA 0.45 μm) in 1- to 10-μl amounts. The filter was submerged in cold 10% trichloroacetic acid (TCA) for a minimum of 10 min followed by a quick rinse in cold distilled water. The filters so treated could be stored at 4°C for up to 2 weeks without introducing error into the protein determination. The protein spots were stained with 0.1% amido black 10B in methanol:acetic acid:distilled water (45:10:45) and destained as described (9). The individual spots were removed from the filter with a cork borer or paper punch and eluted into 200 μl of freshly prepared eluant (25 m*M* NaOH, 50 m*M* EDTA in 50 volume % aqueous ethanol) for concentration estimates at 630 nm. The protein assay was linear from 2 to 40 μg protein/ml and reproducible to a standard error of less than ± 3.3%.

DNA polymerase assays. All enzyme assays were performed in the wells of microtiter trays as previously described (10, 11). Briefly, the assays with DNA were 30 m*M* Tris–HCl (8.0 at 37°C), 2 m*M* dithiothreitol (DTT), 5% ethylene glycol, 20 m*M* KCl, 10 m*M* $MgCl_2$, 0.5 mg/ml "activated" (10) calf thymus DNA (Sigma), 0.2 m*M* dATP, dCTP, dGTP, and 5–6 μ*M* dTTP (4 μ*M* dTTP plus 1–2 μCi of [^{3}H]dTTP, 58 Ci/m*M*, New England Nuclear, or 67 Ci/m*M* International Chicago Nuclear). Standard assay incubations was for 30 min at 37°C.

The assays with poly(A) · oligo(dT) were 30 m*M* Tris–HCl (pH 8.3 at 25°C), 2 m*M* DTT, 5% ethylene glycol, 80 m*M* KCl, 0.35 m*M* $MnCl_2$, 60 μg/ml poly(A) · oligo(dT) (P-L Biochemicals), 0.2 m*M* dATP, and 4 μ*M* dTTP plus 1–2 μCi of [^{3}H]dTTP. The standard assay incubation was for 30 min at 30°C.

The assays with poly(C) · oligo(dG) were 30 m*M* Tris–HCl (pH 8.0 at 40°C), 2 m*M* DTT, 5% ethylene glycol, 0.5 m*M* $MnCl_2$, 10 m*M* KCl, 60 μg/ml poly(C) · oligo(dG), 0.2 m*M* dCTP, and 4 μ*M* dGTP plus 5 μCi of [^{32}P]dGTP (580 Ci/mmole, New England Nuclear). The standard assay incubation was for 30 min at 40°C (10).

The assays of activity with endogenous templates were 30 m*M* Tris–HCl (pH 8.0 at 37°C), 2 m*M* DTT, 5% ethylene glycol, 0.35 m*M* $MnCl_2$, 10 m*M* KCl, 0.2 m*M* dATP, dCTP, and either 0.2 m*M* dGTP and 4 μ*M* dTTP plus 10 μCi of [^{3}H]dTTP or 0.2 m*M* dTTP and 4 μ*M* dGTP plus 5 μCi of [^{32}P]dGTP. The standard assay incubation was for 30 min at 37°C.

DNA products were collected directly into GFC papers (Whatman), acid precipitated, washed, and the radioactivity counted in a liquid scintillation counter as previously described (13). One unit of enzyme activity was equal to 1 fmole of dTTP incorporated in 30 min. Assay variability was less than 10% of the mean for duplicates assayed consecutively over a period of 7 months.

Antigen–antibody studies. Goat antibody against RT purified from Rauscher Leukemia virus (RLV) was previously characterized (10). The anti-RT-RLV IgG, purified by chromatography on protein A Sepharose, was diluted with nonimmune goat IgG to maintain a constant level of total IgG in all assays which also contained 1 mg/ml bovine serum albumin. Antigen and antibody were allowed to react for 18 hr at 4°C in a total volume of 10 μl in a portion of the assay mixture (45 m*M* Tris–HCl, pH 8.3, 2 m*M* DTT, 120 m*M* KCl, 5–10% ethylene glycol, 2 mg/ml BSA, 0.1% NP-40). Residual enzyme activity was measured in the standard assay conditions following the addition of the remaining assay components in a final volume of 15 μl containing 30 m*M* Tris–HCl, pH 8.3, 80 m*M* KCl, 0.5 m*M* $MnCl_2$, 1.5 mg/ml BSA, 0.1 m*M* dATP, 10 μ*M* [^{3}H]dTTP (21 Ci/mMole), 70 μg/ml poly(A) · oligo(dT), 5% ethylene glycol, and 0.08% NP-40. The antibody titers obtained in this way were reproducible to ±15% over a period of several months with IgG preparations stored in 50% ethylene glycol at −20°C.

Results. *Source of the DNA polymerase activity in epididymal fluid.* Initial sperm purification procedures confirmed that the amount of enzyme activity with poly(A) · oligo(dT) remaining in supernatant fluid fractions could not be accounted for by residual sperm or sperm tails. Sperm lysis and release of mitochondrial enzyme into the supernatant fluids was a possibility, although somewhat unlikely in light of the report by Phillippe and Chevallier (3) of the difficulty encountered in solubilizing sperm DNA polymerases. However, to determine whether or not the DNA polymerase activity was being released from sperm in the buffer conditions employed, the integrity of the sperm membranes was assessed by fluorochromasia (7). Following exposure to DCFA, the head-to-tail fluorescence of ≧95% of sperm suspended in buffer A for up to 6 hr at room temperature indicated the sperm membranes were intact. Hence, the enzyme in supernatant epididymal fluid fractions could not be accounted for by sperm degradation.

DEAE–cellulose chromatography of the DNA polymerase activities (Fig. 1) provided additional information that the enzyme ac-

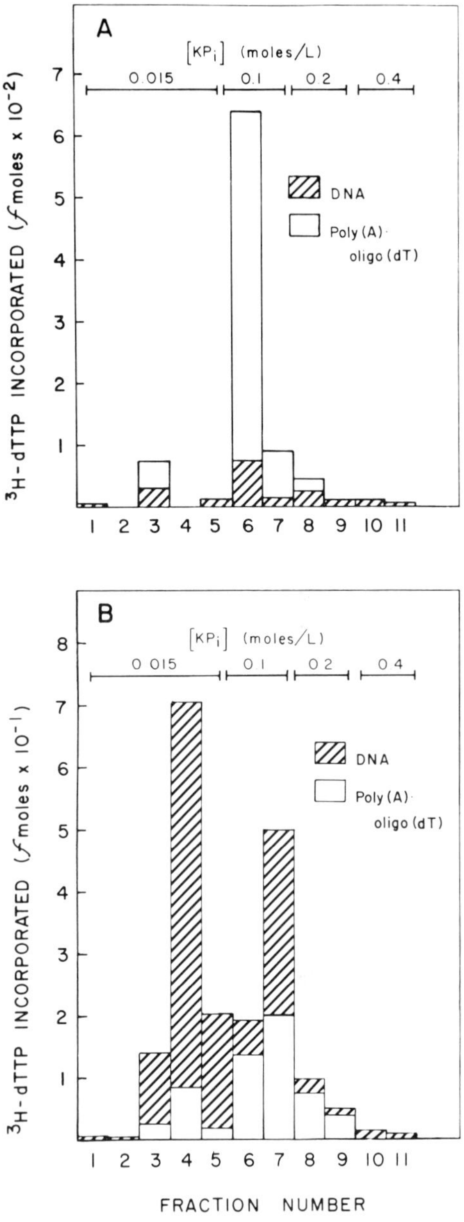

FIG. 1. DEAE–cellulose chromatography of DNA polymerases in NIH Swiss epididymal semen. Epididymal semen from 5–10 mature NIH Swiss males was pooled, separated into fluid and sperm fractions, treated with detergent and reducing agent, and chromatographed as described in Materials and Methods. Supernatant fluid enzyme was chromatographed on column A and pelleted sperm enzyme on column B. Two-microliter aliquots of each fraction (0.5 ml) were assayed for DNA-dependent and poly(A) · oligo(dT)-stimulated DNA polymerase activities. Essentially identical enzyme activity profiles were obtained by chromatography of similar samples from NZB, Balb/c and C57Bl/6 males.

tivity in epididymal supernatant fluid was not due to sperm lysis in the semen preparation. The supernatant fluid DNA polymerase (Fig. 1A) eluted as a single dominant peak of enzyme activity that was more stimulated by poly(A) · oligo(dT) than by DNA. In contrast, the DNA polymerase activities in the pelleted sperm (Fig. 1B) eluted as two dominant peaks that were each more active with DNA than with poly(A) · oligo(dT).

Optimal assay conditions for the epididymal fluid DNA polymerase activity. Mono- and divalent metal ion concentrations for maximal enzyme activity were determined for epididymal fluid DNA polymerase, before and after DEAE–cellulose chromatography, as previously described (10). Briefly, DNA synthesis was measured in each assay of a matrix of Mg^{2+} concentrations at different KCl concentrations with DNA template, and a similar matrix with varying Mn^{2+} and KCl concentrations with poly(A) · oligo(dT) template-primer. The enzyme activity in the epididymal fluid supernatant, and the enzyme activity eluted from the DEAE–cellulose column were maximally active at the same ion concentrations, namely, 10 m*M* Mg^{2+}, 20 m*M* KCl with DNA, and 0.5 m*M* Mn^{2+} and 80 m*M* KCl with poly(A) · oligo(dT). These optimal ion concentrations are the same as those for murine retrovirus RT (10), and unlike those for DNA polymerase γ (12). Optimal incubation temperatures were 37 and 25°C for the assays with poly(A) · oligo(dT) and DNA, respectively.

Buoyant density measurements of the DNA polymerase activity in epididymal fluid. Most of the poly(A) · oligo(dT)-stimulated DNA polymerase activity in the epididymal fluid from Swiss males banded at the buoyant density of retrovirus particles (Fig. 2A) in linear sucrose gradients (8). This was a somewhat surprising finding because of the relatively low incidence of tumors or virus expressed by NIH Swiss, and the males used in this study were members of an active breeding colony with no evidence of disease for their useful lifespan (up to 10–15 months of age). The DNA-dependent DNA polymerase activity at buoyant densities of 1.08–1.10 g/cc did not have the response to poly(A) · oligo(dT) characteristic of RT, and varied in amount relative to the particulate RT activity in each preparation.

In contrast to the Swiss, New Zealand Black (NZB) mice have a high incidence of spontaneous virus expression and the reproductive tract of males has been shown to contain "C"-

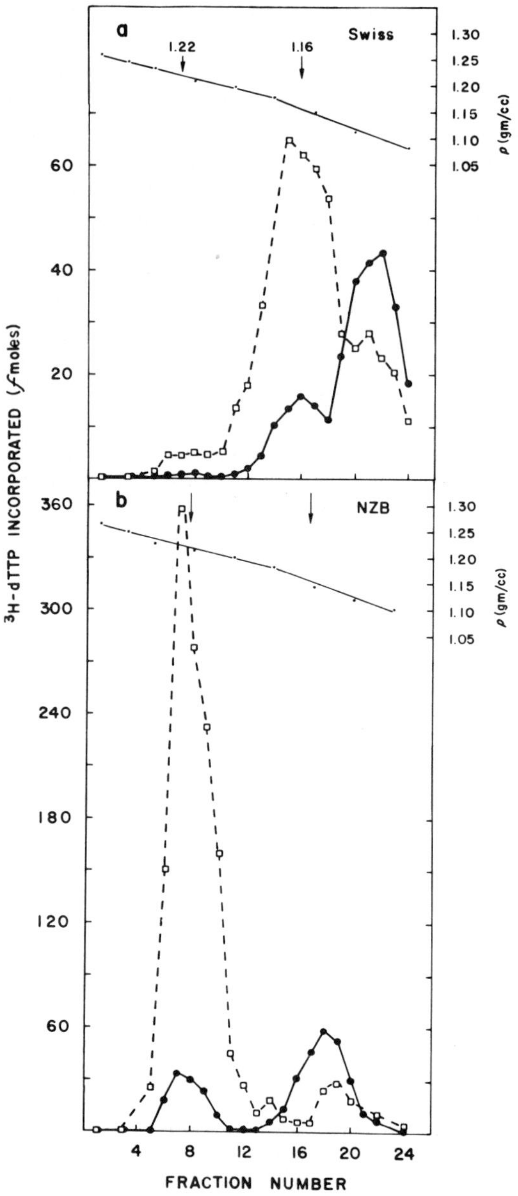

FIG. 2. Isopycnic banding in sucrose density gradients of epididymal fluid DNA polymerases from NIH Swiss and NZB males. Epididymal fluids from five to eight males were pooled and centrifuged to equilibrium as described in Materials and Methods. Three-microliter aliquots of each gradient fraction (0.2 ml) were adjusted to 0.25% NP-40, 5 m*M* DTT, and assayed for enzyme activity with poly(A) · oligo(dT) (□) or DNA (●).

type retrovirus (13). In keeping with these reports, the epididymal fluid from these males contained RT which banded in linear sucrose gradients at the buoyant density of retrovirus particles (Fig. 2B). The measured equilibrium density of 1.22 g/cc was more characteristic of retrovirus particle "cores" that have been freed of outer membrane envelopes. This finding is under further investigation, however, due to the fact that pretreatment with detergent was necessary for expression of peak NZB RT activity in the sucrose density gradients, a characteristic of whole, enveloped virus and unlike the detergent-independent expression of RT activity in virus "cores" (8).

Similar sucrose density gradient measurements of the DNA polymerases in epididymal fluids from Balb/c and C57Bl/6 males revealed multiple peaks of RT activity at buoyant densities below retrovirus particles, between 1.12 and 1.10 g/cc. The enzyme activity was always present in males of these two mouse strains, was stimulated by detergent and reducing agent, but the peaks of activity on the sucrose gradients were not reproducible (data not shown).

Assay characteristics of epididymal fluid DNA polymerases. The responses (Table I) of Swiss epididymal fluid enzyme activity in peak sucrose density gradient fractions confirmed the similarity to RT: the enzyme was more active with synthetic templates, more inhibited by phosphate ion and *N*-ethylmaleimide, and less inhibited by dideoxythymidine, than is characteristic of the DNA polymerase γ class of enzymes (12, 14). In addition, endogenous enzyme activity was detectable in the absence of added exogenous templates; the endogenous activity was not affected by actinomycin D, but was inhibited by ribonuclease, indicating the endogenous template was probably RNA (10). These assay characteristics are indistinguishable from those of murine retrovirus RT and essentially identical results were obtained with similar enzyme fractions from NZB males. C57Bl/6 and Balb/c enzyme responded similarly to the templates, DNA, poly(A) · oligo(dT) and poly(C) · oligo(dG), but activity on endogenous templates was not consistently observed (data not shown).

Molecular weight determinations. Molecular weights in the range of 65,000 to 75,000

TABLE I. ASSAY CHARACTERISTICS OF EPIDIDYMAL FLUID ENZYME

		Enzyme activity (units)[b]		
Assay condition[a]	DNA	Poly(A) · oligo(dT)	Poly(C) · oligo(dG)	Endogenous
Complete	62	202	113	16
−KCL	49	42	—	—
40 m*M* KCl	53	146	—	—
160 m*M* KCl	29	71	—	2
+10 m*M* *N*-ethylmaleimide	27	65	42	3
+25 m*M* ethidium bromide	58	62	—	—
+20 m*M* phosphate	41	124	—	—
+80 m*M* phosphate	23	41	—	—
+d_2TTP	30	61	—	4
−dATP, dCTP, dGTP	19	—	—	5
−oligo dT	—	12	—	—
+Actinomycin D	22	212	111	17
+Ribonuclease	64	—	—	6

[a] Assays were conducted as described in Materials and Methods. Optimal conditions of incubation temperature and assay ingredients were employed for each template-primer. Dideoxythymidine triphosphate (d2TTP) was added at a mole ratio of 1.5 that of the dTTP employed in the assay. Actinomycin D was added at a level of 100 μg/ml and ribonuclease at a level of 20 μg/ml.

[b] One enzyme unit is defined as 1 fmole of total nucleotide incorporated/μg of protein/30 min of incubation at the optimal temperature for the template-primer employed. Each value listed is the average of two to three determinations for each of three enzyme preparations. The standard error for each value was less than ±17% of the mean. The limit of assay sensitivity was 0.5 units, and the assay error in a standard enzyme preparation assayed as a control in each experiment was less than ±8% of the mean. The values reported were determined in the range of linear enzyme response. Enzyme activity in the absence of pretreatment with detergent and reducing agent was 7–33% of the activity with each template-primer tested. Enzyme preparations stored at −20°C exhibited no loss of activity for up to 9 months when adjusted to 50% ethylene glycol, 5 m*M* dithiothreitol (DTT).

Da (data not shown), in good agreement with the molecular weight of murine retrovirus RT (5), were estimated for enzyme from all mouse strains by gel filtration of enzyme fractions that had been partially purified by sucrose density gradients and DEAE chromatography.

Antigenic similarities of epididymal fluid RTs and Moloney murine leukemia virus. The effect of anti-RT antibody on the activity of enzymes from Swiss, NZB, and two retroviruses is shown in Fig. 3. The titration curves of antibody inhibition of the enzyme activity from the Swiss and NZB males were nearly identical to the inhibition curve of M-MuLV RT. The control avian myeloblastosis virus RT was not affected. Balb/c and C57Bl/6 enzyme was inhibited 72 and 66%, respectively, by 200 ng of anti-RLV IgG under the same assay conditions.

Reverse transcriptase activity in epididymal semen fractions from four mouse strains. The concentration of sperm and protein (2.5–3.8 mg protein/10^8 sperm) was comparable for epididymal fluid preparations from the four mouse strains examined (Table II). The level of enzyme activity varied between individual males, but the greater variation was between strains (Table II). Enzyme activity was consistently higher in the supernatant fluid fractions than in the sperm pellets, including the strains with relatively low concentrations of enzyme, Balb/c and C57Bl/6. Pretreatment of enzyme aliquots with detergent and reducing

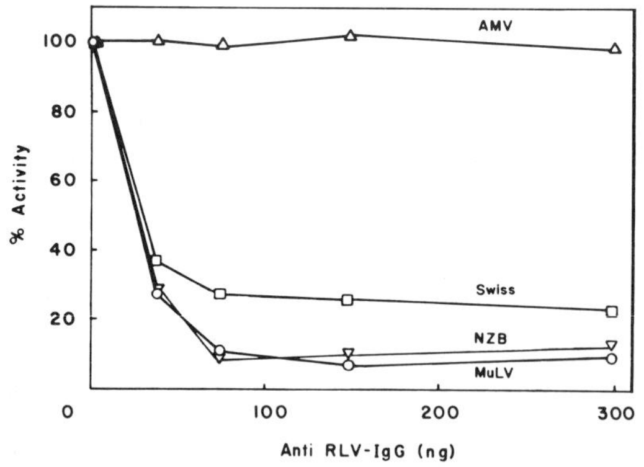

FIG. 3. Titration of epididymal fluid RT activity with goat IgG against RT purified from Rauscher Leukemia virus. Antigen (11 μg, Swiss; 14 μg, NZB; 4 μg MuLV; 8 μg AMV) and antibody were allowed to react overnight and residual enzyme activity assayed as described in Materials and Methods.

TABLE II. REVERSE TRANSCRIPTASE ACTIVITY IN EPIDIDYMAL FLUIDS AND SPERM PELLETS

Mouse strain	Enzyme activity (units)[a] Fluid	Pellet
Balb/c	11 ± 1	10 ± 2
C57Bl/6	14 ± 2	10 ± 3
Swiss	189 ± 37	81 ± 24
NZB	354 ± 104	78 ± 17

[a] Enzyme units and assay conditions are as described in Table I with poly(A) · oligo(dT) template-primer. Values shown are averages of two to three determinations for each of 3–11 enzyme preparations. Enzymes assayed were aliquots of supernatant preparations solubilized with detergent, dithiothreitol, and ethylene glycol (Materials and Methods). Omitting the solubilization reduced measured enzyme activity to 5 to 16% in the Swiss and NZB preparations and 23 to 47% in the Balb/c and C57Bl/6 preparations.

agent (Materials and Methods) was required for maximum expression of enzyme activity in all fractions.

Discussion. These studies provide evidence that RT is present in epididymal fluids of four mouse strains, including high (NZB) and low (C57Bl/6) spontaneous producers of retrovirus. Whether or not the RT is associated with retrovirus remains to be determined, although the known occurrence of C-type retrovirus in NZB males (13) is assumed to account for at least part of the RT activity observed in this strain. The concentration of RT activity in the NZB and Swiss males was equivalent to 10^{11} to 10^{12} virus particles/ml (12) of epididymal fluid, a remarkably high titer for nonmoribund animals. Two possible explanations are (i) the RT is present independent of virus and/or (ii) the RT is associated with endogenous xenotropic virus. The sucrose density gradient profiles of enzyme activity from the Balb/c and C57Bl/6 males support the former possibility as does the work on glycoprotein Gp70, another retrovirus protein known to be present in the male reproductive tract of mice (15, 16). Reports of endogenous xenotropic C-type retrovirus in mouse uteri, particularly NIH Swiss females (17), provides support for the latter possibility, that of xenotropic virus expression in male reproductive tracts. The two possibilities are not mutually exclusive. RT could be present in both viral and nonviral forms simultaneously in the epididymal lumen.

In the context of endogenous virus expression, it is interesting to note that the two strains in this study with the highest level of RT activity in epididymal fluid, NZB and Swiss, are known to express only type III endogenous C-type virus. Proteins of the type III class of virus are expressed in embryo cells of several mouse strains (18). The presence of endogenous virus in both male and female reproductive tracts as well as developing embryos is consistent with the suggestion that the viruses have a normal biological role during embryonic development (19–21). Such circumstantial evidence does not, however, rule out the possibility that virus expression accompanies, but does not influence, cell differentiation.

The contention that reverse transcription of RNA to DNA is a common event in cells of higher organisms is gaining in credibility (22). Whether the process plays a role in cell commitment during early embryogenesis, as originally postulated by Temin (20), and/or serves other roles in cells (23) is under investigation. Although there is evidence that RT is present in normal cells, such as human (8), chick embryo (24), early cleavage stage mouse embryo (25), rabbit uteri (26), and mouse uteri and placenta (27, 28), no unequivocal demonstration of reverse transcription or RT has been associated with normal cell events.

A DNA polymerase with some characteristics of RT was detected in human seminal fluid and sperm (29, 30). The RT activity in epididymal fluids described here is an indication that RT may be associated with the male gametes of mice. Additional information on the presence of virus particles and the site of synthesis of the RT-like enzyme activity present in epididymal fluids is necessary to understand the role of the enzyme and any associated virus in the male reproductive tract of mice. Preliminary findings of electromicrographic studies in progress indicate the presence of retrovirus particles in Swiss and NZB males, but not in the C57Bl/6 males.

I thank C. S. Williams for expert technical assistance. This work was supported by grants from the Medical Research Foundation of Oregon, the National Science Foundation (PCM 8011501), and the American Cancer Society, Oregon Division.

---

1. Hecht NB. A DNA polymerase isolated from bovine spermatozoa. J Reprod Fertil **41**:345–354, 1974.
2. Philippe M, Chevaillier P. Extraction and biochemical characterization of a nuclear DNA polymerase in bull spermatozoa. Biochem J **17**:585–594, 1978.
3. Philippe M, Chevaillier P. Presence of two DNA polymerases in bull spermatozoa. Biochem J **175**:595–600.
4. Witkin SS, Traganos F, Bendich A. Isolation of a nuclear DNA synthesizing complex from human sperm. Biochem Biophys Res Commun **77**:1404–1410, 1977.
5. Sarngadharan MG, Robert-Guroff M, Gallo RC. DNA polymerases of normal and neoplastic mammalian cells. Biochim Biophys Acta **516**:419–487, 1978.
6. Hubscher U, Kuenzle CC, Spadari S. Functional roles of DNA polymerases beta and gamma. Proc Natl Acad Sci USA **76**:2316–2320, 1979.
7. Rotman B, Papermaster BW. Membrane properties of living mammalian cells as studied by enzymatic hydrolysis of fluorogenic esters. Proc Natl Acad Sci USA **55**:134–141, 1966.
8. Kiessling AA, Goulian M. Detection of reverse transcriptase activity in human cells. Cancer Res **39**:2062–2069, 1979.
9. Schaffner W, Weissman C. A rapid, sensitive, and specific method for the determination of protein in dilute solution. Anal Biochem **56**:502–514, 1973.
10. Kiessling AA, Goulian M. A comparison of the enzymatic responses of the DNA polymerases from four RNA tumor viruses. Biochem Biophys Res Commun **71**:1069–1077, 1976.
11. Kiessling AA, Weitlauf HM. DNA polymerase activity in preimplantation mouse embryos. J Exp Zool **208**:347–354, 1979.
12. Bolden A, Noy GP, Weissbasch A. DNA polymerase of mitochondria is a γ-polymerase. J Biol Chem **252**:3351–3356, 1977.
13. Fernandes G, Yunis E, Good RA. Reproductive deficiency of NZB male mice: Possibility of a viral basis. Lab Invest **29**:278, 1973.
14. Edenberg HJ, Anderson S, DePamphilis ML. Involvement of DNA polymerase alpha in SV-40 DNA replication. J Biol Chem **253**:3273–3280, 1978.
15. Elder JH, Jensen FC, Mryant ML, Lerner RA. Polymorphism of the major envelope glycoprotein (gp70) of murine C-type viruses: Virion associated and differentiation antigens encoded by a multi-gene family. Nature (London) **267**:23–28, 1977.
16. DelVillano BS, Lerner RA. Relationship between the oncornavirus gene product gp70 and a major protein secretion of the mouse genital tract. Nature (London) **259**:497–499, 1976.
17. Allen PT, Mullins JA, Saviolakis GA, Strickland JE, Fowler AK, Hellman A. Direct isolation of xenotropic retroviruses from the NIH Swiss mouse uterus. Reprod Biol **79**:239–242, 1977.
18. Aaronson SA, Stephenson JR. Endogenous type-C RNA viruses of mammalian cells. Biochim Biophys Acta **458**:323–354, 1976.
19. Huebner RJ, Kelloff GJ, Sarma PS, Lane WT, Turner

AC, Gilden RV, Oroszlan S, Merer H, Myers DB, Peters RL. Group specific antigen expression during embryogenesis of the genome of the C-type RNA tumor virus: Implications for ontogenesis and oncogenesis. Proc Natl Acad Sci USA **67**:366–376, 1970.
20. Temin HM. The DNA provirus hypothesis. Science **192**:1075–1080, 1976.
21. Hellman A, Fowler AK, Strickland JE, Kouttab NM. A possible physiological function for type C RNA viruses. In: Clemmesen J, Yohn DS, eds. Comparative Leukemia Research 1975, Bibliotheca Haematologica Basel, Karger, Vol 43:pp161–165, 1976.
22. Lewin R. How mammalian RNA returns to its genome. Science **219**:1052–1054, 1983.
23. Bernstein LB, Mount SM, Weiner AM. Pseudogenes for human small nuclear RNA U3 appear to arise by integration of self-primed reverse transcripts of the RNA into new chromosomal sites. Cell **32**:461–462, 1983.
24. Bauer G, Friis RR, Jilek G, Hofschneider PH. Purification and characterization of particles containing RNA-dependent DNA polymerase, in the allantoic fluid of uninfected leukosis virus-free chicken eggs. Biochim Biophys Acta **518**:125–137, 1978.
25. Kiessling AA, Weitlauf HM. Poly(A)·oligo(dT)-stimulated DNA polymerase activity in preimplantation mouse embryos. J Exp Zool **215**:117–120, 1981.
26. Yang WK, Tyndall RL, Daniel JC. DNA- and RNA-dependent DNA polymerases: Progressive changes in rabbit endometrium during pre-implantation stage of pregnancy. Biol Reprod **15**:604–613, 1976.
27. Strickland JE, Fowler AK, Hellman A. Expression of murine leukemia virus DNA polymerase in mouse uterus during pregnancy. Biol Reprod **20**:751–756, 1979.
28. Kalter AA, Heberling RL, Helmke RJ, Panigel M, Smith GC, Kraemer DC, Hellman A, Fowler AK, Strickland JE. A comparative study on the presence of C-type viral particles in placentas from primates and other animals. In: Ito Y, Dutcher RM, eds. Comparative Leukemia Research 1973, Leukemogenesis, Bibliotheca Haematologica, Tokyo, Univ of Tokyo Press/Basel, Karger, Vol 40:pp391–401, 1975.
29. Witkins SS, Bendich A. DNA synthesizing activity in normal human sperm. Exp Cell Res **106**:47–54, 1977.
30. Higgins PJ, Witkin SS, Bendich A. Inhibition of human seminal fluid DNA polymerase by an IgG fraction of seminal plasma from vasectomized men. J Reprod Fertil **54**:97–102, 1978.

Received July 25, 1983. P.S.E.B.M. 1984, Vol. 176.
Accepted March 2, 1984.

PROCEEDINGS OF THE SOCIETY FOR EXPERIMENTAL BIOLOGY AND MEDICINE **176**, 183–186 (1984)

Unstirred Water Layers in Rabbit Intestine: Effects of Pectin (41860)

G. A. GERENCSER, J. CERDA, C. BURGIN, M. M. BAIG, AND R. GUILD

Departments of Medicine and Physiology, College of Medicine, University of Florida, Gainesville, Florida 32610

Abstract. Pectins have been shown to affect the absorption of several different nutrients in clinical studies; however, the mechanisms for decreased absorption have not been defined. A possibility not studied with regards to pectin, but previously demonstrated to be important in absorption, is the effect of change in the unstirred water layer. As the unstirred water layer increases in thickness, the rate of absorption decreases for certain nutrients. The effect of pectin on the unstirred water layer in the lumen of rabbit jejunum was examined by previously described techniques. It was observed that: (1) increases in pectin concentration resulted in an increased thickness of the unstirred water layer; (2) for any stir rate, the addition of pectin increased the thickness of the unstirred water layer; and (3) stir rate is inversely related to the thickness of the unstirred water layer. It was concluded from these results that pectin increases the thickness of the unstirred water layer in rabbit jejunum. This mechanism may explain, in part, the reduction of the rate of absorption of certain nutrients seen following pectin ingestion.

There exists a layer of relatively unstirred water next to all biological membranes through which solute molecules must move by simple diffusion (1). With regards to the small intestine this unstirred water layer consists of a series of water lamellae extending out from the brush border membrane of the absorptive enterocytes, each progressively more stirred, until they blend in with the bulk water phase of the intestinal contents (2). The boundary between the bulk water phase and the unstirred water layer is not stringently defined, but a finite, functional thickness of this layer can be assessed for the evaluation of various absorptive or secretory transport phenomena in the intestine (2, 3). Therefore, during absorptive phenomena in the small intestine, solutes must penetrate both an unstirred water layer and the brush border membrane of the enterocyte. Both of these barriers may exert significant resistance to absorption such that the unstirred water layer may be rate limiting in the overall absorptive process (4).

Pectin is a type of fiber (a large, complex polysaccharide) found in many fruits and vegetables and has been shown in clinical studies to affect the absorption of several different nutrients (5, 6). Previous studies in our laboratory involving possible interaction between bile salts and pectin showed no binding of bile salts to pectin, *in vitro,* but bile salt absorption was reduced in the small intestine (7). The question concerning the role of pectin relative to decreased bile salt absorption prompted us to perform studies using pectin in order to elucidate its effect on the functional thickness of the unstirred water layer.

Materials and Methods. Adult New Zealand rabbits weighing from 2.5 to 4.0 kg were used in this investigation. After the rabbits were sacrificed by decapitation, a segment of jejunum was rapidly removed and placed in a ice-cold (0°C) Krebs–bicarbonate buffer bubbled with 95% O_2:5% CO_2. The jejunum was then opened along the mesenteric border and the mucosal surface was thoroughly flushed with a jet of cold Krebs–bicarbonate buffer from a syringe to remove visible detritus and mucus. Then the intestine was further sectioned into 30 experimental samples and stored in iced (0°C) Krebs–bicarbonate Ringer before preincubation in the various experimental solutions. Preincubation of the intestinal tissue was done in Krebs–bicarbonate Ringer at 37°C containing either 0, 0.25, or 1.0% orange pectin (Sun-Kist Growers Inc.). The jejunal sections were then mounted as a flat sheet in a modified Ussing chamber as first described by Lukie *et al.* (8) and were bathed by the same Krebs–bicarbonate solution (37°C) as in the preincubation step. The incubation solutions were mixed at stirring rates (0, 500, or 1000 rpm) with circular magnetic bars, and stirring rates were precisely adjusted by means of a strobe light (Power Instruments).

0037-9727/84 $1.50

The thickness of the unstirred water layer was measured according to the method of Diamond (9). Briefly, the technique consists of measuring the change in the transmural potential difference (PD) caused when the mucosal surface of the intestine suddenly was exposed to a hyperosmotic solution (Krebs–bicarbonate + 150 m*M* sucrose). The time required to achieve half the new steady-state potential difference, $t_{1/2}$, is a function of the thickness of the unstirred water layer, *d*, and the diffusivity of the molecule used to induce the change in potential difference, *D* (free-diffusion coefficient of sucrose in 150 m*M* NaCl = 6.2×10^{-6} cm^2 sec^{-1}). Thus, the thickness of the unstirred water layer can be calculated from the formula:

$$d = (Dt_{1/2}/0.38)^{1/2}$$

To measure the $t_{1/2}$ values, the PD was monitored continuously by means of KCl bridges placed in the serosal and mucosal compartments of the chamber and connected via calomel half-cells to a voltmeter (Radiometer Inst.) and rapid response chart recorder (Yewtec Corp). To induce a change in the PD, the chamber was rapidly transferred from the incubation solution to another beaker where sucrose had been added to the Krebs–bicarbonate buffer to increase its osmolality. After the new steady-state potential difference was achieved, the chamber was transferred back to the original incubation solution: thus, the $t_{1/2}$ could be measured repeatedly for the build-up and decay of the change in potential difference in the same tissue preparation. These values were used to calculate the effective "*d*" under different experimental conditions and these thicknesses are reported in micrometers (μm).

All data are reported as means ± SEM. Differences between means were analyzed statistically using the nonparametric rank sums test (10). The 0.01 level of probability was used as the criterion of significance.

Results. Figure 1 demonstrates typical examples of different stir rates and pectin concentrations (B, C, D) on the rate of decay of PD (half-times = $t_{1/2}$) from control values (A). As can be seen, the greater the stir rate (B, C, or D) or the less the pectin concentrations in the perfusate (B, C), the less the $t_{1/2}$, which is a direct reflection of the thickness of the unstirred water layer.

Table I summarizes the calculated data of the unstirred water layer thickness relative to concentration of pectin in the perfusate and stirring rate. As can be seen, at 0% pectin concentration the effect of increasing the stirring rate from 0 to 500 rpm significantly decreased the calculated unstirred water layer thickness by 45% ($P < 0.01$), whereas increasing the stirring rate to 1000 rpm further decreased the unstirred layer thickness by 55% compared to control (0% pectin and 0 rpm). At 0.25% pectin concentration, the effect of increasing the stirring rate from 0 to 500 rpm significantly decreased the calculated unstirred water layer thickness by 46% ($P < 0.01$), whereas increasing the stirring rate to 1000 rpm further decreased the unstirred water layer thickness by 58% compared to the concentration-based control (0.25% pectin and 0 rpm). At 1.00% pectin concentration, the effect of increasing

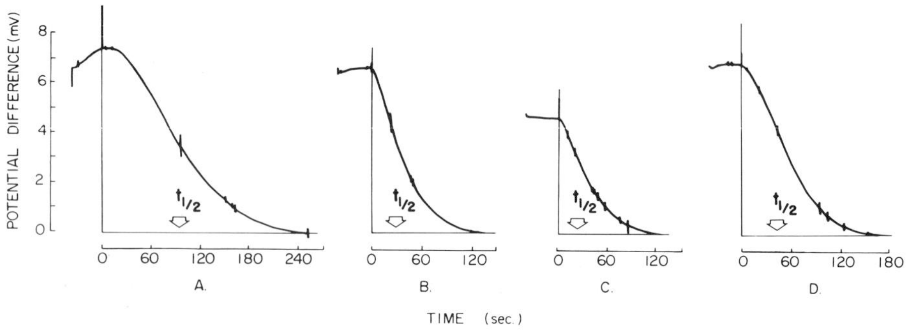

FIG. 1. Representative recordings of potential difference as a function of time in seconds. A: 0 rpm, 1.00% pectin; B: 500 rpm, 0.25% pectin; C: 1000 rpm, 0.25% pectin; D: 1000 rpm, 1.00% pectin.

TABLE I.

	Thickness of unstirred water layer[a]		
Stirring rate[b]	0	500	1000
Concentration of pectin			
0.00%	275.1 ± 12.4 (30)[c]	150.4 ± 8.8 (30)	121.9 ± 2.9 (30)
0.25%	319.6 ± 17.5 (30)	173.7 ± 29.2 (30)	132.7 ± 2.8 (30)
1.00%	385.8 ± 5.3 (30)	189.8 ± 5.7 (30)	156.2 ± 4.1 (30)

[a] Units of unstirred water layer in μm ± SEM.
[b] Stirring rate is expressed in rpm.
[c] Number of observations shown in parentheses.

the stirring rate from 0 to 500 rpm decreased the calculated unstirred water layer thickness by 51%, whereas increasing the stirring rate to 1000 rpm decreased the unstirred water layer thickness by 60% compared to the concentration-based control (1.00% pectin and 0 rpm). As is also observed at 0 rpm stirring rate the thickness of the unstirred water layer of the 0% pectin concentration is significantly less than the thickness of the unstirred water layer at 0.25% pectin ($P < 0.01$), which is significantly less thick than the unstirred water layer in the intestine that is perfused with 1.00% pectin ($P < 0.01$). In addition, the same relationship between thickness of the unstirred water layer and stirring rate at 500 or 1000 rpm hold relative to the control perfusate (0% pectin). In summary, the thickness of the unstirred water layer is directly related to the concentration of luminally perfused pectin and inversely related to the magnitude of the stir rate.

Discussion. As a molecule is actively or passively absorbed from the bulk aqueous solution of the intestinal contents into the cytoplasm of the enterocyte, it must cross two major diffusion barriers: the unstirred water layer external to the cell and the protein lipid membrane of the microvilli. Experiments in the present study were designed to investigate the thickness of the unstirred water layer and how this thickness could be altered. Measurements of the thickness of the unstirred water layer suggested that the diffusion barrier was several hundred micrometers thick (Table I). The intestinal mucosa contains two structural elements, glycocalyx and mucus, overlying the brush border membrane that could conceivably lead to overestimation errors in the determination of the thickness of the unstirred water layer. However, it has been demonstrated that unstirred water layers of similar dimensions have been found in other epithelia, such as gallbladder (9, 11), which have less prominent mucus and glycocalyx layers, and in artificial membranes that have no mucus or glycocalyx at all (12). We have therefore concluded that the diffusion barrier is principally a layer of unstirred water.

The finding that increasing the pectin concentration in the luminal perfusate significantly increased the thickness of the unstirred water layer (Table I) suggests that pectin ingestion can reduce both active and passive nutrient absorption by increasing the external diffusion barrier to that nutrient. However, it is obvious that increasing the stirring rate has an inverse effect on the thickness of the unstirred water layer (Table I), as has also been reported in another intestinal epithelium (13), regardless of pectin concentration. This finding may have little physiological benefit if we equate stirring rate in the *in vitro* situation with intestinal motility in the *in vivo* case for, in that situation, there is a decreased time for nutrient absorption. The opposing effects of decreased absorptive time versus decreased thickness of the unstirred water layer may cancel one another. However, it is difficult to imagine gut motility being as vigorous as the experimentally forced stirring rates in the *in vitro* case and, therefore having similar effects on the thickness of the unstirred water layer. Nonetheless, under pectin-ingestion conditions, the unstirred water layer can become totally rate limiting to the uptake of highly permeant nutrient molecules and significantly reduce their uptake.

A possible cause for the pectin-induced unstirred water layer thickness could be the increase in bulk (bathing) fluid viscosity. Viscosity of the bulk fluid increases nonlinearly with increasing concentrations of pectin (14). This phenomenon is usually due to either dissociation of pectin carboxyl groups, hence increased hydrogen bonding, or complex association of pectinic acid molecules (14). Therefore, intestinal unstirred water layer thickness could be directly related to the increased bathing medium viscosity imparted by luminally perfused pectin. If this premise is true, nutrient absorption by the small intestine is inversely related to luminal fluid viscosity.

This investigation was supported by a grant from the Florida Department of Citrus (Florida Citrus Commission) Grant 78-55 and by Whitehall Foundation Grant 78-156 ck-1.

1. Dainty J. Water relations of plant cells. Advan Botan Res **1**:279–326, 1963.
2. Wilson FA, Dietschy JM. The intestinal unstirred layer: Its surface area and effect on active transport kinetics. Biochim Biophys Acta **363**:112–126, 1974.
3. Westergaard H, Dietschy JM. Delineation of the dimensions and permeability characteristics of the two major diffusion barriers to passive mucosal uptake in the rabbit intestine. J Clin Invest **54**:718–732, 1974.
4. Schiff ER, Small NC, Dietschy JM. Characterization of the kinetics of the passive and active transport mechanisms for bile acid absorption in the small intestine and colon of the rat. J Clin Invest **51**:1351–1362, 1972.
5. Lin TM, Kim KS, Karvinan E, Ivy AC. Effect of dietary pectin, "protopectin" and gum arabic on cholesterol excretion in rats. Amer J Physiol **188**:66–70, 1957.
6. Kritchevsky D, Story JA. Binding of bile salts in vitro by nonnutritive fiber. J Nutr **104**:458–462, 1974.
7. Guild R, Nelson EW, Cerda JJ. Pectin–bile salt interactions. Clin Res **26**:284A, 1978.
8. Lukie BE, Westergaard H, Dietschy JM. Validation of a chamber that allows measurement of both tissue uptake rates and unstirred layer thicknesses in the intestine under conditions of controlled stirring. Gastroenterology **67**:652–661, 1974.
9. Diamond J. A rapid method for determining voltage–concentration relations across membranes. J Physiol **183**:83–100, 1966.
10. Li JCR. Distribution-free methods. In: Li, JCR, ed. Statistical Inference, Ann Arbor, Mich., Edward Bros, pp527–544, 1966.
11. Smulders AP, Wright EM. The magnitude of nonelectrolyte selectivity in the gallbladder epithelium. J Membr Biol **5**:297–318, 1971.
12. Holz R, Finkelstein A. The water and nonelectrolyte permeability induced in thin lipid membranes by the polyene antibiotics nystatin and amphotericin B. J Gen Physiol **56**:125–145, 1970.
13. Wilson FA, Dietschy JM. The effect of unstirred layers on the kinetics of active transport in the rat intestine. Clin Res **20**:783, 1972.
14. Schultz TH, Lotzkar H, Owens HS, Maclay J. Influence of method of deesterification on the viscosity and acid behavior of pectinic acid solutions. J Phys Chem **49**:554–563, 1945.

Received November 7, 1983. P.S.E.B.M. 1984, Vol. 176.
Accepted March 2, 1984.

PROCEEDINGS OF THE SOCIETY FOR EXPERIMENTAL BIOLOGY AND MEDICINE **176**, 187–196 (1984)

Effect of Methoxychlor on Reproductive Systems of the Rat (41861)

HARPAL S. BAL

Department of Veterinary Anatomy, College of Veterinary Medicine, Iowa State University, Ames, Iowa

Abstract. Methoxychlor (MeOCL), a chlorinated hydrocarbon pesticide, was administered by oral gavage for 70 days to male and 14 days to female rats at dose levels of 100 and 200 mg/kg/day of body weight. Methoxychlor inhibited spermatogenesis in the males and folliculogenesis in female rats. The sustentacular (Sertoli) cells showed degenerative fatty changes as a result of which blood–testis barrier could have been affected. Degenerative changes of the spermatogonia and the spermatocytes and transformation of some of these cells into polynucleated and binucleate cells were observed. Myelin figures and degenerate mitochondria were observed in the binucleate cells at the ultrastructural level. Some of the seminiferous tubules were devoid of all cellular elements with the exception of spermatogonia. The epithelium of the ductus epididymis manifested conspicuous cytoplasmic vacuolations, and near the tail, the duct was distended with fluid which compressed the lining epithelium. Atresia of the ovarian follicles was evident with pyknosis and karyorhexis of the granulosa cells.

The original objective of this research project was to study the mutagenic effect of methoxychlor on the rat. The experiment was designed to carry out at least three generation studies on the effect of methoxychlor following the protocols suggested by the U.S. Food and Drug Administration (1). Unfortunately, as a result of the experiment, the treated female rats bred to the treated males did not bear any progeny except the controls.

The histopathological evaluation of testes, epididymis, and ovaries of rats treated orally with 100 and 200 mg/kg of methoxychlor is reported in this study. Although the previous investigators have studied the toxicity effects of methoxychlor, none has reported histopathological changes of the reproductive organs of the animals studied.

Methoxychlor, a chlorinated hydrocarbon insecticide with the chemical structure

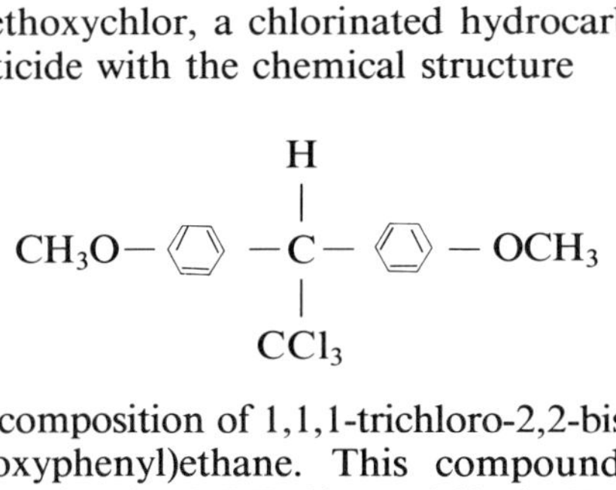

has a composition of 1,1,1-trichloro-2,2-bis(*p*-methoxyphenyl)ethane. This compound is closely related to DDT. Since 1960, the World Health Organization (WHO) has indicated a need for a suitable replacement for DDT because of insect resistance and toxicity to animals (2). Methoxychlor is less toxic than DDT. It has a broad range of effectiveness and long residual action compared to other approved insecticides (3, 4).

The acute LD_{50} of methoxychlor in rats is 6000 mg/kg body weight (4, 5). At dose levels lower than 6000 mg/kg body weight, methoxychlor affects the testes. Weanling rats fed with 1% methoxychlor exhibited histopathological changes in the testes, accessory sex glands, and kidneys (6). In male rats, *exposure* to 1% or more of methoxychlor in feed resulted in pathological changes of the rat testes. No pathological changes in the ovaries of female rats were produced by doses less than 100 mg/kg/day (6–9). Methoxychlor fed 3% in diet for 45 days to adult male rats caused apparent suppression of spermatogenesis, although sustentacular (Sertoli) cells and spermatogonia appeared normal (5). However, methoxychlor fed to rats mixed with Purina Fox Chow meal at a concentration of 0.0025 to 0.16% over a 2-year period had no abnormal effects on the testes.

Osborne–Mendel female rats were fed with 1% methoxychlor in corn oil incorporated in ground commercial laboratory meal at a level of 100 to 500 ppm for 104 weeks. Fifty percent of the female rats developed carcinoma of the ovaries (10).

BALB/c and C3H male mice of 3-weeks age ingested 750 ppm of technical methoxychlor mixed in ground laboratory meal for a

0037-9727/84 $1.50

period of 2 years. Fifty-three percent of the methoxychlor-treated males and 11% of the controls developed carcinoma of the testes. Tumors of mice treated with methoxychlor were more malignant than they were in the controls (10). Other effects of methoxychlor such as carcinoma of the liver in mice and dogs, atrophy of the testes in the rabbit and hyperplasia of the mammary glands and uterus in swine were also reported by the same investigator (10).

Estrogenic activity of methoxychlor *in vivo* and a rare case of anemia in a human after methoxychlor exposure have recently been reported (11–13). Methoxychlor was a recommended pesticide since the 1950s for the control of ectoparasites in dairy cattle, although its excretion in milk did not represent any threat to human health (14). The objective of this investigation was to determine the effect of methoxychlor on the testes and ovaries of the rat.

Materials and Methods. Forty specific-pathogen-free (SPF) rats (10 weeks old), 15 males and 25 females, of Wistar strain (Cesco Lab Co., Omaha, Nebr.) were used in these studies.

Males. The male rats were divided into two treatment groups and a control group of five each. Two dose levels of technical methoxychlor[1] were tested in this investigation. One group of five male rats were given 100 mg/kg/day of methoxychlor (1% solution) suspended in gum tragacanth, and the other group received 200 mg/kg/day (2% solution) of methoxychlor in Mazola corn oil[2] by intubation. Controls were dosed with the vehicle solutions at similar dose levels, respectively. These are the nontoxic vehicles in which methoxychlor is either soluble (corn oil) or can remain suspended as emulsion in water with gum tragacanth. The dosing was continued for a period of 70 days to cover the entire spermatogenic cycle of the male rats.

Females. The female rats were divided into two groups of 10, and each group was administered methoxychlor by intubation at the rate of 100 mg/kg/day in gum tragacanth suspension and 200 mg/kg/day in Mazola corn oil for a period of 3 weeks (four estrous cycles) before mating. Female control rats were divided into two groups of five and each group was given gum tragacanth suspension in water and corn oil at the same dose levels as the treatment groups for the same period of four estrous cycles. The rats were caged individually and provided *ad libitum* with Teklad[3] mouse and rat diet containing 4% fat. Water was available 24 hr/day.

After the treatment period, the male and female groups treated at similar dose levels of 100 and 200 mg/kg/day, respectively, were mated. Similarly the female controls were mated with the male controls. Two females were caged with a male during estrus in the evenings. Vaginal smears were taken the next morning and examined for the presence of sperm under the light microscope. Females with positive sperm in the smear or vaginal plug were considered to have conceived. The day on which coagulated semen (with/without visible sperm) or vaginal plugs were present in the vagina of the female rats was considered as Day 1 of gestation. The matings were continued for a period of 15 days.

Twenty females which were observed to have conceived were put in separate cages. They were dosed daily (100 and 200 mg/kg/day to the respective groups) during the entire period of gestation. Half of the females treated with each respective dose level were killed on Day 13 of gestation in order to examine for the number and distribution of embryos in each uterine horn. The rest of the females were killed after the expiration of the gestation period since they did not litter. Neither viable nor dead embryos and fetuses were observed in the female rats killed on Day 13 of gestation nor in those after the expiration of the gestation period. Viable embryos were present in half the control group of female rats killed on Day 13 of gestation.

Since the methoxychlor-treated females turned out to be barren, it was appropriate to examine the male reproductive organs, especially the testes. The testes (including the epididymis) of half the methoxychlor-treated

[1] Obtained from E. I. Dupont Nemours and Company, Inc., 5725 East River Road, Chicago, Ill. 60631.

[2] Best Foods, Englewood Cliffs, N.J.

[3] Teklad Mills, Winfield, Iowa.

rats, controls and the ovaries of females were fixed in 10% buffered neutral Formalin solution. The parts of the ovaries that needed to be examined were the corpora lutea and the follicles. It was not deemed necessary to study the histopathological changes of the ovaries at the fine structure level since the degenerative changes of the follicles were quite obvious. Two male rats which were unlikely to survive after 9 weeks of treatment with methoxychlor were killed and their tissues were collected for histological evaluation. The ovaries and testes of the rats were embedded in paraffin, sectioned at 6 μm in thickness, and stained with Harris' hematoxylin and eosin.

Electron microscopic technique. The male rats were anesthetized and perfused through the descending aorta with 2% glutaraldehyde solution. The tissues were excised and cut in 1-mm blocks and fixed in 1% OsO_4 (osmium tetroxide) in buffer for at least 2 hrs, washed overnight in cold buffer, dehydrated in ascending grades of ethanol, and embedded in Epon. Poststaining after osmification with 0 to 5% uranyl acetate in acetate buffer was done *en bloc.* Ultrathin sections were cut and stained with uranyl acetate and lead citrate. They were examined and photographed under the Hitachi HU 12A transmission electron microscope at 50 kv.

Results. *Light Microscope Changes. Testes.* There were degenerative changes in the seminiferous tubules of all the treated rats. There was so much deviation in the tubular morphological manifestation from one animal to another that the whole phenomenon can be described as a disorganized picture of the seminiferous tubules. The following histopathological changes were observed in the seminiferous tubules.

Sustentacular (Sertoli) cells. Degeneration of these cells was observed. Large vacuoles appeared in the cytoplasm toward the adluminal compartment of the seminiferous tubules (Fig. 1). In the center of the tubular lumina, fragments of sustentacular cell cytoplasm and pyknotic nuclei of germ cells were observed.

Spermatogonia. The cellular relations within the seminiferous tubules varied between animals and within the same testis. Spermatogonia of A type were observed in mitotic divisions along the periphery of some tubules. Intermediate and B-type spermatogonia were also observed. Seminiferous tubules with advanced degenerative changes were devoid of all cells except a few spermatogonia at the periphery and disfigured sperm (Fig. 2).

Spermatocytes. Primary spermatocytes were disorganized, manifesting a variety of morphological changes. Some of these cells retained their intercellular connections but were displaced. A few appeared to be in the initial stage of the first maturation division. No further advancement toward complete maturation was evident.

Other changes in the seminiferous tubules. Multinucleated and binucleated cells were observed (Figs. 1, 7). Some of these cells appeared in degenerate forms. Degenerated cells and some calcified bodies were seen. A few spermatids were seen scattered and disoriented in some tubules (Fig. 6). Hyaline degenerate bodies, probably of multinucleated cells, were present in tubules exhibiting such changes. Large vacuoles toward the center of the tubules were not uncommon (Fig. 1).

Ductus epididymidis. Ballooning and vacuolation of epithelial cells of the ductus epididymidis were observed (Fig. 4). At about the region of the tail of the ductus epididymidis, there appeared to be some blockage of the flow of the seminal fluid. Here the ductus epididymidis was distended with seminal fluid resulting in compression of the lining epithelium. There were desquamated degenerate epithelial cells in the lumen of the duct.

Ovaries. The ovarian follicles of the female rats treated with methoxychlor were atretic. The granulosa cells of the ovarian follicles exhibited all the initial forms of degenerative changes characterized by pyknosis and karyorhexis of their nuclei. Desquamation of these granulosa cells was also evident (Fig. 3). These degenerative changes in the ovarian follicles probably contributed to failure of ovulation and conception in the females.

Ultrastructural changes in the seminiferous tubules. In sections of the seminiferous tubules of the control rats, the mitochondria in the spermatids were lined along the periphery close to the plasma membrane (Fig. 5). These mitochondria do not have the characteristic cristae but appear as rounded vesicles with a

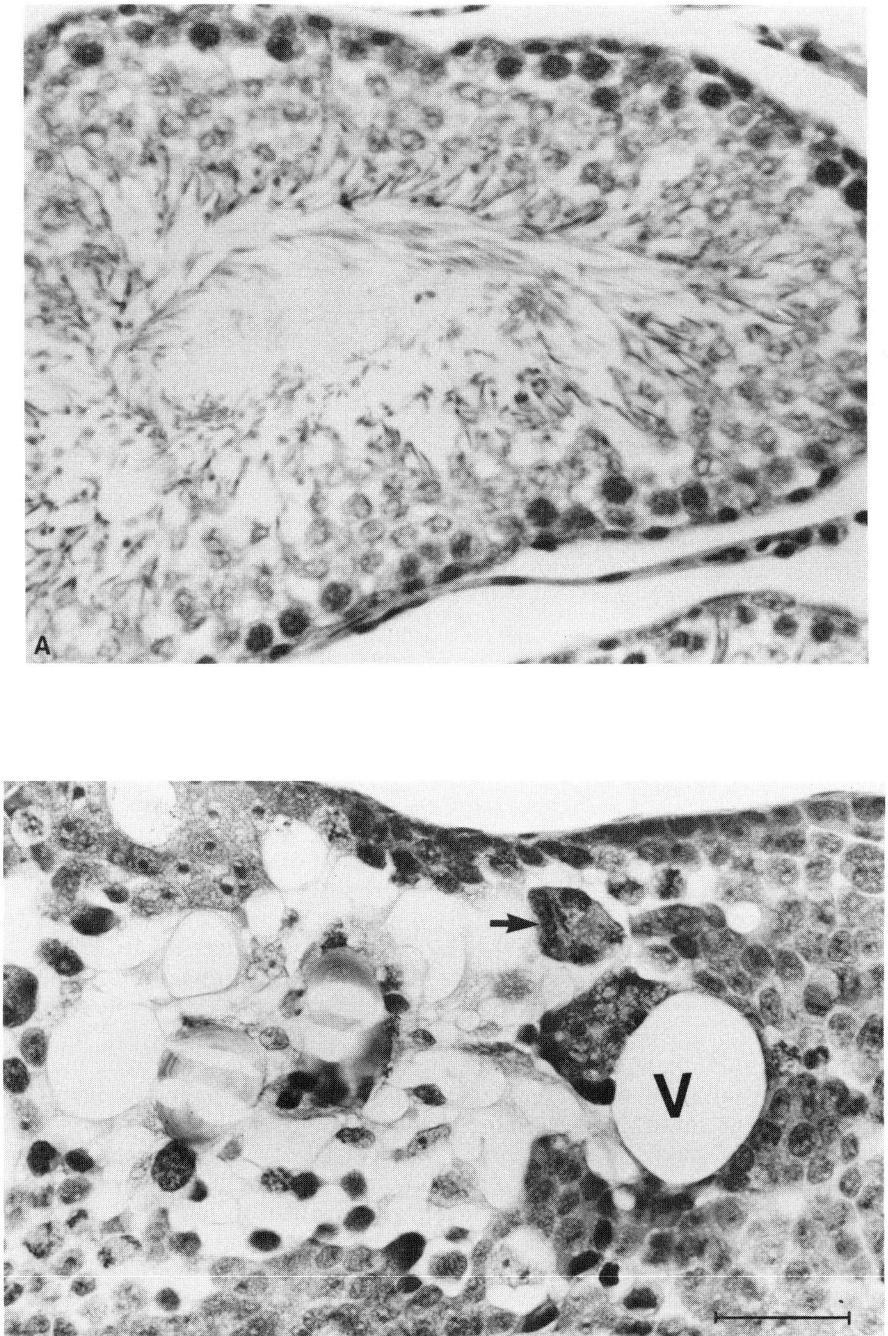

FIG. 1. (A) A section of seminiferous tubule of a control rat showing normal process of spermatogenesis. (B) Section of a seminiferous tubule of methoxychlor-treated rat showing vacuoles (v), multinucleated cells (arrows), and overall disorganization. H & E, ×570.

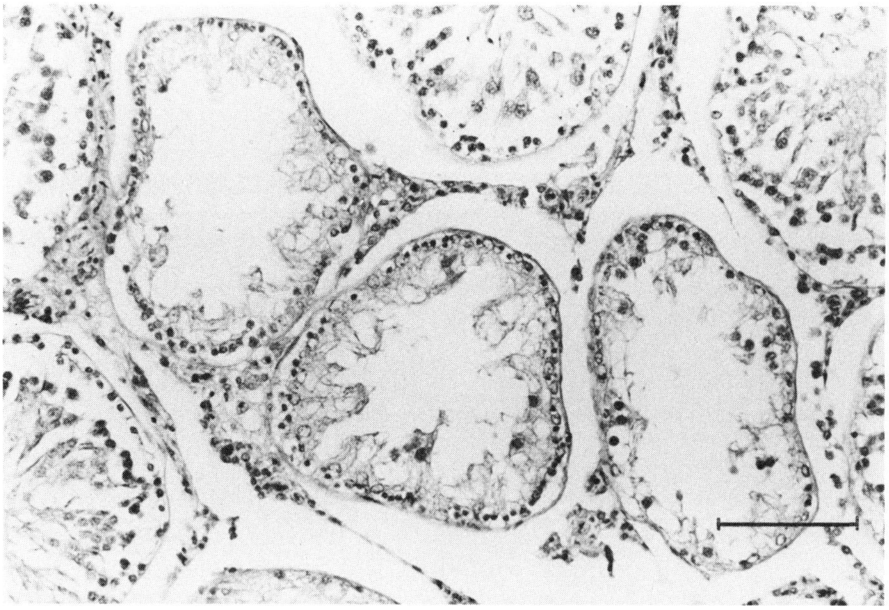

FIG. 2. Section of the testis of methoxychlor-treated rat showing lack of normal spermatogenesis. It appeared that all cell types except spermatogonia have degenerated. H & E, ×143.

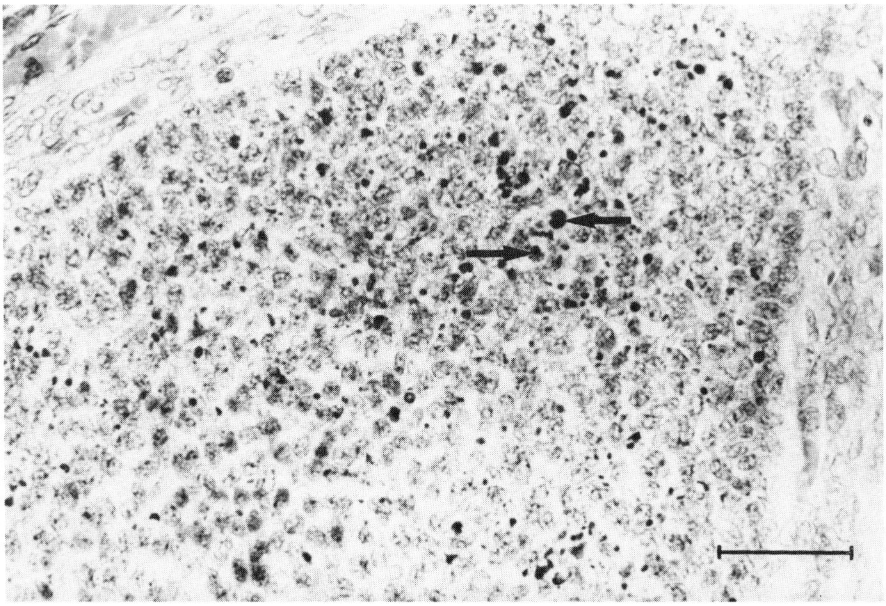

FIG. 3. Section of an ovarian follicle of methoxychlor-treated rat showing degenerative changes (atresia) of the granulosa cells (arrows). H & E, ×360.

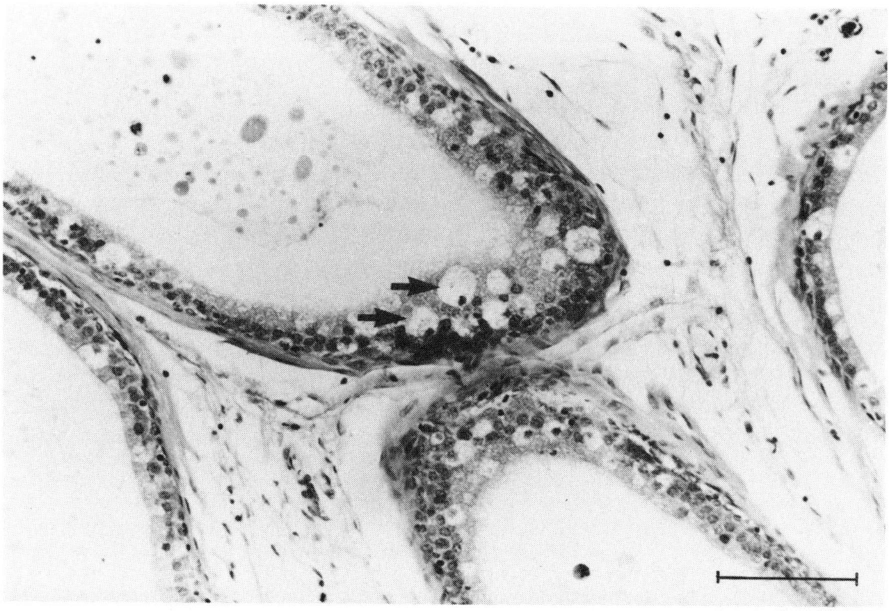

FIG. 4. Section of the ductus epididymidis of methoxychlor-treated rat showing vacuolation and ballooning of the epithelium (arrows). H & E, ×143.

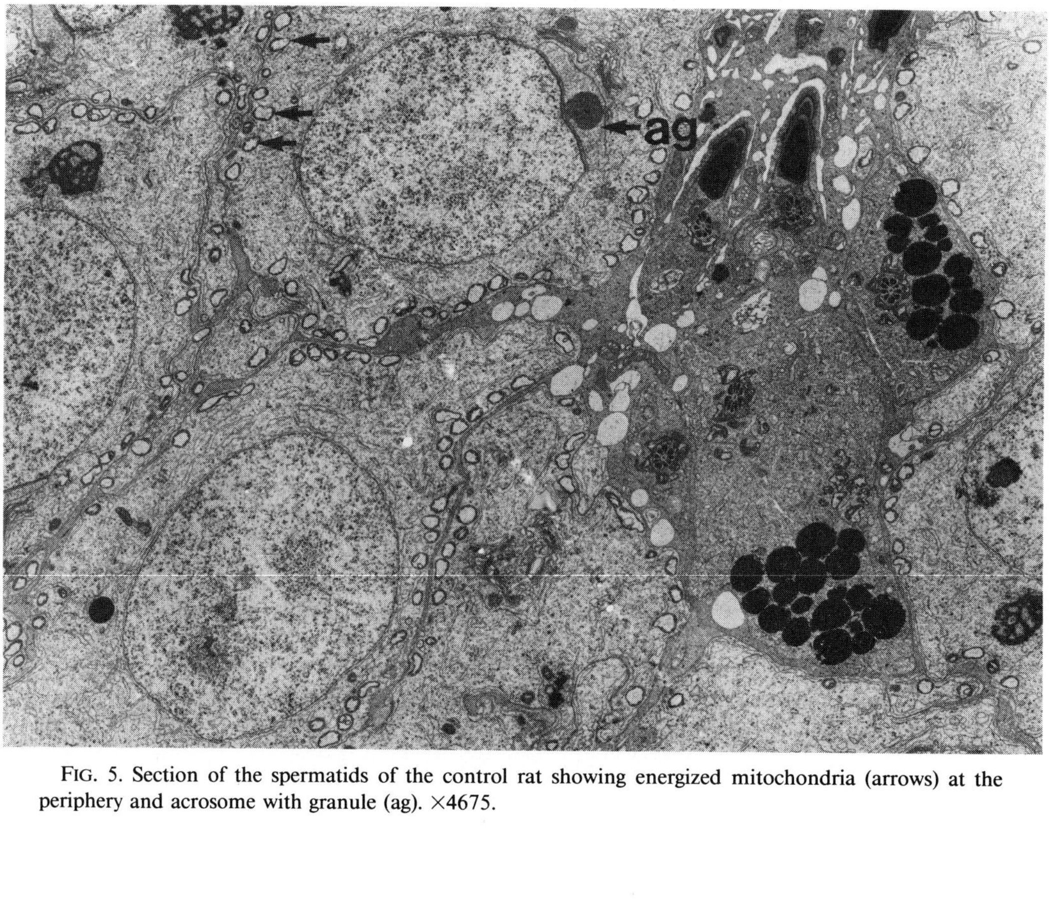

FIG. 5. Section of the spermatids of the control rat showing energized mitochondria (arrows) at the periphery and acrosome with granule (ag). ×4675.

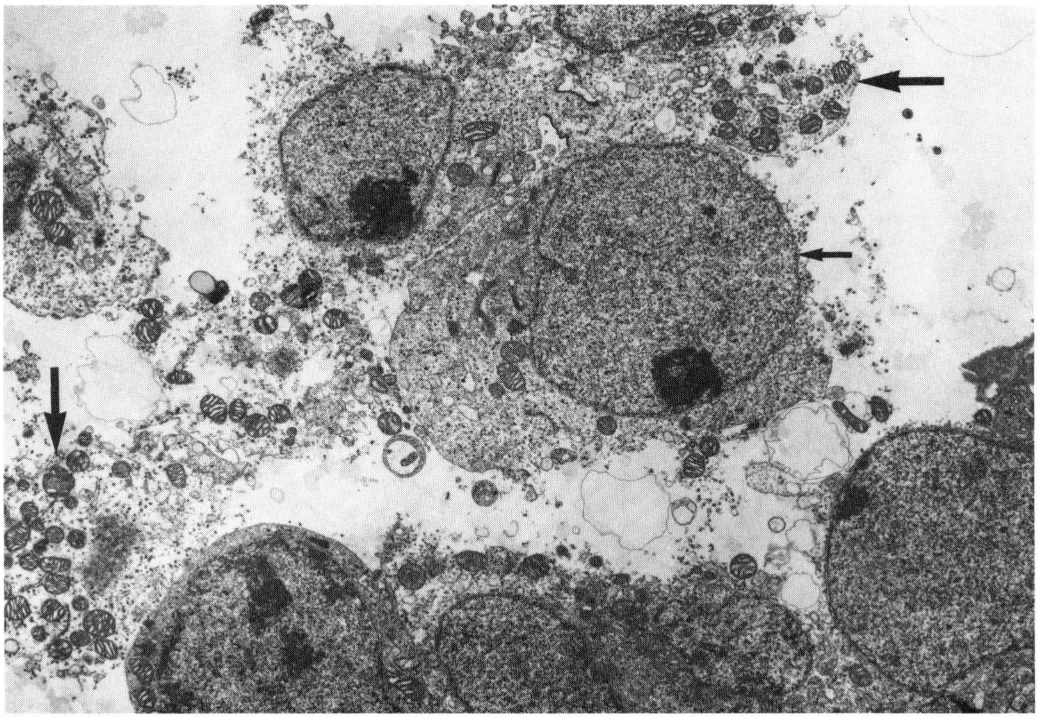

FIG. 6. Section of the seminiferous tubule of methoxychlor-treated rat showing cytoplasmic debris (large arrows) and scattered spermatids (small arrow). ×4675.

double membrane. Such a type of mitochondria manifesting a special functional state has been referred to as energized mitochondria. In those spermatids which had almost completed the process of spermiogenesis, the mitochondria appeared to be reforming their cristae around the flagellum.

In the methoxychlor-treated animals, multinucleated and binucleated cells were seen as in the light microscopic sections of the seminiferous tubules. In these cells, the mitochondria appeared to show degenerative changes with vacuoles around them. A variety of degenerative morphological manifestations of mitochondrial colonies within the binucleated cells was observed (Fig. 7).

In the lighter-appearing multinucleated cells, larger than normal-appearing nucleoli were observed. The multinucleated cells appeared to be the deformed spermatocytes which were fused probably as a result of abnormal cytokinesis. In the normal process of cytokinesis, intercellular bridges are formed in these germ cells and persist up to the spermatid stage.

Degenerating cells were either multinucleated or were surrounded by sustentacular cell cytoplasm. The sustentacular cell cytoplasm had a number of membrane-bound vesicles and other inclusions.

In the sections of the nuclei of some sustentacular cells, there were more than six nucleoli. There appeared some desquamated spermatids and some extracellular organelles in the lumen of the tubules. Occasional macrophages with inclusions and secondary lysosomes were observed. The synchrony of the spermatogenic cycle appeared to be disrupted.

Discussion. From the histopathological changes in the reproductive organs studied in this investigation (testes, epididymis, and ovaries), it is evident that methoxychlor impairs their normal reproductive processes. Previous investigators have used lower doses of methoxychlor in feed (less than 1%) without reporting detailed histopathological changes.

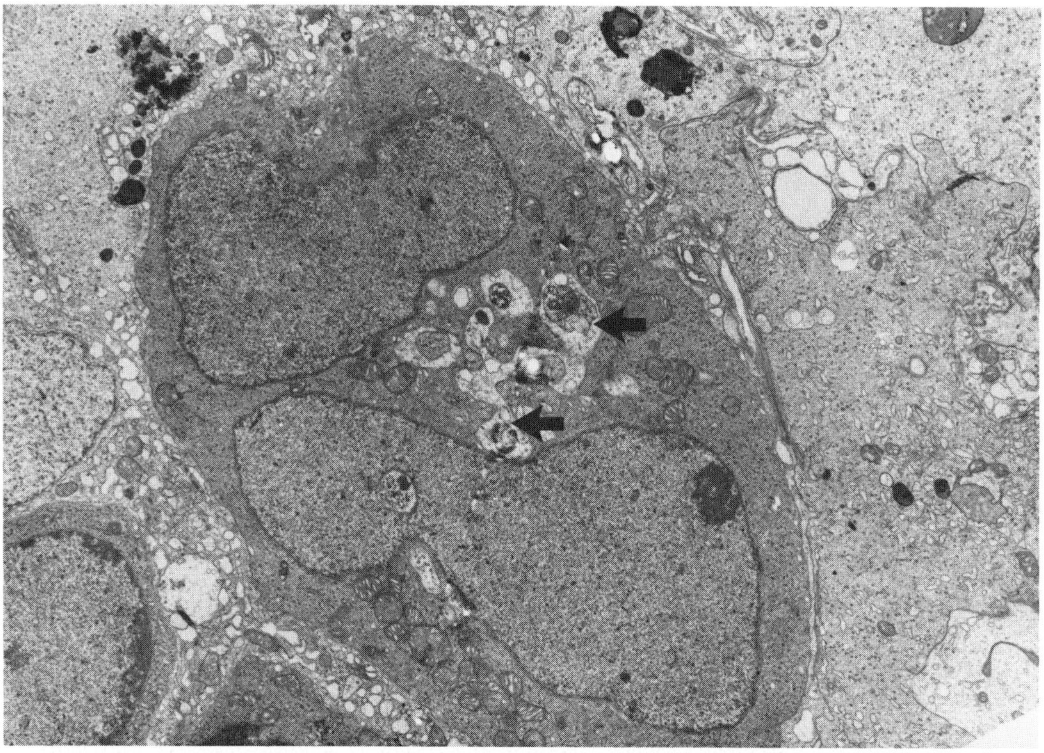

FIG. 7. Section of the seminiferous tubule of methoxychlor-treated rat showing a binucleated cell with degenerating mitochondria (arrows). This cell is almost surrounded by sustentacular cell cytoplasm with many clear membrane bound vesicles. ×5170.

Some have used 3% methoxychlor in diets which did not cover the entire spermatogenic cycle in the male rats (5, 9). It was, therefore, considered appropriate to study the effects of methoxychlor at the dose levels used in this investigation.

The main regulatory cell of the normal process of spermatogenesis is the sustentacular cell with multiple functions (15, 16). In the sections of the methoxychlor-treated rats, large vacuoles in the cytoplasm of the sustentacular cells were observed and manifestations of advanced degenerative changes were also evident. The vacuoles resulting from the removal of lipid during the processing of the tissue from the sustentacular cell cytoplasm could have been from the phagocytosed residual bodies of the germ cells or intracellular fatty changes. The phagocytic ability of the sustentacular cells is established (17). The germ cells which cannot differentiate into sperm would either be phagocytosed by the sustentacular cells or would undergo autolysis. Residual bodies containing lipid and RNA cast off during spermiogenesis are normally phagocytosed by the sustentacular cells (16). As a result of the degenerative changes of the sustentacular cells, the presence of their intercellular junctions which maintain the blood–testis barrier was not observed. Normally the blood–testis barrier is able to develop without the presence of germ cells and in the absence of gonadotrophic hormone stimulation (18). One of the main functions of the blood–testis barrier is to cordon off the primary spermatocytes with a changed genetic composition from the body fluids so that they do not elicit an immune response from the body. Presence of monocyte-like cells have been correlated with the fragmentation of the sustentacular cell junctions (19). Occasional macrophages, which are of monocytic origin, were observed in the seminiferous tubules of the methoxychlor-treated rats.

The binucleated or the multinucleated cells probably resulted due to fusion of the germ cells (primary and secondary spermatocytes, spermatids). The germ cells probably fused because of incomplete cytokinesis during the process of spermatogenesis. Binucleate and multinucleate giant forms are sometimes present among spermatogonia and spermatocytes as a consequence of a peculiar mode of cytokinesis (20). The specific manner in which methoxychlor could have affected the formation of multinucleated cells cannot be explained.

The peripheral distribution of energized mitochondria in relation to the cell membrane of the spermatids of the control rats was observed. Similar morphology and disposition of energized mitochondria in the rat spermatids have been reported (21). Energized mitochondria are seen when energy is being generated much faster than it is dissipated (22). In the experimental rats where the ultimate fate of the germ cells appeared to be death, the energy requirements of the spermatids would be reduced. Therefore, in the methoxychlor-treated rats, the absence of energized mitochondria could be a logical explanation. Degenerate mitochondria were observed in the distorted (binucleate) germ cells.

In this study, the epithelium of the ductus epididymidis exhibited many vesicles and vacuoles. Similar changes in the epididymal epithelium of the rat treated with clomiphene citrate up to 12 weeks were observed (23). Toward the tail of the corpus epididymidis, the lumen of the duct was distended with fluid containing dead cells and disfigured sperm. This distension could have been caused by either obstruction of the duct or stenosis. The epithelial lining of the duct appeared compressed. The blood flow per unit weight through this part of the epididymis is higher than it is for the rest of the epididymis (24).

The sterility of the methoxychlor-treated females was due to the fact that the normal process of folliculogenesis in the ovaries was interrupted, leading to atresia of the ovarian follicles. The granulosa cells exhibited early necrotic changes manifested by pyknosis and karyorhexis of their nuclei. These changes in the ovaries as well as the arrest of normal process of spermatogenesis in the methoxychlor-treated rats could have been due to the estrogenic properties of methoxychlor. Recent studies indicate that metabolites of methoxychlor account for its estrogenic properties *in vivo* (11). Methoxychlor has also been designated as a proestrogen because it requires metabolic activation to achieve its activities (10).

The precise manner in which methoxychlor affects the seminiferous epithelium or the ovarian follicles is not clear. It has been shown that 0.1 μg of diethylstilbestrol has the same estrogenic activity as 1 mg of technical methoxychlor in the rat (25). The estrogenic properties of methoxychlor could surpress the testosterone secretion by the interstitial (Leydig) cells of the testes by inhibiting the release of follicular stimulating hormone (FSH). FSH facilitates the ability of the testes of rats to respond to luteinizing hormone (LH) and secrete testosterone (26). In conclusion, technical methoxychlor does hamper the normal process of spermatogenesis and folliculogenesis. If the effects of methoxychlor on the reproductive systems of the rat are due to its estrogenic properties, further investigations are needed to determine its precise mode of action.

This investigation was supported by the Iowa State University General Research Grant Support, Project Account 430-23-45-00-0211. Appreciation is expressed for the technical assistance of Dr. P. Mungkornkarn, R. Aspengren, and Grace Faber. Gratitude is extended to Glenda Burkheimer and Nancy Brooks for typing this manuscript.

1. Tuchmann-Duplessis H. Teratogenic drug screening. Present procedures and requirements. Teratology **5**:271–286, 1972.
2. Brown AWA. In: White-Stevens R, eds. Pesticides in the Environment. New York, Dekker Vol I, Part II:pp457–552, 1971.
3. Brooks GT. Chlorinated Insecticides. Cleveland, CRC Press, Vol 11:p197, 1974.
4. Meister RT. Farm Chemicals Handbook. Willoughby, Ohio, Meister, p610, 1977.
5. Hodge HC, Maynard EA, Thomas JF, Blanchet HJ, Wilt WG Jr, Mason KE. Short-term oral toxicity tests of methoxychlor in rats and dogs. J. Pharmacol Exp Ther **99**(1):140–148, 1950.
6. Tullner WW, Edgcomb JR. Cystic tubular nephrotomy and decreases in testicular weight in rats following

oral methoxychlor treatment. J Pharmacol Exp Ther **138**:126–130, 1962.
7. Bal HS, Mungkornkarn P. Chronic toxicity effects of methoxychlor on the reproductive system of the rat. International Congress on Toxicology, Toronto, Canada. p4, abstr, 1977.
8. Gellert RJ, Heinrichs WL, Swerdloff R. Effects of neonatally-administered DDT homologs on reproductive function in male and female rats. Neuroendocrinology **16**:84–94, 1974.
9. Hodge HC, Maynard EA, Blanchet EJ Jr. Chronic oral toxicity tests of methoxychlor 2,2-di-(methoxyphenyl) 1,1,1-trichloroethane. J Pharmacol Exp Ther **104**:60–66, 1952.
10. Reuber MD. Carcinogenicity and toxicity of methoxychlor. Environ Health Perspect **36**:205–219, 1980.
11. Kupfer D, Bulgar WH. A novel *in vitro* method for demonstrating proestrogens. Metabolism of methoxychlor and *o,p*-DDT by liver microsomes in the presence of uteri and effects on intracellular distribution of estrogen receptors. Life Sci **25**:975–984, 1979.
12. Ousterhout J, Struck RF, Nelson JA. Estrogenic activities of methoxychlor metabolites. Biochem Pharmacol **30**(20):2869–2871, 1981.
13. Ziem G. Aplastic anemia after methoxychlor exposure. Lancet **11**:1349, 1982.
14. Skaare JV, Berge G, Odegaar S, Grave K. Excretion of methoxychlor in cow milk following dermal application. Acta Vet Scand **23**:16–23, 1982.
15. Hugon J, Borgers M. Ultrastructural and cytochemical changes in spermatogonia and Sertoli cells of whole-body irradiated mice. Anat Rec **155**:15–32, 1966.
16. Lacy D. Light and electron microscopy and its use in the study of factors influencing spermatogenesis in the rat. J R Microsc Soc **79**:209–225, 1960.
17. Burgos MH, VitaleCaipe Aoki A. Fine structure of the testes and its functional significance. In: Johnson AD, Gomes WR, Vandemark NL, eds. The Testes. New York, Academic Press, Vol 1:pp551–649, 1970.
18. Bressler RS. Dependence of Sertoli cell maturation on the pituitary gland in the mouse. Amer J Anat **147**:447–456, 1976.
19. Nagano T, Suzuki F. The postnatal development of junctional complexes of the mouse Sertoli cells as revealed by freeze-fracture. Anat Rec **185**:403–418, 1976.
20. Bloom W, Fawcett DW. A Textbook of Histology. Philadelphia, Saunders pp819–828, 1975.
21. Kaya M, Harrison RG. The ultrastructural relationships between Sertoli cells and spermatogenic cells in the rat. J Anat **121**:279–290, 1976.
22. Baum H. Mitochondria and peroxisomes. In: Beck F, Lloyd JB, eds. The Cell in Medical Science. London, Academic Press, Vol 1:pp183–272, 1974.
23. Flickinger CJ. Effects of clomiphene on the structure of the testis, epididymis and sex accessory glands of the rat. Amer J Anat **149**:533–562, 1977.
24. Reid BL, Cleland RW. The structure and function of the epididymis. 1. The histology of the rat epididymis. Aust J Zool **6**:223–246, 1976.
25. Bitman J, Cecil HC. Estrogenic activity of DDT analogs and polychlorinated biphenyls. J Agric Food Chem **18**:1108–1112, 1970.
26. Odell WD, Swerdloff RS, Jacobs HS, Hescox MA. FSH induction of sensitivity to LH: One cause of sexual maturation in the male rat. Endocrinology **92**:160–165, 1973.

Received December 6, 1983. P.S.E.B.M. 1984, Vol. 176.
Accepted March 2, 1984.

PROCEEDINGS OF THE SOCIETY FOR EXPERIMENTAL BIOLOGY AND MEDICINE **176**, 197–202 (1984)

The Effect of Methylcellulose on Extrarenal Erythropoietin Production (41862)

GARY B. ZUCKERMAN, BRIAN A. NAUGHTON, ANDREA GAITO, ROBERT A. PRETI, AND ALBERT S. GORDON

A. S. Gordon Laboratory of Experimental Hematology, Department of Biology, Graduate School of Arts and Sciences, New York University, New York, New York 10003, and the Department of Medical Laboratory Sciences, School of Health Sciences, Hunter College, New York, New York 10010

Abstract. The macromolecular polymer, methyl cellulose (MC), is a known hepatosplenomegalic agent which promotes a state of experimental hypersplenism in rats. This is characterized by massive splenomegaly, pancytopenia of the blood elements, medullary hypoplasia, and marked gross and histologic alteration of the liver, kidney, adrenals, and lungs. Massive splenomegaly results from storage of this inert material by splenic macrophages. In the present study, chronic MC administration in rats augmented the hepatic Ep response to hypoxia but did not appreciably affect renal production of Ep. Splenectomy resulted in a decrease in the extrarenal Ep response to hypoxia indicating a possible role of the massively enlarged spleen of these MC-treated rats in extrarenal Ep production. The augmentation of extrarenal Ep elaboration may be attributed to a stimulatory effect of MC on the hepatic and splenic macrophages.

The glycoprotein hormone, erythropoietin (Ep), is acknowledged to be the major regulator of erythropoiesis. In mammals, the kidney serves as the primary site of Ep origin (1, 2). Other sites of Ep production exist; the liver is considered to be the major source of extrarenal Ep (3) in the adult mammal. In contrast, the liver is the chief source of Ep in fetal and neonatal animals. In this regard, bilateral nephrectomy (nephrx) of the fetal or neonatal mammal does not significantly alter the Ep response to hypoxia (4) whereas this is almost completely abolished by hepatectomy (hepx) (5).

Liver regeneration following hepx has been shown to be a potent source of Ep (6, 7) when compared to the normal liver. Hepatic regeneration following liver injury evoked by hepatotoxic agents such as CCl_4 (8, 9) or phenylhydrazine (10) results in significant augmentation of hepatic Ep production when compared with normal or saline-injected animals.

The macromolecular polymer, methyl cellulose (MC), is the methylated ether of cellulose (11). It is composed of polymerized dextrose molecules and is an extremely stable entity (11). Chronic administration of MC induces hypersplenism in rats and mice (11–15). In this hypersplenic state there is massive splenomegaly, pancytopenia of the blood elements, and medullary hypoplasia. There is also gross (organomegaly) and histologic (parenchymal cell destruction) alteration of liver, kidney, adrenals, and lungs (11–15). This condition occurs in part due to the sequestration of MC by the splenic macrophages. Hepatic and renal RES elements also engulf MC, although the size of these organs does not change considerably after MC treatment (11). Splenectomy was found to alleviate the anemia associated with MC-induced splenomegaly (19). The ability of MC to induce splenomegaly is apparently species specific. MC produces this effect in rats and mice (11–15) but fails to cause splenomegaly in dogs (16), rabbits (17), or the rhesus monkey (18). Regardless of its ability to promote splenomegaly, MC administration results in significant hematological consequences in mice (14, 15), rats (11–14), dogs (16), rabbits (17), and monkeys (18). MC induces a moderate hemolytic anemia in the monkey (18), although splenic size was not significantly altered. However, treatment with MC significantly lowers the RBC survival time in primates (18) as well as rodents (20). In addition, lymphocytopenia has been reported in the rhesus monkey (18), neutrophilia in the mouse (21), and thrombocytopenia in the rat (13) after MC administration. Several mechanisms of MC-induced anemia have been hypothesized: (i) a humoral factor was reported in the urine of MC-induced hypersplenic rats which caused

0037-9727/84 $1.50

anemia and thrombocytopenia when given intragastrically to normal rats (22), (ii) splenic sequestration and hemolysis of erythrocytes also have been reported to influence this anemia (13, 20, 23), and (iii) renal failure was postulated as a cause of MC-induced anemia. In this regard, MC administration resulted in renal damage symptomized by proteinuria, hypocholesterolemia, and hypoalbuminemia (24).

An augmentation of renal Ep elaboration was noted in rats after repeated MC administration (25), possibly due to concurrent hemolysis. At present, little information exists concerning the role of MC on extrarenal Ep production. The purpose of the following experiments was to study the effects of chronic MC administration on the extrarenal (splenic and hepatic) Ep response to hypoxia.

Materials and Methods. Female Long–Evans rats, initially weighing 150–200 g (Blue Spruce Farms, Altamont, N.Y.) were used. At the termination of the experiment (4 weeks duration) the rats weighed 275–325 g.

Experimental animals were subjected to 4 weeks of chronic injections (ip) of methyl cellulose (Methocel, Dow Chemical Co., Midland, Mich.) at a dosage of 20 mg/100 g body weight. The stock methyl cellulose solution was prepared at a concentration of 5 mg/ml saline. Saline (0.9%) was used as the control substance for each group. Hematocrits were taken via the tail vein on a biweekly basis.

I. Surgical procedures. The following surgical procedures were employed:

(i) Bilateral nephrectomy (nephrx): Two 1-cm incisions were made on the dorsolateral flanks. The kidneys were localized, externalized, ligated with 3-O suture, and removed.

(ii) Splenectomy (splenx): A 2-cm mediolateral incision was made parallel to the costal margin. The spleen was localized, externalized, ligated with 3-O suture, and extirpated. Organs were weighed following removal. The surgical procedures did not evoke significant blood loss and the survival rate was greater than 95%.

II. Experimental protocols. All experimental groups consisted of five to eight rats with three trials performed per data point. In total, eight experimental groups were studied.

(i) Rats were injected with methyl cellulose daily (20 mg/100 g body wt) for 4 weeks. At the end of the fourth week the rats were nephrx and rendered hypoxic in a hypobaric chamber for 6 hr at 0.4 atmospheres (atm) of air. Immediately following hypoxia the rats were exsanguinated via the abdominal aorta, their serum pooled, and assayed for Ep (2) in the exhypoxic polycythemic mouse.

(ii) Animals were splenx initially and injected with methyl cellulose for 4 weeks. At the termination of this period, the animals were nephrx and rendered hypoxic (0.4 atm/6 hr). They were bled and their serum assayed for Ep.

(iii) After chronic methyl cellulose administration over a 4 week period, rats were splenx, nephrx, and rendered hypoxic (0.4 atm/6 hr). Blood was collected from the abdominal aorta, serum prepared, and assayed for Ep.

(iv) These animals were injected with methyl cellulose over a 4 week period. At the end of this time, they were exposed to hypoxia (0.4 atm/6 hr) and blood was collected and assayed for Ep.

(v–viii) Saline (0.9%) was substituted for methyl cellulose for each of the previous groups tested (Groups 1–4) and served as a control.

To eliminate the possible influence of hematocrit variation in these studies, whole blood from normal donor rats of the same sex and approximate age was infused after Hemo-Set filtration, into animals in Groups 1–3 (immediately prior to nephrx) in quantities which were calculated to achieve a hematocrit of 40%. The actual mean hematocrit after infusion and the resulting Ep values are given in Table III.

III. Ep assay procedure. All blood collected was assayed for Ep using the exhypoxic polycythemic mouse. In this procedure BF-1 virgin female mice (Blue Spruce Farms, Altamont, N.Y.) are subjected to discontinuous hypoxia in a hypobaric chamber for 19 hr a day at 0.4 atm of air for 2 weeks. At the end of these 2 weeks the mice are polycythemic and following a 2-day recovery period are particularly sensitive to Ep since they produce little or no endogenous Ep.

The test material was administered on Day 3 and radioiron on Day 5 posthypoxia. Radioiron incorporation into newly formed red blood cells was determined on Day 7 posthypoxia and compared to that of standards obtained with the International Reference Preparation for Ep.

IV. Histological procedures. Representative spleen, liver, and kidney samples were excised from each group of rats, weighed, and frozen in liquid nitrogen prior to cryostat sectioning (5 μm). Sections were fixed on a glass slide and stained with hematoxylin-eosin prior to study.

V. Statistics. Ep values are expressed as the mean (IU/ml) ± 1 standard error of the mean for three separate groups consisting of five to eight animals whose sera was pooled (total, 15–24 rats). Levels of significance (*P* values) are determined using Student's *t* test. Hematocrits are indicated as mean values ±1 standard error of the mean for animals comprising each of the eight experimental groups (i.e., 15–24 rats). Hematocrit values for all animals involved in each of the eight experimental and control groups are given: (i) prior to experimental manipulation and (ii) at the conclusion of the experiment just before sacrifice (Table I).

Results. Splenomegaly was evident in the spleens of MC-treated rats. Mean splenic weight of normal rats was 0.63 g (range 0.55 to 0.67) whereas mean splenic weight of MC-treated animals was 2.51 g (range 1.46 to 3.41), a relative size increase of approximately fourfold. White areas, indicative of MC deposition, were also seen on the surfaces of the MC-treated spleens.

Some degree of hepatomegaly was noted in MC-treated rats (mean normal liver weight of 6.39 g as compared to 7.72 g for MC-treated animals). Livers of these rats were more friable than normal livers and small, localized foci of erythropoiesis were observed but these were not as abundant as those seen after partial hepatectomy (37).

Histological study of the spleen revealed an accumulation of MC in the splenic macrophages and a constriction of the sinusoids. Germinal center sizes diminished but no extramedullary erythropoiesis was noted. In the liver, MC accumulated in Kupffer cells, which underwent a corresponding increase in size and number. Some constriction of the hepatic sinusoids was noted and MC-induced hepatocellular destruction was found in several areas adjacent to engorged Kupffer cells. Splenectomy, when performed at the onset of the experiment, accentuated the Kupffer cell involvement in MC-treated rats.

The appearance of the kidneys of MC-treated rats varied. Kidneys were either normal or anisonephric; however, no correlation was found between hepatic Ep production and the gross appearance of the kidneys of MC-treated rats. MC deposition in the glomerular region was associated with localized necrosis of the renal parenchyma but the frequency of these effects were much lower than those observed with the liver and spleen.

At the termination of the experiment, the MC-treated rats displayed a significantly decreased hematocrit (Table I), when compared to saline-treated animals (Groups 1 and 4 vs

TABLE I. MEAN HEMATOCRITS OF MC- AND SALINE-TREATED ANIMALS[a]

	Mean hematocrit at beginning of experiment	Mean hematocrit at end of experiment
Experimental MC groups		
Group 1. MC, nephrx, hypoxia	41.00 ± 3.28	32.75 ± 1.96
Group 2. splenx, MC, nephrx, hypoxia	43.10 ± 3.01	37.00 ± 3.70
Group 3. MC, nephrx + splenx, hypoxia	40.60 ± 2.43	38.00 ± 2.82
Group 4. MC, hypoxia	43.80 ± 3.50	33.00 ± 3.10
Saline control groups		
Group 5. saline, nephrx, hypoxia	39.40 ± 2.10	39.00 ± 2.60
Group 6. splenx, saline, nephrx, hypoxia	40.00 ± 3.20	40.80 ± 3.91
Group 7. saline, nephrx + splenx, hypoxia	42.00 ± 2.80	41.00 ± 4.02
Group 8. saline, hypoxia	40.00 ± 3.15	40.00 ± 3.00

[a] All values are means ± 1 SEM.

Groups 5 and 8, respectively) ($P < 0.05$). Hematocrits of asplenic MC-treated rats, however, were slightly but not significantly lower than their saline-treated counterparts. This finding is consistent with the previously reported role of the spleen in MC-associated anemia.

Extrarenal Ep production after hypoxia was significantly higher in rats after MC injection when compared to saline-injected controls (Table II: Group 1 vs Group 5) ($P < 0.01$). This was approximately 75% of the renal-Ep response after hypoxia (Table II: Group 1 vs Group 4).

MC-treated rats which were splenx and nephrx prior to hypoxia showed an elevation in hepatic Ep production when compared to saline controls (Table II: Group 2 vs Group 6, Group 3 vs Group 7 ($P < 0.01$), but this response was significantly lower than that observed in the MC-treated anephric hypoxic animals (Table II: Group 1) or in unoperated hypoxic rats (Table II: Group 4) with intact spleens ($P < 0.05$). Splenectomy diminished the extrarenal Ep response to hypoxia regardless of whether it was performed prior to MC administration or after chronic exposure to this substance (Table II: Group 1 vs Groups 2 and 3) ($P < 0.05$). Ep titers in rats rendered anemic by MC were not significantly different than those obtained in similar animals whose hematocrits were raised to normal levels via the infusion of whole blood (Table III). This demonstrates that the influence of hematocrit on the Ep response to acute hypoxia in this animal system was minimal.

TABLE II. MEAN SERUM Ep LEVELS[a]

	Ep (IU/ml)
Experimental MC groups[b]	
Group 1. MC, nephrx, hypoxia	0.77 ± 0.03
Group 2. splenx, MC, nephrx, hypoxia	0.54 ± 0.04
Group 3. MC, nephrx + splenx, hypoxia	0.53 ± 0.06
Group 4. MC, hypoxia	1.14 ± 0.14
Saline control groups	
Group 5. saline, nephrx, hypoxia	0.08 ± 0.01
Group 6. splenx, saline, nephrx, hypoxia	0.06 ± 0.01
Group 7. saline, nephrx + splenx, hypoxia	0.07 ± 0.02
Group 8. saline, hypoxia	1.08 ± 0.10

[a] Values are means ± 1 SEM.
[b] All groups were exsanguinated from the abdominal aorta and assayed for Ep at the conclusion of the hypoxic period.

TABLE III. MEAN SERUM Ep LEVELS[a] AND MEAN HEMATOCRITS IN MC-TREATED TRANSFUSED ANIMALS[b]

	Ep (IU/ml)	Hct
Group 1. MC, nephrx, hypoxia	0.71 ± 0.07	40.9
Group 2. splenx, MC, nephrx, hypoxia	0.40 ± 0.09	39.7
Group 3. MC, nephrx + splenx, hypoxia	0.51 ± 0.05	42.1

[a] Values are means ± 1 SEM.
[b] Whole blood was infused immediately prior to nephrx in volumes which were calculated to raise the Hct for rats in Groups 1–3 into the normal range. Hematocrits immediately prior to infusion are given in Table I, last column; those after infusion are included above.

Discussion. Methyl cellulose is a known hepatosplenomegalic agent which produces a state of experimental hypersplenism in rats (11–13). Our histologic and gross findings agree with previously reported effects of MC on the organs studied. The Kupffer cell, part of the reticuloendothelial system (RES) of the liver, was postulated as the hepatic cellular site of Ep origin (6, 26). Recent studies using immunofluorescence and a purified guinea pig anti-rat Ep have indicated that these cells do indeed store and/or synthesize Ep (27). These macrophages have previously been shown to produce other hematopoietic regulators such as colony stimulating factor for granulopoiesis (28) and several prostaglandins (29).

Methyl cellulose-treated rats display RES stimulation despite storage of MC in macrophages of the liver and spleen (30). This compound was shown to elevate phagocytosis of "RE test emulsion" and colloidal carbon by the liver (30). In addition, splenx resulted in an increase in Kupffer cell phagocytosis of colloidal carbon after MC administration.

The altered hepatic blood flow due to the splenomegaly apparently has little effect on either Kupffer cell phagocytic or secretory functions. In this regard, splenectomy, which significantly retards blood flow, had little effect on the hepatic Ep response to hypoxia in the hepatectomized animal (6). In addition, phenylhydrazine administration, which promotes splenomegaly, actually augments the hepatic Ep response, presumably due to a stimulation of the liver RES.

In the present study, MC treatment augmented the hepatic Ep response to hypoxia but did not appreciably affect renal elaboration of this principle (Table II: Group 1 vs Group 6, Group 4 vs Group 8). Presumably, this is attributable to the previously reported effects of this substance on macrophages (30). The extrarenal response to hypoxia in rats with livers damaged by MC administration (accumulation of MC in Kupffer cells) approximated that in the renal-intact animal (Table II: Group 1 vs Group 4). Kupffer cell cytoplasmic areas and activity have been correlated to the amount of hepatic Ep synthesized or released after hypoxic challenge (31). The increased hepatic Ep response after hypoxia in these MC-treated rats may be associated with macrophage hyperactivity. In addition, hepatic erythropoiesis has been observed after RES activation due to partial hepatectomy (37) and the administration of chemical agents such as glucan (38), phenylhydrazine (39), and MC (19).

Splenx diminished the extrarenal Ep response to hypoxia (Table II: Group 1 vs Groups 2 and 3) ($P < 0.05$) indicating a positive role of the spleen in extrarenal Ep production. MC-activated splenic macrophages may contribute to the increased extrarenal Ep response to hypoxia. The mammalian spleen has been implicated as a possible source of extrarenal Ep (32, 33), although this organ did not appear to contribute to the Ep response to hypoxia in the hepx animal (6). Splenic macrophages also account for most of the erythrophagocytosis in normal animals (34). The sinusoidal macrophages recognize and destroy physically damaged erythrocytes (34), erythrocytes sensitized with metal cations (35), antibody-damaged red cells (36), red blood cells containing inclusions such as Heinz bodies or Howell–Jolly bodies (34), and old erythrocytes so that their iron can be recycled for the production of new hemoglobin (37). Storage and release of iron by these and other RES cells modulating hemoglobin synthesis are recognized as an important function of this system (37).

Chronic administration of MC in rats augmented the production of extrarenal Ep after hypoxia. Most of this was attributed to increased hepatic production of this principle, although splenic Ep elaboration was significant. In contrast to macrophage-rich organs like the liver and spleen, MC had little effect on Ep production in the kidney, which has a relative paucity of these cells. Furthermore, the site of the renal RES (mesangial cells) may preclude any possible direct stimulatory action of MC, due to its ability to occlude the glomerular vasculature (16, 18, 19).

This work was supported by Grant L RO1 HLB03357-23 from the National Heart, Lung, and Blood Institute, NIH, USPHS, and Grant 11-105 from the New York State Health Research Council.

1. Jacobson LO, Goldwasser E, Fried W, Plzak L. Role of the Kidney in erythropoiesis. Nature (London) **179**:633–634, 1957.
2. Gordon AS. Erythropoietin, In: Harris RS, Diszfalusy E, Munson PL, Glover J, eds. Vitamins and Hormones. New York, Academic Press, pp105–174, 1973.
3. Fried W. The liver as a source of extrarenal erythropoietin. Blood **40**:671–676, 1972.
4. Gordon AS, Zanjani ED, Peterson EN, Gidari AS, Lobue J, Camiscoli JF. Studies on fetal erythropoiesis. In: Gordon AS, Condorelli M, Peschle C, eds. First Intern Conf on Hematop Regul of Erythrop. Il Ponte,Milan, pp188–204, 1972.
5. Zanjani ED, Poster J., Burlington J, Mann LI, Wasserman LR. Liver as the primary site of erythropoietin production in the fetus. J Lab Clin Med **89**:640–644, 1977.
6. Naughton BA, Kaplan SM, Roy M, Gordon AS. Hepatic regeneration and erythropoietin production in the rat. Science **196**:301–320, 1977.
7. Anagnostou A, Schade S, Barone J, Fried W. Effect of partial hepatectomy on extrarenal erythropoietin production in rats. Blood **50**:457–462, 1977.
8. Liu P, Naughton BA, Kolks GA, Gordon AS. The effect of hepatoxic agents on hepatic erythropoietin (Ep) production. Anat Rec **196**:224A, 1980.
9. Fried W, Barone J, Schade S, Anagnostou A. Effect of carbon tetrachloride on extrarenal erythropoietin production in rats. J Lab Clin Med **93**:700–705, 1979.
10. Dornfest BS, Naughton BA, Johnson R, Gordon AS. Hepatic production of erythropoietin in a phenylhydrazine-induced compensated hemolytic state in the rat. J Lab Clin Med **102**:274–285, 1983.
11. Hueper WC. Experimental studies in cardiovascular pathology. IV. Methyl cellulose atheromatosis and thesaurosis. Arch Pathol **33**:1–17, 1942.
12. Glomski CA. Experimental hypersplenism and tissue iron distribution. Brit J Exp Pathol **50**:331–339, 1969.

13. Alwmark A, Bengmark S, Bengt B, Gullstrand P. Treatment of hypersplenism. An experimental study in the rat. Eur Surg Res **14**:322–332, 1982.
14. Fiala J, Viktora L. Kotazue transplantace bunek krvetvornych organo u hypersplenickychmysi. Cas Lek Cesk **112**:694–696, 1972.
15. Scheifforth F, Baenkler HW, Peter KH. The kinetics of plaque-forming cells in experimental hypersplenism. Acta Haematol **45**:266–271, 1971.
16. Weissman SM, Waldman TA, Levin E, Berlin NI. An attempt to produce hypersplenism in the dog using methyl cellulose. Blood **17**:632–642, 19xx.
17. Giblett AG, Motulsky FC, Casserd B, Houghton B, Finch CA. Studies on the pathogenesis of splenic anemia. Blood **11**:1118–1131, 1956.
18. Glomski CA, Chung-Faye C, Zuckerman GB. Haemolytic anaemia in rhesus monkeys (*Macaca mulatta*) induced by methyl cellulose. Lab Anim **16**:310–313, 1982.
19. Stang HD, Boggs DR. Effect of methyl cellulose injection on murine hematopoiesis. Amer J Physiol **233**:H234–H239, 1977.
20. Macado E, Lozzio B, Lew V. Erythrocyte destruction induced by methylcellulose. Arch Pathol **82**:590–595, 1966.
21. Tamayo RP, Mejia S. Further studies on the humoral factor(s) of experimental hypersplenism. Exp Mol Pathol **2**:234–242, 1963.
22. Brabeck V, Sebestik V. Survival and sites of sequestration of erythrocytes in normal and hypersplenic rats. Physiol Bohemoslov **23**:119–127, 1974.
23. Rowley DA, Fitch FW, Bye IJ. Anemia produced in the rat by methyl cellulose. Arch Pathol **74**:331–339, 1962.
24. Brabeck V, Neuwirt J. Erythropoietin formation in rats with experimental hypersplenism. Scand J Haematol **14**:86–90, 1975.
25. Peschle C, Marone G, Genovese A, Rappaport IA, Condorelli M. Hepatic erythropoietin. Enhanced production in anephric rats with hyperplasia of Kupffer cells. Brit J Haematol **32**:105–111, 1976.
26. Naughton GK, Naughton BA, Liu P, Piliero SJ, Gordon AS. Localization of erythropoietin in rat liver. Physiologist.
27. Joyce RA, Chervenick PA. Stimulation of granulopoiesis by liver macrophages. J Lab Clin Med **56**:112–117, 1975.
28. Kurland JI, Pelus LM, Ralph P, Bockman RS, Moore MAS. Induction of prostaglandin E synthesis in normal and neoplastic macrophages: Role for colony stimulating factor(s) distinct from effects on myeloid progenitor cell proliferation. Proc Natl Acad Sci USA **76**:2326–2340, 1979.
29. Blickens DA, Diluzio NR. The effect of methyl cellulose on the reticuloendothelial system. J Reticuloendothel Soc **1**:68–76, 1964.
30. Naughton BA, Birnbach DJ, Liu P, Kolks GA, Tung MZ, Piliero SJ, Gordon AS. Reticuloendothelial system (RES) hyperfunction and erythropoietin (Ep) production in the regenerating liver. J Surg Oncol **12**:227–242, 1979.
31. de Franciscas P, de Bella G, Gifaldi S. Spleen as a production site for erythropoietin. Science **150**:1831–1833, 1965.
32. Liotti FS, Giovaninni E, Bruschelli GM. Properties of the erythro-stimulant factors present in the plasma, kidney and spleen of the rabbit. Riv Biol **65**:33–51, 1972.
33. Rifkind RA. Destruction of injured red cells in vivo. Amer J Med **41**:711–718, 1970.
34. Jandl JH, Simmons RL. The agglutination and sensitization of red cells by metallic cations. Brit J Haematol **3**:19–26, 1957.
35. Cutbush M, Mollison PL. Relation between characteristics of blood group antibodies in vitro and associated patterns of red cell destruction in vivo. Brit J Haematol **4**:115–125, 1958.
36. Finch CA, Deubelbeiss K, Cook JD, Eschbach JW, Harker LA, Fund DD, Marsaglia G, Hillman RS, Slichter S, Adamson JW, Gansomi A, Giblett ER. Ferrokinetics in man. Medicine **49**:17–25, 1970.
37. Naughton BA, Kolka GA, Ance JM, Liu P, Piliero SJ, Gordon AS. The regenerating liver: a site of erythropoiesis in the adult rat. Amer J Anat **156**:159–166, 1979.
38. Deimann W, Fahimi HD. Induction of focal hemopoiesis in adult rat liver by glucan, a macrophage activator. Lab Invest **42**:217–228, 1980.
39. Hertzberg C, Orlic D. An electron microscopic study of erythrophagocytosis in the fetal and neonatal rabbit. J Reticuloendothel Soc **28**:15–23, 1980.

Received November 22, 1983. P.S.E.B.M. 1984, Vol. 176.
Accepted March 8, 1984.

PROCEEDINGS OF THE SOCIETY FOR EXPERIMENTAL BIOLOGY AND MEDICINE **176**, 203–207 (1984)

Interaction between Depressor and Pressor Reflexes Arising from the Aorta in Dogs (41863)

T. E. PISARRI AND J. E. KENDRICK

Department of Physiology, University of Wisconsin, Madison, Wisconsin 53706

Abstract. In 18 dogs anesthetized with morphine–chloralose the interaction between the aortic nerve (AN) pressor and depressor reflexes was studied. Low-intensity, high-frequency electrical stimulation of the AN causes large decreases in heart rate and systemic pressure characteristic of baroreflex responses. High-intensity, low-frequency stimulation of the AN causes modest increases in heart rate and systemic pressure similar to the responses observed to intraaortic nicotine. Simultaneous electrical stimulation of these antagonistic reflexes results in much smaller ($P < 0.001$) reductions in heart rate and systemic pressure than can be explained on the basis of simple addition of the individual responses. Similarly the AN depressor reflexes are suppressed during intraaortic infusions of nicotine (40 μg/min). The results suggest that the inhibitory effects of the AN baroreflexes are suppressed by the aortic chemoreflexes. This interaction occurs in the CNS rather than at the level of the heart or vascular smooth muscle.

The aortic nerves in the dog carry afferent fibers arising from both baroreceptors and chemoreceptors of the aortic arch and adjacent arteries. Stimulation of the aortic baroreceptors produces a cardiovascular reflex response qualitatively similar to that produced by carotid baroreceptor stimulation (1); that is, decreased heart rate and ventricular performance (2) and a fall in systemic vascular resistance (3). In contrast, stimulation of aortic chemoreceptors produces a rise in blood pressure and an increased heart rate (4–9). Simultaneous stimulation of both the aortic baroreceptors and chemoreceptors would therefore give rise to antagonistic cardiovascular reflexes that would interact in some manner to determine the ultimate cardiovascular response.

In previous studies (10, 11) we investigated the interaction between the antagonistic responses to stimulation of the pressor afferents in the aortic nerve (AN) and the depressor afferents in the carotid sinus nerve (CSN) in dogs. From these studies we concluded that the aortic chemoreceptor reflex exerts its cardiovascular effects in part by directly increasing sympathetic outflow to the cardiovascular system and in part by suppressing the inhibitory effects of the carotid sinus baroreflexes on the autonomic output. In the present study we have extended these studies to examine the interaction between the aortic pressor afferents and the aortic baroreceptor reflex. The results suggest that the aortic chemoreflex suppresses the cardiovascular effects of the aortic baroreflex in a manner similar to that observed in the interaction with the carotid sinus baroreflex.

Methods. The experiments were conducted on a total of 21 dogs (10–20 kg). All animals were anesthetized with alpha-chloralose (100 mg/kg iv) 30 min after premedication with morphine sulfate (2 mg/kg sc). Anesthesia was maintained by a continuous intravenous drip of chloralose (approx 25 mg/kg/hr). The trachea was intubated and the animals were artificially ventilated with room air or oxygen. This generally eliminated spontaneous breathing movements in response to chemoreflex stimulation. In 8 animals a paralyzing dose of gallamine triethiodide (Flaxedil, 2 mg/kg iv) or pancuronium bromide (Pavulon, 0.2–0.5 mg/kg iv) was given to be certain that respiratory movements were abolished. This caused some reduction in the magnitude of the reflex responses but did not otherwise affect the results. In all animals ventilatory rate was adjusted to maintain end-expiratory CO_2 in the range of 4–5% as monitored by a LB-2 Beckman medical gas analyzer. Arterial pressure was measured from a catheter in a branch of the femoral artery with a Statham pressure transducer and was recorded on a Beckman polygraph. Heart rate was measured with a cardiotachometer triggered from the femoral arterial pulse. A second cannula in the femoral vein was used for intravenous drug infusion.

The AN were identified, carefully isolated, and in most experiments, cut and drawn into

0037-9727/84 $1.50

silver ring electrodes in the manner previously described (11). To exclude reflex changes from the carotid baroreceptors, both carotid sinus nerves were isolated and cut. The AN were stimulated with rectangular pulses from a dual-channel stimulator (Grass S-88). Low-intensity (0.01 msec, 1–3 V) stimuli were delivered to the AN from one channel of the stimulator. These stimuli primarily excite large, low-threshold baroreceptor afferents in the AN and are subthreshold to most of the chemoreceptor afferents (9). High-intensity stimuli (1.0 msec, 1–3 V) were delivered to the AN from the second channel of the stimulator. These stimuli activated both the baroreceptor and small chemoreceptor afferents in the AN. However, as we have shown (9), low-frequency (2 Hz) stimulation of the large baroreceptor afferents in the AN has minimal effects on the cardiovascular system. Thus the predominant reflex effect of low-frequency, high-intensity stimulation of the AN appears to result from the stimulation of chemoreceptor afferents. Similarly the response to low-intensity, high-frequency stimulation of the AN appears to predominantly arise from stimulation of large baroreceptor afferents (9).

In the present experiments, one channel of the stimulator delivered the low-intensity stimulus at high frequency (40 pulses/train, in 100-msec trains at two trains/sec), and the other channel delivered the high-intensity stimulus at low frequency (2 Hz). The strength of the high-intensity stimulus was adjusted to produce an increase of about 15 beats/min in the heart rate. In most experiments the two stimuli were delivered separately and then simultaneously to the same AN through the same electrode. During simultaneous stimulation the high-intensity stimulus was synchronized to the beginning of the low-intensity stimulus train. In six of the experiments, in addition to the usual method of stimulation, the high-intensity stimulus was delivered to one AN while the low-intensity stimulus was delivered to the other AN.

In eight animals, the number of low-intensity stimuli per train was varied in steps from 2 to 60. This series was then repeated with a high-intensity stimulus synchronized to the beginning of each train. The response curves thus obtained were compared.

In three animals intraaortic bolus injections (0.2 ml, 20 μg) or infusions (40 μg/min) of nicotine sulfate were given before cutting the AN. The infusions were made through a catheter placed in the aortic arch through the carotid artery. The response to low-intensity stimulation of one of the intact AN was then obtained in the presence and absence of nicotine infusion. In these experiments and in experiments reported earlier (9, 11) intraaortic nicotine causes variable responses following AN transection. Generally, the cardioacceleration and pressure rise are reduced or abolished but in some cases cardiac slowing and depressor responses occur.

Analysis of data. The sum of the sustained heart rate and blood pressure responses obtained to separate high- and low-intensity stimulation of the AN was compared to the sustained responses obtained during simultaneous stimulation of the AN with both high- and low-intensity stimuli. The standard paired *t* test was used. The 95% level of confidence was selected for significance. All responses are reported as mean values ± SEM.

Results. Figure 1 illustrates the heart rate and blood pressure responses obtained to AN stimulation. In this case, high-intensity, low-frequency stimulation caused an increase in heart rate of 8 beats/min and a systemic pressure rise of 40 mm Hg. This will be referred to as pressor stimulation. Low-intensity, high-frequency stimulation caused heart rate and blood pressure to fall by 84 beats/min and 75 mm Hg, respectively. We will refer to this as depressor stimulation. Simultaneous stimulation with both stimuli (combined stimulation) caused a decrease in heart rate of 42 beats/min and a 7 mm Hg increase in blood

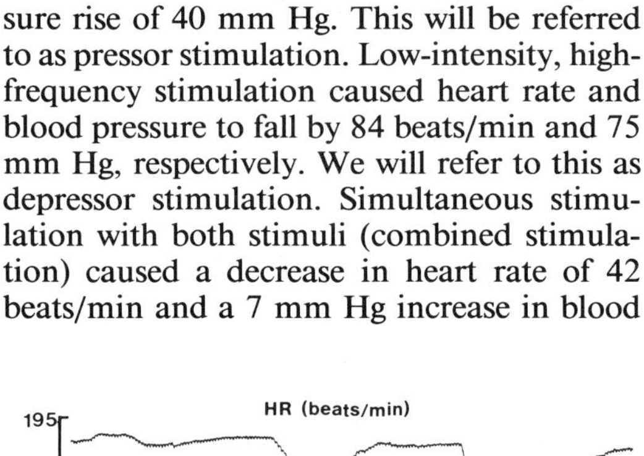

FIG. 1. Heart rate and systemic pressure responses to stimulation of AN pressor afferents (P) and depressor afferents (D) separately and in combination (P&D). Dog paralyzed with pancuronium.

pressure. This response is in contrast to the expected decrease in heart rate of 76 beats/min and a 35 mm Hg fall in pressure that would have occurred if these responses had summed in a simple algebraic manner. The average results of 37 trials in 18 dogs are shown in Fig. 2. Both the heart rate and blood pressure responses to combined stimulation were significantly smaller ($P < 0.001$) than the algebraic sum of the separate reflex responses.

The response curves shown in Fig. 3 illustrate the effect of increasing the frequency of depressor stimulation of the AN before and during simultaneous stimulation with a pressor stimulus. The upper curve illustrates the change in heart rate observed to depressor stimulation during ongoing pressor stimulation of the AN. In this case the initial heart rate was 173 ± 9 beats/min. The lower curve shows the change in heart rate to stimulation with the depressor stimulus alone. The initial heart rate in this case was 152 ± 20 beats/min. Each curve shows the change in heart rate due to depressor stimulation from the initial heart rate for that curve. The difference between these curves illustrates that during ongoing stimulation of the AN pressor reflex the effectiveness of the AN depressor reflexes is reduced over a wide range of stimulation. This difference was significant ($P < 0.05$) at all levels of stimulation above two stimuli per train. If simple addition of the reflex responses had occurred, the degree of slowing would have been the same in both cases and the curves would coincide.

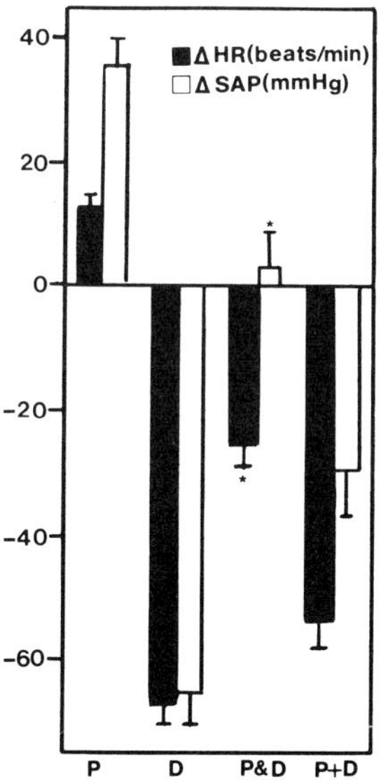

FIG. 2. Average heart rate and systemic pressure responses (±SEM) to separate pressor (P) and depressor (D) stimulation of the AN. The responses to combined stimulation (P&D) are compared to the algebraic sum (P + D) of the separate responses. This difference is significant ($P < 0.001$).

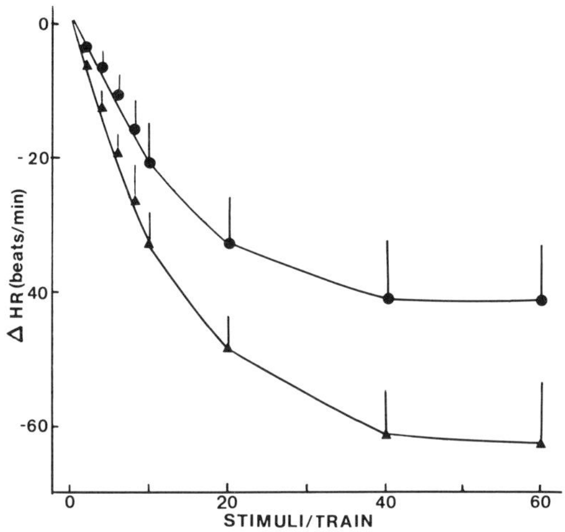

FIG. 3. Heart rate response curves (±SEM) to increasing depressor stimulation of the AN before (triangles) and during simultaneous pressor stimulation of the AN (circles). $N = 8$.

The possibility that the observed interaction was an artifact of two simultaneous stimuli being delivered to the same nerve was tested in six dogs. In these dogs one AN was stimulated with pressor strength stimuli while the other AN was stimulated with depressor strength stimuli. These responses are compared (Table I) to delivery of the pressor and depressor stimuli to the same AN in these dogs. The mode of stimulation had little effect on the results.

Figure 4 illustrates the heart rate responses to intraaortic nicotine (20 μg) before (4A) and during (4B) depressor stimulation of the AN. In the three animals tested in this study, intraaortic nicotine caused small increases in heart rate and systemic pressure. During depressor stimulation of the intact AN heart rate and systemic pressure fell. The responses to intraaortic nicotine were augmented such that they practically or completely offset the bradycardia and fall in systemic pressure. This is

TABLE I. HR RESPONSE TO DEPRESSOR AND PRESSOR STIMULATION OF THE SAME AN VS DEPRESSOR STIMULATION OF ONE AN AND PRESSOR STIMULATION OF THE OTHER AN ($N = 6$)

	Change in heart rate (beats/min ± SEM)			
Pressor stimuli delivered to:	Pressor	Depressor	Combined	Sum of separate pressor and depressor
Same AN as depressor	14 ± 7	−76 ± 9	−31 ± 8	−62 ± 9[a]
Opposite AN from depressor	15 ± 3	−76 ± 9	−36 ± 8[b]	−62 ± 10[a]

[a] Sum of the separate responses different ($P < 0.05$) from the response to combined stimulation.
[b] Not significantly different from response to delivery of both stimuli to the same AN.

further illustrated in Fig. 4C where the depressor response to stimulation of the intact AN is greatly reduced during nicotine infusion. Following transection of the AN, nicotine infusion had no effect on the AN depressor response.

Discussion. The results suggest that the aortic chemoreflex suppresses the inhibitory action of the aortic baroreflex as was previously observed in the interaction between the aortic chemoreflex and the baroreflex from the carotid sinus (10, 11). We recognize that electrical stimulation of the AN may not activate one afferent population in the nerve to the exclusion of all other afferents. However, in this and in our previous study we have obtained similar results with more physiological methods of reflex activation. Nicotine infusion into the aortic arch gives rise to reflex responses similar to those we observe in response to strong electrical stimulation of the AN. Both methods of AN pressor reflex activation reduce the response to stimulation of the aortic baroreflex to a greater degree than can be explained on the basis of simple addition of antagonistic reflexes. This suggests that an interaction between these reflexes is occurring centrally. This interaction is similar to that we have reported between the carotid baroreflexes and the aortic chemoreflexes (10, 11). In our earlier study (11) we suggested that the suppression of the carotid baroreflex occurred at the level of the medulla since this interaction still occurred following transcollicular decerebration. We also concluded that parasympathetic–sympathetic interactions at the heart level could not explain the results. We believe that these earlier arguments remain valid in the present study.

The suppression of the baroreflexes is not a unique action of the aortic chemoreflex. Somatic nerve pressor reflexes have been shown to suppress baroreflexes (12, 13) as have pressor reflexes arising from the thoracic aorta (14) and atrial volume receptors (15, 16). Thus it may be that all reflexes that cause cardioacceleration and vasoconstriction do so in part by suppressing the baroreceptor reflexes. The neuronal mechanisms involved in this suppression remain to be determined.

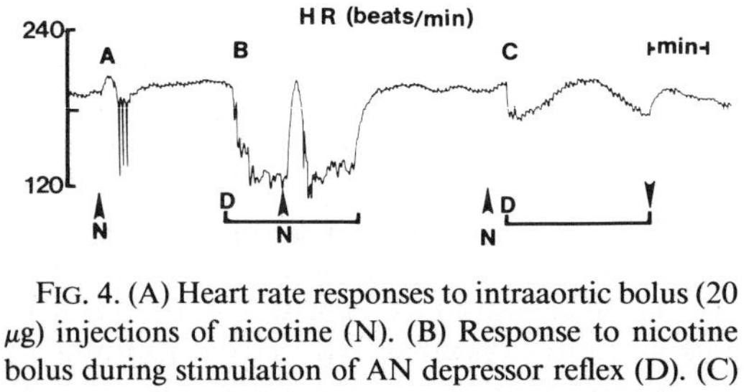

FIG. 4. (A) Heart rate responses to intraaortic bolus (20 μg) injections of nicotine (N). (B) Response to nicotine bolus during stimulation of AN depressor reflex (D). (C) Response to depressor stimulation of the AN during an intraaortic infusion of nicotine (40 μg/min, between arrows).

This work was supported by National Institutes of Health Grant HL 22715.

1. Donald DE, Edis AJ. Comparison of aortic and carotid baroreflex in the dog. J Physiol (London) **215**:521–538, 1971.
2. Levy MN, Ng ML, Zieske H. Cardiac and respiratory effects of aortic arch baroreceptor stimulation. Circ Res **19**:930–939, 1966.
3. Allison JL, Sagawa K, Kumada M. An open loop analysis of the aortic arch barostatic reflex. Amer J Physiol **217**:1576–1584, 1969.
4. Stern S, Rapaport E. Comparison of the reflexes elicited from combined or separate stimulation of the aortic and carotid chemoreceptors on myocardial contractility, cardiac output, and systemic resistance. Circ Res **20**:214–227, 1967.

5. Comroe JH, Mortimer L. The respiratory and cardiovascular responses to temporally separated aortic and carotid bodies to cyanide, nicotine, phenyldiguanide and serotonin. J Pharmacol Exp Ther **146**:33–41, 1964.
6. Biro GP, Hatcher JD, Jennings DB. The role of the aortic body chemoreceptors in the cardiac and respiratory responses to acute hypoxia in the anesthetized dog. Canad J Physiol Pharmacol **51**:249–259, 1973.
7. Karim F, Hainsworth R, Sofola OA, Wood LM. Responses of the heart to stimulation of aortic body chemoreceptors in dogs. Circ Res **46**:77–83, 1980.
8. Edis AJ, Shepherd JT. Selective denervation of aortic arch baroreceptors and chemoreceptors in the dog. J Appl Physiol **30**:294–296, 1971.
9. Kendrick JE, Matson GL. A comparison of the cardiovascular responses to stimulation of the aortic and carotid sinus nerves of the dog. Proc Soc Exp Biol Med **144**:404–411, 1973.
10. Kendrick JE, Matson GL. Interaction between carotid sinus baroreceptor and aortic nerve pressor reflexes in the dog. Amer J Physiol **237** (Heart Circ Physiol **6**):H662–H667, 1979.
11. Pisarri TE, Matson GL, Kendrick JE. Inhibition of baroreflex bradycardia by aortic nerve excitatory afferents in dogs. Amer J Physiol **243** (Heart Circ Physiol **12**):H607–H613, 1982.
12. Quest JA, Gebber GL. Modulation of baroreceptor reflexes by somatic afferent nerve stimulation. Amer J Physiol **222**:1251–1259, 1972.
13. Kumada M, Nogami K, Sagawa K. Modulation of carotid sinus baroreceptor reflex by sciatic nerve stimulation. Amer J Physiol **228**:1535–1541, 1975.
14. Pagani M, Pizzinelli P, Bergamaschi M, Malliani A. A positive feedback sympathetic pressor reflex during stretch of the thoracic aorta in conscious dogs. Circ Res **50**:125–132, 1982.
15. Stinnet HO, Bishop VS, Peterson DF. Reduction in baroreflex cardiovascular responses due to venous infusion in the rabbit. Circ Res **39**:766–772, 1976.
16. Vatner SF, Boettcher DH, Heyndrickx GR, McRitchie RJ. Reduced baroreflex sensitivity with volume loading in conscious dogs. Circ Res **37**:236–242, 1975.

Received July 11, 1983. P.S.E.B.M. 1984, Vol. 176.
Accepted March 8, 1984.

ABSTRACTS

1983 Annual Meeting, Society for Experimental Biology and Medicine: Southeastern Section

Medical College of Virginia, Virginia Commonwealth University, Richmond, Virginia
November 14 and 15, 1983

SECTION OFFICERS

Chairman: DR. JOHN G. CONIGLIO, Vanderbilt University, Nashville, Tennessee

Immediate Past Chairman: DR. KENNETH S. MCCARTY, SR., Duke University Medical Center, Durham, North Carolina

Vice Chairman: DR. LOUIS P. GANGAROSA, SR., Medical College of Georgia, Augusta, Georgia

Secretary–Treasurer: DR. RICHARD B. BRANDT, Medical College of Virginia, Richmond, Virginia

ACKNOWLEDGMENTS

The Southeastern Section of the Society for Experimental Biology and Medicine expresses appreciation to the following organizations for assistance: Society for Experimental Biology and Medicine (National Society); School of Basic Sciences, MCV–VCU; and Massey Cancer Center, MCV–VCU.

0037-9727/84 $1.50

Symposium: Vitamin A, Function and Mechanisms of Action

Tuesday, November 15, 1983
Richmond Academy of Medicine

8:50	Dr. Richard B. Brandt	Introductory Remarks
9:00–9:45	Dr. James A. Olsen Professor and Chairman Department of Biochemistry and Biophysics Iowa State University	"An Overview of Vitamin A Action"
10:00–10:45	Dr. David E. Ong Research Associate Professor Department of Biochemistry Vanderbilt University	"Intracellular Protein in Vitamin A Action"
11:00–11:45	Dr. Luigi DeLuca Chief, Differentiation Control Section National Cancer Institute	"Recent Studies of the Biochemistry of Vitamin A"

Student Competition for Best Scientific Presentation

As a part of its ongoing effort to encourage the development of scientific talent, the Southeastern Section of the Society of Experimental Biology and Medicine sponsors a competition for the best scientific presentation of a paper by a graduate or professional student at the annual fall meeting. Winners in this competition receive a certificate of merit and cash prizes of one hundred, fifty, and twenty-five dollars for first, second, and third place awards respectively.

Winners of the 1983 Student Scientific Presentation competition at the Medical College of Virginia (VCU) meeting were:

First Place—Tie

SCOTT W. N. DUNCAN AND CLIVE M. BAUMGARTEN. Intracellular chloride activity in hypoxic rabbit ventricle. Department of Physiology, Medical College of Virginia, VCU, Richmond, Virginia 23298.

C. H. ROBERTS AND J. F. CHLEBOWSKI. Trypsin modification of *E. coli* alkaline phosphatase. Department of Biochemistry, Medical College of Virginia, VCU, Richmond, Virginia 23298.

Second Place—Tie

CHARLES B. CAIRNS, DREW FILLIPO, AND HERBERT J. PROCTOR. Near infrared spectrophotometry: A non-invasive method for assessing the effects of changes in intracranial pressure on brain metabolism in cats. Trauma Section, Department of Surgery, University of North Carolina, Chapel Hill, North Carolina 27514.

K. A. FOSTER AND J. M. COLLINS. Control of the rates of DNA synthesis through S-phase. Department of Biochemistry, Medical College of Virginia, VCU, Richmond, Virginia 23298.

J. F. RECKELHOFF, R. J. BEYNON, AND J. S. BOND. Degradation of radioiodinated polypeptides by kidney brush borders of meprin-sufficient and meprin-deficient mice. Department of Biochemistry, Medical College of Virginia, VCU, Richmond, Virginia 23298.

Third Place—Tie

MARY D. ELLISON, MARY LEE GIEBEL, AND JOHN T. POVLISHOCK. Quantitative measurements of cerebral capillary permeability in the rat following acute systemic hypertension. Department of Anatomy & Surgery, Medical College of Virginia, VCU, Richmond, Virginia 23298.

JOHN M. KENNEDY AND JAMES L. POLAND. Capillary density and histochemical fiber type in rat skeletal muscle grafts. Department of Physiology & Biophysics, Medical College of Virginia, VCU, Richmond, Virginia 23298.

MARIE H. KOSCO, JOHN G. TEW, AND ANDRAS R. SZAKAL. Cell surface determinants of mouse lymph node follicular dentritic cells (FDSs). Department of Anatomy, Microbiology & Immunology, Medical College of Virginia, VCU, Richmond, Virginia 23298.

D. C. MARSHALL AND J. J. BUCCAFUSCO. Cardiovascular and behavioral changes associated with narcotic withdrawal during the development of physical dependence. Medical College of Georgia/Veterans Administration MC, Augusta, Georgia 30912.

TABLE OF CONTENTS

Page

213 Phase I Safety Studies of Antiviral Iontophoresis .... LP Gangarosa, Sr., JM Hill, J Burris, B Thompson, JP Rissing

213 Δ^9-Tetrahydrocannabinol Decreases Host Resistance to Herpes Simplex Virus Type 2 Vaginal Infection .... E Mishkin, F Marciano-Cabral, GA Cabral

213 Near Infrared Spectrophotometry: A Noninvasive Method for Assessing the Effects of Changes in Intracranial Pressure on Brain Metabolism in Cats .... CB Cairns, D Fillipo, HJ Proctor

214 Cerebral High Energy Phosphate Metabolism after Hypoxic Hypotension: The Role of Ca^{2+} Blockers .... GW Palladino, HJ Proctor, R Sanders

214 Regional Biochemical and Histochemical Differences in Axonal Plasma Membranes in Myelinated Axons from the Bovine Central Nervous System .... PZ Detskey, GH DeVries

214 Cell Surface Determinants of Mouse Lymph Node Follicular Dentritic Cells (FDCs) .... MH Kosco, JG Tew, AK Szakal

215 Prenatal Phenobarbital (PB) Treatment Results in Increased Hepatic *P*-450-Dependent Monooxygenase (MOS) Activity in Adult Rats .... DM Bagley, JR Hayes

215 Development of a Clinical Test for Function of Cranial Nerve ... IR West Fuller, RM Costanzo

215 Quantitative Measurements of Cerebral Capillary Permeability in the Rat following Acute Systemic Hypertension .... MD Ellison, ML Giebel, JT Povlishock

216 Intracellular Chloride Activity in Hypoxic Rabbit Ventricle .... SWN Duncan, CM Baumgarten

216 Cardiovascular and Behavioral Changes Associated with Narcotic Withdrawal during the Development of Physical Dependence .... DC Marshall, JJ Buccafusco

216 Capillary Density and Histochemical Fiber Type in Rat Skeletal Muscle Grafts .... JM Kennedy, JL Poland

217 Acute Changes of Renal Tubular Cells Associated with Nephrotoxicity in the Rat Induced by a Fungicide, *N*-(3,5-Dichlorophenyl) Succinimide .... J Capito, RT Wang, GO Rankin, PI Brown

217 Vitamin A and Stress in the Rat .... BA Doyle, HR Seibel, RB Brandt, WR Burden, JL Poland

217 Is There L-Lactate Dehydrogenase in Mitochondria? .... JE Laux, RB Brandt, ES Kline, SE Spainhour

218 Detection of Aromatase Activity in Mouse Leydig Cell Tumors .... M Brandt, S Zimniski, M Melner, D Covey, D Puett

218 Maturation of *E. coli* Alkaline Phosphatase .... NL Parlet, JF Chlebowski

218 Control of the Rates of DNA Synthesis through S Phase .... KA Foster, JM Collins

219 Properties of Purified 5-Formyltetrahydrofolate Cyclodehydrase from Rabbit Liver .... S Hopkins, L Schirch

219 *In Vitro* Leucine Oxidation Changes by Selected Tissues from Tumor-Bearing Mice .... PZ Detskey, WMY Chan, WL Banks, Jr.

219 Degradation of Radioiodinated Polypeptides by Kidney Brush Borders of Meprin-Sufficient and Meprin-Deficient Mice .... JF Reckelhoff, RJ Beynon, JS Bond

220 Trypsin Modification of *Escherichia coli* Alkaline Phosphatase .... CH Roberts, JF Chlebowski

220 Characterization of a Cysteine Metalloproteinase from Mouse Liver Cytosol .... DL Rosin, JS Bond, SG Bradley

220 Effect of Adenozine Analog Tubercidine (7-Deazanucleoside) on Adenovirus RNA Synthesis in $HeLaS_3$ Cells .... M Speidel

221 Pharmacodynamic Effects of Intravenous Pluronic Polyols F-38, F-68, F-77, F-88, F-108, F-127, and P105: Effects on Serum Lipids and Other Constituents .... JC McPherson, Jr., JC McPherson III

221 Effect of Streptozotocin (STZ)-Induced Diabetes in Rats on Placental Transport and Tissue Uptake of α-Aminoisobutyric Acid (AIB) .... AD Copeland, SP Porterfield

221 Alterations in Rabbit Spinal Cord Structure and Function Produced with Microwave Hyperthermia .... CH Sutton, P Popovic

PHASE I SAFETY STUDIES OF ANTIVIRAL IONTOPHORESIS. L. P. Gangarosa, Sr., J. M. Hill, J. Burris, B. Thompson, and J. P. Rissing. Depts. of Oral Biol.-Pharm., Cell & Molec. Biol., and Medicine, Medical College of Georgia and VA Hospital, Augusta, GA 30912

Normal human subjects volunteered to have iontophoresis of the antiviral drugs 3% Ara-AMP (vidarabine phosphate) and 2% ACV acyclovir to the volar surface of the arm. Three subjects had low (4 mA-min) current dosage (CD), three had medium CD (20 mA-min) and one had high CD (80 mA-min). Blood chemistries were performed before and after (2 and 14 days) drug application. Concentrations of drug were studied in blood samples taken before treatment, one hour after treatment and in a 24 hour urine sample. Urinalysis was also performed on samples taken before treatment and after (48 hr and 14 days). In addition, an allergy challenge was performed by applying the same drug to the same area after 14 days. We found (1) no significant changes in blood chemistries, (2) no significant changes in hematology, (3) no significant changes in urinalysis, (4) no evidence of allergy, (5) no detectable blood level of drug, and (6) no drug (or only traces at higher CD) in the urine. The studies indicate extreme safety in humans of drugs applied by iontophoresis. The low systemic concentration should eliminate any possibility of organ toxicity.
Supported by Grant DE-06136.

DELTA-9-TETRAHYDROCANNABINOL DECREASES HOST RESISTANCE TO HERPES SIMPLEX VIRUS TYPE 2 VAGINAL INFECTION. Mishkin, E.*; Marciano-Cabral, F.; and Cabral, G. A. Sponsored by: S. G. Bradley, Department of Microbiology and Immunology and Department of Pharmacology and Toxicology, The Medical College of Virginia/VCU, Richmond, Virginia 23298

Delta-9-tetrahydrocannabinol (Delta-9-THC), a major psychoactive component of marihuana, elicits suppressive effects on the immune system. This study was undertaken to determine whether Delta-9-THC decreases resistance to herpes simplex virus type 2 (HSV2) genital infection in the guinea pig. The guinea pig was selected as the host since HSV2 induces a spectrum of disease similar to that in humans. Animals inoculated intravaginally with $10^{3.5}$ plaque forming units (PFU) of HSV2 and treated intraperitoneally with 4mg/kg and 10 mg/kg Delta-9-THC exhibited significant increases in lesions and mortalities when compared to nondrug-treated controls. Of infected vehicle-treated animals, 50% exhibited lesions and 33% died. In contrast, 75% of infected animals receiving 4mg/kg Delta-9-THC had lesions and died. Of infected animals treated with 10mg/kg Delta-9-THC, 80% had lesions and 66% died. These results indicate that Delta-9-THC at these doses decreases host resistance to HSV2 vaginal infection in the guinea pig. (Supported by a Center of Excellence Award to MCV/VCU by the Commonwealth of Virginia.)

NEAR INFRARED SPECTROPHOTOMETRY: A NON-INVASIVE METHOD FOR ASSESSING THE EFFECTS OF CHANGES IN INTRACRANIAL PRESSURE ON BRAIN METABOLISM IN CATS. Charles B. Cairns, Drew Fillipo, Herbert J. Proctor. Trauma Section, Department of Surgery, University of North Carolina, Chapel Hill, NC 27514

We report two experiments designed to clarify the role of in vivo near infrared spectrophotometry (niroscopy) for directly measuring the effects of changes in intracranial pressure (ICP) on brain metabolism. Cytochrome a,a_3 redox state, oxyhemoglobin, and deoxyhemoglobin were continuously monitored by niroscopy in adult female cats during experimentally induced increased ICP. In the first experiment (N=10), ICP was markedly increased in 40 mmHg increments from baseline to arterial systolic pressure by cisterna magna infusion of saline. In the second experiment (N=10), a more clinically relevant model was adopted. Subarachnoid infusion of a "mock" CSF solution produced a moderately elevated ICP (18.5 $\pm$ 0.9 mmHg). ICP was monitored via a cisterna magna catheter. The results of both experiments indicate that changes in ICP correlated with a reduction of cyt. a,a_3 redox state ($p<.01$), a monotonic decrease in HbO_2 and a monotonic increase in Hb. These studies suggest the use of niroscopy as a sensitive, non-invasive method for directly monitoring brain metabolic activity during episodes of increased intracranial pressure. (Supported in part by ONR Contract #N00014-79-C-0852 and the Holderness Foundation)

CEREBRAL HIGH ENERGY PHOSPHATE METABOLISM AFTER HYPOXIC-HYPOTENSION: THE ROLE OF CA++ BLOCKERS. G. William Palladino, Herbert J. Proctor, Richard Sanders. Trauma Section, Department of Surgery, University of North Carolina, Chapel Hill, NC 27514

Failure of cerebral cortical high energy phosphate production after hypoxic-hypotension results both from mitochondrial defects and areas of "no reflow". Ca++ blockers might act on either or both of these sites. Thirty rats were subjected to 30 minutes of combined hypoxia (FIO_2 = 7.5%) and hemorrhagic hypotension (MAP = 30 mmHg), and then resuscitated by reinfusion of all shed blood, an equal volume of saline, and restoration of FIO_2 = 30%. Group I received blood and saline alone; Group II received in addition .2 mg/Kg verapamil; and Group III received in addition 10 ug/Kg nifedipine. Rats were sacrificed by liquid nitrogen freezing of their brain 20 and 120 minutes after treatment group allocation/resuscitation. Cerebral cortices were assayed for creatine phosphate (CP), adenosine tri-phosphate (ATP) and lactate (L).

Significantly greater ($p<.01$) I vs. III) concentrations of CP and ATP resulted 20' and 120' after resuscitation in nifedipine treated animals, while no improvement (I vs. II) was noted for verapamil. Blood pressure was restored equally in the three groups, and in view of the more potent vasodilator effects of nifedipine as opposed to verapamil, our results are possibly explainable on the basis of improved cerebral cortical blood flow.

REGIONAL BIOCHEMICAL AND HISTOCHEMICAL DIFFERENCES IN AXONAL PLASMA MEMBRANES IN MYELINATED AXONS FROM THE BOVINE CENTRAL NERVOUS SYSTEM. Peter Zenon Detskey and George H. DeVries, Department of Biochemistry, MCV/VCU, Richmond, VA 23298.

Myelinated axons can be used as a vehicle to isolate the axonal plasma membrane or axolemma (AXL) from normal appearing white matter. We evaluated six distinct regions of bovine white matter as sources for obtaining AXL enriched fractions (FX) containing the least amount of myelin contamination. These areas were: subcortical white matter from the rostral (1), central (2) and caudal (3) regions of the cerebral hemispheres, and white matter from the pons (4), cerebellar peduncle (5) and the cervical region of the spinal cord (6). Myelinated axons were isolated from each source by floatation followed by disruption by mechanical and osmotic shock and separation on a 15%-45% linear sucrose gradient. The levels of 2'3'-cyclic nucleotide-3'-phosphodiesterase (CNP) activity, a marker for myelin related membranes, was 1/3 as high in areas (4,5 and 6) as compared to corresponding FX from areas (1,2 and 3). Acetylcholinesterase (AChE), a marker for AXL had the highest activity in FX derived from areas (4,5 and 6), while similar FX from areas (1 and 2) expressed reduced AChE; area (1) was virtually depleted of AChE. The data suggest that highly myelinated regions (4,5 and 6) yield preparations most enriched in axolemma and least contaminated with myelin and myelin related membranes. (Supported by NIH Grant NS10821).

CELL SURFACE DETERMINANTS OF MOUSE LYMPH NODE FOLLICULAR DENTRITIC CELLS (FDCs). Marie H. Kosco[1], John G. Tew[2], and Andras K. Szakal[1]. Dept's of Anatomy[1], and Microbiology and Immunology[2], Medical College of Virginia, VCU, Richmond, VA 23298.

In order to better understand the mechanism of accessory cell function of FDCs and their derivation, FDCs isolated from passively immunized, horseradish peroxidase (antigen) injected C3H mice were phenotyped for antigenic determinants. Utilizing monoclonal (Mk) antibodies specific for $I\text{-}E^k$ (#14-4-4), $I\text{-}A^k$ (#10-2.16), and $I\text{-}A^b$ (#HB-38) in conjunction with indirect immunofluorescence, the Ia surface Ag's of FDCs were characterized. The results showed that the FDCs were positive for both I-A and E determinants of the k haplotype but negative for I-A of the b haplotype (control). In addition, using the M1/9.3 Mk antibody, the FDCs were shown to bear the leukocyte common antigen (LCA). The reaction of these nonphagocytic, non-MØ-like cells with Mk antibodies specific for surface Ag's of macrophages (MØs) (i.e. Mac-I, Mac II, F4/80), lymphocytes (i.e. M1/69), and dendritic cells (i.e. Ox 2 vs. Ox 4) will also be described. The observation that FDCs are Ia^+ suggests that the mechanism of their accessory cell function may be based on a similar molecular recognition system as that shown for some MØs. The expression of Ia on FDCs could explain T cell requirements for germinal center development in vivo. The presence of LCA on FDCs may suggests that FDCs, similarly to other leukocytes are also bone marrow derived. (Supported by NIH AI 17142)

PRENATAL PHENOBARBITAL (PB) TREATMENT RESULTS IN INCREASED HEPATIC P-450-DEPENDENT MONOOXYGENASE (MOS) ACTIVITY IN ADULT RATS. D. M. Bagley and J. R. Hayes, Dept. of Pharmacology and Toxicology, Medical College of Virginia, Richmond, VA 23298 (Sponsored by J. F. Borzelleca).

At adulthood male rats have higher MOS activities than females, presumably due to endogenous testosterone presence during the neonatal period. This phenomenon has been termed "imprinting". We have previously shown that PB also imprints the MOS during the neonatal period. Here we extend these findings and demonstrate that PB administration to pregnant females during late gestation increases MOS activity in the offspring at adulthood. Pregnant Sprague-Dawley rats were injected i.v. with either 40 mg/kg PB or saline daily on days 17-21 of gestation and allowed to deliver spontaneously. Various MOS activities were measured in 24 day old (weanling) and 105 day old (young adult) offspring. There was no measurable treatment effect in 24-day old rats. In contrast, at 105 days of age there was increased P-450 content and increased ethoxycoumarin-O-deethylase activity in offspring from PB treated mothers. These results support the theory that xenobiotics can imprint the MOS and demonstrates that not only the neonatal period but also the prenatal period is susceptible to PB imprinting. (Supported by a VCU Grants-in-Aid.)

DEVELOPMENT OF A CLINICAL TEST FOR FUNCTION OF CRANIAL NERVE I. **R. West Fuller and Richard M. Costanzo. Dept of Physiol, Med Coll of Virginia, Richmond, VA 23298**

Quantitative measurements of olfactory function are rarely used in a clinical setting despite their usefulness in diagnosing and following disorders of the olfactory nerves (Cranial Nerve I) and cortex. A clinical test that provides quantitative values for both olfactory sensitivity and discrimination was developed and evaluated. Olfactory sensitivity was tested by asking patients to make a forced choice between an array of bottles containing serial dilutions of butanol and a distilled water blank. Ability to identify odors was tested by presentation of 10 common odoriferous substances in unmarked jars; Vicks, ammonia, and wintergreen were included to test trigeminal sensations. Test results from ENT, neurology and head injury patients (N=19) were compared with control subjects (N=18). Test scores successfully confirmed suspected defecits and uncovered some previously unknown undetected pathologies. Additional findings included a head injury patient with loss of odor identification but not sensitivity, suggesting that a central lesion was involved. Preliminary data indicate that the scores obtained from this test are of clinical importance in that they aid diagnosis and monitoring the course of olfactory disorders. (Supported by A.D. Williams Fellowship to RWF and NIH Grant NS16741 to RMC.)

QUANTITATIVE MEASUREMENTS OF CEREBRAL CAPILLARY PERMEABILITY IN THE RAT FOLLOWING ACUTE SYSTEMIC HYPERTENSION. Mary D. Ellison, Mary Lee Giebel, and John T. Povlishock, Depts. of Anatomy and Surgery, Medical College of VA, Richmond,VA 23298

This investigation considers hypertension-induced alterations in blood brain barrier (BBB) status using a technique which applies quantitative autoradiography to the study of the blood-to-brain transfer of a small neutral amino acid, α-amino-isobutyric acid (AIB). AIB, in normal animals, slowly crosses cerebral capillaries, yet once within the brain is rapidly sequestered by brain cells. This process becomes accelerated in pathological states. Using autoradiographic images of brain sections and the integral of arterial plasma activity, a blood-to-brain transfer constant (Ki) for 14C-AIB can be calculated for specific brain loci. In this study, rats were used to evaluate alterations in cerebral capillary permeability following acute hypertension produced by pharmacological agents. Results showed enhanced permeability within cerebral cortices, the thalamus, and the cerebellum. Maximal values for Ki in these loci ranged from 9.56×10^{-5} ml g^{-1} sec-1 in the thalamus to 33.6×10^{-5} ml g^{-1} sec^{-1} in the cerebellum. Control values were less than 2.9×10^{-5} ml g^{-1} sec-1. These results substantiate and extend findings of previous investigations which have suggested increased hypertension-induced BBB permeability to large molecular weight proteins. (Supported by USPH NIH Grant NS 12587)

INTRACELLULAR CHLORIDE ACTIVITY IN HYPOXIC RABBIT VENTRICLE. Scott W.N. Duncan and Clive Marc Baumgarten. Dept of Physiol, Med Coll of Virgina, Richmond, VA 23298

Cl is not passively distributed in cardiac muscle, and Cl/HCO_3 exchange may contribute to Cl accumulation. The effect of hypoxia on Cl activity (a^i_{Cl}) is unknown. Hypoxia may alter Cl/HCO_3 exchange and, therefore, a^i_{Cl}. These experiments measure a^i_{Cl} and access Cl/HCO_3 exchange function during 90 min of hypoxia. Cl ion-selective microelectrodes were made with Corning 477913 liquid ion-exchanger. Muscles were superfused with HEPES-buffered or HCO_3-buffered Tyrode's solution. When HCO_3 was present, a^i_{Cl} was not effected by hypoxia (O_2=19.7 mM, N_2=20.3 mM, P>0.2). In contrast, in HCO_3-free media where Cl/HCO_3 exchange is blocked, hypoxia caused a significant fall in a^i_{Cl} from 24.7 to 20.3 mM (P<0.005). Similarly when Cl/HCO_3 exchange is blocked with 100 μM SITS in the presence of HCO_3, a^i_{Cl} fell significantly from 22.7 to 19.8 mM (P<0.01). E_m was not effected by hypoxia. Under normoxic conditions, removal of HCO_3 caused no significant change in a^i_{Cl} (HEPES=24.7 mM, HCO_3=19.7 mM, P>0.2). The data indicate that Cl/HCO_3 exchange regulates a^i_{Cl} during hypoxia. Under normoxic conditions, however, the importance of the exchanger is less clear. (Supported by grants from NIH (HL-24847), Am Heart Assn (82-792) and EO and PD Sang Foundation. CMB is an Established Investigator of Am Heart Assn.)

Cardiovascular and Behavioral Changes Associated with Narcotic Withdrawal During the Development of Physical Dependence. D.C. Marshall and J.J. Buccafusco, Medical College of Georgia/Veterans Administration MC, Augusta, GA. 30912

Behavioral responses were evaluated along with cardiovascular changes for 60 min following naloxone (N,0.5 mg/kg) administration to freely moving rats, made physically dependent by a constant infusion of morphine at increasing doses (35-300mg/kg) over 7 days. In response to N arterial pressure (AP) increased significantly in a dose and time dependent manner over the infusion schedule (8± 1 - 26±3mmHg). Heart rate changes were similar in magnitude over the course of increasing physical dependence. The frequency of counted behavioral signs increased progressively only for escape attempts (4.2±0.6 - 16.3±4.3/hr), whereas, withdrawal body shakes and writhing peaked early in the dosing schedule and declined to very low levels by day 7. Morphine (50 mg/kg,i.v.) injected during N induced withdrawal significantly reduced the increase in AP by 30%, but was unable to change any behavioral parameters. Injection of N (6 μg) into the lateral cerebral ventricle of dependent rats produced a significantly greater increase in AP (12 ±2 mmHg) as compared with 4th ventricle (6 ± 1mmHg). Thus, the increase in AP during withdrawal may serve as an objective and sensitive measure of the degree of physical dependence. Also sites adjacent to the ventricular system, rostral to the 4th ventricle may mediate the N induced pressor response.

CAPILLARY DENSITY AND HISTOCHEMICAL FIBER TYPE IN RAT SKELETAL MUSCLE GRAFTS. John M. Kennedy and James L. Poland, Dept. of Physiology and Biophysics, Medical College of Virginia, Richmond, Va. 23298

Following transplantation, skeletal muscle degenerates and subsequently regenerates as myogenic cells go through the stages of muscle development. Delivery of metabolic substrates to the regenerated fibers will depend on revascularization of the graft. Reinnervation of the graft will influence metabolism since metabolism reflects muscle fiber type which is under neural control. To study these determinants of metabolism we cross-transplanted two rat muscles of different fiber types. The fast twitch extensor digitorum longus (EDL) muscle was placed in the bed of the slow twitch soleus (SOL) muscle, and vice versa. Following 60 days of regeneration, the grafts and contralateral control muscles were removed and serial sections were subjected to histochemical analysis. Capillary density in either EDL or SOL transplants was similar to the corresponding control EDL or SOL muscles. However, SOL transplants (originally EDL muscles) contained significantly more slow twitch fibers than control EDLs, while the EDL transplants (originally SOL muscles) contained more fast twitch fibers than SOL controls. It is concluded that delivery of metabolic substrates to small skeletal muscle grafts is adequate and that metabolic responses in the grafts will be dictated by the new innervation rather than the original fiber type of the graft.

ACUTE CHANGES OF RENAL TUBULAR CELLS ASSOCIATED WITH NEPHROTOXICITY IN THE RAT INDUCED BY A FUNGICIDE, N-(3,5-DICHLOROPHENYL) SUCCINIMIDE. J. Capito, R.T.Wang, G. O. Rankin, and P. I. Brown. Departs. of Anatomy and Pharmacology, Marshall Univ. Sch. of Med., Huntington, WV 25704

The fungicide N-(3,5-dichlorophenyl)succinimide (NDPS) produces interstitial nephritis with chronic exposure and promotes the carcinogenic effects of many chemicals. This study was to investigate the acute morphological changes of the kidney produced by a single intraperitoneal administration of NDPS (200mg/kg) to male rats. Kidneys were perfused (Na-cacodylate buffer then E. M. fixatives) at 48 hr, removed and processed for light and electron microscopy. Observations revealed extensive damage to the proximal convoluted tubular cells with increased lysosomal accumulation and marked irregularity and sloughing of the luminal brush border. Severe damage to the distal convoluted tubular cells was evident by pronounced distention of the basal infoldings and apical protrusion of the cells. In addition, accumulation of blood cells occurred in the lumen and medullary interstitium suggesting glomerular destruction and leakiness. These observations were supportive of previous studies that functional nephrotoxicity occurs following acute administration of NDPS in rats.
(Supported by NIH Grant AM 31210 and AMA Educational Resources Fund)

VITAMIN A AND STRESS IN THE RAT. B.A. Doyle, H.R. Seibel, R.B. Brandt, W.R. Burden, and J.L. Poland. Depts. of Anatomy, Biochemistry and Physiology, Medical College of Virginia, Virginia Commonwealth University, Richmond, VA 23298

Trauma in humans has been associated with decreased plasma vitamin A concentration. Rat stress models produced by restraint and heat or cold exposure show a similar decrease. In the current research we used a running stress for varying time periods. Biochemical determinations of plasma vitamin A, zinc, albumin and total protein and hepatic vitamin A were conducted. Studies on plasma retinol-binding protein and corticosterone and electron microscopy of liver and other tissues are in progress. During the experimental period, male Sprague Dawley rats were fed normal laboratory chow or a vitamin A-deficient diet (ICN). No significant differences in plasma vitamin A were observed in short-term (1 day) running experiments, however, a significant drop (from 38.5 to 27.8 μg/dl and from 38.5 to 31.6 μg/dl) was observed with a 10-day running routine in both normal and early deficient animals, respectively. Albumin, total protein and zinc levels generally showed no significant changes. In conclusion, we have shown a severe decrease in plasma vitamin A in rats following the stress of a 10-day running routine. Whether this can be prevented by nutritional or other therapy has not yet been addressed.
(Supported by funds from NFCR)

IS THERE L-LACTATE DEHYDROGENASE IN MITOCHONDRIA? J.E. Laux, R.B. Brandt, E.S. Kline, and S.E. Spainhour. Department of Biochemistry, Medical College of Virginia, VCU, Richmond, VA 23298

Previous reports from these laboratories have provided evidence for the oxidation of L-lactate and the reduction of pyruvate in mitochondria (M). We report use of M and cytosol (C) fractions from rat heart, kidney and liver for the assay of NAD+ dependent L-Lactate Dehydrogenase (L-LDH) and Phosphoglucomutase (PGM). PGM was used as a marker of M Contamination by C. The % L-LDH activity, M/C, on a specific activity basis was: liver 2.7; kidney 1.0; heart 0.17. From activity measurements of PGM in M fractions, there was no contamination in any of the tissues assayed. Skilleter & Kun (1974) had previously shown L-LDH in liver M and we extend this to kidney and heart M. Various treatments of M show an increase in L-LDH. Freeze-thawing cycles (10 times) increase the activity two-fold, treatment with 10% Triton X-100 increases the activity by two-fold or greater depending on the tissue. The % L-LDH activity (M/C) increases from 2.7 to 6.2 for liver; 1.0 to 11.4 for kidney and 0.17 to 2.3 for heart with Triton treatment. Sonicated samples show a similar increase. These experiments suggest that there is L-LDH in M not due to C contamination. (Supported by funds from NFCR and ACS)

DETECTION OF AROMATASE ACTIVITY IN MOUSE LEYDIG CELL TUMORS.

Mark Brandt*, Stephen Zimniski*, Michael Melner*, Douglas Covey+, and David Puett*. *Dept. of Biochemistry, Vanderbilt University, Nashville, TN 37232 and +Dept. of Pharmacology, Washington University, St. Louis, MO 63110.

The objective of these experiments was to ascertain the presence of aromatase activity in murine Leydig cell tumors and compare it to that of human placenta. M5480A Leydig cell tumors, maintained by serial transplantation in C57BL/6J mice, were homogenized and microsomes prepared. The crude microsomal preparation was assayed for aromatase activity by following the production of tritiated water from (1β,2β ^{3}H) testosterone by the method of Rabe et al. (J. Steroid Biochem. 17: 305, 1982). The resulting activity was about 1/2000 that of a placental microsome preparation when expressed per mg microsomal protein. The specific aromatase inhibitors, e.g.10-Propargylestr-4-ene-3,17-dione, and its 17 propionate derivative, inhibited the measured enzymic activity in placental and tumor microsomal preparations, thus confirming that the activity can be attributed to aromatase. This is the first report of aromatase activity in this tumor. The role, if any, in tumor growth remains to be elucidated.
(Supported by NIH grants GM07319, HD07043 and AM15838.)

MATURATION OF E.COLI ALKALINE PHOSPHATASE.

N.L. Parlet and J.F. Chlebowski, Department of Biochemistry, Virginia Commonwealth University, Richmond, Virginia 23298.

E.coli alklaine phosphatase (AP), a dimeric periplasmic enzyme, is induced on P_i deprivation of strains with a mutation at the pit 10 locus. The enzyme is transported from the cytoplasm in an elongated precursor form, which is processed (proteolytic cleavage) to yield the mature AP. The mature AP exists in three isozyme forms. Isozyme 1 appears initially in the course of biosynthesis with isozyme 2 and 3 appearing with time. The sequential formation of the isozymes suggests that precursor processing and isozyme formation are distinct processes. Structural variants of AP can be isolated using chromatofocusing methods which rely on differences in protein isoelectric point. Analysis of aliquots of periplasmic proteins isolated during the course of biosynthesis using chromatofocusing reveals species distinct from the mature isozymes, suggesting a complex maturation mechanism. At this time we are certain that the isolated intermediates are forms of AP based on the amino acid composition, AP activity, and cross reaction with the goat antiserum to AP (E.coli). However, there appear to be structural differences between these intermediates based on the kinetic differences and the chromatofocusing profiles (pI). Further structural characterization of these early intermediates is under investigation.

CONTROL OF THE RATES OF DNA SYNTHESIS THROUGH S-PHASE.

K.A. Foster and J.M. Collins. Department of Biochemistry, Medical College of Virginia, Virginia Commonwealth University, Richmond, VA 23298.

DNA synthesis occurs at a discrete period in the life cycle of a cell called S-phase. The rate of DNA synthesis is determined by the number of cells in S-phase, by the rate of polymerization of deoxyribonucleotides, the nature of the DNA template, and the number of replicating units. Our laboratory has demonstrated the use of flow cytometry to obtain quantative rates of DNA synthesis for various parts of the S-phase of synchronized cells. Previously reported data from this laboratory demonstrated that quantitative rates of DNA synthesis are not constant, but rise and fall in a predictable manner specific for the cell line. HeLa cells have a burst of DNA synthesis early in S-phase, a lag period of several hours, and a final burst of DNA synthesis at the end of S-phase. In an attempt to understand how the rates are controlled, we examined the activity of the nuclear DNA polymerases and the activation of the DNA template. Using synchronized HeLa cells we demonstrated that the levels of the polymerases (alpha and beta) rise and fall in a manner directly preceding the rise and fall in the rates of DNA synthesis. Future studies may reveal other factors that are responsible for the discontinuities in the rates of DNA synthesis.
(Supported by NIH Grant No. CA-24158).

PROPERTIES OF PURIFIED 5-FORMYLTETRAHYDROFOLATE CYCLODEHYDRASE FROM RABBIT LIVER.
Sam Hopkins and LaVerne Schirch. Medical College of Virginia, Virginia Commonwealth University, Richmond, VA 23298.
Leucovorin (5-formyltetrahydrofolate) has been implicated in one-carbon metabolism for many years. However, an enzyme utilizing this compound as a substrate has not been isolated in pure form from any source. The focus of our research has been to develop a purification procedure for the enzyme 5-formyltetrahydrofolate cyclodehydrase, which catalyzes the ATP dependent conversion of 5-formyltetrahydrofolate to 5,10 methenyltetrahydrofolate. The enzyme has been purified 5,000-fold. It appears homogenous by SDS polyacrylamide gel electrophoresis and by native gel electrophoresis. Subunit molecular weight determinations from SDS gels yield a value of 25,000. Sephadex G-100 gel filtration, HPLC molecular sieving and equilibrium ultracentrifugation of the native enzyme yield molecular weights of 26,500, 29,000 and 28,000, respectively. The products of the reaction have been verified as being 5,10 methenyltetrahydrofolate, ADP and phosphate. Initial velocity studies yielded K_m values of 0.33 mM for MgATP and 0.5 μM for 5-formyltetrahydrofolate. Dead end and product inhibition studies have established that substrates bind in a random sequential mechanism. (Supported by NIH Grant GM 28143)

IN VITRO LEUCINE OXIDATION CHANGES BY SELECTED TISSUES FROM TUMOR-BEARING MICE.
Peter Zenon Detskey, Winnie M.Y. Chan, and William L. Banks, Jr., Department of Biochemistry and the Massey Cancer Center, MCV/VCU, Richmond, Va., 23298.
Changes in leucine oxidation (LEU ox.) in tumor-bearing (TB) vs. nontumor-bearing (NTB) animals have been described previously. In order to demonstrate the earliest time at which changes occur, the *in vitro* LEU ox. by kidney, liver and skeletal muscle tissues were examined at days 1,2,3,4,5,6,7,14 and 21 after inoculation of Lewis Lung carcinoma cells into mice. LEU ox. rates were measured by counting the $^{14}CO_2$ evolved when tissues were incubated with 1-^{14}C-LEU. A tumor was evident in TB mice at 5-6d., and by 21d. it represented 16% of total host body weight. Statistically significant decreases in the LEU ox. rates in TB vs. NTB mice were noted for the kidney and liver on days 1-3, and for the skeletal muscle on day 1 only. These tissues recovered their ability for LEU catabolism to control levels shortly thereafter. An increase in the LEU ox. rate in skeletal tissue for TB mice was observed on days 14 and 21, after tumor growth was appreciable. The capacity to catabolize LEU by all the tissues examined from TB versus NTB mice was sharply diminished within 24 hrs. of inoculation of tumor cells, even before tumor growth was observed. (Supported by NIH Grant CA26532)

DEGRADATION OF RADIOIODINATED POLYPEPTIDES BY KIDNEY BRUSH BORDERS OF MEPRIN-SUFFICIENT AND MEPRIN-DEFICIENT MICE. J.F. Reckelhoff, R.J. Beynon, J.S. Bond, Medical College of Virginia, VCU, Richmond, Virginia 23298.
A restricted group of inbred mice of the C stock (CBA, C3H, CHI) are deficient in the activity of meprin, a phosphoramidon-insensitive metalloproteinase that is an integral component of the renal brush border membranes of most mouse strains. Brush borders of normal and meprin-deficient mice were compared with respect to the degradation of radioiodinated, physiologically relevant substrates. The relative rates of proteolysis of substrates were the same with both preparations: insulin B-chain > glucagon >> insulin = B_2-microglobulin. Both brush borders degraded substrates more rapidly at pH 7.5 than pH 9.5. There was no difference in absolute rates of degradation when brush borders from a meprin-sufficient strain (C57Bl/6) and a meprin-deficient strain (C3H/HeN) were compared. At least 80% of the degradation by both brush border preparations was attributable to metalloproteinases, but in the meprin-deficient preparation a relatively greater role was assumed by a phosphoramidon-sensitive endopeptidase which is present in all strains.
Supported by NIH Grant AM 19691

TRYPSIN MODIFICATION OF ESCHERICHIA COLI ALKALINE PHOSPHATASE. C.H. Roberts and J.F. Chlebowski, Department of Biochemistry, Virginia Commonwealth University, Richmond, VA 23298.

A tryptic fragment of E.coli alkaline phosphatase (AP) has been isolated, purified, and characterized. The native enzyme, previously thought to be resistant to proteases, shows a loss of 20% of its activity after a 30-min exposure to 10% trypsin. No further loss is seen after 3 h in contrast to apoAP, which loses all activity. A single major peptide is produced, cleaved at the Arg-10 Ala-11 bond, which is purified by chromatofocusing. This modified AP has a V_{max} of 2000 umol h^{-1} mg^{-1} (1 M Tris, pH 8.0, 25°C, 1 mM PNPP), which is 22% less than the V_{max} for the native enzyme (2500). The K_m for PNPP is lower for the peptide than for the native enzyme, 1.9×10^{-5} M and 4×10^{-5} M, respectively. The K_I for P_i for the native enzyme is 1.5×10^{-5} M and for the fragment 1×10^{-5} M. Differential scanning calorimetry results indicate differences in the stabilities of the two species. The fragment has a T_m of 90°C, which is lower than that for the reconstituted apoenzyme (93.5°C) or for the native enzyme (98.5°C). This modified form of AP may prove to be valuable in studies concerning subunit interactions in this system as the deleted decapeptide occurs at the subunit interface region in the native structure.

CHARACTERIZATION OF A CYSTEINE METALLOPROTEINASE FROM MOUSE LIVER CYTOSOL. Diane L. Rosin, Judith S. Bond and S. Gaylen Bradley. Depts. of Microbiology and Immunology and of Biochemistry. Virginia Commonwealth University, Richmond, VA 23298.

There is increasing evidence that extralysosomal proteinases are important in intracellular protein turnover in eukaryotic cells. We have partially purified a cysteine metalloproteinase from C3H mouse liver cytosol that degrades ^{125}I-insulin B chain (IB) at neutral pH values. The enzyme has an estimated mol wt of 190,000. Degradation of IB was inhibited by p-hydroxymercuribenzoate (PHMB) and iodoacetate (cysteine proteinase inhibitors) and by 1,10-phenanthroline and EDTA (metalloproteinase inhibitors). The proteinase also degraded glucagon but was unable to hydrolyze insulin or a number of large proteins. EDTA- and PHMB-inhibitable IB-degrading activity was observed in the cytosolic fractions of brain, liver, lung, kidney, heart and spleen from 4 mouse strains (C3H/HeN, CBA/J, ICR, and C57/Bl6). The activity of the soluble liver proteinase was not altered in C3H mice treated with metal chelators (EDTA, EGTA), bacterial endotoxin, phenobarbital, dexamethasone, or insulin, but the activity was diminished (~40%) in alloxan-induced diabetic mice and in mice starved for 24 or 48 hr. This soluble polypeptide-degrading endopeptidase appears to be ubiquitous in mice and to be regulated by nutritional conditions. (Supported by NCI Grant 5-T32-CA09210-05, NIH Grant AM 19691 and NIH Grant 2 S07RR05697-13.

EFFECT OF ADENOZINE ANALOG TUBERCIDINE (7-DEAZANUCLEOSIDE) ON ADENOVIRUS RNA SYNTHESIS IN $HeLaS_3$ CELLS. Maciej Speidel (Spons. J.C. McPherson, Jr.), Dept. of Cell & Molecular Biology, Medical College of Georgia, Augusta, GA 30912.

Synthesis of nuclear viral HnRNA and virus-associated RNA and methylation of adenovirus-specific RNA in the presence of an adenosine analog, Tubercidine (7-deazanucleoside), late in infection of $HeLaS_3$ has been investigated. Seventeen-eighteen hours after infection for various periods of time, infected cells were exposed to either 100 μCi of [^{3}H]-uridine or 0.5 mCi of orthophosphate [^{32}P] or L[*methyl*-^{3}H] methionine. The initial experiment revealed that optimal dosage effect on nuclear viral HnRNA and virus-associated RNA was 17.5 μg/ml. This dosage reduced HnRNA synthesis by 50% and had no effect on VA-RNA synthesis. Analysis of base composition of HnRNA and cytoplasmic VA-RNA revealed a 4-6.5% and 4.3% incorporation respectively in each type of viral RNA. Incorporation of the analog could not be demonstrated in the 3'-poly (A) segment of mRNA. Experiment using L[*methyl*-^{3}H] methionine, and [^{3}H]-uridine showed no modifications of 5'-termini or internal methylations of cytoplasmic mRNA selected on oligo $(dT)_{10}$ cellulose chromatography column and analized by high voltage electrophoresis after enzymatic digestion. Thus, it appears that synthesis in the presence of this adenosine analog permits appearance in the cytoplasm of viral transcripts with base substitutions in the body of the message.

PHARMACODYNAMIC EFFECTS OF INTRAVENOUS PLURONIC POLYOLS F-38, F-68, F-77, F-88, F-108, F-127 AND P-105: EFFECTS ON SERUM LIPIDS AND OTHER CONSTITUENTS. J.C.McPherson, Jr.(1) and J.C. McPherson, III(2). (1) Dept. of Surgery, Medical College of Georgia, Augusta, GA 30912 and (2) Dept. of Clinical Investigation, Eisenhower Army Medical Center, Fort Gordon, GA 30905.

We have demonstrated that i.v. administered Pluronic polyols show a wide range of responses on the levels of serum lipids with a single dose-time interval. In this study we injected levels of 100, 200, 400, 800, and 1600 mg/kg bd wt in a fixed volume to groups of 10 male rats (300 gm) and blood drawn at 1, 4, 8, or 24 hrs for determination of serum cholesterol, triglyceride, glucose, BUN, creatinine, uric acid and bilirubin. Glucose levels were variable but BUN, creatinine, uric acid and bilirubin levels were within normal ranges for rats in all groups. Cholesterol and TG levels separate the polyols into three groups: (1) those with a minimal response (up to 2 fold increase), F-38 and F-68; (2) those with a moderate response (up to 10 fold increase), F-77 and F-88; and (3) those with a large response (up to 20 fold increase), F-108, F-127, and P-105. At a 400 mg/kg dose level studied at 1, 4, 8, and 24 hrs, the polyols dose response curves fell into the same 3 groups: group 1 - return to normal levels at 24 hrs, group 2 - slight elevation at 24 hrs, and group 3 - marked elevation at 24 hrs.

EFFECT OF STREPTOZOTOCIN (STZ)-INDUCED DIABETES IN RATS ON PLACENTAL TRANSPORT AND TISSUE UPTAKE OF α-AMINO-ISOBUTYRIC ACID (AIB). Albert D. Copeland and Susan P. Porterfield. Dept. of Physiology, Medical College of Georgia, Augusta, GA 30912

This experiment was designed to determine the effects of STZ-induced diabetes in rats on placental transport and tissue uptake of the non-metabolizable amino acid AIB. As a preliminary experiment had shown maternal and fetal serum thyroxine (T_4) were depressed in diabetic rats, a group of STZ animals was treated with T_4 and 3,5 Dimethyl-3'-isopropyl-L-thyronine (DIMIT). STZ was given to 75% of the rats by intracardiac injection (6.5 mg/100g BW) one week prior to mating. The remaining 25% served as intact controls (C). STZ-treated animals were divided into three groups; diabetic (D), diabetic treated with 4 IU/day Lente insulin (DI) and diabetic treated with 1 µg/100g BW/day T_4 days 1-17 of gestation and 2.5 µg/100g BW/day DIMIT days 18-21 (DTD). On day 22 of gestation, animals were injected sq 15 minutes prior to autopsy with 0.50 µCi/100g BW AIB. Mothers were autopsied and tissues collected and solubilized for liquid scintillation counting. T_4 was measured by RIA. Although maternal serum DPM's were not different, fetal serum DPM's were lower in D and DTD groups than C. Whole fetal tissue DPM's were greater in C than D and DTD. More AIB was taken up by fetal liver and fetal brain of C than of D and DTD. Net placental transport of AIB was less in D and DTD than C.

ALTERATIONS IN RABBIT SPINAL CORD STRUCTURE AND FUNCTION PRODUCED WITH MICROWAVE HYPERTHERMIA. Carl H. Sutton and Pava Popovic. Div. of Neurosurg., Univ. of So. FL and VA Hosp., Tampa, FL 33612, and Dept. of Physiol., Emory Univ., Atlanta, GA 30345

The use of a variety of injury models in different species to produce spinal cord lesions by trauma or ischemia has often given rise to conflicting or inconclusive data. A new model has been developed in rabbits. Spinal cord lesions were produced in selected spinal cord segments of Male New Zealand white rabbits by non-invasive irradiation with microwaves in the near field at 915 MHz. Graded injuries of predictable severity can be produced by the non-invasive induction of moderate hyperthermia in the thoracic spinal cord at precise dosage levels of temperature elevation and duration. Histological changes in microwave-induced hyperthermia closely parallel those seen in traumatic lesions of the human spinal cord, as well as those produced in animals with the classical weight drop method of Allen. In addition to grading the spinal cord lesions with respect to residual neurological function, dose-response observations, utilizing somatosensory evoked responses, blood-spinal cord barrier tracers, and neurohistological and enzyme histochemical preparations, suggest that it will be possible to use this approach to develop a standardized, calibrated model in rabbits to evaluate the efficacy of new therapeutic modalities for the treatment of spinal cord injury.

Maurice B. Visscher
(1901–1983)

PROCEEDINGS OF THE SOCIETY FOR EXPERIMENTAL BIOLOGY AND MEDICINE **176**, 223–225 (1984)

IN MEMORIAM

Maurice B. Visscher (1901–1983)

It is most fitting that the Society for Experimental Biology and Medicine, which by virtue of its efforts to enroll young scientists to its membership has encouraged scientific investigation by young people, pay tribute to the memory of Maurice B. Visscher, one of its former Presidents (1968–1969). In his long and distinguished career in biomedical science, he did much to foster the entrance of young people into scientific careers.

In addition to being a world renowned scientist, Dr. Visscher was a preeminent humanitarian, philosopher, educator, and political reformer who had made seminal contributions in each of these fields, marking him as a true Renaissance man. Regarding his scientific contributions, he was perhaps best known for his work in cardiovascular physiology that began with a postdoctoral fellowship with Ernest Starling resulting in an important paper on the regulation of the energy output of the heart, an area he was to pursue for some years and which caused his name to become inextricably linked with "Starling's Law of the Heart." However, he felt his greatest contribution had been to the field of material transport. By means of a series of cleverly designed experiments, he proved that certain ions were actively transported across the intestinal mucosa, as well as the bidirectional movement of water across it. As Charles Code, the noted gastrointestinal physiologist who had been a postdoctoral student in Visscher's laboratory and who remained a lifelong friend so aptly put it, "There is no area in his multifaceted career in which Visscher's virtuosity was more brilliantly displayed than in his studies of intestinal transport. He was really plowing new ground—all alone."

In addition to the primary areas of cardiovascular and gastrointestinal physiology, Maurice Visscher made fundamental contributions to a remarkable number of other widely different areas of physiology including nutrition, pulmonary function, cancer biology, chronobiology, renal physiology (tubular transport), oximetry, pulmonary edema, endotoxin shock, and aging. At least several publications, spread out over a number of years, were generated in each of these areas, evidence of his continuing deep interest in them.

A scientist leaves his mark not only through his scientific work but also through the students and co-workers whose careers he has influenced by contact with them in the laboratory. Here again Maurice Visscher excelled, having had as students or collaborators a large number of basic and clinical scientists, most of whom reached professorial rank and attained national and international stature, which is probably a better measure of his influence on biomedical science than the number of his scientific publications, which, however, was enormous, considering the care with which each one was prepared. Thus it is clear that he had earned his scientific credentials the hard way and left us a legacy of a large number of outstanding students and collaborators to disseminate and perpetuate his approach to scientific problems as well as his ideals.

However, Dr. Visscher's prodigious and highly innovative scientific contributions and the numerous honors stemming therefrom merely served as a vehicle permitting him to exercise his deeply felt civic and humanitarian obligations. It is difficult, at this point, to determine whether the scientific or the civic and humanitarian activities took precedence in his mind, which in itself tells us much about the man. What is clear is that he eagerly pursued a wide variety of humanitarian and civic activities at the expense of his scientific productivity, and there is no telling what great scientific

0037-9727/84 $1.50

insights he sacrificed selflessly in order to be of help to his fellow man. It is simply impossible even to list the myriad of science policy, civic, and humanitarian activities in which he participated, so that a highly abbreviated selected sample will have to suffice.

Years ago, as department chairman at an early age successively at the Universities of Tennessee, Southern California, Illinois, and Minnesota, he astutely foresaw the magnitude of the threat to experimental biology and medicine posed by the antivivisectionists and consequently devoted a great deal of effort over his entire lifetime to this important cause, the true significance of which scientists in certain parts of our country have only recently come to appreciate, as they lost access to inexpensive experimental animals in favor of the senseless destruction of these animals in the pounds.

As a humanitarian, in an effort to make medical care available to the working poor, he helped to found the first health maintenance organization (HMO) in Minnesota, one of the first in the country, whose existence engendered great enmity toward him in the medical community. He served as scientific head of a post-World War II UN and Unitarian relief mission to Italy. A long-time proponent of worldwide nuclear disarmament, he was among the first in this country to warn against the danger of radioactive contamination of our food chain from above-ground nuclear explosive testing. As chairman of the Special Committee on Civil Liberties of the AAAS, which he caused to be set up, he fought the tyrannical witch-hunting harassment of scientists of the Joe McCarthy–House Unamerican Activities Committee era, at the cost of having his own loyalty to his country called into question by what have now clearly become known to have been demagogic power-hungry legislators. The cost of this dark episode in our history in damaged careers and lives and in curtailed productivity in science and in the arts, already recognized by Visscher long ago, is just being appreciated by the public at large.

Visscher also made major contributions to the identification of the problems and to the outlining of their solution in the important area of scientific communication, problems stemming largely from the unprecedented support for biomedical research in the last quarter of a century. In a relatively recent article he decried the current chaotic "nonsystem" of scientific publication for its "editorial censorship" and for publisher's attempts to restrict journal article reproduction rights, neither of which is in the interest of the scientist–author nor of the public at large, which ultimately paid for the research being communicated. He had the courage to question the wisdom of the current censorship system that is intended to "protect the authors against themselves" rather than permitting readers to make their own evaluations and ignores "the personal biases or even the selfish interests of the referees," which may be the basis for the rejection of manuscripts. His interim remedy was the substitution of informative abstracts with a national repository making available copies of the complete manuscripts, with an international computerized storage and retrieval system as the ultimate solution.

Turning now to Maurice Visscher, the man. He was a quiet, thoughtful man of great compassion. He would take the time to help anyone who needed it, and no request for help was ever turned down. In discussing scientific matters, despite his vast knowledge, he was not at all intimidating, so that no one felt constrained to hold back ideas or judgments, with the end result that no new thought or idea probably was ever lost on his account. His brilliant insights, coupled with his selfless devotion, made the beleaguered participants of what appeared initially to be hopeless causes, such as the anti-Vietnam War effort, feel that their labors were not wasted. And he was often successful, in spite of the odds. The same restrained courage which permitted him to stand apart from the crowd and go against current dogma in scientific matters pervaded all of his actions. When he thought something was the right thing to do, he was unshakeable and the greater the size of the opposition, its social rank, or political power, the more tenacious and steadfast he became in his beliefs. The foregoing is not intended to cloak him in a mantle of righteous infallibility, for he did make mistakes, but most frequently these grew out of a kindly desire to help someone in difficulty. His friendship was warm and genuine, and he could always be counted on for encouragement and support in times of stress. Rather than list the numerous honors he was awarded, it is considered preferable to have detailed the reasons he deserved them. The thought I would most like to leave with the reader is that to every endeavor that he undertook throughout his life, and these were legion, he made major and unique contributions because of his incisive intellect, the extremely wide range of his knowledge, and his abiding humanity. At the end he said he had no regrets—he had had a full life, the companionship of a wonderful family, and had been fortunate in many other respects. Since one cannot imagine him refusing assistance to anyone or permitting injustice anywhere on the globe to go unchallenged, all the world's people have lost a friend. We will not see his like again soon.

IRWIN J. FOX
Professor of Physiology
University of Minnesota

PROCEEDINGS OF THE SOCIETY FOR EXPERIMENTAL BIOLOGY AND MEDICINE **176**, 226–237 (1984)

MINIREVIEW

Autoimmune Diseases of the Kidney (41864)

GIUSEPPE A. ANDRES AND JAN R. BRENTJENS

Departments of Microbiology, Pathology, and Medicine, School of Medicine, State University of New York, Buffalo, New York 14214, and the Renal Research Laboratory of the Buffalo General Hospital, Buffalo, New York 14203

Autoimmune diseases are due to a breakdown of the tolerant state to autologous constituents. Some autoimmune diseases, including kidney diseases, can occur spontaneously in man. Our present understanding of the pathogenesis of human autoimmune diseases, however, is based mainly on the results of studies of diseases induced in laboratory animals by appropriate immunization. These diseases usually involve strong immunization such as incorporation of autologous tissue in "adjuvants," like Freund's adjuvant, or immunization of animals with a similar tissue from a different species that shares cross-reactive antigens.

Autoimmune reactions can be manifested by the production of autoantibodies and/or of autoreactive T cells. Thus, tissue damage may result from the reaction of antibodies with antigens present in the kidney, from tissue deposition of circulating immune complexes, and from cellular immune processes (1, 2). These mechanisms of hypersensitivity are not mutually exclusive. It is only for didactic reasons that we arbitrarily classify the various autoimmune renal diseases as if they were induced by a single pathogenic mechanism (Table I). In this review two groups of animal models of nephritis will be described. In the first group kidney lesions are induced by autoantibodies reacting with structural kidney antigens such as those of basement membranes or those present on the surface of cells. In immunofluorescence microscopy the immune reactants may be found along basement membranes in either a linear (e.g., in anti-basement membrane nephritis) or a granular pattern (e.g., in Heymann glomerulonephritis). In the second group the nephropathies are conceivably the result of deposition in the kidney of circulating autologous immune complexes. The immune complexes accumulate in a granular pattern.[1] Where possible, we will present evidence that similar diseases occur in man. Because insufficient solid data are available, a separate discussion of the role of autoreactive T cells in the development of kidney diseases is not included in this review.

I. Injury Resulting from the Interaction of Autoantibodies with Structural Antigens of the Kidney. *1. Glomerulonephritis Mediated by Antibodies to Glomerular Basement Membrane (GBM). a. Animal models. i. Glomerulonephritis resulting from immunization with GBM antigens.* Steblay and his associates have shown that sheep immunized with either heterologous (human) or homologous GBM in complete Freund's adjuvant develop GBM antibodies and a rapidly progressive, crescentic glomerulonephritis (3). Some of the antibodies are clearly autoantibodies because they react with autologous GBM. Study by direct immunofluorescence microscopy shows characteristic linear deposits of sheep IgG along the GBM. C3 may be bound to GBM in a similar pattern. Antibodies eluted from diseased kidneys react *in vitro* with sheep and human GBM, as well as with alveolar basement membranes (ABM) (4). The antibodies eluted from kidneys of sheep with Steblay's glomerulonephritis react with structural components localized mainly in the lamina rara interna of the GBM. This reaction is completely inhibited by prior absorption of the antibodies with collagenase-digested human GBM. Furthermore, the antibodies eluted from kidneys of nephritic sheep inhibit the

[1] The term "immune complex nephritis" has been traditionally used to encompass all those nephropathies in which granular immune deposits are found irrespective of whether these deposits are formed locally or from circulating immune complexes. Therefore, this term will only seldom be used in this review.

0037-9727/84 $1.50

TABLE I. KIDNEY DISEASES WITH AN AUTOIMMUNE PATHOGENESIS

I. *Injury resulting from the interaction of autoantibodies with structural antigens of the kidney*
 1. Glomerulonephritis mediated by antibodies to glomerular basement membrane (GBM)
  a. Animal models
   i. Glomerulonephritis resulting from immunization with GBM antigens
   ii. Glomerulonephritis induced by mercuric chloride
   iii. Spontaneous glomerulonephritis
  b. Human glomerulonephritis
 2. Glomerulonephritis mediated by antibodies to glomerular epithelial antigens
  a. Animal models
   i. Heymann glomerulonephritis
  b. Human glomerulonephritis (?)
 3. Tubulo-interstitial nephritis mediated by antibodies to tubular basement membrane (TBM)
  a. Animal models
   i. Tubulo-interstitial nephritis resulting from immunization with TBM antigens
   ii. Anti-TBM antibodies following kidney transplantation
  b. Human tubulo-interstitial nephritis
 4. Tubular injury mediated by antibodies to tubular epithelial antigens
  a. Animal models
  b. Tubular injury in man (?)
II. *Injury presumably resulting from deposition in the kidney of circulating autologous immune complexes*
 1. Glomerulonephritis
  a. Animal models
   i. Glomerulonephritis induced by graft-versus-host or host-versus-graft reactions
   ii. Glomerulonephritis induced by thyroglobulin or sperm antigens
   iii. Glomerulonephritis induced by antigens of basement membranes and of the collagen matrix
   iv. Glomerulonephritis in mice with spontaneous lupus-like syndrome
  b. Human diseases
   i. Systemic lupus erythematosus nephritis
   ii. Other types of glomerulonephritis
 2. Tubulo-interstitial nephritis
  a. Animal models
  b. Human diseases

reaction of Goodpasture's antibodies (see Sect. I1b) with human GBM, suggesting that common antigenic determinants of the GBM react with Steblay's and Goodpasture's antibodies (5). Steblay's glomerulonephritis can be passively transferred with antibody to sheep, which develop a glomerulonephritis identical to that of the donor animal (4). Sheep passively or actively immunized do not develop autoimmune hemorrhagic pneumonitis despite the presence in the circulation of elevated levels of antibodies capable of reacting with sheep ABM *in vitro*. It is conceivable that, in addition to antibodies, other factors increasing the permeability of the alveolar capillary wall may be required for the development of lung injury (6). In the sheep model the precise role of the mediators of the inflammatory reaction is not well established. The exudative lesions are characterized by accumulation of bloodborne macrophages which contribute to the formation of crescents (2).

Anti-GBM glomerulonephritis can be induced by both xeno- and allo-immunization of rats, rabbits, mice, guinea pigs, and monkeys (2). The urine of normal rabbits contains GBM antigens that, when used for immunization of rabbits, induce anti-GBM glomerulonephritis. In guinea pigs complement activation does not seem important for the development of proteinuria. Mice immunized with human GBM develop a conspicuous expansion of the lamina rara externa and large "spikes." The eluates from kidneys of nephritic mice contain all IgG subclasses but only IgG_1 binds to normal mouse GBM. This finding was interpreted as indicating that *in vivo* fixation to the GBM of IgG subclasses other than IgG_1 results from synthesis of antibodies to abnormal GBM components generated as a consequence of the initial injury induced by GBM antibodies of the IgG_1 subclass (7).

ii. Glomerulonephritis induced by mercuric chloride ($HgCl_2$). New Zealand rabbits injected intramuscularly with $HgCl_2$ develop a biphasic, systemic disease first characterized by autoantibodies reactive to basement membranes and collagen matrix and, then, by antigen–antibody complexes containing the same kind of antibodies (8). A similar biphasic disease occurs in Brown-Norway rats (9, 10). In these animals the autoimmune response depends upon two or three genes, one of which is H-1 linked (11). Other studies have shown that $HgCl_2$ induces a polyclonal B-cell activation (12) and, possibly, a loss of T-cell suppression function (13). In the rat a proliferative and exudative glomerulonephritis can be observed 10 to 15 days after the beginning of administration of $HgCl_2$. In the rabbit this initial inflammatory injury was not described. In a later stage of $HgCl_2$ injection both rabbits and rats develop a systemic immune complex disease, including membranous glomerulonephritis (Sect. II1a.iii), presumably as a consequence of tissue deposition of circulating immune complexes (10, 14).

iii. Spontaneous glomerulonephritis. A glomerulonephritis induced by antibodies to GBM was described in the horse (15).

b. Human glomerulonephritis. Lerner *et al.* (16) have shown that human renal disease may infrequently (1.5–2% of the nephritic population) result from autoantibodies directed against constituents of the GBM. Anti-GBM glomerulonephritis is usually characterized by extensive crescent formation and rapid deterioration of renal function. Because of antigenic similarities among GBM, TBM, and ABM, anti-GBM glomerulonephritis may be associated with tubulo-interstitial nephritis and/or with hemorrhagic pneumonitis. A number of clinical syndromes can result. "Anti-renal basement membrane nephritis" is characterized by the presence of antibodies to GBM and TBM. In "Goodpasture's disease" or "anti-GBM glomerulonephritis with hemorrhagic pneumonitis" antibodies binding to GBM and ABM are found. The antigens responsible for the immune response occurring in Goodpasture's disease and in some cases of isolated rapidly progressive glomerulonephritis are contained in the noncollagenous fractions of the GBM (2) and, especially, in their most cationic 25- and 45-kDa components (17). One of the antigenic sites is located on a polypeptide with a molecular weight of 26,000 (18). Immunocytochemical studies have shown that these antigenic components are restricted to the lamina rara interna of the GBM (19).

The basic pathogenetic mechanism responsible for anti-GBM glomerulonephritis or Goodpasture's disease is, at least partially, known. The demonstration that anti-GBM antibodies are responsible for the development of the disease is based on the following evidence: first, linear deposits of IgG, frequently but not always associated with C3, are present along the basement membranes; second, antibodies to GBM can be detected in the circulation, especially after bilateral nephrectomy; third, the immunoglobulins eluted from diseased kidneys contain antibodies, that, upon intravenous injection into monkeys, bind in a linear pattern to the GBM and induce a proliferative and exudative glomerulonephritis and proteinuria; and, fourth, anti-GBM glomerulonephritis may recur in a renal graft if transplantation is performed when antibodies are still present in the circulation of the recipient (2, 20).

The demonstration of linear deposits of IgG in ABM of patients with Goodpasture's disease together with the observation that anti-ABM antibodies cross-react with GBM suggests that the immunological mechanisms inducing injury in the lung and in the kidney are identical. Although etiologic factors are not known, three hypotheses may be considered. First, exogenous antigens, cross-reacting with GBM and ABM, could initiate autoantibody formation. Second, endogenous GBM or ABM, secreted in increased amounts or altered in composition, could be the immunogenic stimulus. Third, an abnormality of the immune response, involving polyclonal B-cell activation and other alterations of stimulatory or inhibitory signals, may predispose individuals carrying the HLA-DRW2 allotype to develop basement membrane antibodies. The chief difference between experimental and human anti-GBM glomerulonephritis is the absence of lung hemorrhage in laboratory animals. The observation that in patients with anti-GBM nephritis lung disease may be absent despite the presence in the circulation of antibodies cross-reacting *in vitro* with ABM and the demonstration that the titer of circulating antibodies does not correlate with the severity of lung involvement in patients with Goodpasture's disease suggest that, besides antibodies, additional factors are needed for lung disease to occur (6, 21).

2. Glomerulonephritis Mediated by Antibodies to Glomerular Epithelial Antigens. a. Animal models. i. Heymann glomerulonephritis. Heymann and his associates (22) described the development of nephrotic syndrome in rats immunized with homogenates of homologous kidney in Freund's adjuvant. The massive proteinuria is caused by glomerular lesions characteristic of membranous nephropathy. The disease is associated with the formation of autoantibodies reactive with antigens present on the cells of proximal tubules (a cellular fraction called F × 1A) (23) and also expressed on glomerular visceral epithelial cells. More recently the antigen has been characterized as a glycoprotein (gp 330) concentrated mainly in the "coated pits" of the plasma membrane of the apical part of the proximal tubule cells, and in the plasma membrane of glomerular visceral epithelial cells, and of other absorptive epithelia (24).

An immune complex disease similar to active Heymann nephritis develops in rats soon after passive transfer of homologous F × 1A antibodies (25). A comparable membranous nephropathy can also be induced by passive transfer of heterologous F × 1A antibody (26). Since perfusion of isolated rat kidney with heterologous antibody to F × 1A is followed by formation of granular immune deposits along the epithelial side of GBM, it is conceivable that the granular immune deposits of IgG found along GBM arise by the reaction of the perfusing antibodies with the gp 300 antigen present in glomeruli (27, 28). Whether *in situ* formation of immune complexes plays an exclusive role in the pathogenesis of active Heymann nephritis remains a matter of debate.

The development of Heymann nephritis is genetically controlled. Five different inbred rat strains, representing three haplotypes of the major histocompatibility locus H-1, were studied. It was found that Lewis, AS (H-1), and Lewis × BDV (H-1d) were highly susceptible to disease stimulation, whereas Brown-Norway and Lewis × Brown-Norway were resistant or only slightly susceptible. These findings indicate that the expression of the disease is linked to genes of the major histocompatibility complex (29).

b. Human glomerulonephritis (?). Tubular antigens, similar to those responsible for Heymann glomerulonephritis, were tentatively identified in Japan in a few patients with membranous glomerulonephritis. Outside Japan, these observations were not confirmed (2), with the exception of one patient with glomerulonephritis and tubulo-interstitial nephritis that appeared to have analogies with Heymann nephritis (30). It is conceivable, however, that in patients with idiopathic membranous nephropathy autoantibodies have reacted *in situ* with structural glomerular capillary wall components other than the Heymann antigen.

3. Tubulo-interstitial Nephritis Mediated by Antibodies to Tubular Basement Membrane (TBM). a. Animal models. i. Tubulo-interstitial nephritis resulting from immunization with TBM antigens. The first laboratory model of tubulo-interstitial nephritis induced by antibody reactive with TBM was described by Steblay and Rudofsky in guinea pigs immunized with rabbit TBM (31). The animals develop a severe renal disease as well as autoantibodies that react with the guinea pig's own TBM to form continuous linear deposits of IgG, detectable by direct immunofluorescence tests, along the basement membrane of proximal tubules. C3 is also bound to TBM in the same pattern. The kidneys of immunized guinea pigs become swollen and petechiae are visible at the surface. Examination by light and electron microscopy reveals interstitial mononuclear cell infiltrates and formation of giant cells which surround and destroy the tubules. The glomeruli exhibit little or no pathologic changes despite the presence of weak IgG deposits along GBM. Absorption studies with renal eluates reveal that TBM shares antigens with GBM, although some TBM determinants are distinct from those of GBM. Guinea pigs of strain 13 develop tubulo-interstitial nephritis with conditions of immunization that usually do not generate a comparable disease in strain 2. The increased susceptibility to develop anti-TBM antibody appears to be inherited as a single dominant or codominant trait, linked to the major histocompatibility complex (32). With larger immunizing doses of TBM antigens, strain 2 animals develop tubulo-interstitial nephritis indistinguishable from that seen in strain 13 and outbred Hartley guinea pigs, although longer time is required for the full expression of severe disease in strain 2. The disease can be transferred to animals of the same species with serum or renal eluates or with autoantibodies of the IgG_1 or IgG_2 isotype. If transferred by IgG_1 or by IgG_2 autoantibodies, the recipient guinea pigs generate antibodies of the isotype that had not been transferred and higher titers than expected of the isotype that had been transferred (33). This "autoimmune amplification," similar to that described in autoimmune hemolytic anemia, could have importance in the self-perpetuation of the disease.

Anti-TBM tubulo-interstitial nephritis can be induced in guinea pigs genetically deficient in C4. Passive transfer of tubulo-interstitial nephritis by serum can be inhibited by depletion of complement, using cobra venom factor, or by depletion of leukocytes with irradiation. Furthermore, an inhibition of the autoimmune anti-TBM response and the ensuing disease is achieved by injection of heterologous antibodies to the anti-TBM antibodies. This inhibition may be caused by idiotype suppression (34). The disease cannot be transferred by sensitized lymphocytes.

Another model of anti-TBM tubulo-interstitial nephritis was described in Brown-Norway and Lewis × Brown-Norway rats immunized with Sprague–Dawley rat kidney homogenate in complete Freund's adjuvant and pertussis vaccine (35). The evidence supporting a primary pathogenetic role for anti-TBM autoantibodies in this model consists of: first, presence of linear deposits of rat IgG and C3 along TBM; second, presence of anti-TBM antibodies in the serum and in renal eluates of immunized rats; and third, transfer of the disease to normal rats with serum or renal eluates of nephritic rats. The histopathology of the tubulo-interstitial nephritis observed in rats is similar to that seen in guinea pigs. However, several weeks after the onset of tubulo-interstitial nephritis, Heymann nephritis may also appear, with characteristic granular deposits of IgG and C3 along glomerular capillary walls.

Anti-TBM tubulo-interstitial nephritis in Brown-Norway or Lewis × Brown-Norway F_1 hybrid rats has been produced by immunization with bovine TBM (36). The analysis of the various antibodies generated in this animal model shows that only the antibodies reactive with autologous collagenase solubilized TBM are deposited in the kidneys of nephritic rats and play a major role in the development of inflammatory injury. Studies of cross-absorption indicate that these antibodies are induced by an immune response to bovine TBM antigens cross-reactive with the TBM of BN rats (37).

ii. Anti-TBM antibodies following kidney transplantation. Anti-TBM antibodies may be generated by renal allograft implantation [for review see Ref. (38)]. In one study, however, the anti-TBM response was shown not to be autoimmune in nature. Lewis rats receiving Lewis × Brown-Norway F_1 hybrid kidneys develop anti-TBM antibodies which bind to kidneys of the donor, but not of the recipient, strain. In contrast, Brown-Norway rats receiving Lewis × Brown-Norway F_1 hybrid kidneys do not make anti-TBM antibodies. The observations indicate that the antibody response is generated by a TBM alloantigen introduced by transplantation (39).

Renal alloantibody formation was studied in Lewis rats immunized with DA rat kidney homogenates or receiving DA renal allografts. Using a ^{125}I anti-IgG binding assay with kidney homogenate as target tissue, it was found that the alloantigen is present in the TBM of proximal convoluted tubules and in Bowman's capsule, that the locus coding for this alloantigen is not linked to the major histocompatibility complex, and that the immune response to the TBM alloantigen does not induce detectable graft damage (40).

b. Human tubulo-interstitial nephritis. There is convincing evidence that anti-TBM disease occurs in man, although it is rare. Anti-TBM tubulo-interstitial nephritis is well documented in association with anti-GBM glomerulonephritis (2, 17, 38). The presence of anti-TBM antibodies is indicated by linear deposits of IgG, and occasionally of C3, along TBM. As the eluates of renal tissue contain antibodies which react with GBM, TBM, and ABM, the autoantibodies appear to be directed against antigenic determinants shared by these three structures. In order to evaluate the pathogenic role of anti-TBM antibodies, a comparative immunopathologic study was performed in three groups of patients: one with anti-GBM glomerulonephritis, another with anti-GBM and anti-TBM nephritis, and still another with nephritides not associated with autoantibodies to renal basement membranes. The results showed that tubulo-interstitial nephritis is most frequent and severe when anti-TBM autoantibodies are detectable. It was concluded that autoantibodies to TBM contribute to the development of tubulo-interstitial lesions (41).

Anti-TBM antibodies have been detected in the sera and in TBM of a few patients with severe acute tubulo-interstitial nephritis apparently not associated with concomitant factors (2, 38). Attempts to transfer the disease to BN rats or to other mammals by iv injections of serum antibodies have been unsuccessful and only minimal binding of human IgG to TBM was found, suggesting that the antigen is not readily available to circulating IgG (personal observations). Anti-TBM antibodies may occur in recipients of renal allografts (2, 38). In some of these patients the antibodies react with the TBM of both the graft and the native kidneys and, therefore, behave as autoantibodies. In other patients, however, the antibodies react only with the TBM of the grafted kidney, suggesting that they may have been generated by an alloimmune response to a foreign TBM antigen present in the graft but not in the recipient. Anti-TBM antibodies have also been described in association with immune complex glomerulonephritis and in some patients with tubulo-interstitial nephritis associated with administration of methicillin.

4. Tubular Injury Mediated by Antibodies to Tubular Epithelial Antigens. a. Animal models. In rats with Heymann nephritis autoantibodies bind *in vivo* to antigens of the apical part of the cells of the proximal tubules during the first week of proteinuria. Antibodies with similar reactivity are found in the urine. Concomitantly, an extensive loss of microvilli together with degeneration and proliferation of epithelial cells of proximal tubules are observed. The results of indirect immunofluorescence tests using Heymann antibodies on kidneys of rats with Heymann nephritis confirm the loss of antigens from the tubules. In rats with Heymann nephritis of long duration, which have little or no circulating antibodies and persistent proteinuria, a partial recovery of tubular epithelia is seen. Direct evidence of the cytotoxic action of these autoantibodies on proximal tubule cells has been obtained from passive transfer experiments (42).

Tamm–Horsfall protein is an antigen present in the plasma membrane of the cells of the thick ascending limb of Henle's loop (43). When rats are immunized with Tamm–Horsfall protein, they develop granular immune deposits, containing this antigen, immunoglobulin, and complement, at the base of the epithelium of the thick ascending limb. Infiltration of leukocytes is observed around these segments of the nephron. These lesions are induced by *in situ* formation of immune complexes that originate from a reaction between plasma membrane antigens and circulating antibodies (44).

b. Tubular injury in man (?). Granular deposits of immunoglobulin along the TBM of proximal convoluted tubules have been described in one patient with membranous glomerulonephritis that appeared to be analogous to Heymann nephritis (30). If, however, a tubular injury comparable to Heymann nephritis occurs in man, its frequency is very rare. Antibodies reacting with the apical part of the cells of proximal convoluted tubules have been detected in the sera of patients with renal allografts (45). Proof that these antibodies contribute to the development of tubular damage is still lacking.

Antibodies to Tamm–Horsfall protein are frequently detected in the sera of patients with urinary tract obstruction, infection, and vesicoureteral reflux. In some patients with tubulo-interstitial nephritis deposits of Tamm–Horsfall protein are found sequestered in the renal interstitium where they should have the potential for eliciting inflammatory and immunologic responses (46, 47). However, a precise correlation between Tamm–Horsfall antibodies, abnormal interstitial deposits, and tubulo-interstitial nephritis has not been established.

II. Injury Presumably Resulting from Deposition in the Kidney of Circulating Autologous Immune Complexes. *1. Glomerulonephritis. a. Animal models. i. Glomerulonephritis induced by graft-versus-host or host-versus-graft reactions.* One of the most common pathologic events in F_1 mice with chronic graft-versus-host reaction (GVHR) is membranous glomerulonephritis (48). The disease has all the characteristic immunopathologic features of immune complex injury. In the initial experiments it was assumed that the nephritogenic antibodies were anti-H-2 alloantibodies produced by donor B cells (49). Later, however, it became evident that autoreactive B cells normally exist and can be triggered by a number of mechanisms, including GVHR. It was found that F_1 mice with GVHR develop a disease resembling murine lupus with host-derived autoantibodies against erythrocytes, and nuclear antigens. The underlying mechanism of the autoimmune response in GVHR is thought to consist of an abnormal cooperation between alloreactive helper T cells of the donor and the normally existing (auto)reactive B cells of the recipient (50).

A similar membranous glomerulonephritis occurs in mice perinatally inoculated with related F_1 hybrid spleen cells (51). The model of host-versus-graft reaction is characterized by a rapid fatal evolution with severe depletion of T lymphocytes in lymphoid organs, influx of polymorphonuclear leukocytes, early activation of the B-cell system with hypergammaglobulinemia and immune complex disease, disseminated intravascular coagulation, hepatic necrosis, and intestinal hemorrhage. The disease does not appear to be related to any special H-2 incompatibility between host and F_1 donor. Other studies of host-versus-graft reaction induced by perinatal injection of semi-allogeneic F_1 hybrid spleen cells show that mice develop a lupus-like autoimmune disease characterized by hypergammaglobulinemia, autoantibodies, especially rheumatoid factor-like and anti-single-stranded DNA antibodies, systemic immune complex injury, and transplantation tolerance, as assessed by the inability of the recipient's spleen cells to generate cytolytic responses to donor alloantigens (52). The antinuclear antibodies bear allotypes specific of the F_1 donor as well as the parental host, indicating that the autoantibodies are of both donor and host origin. The mechanisms that stimulate autoreactive B cells are not firmly established but could involve a stimulus from T helper cells, a T-cell-independent polyclonal B-cell activation, or an impairment of the function of suppressor T cells.

ii. Glomerulonephritis induced by thyroglobulin or sperm antigens. Autologous thyroglobulin or sperm acrosomal antigens may induce a mild immune complex glomerulonephritis. Rabbits immunized with thyroglobulin develop glomerular lesions when the amount of thyroglobulin available for immune complex formation is artificially increased (53). Likewise, granular deposits of immune complexes are found in glomeruli of some vasectomized rabbits with persistent high concentrations of circulating anti-sperm antibodies. As immunoglobulins eluted from the kidneys of these rabbits bind to acrosomes, it is possible that the glomerular lesions result from a local deposition of circulating antigen–antibody complexes (54).

iii. Glomerulonephritis induced by antigens of basement membranes and of the collagen matrix. If administered in large amounts, compounds containing mercury are nephrotoxic and cause tubular lesions. When injected in small doses into rabbits or Brown-Norway rats, however, $HgCl_2$ induces a membranous glomerulonephritis (55). As mentioned in Section I1a.ii the autoimmune response is first characterized by formation of antibodies reactive with rabbit or rat basement membranes and collagen matrix and, later, by circulating antigen–antibody complexes, containing the same kind of autoantibodies detected during the first stage of disease (8–10, 14). Studies performed with the aid of syngeneic kidney transplantation have shown that the renal lesions are due to an alteration of the immune response rather than to direct renal injury. Furthermore, these studies have demonstrated that the membranous glomerulonephritis occurs only when antigen–antibody complexes are detectable in the circulation. This finding is consistent with the interpretation that in the $HgCl_2$ model the granular immune deposits seen in the subepithelial part of the GBM are not, or not exclusively, formed *in situ* (56).

iv. Glomerulonephritis in mice with spontaneous lupus-like syndrome. Mice with lupus-like syndrome provide a useful model for the study of a generalized autoimmune disease that includes a glomerulonephritis characterized by granular deposits of antigen–antibody complexes, containing native (57) and single-stranded (58) DNA. The possibility that part of these immune deposits may be formed *in situ* is a matter of debate (59). The most studied strains are NZB, NZB/NZW F_1, MRL, and the BXSB mice. All these animals develop hypergammaglobulinemia, anti-DNA and other antinuclear antibodies, anti-retroviral gp 70 antibodies, circulating immune complexes, and glomerulonephritis, the most common cause of death (60). The features of the disease, however, are different from strain to strain and concern the amounts and specificities of the autoantibodies, the rapidity of progress of nephritis, the influence of sex on the severity of the disease, and the extent and nature of lymphoid hyperplasia (60). NZB/NZW F_1 females, BXSB males, and MRL/Mp-*lpr/lpr* develop immunopathological abnormalities a few weeks after birth and significant mortality within the first 6 months of life. MRL/Mp-*lpr/lpr* also have necrotizing polyarteritis and a rheumatoid arthritis-like disease associated with rheumatoid factors in the serum, anti-Sm antibodies, and frequently monoclonal γ-globulins of the IgG_1 and IgG_{2a} varieties. In contrast, in NZB, BXSB females, and MRL/Mp the disease occurs in the second year of life. In $(NZB \times BXSB)F_1$ the incidence of coronary vascular disease and myocardial infarction is as high as 75% (61). In all mouse strains the development of overt systemic disease is associated with enhanced production of polyclonal autoantibodies and a switch from IgM to IgG antibody production, with subsequent formation of pathogenic antigen–antibody complexes (61).

Studies of appropriate bone marrow, spleen, or fetal liver cell chimeras show that the autoimmune disease is not induced by abnormal autoantigens but rather by abnormalities of the lymphoid-precursor cells, related to the genetic background (61). The autosomal recessive *lpr* (lymphoproliferation) gene in MRL-*lpr/lpr* mice, a Y-chromosome-linked gene in BXSB males, and females hormones in NZB/NZW F_1 are responsible for the early development and for the particular severity of the disease. The abnormality of the lymphoid-precursor cells is mainly expressed by a B-cell hyperactivity manifested by increased numbers of IgG-containing and/or Ig-secreting cells, increased numbers of cells which spontaneously form antibodies to incidental antigens, such as haptens, and increased numbers of colony-forming B cells. The cause of B-cell hyperactivity has not been definitively established. It could be due to an intrinsic B-cell defect, abnormal levels of suppressor or helper T cells, or abnormalities in the way B cells respond to accessory signals from suppressor or helper T cells (61). The data presently available argue against any consistent alteration related to suppressor T cells as the responsible factor. In contrast, they support the interpretation that an abnormal response to, and/or production of, T-cell-derived B-cell activating factors may have a central role in the pathogenesis of the autoimmune disease (62). B cells from BXSB and NZB/NZW strains, once triggered by the usual signals, give abnormally high responses. In contrast, B cells from MRL-*lpr/lpr* respond normally but are exposed to an increased help provided by T cells. This helper function, which is not antigen specific, is induced by a soluble B-cell differentiation factor promoting a switch from IgM to IgG antibody production with predominant secretion of IgG_2 antibodies, the primary subclass of IgG involved in autoantibody and immune complex formation in mice with lupus-like disease (62).

b. Human diseases. i. Systemic lupus erythematosus (SLE) nephritis. The best example of autoimmune immune complex glomerulonephritis in man is nephritis in SLE. In that disease, nuclear antigens including native (63) and denatured DNA (64) (presumably of endogenous nature), antinuclear antibodies, and complement components, including the membrane attack complex (65), are found in glomeruli. Additional antigen–antibody systems, such as IgG–anti-IgG complexes may also be important in the pathogenesis of the disease (66). A wide spectrum of histologic lesions is found in glomeruli and in tubulo-interstitial structures. There is evidence that the type and severity of glomerular lesions may depend on the quantity and quality of the antibodies. As for possible analogies between the features of human and murine lupus, the disease manifestation in NZ mice parallels that in humans in the sex distribution and the immunopathological aspects of the disease. The BXSB males could be the counterpart of a recently described lupus that affects primarily fathers and sons. In contrast, the disease in MRL-*lpr/lpr* has no apparent human counterpart (61, 62).

ii. Other types of glomerulonephritis. Immune deposits have been identified in the glomeruli of patients with thyroiditis and glomerulonephritis (67, 68). Anti-thyroglobulin antibodies are usually present in great excess in the circulation during thyroiditis. Therefore, nephritogenic immune complexes in equivalence or in slight antigen excess are seldom found. Therapeutic manipulation, such as radioiodine therapy or irradiation, may either increase the amount of antigen available in the circulation or decrease the antibody concentration, leading to formation of nephritogenic immune complexes.

IgG–anti-IgG complexes, of rheumatoid factor type, have been considered as possible nephritogenic agents in several glomerulonephritides including SLE (66), post-streptococcal glomerulonephritis (69), and essential cryoglobulinemia (70). It is unknown whether an antigen, besides IgG, is present in these immune complexes. Other complexes present in glomerular immune deposits might be formed by specific IgG antigenic determinants (idiotypes) and by anti-idiotype antibodies (71, 72).

During the course of GVHR induced by bone marrow allotransplantation, some patients develop autoantibodies and immune complex glomerulonephritis (73). It is conceivable that the pathogenesis of this renal injury is similar to that occurring in non-autoimmune strains of mice undergoing experimentally induced GVHR (see Sect. II1a.i). Nephrotic syndrome, possibly due to immune complex glomerulonephritis, has been observed in children successfully treated with fetal liver transplantation for severe combined immunodeficiency (74). In these patients the possibility of an unusual chronic form of GVHR, induced by the transplantation of healthy stem cells, cannot be excluded.

2. Tubulo-interstitial Nephritis. a. Animal models. The first description of autologous immune complex tubulo-interstitial nephritis was in rabbits injected with preparations of homologous renal tissue (75) or given repeated renal allografts (76). The rabbits develop granular deposits of IgG and C3 along TBM of proximal tubules, interstitial fibrosis, tubular cell damage, and thickening or splitting of TBM. Mild and focal interstitial infiltration of mononuclear cells is present. Some rabbits have glucosuria and aminoaciduria. The immunoglobulins eluted from diseased kidneys react with the deposits present along TBM in the diseased kidneys and with the cytoplasm of the epithelial cells of proximal tubules of normal rabbits. It seems, therefore, that the immune deposits along TBM result from the reaction of circulating autoantibodies with autologous antigens as they move out of tubular cells (77). A similar mechanism may be responsible for the immune deposits observed at the epithelial side of the basement membrane of proximal tubules of rats with active Heymann nephritis.

b. Human diseases. Granular deposits of IgG and C3 along TBM, usually associated with tubulo-interstitial nephritis, are found in 50–60% of patients with proliferative SLE glomerulonephritis. The deposits have been shown to react with fluorescein-conjugated antibody to thymidine and cytidine, indicating that DNA is a constituent of the immune deposits (78, 79).

Aside from those found in SLE nephritis, extraglomerular immune deposits in the kidney are rare in patients with glomerulonephritis. Patients with renal allografts may occasionally develop granular deposits of IgG and C3 along TBM, similar to those described in rabbits receiving multiple renal allografts (80). It is unknown, however, if these tubular immune deposits result from *in situ* formation of autologous immune complexes.

This study was sponsored by Grant AI-10334 of the National Institute of Allergy and Infectious Diseases, U.S. Public Health Service.

1. Dixon FJ. The pathogenesis of glomerulonephritis. Amer J Med **44**:493, 1968.

2. Wilson CW, Dixon FJ. The renal response to immunological injury. In: Brenner BM, Rector FC, eds. The Kidney. Philadelphia, Saunders pp1234–1350, 1981.
3. Steblay RW. Glomerulonephritis induced in sheep by injections of heterologous glomerular basement membrane and Freund's complete adjuvant. J Exp Med **116**:253–272, 1962.
4. Steblay RW. Anti-glomerular basement membrane glomerulonephritis. Amer J Pathol **96**:875–878, 1979.
5. Jeraj K, Michael AF, Fish AJ. Immunologic similarities between Goodpasture's and Steblay's antibodies. Clin Immunol Immunopathol **23**:408–413, 1982.
6. Jennings L, Roholt O, Pressman D, Blau M, Andres G, Brentjens J. Experimental anti-alveolar basement membrane antibody-mediated pneumonitis. I. The role of increased permeability of the alveolar capillary wall induced by oxygen. J Immunol **127**:129–134, 1981.
7. Bolton WK, Benton FR, Sturgill BC. Autoimmune glomerulotubular nephropathy in mice. Clin Exp Immunol. **33**:463–473, 1978.
8. Roman-Franco AA, Turiello M, Albini B, Ossi E, Andres G. Anti-basement membrane antibody (A-BM Ab) and immune complexes (IC) in rabbits injected with mercuric chloride ($HgCl_2$). Kidney Int **10**:549, 1976.
9. Sapin C, Druet E, Druet P. Induction of anti-glomerular basement membrane antibodies in the Brown-Norway rat by mercuric chloride. Clin Exp Immunol **28**:173–179, 1977.
10. Druet P, Druet E, Potdevin F, Sapin C. Immune type glomerulonephritis induced by $HgCl_2$ in the Brown Norway rat. Ann Immunol (Inst Pasteur) **129C**:777, 1978.
11. Druet E, Sapin C, Gunther E, Feingold N, Druet P. Mercuric chloride-induced anti-glomerular basement membrane antibodies. Eur J Immunol **7**:348–351, 1977.
12. Hirsch F, Couderc J, Sapin C, Fournie G, Druet P. Polyclonal effect of $HgCl_2$ in the rat, its possible role in an experimental autoimmune disease. Eur J Immunol **12**:620–625, 1982.
13. Weening JJ, Hoedemaeker J, Bakker WW. Immunoregulation and anti-nuclear antibodies in mercury-induced glomerulopathy in the rat. Clin Exp Immunol **45**:64–71, 1981.
14. Roman-Franco AA, Turiello M, Albini B, Ossi E, Milgrom F, Andres GA. Anti-basement membrane antibodies and antigen–antibody complexes in rabbits injected with mercuric chloride. Clin Immunol Immunopathol **9**:464–481, 1978.
15. Banks KL, Henson JB. Immunologically-mediated glomerulonephritis of horses. II. Antiglomerular basement membrane antibody and other mechanisms in spontaneous disease. Lab Invest **26**:708–715, 1972.
16. Lerner R, Glassock RJ, Dixon FJ. The role of anti-glomerular basement membrane antibody in the pathogenesis of human glomerulonephritis. J Exp Med **126**:989–1004, 1967.
17. Yoshioka K, Kleppel M, Price RG, Michael AF, Fish AJ. Characterization of Goodpasture (GP) antigen(s) by high resolution two-dimensional electrophoresis. Amer Soc Nephrol p84A, 1983 (abstr).
18. Wieslander J. Glomerular Basement Membrane Antigens and Goodpasture's Syndrome. Thesis, University of Lund, 1983.
19. Sisson S, Dysart NK, Fish AJ, Vernier RL. Localization of the Goodpasture antigen by immunoelectron microscopy. Clin Immunol Immunopathol **23**:414–429, 1982.
20. Wilson CB, Dixon FJ. Anti-glomerular basement membrane antibody-induced glomerulonephritis. Kidney Int **3**:74–89, 1973.
21. Wilson CB, Dixon FJ. Renal injury from immune reactions involving antigens in or of the kidney. In: Brenner BM, Stein JH, eds. Immunologic Mechanisms of Renal Disease, Contemporary Issues in Nephrology. New York, Churchill Livingstone, Vol 3:p35, 1979.
22. Heymann W, Hackel DB, Harwood S, Wilson SGF, Hunter JLP. Production of nephrotic syndrome in rat by Freund's adjuvant and rat kidney suspension. Proc Soc Exp Biol Med **100**:660–664, 1959.
23. Edgington TS, Glassock RJ, Dixon FJ. Autologous immune complex nephritis induced with renal tubular antigens. I. Identification and isolation of the pathogenetic antigen. J Exp Med **127**:555–572, 1968.
24. Kerjaschki D, Sacktor B, Reiss U, Farquhar MG. Microdomains of distinctive glycoprotein composition in the kidney proximal tubule brush border. J Cell Biol **97**:178a, 1983 (abstr).
25. Sugisaki T, Klassen J, Andres GA, Milgrom F, McCluskey RT. Passive transfer of Heymann nephritis with serum. Kidney Int **3**:66–73, 1973.
26. Barabas AZ, Lannigan R. Induction of autologous immune complex glomerulonephritis in the rat by intravenous injection of heterologous anti-rat kidney tubular antibody. I. Production of chronic progressive immune complex glomerulonephritis. Brit J Exp Pathol **55**:47–55, 1974.
27. Van Damme BJC, Fleuren GJ, Bakker WW, Vernier RL, Hoedemaeker PhJ. Experimental glomerulonephritis in the rat induced by antibodies directed against tubular antigens. Lab Invest **38**:502–509, 1978.
28. Couser WG, Steinmuller DR, Stilmant MM, Salant DJ, Lowenstein LM. Experimental glomerulonephritis in the isolated perfused rat kidney. J Clin Invest **62**:1275–1287, 1978.
29. Stenglein B, Thoenes GH, Günther E. Genetic control of susceptibility to autologous immune complex glomerulonephritis in inbred rat strains. Clin Exp Immunol **33**:88–94, 1978.
30. Douglas MFS, Rabideau D, Schwartz MM, Lewis EJ.

Evidence of autologous immune-complex nephritis. N Engl J Med **305**:1326–1329, 1981.
31. Steblay RW, Rudofsky U. Renal tubular disease and autoantibodies against tubular basement membrane induced in guinea pigs. J Immunol **107**:589–594, 1971.
32. Hyman LR, Colvin RB, Steinberg AD. Immunopathogenesis of autoimmune tubulo-interstitial nephritis. I. Demonstration of different susceptibility in strain II and strain XIII guinea pigs. J Immunol **116**:327–335, 1976.
33. Hall CL, Colvin RB, Carey K, McCluskey RT. Passive transfer of autoimmune disease with isologous IgG_1 and IgG_2 antibodies to the tubular basement membrane in strain XIII guinea pigs. J Exp Med **146**:1246–1260, 1977.
34. Brown AC, Carey K, Colvin RB. Inhibition of autoimmune tubulointerstitial nephritis in guinea pigs by heterologous antisera containing anti-idiotype antibodies. J Immunol **123**:2102–2107, 1979.
35. Sugisaki T, Klassen J, Milgrom F, Andres GA, McCluskey RT. Immunologic study of an autoimmune tubular and interstitial renal disease in Brown Norway rats. Lab Invest **28**:658–671, 1973.
36. Lehman DH, Wilson CB, Dixon FJ. Interstitial nephritis in rats immunized with heterologous tubular basement membrane. Kidney Int **5**:187–195, 1974.
37. Zanetti M, Wilson CB. Analysis of anti-tubular basement membrane (TBM) antibodies (Ab) in Brown Norway (BN) rats. Kidney Int **21**:208, 1982 (abstr).
38. Andres GA, McCluskey RT. Tubular and interstitial renal disease due to immunologic mechanisms. Kidney Int **7**:271–289, 1975.
39. Lehman DH, Lee S, Wilson CB, Dixon FJ. Induction of antitubular basement membrane antibodies in rats by renal transplantation. Transplantation **17**:429–455, 1974.
40. Hart DNJ, Fabre JW. Kidney-specific alloantigen system in the rat. Characterization and role in transplantation. J Exp Med **151**:651–666, 1980.
41. Andres G, Brentjens J, Kohli R, Anthone R, Anthone S, Baliah T, Montes M, Mookerjee BK, Prezyna A, Sepulveda M, Venuto R, Elwood C. Histology of human tubulo-interstitial nephritis associated with antibodies to renal basement membranes. Kidney Int **13**:480–491, 1978.
42. Noble B, Mendrick DL, Brentjens JR, Andres G. Antibody mediated injury in proximal tubules in the rat kidney induced by passive transfer of homologous anti-brush border serum. Clin Immunol Immunopathol **19**:289–301, 1981.
43. Hoyer JR, Sisson SP, Vernier RL. Tamm–Horsfall glycoprotein. Ultrastructural immunoperoxidase localization in rat kidney. Lab Invest **41**:168–171, 1979.
44. Hoyer JR. Tubulointerstitial immune complex nephritis in rats immunized with Tamm–Horsfall protein. Kidney Int **17**:284–292, 1980.
45. Paul LC, Stuffers-Heiman M, van Es LA, de Graeff J. Antibodies directed against brush border antigens of proximal convoluted tubules in renal allograft recipients. Clin Immunol Immunopathol **14**:238–243, 1979.
46. Zager RA, Cotran RS, Hoyer JR. Pathologic localization of Tamm–Horsfall protein in interstitial deposits in renal disease. Lab Invest **38**:52–57, 1978.
47. Resnick JS, Sisson S, Vernier RL. Tamm–Horsfall protein. Abnormal localization in renal disease. Lab Invest **38**:550–555, 1978.
48. Lewis RM, Armstrong MYK, André-Schwartz J, Muftuoglu A, Beldotti L, Schwartz RS. Chronic allogeneic disease. I. Development of glomerulonephritis. J Exp Med **128**:653–680, 1968.
49. Kano K, Beldotti L, Milgrom F, Schwartz RS. Glomerulonephritis in the graft-vs-host reaction: Serologic demonstration of anti-host antibodies. J Immunol **112**:410–412, 1974.
50. Rolink AG, Gleichmann H, Gleichmann E. Diseases caused by reactions of T lymphocytes to incompatible structures of the major hystocompatibility complex. J Immunol **130**:209–215, 1983.
51. Hard RC, Moncure CW, Still WJS. Renal lesions with organized deposits and lipid as part of the host versus graft syndrome in parent/F_1 mouse chimeras. Lab Invest **28**:468–476, 1973.
52. Goldman M, Feng H-M, Engers H, Hochman A, Louis J, Lambert P-H. Autoimmunity and immune complex disease after neonatal induction of transplantation tolerance in mice. J Immunol **131**:251–258, 1983.
53. Weigle WO, Nakamura RM. Perpetuation of autoimmune thyroiditis and production of secondary renal lesions following periodic injections of aqueous preparations of altered thyroglobulin. Clin Exp Immunol **4**:645–657, 1969.
54. Bigazzi PL, Kosuda L, Hsu KC, Andres GA. Immune complex orchitis in vasectomized rabbits. J Exp Med **143**:382–404, 1976.
55. Bariety J, Druet P, Laliberte F, Sapin C. Glomerulonephritis with γ and B_1c globulin deposits induced in rats by mercuric chloride. Amer J Pathol **65**:293–302, 1971.
56. Houssin D, Druet E, Hinglais N, Verroust P, Grossetete J, Bariety J, Druet P. Glomerular and vascular IgG deposits in $HgCl_2$ nephritis: Role of circulating antibodies and of immune complexes. Clin Immunol Immunopathol **29**:167–180, 1983.
57. Lambert P-H, Dixon FJ. Pathogenesis of the glomerulonephritis of NZB/W mice. J Exp Med **127**: 507–522, 1968.
58. Seegal BC, Accinni L, Andres GA, Beiser SM, Christian CL, Erlanger BF, Hsu KC. Immunologic studies of autoimmune disease in NZB/NZW F_1 mice. I. Binding of fluorescein-labeled antinucleoside antibodies in lesions of lupus-like nephritis. J Exp Med **130**:203–216, 1969.
59. Izui S, Lambert P-H, Miescher PA. In vitro dem-

onstration of a particular affinity of glomerular basement membrane and collagen for DNA: A possible basis for a local formation of DNA–anti-DNA complexes in systemic lupus erythematosus. J Exp Med **144**:428–443, 1976.
60. Andrews BS, Eisenberg RA, Theofilopoulos AN, Izui S, Wilson CB, McConahey PJ, Murphy ED, Roths JB, Dixon FJ. Spontaneous murine lupus-like syndromes: Clinical and immunopathological manifestations in several strains. J Exp Med **148**:1198–1215, 1978.
61. Theofilopoulos AN, Prud'homme GJ, Fieser TM, Dixon FJ. B-Cell hyperactivity in murine lupus. I. Immunological abnormalities in lupus-prone strains and the activation of normal B cells. Immunol Today **4**:287–291, 1983.
62. Theofilopoulos AN, Prud'homme GJ, Fieser TM, Dixon FJ. B-Cell hyperactivity in murine lupus. II. Defects in response to and production of accessory signals in lupus-prone mice. Immunol Today **4**:317–319, 1983.
63. Koffler D, Schur P, Kunkel H. Immunological studies concerning the nephritis of systemic lupus erythematosus. J Exp Med **126**:607–624, 1967.
64. Andres G, Accinni L, Beiser S, Christian C, Cinotti C, Erlanger B, Hsu K, Seegal BC. Localization of fluorescein-labeled antinucleoside antibodies in glomeruli of patients with active systemic lupus erythematosus. J Clin Invest **49**:2106–2118, 1970.
65. Biesecker G, Katz SM, Koffler D. Renal localization of the membrane attack complex in systemic lupus erythematosus nephritis. J Exp Med **154**:1779–1794, 1981.
66. Cochrane CG, Koffler D. Immune complex disease in experimental animals and man. Adv Immunol **16**:185–264, 1973.
67. O'Regan S, Fong JSC, Kaplan BS, de Chadarevian JP, Lapointe N, Drummond KN. Thyroid antigen–antibody nephritis. Clin Immunol Immunopathol **6**:341–346, 1976.
68. Ploth DW, Fitz A, Snetzler D, Seidenfeld J, Wilson CB. Thyroglobulin–antithyroglobulin immune complex glomerulonephritis complicating radioiodine therapy. Clin Immunol Immunopathol **9**:327–334, 1978.
69. McIntosh RM, Griswold WR, Chernack WB, Williams G, Strauss J, Kaufman DB, Koss MN, McIntosh JR, Cohen R, Veill R III. Further studies on the nature, incidence, clinical diagnostic, prognostic, and immunopathologic significance of cryoproteins in renal disease. Q J Med **174**:285–307, 1975.
70. Meltzer M, Franklin EC, Elias K, McCluskey RT, Cooper N. Cryoglobulinemia—A clinical and laboratory study. II. Cryoglobulins with rheumatoid factor activity. Amer J Med **40**:837–856, 1966.
71. Goldman M, Rose LM, Hochmann A, Lambert P-H. Deposition of idiotype–antiidiotype immune complexes in renal glomeruli after polyclonal B cell activation. J Exp Med **155**:1385–1399, 1982.
72. Zanetti M, Wilson CB. Participation of auto-anti-idiotypes in immune complex glomerulonephritis in rabbits. J Immunol **131**:2781–2783, 1983.
73. Shulman HM, Sullivan KM, Weiden PL, McDonald GB, Striker GE, Sale GE, Hackman R, Tsoi M-S, Storb R, Thomas ED. Chronic graft-versus-host syndrome in man. Amer J Med **69**:204–217, 1980.
74. Keightley RG, Lawton AR, Cooper MD. Successful fetal liver transplantation in a child with severe combined immunodeficiency. Lancet **2**:850–853, 1975.
75. Klassen J, McCluskey RT, Milgrom F. Nonglomerular renal disease produced in rabbits by immunization with homologous kidney. Amer J Pathol **63**:333–350, 1971.
76. Klassen J, Milgrom F. Autoimmune concomitants of renal allografts. Transplant Proc **1**:605–608, 1969.
77. Klassen J, Milgrom F, McCluskey RT. Studies of the antigens involved in an immunologic renal tubular lesion in rabbits. Amer J Pathol **88**:135–141, 1977.
78. Brentjens J, Sepulveda M, Baliah T, Bentzel C, Erlanger B, Elwood C, Montes M, Hsu K, Andres G. Interstitial immune complex nephritis in patients with systemic lupus erythematosus. Kidney Int **7**:342–350, 1975.
79. Lehman DH, Wilson CB, Dixon FJ. Extraglomerular immunoglobulin deposits in human nephritis. Amer J Med **58**:765–786, 1975.
80. Andres GA, Accinni L, Hsu KC, Penn I, Porter KA, Randall JM, Seegal BC, Starzl TE. Human renal transplants III. Immunopathologic studies. Lab Invest **22**:588, 1970.

PROCEEDINGS OF THE SOCIETY FOR EXPERIMENTAL BIOLOGY AND MEDICINE **176,** 238–242 (1984)

Inhibition of Ovulation in Rats with Epostane, an Inhibitor of 3β-Hydroxysteroid Dehydrogenase (41865)

B. W. SNYDER, G. D. BEECHAM, AND H. P. SCHANE

Sterling–Winthrop Research Institute, Rensselaer, New York 12144

Abstract. Epostane (Win 32729), an inhibitor of the 3β-hydroxysteroid dehydrogenase enzyme system, inhibited both spontaneous and pregnant mare's serum/human chorionic gonadotropin-induced ovulation in rats. When administered on the morning of proestrus, the drug blocked pregnancy in females that were inseminated that evening. The blockage of pregnancy occurred at a dose of 200 mg/kg but not at 50 mg/kg. Similarly, when administered on the morning of proestrus at a dose of 200 mg/kg, epostane inhibited the appearance of ova in the oviducts the next day. In gonadotropin-primed immature rats, epostane inhibited ovulation in a dose-related fashion with an ED_{50} between 25 and 50 mg/kg. The drug also decreased plasma progesterone levels in these animals. The inhibitory effect of epostane on gonadotropin-stimulated ovulation was reversed by injections of progesterone at a total daily dose of 6.25 mg/rat or greater. These results support the contention that steroidogenesis, specifically progesterone synthesis, is a prerequisite to ovulation.

A preovulatory rise in progesterone levels has been observed during the proestrous phase of the rat estrous cycle (1) and several lines of evidence indicate that this rise is necessary for the ensuing ovulation that occurs that night. For example, Lipner and Greep (2) showed that aminoglutethimide and cyanoketone, drugs that block the synthetic pathway to progesterone, prevented ovulation in immature rats injected with gonadotropins. Further evidence in support of a role for progesterone in the ovulatory process comes from the experiments of Mori *et al.* (3) who demonstrated that injection of an antiserum directed against progesterone inhibited the induction of ovulation in immature rats. Thus, agents that block either the synthesis or action of progesterone inhibit ovulation in rats.

Luteinizing hormone (LH) is also known to play a role in the ovulatory process. Rondell (4, 5) demonstrated that follicular wall tissue underwent increases in distensibility immediately before rupture of the follicle and this effect could be duplicated in follicular strips maintained in tissue culture by treatment with either LH or progesterone; cyanoketone was shown to inhibit the increased distensibility induced by LH but not by progesterone. Takahashi *et al.* (6) presented evidence for the occurrence of a two-step process on the afternoon of proestrus that leads to ovulation; the first step requires a short exposure to LH and the second an exposure to progesterone. These studies are consistent with the concept that the ovulatory surge of LH stimulates progesterone production which, in turn, activates the ovulatory process.

In contrast, Bullock and Kappauf (7) claimed to have dissociated the preovulatory rise of progesterone from ovulation by administration of cyanoketone or aminoglutethimide in doses that blocked one of these physiological events but not the other. These authors concluded that follicular changes leading to ovulation were not initiated by steroidogenesis.

In this paper, we examine the ability of a new inhibitor of the 3β-hydroxysteroid dehydrogenase enzyme system, epostane [Win 32729, (4α,5α,17β)-4,5-epoxy-3,17-dihydroxy-4,17-dimethylandrost-2-ene-2-carbonitrile], to block ovulation in mature rats and gonadotropin-stimulated immature rats. The structure of epostane is shown in Fig. 1. The compound has recently been shown to lower plasma progesterone levels and terminate pregnancy in rats and rhesus monkeys (8).

Materials and Methods. *Animal procedures.* Rats used in these experiments were of the Sprague–Dawley strain obtained from Taconic Farm Breeding Laboratories, Inc., Germantown, New York. They were housed in an air-conditioned room with a 12-hr light:dark

0037-9727/84 $1.50

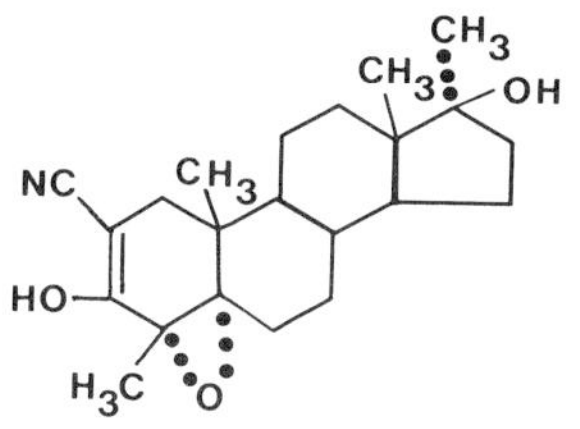

FIG. 1. Structure of epostane.

schedule. Rat chow and water were provided *ad libitum.*

Mature rats to be used for mating were subjected to daily vaginal smears. Animals with two consecutive 4-day cycles were administered vehicle or epostane, orally, on the morning of proestrus of the third cycle. After medication, each rat was caged overnight with a proven breeding male. The following day (expected day of estrus), the female rats were separated from the males and vaginal smears were made and examined microscopically for the presence of sperm. Nine days after mating, the animals were killed with an overdose of sodium pentobarbital and their uteri excised and examined for evidence of implantation.

Ovulation was assessed in regularly cycling mature female rats that were treated with vehicle or drug by sacrificing the animals on the expected day of ovulation and excising their oviducts for inspection. The oviducts were gently pressed between two glass slides and the ova were visualized and counted with the aid of a dissecting microscope (40×).

Immature female rats approximately 22 days of age were induced to ovulate with a subcutaneous injection of 12.5 IU pregnant mare's serum (PMS) followed 48 hr later by an intraperitoneal injection of 20 IU human chorionic gonadotropin (HCG). Oral administration of epostane or vehicle occurred at the time of HCG medication. In one experiment progesterone was injected subcutaneously in equally divided doses 6 hr prior to and at the time of HCG and drug administration. The total daily dose of progesterone administered in these experiments ranged from 1.56 to 50 mg/rat.

Blood samples for plasma progesterone determinations were obtained by cardiac puncture from unanesthetized rats. Progesterone levels were measured by radioimmunoassay as supplied by Pantex Inc. (Method 037). The sensitivity of the assay was 0.2 ng/ml and the coefficient of variation was 6.8% within an assay and 11.6% between assays. The cross-reactivities of related steroids to the progesterone antibody were (progesterone equals 100%): desoxycorticosterone, 1.5%; 17α-hydroxyprogesterone, 0.18%; pregnenolone, 17-hydroxypregnenolone, and corticosterone, <0.01%. The assay of increasing volumes of serum remained parallel to the standard.

Solutions. PMS and HCG (Sigma Chemical Co., St. Louis, Mo.) were diluted with 1% bovine serum albumin (Sigma) in saline to an injectable volume of 0.1 ml/rat. Epostane was prepared as a solution/suspension in absolute ethanol:cottonseed oil (1:9 v/v) and administered orally (po) at a volume of 0.5 ml/rat in immature rats and 1.0 ml/100 g in mature rats. Progesterone (Sigma) was prepared as a solution/suspension in absolute ethanol:-cottonseed oil (1:9 v/v) and administered subcutaneously (sc) at a volume of 0.2 ml/rat.

Statistical evaluation. Comparisons between treatment and control values were made using Fisher's exact test except for the data in Table V where Student's t test was used.

Results. Table I illustrates the effect of epostane when administered orally to regularly cycling female rats on the morning of proestrus. One hundred percent of the mated animals treated with either vehicle alone or the low dose of epostane (50 mg/kg) were pregnant when autopsied 9 days later. In contrast, none of the mated animals treated with 200 mg/kg of epostane had implantation or resorption sites 9 days after mating. Epostane did not adversely affect mating success since the percentage of females that mated did not differ between the high drug dose (200 mg/kg) group and the vehicle control group.

TABLE I. EFFECT OF EPOSTANE ON PREGNANCY IN MATURE RATS

Epostane (mg/kg po)	Proportion mating (%)	No. pregnant at autopsy	Sites/ uterus[a]
0	15/26 (58)	15/15	11.9 ± 0.3
50	11/13 (85)	11/11	10.6 ± 0.8
200	6/14 (43)	0/6[b]	0

[a] Mean ± SE.
[b] $P < 0.01$ compared to the vehicle control.

To investigate the possibility that epostane may be inhibiting a postovulatory event (e.g., implantation), a direct measurement of ovulation was employed. The oviducts of mature regularly cycling rats were excised and examined for the presence of tubal ova 24 hr after proestrus treatment with epostane or vehicle. Epostane did not alter the proportion of animals having cornified vaginal smears on the expected day of estrus. Ova were not observed in females treated with epostane (200 mg/kg), whereas 9 of 14 vehicle-treated animals ovulated (Table II).

An experiment was performed to determine whether the ovulation inhibition effect of epostane was due to an inhibition of gonadotropin secretion. Immature female rats were induced to ovulate with injections of PMS followed 24 hr later by concomitant administration of HCG and either epostane or vehicle. The results of this experiment, shown in Table III, illustrate that epostane inhibited the number of rats ovulating in a dose-related fashion. A dose of 50 mg/kg significantly reduced the number of rats that ovulated while the 100 and 200 mg/kg doses of epostane inhibited ovulation in all the animals treated. Doses of less than 50 mg/kg were not effective in inhibiting ovulation.

Progesterone was administered to determine whether it could reverse the inhibition of ovulation observed after treatment with epostane. Progesterone was injected subcutaneously at various doses into gonadotropin-primed immature female rats given an oral medication of epostane at 50 mg/kg. Progesterone injected twice on the same day as oral administration of epostane overcame the inhibition of ovulation in a dose-related fashion (Table IV). Reversal of epostane inhibition of ovulation occurred at a total progesterone dose of 6.25 mg/rat or greater, whereas a lower dose of 1.56 mg/rat was ineffective in blocking the epostane effect.

The effect of epostane on circulating progesterone levels is presented in Table V. Plasma samples for progesterone determination were obtained 4 hr after oral administration of epostane. Dose levels of drug as low as 12.5 mg/kg lowered plasma progesterone significantly below vehicle control levels even though ovulation was not inhibited at this dose. Epostane at doses of 25 mg/kg and greater inhibited ovulation as well as decreased plasma progesterone concentrations.

Discussion. This study supports the concept that steroidogenesis is a prerequisite for the process of ovulation since an agent that interfered with the synthesis of steroids also blocked ovulation. Epostane blocked ovulation in cycling rats as evidenced by inhibition

TABLE II. EFFECT OF EPOSTANE ON SPONTANEOUS OVULATION IN THE MATURE RAT

Epostane (mg/kg po)	Proportion ovulating	Ova/rat[a]
0	9/14	9.0 ± 0.8
200	0/17[b]	0

[a] Mean ± SE.
[b] $P < 0.001$ compared to vehicle control.

TABLE III. DOSE-RELATED EFFECT OF EPOSTANE ON OVULATION IN THE GONADOTROPIN-PRIMED IMMATURE RAT

Epostane (mg/kg po)	Proportion ovulating	No. of ova/ ovulatory rat[a]
0	18/20	13.8 ± 2.3
12.5	10/10	9.8 ± 1.8
25.0	10/10	19.4 ± 3.4
50.0	2/20[b]	2.0 ± 1.0
100.0	0/10	—
200.0	0/10	—

[a] Mean ± SE.
[b] $P < 0.001$ compared to vehicle control.

TABLE IV. EFFECT OF EPOSTANE ON OVULATION IN GONADOTROPIN-PRIMED AND PROGESTERONE-SUPPLEMENTED IMMATURE RATS

Treatment			
Epostane (mg/kg po)	Total daily progesterone (mg/rat sc)	Proportion ovulating	Ova/ ovulatory rat[a]
0	0	16/20	27.9 ± 3.0
50	0	0/20	0
50	1.56	0/10	0
50	6.25	8/10	13.4 ± 3.7
50	12.5	8/10	16.3 ± 4.4
50	25	7/10	12.3 ± 3.8
50	50	19/20	28.4 ± 3.3
0	50	7/9	25.9 ± 4.6

[a] Mean ± SE.

TABLE V. EFFECT OF EPOSTANE ON OVULATION AND PROGESTERONE PLASMA CONCENTRATION IN THE GONADOTROPIN-PRIMED IMMATURE RAT

Epostane (mg/kg po)	Proportion ovulating (%)	Ova/ovulating rat (mean ± SE)	Plasma progesterone[a] (ng/ml)	n[b]
0	24/25 (96)	27.8 ± 2.7	33.3 ± 2.4	13
12.5	9/10 (90)	36.0 ± 4.0	4.6 ± 0.8[c]	6
25	5/24 (21)	11.4 ± 3.5	2.8 ± 0.3	14
50	2/10 (20)	13.0 ± 12.0	1.6 ± 0.2	6
100	0/15 (0)	—	1.5 ± 0.2	8
200	0/15 (0)	—	1.4 ± 0.2	7

[a] Mean ± SE.
[b] No. of rats randomly chosen for progesterone determination.
[c] $P < 0.001$ compared to the vehicle control.

of pregnancy in mated animals and more specifically by lack of ova in the oviducts on the morning of estrus. A direct effect of epostane on the ovary is likely since the drug also inhibited the induction of ovulation in immature animals treated with PMS and HCG.

Epostane has been shown to inhibit the 3β-hydroxysteroid dehydrogenase enzyme system. *In vitro* preparations of this enzyme from rat adrenal (8) and human placenta (9) were competitively inhibited by epostane. When administered orally, epostane terminated pregnancy in rats and rhesus monkeys and this effect was overcome by injections of progesterone (8). In rats epostane was equipotent as an inhibitor of adrenal and ovarian steroidogenesis, but in rhesus monkeys the drug interrupted pregnancy at doses that did not inhibit adrenal steroidogenesis (8). Epostane has no apparent hormonal activity in a number of standard test systems.

In this study, epostane sharply reduced circulating progesterone levels in rats injected with PMS and HCG and, at the same time, inhibited ovulation. Progesterone injections reversed the inhibitory effects of epostane on ovulation. Lipner and Greep (2) used cyanoketone to inhibit ovulation but were unable to override this inhibition with a single injection of 4 mg progesterone. The failure to overcome the inhibitory effects of cyanoketone on ovulation may have been due to administration of insufficient amounts of progesterone since in the present study, two successive injections of 3.1 mg of progesterone were required to restore the proportion of ovulating animals to normal. Even higher doses were required to return the number of ova shed per rat to the control levels. Perhaps high doses of exogenous progesterone are required to raise intrafollicular concentrations to the levels that are needed for ovulation.

Bullock and Kappauf (7) claimed to have disassociated the effects of cyanoketone and aminoglutethimide on ovulation and steroidogenesis. By administering the appropriate dose, they showed that aminoglutethimide decreased HCG-elevated progesterone levels without inhibiting ovulation. In contrast, cyanoketone was shown to partially block ovulation without having a significant effect on progesterone levels. In this study, we observed that low doses of epostane also lowered circulating progesterone levels without blocking ovulation (see Table V). However, we do not believe that these observations preclude the involvement of progesterone in the ovulatory process. One possibility is that progesterone levels within the follicle may differ significantly from levels measured peripherally. Second, progesterone levels in this study, as well as the Bullock and Kappauf (7) study, were measured at only a single time point after drug administration and it is possible that, at a later critical time point, progesterone levels had increased sufficiently to facilitate ovulation.

A preovulatory increase in progesterone has been observed in primates but the significance of this rise to ovulation is not clear. Plasma progesterone levels were shown to rise abruptly on the day prior to ovulation in rhesus monkeys (10, 11) and about 12 hr before the midcycle LH surge in humans (12, 13). The preovulatory progesterone rise in women has been shown to increase the duration of the midcycle LH surge (14), an effect that could facilitate ovulation. It is not known whether the preovulatory rise of progesterone in primates facilitates ovulation by a direct effect on the ovary. These observations suggest that studies are warranted to determine whether epostane will inhibit ovulation in primates.

We thank J. L. Houghtling for expert technical assistance in the execution of these studies and N. L. Valcik for typing assistance.

---

1. Hashimoto I, Hendricks DM, Anderson LL, Melampy RM. Progesterone and preg-4-ene-20α-ol-3-one in ovarian venous blood during various reproductive states in the rat. Endocrinology **82**:333–341, 1968.
2. Lipner H, Greep RO. Inhibition of steroidogenesis at various sites in the biosynthetic pathway in relation to induced ovulation. Endocrinology **88**:602–607, 1971.
3. Mori T, Suzuki A, Nishimura T, Kambegawa A. Inhibition of ovulation in immature rats by anti-progesterone antiserum. J Endocrinol **73**:185–186, 1977.
4. Rondell P. Follicular processes in ovulation. Fed Proc **29**:1875–1879, 1970.
5. Rondell P. Role of steroid synthesis in the process of ovulation. Biol Reprod **10**:199–215, 1974.
6. Takahashi M, Ford JJ, Yoshinaga K, Greep RO. Induction of ovulation in hypophysectomized rats by progesterone. Endocrinology **95**:1322–1326, 1974.
7. Bullock DW, Kappauf BH. Dissociation of gonadotropin-induced ovulation and steroidogenesis in immature rats. Endocrinology **92**:1625–1628, 1973.
8. Creange JE, Anzalone AJ, Potts GO, Schane HP. Win 32729, a new, potent interceptive agent in rats and rhesus monkeys. Contraception **24**:289–299, 1981.
9. Rabe T, Kiesel L, Kellermann J, Weidenhammer K, Maletz-Kehry W, Runnebaum B. Inhibition of human placental progesterone synthesis by synthetic steroids in vitro. Acta Endocrinol **99**(Suppl. 246):24, 1982.
10. Johansson EDB, Neill JD, Knobil E. Periovulatory progesterone concentration in the peripheral plasma of the rhesus monkey with a methodologic note on the detection of ovulation. Endocrinology **82**:143–148, 1968.
11. Resko JA, Koering MJ, Goy RW, Phoenix CH. Preovulatory progestins: Observations on their source in rhesus monkeys. J Clin Endocrinol Metab **41**:120–125, 1975.
12. Hoff JD, Quigley ME, Yen SSC. Hormonal dynamics at midcycle: A reevaluation. J Clin Endocrinol Metab **57**:792–796, 1983.
13. Laborde N, Carril M, Cheviakoff S, Croxatto HD, Pedroza E, Rosner JM. The secretion of progesterone during the periovulatory period in women with certified ovulation. J Clin Endocrinol Metab **43**:1157–1163, 1976.
14. Liu JH, Yen SSC. Induction of midcycle gonadotropin surge by ovarian steroids in women: a critical evaluation. J Clin Endocrinol Metab **57**:797–802, 1983.

Received January 12, 1984. P.S.E.B.M. 1984, Vol. 176.
Accepted March 9, 1984.

PROCEEDINGS OF THE SOCIETY FOR EXPERIMENTAL BIOLOGY AND MEDICINE **176**, 243–248 (1984)

Effects of Immunization of Heifers against Estradiol on Growth, Reproductive Traits, and Carcass Characteristics (41866)

T. WISE AND C. FERRELL

U.S. Department of Agriculture,[1] Agricultural Research Service, U.S. Meat Animal Research Center, P.O. Box 166, Clay Center, Nebraska 68933

Abstract. An experiment was performed to evaluate the effects of active immunization of heifers against estradiol on feedlot performance (growth and efficiency), carcass characteristics, and reproductive functions. Seventy-two crossbred heifers were divided into four equal treatment groups consisting of controls, ovariectomized heifers, and heifers actively immunized against keyhole limpet–estradiol antigen and bovine serum albumin–estradiol antigen. Heifers were fed *ad libitum* for 170 days. Both groups of heifers immunized against estradiol had higher ($P < 0.05$) average daily gains than controls. Heifers immunized against bovine serum albumin–estradiol had increased feed efficiency ($P < 0.05$) over controls. Ovariectomized heifers did not perform at levels sufficient to compensate for the initial setback from surgery. No differences were noted in carcass grade, quality, or concentration of water, fat, or protein. Uterine weights were increased in estrogen-immunized animals but were not significantly greater than controls. Ovarian weights and numbers of large follicles (>9 mm diam) in immunized animals were significantly greater than in controls. Twenty-eight percent of the animals ($n = 5$) in the bovine serum albumin–estradiol-immunized group had cystic follicles (>20 mm diam) and 50% ($n = 9$) of this group had no detectable corpus luteum. Low titer (1:100) systemic binding of estrogens may act as a steroid reservoir in which systemic estrogen clearance is decreased and availability to target tissues is increased.

Estrogens and related estrogenic compounds (diethylstilbestrol) have been proven to be excellent anabolic growth promotants for ruminants. These compounds improve both growth rate and feed conversion (1–3). The administration of diethylstilbestrol to steers in the feedlot increases the carcass protein and moisture content, and retail yield (2, 3). Growth rate and feed conversion are generally lower for heifers than steers.

Estrogen levels in animals immunized against estrogens are considerably elevated (4–6) and may produce an *in vivo* estrogenic growth effect depending on how much of the bound estrogen is available to target tissue. The goals of this experiment were to evaluate the effects of active immunization against estradiol on (1) feedlot performance, (2) reproductive effects, and (3) carcass characteristics in heifers.

Materials and Methods. *Animals and treatments.* Seventy-two crossbred heifers were randomized by breed and weight to four groups: Group I ($n = 18$) contained controls injected with 1 ml saline (9 g NaCl/liter); Group II ($n = 18$) contained ovariectomized animals injected with 1 ml saline; Group III ($n = 18$) animals were immunized against 1,3,5,(10)-estratrien-3,17β-diol-6-one carboxymethoxime (Steraloids, Inc., Wilton, N.H.) conjugated to keyhole limpet hemocyanin (KLH; Calbiochem, La Jolla, Calif.); and Group IV ($n = 18$) animals were immunized against 1,3,5,(10)-estratrien-3,17β-diol-6-one carboxymethoxime conjugated to bovine serum albumin (BSA). Steroids were coupled to the carrier protein (KLH or BSA) by the carbodiimide method of Goodfriend *et al.* (7).

Animals were injected along the tailhead with 5 mg antigen for Group III and 1 mg of antigen for Group IV in 1 ml of Freund's complete adjuvant:saline (1:1 v/v) and 0.5 ml each of diphtheria, tetanus, and pertussis toxoids (Wyeth Lab, Marietta, Pa.). Booster injections were given in Freund's incomplete adjuvant 60 and 90 days after the initial injection. Animals were weighed at the time of each injection.

[1] Mention of trade names or companies does not constitute an implied warranty or endorsement by the U.S. Department of Agriculture or the authors.

0037-9727/84 $1.50

Serum obtained at slaughter was submitted to dextran–charcoal radioassay to measure the estradiol binding titer (8). Aliquots of diluted serum (1:100, 1:1000 in phosphate-buffered saline) were incubated with 20,000 dpm of [1,2,6,7,16,17-^{3}H]estradiol-17β (sp act 137 Ci/mmole; New England Nuclear Corp., Boston, Mass.). At the time of slaughter, the reproductive tract was removed; then ovarian, corpora luteal, and uterine weights were recorded. Ovarian surface follicles were counted and divided into three size groups: small ($\leq$4 mm diam), medium (5–8 mm diam), and large (>9 mm diam).

Feeding regime and carcass analysis. Six heifers within each treatment were randomly assigned to each of three pens (total of 12 pens) and fed the diet indicated in Table I *ad libitum* for 170 days. Mean (±SE) heifer age at the initiation of the study was 307 ± 1.2 days (range 288–324). Heifers were weighed on two consecutive days at the beginning and end of the study and at 28-day intervals during the study. Feed samples were taken and frozen daily throughout the diet study, composited for each 28-day period, and subsequently analyzed for dry matter and crude protein. Weights of orts were recorded weekly. Heifers were slaughtered at the research center abattoir at the end of the study. Hot carcass weight was obtained. Fat thickness at the 12th rib and longissimus muscle area were determined; marbling score and percentage kidney, heart, and pelvic (KHP) fat were subjectively evaluated approximately 24 hr after slaughter.

TABLE I. DIET DRY MATTER COMPOSITION

Ingredient	Percentage of diet dry matter[a]
Corn silage	25.00
High moisture corn	71.67
Supplement	3.33
Urea	30.63
Dicalcium phosphate	15.63
Limestone	36.34
Salt	15.00
Chelated trace mineral	0.60
Vitamins A, D, and E[b]	1.80

[a] Diet contains 2.99 Mcal ME/kg, 12.1% crude protein, 0.61% calcium, and 0.40% phosphorus.

[b] Vitamin A, D, and E supplements contained 2.65 g vitamin A, 22 mg vitamin D, and 88 g vitamin E per kilogram.

Carcass water, fat, and protein concentrations were estimated from fat thickness, longissimus area, marbling score, and KHP fat (9).

Statistical analysis. Data were analyzed by analysis of variance and χ^2 to determine effects of treatment. When analysis of variance indicated differences, means were compared by Student's t test. Feed intake and efficiency of feed conversion were calculated on a pen basis (n = 6/pen; 3 pens/treatment). Linear and quadratic relationships between weight and time, cumulative feed intake and time, and weight and cumulative feed intake were evaluated by least-squares procedures.

Results. *Antibody response.* The pattern of anti-estradiol titer increased in immunized animals to 1:10 at the 60-day booster and approached a 1:100 dilution by the 90-day booster. At slaughter time, the titer of anti-estradiol was 1:100 (2–90% binding) in all immunized animals. Animals immunized against the BSA–estradiol antigen had a final average serum binding of 44% at 1:100 and those immunized against KLH–estradiol bound 31% (1:100). Control and ovariectomized animals bound less than 1% at 1:100 dilution. The cross-reactivity for estrone was 5% for the KLH–estradiol antigen and less than 1% for the BSA–estradiol antigen (determined by mass of steroid required for 50% displacement of [^{3}H]estradiol).

Feedlot performance. Of the animals immunized against estradiol (KLH–estradiol and BSA–estradiol), 50% had average daily gains greater than 1 kg/day whereas only 14% of the controls reached this level. Animals immunized against the BSA–estradiol antigen had a higher average daily gain and feed efficiency over the 170-day feeding period than the other treatment groups and controls (Table II). Heifers immunized against the KLH–estradiol antigen had a higher average daily gain than controls (Group I) but efficiency (gain/feed intake) did not differ significantly. Animal variation is high in response both to the immunization procedure (titers developed) and to the possible growth effects from the sequestered estrogen. Many animals with low binding (1–2% at 1:100) had good average daily weight gains (1.2–1.3 kg/day) whereas others with 60–80% estradiol binding (1:100) gained less than 0.7 kg/day. Ovariectomized heifers gained weight at a similar rate as con-

TABLE II. PERFORMANCE CHARACTERISTICS OF CONTROL, OVARIECTOMIZED, AND IMMUNIZED CROSSBRED HEIFERS DURING A 170-DAY POSTWEANING FEEDING PERIOD

Trait	Group I (control)	Group II (ovariectomized)	Group III (KLH–estradiol)	Group IV (BSA–estradiol)	SE
Initial weight (kg)	304^{b}	278^{a}	296^{b}	296^{b}	2.2
Final weight (kg)	$446^{a,b}$	429^{a}	457^{b}	461^{b}	4.2
Daily gain (kg)	0.83^{a}	$0.88^{a,b}$	$0.95^{b,c}$	0.97^{c}	0.017
Dry matter intake (kg/day)	7.12	6.45	7.49	6.79	0.27
Gain/feed consumption (g/kg)	118^{a}	140^{b}	$126^{a,b}$	142^{b}	1.9

$^{a-c}$ Means within a row with different superscripts differ ($P < 0.05$).

trol heifers but were more efficient; final weights were lower due to the initial setback from the surgery. When initial weight was included as a covariate in the statistical model, final weight and average daily gain were significantly higher in Groups III and IV than in controls, and these values in ovariectomized heifers were intermediate between those of immunized and control heifers. When animals were adjusted for initial body weight, feed efficiency did not differ significantly among treatments but tended to be greater for heifers immunized against the BSA–estradiol antigen (144 g/kg) than for other heifers (128 g/kg; residual standard deviation = 11, error $df = 6$).

Figure 1 shows the regression of live weight on cumulative feed intake. These relationships were curvilinear ($P < 0.05$) for control and ovariectomized animals but linear for immunized animals, suggesting that efficiency decreased for the control and ovariectomized heifers but was constant for immunized heifers during the study. Not only were ovariectomized animals penalized at the beginning of the experiment from the surgery, but also apparently matured more rapidly than other heifers.

Carcass characteristics. Ovariectomized heifers had lower carcass weights and longissimus muscle areas than other heifers due to lower final weights in the feedlot (Table III). Ovariectomized heifers had greater ($P < 0.01$) marbling scores and tended ($P = 0.10$) to have more KHP fat than controls. No differences were noted in relation to estimated carcass water, fat, or protein concentrations among the four treatment groups. Ovariectomized heifers had greater ($P < 0.05$) marbling scores, higher concentrations of fat, and lower concentrations of water and protein than other heifers when carcass data were evaluated at

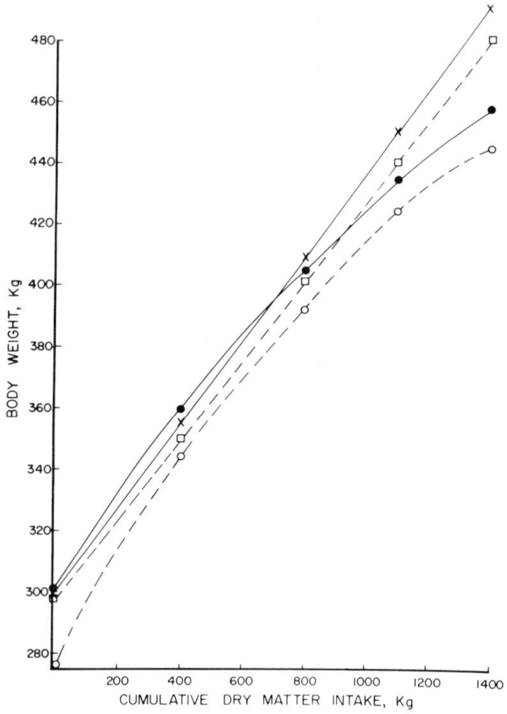

FIG. 1. Regression of live weight (kg) on cumulative dry feed intake (kg) for control (●), ovariectomized (○), BSA–estradiol-immunized (×), and KLH–estradiol-immunized (□) groups of heifers. Control ($Y = 301 + 0.16X - 0.000034X^2$, $r = 0.97$) and ovariectomized ($Y = 277 + 0.186X - 0.000047X^2$, $r = 0.98$) are quadratic ($P < 0.05$) whereas BSA–estradiol ($Y = 299 + 0.137X$, $r = 0.99$) and KLH–estradiol ($Y = 298 + 0.13X$, $r = 0.97$) are linear ($P < 0.05$).

TABLE III. CARCASS CHARACTERISTICS OF CONTROL, OVARIECTOMIZED, AND IMMUNIZED CROSSBRED HEIFERS

	Group I (control)	Group II (ovariectomized)	Group III (KLH–estradiol)	Group IV (BSA–estradiol)	SE
Carcass weight (kg)	282[b,c]	266[b]	289[c]	290[c]	3.5
Fat thickness (cm)	0.84	0.84	0.79	0.83	0.033
Adjusted fat thickness (cm)	0.78	0.76	0.73	0.76	0.030
Longissimus area (cm^2)	77.7[c]	72.2[b]	74.5[b,c]	76.5[c]	0.87
Kidney, heart, and pelvic fat	3.65[b]	3.88[b,c]	3.75[b,c]	3.92[c]	0.05
Marbling score[a]	4.10[b]	4.88[c]	4.36[b,c]	4.42[b,c]	0.11
Water (g/kg)	520	511	519	515	2.6
Fat (g/kg)	321	334	323	328	3.4
Protein (g/kg)	158	154	157	156	0.86

[a] Marbling score: 4.0 = small, 5.0 = modest.
[b,c] Means within a row with different superscripts differ ($P < 0.05$).

constant carcass weight by covariate analysis.

Reproductive effects. Differences in reproductive tissues at slaughter were monitored as a biological index of increased estrogens due to the binding antibodies. Uterine weights tended to be greater in immunized groups (Table IV) but were not significantly different from controls. Ovarian weight and numbers of large follicles on the ovary were significantly greater in controls than in the estradiol-immunized groups. Two animals in each estradiol-immunized group had double ovulations. Fifty percent ($n = 9$) of the BSA–estradiol group were acyclic as no corpora lutea were noted and 22% ($n = 5$) had cystic follicles (>20 mm diam). No differences were noted between the control and KLH–estradiol groups in relation to number of corpora lutea or cystic follicles.

Discussion. The increased growth rate and efficiency noted in animals immunized against estradiol may be related not only to the mitogenic effects estrogen has at the cellular level but also to augmentation by growth hormone. Although growth hormone relationships with improved gain and efficiency have not been consistent (10–12), increased growth hormone secretion has been accepted as the general mode of action by which estrogenic anabolic agents improve the rate of gain and feed con-

TABLE IV. REPRODUCTIVE TRAITS OF CONTROL, OVARIECTOMIZED, AND IMMUNIZED CROSSBRED HEIFERS

	Group I (control)	Group II (ovariectomized)	Group III (KLH–estradiol)	Group IV (BSA–estradiol)	SE
Uterus weight (g)	192[b]	55[a]	208[b]	211[b]	5.2
Ovary weight (g)	13.2[a]	—	20.6[b]	19.8[b]	1.3
No. corpus luteum	0.83[b]	—	0.96[b]	0.50[a]	0.08
No. large follicles (>9 mm diam)	1.7[a]	—	2.3[a,b]	2.7[b]	0.2
No. medium follicles (5–8 mm diam)	5.6	—	7.0	5.7	0.7
No. small follicles (≤4 mm diam)	39.0	—	50.0	52.0	4.2
No. cows with follicles >20 mm (cystic)	0.0[a]	—	1.0[a]	5.0[b]	0.03
Percentage estradiol serum binding at 1:100 dilution	0.39[a]	0.42[a]	31.0[b]	43.5[c]	2.4

[a–c] Means within a row with different superscripts differ ($P < 0.05$).

version of ruminants (3). Increased feed efficiency from anabolic steroids is thought to be due to increased cellular protein accretion and reduced turnover rates (13). A major effect of the anti-estradiol titers upon feedlot performance may be interpreted as an extended growth phase, whereas control and ovariectomized animals matured at a lower body weight (Fig. 1).

Since animals were in unknown stages of the estrous cycle throughout the study, systemic estrogens were not quantitated. Interpretation of blood estrogen concentrations and growth rate is difficult when the data are confounded with the stage of the estrous cycle. Uterine and ovarian weights (Group I, III, IV) provide a method of estimating estrogen activity on known target tissues (14, 15) and indicate that immunized animals have a greater availability of estrogens at target tissues. Animals given diethylstilbestrol have increased uterine weights (16–18) but not necessarily ovarian weights (16, 18). The increased ovarian weights in immunized animals may indicate that the mechanism of action of the animal's own estrogen bound to antibodies may not be exactly the same as that of exogenously administered estrogenic growth stimulants. Increased ovarian function from estrogen immunization has been observed in ewes by Scaramuzzi *et al.* (6). The correlation of ovarian and uterine weights with average daily gain ($r = 0.39$ and 0.21; $P < 0.05$, respectively) may indicate that estrogen affected other body tissues as well as reproductive tissues.

Changes in sex-binding globulins can regulate steroid clearance because hepatic clearance of gonadal steroids is proportional to the extent bound (19). The rate of steroid clearance and metabolism to more polar metabolites is inhibited in immunized animals (20). The mode of action by which immunization against estradiol increases animal feedlot performance is unknown, but may involve behavior aspects (e.g., decreased estrous activity) due to antibody-bound estrogens being less available to the higher brain centers (19). As noted in this study (the BSA–estradiol-immunized animals), animals with high titers become anovulatory (4, 5, 21) and thus may be more efficient under feedlot conditions because of diminished estrous activity.

At the anti-estradiol titers generated in this study, the antibody may act as a mass-action reservoir for estrogens that functions to increase estrogen availability to target tissues (8). Alternatively, as the antibody binding of estrogen increases, albumin-bound estrogen decreases and total hormone concentration may increase to offset the decrease in the albumin-bound fraction (19). This may not only decrease the clearance rate of bound estrogen, but also elevate the quantity of hormone available to target tissues.

Earlier studies have shown that little advantage accrues from ovariectomizing heifers that are going into the feedlot (22–24) but the decreases in rate of gain or feed efficiency in ovariectomized animals noted in the above studies were not observed in this experiment (Table II). The decreased performance of ovariectomized animals observed in this study was most likely due to the trauma of ovariectomy and the fact that ovariectomized animals seemed to reach maturity at a lower weight (Fig. 1). The initial weight loss due to surgery and lack of full compensation in the feedlot as well as carcass differences suggest that disadvantages probably offset the advantages of the procedure.

The influence of estrogenic growth stimulants on carcass composition of castrated male ruminants is to increase carcass protein and water content and decrease carcass fat (2, 11, 25, 26). However, in female ruminants, estrogenic growth stimulants appear to have less effect on carcass composition (2, 24) though estrogenic effects upon ovariectomized animals are unknown. The increased utilization of the animals' own estrogen to increase growth and efficiency from the active immunization against estrogens may provide the beef industry with a useful management tool.

1. Burgess TD, Lamming GE. The effect of diethylstilboestrol, hexoestrol and testosterone on the growth rate and carcass quality of fattening beef steers. Anim Prod **2**:93–103, 1960.
2. Galbraith H, Topps JH. Effect of hormones on the growth and body composition of animals. Nutr Abstr Rev, Ser B **51**:521–540, 1981.
3. Preston RL. Biological responses to estrogen additives in meat producing cattle and lambs. J Anim Sci **41**:1414–1430, 1975.
4. Elsaesser F. Effects of active immunization against oestradiol-17β, testosterone or progesterone on re-

ceptivity in the female rabbit and evaluation of specificity. J Reprod Fert **58**:213–218, 1980.
5. Martin TE, Henricks DM, Hill JR Jr, Rawlings NC. Active immunization of the cow against oestradiol-17β. J Reprod Fert **53**:173–178, 1978.
6. Scaramuzzi RJ, Martensz ND, Van Look PFA. Ovarian morphology and the concentration of steroids, and of gonadotrophins during the breeding season in ewes actively immunized against oestradiol-17β or oestrone. J Reprod Fert **59**:303–310, 1980.
7. Goodfriend TL, Levine L, Fasman GD. Antibodies to bradykinin and angiotensin: A use of carbodiimides in immunology. Science **144**:1344–1346, 1964.
8. Wise TH, Schanbacher BD. Reproductive effects of immunizing heifers against androstenedione and oestradiol-17β. J Reprod Fert **69**:605–612, 1983.
9. Crouse JD, Dikeman ME. Methods of estimating beef carcass chemical composition. J Anim Sci **38**:1190–1196, 1974.
10. Davis SL, Ohlson DL, Klindt J, Anfinson MS. Episodic growth hormone secretory patterns in sheep: Relationship to gonadal steroid hormones. Amer J Physiol **233**:E519–E523, 1977.
11. Muir LA, Wien S, Duquette PF, Rickes EL, Cordes EH. Effects of exogenous growth hormone and diethylstilbestrol on growth and carcass composition of growing lambs. J Anim Sci **56**:1315–1323, 1983.
12. Swan H, Bolt DJ, Miller LR, Oltjen RR, Rumsey TS, Moe PW. Feed intake and DES on growth hormone and prolactin in steers. J Anim Sci **35**:276, 1972 (abstr).
13. Heitzman RJ. Anabolic agents in beef production: Their action as growth promoters. In: de Boer H, Martin J, eds. Patterns of Growth and Development in Cattle. Boston, Martinas Nijhoff, pp353–359, 1978.
14. Emmens CW. Estrogens. In: Dorfman RI, ed. Methods in Hormone Research. New York, Academic Press, Vol. II:pp93–100, 1962.
15. Louvet JP, Harman SM, Ross GT. Effects of human chorionic gonadotropin, human interstitial cell stimulating hormone and human follicle-stimulating hormone on ovarian weights in estrogen-primed hypophysectomized immature female rats. Endocrinology **96**:1179–1186, 1975.
16. Preston RL, Burroughs W. Physiological actions of diethylstilbestrol in lambs fed varying levels of protein and energy. J Appl Physiol **15**:97–100, 1960.
17. Reuber HW, Pearson CC, Pope LS. Genital effects of implanted and oral diethylstilbestrol on heifers. J Amer Vet Med Assoc **138**:72–77, 1961.
18. Taylor B, Hale WH, Burroughs W. Growth and fattening stimulation in ewe lambs by certain androgenic and estrogenic compounds. J Anim Sci **16**:294–306, 1957.
19. Pardridge WM. Transport of protein-bound hormones into tissues *in vivo*. Endocrine Rev **2**:103–123, 1981.
20. Sundaram K, Tsong YY, Hood W, Brinson A. Effect of immunization with estrone-protein conjugate in rhesus monkeys. Endocrinology **93**:843–847, 1973.
21. Ferin M, Dyrenfurth I, Cowchock S, Warren M, Vande Wiele RL. Active immunization to 17β-estradiol and its effects upon the reproductive cycle of the rhesus monkey. Endocrinology **94**:765–776, 1974.
22. Dinusson WE, Andrews FN, Beeson WM. The effects of stilbestrol, testosterone, thyroid alteration and spaying on the growth and fattening of heifers. J Anim Sci **9**:321–330, 1950.
23. Ray DE, Hale WH, Marchello JA. Influence of season, sex and hormonal growth stimulants on feedlot performance of beef cattle. J Anim Sci **29**:490–495, 1969.
24. Saul GR, Baud SR, McDonald JW, McRae C, Clark AJ. A comparison of the growth rate and carcass characteristics of steers and heifers when entire, spayed, pregnant or fitted with an intravaginal device. Aust J Exp Agric Anim Husb **22**:258–263, 1982.
25. Gassner FX, Reifenstein EC Jr, Alego JW, Mattox WL. Effects of hormones on growth, fattening and meat production potential of livestock. Rec Progr Horm Res **41**:183–217, 1958.
26. Rumsey TS, Tyrell HF, Dinius DA, Moe PW, Cross HR. Gain and body composition of beef steers fed DES. J Anim Sci **45**(Suppl. 1):254, 1977 (abstr).

Received January 12, 1984. P.S.E.B.M. 1984, Vol. 176.
Accepted March 15, 1984.

PROCEEDINGS OF THE SOCIETY FOR EXPERIMENTAL BIOLOGY AND MEDICINE **176,** 249–256 (1984)

Glutathione Levels during the Mosquito Life Span with Emphasis on Senescence (41867)

GEORGE A. HAZELTON AND CALVIN A. LANG

Department of Biochemistry, University of Louisville School of Medicine, Louisville, Kentucky 40292

Abstract. Glutathione levels were determined in mosquitoes of all ages of the life span. Specific analyses for reduced (GSH) and oxidized (GSSG) glutathione were used and validated to ensure minimal autoxidation of GSH and conversion of these forms. Indeed GSH accounted for >97% of the total glutathione (GSH + GSSG) content in all samples. Marked changes occurred during the life span, and the highest levels of GSH and total glutathione were found during larval growth and metamorphosis ($P < 0.001$). Thereafter the levels decreased in the early adult, plateaued in the mature, and decreased 46% in the old and very old mosquito ($P < 0.001$). This aging-specific decrease was a general phenomenon, for it occurred in all body regions of both sexes. Starvation up to 3 days did not affect the GSH levels. The importance of these changes in glutathione is its relationship to the reducing and biosynthetic capacities of different life span stages. Of special interest is the senescence decrease which can lead to lower biosynthetic activity and also impaired detoxification capacity.

The high levels of glutathione in many animal and plant cells suggest it may have important biological functions. Indeed, this tripeptide (L-γ-glutamyl-L-cysteinyl-glycine) is the most abundant thiol reducing agent in tissues. Glutathione participates in a variety of biosynthetic and detoxification reactions as described in a number of reviews (1–7).

Glutathione has been implicated in the growth and development of a number of organisms. Changes in levels were observed during fetal development in mouse liver (8), the postnatal growth of rat liver (9), the asexual life cycle of neurospora (10), and the embryonic development of the sea urchin (11).

A possible role of glutathione in the aging process was demonstrated by our finding that aging-specific decreases in glutathione status occurred in various tissues of the mouse. In erythrocytes marked decreased in GSH content, free thiol groups, and GSSG reductase activity were observed as a function of cell age as well as mouse age (12). Recently similar aging-specific decreases in GSH and also total glutathione concentrations were found in other, more typical tissues (13).

There has been no systematic investigation of glutathione during the growth and aging stages of a multicellular eukaryote throughout its life span. To this end we selected the mosquito as an appropriate model since it has the following advantages. First, it is a multicellular organism that resembles mammals in its biochemical composition and nutritional requirements for growth. Second, it has discrete, synchronizable life span stages of growth, maturity, and aging, which have been characterized biochemically. Third, it can be cultured axenically and aged under controlled and defined nutritional conditions. Fourth, its short life span enables the study of the entire life cycle in 6 weeks.

Our current hypothesis is that glutathione content is related to the level of biosynthetic activity and the age of the organism. Thus the objective of this investigation was to determine the GSH and GSSG levels in tissue samples at different stages of the life span that differ in biosynthetic level. The biochemical basis for this approach was the high DNA content and biosynthetic activity found in mosquito larvae and the low values in the mature and senescent adult (14, 15). A preliminary account of this work has been presented (16).

Materials and Methods. *Experimental organism and its culture.* The experimental organism was the yellow fever mosquito, *Aedes aegypti* (Louisville), which has been colonized in this laboratory for over 17 years amounting to about 250 generations. Under our standard conditions, the larval period lasts approximately 7 days, and the pupal period, 2 days.

The chronological and biological ages of adult mosquitoes were as follows: 0–5 days,

0037-9727/84 $1.50

late metamorphosis; 6–22 days, mature; 23–35 days, old; 35+ days, very old. These age periods were characterized from survival curves and from DNA and protein profiles (14) of cohort populations that were cultured and aged under our standard conditions. The median survival time for these mosquitoes was 29 ± 2 days, a value which has been reproducible for several decades.

Standard culture. Our standardized culture procedure was used to produce mosquitoes of all ages of the life span (17). The procedure is outlined as follows: Eggs stored at 29°C for less than 1 month were hatched by agitating them for several minutes in distilled water on a Vortex mixer. Almost all larvae emerged within 15 min and were transferred to pans containing distilled water with a mineral supplement corresponding to that in axenic media. An aqueous 19% (w/v) suspension of desiccated hog liver (Teklad, Madison, Wisc.) was added daily to maintain a bacterial infusion which is the principal source of nutrients for the growing larvae.

Pupae were transferred to distilled water for adult emergence. Adult mosquitoes were fed a 10% (w/v) sucrose solution on cotton pads. No blood meals were offered to the experimental groups, and thus ovarian development was prevented. An environmental temperature of 29°C was maintained throughout the life span.

Axenic culture. Mass cultures of mosquito larvae were grown axenically on a defined medium as described by Lang *et al.* (18). Both axenic and standard, nonaxenic mosquitoes have the same rates of growth, pupation, and adult emergence under these conditions.

Tissue preparation. The protocol for each daily experiment included samples from different age groups. To determine total glutathione (GSH + GSSG), homogenates (9% w/v) of cold-inactivated larvae or adult mosquitoes were prepared in ice-cold 5% (w/v) *meta*-phosphoric acid using an all-glass, Ten-Broeck homogenizer. The actual total weights of mosquitoes used varied from 90 to 300 mg. Portions of the homogenates (1.0 ml) were centrifuged at 14,000*g* for 15 min in a Lourdes LRA centrifuge with a 9RA rotor. The supernatants were then diluted with 0.1 *M* sodium phosphate/0.005 *M* EDTA, pH 7.5.

A different process was used for GSSG. Mosquitoes were homogenized in ice-cold 0.01 *M* *N*-ethylmaleimide and incubated for 5–10 min at 4°C. Then metaphosphoric acid was added to a final concentration of 5% (w/v), and the homogenate was centrifuged. Excess *N*-ethylmaleimide was removed by extracting eight times with equal volumes of ether, and residual ether was removed by bubbling air through the samples for 20–30 min.

For recovery experiments known amounts of GSH or GSSG were added to different samples before homogenization. Each sample consisted of 40–50 mosquitoes for GSH determination and 90–100 for GSSG.

Samples of head, thorax, and abdomen were obtained from cold-inactivated mosquitoes which were trisected at the head–thorax and thorax-abdomen junctions with stainless-steel needles. Pooled samples of each body region were processed as described above.

Glutathione assay. Total glutathione and GSSG were assayed by a modification of the enzymatic cycling method of Tietze (19) and Owens and Belcher (20) in which the rate of 5,5′-dithiobis(2-nitrobenzoic acid) (DTNB) reduction is proportional to the amount of either GSH or GSSG present. Tissue extracts (volume 25–100 μl) were added to an assay medium containing 0.5 EC unit of yeast glutathione reductase (1 unit will reduce 1.0 μmole GSSG/min at pH 7.6 at 25°C), 0.5 μmole of DTNB, and 0.1 *M* sodium phosphate/0.005 *M* EDTA buffer, pH 7.5, in a volume of 0.9 ml. This reaction mixture was preincubated for 2 min at 20–22°C to allow thiol components in the tissue extract to interact with DTNB. Then the enzymatic cycling reaction was initiated by the addition of 0.1 ml of NADPH equivalent to 0.2 μmole, and the rate of DTNB reduction was determined from the increase in A_{412} using a Zeiss PMQ II spectrophotometer. This rate was corrected for the reaction of DTNB with glutathione reductase without tissue sample. Each sample was analyzed at two or more concentrations to ensure that the initial rates were proportional to sample size for all tissues. Also, every daily assay included standard curves using known amounts of GSH and GSSG. GSH was calculated from the difference between the total glutathione and GSSG values.

Chemicals. NADPH of 98% purity, yeast glutathione reductase [NAD(P)H-GSSG glutathione oxidoreductase, EC 1.6.9.2] (200 units/ml). GSH, GSSG, 5,5′-dithiobis(2-nitrobenzoic acid), and *N*-ethylmaleimide were obtained from the Sigma Chemical Company (St. Louis, Mo.). Solutions of these reagents were prepared in 0.1 *M* sodium phosphate/EDTA buffer, pH 7.5. Other chemicals were reagent grade, and double-distilled water was used.

Statistical methods. Student's *t* test was used for statistical comparisons (21). Statistical procedures were facilitated by use of a Hewlett–Packard minicomputer.

Results. *Validation of the method.* An important aspect of this investigation was the use of an analytical method specific for both GSH and GSSG. The enzymatic cycling method of Tietze (19) was selected and evaluated for mosquito samples by determining optimal assay conditions and by recovery experiments.

The measurement of glutathione was based on the initial rates and time courses of the enzymatic reduction of DTNB. For the assay of either total glutathione or GSSG in larval or adult samples, A_{412} was proportional to time for the initial 2.0 min. Thus for routine assays the initial rates were determined within the first 1.5 min. Also, several concentrations of each sample were assayed to ensure proportionality between initial rates and sample size. In addition, mixing experiments with samples of high and low levels were performed to detect the presence of any endogenous inhibitors or activators. None was found, for the results were additive.

Recovery experiments were carried out by adding known amounts of GSH or GSSG to mosquito samples before homogenization (Table I). The recoveries of GSH or GSSG were quantitative and ranged from 92 to 108% with various added amounts and with different ages of organisms. This evidence indicated that the processing and analytical methods were valid for the quantitative determination of both GSH and GSSG.

Glutathione levels. The levels of GSH, GSSG, and total glutathione during the life span of the mosquito are shown in Table II. The data are expressed per milligram of fresh tissue since our previous studies showed that weight, DNA, and protein contents are equivalent biochemical parameters of cell size and number during all stages of the life span (14, 15). Throughout the life span the GSH content was greater than 97% of the total glutathione. Thus the GSH profile was essentially identical to the total glutathione profile.

The relative GSH content during the different stages of the mosquito are presented in Fig. 1. GSH was found in the newly hatched larva and thus was present in the diapausing mosquito embryo. During larval development the GSH content increased two-fold and reached a maximum in the 3-day-old larva.

TABLE I. RECOVERY OF GLUTATHIONE ADDED TO MOSQUITO SAMPLES

Stage	Expt	GSH or GSSG (neq of GSH/ sample)	GSH: neq of GSH added	GSH: Recovery (%)	GSSG: neq of GSH added	GSSG: Recovery (%)
Larval	1	208 (GSH)	162	103	—	—
			324	99.1	—	—
	2	6.00 (GSSG)	—	—	6.48	108
					13.0	94.7
Adult	1	204 (GSH)	162	98.1	—	—
			324	93.7	—	—
	2	149 (GSH)	162	93.1	—	—
			324	102	—	—
	3	3.24 (GSSG)	—	—	6.48	92.5
			—	—	13.0	98.5

Note. Known amounts of GSH or GSSG were added to different samples before homogenization and further tissue processing. The results are expressed as percentage of added glutathione recovered compared with the calculated amounts. The methods used are described in the text.

TABLE II. GLUTATHIONE CONTENT IN THE MOSQUITO DURING ITS LIFE SPAN

Stage	Age (days)	No. of samples	Glutathione (neq of GSH/mg of tissue) GSH	GSSG	Total
Larval	0	1	0.898	0.0146	0.913
	3	4	1.68 ± 0.0368	0.0169 ± 0.00193	1.70 ± 0.0371
	5	4	1.44 ± 0.0321	0.0196 ± 0.00159	1.46 ± 0.0329
	7	4	1.26 ± 0.0394	0.0152 ± 0.00231	1.27 ± 0.0407
Pupa	1	3	1.28 ± 0.0515	0.0164 ± 0.00196	1.30 ± 0.0524
Adult	0.5	6	1.41 ± 0.0241	0.0156 ± 0.00121	1.43 ± 0.0243
	5	6	1.09 ± 0.0338	0.0178 ± 0.00275	1.11 ± 0.0355
	12	6	1.07 ± 0.0338	0.0184 ± 0.00252	1.09 ± 0.0332
	15	6	0.990 ± 0.0270	0.0126 ± 0.00103	1.01 ± 0.0329
	21	7	0.821 ± 0.0287	0.0155 ± 0.00198	0.834 ± 0.0292
	25	5	0.655 ± 0.0472	0.0176 ± 0.00165	0.681 ± 0.0450
	32	6	0.593 ± 0.0381	0.0151 ± 0.00358	0.609 ± 0.0394
	47	5	0.566 ± 0.0407	0.0171 ± 0.00554	0.583 ± 0.0435

Note. Larvae, pupae, and adults of different ages were analyzed for glutathione content by the procedures described in the text. The 0-day larvae were hatched synchronously and analyzed within 30 min. The larvae and pupae were obtained by axenic culture, and adults were obtained by standard culture. The results are expressed as the means ± SEM of the indicated number of samples. Each sample consisted of 20–30 mosquitoes. The exceptions are the GSH and GSSG values for 0-day larvae, which were obtained from only one sample of ≃22,000 mosquitoes.

Thereafter the GSH levels decreased 66% in an irregular pattern during the remaining larval, pupal, and adult stages.

These changes were analyzed statistically by planned comparisons among class means of the developmental periods (21). The highest values which occurred during larval growth and metamorphosis were different from those for the mature adult period (5–21 days) which in turn were different from those for the senescent adult (25–47 days) ($P < 0.001$).

Of special importance was the close relationship between GSH content and the biological ages of the adult mosquito as shown by the superimposed GSH and survival curves in Fig. 2. After the fifth day of adult life when maturity was attained, GSH levels decreased 46% ($P < 0.001$) and the GSH profile was

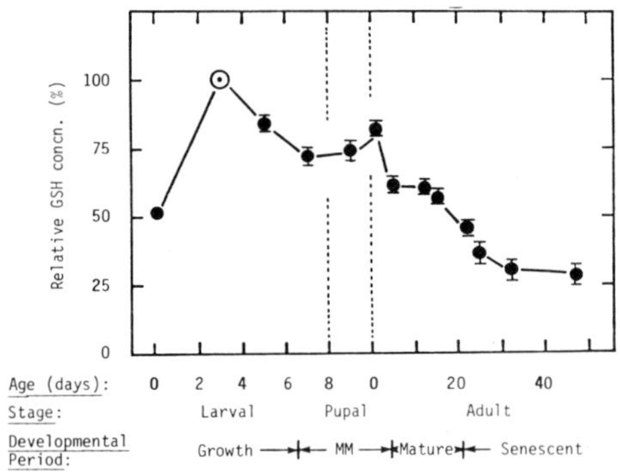

FIG. 1. Relative GSH content during the mosquito life span. Larvae, pupae, and adults of different ages were analyzed for glutathione content as described in Table II. The relative GSH content was based on the 3-day larval value, 1.68 neq GSH/mg tissue, expressed as 100%. MM denotes the metamorphosis stage.

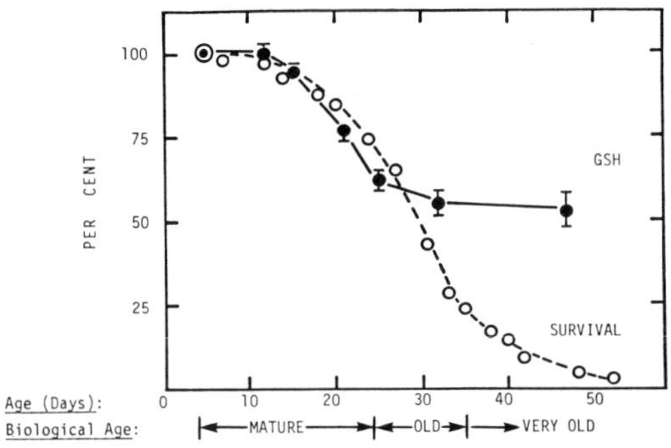

FIG. 2. The relationship of GSH content and percentage survival of the adult mosquito. Adult mosquitoes of different ages were analyzed for GSH content as described in Table II. Both the glutathione profile and the mosquito survival curve were based on their 5-day values expressed as 100%. The median survival time was 29.1 days.

TABLE III. LACK OF SEX DIFFERENCE IN GLUTATHIONE CONTENT OF MATURE AND OLD ADULT MOSQUITOES

Sex	Adult age	Weight (mg per mosquito)	Glutathione (neq of GSH) Per mg	Per mosquito
Male	Mature, 12 days	1.14 ± 0.120	0.990 ± 0.0463	1.12 ± 0.0508
	Old, 27 days	1.01 ± 0.103	0.639 ± 0.0255	0.640 ± 0.0395
Female	Mature, 12 days	2.23 ± 0.0427	1.04 ± 0.0234	2.33 ± 0.0298
	Old, 33 days	2.19 ± 0.0511	0.549 ± 0.0139	1.20 ± 0.0247

Note. Adult mosquitoes raised under our standard conditions were sexed by visual examination of antennae. Biologically mature (12 days) and old (27–33 days) mosquitoes were compared. Pooled samples of 50–75 males or females were analyzed for glutathione content as described in the text. The results are expressed as the means ± SEM of three to eight samples. The GSH contents of the old groups were statistically different from those of the mature groups ($P < 0.005$).

superimposed on the survival curve until 32 days of age ($r = 0.997$). This decrease was aging specific and coincided with the rapid decrease in survivors occurring at that time. Of special note was the constant GSH content in the biologically old and very old adults (25–47 days) which suggested a critical level for survival.

GSSG contents, unlike GSH, were less than 3% of the total glutathione and were constant through the life span including the aging period.

To explore possible sex differences, adult male and female mosquitoes of mature (12 days) and old (27–33 days) biological ages were compared (Table III). The data indicated the same GSH levels in both sexes despite the twofold greater weight of the female. Also, a similar 33–49% ($P < 0.005$) aging-specific decrease in GSH content occurred in both sexes.

To determine whether the GSH changes were localized or general, different body regions of mosquito larvae and adults were analyzed. GSH was found in all body regions of both the larva and the adult with approximately 50% of the total GSH of the organism localized in the abdomen. In the 6-day-old larva the highest GSH level was found in the head (1.69 neq GSH/mg tissue), followed by the thorax (1.17 neq GSH/mg tissue) and abdomen (1.09 neq GSH/mg tissue).

In adults of all ages the highest GSH content was also in the head. However, in contrast to the larva, the content in the thorax was ~45% lower than that in the abdomen.

During adult aging GSH changes occurred in the body regions of the mosquito (Table IV). When the mature (10-day-old) and senescent (33-day-old) adults were compared, the decreases in GSH content in each body region (36–41%) were similar to that in the whole organism (38%). Also, when the GSH levels were expressed per milligram of protein or DNA, similar decreases occurred in all body regions, as well as the whole organism. Thus the decrease in GSH content during the adult

TABLE IV. AGING CHANGES IN GLUTATHIONE CONTENT IN BODY REGIONS OF THE MOSQUITO

Adult age	Region	Glutathione concentration neq/mg tissue	% of mature
Young, 1 day	Head	1.86	131
	Thorax	1.00	138
	Abdomen	1.45	109
	Whole organism	1.26	128
Mature, 10 days	Head	1.42	(100)
	Thorax	0.727	(100)
	Abdomen	1.33	(100)
	Whole organism	0.986	(100)
Old, 33 days	Head	0.889	62.6
	Thorax	0.431	59.3
	Abdomen	0.846	63.6
	Whole organism	0.608	61.6

Note. Adult female mosquitoes of different ages were used as whole organisms or were trisected into head, thorax, and abdominal regions. Each sample consisted of 100–150 mosquitoes. The dissection procedure and determination of glutathione content are described in the text. The percentage glutathione contents were based on the 10-day adult concentrations as 100%.

aging period was a general phenomenon and not restricted to a specific body region.

Previous investigators have demonstrated changes in the GSH content of tissues in the rat with starvation (22, 23). To determine whether starvation was the causative factor for the aging decrease, mature and old adults were maintained on water alone for several days. At intervals mosquito samples were removed and analyzed for GSH content (Fig. 3). The content for both mature and old adults remained at the prestarvation level. Similar results were observed when GSH content was expressed per milligram of tissue or per organism. Thus the aging decrease in GSH content was not due to starvation.

Discussion. This investigation is the first systematic study of GSH, GSSG, and total glutathione contents during the life span of a multicellular, eukaryotic organism. Our results demonstrated that changes in GSH and total glutathione content occurred during the different biological stages of the mosquito, while GSSG levels were very low and unchanged.

GSH content and biosynthetic activity were correlated during the development periods for there were high GSH levels during larval growth and during metamorphosis which occurs in the pupal and the early adult stages. The maximal GSH level on the third day of larval growth coincided with maximal values of DNA, RNA, and protein contents (14) and of DNA biosynthesis (15). Also, the high GSH content in early adult life was related to high levels of protein, DNA, and electron transport enzymes occurring at that time (15, 24, 25).

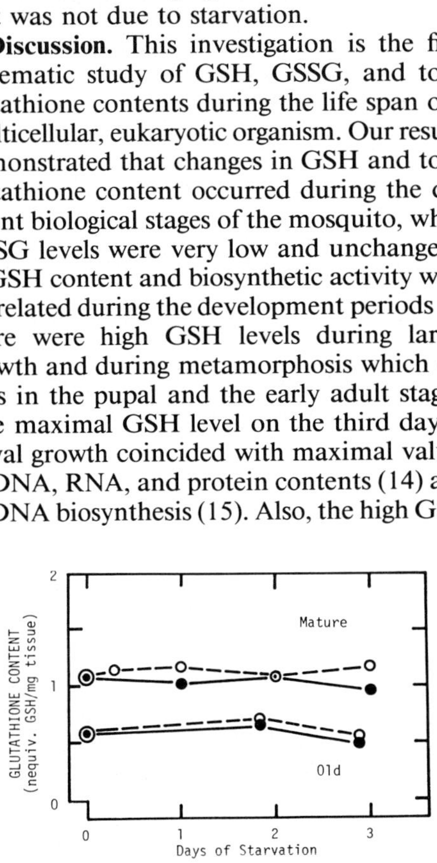

FIG. 3. Lack of starvation effect on the glutathione content of mature and old mosquitoes. Mature (13 days) and old (33 days) mosquitoes were starved by replacing their sucrose diet with water. Glutathione content was analyzed by procedures in the text. Each point is the mean of two or three samples of 15–25 mosquitoes. The exceptions are the 0.25-day-old mature, starved point and the 3-day-old, control point which consists of a single sample. ●, control; ○, starved.

GSH has been implicated in several growth processes which may explain its correlation with high biosynthetic activity. During cell division a structural function of GSH was proposed for the formation of the mitotic apparatus in sea urchin eggs but definite information is lacking (11, 26, 27). Also, the assembly and disassembly of cytoplasmic microtubules *in vitro* were related to cellular GSH content (28).

Of special importance was the GSH decrease during senescence. This change was aging specific, for it coincided with the biologically old period during which there was a marked decrease in survival. Also this GSH decrease is unusual, for the biochemical parameters of cell size and number such as weight, DNA, RNA, and protein and the free amino acid concentrations are constant in the aging mosquito (14, 29). Moreover, starvation did not affect the GSH level. Our recent evidence indicates that impaired GSH synthesis is probably the causal mechanism for the GSH decrease (29).

Equally important was our finding that the GSH content plateaus in the long-lived (<50% survivorship), senescent adult. This indicated that there may be a critical level for survival, in view of the fact that only live organisms were sampled. To prove this a longitudinal study is needed but not possible. However, it should be noted that our study is pseudo-longitudinal, since the mosquitoes were near-identical due to their relative genetic homogeneity through several hundred generations of standardized inbreeding and rigorous environmental control. Thus the determination of GSH content in mosquito samples of different ages is equivalent to repeated measurements of a single aging organism.

The decrease in GSH may be a general characteristic of many aging tissues for several reasons. First, our values were obtained initially with samples of whole organisms, and thus the decrease reflected a general aging phenomenon of most cells and not of an isolated and perhaps atypical cell type. Further our subsequent evidence showed that this GSH decrease occurred in different body regions. Second, our finding of a 37% decrease in GSH content in the aging mosquito is similar to the decrease of 20–34% found in aging mouse and man (12, 13, 30–32).

The significance of our observation that GSH decreases with aging is exemplified by the central role GSH plays in a variety of metabolic processes. Indeed, the GSH decrease could have profound effects on the level of biosynthetic activity in cells through the regulation of enzyme activities, the synthesis of macromolecules, and the activity of the pentose phosphate cycle (6, 33–37).

Evidence for this view are our findings in the aging mosquito of marked decreases in protein and DNA synthetic rates, $NADP^+$-linked enzyme activities, and NADPH/$NADP^+$ ratios (15, 25, 38, 39). These results formed our hypothesis that a lower reducing capacity, or GSH status, occurs in aging tissue.

Another major consequence of the aging-specific decrease in GSH content is a decrease in GSH-linked detoxification capacity. Thus, old organisms could be at risk and more susceptible to toxicants. Support for this view comes from our recent findings that the toxicity of acetaminophen, a model compound for GSH conjugation reactions, was sevenfold greater in senescent compared to mature mosquitoes. Also there was a very high correlation ($r = 0.99$) between GSH content and the LD_{50} for acetaminophen (40). Further the GSH content is critical since a major function is the detoxification of peroxides produced by normal lipid metabolism and of xenobiotics via glutathione *S*-transferase, which we also found to decrease in the aging mosquito (41).

Our results indicate that GSSG levels in the mosquito are low and constant through the life span. Similar low GSSG values were found in mammalian tissues (13, 19, 42, 43). This is in contrast to the result of others who reported markedly higher concentrations (44–47). These discrepancies are most likely due to faulty methodology, for erroneously high GSSG values will be obtained due to autoxidation of GSH during sample processing and storage unless precautions are taken. In this regard Wendell (42) has pointed out the shortcomings of measuring GSSG by difference from the amount of GSH assayed before and after chemical reduction, because autoxidation of even a small proportion of GSH will appear as a large increase in GSSG.

Special thanks are due to Dr. Betty Jane Mills for her generous advice at all stages of this work, to Mrs. Helen Shields and Mr. John Richie, Jr., for their technical assistance, and to Mrs. Ellen Ford for preparation of the manuscript. This work was supported by grants from the Sigma Kappa Foundation, the U.S. Environmental Protection Agency, and Swift and Company.

1. Jocelyn PC. Biochemistry of the SH Group. New York, Academic Press, 1972.
2. Flohé L, Benöhr H Chr, Sies H, Waller HD, Wendell A, eds. Glutathione. New York, Academic Press, 1974.
3. Meister A. Biochemistry of glutathione. In: Greenberg DM, ed. Metabolism of Sulfur Compounds, New York, Academic Press, Vol. VII: pp101–188, 1975.
4. Meister A, Tate SS. Glutathione and related γ-glutamyl compounds: Biosynthesis and utilization. Annu Rev Biochem **45**:559–604, 1976.
5. Arias IM, Jakoby WB, eds. Glutathione: Metabolism and Function. New York, Raven Press, 1976.
6. Kosower NS, Kosower EM. Glutathione status of cells. Int Rev Cytol **54**:109–160, 1978.
7. Sies, H, Wendel A, eds. Functions of Glutathione in Liver and Kidney. New York, Springer-Verlag, 1978.
8. Lambert GH, Thorgeirsson SS. Glutathione in the developing mouse liver: Developmental curve and depletion after acetaminophen treatment. Biochem Pharmacol **25**:1777–1781, 1976.
9. Harisch G, Schole J. Der Glutathionstatus der Rattenleber in Abhängigkeit vonn Lebensalter und von Akuter Belastung. Z Naturforsch **29**:261–266, 1974.
10. Fahey RC, Brody S, Mikolajczyk SD. Changes in the glutathione thiol-disulfide status of *Neurospora crassa* coinidia during germination and aging. J Bacteriol **121**:141–151. 1975.
11. Fahey RC, Mikolajczyk SD, Meier GP, Epel D, Carroll EJ Jr. The glutathione thiol-disulfide status in the sea urchin egg during fertilization and the first cell division cycle. Biochim Biophys Acta **437**:445–453, 1976.
12. Abraham EC, Taylor JF, Lang CA. Influence of mouse age and erythrocyte age on glutathione metabolism. Biochem J **174**:819–825, 1978.
13. Hazelton GA, Lang CA. Glutathione contents of tissues in the aging mouse. Biochem J **188**:25–30, 1980.
14. Lang CA, Lau HY, Jefferson DJ. Protein and nucleic acid changes during growth and aging in the mosquito. Biochem J **95**:372–377, 1965.
15. Mills BJ, Lang CA. The biosynthesis of DNA during the life span of the mosquito. Biochem J **154**:481–490, 1976.
16. Hazelton GA, Lang CA. Glutathione determination in the mosquito. Fed Proc **37**:No 6, Abstr 2378, 1978.
17. Kao PC, Beyer CF, Lang CA. A DNA replication intermediate in the growing mosquito. Biochem J **154**:471–480, 1976.
18. Lang CA, Basch KJ, Story RF. The growth, composition and longevity of the axenic mosquito. J Nutr **102**:1057–1066, 1972.

19. Tietze F. Enzymic method for quantitative determination of nanogram amounts of total and oxidized glutathione: Applications to mammalian blood and other tissues. Anal Biochem **27**:502–522, 1969.
20. Owens CWI, Belcher RV. A colorimetric micromethod for the determination of glutathione. Biochem J **94**:705–711, 1965.
21. Snedecor GW, Cochran WG. Statistical Methods, 7th ed., Ames, Iowa State College Press, 1980.
22. Higashi T, Tateishi N, Naruse A, Sakamoto Y. A novel physiological role of liver glutathione as a reservoir of L-cysteine. J Biochem **82**:117–124, 1977.
23. Tateishi N, Higashi T, Nakashima ANK, Shiozaki H, Sakamoto Y. Rat liver glutathione: Possible role as a reservoir of cysteine. J Nutr **107**:51–60, 1977.
24. Lang CA. Cytochrome c reductase activities during development. Exp Cell Res **17**:516–518, 1959.
25. Smith ER. Protein Metabolism in the Aging Mosquito. Ph.D. dissertation, University of Louisville School of Medicine, 1971.
26. Mazia D. SH and growth. In: Colowick S, Lazarow A, Racker, E, Schwarz DR, Stadtman E, Waelsch H, eds. Glutathione: A Symposium. New York, Academic Press, pp209–223, 1954.
27. Rapkine L. Sulfhydryl groups in sea urchin egg cell division. Ann Physiol Physicochim Biol **7**:382–417, 1931.
28. Oliver JM, Albertini DF, Berlin RD. Effects of GSH-oxidizing agents on microtubule assembly and microtubule-dependent surface properties of human neutrophils. J Cell Biol **71**:921–932, 1976.
29. Hazelton GA, Lang CA. Glutathione biosynthesis in the aging adult yellow-fever mosquito [*Aedes aegypti* (Louisville)]. Biochem J **210**:289–295, 1983.
30. Harding JJ. Free and protein-bound glutathione in normal and cataractous human lenses. Biochem J **117**:957–960, 1970.
31. Waller HD, Birke G, Tiggs FJ, Benöhr H Chr. Glutathiongehalt und Glutathion reduzierende enzyme in erythrocyten verschiedenen alters. Klin Wochenschr **52**:179–184, 1974.
32. Naryshkin S, Miller L, Lindeman R, Lang CA. Blood glutathione: A biochemical index of human aging. Fed Proc **40**:No 3, Abstr 3179, 1981.
33. Hosoda S, Nakamura W. Role of glutathione in regulation of hexose monophosphate pathway in Ehrlich ascites tumor cells. Biochim Biophys Acta **222**:53–64, 1970.
34. Hochstein P, Utley H. Hydrogen peroxide detoxification by glutathione peroxidase and catalase in rat liver homogenates. Mol Pharmacol **4**:575–581, 1968.
35. Jacob HS, Jandl JH. Effects of sulfhydryl inhibition on red blood cells. J Biol Chem **241**:4243–4250, 1966.
36. Rodriguez-Segade S, Freire M, Carrion A. Regulation of the oxidative phase of the pentose phosphate cycle in mussels. Biochem J **170**:577–582, 1978.
37. Eggleston LV, Krebs HA. Regulation of the pentose phosphate cycle. Biochem J **138**:425–435, 1974.
38. Lang CA, Stephan JK. Nicotinamide adenine dinucleotide phosphate enzymes in the mosquito during growth and aging. Biochem J **102**:331–338, 1967.
39. Lang CA, Acree DW. Nicotinamide adenine dinucleotide phosphate coenzyme levels during the life span of the mosquito. Gerontologist **7**:13, Abstr, 1967.
40. Richie JP Jr, Lang CA. Correlation of acetaminophen toxicity and glutathione levels in senescence. Pharmacologist **24**:No 41, 1982.
41. Hazelton GA, Lang CA. Glutathione S-transferase activities in the yellow-fever mosquito [(*Aedes aegypti* (Louisville)] during growth and aging. Biochem J **210**: 281–287, 1983.
42. Wendell PL. Measurement of oxidized glutathione and total glutathione in the perfused rat heart. Biochem J **117**:661–665, 1970.
43. Griffith OW. Determination of glutathione and glutathione disulfide using glutathione reductase and 2-vinylpyridine. Anal Biochem **106**:207–212, 1980.
44. Lipke H, Chalkley J. Glutathione, oxidized and reduced, in some Dipterans treated with 1,1,1-trichloro-2,2-di-(p-chlorophenyl)-ethane. Biochem J **85**:104–109, 1962.
45. Ilvicky J, Agosin M. Glutathione turnover in *Triatoma infestans* treated with 2,2-bis-(p-chlorophenyl)-1,1,1-trichloroethane. J Exp Parasitol **20**:345–356, 1967.
46. Oeriu S. Proteins in development and senescence. Adv Gerontol Res **1**:23–85, 1964.
47. Oeriu S, Tigheciu M. Oxidized glutathione as a test of senescence. Gerontologia **9**:9–17, 1964.

Received October 19, 1982. P.S.E.B.M. 1984, Vol. 176.
Accepted March 19, 1984.

PROCEEDINGS OF THE SOCIETY FOR EXPERIMENTAL BIOLOGY AND MEDICINE **176**, 257–260 (1984)

Interactive Effects of Ethanol and Silver on Sodium Transport across Toad Skin (41868)

GEORGE A. GERENCSER, STANLEY Y. LOO, AND KUULEIALOHA M. CORNETTE

Department of Physiology, College of Medicine, University of Florida, Gainesville, Florida 32610, and Department of Physiology, School of Medicine, University of Hawaii, Honolulu, Hawaii 96822

Abstract. Both ethanol and silver ions have been shown to affect ion transport across various epithelia. This investigation was principally undertaken to further define mechanisms of silver ions and ethanol, and their possible interactions, on sodium transport across toad skin. Isolated toad skin, mounted between identical oxygenated amphibian bicarbonate Ringer solutions, maintained stable transepithelial potential differences (serosa positive) and short-circuit currents for several hours at 25°C. It was observed that (1) ethanol inhibited the active transcellular component of sodium absorption and this effect was reversible; (2) inhibition of sodium transport by ethanol was directly proportional to the applied concentration; (3) pretreatment with silver ions prevented any ethanol effects; and (4) pretreatment with ethanol prevented any silver ion effects. It was concluded from these results that ethanol induced its inhibitory effects on membrane phospholipids thereby perturbing the function of a sulfhydryl ligand, while silver ion or silver chloride complex binding to this ligand would maintain its function in sodium transport despite the presence of ethanol.

Silver–silver chloride (Ag–AgCl) electrodes immersed directly or connected via electrolytic bridges in the bathing media of isolated epithelia have been extensively used in the measurement of transepithelial bioelectric phenomena such as transepithelial potential difference (PD) and short-circuit current (SCC). The first observation of silver on these bioelectric characteristics was made by Nedergaard and Ussing (1). They demonstrated a silver-induced SCC across frog skin. Using direct immersion Ag–AgCl electrodes, Clarkson and Toole (2) described a transient increase in SCC across rat ileum that gradually decreased over a 1-hr period. They proposed that Ag^+ from the Ag–AgCl electrodes increased mucosal membrane permeability of the rat enterocytes to Na^+ which resulted in an increased Na^+ transport pool and, consequently, an increased active Na^+ efflux across the basolateral membrane. Walser (3) demonstrated a stimulation of SCC by Ag–AgCl immersion electrodes in isolated toad bladder using electrolytic bridge systems as controls. In fact, SCC was increased when a non-current-carrying Ag–AgCl wire was immersed in the mucosal bathing solution of the control system. Curran (4) demonstrated that Ag^+ addition to the outside bathing medium of isolated frog skin resulted in a sharp transient rise in SCC followed by a decrease. Through mannitol, Na^+, and K^+ flux studies, Curran concluded that Ag^+ affected both shunt and cellular permeability properties for Na^+. Boyett and Van Bruggen (5) demonstrated a concentration-dependent inhibition of ethanol on Na^+ transport across isolated frog skin. The present study was therefore undertaken to further define mechanisms of Ag^+ and ethanol, and their possible interactions, on Na^+ transport across toad skin.

Materials and Methods. Toads, *Bufo marinus,* of either sex were caught around Manoa Valley (Honolulu, Hawaii) and around Lake Alice (Gainesville, Fla.). They were kept fasting at room temperature (25°C) prior to experimentation. Adult animals were used in these experiments.

The toad was stunned by a blow on the head and its ventral skin was removed and mounted between two Lucite chambers as a flat sheet having an area of 3.14 cm^2 for the determination of electrical characteristics. The skin was aerated and bathed by amphibian bicarbonate Ringer of the type described by Gerencser *et al.* (6) having a total osmolality of 235 mosmol/liter and a pH of 7.8 at 25°C. The chambers employed were equipped with two sets of electrodes and were similar in design to those described by Ussing and Zerahn

0037-9727/84 $1.50

(7). PD and SCC were measured by methods similar to those employed by Schultz and Zalusky (8) except that both Ag–AgCl and agar salt bridges were used to apply external current to the system. A voltage clamp device was used to maintain short-circuit conditions as described by Rothe *et al.* (9). The electrolyte content of the agar salt bridges was identical to that of the bathing solution. The agar bridges from the potential-sensing electrodes contained saturated KCl. To minimize potential offset between these electrodes, the ends of these bridges were preequilibrated with the bathing solution for several hours before the experiments. Offset between the potential-sensing electrodes was measured at the beginning of the experiment and again at the end of the run following removal of the tissue and replacement of the bathing fluid.

Each mirror-image compartment of the chamber had a volume of 20 ml. The addition of 0.48 ml of a 95% ethanol solution (20.62 *M*) to one compartment gave a final concentration of 0.50 *M* ethanol, whereas 0.24 ml of the same solution gave a final concentration of 0.25 *M* ethanol. The opposite compartment of the chamber received an equivalent volume of amphibian Ringer solution, thereby preventing the development of a hydrostatic gradient across the tissue.

The application of radiotracer technique for the determination of the unidirectional fluxes of $^{22}Na^+$ under short-circuited conditions was as described by Quay and Armstrong (10).

All data are reported as means ± SE. Differences between means were analyzed statistically using Student's *t* test.

Results. When ethanol was added to the outside bathing solution of isolated toad skin (0.5 *M*, final concentration), the SCC immediately decreased to a new level and remained steady for several hours. Rinsing and replacing ethanol with an ethanol-free Ringer solution promptly restored the SCC of the skin to control levels (Fig. 1). The SCC response to the addition of ethanol was proportional to the concentration of ethanol (Table I). Maximal inhibition of SCC was obtained with 0.5 *M* ethanol while 0.25 *M* ethanol elicited 50% inhibition. The skin resistance (PD/SCC) was not changed significantly by ethanol addition to the outside bathing solution. The addition of ethanol (0.5 *M*, final concentra-

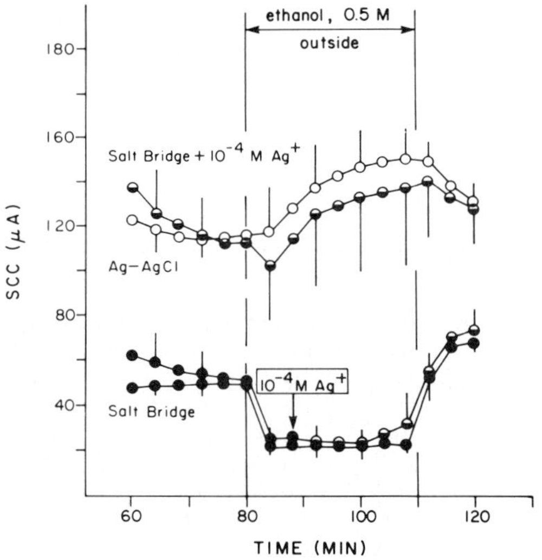

FIG. 1. Comparison between the inhibitory effect of ethanol on SCC in a salt bridge-driven system with and without 10^{-4} *M* Ag^+ in the medium and Ag–AgCl immersion electrodes. Open circles (○) represent Ag–AgCl electrode, closed circles (●) represent salt bridge-driven systems, whereas half-closed circles (◒) represent salt bridge + 10^{-4} *M* Ag^+. Each point represents the mean of seven experiments. Vertical bars represent the SEM.

tion) to the inside bathing medium had no significant effect on SCC ($N = 3$). The addition of sucrose (0.5 *M*, final concentration) to the outside ($N = 3$) or inside ($N = 2$) bathing solutions had no significant effect on SCC.

The next series of experiments examined the interactive effects of Ag^+ and ethanol on SCC. Figure 1 shows matched comparisons of SCC using three skin preparations from the same animal. As can be seen ethanol had no significant effect on SCC in the skin preparations exposed to Ag^+ (salt bridge + 10^{-4} *M* $AgNO_3$ or Ag–AgCl current-driving system). The Ag^+-induced increase in mean SCC, however, had considerable variation due to each skin responding differently to the given concentration of Ag^+. Rinsing and replacing the outside bathing medium with ethanol-free Ringer solution had no significant effect on SCC in those preparations exposed to Ag^+. Similarly, replacing Ag^+ with 0.5 m*M* *p*-chloromercurobenzoate (*p*-CMB) in the inside bathing solution prevented any subsequent SCC inhibition by 0.5 *M* ethanol added to the outside bathing solution ($N = 4$). The addition of 10^{-4} *M* $AgNO_3$ to a 0.5 *M* ethanol-inhib-

TABLE I. BASAL AND ETHANOL-INHIBITED SCCs

	SCC (μA/cm^2)		
	Basal	0.25 *M* ethanol	0.5 *M* ethanol
Electrolytic agar bridge	14.3 ± 2.5 (5)	8.9 ± 1.8 (5)	2.7 ± 0.5 (5)

Note. Average values ± SEM are given for the number of experiments shown in parentheses.

ited SCC had no effect on the reduced SCC (Fig. 1).

In order to discern the mechanism and ionic nature of the ethanol-induced SCC, an assessment of the unidirectional outside-to-inside (J_{OI}) and inside-to-outside (J_{IO}) Na^+ fluxes was made using $^{22}Na^+$ in three preparations from the same animal when their respective Ag–AgCl or salt bridge-driven short-circuit currents matched. As shown in Table II the mean J_{OI}^{NET} ($J_{OI} - J_{IO}$) of Na^+, in both Ag^+-exposed and Ag^+-free tissues, respectively, was not significantly different from the mean SCC in the presence of ethanol (0.5 *M*). Ethanol had no significant effect on J_{IO} of Na^+ whether the tissue was exposed to Ag^+ or not. However, ethanol significantly reduced ($P < 0.05$) the J_{OI} of Na^+ in the Ag^+-free preparation but had no significant effect on the J_{OI} of Na^+ in the Ag^+-exposed skin preparations.

Discussion. The present results indicate that ethanol inhibits active Na^+ transport across the toad skin and are similar to the results of Boyett and Van Bruggen (5) in frog skin. The finding that ethanol inhibited SCC proportional to the dose administered (Table I) attests to its inhibiting the active Na^+ transport pathway because the mean SCC was identical to the mean net J_{OI}^{NET} of Na^+ in the absence or presence of ethanol (Table II). The finding that 0.5 *M* ethanol or 0.5 *M* sucrose, added to either compartment, had no significant effect on the J_{IO} of Na^+ or SCC, respectively, strongly suggests that the ethanol-induced effect was not osmotic in origin (11).

The previous findings by Gerencser *et al.* (6, 12, 13) and the present observation (Table II) that Ag^+ addition to the bathing medium, or Ag–AgCl immersion electrodes, stimulates SCC that is identical to the active Na^+ absorptive flux across the toad skin indicates that the Ag^+-induced effects are Na^+ specific. The effects observed by Ag^+ addition are probably caused by Ag^+Cl^- complexes, rather than the Ag^+, as suggested by Gerencser *et al.* (6). Previous observations also demonstrated that Ag^+ addition had no effect on J_{IO} of Na^+, therefore eliminating any paracellular effects of this ion on Na^+ transport (6, 12). The finding that there was no significant change in the Ag^+ or *p*-CMB-induced SCC by ethanol addition (Fig. 1) or in either J_{OI} or J_{IO} of Na^+ during ethanol administration (Table II) suggests that the ethanol-induced inhibition of active Na^+ transport acts on the same site as does Ag^+ or Ag^+Cl^- complexes in stimulating active Na^+ transport across the toad skin. Buttressing this argument is the observation that

TABLE II. SODIUM FLUXES IN TOAD RINGER

	J_{OI} (neq/cm^2/min)	J_{IO} (neq/cm^2/min)	SCC (neq/cm^2/min)
Salt bridge			
Before ethanol addition	10.2 ± 3.1 (5)	1.9 ± 0.7 (5)	10.3 ± 2.6 (5)
After ethanol addition	4.3 ± 1.6 (5)	2.1 ± 0.6 (5)	3.4 ± 1.6 (5)
Ag–AgCl electrode			
Before ethanol addition	21.6 ± 4.2 (5)	2.8 ± 0.7 (5)	19.8 ± 4.6 (5)
After ethanol addition	23.2 ± 5.6 (5)	3.6 ± 1.6 (5)	18.1 ± 5.3 (5)

Note. Average values ± SEM are given for the number of experiments shown in parentheses.

Ag^+ or Ag^+Cl^- complexes could not alter the inhibition of Na^+ transport induced by ethanol. These conclusions concur with those of Boyett and Van Bruggen (5) and Curran (4) who speculated that ethanol and Ag^+, respectively, had effects on cellular ionic permeability in frog skin.

Gerencser *et al.* (6, 12, 13) suggested that Ag^+ or Ag^+Cl^- complexes and *p*-CMB induced their effects on toad skin by interacting with sulfhydryl groups of the cells that permit active transport of Na^+ which was in concert with the conclusions of Curran (4) and Benos *et al.* (14) in frog skin. Since ethanol had no effect on Na^+ transport in the presence of Ag^+ or *p*-CMB, it is not unreasonable to speculate that all three chemical species affect the same sulfhydryl ligand, Ag^+ or Ag^+Cl^- complexes and *p*-CMB binding to it directly, whereas ethanol perturbing it indirectly by its effects on surrounding membrane phospholipids as postulated by Gutknecht and Tosteson (15). These chemically induced effects, both direct and indirect, probably alter Na^+ channel conductive properties (16). It seems more feasible that ethanol affected Na^+ translocation at the outer membrane of the transporting cell rather than affecting ($Na^+ + K^+$) ATPase at the inner membrane because ethanol applied to the inside bathing medium had no significant effect on SCC. These conclusions are in accordance with those of Boyett and Van Bruggen (5) for ethanol effects on frog skin and are in contrast with those studies on a partially purified ($Na^+ + K^+$) ATPase preparation (17).

This work was supported by a Nephrology Training Grant from the National Institute of Arthritis and Metabolic Diseases (1-T01-AM-05697-02 and -03) and by Whitehall Foundation Grant 78-156 ck-1 DSR.

1. Koefoed-Johnsen V, Ussing HH. Ion transport. In: Comar CL, Bronner F. eds. Mineral Metabolism. New York, Academic Press, pp169–203, 1960.
2. Clarkson TW, Toole SR. Measurement of short-circuit current and ion transport across the ileum. Amer J Physiol **206**:658–668, 1964.
3. Walser M. Calcium transport in the toad bladder: Permeability to calcium ions. Amer J Physiol **218**:582–589, 1970.
4. Curran PF. Effect of silver ion on permeability properties of frog skin. Biochim Biophys Acta **228**:90–97, 1972.
5. Boyett JD, Van Bruggen JT. The effect of ethanol on ion transport in frog skin. Biochim Biophys Acta **436**:686–695, 1976.
6. Gerencser GA, Cornette KM, Loo SY, Hong SK. Effect of silver chloride on the short-circuit current across the isolated toad skin. Life Sci **20**:1883–1890, 1977.
7. Ussing HH, Zerahn K. Active transport of sodium as the source of electric current in the short-circuited isolated frog skin. Acta Physiol Scand **23**:110–127, 1951.
8. Schultz SG, Zalusky R. Ion transport in isolated rabbit ileum. I. Short-circuit current and Na^+ fluxes. J Gen Physiol **47**:567–584, 1964.
9. Rothe CF, Quay JF, Armstrong WMcD. Measurement of epithelial electrical characteristics with an automatic voltage clamp device with compensation for solution resistance. IEEE Trans Biomed Eng **16**:160–164, 1969.
10. Quay JF, Armstrong WMcD. Sodium and chloride transport by isolated bullfrog small intestine. Amer J Physiol **217**:694–702, 1969.
11. Desjeux JF, Tai YH, Curran PF. Characteristics of sodium flux from serosa to mucosa in rabbit ileum. J Gen Physiol **64**:274–292, 1974.
12. Gerencser GA, Loo SY, Cornette KM. Drug modification of silver-induced sodium transport across toad skin. Experientia **38**:956–957, 1982.
13. Gerencser GA, Loo SY, Cornette KM. Effect of silver on sodium transport across toad skin. Comp Biochem Physiol C **75**:337–341, 1983.
14. Benos DJ, Mandel LJ, Simon SA. Effects of chemical group specific reagents on sodium entry and the amiloride binding site in frog skin: Evidence for separate sites. J Membrane Biol **56**:149–158, 1980.
15. Gutknecht J, Tosteson DC. Ionic permeability of thin lipid membranes. Effects of n-alkyl alcohols, polyvalent cations, and a secondary amine. J Gen Physiol **55**:359–374, 1970.
16. Dick HJ, Lindemann B. Saturation of Na-current into frog skin epithelium abolished by PCMB. Pflueger's Arch **355**:R72, 1975.
17. Hegyvary C. Effects of some organic solvents on the reactivity of sodium plus potassium ion transport ATPase. Biochim Biophys Acta **311**:272–291, 1973.

Received December 12, 1983. P.S.E.B.M. 1984, Vol. 176.
Accepted March 27, 1984.

PROCEEDINGS OF THE SOCIETY FOR EXPERIMENTAL BIOLOGY AND MEDICINE **176,** 261–267 (1984)

Relationship between the Severity of Experimental Diabetes and Altered Lung Phospholipid Metabolism (41869)

MICHAEL J. ENGLE, ROBERT H. PERELMAN, KATHLEEN E. MCMAHON, SUSAN M. LANGAN, AND PHILIP M. FARRELL

Department of Pediatrics, University of Wisconsin, Madison, Wisconsin 53792

Abstract. Glucose intolerance was induced in rats by iv infusion of streptozotocin (STZ) in doses of 30, 40, 50, and 100 mg/kg. Serum glucose concentrations were elevated versus controls and weight gains were reduced in a dose-dependent fashion up to 50 mg/kg. Urine outputs and blood urea nitrogen (BUN) values were higher than control values in the animals treated with 40 and 50 mg/kg and serum albumin concentrations were decreased after infusion with 50 mg STZ/kg. Lung phosphatidylcholine (PC) concentrations and dry-to-wet weight ratios were unchanged by STZ treatment, while lung protein and disaturated phosphatidylcholine (DSPC) concentrations were depressed in the 50-mg/kg group. Animals surviving treatment with 100 mg/kg demonstrated increased fasting blood glucose levels, BUN values, and 48-hr urine outputs, and decreased lung protein levels. However, these alterations were less than those found in the 50-mg/kg animals. Pulmonary concentrations of PC, DSPC, and lung dry-to-wet weight ratios were unchanged. It was found advantageous to express the results relative to fasting blood glucose levels. This demonstrated that urine output and BUN values increased and weight gain decreased with rising glucose concentrations, but serum albumin decreased only in moderate and severe hyperglycemia. Fasting glucose concentrations greater than 400 mg/dl were associated with reduced lung DSPC and protein levels, while pulmonary PC and dry-to-wet weight ratios demonstrated no change with increasing hyperglycemia.

In order to study the metabolic effects of diabetes mellitus, several methods have been developed to produce glucose intolerance, but streptozotocin (STZ) is now generally used as the preferred agent (1–4). STZ causes β-cell destruction and disruption of islet architecture (1, 5, 6), leading to insulin insufficiency (7–9), increased urine output (7–9), glycosuria (1, 7–9), and abnormal kidney and liver function (10, 11). Chemically induced diabetic animals also demonstrate impaired pulmonary carbohydrate metabolism (12), altered lung ultrastructure, as evidenced by changes in Type II pneumocyte and Clara cell morphology (13, 14), and disturbed pulmonary lipid and surfactant synthesis (11, 15–17). Thus, STZ-induced diabetes is a useful model for studying the effects of carbohydrate intolerance in a variety of organ systems. The studies performed to date, however, have employed a wide range of drug dosages; also, the duration of the experimental diabetes has varied greatly. These and other differences in methodology make it difficult to compare results between studies. Experimental protocols also differ with respect to species, age, and sex of animals analyzed. Furthermore, there have been very few reports which attempt to relate the effects of STZ to specific blood glucose levels. These experiments were therefore undertaken in order to define a dose–response relationship between STZ and the severity of the resultant diabetes, as judged by its effects on several organ systems in the rat. These studies were also designed to correlate these effects with blood glucose levels in fasting animals. The responses of lung metabolism to these varying levels of chemically induced diabetes were then examined to further investigate the effects of diabetes on pulmonary carbohydrate and phospholipid metabolism.

Materials and Methods. Glucose intolerance was induced in 150- to 200-g male Sprague–Dawley rats (Harlan Sprague–Dawley, Inc., Indianapolis, Ind.) after an overnight fast by the intravenous infusion of STZ via the tail vein in doses of 30, 40, 50, or 100 mg/kg. Streptozotocin was a gift of Dr. W. A. Dulin, Upjohn Company, Kalamazoo, Michigan. The volume of the STZ infusions was kept constant at 0.5 ml. On the same day that STZ infusions were performed, control rats

0037-9727/84 $1.50

received an equal volume of diluent (0.4 *M* citrated saline, pH 4.5). A second control group consisted of rats that received no infusion. Because the effects of STZ are generally manifest by 48 hr, the urine output of the experimental animals was measured on Days 2 and 4 following STZ treatment. The urine volumes were used as a crude estimate of the effectiveness of the infused agent and a monitor of the severity of the diabetes-like state. Urine volumes were used because they were easily obtained, readily measured, and noninvasive. Urine outputs were obtained by placing the animals in individual metabolic cages for overnight urine collection. Urine volume was subsequently measured and the presence of glucose and ketones in urine was determined semiquantitatively with Labstix Reagent Strips (Ames Co., Elkhart, Ind.).

One week after infusion, overnight fasted rats were anesthetized with sodium pentobarbital (50 mg/kg) and weighed. Blood samples were drawn via cardiac puncture, and the lungs quickly removed and frozen in liquid nitrogen. Lung samples were stored at −70°C until used for biochemical assays. Serum samples were analyzed for blood urea nitrogen (urea nitrogen diagnostic kit No. 535, Sigma Chemical Co., St. Louis, Mo.) and albumin (albumin diagnostic kit No. 630, Sigma). Serum glucose concentrations were measured by the glucose oxidase method on a Beckman Glucose II analyzer (Beckman Instrument Company, Fullerton, Calif.).

Lung protein was measured according to the method of Hartree (18), with bovine serum albumin as standard. Lung dry-to-wet weight ratios were determined in the following manner. Approximately 50–75 mg of lung tissue was placed in a weighing vial and dried in a 110°C oven. After 72 and 96 hr, dry weight values were obtained. Dry weights were utilized when values on two consecutive days were within 0.5 mg. The lipids from whole lung were extracted with chloroform:methanol (2:1 v/v) and washed to remove nonlipid contaminants (19). Further separation of the lipid compounds into separate phospholipid classes was achieved by thin-layer chromatographic methods (20). Saturated phosphatidylcholine was measured after osmic acid treatment as described by Mason *et al.* (21). Recovery of phosphatidylcholine and disaturated phosphatidylcholine from whole lung was routinely assessed by adding [^{14}C]dipalmitoyl phosphatidylcholine (Applied Science Co., State College, Pa.) at the time of extraction of lung tissue samples. This permitted the correction for any losses during processing and allowed ongoing assessment of quality control. The appropriate lipid spots were scraped from the plates and the phospholipids extracted from the gel by the method of Bligh and Dyer (22). Lipid phosphorus determinations (23) were performed on each fraction and the amount of radioactivity in each phospholipid was measured by liquid scintillation counting techniques in a Beckman LS 7000 liquid scintillation counter.

The responses of the controls, treated animals, and fasting blood glucose groupings were compared in a one-way analysis of variance (24), using routines in the BMDP computer package (25). The mean response at each dose or grouping was compared with the mean of the appropriate controls and tested for significance.

Results. All of the animals in the control, 30-mg/kg, and 40-mg/kg treatment groups and 90% of the 50-mg/kg group survived the 7-day experimental period. In contrast, only 55% of the 100-mg/kg STZ-treated rats survived. The deaths in this latter group occurred within 48–96 hr of STZ infusion.

Table I presents the data on the effects of STZ on blood chemistry, growth, and urine output as a function of STZ dose. Since the two control groups did not differ significantly in any of the indices examined, they were combined and represent the normal population in this study. The serum glucose concentrations in rats injected with 30, 40, and 50 mg/kg STZ were all significantly different from those of the control group. The administration of 100 mg/kg STZ also produced significant hyperglycemia, although the average of the fasting blood glucoses of the survivors in this group was less than that found in the group injected with 50 mg/kg.

Table I also demonstrates that infusion of STZ produced a reduction in weight gain that generally paralleled increasing STZ dose. The reduction in weight gain is significant in all treatment categories with the exception of the 100-mg/kg group. As was found with fasting blood glucose, the reduction in weight gain in

TABLE I. STREPTOZOTOCIN DOSE RESPONSE[a]

Effect on	Controls	30 mg/kg	40 mg/kg	50 mg/kg	100 mg/kg
Fasting blood glucose (mg/dl)	88.0 ± 4.4 (20)	129.6 ± 9.4 (20)	159.9 ± 16.3 (20)	388.7 ± 25.2 (18)	213.2 ± 49.3 (11)
P value[b]	—	<0.05	<0.001	<0.001	<0.001
Blood urea nitrogen (mg/dl)	12.48 ± 0.45 (20)	16.44 ± 1.01 (20)	19.44 ± 1.74 (20)	43.35 ± 3.15 (18)	30.91 ± 7.85 (11)
P value[b]	—	N.S.	<0.05	<0.001	<0.001
Albumin (g/dl)	3.27 ± 0.05 (20)	3.63 ± 0.05 (20)	3.44 ± 0.07 (20)	2.53 ± 0.06 (18)	2.70 ± 0.13 (11)
P value[b]	—	N.S.	N.S.	<0.01	N.S.
Weight gain (g)[c]	55.9 ± 2.7 (20)	38.1 ± 2.8 (20)	31.3 ± 4.0 (20)	8.2 ± 4.6 (18)	36.9 ± 8.6 (11)
P value[b]	—	<0.05	<0.001	<0.001	N.S.
Urine output (ml/100 g/24 hr) 48 hr post-STZ	4.4 ± 0.3 (19)	7.7 ± 1.1 (20)	15.8 ± 2.4 (20)	34.7 ± 2.2 (20)	15.5 ± 4.0 (15)
P value[b]	—	N.S.	<0.001	<0.001	<0.01
96 hr post-STZ	4.3 ± 0.2 (19)	9.7 ± 1.6 (20)	19.9 ± 3.1 (20)	50.8 ± 2.7 (18)	21.6 ± 8.9 (11)
P value[b]	—	N.S.	<0.001	<0.001	N.S.

[a] Values represent the means ± SE for (*n*) determinations.
[b] *P* vs controls; N.S., not significant.
[c] The weight gain represents the amount of weight gained during the 1-week experimental period.

this group was less than would be expected. Furthermore, due to the wide range of weight gains in the animals receiving 100 mg/kg STZ, they did not differ significantly from the controls. Urine volumes 48 and 96 hr after STZ administration were significantly higher than control values in the 40- and 50-mg/kg groups. The urine volume of the 30-mg/kg group is somewhat higher than that found in the control group, although the difference is not statistically significant. The 100-mg/kg group produced urine volumes that were generally higher than those found in controls, but due to the large range of volumes encountered these values were statistically significant only at the 48-hr collection.

Serum albumin and blood urea nitrogen (BUN) concentrations were determined as laboratory indices of liver and kidney function. Table I demonstrates that BUN values in the 30-mg/kg group were similar to those found in the controls, while the 40-, 50-, and 100-mg/kg groups had values significantly higher than those of the control group. Although the BUN concentrations generally increased with drug dosage, the 100-mg/kg animals had an average value intermediate between that found for the 40- and 50-mg/kg groups. Serum albumin concentrations, in contrast, were significantly different from controls only in the 50-mg/kg group. The 100-mg/kg group showed serum albumin concentrations which were higher than those in the 50-mg/kg group, but lower than those found in the 40-mg/kg group.

The effects of STZ-induced diabetes on lung tissue are shown in Table II. Total lung phosphatidylcholine concentrations and dry-to-wet weight ratios were unchanged in any of the treatment groups. In contrast, the disaturated phosphatidylcholine levels were significantly depressed in the 50-mg/kg group. This lowered level of disaturated phosphatidylcholine resulted in a 30% decrease in the disaturated phosphatidylcholine-to-total lung phosphatidylcholine ratio. The animals that survived treatment with 100 mg STZ/kg generally had lower levels of disaturated phosphatidylcholine than controls. However, these two groups were not statistically different, due to the wide variability of disaturated phosphatidylcholine concentrations found in the 100-mg/kg group. Lung protein concentrations were also affected by the administration of STZ and demonstrated significant reductions after treatment with 50 and 100 mg/kg.

Although the fasting blood glucose levels generally increased with increasing STZ dos-

TABLE II. EFFECTS OF STREPTOZOTOCIN DOSE ON LUNG BIOCHEMISTRY[a]

Effect on	Controls	30 mg/kg	40 mg/kg	50 mg/kg	100 mg/kg
Phosphatidylcholine (μmole/g wet wt.)	10.66 ± 0.33 (14)	11.57 ± 0.27 (20)	11.11 ± 0.32 (19)	11.37 ± 0.47 (16)	11.02 ± 0.57 (11)
P value[b]	—	N.S.	N.S.	N.S.	N.S.
Disaturated phosphatidylcholine (μmol/g wet wt)	5.32 ± 0.21 (14)	5.76 ± 0.09 (19)	5.46 ± 0.14 (19)	3.94 ± 0.33 (18)	4.58 ± 0.43 (8)
P value[b]	—	N.S.	N.S.	<0.01	N.S.
Protein (mg/g wet wt)	133.79 ± 3.67 (10)	134.78 ± 2.80 (20)	136.64 ± 2.60 (20)	115.50 ± 1.88 (18)	117.52 ± 3.46 (11)
P value[b]	—	N.S.	N.S.	<0.005	<0.05
Dry/wet wt ratio	0.2078 ± 0.0037	0.2008 ± 0.0021	0.2006 ± 0.0029	0.2018 ± 0.0023	0.1952 ± 0.0031
P value[b]	N.S.	N.S.	N.S.	N.S.	N.S.

[a] Values represent the means ± SE for (*n*) determinations.
[b] *P* vs controls; N.S., not significant.

age, there was considerable overlap between the groups. Therefore, in order to correlate the effects of STZ-induced diabetes with hyperglycemia, the data are presented in Tables III and IV as a function of the final fasting blood glucose concentration. For these analyses, animals with fasting blood glucose concentrations of 100 mg/dl or less were used as the normal group for statistical comparisons. Table III shows that weight gain and 96-hr urine output were significantly different from controls in all animals with fasting glucose

TABLE III. CORRELATION OF EFFECTS OF STREPTOZOTOCIN-INDUCED HYPERGLYCEMIA WITH FASTING BLOOD GLUCOSE (mg/dl)[a]

	Fasting blood glucose (mg/dl)					
Effect on	⩽100	101–125	126–150	151–200	201–400	>400
Mean fasting blood glucose (mg/dl)	83.8 ± 3.0 (23)	112.0 ± 1.5 (22)	138.7 ± 2.3 (12)	171.3 ± 3.4 (7)	284.3 ± 20.3 (10)	452.9 ± 10.6 (15)
P value[b]	—	<0.001	<0.001	<0.001	<0.001	<0.001
Blood urea nitrogen (mg/dl)	11.89 ± 0.39 (23)	14.98 ± 0.76 (22)	17.44 ± 0.81 (12)	24.36 ± 0.95 (7)	30.79 ± 2.90 (10)	53.12 ± 3.65 (15)
P value[b]	—	<0.05	<0.001	<0.001	<0.001	<0.001
Albumin (g/dl)	3.42 ± 0.08 (23)	3.42 ± 0.08 (22)	3.53 ± 0.08 (12)	3.40 ± 0.13 (7)	2.93 ± 0.13 (10)	2.49 ± 0.08 (15)
P value[b]	—	N.S.	N.S.	N.S.	<0.01	<0.001
Weight gain (g)	54.3 ± 2.0 (23)	49.6 ± 2.6 (22)	35.0 ± 2.6 (12)	16.3 ± 3.8 (7)	18.5 ± 4.6 (10)	0.1 ± 4.1 (15)
P value[b]	—	N.S.	<0.001	<0.001	<0.001	<0.001
Urine output (ml/100 g/24 hrs) 96 hr post-STZ	4.5 ± 0.3 (22)	6.9 ± 1.1 (22)	9.7 ± 2.2 (12)	31.5 ± 3.6 (7)	41.9 ± 3.0 (10)	54.4 ± 3.9 (15)
P value[b]	—	N.S.	<0.005	<0.001	<0.001	<0.001
Glucose in urine, 96 hr, post-STZ	0/22	6/22	7/12	7/7	10/10	15/15
Ketones in urine, 96 hr, post-STZ	0/22	0/22	0/12	0/7	0/10	3/15

[a] Values represent the means ± SE for (*n*) determinations.
[b] *P* vs ⩽100 mg/dl glucose group; N.S., not significant.

TABLE IV. CORRELATION OF EFFECTS OF STREPTOZOTOCIN-INDUCED GLUCOSE INTOLERANCE ON PULMONARY BIOCHEMISTRY WITH FASTING BLOOD GLUCOSE[a]

	Fasting blood glucose (mg/dl)					
Effect on	⩽100	101–125	126–150	151–200	201–400	>400
Phosphatidylcholine	11.10 ± 0.29	11.10 ± 0.33	11.14 ± 0.45	11.54 ± 0.42	11.05 ± 0.77	11.36 ± 0.43
(μmol/g)[b]	(18)	(20)	(12)	(7)	(9)	(14)
P value[c]	—	N.S.	N.S.	N.S.	N.S.	N.S.
Disaturated	5.41 ± 0.19	5.58 ± 0.14	5.32 ± 0.25	4.70 ± 0.54	4.87 ± 0.39	4.12 ± 0.40
phosphatidylcholine	(18)	(17)	(12)	(7)	(10)	(14)
(μmole/g)						
P value[c]	—	N.S.	N.S.	N.S.	N.S.	~0.01
Protein (mg/g)	132.8 ± 2.9	127.1 ± 3.3	138.5 ± 3.4	134.3 ± 4.9	125.4 ± 5.8	116.1 ± 1.7
	(16)	(19)	(12)	(7)	(10)	(15)
P value[c]	—	N.S.	N.S.	N.S.	N.S.	<0.01
Dry/wet wt ratio	0.2031 ± 0.0022	0.2013 ± 0.0030	0.1992 ± 0.0027	0.1986 ± 0.0037	0.2006 ± 0.0054	0.2015 ± 0.0026
	(16)	(19)	(12)	(7)	(9)	(15)
P value[c]	—	N.S.	N.S.	N.S.	N.S.	N.S.

[a] Values represent the means ± SE for (*n*) determinations.
[b] All data are expressed per wet weight of tissue.
[c] *P* vs ⩽100 mg/dl group; N.S., not significant.

levels higher than 126 mg/dl. Blood urea nitrogen values rose with increasing glucose concentration, while albumin concentrations remained relatively steady at glucose concentrations less than 200 ml/dl. Above this value the albumin concentrations declined to appreciably lower levels. Glucose could be detected in the urine of a limited number of animals with blood glucose values in the range 101–125 mg/dl, but was found in all urine samples from animals with levels greater than 151 mg/dl. Ketonuria, on the other hand, rarely occurred in animals with STZ-induced experimental diabetes.

Table IV documents the relationship between increasing hyperglycemia and lung disaturated phosphatidylcholine concentrations and illustrates that the concentrations of this phospholipid decreased with increasing blood glucose values, but only reached statistically lower concentrations at glucose levels greater than 400 mg/dl. Lung protein concentrations remained relatively constant up to fasting glucose levels of 400 mg/dl; above this concentration lung proteins were decreased approximately 13%. Total lung phosphatidylcholine and pulmonary dry-to-wet weight ratios, on the other hand, demonstrated no change with increasing hyperglycemia.

Discussion. In this study intravenous injection of STZ in a dose of 30 mg/kg or greater produced carbohydrate intolerance in the rat, and fasting blood glucose levels increased coincident with increased drug dose. Higher STZ dosages also resulted in increased urine outputs, decreased weight gains, and perturbed kidney function, as assessed by blood urea nitrogen concentrations. Liver function, as represented by serum albumin levels, was affected only in the 50-mg/kg STZ group. The administration of 100 mg STZ/kg resulted in a diabetes-like state that was less severe than anticipated; this may result from the death of this group's markedly abnormal animals within 96 hr after STZ infusion. In general, the effects on urine output, weight gain, and kidney and liver function reported here are similar to previous findings (4, 8–10, 26–28). The fasting blood glucose levels, however, differ from those reported previously, a variance most likely due to different experimental techniques and/or variability in STZ potency (29).

This study also indicates that alterations in adult lung metabolism are dependent on the extent of the diabetic condition. This is exemplified by the decreased concentrations of pulmonary protein and disaturated phosphatidylcholine found in animals treated with 50–100 mg/kg STZ. Since insulin is recognized as an anabolic hormone, the decreased protein concentrations found in severe diabetes were not unexpected. The decreased levels of disaturated phosphatidylcholine, however, may not be attributable solely to the general catabolic effects of diabetes, since total lung phosphatidylcholine concentrations were not affected in any of the treatment groups. This preferential decrease in disaturated phosphatidylcholine may indicate that diabetes selectively affects the pathways leading to the formation of the disaturated phospholipids that are particularly characteristic of lung surfactant. The results from the dose–response relationships support and extend those of previous findings, where only large doses of STZ were employed (11–17).

Although the fasting blood glucose levels generally increased with increasing STZ dosages, there was considerable overlap between the groups. Therefore, the data were also analyzed as a function of the fasting blood glucose concentration at the time of sacrifice in order to directly compare the severity of the effects of chemically induced diabetes to the severity of glucose intolerance. Also, the effects of STZ-induced hyperglycemia based on fasting blood glucose concentrations may be a more sensitive indicator of the deleterious effects of diabetes on different organ systems that STZ dose alone. Thus, increasing hyperglycemia is accompanied by decreased weight gains and serum albumin levels and elevated blood urea nitrogen concentrations and urine outputs. Pulmonary protein concentrations remain unchanged until hyperglycemia becomes pronounced, then drop to a significantly lower level. Disaturated phosphatidylcholine content appears to decline with increasing hyperglycemia, but can be differentiated statistically from controls only when fasting blood glucose concentrations are greater than 400 mg/dl. This relationship is further support for the notion that the severity of diabetes is an important variable in studies of adult lung metabolism in diabetic animal models.

Using fasting blood sugar levels as a reference base for data analysis is useful because it reveals that some organ systems are sensitive to even mild or moderate glucose intolerance and deteriorate as the carbohydrate intolerance worsens. Other tissue characteristics, however, are apparently more resistant to the disabling effects of diabetes and are affected only in the severest cases, if at all. The relative sensitivity of different tissues and metabolites should be taken into account when using animal models for the study of diabetes mellitus. These results also indicate the importance of reporting blood glucose levels (preferably in fasted animals) in any study involving experimental diabetes. The necessity of establishing the appropriate level of glucose intolerance has been underscored in several publications concerning the effects of maternal diabetes on fetal development (30–32). These investigators have reported that fetal size, fetal insulin, and fetal glucose concentrations are dependent on the degree of maternal carbohydrate imbalance.

The authors thank Dr. W. J. Raynor for the statistical analyses used in this manuscript. This work was supported in part by grants from the National Institutes of Health, Pulmonary SCOR P50-HL-27358, and the Juvenile Diabetes Foundation, 79R263. Dr. M. J. Engle is the recipient of Research Career Development Award KD4-HD-00350.

1. Rakieten N, Rakieten ML, Nadkarni MV. Studies on the diabetogenic action of streptozotocin (NSC-37917). Cancer Chemother Rep **29**:91–98, 1963.
2. Brosky G, Logothetopoulos J. Streptozotocin diabetes in the mouse and guinea pig. Diabetes **18**:606–611, 1969.
3. Schein PS, Cooney DA, Vernon ML. The use of nicotinamde to modify the toxicity of streptozotocin diabetes without loss of antitumor activity. Cancer Res **27**:2324–2332, 1967.
4. Pitkin RM, Reynolds WA. Diabetogenic effects of streptozotocin in rhesus monkeys. Diabetes **19**:85–90, 1970.
5. Ganda OP, Rossini AA, Like AA. Studies on streptozotocin diabetes. Diabetes **25**:595–603, 1976.
6. Jones CW, Reynold WA, Hoganson GE. Streptozotocin diabetes in the monkey. Diabetes **29**:536–546, 1980.
7. Junod A, Lambert AE, Orci L, Pictet R, Gonet AE, Renold AE. Studies of the diabetogenic action of streptozotocin. Proc Soc Exp Biol Med **126**:201–205, 1967.
8. Junod A, Lambert AE, Stauffacher W, Renold AE. Diabetogenic action of streptozotocin: Relationship of dose to metabolic response. J Clin Invest **48**:2129–2139, 1969.
9. Kemnitz JW, Engle MJ, Perelman RH, Farrell PM. An experimental model for studies of fetal maldevelopment in the diabetic pregnancy. Pediatrics, in press.
10. Levine JH, Buse MG, Leaming AB, Raskin P. Effect of streptozotocin-induced diabetes on renal ornithine decarboxylase activity. Diabetes **29**:532–535, 1980.

11. Das DK, Kumar S. Nutritional and hormonal variations alter *de novo* fatty acid synthesis in mammalian lung. Fed Proc **34:**673, 1975.
12. Morishige WK, Uetake C, Greenwood FC, Akaka J. Pulmonary insulin responsivity: *In vivo* effects of insulin on the diabetic rat lung and specific insulin binding to lung receptors in normal rats. Endocrinology **100:**1710–1722, 1977.
13. Plopper CG, Morishige WK. Alterations in granular (Type II) pneumocyte ultrastructure by streptozotocin-induced diabetes in the rat. Lab Invest **38:**143–148, 1978.
14. Plopper CG, Morishige WK. Alterations in the ultrastructure of nonciliated bronchiolar epithelial (Clara) cells by streptozotocin-induced diabetes in rats. Amer Rev Resp Dis **120:**1137–1143, 1979.
15. Reinila A, Koivisto VA, Akerblom HK. Lipids in the pulmonary artery and the lungs of severely diabetic rats. Diabetologia **13:**305–310, 1977.
16. Moxley MA, Longmore WJ. Studies on the effects of alloxan and streptozotocin induced diabetes on lipid metabolism in the isolated perfused rat lung. Life Sci **17:**921–926, 1975.
17. Moxley MA, Longmore WJ. Effects of experimental diabetes and insulin on lipid metabolism in the isolated perfused rat lung. Biochim Biophys Acta **488:**218–224, 1977.
18. Hartree AS. A modification of the Lowry method that gives a linear photometric response. Anal Biochem **48:**422–427, 1972.
19. Radin NS. Preparation of lipid extracts. In: Lowenstein JM, ed. Methods in Enzymology. New York, Academic Press, Vol 14:pp245–254, 1969.
20. Engle MJ, Sanders RL, Longmore WJ. Phospholipid composition and acyltransferase activity of lamellar bodies isolated from rat lung. Arch Biochem Biophys **173:**586–595, 1976.
21. Mason RJ, Nellenbogen J, Clements JA. Isolation of disaturated phosphatidylcholine with osmium tetroxide. J Lipid Res **17:**281–284, 1976.
22. Bligh EG, Dyer WJ. A rapid method of total lipid extraction and purification. Canad J Biochem Physiol **37:**911–917, 1959.
23. Ames BN, Dubin DT. The role of polyamines in the neutralization of bacteriophage deoxyribonucleic acid. J Biol Chem **235:**769–775, 1960.
24. Kleinbaum DG, Kupper LL. Applied Regression Analysis and Other Multivariable Methods. North Scituate, Mass., Duxbury Press, 1978.
25. Dixon WJ, Brown MB, Engleman L, Frane JW, Hill MA, Jennrich RI, Toporer JD. BMDP Statistical Software, Berkeley, Univ. of California Press, 1981.
26. Somani P, Singh HP, Saini RK, Rabinovitch A. Streptozotocin-induced diabetes in the spontaneously hypertensive rat. Metabolism **28:**1075–1077, 1979.
27. Schein PS, Rakieten N, Cooney DA, Davis R, Vernon ML. Streptozotocin diabetes in monkeys and dogs, and its prevention by nicotinamide. Proc Soc Exp Biol Med **143:**514–518, 1973.
28. Sadoff L. Nephrotoxicity of streptozotocin (NSC-85998). Cancer Chemother Rep **54:**457–459, 1979.
29. Rossini AA, Like AA, Dulin WE, Cahill GF Jr. Pancreatic beta cell toxicity by streptozotocin anomers. Diabetes **26:**1120–1124, 1977.
30. Pitkin RM, Van Orden DE. Fetal effects of maternal streptozotocin-diabetes. Endocrinology **94:**1247–1253, 1974.
31. Kervran A, Guillame M, Jost A. The endocrine pancreas of the fetus from diabetic pregnant rat. Diabetologia **15:**387–393, 1978.
32. Eriksson W, Andersson A, Efendic S, Elde R, Hellerstrom C. Diabetes in pregnancy: Effects on the fetal and newborn rat with particular regard to body weight, serum insulin concentration and pancreatic contents of insulin, glucagon, and somatostatin. Acta Endocrinol **94:**354–364, 1980.

Received July 11, 1983. P.S.E.B.M. 1984, Vol. 176.
Accepted March 26, 1984.

PROCEEDINGS OF THE SOCIETY FOR EXPERIMENTAL BIOLOGY AND MEDICINE **176**, 268–275 (1984)

Anesthesia and Stimulation of Pituitary β-Endorphin Release in Rats (41870)

SHARON MAIEWSKI, SHEILA MULDOON,* AND GREGORY P. MUELLER

*Departments of Physiology and *Anesthesiology, Uniformed Services University of the Health Sciences, 4301 Jones Bridge Road, Bethesda, Maryland 20814*

Abstract. The effects of several anesthetic drugs and artificial respiration on the release of pituitary β-endorphin-like immunoreactivity (β-END-LI) were examined in rats. Plasma β-END-LI responses to halothane and pentobarbital were similar in magnitude and duration, being maximal (2- to 3-fold) by 10 min and returning to control values by 30 min after induction. Urethane anesthesia was associated with an 8-fold increase in plasma β-END-LI throughout the 30-min treatment period. In comparison to anesthesia alone, anesthesia plus intubation with artificial respiration (standard parameters) was associated with considerably greater elevations in plasma β-END-LI (up to 30-fold). Further, intubation and artificial respiration appear to have contributed separately, and in an additive fashion, to the overall β-END-LI responses observed. As compared to halothane anesthesia alone, intubation evoked a 4-fold increase in circulating β-END-LI, whereas intubation plus ventilation was associated with a 12-fold increase. Treatment with morphine (1 or 5 mg/kg), but not pancuronium (0.3 mg/kg), attenuated the plasma β-END-LI response to mechanical ventilation, suggesting that a subconscious phenomenon, perhaps related to pain, was partially responsible for the profound release of pituitary β-END-LI associated with artificial respiration. Chromatographic analysis of the molecular forms of β-END-LI released into plasma revealed that both β-END- and β-lipotropin (β-LPH)-sized peptides were secreted under the present experimental conditions. Since the analgesic form of β-END (β-END_{1-31}) is cosecreted with β-LPH from the pars distalis, increases in the fraction of plasma β-END-LI corresponding to β-END in size were probably due to the release of opiate active β-END_{1-31}.

Various theories have been proposed describing the analgesic mechanism of anesthetic drugs. Several groups of investigators have suggested that anesthetic analgesia may be mediated through the release of endogenous opiate peptides (1–3). Evidence supporting this hypothesis includes findings that the opiate receptor antagonist, naloxone, partially reversed the analgesia (1, 2, 4, 5) and attenuated the circulatory (6, 7) and hypnotic (6) effects of inhalation anesthetics in laboratory animals. Also, Berkowitz (8) reported a cross-tolerance between nitrous oxide and morphine in rats. In man, nitrous oxide decreased the perception of pain (subjective reports) (3, 9) and reduced the amplitude of cerebral evoked potentials to painful tooth pulp stimulation (9). Importantly, both these responses were partially reversed by naloxone (3, 9), again suggesting a role for endogenous opiate peptides in anesthetic analgesia. By contrast, results of several comparable studies do not support this conclusion. For example, Harper *et al.* (10) observed that naloxone had little influence on the anesthetic requirement for halothane in rats. Also, Way *et al.* (11) failed to observe an increase in cerebral spinal fluid β-endorphin (β-END) following thiopental–nitrous oxide–halothane anesthesia in humans. Although these findings suggest that the effects of anesthetics may not be mediated through the release of endogenous opiate peptides within the central nervous system (CNS), the possible release of pituitary β-END into blood and its contribution to the development of anesthesia remain to be determined. Accordingly, we have investigated the effects of halothane, pentobarbital, and urethane on the secretion of pituitary β-END in rats. The present findings indicate that all three agents increase plasma levels of β-END-like immunoreactivity (β-END-LI); however, these responses are modest in comparison to the release of pituitary β-END-LI evoked by anesthesia plus artificial respiration. Chromatographic analysis suggests that the molecular form of β-END released under the present condition is, indeed, the analgesic form β-END_{1-31}.

Materials and Methods. *Animals and treatments.* Male Sprague–Dawley rats (Taconic Farms, Inc., Germantown, Pa.) weighing 300 to 500 g were housed at 22°C with lights on

0037-9727/84 $1.50

from 0600 to 1800 hr having free access to standard rat chow and tap water. Sodium pentobarbital (50 mg/kg, Sigma Chemical Co., St. Louis, Mo.), urethane (1.5 g/kg, Sigma), or morphine (1 and 5 mg/kg, Mallinckrodt Chemical Works, St. Louis, Mo.) were injected intraperitoneally in a volume of 0.4 ml; control animals received injections of 0.9% NaCl vehicle. Pancuronium bromide (0.3 mg/kg, Organon, Inc., West Orange, N.J.) was injected via a tail artery cannula 8 to 10 min after pentobarbital administration; a maintenance dose of 0.1 mg/kg was given 14 min after the first injection of pancuronium. Control animals received corresponding vehicle injections. Halothane was administered in room air at a flow rate of 7.5 liters/min via a vaporizer (Flotec MK2, Cyprane Ltd., Keighley, England). Halothane induction was carried out in a plastic chamber having an atmosphere of 4% halothane; control animals were handled similarly but were not exposed to halothane. Anesthetized rats were maintained on 1.5% halothane administered via a nose cone. Mechanical ventilation (Rodent Respirator, Harvard Apparatus, South Natick, Mass.) was performed via an endotracheal tube using a stroke volume (5.5 cm^3) and frequency (60 cycles/min) determined to maintain blood gases (pO_2, pCO_2) and pH within the normal ranges. Colonic temperatures were monitored (Yellow Springs Instrument Co., Yellow Springs, Ohio) and maintained between 36 and 38°C by a heated water pad (Hamilton Industries, Cincinnati, Ohio). Additional details for treatments within individual experiments are presented under Results.

Blood collection, radioimmunoassay, and gel filtration chromatography. Serial blood samples (0.8 to 1.0 ml) were collected via tail artery cannulae (PE-90, Clay Adams) into plastic syringes containing 40 μl of 10% EDTA and 5 mg% bacitracin; cannulations were completed within 10 min after exposure to anesthetic. The cells and fluid volume removed were returned (in 0.9% NaCl) immediately following each collection. Decapitation blood samples (approximately 6 ml) were collected into plastic tubes containing 600 μl of 10% EDTA and 5 mg% bacitracin and placed on ice. Plasmas were prepared by centrifugation and stored at −70°C until assayed. It was determined that within the same anesthetic treatment group, the two methods for blood collection yielded comparable plasma hormone values, indicating that cannulation and blood sampling, per se, did not affect circulating levels of β-END-LI.

Plasma levels of β-END-LI were measured by radioimmunoassay using a rabbit antiserum (C-55) raised against camel β-END$_{1-31}$. As previously described by Mueller (12), this antibody recognizes the C-terminal portion of β-END$_{1-31}$ and reacts equally with shorter and α-*N*-acetylated β-endorphins, as well as β-lipotropin (β-LPH). The antibody does not recognize α-endorphin, the enkephalins, or other peptides structurally related to the N-terminal sequence of β-END$_{1-31}$. Similarly, non-opiate hormones of the hypothalamus, pituitary, and gastrointestinal tract are not recognized by this assay. Because more than one molecular form of β-END-LI is detected, data are expressed in picograms per milliliter based on the camel β-END$_{1-31}$ standard used (Peninsula Laboratories, Inc., Belmont, Calif.).

To determine the relative contribution of β-END- and β-LPH-sized material to total circulating β-END-LI under the various conditions reported here, treatment group pools of plasma (5.0 to 10.0 ml each) were chromatographed at 4°C on a Sephadex G-50 (superfine, Pharmacia, Inc., Piscataway, N.J.) column (2.5 × 80 cm) using 0.1 *N* acetic acid containing 0.05% BSA, 0.02% sodium azide, and 5 mg% bacitracin as the mobile phase. Aliquots of each 7.0-ml fraction were lyophilized, resuspended in assay buffer, and immunoassayed for β-END-LI. Recovery of applied β-END-LI averaged 87 ± 7% for all the runs ($N = 7$). Purified preparations of human β-LPH (gifts of D. Orth and A. Parlow) and rat β-LPH (prepared in house), as well as synthetic β-END$_{1-31}$, were used to characterize the column.

Statistical analysis. Data were analyzed statistically using an analysis of variance and Duncan's multiple range test; differences were considered significant at the level of $P < 0.05$.

Results. Shown in Fig. 1 are the time course effects of pentobarbital, urethane, and halothane on plasma β-END-LI levels in spontaneously breathing and mechanically ventilated rats. When given alone, pentobarbital

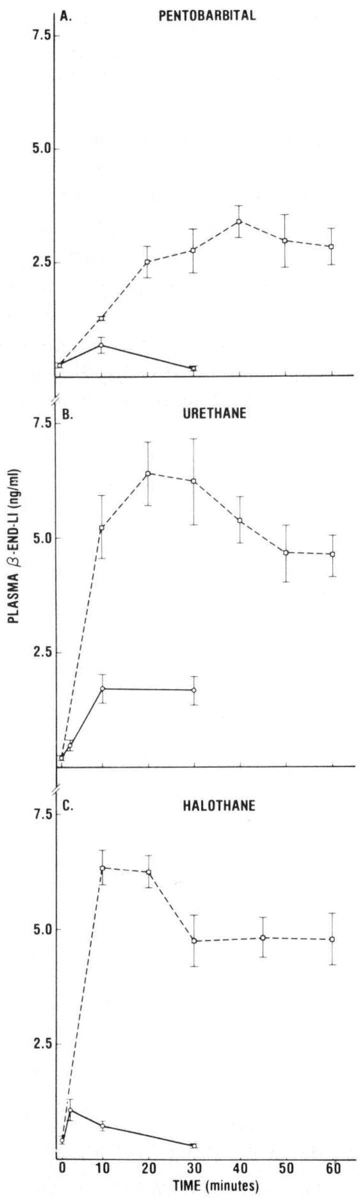

FIG. 1. The time course effects of pentobarbital (50 mg/kg), urethane (1 mg/kg), and halothane (induction with 4%, maintenance with 1.5%) on plasma levels of β-END-LI in spontaneously breathing (O —— O) and mechanically ventilated (O --- O) rats. Serial blood samples were collected in the ventilated groups; decapitation samples in the anesthetized spontaneously breathing and unanesthetized control groups. Mean plasma β-END-LI values for the unanesthetized control groups of the pentobarbital, urethane, and halothane experiments were 253 ± 29, 209 ± 38, and 434 ± 80 pg/ml, respectively. Values are group means ± SEM (N = 6–10). All values are significantly different ($P < 0.05$) from 0 time control values with the exception of the 30-min means in spontaneously breathing rats anesthetized with either pentobarbital or halothane.

and halothane evoked rapid but small increases in circulating β-END-LI as compared to 0 time control values ($P < 0.05$). Plasma β-END-LI responses to both anesthetics were similar in magnitude (2- to 3-fold) and duration (maximal by 10 min; return to control values by 30 min following induction). Urethane anesthesia resulted in a more prolonged (30 min) 8-fold increase in plasma β-END-LI in spontaneously breathing animals. Though significant, the increases in plasma β-END-LI evoked by pentobarbital, halothane, and urethane in spontaneously breathing animals were modest as compared to the rises observed in anesthetized animals receiving mechanical ventilation. Anesthesia plus intubation with mechanical ventilation was associated with dramatic 15- to more than 30-fold elevations in plasma levels of β-END-LI over normal control values.

Although tail artery cannulation and serial blood sampling did not produce any noticeable physical or hormonal responses (data not shown), endotracheal intubation characteristically resulted in a brief physical response (generalized muscle contraction with irregular breathing and gagging) in spite of a surgical plane of anesthesia. To examine the possibility that the intubation procedure might contribute separately to marked release of β-END-LI in artificially respirated animals, the experiment presented in Fig. 2 was conducted. Under halothane anesthesia, intubation resulted in significant elevations in plasma β-END-LI (10 to 30 min) over values measured in rats receiving just anesthetic; a maximal 4-fold response was elicited 10 min following endotracheal intubation. Mechanical ventilation in combination with intubation further increased circulating levels of β-END-LI to a value which was 11-fold greater than that observed in animals under anesthesia alone.

As painful stimuli are potent stimulators of pituitary β-END release in laboratory animals (13–15), it is possible that some effect related to pain caused the dramatic plasma β-END-LI increases associated with intubation and mechanical ventilation (Fig. 1). Accordingly,

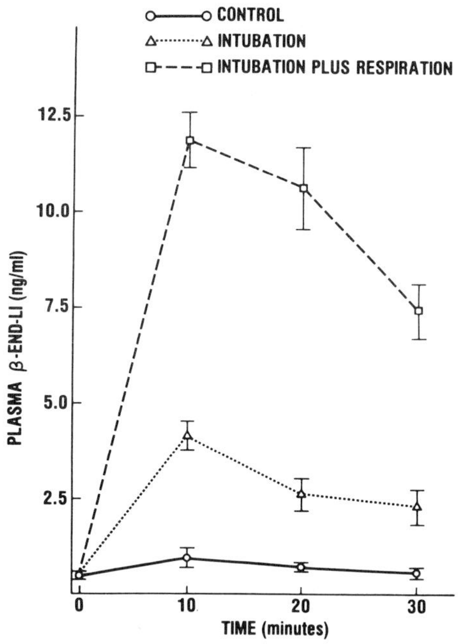

FIG. 2. Effects of endotracheal intubation and intubation plus mechanical ventilation on plasma levels of β-END-LI in rats anesthetized with halothane. Following induction groups of animals were intubated or intubated and ventilated; all anesthetized animals were rapidly cannulated for blood collection (completed within 5 min of induction). The 0 time control value (493 ± 107 pg/ml) represents plasma β-END-LI in normal rats sacrificed by decapitation; the 10-, 20-, and 30-min control values represent plasma β-END-LI in rats treated with halothane alone. Data plotted are group means ± SEM (N = 6 or 7). Plasma β-END-LI values in intubated rats are significantly greater ($P < 0.05$) than values in animals treated with halothane alone. Intubation plus respiration significantly elevated ($P < 0.05$) plasma β-END-LI above values observed in intubated animals.

we examined the sensitivity of the plasma β-END-LI response to pretreatment with morphine. Under pentobarbital anesthesia, artificially respirated animals had plasma β-END-LI concentrations which averaged 7-fold higher than those of spontaneously breathing animals by 10 to 30 min after anesthetic administration (Fig. 3). Morphine (1 mg/kg, ip), administered concurrently with pentobarbital, significantly attenuated the plasma β-END-LI response to artificial respiration at 30 min but not at earlier time points (10 and 20 min). A higher dose of morphine (5 mg/kg, ip) given 10 min prior to pentobarbital almost completely prevented the stimulated release of β-END-LI at all time points (Table I). By contrast, neuromuscular blockade by pancuronium (0.3 mg/kg, iv) was without effect on the time-related increases in plasma β-END-LI associated with mechanical ventilation (data not shown).

Gel filtration chromatographic analysis revealed that anesthesia along or together with mechanical ventilation resulted in elevated levels of β-END-LI (Figs. 1–3) resembling both β-END_{1-31} and β-LPH standards in molecular size (Table II). Some variation in the ratio of

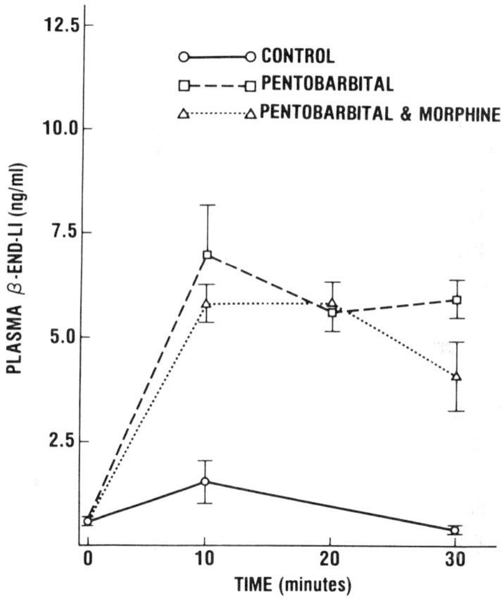

FIG. 3. Effects of morphine treatment on plasma β-END-LI in anesthetized and mechanically ventilated rats. Morphine (1 mg/kg, ip) was administered following induction of pentobarbital (50 mg/kg) anesthesia and just prior to intubation. The 0-min control value (595 ± 10 pg/ml) represents plasma β-END-LI in untreated rats; the 10-, 20-, and 30-min control samples were collected from animals anesthetized but not ventilated (○ —— ○). The groups designated pentobarbital (□ --- □) and pentobarbital morphine (△ · · · △) were mechanically ventilated. Serial blood samples were collected in the ventilated groups; decapitation samples in the spontaneously breathing groups. Values are group means ± SEM (N = 5 or 6). Circulating β-END-LI levels in both groups of respirated animals were significantly greater ($P < 0.05$) than those observed in control animals. Morphine significantly attenuated the plasma β-END-LI response to mechanical ventilation at the 30-min time point.

TABLE I. EFFECTS OF MORPHINE (5 mg/kg) PRETREATMENT ON PLASMA LEVELS OF β-END-LI IN MECHANICALLY VENTILATED RATS

Treatment	β-END-LI (pg/ml)
Control	180 ± 18
Pentobarbital	
10 min	914 ± 131[a]
20 min	983 ± 162[a]
30 min	1275 ± 229[a]
Pentobarbital plus morphine:	
10 min	381 ± 45[a,b]
20 min	276 ± 37[b]
30 min	187 ± 30[b]

Note. Control animals received vehicle injections; all animals receiving pentobarbital were mechanically ventilated. Values stated are group means ± SEM (N = 7 or 8).

[a] Significantly different from control values, $P < 0.05$.

[b] Significantly different from values of pentobarbital-treated animals at corresponding time, $P < 0.05$.

β-END- to β-LPH-sized immunoreactivity was observed though not quantitated precisely because the chromatographic procedure used required that large volumes of plasma be run in order to fractionate measurable amounts of β-END-LI in an elution profile. Accordingly, no more than two runs could be made with each treatment group plasma pool. It is important to note, however, that β-LPH, a marker for the release of opiate active β-END_{1-31} from the par distalis, was generally increased under conditions examined here (see Discussion).

Discussion. The present findings indicate that pentobarbital, halothane, and urethane all evoke rapid and significant increases in bloodborne β-END-LI in rats. As previously observed with ether anesthesia (15), stimulation of pituitary β-END-LI release by pentobarbital or halothane is of shorter duration (5–20 min) and reduced magnitude (2- to 3-fold) as compared to that caused by a variety of physical stimuli (e.g., physical immobilization) known to increase β-END-LI secretion in this species (13–15). Urethane, a commonly used anesthetic in rodents, was more effective than pentobarbital, halothane, or ether [see Ref. (15)] in stimulating pituitary β-END-LI release. Perhaps a more generalized depression of CNS function, as may have resulted from the carbamate administration (16), produced the enhanced plasma β-END-LI response to urethane. The ability of each anesthetic, however, to stimulate pituitary β-END-LI release indicates that a rise in circulating opiates may

TABLE II. EFFECTS OF HALOTHANE, URETHANE, PENTOBARBITAL, AND MECHANICAL VENTILATION ON THE DIFFERENT MOLECULAR FORMS OF IMMUNOREACTIVE β-END IN RAT BLOOD

Treatment	Total plasma β-END-LI per pool[a] (pg/ml)	% β-END	% β-LPH	β-END/β-LPH ratio
Control	299	83	17	4.9
Halothane				
Spontaneous breathing	682	69	31	2.2
Mechanically ventilated	5402	60	40	1.5
Urethane				
Spontaneous breathing	1289	54	42	1.3
Mechanically ventilated	5481	81	19	4.3
Pentobarbital				
Spontaneous breathing	418	84	16	5.2
Mechanically ventilated	2718	71	24	3.0

[a] Treatment group plasma pools (5–10 ml) were chromatographed on Sephadex G-50 superfine resin. The plasma pools and elution profiles were immunoassayed for β-END-LI and the relative contribution of β-END- and β-LPH-sized immunoreactivity to total plasma β-END-LI are presented as percentages. Where their combined amounts do not equal 100%, a small portion of total plasma β-END-LI (≤5%) eluted in the void volume, suggesting the presence of a high-molecular-weight precursor for β-END. The β-END/β-LPH ratio indicates the β-END-sized material is the predominant form of circulating β-END-LI under most conditions.

be a common phenomenon associated with most, if not all, anesthetics. This relationship between anesthesia and pituitary β-END-LI release points to the possible role(s) for endogenous opiates in anesthetic analgesia. Caution, however, must be taken when considering this possibility [see Ref. (17)]. Although numerous reports indicate that opiate antagonists (naloxone and naltrexone) diminish various *in vivo* effects of a number of anesthetics (1–7, 9, 17–19), comparable experiments have failed to demonstrate such actions for the antagonists in both man (20, 21) and laboratory animals (10, 22–25). That these differences exist raises question as to the importance of endogenous opiates in mediating the anesthesia produced by anesthetic drugs. It is possible, however, that β-END and related opiate peptides influence anesthesia through actions on receptors which do not readily recognize naloxone or naltrexone. If so, these actions would be little affected by the two opiate antagonists. Compelling evidence to support this conclusion is presently lacking but may emerge as the pharmacology of multiple opiate receptors is better elucidated (26). The findings reported here do demonstrate that anesthesia, as produced by a number of agents, is associated with the activation of at least one intrinsic opiate peptide system, the release of pituitary β-END-LI into blood. Whether this occurs as a consequence of the anesthesia or participates in the development of the anesthetic state remains to be determined. Similar to pituitary β-END, release of opiate peptides by neurons within the CNS (27) or from the adrenal medulla (28) may also occur during anesthesia and contribute to the CNS and/or peripheral effects produced by anesthetic drugs.

Reported here are dramatic plasma β-END-LI responses to endotracheal intubation and mechanical ventilation which occur in animals under general anesthesia (Figs. 1–3). The time courses of these hormonal responses suggest mediation via a neuroendocrine reflex mechanism initiated by physical distention and/or trauma of the trachea and upper airways. Interestingly, morphine treatment (1 mg/kg, Fig. 3; 5 mg/kg, Table I) does attenuate this release of pituitary β-END-LI. This suggests the possibility that a morphine sensitive, yet subconscious, phenomenon is involved in the sequence of events leading to the greatly stimulated β-END-LI release. Similar observations have also been made in man. DuBois and coworkers (29) recently reported that pituitary β-END-LI responses occur in anesthetized humans (in response to laparotomy) and these, too, are diminished by administration of an opiate (fentanyl). Unlike the narcotic analgesics, the neuromuscular blocking drug pancuronium (30) (0.3 kg/mg) does not effect the plasma β-END-LI response to mechanical ventilation in rats (data not shown). Therefore, under the present conditions, the release of pituitary β-END-LI is probably not associated with neuromuscular activity in the chest wall or elsewhere in the body.

Gel filtration analysis revealed that the anesthetic drugs investigated here, as well as the procedures of intubation and mechanical ventilation, generally increased circulating β-END-LI resembling both β-END and β-LPH in molecular size. Although β-LPH is not analgesic, it does serve as a marker for β-END-LI secretion from corticotrophs of the pars distalis (31–34). Since opiate active β-END_{1-31} is cosecreted with β-LPH by corticotrophs *in vitro* (32–34), it is reasonable to conclude that increases in β-END_{1-31} also accompany rises in plasma β-LPH *in vivo*. This point may be of importance since only β-END_{1-31} is analgesic (31), whereas the modified forms of β-END_{1-31} (shorter and/or acetylated) released by the melanotrophs of the pars intermedia are not active at known opiate receptors (31–33).

In summary, we have demonstrated that the anesthesia produced by several commonly used anesthetics is associated with the release of pituitary β-END-LI in rats. The amounts released, however, are quite modest as compared to those evoked by intubation or mechanical ventilation. In all cases, however, the data indicate that concentrations of circulating β-END_{1-31}, the analgesic form of β-END, are elevated suggesting the possible involvement of endogenous opiate peptides in anesthesia. The considerable variability in the reported effects of opiate antagonists on anesthesia and anesthetic analgesia [see Ref. (17)], however, indicates that the released pituitary β-END_{1-31} probably does not mediate the predominant effects of general anesthetics. Possible actions of endogenous opiate peptides mediated through receptors which do not recognize naloxone or naltrexone should be considered in light of the increasing number of pharmacologically distinct receptors to which β-END_{1-31} and related peptides are reported to bind. At present, the physiologic functions of pituitary β-END released in response to anesthetic drugs and mechanical ventilation remain to be determined as do the specific receptors with which this class of peptides may interact.

1. Berkowitz BA, Ngai SH, Finck AD. Nitrous oxide "analgesia": Resemblance to opiate action. Science **194**:967–968, 1976.
2. Finck AD, Ngai SH, Berkowitz BA. Antagonism of general anesthesia by naloxone in the rat. Anesthesiology **46**:241–245, 1976.
3. Yang JC, Clark WC, Ngai SH. Antagonism of nitrous oxide analgesia by naloxone in man. Anesthesiology **52**:414–417, 1980.
4. Berkowitz BA, Finck AD, Ngai SH. Nitrous oxide analgesia: Reversal by naloxone and development of tolerance. J Pharmacol Exp Ther **203**:539–547, 1977.
5. Lawrence D, Livingston A. Opiate-like analgesic activity in general anaesthetics. Brit J Pharmacol **73**:435–442, 1981.
6. Arndt JO, Freye E. Perfusion of naloxone through the fourth cerebral ventricle reverses the circulatory and hypnotic effects of halothane in dogs. Anesthesiology **51**:58–63, 1979.
7. Arndt JO, Freye E. Opiate antagonist reverses the cardiovascular effects of inhalation anesthesia. Nature (London) **277**:399–400, 1979.
8. Berkowitz BA, Finck AD, Hynes MD, Ngai SH. Tolerance to nitrous oxide analgesia in rats and mice. Anesthesiology **51**:309–312, 1979.
9. Chapman CR, Benedetti C. Nitrous oxide effects on cerebral evoked potential to pain: Partial reversal with a narcotic antagonist. Anesthesiology **51**:135–138, 1979.
10. Harper MH, Winter PM, Johnson BH, Eger EI. Naloxone does not antagonize general anesthesia in the rat. Anesthesiology **49**:3–5, 1978.
11. Way WL, Hosobuchi Y, Eger EI, Johnson BH. Anesthesia does not increase cerebrospinal fluid opioid peptides in humans. Anesth Analg (Cleveland) **61**:223, 1982.
12. Mueller GP. Attenuated pituitary β-endorphin release in estrogen-treated rats. Proc Soc Exp Biol Med **165**:75–81, 1980.
13. Guillemin R, Vargo T, Rossier J, Minck S, Ling N, Rivier C, Vale W, Bloom F. β-Endorphin and adrenocorticotropin are secreted concomitantly by the pituitary gland. Science **197,** 1367–1369, 1977.
14. Rossier J, French E, Rivier C, Shibasaki T, Guillemin R, Bloom F. Stress-induced release of prolactin: blockade by dexamethasone and naloxone may indicate beta-endorphin mediation. Proc Natl Acad Sci USA **77**:666–669, 1980.
15. Mueller GP. Beta-endorphin immunoreactivity in rat plasma: Variations in response to different physical stimuli. Life Sci **29**:1669–1674 and 2673, 1980.
16. Harvey SC. Hypnotics and sedatives. In: Goodman LS, Gilman A, eds. The Pharmacologic Basis of Therapeutics. New York, Macmillan, p126, 1975.
17. Yaksh TL, Howe JR. Opiate receptors and their definition by antagonists. Anesthesiology **56**:246–249, 1982.
18. Fürst Z, Foldes FF, Knoll J. The influence of naloxone on barbiturate anesthesia and toxicity in the rat. Life Sci **20**:921–926, 1977.
19. Gilbert PE, Martin WR. Antagonism of the effects of pentobarbital in the chronic spinal dog by naltrexone. Life Sci **20**:1401–1406, 1977.
20. Levine JD, Gordon NC, Fields HL. Naloxone fails to antagonize nitrous oxide analgesia for clinical pain. Pain **13**:165–170, 1981.
21. Duncalf D, Nagashim H, Duncalf RM. Naloxone fails to antagonize thiopental anesthesia. Anesth Analg (Clevelend), **87**:558–562, 1978.
22. Smith RA, Wilson M, Miller KW. Naloxone has no effect on nitrous oxide anesthesia. Anesthesiology **49**:6–8, 1978.
23. Bennett PB. Naloxone fails to antagonize the righting response in rats anesthetized with halothane. Anesthesiology **49**:9–11, 1979.
24. Artru AA, Steen PA, Michenfelder JD. Cerebral metabolic effects of naloxone administered with anesthetic and subanesthetic concentrations of halothane in the dog. Anesthesiology **52**:217–220, 1980.
25. Pace NL, Wong KC. Failure of naloxone and natrexone to antagonize halothane anesthesia in the dog. Anesth Anal (Cleveland) **58**:36–39, 1979.
26. Simon EJ, Bonnet KA, Crain SM, Groth J, Hiller JM, Smith JR. Recent studies on interaction between opioid peptides and their receptors. In: Costa E, Trabucchi M, eds. Neural Peptides and Neuronal Communication. New York, Raven Press, pp335–346, 1980.
27. Bloom F, Battenberg E, Rossier J, Ling N, Guillemin R. Neurons containing β-endorphin in rat brain exist separately from those containing enkephalin: Immunocytochemical studies. Proc Natl Acad Sci USA **75**:1591–1595, 1978.
28. Stern AS, Jones BN, Shively JE, Stein S, Udenfriend S. Two adrenal opioid polypeptides: Proposed intermediates in the processing of proenkephalin. Proc Natl Acad Sci USA **78**:1962–1966, 1981.

29. Dubois M, Pickar D, Cohen M, Gradde P, Macnamara TE, Bunney WE. Effects of fentanyl on the response of plasma beta-endorphin immunoreactivity to surgery. Anesthesiology **57**:468–472, 1982.
30. Koelle GB. Neuromuscular blocking agents. In: Goodman LS, Gilman A, eds. The Pharmacologic Basis of Therapeutics. New York, Macmillan, p576, 1975.
31. Smyth DG, Massey DE, Zakarian S, Finnie MDA. Endorphins are stored in biologically active and inactive forms: Isolation of alpha-N-acetyl peptides. Nature (London) **279**:252–254, 1979.
32. Mains R, Eipper BA. Differences in the post-translational processing of beta-endorphin in rat anterior and intermediate pituitary. J Biol Chem **256**:5683–5688, 1981.
33. Liotta AS, Yamaguchi H, Krieger DT. Biosynthesis and release of beta-endorphin-, N-acety beta-endorphin-, beta-endorphin-(1-27)-, and N-acety beta endorphin-(1-27)-like peptides by rat pituitary neurointermediate lobe: Beta-endorphin is not further processed by anterior lobe. J Neurosci **1**:585–595, 1981.
34. Pettibone DJ, Mueller GP. Evidence for independent secretion of β-endorphin immunoreactivity from rat pars distalis *in vivo*. Endocrinology **110**:469–473, 1982.

Received December 2, 1983. P.S.E.B.M. 1984, Vol. 176.
Accepted March 20, 1984.

PROCEEDINGS OF THE SOCIETY FOR EXPERIMENTAL BIOLOGY AND MEDICINE **176**, 276–284 (1984)

Changes in Plasma, Tissue, and Urinary Nitrogen Metabolites Due to an Inflammatory Challenge (41871)

K. C. KLASING[1] AND R. E. AUSTIC

Department of Poultry and Avian Sciences, and Division of Nutritional Sciences, Cornell University, Ithaca, New York 14853

Abstract. Studies were undertaken to define the changes in protein metabolism that result from stimulation of the immune system by noninfectious inflammatory agents. Chicks were injected with inflammatory agents and metabolite concentrations were determined between 4 and 48 hr postchallenge. Inflammatory agents resulted in a generalized decrease in the concentration of plasma nitrogen metabolites, including ammonia, uric acid, urea, and several amino acids. *Escherichia coli* and sheep red blood cell (SRBC) injections induced changes in the concentrations of tissue-free amino acids at 16 hr postchallenge. After *E. coli* injections, free amino acid concentrations were increased by 175% in muscle and decreased by approximately 25% in liver, spleen, and bursa. A SRBC challenge resulted in similar decreases in free amino acid concentrations in the spleen and bursa as did *E. coli;* however, muscle and liver free amino acid concentrations were mostly unchanged. Urinary ammonia was increased, urinary uric acid was decreased, and urinary amino acids were not affected by *E. coli* injection. These findings indicate that stimulation of the immune system by noninfectious inflammatory agents induces tissue-specific changes in nitrogen metabolism. Changes in amino acid pool sizes in various tissues suggest alterations in rates of protein synthesis or degradation.

The immune system is dependent upon protein synthesis and, therefore, amino acids for the turnover of existing proteins and the synthesis of new proteins involved in an immune response. Nucleotides are required for the RNA and DNA synthesis which accompanies cell division. The nitrogen requirement for an optimal immune response and the homeostatic mechanisms which come into play to meet these demands have received little attention.

It is possible that changes in protein metabolism, which occur when the immune system is stimulated, are homeostatic in nature and serve to meet the new demands of the cells involved in the immune response. Infection-induced changes in the protein metabolism of muscle and liver have been examined and suggest that sizable changes occur. For example, infection results in decreased protein synthesis in muscle (1) and an increase in the utilization of amino acids in liver for synthesis of acute phase plasma globulins (2, 3). In studies which have examined infection, the metabolic changes due to stimulation of the immune system are confounded by changes due to the pathological invasiveness of the infectious organism and its toxins. The present study was undertaken to define the changes in protein metabolism due to stimulation of the immune system using noninfectious inflammatory agents.

Materials and Methods. *Animals.* Male Single-Comb White Leghorn chicks of the Cornell K strain were used in all experiments. Chicks were raised in environmentally controlled battery brooders and exposed to 15 hr of light daily from 0700 to 2200 hr. Chicks were fed a commercial chick starter (Beacon Milling Co., Cayuga, N.Y.) until they were used for experimentation at 600–900 g. Chicks were allowed to adjust to their cages and cage mates for at least 48 hr before experiments were initiated.

Inflammatory agents. Sheep red blood cells (SRBC) and *Escherichia coli* 263 (08:K87, 88ab, H19) were washed three times with and then suspended in phosphate-buffered saline (PBS). Keyhole limpet hemocyanin (KLH) was obtained from Sigma Chemical Company (St. Louis, Mo.). Inflammatory agents were prepared to give a 1% suspension of SRBC or *E. coli* and a 0.05% suspension of KLH in PBS. Chicks were injected ip with 1 ml of

[1] Present address: Department of Animal Science, University of Illinois, Urbana, Ill. 61801.

0037-9727/84 $1.50

either inflammatory agent or PBS (control) at a time which would allow tissue sampling to begin at 1000 hr. In experiments which included secondary injections, the priming dose was given 10 days prior to the experiment. Except in the first experiment, chicks were fasted or pair-fed the amount of feed consumed by the *E. coli*-treated group after injection.

Tissue collection. Blood was collected by heart puncture. Proteins were precipitated from plasma by adding 0.5 ml of 6% sulfosalicylic acid per milliliter plasma. The deproteinized plasma was frozen until analysis. After bleeding, chicks were killed by cervical dislocation. Tissues were immediately removed and frozen. Before analysis, the tissues were thawed, and the thymus, bursa, and spleen were placed in 5 ml cold PBS. The capsule and connective tissue stroma were removed by teasing with a scalpel and forceps. The cellular mixtures were then filtered through a 200-mesh nylon screen into cold centrifuge tubes. Red blood cells were removed from the spleen by the method of Rao and Glick (4). Pectoralis muscle and liver samples were scissor-minced. One-gram tissue samples were homogenized in 3 ml PBS utilizing a tightly fitting Potter–Elvehjem tissue homogenizer submerged in ice. Proteins were precipitated from the homogenate with 3 ml of 8% sulfosalicylic acid. Deproteinized tissue and plasma samples from two birds per treatment were pooled for amino acid analysis, resulting in five pooled samples per treatment per tissue.

Urine collection. The collection of urine separate from feces was accomplished by exteriorizing the section of the cloaca in which the ureters terminate, utilizing blunt forceps. A suture (size: OO) was inserted into the cloacal epithelium immediately distal to the ureters. The ends of the suture were threaded through a 1-ml disposable pipet tip. The pipet tip was pulled snugly against the cloaca and acted as a funnel to collect the urine as it was excreted. Two 1.5-ml samples were collected from each bird; one sample was collected into an empty centrifuge tube and analyzed for urea and uric acid, and one sample was collected into a centrifuge tube containing 0.1 ml of 0.1 *N* HCl and analyzed for ammonia.

Metabolite concentrations. An automated amino acid analyzer (Technicon Instruments, Tarrytown, N.Y.) was used to resolve amino acids in 50–200 μl of diluted deproteinized plasma, urine, or tissues. Urea was determined by the method of Skeggs (5). Plasma uric acid was determined by phosphotungstic acid reduction (6). Ammonia and urinary uric acid concentrations were determined enzymatically (Sigma, St. Louis, Mo.).

Sterility test. Whole blood was collected by heart puncture and peritoneal washings were collected after first injecting 20 ml sterile PBS into the peritoneal cavity. These fluids were spread onto nutrient agar plates. After 24 hr incubation at 37°C, bacterial colonies were counted.

Analysis of variance followed by Duncan's multiple-range test was used for data analysis.

Results. The injection of inflammatory agents resulted in a reduction of feed intake (Fig. 1). In the case of SRBC, this reduction was significant at 4 hr postinjection and returned to normal between 8 and 16 hr. *E. coli* injection resulted in a reduction in feed intake which was longer in duration and quantitatively greater than that due to SRBC. Feed intake was less than 20% of control levels at 4 hr and did not return to normal until 24 hr after *E. coli* injection. In this experiment, the control birds were sham-injected with PBS and otherwise handled in the same manner as treatment-injected birds. For this reason the depressed feed intake resulting from SRBC or *E. coli* injection cannot be attributed to the injection process or related stress.

The injection of inflammatory agents resulted in a generalized depression in the concentration of plasma nitrogen metabolites (Table I). The extent of change was dependent

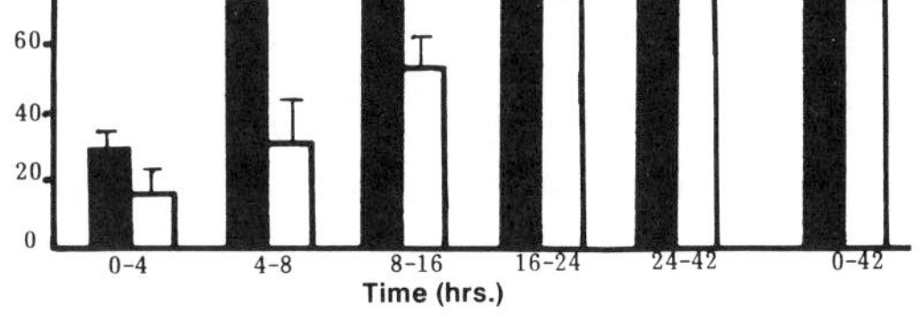

FIG. 1. The effect of antigenic challenge on feed consumption (% of controls fed *ad libitum*). Bars represent four replications of four birds ±SEM.

TABLE I. PLASMA UREA, URIC ACID, AND AMMONIA[a,b]

		Hours postinjection					
Metabolite	Treatment	4	8	12	24	36	48
Uric acid (mg/100 ml)	Control	5.70 ± 0.88	4.60 ± 0.51[c]	5.23 ± 0.62[c]	5.98 ± 0.61[c]	5.74 ± 0.58[c,d]	6.26 ± 0.86[c]
	SRBC 1	4.38 ± 0.54	5.23 ± 0.79[c]	4.20 ± 0.48[c,d]	3.23 ± 0.42[d]	7.60 ± 0.88[d]	6.63 ± 1.0[c]
	SRBC 2	6.00 ± 0.83	5.33 ± 0.42[c]	3.86 ± 0.37[d]	3.13 ± 0.23[d]	4.70 ± 0.67[c]	4.88 ± 0.61[c,d]
	E. coli 1	5.17 ± 0.98	3.07 ± 0.43[d]	6.22 ± 7.4[c]	3.81 ± 0.49[d]	6.93 ± 1.0[c,d]	3.38 ± 0.55[d]
	E. coli 2	5.57 ± 0.33	3.35 ± 0.41[d]	6.00 ± 1.2[c]	6.32 ± 1.0[c]	5.77 ± 0.41[c,d]	5.17 ± 0.92[c,d]
	KLH	5.95 ± 0.89	5.05 ± 0.91[c]	4.55 ± 0.34[c,d]	4.27 ± 0.11[c,d]	4.86 ± 0.73[c]	3.65 ± 0.77[d]
Urea (mg/100 ml)	Control	1.21 ± 0.16	1.25 ± 0.13[c]	1.37 ± 0.11[c,d]	1.22 ± 0.10[c]	1.30 ± 0.17	1.28 ± 0.10
	SRBC 1	0.833 ± 0.18	1.16 ± 0.23[c,d]	1.18 ± 0.18[c]	0.780 ± 0.07[d]	1.17 ± 0.19	1.21 ± 0.11
	SRBC 2	1.09 ± 0.16	1.23 ± 0.19[c]	1.34 ± 0.18[c,d]	1.28 ± 0.18[c]	1.52 ± 0.27	1.32 ± 0.16
	E. coli 1	1.29 ± 0.19	0.908 ± 0.06[d]	1.58 ± 0.09[c,d]	1.28 ± 0.15[c]	1.18 ± 0.10	1.24 ± 0.10
	E. coli 2	0.975 ± 0.11	0.675 ± 0.15[d]	1.72 ± 0.21[d]	1.16 ± 0.19[c,d]	1.23 ± 0.14	1.36 ± 0.12
	KLH	1.36 ± 0.24	1.37 ± 0.33[c]	1.60 ± 0.25[d]	1.17 ± 0.21[c,d]	1.16 ± 0.14	1.42 ± 0.17
Ammonia (μg/ml)	Control	2.88 ± 0.28[c,e]	0.837 ± 0.33[c]	2.27 ± 0.33[c]	3.68 ± 0.28[c]	2.59 ± 0.19[c]	1.43 ± 0.49[c]
	SRBC 1	1.21 ± 0.05[c,d]	0.720 ± 0.12[c]	1.86 ± 0.55[c,d]	1.05 ± 0.23[d]	0.881 ± 0.21[d]	0.300 ± 0.06[d]
	E. coli 1	0.638 ± 0.31[d]	0.301 ± 0.01[c]	1.99 ± 0.42[c]	1.11 ± 0.36[d]	0.567 ± 0.17[d]	0.339 ± 0.05[d]
	KLH	4.13 ± 0.37[e]	2.24 ± 0.26[d]	0.399 ± 0.10[d]	0.984 ± 0.24[d]	0.611 ± 0.15[d]	0.361 ± 0.09[d]

[a] Feed intake was equalized by pair feeding all chicks to the amount consumed by the chicks receiving *E. coli* 1 during each 4-hr period.

[b] Values represent means ± SEM of six chicks.

[c,d,e] Means in column within metabolites with different superscripts are significantly different ($P < 0.05$).

upon the stimulus, time period, and metabolite considered. Plasma ammonia concentrations were drastically affected by inflammatory agents. As compared to controls, a primary injection of either SRBC (SRBC 1) or *E. coli* (*E. coli* 1) resulted in depressed ammonia concentrations. These decreases were significant at 4, 24, 36, and 48 hr for *E. coli* 1 and at 24, 36, and 48 hr for SRBC 1; at each of these time periods, *E. coli* 1 and SRBC 1 injection resulted in plasma ammonia concentrations which were less than 40% of control values. KLH resulted in an initial increase (8 hr) followed by a significant decrease in ammonia concentrations at 12, 24, 36, and 48 hr.

Uric acid concentrations were depressed maximally to 54 and 52% of controls at 24 hr for SRBC 1 and a secondary injection of SRBC (SRBC 2), respectively, and to 54% at 48 hr and 73% of controls at 8 hr for *E. coli* 1 and a secondary injection of *E. coli* (*E. coli* 2), respectively. KLH resulted in a significant decrease in uric acid (58% of control) 48 hr postinjection.

Changes in plasma urea were variable; however, urea concentrations were significantly decreased from control values at 8 hr due to *E. coli* 1 and *E. coli* 2 and at 24 hr due to SRBC 1.

Glu and Gln concentrations were also affected by inflammatory agents (Table II). SRBC 2 decreased Glu at 12 and 24 hr postinjection while SRBC 1 significantly decreased Glu only at 36 hr. A similar pattern was observed after *E. coli* injection; *E. coli* 2 decreased Glu at 12 and 24 hr, whereas *E. coli* 1 did not result in decreased values until 24 hr postinjection. All five antigen treatments decreased Gln concentrations at 24 hr, relative to control values.

It is known that plasma Zn concentrations are decreased by infection (7). In this experiment all four treatments significantly depressed ($P < 0.05$) Zn concentrations as compared to controls (data not shown).

The *in vivo* viability of the *E. coli* used to challenge the chicks was also determined in this experiment. At 4, 8, and 12 hr postinjection, whole blood and peritoneal washings were tested for sterility. *E. coli* 1- and *E. coli* 2-injected birds as well as control birds had no detectable bacterial populations in their body fluids, demonstrating the lack of viability

TABLE II. PLASMA Glu AND Gln CONCENTRATIONS[a,b]

	Hours postinjection					
	12		24		36	
Treatment	Glu	Gln	Glu	Gln	Glu	Gln
Control	31.0 ± 1.2[c]	56.6 ± 8.6	37.2 ± 2.0[c]	40.7 ± 2.0[c]	34.2 ± 1.5[c]	55.6 ± 4.1[c]
SRBC 1	32.1 ± 2.2[c]	48.7 ± 5.9	30.6 ± 2.1[c,d]	30.1 ± 1.7[d]	21.6 ± 1.3[d]	35.1 ± 2.0[d]
SRBC 2	26.2 ± 1.4[d]	38.1 ± 7.9	25.1 ± 1.2[d]	32.7 ± 1.5[d]	29.7 ± 2.6[c]	49.5 ± 7.3[c]
E. coli 1	30.6 ± 2.7[c,d]	37.3 ± 4.6	25.3 ± 1.5[d]	27.6 ± 1.8[d]	30.3 ± 2.1[c]	47.5 ± 5.1[c]
E. coli 2	26.2 ± 1.1[d]	40.1 ± 7.2	27.4 ± 1.1[d]	25.0 ± 2.2[d]	29.7 ± 1.9[c]	63.5 ± 2.9[c]
KLH	36.4 ± 2.4[c]	35.2 ± 5.5	29.1 ± 2.2[c,d]	31.1 ± 1.6[d]	34.6 ± 3.2[c]	39.0 ± 4.7[c]

[a] Feed intake was equalized by pair feeding all chicks to the amount consumed by the chicks receiving *E. coli* during each 4-hr period.
[b] Values are expressed in μmol/dl and are the mean ± SEM of six chicks.
[c,d] Means in a colum with different superscripts are significantly different ($P < 0.05$).

of the injected *E. coli* and the lack of contamination due to the injection procedure.

The effect of SRBC and *E. coli* on free amino acid concentrations 16 hr postinjection are summarized in Tables III and IV. *E. coli* injection resulted in decreased concentrations of many of the nonessential amino acids; Asp, Ser, Glu, Gln, and Tyr were significantly decreased in concentration as compared to values from PBS-injected controls. Of the essential amino acids, Met was decreased while the branched chain amino acids, Ile, Leu, and Val, as well as Phe were elevated as a result of *E. coli* injection. SRBC injection resulted in decreased Glu, Gln, and Tyr and increased Met concentrations as compared to controls.

Changes in muscle-free amino acids did not reflect changes in plasma. *E. coli* injection resulted in a substantial increase in the concentration of most of the free amino acids in the muscle. This represents an increase in total amino acid concentrations of 175% over control values. SRBC injection caused an increase in only ASP concentrations; no other amino acid was affected significantly.

The concentrations of many of the free amino acids in the liver were decreased due to *E. coli* injection, whereas SRBC injection did not result in any significant changes. *E. coli* injection resulted in a 24% decrease in the total concentration of free amino acids as compared to controls.

The concentration of free amino acids in the tissues involved in the immune response were also affected by the injection of inflammatory agents. Both SRBC and *E. coli* exerted their largest effect on the bursa. SRBC and *E. coli* injection resulted in a significant depression in the concentrations of 10 and 7 amino acids, respectively. In this tissue, none of the amino acids were increased in concentration 16 hr after the injection of either SRBC or *E. coli*. Both treatments resulted in an approximately 25% reduction in total free amino acids in the bursa.

The results observed in the spleen were similar to those in the bursa. Six and seven amino acids were decreased in concentration as a result of *E. coli* and SRBC, respectively. Again, both treatments resulted in an approximately 25% depression in total free amino acids when compared to controls.

The thymus responded to the injection of inflammatory agents differently than the bursa and spleen. In this tissue, several amino acids were increased in concentration due to *E. coli* or SRBC injection. No amino acid was significantly decreased. Total free amino acid concentrations were not significantly elevated by either treatment; however, they tended to be increased by about 12% over control values.

The urinary concentrations of ammonia, urea, and uric acid are shown in Table V. *E. coli* injection resulted in increased urinary ammonia concentrations as compared to controls. This increase was statistically significant ($P < 0.05$) at 12 hr. Urinary urea concentra-

TABLE III. FREE AMINO ACID CONCENTRATIONS[a]

Tissue	Treatment	Amino acid																
		Asp	Thr	Ser	Glu	Gln	Pro	Gly	Ala	Val	Met	Ile	Leu	Tyr	Phe	Lys	His	Arg	Total
Plasma[b]	Control	5.7	43.5	78.0	30.8	26.2	34.4	50.9	54.1	22.0	9.5	17.3	23.0	23.5	12.1	47.7	9.5	36.2	524
	SRBC	5.5	43.0	79.2	23.3*	17.2*	42.9	46.2	47.1	28.6	6.0*	17.1	28.5	17.0*	15.1	34.3	11.1	29.0	491
	E. coli	3.7*	43.8	47.2*	21.4*	13.4*	27.3	38.1	36.6	47.3*	5.4*	30.1*	44.9*	11.4*	20.0*	37.9	9.6	29.9	468
	SEM	0.5	2.7	6.3	1.5	1.3	7.4	4.5	5.6	4.6	0.8	2.8	3.2	0.8	1.3	3.7	1.6	1.2	16.7
Muscle[c]	Control	48.3	32.1	55.0	66.5	42.4	17.5	56.0	64.7	24.8	10.5	20.9	25.5	23.8	15.0	17.9	10.8	16.8	549
	SRBC	64.2*	33.3	66.1	57.1	44.4	20.1	43.5	63.1	24.3	7.62	15.3	24.1	18.8	11.7	20.4	8.92	17.2	550
	E. coli	41.5	61.8*	80.6*	73.8*	96.4*	30.1*	122**	110**	58.2**	20.7**	42.2**	58.4**	29.2	28.6*	48.2**	26.4**	32.0**	960*
	SEM	3.1	2.3	2.6	2.6	8.4	2.8	6.0	5.7	1.7	1.0	1.5	1.9	2.2	1.4	2.6	1.2	1.8	30.3
Liver[c]	Control	65.6	34.7	58.7	86.3	31.6	26.3	73.1	64.3	22.2	14.3	16.1	35.3	19.4	12.0	34.9	14.6	31.5	640
	SRBC	72.3	38.7	56.8	91.4	40.9	28.6	76.9	71.1	26.2	16.9	19.4	39.3	20.2	14.5	37.9	16.6	36.7	704
	E. coli	54.4	26.0*	40.1	89.7	23.8*	21.3	50.6*	47.6	17.9	9.32	15.1	23.7*	12.3*	7.69*	21.3*	11.4	19.9*	491*
	SEM	5.6	2.0	5.4	4.7	2.1	2.1	5.4	6.2	1.9	1.4	2.0	2.8	1.3	1.0	3.0	4.4	2.3	26.7

[a] Chicks were fasted postinjection and killed after 16 hr. [b] Values expressed as μmol/100 ml. [c] Values expressed as μmol/10 g tissue.
* Significantly different from controls ($P < 0.05$). ** Significantly different from controls ($P < 0.01$).

TABLE IV. FREE AMINO ACID CONCENTRATIONS[a]

Tissue	Treatment	Amino acid															
		Asp	Thr	Ser	Glu	Gln	Gly	Ala	Val	Met	Ile	Leu	Try	Phe	Lys	His	Arg	Total
Thymus	Control	50.9	13.7	22.6	90.4	10.3	47.2	24.2	7.22	4.63	5.07	11.0	4.66	4.43	6.69	2.76	5.64	311
	SRBC	62.8*	16.4*	24.6	99.0	14.4	48.9	29.1*	7.22	4.91	5.62	12.1	5.06	4.97	6.42	4.48	6.41	352
	E. coli	59.7	15.9	21.5	95.6	11.6	48.9	25.9	9.44	6.96**	6.07	12.6	5.13	5.82*	9.41*	3.56	8.00*	346
	SEM	3.2	0.9	1.1	4.9	2.3	1.9	1.0	1.0	0.4	0.4	0.5	0.2	0.3	0.5	0.8	0.5	14.7
Bursa	Control	32.9	14.3	28.2	89.4	15.6	68.0	30.1	10.9	6.38	6.96	14.2	6.89	6.32	10.8	4.29	10.9	377
	SRBC	26.2*	11.5	21.9*	81.2	7.81*	56.3*	21.4	8.27	4.27*	5.57	9.58*	4.24	4.04*	7.16*	3.12*	6.52*	279*
	E. coli	22.9**	13.7	20.6*	85.4	11.0	54.1*	24.4	10.7	4.44*	4.98*	10.8	4.23	4.68	7.55*	2.90*	7.26	290*
	SEM	0.8	0.8	1.2	4.8	1.7	2.4	2.7	1.0	0.5	0.4	0.9	0.7	0.6	0.5	0.2	0.7	12.0
Spleen	Control	61.2	22.6	36.9	107.7	26.0	71.9	37.5	19.3	11.8	9.81	20.0	10.5	8.22	27.2	6.01	16.6	493
	SRBC	41.0*	20.6	30.2	88.4	12.6**	62.6	24.2*	15.0	11.8	5.67*	15.1	5.11*	4.79*	20.1	6.44	12.8*	376
	E. coli	30.2*	21.8	27.9	93.5	20.0	43.8*	29.1	11.6*	10.1	5.25*	14.8	5.99*	6.79	21.3	7.30	11.7*	361*
	SEM	2.9	2.0	3.1	7.4	1.8	4.3	2.6	1.1	1.2	0.4	1.4	0.5	0.6	1.7	0.5	1.0	25.3

[a] Values expressed as μmole/10 g. Chicks were fasted postinjection and killed after 16 hr.
* Significantly different from controls ($P < 0.05$). ** Significantly different from controls ($P < 0.01$).

TABLE V. URINARY NITROGEN[a]

Hours postinjection	Treatment	Ammonia (μg/ml)	Urea (mg/100 ml)	Uric acid (mg/ml)	Total amino acids[b] μmole/ml
12	Control	102 ± 14[c,d]	14.2± 1.4	7.11 ± 0.58	0.514
	SRBC	138 ± 9.1[d]	14.6 ± 0.51	7.16 ± 0.26	0.501
	E. coli	184 ± 13[e]	13.6 ± 1.1	5.74 ± 0.23	0.513
24	Control	85.3 ± 13	10.7 ± 1.2	5.85 ± 0.26[d]	0.477
	SRBC	98.0 ± 13	11.2 ± 0.91	5.11 ± 1.07[d]	0.508
	E. coli	113 ± 22	8.0 ± 1.1	3.06 ± 0.59[e]	0.461

[a] Chicks were fasted after injection.
[b] From analysis of a sample pooled from all four chicks in each treatment. Individual amino acid concentrations were similar among treatments.
[c] Means ± SEM of four chicks.
[d,e] Means in a column within the same time period followed by different superscripts are significantly different ($P< 0.05$).

tions were not significantly affected at either 12 or 24 hr postinjection. Urinary uric acid concentrations tended to be depressed at 12 hr and were significantly decreased at 24 hr postinjection by *E. coli* but not SRBC. Total amino acid concentrations in the urine were not affected by either SRBC or *E. coli* injection.

Discussion. Inflammatory agents alter feed intake and many aspects of nitrogen metabolism, the changes occurring relatively quickly after injection. The extent of change is largely influenced by the type of stimulus. *E. coli* resulted in larger perturbations in most parameters than the nonmicrobial agents SRBC and KLH.

It is well documented that infection results in depressed appetite and consequently depressed feed intake (8). Berry and Smythe (9) observed a depression in feed intake after the injection of either viable or heat-killed *S. typhimurium*. Their work demonstrates that the development of an infectious process is not an obligatory prerequisite for a reduction in feed intake. The present studies demonstrate that a noninfectious and rapidly cleared strain of *E. coli* also results in reduced feed intake; in addition, SRBC, which contains no toxins but are rapidly phagocytized, depress feed intake. It is apparent that feed intake must be equalized between treatments so that effects on metabolism resulting from the inflammatory agents are not confounded by diet. This was accomplished in the present studies by withholding feed or pair feeding after injection.

The presence of foreign organisms during infection stimulates the immune system. Consequently, studies investigating changes in nitrogen metabolism during infection may be compared to this present study. In making these comparisons, several factors should be considered. First, measurements of nitrogen metabolism during infection are typically made several days after the organism is introduced. In this present study observations were made closer to the time of challenge. Second, pathological changes resulting from the infectious organism may induce alterations in nitrogen metabolism which are unrelated to those changes induced by the immune response to those organisms. Third, this study utilizes chickens which differ from mammals in several important aspects of nitrogen metabolism, including uric acid excretion, lack of a functional urea cycle, and tissue distributions of amino acid catabolizing enzymes.

Studies of changes in nitrogen metabolism due to noninfectious bacteria or nonmicrobial antigens have not been reported.

Infection in humans and experimental animals results in a negative nitrogen balance as evidenced by increased nitrogen excretion as urea ammonia, creatine, and uric acid (10, 11). This increase begins about 4 days postinfection. In experiments reported here, urinary nitrogen concentrations were reduced during the first day after *E. coli* injection; uric acid concentrations in particular were depressed. The increase in ammonia concentration due to *E. coli* (64 and 22 μg N/ml urine at 12 and 24 hr, respectively) is a relatively small change compared to the decrease in nitrogen concentrations as uric acid (375 and 764 μg N/ml at 12 and 24 hr, respectively). Some of the decrease in urinary uric acid concentrations may be a result of increased excretion of nitrogen as ammonia. Most of the decrease in urinary and plasma uric acid concentrations may represent an increase in utilization of nitrogen for synthesis of nucleic acids and/or a decrease in nitrogen production by amino acid catabolism.

The increase in urinary ammonia together with decreased plasma glutamine may be indicative of increased renal glutaminase activity. Since plasma ammonia levels are also decreased, ammonia secretion into the kidney tubules also may be increased. Regardless of the mechanism, the increased urinary ammonia is indicative of acidification of the urine. It is not clear if this is due to an *E. coli*-induced acidosis or if the increased ammonia excretion reflects a renal alkalosis.

Due to the lack of a functioning urea cycle, arginine is not synthesized in the chick (12). Urea is a reflection of arginase activity in kidney. These experiments indicate that arginine degradation was unaffected by treatment.

Plasma nonessential amino acid concentrations represent a balance between the influx of amino acids into plasma due to dietary intake and amino acid synthesis in the tissues, and the loss of amino acids from plasma due to catabolism, excretion, or use for protein synthesis. In the present experiments, dietary intake was equalized between treatments, and urinary amino acid concentrations were not increased. Therefore, the changes in plasma nonessential amino acids may be due to a relative increase in the rate of deamination versus amino acid synthesis in the tissues or to an increased utilization for nucleic acid or protein synthesis. A net increase in protein synthesis is unlikely because it would result in a depression in the essential amino acids as well. Essential amino acids are not synthesized *in vivo,* so their plasma concentrations must reflect the balance between whole body protein synthesis and catabolism. Since the plasma concentrations of most of the essential amino acids were unchanged, except the branched chain amino acids which were increased, it is doubtful that the antigen-challenged chicks were in a net protein anabolic state. The depressed nonessential amino acid concentrations may be a result of deamination coupled with increased shunting of nitrogen into another pool. The fate of the nitrogen cannot be determined from these data but may consist of nucleotide synthesis and ammonia excretion.

The change in concentrations of amino acids in various tissues in response to an inflammatory challenge may explain some of the changes in plasma. Changes in tissue free-amino acid concentrations reflect changes in transport, amino acid catabolism, amino acid synthesis, and the relative rates of protein synthesis and protein catabolism. In this latter case, an increase in tissue free-amino acid concentrations would represent net protein catabolism or amino acid liberation, and a decrease would represent net protein synthesis or amino acid utilization. This is particularly true for those amino acids which are neither synthesized nor catabolized in the tissue being considered, i.e., phenylalanine in muscle or arginine in liver. Based on this interpretation of tissue amino acid concentrations and assuming that variations in amino acids are not mediated by transport phenomenon, *E. coli* resulted in a net liberation of amino acids in the muscle and possibly the thymus and a net utilization by the spleen, liver, and bursa. SRBC resulted in similar effects in the spleen and bursa but little, if any, change in the muscle and liver.

The increased plasma branched chain amino acids after *E. coli* injection may be due to release of these amino acids from muscle at a faster rate than they are used for protein synthesis in the liver, bursa, and spleen.

It should be emphasized that assigning metabolic significance to static measurements of amino acid concentrations or pool sizes is difficult because of the complexity of factors and magnitude of the fluxes involved.

Squibb (13) has reported a depression in liver lysine, histidine, arginine, aspartic acid, alanine, valine, and leucine concentrations in the chick liver due to the Newcastle disease virus. This was attributed to increased protein synthesis as demonstrated by increased total liver RNA and protein. Depressions of plasma amino acids occur in experimental infection of humans, regardless of etiology (14). This depression occurs on the first day after infection before the onset of clinical signs such as fever or anorexia.

In the experiments reported here, it is not clear whether the alterations in nitrogen metabolism are due to a specific immune response. The antibody titer of chicks to *E. coli* 263 should be high due to cross-reactivity with the normal indiginous microbial flora. Chicks, however, have very low, if any, antibody titers to SRBC or KLH at the time of their first exposure. It was demonstrated that prior exposure to antigens did not increase the perturbations in nitrogen metabolism. This indicates that nonspecific factors mediate these changes. Phagocytosis by macrophages and polymorphonuclear leukocytes is a nonspecific immune response to particulate antigens such as those utilized in this study. These phagocytic cells may elaborate a substance which induces the wide-ranging changes in nitrogen metabolism. Leukocyte endogenous mediator (LEM), one such substance, has been shown to induce a change in the transport of nonmetabolizable amino acids in the liver and muscle (15). LEM, also referred to as interleukin 1, stimulates muscle protein degradation (16).

E. coli resulted in quantitatively greater perturbations in most of the parameters measured than did the nonmicrobial agents, SRBC and KLH. This may be due to several factors. First, the onset of metabolic changes occurs later after KLH or SRBC as compared to *E. coli* injection. This is particularly true for Zn, ammonia, and uric acid. The lower response of plasma and tissue amino acids to SRBC as compared to *E. coli* may be due to the relatively early time periods during which measurements were taken.

After injection, both SRBC and *E. coli* would be eliminated by phagocytosis; however, microbial antigens, particularly *E. coli* endotoxin (present in strain 263), potentiate the phagocytic process and initiate other immune responses. These include an increase in neutrophil and macrophage chemotaxis to the site of injection, macrophage production of macrophage colony-stimulating factor, lymphocyte-stimulating factor, and endogenous pyrogen and the stimulation of polyclonal B-lymphocyte proliferation (17). One of these mechanisms may be responsible for the quicker onset and quantitatively greater change in nitrogen metabolism induced by *E. coli* as compared to SRBC.

This study demonstrates that stimulation of the immune system by noninfectious inflammatory agents induces tissue-specific changes in nitrogen metabolism. There is a change in the amino acid pool size of various tissues, suggesting an alteration in protein synthesis or degradation. It is possible that some of these changes represent a homeostatic mechanism responsible for the shunting of amino acids between tissues to support an immune response.

1. Young VR, Chen SC, Newberne PM. Effect of infection on skeletal muscle ribosomes in rats fed adequate or low protein. J Nutr **94**:361–368, 1968.
2. Bostian KA, Blackburn BS, Wannemacher RW Jr, McGrann VG, Beisel WR, DuPont HL. Sequential changes in the concentration of specific serum proteins during typhoid fever infection in man. J Lab Clin Med **87**:577–585, 1976.
3. Powanda MC, Wannemacher RW Jr, Cockerell GL. Nitrogen metabolism and protein synthesis during pneumococcal sepsis in rats. Infect Immun **6**:226–271, 1972.
4. Rao DSVS, Glick B. The production of a lymphocyte inhibitory factor (LyIF) by bursal and thymic lymphocytes. In: Benedict AA, ed. Avian Immunology. New York, Plenum, pp87–98, 1977.
5. Skeggs LT. An automatic method for colorimetric analysis. Amer J Clin Pathol **28**:311–322, 1957.
6. Oser BL. Hawks physiological chemistry. New York, McGraw–Hill, pp1046–1047, 1965.
7. Wannemacher RW Jr, DuPont HL, Pekarek RS, Powanda MC, Schwartz A, Hornick RB, Beisel WR. An endogenous mediator of depression of amino acids and trace metals in serum during typhoid fever. J Infect Dis **126**:77–86, 1972.
8. Murray MJ, Murray AB. Anorexia of infection as a mechanism of host defense. Amer J Clin Nutr **32**:593–596, 1979.
9. Berry LJ, Symthe DS. Some metabolic aspects of host-parasite interactions in the mouse typhoid model. Ann NY Acad Sci **88**:1278–1286, 1960.
10. Beisel WR. Magnitude of host nutritional response to infection. Amer J Clin Nutr **30**:1236–1247, 1977.

11. Rapoport MI, Beisel WR, Hornick RB. Tryptophan metabolism during infectious illness in man. J Infec Dis **122**:159, 1970.

12. Tamir H, Ratner S. Enzymes of arginine metabolism in chicks. Arch Biochem Biophys **102**:249–258, 1963.

13. Squibb RL. Nutrition and biochemistry of survival during Newcastle disease virus infection. III. Relation of dietary protein to nucleic acid and free amino acids of avian liver. J Nutr **82**:427–431, 1964.

14. Wannemacher RW. Key role of various individual amino acids in host response to infection. Amer J Clin Nutr **30**:1269–1280, 1977.

15. Wannemacher RW Jr, Pekarek RS. A hormone-like mediator which is capable of regulating amino acid transport and hepatic protein synthesis. Fed Proc **32**:953, 1973.

16. Baracos V, Rodemann HP, Dinarello CA, Goldberg AL. Stimulation of muscle protein degradation and prostaglandin E_2 release by leukocytic pyrogen (interleukin-1). N Engl J Med **308**:553–558, 1983.

17. Rosentreich DL. The Macrophage. In: Oppenheim JJ, Rosentreich DL, Potter DL, eds. Cellular Functions in Immunity and Inflammation. New York, Elsevier/North-Holland, pp127, 1981.

Received September 6, 1983. P.S.E.B.M. 1984, Vol. 176.
Accepted March 30, 1984.

PROCEEDINGS OF THE SOCIETY FOR EXPERIMENTAL BIOLOGY AND MEDICINE **176,** 285–291 (1984)

Changes in Protein Synthesis Due to an Inflammatory Challenge (41872)

K. C. KLASING[1] AND R. E. AUSTIC

Department of Poultry and Avian Sciences and Division of Nutritional Sciences, Cornell University, Ithaca, New York 14853

Abstract. Rates of protein synthesis in various chick tissues were examined 16 hr after an inflammatory challenge. Protein synthetic rates were calculated from the rate at which [^{14}C]leucine was incorporated into protein and the specific activity of [^{14}C]leucine in the precursor pool. An injection of either *Escherichia coli* or sheep red blood cells (SRBC) decreased the rate of protein synthesis in the gastrocnemius muscle, and increased the rate in liver, bursa, spleen, and thymus. *E. coli,* but not SRBC, decreased protein synthesis in the pectoralis muscle. *E. coli* significantly decreased the aggregation of pectoralis muscle polysomes and increased the aggregation of polysomes in the thymus, bursa, and spleen. *E. coli* increased the aggregation of free, but not bound, polysomes in liver, suggesting an increase in synthesis of export proteins. SRBC significantly increased polysomal aggregation in bursa and spleen only. A crude preparation of leukocyte endogenous mediator, isolated from peritoneal macrophages, decreased muscle-polysomal aggregation. These studies indicate that tissue-specific changes in protein synthesis occur after a noninfectious inflammatory challenge. These changes may be part of a homeostatic mechanism which supports the immune response.

The tissue-specific changes in protein metabolism induced by an immune response and the homeostatic processes by which these changes occur are not well characterized. Characterization of these changes may help elucidate the mechanisms by which environmental factors such as nutrition and stress, which also affect protein metabolism, exert their effects upon immunocompetence.

Inflammation-induced changes in the concentrations of free amino acids of various tissues, described previously (1), suggest that exposure to antigens causes changes in the relative rates of protein synthesis and degradation in several tissues. That these changes in free amino acid concentrations are due, in part, to changes in protein synthesis was examined in these experiments.

Methods. Chicks were housed, inflammatory agents were prepared, and tissues were collected as described previously (1), unless otherwise noted.

Fractional synthetic rate (FSR). The effect of an inflammatory challenge on the rates of protein synthesis in various tissues was estimated from the incorporation of [^{14}C]leucine into protein after a pulse dose. Nine birds per treatment were injected ip with 1 ml of either PBS, 0.5% SRBC, or 0.5% *Escherichia coli.* At 0.5, 1, or 2 hr before sacrifice, three chicks per treatment were injected iv with 3 μCi/100 g of [1-^{14}C]leucine (Amersham, Arlington Heights, Ill.). Feed was withheld after injection; water was provided *ad libitum.* Birds were killed 16 hr postinjection, and tissues were sampled immediately and frozen in liquid nitrogen. Frozen muscle and liver samples were minced using scissors, and 1-g samples were homogenized in 4 ml cold double-distilled water. To a 1.8-ml aliquot of the homogenate, 0.2 ml cold, 30% sulfosalicylic acid (SSA) was added to precipitate proteins. The supernatant was saved for analysis of the specific activity of the precursor pool.

An additional 1.25-ml aliquot of the homogenate was used to isolate protein and RNA. This was accomplished by the following steps. Macromolecules were precipitated from the homogenate by the addition of 2.5 ml cold, 0.3 N $HClO_4$. After standing for 10 min (3°C), the mixture was centrifuged at 2000g and 3°C for 15 min. The supernatant was discarded and the precipitate was washed twice with cold 0.2 N $HClO_4$. After the final washing, the precipitate was drained over a paper towel. The lipids were separated from the precipitate by extraction for 15 min with each of the following in succession: K-acetate-saturated ab-

[1] Present address: Department of Animal Science, University of Illinois, Urbana, Ill. 61801.

0037-9727/84 $1.50

solute ethanol, ethanol–ether 3:1, and anhydrous ether.

RNA was then separated from the precipitate by differential hydrolysis. To accomplish this, the precipitate was resuspended in 4 ml of 0.3 *N* KOH and incubated for 1 hr at 37°C. The suspension was cooled in ice, and the protein was precipitated with 2.5 ml of 1.2 *N* $HClO_4$. After 10 min, the samples were centrifuged at 2000*g* and 3°C for 15 min, and the supernatant was separated and saved. The precipitate was washed twice with 0.5 ml of 0.2 *N* $HClO_4$ and the washing combined with the supernatant. The washings and supernatant were diluted to a known volume and $HClO_4$ concentration with water. The RNA concentrations were determined by absorbance at 260 n*m*. Torula yeast RNA was used as a standard.

The remaining pellet was hydrolyzed in a sealed tube with 4 ml of 6 *N* HCl for 20 hr at 110°C. The hydrolysate was concentrated in a vacuum oven at 50°C. The pH of the final concentrate was raised to 2.0 with sodium hydroxide.

The specific activity of leucine in the SSA-soluble fraction (precursor pool) and the hydrolyzed protein was determined by counting 0.5 ml of the sample in 10 ml of scintillation cocktail and determining the leucine concentration of a separate aliquot by automated amino acid analysis. Cells isolated from thymus, spleen, and bursa as previously described (1) were weighed and treated in the same manner as minced muscle and liver.

FSR can be derived from the simultaneous measurements of radioactivity in the precursor pool and the protein molecules according to the equation

$$dP^*/dt = k_s F^* - k_d P^*$$

where P^* is the specific activity of leucine in the protein molecules, F^* is the specific activity of leucine in the precursor pool, and k_s and k_d represent the rate contant for protein synthesis and degradation, respectively (2). The rate of increase in radioactivity in the protein molecule at any given time is given by the difference between radioactivity entering from the precursor pool ($k_s F^*$) and that leaving due to protein degradation ($k_d P^*$). This equation can be integrated between two times after isotope administration, t_1 and t_2, to give

$$P^*t_2 - P^*t_1 = k_s \int_{t_1}^{t_2} F^*(t)dt - k_d \int_{t_1}^{t_2} P^*(t)dt.$$

In this experiment t_2 = 2 hr and t_1 = 0.5 hr after isotope injection. Since protein synthesis was examined very soon after isotope injection, values for $P^*(t)dt$ were insignificant as compared to $F^*(t)dt$ and the equation becomes

$$\text{FSR} = k_s = \frac{P^*t_2 - P^*t_1}{\int_{t_1}^{t_2} F^*(t)dt}.$$

The calculated FSR value has the units hours^{-1} and can be expressed as percentage per day by the conversion factor of 2400. Since all of the chicks in each treatment were required to estimate $\int_{.5}^{2} F^*(t)$, no estimate of variation is available for statistical analysis of the precursor-pool-specific activity and, therefore, the FSR.

Polysomal aggregation. Protein synthesis was further examined by the use of polysomal profiles. Chicks were injected and killed 16 hr later. Feed was removed at the time of injection. The aggregation of polysomes was determined using fresh tissue from three birds per treatment. Cells from thymus, bursa, and spleen were isolated as described previously (1) except red blood cells were not removed from the spleen.

Muscle polysomes were analyzed by the method of Heywood *et al.* (3). The free and bound polysomes in liver were separated according to the method of Ramsey and Steele (4).

Polysomes from the cells obtained from the thymus, bursa, and spleen were prepared as follows. The tissue sample was homogenized in 3 vol of polysome buffer (4) with 250 m*M* sucrose and 0.25% Triton X-100 by the procedure described for muscle (3). The homogenate was centrifuged at 10,000*g* for 5 min, and the supernatant was decanted. Triton X-100 was added to the supernatant to give a 1% solution. This was layered onto a 6–21% continuous gradient containing 75 m*M* KCl, 5 m*M* $MgCl_2$, and 0.5 m*M* EDTA and centrifuged at 131,000*g* for 105 min at 3°C.

The sucrose gradients were drained by puncturing the bottom of the centrifuge tube utilizing a Buchler gradient siphon. The rate of drainage was limited to 3 ml/min by a polystalic pump. Optical density was continuously recorded at 254 nm using a flow-through spectrophotometer with a 10-in. chart recorder. To prevent interference due to mixing vortex lines, the flow cell and delivery tubes were first equilibrated with the heaviest density sucrose. The absorbance curves were divided into a subunit plus small polysome segment (light) and a polysome segment (heavy).

Preparation of soluble mediators. Polymorphonuclear (PMN) leukocytes and macrophages were isolated from the peritoneal cavity. To accomplish this adult birds were injected ip with 150 ml of 0.4% oyster glycogen in sterile physiologic saline containing 100,000 U/liter of penicillin G and 0.5 g/liter streptomycin. An additional 100 ml of sterile saline was injected 14 hr later, and peritoneal exudates were aspirated into the iced vacuum flask containing heparin (20 IU/100 ml exudate). The exudate was centrifuged at 800*g* for 10 min at 4°C, washed with saline, and resuspended at a concentration of 10^5 cells/ml with sterile saline. The cells were incubated immediately for 4 hr with gentle shaking at 37°C. The supernatant was separated by centrifugation (800*g* for 10 min) and sterilized by membrane filtration. The protein content of this preparation was 0.7 mg/ml as determined by the method of Lowry *et al.* (5). An aliquot was heated at 90°C for 30 min and served as a heat-denatured control. To prevent contamination with pyrogens, all glassware was acid washed and autoclaved at 120°C for 15 min. The preparation of these soluble mediators is similar to the methods used by others (6, 7) to isolate a mediator termed leukocyte endogenous mediator (LEM). For this reason the leukocyte product utilized in this experiment will be referred to as LEM. It must be recognized that in this report LEM does not refer to a purified mediator.

Results. In experiment 1, the incorporation of [^{14}C]leucine into protein between 0.5 and 2 hr after isotope injection was examined. Since leucine-specific activity was examined shortly after isotope injection, F^* was considerably higher than P^* and the proteins in the body were accumulating label. The FSR, absolute increase in P^*, and average F^* are presented in Table I. SRBC and *E. coli* exposure did not appear to affect the specific activity of the precursor pool in the gastrocnemius muscle but did decrease leucine incorporation into protein as compared to the control, resulting in decreased FSR. In the pectoralis muscle, leucine incorporation into protein tended to be equally depressed due to SRBC and *E. coli* exposure, as compared to control birds; however, the changes in the specific activity of the precursor pool resulted in little change in FSR due to SRBC and a 24% decrease due to *E. coli.* In the liver, SRBC and *E. coli* exposure resulted in an increase in the specific activity of the precursor pool but proportionally greater increases in leucine incorporation into protein yielded an increase in the FSR. The FSR of protein in the bursa was increased by 43 and 240% over control values due to SRBC and *E. coli* and by 17 and 51%, respectively, in the spleen. In both the bursa and spleen, an inflammatory challenge resulted in depressed specific activity of the precursor pool, yet increased rates of leucine incorporation into protein were observed. The FSR of protein was also increased in the thymus due to both SRBC and *E. coli* injection.

Tissue RNA concentrations were not affected by treatments except in the spleen where *E. coli* resulted in a significant increase as compared to controls (Table I).

The aggregation of polysomes in various tissues was examined in the second experiment. These results are summarized in Table II. *E. coli* resulted in an increase in the aggregation of polysomes, as indicated by decreased ratios of light versus heavy polysomes, in the thymus, bursa, spleen, and liver (bound) as compared to controls. *E. coli* did not result in a significant change in the aggregation of the free polysomes of liver and resulted in decreased aggregation in muscle. SRBC resulted in a significant change in polysomal aggregation as compared to controls only in the spleen. Polysomes tended to be more aggregated, due to SRBC, in the liver (bound), thymus, and bursa and less aggregated in the muscle; however, these changes were not statistically significant ($P < 0.05$).

Soluble factors (LEM) produced by leukocytes resulted in decreased muscle-poly-

TABLE I. THE EFFECT OF SRBC AND *E. coli* ON TISSUE PROTEIN SYNTHESIS AND RNA

Tissue	Treatment	RNA (mg/g)	Specific activity (dpm/μmole) Precursor[a]	Specific activity (dpm/μmole) Protein[b]	Fractional synthetic rate
Gastrocnemius muscle	Control	1.37 ± 0.064[c]	35,344	346	23.4
	SRBC	1.44 ± 0.093	34,313	243	17.0
	E. coli	1.35 ± 0.068	35,441	237	16.1
Pectoralis muscle	Control	1.28 ± 0.073	27,191	288	25.4
	SRBC	1.24 ± 0.051	22,939	259	27.1
	E. coli	1.26 ± 0.105	32,538	263	19.4
Liver	Control	9.65 ± 0.221	14,905	256	41.3
	SRBC	10.5 ± 0.364	18,863	424	53.9
	E. coli	10.7 ± 0.168	20,072	411	49.3
Bursa	Control	6.62 ± 0.422	21,429	654	73.2
	SRBC	8.12 ± 0.423	18,273	803	105.0
	E. coli	7.26 ± 0.463	13,286	1380	249.0
Spleen	Control	6.68 ± 0.311	20,259	513	60.8
	SRBC	7.41 ± 0.301	16,941	502	71.1
	E. coli	8.01 ± 0.299[d]	16,910	648	92.1
Thymus	Control	6.90 ± 0.495	8,812	175	47.7
	SRBC	7.17 ± 0.336	8,422	202	57.6
	E. coli	6.72 ± 0.293	7,055	176	59.9

[a] $\int_{0.5}^{2} F^*(t)dt$.
[b] $P_2^* - P_{0.5}^*$.
[c] Means ± SEM of six chicks.
[d] Significantly different from control ($P < 0.05$).

somal aggregation (Table III) as compared to saline- and heat-denatured LEM controls or *E. coli.* Zinc concentrations were decreased by both LEM and *E. coli* in comparison to saline- and heat-denatured LEM controls. *E. coli* probably did not result in reduced aggregation of muscle polysomes because of the short time interval between dosing and sampling (5 hr).

Discussion. The rates of muscle protein synthesis determined by the pulse dose technique in these experiments are similar to the results determined in the same muscles by Maruyama *et al.* (8) in chicks. These authors administered [^{14}C]tyrosine in the diet and found the FSR of gastrocnemius and pectoralis muscles to be 22.3 and 18.5% per day, respectively. Quantitative data on protein syn-

TABLE II. POLYSOMAL PROFILES[a]

Tissue	Treatment: Control[b]	Treatment: SRBC[b]	Treatment: *E. coli*[b]
Pectoralis	1.67 ± 0.21[c]	2.14 ± 0.41[c,d]	3.28 ± 0.40[d]
Liver (free)	0.640 ± 0.07	0.575 ± 0.09	0.597 ± 0.05
Liver (bound)	1.05 ± 0.10[c]	0.83 ± 0.08[c,d]	0.65 ± 0.11[d]
Thymus	0.680 ± 0.02[c]	0.624 ± 0.02[c,d]	0.550 ± 0.03[d]
Bursa	0.855 ± 0.04[c]	0.760 ± 0.07[c]	0.538 ± 0.04[d]
Spleen	0.661 ± 0.03[c]	0.515 ± 0.02[d]	0.504 ± 0.02[d]

[a] Ratio of light to heavy polysomes.
[b] Means ± SEM of three profiles.
[c,d] Means in the same row with different superscripts are significantly different ($P < 0.05$).

TABLE III. MUSCLE POLYSOMAL PROFILES AND PLASMA ZINC[a]

Treatment	Aggregation (light/heavy)	Zinc (μg/ml)
Control	1.97 ± 0.10[b]	1.55 ± 0.06[c]
LEM	3.11 ± 0.31*	0.86 ± 0.13*
Heated LEM	2.14 ± 0.17	1.64 ± 0.05
E. coli	2.11 ± 0.20	0.57 ± 0.08*

[a] Chicks were killed 5 hr postinjection. Feed was withdrawn after injection.
[b] Means ± SEM of three chicks per treatment.
[c] Means ± SEM of four chicks per treatment.
* Significantly different from Controls ($P < 0.05$).

thetic rates in chick liver, thymus, bursa or spleen have not been reported. The FSR of protein synthesis in the chick liver appears to be slightly less than values reported for the rat utilizing constant infusion techniques (9). The immune tissue, and in particular the bursa and spleen, had very high FSR values. This may reflect increased mitosis in cell populations from these tissues.

In the experiments reported here, the cells of the immune tissue were separated from the connective tissue matrix but were not a homogeneous population. The thymus, bursa, and spleen consist predominantly of lymphocytes but also contain other cell types such as epithelial reticular cells, fibroblasts, and macrophages.

Inflammation-induced decreases in the protein synthetic rate of gastrocenemius muscle suggest a role of muscle in supplying amino acids for use in the liver and immune tissues, which have increased demand for these substrates. The absolute decrease in muscle FSR is relatively small in comparison to the increases in liver and the immune tissue. However, in rats the muscle contributes approximately 40% to the whole body protein pool whereas the immune tissue and liver contribute 2 and 4%, respectively (10). It is possible that the relatively small decrease in muscle FSR is compensated by the large amount of protein in this tissue, allowing the muscle to supply adequate quantities of amino acids to the liver and immune tissue.

Both *E. coli* and SRBC challenge resulted in increased FSR in the liver, spleen, thymus, and bursa. In most cases, the decrease in tissue free amino acid concentrations reported previously (1) corresponded with increased protein synthesis. It is likely that the increased use of amino acids for protein synthesis is responsible for the depressed tissue amino acid concentrations. SRBC did not result in depressed liver free amino acid concentration but did increase the FSR. In addition, both SRBC and *E. coli* resulted in increased thymic FSR accompanied by increased free amino acid concentrations. These discrepancies may be due to either an increase in the rate of amino acid transport to match or exceed the increased demand for protein synthesis or an increase in protein catabolism which is relatively greater than the increase in synthesis.

The determination of polysomal aggregation is a useful method to detect changes in protein synthesis. An increase in aggregation of polysomes represents a greater number of ribosomes translating each individual mRNA and increased protein synthesis whereas a decrease in aggregation represents reduced synthetic activity as a result of fewer translating ribosomes. This interpretation of polysomal aggregation is only valid when changes in the rate of protein synthesis are regulated by initiation. Since the regulation of protein synthesis is often due to or accompanied by changes in the initiation step (11), polysomal aggregation is a good measure of protein synthesis. This method can be misleading when regulation of protein synthesis occurs at transcription or at other steps of translation. However, when the change in rate of protein synthesis is known, the corresponding change in polysomal aggregation indicates the point of control for this change (11).

In these experiments, the general correlation between the rates of protein synthesis, as measured by isotope incorporation, with the extent of polysomal aggregation indicates two points. First, both methods are accurate methods for the detection of changes in protein synthesis resulting from inflammatory agents; however, the isotopic method is quantitative and possibly more sensitive. Second, the changes in rates of protein synthesis are regulated, at least in part, at the initiation step.

RNA concentrations were not affected by treatment in any tissue except the spleen. Since mRNA constitutes 80 to 90% of the total RNA (12, 13), it appears that with the exception of the spleen, protein synthesis is not controlled by changes in the availability of mRNA.

The control of inflammation-induced changes in protein synthesis in the thymus, bursa, and spleen appears to be similar to the control of protein synthesis after lymphocyte stimulation. Mitogen-induced increases in protein synthesis do not appear to be dependent upon the synthesis of new ribosomes, and there is no change in the rate at which individual protein molecules are synthesized (14). There is, however, a large increase in the proportion of lymphocyte ribosomes translating mRNA, indicating an increase in the rate of initiation (15, 16). Furthermore, it appears that unstimulated lymphocytes contain a translation inhibitor which reduces protein synthesis by inhibiting initiation factors (17).

Young *et al.* (18) have demonstrated depressed incorporation of [^{14}C]leucine into protein by muscle ribosomes *in vitro,* together with a disaggregation of polysomes after *Salmonella typhimurium* injection in rats. This, in conjunction with the present studies, demonstrates reduced protein synthesis in muscle due to decreased initiation after both infectious and noninfectious bacterial challenges as well as SRBC.

The increase in FSR in the liver is a result of an increase in the synthesis of protein synthesized on membrane-bound polysomes. This suggests that there is an increase in the synthesis of proteins destined for export from this tissue (i.e., plasma proteins) and/or membrane or organelle proteins. After experimental infections in rats, labeled amino acids are incorporated into plasma proteins at a much faster rate than in noninfected controls (19). Infection as well as LEM from stimulated leukocytes appeared to induce similar biochemical changes in liver (7). These include increases in the rate of amino acid transport and amino acid incorporation into protein. These changes occur in adrenalectomized, thyroidectomized, hypophysectomized, or diabetic rats. Interpretation of these experiments is difficult because the specific activity of the precursor pool was not determined.

LEM, also known as endogenous pyrogen and interleukin-1, has been shown to reduce plasma iron and zinc concentrations in several species including mouse, rat, and man (20, 21). These results suggest that LEM also lowers the plasma zinc concentration in the chick. Another possible function of LEM is to reduce the rate of protein synthesis in muscle. This may result in the release of amino acids from muscle for use in other tissues. The reduction in protein synthesis due to LEM occurred quickly, within 5 hr, which was much less than the time for an *E. coli*-induced reduction. This suggests that these changes are caused by a regulatory property of LEM and not an antigenic or inflammatory property.

Since LEM resulted in similar changes in muscle protein synthesis as did *E. coli,* it is possible that this mediator is responsible for the changes induced by *E. coli.* It is known that endotoxin is a potent inducer of LEM release (22). From this study, it cannot be determined if LEM directly interacted with muscles to decrease rates of protein synthesis or if the effects are induced by a hormone or other mediator which is released as a result of LEM. Baracos *et al.* (23) have demonstrated that leukocytic pyrogen (LEM) stimulates protein degradation but does not influence rates of protein synthesis in muscles incubated *in vitro.*

---

1. Klasing KC, Austic RE. Changes in plasma, tissue and urinary nitrogen metabolites due to an inflammatory challenge. Proc Soc Exp Biol Med **176**:276–284, 1984.
2. Zak R, Martin AF, Blough R. Assessment of protein turnover by use of radioisotopic tracers. Physiol Rev **59**:407–447, 1979.
3. Heywood SM, Dowben RM, Rich A. The identification of polyribosomes synthesizing myosin. Proc Natl Acad Sci USA **57**:1002–1009, 1967.
4. Ramsey JC, Steele WJ. A procedure for the quantitative recovery of homogeneous populations of undegraded free and bound polysomes from rat liver. Biochemistry **15**:1704–1712, 1976.
5. Lowry OH, Rosenbrough NJ, Farr AL, Randall RJ. Protein measurement with the Folin phenol reagent. J Biol Chem **193**:265–275, 1951.
6. Kampschmidt RF, Upchurch HF. Effect of leukocytic endogenous mediator on plasma fibrinogen and haptoglobin. Proc Soc Exp Biol Med **146**:904–907, 1974.
7. Wannemacher RW Jr, Pekarek RS, Thompson WL, Curnow RT, Beall FA, Zenser TV, DeRertis FR, Beisel WR. A protein from polymorphonuclear leukocytes (LEM) which affects the rate of hepatic amino acid transport and synthesis of acute phase globulins. Endrocrinology **96**:651–661, 1975.
8. Maruyama K, Sunde ML, Swick RW. Growth and muscle protein turnover in the chick. Biochem J **176**:573–582, 1978.

9. Waterlow JC, Garlick PJ, Millward DJ, eds. Protein Turnover in Mammalian Tissues and in the Whole Body. New York, North-Holland, 1978.
10. Waterlow JC, Stephen JML. Adaptation of the rat to a low protein diet: The effect of a reduced protein intake on the pattern of incorporation of L-(^{14}C)lysine. Brit J Nutr **20**:461–484, 1966.
11. Pain VM, Clemens MJ. Protein synthesis in mammalian systems. In: Florkin M, Neuberger A, Van Deenen L, eds. Comprehensive Biochemistry. Amsterdam, Elsevier, Vol 19B, 1980.
12. Whelly RW, Barker KL. Early effect of estradiol on the peptide elongation rate by uterine ribosomes. Biochemistry **13**:341–346, 1974.
13. Mathews RW, Haschemeyer AEV. Liver protein synthesis. Biochim Biophys Acta **425**:220–228, 1976.
14. Kay JE, Ahern T, Lindsay VJ, Sampson J. The control of protein synthesis during the stimulation of lymphocytes by phytohaemaglutinin. Biochim Biophys Acta **378**:241–250, 1975.
15. Kay JE, Ahern T, Lindsay VJ, Sampson J. Control of protein synthesis during the activation of lymphocytes by phytohaemaglutinin. Biochim Biophys Acta **247**:322–334, 1971.
16. Cooper HL, Braverman R. Free ribosomes and growth stimulation in human peripheral lymphocytes. J Cell Physiol **93**:213–226, 1977.
17. Kay JE, Wallace DM, Benzie CR, Jagus R. Regulation of protein synthesis during lymphocyte activation by phytohaemaglutinin. In: Quastel MR, ed. Cell Biology and Immunology of Leukocyte Function. New York, Academic Press, 1979.
18. Young VR, Chen SC, Newberne PM. Effect of infection on skeletal muscle ribosomes in rats fed adequate or low protein. J Nutr **94**:361–368, 1968.
19. Powanda MC, Wannemacher RW Jr, Cockerell GL. Nitrogen metabolism and protein synthesis during pneumococcal sepsis in rats. Infect Immun **6**:226–271, 1972.
20. Kampschmidt RF, Pulliam LA, Upchurch HF. The activity of partially purified leukocytic endogenous mediator in endotoxin-resistant C3H/He J mice. J Lab Clin Med **95**:616–623, 1980.
21. Wannemacher RW Jr, DuPont HL, Pekarek RS, Powanda MC, Schwartz A, Hornick RB, Beisel WR. An endogenous mediator of depression of amino acids and trace metals in serum during typhoic fever. J Infect Dis **126**:77–86, 1972.
22. Rafter GW. Stimulation of pyrogen production by lipopolysaccharide–leukocyte interactions. In: Schlesinger D, ed. Microbiology 1980. Washington DC, Amer Soc Microbiol, p154, 1980.
23. Baracos V, Rodemann HP, Dinarello CA, Goldberg AL. Stimulation of muscle protein degradation and prostaglandin E_2 release by leukocytic pyrogen (interleukin-1). N Engl J Med **303**:553–558, 1983.

Received September 6, 1983. P.S.E.B.M. 1984, Vol. 176.
Accepted March 30, 1984.

PROCEEDINGS OF THE SOCIETY FOR EXPERIMENTAL BIOLOGY AND MEDICINE **176**, 292–296 (1984)

Changes in Protein Degradation in Chickens Due to an Inflammatory Challenge (41873)

K. C. KLASING[1] AND R. E. AUSTIC

Department of Poultry and Avian Sciences, and Division of Nutritional Sciences, Cornell University, Ithaca, New York 14853

Abstract. Tissue-specific changes in protein catabolism were examined in chicks 16 hr following an inflammatory challenge. It was determined that tyrosine was not catabolized or converted to phenylalanine in muscle, thymus, bursa, or spleen. Therefore, rates of tyrosine release from protein were used to estimate rates of protein catabolism in these tissues. Arginine was not catabolized to urea by chick liver; consequently, arginine release from liver protein was used to measure protein catabolism in this tissue. An injection of sheep red blood cells (SRBC) or *Escherichia coli* did not change rates of protein catabolism in liver or bursa as compared to saline-injected controls. SRBC significantly increased protein catabolism in muscle and spleen by 29 and 15%, respectively. *E. coli* resulted in significant increases in muscle, spleen, and thymus of 43, 30, and 34%, respectively. These changes in protein catabolism, together with known changes in protein synthesis, suggest that an inflammatory response to SRBC and *E. coli* result in increased protein accretion in the bursa and liver, and net protein loss from muscle.

Net protein accretion or liberation in a tissue is determined by the balance between protein synthesis and degradation. The rates of protein synthesis in various tissues and the effect of inflammatory agents on these rates were described previously (1). In this report the relative rates of protein degradation were examined. Tissue-specific changes in protein accretion or liberation following stimulation of the immune system may represent a homeostatic response involved in the support of the immune response.

Investigations of protein degradation have been limited by methodological difficulties. Most studies have utilized intact animals and followed the disappearance of radioactively labeled proteins. These studies are subject to a number of artifacts such as those due to reutilization of the labeled amino acids (2). In order to analyze relative rates of protein degradation under carefully controlled conditions, the *in vitro* method of Fulks *et al.* (3) was employed. With this technique, the rate of liberation of an amino acid which is neither synthesized nor catabolized in the tissue being considered is determined.

Materials and Methods. *General.* All experiments utilized 600-g male, Single-Comb White Leghorn chicks (Cornell K-strain) except in experiments examining muscle where 350-g chicks were utilized. Chicks were reared and inflammatory agents were prepared as described previously (4). Chicks were injected with either 1% *Escherichia coli* (263,08: K87,88ab:H19), 1% sheep red blood cells (SRBC), or phosphate-buffered saline (control). Feed was removed at the time of injection and the chicks were killed after 16 hr.

Tissue preparation. Thymus, bursa, and spleen cells were separated from connective tissue as described previously (4). Liver slices were prepared by the method of Stadie and Riggs (5), which employs a razor blade microtome and results in slices which are about 0.5 mm thick. The extensor digitus longus muscle (EDL) was dissected from the lower leg without damage to the fibers and with the tendons intact at each end of the muscle. This was accomplished by separating the EDL from surrounding muscles (tibialis anterior) by blunt dissection and severing the tendons from the points of origin and insertion with a scapel. Tissue samples approximately 100 mg were utilized. The EDL from 350-g chicks weighed about 100 mg. It was important to limit muscle size to 100 mg in order to maintain viability, which is limited by O_2 and nutrient diffusion (6).

Conditions for incubation. Tissues were incubated in a manner similar to that described by Fulks *et al.* (3). Immediately after collection (muscle), slicing (liver), or isolation of cells

[1] Present address: Department of Animal Science, University of Illinois, Urbana, Ill. 61801.

0037-9727/84 $1.50

(thymus, bursa, and spleen), tissues were placed in 25-ml Erlenmeyer flasks. The flasks contained 5 ml of Krebs–Ringer bicarbonate (KRB) buffer (104 m*M* NaCl, 5 m*M* KCl, 3 m*M* $CaCl_2$, 1 m*M* $MgSO_4$, 1 m*M* KH_2PO_4, and 25 m*M* $NaHCO_3$, pH 7.4, at 37°C) with glucose (10 m*M*), amino acids (Table I), and chloramphenicol (0.3 mg/liter) and saturated with a 95% O_2–5% CO_2 gas mixture. The flasks were stoppered and re-equilibrated with the gas mixture. The O_2-charged flasks were preincubated for 30 min at 37°C with shaking. The tissues were then transferred to flasks containing fresh O_2-saturated KRB, chloramphenicol, glucose, amino acids, and 0.5 m*M* cycloheximide. Tissues were incubated an additional 3 hr at 37°C with shaking, and the reaction was terminated by the injection of 1 ml of 30% trichloroacetic acid solution. The concentration of tyrosine in the media was determined by the method of Waalkes and Udenfriend (7). Arginine concentrations were determined by automated amino acid analysis.

Amino acid catabolism. To measure protein catabolism by amino acid release, it is assumed that the marker amino acid is not catabolized to an unmeasured form after its release from protein. This was confirmed for the amino acids used in this study by the addition of ^{14}C-labeled amino acid to the incubation mixture and examining ^{14}C in the metabolic end products.

TABLE I. AMINO ACID COMPOSITION OF BUFFER

Amino acid	Concentration (μmole/liter)[a]
Asp	100
Thr	400
Ser	600
Glu	300
Gln	250
Gly	500
Ala	450
Cys	100
Val	220
Met	80
Ile	180
Leu	250
Tyr	180[b]
Phe	130
Pro	400
Lys	450
His	120
Arg	300[c]
Trp	80

[a] Concentrations reflect the normal plasma amino acid values of 600-g chicks fasted for 16 hr.

[b] Tyr was omitted in experiments examining Tyr catabolism and protein catabolism (except in liver).

[c] Arg was omitted in experiments examining Arg or protein catabolism in the liver.

Tyrosine catabolism. Muscle, thymus, bursa, and spleen were incubated wth 0.06 μCi/ml L-[U-^{14}C]tyrosine. The incubation was terminated by the injection of 1 ml 30% TCA into the incubation media. CO_2 was collected by injecting 90 ml of air into the flask while collecting the displaced gas via a hypodermic needle placed through the serum stopper. $^{14}CO_2$ was trapped in 25 ml of a 1:2 solution of 2-aminoethanol (ethanolamine):ethylene glycol monomethyl ether. Three milliliters of the trapping solution was counted in 12 ml of scintillation cocktail (Amersham, Arlington Heights, Ill.).

Arginine catabolism. Livers from chicks and rats (positive control) were incubated with 0.1 μCi/ml L-guanidino[^{14}C]arginine. The incubation was terminated with 1 ml 30% sulfosalicylic acid (SSA). Urea and arginine were isolated by collecting the effluent from an automated amino acid analyzer (Technicon Instruments Co., Terrytown, N.Y.). The [C^{14}]urea and [^{14}]arginine were determined by scintillation counting.

Conversion of phenylalanine to tyrosine. Tissues were incubated with 0.1 μCi/ml L-phenylalanine (side chain-^3H; ICN Pharmaceuticals, Inc., Irvine, Calif.). The incubation was terminated with 1 ml 30% SSA. Initial phenylalanine and final tyrosine concentrations were determined by automated amino acid analysis and the radioactivity of fractions containing the isolated amino acid was determined.

Results and Discussion. It is known that the kidney and liver can catabolize tyrosine; however, the tissue distribution of the enzymes of tyrosine catabolism has not been examined in detail (8). It was found that the spleen, bursa, and thymus catabolize very little tyrosine as compared to liver (Table II). The extent of tyrosine catabolism in these tissues was similar to that in muscle.

In comparison to rat liver, chick liver catabolized very little arginine. Since chick liver does not possess a functional urea cycle and

TABLE II. TISSUE AMINO ACID CATABOLISM

Tissue	Amino acid	Percentage catabolized per hour[a]
Liver	Tyr	0.92[b]
Muscle	Tyr	0.04
Bursa	Tyr	0.08
Thymus	Tyr	0.01
Spleen	Tyr	0.04
Liver	Leu	0.26
Liver	Arg	0.01
Liver (rat)	Arg	0.97

[a] cpm CO_2 or urea/initial cpm buffer.
[b] Means of two determinations.

has only trace arginase activity (9), arginine can be neither synthesized nor catabolized in chick liver. In this study and the study by Tamir and Ratner, chick arginase activity was about 1% of that in the rat.

In rats, the conversion of phenylalanine into tyrosine by phenylalanine hydroxylase occurs only in the liver and the adrenal medulla (10, 11). The inability of chick muscle, spleen, thymus, and bursa to synthesize tyrosine from phenylalanine is demonstrated in Table III. The chick liver exhibited active phenylalanine hydroxylase activity.

When protein synthesis is blocked and a tissue can neither synthesize nor catabolize a particular amino acid, the rate of increase in the concentration of that amino acid is indicative of this liberation due to protein catabolism. Tyrosine meets these requirements in the muscle, thymus, spleen, or bursa, and arginine meets the requirements in the liver. The release of these amino acids can be used to determine the rates of protein catabolism.

In this study, SRBC and *E. coli* did not affect protein catabolism in the liver or bursa as compared to controls (Table IV). SRBC significantly increased protein catabolism in the muscle and spleen by 29 and 15%, respectively. *E. coli* resulted in significant increased in the muscle, spleen, and thymus of 43, 30, and 34%, respectively.

Since rates of protein degradation were not affected by treatments in the liver and bursa, increases in protein synthesis reported previously (1) indicate that these tissues undergo net protein accretion. In muscle, rates of protein degradation and synthesis were changed in opposite directions after exposure to inflammatory agents. Consequently, protein is catabolized in muscle and amino acids are liberated.

Interpretation of the net change in protein metabolism in the thymus and spleen is difficult since the rates of synthesis (1) and degradation are both increased. The *in vitro* measurement of protein degradation by amino acid release is useful for determining qualitative, but not quantitative, changes. The quantitative limitations of this technique have been explored in muscle (3). When skeletal muscles from growing rats are incubated in unsupplemented KRB, they undergo net protein breakdown. Glucose and amino acids inhibit protein degradation, but the balance between protein synthesis and degradation is still very negative. Insulin also inhibits protein degradation and improves the nitrogen balance of incubated muscles; however, all of these factors together do not prevent net protein catabolism. Since glucose and amino acids, but not insulin, were provided in the incubation media in this study, it is apparent that the incubating muscle would have rates of protein degradation which are higher than

TABLE III. TISSUE-SPECIFIC CONVERSION OF Phe TO Tyr

Tissue	Percentage converted[a]
Liver	6.70[b]
Muscle	0.00
Spleen	0.35
Thymus	0.01
Bursa	0.01

[a] cpm/μmole Tyr at 3 hr/initial cpm/μmole Phe $\times$ 100.
[b] Means of two determinations.

TABLE IV. TISSUE PROTEIN CATABOLISM[a]

Tissue	*N*	Control	SRBC	*E. coli*
Liver	3	382 ± 11[b]	383 ± 17	410 ± 12
Muscle	8	224 ± 9[c]	288 ± 11[d]	321 ± 16[d]
Thymus	4	545 ± 14[c]	612 ± 34[c,d]	732 ± 54[d]
Spleen	4	820 ± 22[c]	942 ± 35[d]	1070 ± 41[d]
Bursa	4	649 ± 44	663 ± 46	790 ± 46

[a] Picomoles tyrosine or arginine (liver) released per gram of tissue in 3 hr of incubation.
[b] Mean ± SEM.
[c,d] Means in the same row with different superscripts are significantly different ($P < 0.05$).

in vivo rates. If the *in vitro* incubation of the spleen and thymus results in similar perturbations in nitrogen balance as that which has been reported in muscle, then changes in tyrosine release due to inflammatory agents cannot be considered as reliable quantitative measurements of protein degradation *in vivo*. For this reason the variable, milligrams protein degraded per unit time, which can be calculated from the moles of tyrosine released per unit time, would have little physiological significance. Therefore, comparison of the fractional synthetic rates reported previously (1) with degradation values in order to determine net protein production or loss is not valid.

From the consideration of the changes in free amino acid concentrations in these tissues after exposure to inflammatory agents (4), it appears that the spleen is in a state of net protein synthesis, whereas the thymus undergoes amino acid liberation and, therefore, net protein catabolism. This may indicate that the protein synthetic rate was greater than the degradative rate in the spleen but less in the thymus.

Most conditions which cause amino acid liberation from the muscle, such as food deprivation, denervation, disuse, or glucocorticoids, are a result of decreased protein synthesis and increased protein degradation (12). Inflammation-induced net protein degradation in muscle appears to be another example of amino acid liberation due to complementary changes in protein synthesis and degradation. Net protein accretion in muscle is also accompanied by increased protein degradation, but protein synthetic rates increase to a greater extent (13). This situation occurred in the spleen. It has been suggested that the high rates of protein degradation which occur simultaneously with growth allow the remodeling of structural proteins to accommodate the growth of the cell (13).

Increased liver protein accumulation is usually a result of decreased degradation with little change in synthesis (14); however, the increase in production of export proteins upon refeeding is a result of increased synthesis with little change in degradation (15). The inflammation-induced increase in liver protein synthesis is predominantly due to increased export protein (1) and has similar basis as an increase due to refeeding.

From the consideration of both protein synthesis (1) and catabolism, it is evident that the bursa, spleen, and liver respond to an ip injection of SRBC or *E. coli* by increasing their net rate of protein synthesis. This is not unexpected since it is the cells of the immune system which respond to antigenic stimuli, and the liver produces many of the immunologically active plasma proteins. It is well recognized that the spleen is an important secondary lymphatic tissue which is active during both systemic and localized infections. The ability of the bursa to process and respond to antigens has been recognized recently (16). It cannot be determined from these data if the increased protein synthesis in the bursa is due to an immune response in this tissue or to an increase in the synthesis of new cells which migrate to secondary lymphatic tissues.

The increased demand for amino acids for protein synthesis in the immune tissue and the liver appears to be satisfied by the release of amino acids from the muscle. The absolute increase in protein catabolism in this tissue due to exposure to inflammatory agents may not be great; however, the large size of this tissue apparently allows sufficient release of amino acids. This is demonstrated by the maintenance of essential amino acid concentrations in plasma after injection of inflammatory agents (4). It is possible that changes in protein degradation observed in this study are induced by mediators released from phagocytes stimulated by the inflammatory agents. Endogenous pyrogen, also known as interleukin-1 and leukocyte endogenous mediator, stimulates protein degradation in rat muscle incubated *in vitro* (17). A leukocyte-derived mediator also stimulates a change in the concentration of the nonmetabolizable amino acid, cycloleucine, in liver, suggesting the utilization of amino acids by liver (18).

1. Klasing KC, Austic RE. Changes in protein synthesis due to an inflammatory challenge. Proc Soc Exp Biol Med **176**:285–291, 1984.
2. Waterlow JC, Garlick PJ, Millward DJ. Protein Turnover in Mammalian Tissues and in the Whole Body. New York, North-Holland, pp 376–388, 1978.
3. Fulks RM, Li JB, Goldberg AL. Effects of insulin, glucose and amino acids on protein turnover in rat diaphragm. J Biol Chem **250**:290–298, 1975.
4. Klasing KC, Austic RE. Changes in plasma, tissue

and urinary nitrogen metabolites due to an inflammatory challenge. Proc Soc Exp Biol Med **176**:276–284, 1984.
5. Stadie WC, Riggs BC. Microtome for the praparation of tissue slices for metabolic studies of tissues in vitro. J Biol Chem **154**:1101, 1944.
6. Pain VM, Clemens MJ. Protein synthesis in mammalian systems. In: Florkin M, Neuberger A, eds. Comprehensive Biochemistry. Amsterdam, Elsevier, Vol 19B, pp 1–76, 1980.
7. Waalkes TP, Udenfriend S. A fluorometric method for the estimation of tyrosine in plasma and tissues. J Lab Clin Med **50**:733–736, 1957.
8. Meister A. Biochemistry of Amino Acids. New York, Academic Press, Vol 2, pp 884–928, 1965.
9. Tamir H, Ratner S. Enzymes of arginine metabolism in chicks. Arch Biochem Biophys **102**:249–258, 1963.
10. Udenfriend S, Cooper JR. The enzymatic conversion of phenylalanine to tyrosine. J Biol Chem **194**:503–511, 1952.
11. Fellman JH, Devlin MK. Concentration and hydroxylation of free phenylalanine in adrenal glands. Biochim Biophys Acta **28**:328–332, 1958.
12. Goldberg AL, Howell EM, Li JB, Martel SB, Prouty WF. Physiological significance of protein degradation in animal and bacterial cells. Fed Proc **33**:1112–1120, 1974.
13. Millward DJ. Protein turnover in skeletal and cardiac muscle during normal growth and hypertrophy. In: Wildenthal K, ed. Degradative Processes in Heart and Skeletal Muscle. New York, Elsevier, pp 161–224, 1980.
14. Mortimore GE, Ward WF. In: Dingle JT, Dean RT, eds. Lysosomes in Biology and Pathology. Amsterdam, North-Holland, Vol 5:pp157–184, 1976.
15. Morgan EH, Peters T. The biosynthesis of rat serum albumin. J Biol Chem **246**:3500–3505, 1971.
16. Van Alten PJ, Muehlman C. The role of the bursa of Fabricius in localized immunity and as a modulator of systemic immune responses. In: Solomon JB, ed. Aspects of Developmental and Comparative Immunology. New York, Pergamon Press, pp 253–257, 1980.
17. Baracos V, Rodemann MP, Dinarello CA, Goldberg AL. Stimulation of muscle protein degradation and prostaglandin E_2 release by leukocytic pyrogen (interleukin-1). N Engl J Med **308**:553–558, 1983.
18. Wannemacher RW, Pekarek RS, Beisel WR. Mediator of hepatic amino acid flux in infected rats. Proc Soc Exp Biol Med **139**:128–132, 1972.

Received September 6, 1983. P.S.E.B.M. 1984, Vol. 176.
Accepted March 30, 1984.

PROCEEDINGS OF THE SOCIETY FOR EXPERIMENTAL BIOLOGY AND MEDICINE **176**, 297–301 (1984)

Dimethyl Sulfoxide-Induced Inhibition of the Immunosuppressive Activity of Cultured Friend Erythroleukemia Cells (41874)

STEVEN SPECTER, WILLIAM I. COX,[1] AND HERMAN FRIEDMAN

Department of Medical Microbiology and Immunology, University of South Florida College of Medicine, Tampa, Florida 33612

Abstract. Two Friend leukemia virus-induced tumor cell lines lost their immunosuppressive properties *in vitro* when treated with dimethyl sulfoxide (DMSO), a known cellular differentiation agent. Incubation of the cell lines, GM 979 and GM 86, with DMSO for 4 days or longer, inhibited their ability to suppress the antibody forming capacity of normal murine spleen cells immunized *in vitro* with sheep red blood cells. Suppression of the inhibitory capability of the tumor cell lines by DMSO was time dependent. Three days incubation caused only slight, if any, inhibition, while a shorter period of treatment had no effect. Inhibition of the immunosuppressive properties of the tumor cell lines was not due to a decrease in tumor cell viability. The development of previously reported metabolic alterations in the treated cells, such as increased hemoglobin synthesis and other physicochemical alterations, paralleled cellular differentiation, and loss of immunosuppressive properties.

Oncogenic retroviruses such as the Friend leukemia virus (FLV) complex are known to have marked immunodepressive activities in susceptible mice (1–3). Acquired immunodeficiency induced in genetically susceptible animals by leukemia viruses is characterized by markedly depressed antibody responses following immunization with a wide variety of T-cell-dependent or -independent antigens. Cell-mediated immune responses also may be depressed in susceptible animals infected with such viruses. Leukemia virus-transformed cell lines have been established and are widely utilized in studies concerning the mechanisms of leukemogenesis. In this regard, a number of FLV-induced cell lines have been characterized in depth in terms of their biologic and physiologic activities (4, 5). Several of these cell lines, when incubated with relatively small concentrations of dimethyl sulfoxide (DMSO), a known differentiation agent, acquire some of the characteristics of normal erythroblastoid cells, including the ability to produce hemoglobin (6–9). DMSO treatment of such leukemic cells for 4 days results in differentiation of the cells and loss of many of their tumorigenic properties. Previous studies in this laboratory had shown that FLV-induced erythroleukemia cells from mouse spleens, when injected into normal susceptible animals or added to cultures of normal mouse spleen cells, markedly depressed antibody responses to antigens such as sheep red blood cells (2, 3). As shown in the present study, incubation of FLV induced cell lines with DMSO reversed their immunosuppressive properties for normal mouse spleen cells.

Methods and Procedures. *Animals.* BALB/c mice, 6–8 weeks old, were purchased from Jackson Laboratories, Bar Harbor, Maine. They were fed Purina mouse pellets and water *ad libitum* and kept in groups of 6–8 in plastic mouse cages.

Antibody assay. The *in vitro* induction of antibody-forming cells was performed as described previously (10). In brief, dispersed spleen cell suspensions were prepared in RPMI 1640 medium, fortified with 10% fetal bovine serum, plus 100 U penicillin and 100 μg streptomycin/ml medium (complete RPMI). The cells were washed once by centrifugation at 500*g* for 10 min at 4°C and suspensions of 5 $\times 10^6$ nucleated spleen cells were placed in 1.0 ml of medium in individual wells of Linbro 24-well culture plates. To each culture was added 0.2 ml of a 0.1% suspension of washed sheep red blood cells (SRBC) so that each culture was immunized with 2×10^6 erythrocytes. The plates were incubated in an atmosphere of 5% CO_2, 95% air in a humidified chamber at 37°C for 5 days. At that time the number

[1] Current Address: ImmunoMed Corp., Tampa, Fla. 33630-3125.

0037-9727/84 $1.50

of antibody plaque-forming cells (PFC) in each well was determined by a standard Cunningham plaque assay (11). The average number of PFC per culture for three or more cultures was calculated.

Leukemic cells. FLV-induced leukemia cells, i.e., cell line GM 979 and cell line GM 86, were obtained initially through the courtesy of Dr. Gary Lyman, Division of Oncology, University of South Florida College of Medicine. The cell cultures were maintained *in vitro* by frequent passage in complete RPMI medium. Graded concentrations of each cell suspension were added to cultures of normal mouse spleen cells being immunized with SRBC. For differentiation, cell cultures were incubated at a concentration of 1×10^5 nucleated leukemic cells per milliliter in complete RPMI containing 2% DMSO for the various time periods defined in each experiment. Following treatment with DMSO, the cells were washed three times by centrifugation at 250*g* for 10 min at 4°C with medium and resuspended to the appropriate concentration in complete medium without DMSO.

Experimental design. The effect of DMSO on the ability of the leukemia cells to depress the antibody response of normal spleen cells was determined by coculturing the tumor cells in graded numbers with optimum numbers of normal spleen cells being immunized with SRBC. The effect of length of incubation of the tumor cells with DMSO on their immunosuppressive properties was determined. Following DMSO treatment, the tumor cell lines were examined for viability by microscopic examination, using trypan blue dye exclusion and a hemocytometer.

Experimental Results. The two leukemia cell lines used for the study were markedly immunosuppressive for normal mouse spleen cells *in vitro.* As is evident in Table I, coculture of graded numbers of GM 979 or GM 86 cells with 5×10^6 normal mouse spleen cells resulted in a dose-related suppression of the expected antibody response. Whereas normal spleen cell cultures, without added leukemia cells, developed large numbers of PFC when immunized *in vitro* with SRBC, cultures containing as few as 10^5 tumor cells (a ratio of 1 tumor cell to 50 normal cells) showed a consistent but noticeable depression in the expected number of PFC. A 5- to 10-fold larger number of tumor cells (ratios of 1:10 or 1:5) decreased the antibody response consistently to levels that were significantly lower than

TABLE I. ALTERATION OF *IN VITRO* ANTI-SRBC RESPONSE OF NORMAL MOUSE SPLEEN CELLS COCULTURED WITH FRIEND ERYTHROLEUKEMIA CELLS

	Antibody response[b]			
	Experiment No. 1		Experiment No. 2	
Addition to cultures[a]	PFC/culture	Percentage of control	PFC/culture	Percentage of control
None (control)	50 ± 17	—	88 ± 38	—
SRBC only	492 ± 82	—	1575 ± 139	—
Plus GM 979 10^4	613 ± 338	125	1100 ± 118	70
5×10^4	—	—	950 ± 201	62
10^5	513 ± 38	104	900 ± 113	57 (<0.002)
5×10^5	50 ± 5	10 (<0.05)[c]	267 ± 96	17 (<0.005)
10^6	0	0 (<0.02)	0	0 (<0.001)
Plus GM 86 10^4	325 ± 50	68	1542 ± 137	98
5×10^4	113 ± 38	23 (<0.05)	1540 ± 186	98
10^5	100 ± 50	20 (<0.005)	1467 ± 131	93
5×10^5	13 ± 13	3 (<0.02)	533 ± 145	34 (<0.001)
10^6	13 ± 10	3 (<0.02)	33 ± 8	2 (<0.001)

[a] Cultures of 5×10^6 spleen cells from normal mice immunized *in vitro* with 2×10^6 SRBC and incubated with indicated number of leukemia cells.

[b] Average PFC response, ±SD, for three cultures per group 5 days after *in vitro* culture initiation.

[c] Significance determined by Student's *t* test (two tailed).

controls. In contrast, when up to 10^6 tumor cells which were cultured for 4 days with 2% DMSO were added to normal spleen cell cultures, many more PFC developed (Table II). For example, addition of 10^5 DMSO-treated leukemia cells of either cell line to normal spleen cell cultures resulted in essentially no decrease in the number of antibody producing normal splenocytes. Although 10^6 untreated GM 979 cells severely suppressed the antibody response of normal spleen cell cultures, after treatment for 4 days *in vitro* with DMSO the same number of GM 979 cells had no depressive effect and actually resulted in some enhancement of the response (Table II). Although the GM 86 cells before treatment with DMSO were also markedly immunosuppressive, after treatment with DMSO they only partially suppressed the antibody response.

No difference between the number of viable leukemic cells was noted in either tumor cell preparation, regardless of whether or not they were first treated with DMSO. Although the GM 979 cell line appeared to be somewhat more suppressive in some experiments, both tumor cell lines had similar suppressive effects for normal spleen cells, since larger numbers completely suppressed antibody forming capacity of normal spleen cells while smaller numbers had less effect.

The ability of DMSO to reverse the suppressive effects of the leukemia cells depended upon the length of time the cells were exposed to this agent. Previous studies had shown that 2% DMSO was an optimum concentration for inducing cellular differentiation and hemoglobin formation (4). In the present study, hemoglobin was induced to a sufficient concentration so that cell pellets were light red after 4 days in 2% DMSO. Lesser amounts had little or no effect, while larger concentrations did not increase the effect. Similarly, previous studies had shown that DMSO treatment required a minimum of 3–4 days to result in normal amounts of hemoglobin synthesis and loss of tumorigenic properties. As is evident in Fig. 1, cultures treated for 4 days or longer *in vitro* with DMSO had the least immunosuppressive activity when added to normal spleen cells *in vitro*. Incubation of cultures with DMSO for 3 days resulted in much less or no effect on the immunosuppressive activity of the cells. Incubation of the tumor cells for 4–6 days resulted in the greatest loss of suppressive activity when treated leukemic cells were cocultured with normal spleen cells.

Discussion. FLV induced cell lines GM 979 and GM 86 were markedly immunosuppressive for normal spleen cells immunized *in vitro* with SRBC. DMSO resulted in a loss of their

TABLE II. EFFECT OF DMSO-INDUCED DIFFERENTIATION OF FRIEND ERYTHROLEUKEMIA CELLS ON *IN VITRO* SUPPRESSION OF ANTI-SRBC PFC RESPONSES OF NORMAL MOUSE SPLEEN CELLS

Addition to cultures[a]		Antibody response[b]: Untreated PFC/culture	Untreated Percentage of control	DMSO-treated PFC/culture	DMSO-treated Percentage of control
None (control)		467 ± 82	—	—	—
SRBC only		1910 ± 21	100	—	—
Plus GM 979	10^4[c]	2692 ± 448	144	2259 ± 412	118
	10^5	1596 ± 176	84	1971 ± 264	103 (<0.005)[d]
	10^6	63 ± 31	3	2521 ± 364	131 (<0.025)
Plus GM 86	10^4	2321 ± 216	122	2117 ± 178	111
	10^5	879 ± 214	46	1829 ± 170	96 (<0.05)
	10^6	4 ± 4	1	584 ± 4	31 (<0.001)

[a] Indicated numbers of Friend leukemia cells added to cultures of 5×10^6 normal mouse spleen cells immunized *in vitro* with 2×10^6 SRBC.

[b] Average number of PFC, ±SD, for three cultures per group 5 days after *in vitro* culture initiation.

[c] Friend erythroleukemia cells cultured for 4 days with 2% DMSO.

[d] Significance determined in comparison to responses of cultures incubated with untreated leukemia cells by Student's *t* test (two tailed).

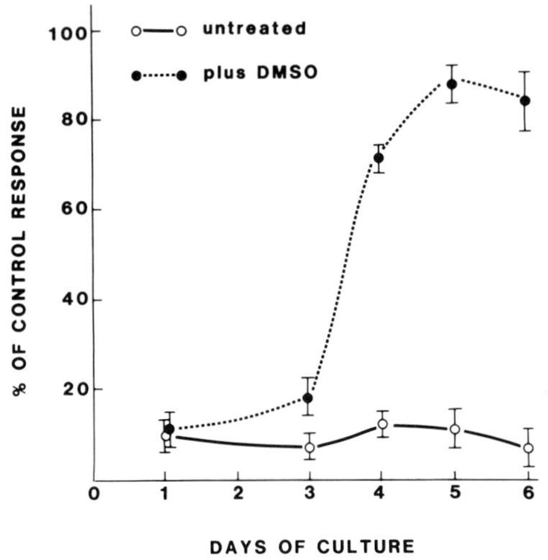

FIG. 1. Effect of DMSO treatment on GM 979 cell line *in vitro* for various lengths of time on immunosuppressive activities for normal mouse spleen cells. Each point represents the average anti-SRBC PFC response ± SD, 5 days after *in vitro* immunization of cultures of 5×10^6 spleen cells from normal mice incubated with 10^5 GM 979 cells, either untreated (solid line) or cultured for the indicated number of days with 2% DMSO (dashed line).

ability to suppress the antibody-forming capacity of normal spleen cell cultures. Previous studies had shown that DMSO treatment of various leukemia cell lines caused differentiation of the cells; hemoglobin synthesis became evident and histologically the cells appeared to be more like those of normal erythroblastoid cells (6, 7). Similarly, DMSO treatment of leukemic cells for 4 days or longer *in vitro* resulted in loss of leukemogenic properties as assessed by subsequent transfer of the cells into syngeneic animals, which failed to develop a tumor (unpublished observation). Normally a tumor results upon injection of these cell lines into susceptible syngeneic recipient mice.

Previous studies also showed that when mouse splenic FLV-induced leukemia cells were added to normal spleen cell cultures, even at ratios as low as 1:20 or 1:50, marked immunosuppression occurred (3). This was evident in the present experiments where a dose-related suppression of the normal immune response occurred. This suppression did not appear due merely to "overgrowth" of the normal lymphoid cells by the leukemia cells. Previous studies had shown that cell-free extracts or culture supernatants from the GM 979 cell line (unpublished observations) as well as from FLV-infected spleen cells per se, were markedly immunosuppressive (3). Thus, immunosuppression appeared to be associated with soluble factor(s) released from the tumor cells or possibly the virus itself. Furthermore, in coculture experiments with Millipore membranes it was evident that when the leukemia cells were grown in one chamber, separated by a cell-impermeable membrane from normal spleen cells being immunized with SRBC in a separate chamber, marked immunosuppression still occurred (12). Thus, Friend erythroleukemia tumor cells had the property of directly suppressing normal spleen cells *in vitro,* similar to the suppression induced by tumor cells or virus *in vivo.* It is interesting to note that GM 979 when examined by transmission electron microscopy, contain C-type virus particles, yet cell-free extracts do not cause leukemia in FLV-susceptible mice. This suggests that either the particles are not FLV or that they are not infectious virus. In addition, 2% DMSO treatment increased the number of particles visible by TEM (unpublished observations). Thus, it seems unlikely that the effect of DMSO was to inhibit production of virus.

In the present study it was evident that prior treatment of the leukemia cells with DMSO similar to the treatment which induces differentiation also diminished the immunosuppressive properties of the cells. It is not clear, however, whether this reduction in immunosuppressive activity was due to direct or indirect effects on virus infection of the cells, production or release of other intermediary factors, or alteration of a cell membrane component. Nevertheless, it is evident from the results of this study that differentiating leukemia cells after treatment with DMSO lost the ability to suppress antibody formation. It is possible that important metabolic activities of the leukemic cells could have been altered following treatment with DMSO or that the DMSO-treated leukemic cells became more susceptible to cell mediated lysis, even *in vitro* (13). Whether the effect of DMSO is due to cell differentiation or some other phenomenon is unclear. Thus, it will be of interest to determine whether other differentiating agents such as butyric acid have similar effects on the immunosuppressive properties of viral induced leukemic cells.

1. Notkins AL, Mergenhagen SE, Howard RJ. Effect of virus infections on function of the immune system. Annu Rev Microbiol **24**:525–538, 1970.
2. Friedman H. Immunosuppression by murine leukemia viruses. In: Koprowska C, Koprowski H, eds. Viruses and Immunity. New York, Academic Press, pp27–47, 1975.
3. Specter S, Friedman H. Viruses and the immune response. Pharmacol Therap (Part A) **2**:595–622, 1978.
4. Friend C, Sher W, Holland JG, Sato T. Hemoglobin synthesis in murine virus induced leukemia cells in vitro: Stimulation of erythroid differentiation by dimethyl sulfoxide. Proc Natl Acad Sci USA **68**:378–382, 1971.
5. Plata F, Goodenow MM, Lilly F. Studies of cloned Friend erythroleukemia tumor cells. Modulation of the tumor specific cytotoxic T-lymphocyte response by infectious Friend virus production in vitro. J Exp Med **151**:726–742, 1980.
6. Ross J, Ikawa Y, Leder P. Globin messenger-RNA induction during erythroid differentiation of cultured leukemia cells. Proc Natl Acad Sci USA **69**:3620–3623.
7. Conkie D, Affara N, Harrison PR, Paul J, Jones K. In situ localization of globin messenger RNA formation. II. After treatment of Friend virus-transformed mouse cells with dimethyl sulfoxide. J Cell Biol **63**:414–419, 1974.
8. Ebert PS, Ikawa Y. Induction of δ-aminolevulinic acid synthetase during erythroid differentiation of cultured leukemia cells. Proc Soc Exp Biol Med **146**:601–604, 1974.
9. Sabban EL, Sabatini DD, Marchesi VT, Adesnik M. Biosynthesis of erythrocyte membrane protein band 3 in DMSO-induced Friend erythroleukemia cells. J Cell Physiol **104**:261–268, 1980.
10. Kamo I, Pan SH, Friedman H. A simplified procedure for in vitro immunization of dispersed spleen cell cultures. J Immunol Methods **11**:55–62, 1976.
11. Cunningham AJ, Szenberg A. Further improvements in the plaque technique for detecting single antibody forming cells. Immunol **14**:599–600, 1968.
12. Specter S, Patel C, Friedman H. Immunosuppression induced in vitro by cell-free extracts of Friend leukemia virus infected splenocytes. J Natl Cancer Inst **56**:143–147, 1976.
13. Cox WI, Specter S, Friedman H. Susceptibility of Friend erythroleukemia cells to natural cytotoxicity after *in vitro* treatment with dimethyl sulfoxide. Proc Soc Exp Biol Med **169**:337–342, 1984.

Received January 26, 1984. P.S.E.B.M. Vol. 176, 1984.
Accepted March 30, 1984.

PROCEEDINGS OF THE SOCIETY FOR EXPERIMENTAL BIOLOGY AND MEDICINE **176**, 302–308 (1984)

An *in Vitro* Model of Fibroplasia: Simultaneous Quantification of Fibroblast Proliferation, Migration, and Collagen Synthesis[1] (41875)

MARTIN F. GRAHAM,* ROBERT F. DIEGELMANN,† AND I. KELMAN COHEN†

*†Division of Plastic Surgery and *Department of Pediatrics, Children's Medical Center, Medical College of Virginia/Virginia Commonwealth University, Richmond, Virginia 23298*

Abstract. Previous studies of fibroblast proliferation, migration, and collagen synthesis have been limited in their ability to define the interrelationship among these events in response to various inflammatory mediators. We have now defined an *in vitro* tissue culture model for the synchronous quantification of these parameters of fibroplasia. Biopsies (2 mm) of chicken flexor tendons are embedded in a fibrin matrix and exposed to various factors for 5 days in tissue culture. The availability of the fibrin matrix surrounding the tendon biopsy satisfies the need for a solid support medium for fibroblast migration. Multiple measurements of tendon fibroblast proliferation, migration into the fibrin matrix, and relative collagen synthesis are then made on these preparations. Fetal calf serum stimulated tendon fibroblast proliferation and migration in a dose responsive fashion, whereas the selective expression of collagen synthesis was decreased. Platelet lysate stimulated fibroblast proliferation at low concentration, but migration only at high concentration and was without effect on relative collagen synthesis. This model now provides a means of more clearly defining the influence of various inflammatory factors on the events of fibroplasia.

The "healing" response of tissue to injury involves complex interactions between inflammatory cells, their products, coagulation factors, hormonal and nutritional plasma elements, and the collagen-producing cells (1–4). These interactions are thought to induce the fibroblasts to move into the area of inflammation, to proliferate there, and to lay down new connective tissue protein. The precise relationship between the various inflammatory cells and their factors and the different components of the connective tissue response has been difficult to discern *in vivo* and in cell culture. *In vivo* studies are difficult to control and cell culture studies employ diverse techniques to study different phenomena. For example, *in vitro* studies employ a Boyden chamber for migration (5), a culture dish for proliferation (6), and usually a different set of defined conditions for the measurement of collagen and protein synthesis (7). In recent years, evidence has accumulated that the behavior of connective tissue cells is influenced, to a large extent, by their extracellular environment (8)—one that is highly variable under cell culture conditions. We have thus designed a tissue culture model that mimics to a limited degree the wound environment and also permits synchronous study of the events of fibroplasia within that environment.

Explants of chicken flexor tendons are embedded in a fibrin matrix and are then incubated in culture medium containing various inflammatory mediators. The fibrin matrix serves as a solid support into which the tendon fibroblasts can migrate. Tendon fibroblast migration, proliferation, and collagen synthesis are then all quantified under the same experimental conditions. Approximately 80 explants are procured from each set of tendons from a single chicken permitting quantification of replicates of each culture condition.

This paper describes the details of this *in vitro* model of fibroplasia, and how in initial studies, it has been used to discern the disparate effect of two inflammatory mediators on fibroblast migration, proliferation, and collagen synthesis.

Materials and Methods. *Experimental model.* Flexor digitorum profundus tendons were removed from the long digits of female White Leghorn chickens (2.5–3 kg) in sterile fashion, rinsed in Dulbecco's Modified Eagle's Medium (DMEM), and dissected to ensure complete removal of all sheath and other sy-

[1] Presented in part at the Federation of American Societies for Experimental Biology Annual Meeting (Fed Proc **41**:439, 1982, and Fed Proc **42**:1298, 1983).

0037-9727/84 $1.50

novial components. Plugs 2 mm in diameter were cut from the excised tendons with a dermal trephine and placed in multi-well culture plates (Costar No. 3524, Cambridge, Mass.). The tendon plugs were covered first by 10 μl thrombin solution (2 mg/ml DMEM) and then by 50 μl fibrinogen solution (KABI, Grade L, Stockholm, Sweden; 3 mg/ml). The fibrin matrix was allowed to mature at 37°C for 30 min in a humidified atmosphere after which 1 ml of DMEM supplemented with glycl-histidyl-lysine (200 ng/ml) (9), aprotinin (100 KIU/ml, Trasylol, Mobay Chemical Corp., New York), and fresh ascorbate (0.1 m*M*) were added to each well. The tripeptide, glycyl-histidyl-lysine, was used to maintain the viability of the tendon fibroblasts in the absence of exogenous serum or growth factors (9) and the aprotinin was used to ensure the stability of the fibrin matrix against breakdown by tissue proteases. This medium will be referred to as "DMEM base." After a 48-hr period of quiescence in DMEM base, various exogenous factors to be assayed were added to the medium and incubation was continued for an additional 5 days. This was the period determined in an earlier study, necessary to achieve maximal fibroblast proliferation (10). Medium supplemented with fresh ascorbate was replaced every 24 hr.

Tendon fibroblast migration. In a stimulated system (10% fetal calf serum) fibroblasts can be observed migrating into the fibrin matrix after 48 hr (10, 11). After 5 days incubation in the presence of 10% fetal calf serum, the fibroblasts have migrated out of the tendon plug into an area 5–8 mm^2 (10). Projection of the radiating fan of migrating cells onto paper then permits measurement of the area of migration using a Zeiss MOPP III automatic planimeter.

Tendon fibroblast proliferation. Incorporation of [^{125}I]iododeoxyuridine (^{125}IUDR, 2,000 Ci/mmole, New England Nuclear, Boston, Mass.) into dividing fibroblasts was used to quantitate DNA synthesis as an index of proliferation (12). After 5 days of incubation in factor-supplemented medium, the specimens were pulsed with ^{125}IUDR (1 μCi/ml) and 10^{-5} *M* 5-fluorodeoxyuridine (FUDR, Sigma, St. Louis, Mo.) for 12 hr. The duration of this pulse was determined by a time-course experiment of ^{125}IUDR incorporation into the tendon fibroblasts (Fig. 1). The FUDR enhanced ^{125}IUDR uptake by providing a specific inhibition of endogenous thymidine synthesis (13). Following the incubation, the radioactive medium was removed, the wells were rinsed three times with phosphate-buffered saline, and the contents of the wells were dissolved completely in 1 ml of 1 *N* sodium hydroxide at 37°C for 24 hr. The sodium hydroxide solution contained 2 mg of carrier DNA (Type I, calf thymus, Sigma Chemical Co., St. Louis, Mo.) to ensure complete recovery of the radioactive tendon fibroblast DNA. The alkaline treatment was used to facilitate complete tissue solubilization, hydrolyze ribonucleic acid, and destroy nucleases (14, 15). In addition, DNA is more readily precipitated by acid following alkali treatment (16).

After neutralization with 0.5 ml of 2 *N* hydrochloric acid, the samples were chilled to 4°C and protein and DNA were precipitated by the addition of 0.15 ml of 50% trichloroacetic acid (TCA) to give a final concentration of 5%. Micro stir bars (8 × 1.5 mm) were placed in each well and the culture plate was placed on a stir plate to allow adequate mixing

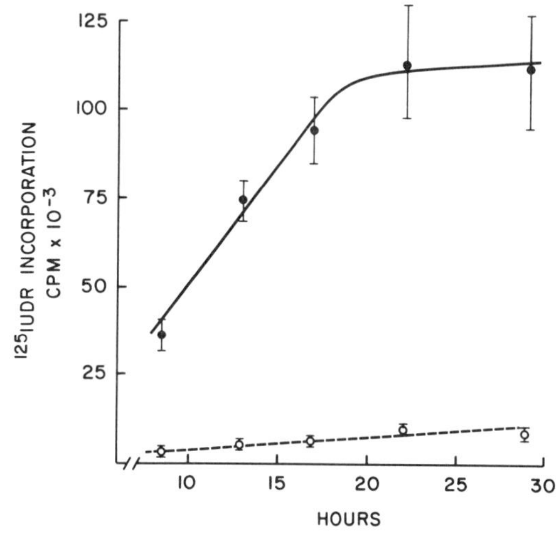

FIG. 1. Time course of ^{125}IUDR incorporation into tendon fibroblast DNA. Cultures were incubated for 5 days in the presence of 10% FCS. Solid line represents isotope incorporation for the duration of hours indicated. The dashed line represents the background activity in control specimens incubated in the presence of 25 m*M* hydroxyurea during the isotope pulsing period. The error bars represent the SEM of six replicates.

during these additions. The precipitated DNA was washed four times with 1 ml of 5% TCA in the cold to remove unincorporated isotope. To facilitate this procedure, the 24-well culture plates were centrifuged (300*g*) using microtiter centrifuge carriers (Cooke System, Dynatech Laboratories Inc., Alexandria, Va.). After the last wash, the stir bars were removed, the final precipitate was dried, and the wells were sprayed with clear plastic. The wells were then cut out of the plate with a band saw, and counted for ^{125}I radioactivity in a gamma spectrometer (12). Control specimens were preincubated for 2 hr with hydroxyurea (25 m*M*) to allow sufficient time for the DNA synthesis inhibitor to penetrate through the fibrin matrix and into the tendon fibroblasts. The use of hydroxyurea as a specific inhibitor of DNA synthesis (17) allows determination of background nonspecific binding of isotope which is then subtracted from the test samples.

IUDR is deoxythymidine with iodine substituted for a methyl group in the fifth position of the nucleotide ring. The use of ^{125}IUDR to measure DNA synthesis was chosen because with gamma radioactive counting, samples do not need to be transferred from the multi-well culture plates for analysis. In addition, the cost associated with scintillation vials and fluors needed for [^{14}C]- or [^{3}H]thymidine usage is also avoided. Iododeoxyuridine equilibrates with the thymidine pool and its incorporation into DNA can be blocked by thymidine competition (18). The use of ^{125}IUDR as a specific DNA precursor is gaining acceptance and the rate of incorporation of this isotope has been shown to be directly related to cell proliferation (19–21).

Tendon fibroblast collagen synthesis. These studies were performed on tendon cultures incubated in parallel with those used for proliferation and migration studies. Collagen synthesis was quantitated by a technique based upon the susceptibility of newly synthesized radioactive protein to be digested by purified bacterial collagenase (22). After 5 days of factor-supplemented incubation, tendon explants were incubated with the appropriate medium containing fresh ascorbate (0.1 m*M*) and 10 μCi of [^{3}H]proline (43 Ci/mmole, Schwarz/Mann, Orangeburg, N.J.). After 6 hr, the incubation was stopped by removing the radioactive medium and then rinsing the culture plate wells twice with phosphate-buffered saline (4°C). The explants, complete with fibrin matrix, were removed and placed into centrifuge tubes on ice. The wells were rinsed with 1 ml of deionized water which was added to the tissue samples. The samples were then heated to 90°C for 10 min to destroy any proteolytic enzyme activity and then frozen until time of analysis. Specimens from two wells were pooled and analyses were done in triplicate. After thawing, the radioactive protein was precipitated in the cold with TCA (5%) prior to digestion with a highly specific bacterial collagenase as previously described (22). After digestion of the collagen, the noncollagenous protein was reprecipitated with 5% TCA–0.25% tannic acid. Supernatants containing collagen-derived peptides and pellets containing the noncollagenous protein were then counted separately for radioactivity. Radioactivity released by collagenase is represented by the value in the numerator and the percentage collagen synthesized relative to total protein synthesis is calcualted according to the following formula:

$$\%\ \text{collagen synthesis} = \frac{\text{cpm in collagen}}{(\text{cpm in noncollagen protein} \times 5.4) + \text{cpm in collagen}} \times 100.$$

The factor of 5.4 corrects for the enriched content of proline and hydroxyproline in collagen versus only proline in noncollagen protein (23).

Effect of various trophic factors on fibroblast proliferation, migration, and collagen synthesis. After 48 hr incubation in DMEM base, various concentrations of fetal calf serum (FCS) and platelet lysate (PL) with 5% platelet-poor plasma (PPP) were added to the incubation medium. After 5 days of additional incubation, fibroblast proliferation, migration, and collagen synthesis were determined as described above. The FCS was purchased from GIBCO Laboratories (Grand Island, N.Y.). Platelet lysate (PL) and PPP were prepared as previously described by Pledger *et al.* (24). Expired human platelets were obtained from the Medical College of Virginia blood bank and washed three times in phosphate-buffered saline. The platelet suspension was then frozen, thawed, and heated to 100°C for 5 min.

The cell debris was removed by centrifugation and the supernatant was used as the platelet lysate. The protein concentration in the lysate was estimated by 260–280-nm determinations (25).

For the preparation of PPP, freshly obtained human plasma was collected in citrated tubes and centrifuged at 3500*g*. The supernatant was collected and defibrinated by heating at 56°C for 30 min. The plasma was then centrifuged at 27,000*g* for 30 min and sterile-filtered (0.45 μm) prior to use (24).

Results. *Time course of* ^{125}*IUDR incorporation into tendon fibroblasts.* Incubation of tendon explants with ^{125}IUDR at intervals from 8 to 28 hr on the fifth day of incubation with 10% FCS showed a linear incorporation of isotope from 8 to 16 hr (Fig. 1). In subsequent studies, the level of background radioactivity in the hydroxyurea blanks was subtracted from the test specimens. The background value was normally less than 5% of the radioactivity incorporated into the non-hydroxyurea-treated specimens. A 12-hr pulse was, therefore, used in all subsequent experiments.

Effect of fetal calf serum on fibroblast proliferation, migration, and collagen synthesis. Both fibroblast proliferation and migration responded in a dose-related fashion to increasing concentrations of fetal calf serum in the culture medium and were maximal at the highest concentration tested (10%). In contrast, collagen synthesis, relative to total protein synthesis, was maximal at low concentrations of fetal calf serum (8–10% of total protein synthesized) and with increasing concentrations, became minimal at the 10% concentration (3.5% of total protein synthesized) (Fig. 2). When these collagen synthesis data were calculated on an absolute basis (per tendon explant), it became apparent that there was an increase in the synthesis of collagen (2.6-fold, from 0.1 to 10% fetal calf serum) but this was overshadowed by the increase in the synthesis of noncollagen protein (6.5-fold) (Table I). Therefore, the net effect resulted in a decrease in relative collagen synthesis in response to increasing concentrations of fetal calf serum.

Effects of platelet lysate on fibroblast proliferation, migration, and collagen synthesis. The addition of platelet lysate to medium containing 5% platelet-poor plasma resulted in a proliferative response at low concentrations of lysate (5 μg/ml), approaching a maximal response at 20 μg/ml (Fig. 3). A migratory response, in contrast, did not occur at low concentrations of platelet lysate and was elicited only at the highest concentration of platelet lysate tested (100 μg/ml). This disparity

TABLE I. INFLUENCE OF FETAL CALF SERUM ON THE SYNTHESIS OF COLLAGEN AND NONCOLLAGEN PROTEIN BY TENDON EXPLANT CULTURES

Percentage fetal calf serum	Collagen (cpm/tendon culture)[a]	Noncollagen protein (cpm/tendon culture)[a]	Relative collagen synthesis (%)
0	106 ± 26	245 ± 93	8.1
0.1	229 ± 11	490 ± 50	8.1
0.5	180 ± 27	291 ± 31	10.3
1.0	241 ± 51	467 ± 137	9.4
2.0	246 ± 37	970 ± 185	4.8
10.0	606 ± 168	3183 ± 963	3.5

[a] Data expressed as mean ± SEM; *N* = 3. Cultures were incubated for 6 hr with [^{3}H]proline (10 μCi/ml) and two tendon explants were pooled for each analysis. Collagen was specifically digested by purified bacterial collagenase and the radioactivity released into the supernatant was measured whereas noncollagen protein was reprecipitated and measured in the pellet (22). The percentage collagen synthesis was calculated after correcting for the enriched amino acid content of collagen (23).

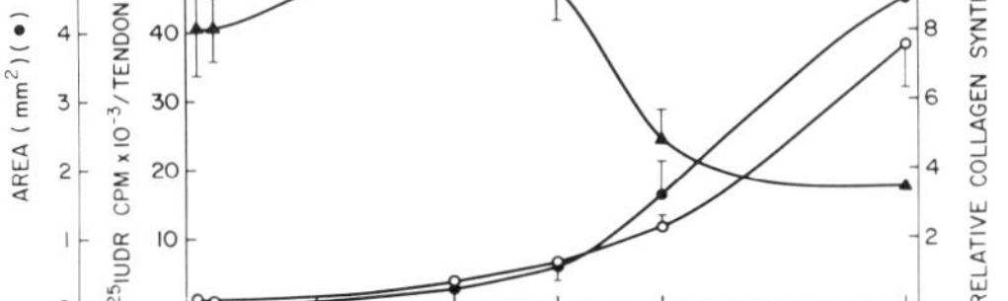

FIG. 2. Effect of FCS on fibroplasia. Various concentrations of whole FCS were used to determine the effect on fibroblast proliferation, migration, and collagen synthesis. Cultures were incubated for 5 days with the indicated concentrations of FCS. Fibroblast proliferation as measured by ^{125}IUDR incorporation into DNA was made on four replicate specimens and the background radioactivity observed in the hydroxyurea blanks (two replicates) was subtracted. Relative collagen synthesis was measured in triplicate and migration was measured using six replicates. The error bars indicate the SEM.

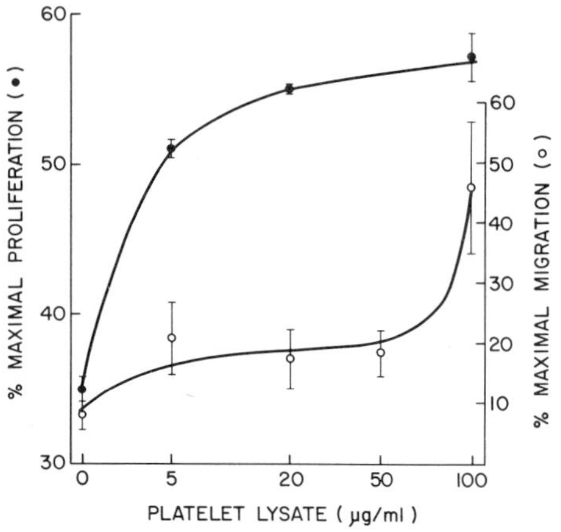

FIG. 3. Effect of PL on fibroblast proliferation and migration. Cultures were incubated for 5 days with the indicated concentrations of PL. fibroblast proliferation was measured by ^{125}IUDR incorporation into DNA (four replicate specimens) and a hydroxyurea blank value (two replicates) was subtracted. Migration was measured using six replicates and error bars indicate the SEM. Data are expressed as percent maximal proliferation observed using 10% FCS (37×10^{-3} cpm/tendon biopsy) and maximal migration observed using 10% FCS (5.1 mm^2).

between proliferative and migratory responses contrasted sharply with the marked similarity between these two events in response to fetal calf serum (Fig. 2). There was no significant effect of varying concentrations of PL on either absolute or relative collagen synthesis in these experiments. Incubation with 10% FCS (positive control) resulted in a relative collagen synthesis value of 6.7% whereas the mean value for PL from 0 to 100 µg/ml was 6.1 ± 0.4%.

Discussion. The most realistic setting for the study of fibroplasia in response to inflammation is obviously an *in vivo* one. However, the multiplicity of factors involved and cellular events occurring precludes that system from being a controllable one for study. Currently, there is considerable debate concerning the validity of cell culture techniques for such studies (26–28). The controversy hinges on the appreciation now that the behavior of fibroplastic cells is governed to a great extent by their extracellular environment and surrounding matrix (8). Any aberration in this environment will undoubtedly affect the cellular events being studied, and hence influence the particular response being documented. In addition, many essential wound elements are not present in the culture dish, again modifying the results. The design of this model for the study of the interrelationship between inflammatory factors and fibroplastic events endeavored to satisfy three criteria: (i) the fibroplastic cells under study should be within their native tissue matrix; (ii) the cells should be exposed to an inflammatory environment that contains the essential elements of a wound; and (iii) all three fibroblast events—proliferation, migration, and collagen synthesis—should be studied under identical conditions, hence permitting a determination of the interrelationship between the events.

The first criterion was satisfied by using tissue explants in culture. The problem of controlling for the different cell types in whole tissue was resolved by employing tendon tissue for the model. Tendon was ideal as it is constituted by a matrix rich in highly organized collagen and a single homogeneous population of fibroplastic cells—tenoblasts. All cellular events observed can thus be attributed to the tendon fibroblasts.

The second criterion was met by surrounding the tissue with a fibrin matrix. Previous studies using this model demonstrated that fibrin was an essential constituent of the plasma clot needed for the rapid migration of tendon fibroblasts out of the tissue (10, 11). The presence of a fibrin matrix resulted in a 54% increase in tendon fibroblast proliferation and a 7- to 10-fold increase in cell migration from the tendon explant (10, 11). Fibroblasts normally migrate on a solid, collagenous, or fibrous matrix of connective tissue or plasma clot and, therefore, their movements should be studied in a solid medium. The peri-explant fibrin matrix employed in this model provides this necessary "scaffold" and we think is an essential component of the cellular environment in studies of this nature.

The third criterion has been satisfied by the model design. Adaptation of established assays for DNA (12, 18–21) and collagen synthesis (22) and an innovative assay for quantifying the area of migration out of the tissue explant allow all three cellular events to be studied in the same preparation (10). This capacity to assay three separate fibroplastic events under identical conditions has provided a valuable insight into their interrelationships and has also demonstrated their individualistic modes of response. Low concentrations of fetal calf serum (0.1 to 0.5%) favored production of collagen relative to total protein synthesis but were suboptimal for tendon fibroblast proliferation and migration (Fig. 2). In contrast, 10% fetal calf serum was highly stimulatory for proliferation and migration at the expense of differential collagen synthesis (Table I).

The decrease in relative collagen synthesis at high concentration of FCS has been previously reported (27, 28) but was not analyzed by those investigators in relation to maximal fibroblast proliferation or migration. It is understandable that during maximal proliferation and migration, utilization of energy and precursors for synthesis of various cellular components (DNA and cytosol elements) may occur at the expense of other specialized cellular functions (collagen synthesis). It is interesting that in this specialized collagen-producing cell, synthesis of noncollagen protein takes precedence over collagen synthesis in response to 10% fetal calf serum (Table I). In the wound setting, it is likely, however, that despite the decrease in the relative commitment of protein synthesis to collagen, the total amount of collagen being produced is actually increased due to (i) increase in collagen synthesis per cell, (ii) the recruitment of fibroblasts into the area, and (iii) their proliferation.

Platelet-derived growth factor, a known commitment factor for cell proliferation (29–31), was demonstrated to have an effect on fibroblast proliferation at relatively low concentrations, but a migratory effect only at higher concentrations (Fig. 3). The discordance of the proliferative and migratory responses demonstrates either the coexistence of two separate response mechanisms for the two events, or the presence of two distinct proliferative and migratory factors in the platelet lysate. Platelet lysate and platelet-derived growth factor have been shown to be chemotactic for smooth muscle cells (32) and fibroblasts (33) using the Boyden chamber assay. Evidently, platelet lysate, as tested under the conditions in this model, does not contain factors affecting collagen or total protein synthesis.

We present here a model for the study of fibroplasia that now provides a means of defining more clearly the influence of various inflammatory cells and their products on fibroplastic events. Based upon these initial studies, it has become apparent that the mode and the degree of the response of the fibroplastic cells are dependent both on the nature and concentration of the inflammatory factors and possibly a reciprocal relationship between the different cellular events.

This work was supported by NIH Grant GM-20298. The authors thank Fay Akers and Rae Carole Spivey for expert secretarial assistance in preparing the manuscript and to Mrs. Patricia S. Keathley for fine technical assistance.

1. Ross R. The fibroblast and wound repair. Biol Rev **43**:51–95, 1968.
2. Ross R. Wound healing. Sci Amer **220**:40–50, 1969.
3. Schilling J. Wound healing. Surg Clin N Amer **56**:859–874, 1976.
4. Hunt TK, Halliday B. Inflammation in wounds: From "laudable pus" to primary repair and beyond. In: Hunt TK, ed. Wound Healing and Wound Infection. New York, Appleton–Century–Crofts, pp281–293, 1980.
5. Boyden S. The chemotactic effect of mixtures of antibody and antigen on polymorphonuclear leukocytes. J Exp Med **115**:453–466, 1962.
6. Leibovich SJ, Ross R. A macrophage-dependent factor that stimulates the proliferation of fibroblasts *in vitro*. Amer J Pathol **84**:501–513, 1976.
7. Wahl SM, Whal LM, McCarthy JB. Lymphocyte-mediated activation of fibroblast proliferation and collagen production. J Immunol **121**:942–946, 1978.
8. Hay ED. Cell Biology of Extracellular Matrix. New York, Plenum, 1981.
9. Pickart L. The use of glycylhistidyl-lysine in culture systems. In Vitro **17**:459–466, 1981.
10. Graham MF, Becker H, Cohen IK, Merritt W, Diegelmann RF. Intrinsic tendon fibroplasia: Documentation by *in vitro* studies. J Orthop Res **1**:251–256, 1984.
11. Becker H, Graham MF, Cohen IK, Diegelmann RF. Intrinsic tendon cell proliferation in tissue culture. J Hand Surg **6**:616–619, 1981.
12. Cohen AM, Burdick JE, Ketcham AS. Cell-mediated cytotoxicity: An assay using ^{125}iododeoxyuridine-labeled target cells. J Immunol **107**:895–898, 1971.
13. Hartmann KV, Heidelberger CJ. Studies on fluorinated pyrimidine: XIII. Inhibition of thymidylate synthetase. J Biol Chem **236**:3006–3013, 1961.
14. Munro HN, Fleck A. The determination of nucleic acids. In: Glick D, ed. Methods of Biochemical Analysis. New York, Wiley, pp113–176, 1966.
15. Schmidt G, Tanhauser SJ. A method for the determination of deoxyribonucleic acid, ribonucleic acid

and phosphoproteins in animal tissues. J Biol Chem **161**:83–89, 1945.
16. Mathieson AR, Porter MR. Fractional precipitation of nucleic acid. Nature (London) **173**:1190–1191, 1954.
17. Pfeiffer SE, Tolmach LJ. Inhibition of DNA synthesis in HeLa cells by hydroxyurea. Cancer Res **27**:124–129, 1967.
18. Commerford SL. Biological stability of 5-iodo-2′-deoxyuridine labeled with iodine-125 after its incorporation into the deoxyribonucleic acid of the mouse. Nature (London) **205**:949–950, 1965.
19. Seigers MP, Feinendegen LE, Lahiri S, Cronkite E. Proliferation kinetics of early hemopoietic precursor cells with self-sustaining capacity in the mouse, studied with 125-I-labeled iodo-deoxyuridine. Exp Hematol **7**:469–482, 1979.
20. Diegelmann RF, Cohen IK, Kaplan AM. Effect of macrophages on fibroblast DNA synthesis and proliferation. Proc Soc Exp Biol Med **169**:445–451, 1982.
21. Inoue T, Bullis JE, Cronkite EP, Hüber GE. Relationship between number of spleen colonies and ^{125}IdUrd incorporation into spleens and femur. Proc Natl Acad Sci USA **80**:435–438, 1983.
22. Peterkofsky B, Diegelmann RF. The use of a mixture of proteinase-free collagenases for the specific assay of radioactive collagen in the presence of other proteins. Biochemistry **10**:988–994, 1971.
23. Diegelmann RF, Peterkofsky B. Collagen biosynthesis during connective tissue development in chick embryo. Dev Biol **28**:443–453, 1972.
24. Pledger WJ, Stiles CD, Antoniades HN, Scher CD. Induction of DNA synthesis in BALB/c 3T3 cells by serum components: Re-evaluation of the commitment process. Proc Natl Acad Sci USA **74**:4481–4485, 1977.
25. Warburg O, Christian W. Isolienung und kristallisation des gärungsferments enolase. Biochem Z **310**:384–442, 1941.
26. Peterkofsky B, Prather WB. Increased collagen synthesis in Kirsten sarcoma virus-transformed BALB 3T3 cells grown in the presence of dibutyryl cyclic AMP. Cell **3**:291–299, 1974.
27. Schwarz R, Colarusso L, Doty P. Maintenance of differentiation in primary cultures of avian tendon cells. Exp Cell Res **102**:63–71, 1976.
28. Schwarz RI, Bissell MJ. Dependence of the differential state on the cellular environment: Modulation of collagen synthesis in tendon cells. Proc Natl Acad Sci USA **74**:4453–4457, 1977.
29. Balk SD. Calcium as a regulator of the proliferation of normal but not of transformed chicken fibroblasts in a plasma-containing medium. Proc Natl Acad Sci USA **68**:271–275, 1971.
30. Kohler N, Lipton A. Platelets as a source of fibroblast growth-promoting activity. Exp Cell Res **87**:297–301, 1974.
31. Rutherford RB, Ross R. Platelet factors stimulate fibroblasts and smooth muscle cells quiescent in plasma serum to proliferate. J Cell Biol **69**:196–203, 1976.
32. Grotendorst GR, Seppä HEJ, Kleinman HK, Martin GR. Attachment of smooth muscle cells to collagen and their migration toward a platelet-derived growth factor. Proc Natl Acad Sci USA **78**:3669–3672, 1981.
33. Seppä H, Grotendorst G, Seppä S, Schiffman E, Martin GR. Platelet-derived growth factor is chemotactic for fibroblasts. J Cell Biol **92**:584–588, 1982.
34. Graham MF, Diegelmann RF, Cohen IK. Effects of inflammation on wound healing. I. In vitro studies. In: Hunt TK, Heppenstall RB, Pines E, Rovee D, Eds. Soft and Hard Tissue Repair: Biological and Clinical Aspects. New York, Prager, Chap 20, 1984.

Received September 8, 1983. P.S.E.B.M. 1984, Vol. 176.
Accepted March 27, 1984.

PROCEEDINGS OF THE SOCIETY FOR EXPERIMENTAL BIOLOGY AND MEDICINE **176**, 309–312 (1984)

Alloimmunization Induces an Autoantibody Reactive with a Common, Cryptic Antigen (41876)

JERALD J. KILLION

Department of Physiology, Schools of Medicine and Dentistry, Oral Roberts University, Tulsa, Oklahoma 74171

Abstract. C57BL/6 mice (haplotype H-2^b) were alloimmunized by a classical protocol using repeated injections of DBA/2 spleen and liver cells (H-2^d). The resulting polyclonal, hyperimmune antisera were highly cytotoxic to untreated and neuraminidase- (VCN)-treated DBA/2 spleen cells. An unexpected result was that the anti-H-2^d sera were also cytotoxic to VCN-treated C57BL/6 spleen cells. The cytotoxicity was limited to an IgM antibody and could be evoked by a single alloimmunization. The results demonstrate a new feature of the classical immune response, autoantibodies against a common, though cryptic murine antigen, designated Mo1.

Tissue grafts between murine strains of disparate haplotypes provokes both humoral and cellular immunity. Immune processing of allogeneic grafts probably involves the discrimination between self and non-self molecular domains of both the foreign tissue and host lymphoid cells. This recognition of self-antigens may lead to normal regulatory events, although an abberant response may generate autoreactive T and B cells (1). The induction of both autoantibody and autoreactive lymphocytes against self H-2 determinants has recently been reported (2, 3). I describe here the appearance of an autoantibody, detected by the lysis of neuraminidase-treated syngeneic cells, in the serum of C57BL/6 (H-2^b) mice following immunization to DBA/2 (H-2^d) strain tissue. This antibody is reactive with a cryptic, carbohydrate-containing antigen that is found on spleen cells from several mouse strains, and has been designated Mo1 for "common mouse antigen 1."

Materials and Methods. *Animals.* C57BL/6, DBA/2, B6D2F1, Balb/c, and SJL mice were purchased from the Jackson Laboratory, Bar Harbor, Maine. CD1 mice were obtained from the Biomedical Research Center, Oral Roberts University.

Serum preparation. Normal C57BL/6 serum was obtained by bleeding 2- to 6-month-old female cagemates. The blood was collected on ice and pooled; the serum was isolated by centrifugation, aliquoted, and stored at −80°C. Hyperimmune, polyclonal C57BL/6 anti-DBA/2 serum was raised by a minimum of four ip injections of 3- to 6-month-old female C57BL/6 mice with 10^6 washed DBA/2 spleen and liver cells every 2 weeks. Four different batches of anti-DBA/2 serum were prepared in this manner and denoted anti-H-2^d serum. Preliminary studies showed that all anti-H-2^d serum produced >50% lysis of H-2^d-positive cells when tested at a dilution of 64-fold.

Serum fractionation. The hyperimmune serum was separated into two fractions by protein A–Sepharose CL4B chromatography, according to the method of Goding (4). The IgM-containing fraction (unbound and washed through the column by buffered saline, pH 8.2) and IgG fraction (eluted from the column by 1 *M* acetic acid in normal saline, pH 4.3) were reconstituted to original protein concentrations by positive-pressure dialysis. In addition, the hyperimmune serum was separated by Sephacryl S-300 gel filtration. One milliliter of serum was applied to a 1.5 × 116-cm column (flow rate, 13 ml/hr in PBS; room temperature) and the peaks corresponding to molecular weights of IgM (void volume) and IgG (150,000) were concentrated by positive-pressure dialysis back to the original serum volume. Double radial immunodiffusion of the peaks against class-specific antiserum (Cappel Laboratories, Cochranville, Pa.) showed that the void volume peak contained only IgM and the IgG peak contained IgG and some IgA immunoglobulin. These peaks were tested for cytotoxicity against untreated and neuraminidase-treated cells.

Cytotoxicity assay. The lysis of sham-treated and neuraminidase-treated cells was determined by a modified NIH technique, using trypan blue dye (2). Target spleen cells were washed twice in RPMI 1640 medium (containing 1% heat-inactivated fetal bovine serum, denoted 1% medium) followed by in-

0037-9727/84 $1.50

cubation in acetate buffer, pH 5.6, 37°C for 1 hr, with or without the presence of *Vibrio cholerae* neuraminidase (VCN) (Grand Island Biological Co., Grand Island, N.Y.) at 1 unit per 10^6 cells as previously described (8). Sham-treated cells were incubated in an equal volume of acetate buffer. The cells were then washed twice in 1% medium and 10^5 cells in 50 μl were added to 50 μl of serially diluted serum (or serum fractions), incubated for 45 min, 37°C followed by the addition of 5 μl of guinea pig serum (source of complement). All reactions required the presence of complement. After incubation of 1 hr, 25 μl of a 0.4% trypan blue solution was added to each well and a minimum of 200 cells were scored for viability. In the present study, our interest focused upon merely the presence or absence of significant cell lysis, due to the test sera compared to the cell lysis observed for cells incubated in the presence of complement alone. Hence, the percentage lysis is indicated in ranges of ten for simplicity of presentation. The lysis due to presence of complement alone was always less than 10%. χ^2 analysis of viable cell counts required that a minimum of 10–15% difference between samples be observed for significance at a level of $P < 0.05$. Intraassay variation between replicates was less than 8%. Maximum lysis of the VCN-treated C57BL/6 cells usually occurred at a twofold dilution of serum; hence all cell lysis was scored at this serum dilution.

Results. The data of Table I demonstrate the autoreactive phenomena. As expected, the sera of normal (nonimmunized) C57BL/6 did not possess cytolytic activity for either untreated or VCN-treated spleen cells obtained from C57BL/6, DBA/2, and B6D2F1 mice. Hyperimmune, polyclonal anti-DBA/2 sera (different batches) were cytotoxic to spleen cells from mice bearing the H-2^d haplotype (DBA/2; BALB/c, H-2^d; B6D2F1, H-$2^{b/d}$). However, these same sera were also cytotoxic to VCN-treated cells from C57BL/6; indeed, the sera lysed all VCN-treated spleen cells tested (SJL, H-2^s; CD1, outbred; C57BL/6, DBA/2, BALB/c, B6D2F1).

The cytolytic activity of these sera toward VCN-treated cells could be dissociated from the strong anti-H-2^d titer (usually greater than 1:64 for 50% cell death). The data of Figs. 1a–c demonstrate the removal of the anti-H-2^d activity of the hyperimmune sera after sequential absorption with 8, 12, and 16 × 10^8 DBA/2 spleen cells/ml of sera. However, in spite of this loss of alloreactive antibody, the absorbed sera retained the same level and titer of cytotoxicity against VCN-treated C57BL/6 cells (the use of the VCN-treated DBA/2 as target cells with absorbed sera is shown in Fig. 1d). This observation is consistent with the notion that the antigenic moiety of the VCN-treated H-2^b cell was not related to the H-2^d antigen(s). This idea was further strengthened by fractionating the antisera into IgM-containing and IgG fractions, using protein A–Sepharose chromatography. These fractions were tested for cytotoxicity against VCN-treated H-2^d cells (for clarity or comparison,

TABLE I. PRESENCE OF ANTI-C57BL/6 ANTIBODIES IN SERA OF ALLOIMMUNIZED C57BL/6 MICE

	Target cell lysis (%)							
C57BL/6 serum	C57BL/6	VCN-C57BL/6	DBA/2	VCN-DBA/2	B6D2F1	VCN-B6D2F1	CD1	VCN-CD1
Normal	<10	<10	<10	<10	<10	<10	<10	<10
Anti-DBA/2 (1)[a]	<10	>90	>80	>80	>80	>80	<10	>80
Anti-DBA/2 (2)	<10	>60	>80	>80	>80	>80	<10	>80

	VCN-C57BL/6	VCN-Balb/c	VCN-B6D2F1	SJL	VCN-SJL
Normal	<10	<10	<10	<10	<10
Anti-DBA/2 (1)	>80	>80	>80	<10	>80
Anti-DBA/2 (2)	>80	>80	>80	<10	>80
Anti-DBA/2 (3)	>80	>80	>80	<10	>80
Anti-DBA/2 (4)	>80	>80	>80	<10	>80

[a] Numbers denote different batch preparation of serum. Target cell lysis (%) was rounded to the nearest 10% for clarity of presentation.

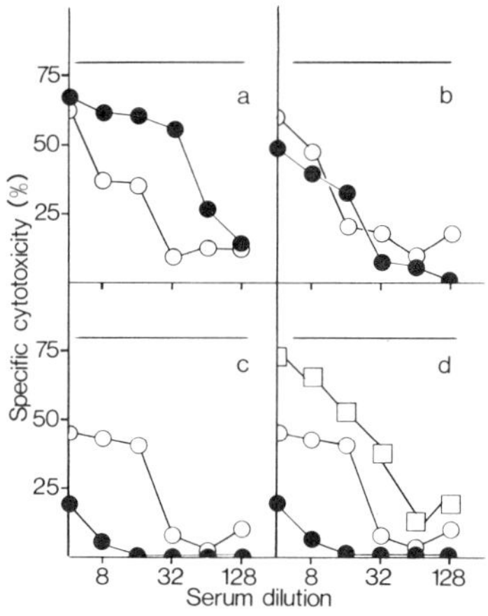

FIG. 1. The removal of the anti-H-2^d antibodies from the hyperimmune, polyclonal C57BL/6 anti-DBA/2 serum (a–c). ●, Cytotoxicity of anti-H-2^d serum toward untreated DBA/2 target cells after absorption with 8 (a), 12 (b), and 16 (c) × 10^8 DBA/2 cells/ml of serum. DBA/2 spleen cells were washed twice in normal saline and incubated in the above ratio for 2 hr, 4°C. The solid line indicates the lysis observed for an aliquot of unabsorbed serum. Cytotoxicity due to complement alone was less than 10%. ○, Cytotoxicity of absorbed serum toward VCN-C57BL/6 spleen cells. (d) □, Retention of cytotoxicity of absorbed serum toward VCN-DBA/2 spleen cells.

only the data for VCN-treated cells are shown) and the results are shown in Fig. 2. The specific cytotoxicity of the IgM fraction was somewhat lower than that of the unfractionated serum, evidently due to preparative procedures. The VCN-treated H-2^d cell was lysed by both the IgM and IgG antibody fractions of the anti-H-2^d sera. In contrast, only the IgM fraction was cytotoxic for the VCN-treated H-2^b cell, again suggesting the presence of autoantibodies having no specificity, per se, for the allogeneic cells. These results were confirmed by fractionation of the hyperimmune serum using Sephacryl S-300 gel filtration, and the results are shown in Table II. The IgM fraction was highly cytotoxic toward VCN-treated DBA/2, VCN-treated C57BL/6, and untreated DBA/2 cells, whereas the IgG fraction was cytotoxic for the allogeneic DBA/2 cells. Other studies (not shown) have determined that this IgM-mediated cytotoxicity can be blocked by D-galactosamine and D-glucosamine. The data of Table III show that a single injection of allogeneic cells was sufficient to induce detectable levels of the autoantibody in about 20 days.

Discussion. These data have shown that the allogeneic graft of H-2^d cells to the H-2^b recipient resulted in the induction of an autoantibody having specificity for a cryptic antigen, Mo1, the expression of which was not limited to H-2^b cells. The generality of the phenomenon is currently being determined, e.g., the tissue distribution of Mo1 and the presence of the antigen among many inbred murine strains. The induction of the autoantibody is not associated with immune reactivity, per se, since high-titer C57BL/6 antisera to either sheep red blood cells of E1 strain measles virus did not contain autoreactive antibody (data not shown). The data are consistent with the notion that the lytic factor against VCN-treated C57BL/6 cells was IgM antibody since (a) cytotoxicity was complement dependent, (b) the cytotoxicity was abolished by treatment of the serum with 0.2 *M* mercaptoethanol, (c) the factor did not bind protein A, and (d) cytotoxicity eluted in the void volume of a Sephacryl S-300 column. The phenomenon described here is reminiscent of blood group reactivity (carbohydrate inhibition, IgM antibody), especially the T-antigen system reported by Springer and colleagues (5). They have described sialic acid-containing structures on a variety of normal and malignant tissue which serve as cryptic antigens of the M and N structures (T antigen) and most human sera contain naturally occurring antibodies to these normally hidden

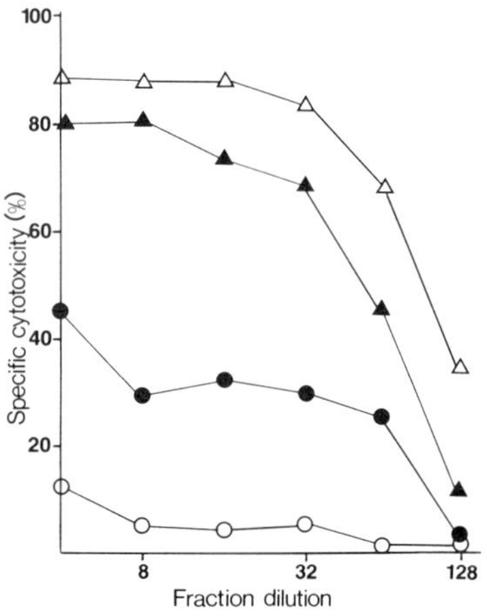

FIG. 2. Cytotoxicity of the IgG (open symbols) and IgM (closed symbols) fractions of hyperimmune, polyclonal C57BL/6 anti-DBA/2 serum toward VCN-treated DBA/2 (△, ▲) and VCN-treated C57BL/6 (○, ●) spleen cells.

TABLE II. FRACTIONATION OF C57BL/6 ANTI-DBA/2 SERUM BY SEPHACRYL S-300 GEL FILTRATION

	Target cell lysis (%)			
	C57BL/6	VCN-C57BL/6	DBA/2	VCN-DBA/2
Whole serum	<10	>80	>90	>90
IgM fraction	<10	>80	>80	>80
IgG fraction	<10	<10	>90	>90

Note. Values for percentage lysis represent nearest, lower whole number (in tens) for simplicity of presentation. Lysis due to complement alone was less than 10%. All values were from 1:4 dilutions of the indicated serum or fraction, although full-strength solutions and 1:2 and 1:8 dilutions gave the same results.

moieties. Indeed, the present results suggest that such antibodies may be a result of normal immune reactions.

Although autoantibodies are not uncommon in mice (6, 7), the autoantibody reported here has not been previously reported. At the present time, it is difficult to demonstrate the role of either this autoantibody or autoantigen, since the method of detection does not involve untreated lymphoid cells. The antibody may only react with a subpopulation of cells that express Mo1 in a noncryptic manner. There are two other circumstances that lead to the production of autoantibodies that have the properties described above (cytolytic to only VCN-treated cells, lack of H-2 specificity, presumably IgM class, carbohydrate inhibited): the genetically determined NZB autoimmune disease (unpublished observations) and the graft of the DBA/2 lymphoma L1210 into either the DBA/2 host or the B6D2F1 hybrid (8).

At the present time, the Mo1 autoantigen remains defined solely by serological methods. Efforts are currently directed to design experiments that demonstrate a functional (regulatory?) role for such autoantibodies and to biochemically characterize the Mo1 antigen.

TABLE III. PRODUCTION OF ANTI-C57BL/6 AND ANTI-DBA/2 ANTIBODIES WITH TIME FOLLOWING ALLOIMMUNIZATION OF C57BL/6 MICE

Donor C57BL/6		Target cell lysis (%)	
Injections	Bleed	VCN-BL/6	DBA/2
0	—	<10	<10
>4	—	>90	>90
1	Day 7	<10	>40
1	Day 14	<10	>50
1	Day 21	>80	<10
1	Day 42	>90	<10
2	Day 42	>70	>70

Note. Values for percentage lysis represent nearest, lower whole number (in tens) for simplicity of presentation. A group of C57BL/6 mice received ip injections of 10^6 DBA/2 spleen and liver cells; then separate groups of 3–5 mice were bled on Days 7, 14, 21, and 42. One group of five animals received a second ip injection of 10^6 DBA/2 cells on Day 14, and were bled on Day 42.

This study was supported in part by an ORU Intramural Grant.

1. Cohn M. Conversations with Niels Kaj Jerne on immune regulation: Associative versus network recognition. Cell Immunol **61**:425–433, 1981.
2. Risser R, Grunwald DJ. Production of anti-self H-2 antibodies by hybrid mice immune to a viral tumor. Nature (London) **289**:563–568, 1981.
3. Nakano K, Nakamura I, Cudkowicz G. Generation of F1 hybrid cytotoxic T lymphocytes specific for self H-2. Nature (London) **289**:559–562, 1981.
4. Goding JW. Conjugation of antibodies with fluorochromes: Modifications to the standard methods. J Immunol Methods **13**:215–226, 1976.
5. Springer GF, Desai R, Scanlon EF. Blood group MN precursors as human breast carcinoma-associated antigens and "naturally" occurring human cytotoxins against them. Cancer **37**:169–176, 1976.
6. Steele EJ, Cunningham AJ. High proportion of Ig-producing cells making autoantibody in normal mice. Nature (London) **274**:483–484, 1978.
7. Dresser DW. Most IgM-producing cells in the mouse secrete auto-antibodies (rheumatoid factor). Nature (London) **274**:484–486, 1978.
8. Killion JJ, Baker JR. Autoreactive factors identify tumor-host heterogeneity and responsiveness to immunotherapy. Cancer Immunol Immunother **12**:111–117, 1982.

Received November 14, 1983. P.S.E.B.M. 1984, Vol. 176.
Accepted April 6, 1984.

PROCEEDINGS OF THE SOCIETY FOR EXPERIMENTAL BIOLOGY AND MEDICINE **176**, 313–321 (1984)

Spermine-Enhanced Protein Phosphorylation in Human Placenta (41877)

JOHN J. MOORE, RICHARD C. CARDAMAN, AND DAVID W. LUNDGREN

Newborn Division, Department of Pediatrics, and Department of Obstetrics and Gynecology, Case Western Reserve University School of Medicine, Cleveland Metropolitan General Hospital, 3395 Scranton Road, Cleveland, Ohio 44109

Abstract. Polyamines are known to have a role in cell proliferation, differentiation, and protein synthesis. During pregnancy, major changes in polyamine levels occur in maternal serum, amniotic fluid, and placental tissue. Polyamine-activated phosphorylation has recently been proposed as a mechanism by which polyamines may regulate metabolic processes in target tissues. Polyamine-activated protein phosphorylation has not been studied in placenta. Homogenate membrane and cytosol fractions from human placenta were subjected to an endogenous protein phosphorylation assay using [γ-^{32}P]ATP in the presence and absence of the polyamines, spermine and spermidine, and the diamine, putrescine. Protein phosphorylation was assessed by sodium dodecyl sulfate–polyacrylamide gel electrophoresis and autoradiography. When compared to basal levels, spermine (10^{-3} *M*) significantly ($P < 0.001$) stimulated ^{32}P incorporation into phosphoproteins having molecular weights of 55,000 and 105,000. At this concentration spermidine and putrescine failed to stimulate phosphorylation. Half-maximal ^{32}P incorporation was observed with $3.7 \pm 1.25 \times 10^{-4}$ *M* spermine. Polylysine enhanced the phosphorylation of phosphoproteins of the same molecular weight as those enhanced by spermine. Heparin and high Mg^{2+} inhibited spermine-induced phosphorylation. cAMP and Ca^{2+} did not stimulate phosphorylation of the spermine-dependent phosphoproteins. Spermine, however, acted as an antagonist for cAMP-dependent phosphorylation of a M_r 45,000 phosphoprotein.

The biochemistry and physiology of the polyamines, spermine and spermidine, and their biosynthetic precursor putrescine have been extensively reviewed (1–4). Requirement for these aliphatic amines for growth and differentiation has been established in several systems, and data supporting their roles in DNA, RNA, and protein biosynthesis and/or regulation are extensive. In addition, numerous hormones increase polyamine biosynthesis in specific target tissues, suggesting that polyamines may in part function as mediators of hormone action.

Polyamine concentrations increase during human pregnancy in both plasma (5, 6) and urine (5) as well as fluctuate in placenta (7) and amniotic fluid (5) as a function of gestational age (8, 9). However, the specific targets of enhanced polyamine biosynthesis during pregnancy remain to be established. Since the placenta plays a central role in fetal growth and development, this tissue could be a primary target for the increased polyamine biosynthesis seen in pregnancy.

Recent studies indicate that polyamines stimulate the phosphorylation of specific proteins and could thereby act as regulators of intracellular metabolism (10, 11). Accordingly, we have examined the ability of polyamines to alter phosphorylation of placental proteins. In this study we describe for the first time that spermine selectively stimulates the phosphorylation of several placental proteins.

Materials and Methods. *Materials.* [γ-^{32}P]ATP (35 Ci/mmole) was purchased from New England Nuclear Corporation (Boston, Mass.). Spermine, spermidine, putrescine, polylysine, cAMP, and other reagents were purchased from Sigma Chemical Company (St. Louis, Mo.). All other reagents were obtained from Fisher Scientific Company.

Tissue preparation. Placentas from uncomplicated pregnancies were obtained at delivery and processed immediately. Cotyledons to be used were perfused free of blood with normal saline. Decidual tissue was removed by sharp dissection. The remaining tissue was then washed in iced buffer containing 0.25 *M* sucrose and 10 m*M* Tris–HCl (pH 7.2). Throughout the remainder of the preparation procedure the tissue was maintained at 4°C. Approximately 30 g of washed tissue was then homogenized with a Tekmar Tissuemizer (Tekmar Co., Cincinnati, Ohio) in 300 ml of

0037-9727/84 $1.50

the sucrose buffer (3 × 10 sec at high setting). The homogenate was poured through four layers of cheesecloth. Aliquots were then removed and used as the crude homogenate preparation. The remaining material was centrifuged at 5000*g* for 10 min. The pellet was discarded and aliquots of the supernatant served as the 5000*g* supernatant fraction. The rest of the supernatant was centrifuged at 100,000*g* for 60 min. The supernatant of this centrifugation was used as the placental cytosol preparation. The 100,000*g* pellet was washed twice by resuspension in equal amounts of the sucrose buffer and finally resuspended in sucrose buffer to give a protein concentration of 2–3 mg/ml. Placental fractions were assayed on the day of preparation or after freezing and storage at −70°C. No differences were seen in fresh and frozen preparations under these conditions. Protein concentrations were determined by the method of Lowry *et al.* (12).

Gel electrophoresis and autoradiography. Phosphorylated substrates were identified by incubation of placental fractions with [γ-^{32}P]ATP followed by gel electrophoresis and autoradiography. The reaction mixture (total volume 0.2 ml) consisted of the protein sample (5–10 μg), 5 μM [γ-^{32}P]ATP (5–20 cpm/pmole), 20 mM Tris–HCl (pH 7.2), 5 mM $MgCl_2$, 10 mM EGTA, and 10 mM NaF. Potential effector compounds were added as indicated. In some assays cAMP or $CaCl_2$ was added. The amount of $CaCl_2$ required to give specific free Ca^{2+} concentrations was calculated by a computer program according to the method of Sillin and Martell (13). Assays were initiated by addition of [γ-^{32}P]ATP and incubated for 6 min at 30°C in a water bath. The reaction was terminated by the addition of 100 μl of ice-cold 12% trichloroacetic acid (TCA). The protein was then precipitated by centrifugation in a Beckman B microfuge for 5 min and the pellet washed twice with 350 μl H_2O. The pellet was dissolved in a solution (60 μl) containing 2% SDS, 10% glycerol, 5% β-mercaptoethanol, and 0.001% bromophenol blue and boiled for 5 min. Samples were then loaded on an SDS–polyacrylamide gel (4.3% stacking, 10% running) for electrophoresis according to the method of Laemmli (14). The molecular weight standards used included myosin (205,000), β-galactosidase (116,000), phosphorylase b (97,400), BSA (66,000), ovalbumin (45,000), and carbonic anhydrase (29,000). The gels were fixed overnight in 50% methanol and 7.5% acetic acid, stained with Coomassie blue, and destained. Gels were dryed on Whatman Grade 3 filter paper, autoradiographed on Kodak XR film, and developed for the desired length of time (24 hr to 2 weeks) to demonstrate the phosphorylated proteins. The autoradiographs were then scanned at 550 nm with a Beckman Du-8 spectrophotometer with slab gel scanner attachment.

Where indicated, after destaining, the gels were cut into 1-mm slices, dissolved in 3% Protosol (New England Nuclear), and counted by standard scintillation technique.

Phosphate bond analysis. To demonstrate that phosphate was incorporated into proteins and to establish the type of phosphate bond formed, the following experiments were performed: Protein phosphorylation was performed exactly as described in the preceding paragraph except that two tubes each containing 50 μg of cytosol protein in total incubation volumes of 2 ml were used. One contained 10^{-3} M spermine and the other contained no spermine. After protein precipitation with a comparable amount of 12% TCA, the 2.0-ml samples were each divided into seven 200-μl aliquots (a–g) and treated as follows: (a) The first aliquot was centrifuged and the pellet extracted three times with acetone (350 μl). The resulting pellet was then placed in a 60-μl solution (Laemmli) containing 2% SDS, 10% glycerol, 5% β-mercaptoethanol, and 0.001% bromophenol blue and boiled for 5 min. (b) The second tube was treated identically as (a) except that the pellet was extracted three times with chloroform/methanol (2/1) immediately following the acetone step. (c) The third tube was treated like (a) except that following the initial centrifugation and prior to the acetone extraction, the pellet was resuspended in ice-cold 0.5 M NaOH for 5 min and then precipitated in 5% TCA (350 μl). (d) The fourth was exactly as (c) except that the NaOH solution was boiled for one of the 5 min. (e) The fifth was as in (a) except that following the 12% TCA addition, the solution was boiled for 1 min prior to centrifugation. (f, g) These were treated as in (a) except that following addition of the Laemmli solution they were exposed to Pronase (0.01 mg) and ribonuclease A (0.01 mg), respectively, for 10 min at 37°C. All of the boiled samples were then loaded on gels and processed exactly as in the preceding paragraph.

Results. Spermine (10^{-3} M) activated protein phosphorylation of several endogenous proteins in human placental cytosol. Phosphoproteins of M_r 55,000 and 105,000 consistently demonstrated polyamine-dependent phosphorylation in ten different placental preparations (Fig. 1). Densitometer scans of autoradiographs of SDS–polyacrylamide gels of placental cytosol in the presence or absence of spermine (10^{-3} M) demonstrated significant differences ($P < 0.001$) in each of these polyamine-activated phosphoproteins. Densitometer readings were 0.504 ± 0.19 and 0.868 ± 0.22 (arbitrary unit) for the 105,000 and 55,000 M_r phosphoproteins, respectively, in the absence of spermine, and 1.459 ± 0.30 and 1.059 ± 0.31 in the presence of 10^{-3} M spermine. Gels which were sliced into 1-mm sections also demonstrated spermine-induced incorporation of ^{32}P into proteins of the same molecular weight (Table I). In many preparations phosphoproteins of M_r 205,000, 150,000, 116,000 99,000, 85,000, 64,000, 52,000, and 46,000 also appeared to incorporate additional ^{32}P in the presence of spermine (10^{-3} M). However, augmented phosphorylation of these proteins was not as pronounced and/or consistent as that observed for the M_r 55,000 and 105,000 proteins. In membrane containing crude placental homogenate and 5000g supernatant fractions spermine (10^{-3} M) increased phosphorylation of the proteins of the same molecular weight as those seen in placental cytosol. Phosphorylation in these fractions was not as pronounced nor were additional spermine-induced phosphoproteins detected in the membrane containing fractions (data not shown).

The nature of the phosphate bond was studied by exposure of the phosphorylated cy-

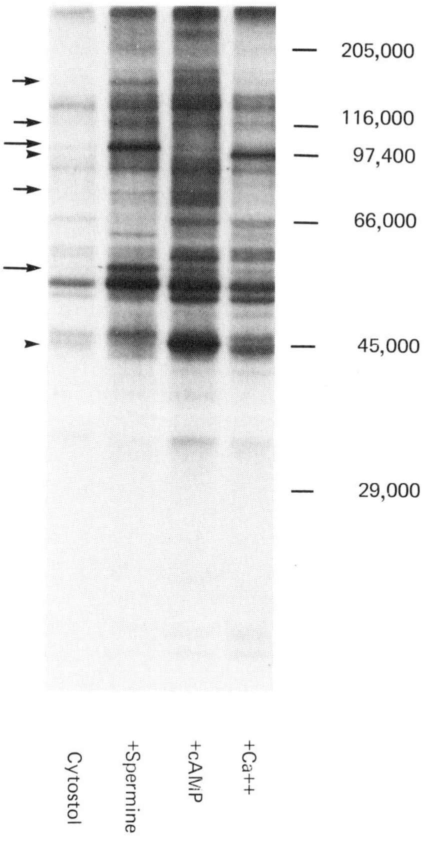

FIG. 1. Autoradiograph of phosphorylated proteins in placental cytosol. Placental cytosol was incubated as described under Materials and Methods with no effector, cAMP (10^{-6} M), spermine (10^{-3} M), or calcium (10^{-5} M) as indicated. The arrows (to the left) indicate proteins differentially phosphorylated by spermine (large arrows indicate phosphoproteins seen in all preparations; small arrows indicate those seen in many preparations). Arrowheads alone indicate those proteins stimulated by cAMP or calcium. The positions of the marker proteins are indicated at the right. The results shown are representative of gels from placental cytosol of ten placentas (n = 10).

TABLE I. ^{32}P INCORPORATION INTO SPERMINE-DEPENDENT PHOSPHOPROTEINS

	^{32}P Incorporation (pmole PO_4/mg cytosol protein)	
Spermine-dependent phosphoprotein (M_r)	+ Spermine	− Spermine
105,000	0.96 ± 0.1*	0.28 ± 0.2
55,000	1.45 ± 0.2*	0.51 ± 0.2

Note. Phosphorylation and gel electrophoresis of placental cytosol were performed as described under Materials and Methods. The gels were then cut into sequential 1-mm slices which were dissolved in 3% Protosol (New England Nuclear) at 37°C overnight and then counted by standard scintillation technique. For each of the spermine-dependent phosphoproteins, the increase in ^{32}P incorporation induced by spermine (10^{-3} M) is listed (n = 3). Values are means ± SD.

* $P < 0.001$ by a paired Student t test.

tosol to hot and cold TCA, hot and cold 0.5 *N* NaOH, Pronase, ribonuclease A, acetone, and chloroform/methanol (see Material and Methods). As illustrated in Table II, none of these treatments had major effects on the incorporation of ^{32}P into polyamine-dependent phosphorylated proteins except hot NaOH and Pronase. Treatment with hot NaOH or Pronase removed the proteins as well as the ^{32}P label from the gel. The results of these experiments indicate that the ^{32}P associated with the two proteins whose phosphorylation is stimulated by spermine was incorporated into protein rather than lipid or nucleic acid. In addition the stability of these phosphorylated compounds in base at low temperatures, and in trichloroacetic acid at elevated temperatures, indicates that the bonds are of the phosphoester rather than acylphosphate type (15).

Spermine, at concentrations above 10^{-5} *M*, induced dose-dependent increases in the phosphorylation of specific phosphoproteins. Dose–responsive phosphorylation analysis of the M_r 105,000 protein showed that half-maximal phosphorylation occurred at approximately $3.7 \pm 1.3 \times 10^{-4}$ *M* spermine (Fig. 2). In contrast to spermine, neither spermidine nor putrescine at 10^{-3} *M* caused detectable enhancement of protein phosphorylation. Spermidine, however, at nonphysiological concentrations (10^{-2} *M*) did enhance phosphorylation of the spermine-activated phosphoproteins comparable to that seen with 10^{-4} *M* spermine (Fig. 2). In contrast, the diamine putrescine did not enhance protein phos-

TABLE II. PHOSPHATE BOND ANALYSIS EXPERIMENTS

Treatment	Arbitrary density units + Spermine	− Spermine
1. Acetone	1.237	0.596
2. Chloroform/methanol	1.469	0.673
3. NaOH (cold)	1.225	0.505
4. NaOH (boiling)	—	—
5. TCA (boiling)	1.292	0.548
6. Pronase	—	—
7. Ribonuclease A	1.425	0.608

Note. Phosphorylation of placental cytosol was performed with the after treatment listed in the table as described under Materials and Methods. For each treatment the densitometer scanner reading in arbitrary units of the M_r 105,000 spermine-dependent phosphoprotein is given (n = 2).

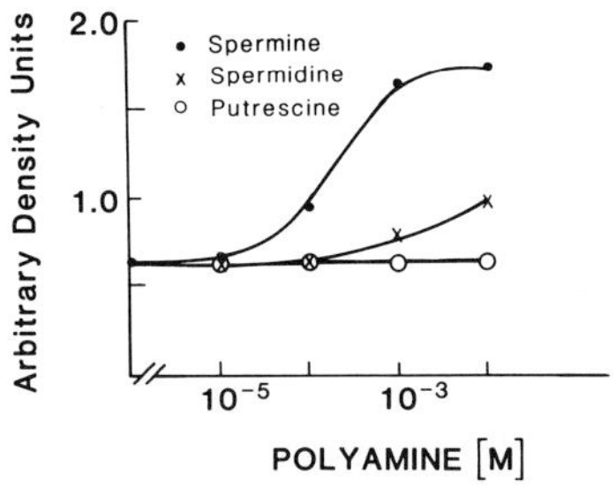

FIG. 2. Dose response of phosphorylation of the M_r 105,000 protein. The degree of phosphorylation of the M_r 105,000 protein (arbitrary units) as determined by densitometer scanning of autoradiographs (vertical axis) is shown versus concentration (*M*) of added spermine, spermidine, or putrescine. The results are representative of three experiments (n = 3).

phorylation even at 10^{-2} *M* concentrations. Putrescine, however, inhibited spermine-induced phosphorylation in a dose-dependent manner (Figs. 3a, b). The synthetic polycation, polylysine, stimulated phosphorylation of the spermine-dependent phosphoproteins at concentrations as low as 10^{-6} *M* (data not shown).

The effect of polyamines on cAMP and Ca^{2+}-activated phosphorylation in placental cytosol was also examined. The cAMP and Ca^{2+}-dependent phosphoproteins were distinct from those whose phosphorylation was augmented by polyamines (Fig. 1). Spermine, however, caused a dose-dependent inhibition of cAMP-dependent phosphorylation. Several cAMP-dependent phosphoproteins including the major M_r 45,000 phosphoprotein were inhibited by spermine (Figs. 4a, b). Inhibition of cAMP-induced phosphorylation occurred at concentrations of spermine 10-fold lower than that required for detectable spermine-activated phosphorylation. At higher spermine concentrations, inhibition of Ca^{2+}-dependent phosphorylation was also seen (data not shown).

Magnesium at low concentrations (>1 m*M*) was necessary for polyamine-enhanced phosphorylation. At higher, nonphysiological concentrations (Mg >20 m*M*), magnesium alone caused phosphorylation of proteins which comigrated with the polyamine-induced proteins. Addition of 10^{-3} *M* spermine resulted in less phosphorylation of these proteins than with the high magnesium alone (Fig. 5). Sodium chloride (>60 m*M*) and heparin inhib-

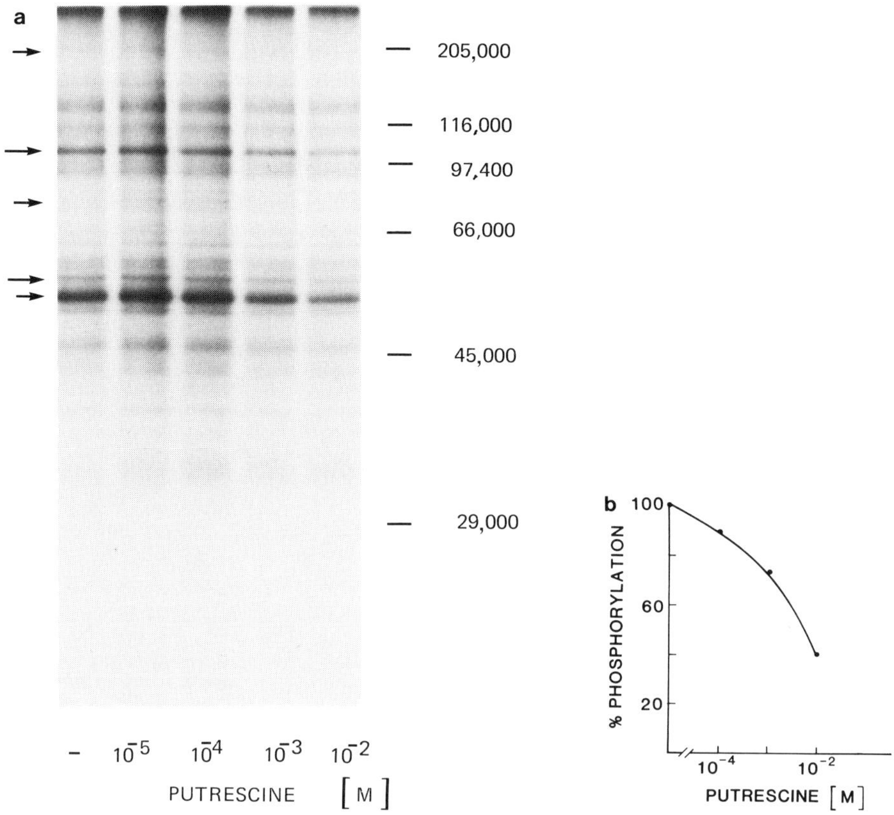

FIG. 3. Inhibition of spermine-dependent phosphorylation by putrescine. A representative autoradiograph demonstrating the effect of increasing concentrations of putrescine (10^{-5} to 10^{-2} *M*) upon phosphorylation of proteins by spermine (10^{-3} *M*). Phosphorylated proteins (left) and standards (right) are indicated as in Fig. 1. (b) Densitometer readings (arbitrary units) of the degree of phosphorylation of the spermine-dependent 105,000 M_r protein (vertical axis) are plotted against the spermine concentration (*M*). These results are representative of three experiments (n = 3).

ited spermine-dependent phosphorylation in placental cytosol as well as many non-spermine-dependent phosphoproteins (data not shown).

Discussion. The central finding in this study is that the phosphorylation of a select group of proteins in human placenta extracts is influenced by polyamines. These observations raise the possibility that polyamines, or their metabolic products, are primary effector compounds for specific cascade systems and, thereby, participate in the regulation of one or more metabolic processes associated with pregnancy. Polyamine biosynthesis shows marked changes during pregnancy: In human pregnancy, polyamine levels increase significantly in maternal blood (5) and urine (5, 6), as well as fluctuate in placenta (7) and amniotic fluid (5) as a function of gestational age. Amniotic fluid polyamine concentrations in some types of high-risk pregnancies (e.g., intrauterine growth retardation) deviate significantly from concentrations observed in normal pregnancies (16). Polyamine fluctuation in the pregnant rat has been more extensively studied: Serum polyamine concentrations are elevated (17, 18) and placental tissue and fetal tissue polyamine levels change with gestational age (19, 20). Further, the specific activity of ornithine decarboxylase, the rate-limiting step in polyamine biosynthesis, changes in placenta and fetal tissue during gestation (19, 20) and is elevated in maternal liver (17). As polyamines are recognized as important metab-

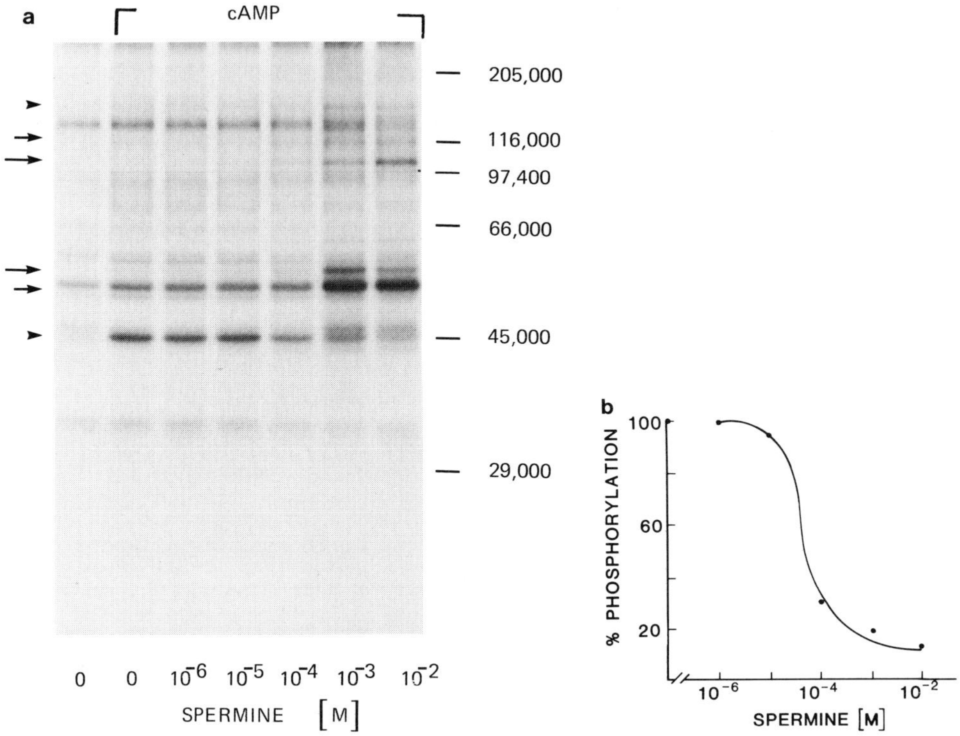

FIG. 4. Inhibition of cAMP-dependent phosphorylation by spermine. A representative autoradiograph demonstrating the effect of increasing concentrations of spermine (10^{-6} to 10^{-2} *M*) upon phosphorylation of proteins by cAMP (10^{-6} *M*). The major cAMP-dependent phosphoprotein (M_r = 45,000) is indicated by an arrowhead on the left; spermine-enhanced phosphoproteins (left) and standards (right) are indicated as in Fig. 1. (b) Densitometer readings (arbitrary units) of the degree of phosphorylation of the cAMP-dependent 45,000 M_r protein (vertical axis) are plotted against the spermine concentration (*M*). These results are representative of three experiments (n = 3).

olites in growth and differentiation (1–4), the increased polyamine concentrations observed during pregnancy are, at least in part, a reflection of the rapidly growing fetus. Nevertheless specific targets of the elevated polyamine concentrations during pregnancy remain to be determined.

Placental cytosol contains a protein kinase which is activated by spermine to phosphorylate proteins of M_r 55,000 and 105,000. However, spermine also activates phoshorylation of eight other proteins in many preparations. In addition, the resolving ability of the gel system used in these studies is limited. Therefore, although the M_r 55,000 and 105,000 proteins are discussed here as single proteins, they may represent several proteins of similar size. A final listing of spermine-activated phosphoproteins in placenta must await further studies in which individual proteins are identified.

The effects of four polyamines upon placental cytosol phosphorylation was examined. The potency order of the three naturally occurring polyamines, spermine $\gg$ spermidine $\gg$ putrescine, was similar to that seen in rat adrenocortical tissue extracts (21, 22). This potency order parallels the placental tissue levels of these polyamines at term gestation (7). The spermine concentration required for half-maximal ^{32}P incorporation into the M_r 105,000 phosphoprotein was demonstrated to be $3.7 \pm 1.3 \times 10^{-4}$ *M*. This concentration is within the physiological range of many human and animal tissues (16). More specifically, human placental spermine concentrations have been reported to vary from a low of 210 ± 9.8 nmol/g wet wt at 8–10 weeks pregnancy to

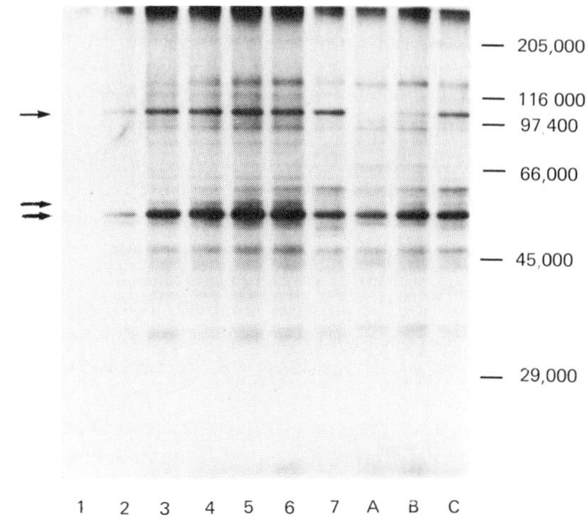

FIG. 5. Effect of Mg^{2+} upon spermine-dependent phosphorylation. Effect of increasing concentrations of Mg^{2+} (no added Mg^{2+} to 50 m*M*) upon spermine (10^{-3} *M*)-dependent phosphorylation is shown in the first seven (1–7) lanes. The three remaining lanes (A–C) show the effect of Mg^{2+} without spermine. The spermine-dependent proteins are designated by arrows to the left (as in Fig. 1) and marker proteins are shown on the right. The results are representative of three experiments ($n = 3$). The components of individual wells are shown below.

	1	2	3	4	5
Cytosol	+	+	+	+	+
[Mg^{2+}] (m*M*)	–	0.5	1.5	5.0	10
Spermine	+	+	+	+	+

	6	7	A	B	C
Cytosol	+	+	+	+	+
[Mg^{2+}] (m*M*)	20	50	5.0	20	50
Spermine	+	+	–	–	–

356 ± 17.2 nmol/g wet wt at term gestation (7).

The spermine-induced phosphoproteins in human placenta are distinct from both cAMP (M_r 25,000, 27,000, 39,000, 45,000, 52,000, 58,000, and 73,000) and Ca^{2+}-induced (M_r 97,000, 90,000, 20,000, 19,000) phosphoproteins (23) in placental cytosol. Although spermine does not activate phosphorylation of cAMP or Ca^{2+}-dependent phosphoproteins, spermine inhibits cAMP and Ca^{2+}-dependent phosphorylation in the placenta. This is consistent with reports that spermine inhibits the catalytic subunit of cAMP-dependent protein kinase and Ca^{2+}/calmodulin kinases in other systems (24–26). The evidence for cAMP-mediated effects on placental metabolism is abundant (27–31). The complete cascade for such effects including β-adrenergic receptors, catecholamine-sensitive adenylate cyclase, cAMP-dependent protein kinase, and specific cAMP-dependent phosphoproteins has also been described in human placenta (32–35). At this time, there is no evidence for a Ca^{2+}-mediated pathway in placenta; however, specific Ca^{2+}-dependent phosphoproteins have been demonstrated (23). Polyamines may therefore act both directly, by mediating phosphorylation of specific polyamine-dependent proteins, and indirectly, by inhibiting phosphorylation induced by other known secondary messengers.

The effects of magnesium, sodium, heparin, and polylysine upon polyamine-enhanced phosphorylation in placental cytosol were examined to determine whether they would modulate phosphorylation of placental cytosolic proteins similarly to polyamine-dependent casein G kinase seen in other tissues (36–38). Mg^{2+} at low levels was required for kinase activity but at higher levels (>20 m*M*) it inhibited polyamine-induced phosphorylation. Nonphysiological concentrations of Mg^{2+} (>50 m*M*) resulted in phosphorylation of the two spermine-induced phosphoproteins in the absence of the polyamines. Heparin and sodium chloride resulted in inhibition of polyamine-induced phosphorylation while polylysine was able to substitute for spermine. All are consistent with the reported characteristics of the casein G kinase I (11).

Results in this study reinforce previous suggestions that polyamines may exert some of their effects during growth and differentiation by mediating protein phosphorylation in one or more cascade systems. Confirmation of the physiological significance of these observations, however, must await identification of specific proteins whose phosphorylation is enhanced and demonstration that increases in the phosphorylation of these proteins are paralleled by increases in polyamine biosynthesis in an *in vivo* system and are accompanied by specific metabolic changes *in vivo*. Phosphorylation studies in human placental cells in culture are now in progress to examine these criteria.

1. Heby O. Role of polyamines in the control of cell proliferation and differentiation. Differentiation **19:**1–20, 1981.
2. Williams A, Shman HG, Canellakis ZN. Polyamines in mammalian biology and medicine. Perspect Biol Med **22:**421–453, 1979.
3. Pegg AE, Hisbasami H, Matsui I, Bethell DR. Formation and interconversion of putrescine and spermidine in mammalian cells. Adv Enzyme Regul **19:**427–451, 1981.
4. Pegg AE, McCann PP. Polyamines metabolism and function. Amer J Physiol **243:**212–221, 1982.
5. Russell DH, Giles HR, Christian CD, Campbell JL. Polyamines in amniotic fluid, plasma, and urine during normal pregnancy. Amer J Obstet Gynecol **132:**649–652, 1978.
6. Hiramatsu Y, Eguchi K, Yonezaw M, Hayase R, Sekeba K. Alterations of red blood cells polyamines during pregnancy and neonatal period. Biol Neonate **40:**136–144, 1981.
7. Porta R, Servillo L, Abbruzzese A, Pietra DG. Automated chromatographic analyses of human placenta polyamines. Biochem Med **19:**143–147, 1978.
8. Gunada K, Sheth A, Gunada C, Rao C. Concentrations of putrescine & polyamines during the development of rat placenta. Indian J Biochem Biophys **10:**134–135, 1973.
9. Gunada C, Sheth A, Gunada K, Rao C. Polyamines in the human placenta. Indian J Biochem Biophys **9:**272–274, 1972.
10. Cochet C, Chambaz E. Polyamine-mediated protein phosphorylation: A possible target for intracellular polyamine action. Mol Cell Endocrinol **30:**247–266, 1983.
11. Kuehn G, Atmar V. New perspectives on polyamine-dependent protein kinase and the regulation of ornithine decarboxylase by reversible phosphorylation. Adv Polyamine Res **4:**615–629, 1983.
12. Lowry OH, Rosebrough NJ, Farr AL, Randall RJ. Protein measurement with the Folin phenol reagent. J Biol Chem **193:**265–275, 1951.
13. Sillen L, Martell A. In: Stability Constants of Metal–Ion Complexes, 2nd ed., Ser Pub No 17, Chem Soc, Burlington House, London, 1961.
14. Laemmli U. Cleavage of structural proteins during the assembly of the head of bacteriophage T4. Nature (London) **227:**680–685, 1951.
15. Garrison J. The effects of glucagon, catecholamines, and the calcium ionophore A23187 on the phosphorylation of rat hepatocyte cytosolic proteins. J Biol Chem **253:**7091–7100, 1978.
16. Russell HD. Clinical relevance of polyamines. CRC Crit Rev Clin Sci **18:**261–311, 1983.
17. Lundgren DW, Oka T. Alterations in polyamine levels in rat blood during pregnancy and lactation. Amer J Physiol **234:**451–456, 1978.
18. Anderson AC, Henningson S. On the biogenesis of diamines and polyamines in the pregnant rat. Acta Endocrinol **98:**456–463, 1981.
19. Hoshiae H, Lin YC, Loring JM, Perelle BA, Villee CA. Ornithine decarborylase activity and polyamine content of placenta and decidual tissue in rat. Placenta **2:**105–116, 1981.
20. Guha SK, Fanne J. The synthesis and accumulation of polyamines in reproductive organs of rat during pregnancy. Biochim Biophys Acta **437:**244–252, 1976.
21. Cochet C, Job D, Pirollet F, Chambaz E. Cyclic nucleotide independent casein kinase (G type) in bovine adrenal cortex. Biochim Biophys Acta **658:**191–201, 1981.
22. Morishita Y, Akogyeram C, Deu B, Criss W. Regulation of polyamine-responsive protein kinase by certain highly specific polyamines and charged carbohydrates. Biochim Biophys Acta **755:**358–362, 1983.
23. Moore J. Protein phosphorylation by hormonal second messengers in human placenta. Pediat Res, 1984, in press.
24. Hochman J, Katz A, Bachrach U. Polyamines and protein kinase. II. Effect of polyamines on cyclic AMP-dependent protein kinase from rat liver. Life Sci **22:**1481–1484, 1978.
25. Murray A, Froscio M, Rogers A. Effect of polyamines on cyclic AMP-dependent and independent protein kinases from mouse epidermis. Biochem Biophys Res Commun **71:**1175–1181, 1976.
26. Wise B, Glass D, Chou C-H, Raynor R, Katoh N, Schatzman R, Turner R, Kibler R, Kou J. Phospholipid-sensitive Ca^{2+}-protein kinase from heart. II. Substrate specificity and inhibition by various agents. J Biol Chem **257:**8489–8495, 1982.
27. Hussa R, Story M, Pattillo R. Cyclic adenosine monophosphate stimulates secretion of human chorionic gonadotropin and estrogens by human trophoblast in vitro. J Clin Endocrinol Metab **38:**338–340, 1974.
28. Handwerger S, Barrett J, Tyrey L, Schomberg D. Differential effects of cyclic adenosine monophosphate on the secretion of human placental lactogen and human chorionic gonadotropin. J Clin Endocrinol Metab **36:**1268–1270, 1978.
29. Hussa R, Pattillo R, Ruckert A, Scheuermann K. Effects of butyrate and dibutyryl cyclic AMP on hCG-secreting trophoblastic and non-trophoblastic cells. J Clin Endocrinol Metab **46:**69–76, 1978.
30. Chou J. Establishment of clonal human placenta cells synthesizing human choriogonadotropin. Proc Natl Acad Sci USA **75:**1854–1858, 1978.
31. Yarimagan H, Bor N. The effects of epinephrine on guinea pig placental glycogen metabolism and on cellular cyclic AMP. Biochem Med **25:**125–134, 1981.
32. Whitsett J, Johnson C, Noguchi A, Darovec-Beckerman C, Costello M. β-Adrenergic receptors and cat-

echolamine sensitive adenylate cyclase of the human placenta. J Clin Endocrinol Metab **50**:27–32, 1980.
33. Moore J, Whitsett J. The β-adrenergic receptor in human placenta: Receptor subtype analysis (β_1 and β_2) and partial characterization of the solubilized receptor. Placenta Suppl **3**:103–113, 1981.
34. Moore J, Workman L, Whitsett J. Trophoblast cells of the hydatidiform mole contain a β_1 subtype adrenergic receptor. J Clin Endocrinol Metab **55**:341–346, 1982.
35. Moore J, Baker J, Whitsett J. Adenosine 3′,5′ monophosphate (cAMP)-binding protein and cAMP-dependent protein kinase in human placenta. J Clin Endocrinol Metab **56**:1035–1041, 1983.
36. DePaoli-Roach A, Roach P. Heparin inhibition and polyamine stimulation of a glycogen synthase kinase ($PC_{0.7}$) from rabbit skeletal muscle. Arch Biochem Biophys **217**:305–311, 1982.
37. Meggio F, Deana A, Pinna L. Endogenous phosphate acceptor proteins for rat liver cytosolic casein kinases. J Biol Chem **256**:11,958–11,961, 1981.
38. Kuehn G, Atmar V. New perspectives on polyamine-dependent protein kinase and the regulation of ornithine decarboxylase by reversible phosphorylation. Adv Polyamine Res **4**:615–629, 1983.

Received February 13, 1984. P.S.E.B.M. 1984, Vol. 176.
Accepted April 6, 1984.

PROCEEDINGS OF THE SOCIETY FOR EXPERIMENTAL BIOLOGY AND MEDICINE **176**, 322–326 (1984)

Effect of cAMP and Calmodulin Inhibitors on Water Absorption in Rat Proximal Tubule (41878)

EDWARD J. WEINMAN, STEPHEN C. BENNETT, RICHARD C. BRADY, JEFFREY F. HARPER, MICHAEL K. HISE, AND ANDREW M. KAHN

Department of Internal Medicine, Division of Nephrology and Division of Endocrinology, University of Texas Medical School, Houston, Texas 77025

Abstract. The possible role of calmodulin in solute transport was examined in the kidney of the rat. Utilizing a radioimmunoassay, calmodulin was identified and quantitated in homogenates of the cortex of the kidney. The physiologic significance of these findings was examined utilizing *in vivo* microperfusion techniques applied to the proximal convoluted tubule of the thyroparathyroidectomized rat. The addition of dibutyryl cyclic adenosine monophosphate (cAMP) to the luminal perfusion solution resulted in a lower rate of water absorption of 1.67 ± 0.09 nl min^{-1} mm^{-1} as compared to 2.46 ± 0.11 in controls. The addition of either of two compounds with affinity for calmodulin, trifluoperazine (TFP) or W-13, reversed the cAMP-induced inhibition of water absorption. In the absence of cAMP, neither agent affected water absorption. Analogs of TFP and W-13 with lower binding affinities for calmodulin had no effect on water absorption and did not reverse the cAMP effect. None of the above experimental maneuvers affected the absorption of phosphate. These results demonstrate the presence of calmodulin in the kidney of the rat and suggest that calmodulin may be involved in cAMP-associated inhibition of water and electrolyte transport in the proximal tubule of the rat.

Calmodulin has been identified as a major calcium binding protein and has been implicated as a modulator of an impressive number of intracellular events. The protein itself has been identified in many species of animals and in many organs. Several recent reviews have cataloged the species and organs in which calmodulin has been identified (1, 2). These reviews also list the physiologic processes for which a role for calmodulin has been suggested (1, 2). Prior reports have documented the presence of calmodulin in renal tissue (3–5). Although a role for calmodulin in solute transport has been suggested in nonrenal tissue, we are unaware of reports implicating a role for this protein in the transport of electrolytes and water in the mammalian kidney (6, 7). The present studies provide evidence that calmodulin is present in the kidney of the rat. *In vivo* microperfusion studies indicate that the inhibition of water absorption by cyclic adenosine monophosphate (cAMP) in the proximal tubule of the rat is blocked by drugs which have affinity for calmodulin in other tissue systems. The results, then, implicate a role for a calmodulin-dependent step in electrolyte and water transport in the mammalian kidney.

Methods. Studies were performed on male Sprague–Dawley rats with free access to food and water prior to study.

Calmodulin determinations. The calmodulin concentration of homogenates of kidney cortex and brush border membranes was determined by radioimmunoassay (8). The preparation of the homogenates of kidney cortex and of brush border membranes by a modification of a magnesium aggregation method have previously been described (9). The methodology and characterizations of these membranes have also been reported from our laboratories (10). In brief, the brush border membranes as compared to the whole homogenate were enriched in alkaline phosphatase 10- to 13-fold but not enriched in the basolateral membrane marker Na^+–K^+ ATPase (10).

Micropuncture studies. Animals were anesthetized with pentobarbital sodium (50 mg/kg body wt) injected intraperitoneally. A thyroparathyroidectomy was performed utilizing electric cautery following which the animals were prepared for micropuncture. Two hours were permitted to elapse after thyroparathyroidectomy before the experiments were started. In all animals, the measured fractional

0037-9727/84 $1.50

excretion of phosphate was less than 2%, confirming adequate removal of all parathyroid tissue. Each animal received a volume of isotonic saline equal to 1% of body weight to replace surgical losses of fluid and a sustaining intravenous infusion of saline at a rate of 1.2 ml/hr for the duration of the study.

In vivo microperfusion studies were performed in the proximal convoluted tubule by methods previously described (11). The microperfusion solution (pH 7.4) contained sodium, 139 mmole/liter; chloride, 119 mmole/liter; bicarbonate, 25 mmole/liter; potassium, 4 mmole/liter; and calcium 0.5, mmole/liter. NaH_2PO_4 was added to the solution to a final concentration of 2 m*M*. [*methoxy*-^{3}H]Inulin and [^{32}P]orthophosphate (New England Nuclear Corp., Boston, Mass.) were added in amounts sufficient to permit accurate isotope counting. Where examined, dibutyryl cAMP (10^{-6} *M*), (Sigma, St. Louis, Mo.) and/or trifluoperazine (TFP) (30 μM), TFP oxide (30 μM), *N*-(4-aminobutyl)-5-chloro-2-naphthalenesulfonamide (W-13, 30 μM; CAABCO, Inc., Houston, Tex.) or *N*-(4-aminobutyl)-2-naphthalenesulfonamide W-12, 30 μM; (CAABCO) were added to the microperfusion solution. At the conclusion of each microperfusion, the tubule was filled with latex and the distance between perfusion and collection sites determined subsequently by microdissection. Generally, only one solution was examined in any individual animal and two to four microperfusion collections were obtained per animal. The procedures for processing of the microperfusion samples have previously been described (11). For each microperfusion, the perfusion rate, the rate of water absorption, and the rate of phosphate absorption were determined from standard formulas. All values are expressed as the means ± SEM for all tubules studied. The results were not different when calculated as the mean of means from individual animals. Statistical significance was determined by the *t* test for unpaired data.

In order to determine if the drugs directly affected cAMP, the perfusion solutions were tested in a cAMP-dependent, calmodulin-independent system. cAMP-dependent protein kinase was partially purified from the parotid glands of the rat and its activity was assayed by a modification of the method of Livesey *et al.* (12). cAMP-stimulated protein kinase activity was determined in the presence of the same concentrations of the drugs as used in the microperfusion studies.

Results. The concentration of calmodulin was determined in homogenates of kidney cortex and in brush border membranes prepared from these homogenates. The calmodulin concentration in the whole homogenates averaged 60.1 ± 17.1 ng/mg protein (n = 3); the calmodulin concentration in the brush border membranes averaged 44.3 ± 18.8 ng/mg protein (n = 3). The ratio of calmodulin concentration in the brush border membranes as compared to the whole homogenate was 0.73.

Under control conditions, water absorption averaged 2.46 ± 0.11 nl min^{-1} mm^{-1} (Table

TABLE I. WATER AND PHOSPHATE ABSORPTION IN THE PROXIMAL TUBULE OF THE RAT

Perfusion solution	n	L (mm)	PR (nl min^{-1})	J_v (nl min^{-1} mm^{-1})	J_{PO_4-2} (pmole min^{-1} mm^{-1})
Control	19	1.3 ± 0.1	18.7 ± 0.4	2.46 ± 0.11	10.7 ± 0.8
cAMP	15	1.5 ± 0.1	18.6 ± 0.6	1.61 ± 0.12*	9.1 ± 0.6
cAMP + TFP	19	1.3 ± 0.1	18.5 ± 0.6	2.40 ± 0.09	11.3 ± 1.1
cAMP + TFP oxide	17	1.2 ± 0.1	18.3 ± 0.8	1.67 ± 0.09*	10.9 ± 0.8
cAMP + W-13	16	1.6 ± 0.2	18.4 ± 0.8	2.48 ± 0.21	9.4 ± 1.1
cAMP + W-12	16	1.5 ± 0.1	17.2 ± 1.0	1.88 ± 0.14*	10.8 ± 0.7
TFP	10	1.1 ± 0.1	18.5 ± 1.0	2.36 ± 0.07	12.6 ± 1.4
TFP oxide	11	1.5 ± 0.2	18.1 ± 1.0	2.39 ± 0.17	10.8 ± 1.1
W-13	12	1.5 ± 0.2	17.5 ± 1.0	2.55 ± 0.17	12.8 ± 1.5
W-12	14	1.5 ± 0.1	17.2 ± 0.6	2.67 ± 0.26	11.02 ± 1.3

Note. Values are expressed as the means ± SEM n = number of tubules; L = length of perfused tubule; PR = perfusion rate; J_v = water absorption; and J_{PO_4-2} = phosphate absorption. *$P < 0.02$ as compared to controls.

I). The addition of 10^{-6} *M* cAMP to the perfusion solution resulted in a significantly lower rate of water absorption of 1.61 ± 0.12 nl min^{-1} mm^{-1}. The addition of either TFP or W-13 to the microperfusion solution containing cAMP resulted in rates of water absorption of 2.40 ± 0.09 and 2.48 ± 0.21 nl min^{-1} mm^{-1}, respectively, values significantly higher than that obtained with cAMP alone and not significantly different from those of controls. By contrast, the addition of analogs of TFP and W-13 with lower affinities for binding of calmodulin (TFP oxide and W-12) to the microperfusion solution containing cAMP did not significantly affect the rates of absorption of water. TFP, TFP oxide, W-13, or W-12 when added to the control microperfusion solution not containing cAMP resulted in rates of water absorption not significantly different from those of controls.

The ability of cAMP to activate a protein kinase derived from the parotid gland of the rat was examined in the presence of the drugs in order to determine if the drugs were binding cAMP, inactivating cAMP, or otherwise inhibiting the action of cAMP on protein kinase. The activity of cAMP-dependent protein kinase, expressed as a percentage of activity stimulated by cAMP alone, as determined in three separate assays, did not differ by more than ±10% with the addition of any of the drugs.

Discussion. Recent reviews have cataloged the number of species and organs in which calmodulin has been identified (1, 2). In the present studies, a sensitive radioimmunoassay was utilized which confirms that calmodulin is present in the kidney (3–5). The mere presence of protein, however, allows no insight into the role of calmodulin in transport processes. In addition, the radioimmunoassay utilized measures total calmodulin and not calmodulin activity. In a variety of test systems, a putative role for calmodulin in physiologic processes has been deduced from the effects of drugs or agents which have affinity for calmodulin and block its activity. This strategy was employed in the present experiments.

TFP and W-13 have both been found to have binding affinities for calmodulin in other tissue systems (13–16). The concentration of these agents employed in the present studies approximates the IC_{50} determined in these other systems (13, 14). Both agents reversed the cAMP-induced inhibition of water absorption in the proximal convoluted tubule of the rat. These findings are consistent with the conclusion that calmodulin is required for the expression of cAMP-associated inhibition of water absorption. The validity of such a conclusion, however, must be tempered in view of the uncertainty regarding the specificity of the drugs. It has been suggested that TFP and perhaps other drugs thought to be calmodulin antagonists may directly affect other facets of cell function by a mechanism unrelated to calmodulin and that the effects of TFP cannot be taken, a priori, to indicate a calmodulin-mediated reaction (17, 18). These nonspecific effects of the calmodulin antagonists may relate to the hydrophobic properties of the drugs. It has been reported, for example, that TFP may limit mitochondrial energy production and inhibit Na^+–K^+ ATPase activity by calmodulin-independent mechanisms (17, 18). Several lines of evidence in the present studies would indicate that the effects of the drugs were not the result of such nonspecific effects. First, in the absence of cAMP none of the drugs exerted an effect on water absorption. Moreover, the absorption of phosphate was not influenced by the drugs. Thus, if TFP or W-13 were changing the characteristics of the membrane, limiting mitochondrial energy production, or decreasing Na^+–K^+ ATPase activity, it would be anticipated that some response would be evident even in the absence of cAMP in the luminal perfusate. Second, analogs of TFP and W-13 with lesser binding affinities for calmodulin had no effect on water absorption and did not reverse the cAMP-associated inhibition of water transport (15, 16). Finally, TFP and W-13 are structurally different from one another. Findings in the present study also indicate that the drugs themselves did not inactivate cAMP or prevent its binding to a receptor. While the above considerations are suggestive that the effects of TFP and W-13 are not a nonspecific response, the findings do not totally exclude such a possibility. In view of these uncertainties, the most cautious interpretation of the results of the present studies is that TFP and

W-13 block the cAMP-associated inhibition of water absorption. The findings of the present studies are consistent with but do not unequivocally prove that the cAMP-induced inhibition of water transport in this nephron segment involves an interaction with calmodulin.

Prior studies have demonstrated that parathyroid hormone or cAMP inhibits the transport of water and phosphate in the proximal tubule (19–21). Recent studies have indicated that PTH and cAMP inhibit the absorption of water by altering the activity of the sodium-proton counter exchanger located in the brush border membrane of the proximal convoluted tubule (22, 23). In the present studies the transport of water but not phosphate was inhibited by cAMP. The reasons for these differences are unknown at present. It is possible then that the failure to discern a change in phosphate transport may reflect perfusion of segments of the proximal tubule in which phosphate transport is not influenced by cAMP (20, 24). Additional studies will be required to clarify this issue. Thus, while a role for calmodulin in the expression of the inhibitory effects of cAMP on the absorption of water is suggested from the results of the present experiments, no definitive statement can be made as to the possible role of calmodulin on the effect of cAMP on the transport of phosphate.

The authors wish to acknowledge the assistance of Ms. Toña Larkin in the preparation of this manuscript and Dr. John Dedman who provided valuable consultation in the performance of these experiments.

1. Means AR, Tash JS, Chafouleas JG. Physiologic implications of the presence, distribution and regulation of calmodulin in eukaryotic cells. Phys Rev **62**:1–30, 1982.
2. West WL. Calmodulin-regulated enzymes: Modification by drugs and disease. Fed Proc **41**:2251–2252, 1982.
3. Morgan DW, Kim S, Campbell BJ, Cheung WY, Lynch T. Purification and characterization of calmodulin from porcine renal medulla. Arch Biochem Biophys **205**:510–519, 1980.
4. Smoake JA, Song S, Cheung WY. Cyclic 3′,5′-nucleotide phosphodiesterase. Distribution and developmental changes of the enzyme and its protein activator in mammalian tissues and cells. Biochim Biophys Acta **341**:402–411, 1974.
5. Yerna MJ, Harthshore D, Goldman RD. Isolation and characterization of baby trimoter kidney (BHK-21) cell modulator protein. Biochemistry **18**:673–678, 1979.
6. Akyempon CK, Roufogalis BD. The stoichiometry of the Ca^{+2} pump in human erthrocyte vesicles: Modulation by Ca^{+2} Mg^{+2} and calmodulin. Cell Calcium **3**:1–17, 1982.
7. Hyun CS, Kimmich GA. Effect of cholera toxin on cAMP levels and Na^+ influx in isolated intestinal epithelial cells. Amer J Physiol **243**(Cell Physiol 12):C107–C115, 1982.
8. Chafouleas JG, Dedman JR, Mungaal RP, Means AR. Calmodulin: Development and application of a sensitive radioimmunoassay. J Biol Chem **254**:10,262–10,267, 1979.
9. Booth AG, Kenny AJ. A rapid method for the preparation of microvilli from rabbit kidney. Biochem J **142**:575–581, 1974.
10. Kahn AM, Branham S, Weinman EJ. Mechanism of urate and PAH transport in rat renal microvillus membrane vesicles. Amer J Physiol **245**(Renal Fluid and Electrolyte Physiology 14):F151–F158, 1983.
11. Knight TF, Senekjian HO, Sansom S, Weinman EJ. Influence of D-glucose on phosphate absorption in the rat proximal tubule. Mineral Electrolyte Metab **4**:37–42, 1980.
12. Roskoski R. Assays of protein kinases. In: Corbin JD, Hardman JG, eds. Methods in Enzymology. Academic Press, New York, Vol 99:pp3–6.
13. Chafouleas JG, Bolton WE, Hidaka H, Boyd AE III, Means AR. Calmodulin and the cell cycle: Involvement in regulation of cell-cycle progression. Cell Vol **28**:41–50, 1982.
14. Schubart UK, Erlichman J, Fleischer N. Insulin release and protein phosphorylation: Possible role of calmodulin. Fed Proc **41**:2278–2282, 1982.
15. Tanaka T, Ohmura T, Hidaka H. Hydrophobic interaction of the Ca^{2+}–calmodulin complex with calmodulin antagonists: Naphthalenesulfonamide derivatives. Mol Pharmacol **22**:403–407, 1982.
16. Levin RM, Weiss B. Selective binding of the antipsychotics and other psychoactive agents to the calcium-dependent activator of cyclic nucleotide phosphodiesterase. J Pharmacol Exp Ther **208**:454–495, 1979.
17. Luthra MG. Trifluoperazine inhibition of calmodulin-sensitive Ca^{+2}-ATPase and calmodulin insensitive ($Na^+ + K^+$) and Mg^{+2}-ATPase activities of human and rat blood cells. Biochim Biophys Acta **692**:271–277, 1982.
18. Ruben L, Rasmussen H. Phenothiazines and related compounds disrupt mitochondrial energy production by a calmodulin-independent reaction. Biochim Biophys Acta **637**:415–422, 1981.
19. Agus AZ, Puschett JB, Senesky D, Goldberg M. Mode of action of parathyroid hormone and cyclic adenosine

3′-5′ monophosphate on renal tubular phosphate reabsorption in the dog. J Clin Invest **50**:617–626, 1971.
20. Bank N, Aynedjian HS, Weinstein SW. A microperfusion study of phosphate reabsorption by the rat proximal renal tubule. Effect of parathyroid hormone. J Clin Invest **54**:1040–1048, 1974.
21. Baumann K, Chan YL, Bode F, Papvassiliou F. Effect of parathyroid hormone and cyclic adenosine 3′-5′ monophosphate on isotonic fluid reabsorption: Polarity of proximal tubular cells. Kidney Int **11**:77–85, 1977.
22. Cohn DE, Klahr S, Hammerman MR. Metabolic acidosis and parathyroidectomy increase Na^+/H^+ exchange in brush border vesicles. Amer J Physiol. **245**(Renal Fluid Electrolyte Physiol. 14):F217–F222, 1983.
23. Kahn AM, Dolson GM, Bennett SC, Weinman EJ. cAMP and PTH inhibits Na^+/H^+ exchange in brush border membrane vesicles (BBM) derived from a suspension of rabbit proximal tubules. Kidney Int **25**:289, 1984 (Abstr).
24. Dennis W, Bello-Reuss E, Robinson R. Response of phosphate transport to parathyroid hormone in segments of rabbit nephron. Amer J Physiol. (Renal Fluid Electrolyte Physiol.) **2**(1):F29–F38, 1977.

Received December 19, 1983. P.S.E.B.M. 1984, Vol. 176.
Accepted April 6, 1984.

PROCEEDINGS OF THE SOCIETY FOR EXPERIMENTAL BIOLOGY AND MEDICINE **176**, 327–336 (1984)

ABSTRACTS

1983 Annual Meeting, Society for Experimental Biology and Medicine: Northwest Section

Joint Center for Graduate Studies, Richland, Washington
October 29, 1983

SECTION OFFICERS

Chairman: DR. M. R. SIKOV, Biology Department, Battelle Northwest Laboratories, Richland, Washington
Secretary–Treasurer: DR. FRANK P. HUNGATE, Biology and Chemistry Department, Battelle Northwest Laboratories, Richland, Washington

0037-9727/84 $1.50

The annual meeting of the Section was held on Saturday, October 29, 1983, at the Joint Center for Graduate Studies, Richland, Washington, with an attendance of over 40 members and guests. The meeting was preceded by a social evening on Friday, October 28. Nature continued to favor our selection of meeting dates with warm and sunny weather, as has been the case for the last several years.

Seventeen papers were presented throughout the day and covered a wide diversity of subjects. They were grouped in a series of four sessions, generally fitting into categories of Microbiology, Physiology, Biochemistry, and Developmental Biology. The award for the best paper presented by a junior postdoctoral scientist went to Dr. Karen Carlberg, from Eastern Washington University, for her paper "Pain Sensitivity in Exercise-Trained Rats" (coauthored by M. J. Fregly from the University of Florida). The award for the best paper presented by a predoctoral scientist went to Cathleen L. Rawson, from Oregon State University, for her paper "Denervation Supersensitivity-Like Response Assessed in Rat Caudal Arteries" (coauthored by Robert E. Larson).

The organization and academic program at the Joint Center for Graduate Studies was described to the attendees by Dr. Jim Hampton, Associate Dean of the Center (and a former chairman of our Section). Jim also described opportunities for undergraduate, graduate, and faculty participation in R&D programs offered by the Northwest College and University Association for Science (NORCUS) program. At the section business meeting, Dr. James Carlson, Washington State University, was elected Chairman and Dr. Robert Larson, Oregon State University, was elected Secretary/Treasurer of the Section for 1983–1984. In other items of business it was reported that the Section is solvent, largely due to Institutional support for the last few years; those wishing to pay dues should send them to Dr. Larson. We continue to have substantial interest from the membership, including those not able to attend. It was decided that it would be advisable to reinstitute the concept of a counselor representing each of the several institutions represented in the Section. We encourage the membership at each institution to select a colleague who will serve as counselor and as focal point for communications and stimulation of interest. Members should indicate nominees to Dr. Carlson or Dr. Larson, so that they may communicate with them in setting up next year's meeting.

By way of further information, Frank Hungate provided the National Office with a report of our 1982 meeting which appeared in the *Proceedings.* Frank also secured a supply of abstract forms which were supplied to presenters and the abstracts are being submitted for publication in the *Proceedings.* We hope that this is a practice which will continue.

The Section accepted an invitation to hold the 1984 annual meeting in Pullman, Washington. The date for that meeting has been scheduled for October 13. The call for abstracts and further information will be issued by Jim Carlson. We hope that many of you will begin planning for attendance and presentation, and we hope to see you there.

TABLE OF CONTENTS

Page

331 Involvement of a Protease in Extracellular Enzyme Induction of *Neurospora crassa* .... RA Lindberg, H Drucker

331 A Defined Medium for Toxin Synthesis Related Nutritional Studies of *Corynebacterium diphtheriae* .... JF Jones, HN Lightfoot

331 Plasmid DNA Isolated from Phase I and Phase II *Coxiella burnetii* .... JE Samuel, ME Frazier, LP Mallavia, L Thomashow, ML Kahn

332 Denervation Supersensitivity-Like Response Assessed in Rat Caudal Arteries .... CL Rawson, RE Larson

332 Pain Sensitivity in Exercise-Trained Rats .... KA Carlberg, MJ Fregly

332 Species Differences in Neuropeptides in Slugs .... AW Martin, I Deyrup-Olsen

333 Lung Clearance, Translocation, and Toxicity of Metal Oxides Deposited in Rat Lung .... K Rhoads, CL Sanders

333 The Relationship between Glutathione Conjugation and Organic Anion Excretion during Drug-Induced Cholestasis in Rats .... DG Hoyt, RE Larson

333 Prenatal and Postnatal Effects of *in Utero* Exposure to Solvent Refined Coal Materials in Rats .... RL Rommereim, PL Hackett, DL Springer, DD Mahlum, MR Sikov

334 Hormonal Changes in Rats Given Alcohol prior to and during Gestation .... M Lee, K Wakabayashi

334 Transient Lipoprotein Deficiency at Birth: A Cause of Low Levels of Vitamin E in the Newborn .... ID Desai, FE Martinez, JE Dos Santos, JE Dutra de Oliveira

334 Placental Mineralization in Miniature Swine .... DN Rommereim, RA Miller, RL Buschbom, MR Sikov

335 Synthesis of Acyl-CoA Carboxylase, Malonyl-CoA Decarboxylase, and Fatty Acid Synthase during Development of Uropygial Gland of Goose .... AJ Poulose, L Rogers, PE Kolattukudy

335 The Simultaneous Determination of Cytochrome *P*-450 *O*-Deethylase and *N*-Demethylase Activity by High-Performance Liquid Chromatography .... EJ Jarvi, JC Stolzenbach, RE Larson

335 Drug Induced Decreases in Rat Liver Cytochrome *P*-450 Content and Alterations in Hepatic Heme Metabolism .... JC Stolzenbach, RE Larson

336 Effect of Ethanol and 2-Chloroadenosine on High Affinity Choline Uptake in Rat Brain .... P Szot, RE Larson, TF Murray

336 *In Vivo* Analysis of Ethanol and Acetaldehyde Inhibited Drug Metabolism .... S LaFollette, RE Larson

INVOLVEMENT OF A PROTEASE IN EXTRACELLULAR ENZYME INDUCTION OF NEUROSPORA CRASSA

Richard A. Lindberg and H. Drucker. Pacific Northwest Laboratory, Richland, WA 99352 (Introduced by M. R. Sikov)

The regulatory mechanisms that control extracellular hydrolases of Neurospora crassa were investigated. N. crassa synthesizes and secretes several proteases and nucleases in response to limitation of the elemental nutrients obtainable from nucleic acids and proteins. An additional requirement for synthesis of these enzymes is the presence of exogenous protein, but the mechanisms of this form of induction remain obscure. Induction during carbon derepression also requires exogenous proteolytic activity, which is not required for sulfur, nitrogen, or phosphorus derepression. In order to explain this phenomenon, minor extracellular proteases were investigated and results showed that an N. crassa protease may be involved in the inductive process. The protease is not present in an active form under carbon starvation; presumably, the exogenous proteolytic activity substitutes for it. The conversion to active form is pH-dependent and does not occur at the high pH caused by secretion of ammonia when N. crassa utilizes amino acids as a carbon source. (This work was supported by the U.S. Department of Energy under Contract #DE-AC06-76RLO 1830).

A DEFINED MEDIUM FOR TOXIN SYNTHESIS RELATED NUTRITIONAL STUDIES OF CORYNEBACTERIUM DIPHTHERIAE.

Jean F. Jones, Haideh N. Lightfoot. Eastern Washington University, Cheney, WA 99004.

Studying toxin synthesis by C. diphtheriae requires a culture medium which can be manipulated, enabling specific nutritional studies and incorporation of radioisotopes into cellular constituents. We have developed a defined medium containing per liter, 20 mg of each amino acid, 1.0 ml of Mueller's solution II, 0.5 mg calcium pantothenate and 2.5% maltose in 50 mM sodium-potassium phosphate buffer, pH 7.2. When assayed by ADP-ribosylation of elongation factor-2 and rabbit skin test, toxin synthesis by exponentially growing cells which have been transferred to this medium, is continuous for up to 24 hr. Toxin synthesis was arrested by the addition of iron. Production of Btox+ phage by $C_7(-)$ host strain is similar to that in complex media. C. diphtheriae cells do not appear to multiply in this medium however, protein and RNA synthesis remain active as indicated by the uptake of radioisotope labeled bases and amino acids. ^{3}H-uridine and ^{14}C-amino acids are incorporated at an increased rate of approximately 10 times compared with complex media. Therefore, high specific labeling of macromolecules during short pulse times was obtained. Currently we are using modified forms of this medium to study nutritional requirements of C. diphtheriae in relation to toxin synthesis. (Supported by USPHS Grant AI-18159)

PLASMID DNA ISOLATED FROM PHASE I AND PHASE II COXIELLA BURNETII.

J. E. Samuel[1], M. E. Frazier[2], L. P. Mallavia[1], L. Thomashow[1]. and M. L. Kahn[1]. [1]Department of Bacteriology and Public Health, Washington State University, Pullman, WA 99163 and [2]Biology and Chemistry Department, Battelle Northwest Laboratories, Richland, WA 99352. (Introduced by F. P. Hungate)

A multiple copy plasmid was isolated from the Nine Mile Phase I strain of Coxiella burnetii. The plasmid DNA was subjected to digestion using a number of restriction endonucleases. Analysis of the restriction fragments generated in these studies indicated that a single 36 Kb plasmid was present. Four enzymes (PstI, XbaI, KpNI and SalI) were subsequently used in double digestion studies to derive a restriction map of the plasmid, designated QphI. Isolation of DNA from phase II organisms yielded a similar plasmid. A comparison of restriction enzyme digestion patterns revealed no major differences between the phase I and phase II plasmid. In addition, phase I Nine Mile organisms maintained in cell culture also contain plasmid sequences as determined using Southern hybridization techniques. Studies confirm the plasmid is of rickettsial origin and not due to contamination. The plasmid has been cloned into E. coli RR1 using pACYC 177 as a vector. (This work was supported by Battelle Northwest Laboratories and NIH Grant Number 1 R01 A12019001.

Denervation Supersensitivity-Like Response Assessed In Rat Caudal Arteries. Cathleen L. Rawson and Robert E. Larson, College of Pharmacy Oregon State University, Corvallis, OR 97331.

Other toxicity studies suggested cardiovascular effects of the carcinostatic alkylating drug 1,3-bis (2-chloroethyl) -1-nitrosourea (BCNU). Some alkylating agents are known to be strong α-adrenergic blockers. The effects of BCNU (15-25 mg/kg ip) were studied in caudal artery segments taken from male rats 1-28 days after treatment. Arterial segments were doubly cannulated and perfused intraluminally and bathed in Krebs-bicarbonate solution. Periarterial nerve stimulation via bipolar platinum ring electrodes over a range of 1.4-10.0 Herz (Hz) established frequency-response relationships for the neurogenic response. The vascular smooth muscle responsiveness was evaluated by perfusion with norepinephrine, (NE, $5.6X10^{-8}$ - 10^{-6}M). BCNU depressed the neurogenic response in a frequency dependent manner between 1 and 7 days after treatment. Recovery occurred by day 10 followed by an increase responsiveness manimizing to 140% of control by day 14. The responsiveness to NE never diminished and increased steadily to a maximum of 150% of control between 10 and 14 days. These findings suggest a reversible neuronal toxicity of BCNU which results in a denervation supersensitivity type response of vascular smooth muscle. (Supported by institutional funds as an OSU Tartar Fellowship).

PAIN SENSITIVITY IN EXERCISE-TRAINED RATS. K. A. Carlberg and M. J. Fregly. East. Wash. Univ., Cheney, WA 99004 and Univ. of Fla., Gainesville, FL 32610.

Exercise may stimulate secretion of endogenous opiates (EO), particularly beta-endorphin. EO are believed to reduce pain sensitivity. Thus we examined effects of exercise, acute and chronic, on pain sensitivity in rats, and reversibility of those effects by the opiate antagonist naloxone (NAL). Ten rats were exercised daily for 10 wk in motor-driven exercise wheels. Nine sedentary rats were handled daily. Pain sensitivity was evaluated by the tail flick latency (TFL) test, which measures length of time for a rat to flick its tail after a hot light is focused on the tail. A long latency indicates reduced pain sensitivity. When tested immediately after an exercise bout, TFL was longer in exercise rats than in sedentary rats (E: 11.7 sec $\pm$ 0.8 SE; S: 7.9 $\pm$ 1.5; $p<0.025$). The difference was abolished by NAL (10 mg/kg, s.c.). At 5-8 hr after exercise, TFL was still longer in the exercise rats (E: 8.9 sec $\pm$ 1.0; S: 5.5 $\pm$ 1.0, $p<0.05$). When tested 28-31 hr after the last exercise bout, TFL was actually reduced in the exercise rats (E: 4.7 sec $\pm$ 0.8; S: 7.9 $\pm$ 1.8) although large variability precluded significance. This suggests "withdrawal" from "opiate addiction" accompanying exercise training. We conclude that there is an opiate-mediated reduction in pain sensitivity for at least 8 hr after exercise in rats, and that exercise training may produce tolerance to EO. (Amer Heart Assoc, Suncoast)

SPECIES DIFFERENCES IN NEUROPEPTIDES IN SLUGS. A. W. Martin and I. Deyrup-Olsen. Department of Zoology, University of Washington, Seattle, WA 98195

We described a preparation of slug body wall (posterior chamber, PC) that responds to stimulation and to injection of transmitters by exuding fluid (Deyrup-Olsen and Martin, Comp. Biochem. Physiol. 72 C, 45-51, 1982). Arginine vasotocin (AVT) was the most active agent in *Ariolimax columbianus* (*Ac*). AVT was tested on other slugs. Limacidae *Limax flavus* (*Lf*) and *Limax maximus* (*Lm*) responded well to AVT; the Arionidae *Arion ater* (*Aa*) and *Prophysaon foliolatum* (*Pf*) gave little response.

Ganglionic extracts contain AVT-like substances and stimulate PCs like AVT (Sawyer, et al. 9th International Sym. Comp. Endocrinol., 1981). We have tested ganglionic extracts from several species of land slugs. Each species PC responded to an extract of its own ganglia except *Pf*, which also failed to respond to any other species extract. PCs of *Ac* responded to extracts of *Pf*, and to those of the other three species tested. *Aa* PCs responded only to extracts from *Aa* and from *Pf*. We conclude that there is diversity among slugs in the composition of their ganglionic neuropeptides.

LUNG CLEARANCE, TRANSLOCATION, AND TOXICITY OF METAL OXIDES DEPOSITED IN RAT LUNG. K. Rhoads and C. L. Sanders (Sponsor: M. R. Sikov), Battelle, Pacific Northwest Laboratory, Richland, WA 99301

Power production in nuclear or fossil-fueled plants may release a number of oxidized heavy metals to the environment. We have studied the behavior and toxicity of arsenic, beryllium, cadmium, cobalt, lead, selenium, vanadium and ytterbium oxides deposited in rat lungs via inhalation or intratracheal instillation. Translocation to other organs was followed by serial sacrifices for several weeks to months after exposure. Be, Co, and Yb were relatively insoluble in the lung and showed minimal translocation to extrapulmonary tissues. As, Cd, Pb, Se, and V cleared the lung rapidly and were retained at other sites in the body, especially bone, kidney, liver, and muscle. Of those compounds tested for acute lethality, cadmium oxide was most toxic, followed by selenium, vanadium and arsenic oxides. In a study of interactions between different metals, Cd slowed the clearance of selenium and plutonium oxides from the lung when both were deposited together. Aqueous solubility in vitro was a poor predictor for the behavior of many of these compounds in the lung because of their interaction with various metabolic processes.

(Work Supported by the U.S. Department of Energy Contract DE-AC06-76RLO-1830)

The Relationship Between Glutathione Conjugation and Organic Anion Excretion During Drug-Induced Cholestasis In Rats. Dale G. Hoyt and Robert E. Larson, College of Pharmacy, Oregon State University, Corvallis, OR 97331.

Previous experiments in rats showed that 1,3 bis(2-chloroethyl)-1-nitrosourea BCNU-induced intrahepatic cholestasis was characterized by a specific reduction of the bile salt independent bile flow. Before and during cholestasis, sulfobromopthalein (BSP) excretion rate and biliary concentration were reduced while bile salt concentration was elevated. Since BSP excretion is facilitated by conjugation with glutathione (GSH), the possibility that BSP metabolism was inhibited was investigated in male rats by determining the effect of BCNU (20 mg/kg ip in corn oil) on cytosolic GSH-S-transferase activity in the liver. Also, the effect of BCNU on the excretion of the non-metabolized dye, indocyanine green (ICG), was determined. The in vitro activity of GSH-S-transferase toward BSP was not altered by BCNU pretreatment. The conjugation of 1-chloro-2,4-dinitrobenzene was reduced 24 hours after BCNU treatment, but activity returned by 48 hours. ICG excretion rate and biliary concentration were reduced by BCNU. These results imply that reduced organic anion excretion was due to a decrease in net flux across the canalicular membrane. (Supported by institutional funds and a gift from the Chiles Foundation.)

PRENATAL AND POSTNATAL EFFECTS OF IN UTERO EXPOSURE TO SOLVENT REFINED COAL MATERIALS IN RATS. R.L. Rommereim, P.L. Hackett, D.L. Springer, D.D. Mahlum, and M.R. Sikov. Developmental Toxicology Section, Biology and Chemistry Dept.,Pacific Northwest Laboratory, Richland, WA 99352.

Studies performed by administering materials from solvent refined coal processes (SRC) to pregnant rats indicated that high-boiling mixtures were embryotoxic and teratogenic. The most commonly observed dose-related fetal morphologic lesion was "small lung," often accompanied by cleft palate or diaphragmatic hernia. In studies, to be reported here, we determined (1) influence of embryonic development at exposure; (2) fetal and maternal responses to boiling range cuts of crude materials; and (3) postnatal consequences of in utero exposure to process material. For these studies, rats were dosed by intragastric intubation at intervals between 12 and 16 days of gestation (dg) with a process material (designated as HPS) or with mixtures of five boiling-range cuts. The incidence of small fetal lungs was highest following exposure to HPS on 12 or 13 dg and cleft palate occurred more frequently following exposure on 13 dg. No adverse effects were produced by the administration of complex mixtures boiling below 700°; boiling range cuts above 700°F increased mortality and the incidence of small lungs. Over 50% mortality occurred in the HPS-exposed pups within 3 days of birth. (Work supported by the US Dept. of Energy, Contract No. DE-AC06-76RLO-1830)

HORMONAL CHANGES IN RATS GIVEN ALCOHOL PRIOR TO AND DURING GESTATION

Melvin Lee, Univ. British Columbia, Vancouver, B.C., Canada and
K. Wakabayashi, Inst. Endocrinology, Gunma Univ., Maebashi, Japan

Pituitary LH and FSH and serum LH, FSH, progesterone and testosterone were measured in rats exposed to alcohol prior to and throughout gestation Fetuses of alcohol-fed rats were significantly smaller and placentae were significantly larger than those of pair-fed (PF) or ad libitum-fed (C) rats. Progesterone was depressed in alcohol-fed rats on day 17, but testosterone did not differ among the three groups. Serum LH was lower in the A and PF groups, but serum FSH and pituitary LH did not differ in the three groups. It is suggested that low progesterone levels may play some role in placental enlargement of fetal alcohol syndrome, but that changes in LH and FSH do not seem to be responsible for the reduction in progesterone. Low serum LH may be a response to moderate caloric restriction accompanying alcohol ingestion.

TRANSIENT LIPOPROTEIN DEFICIENCY AT BIRTH: A CAUSE OF LOW LEVELS OF VITAMIN E IN THE NEWBORN. I.D. Desai, F.E. Martinez, J.E. Dos Santos, J.E. Dutra de Oliveira. Division of Human Nutrition, University of British Columbia, Vancouver, B.C., Canada V6T 1W5 and Faculty of Medicine, University of Sao Paulo, 14100 Ribeirao Preto, Brazil.

In newborns, the level of vitamin E in blood is very low as compared to that of placental intervillous blood and maternal blood. In our attempt to investigate the role of placenta in the transfer of vitamin E from the maternal to the newborn circulation, we have discovered that vitamin E is able to enter placental blood but is not being efficiently transferred from the placental to the newborn circulation. It appears from our preliminary study that the most limiting factor in the transfer of vitamin E from the placental to the newborn circulation is the transient deficiency of prebeta lipoprotein in the newborn blood at birth. A transient lipoprotein deficiency is implicated as a cause of low levels of vitamin E in the newborn.

PLACENTAL MINERALIZATION IN MINIATURE SWINE. D.N. Rommereim, R.A. Miller, R.L. Buschbom, and M.R. Sikov. Battelle, Pacific Northwest Laboratory, Richland, WA 99352.

During a developmental toxicology study, we incidentally observed opaque white deposits in placentas of Hanford Miniature swine examined at 100 days of gestation. Initially, presence of deposits was simply noted, but subsequently their extent was scored; neither measure was treatment related, suggesting that the deposits developed spontaneously. Deposits were present in the placentas of 52 of 149 fetuses, representing 19 of 30 litters, and ranged in size from barely visible to massive. They tended to be more frequent in placentas of fetuses with more advanced development, but we could not establish statistically significant associations with fetal weight, or with radiographic skeletal opacity or numbers of sternal and carpal ossification centers. The deposits were dissolved in specimens fixed in neutral buffered formalin. Examination of frozen sections demonstrated that they were located in the chorion, did not elicit an inflammatory response, and showed positive reactions to Alizarin red and vonKossa's stains. Neither incidence nor extent was related to calcium or phosphate levels in maternal serum. Similar deposits have been anecdotally reported previously, and may relate to calcification in human placentas. (Research supported by the Electric Power Research Institute)

SYNTHESIS OF ACYL-CoA CARBOXYLASE, MALONYL-CoA DECARBOXYLASE AND FATTY ACID SYNTHASE DURING DEVELOPMENT OF UROPYGIAL GLAND OF GOOSE. A.J. Poulose, Linda Rogers and P.E. Kolattukudy, Institute of Biological Chemistry and Biochemistry/Biophysics Program, Washington State Univ., Pullman, WA 99164. (Sponsored by J.R. Carlson, Dept. of Animal Science, Washington State Univ., Pullman, WA 99164.)

Uropygial gland of waterfowl produces large quantities of methyl-branched fatty acids. The coordinated action of an acyl-CoA carboxylase which carboxylates both acetyl-CoA and propionyl-CoA, a fatty acid synthase which utilizes both malonyl-CoA and methylmalonyl-CoA and a malonyl-CoA decarboxylase results in the production of methyl-branched fatty acids. In this study, the levels of these enzymes were determined during development by measurement of, a) activity of the enzymes, b) immunologically cross reacting material with specific antibodies and c) level of mRNA for malonyl-CoA decarboxylase by hybridization with labeled cDNA probe. The results showed that significant amounts of fatty acid synthase and malonyl-CoA decarboxylase appeared in the gland 4 days before hatching while acyl-CoA carboxylase appeared only 4 days after hatching but before production of large amounts of lipids. Thus it appears that malonyl-CoA decarboxylase is synthesized sufficiently early in the development of this gland to regulate the malonyl-CoA level to ensure the production of methyl-branched lipids. (Supported in part by USPH NIH Grant GM-18278).

The Simultaneous Determination of Cytochrome P-450 O-deethylase and N-demethylase Activity By High Performance Liquid Chromatography. Eric J. Jarvi, James C. Stolzenbach, and Robert E. Larson, Oregon State University, College of Pharmacy, Corvallis, OR 97331.

The measurement of cytochrome P-450 O-deethylase and N-demethylase activity has previously required a thin layer chromatographic separation of the products obtained from a radiolabeled substrate. This reported HPLC method utilizes a commercial counter-ion which permits the detection and quantitation of all potential products of *in vitro* P-450 mediated ethylmorphine metabolism: normorphine, morphine, and norethylmorphine. The procedure requires a one step extraction of the enzyme reaction mixture, has a detection limit of 5 μg/ml, and is linear over the range of 5 to 500 μg/ml for all three reaction products. We used this new method to measure P-450 activity in liver microsomal preparations from control and phenobarbital induced male Sprague Dawley rats. The sensitivity and specificity of this method offers distinct advantages over the Nash reaction and it does not suffer the inherent problems associated with the radiolabeled TLC procedure. (Supported by institutional funds, an OSU Tartar fellowship, and by a gift from the Chiles Foundation.)

Drug Induced Decreases In Rat Liver Cytochrome P450 Content and Alterations in Hepatic Heme Metabolism. James C. Stolzenbach and Robert E. Larson, College of Pharmacy, Oregon State University, Corvallis, OR 97331.

Previous experiments have described decreases in rat liver cytochrome P450 content and activity following a single ip injection of the antitumor agent 1,3 bis-(2-chloroethyl)-1-nitrosourea, (BCNU). The current investigation measured the effect of BCNU on general microsomal heme metabolism in attempts to relate it to these alterations in P450. Spectrophotometric techniques were utilized to measure δ-aminolevulinic acid (ALA) synthetase activity. Heme degradation was monitered through the activity of heme oxygenase. Total microsomal heme content was also measured. Male rats were given single ip injections of 20 mg/kg BCNU and sacrificed after 14 days for enzyme determinations and comparison to controls. Results demonstrate decreases (67% of controls) in ALA synthetase activity and corresponding increases (130% of controls) in activity of heme oxygenase. Total heme content was unaltered. From these data it is postulated BCNU causes an increase in unincorporated heme by decreasing demand for P450 synthesis which activates the oxygenase and feedback inhibition of heme synthesis. (Supported by institutional funds, an OSU Tartar fellowship and by a gift from the Chiles Foundation.)

Effect Of Ethanol And 2-Chloroadenosine On High Affinity Choline Uptake In Rat Brain.
Patricia Szot, Robert E. Larson and Thomas F. Murray. Department of Pharmacology, Oregon State University, Corvallis, OR 97331.

Ethanol has been reported to decrease both acetylcholine release and the high affinity choline uptake system of rat brain following oral administration. We have attempted to further characterize this effect of ethanol on cholinergic neurotransmission using an improved assay methodology for measuring hemicholinium-3-sensitive high affinity choline uptake (HACU) in rat brain synaptosomes. The acute administration of ethanol elicited a 50% reduction in the HACU in the hippocampus. As this dose of ethanol also elicits a significant hypothermic effect in rats, we evaluated the potential role of this hypothermia in ethanol's effect on hippocampal HACU. Where the animals body temperature was maintained at 37°C the ethanol induced reduction in HACU was prevented. 2-Chloroadenosine in a dose which produced hypothermia, also decreased the HACU in hippocampus. The decrease in HACU in the hippocampus elicited by 2-chloroadenosine was 31%, however in animals whose body temperature was maintained at 37°C the HACU was decreased by 51%. Therefore, the reduction in HACU by high doses of ethanol appears to be the result of hypothermia. In contrast, the decrease in HACU elicited by 2-chloroadenosine appears to be independent of the hypothermia. (Supported by funds provided by the State of Washington Initiative Measure No. 171.)

In Vivo Analysis of Ethanol and Acetaldehyde Inhibited Drug Metabolism.
Sharron LaFollette and Robert E. Larson, College of Pharmacy, Oregon State University, Corvallis, OR 97331.

The inhibition of mixed-function oxygenase activity by ethanol and acetaldehyde was examined *in vivo* by monitoring changes in salivary half-life of antipyrine and aminopyrine in adult male rats. Ethanol (22-130 mmol/kg po) or acetaldehyde (4-8 mmol/kg ip) was administered 20 minutes prior to antipyrine (100 mg/kg, ip) or aminopyrine (80 mg/kg, ip). Ethanol increased the half-life of antipyrine in a dose-dependent manner over the control value of 166 $\pm$ 5 min. Acetaldehyde inhibition was less dramatic and not dose-dependent. Aminopyrine half-life remained statistically unchanged from control (68 $\pm$ 7 min) with either treatment. Thus, heterocyclic hydroxylation (antipyrine) but not N-demethylation (aminopyrine) appears to be inhibited *in vivo* by ethanol and acetaldehyde. (Supported by institutional funds and an OSU Tartar fellowship.)

PROCEEDINGS OF THE SOCIETY FOR EXPERIMENTAL BIOLOGY AND MEDICINE **176**, 337–341 (1984)

MINIREVIEW

The Lupus Anticoagulant (41879)

NORBERTO PERICO, FIORENZA PUSINERI, AND GIUSEPPE REMUZZI[1]

Istituto di Ricerche Farmacologiche "Mario Negri," Bergamo, and Divisione Nefrologia e Dialisi, Ospedali Riuniti, Bergamo, Italy

Lupus-like anticoagulant (LLAC) is the term used to identify an acquired inhibitor (1) of blood coagulation, first described by Conley and Hartmann in patients with systemic lupus erythematosus (SLE) (2). A circulating "lupus-like" anticoagulant has been detected in 5–10% of all SLE patients. A lupus anticoagulant is also found in other diseases including immunologic, oncologic, gynecologic, and neurologic disorders (3–12). In autoimmune diseases a lupus anticoagulant may occur in families, suggesting a genetic predisposition (13–15). Methods now available can distinguish between lupus anticoagulant and other inhibitors of coagulation (i.e., agonist factor VIII, IX, X, XI, and XII) occurring in SLE (16–19) and, more generally, in autoimmune diseases. In fact, in mixtures of LLAC plasma and normal plasma an immediate inhibition can be observed which is not increased by prolonging the incubation period, in contrast to the gradual time-dependent inhibition that occurs in patients with other types of coagulation inhibitors.

Phospholipid and Lupus Anticoagulant Interaction. Only in the last few years have significant advances been made in our understanding of the lupus anticoagulant mechanism of action. The thromboplastin generation test using diluted plasma or serum from a patient with a "lupus anticoagulant" is normal, suggesting that the lupus inhibitor does not interfere with the generation of intrinsic prothrombin (1, 20–22). However, the abnormality can be revealed when the patient's plasma is used, instead of normal plasma, as source of prothrombin and fibrinogen (1, 20, 22). These findings suggest that lupus anticoagulant interferes with the activation of prothrombin, acting at the junction between intrinsic and extrinsic coagulation pathways. In other words, the anticoagulant inhibits the "prothrombin activator complex" (factor Xa, factor V, calcium, and phospholipids) and, more particularly, seems to be directed against the phospholipid fraction of the complex (3, 4, 23). This possibility is suggested by the observation that the inhibitory effect is considerably potentiated by reducing the phospholipid content of clotting mixtures (23–25). Moreover, the abnormal "prothrombin consumption" of blood containing the lupus anticoagulant can be corrected by adding a phospholipid mixture as a source of platelet factor 3-like activity (26). Recently, Thiagarajan *et al.* (27), using a specific immunologic interaction with negatively charged phospholipids, reported that this inhibitor is able to block the calcium ion-dependent binding of prothrombin and factor X to phospholipid micelles. In patients with "systemic lupus" the incidence of false-positive tests for syphilis is considerably higher when the anticoagulant is present. This observation further supports the possibility of an interaction between phospholipids and the lupus anticoagulant (28–30).

The Nature of Lupus Anticoagulant. Whether a cofactor in normal plasma, either prothrombin (31) or a gamma globulin (32), potentiates the LLAC inhibitory activity under appropriate experimental conditions is uncertain. More recent work characterized the cofactor as heat labile and different from complement (10), poorly absorbed by $BaSO_4$ or $Al(OH)_3$, with an approximate molecular weight of 200,000 on gel filtration (33). Moreover, it is possible that an artifact, due to the presence of traces of thrombin or platelet fragments in the test plasma (34), could account for all the findings suggesting the existence of a cofactor. In the past 15 years, much work has been done to identify the nature of lupus anticoagulant which is either an IgG (4, 32, 35–37), an IgM (4, 8, 27, 38), or a mixture of both (4, 8, 36, 39, 40). Thiagarajan and co-

[1] To whom reprint requests should be addressed at: Istituto di Ricerche Farmacologiche "M. Negri" via Gavazzeni 11 24100 Bergamo, Italy.

0037-9727/84 $1.50

workers (27) identified the Fab μ tryptic fragment in monoclonal IgM paraprotein as the component responsible for lupus-like anticoagulant activity in a patient affected by Waldenstrom's disease. They also demonstrated that IgM reacted with phosphatidylserine and, to a lesser extent, with phosphatidic acid, but not with phosphatidylcholine or phosphatidylethanolamine. Phosphatidylserine seems to be located exclusively on the inner aspect of the platelet membrane (41). This could explain why the patient's radiolabeled Fab μ fails to bind to platelets, unless they have been previously activated with thrombin. Furthermore, this interpretation fits with the observation that platelets, if used as a source of phospholipids in a test system, support normal coagulation even in the presence of lupus anticoagulant (27). More recently, Lafer and co-workers (42), using monoclonal autoantibodies, demonstrated that anti-DNA antibodies, including antibodies with the characteristics of LLAC, can be serologically polymorphic having the capacity to bind to different structures containing phosphate ester. They also found that the same monoclonal anti-DNA antibodies binding polynucleotides can both react with phospholipids and mimic the *in vitro* action of LLAC.

Diagnosis of Lupus Anticoagulant. The prothrombin time is usually normal or slightly prolonged in patient with the lupus anticoagulant (3, 23). In contrast, a prolonged activated partial thromboplastin time (APTT), which is not corrected by adding normal plasma in mixing experiments, allows one to diagnose the presence of a lupus anticoagulant rather than a factor deficiency and represents the most widely employed screening test (3, 10, 32, 36, 39, 43, 44).

Differences in APTT values obtained using different commercial reagents have been attributed to the concentration of the platelet substitute in the preparation (25). Since the anticoagulant interferes with negatively charged phospholipids, the most sensitive tests used to detect LLAC are those with a reduced phospholipid content, such as the prothrombin time performed with dilute thromboplastin (1, 3, 9, 10, 23, 25, 28, 44).

Another test believed to be sensitive enough to detect lupus anticoagulant is the kaolin clotting time (KCT). Using this test, Exner and associates (34) indicated that the presence of an anticoagulant can be predicted when aliquots of the test plasma prolonged the KCT of normal plasma more than would be expected on the basis of dilution alone. Moreover, the same authors suggest that the KCT allows distinguishing between the classical "lupus inhibitor" alone and the presence of an associated coagulation factor deficiency on the basis of different mixing patterns. In this context, it must be remembered that because of the PTT sensitivity to the effects of the anticoagulant, factors such as VIII, IX, XI, or XII may appear deficient although being present in normal amounts when assayed by a two-stage assay (5, 6, 8, 10, 25). Despite these abnormalities, patients with lupus anticoagulant are not affected by a bleeding tendency (3, 4, 10, 29, 37, 44, 45), nor do they bleed excessively when undergoing surgery (1, 3, 23, 29, 37, 44, 46) unless another abnormality of the hemostatic system, such as thrombocytopenia, is present (7, 20, 39, 47).

Thrombosis and Lupus Anticoagulant. Paradoxically, such patients suffer from a still poorly understood thrombotic tendency (8, 23, 26, 48–52). Mueh *et al.* (29) have recently reported the occurrence of thrombosis in 8 out of 35 patients having a "circulating lupus anticoagulant." An explanation for the fact that these patients do not bleed could be that the phospholipid moiety of platelet membrane is not accessible to the antiphospholipid gamma globulin which might express its activity only against the artificial source of phospholipids used during "*in vitro*" tests. The effect of anticoagulant "*in vivo*" can also be minimized by the high affinity factor Xa binding receptor present on the platelet surface which promotes thrombin formation even in the absence of added phospholipids (53). Given the fact that these patients do not bleed, why should they be at increased risk of developing thrombosis? Rather unconvincing explanations were advanced which involved an excessive generation of thromboplastin as a "compensatory phenomenon" to the presence of a circulating anticoagulant (26) or abnormalities of the fibrinolytic system (54, 55). More recently, a functional abnormality in antithrombin III was suggested as a possible explanation of recurrent thrombosis in patients with circulating LLAC (56).

A very interesting study by Carreras and co-workers (35) in a young woman with a lupus anticoagulant and a history of recurrent abortions with multiple arterial thrombosis demonstrated that the IgG plasma fraction from this patient reduced the release of PGI_2 in an "*in vitro*" system. This defect could be by-passed when the prostaglandin precursor, arachidonic acid, was exogenously added to the system. It seems reasonable, therefore, to postulate an interference of the "anticoagulant" gamma globulin with the mechanism involved in arachidonic acid release from endothelial cell membrane phospholipids. As PGI_2 is the most potent vascular inhibitor of platelet aggregation (57), its impaired release could contribute to the thrombotic tendency. This hypothesis is now the subject of numerous investigations (58, 59). Moreover, the repeatedly reported intrauterine deaths in these patients (5, 35, 60–65) appear to identify a new syndrome that might be explained by the inhibitory effect of the patients' IgG on PGI_2 production by tissues other than endothelium. A therapeutic approach to patient with lupus anticoagulant makes use of steroids and usually leads to amelioration of the primary disease and disappearance of the "anticoagulant" activity (37, 39, 66, 67).

Since bleeding is not a clinical problem in these patients, there is no need to treat a laboratory abnormality. When heparin or warfarin have been used to treat thrombotic complications in patients with lupus anticoagulant, the risk of bleeding related to these drugs has been comparable to the normal population (29, 48, 51, 61). Effective prevention of further thrombosis has been achieved by Mueh *et al.* (29) with continuous intravenous infusion of heparin at an average dose of 1000 IU/hr. None of the seven patients with lupus anticoagulant bled while being treated on this schedule. If a selective inhibitor of platelet aggregation becomes available, this should have a place in the future management of patients with reduced vascular PGI_2 associated with thrombi consisting almost entirely of platelets (58).

We wish to thank Professor J. C. McGiff and Professor J. S. Cameron for their critical discussion of this manuscript. We are also grateful to Donna Centi, Shirley Klein, Pam Blank, and Sallie McGiff for their help in its preparation.

1. Margolius A Jr, Jackson DP, Ratnoff OD. Circulating anticoagulants: Study of 40 cases and review of literature. Medicine **40**:145–202, 1961.
2. Conley CL, Hartmann RC. A hemorrhagic disorder caused by circulating anticoagulant in patients with disseminated lupus erythematosus. J Clin Invest **31**:621–622, 1952.
3. Feinstein DI, Rapaport SI. Acquired inhibitors of blood coagulation. In: Spaet TH, ed. Progress in Haemostasis and Thrombosis. New York, Grune & Stratton, pp75–95, 1972.
4. Lechner K. Acquired inhibitors in non-hemophilic patients. Haemostasis **3**:65–93, 1974.
5. Nilsson IM, Astedt B, Hedner U, Berezin D. Intrauterine death and circulating anticoagulant ("antithromboplastin"). Acta Med Scand **197**:153–159, 1975.
6. Rapp Y, Miller SP, Schwartz AR. Subepidermal bullous disease with a circulating anticoagulant. Arch Dermatol **99**:161–169, 1969.
7. Frick PG. Acquired circulating anticoagulants in systemic "collagen disease." Auto-immune thromboplastin deficiency. Blood **10**:691–706, 1955.
8. Lechner K. A new type of coagulation inhibitor. Thromb Diath Haemorrh **21**:482–499, 1969.
9. Mueller JF, Ratnoff OD, Heinle RW. Observations on the characteristics of an unusual circulating anticoagulant. J Lab Clin Med **38**:254–261, 1951.
10. Schleider MA, Nachman RL, Jaffe EA, Coleman M. A clinical study of the lupus anticoagulant. Blood **48**:499–509, 1976.
11. Carreras LO, Vermylen J. "Lupus" anticoagulant and prostacyclin. Lancet **1**:665, 1981.
12. Bernhardt B, Valletta M. Lupus anticoagulant in myelofibrosis. Amer J Med Sci **272**:229–231, 1976.
13. Exner T, Barber S, Kronenberg H, Rickard KA. Familial association of the lupus anticoagulant. Brit J Haematol **45**:89–96, 1980.
14. Hermansky F, Demjal S. Anticoagulant familial a activite antithromboplastique. Nouv. Rev. Fr. Hematol. **14**:12–25, 1959.
15. Rouget JP, Goudemand J, Montreuil G, Cosson A, Jaillard J. Lupus anticoagulant: A familial observation. Lancet **2**:105, 1982.
16. Breckenridge RT, Ratnoff OD. Studies on the site of action of a circulating anticoagulant in disseminated lupus erythematosus. Evidence that this anticoagulant inhibits the reaction between activated Stuart factor (factor X) and proaccelerin (factor V). Amer J Med **35**:813–819, 1963.
17. Castro O, Farber LR, Clyne LP. Circulating anticoagulants against factors IX and XI in systemic lupus erythematosus. Ann Intern Med **77**:543–548, 1972.
18. Cronberg S, Nilsson IM. Circulating anticoagulants against factors XI and XII together with massive spontaneous platelet aggregation. Scand J Haematol **10**:309–314, 1973.
19. Biggs R, Denson KWE. The mode of action of a

coagulation inhibitor in the blood of two patients with DLE. Brit J Haematol **10**:198–216, 1964.
20. Lee SL, Sanders M, Kahny HM. A disorder of blood coagulation in systemic lupus erythematosus. J Clin Invest **34**:1814–1822, 1955.
21. Medal LS, Lisker R. Circulating anticoagulants in disseminated lupus erythematosus. Brit J Haematol **5**:284–293, 1959.
22. Douglas AS, Clatanoff DV, McNicol GP, Bailey PAM. An atypical circulating anticoagulant. Scand J Haematol **3**:49–58, 1966.
23. Veltkamp JJ, Kerkhoven P, Loeliger EA. Circulating anticoagulant in disseminated lupus erythematosus. Haemostasis **2**:253–259, 1973/1974.
24. Exner T, Rickard KA, Kronenberg H. Studies on phospholipids in the action of a lupus coagulation inhibitor. Pathology **7**:319–328, 1975.
25. Mannucci PM, Canciani MT, Mari D, Meucci P. The varied sensitivity of partial thromboplastin and prothrombin time reagents in the demonstration of the lupus-like anticoagulant. Scand J Haematol **22**:423–432, 1973.
26. Bowie EJW, Thompson JH, Pascuzzi CA, Owen CA Jr. Thrombosis in systemic lupus erythematosus despite circulating anticoagulant. J Lab Clin Med **3**:416–430, 1963.
27. Thiagarajan P, Shapiro SS, DeMarco L. Monoclonal immunoglobulin M coagulation inhibitor with phospholipid specificity. Mechanism of a lupus anticoagulant. J Clin Invest **66**:397–405, 1980.
28. Laurell A, Nilsson IM. Hyperglobulinemia, circulating anticoagulant and biologic false positive Wassermann reaction. J Lab Clin Med **49**:694–707, 1957.
29. Mueh JR, Herbst KD, Rapaport SI. Thrombosis in patients with the lupus anticoagulant. Ann Intern Med **92**:156–159, 1980.
30. Gazengel C, Dougados M, Kremp O, Tron F. Anticoagulants circulants d'activite antiprothrombinase au cours du lupus erythemateux dissemine. Nouv Presse Med **9**:2325–2328, 1980.
31. Loeliger A. Prothrombin as cofactor of circulating anticoagulant in systemic lupus erythematosus. Thromb Diath Haemorrh **3**:237–256, 1959.
32. Yin ET, Gaston LW. Purification and kinetic studies on a circulating anticoagulant in a suspected case of lupus erythematosus. Thromb Diath Haemorrh **14**:88–115, 1965.
33. Rivard GE, Schiffman S, Rapaport SI. Cofactor of the "Lupus Anticoagulant." Thromb Diath Haemorrh **32**:554–563, 1974.
34. Exner T, Rickard KA, Kronenberg H. A sensitive test demonstrating lupus anticoagulant and its behavioral patterns. Brit J Haematol **40**:143–151, 1978.
35. Carreras LO, Defreyn G, Machin SJ, Vermylen J, Deman R, Spitz B, Vas Assche A. Arterial thrombosis, intrauterine death and "lupus" anticoagulant: Detection of immunoglobulin interfering with prostacyclin formation. Lancet **1**:244–246, 1981.
36. Regan MG, Lachner H, Karpatkin S. Platelet function and coagulation profile in lupus erythematosus: Studies in 50 patients. Ann Intern Med **81**:462–468, 1974.
37. Green D. Circulating anticoagulants. Med Clin N Amer **56**:145–151, 1972.
38. Houbouyan L, Soria J, Goguel A. Analysis of an autoimmune antibody (IgM class) in a case of chronic lymphocytic leukemia. Haemostasis **3**:171–182, 1974.
39. Gonyea L, Herdman R, Bridges RA. The coagulation abnormalities in systemic lupus erythematosus. Thromb Diath Haemorrh **20**:457–464, 1968.
40. Lechner K. Acquired inhibitors in auto- and isoimmune disease. Thromb Diath Haemorrh (Suppl) **45**:227–241, 1971.
41. Schick PK, Kurica KB, Chacko GK. Localization of phosphatidylethanolamine and phosphatidylserine in the human platelet plasma membrane. J Clin Invest **57**:1221–1226, 1976.
42. Lafer EM, Rauch J, Andrzejewski C Jr, Mudd D, Furie B, Furie B, Schwartz RS, Stollar BD. Polyspecific monoclonal lupus autoantibodies reactive with both polynucleotides and phospholipids. J Exp Med **153**:897–909, 1981.
43. Shapiro SS, Hultin M. Acquired inhibitors to blood coagulation factors. Semin Thromb Hemostasis **1**:336–385, 1975.
44. Boxer M, Ellman L, Carvalho A. The lupus anticoagulant. Arthritis Rheum **19**:1244–1248, 1976.
45. Edwards RL, Rick ME, Wakem CJ. Studies on a circulating anticoagulant in procainamide-induced lupus erythematosus. Arch Intern Med **141**:1688–1690, 1981.
46. Shaulian E, Shoenfeld Y, Berliner S, Shaklai M, Pinkhas J. Surgery in patients with circulating lupus anticoagulant. Int Surg **66**:157–159, 1981.
47. Corrigan J, Patterson JH, May NE. Incoagulability of the blood in systemic lupus erythematosus. Amer J Dis Child **119**:365–369, 1970.
48. Williams H, Laurent R, Gibson T. The lupus coagulation inhibitor and venous thrombosis: A report of four cases. Clin Lab Haematol **2**:139–144, 1980.
49. Alexandre P, Andre E, Briquel ME, Labrude P, Streiff F. Inhibiteurs acquis de la coagulation. Nouv Presse Med **9**:2901–2904, 1980.
50. Peck B, Hoffman GS, Franck WA. Thrombophlebitis in systemic lupus erythematosus. JAMA **240**:1728–1730, 1978.
51. Manoharan A, Gibson L, Rush B, Feery BJ. Recurrent venous thrombosis with a "lupus" coagulation inhibitor in the absence of systemic lupus. Aust NZ Med J **7**:422–426, 1977.
52. Clauvel JP, Sultan Y. Anticoagulant circulant, et syndrome de Willebrand au cours du lupus erythemateux dissemine. Actual. Hematol **11**:109–121, 1977.
53. Milelich JP, Jackson CM, Majerus PW. Properties of the factor Xa binding site on human platelets. J Biol Chem **253**:6908–6916, 1978.
54. Johansson EA, Niemi KM, Mustakallio KK. A pe-

ripheral vascular syndrome overlapping with systemic lupus erythematosus. Dermatologica **155**:257–267, 1977.
55. Sanfelippo MJ, Drayna CJ. Prekallikrein inhibition associated with the lupus anticoagulant. Amer J Clin Pathol **77**:275–279, 1982.
56. Cosgrift TM, Martin BA. Low functional and high antigenic antithrombin III level in a patient with the lupus anticoagulant and recurrent thrombosis. Arthritis Rheum **24**:94–96, 1981.
57. Moncada S, Higgs EA, Vane JR. Human arterial and venous tissues generate prostacyclin (prostaglandin X), a potent inhibitor of platelet aggregation. Lancet **1**:18–20, 1977.
58. Slater D. "Lupus" and prostacyclin formation. Lancet **1**:393, 1981.
59. Marchesi D, Parbtani A, Frampton G, Livio M, Remuzzi G, Cameron JS. Thrombotic tendency in systemic lupus erythematosus. Lancet **1**:719, 1981.
60. Carreras LO, Vermylen J, Spitz B, Van Assche A. "Lupus" anticoagulant and inhibition of prostacyclin formation in patients with repeated abortion, intrauterine growth retardation and intrauterine death. Brit J Obstet Gynaecol **88**:890–894, 1981.
61. Soulier JP, Boffa MC. Avortements a repetition thromboses et anticoagulant circulant anti-thromboplastine. Nouv Presse Med **9**:859–864, 1980.
62. DeWolf F, Carreras LO, Moerman P, Vermylen J, Van Assche A, Renaer M. Decidual vasculopathy and extensive placental infarction in a patient with repeated thromboembolic accidents, recurrent fetal loss and a lupus anticoagulant. Amer J Obstet Gynecol **142**:829–834, 1982.
63. Duran-Suarez JR, Pigrau-Serrallach C, Bosch-Gil J, Ordi-Ros J, Triginer-Boixeda J. Possible relationship between circulating anticoagulants and recurrent abortion. Haematologica **67**:320–321, 1982.
64. Gabriel L, Samama M, Conard J, Horellou MH, Servelle M. Anticoagulant circulant antiprothrombinase thromboses et avortements spontanes, une nouvelle observation. Nouv Presse Med **9**:2159, 1980.
65. Firkin BG, Howard MA, Radford N. Possible relationship between lupus inhibitor and recurrent abortion in young women. Lancet **2**:366, 1980.
66. Ramot B, Singer K. An unusual circulating anticoagulant in systemic lupus erythematosus. Acta Haematol (Basel) **16**:158–169, 1956.
67. Rapaport SI, Ames SB, Duvall BJ. A plasma coagulation defect in systemic lupus erythematosus arising from hypoprothrombinemia combined with antiprothrombinase activity. Blood **15**:212–227, 1960.

P.S.E.B.M. Vol. 176, 1984.

PROCEEDINGS OF THE SOCIETY FOR EXPERIMENTAL BIOLOGY AND MEDICINE **176**, 342–345 (1984)

Mineralization in Rat Metaphyseal Bone Exhibits a Circadian Stage Dependency[1] (41880)

JEAN E. RUSSELL, BRENT GRAZMAN, AND DAVID J. SIMMONS

Washington University School of Medicine, Department of Surgery, Division of Orthopedic Surgery, St. Louis, Missouri 63110

Abstract. Density gradient fractionation analysis of rat metaphyseal bone was used to delineate the biorhythmic changes in bone matrix mineralization. Seventy-two 4-week-old rats were entrained to 12-hr light, 12-hr dark cycles (light, 0800–2000 hr; darkness, 2000–0800 hr) for 4 weeks. All animals were fed *ad lib.* on Purina laboratory rat chow and tap water. Groups of 10–12 rats were killed by cervical dislocation at 4-hr intervals during a 24-hr period, and the tibias were then biopsied and frozen in liquid N_2. Metaphyseal bone was fractionated via bromoform–toluene density gradients into specific gravity fractions ranging from 1.7 to 2.8. Density gradient fractions were analyzed for concentrations of calcium and inorganic phosphorus.

Chronograms indicated that the accumulation of both calcium and inorganic phosphorus into the newly forming/least-dense mineral moieties of bone (1.3–1.7 sp grav) showed a single peak in the biorhythm of the rat. A statistically significant circadian rhythm of mineralization was detected for calcium ($P < 0.001$) and inorganic phosphorus ($P < 0.039$), with peaks during the environmental dark span. These results suggest that the physiological phasing of bone mineralization in the light–dark synchronized rat, is similar to that previously noted for cartilage mineralization and is antiphasal to the midday peak in bone collagen synthesis.

Circadian rhythms are a characteristic feature of the physiology of most tissues in the body. In a general sense, this means that physiological functions have excursions in activity that often range from two- to fourfold, with a single peak (acrophase) and minimum (nadir) during the course of a 24-hr day (if sampling is performed at 3- to 4-hr intervals). There is a growing awareness that these biorhythms are not only intrinsically interesting, but also can have a practical impact on physiological/endocrinological investigations (1, 2).

Our laboratory has focused its efforts on the chronobiology of the skeleton and has examined a spectrum of normal metabolic rhythms in bone and cartilage (3–5). Most recently we have asked how the timing of these changes is related to the timing of mineralization in rat epiphyseal cartilage (4), and the data suggested that the mineralization of the epiphyseal cartilage occurs most actively at night. Since this mineralization of cartilage is antiphasal to the rhythm of net collagen synthesis in both epiphyseal cartilage (3) and bone (5), and since a lag-time between matrix formation and mineralization has been demonstrated in bone (6, 7) as well as cartilage (4), this study was undertaken to more fully delineate the biorhythmic changes in bone matrix mineralization.

Materials and Methods. During the spring months, 72 young male rats (Sprague–Dawley; 4 weeks of age; 100–120 g body wt) were conditioned to a 12-hr/12-hr LD cycle for 4 weeks (light, 0800–2000 hr; darkness, 2000–0800 hr). All animals were fed Purina laboratory rat chow *ad lib.* and tap water. The animals (275 ± 25 g body wt) were then randomized into groups of 10–12, and a different group was killed (cervical dislocation) every 4 hr throughout a single 24-hr time span. The tibias were recovered at autopsy, frozen in liquid N_2, lyophilized, and stored at −80°C. The proximal metaphyseal bone trabecular region was dissected from each tibia at the time of use.

Mineral maturation profiles. The status of metaphyseal bone matrix mineralization was assessed by a bromoform–toluene density gradient fractionation technique as previously used in this (8, 9) and other laboratories (10, 11). The bone was ground to a 40 μm particle size in a Spex Mill, and separated into four

[1] Work supported by USPHS Grant AM16391.

0037-9727/84 $1.50

specific gravity fractions (1.3–1.7, 1.8–1.9, 2.0–2.1, and 2.2–2.8 sp grav). The amount of calcium (Ca) or inorganic phosphorus (P_i) in each specific gravity fraction was analyzed by methods previously described (8), and the data were expressed as a percentage of the total Ca and P_i. It has already been established that this gradient profile of bone reflects states of mineral–collagen maturation/mineralization (8, 10, 12). The lowest density, least mature fraction (1.3–1.7) is synonymous with newly mineralizing moieties of bone (10, 12). Specific gravity fractions above 1.7 are not correlated with the newly forming bone mineral.

Statistics. The presence or absence of a significant circadian rhythm was assessed by the Cosinor method of Halberg (13). This is a least-squares analysis using a cosine function and is usually fitted to a 24-hr time interval. The test provides a P value which indicates the significance of the fit of the cosine curve to the data, and thus it is a way to detect the presence of statistically significant rhythms. The analyses also provide information about the time in the rhythm when the peak value in the curve (acrophase) would be expected to occur.

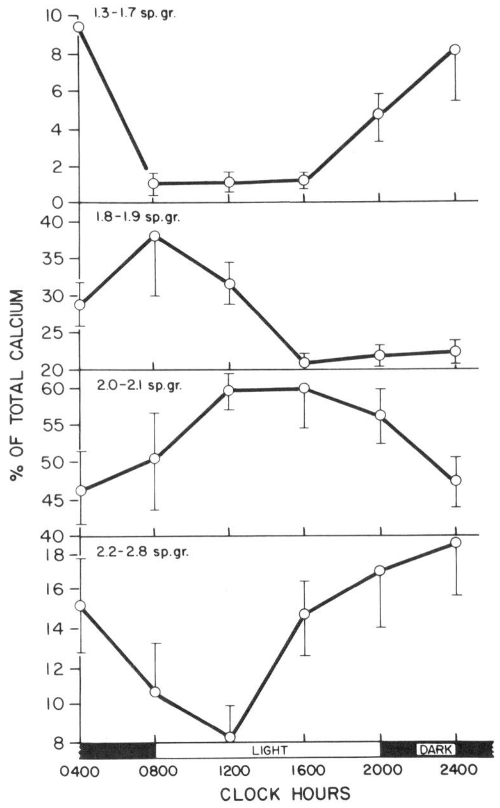

FIG. 1. Plot of the circadian changes in rat metaphyseal calcium: the bone was fractionated into four specific gravity fractions on bromoform–toluene density gradients as described (8). $N = 6$ for each point of observation, and each point represents the mean ± SEM. The statistical significance of each of the rhythms and their acrophase times are reported in Table I.

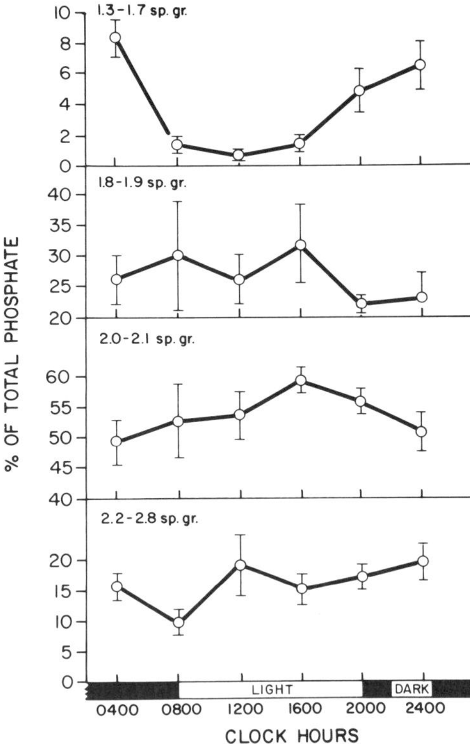

FIG. 2. Plot of the circadian changes in rat metaphyseal inorganic phosphorus: the bone was fractionated into four specific gravity fractions on bromoform–toluene density gradients as described (8). $N = 6$ for each point of observation, and each point represents the mean ± SEM. A statistically significant rhythm as defined by the cosinor method was only found for the 1.7-sp grav fraction (see Table I).

Results. Density gradient analysis of the rat tibial metaphyseal bone from rats revealed that there were striking changes in the mineral profiles at different times in the 24-hr body rhythm (Figs. 1 and 2). In normal 8-week-old male rats, the percentage of the total bone mineral in the lowest density gradient fraction (1.3–1.7 sp grav) was highest during the daily

TABLE I. COSINOR ANALYSIS OF THE BIORHYTHMICITY OF BONE CALCIUM AND INORGANIC PHOSPHORUS LEVELS: CHARACTERIZATION VIA DENSITY GRADIENT FRACTIONATION

Measurement	Density gradient fraction (sp grav)	P^a	N	Peak or acrophase in clock hours (±95% CL)
Calcium (% of total)	1.7	0.001	36	1.18 ± 0.86
	1.8–1.9	0.010	33	8.13 ± 1.16
	2.0–2.1	0.020	35	15.08 ± 1.28
	2.2–2.8	0.009	34	22.74 ± 1.13
Inorganic phosphorus (% of total)	1.7	0.039	36	24.44 ± 1.40
	1.8–1.9	NS	36	—
	2.0–2.1	NS	36	—
	2.2–2.8	NS	36	—

[a] P value was determined according to the Cosinor statistical analysis as described under Materials and Methods. In the absence of a significant fit of the data to a cosine curve, no peak or acrophase time can be ascribed to the data.

dark span when it accounted for as much as 8–10% of the total bone calcium or inorganic phosphorus. The 1.3- to 1.7-sp grav fraction accounted for only 1.0% of total bone Ca and P_i during the daily 12-hr light span. Cosinor analysis of the data (Table I) revealed that the distribution of Ca and P_i within the 1.3- to 1.7-sp grav fraction did show a significant circadian rhythmicity. The peak time (acrophases) of Ca accumulation in this low-density fraction was 0100 hr, while that for P_i was 2400 hr. These changes in the mineral distribution throughout the 24-hr period were not accompanied by alterations in either total bone Ca or P_i (data not shown). The average metaphyseal calcium level was 186.03 ± 3.54 mg/g dry wt of bone and inorganic phosphorus was 95.52 ± 2.93 mg/g dry wt of bone.

The profiles in Figs. 1 and 2 also suggest a time-related shift of Ca and P_i into progressively higher specific gravity (more dense/mature mineral) fractions. The variations within each clock-hour group were less for bone Ca than P_i (see P values for different specific gravity fractions in Table I).

Discussion. The intent of this study was to extend our observations about the normal biorhythmic changes of rat tibial bone metabolism. Previously, we and others have demonstrated that in light–dark (LD) synchronized *ad lib.*-fed rats, the levels of bone and cartilage matrix production peak during the early hours of the light span (daytime period) (3, 5, 14). In such animals, epiphyseal cartilage mineralization appeared to progress most actively during the environmental dark span (nighttime), but we had no firm information about the time in the body rhythm when the rat tibiae mineralized. However, given the synchrony of matrix biosynthesis in cartilage and bone and the fact that a mineralization lag time has been documented in both tissues (3, 4, 6, 7), it seemed reasonable to anticipate that the most active period of new bone mineralization would occur at night. The data developed in this study by the density gradient fractionation technique affirmed that inference. The mineral maturation profiles showed that the highest percentage of newly deposited mineral (1.3–1.7 sp grav) occurred during the nocturnal hours of the 24-hr period. Thus, it appears that the pace of cartilage and bone mineralization is antiphasal to the pace of matrix biosynthesis in the *ad lib.*-fed, LD-synchronized rat (4, 5).

While the density gradient fractionation method has provided valuable information about how metabolic disorders of bone affect mineral maturation (8, 9, 15–18), this study demonstrates for the first time that the precise profiles are circadian stage-dependent. The shifts in mineralization profiles across the 24-hr time span call attention to the need to observe basic chronobiological principles in experimental design and interpretation of laboratory results.

1. Vazquez AM, Schutt-Aine J, Drash AL, Kenny FM, Richards C, Anthony D. Diurnal patterns of secretion of cortisol and growth hormone in normal adolescents, in patients with exogenous growth hormone, in patients with exogenous and endogenous Cushing's syndromes, in patients with diabetes mellitus, and in a fasting subject. J Pediatr **83**:578–586, 1973.
2. Riggs BL, Arnaud CD, Goldsmith RS, Taylor FH. Plasma kinetic and acute effects of pharmacologic doses of porcine calcitonin in man. J Clin Endocrinol Metab **33**:115–127, 1971.
3. Simmons DJ, Whiteside LA, Whitson SW. Biorhythmic profiles in the rat skeleton. Metab Bone Dis Rel Res **2**:49–64, 1979.
4. Simmons DJ, Arsenis C, Whitson SW, Kahn SE, Boskey AL, Gollub N. Mineralization of rat epiphyseal cartilage: A circadian rhythm. Min Electrolyte Metab **9**:28–37, 1983.
5. Russell JE, Simmons DJ, Huber B, Roos BA. Meal timing as a zeitgeber for skeletal deoxyribonucleic acid and collagen synthesis rhythms. Endocrinology **113**:2035–2042, 1983.
6. Wergedal JE, Baylink DJ. Electron microprobe measurements of bone mineralization rate. Amer J Physiol **226**:345–352, 1974.
7. Heersche JNM, Tam CS, Jones G. Measurement of the apposition rate of mineralized bone matrix and osteoid in normal, D-restricted and D-repleted rats using simultaneous labelling with ^{3}H proline and tetracycline. In: Vies A, ed. The Chemistry and Biology of Mineralized Connective Tissues. New York, Elsevier/North-Holland, pp 313–315, 1981.
8. Russell JE, Avioli LV. Effect of experimental chronic renal insufficiency on bone mineral and collagen. J Clin Invest **51**:3072–3079, 1972.
9. Russell JE, Termine JD, Avioli LV. Experimental renal osteodystrophy: The response to 25-hydroxycholecalciferol and dichloromethylene diphosphonate therapy. J Clin Invest **56**:548–554, 1975.
10. Quinaux N, Richelle LO. X-ray diffraction and infrared analysis of bone specific gravity fraction in the growing rat. Isr J Med Sci **3**:677–690, 1967.
11. Letteri JM, Biltz RM, Ellis KJ, Martino A, Yatsumura S, Brook D, Cohn SH, Pellegrino ED. Arrested bone growth and mineral maturation in subtotally nephrectomized rats. Clin Sci Mol Med **53**:479–484, 1977.
12. Herman H, Richelle L. Le calcium exchangeable de la substance minerale de l'os etudiee a l'aide de ^{45}Ca. Activite comparee de fractions d'os totale de densite differente. Bull Soc Chim Biol **43**:273–282, 1961.
13. Halberg F, Carandente F, Cornelissen G, Katinas G. Glossary of chronobiology. Chronobiologia **4**(Suppl 1):1–189, 1977.
14. Hansson LI, Stenstrom A, Thorngren K-G. Diurnal variation of longitudinal bone growth in the rabbit. Acta Orthop Scand **45**:499–507, 1974.
15. Dickson IR, Kodicek E. Effect of vitamin D deficiency on bone formation in the chick. Biochem J **182**:429–435, 1979.
16. Lian JB, Glimcher MJ, Roufosse AH, Hauschka PV, Gallop PM, Cohen-Solal L, Reit B. Alterations of the γ-carboxyglutamic acid and osteocalcin concentrations in vitamin D-deficient chick bone. J Biol Chem **257**:4999–5003, 1982.
17. Simmons DJ, Russell JE, Winter F, Tran Van P, Vignery A, Baron R, Rosenberg GD, Walker WV. The effect of spaceflight on the non-weight bearing bones of the rat skeleton. Amer J Physiol **244**:R319–R326, 1983.
18. Simmons DJ, Chang S-L, Russell JE, Grazman B, Webster D, Oloff C. The effect of protracted tetracycline treatment on bone growth and maturation. Clin Orthop Relat Res **180**: 253–259, 1983.

Received January 23, 1984. P.S.E.B.M. 1984, Vol. 176.
Accepted April 10, 1984.

PROCEEDINGS OF THE SOCIETY FOR EXPERIMENTAL BIOLOGY AND MEDICINE **176**, 346–349 (1984)

In Vitro Response of Hepatic Lysosomes to Endogenous and Exogenous Cationic Compounds (41881)

JAMES H. POWELL AND MARCUS M. REIDENBERG

Departments of Pharmacology and Medicine, Cornell University Medical College, 1300 York Avenue, New York, New York 10021

Abstract. An investigation of the effect of four cationic compounds on rat liver lysosomes was carried out. Lysosomes from homogenized rat liver were isolated by differential centrifugation at 0–5°C in 0.3 *M* sucrose. These lysosomes were then incubated for 1 hr at 37°C in 0.25 *M* glycine solution containing widely varied concentrations of the test agent. The lysosomes were resedimented and the *N*-acetyl-*β*-glucosaminidase (NAG) activity was measured in the supernatant and in the remaining pellet after disruption. Spermine, ferric ion, mepacrine, and gentamicin all produced dose-dependent effects on these lysosomes. Low concentrations of these compounds inhibited the release of NAG into the supernatant while high concentrations enhanced the release of NAG. This effect of these cationic compounds on the lysosomal membrane may be a mechanism by which they produce cellular toxicity with the organ or tissue selectivity being related to the distribution of the cation.

Since the discovery of the lysosome by de Duve and co-workers (1), the functional integrity of the membrane of this organelle has been accepted as essential to its definition. This is primarily due to the ability of enzymes contained within lysosomes to digest nearly all cellular constituents. The lysosomal membrane is known to be composed, to a large degree, of lipids (3, 4). Consistent with this, other investigators have demonstrated lysosomal membrane stability to be inversely related to lipolytic activity (5) and, but less sensitive, to the actions of proteases (6).

We have recently published data showing effects of cations on renal cortical lysosomes and suggested that cationic compounds which reach the proximal renal tubular lysosomes can cause renal injury by decreasing lysosomal phospholipase activity (7, 8). In this study, we examined the response of lysosomes from hepatic tissue to endogenous and exogenous cationic compounds to determine if lysosomes from other types of cells might respond in a manner similar to lysosomes from kidney cells.

Materials and Method. Spermine and gentamicin sulfate were purchased from Sigma Chemical Company, St. Louis, Missouri. Mepacrine hydrochloride was purchased from ICN Pharmaceuticals Inc., Plainview, New York.

Male Fisher 344 rats weighing between 200 and 250 g were anesthetized with subcutaneous sodium pentobarbital. Rats were perfused transcardially with 10 ml of cooled 0.3 *M* sucrose containing 1 m*M* EDTA at pH 7.0 (hypertonic sucrose). Livers were removed and placed in a rinsing bath of hypertonic sucrose at 0–5°C. The entire homogenization and isolation procedure was carried out at 0.5°C. After rinsing, the livers were homogenized in hypertonic sucrose with 5 strokes of a manual all glass Dounce homogenizer and 5 strokes of a Potter–Elvejehm homogenizer with Teflon pestle rotating at 1500 rpm. The homogenate was then centrifuged twice in a Sorvall RC-2B centrifuge with an SS-34 rotor at 750*g* for 10 min. The sediment was discarded. The supernatants were recentrifuged at 10,000*g* for 10 min. The supernatant and other cellular debris overlying the light brown crude lysosomal–mitochondrial pellet (lysosomal pellet) was discarded. The lysosomal pellet was then resuspended in 3 ml of hypertonic sucrose and resedimented as a wash procedure and the supernatant was discarded.

A pH 7.0 solution of 0.25 *M* glycine (isotonic glycine) was prepared and compounds to be tested were dissolved at 10 times a final concentration in isotonic glycine. The lysosomal pellet was also resuspended in isotonic glycine. Two-tenths milliliter of drug/glycine solution was added to 1.8 ml of lysosomal suspension (incubation mixture) in separate centrifuge tubes, gently vortexed, and incu-

0037-9727/84 $1.50

bated for 1 hr at 37°C in a gently shaking water bath. Two-tenths milliliter of isotonic glycine containing no drug was added to 1.8 ml of lysosomal suspension and incubated as a control. Immediately after incubation, the incubation mixtures were cooled, resedimented, and the supernatants were removed. The remaining pellets were disrupted in 2 ml of 0.1% Triton X-100 containing 100 m*M* KCl.

Supernatants and disrupted pellets were diluted appropriately and assayed for the activity of the lysosomal enzyme *N*-acetyl-β-glucosaminidase (EC 3.2.1.30) (NAG) by our previously published method (7). The percentage NAG released was calculated as the ratio of the NAG activity in the supernatant to the total NAG activity in the supernatant and the pellet multiplied by 100.

Results and Discussion. Hepatic lysosomes incubated in the presence of ferric ion or spermine in isotonic glycine demonstrated the responses shown in Fig. 1. Low concentrations of these compounds inhibited NAG release while high concentrations enhanced NAG release. A similar response was observed when mepacrine or gentamicin was added to the incubation mixture (Fig. 2).

These effects on liver lysosomes are similar to those produced by aminoglycosides (7) and other cations (8) on kidney lysosomes. Other investigators have shown mepacrine (9), the polyamino compounds gentamicin (10, 11) and spermine (12), as well as ferric ions and other metal ions (13), to be phospholipase inhibitors. These compounds appear to have little in common except for the mechanism by which they are thought to inhibit phospholipase enzymes. These cations appear to bind to the negative charge of the phospholipid substrate thereby inhibiting phospholipase enzyme–substrate interaction (9, 10, 12, 13). This is a mechanism of phospholipase inhibition that has been described for many cationic compounds (9, 14).

We have used ferric ion and spermine as examples of endogenous compounds and gentamicin and mepacrine as examples of exogenous compounds. These compounds are not degraded by lysosomal enzymes so they can remain intact in the lysosome. This is in contrast to albumin and some other proteins which can inhibit lysosomal phospholipases (5) but are degraded by lysosomal enzymes, a process which disinhibits the phospholipase. Amino acid hydrolysis products of proteins permeate the lysosomal membrane poorly, (15, 16) and have been suggested to diffuse out of the lysosomes through pores in the membrane which are dependent on phospho-

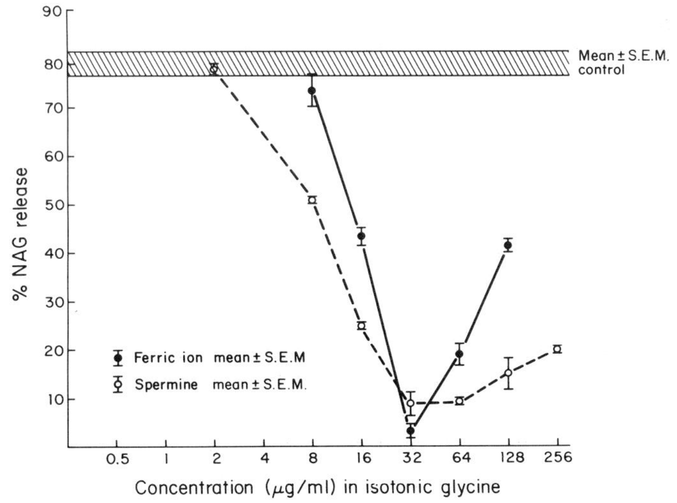

FIG. 1. The percentage NAG release from hepatic lysosomes as a function of the concentration of ferric ion or spermine in isotonic glycine. Values are means ± SEM of four replicate determinations at each drug concentration except for 128 μg/ml ferric ion and 2, 8, 16, and 64 μg/ml spermine which were done in duplicate.

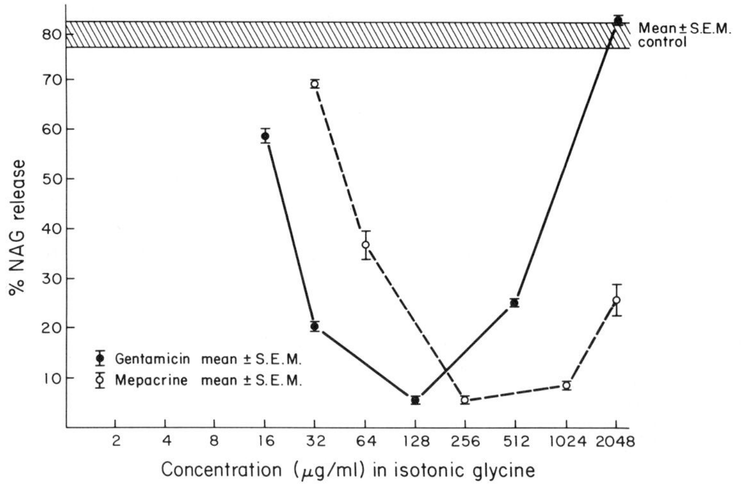

FIG. 2. The percentage NAG release from lysosomes as a function of the concentration of gentamicin or mepacrine in isotonic glycine. Values are means ± SEM of four replicate determinations at each drug concentration except for 8 and 6 μg/ml gentamicin and 8, 32, and 256 μg/ml mepacrine which were done in duplicate.

lipase activity as described by Lucy (4). Support for this mechanism of efflux is the failure to demonstrate carrier-mediated processes for transport of amino acids out of lysosomes (15). If phospholipase activity is inhibited, then these osmotically active hydrolysis products will remain inside the lysosome drawing water into the organelle. This should cause it to swell and even eventually rupture. Stimulation of endogenous proteolysis has been shown to transiently increase the swelling, fragility, and osmotic sensitivity (17, 18) of lysosomes as well as decrease their density (18). In addition to this, the compounds we examined, spermine (19), gentamicin (20), mepacrine (21), and iron (22) have been associated with lysosomal swelling and lipid accumulation in animals. Lysosomes which have accumulated gentamicin (23) and iron (24) have also been associated with increased lysosomal fragility as well as lysosomal enzyme accumulation. This accumulation of enzymes may be related to the inhibition of secretion caused by stabilization of lysosomes (4, 8).

The four compounds tested have little structural similarity. Yet these compounds appear to produce similar effects on lysosomes from renal (7, 8) and hepatic tissue. The selective toxicity of aminoglycosides (20), polyamines (19), iron (24), and the cationic amphiphillic class of drugs (of which mepacrine is a prototype) to specific types of cells may be related to differences in mechanisms by which these compounds distribute to or are accumulated by different cell types. Iron may reach high concentrations in lysosomes through sequestration of heme-containing proteins in overload states (25). Gentamicin seems to accumulate through pinocytosis by proximal renal tubular cells (26) but probably less so by other cells in which it would have to compete with serum proteins for pinocytotic uptake (27). Mepacrine, as well as other cationic amphiliphillic drugs, appears to accumulate by simple diffusion and ion trapping of the weak bases at the low pH of lysosomes (9, 21). Accumulation of spermine by lysosomes has not been shown. However, in situations where spermine is pathologically increased in extracellular fluid, several pathways might be utilized. Spermine may bind to sites for pinocytosis as in renal cells (28). Since it also binds covalently to some serum proteins (29) it may be pinocytosed as a part of this structure and released inside the lysosome with hydrolysis of the protein (29).

In summary, the cationic compounds, ferric ion, spermine, mepacrine, and gentamicin, produce a biphasic effect on hepatic lysosomes, *in vitro,* just as cationic compounds affect kidney lysosomes *in vitro* (7, 8). Low concentrations of these compounds stabilize lysosomes while high concentrations disrupt them. This lysosomal effect may be a mechanism by which cationic compounds injure cells. The organ or tissue selectivity by the particular chemical would then be related to the distribution of the chemical to the lysosomes of the specific cells involved.

We thank Dr. B. Robert Meyer and Kathleen Restivo for their helpful criticism and assistance. This work was supported in part by Grant AG01441 of the NIH. Dr. Powell is the recipient of a fellowship award from NIH Grant 5-T32-GM07488 and a grant from Merck and Company.

1. de Duve C, Pressman BC, Gianetto R, Wattiaux R, Appelmans F. Tissue fractionation studies. Biochem J **60**:604–617, 1955.
2. Sawant PL, Desai ID, Tappel AL. Digestive capacity of purified lysosomes. Biochim Biophys Acta **85**:93–102, 1964.
3. Dean RT, Barret AJ. Lysosomes. Essays Biochem **12**:1–40, 1976.
4. Lucy JA. Lysosomal membranes. In: Dingle JT, Fell HB, eds. Lysosomes in Biology and Pathology. Amsterdam, North-Holland, Vol 2:p313, 1969.
5. Weglicki WB, Ruth RC, Owens K, Griffin HD, and Waite BM. Changes in lipid composition of triton filled lysosomes during lysis. Biochim Biophys Acta **337**:145–152, 1974.
6. Romeo D, Stagni N, Sottocasa GL, Pugliarello MC, De Bernard B, Vittar F. Lysosomes in heart tissue. Biochim Biophys Acta **130**:64–80, 1966.
7. Powell JH, Reidenberg MM. In vitro response of rat and human kidney lysosomes to aminoglycosides. Biochem Pharmacol **31**:3447–3453, 1982.
8. Powell JH, Reidenberg MM. Further studies of the response of kidney lysosomes to aminoglycosides. Biochem Pharmacol **32**:3213–3220, 1983.
9. Kunz H, Hesse B, Bohn E. Effects of antimalarial drugs on several rat-liver lysosomal enzymes involved in phosphatidylethanolamine catabolism. Biochim Biophys Acta **713**:112–117, 1982.
10. Hostetler KY, Hall LB. Inhibition of kidney lysosomal phospholipases A and C by aminoglycoside antibiotics. Proc Natl Acad Sci USA **79**:1663–1667, 1982.
11. Feldman S, Wang WY, Kaloyanides GJ. J Pharmacol Exp Ther **220**:514–520, 1981.
12. Sechii AM, Cabrini L, Landi L, Pasquali P, Lenaz G. Inhibition of phospholipase A2 and phospholipase C by polyamines. Arch Biochem Biophys **186**:248–254, 1978.
13. Waite M, Griffin HD, Franson R. The phospholipases A of lysosomes. In: Dingle JT, Dean RT, eds. Lysosomes in Biology and Pathology. Amsterdam, North-Holland, Vol 5:p257, 1976.
14. Bangham AD, Dawson RMC. Control of lecithinase activity by the electrophoretic charge on its substrate surface. Nature (London) **182**:1292–1293, 1958.
15. Reeves J. Accumulation of aminoacids by lysosomes incubated with amino acid methyl esters. J Biol Chem **254**:8914–8921, 1979.
16. Reijngoud DJ, Tager JM. The permeability properties of the lysosomal membrane. Biochim Biophys Acta **472**:419–449, 1977.
17. Mortimore GE, Ward WF. Behavior of the lysosomal system during organ perfusion. In: Dingle JT, Dean RT, eds. Lysosomes in Biology and Pathology. Amsterdam, North-Holland, Vol 5:p157, 1975.
18. Deter RL, de Duve C. Influence of glucagon, an inducer of cellular autophagy, on some physical properties of rat liver lysosomes. J Cell Biol **33**:437–449, 1967.
19. Fisher ER, Rosenthal SM. Pathology and pathogenesis of spermine-induced renal disease. Arch Pathol **57**:244–253, 1951.
20. Kaloyanides GJ, Pastoriza-Munoz E. Aminoglycoside nephrotoxicity. Kidney Int **18**:571–582, 1980.
21. Lullman-Rauch R. Drug induced lysosomal storage disorders. In: Dingle JT, Jaques DJ, Shaw IW, eds. Lysosomes in Applied Biology and Therapeutics. Amsterdam, North-Holland, Vol 6:p49, 1979.
22. Miller F. Hemoglobin absorption by the cells of the proximal convoluted tubule in mouse kidney. J Biophys Biochem Cytol **8**:689–718, 1960.
23. Meisner H. Effect of gentamicin on the subcellular distribution of renal *β-N*-acetylglucosaminidase activity. Biochem Pharmacol **30**:2949–2952, 1981.
24. Peters TJ, Seymour CA. Acid hydrolase activities and lysosomal integrity in liver biopsies from patients with iron overload. Clin Sci Mol Med **50**:75–78, 1976.
25. Selden C, Owen M, Hopkins JMP, Peters TJ. Studies on the concentration and intracellular localization of iron overload with special reference to their role in lysosomal disruption. Brit J Haematol **44**:593–603, 1980.
26. Just M, Erdmann G, Habermann E. The renal handling of polybasic drugs. Naunyn-Schmiedebergs' Arch Pharmacol **300**:57–66, 1977.
27. Tulkens P, Aubert-Tulkens G, Van Hoof F, Trouet A. The lysosomal toxicity of aminoglycosides. In: Fillastre JP, ed. Nephrotoxicity. New York, Masson, p231, 1978.
28. Just M, Habermann E. The renal handling of polybasic drugs. Naunyn-Schmiedebergs' Arch Pharmacol **300**:67–76, 1977.
29. Aigner-Held R, Daves GD. Polyamine metabolites in man and higher animals—A review of the literature. Physiol Chem Phys **12**:389–400, 1980.

Received December 2, 1983. P.S.E.B.M. 1984, Vol. 176.
Accepted April 13, 1984.

PROCEEDINGS OF THE SOCIETY FOR EXPERIMENTAL BIOLOGY AND MEDICINE **176**, 350–355 (1984)

Dopaminergic and Cholinergic Muscarinic Receptor Effects of L-Alphacetylmethadol (LAAM) and Its Metabolites[1] (41882)

ALBERT E. LANGLEY,[2] STEPHEN G. SMITH, AND ROBERT L. ZEID

Department of Pharmacology and Toxicology, Wright State University School of Medicine, Dayton, Ohio 45435

Abstract. In isolated rat hearts L-alphacetylmethadol (LAAM) produced a concentration-dependent decrease in the spontaneous beating rate. This effect was completely prevented by 1.0 μM atropine. Chronic treatment of rats with LAAM increased the number of striatal dopamine receptors measured by [^{3}H]spiroperidol binding. The affinity of these binding sites for [^{3}H]spiroperidol was unchanged by LAAM treatment. There were no significant changes in the number or affinity of binding sites for the labeled muscarinic antagonist [^{3}H]quinuclidinyl benzilate ([^{3}H]QNB) with chronic LAAM treatment. The ability of LAAM, nor-LAAM, or dinor-LAAM to antagonize the binding of [^{3}H]spiroperidol (40 pM) or [^{3}H]QNB (125 pM) to striatal membrane fragments was tested. The measured affinity constants for LAAM and metabolites were 100–3000 times higher than the affinity constants of unlabeled spiroperidol at [^{3}H]spiroperidol binding sites. The affinity constants of LAAM and metabolites at muscarinic binding sites were 10–20 times higher than pilocarpine and 5000–8000 times higher than atropine. These results suggest that LAAM can produce some of its effects by acting as a weak agonist at muscarinic receptor sites.

Stickney (1) reported that L-alphacetylmethadol (LAAM) produced an atropine-sensitive slowing of guinea pig isolated atria. We confirmed this bradycardic effect in isolated perfused guinea pig hearts (2). Atropine blocked LAAM-induced negative chronotropy during the period prior to nerve stimulation. Atropine also prevented the LAAM-induced depression of peak heart rate and the inhibition of norepinephrine release in response to nerve stimulation. We have concluded from these data that LAAM can activate both postsynaptic and presynaptic muscarinic receptors in guinea pig hearts. We attempted to confirm the muscarinic receptor mediated cardiac slowing effect of LAAM in rat hearts.

We previously reported that chronic treatment of mice and guinea pigs with LAAM resulted in changes in the striatal dopamine system (3). These changes consisted of augmented apomorphine induced stereotypy scores and increased numbers of [^{3}H]spiroperidol binding sites in striatal slices from LAAM-treated mice and guinea pigs.

Using diverse experimental approaches, the present study was designed to test the possibility that muscarinic receptors were involved in the striatal dopaminergic and peripheral cardiac actions of LAAM in rats.

Methods. *Treatment of rats with LAAM.* Male Wistar rats (250–350 g) were treated on alternate days for 40 days with 20 mg/kg po LAAM. The dose was determined to be effective in suppressing withdrawal signs for 24 hr in morphine-dependent rats (4).

Dosing was discontinued 4 days prior to sacrifice in order to allow sufficient time to completely eliminate residual LAAM and its active metabolites from the body (5).

Isolation and preparation of rat hearts. Hearts from rats (250–350 g) were isolated and perfused as previously described for guinea pigs (2, 6). The animals were sacrificed by decapitation and a flap of the thorax around the sternum was removed. A cannula was inserted into the ascending aorta and the heart perfused *in situ* at 34°C with a Krebs–Henseleit solution containing 0.2% bovine serum albumin and aerated with 95% O_2, 5% CO_2. A small incision was made in the pulmonary artery to allow the perfusate from the coronaries to escape and the inferior vena cava was severed near the diaphragm. The heart was removed from the thorax and suspended

[1] This work was supported by research grants from the Miami Valley Chapter of the American Heart Association and the National Institute of Drug Abuse (DAO2004).

[2] To whom correspondence should be addressed.

0037-9727/84 $1.50

from a stand via the aortic cannula and allowed to stabilize for 20 min. A PE-200 catheter inserted into the right ventricle via the pulmonary artery and connected to a Statham P-23D pressure transducer detected the heart rate, which was recorded on a Brush model 2400 electronic recorder. Perfusion was maintained at a constant rate of 7 ml/min. The effect of *in vitro* perfusion with LAAM (1×10^{-6}, 5×10^{-6}, 1×10^{-5}, 5×10^{-5}, and 1×10^{-4} *M*) on heart rate was tested.

The ability of a single concentration of atropine (1×10^{-6} *M*) to antagonize the effects of LAAM was tested in separate experiments. Perfusion with atropine was initiated 1 min prior to the start of LAAM infusion and continued through the end of the experiment.

[^{3}H]Spiroperidol binding. Changes in the binding of [^{3}H]spiroperidol to dopamine receptors were assessed 4 days following termination of LAAM dosing. The striata were homogenized in 100 vol (w/v) of cold 0.5 *M* Tris buffer, pH 7.7, with a Brinkman polytron. The tissue homogenates were centrifuged twice at 25,000 rpm (Sorvall OTD-2) for 15 min. The final pellet was homogenized in 150 vol of cold 0.05 *M* Tris buffer containing 0.1% ascorbic acid, 120 m*M* NaCl, 5 m*M* KCl, 1 m*M* $CaCl_2$, pH 7.1, at 37°C for 10 min and returned to ice (7).

The incubation tubes contained varying concentrations of [^{3}H]spiroperidol in a volume of 0.1 ml, 0.1 ml of 0.1% ascorbic acid with or without 1.0 μ*M* apomorphine, and 1.8 ml of tissue homogenate. Tubes were incubated for 20 min at 37°C and filtered through Whatman GF/B glass microfilters under vacuum, using the rapid filtration method of Creese *et al.* (7). The tubes were rinsed and the filters were washed with 3 × 5-ml aliquots of Tris buffer. The filters were placed into liquid scintillation vials containing Aquasure and counted on a Packard Prias Tri-Carb scintillation counter with counting efficiencies ranging from 53 to 63%. The specific binding to dopaminergic receptors was estimated as the difference of binding in the absence and presence of 1 μ*M* apomorphine. The kinetics of [^{3}H]spiroperidol binding was determined using Scatchard analysis and subjected to a Student's *t* test for significance. Protein was measured by the Lowry method.

[^{3}H]QNB binding. Saturation binding of [^{3}H]QNB was carried out according to the method of Hulme *et al.* (8). Striata from three rats were homogenized on ice in 10 vol of 0.32 *M* sucrose. The homogenate was centrifuged at 1000*g* for 10 min and the pellet was discarded. The supernatant was centrifuged at 10,000*g* for 20 min. The resulting pellet was resuspended in Krebs–Henseleit buffer (pH 7.4) to a final protein concentration of 1.0 mg/ml. The membrane suspension was preincubated at 30°C for 15 min. Eight-hundred-microliter aliquots were pipetted into 7-ml plastic scintillation vials which contained 50 μl of [^{3}H]QNB and 50 μl of either Krebs–Henseleit (K–H) buffer or atropine in K–H buffer. The reaction was incubated for 15 min at 30°C and terminated by centrifugation at 14,000*g* for 15 min. The supernatant was discarded and the pellets were gently washed three times with 1.5 ml of Krebs–Henseleit buffer. The vials were allowed to air dry. Five milliliters of liquid scintillation cocktail was added to each vial, the vials were shaken by hand, and counted by liquid scintillation spectrometry.

Binding assays were carried out which tested the ability of different drugs to displace a single concentration of [^{3}H]spiroperidol (40 p*M*) from dopamine binding sites or a single concentration of [^{3}H]QNB (125 p*M*) from muscarinic binding sites. The assay conditions were the same as described in saturation binding experiments. Cold spiroperidol, LAAM, nor-LAAM, and dinor-LAAM were used to antagonize [^{3}H]QNB. Probit analysis was used to determine the concentration of drug necessary to displace 50% of the ^{3}H-labeled ligand (EC_{50}).

Results. *In vitro effect of LAAM on isolated rat hearts.* Perfusion of isolated rat hearts with LAAM produced a decrease in heart rate (Fig. 1). This cardiac slowing effect of LAAM was statistically significant at all tested concentrations of LAAM. The highest concentration, 100 μ*M* LAAM, decreased heart rate by 61% (190 to 74 bpm). In seven hearts atropine (1.0 μ*M*) was infused beginning 1 min prior to the infusion of the first concentration of LAAM and continued to the end of the experiment. The negative chronotropic effect of LAAM was completely inhibited in these experiments.

[^{3}H]Spiroperidol and [^{3}H]QNB binding. Scatchard analysis of [^{3}H]spiroperidol binding

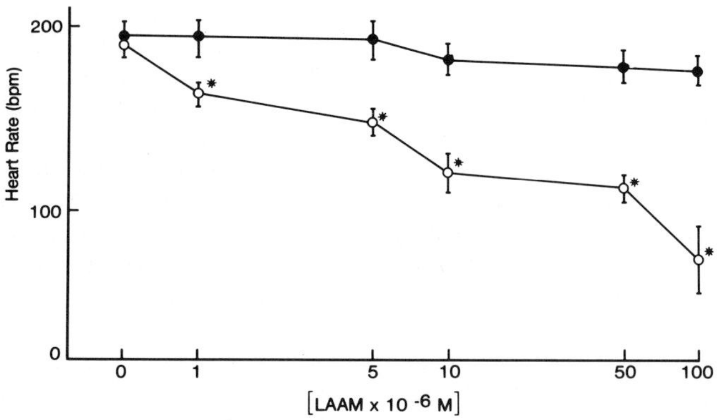

FIG. 1. Effect of LAAM alone (○, $N = 8$) or LAAM in the presence of 1×10^{-6} M atropine (●, $N = 7$) on the beating rate of isolated rat hearts. *LAAM significantly less than atropine + LAAM $P < 0.05$ (Student's t test).

showed no change in the apparent affinity constant with chronic LAAM treatment (control $K_D = 40 \pm 5.1$ pM vs LAAM $K_D = 37 \pm 8.8$ pM) (Fig. 2). The maximum number of binding sites was significantly greater in striata from LAAM treated rats (control $B_{max} = 75.1 \pm 3.2$ fmole/mg protein vs LAAM $B_{max} = 94.2 \pm 6.1$ fmole/mg protein).

The binding of the muscarinic antagonist [^{3}H]QNB to striatal membranes was unchanged by chronic LAAM treatment (Fig. 3). The maximum number of binding sites was identical in striatal membrane fragments from both control and LAAM treated rats (control $B_{max} = 750 \pm 37$ fmole/mg protein vs LAAM $B_{max} = 752 \pm 60$ fmole/mg protein). There was no significant difference in the affinity of [^{3}H]QNB for its binding sites (control $K_D = 0.15 \pm 0.03$ nM vs LAAM $K_D = 0.11 \pm 0.04$ nM).

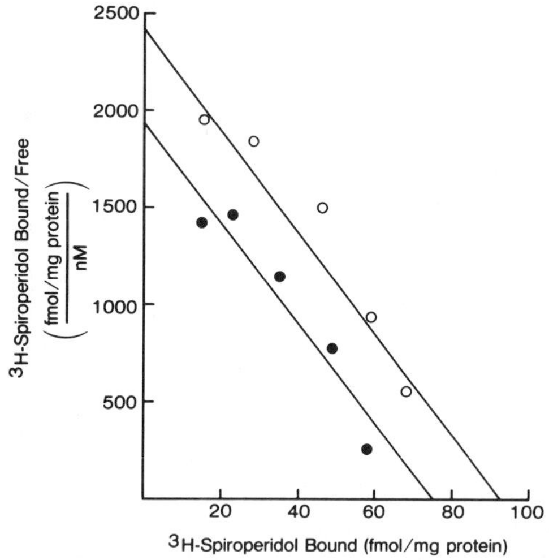

FIG. 2. Scatchard plots of [^{3}H]Spiroperidol binding to rat striatal membrane fragments. The number of binding sites was significantly increased by chronic LAAM treatment ($P < 0.05$ Student's t test). Control (●, $N = 8$); LAAM treated (○, $N = 9$). Linear regression analysis was used to determine the line of best fit.

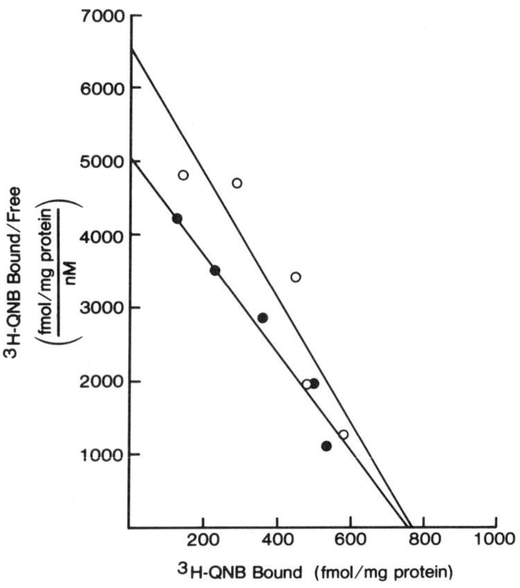

FIG. 3. Scatchard plots of [^{3}H]QNB binding to rat striatal membrane fragments. There were no significant differences in the apparent affinity constant or number of binding sites ($P > 0.05$ Student's t test). Control (●, $N = 8$); LAAM-treated (○, $N = 8$).

Antagonism of [^3H]spiroperidol and [^3H]-QNB binding. LAAM, nor-LAAM, and dinor-LAAM were tested for their ability to antagonize the binding of a single concentration of either [^{3}H]spiroperidol (40 p*M*) or [^{3}H]QNB (125 p*M*) to rat striatal membranes. The metabolites of LAAM show a higher affinity than the parent compound for [^{3}H]spiroperidol binding sites, but all three were significantly less potent than cold spiroperidol at displacing [^{3}H]spiroperidol from striatal binding sites (Table I).

The potencies of LAAM, nor-LAAM, and dinor-LAAM were similar vs the binding of [^{3}H]QNB to striatal membranes but slightly less potent than pilocarpine and much less potent than atropine. Pilocarpine had an affinity 10–20 times greater and atropine had an affinity 5000–8000 times greater than LAAM and metabolites for [^{3}H]QNB binding sites (Table I).

Discussion. An earlier report from our laboratory demonstrated that chronic treatment with LAAM altered dopaminergic mechanisms in the striata of mice and guinea pigs (3). Other narcotic agonists like morphine or methadone have been shown to produce changes in the striatal dopamine system similar to those produced by chronic treatment with neuroleptics (9–12). These changes were thought to be due to long-term blockade of dopamine receptors by the narcotics (13). In the present study, we attempted to determine if the increased number of [^{3}H]spiroperidol binding sites following chronic LAAM treatment was due to the ability of LAAM to block striatal dopamine receptors or resulted from some other section of LAAM.

Treatment of rats with LAAM (20 mg/kg po for 40 days) resulted in a change in [^{3}H]spiroperidol binding to striatal membranes similar to that seen in mice and guinea pigs (3). Scatchard analysis of saturation binding data demonstrated that the maximum number of bindings sites was significantly increased with no change in the apparent affinity constant (Fig. 1). The micromolar concentrations of LAAM and its metabolites which were required to antagonize a 40 p*M* concentration of [^{3}H]spiroperidol indicate that the drugs are probably not acting as antagonist at these sites (Table I). While there appeared to be increased affinity for [^{3}H]spiroperidol binding sites with successive metabolism of LAAM to nor-LAAM and then to dinor-LAAM, the EC_{50} values were 100–3000 times higher than for cold spiroperidol. These data cast doubt on a dopaminergic antagonist action for LAAM or its major metabolites.

We have previously reported that LAAM produced a negative chronotropic effect in isolated guinea pig hearts. In addition, LAAM inhibited the release of norepinephrine from cardiac sympathetic nerves induced by nerve stimulation. These effects were not blocked by 10 μM naltrexone but could be antagonized by 1.0 μM atropine. It was concluded that these actions of LAAM were mediated by atrial (postsynaptic) and nerve terminal (presynaptic) muscarinic receptors, respectively (2). In the present study, LAAM produced a similar negative chronotropic response in isolated rat hearts and this response was completely antagonized by 1.0 μM atropine (Fig. 2). These actions at peripheral synapses and the fact that the striatum contains muscarinic receptors which influence dopamine neurons (20, 1) led us to examine the possibility that the striatal effects of LAAM might be mediated by stimulation of muscarinic receptors.

In order to test this possibility, we measured the binding of [^{3}H]QNB to rat striatal membranes following chronic treatment with LAAM (20 mg/kg po alternate days for 40 days). No significant changes in the binding affinity or the maximum number of binding sites occurred (Fig. 3). It has been reported that prior exposure to agonists can desensitize muscarinic receptors in smooth muscle (14) but not in rat brain (15). Additional experiments were performed on striatal membranes from untreated rats which tested the ability

TABLE I. CONCENTRATION OF DIFFERENT DRUGS (MICROMOLAR) REQUIRED TO DISPLACE 50% OF 40 p*M* [^{3}H]SPIROPERIDOL OR 125 p*M* [^{3}H]QNB FROM RAT STRIATAL MEMBRANE FRAGMENTS

	EC_{50} (μM) vs [^{3}H]Spiroperidol	EC_{50} (μM) vs [^{3}H]QNB
LAAM	30	42
Nor-LAAM	4.8	35
Dinor-LAAM	1.5	24
Spiroperidol	0.01	—
Pilocarpine	—	2.3
Atropine	—	0.005

of LAAM, nor-LAAM, or dinor-LAAM to antagonize the binding of 125 p*M* [^{3}H]QNB (Table I). There were no differences in the affinities of LAAM or its metabolites for the [^{3}H]QNB binding sites. The EC_{50} values for pilocarpine and atropine were similar to those previously reported (16). The concentration of LAAM and its metabolites necessary to displace 50% of 125 p*M* [^{3}H]QNB were 10–20 times higher than pilocarpine and 5000–8000 times higher than atropine. These data indicate that LAAM, nor-LAAM, and dinor-LAAM have low affinities for striatal muscarinic binding sites. In spite of a relatively low affinity, LAAM may produce some of its effects through stimulation of muscarinic receptors in the striatum. Activation of guanylate cyclase in a neuroblastoma clone has been reported to be due to stimulation of a population of low-affinity muscarinic receptors (17). The mechanism by which this muscarinic action of LAAM would produce a supersensitivity of dopamine receptor sites is unclear since most published reports indicate that dopamine neurons synapse on cholinergic neurons in the striatum rather than the reverse (18, 19). It is possible that the muscarinic receptors stimulated by LAAM reside on dopamine nerve terminals. Evidence has been presented supporting the possible existance of presynaptic cholinergic receptors on dopamine nerve endings in the rat striatum (20, 21). Nomura *et al.* (22) reported that destruction of dopaminergic neurons in the striatum and mesolimbic areas of the rat brain by 6-hydroxydopa reduced the number of muscarinic receptor sites measured by [^{3}H]QNB binding without changing the affinity constant indicating a nerve terminal locus for these receptors. Giorguieff *et al.* (23) demonstrated the presence of nicotinic and muscarinic receptors on dopamine nerve terminals in superfused rat striatal slices. Both types of cholinergic receptors enhanced the spontaneous release of dopamine. De Belleroche and Bradford (24) on the other hand have reported presynaptic muscarinic receptors which inhibit the release of dopamine from striatal terminals during nerve stimulation. Such an inhibition of dopamine release would lead to a postsynaptic dopamine receptor supersensitivity (up regulation) like that observed in our experiments. A possible explanation for the lack of measurable change in striatal muscarinic receptors following chronic treatment with LAAM is that the presynaptic receptors represent a small percentage of the total pool of striatal muscarinic receptors.

1. Stickney JL. Cardiac effect of α-acetylmethadol chronotropic effects in vitro. Toxicol Appl Pharmacol **40**:23–32, 1977.
2. Langley AE, Lehman TM, Kirlangitis J, Zeid, R. Cardiac and autonomic nervous system effect of *l*-alphacetylmethadol (LAAM) Arch Int Pharmacodyn **259**:250–258, 1982.
3. Langley AE, Kirlangitis J, Lehman T. Stereotypy and striatial dopamine receptor changes with *l*-α-acetylmethadol (LAAM) Pharmacol Biochem Behav **14**:753–756, 1981.
4. Dixon WJ. The up-and-down method for small samples. J Amer Stat Assoc **60**:967–978, 1965.
5. Henderson GL, Wilson BK, Law DHM. Plasma *l*-α-acetylmethadol (LAAM) after acute and chronic administration. J Pharmacol Exp Ther **21**:16–25, 1977.
6. Langley AE, Weiner N. Enhanced exocytotic release of norepinephrine consequent to nerve stimulation by low concentrations of cyclic nucleotides in the presence of phenoxybenzamine. J Pharmacol Exp Ther **205**:426–432, 1978.
7. Creese I, Schneider R, Snyder SH. ^{3}H-Spiroperidol labels dopamine receptors in pituitary and brain. Eur J Pharmacol **46**:37;7–381, 1977.
8. Hume EC, Birdsall NJM, Burgen ASV, Mehta P. The binding of antagonists to brain muscarinic receptors. Mol Pharmacol **14**:737–750, 1978.
9. Carlson KR, Almasi J. Behavioral supersensitivity to apomorphine following chronic narcotic treatment in the guinea pig. Psychopharmacology **57**:273–277, 1978.
10. Carlson KR, Almasi J. Time course of dopaminergic hypersentivity following chronic narcotic treatment. Pharmacol Biochem Behav **11**:283–287, 1979.
11. De la Baume S, Patey G, Marcais H, Protais P, Constentin J, Schwartz JC. Changes in dopamine receptors in mouse striatum following morphine treatments. Life Sci **24**:2333–2342, 1979.
12. Lal H. Narcotic dependence, narcotic action and dopamine receptors. Life Sci **17**:483–496, 1976.
13. Sasame HA, Perez-Cruet J. Evidence that methadone blocks dopamine receptors in the brain. J Neurochem **19**:1953–1957, 1972.
14. Young JM. Desensitization and agonist binding to cholinergic receptors in intestinal smooth muscle. FEBS Lett **46**:354–356, 1974.
15. Birdsall NJ, Burgen, ASV, Hulme EC. The binding of agonists to brain muscarinic receptors. Mol Pharmacol **14**:723–736, 1978.
16. Yamamura HI, Snyder SH. Muscarinic cholinergic

binding in rat brain. Proc Natl Acad Sci **71**:1725–1729, 1974.
17. Birdsall NJ, Burgen ASV, Hulme EC. Correlation between the binding properties and pharmacological responses of muscarinic receptors. In: Jenden DJ, ed. Cholinergic Mechanisms in Psychopharmacology. New York, Plenum, pp 25–33, 1977.
18. Koide T, Matsushita H. An enhanced sensitivity of muscarinic cholinergic receptor associated with dopaminergic receptor subsensitivity after chronic antidepressant treatment. Life Sci **28**:1139–1145, 1981.
19. Robinson EE, Malthe-Sorenssen D, Wood, PL, Commission J. Dopaminergic control of the septal–hippocampal cholinergic pathway. J Pharmacol Exp Ther **208**:476–479, 1979.
20. Butcher L. Nature and mechanisms of cholinergic–monaminergic interactions in the brain. Life Sci **21**:1207–1229, 1977.
21. Butcher LL, Woolf NJ. Monaminergic–cholinergic relationships and the chemical communication matrix of the substantia nigra and neostriatum. Brain Res Bull **9**:475–492, 1982.
22. Nomura Y, Kajiyama H, Nakata Y, Segewa T. Muscarinic cholinergic binding in striatal and mesolimbic areas of the rat: reduction by 6-hydroxydopa. Eur J Pharmol **58**:125–131, 1979.
23. Giorguieff MF, LeFloc'H ML, Glowinski J, Beeson MJ. Involveent of cholinergic presynaptic receptors of nicotinic and muscarinic types in the control of the spontaneous release of dopamine from striatal dopaminergic terminals in the rat. J Pharmacol Exp Ther **200**:535–544, 1977.
24. De Belleroche J, Bradford HF. Biochemical evidence for the presence of presynaptic receptors on dopaminergic nerve terminals. Brain Res **142**:53–68, 1978.

Received June 30, 1983. P.S.E.B.M. 1984, Vol. 176.
Accepted April 13, 1984.

PROCEEDINGS OF THE SOCIETY FOR EXPERIMENTAL BIOLOGY AND MEDICINE **176**, 356–365 (1984)

Effect of Albumin on the *in Vitro* Conjugation of Bilirubin by Rat Liver Microsomes (41883)

NICOLA TAVOLONI, MARY JANE T. JONES, LUIS M. J. ISOLA, AND PAUL D. BERK

The Polly Annenberg Levee Hematology Center and the Hepatic Research Group (Department of Medicine) and the Department of Physiology, Mount Sinai School of Medicine, New York, New York 10029

Abstract. These studies were carried out to determine whether bovine serum albumin (BSA), which is usually included in the incubation mixture for the *in vitro* determination of bilirubin-UDP-glucuronyl transferase (GT) activity, affects GT activity. Using bilirubin as substrate, addition of BSA to the enzyme reaction mixture at concentrations varying from 2 to 30 mg/ml resulted in a dose-related inhibition of "native" GT activity of rat liver microsomes. When detergent-activated enzyme was employed, increasing concentrations of BSA also required higher concentrations of deoxycholate, digitonin, or Triton X-100 to produce maximal bilirubin conjugation. Low BSA concentrations (2 mg/ml) prevented enzyme activation by both detergents and UDP-*N*-acetyl glucosamine. When BSA was omitted and bilirubin dissolved in dimethyl sulfoxide, UDP-*N*-acetyl glucosamine failed to enhance GT activity, and activation by detergents was only 15–25% of that observed in the presence of optimal concentrations of BSA. When rat albumin was substituted for BSA, a similar dose-related inhibition of *in vitro* bilirubin conjugation by untreated microsomes was observed, although at any given albumin concentration, GT activity was lower with rat than with bovine albumin. Additionally, both detergents and UDP-*N*-acetyl glucosamine produced similar GT activation regardless of the rat albumin concentration. Finally, these effects of BSA and rat albumin could not be reproduced when β-lactoglobulin was employed and/or when *p*-nitrophenol was the acceptor substrate of GT. These findings indicate that albumin, in particular BSA, profoundly and selectively influences the *in vitro* activity of microsomal GT toward bilirubin as the acceptor substrate.

UDP-glucuronyl transferase (GT) denotes the group of enzymes responsible for the addition of glucuronic acid to a variety of aglycones of endogenous and exogenous origin. Accordingly, the *in vitro* activity of GT can be measured using a number of acceptor substrates, and several systems have been described for its assay (1–8).

A specific bilirubin GT has been isolated, and detailed studies of its enzymologic properties have been reported (9). Nevertheless, in certain clinical settings, especially in puzzling cases of unconjugated hyperbilirubinemia, assay of bilirubin GT is still frequently performed employing crude homogenates of biopsy samples of liver tissue (10) or, when larger samples are available, partially purified microsomal preparations (1, 2). Several authors have noted the wide variation in assay results produced by superficially similar methods (1, 2, 10), and the apparent discrepancy in many situations between the bilirubin GT activity and the serum concentration of unconjugated bilirubin (11, 12). The reasons for the discrepancies have not been fully elucidated.

When bilirubin is employed as the acceptor substrate, determination of GT activity usually involves the introduction into the enzyme incubation mixture of a certain amount of albumin (4–8 mg/ml), most often bovine serum albumin (BSA) (1, 2, 10). This is required because at the optimal pH of the enzyme reaction (7.7 at 37°C (1, 2, 10, 13)), bilirubin is virtually insoluble in the aqueous phase (14, 15) and must be bound to albumin to avoid precipitation. However, despite this commonly used procedure, no studies have systematically examined whether the presence of albumin influences the enzyme activity. In this report we describe the effects of albumin on the *in vitro* conjugation of bilirubin by rat liver microsomes. Similar considerations may apply to the assay of human bilirubin GT, although limited access to fresh human liver tissue has thus far prevented direct confirmation of these findings in man.

0037-9727/84 $1.50

Methods. *Chemicals and solutions.* All chemicals including proteins used in these studies were reagent grade and, unless otherwise indicated, were purchased from Sigma (St. Louis, Mo.). Bovine serum albumin (BSA) was fatty acid free as defined by the supplier. The original source of β-lactoglobulin (folate binding protein, containing both A and B fractions) was cow's milk. Rat albumin was Fraction V. Proteins were generally used as furnished by the supplier. However, in selected studies, they were first dialyzed for 18 hr at 4°C against 20 vol of 0.1 *M* sodium bicarbonate, pH 8.6. Most reagent solutions for the GT assay were prepared immediately before use; the reader is referred to our previous report for detailed information (13). Bilirubin (E_{450} = 59,000–61,000; >92% IXα by thin layer chromatography (16)) was dissolved first in a few drops of NaOH (0.25 *M*) and subsequently added to a solution of BSA, rat albumin, or β-lactoglobulin. The resulting stock solution contained the desired concentration of unconjugated bilirubin (0.856 m*M* or 0.5 mg/ml for standard enzyme assay) and 8 mg/ml of one of the above-mentioned proteins. This solution was adjusted to a pH of 7.9 at 22°C (7.7 at 37°C) and was invariably used within 6 hr of preparation, over which it was stable with no evidence of either precipitation or colloid formation. When unconjugated bilirubin was dissolved in dimethyl sulphoxide (DMSO) (Fisher, Pittsburgh, Pa.), the pigment was added directly to the solvent to achieve a concentration of 0.856 m*M*. Chromatographically pure bilirubin diglucuronide was isolated from rat bile as previously described (17), stored *in vacuo* and in the dark at −20°C, and dissolved just prior to use. All the procedures for the preparation of the bilirubin solutions as well as those for measuring GT activity were carried out in the presence of subdued light.

Animals and microsome preparation. Male Sprague–Dawley rats (260–280 g) were purchased from Perfection Breeders (Douglasville, Pa.) and kept for at least 1 week in a temperature-controlled room (22°C) with alternating 12-hr light–dark cycles prior to being used. Except where otherwise noted, hepatic microsome fractions were prepared in 0.25 *M* sucrose containing 1 m*M* EDTA (pH 7.4) by a conventional ultracentrifugation procedure as reported in detail elsewhere (13). Microsome pellets were stored at −20°C and resuspended in an appropriate volume of sucrose–EDTA so that the microsomes isolated from 1 g of liver were contained in a 4-ml suspension. For a limited number of comparison studies, microsomes prepared, stored, and resuspended in 150 m*M* KCl (2) were employed.

Enzyme activation. GT activity toward bilirubin or *p*-nitrophenol as the acceptor substrate was measured in microsome suspensions in which the enzyme was either in its "native" form or activated with a variety of detergents or with the sugar nucleotide UDP-*N*-acetyl glucosamine (UDPNAG). The source of "native" enzyme was a suspension of microsomes obtained from 1 g of liver in 8 ml of sucrose–EDTA, which was obtained by diluting 1 vol of the original suspension (4 ml) with 1 vol of sucrose–EDTA. Similarly, the detergent-activated enzyme was prepared by adding 1 vol of the original microsome suspension to 1 vol of sucrose–EDTA containing the desired concentration of the detergent used. Both untreated and detergent-treated microsome suspensions were incubated at 0°C for 30 min before being added to the reaction mixture. When GT was activated by UDPNAG, the latter was added directly to the reaction mixture.

GT activity determination. The activity of GT was measured aerobically at 37°C using either bilirubin or *p*-nitrophenol as the acceptor substrate. When bilirubin was employed, the standard incubation mixture contained: Tris (pH 7.7 at 37°C), 250 m*M;* MgCl, 10 m*M;* UDP-glucuronic acid, 5.17 m*M;* microsomal protein, 0.25–0.35 mg; bilirubin, 0.214 m*M;* and the desired concentration of BSA, rat albumin, or β-lactoglobulin. When applicable, UDPNAG was included at the desired concentration (see below). In studies omitting BSA, rat albumin, and β-lactoglobulin, bilirubin was dissolved in DMSO, at a final concentration in the incubation mixture of 2.5 *M*. Similar incubation mixtures were prepared when *p*-nitrophenol was the acceptor substrate, except that Tris, pH 7.4, was used instead of Tris, pH 7.9, and *p*-nitrophenol (0.75 m*M*) was substituted for bilirubin. In both assays, the final volume of the reaction mixture was 1 ml and all components were added to a 10 ml Erlenmeyer flask which was kept on ice until incubation was initiated. In the bilirubin GT assay, incubations were done for 30 min, whereas in the *p*-nitrophenol GT assay, samples were incubated for 10 min. The activity of GT toward bilirubin and *p*-nitrophenol was measured by minor modifications of the methods of Strebel and Odell (2) and Isselbacher *et al.* (3), respectively, as previously described (18). Protein concentration was determined by the Lowry method (19) using BSA as standard.

Effect of BSA on the extraction and diazotization of conjugated bilirubin. Determination of GT activity by the procedure used in the present studies involves coupling of the conjugated bilirubin with diazotized sulfanilic acid, after its extraction from the unconjugated pigment by solvent partitioning (lactic acid–ethyl acetate:chloroform), according to a modification of the method of Weber and Schalm (20). The validity of applying this partition method to the extraction of bile pigments from tissue-derived preparations, such as the enzyme incubation mixture, previously demonstrated in our laboratory (21), was again confirmed; ≥91% of added radiolabeled bilirubin mono- and diglucuronides was invariably recovered in the polar, upper layer of the partition system, and >95% of labeled unconjugated bilirubin in the nonpolar, lower chloroform layer. Nevertheless, it was essential to ascertain that any observed effects of BSA on GT activity were not related to technical artifacts introduced into the extraction and/or diazotization procedures, but reflected real changes in enzyme activity. Accordingly, conversion of the measured extinction values into units of enzyme activity was made using as standards modified incubation mixtures which contained two different concentrations of BSA (2 or 18 mg/ml) and known amounts of pure bilirubin diglucuronide (17). UDP-glucuronic acid and UDPNAG were omitted and these preparations were kept on ice prior to determination of extinction.

Estimation of the influence of albumin on free bilirubin concentration. To examine the hypothesis that albumin influences GT activity simply through its effect on the concentration of free bilirubin in the reaction mixture, the free bilirubin concentrations present in solutions containing 0.214 m*M* total bilirubin and 0.029 m*M* to 0.441 m*M* bovine or rat albumin (bilirubin:albumin molar ratio 7.3–0.49) were estimated. The estimation was done using published bilirubin–albumin association constants for multiple binding sites, determined for rat and bovine albumin by various techniques (16, 22). Particular comparisons were made for binding constants obtained by a standard fluorescence technique (22), the only method for which BSA and rat albumin were studied under comparable conditions. Computation of the free bilirubin concentration was done employing the algorithm published by Wosilait and associates (23), adapted in MINC–BASIC for use on a MINC-11 digital minicomputer (Digital Equipment, Maynard, Mass.).

Results. *Validation of methods.* Irrespective of the albumin concentration in the reaction mixture, conjugated bilirubin formation increased linearly with time for at least 30 min whether native, detergent activated (digitonin, deoxycholate), or UDPNAG-activated microsomes were employed (Fig. 1). In addition, as we have reported previously, quantitation of conjugated bilirubin formation yielded identical results whether measured by the solvent extraction method of Weber and Schalm, or by selective diazotization with ethyl anthranilate at pH 2.7 (13). Glucuronidation of *p*-nitrophenol has also been shown to be linear over the initial 10 min of the reaction (18).

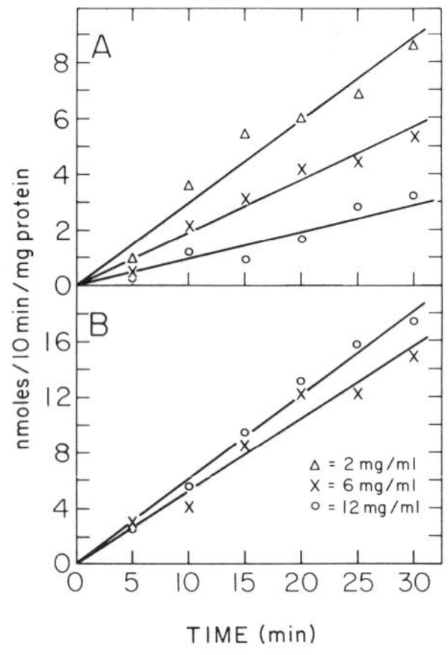

FIG. 1. Formation of conjugated bilirubin by native (A) and 0.1% deoxycholate-activated (B) rat liver microsomes at three different concentrations of albumin. Figure illustrates linearity of the reaction over the initial 30 min of incubation. Similar linearity was observed with digitonin- or UDPNAG-activated microsomes.

In view of the established linearly of the conjugation of both substrates investigated in this report, measurement of product formation at any point within the linear period provides equivalent information to determination of initial reaction rates.

Effect of bilirubin concentration on bilirubin GT activity. As already reported by other investigators (1, 2), increasing concentrations of unconjugated bilirubin in the enzyme incubation mixture produced a biphasic effect on the bilirubin glucuronidation rate: an initial increase followed by a decrease. As illustrated in Fig. 2, however, the activating effect of bilirubin was dependent on the amount of BSA present in the incubation mixture, and proportionally higher concentrations of bilirubin were necessary to produce maximal GT activity when increasing concentrations of BSA were included. Thus, in the presence of 2, 6, and 12 mg/ml BSA, the highest GT activity with digitonin-activated microsomes was obtained with 0.086, 0.214, and 0.342 m*M* bilirubin, respectively. This effect of BSA was similarly observed when "native" enzyme or enzyme activated by UDPNAG or deoxycholate was employed.

Effect of BSA on bilirubin GT activity. When a constant concentration of unconjugated bilirubin (0.214 m*M*) was included in the enzyme incubation mixture, the apparent activity of bilirubin GT in untreated microsomes ("native" enzyme) varied inversely as a logarithmic function of the BSA concentration. The highest GT activity, which ranged from 7.8 to 10.2 nmoles/10 min/mg protein, was observed with the lowest BSA concentration (2 mg/ml), and proportionally lower enzyme activities were obtained as the BSA concentration was increased up to 30 mg/ml (Fig. 3). With 30 mg/ml BSA, the rate of bilirubin glucuronidation averaged 1.25 nmoles/10 min/mg, a value which represented roughly 10–15% of that observed with 2 mg/ml BSA. Virtually identical data were obtained when dialyzed albumin was employed.

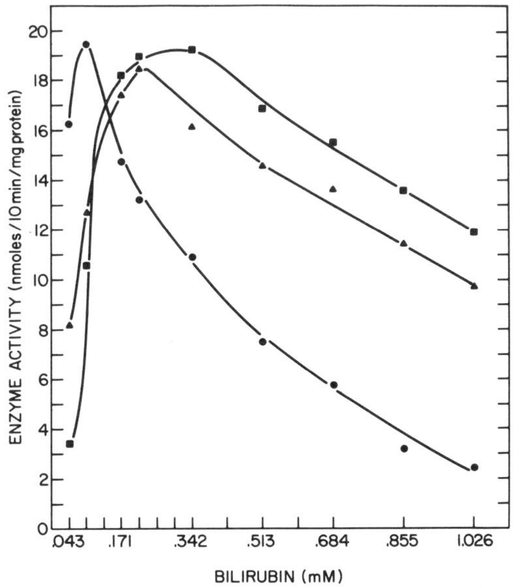

FIG. 2. Effect of unconjugated bilirubin on bilirubin GT activity in presence of 2 (●), 6 (▲), and 12 (■) mg/ml bovine serum albumin.

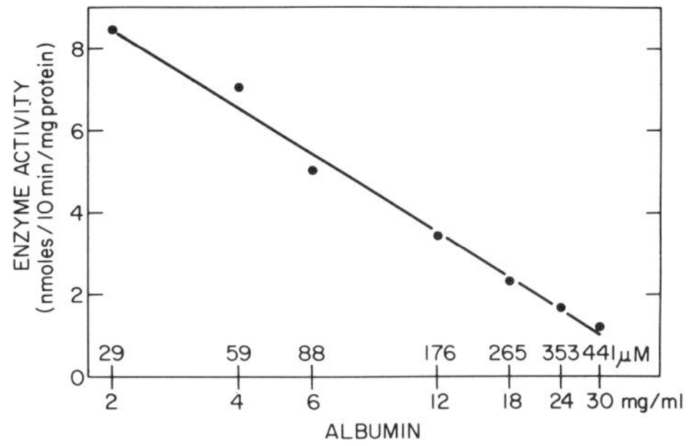

FIG. 3. Effect of bovine serum albumin on "native" bilirubin GT activity.

The concentration of BSA in the incubation mixture influenced not only the activity of the "native" GT, but also that of the detergent-activated enzyme. Figure 4 illustrates the GT activation profile by deoxycholate in the presence of 2, 6, and 18 mg/ml BSA. With 2 mg/ml BSA, little or no activation by deoxycholate was observed, and only an inhibitory effect on GT activity was obtained with concentrations of the detergent greater than 0.075–0.10%. Conversely, when BSA was included at a concentration of 6 mg/ml or greater, the typical biphasic effect of deoxycholate was observed, which consisted of an initial activation followed by inhibition of GT activity. However, as the presence of BSA also resulted in buffering the activating as well as the inhibitory effect of the detergent, proportionally higher concentrations of deoxycholate were necessary to produce maximal GT activation when increasing BSA concentrations were included. Thus, in the presence of 6, 18,

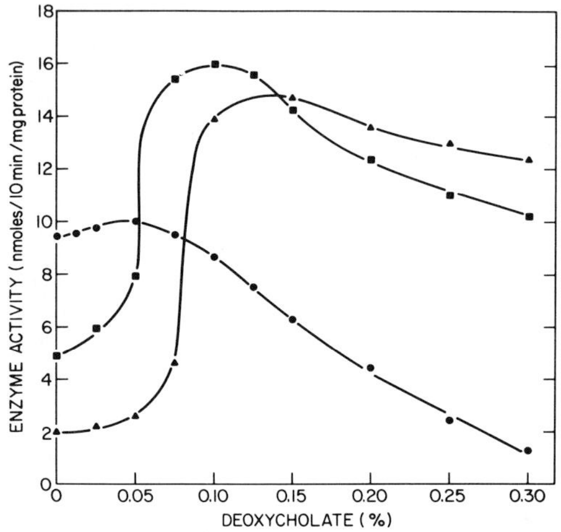

FIG. 4. Effect of deoxycholate on bilirubin GT activity in presence of 2 (●), 6 (■), and 18 (▲) mg/ml bovine serum albumin.

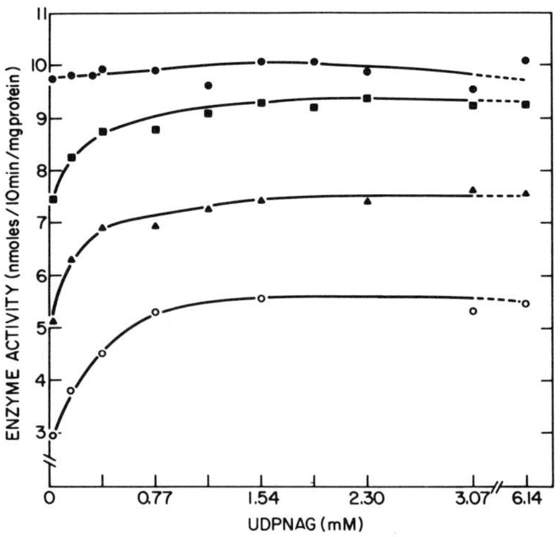

FIG. 5. Effect of UDPNAG on bilirubin GT activity in presence of 2 (●), 4 (■), 6 (▲), and 12 (○) mg/ml bovine serum albumin.

and 30 mg/ml BSA, maximal GT activity was obtained with 0.1, 0.15, and 0.2% deoxycholate, respectively. These effects of BSA on the activation profile of bilirubin GT by deoxycholate were similarly observed when other detergents, both neutral (digitonin) and cationic (Triton X-100), were employed.

When UDPNAG was used to activate bilirubin GT, it produced no increase in enzyme activity when employed with concentrations of BSA below 3–3.5 mg/ml. However, introduction of BSA at or above 4 mg/ml resulted in GT activation by UDPNAG (Fig. 5). If the activated GT activity was expressed as a percentage of the "native" value, UDPNAG enhanced enzyme activity in a fashion linearly related to the BSA concentration. Thus, with 4, 6, and 12 mg/ml BSA, UDPNAG enhanced GT activity by 26, 44, and 86%, respectively.

All of these effects of BSA on "native," and detergent- and UDPNAG-activated bilirubin GT were fully reproduced when microsomal fractions were prepared and resuspended in 150 mM KCl. Under comparable enzyme incubation conditions, however, the bilirubin GT activity in microsomes isolated in KCl was always lower (20–30%) than that observed in microsomes prepared in sucrose–EDTA.

Finally, when unconjugated bilirubin (0.214 mM) was dissolved in DMSO and no BSA was included in the enzyme incubation mixture, the activation profile of GT differed significantly from that observed in the presence of BSA. Thus, although "native" GT values in this situation approximated those seen with 6 mg/ml BSA (4.05 nmole/10 min/mg), no activation was produced by UDPNAG (Fig. 6). Detergents, including deoxycholate, digitonin and Triton X-100, enhanced GT activity (Fig. 6), but the optimal activating effect (50–100%) was far lower than that observed when bilirubin was dissolved in BSA (300–500%) (Fig. 4).

To determine whether these effects of BSA were due to technical artifacts during the extraction and/or diazotization procedure,

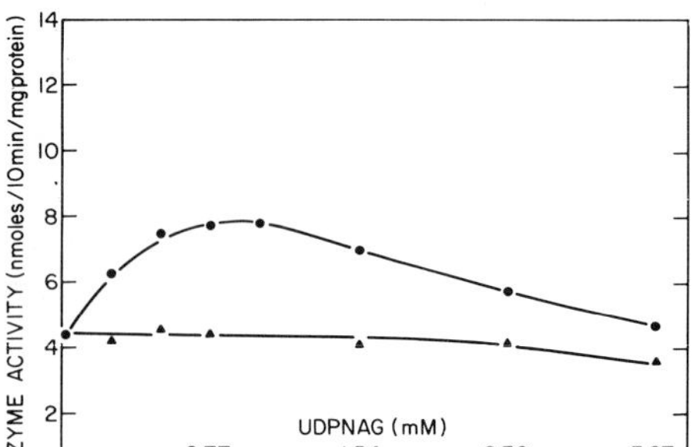

FIG. 6. Effect of UDPNAG (▲) or digitonin (●) on bilirubin GT activity when DMSO (2.5 M) was included in the enzyme incubation mixture. No albumin was present.

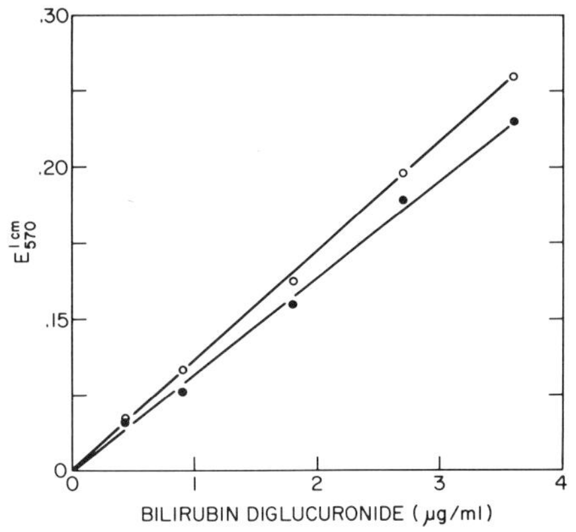

FIG. 7. Relationship between the concentration of sulfanilic acid azopigments derived from bilirubin diglucuronide and their extinction of 570 nm in presence of 2 (○) and 18 (●) mg/ml bovine serum albumin.

known amounts of bilirubin diglucuronide were extracted and diazotized (see Methods) in the presence of 2 or 18 mg/ml BSA. Under these conditions, formation of sulfanilic acid azopigment of bilirubin diglucuronide was essentially the same in the presence of either BSA concentration (Fig. 7). The E_{570} values with 2 and 18 mg/ml BSA were, respectively, 38.1 and 37.2 × 10^3 M^{-1}, cm^{-1}.

Effect of rat albumin on bilirubin GT activity. When rat albumin was substituted for BSA, only part of the previously described effects were observed. "Native" bilirubin GT activity was similarly influenced by the presence of rat albumin and, as observed with BSA, the highest GT activity was observed with the lowest albumin concentration (2 mg/ml). However, GT activity of untreated microsomes in the presence of 2 mg/ml rat albumin accounted for only 60–70% of that found with similar concentrations of BSA, and could be enhanced by both detergents and UDPNAG. Thus, as illustrated in Fig. 8 and Table I, treatment of microsomes with deoxycholate resulted in GT activation, which was essentially the same when 2 or 6 mg/ml rat albumin were included. With 6 mg/ml, however, deoxycholate enhanced the "native" GT activity by 330–400% when BSA was used and 230–300% in the presence of rat albumin. Similarly, UDPNAG produced the same degree of activation in the presence of 2 or 6 mg/ml rat albumin (Fig. 9 and Table I). Dialysis did not alter the observed effects of rat albumin.

Influence of free bilirubin concentration on bilirubin GT activity. Calculated unbound bilirubin concentrations in solutions containing 0.214 m*M* bilirubin and 2–30 mg bovine or rat serum albumin (bilirubin:albumin molar ratio 0.49–7.3) are illustrated in Fig. 10. Although, in general, GT activity increases as the free bilirubin concentration increases, there is no simple relation between the free bilirubin concentration and measured values for GT. Moreover, at any given bilirubin:albumin molar ratio, GT activity of native microsomes is greater in the presence of bovine than rat albumin, although the estimated free bilirubin concentration is lower with bovine-derived proteins.

Effect of β-lactoglobulin on bilirubin GT activity. Replacement of albumin with β-lactoglobulin failed to reproduce the typical effects of BSA or rat albumin on bilirubin conjugation. "Native" GT activity (9–11 nmol/10 min/mg) was similar when 2 or 6 mg/ml of β-lactoglobulin were included and roughly resembled that obtained with 2 mg/ml BSA. Furthermore, GT activity in untreated microsomes could not be enhanced by either detergents or UDPNAG, regardless of the concentration of β-lactoglobulin present. On the contrary, addition of either UDPNAG (1.54–6.14 m*M*) or deoxycholate (0.05–0.2%) invariably resulted in inhibition of GT activity (Table I).

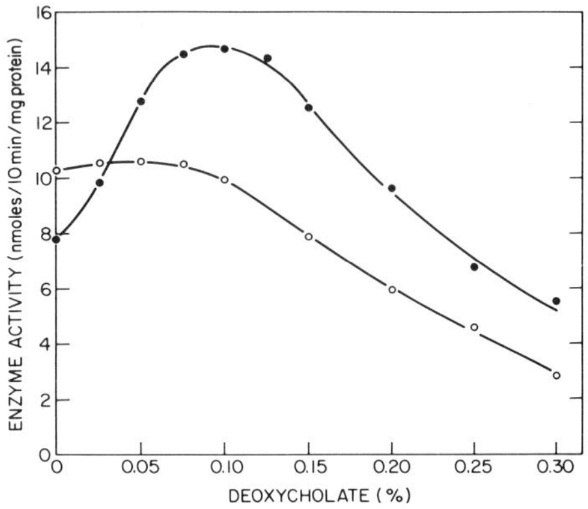

FIG. 8. Effect of deoxycholate on bilirubin GT activity in presence of 2 mg/ml bovine (○) or rat (●) serum albumin.

TABLE I. EFFECT OF BOVINE SERUM ALBUMIN, RAT ALBUMIN, AND β-LACTOGLOBULIN ON THE *IN VITRO* CONJUGATION OF BILIRUBIN BY RAT LIVER MICROSOMES

	Albumin (mg/ml)				β-Lactoglobulin (mg/ml)	
	Bovine		Rat			
Enzyme preparation	6	2	6	2	6	2
"Native"	100[a]	180	80	130	200	200
UDPNAG[b]	150	180	120	170	180	190
Deoxycholate[c]	350	170	240	270	160	170

[a] Values are percentages of the "native" enzyme activity obtained when bovine serum albumin was included in the enzyme incubation mixture of 6 mg/ml (88 μM).

[b] Maximal activation obtained (usually observed with 3.07 mM UDPNAG).

[c] Maximal activation obtained (usually observed with 0.10% deoxycholate at these concentrations of albumins).

Lineweaver–Burk plot of "native" enzyme activity against UDP-glucuronic acid concentration in the presence of 6 mg/ml BSA or β-lactoglobulin (which resembled that obtained with 2 mg/ml BSA) revealed that Michaelis–Menten kinetics were followed in both of these situations. Similar apparent K_m values were obtained (5.43 and 5.68 mM with BSA and β-lactoglobulin, respectively) (Fig. 11).

Effect of BSA on p-nitrophenol GT activity. To determine whether these effects of BSA were also observed when another acceptor substrate of GT was employed, *p*-nitrophenol GT activity was measured in the presence of 2 and 12 mg/ml BSA. As illustrated in Fig. 12, both "native" and UDPNAG- or deoxycholate-activated enzyme activities were unaffected by different concentrations of BSA. As expected, the inhibitory effect of high concentrations of deoxycholate was buffered when 12 mg/ml BSA were included.

Discussion. The results of these studies have demonstrated that the presence of BSA in the reaction mixture profoundly influences the rate of *in vitro* conjugation of bilirubin by rat liver microsomes. Specifically, our studies have shown that when increasing concentra-

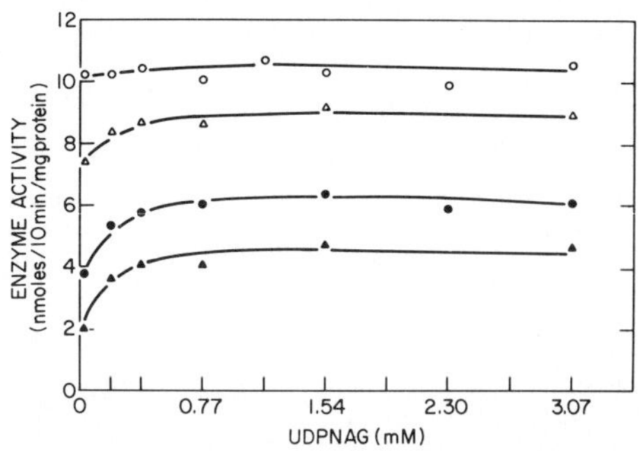

FIG. 9. Effect of UDPNAG on bilirubin GT activity in presence of bovine (circles) or rat (triangles) serum albumin at 2 (open symbols) and 6 (closed symbols) mg/ml.

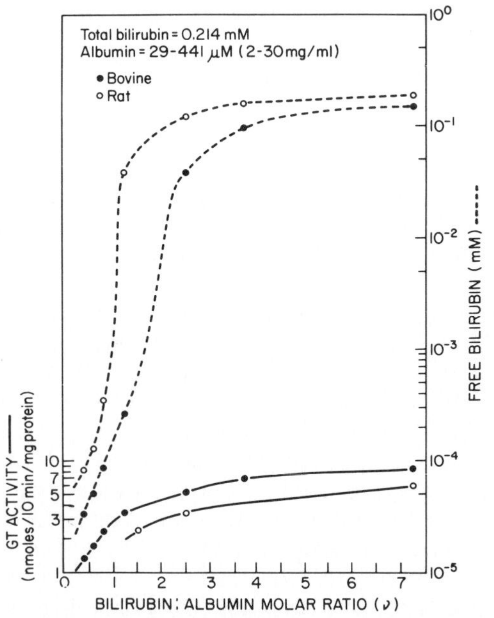

FIG. 10. Influence of bilirubin:albumin molar ratio (ν) on free bilirubin concentration and bilirubin GT activity in incubations containing 0.214 mM bilirubin and either bovine or rat albumin.

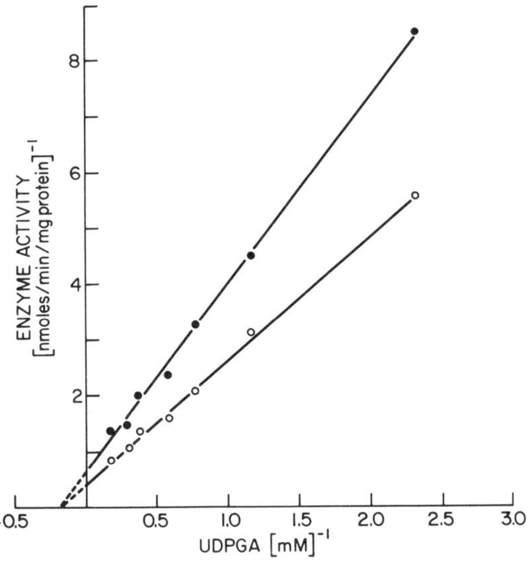

FIG. 11. Double-reciprocal plots of bilirubin GT activity against UDPGA concentration in presence of 6 mg/ml bovine serum albumin (●) or β-lactoglobulin (○).

tions of BSA are added to the incubation mixture proportionally higher concentrations of unconjugated bilirubin are necessary to produce optimal GT activity, and proportionally less conjugated bilirubin is formed when untreated microsomes are used. Higher concentrations of BSA require higher concentrations of detergents to produce maximal GT activation, whereas low concentrations (2 mg/ml) prevent enhancement of bilirubin conjugation by both detergents and UDPNAG. These effects were observed only in part when rat albumin was substituted for BSA and could not be reproduced when BSA was replaced by β-lactoglobulin. None of these effects of BSA on bilirubin conjugation could be demonstrated when *p*-nitrophenol was employed as the acceptor substrate for GT. Thus, it appears that BSA selectively interferes with the process of bilirubin conjugation *in vitro* by rat liver microsomes. Since in the liver cell, prior to its conjugation, bilirubin is bound to ligandin (24) rather than albumin, the relevance of these findings to its *in vivo* conjugation is unknown.

In attempting to explain these findings, an obvious hypothesis is that the effects on bilirubin GT activity of the various proteins studied are determined by their influence on the "free," or available substrate concentration. However, no obvious direct relationship between GT activity and the free bilirubin concentration was evident. Indeed, as noted above, at any molar ratio of bilirubin to albumin, the calculated free bilirubin concentration is lower with BSA than with rat albumin, although bilirubin GT activity is higher in the former case than the latter. Hence, the effects of different proteins in the incubation mixtures do not appear to be mediated solely by alterations in the free bilirubin concentration. This latter conclusion must be considered somewhat tentative, as the free bilirubin concentrations were calculated from binding constants highly dependent on methodology (16, 22, 25), using a simple mathematical model which ignores the binding of bilirubin to microsomes (26) and other trace constituents of the reaction mixture. A rigorous calculation of the free bilirubin concentration in the initial reaction mixture does not appear feasible at this time, both because of the complexities of the model, and the uncertainties in the various binding parameters.

That the precise basis for the observed effects of BSA remains obscure may reflect the complexity of the processes taking place in the microsomal reaction mixture, and the in-

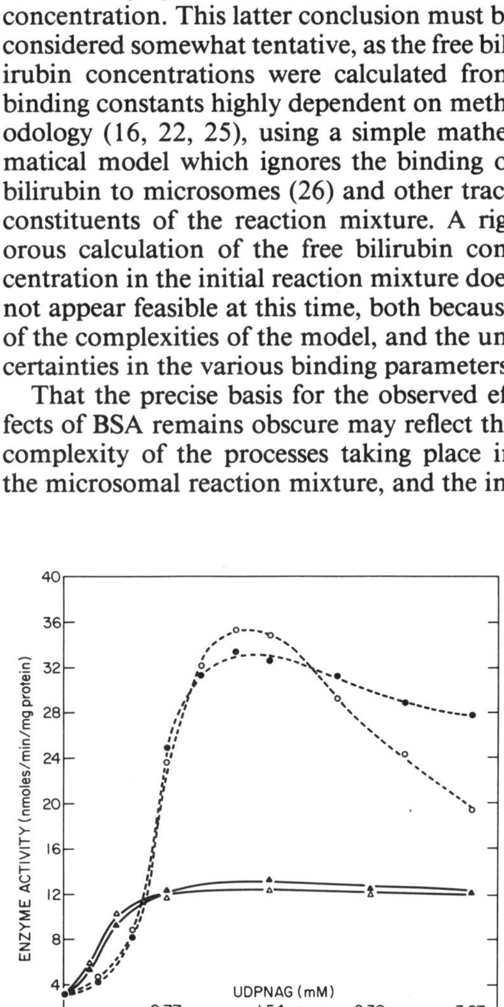

FIG. 12. Effect of UDPNAG (triangles) or deoxycholate (circles) on p-nitrophenol GT activity in presences of 2 (open symbols) and 12 (closed symbols) mg/ml bovine serum albumin.

adequacy of the relatively crude endpoint employed for their quantitation. Thus, bilirubin conjugation involves the formation of two isomeric (C_8, C_{12}) bilirubin monoglucuronides, as well as bilirubin diglucuronide, each of which may be formed at a different rate. Twice as much cosubstrate (UDPGA) is consumed per mole of bilirubin diglucuronide formed as per mole of bilirubin monoglucuronide, yet the extraction/diazotization procedure employed to quantitate conjugation does not distinguish between the formation of diconjugated and monoconjugated products.

Studies from our laboratory and others have demonstrated the formation of both bilirubin mono- and diglucuronides by native UDPNAG- and digitonin-activated rat liver microsomes (27). To accurately define the effect of BSA on these processes, the use of purified enzyme rather than microsomal preparations (9), and of high-performance liquid chromatography to determine the rates of formation of individual products (28) would be essential. While such studies are now becoming technically feasible in the basic biochemistry laboratory, they remain impractical in the setting of a clinical enzyme assay. Hence, studies of the sort described above will continue to be performed for some years to come, employing homogenates of microsomal preparations from very small samples of human liver and extraction and diazotization produces to estimate the overall rate of formation of conjugated products.

The present studies indicate that BSA profoundly affects the *in vitro* glucuronidation of bilirubin by rat liver microsomes, and, presumably by human liver when employed in analogous assay procedures. Because of the widespread use of BSA in *in vitro* measurements of bilirubin GT activity in human liver biopsy specimens, the importance of these results must be kept in mind. Caution will be necessary when comparing bilirubin GT activities from different laboratories, both with respect to its "native" and activated values, as different assay procedures may include different concentrations of BSA in the enzyme reaction mixture. Additionally, special consideration of the present findings is warranted in those studies which utilize DMSO to dissolve bilirubin (29), as the bilirubin GT activities, at least following activation by detergents or UDPNAG, may provide information considerably different from that obtained in the presence of albumin.

The authors sincerely thank Ms. Annette Seaborough for her devotion in the preparation of the manuscript. This work was supported by Grant AM-26438 from the National Institute of Arthritis, Diabetes, Digestive and Kidney Diseases, by Grant HD-17556 from the National Institute of Child Health and Human Development, and by generous gifts from the Jack Martin Fund and the Polly Annenberg Levee Charitable Trust. Portions of this study were published in abstract form (Hepatology **2**:717, 1982).

---

1. Van Roy FP, Heirwegh KPM. Determination of bilirubin glucuronide and assay of glucuronyl transferase with bilirubin as acceptor. Biochem J **107**:507–518, 1968.
2. Strebel L, Odell GB. Bilirubin uridine diphosphoglucuronyl transferase in rat liver microsomes: Genetic variation and maturation. Pediatr Res **5**:548–559, 1971.
3. Isselbacher KJ, Chrabas MF, Quinn RC. The solubilization and partial purification of a glucuronyl transferase from rabbit liver microsomes. J Biol Chem **237**:3033–3036, 1962.
4. Dutton GJ. The biosynthesis of glucuronides. In: Dutton GJ, ed. Glucuronic Acid: Free and Combined. New York, Academic Press, p185, 1966.
5. Rao GS, Hauter G, Rao ML, Breuer H. An improved assay for steroid glucuronyl transferase in rat liver microsomes. Anal Biochem **74**:35–40, 1976.
6. Sanchez E, Tephly TR. Morphine metabolism. I. Evidence for separate enzymes in the glucuronidation of morphine and p-nitrophenol by rat hepatic microsomes. Drug Metab Dispos **2**:247–253, 1974.
7. Bock KW, von Clausbruch VC, Josting D, Ottenwalder H. Separation and partial purification of two differentially inducible UDP-glucuronyl transferases from rat liver. Biochem Pharmacol **26**:1097–1110, 1977.
8. Otani G, Abou-El-Makarem MM, Bock KW. UDP-glucuronyl-transferase in perfused rat liver and in microsomes. III. Effects of galactosamine and carbon tetrachloride on the glucuronidation of 1-naphtol and bilirubin. Biochem Pharmacol **25**:1293–1297, 1976.
9. Burchell B. Bilirubin UDP-glucuronyl transferase. In: Jacoby WB, ed. Methods in Enzymology. New York, Academic Press, p188, 1981.
10. Black M, Billing BH, Heirwegh KPM. Determination of bilirubin UDP-glucuronyltransferase activity in needle-biopsy specimens of human liver. Clin Chim Acta **29**:27–35, 1970.
11. Black M, Billing BH. Hepatic bilirubin UDP-glucuronyl transferase activity in liver disease and Gilbert's syndrome. N Engl J Med **280**:1266–1271, 1969.
12. Felsher BF, Carpio NM. Chronic persistent hepatitis

and unconjugated hyperbilirubinemia. Gastroenterology **76**:248–252, 1979.
13. Tavoloni N, Jones MJT, Wittman R, Kiang C-L, Berk PD. Comparison of different activators and diazotization procedures in the assay of bilirubin-UDP-glucuronyl transferase activity in rat liver. Clin Chim Acta **128**:209–221, 1983.
14. Brodersen R, Theilgaard J. Bilirubin colloid formation in neutral aqueous solution. Scand J Clin Lab Invest **24**:395–398, 1969.
15. Lee K, Gartner LM. Spectrophotometric characteristics of bilirubin. Pediatr Res **10**:782–788, 1976.
16. McDonagh AF. Bile pigments: Bilatrienes and 5,15-bilatrienes. In: Dolphin D, ed. The Porphyrins. New York, Academic Press, Vol 6:p293, 1979.
17. Berk PD, Kiang C-L, Stremmel W, Tavoloni N. A simple procedure for the isolation of bilirubin monoglucuronide and diglucuronide from bile. J Lab Clin Med **99**:559–547, 1982.
18. Tavoloni N, Jones MJT, Berk PD. Effect of low-dose phenobarbital on hepatic microsomal UDP-glucuronyl transferase activity. Biochem Pharmacol **32**:2143–2147, 1983.
19. Lowry OH, Rosebrogh NJ, Farr AL, Randall RJ. Protein measurement with the Folin phenol reagent. J Biol Chem **193**:265–275, 1951.
20. Weber AP, Schalm L. Quantitative separation and determination of bilirubin and conjugated bilirubin in human serum. Clin Chim Acta **7**:805–810, 1962.
21. Wolkoff AW, Ketley JN, Waggoner JG, Berk PD, Jacoby W. Hepatic accumulation and intracellular binding of conjugated bilirubin. J Clin Invest **61**:142–149, 1978.
22. Chen RF. The fluorescence of bilirubin–albumin complexes. In: Thaer AA, Sernetz M, eds. Fluorescence Techniques in Cell Biology. New York, Springer, p273, 1973.
23. Wosilait WD, Nagy P. A method of computing drug distribution in plasma using stepwise association constants: Clofibrate acid as an illustrative example. Comput Programs Biomed **6**:142–148, 1976.
24. Levi AJ, Gatmaitan Z, Arias IM. Two hepatic cytoplasmic protein fractions, Y and Z, and their possible role in the hepatic uptake of bilirubin, sulphobromophthalein, and other anions. J Clin Invest **48**:2156–2167, 1969.
25. Lee K, Gartner LM. Bilirubin binding by plasma proteins: A critical evaluation of methods and clinical implications. Rev Perinat Med **2**:319–343, 1978.
26. Vessey DA, Goldenberg J, Zakim D. Differentiation of homologous forms of hepatic microsomal UDP-glucuronyl transferase. II. Characterization of the bilirubin conjugating form. Biochim Biophys Acta **309**:75–82, 1973.
27. Blanckaert N, Gollan J, Schmid R. Bilirubin diglucuronide synthesis by a UDP-glucuronic acid-dependent enzyme system in rat liver microsomes. Proc Natl Acad Sci USA **76**:2037–2041, 1979.
28. Gordon ER, Goresky CA. A rapid and quantitative high performance liquid chromatographic method for assaying bilirubin and its conjugates in bile. Canad J Biochem **60**:1050–1057, 1982.
29. Odell GB, Cuckier JO, Gourley GR. The presence of microsomal UDP-glucuronyl transferase for bilirubin in homozygous jaundiced Gunn rats and in the Crigler–Najjar syndrome. Hepatology **2**:307–315, 1981.

Received October 14, 1983. P.S.E.B.M. 1984, Vol. 176.
Accepted April 17, 1984.

PROCEEDINGS OF THE SOCIETY FOR EXPERIMENTAL BIOLOGY AND MEDICINE **176**, 366–370 (1984)

Muramyl Dipeptide-Induced Enhancement of Phagocytosis of Antibiotic Pretreated *Escherichia coli* by Macrophages (41884)

HERMAN FRIEDMAN AND GEORGE WARREN

Department of Medical Microbiology and Immunology, University of South Florida College of Medicine, Tampa, Florida, and Department of Microbiology, Thomas Jefferson University School of Medicine, Philadelphia, Pennsylvania 19107

Abstract. Treatment of mice with muramyl dipeptide, a known immunoadjuvant, resulted in marked augmentation of the phagocytic activity of peritoneal macrophages incubated *in vitro* with *Escherichia coli.* Even greater phagocytosis occurred when the *E. coli* were pretreated for 2 hr with subinhibitory concentrations of the semisynthetic penicillins cyclacillin or ampicillin, but not penicillin G to which they were resistant. The antibiotic-pretreated *E. coli* were more rapidly ingested by the macrophages derived from MDP-treated mice as compared to similar cells from normal mice. Optimum augmentation of phagocytosis of untreated or antibiotic-pretreated *E. coli* occurred 2 to 3 days after administration of MDP to the mice. Similar augmentation of phagocytosis occurred by treating cultures of peritoneal macrophages from normal mice *in vitro* with MDP prior to incubation with the antibiotic-pretreated bacteria. These results indicate that macrophages from MDP stimulated mice interact with antibiotic-pretreated bacteria to a greater extent than with untreated *E. coli,* resulting in increased phagocytosis and killing of the bacteria.

A wide variety of substances stimulate increased phagocytic activity of macrophages, either *in vivo* or *in vitro* (1–4). In this regard, purified bacterial cell wall products, as well as synthetic analogs of the adjuvants of such cell walls are strong immunologic stimulators and macrophage activators (5, 6). A large number of studies have shown that substances such as muramyl dipeptide (MDP), widely studied as a synthetic analog of the cell wall adjuvant derived from microorganisms such as mycobacteria, activate macrophages and increase their phagocytic activity (4–12). Previous studies in this laboratory, as well as others, have shown that bacteria such as staphylococci or *Escherichia coli,* when incubated *in vitro* with an antibiotic which inhibits cell wall synthesis, become extremely susceptible to killing by phagocytic cells such as macrophages, polymorphonuclear cells, neutrophils, etc. (13–22). In the present study *E. coli,* when incubated with semisynthetic penicillins such as cyclacillin or ampicillin, but not with penicillin G to which they were resistant, became much more susceptible to phagocytosis not only by macrophages from normal mice, but also from animals pretreated with the macrophage stimulator MDP.

Experimental Methods and Procedures. *Bacteria.* A penicillin-resistant strain of *E. coli* was utilized for the study (13, 16). The bacteria were cultured for 18 hr in brain–heart infusion broth at 37°C, washed by centrifugation at 10,000*g* with sterile saline and resuspended to a concentration of 10^8 bacteria per milliliter saline as determined by standard plate counting. The bacteria were resistant to at least 500 U penicillin/ml but were susceptible to cyclacillin and ampicillin, with an MIC of 5–10 μg/ml.

Animals. Inbred BALB/c mice weighing 16–18 g each were obtained from The Jackson Laboratory (Bar Harbor, Me.). They were maintained in groups of five to six in plastic mouse cages and fed Purina mouse pellets and water *ad libitum.*

Phagocytic assay. Cells from the peritoneum of unstimulated mice were obtained by lavage with 5 ml sterile Medium 199. The cells in the lavage fluid were pelleted by centrifugation at 1000*g*, and resuspended in Medium 199 containing 10% fetal calf serum. The percentage of macrophages in the cell suspensions was ascertained by microscopic examination after Giemsa staining. Over 90% of the cells readily phagocytized latex particles within 15 min at 37°C as determined by microscopic examination. For phagocytic studies, a suspension of 10^6 nucleated cells in 0.5 ml medium were incubated for up to 4 hr at 37°C

0037-9727/84 $1.50

with 10^7 or 10^8 bacteria. The number of phagocytizing cells per 100 macrophages was determined by microscopic examination, usually with triplicate samples, and the average number of phagocytizing cells per culture calculated.

Muramyl dipeptide. MDP was obtained as a kind gift from the Pasteur Institute, Paris, France, through the courtesy of Dr. Louis Chedid. The adjuvant was suspended in saline at varying concentrations and injected into animals or added to cultures as needed.

Antibiotics. Cyclacillin, ampicillin, and penicillin G were obtained from Wyeth Laboratories and resuspended in saline in the appropriate concentrations (16).

Experimental design. Dispersed macrophage preparations were obtained from normal or MDP-pretreated mice and suspensions of 10^6 washed cells were placed in test tubes to which were added graded numbers of viable *E. coli,* either untreated or previously treated for 2 hr with the indicated concentration of antibiotic. Following further incubation of the bacteria–cell mixture for 30 min to 4 hr, aliquots of the cell samples were washed, the supernatants plated for bacteria, and the pelleted cells examined microscopically, after staining with gram stain, for the numbers of bacteria per cell. In some experiments the pelleted cells, after washing, were frozen and thawed three times and the numbers of bacteria determined by standard plate counting. In all cases at least 100 macrophages were examined for phagocytic activity per slide.

Experimental Result. As is apparent in Table I, peritoneal macrophages from MDP-treated mice had approximately twice as much phagocytic activity as those from normal mice after incubation with untreated *E. coli.* However, when the *E. coli* were pretreated for 2 hr with graded amounts of cyclacillin, ampicillin, or penicillin, and then washed before incubation with the macrophage cultures, marked differences in the percentage of phagocytizing cells occurred. Those *E. coli* which had been preincubated with cyclacillin or ampicillin were much more readily phagocytized by macrophages from both normal as well as MDP-treated mice. In general, macrophages from the MDP-treated mice phagocytized twice as many antibiotic-pretreated bacteria as did the macrophages from normal

TABLE I. EFFECT OF MDP PRETREATMENT OF MICE ON PHAGOCYTIC ACTIVITY OF PERITONEAL MACROPHAGES INCUBATED WITH ANTIBIOTIC-PRETREATED *E. coli*

Antibiotic pretreatment of *E. coli*[a]	Macrophage source for phagocytosis[b]: Normal mice	MDP pretreated[c]	P^d
None (control)	5.2 ± 1.3	11.3 ± 2.1	<0.05
Cyclacillin (μg)			
10.0	15.3 ± 2.4	30.5 ± 2.6	<0.01
5.0	18.5 ± 3.1	32.6 ± 3.8	<0.01
1.0	12.3 ± 1.2	25.2 ± 1.9	<0.01
Ampicillin (μg)			
10.0	12.3 ± 2.1	28.3 ± 3.1	<0.01
5.0	15.9 ± 3.1	31.1 ± 2.7	<0.01
1.0	16.1 ± 2.9	25.2 ± 3.2	<0.01
Penicillin G (U)			
200	6.1 ± 0.8	10.3 ± 1.2	<0.05
50	5.8 ± 0.7	11.5 ± 0.9	<0.05

[a] Indicated antibiotic incubated with 10^8 *E. coli* for 2 hr at 37°C before assay.

[b] Average percentage ± SD of macrophages taking up two or more *E. coli* after incubation for 2 hr at 37°C with 10^8 *E. coli.*

[c] Mice injected 2 days earlier with 50.0 μg MDP.

[d] Probability determined by Student's *t* test (probability between MDP pretreated vs control for each group).

control mice. It was apparent, however, that when *E. coli* were pretreated with penicillin, either a high or low dose, there was essentially no difference in their uptake by macrophages as compared to the uptake of untreated bacteria.

In other experiments (data not shown) it was found that greater killing of the bacteria occurred with macrophages from MDP-treated mice as compared to normal mice. Following incubation with the bacteria for 2 hr fewer organisms were recovered in the supernatant or cell-free lysates from cultures of macrophages derived from MDP-pretreated mice as compared to control cultures, using *E. coli* pretreated with cyclacillin or ampicillin, but not penicillin.

The time of administration of MDP to mice markedly affected the ability of the peritoneal cells to phagocytize either untreated or antibiotic-pretreated *E. coli* (Table II). Maximum augmentation of phagocytosis occurred when peritoneal cells were obtained from mice given MDP 2 days earlier. Increased phagocytosis

TABLE II. EFFECT OF TIME OF ADMINISTRATION OF MDP TO MICE ON ABILITY OF PE MACROPHAGES TO PHAGOCYTIZE UNTREATED OR ANTIBIOTIC-PRETREATED *E. coli*

	Phagocytosis of *E. coli*[b]		
Day of injection[a]	None	Cyclacillin (2.0 μg)	Penicillin (100 U)
None	4.2 ± 0.8	14.1 ± 2.3*	5.3 ± 1.1
MDP			
1	9.1 ± 1.2	22.6 ± 2.1*	8.1 ± 1.2
2	11.3 ± 1.6	30.1 ± 3.2*	12.3 ± 1.9
4	7.2 ± 0.8	17.8 ± 1.9*	6.7 ± 0.7
8	5.1 ± 1.1	15.3 ± 2.1*	8.2 ± 1.1
15	4.3 ± 0.7	13.8 ± 1.7*	5.3 ± 0.8

[a] Mice injected ip with 50 μg MDP on day indicated before assay for phagocytosis.

[b] Average percentage ± SD of PE macrophages phagocytizing two or more *E. coli* after 2-hr incubation at 37°C with 10^8 *E. coli* either untreated or after 2-hr pretreatment with indicated antibiotic.

* $P < 0.02$ determined by Student's *t* test for phagocytosis of cyclacillin vs untreated bacteria.

also occurred, but to a lesser extent, when the macrophages were obtained 1 day after MDP administration. However, by the third to fourth day after MDP administration there was only a slight or marginal effect on phagocytic activity. By 8 to 15 days after MDP pretreatment there was essentially no detectable effect.

MDP addition to cultures of normal macrophages increased their ability to phagocytize *E. coli,* either untreated or pretreated with cyclacillin (Table III). Addition of 1–10 μg MDP to cultures of normal macrophages 2 hr prior to addition of the *E. coli* resulted in marked stimulation of the ability of the macrophages to phagocytize the bacteria. In other experiments (data not shown) addition of MDP at the time of culture initiation had marginal, if any effect on the uptake of the bacteria.

Discussion and Conclusions. Results of this study indicate that macrophages obtained from the peritoneum of mice stimulated with a known macrophage activator, i.e., MDP, showed enhanced ability to phagocytize and kill *E. coli in vitro.* The total number of phagocytized *E. coli* in the macrophages and the percentage of macrophages showing uptake of two or more *E. coli* increased markedly when these cells were obtained from MDP-treated mice. Furthermore, addition of MDP to cultures of macrophages *in vitro* resulted in markedly stimulated phagocytosis of both untreated and cyclacillin or ampicillin-pretreated *E. coli.*

Previous studies had shown that semisynthetic penicillins, i.e., cyclacillin and ampicillin, markedly increased the susceptibility of *E. coli* to killing by antibody and complement *in vitro* or by macrophages (13–16). It seemed likely that a subinhibitory dose of the anti-

TABLE III. EFFECT OF MDP ADDITION TO CULTURES OF NORMAL MOUSE PERITONEAL MACROPHAGES ON PHAGOCYTOSIS OF ANTIBIOTIC-PRETREATED *E. coli*

	Antibiotic pretreatment of *E. coli*[b]			
		Cyclacillin[c]		
MDP addition to cultures[a]	None	5.0 μg	1.0 μg	Penicillin (100 U)[c]
None	5.2 ± 1.2	15.1 ± 2.5*	17.3 ± 2.1*	6.1 ± 0.9
MDP (μg)				
100	12.1 ± 2.2	24.4 ± 1.9*	31.4 ± 2.4*	11.3 ± 1.2
5.0	11.3 ± 1.9	28.5 ± 2.6*	30.5 ± 3.1*	10.1 ± 2.2
1.0	6.5 ± 0.5	20.1 ± 2.5*	27.6 ± 1.3*	8.3 ± 1.3
0.5	7.2 ± 0.9	14.5 ± 2.2*	20.3 ± 2.1*	7.5 ± 0.9

[a] Indicated amount of MDP added to cultures of 10^6 peritoneal macrophages from normal mice 2 hr before assay for phagocytosis.

[b] Average percentage ± SD of macrophages in 3–4 cultures phagocytizing two or more *E. coli* after incubation for 2 hr with 10^8 *E. coli* at 37°.

[c] *E. coli* pretreated for 2 hr culture with indicated antibiotic at 37°C before washing and phagocytosis assay.

* $P < 0.02$ for phagocytosis of cyclacillin vs untreated bacteria.

biotic altered the surface of the bacteria sufficiently so they would be more readily recognized by host immune factors such as antibody or phagocytes. Studies from a number of laboratories have shown that filaments are formed when *E. coli* or other bacteria are exposed *in vitro* for even relatively short periods of time with a subinhibitory concentration of an antibiotic (26). Furthermore, other studies in this laboratory showed a greater immunogenicity of antibiotic-pretreated *E. coli* as determined by appropriate injection of extracts of macrophages cultured *in vitro* with the bacteria (6).

The results of this study support the view that even a subinhibitory concentration of an antibiotic, which does not kill the bacteria, may alter the susceptibility of a bacterium to host factors, possibly by exposure of new antigenic determinant(s) on the surface or increasing the amount of somatic antigens. Such bacteria undoubtedly become much more readily recognizable by cells such as macrophages. The results of the present study further show that activated macrophages, i.e., those obtained from MDP-pretreated mice, can recognize such antibiotic-pretreated bacteria to a greater extent than untreated bacteria and thus result in increased phagocytosis and killing of the bacteria. Such synergism between antibiotic pretreatment of bacteria and enhancement of phagocytic activity by an adjuvant may be a useful strategy for increasing the immunologic competence of immunosuppressed individuals who are susceptible to opportunistic microorganisms such as gram-negative bacteria. The combination of antibiotic therapy and immunostimulation should be useful for overcoming heightened susceptibility to infection by individuals with immunologic deficiencies.

1. Klebanoff SJ, Haman CB. Antimicrobial systems of mononuclear phagocytes. In: von Furth R, ed. Mononuclear Phagocytes in Immunity, Infection and Immunopathology. Oxford, pp507–529, 1975.
2. Nelson DS, ed. Immunobiology of Macrophages. New York, Academic Press, 1978.
3. Cohn ZA. The activation of mononuclear phagocytes: Fact, fancy and future. J Immunol **121**:813–820, 1978.
4. Sone S, Fidler IJ 1981. In vitro activation of tumoricidal properties in rat alveolar macrophages by synthetic muramyl dipeptide encapsulated in liposomes. Cell Immunol **57**:42–50, 1981.
5. Friedman H, Specter S, Butler C. Stimulation of immunostimulatory factors by bacterial endotoxin or nontoxic polysaccharides. In: Nowotny A, ed. Beneficial Aspects of Endotoxin. New York, Plenum, pp273–282, 1983.
6. Friedman H. Immunomodulation by small molecular weight bacterial products. Adv Exp Biol Med **166**:199–214, 1983.
7. Lederer E. Immunomodulation by muramyl peptides; Recent developments. Clin Immunol Newslett **3**:83–85, 1982.
8. Yamamura Y, Zuma I. Immunostimulation in cancer patients by biological response modifiers. Adv Exp Med Biol **166**:1–13, 1982.
9. Chedid L, Audibert F, Johnson AG. Biological activities of muramyl dipeptide, a synthetic glycopeptide analogous to bacterial immunoregulating agents. Progr Allergy, **25**:13–79, 1978.
10. Chedid L, Parant M, Audibert F, Lefrancier F, Chocy J, Sela M. Enhancement of certain biological activities of muramyl dipeptide derivatives after conjugation to a multipoly (DL-alanine)-poly (L-lysine) carrier. Proc Natl Acad Sci USA **76**:6557–6561, 1979.
11. Humphres RC, Henika PR, Ferraresis RW, Krahoubuhl JC. Effects of treatment with muramyl dipeptide and certain of its analogs on resistance to Listeria monocytogenes in mice. Infect Immun **30**:462–466, 1981.
12. Kierszenbaum F, Ferraresis RW. Enhancement of host resistance against *Trypanosoma cruzi* infection by immunoregulatory agent muramyl dipeptide. Infect Immun **25**:273–278, 1979.
13. Friedman H, Warren GH. Antibacterial activity of cyclacillin in vivo and in vitro: Effects on gram-negative organisms. Progr Chemother **2**:119–126, 1974.
14. Friedman H, Warren GH. Enhanced susceptibility of penicillin-resistant staphylococci to phagocytosis after in vitro incubation with low doses of nafcillin. Proc Soc Exp Biol Med **146**:707–711, 1974.
15. Friedman H, Warren GH. Antibody mediated bacteriolysis: Enhanced killing of cyclacillin-treated bacteria. Proc Soc Exp Biol Med **153**:301–304, 1976.
16. Friedman H, Warren GH. Cyclacillin-induced potentiation of *Escherichia coli* immunogenicity in vivo and in vitro. Chemotherapy **23**:324–336, 1977.
17. Friedman H, Warren G. Increased phagocytosis of *Escherichia coli* pretreated with subinhibitory concentrations of cyclacillin or ampicillin. Proc Soc Exp Biol Med **169**:301–305, 1982.
18. Ofeki I, Beeckery EH, Seisenstein BI, Alkan ML, Shann N. Suppression of bacterial adherence by sublethal concentration of B-lactan and aminoglycoside antibiotics. Rev Infect Dis **1**:832–837, 1979.
19. Germmell CG, Petersen PK, Schmalling D, Kim Y, Malteus J, Wannanaker L, Quie PG. Potentiation of opsonication of phagocytosis of *Streptococcus pyogenes* following growth in the presence of clindamycin. J Clin Invest **67**:1249–1256, 1981.

20. Vosbeck K, Handschin H, Merge EB, Zak G. Effects of subinhibitory concentration of antibiotics on adhesiveness of *Escherichia coli* in vitro. Rev Infect Dis **1**:845–851, 1979.

21. Forsgen AG, Banck H, Beckman A, Belhoshene. Antibiotic–host defense interactions in vitro and in vivo. Scand J Infect Dis Suppl **24**:195–203, 1980.

22. Mandell LA. Effects of antimicrobial and antineoplastic drugs on the phagocytic and microbicidal function of the polymorphonuclear leukocyte. Infect Dis Rev **4**:683–687, 1982.

23. McDonald PJ, Wetherall BL, Prinel H. Post antibiotic leukocyte enhancement. Increased susceptibility of bacteria pretreated with antibiotic to activity of leukocytes. Rev Infect Dis **3**:38–44, 1981.

24. Horne D, Tomasz D. Hypersusceptibility of penicillin treated group B streptococci to bactericidal activity of human polymorphonuclear leukocytes. Antimicrob Agents Chemother **19**:745–753, 1981.

25. Root RK, Istnonz R, Molavs A, Metcalf JA, Maleck HL. Interaction between antibiotics and human neutrophils in the killing of staphylococci; studies with normal and cytochalasin B treated cells. J Clin Invest **67**:247–259, 1981.

26. Gillissen G. Antibiotics and immune responses, concomitant effects of chemotherapy. Immun Infek **8**:79–88, 1980.

27. Munster AM, Loodholdt CB, Leary AG, Barnes MA. Effect of antibiotics on cell-mediated immunity. Surgery **81**:692–695, 1977.

Received January 30, 1984. P.S.E.B.M. 1984, Vol. 176.
Accepted April 18, 1984.

PROCEEDINGS OF THE SOCIETY FOR EXPERIMENTAL BIOLOGY AND MEDICINE **176**, 371–377 (1984)

Pulsed Electromagnetic Fields Increase the Rate of Rat Liver Regeneration after Partial Hepatectomy (41885)

V. OTTANI,* M. G. MONTI,† G. PICCININI,† L. PERNECCO,† P. ZANIOL,‡
A. RUGGERI,* AND B. BARBIROLI†

**Istituto di Anatomia Umana Normale, Via Irnerio 48, 40126 Bologna, †Istituto di Chimica Biologica, Via Campi 287, 41100 Modena, and ‡Istituto di Radiologia, Via del Pozzo, 41100 Modena, Italy*

Abstract. Pulsed extremely low-frequency electromagnetic fields interact with rat liver regeneration following partial hepatectomy when delivered to the rats immediately after the operation and every 12 hr thereafter. This interaction results first in an increased ornithine decarboxylase activity, an enzyme used as an early marker of cell growth. The rate of labeled thymidine incorporation into DNA is also increased by the treatments with magnetic fields during the early phases of liver regeneration. Glycogen depletion and lipid accumulation, two well-known early peculiar phenomena of liver regeneration following partial hepatectomy, are quantitatively decreased by the treatments with electromagnetic fields. The recovery to normal glycogen and lipid contents is completed within 5 days after surgery, instead of 7 days as found in control rats.

It is known that extremely low-frequency (ELF, 1–1000 Hz) pulsed electromagnetic fields interact with the living organisms and are able to modify several metabolic parameters of the cell (1–6). They are also being used to stimulate ligament (7) and bone healing (8) and to treat successfully several human bone diseases (9). However, very little is known not only of their mode of action but also of their precise effects on mammalian soft tissues.

A potentially fruitful approach to gain some insights into this problem would be the study of the effects of ELF electromagnetic fields on rat liver regeneration after partial hepatectomy. In fact this is a model for the study of controlled growth *in vivo* and a useful comparative system to study uncontrolled growth (10).

In this paper we report a remarkable increase of ornithine decarboxylase activity, an early marker of cell growth (11), induced in the regenerating rat liver by ELF pulsed electromagnetic fields. We show further that the same treatment induces an increase of the rate of DNA synthesis. Other parameters, such as glycogen and lipid contents, studied by stereological procedures performed on electron micrographs, show that treatment with pulsed electromagnetic fields determines a faster recovery of liver toward a normal metabolism.

Materials and Methods. Four-month-old male albino Wistar rats (350–370 g) were used in these experiments. Partial hepatectomy was performed under ether anesthesia with removal of the main lobes (68–70% of the liver) as described by Higgins and Anderson (12). All operations were performed at the same time of day (i.e., between 8:00 and 9:00 AM) after a fasting period of 12 hr. The portions of liver excised were employed to evaluate at zero time the parameters studied.

At the time intervals indicated in the single experiments, groups of rats were killed by decapitation, the livers were removed, rinsed in cold saline, blotted with absorbent tissue, and weighed.

Treatment to the animals. A pulsing electromagnetic field, homogeneous in a cylindrical volume of 30-cm diameter × 20-cm length, and generated by an apparatus made by one of us (P.Z.) was used. The shape of the pulse was a major sinusoidal halfwave (50 Hz, 6 mT) followed by few cycles of different frequency (400 Hz) and intensity (0.6 mT), as shown in Fig. 1. Thirty-minute treatments were delivered to the animals immediately after surgery and thereafter every 12 hr or as indicated in the single experiments. Control rats were left for the same length of time in the apparatus after having switched it off.

Ornithine decarboxylase activity. The livers were homogenized in 0.25 *M* sucrose with a Potter–Elvehjem homogenizer fitted with Teflon pestle. The homogenates (15% w/v) were centrifuged for 90 min at 105,000*g*. The resulting supernatant fraction was used for assay of ornithine decarboxylase activity.

Ornithine decarboxylase activity was mea-

0037-9727/84 $1.50

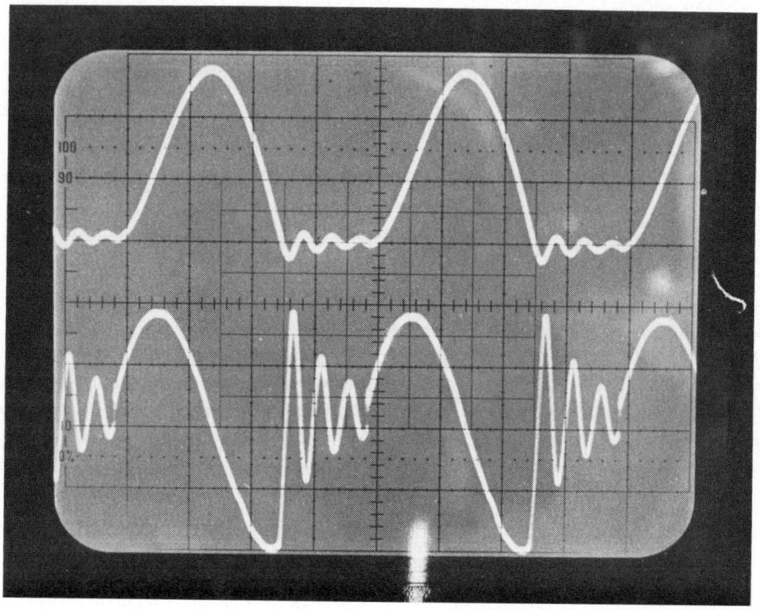

FIG. 1. Oscilloscopic traces of the pulsed electromagnetic field generated by the apparatus used in these experiments. Upper trace [$B(t)$] has been obtained by monitoring the pulsing electromagnetic field in air with a Hall probe connected to a Tektronic 466 oscilloscope (vert.: 20 G/div.; hor.: 5 msec/div.). Lower trace $\left[\frac{d\phi_B}{dt}\right]$ has been obtained by monitoring the pulsing electromagnetic field in air with a coil probe made of 50 turns of copper wire, i.d. 5 mm, length 15 mm, connected to a Tektronic 466 oscilloscope (vert.: 1 mV/div.; hor.: 5 msec/div.).

sured as previously described (13). The standard incubation mixture contained in a final volume of 0.5 ml: 25 μmole of Tris–HCl buffer, pH 7.1; 0.05 μmole of pyridoxal-5-phosphate; 1.25 μmole of dithiothreitol; 0.3 μmole of L-ornithine; 0.25 μCi of DL-[1-^{14}C]ornithine (New England Nuclear (NEN) Chemicals, GmbH, Frankfurt, Main, Germany; sp act 47.2 mCi/mmole), and 0.2 ml of liver extract. The incubations were carried out in vials fitted with a disposable polypropylene center well attached to a rubber stopper for 60 min in a shaking water bath at 37°C. The released $^{14}CO_2$ was trapped into 0.2 ml of 1 *M* hyamine hydroxide in the center well. The reaction was stopped by injecting 1 ml of 10% (w/v) trichloroacetic acid into the reaction mixture, and the vials were left for an additional 15 min at 37°C to ensure the release of all $^{14}CO_2$ from the acidified medium. The center well and its contents were put directly into a scintillation vial containing 10 ml of toluene-base scintillation fluid and counted in a Packard Tri-Carb liquid scintillation spectrometer. Protein was assayed by the method of Lowry *et al.* (14).

Incorporation of thymidine into DNA and measurement of haploid genomes. To evaluate DNA synthesis, the rats of each group were injected intraperitoneally with 50 μCi/100 g body wt of methyl[^{3}H]thymidine (NEN; sp act 16.2 Ci/mmole) in 1 ml of saline and killed by decapitation exactly 1 hr after the injection (15). The livers were quickly removed, dropped into cold saline, and blotted with filter paper, and then homogenized in 9 vol of distilled water. Perchloric acid was added to an aliquot of the homogenate to a final molarity of 0.5. After centrifugation the supernatant was saved and the residue was washed once with cold 0.2 *M* perchloric acid. The supernatants were combined and designated as the "acid-soluble fraction." The DNA in the pellet was separated from the RNA (16) and was assayed for radioactivity.

The DNA extracted as described was quantitatively assayed (17). The number of haploid genomes was calculated considering 3.25 $\times 10^{-12}$ g of DNA the weight of one rat liver haploid genome.

Electron microscopy and stereological procedure. Perfusion *via* the hepatic portal vein (18), as well as immersion fixation were carried out for every single experiment using 2% glutaraldehyde in 0.1 *M* phosphate buffer, pH 7.4. In both fixations, segments from the tip of the lobus caudatus of unoperated animals and from regenerating lobes of hepatectomized rats, either treated or untreated, were removed. The segments were cut into 1-mm^3 blocks and immersed for 2 hr in 2% glutaraldehyde. After a rapid washing in phosphate buffer, the specimens were postfixed in 1% OsO_4 in 0.1 *M* phosphate buffer, pH 7.4, and then dehydrated in graded ethanols and embedded in Araldite. Thin sections were examined at the electron microscope and photographed at a primary magnification of 4000. Pictures to be used for stereological analysis were randomly selected from specimens either fixed in glutaraldehyde or in OsO_4. Areas to be analyzed by stereological analysis (19) were randomly selected choosing the upper left corner of the grid square and photographically enlarged to 1200×. Two square lattice systems were superimposed on the electron micrographs: the first, 11 × 11 cm, having a total number of 256 test points with a point spacing of 0.7 cm; the second, a double lattice 11 × 11 cm, having a total number of 1024 test points with a point spacing of 0.3 cm.

Results and Discussion. When partially hepatectomized rats are exposed, immediately after the operation, for 30 min to the electromagnetic field described, liver ornithine decarboxylase (ODC) activity shows a striking increase compared with the control rats (Fig. 2). In fact 3 and 6 hr after the operation the enzyme activity is, respectively, 234 and 250% of the corresponding values obtained from the untreated rats. This effect appears to be transient in nature as 9 and 12 hr after the operation no difference in the enzyme activity was observed between control and treated rats. However, if the same treatment is repeated 8.5 hr after the operation, a second increase of liver ODC activity is observed 3 hr later. This increase is of a smaller magnitude, i.e., 139% of the values observed either in un-

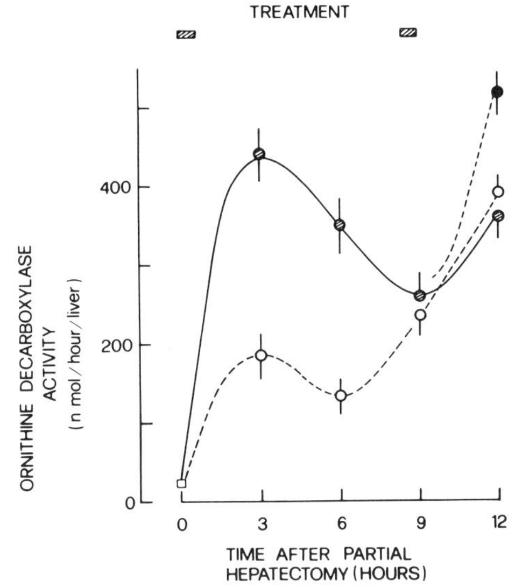

FIG. 2. Effect of ELF pulsing electromagnetic fields on ornithine decarboxylase activity of rat liver during early phases of regeneration following partial hepatectomy. Rats were treated with the electromagnetic field described in the text for 30 min, and treatment repeated 8.5 hr after surgery. Control rats (○); rats treated only once after surgery (◍); rats treated twice (●). Each point is the average of at least 9 rats and vertical bars represent the SEM.

treated rats or rats treated only once immediately after the operation (Fig 2). Exposure to the same electromagnetic field did not have any effect on liver enzyme activity in intact or sham-operated rats (data not reported).

ODC activity is induced by many hormones in their target tissues, the highest ODC levels paralleling the period of most rapid cellular growth and replication in a number of animal tissues. Direct evidence for the correlation of ODC activity and neoplastic growth has been obtained by comparing enzyme activity in normal and virus-transformed cells (for a recent review see Ref. (11)). Therefore it has been suggested that the mechanisms that regulate the ODC activity are an integral part of growth-control machinery. Furthermore, the extremely short half-life of ODC has suggested that this enzyme also plays a role in the regulation of growth. In this light our present results indicate that ELF pulsed electromagnetic fields are able either to amplify the regeneration of liver or to cause completion of regeneration to be reached in a shorter time.

To test these possibilities, we have studied

TABLE I. EFFECT OF PULSED ELF ELECTROMAGNETIC FIELDS ON THE INCORPORATION OF LABELED THYMIDINE INTO LIVER DNA DURING REGENERATION FOLLOWING PARTIAL HEPATECTOMY

Time after partial hepatectomy (days)	Total uptake (dpm/100 mg liver × 10^{-3})		Radioactivity in DNA (% of total uptake)	
	Control	Treated	Control	Treated
0	40 ± 1.2	—	ND	—
1	132 ± 2.9	289 ± 7.8	8.1 ± 0.3	18.3 ± 0.8
3	143 ± 3.5	324 ± 11.1	20.5 ± 1.1	31.6 ± 1.3
5	186 ± 6.0	263 ± 7.3	18.7 ± 0.8	21.4 ± 0.9
7	80 ± 2.9	180 ± 5.1	5.6 ± 0.2	ND

Note. Rats were injected ip with [^{3}H]thymidine and pulsed for 60 min. Rats were treated with the electromagnetic field described in the text for 30 min every 12 hr, beginning immediately after surgery. Control rats were put, for the same length of time, into the apparatus which was switched off. Data are expressed as percentage of total uptake, defined as the sum of the radioactivities in DNA and in acid-soluble fraction at 1 hr after injection (15). Figures represent the average of at least six determinations performed on different occasions ± SEM (ND = not detectable).

the later phases of regeneration by measuring the rate of DNA synthesis and the number of haploid genomes from Day 1 to Day 7 after partial hepatectomy. Rats have been treated with the same pulsed electromagnetic field for 30 min every 12 hr, receiving the first treatment immediately after surgery.

The rate of DNA synthesis has been measured by the incorporation of labeled thymidine into DNA, and data are expressed as percentage of total uptake, defined as the sum of the radioactivities in DNA and in acid-soluble fraction at 1 hr after injection (15). This minimizes the changes in uptake of labeled thymidine due to permeability of cellular membrane which in turn would alter the specific activity of the TTP precursor pool for DNA.

Indeed, the pulsed electromagnetic fields used in these experiments have a positive effect on the rate of DNA synthesis. In fact, 1 day after the operation the labeled thymidine incorporated into DNA is 18.3% of total uptake in treated rats, while control rats had only an 8.1% label in the DNA (Table I). A smaller difference is found 3 days after the operation, and at the 5th day the rate of DNA synthesis is almost the same in both control and treated rats. Seven days after the operation the control animals are still synthesizing DNA, while the treated ones do not show any detectable label in DNA. These different patterns of the rate of DNA synthesis find direct confirmation from the accumulation patterns of total liver genomes (Fig. 3). In fact control rats show a constant increase of liver total genomes from the operation to Day 7, while in treated rats the accumulation is faster during the first postoperative days. The largest difference is

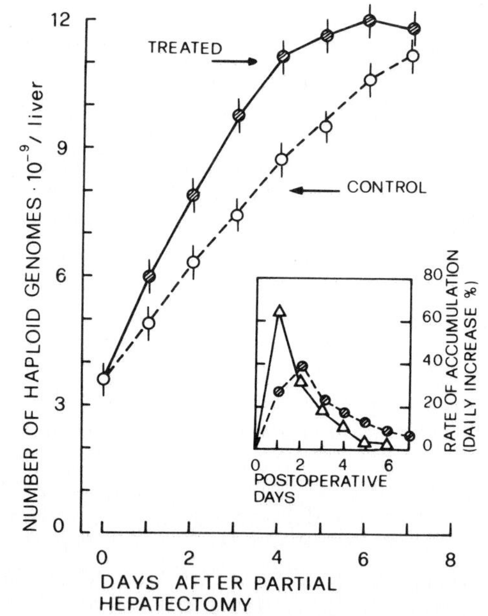

FIG. 3. Effect of pulsed ELF electromagnetic fields on the number of liver haploid genomes during regeneration following partial hepatectomy. For experimental details and treatments see legend to Table I and Materials and Methods. One liver haploid genome is considered 3.25 × 10^{-12} g of DNA. Each point represents the average of at least six determinations performed on different occasions. Vertical bars represent the SEM. The number of haploid genomes in the liver of intact rats was 13.1 ± 0.4 × 10^{-9} (average of eight determinations). The insert shows the rate of change during regeneration.

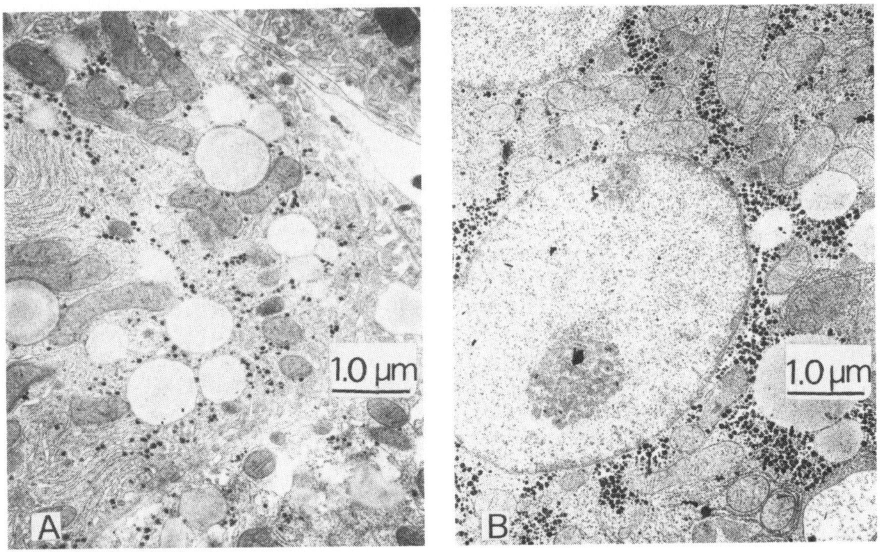

FIG. 4. Regenerating rat liver 1 day after partial hepatectomy. (A) Untreated controls; (B) rats treated with pulsed electromagnetic fields.

observed at the 4th day after surgery, and 3 days later the difference between the two groups is very small, if any. The total amount of labeled TdR (acid-soluble plus acid-insoluble counts) taken up by the cell during the pulse is remarkably increased by the treatments (Table I). This shows that magnetic fields used in these experiments have an influence on the accumulation of this molecule into the cell and hence possibly on its transport across cell membrane.

From a metabolic point of view the most striking and peculiar features of liver regeneration after partial hepatectomy are the gly-

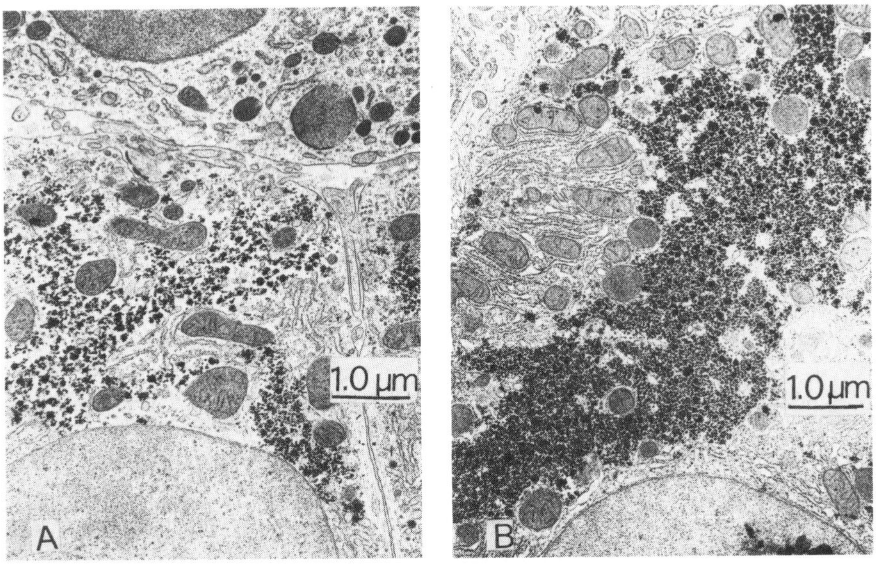

FIG. 5. Regenerating rat liver 5 days after partial hepatectomy. (A) Untreated controls; (B) rats treated with pulsed magnetic fields.

TABLE II. EFFECT OF PULSED ELF ELECTROMAGNETIC FIELDS ON GLYCOGEN AND LIPID CONTENTS OF RAT LIVER DURING REGENERATION FOLLOWING PARTIAL HEPATECTOMY

Time after partial hepatectomy (days)	Glycogen volume density (cm^3/cm^3)		Lipid volume density (cm^3/cm^3)	
	Control	Treated	Control	Treated
0	0.201 ± 0.32	—	0.004 ± 0.05	—
1	0.044 ± 0.05	0.082 ± 0.07	0.084 ± 0.01	0.043 ± 0.05
5	0.149 ± 0.17	0.195 ± 0.10	0.021 ± 0.04	0.006 ± 0.02

Note. Rats were treated with electromagnetic fields as described in the legend to Table I and under Materials and Methods. Glycogen and lipid contents were determined by stereological analysis carried out on electron photomicrographs and are expressed as volume density. Figures represent the average of at least six determinations ± SEM.

cogen depletion during the first 24 hr after the operation and the almost parallel accumulation of lipid droplets within the same time (20–22). In order to ascertain whether the pulsed electromagnetic fields used in these experiments are able to influence also these metabolic parameters, we have studied liver glycogen and lipid contents by means of stereological analysis performed on electron micrographs. Examples of ultrastructural pictures used to perform these measurements are reproduced in Figs. 4 and 5 and data are reported in Table II.

One day after the operation both phenomena, i.e., glycogen depletion and lipid accumulation, are present in a more limited extent in the liver of rats treated with pulsed electromagnetic fields. Furthermore, the treated rats at the 5th day after surgery have already reached the zero time values, whereas control rat livers still have a lower glycogen and a higher lipid content.

Electromagnetic fields have been shown to have different and often contradictory effects on the living organisms including acceleration (23) of growth and its inhibition (24). However, it is important to stress that all results must be interpreted in strict relation to the particular intensity, frequency and wave form of the magnetic field and the treating protocol used.

In our experimental conditions the electromagnetic fields used have been shown to be able to increase the rate of liver regeneration following partial hepatectomy, apparently without interfering with the control mechanisms which regulate the end-point of regeneration.

1. Bawin SM, Adey WR. Sensitivity of calcium binding in cerebral tissue to weak environment electric fields oscillating at low frequency. Proc Natl Acad Sci USA **73**:1999–2003, 1976.
2. Tabrah FL, Guernsey DL, Chou SC, Batkin S. Effect of alternating magnetic fields (60–100 gauss, 60 Hz) on *Tetrahymena pyriformis.* Tower Int Technicomedical J Life Sci **8**:73–77, 1978.
3. Chiabrera A, Hinsenkamp M, Pilla AA, Ryaby J, Ponta A, Belmont A, Beltrame F, Grattarola M, Nicolini C. Cytofluorometry of electromagnetically controlled cell differentiation. J Histochem Cytochem **27**:375–381, 1979.
4. Grisset JD. Biological effects of electric and magnetic fields associated with ELF communications systems. Proc IEEE **68**:98–104, 1980.
5. Adey WR. Tissue interactions with nonionizing electromagnetic fields. Physiol Rev **61**:435–514, 1981.
6. Greenebaum B, Goodman ZM, Marrow MT. Magnetic field effects on mitotic cycle length in Physarum. Eur J Cell Biol **27**:156–160, 1982.
7. Frank C, Schachar N, Dittrich D, Shrive N, Dehaas W, Edwards G. Electromagnetic stimulation of ligament healing in rabbits. Clin Orthop **175**:263–272, 1983.
8. Barker AT, Lunt MJ. The effects of pulsed magnetic fields on the type used in stimulation of bone fracture healing. Clin Physiol P **4**:1–27, 1983.
9. Bassett CAL. Pulsing electromagnetic fields: A new method to modify cell behavior in calcified and noncalcified tissues. Calcif Tissue Int **34**:1–8, 1982.
10. Bresnick E. Regenerating liver: An experimental model for the study of growth. Methods Cancer Res **6**:347–397, 1971.
11. Bachrach U. The induction of ornithine decarboxylase in normal and neoplastic cells. In: Gaugas JM, ed. Polyamines in Biomedical Research. Chichester, Wiley, pp81–107, 1980.
12. Higgins GM, Anderson RM. Experimental pathology of liver. I. Restoration of liver of white rat following

partial surgical removal. Arch Pathol **12**:186–190, 1931.
13. Barbiroli B, Moruzzi MS, Tadolini B, Monti MG. Ornithine decarboxylase activity in regenerating liver from rats adapted to controlled feeding schedules. J Nutr **105**:408–412, 1975.
14. Lowry OH, Rosebrough NJ, Farr AL, Randall RJ. Protein measurement with the folin phenol reagent. J Biol Chem **193**:265–275, 1951.
15. Barbiroli B, Potter VR. DNA synthesis and interaction between controlled feeding schedules and partial hepatectomy in rats. Science **172**:738–741, 1971.
16. Munro HN, Fleck A. The determination of nucleic acids. Methods Biochem Anal **14**:113–176, 1966.
17. Hopkins HA, Flora JB, Schmidt RR. Periodic DNA accumulation during the cell cycle of a termophilic strain of *Chlorella pyrenoidosa.* Arch Biochem Biophys **153**:845–849, 1972.
18. Wisse E. An electron microscopic study of the fenestrated endothelial lining of rat liver sinusoids. J Ultrastruct Res **31**,125–150, 1970.
19. Weibel ER. Stereological Methods. Vol. I. Practical Methods for Biological Morphometry. London, Academic Press, 1979.
20. Bucher NLR, Malt RA. In: Regeneration of Liver and Kidney. New England J Medicine, Medical Progress Series. Boston, Little, Brown, 1971.
21. Marks C, Markey C, Dyer R, Vaupel MR. An electron microscopic study of the effects of portacaval shunts on the ultrastructure of the rat liver after partial hepatectomy. Amer J Surg **129**:156–162, 1975.
22. Bartel H, Orkisz S, Kmiec B. Ultrastructure of hepatocyte in regenerating rat liver. Folia Morphol Warsz **4**:367–372, 1977.
23. Aarholt E, Flinn EA, Smith CW. Effects of low-frequency magnetic fields on bacterial growth rate. Phys Med Biol **26**:613–621, 1981.
24. Neurath PW. High gradient magnetic fields inhibits embryonic development of frogs. Nature (London) **219**:1358–1359, 1969.

Received September 6, 1983. P.S.E.B.M. 1984, Vol. 176.
Accepted April 18, 1984.

PROCEEDINGS OF THE SOCIETY FOR EXPERIMENTAL BIOLOGY AND MEDICINE **176**, 378–383 (1984)

Strain Differences in Testes Degeneration, Myopathy, and the Lymphocyte Mitogen Response in Vitamin E-Deficient Rats (41886)

EDDA GABRIEL, ADRIANNE BENDICH,[1] AND LAWRENCE J. MACHLIN

Vitamins and Clinical Nutrition, Hoffmann-La Roche, Nutley, New Jersey 07110

Abstract. The differences in sensitivity to vitamin E deficiency were examined in two genetically related inbred strains of rat, the spontaneously hypertensive rat and its genetic ancestor, the Wistar–Kyoto rat, as well as in the outbred Sprague–Dawley strain. The three strains showed differences in growth rate, myopathy, testes degeneration, and immunological responses in response to vitamin E deficiency with the spontaneously hypertensive rat showing the greatest sensitivity to the deficiency.

We have previously reported that tissue vitamin E levels in the spontaneously hypertensive rat (SHR) fed a commercial rodent diet were lower than in the ancestral, normotensive Wistar–Kyoto (W/K) strain (1). This was also the case when vitamin E was administered *per os* to SHR and W/K fed vitamin E-deficient diets (2). These findings suggested that there may be a difference in absorption, depletion, utilization, and/or requirement for vitamin E between these two strains. Furthermore, the data raised the questions as to whether the hypertension and depressed immune responses (3) in the SHR were related to the physiological consequences of lower tissue vitamin E and whether the SHR would be more sensitive to vitamin E deficiency than other rat strains.

In the study reported here, we compare the responses of the SHR, W/K, and the well-characterized Sprague–Dawley (SD) rat to vitamin E deficiency or supplementation by measuring several classical symptoms of vitamin E deficiency (growth rate, myopathy, and testes degeneration) as well as blood pressure and immune responses.

Materials and Methods. *Animals.* Weanling male SHR, W/K, and SD[2] were randomly separated into two groups. One group received a vitamin E-deficient casein-based semipurified diet (4) modified by substituting 10% stripped lard for corn oil.[3] The second group received the identical diet supplemented with 200 mg/kg of *all-rac-α*-tocopheryl acetate, hereafter referred to as vitamin E.

All animals were given food and water *ad libitum* and kept on a 12-hr light/dark cycle. Animals were caged in plastic containers until 6 weeks of age and then placed in stainless-steel wire-floored cages with six animals/cage. All animals remained on their respective diets until 20 weeks of age.

Body weights were measured bimonthly. Blood pressures were measured by indirect tail cuff method (5). After 5, 8, and 17 weeks on the diet, 6–12 animals from each dietary group were anesthetized with Metofane[4] and blood collected by cardiac puncture using 5% EDTA as anticoagulant. The plasma was separated and pyruvate kinase (PK) levels determined (6, 7). At the termination of the experiment, plasma, liver, testes, and gastrocnemius muscles were removed from the supplemented groups for vitamin E analysis (2).

Spleens were removed aseptically and prepared for measurement of *in vitro* mitogen activity (8). Specifically, individual spleens were evaluated for activity against the T-cell mitogens Concanavalin A (Con A), and phytohemagglutinin (PHA), and the B-cell mitogen, lipopolysaccharide from *Escherichia coli* (LPS). Single cell suspensions were prepared in RPMI 1640 tissue culture medium with 25 mM Hepes buffer supplemented with 5×10^{-5} *M* 2-mercaptoethanol, 2 m*M* glutamine, and 5.0 μg/ml gentamicin. Spleen cells (5×10^{6} cells/ml) were placed in 96-well mi-

[1] To whom correspondence should be addressed.

[2] Charles River, Wilmington, Mass.

[3] Prepared by Dyets, Bethlehem, Pa.

[4] Pitman-Moore Inc., Washington Crossing, N.J.

0037-9727/84 $1.50

crotiter plates, incubated at 37°C in a humidified 5% CO_2 incubator for 24 hr, pulsed with 1.0 μCi of [^{3}H]thymidine (sp act 2 Ci/mmole)[5] and harvested 24 hr later using a Ph.D. cell harvester.[6] The glass fiber filter disks were suspended in Liquifluor[5] and counted in a liquid scintillation counter. Data are presented as counts/minute (cpm).

In an effort to determine the reason for the more rapid onset of vitamin E deficiency symptoms of the SHR, a comparison was made of the depletion rates of the vitamin between SHR and W/K. Twenty male weanling SHR and W/K were fed the vitamin E-deficient diet for 4 weeks. At 0, 1, 2, and 4 weeks, 5 animals from each strain were sacrificed and testes and leg muscles were analyzed for vitamin E content.

Statistical analyses by Student's t test were performed to determine the effect of the dietary vitamin E level on the body weight, organ weight, and mitogenic responses within strains. Comparisons among strains were determined for the plasma PK and tissue vitamin E levels.

Results. *1. Effect of vitamin E deficiency on body weight.* After 17 weeks on the vitamin E-deficient diet, all three strains had lower body weights compared to their vitamin E-replete controls. However, this difference did not become manifest in the SD until 14 weeks on the diet (Fig. 1). In contrast, the W/K showed consistent weight differences after 3 weeks, and the SHR showed consistent weight differences after 9 weeks on the deficient diet. The SD was heavier than either SHR or W/K in both the deficient and replete groups throughout the experiment.

2. Myopathy. Following 5 weeks on the vitamin E-deficient diet, the PK of SHR was more than two times higher than that of W/K ($P < 0.01$), indicating the SHR's earlier onset of myopathy (Fig. 2). However, the degree of myopathy which eventually developed in all three strains was equivalent, as shown by PK levels following 8 or 17 weeks on the vitamin E-deficient diet.

3. Testicular degeneration and splenomegaly. The testes of SHR showed macroscopic degeneration (cyanotic appearance, decreased

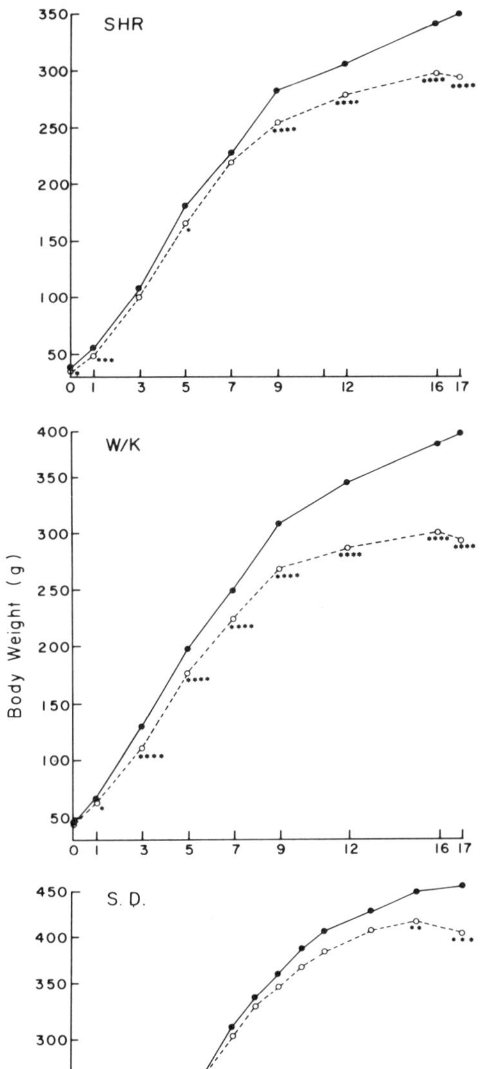

FIG. 1. Growth curves of SHR, W/K, and SD rats fed a vitamin E-deficient diet or the deficient diet supplemented with 200 mg/kg all-rac-α-tocopheryl acetate from weanling for 17 weeks. Statistical comparisons are between the vitamin E-deficient and vitamin E-supplemented animals of each strain.

[5] New England Nuclear, Boston, Mass.

[6] Cambridge Technology, Cambridge, Mass.

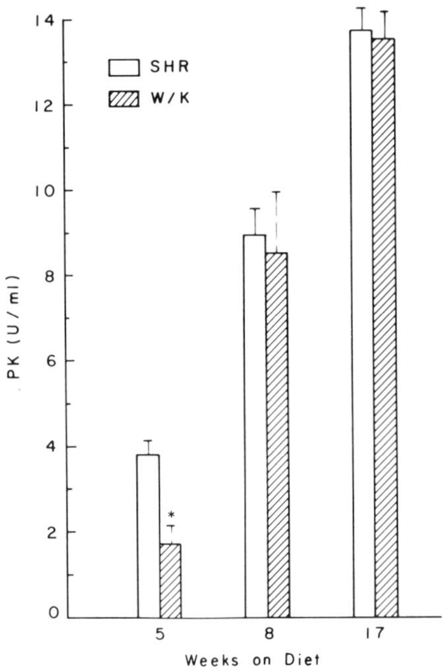

FIG. 2. Plasma pyruvate kinase levels of vitamin E-deficient SHR and W/K measured after 5, 8, and 17 weeks on the diet (*$P < 0.01$).

size and weight) after 17 weeks on a vitamin E-deficient diet. The W/K and SD showed none of these testicular changes following 17 weeks on the deficient diet (Table I). The higher testes/BW ratio seen in the W/K fed the vitamin E-deficient diet compared to the W/K fed the diet with vitamin E was due to the lower body weight of the vitamin E-deficient W/K. All three strains exhibited statistically significant splenomegaly on the deficient diet. Splenomegaly was more pronounced in the SHR and W/K than in the SD.

4. *Blood pressure.* The presence or absence of vitamin E in the diet had no effect on the systolic blood pressure of the SHR which was approximately 210 mm Hg at 20 weeks of age for both dietary groups. Blood pressures were not measured in the normotensive W/K and SD.

5. *Mitogenic responses.* All three rat strains fed the vitamin E-deficient diet had depressed splenic mitogen responses compared to animals fed the diet containing vitamin E (Fig. 3). SD splenocytes showed consistently higher mitogenic responses to both T- and B-cell mitogens than splenocytes from either SHR or W/K on either diet. Both the SHR and W/K mitogenic responses to Con A and PHA were significantly enhanced when animals were fed the diet with vitamin E compared to SHR and W/K fed the vitamin E-deficient diet. Mitogenic responses of SD were increased, but to a lesser extent, by addition of vitamin E to the diet. In all three strains there was an increase in splenic mitogen response to LPS with the addition of vitamin E to the diet.

6. *Tissue vitamin E levels and depletion rates.* When both SHR and W/K were fed the semipurified diet containing 200 mg/kg vitamin E, the plasma, liver, and testes of the

TABLE I. TESTES AND SPLEEN WEIGHTS OF RATS FED VITAMIN E-DEFICIENT OR -SUPPLEMENTED DIETS FOR 17 WEEKS

Rat strain[a]	Dietary vitamin E (mg/kg)	Testes (g)	Testes (mg/kg body wt)	Spleen (g)	Spleen (mg/g body wt)
SHR	0	1.6 ± 0.2[b]	0.56 ± 0.07	0.79 ± 0.04	0.27 ± 0.01
	200	2.9 ± 0.1***[c]	0.82 ± 0.03*	0.63 ± 0.02**	0.18 ± 0.01***
W/K	0	2.5 ± 0.1	0.87 ± 0.01	0.96 ± 0.06	0.33 ± 0.02
	200	2.7 ± 0.1*	0.70 ± 0.01***	0.79 ± 0.04*	0.20 ± 0.01***
SD	0	3.5 ± 0.1	0.88 ± 0.02	0.92 ± 0.04	0.23 ± 0.01
	200	3.6 ± 0.1	0.84 ± 0.04	0.78 ± 0.03**	0.18 ± 0.01***

[a] SHR = spontaneously hypertensive rat; W/K = Wistar–Kyoto; SD = Sprague–Dawley.
[b] Mean ± SE, from eight animals/strain.
[c] Statistical comparisons are between the vitamin E-deficient and -replete animals within each strain.
* $P < 0.05$.
** $P < 0.01$.
*** $P < 0.001$.

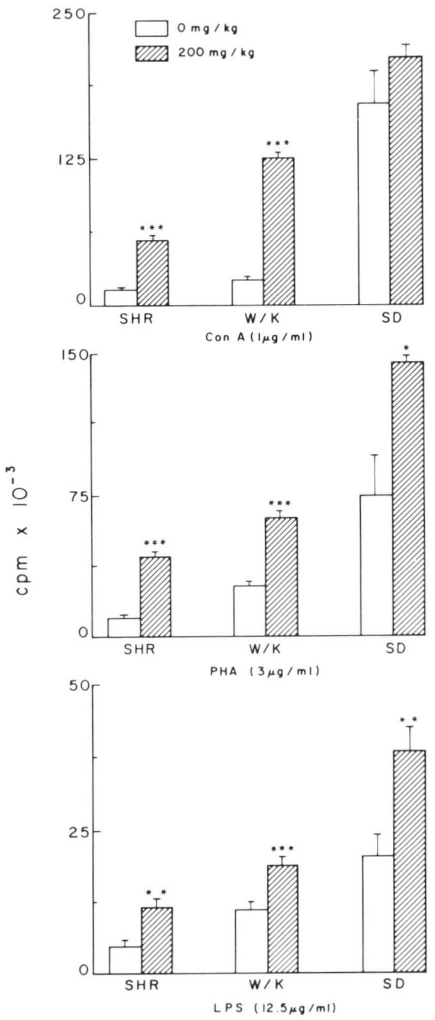

FIG. 3. Mitogen responses of SHR, W/K, and SD rat splenocytes fed either the vitamin E-deficient diet or the identical diet supplemented with 200 mg/kg all-rac-α-tocopheryl acetate for 17 weeks. Data represent responses to the optimal concentration of each mitogen. Details of culturing procedure are discussed under the Materials and Methods section. Data represent means ± SE from three experiments. Comparisons for statistical significance are between the two dietary groups in each strain for each mitogen examined (*$P < 0.05$, **$P < 0.01$, ***$P < 0.001$).

SHR still had significantly lower vitamin E levels than the W/K (Table II). There was no difference in the vitamin E level of skeletal muscle. Plasma of the SD had a level of vitamin E intermediate between the SHR and W/K which was significantly different from both. The level in the testes of the SHR and SD was identical and significantly lower than the W/K. The level of vitamin E in the muscle of SD was not different from the SHR, but was significantly higher than the W/K. The depletion rates of vitamin E from testes and muscle of the SHR and W/K fed a vitamin-E deficient diet were the same over a 4-week period (Fig. 4).

Discussion. Based on testes degeneration, body weight, and plasma PK, the SHR fed a vitamin E-deficient diet from weaning developed vitamin E deficiency signs more rapidly than the W/K or SD rats fed the identical vitamin E-deficient diet. Both of the inbred strains showed weight reduction earlier than the SD. In addition, the vitamin E-deficient SHR had the lowest response of all three strains to mitogen stimulation of splenocytes. The SHR has been shown to have lower mitogen responses than the W/K (3). In this study, we have demonstrated that all three rat strains had responses to mitogens which were modulated by dietary vitamin E, and that even on a vitamin E-deficient diet, the strain difference in mitogen responses between the SHR and W/K remained.

The lymphocyte mitogen response was enhanced to a greater extent by vitamin E in both the SHR and W/K rats than in the SD (Fig. 3). The SD is an outbred strain and splenocytes from this strain demonstrated the strongest responses to the mitogens tested. B-cell responses to the mitogen LPS were enhanced equally in all three strains by dietary vitamin E when compared to animals fed a vitamin E-deficient diet (Fig. 3).

Thus, depending upon the parameter measured, there are distinct strain differences in the sensitivity to a vitamin E-deficient state, with the SHR being most sensitive and the SD the least sensitive. However, it is not possible to correlate tissue levels of vitamin E following ingestion of a diet containing 200 mg/kg of the vitamin for 17 weeks with the variation in sensitivity to vitamin E deficiency. For example, although the SHR developed myopathy (as indicated by plasma PK) earlier than the W/K, the muscle tocopherol levels of SHR and W/K fed diets containing 200 mg/kg vitamin E were the same (Table II). Similarly, although the vitamin E-deficient SHR developed testes degeneration earlier than the vitamin E-deficient SD, the testes

TABLE II. TISSUE α-TOCOPHEROL LEVELS OF SHR, W/K, AND SD AFTER 17 WEEKS ON DIETS CONTAINING 200 mg/kg VITAMIN E

	Strain		
Tissue	SHR	W/K	SD
Plasma (μg/ml)	9.3 ± 0.3[a]	15.8 ± 0.7[b]	11.3 ± 0.7[c]
Liver (μg/g)	43.8 ± 2.0[a]	55.6 ± 4.0[b]	49.8 ± 2.3[a,b]
Testes (μg/g)	24.2 ± 0.4[a]	31.1 ± 0.5[b]	23.2 ± 0.7[a]
Gastrocnemius muscle (μg/g)	14.3 ± 0.8[a,b]	13.4 ± 0.5[a]	16.1 ± 1.1[b]

Note. Data represent the means ± SE of tissue tocopherol levels from eight animals/strain. Means with the same letter superscript are not different statistically ($P > 0.05$).

tocopherol levels were the same when both strains were fed 200 mg/kg vitamin E in the diet.

Measurement of vitamin E content of a tissue at a single time point (after 17 weeks on the diet) does not indicate rate of uptake. In addition, Tengerdy and Brown (9) have indicated that certain tissues may have an upper limit for the capacity for storing vitamin E. This may be the case for the muscle and testes of the rat. Our data (Fig. 4) show that the relative rates of depletion between SHR and W/K strains are the same. Thus, depletion rates cannot account for the difference in time of onset of vitamin E deficiency symptoms between these two strains. Moreover, although at 4 weeks the SHR had elevated plasma PK levels (data not shown), the tocopherol content was not different from skeletal muscle of the W/K whose plasma PK was normal. This suggests that the more rapid onset of myopathy in the SHR may not be directly related to tocopherol status.

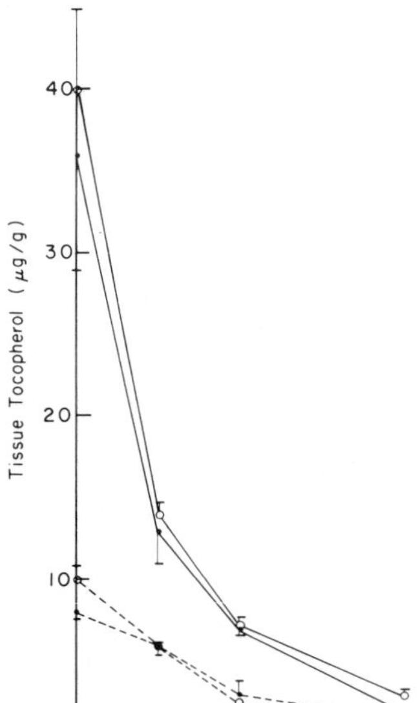

FIG. 4. Depletion of muscle and testes tocopherol from SHR and W/K over 4 weeks. SHR testes (● —— ●); SHR muscle (● -- ●); W/K testes (O —— O); W/K muscle (O - - - O).

It would therefore appear that strain differences in sensitivity to a vitamin E deficiency are not solely related to tocopherol status of the tissue, but may involve other metabolic variables which could influence the onset of pathology in the different tissues. It is likely that such processes are induced by free radicals. Therefore, the relative concentration of other agents involved in protecting the cell against free radical damage, such as superoxide dismutase, catalase, glutathione peroxidase, or ascorbic acid could influence the relative sensitivity to a vitamin E deficiency. Similarly, metabolites which might enhance free radical formation, such as ferrous ion or polyunsaturated fatty acids, might also alter sensitivity of a tissue to vitamin E deficiency. Differences in the utilization of dietary selenium and polyunsaturated fatty acids could certainly influence the sensitivity of the animal to a vitamin E deficiency. Finally, there are diffuse structural alterations in the membranes of cells from the SHR compared to the W/K which could lead to a less stable structure (10). Higher amounts of tocopherol may therefore be needed to stabilize such membranes.

The present study clearly demonstrates that differences in sensitivity to vitamin E deficiency can occur among strains of animals within species. Similar strain differences have been reported for owl monkeys (11). Furthermore, we have developed inbred rats which are sensitive or resistant to a vitamin E deficiency by selective breeding (12). The biochemical basis for these strain differences remains to be established.

1. Bendich A, Gabriel E, Machlin LJ. Low concentrations of vitamin E in the tissues of spontaneously hypertensive rats (SHR). Fed Proc **41**:344, 1982.
2. Bendich A, Gabriel E, Machlin LJ. Differences in vitamin E levels in tissues of the spontaneously hypertensive and Wistar–Kyoto rats. Proc Soc Exp Biol Med **172**:277–300, 1983.
3. Bendich A, Belisle EH, Strausser HR. Immune system modulation and its effect on the blood pressure of the SHR. BBRC **99**:600–607, 1981.
4. Draper HA, Bergan JG, Chiu M, Csallany AS, Board AV. A further study of the specificity of the vitamin E requirement for reproduction. J Nutr **84**:395–400, 1964.
5. Williams JR, Harrison TR, Grollman A. A simple method for determining the systolic blood pressure of the unanesthetized rat. J Clin Invest **18**:373–376, 1939.
6. Beutler E. In: A Manual of Biochemical Methods. New York, Grune & Stratton, p58, 1965.
7. Machlin LJ, Gabriel E, Spiegel HE, Horn LR, Brin M, Nelson J. Plasma activity of pyruvate kinase and glutamic oxalacetic transaminase as indices of myopathy in the vitamin E deficient rat. J Nutr **108**:1963–1968, 1978.
8. Bendich A, Gabriel E, Machlin LJ. Effect of dietary level of vitamin E on the immune system of the spontaneously hypertensive (SHR) and normotensive Wistar–Kyoto (WKY) rat. J Nutr **113**:1920–1926, 1983.
9. Tengerdy RP, Brown JC. Effect of vitamin E and A on humoral immunity and phagocytosis in *E. coli* infected chickens. Poultry Sci **56**:957–963, 1977.
10. Derynck MA, Pernollet MG, Nunez AM, Aragm I, Montenay-Garestier T, Helene C, Meyer P. Diffuse structural alterations in cell membranes of spontaneously hypertensive rats. Proc Natl Acad Sci USA **79**:5057–5060, 1982.
11. Walsh FX, Nicolosi RJ, Meydane SN, Sehgal PK, Hayes KC. Hemolytic anemia of owl monkeys: red blood cell lipid alterations. Proc Soc Exp Biol Med **169**:253–259, 1982.
12. Gabriel E, Machlin LJ. Selection of rats for high and low susceptibility to vitamin E deficiency. Fed Proc **41**:344, 1982.

Received January 24, 1984. P.S.E.B.M. 1984, Vol. 176.
Accepted April 19, 1984.

PROCEEDINGS OF THE SOCIETY FOR EXPERIMENTAL BIOLOGY AND MEDICINE **176**, 384–391 (1984)

Nonalgebraic Interaction between Pressor and Depressor Reflexes in Dogs: Evidence for a Central Site of Action (41887)

P. M. LALLEY, J. E. KENDRICK, AND G. L. MATSON

Department of Physiology, University of Wisconsin, Madison, Wisconsin 53706

Abstract. In a previous study (Kendrick, JE and Matson, G 1979, Amer J Physiol **327**:H662–H667) we demonstrated that the vascular responses in dogs to electrical stimulation of aortic nerve (AN) pressor and carotid sinus nerve (CSN) depressor afferents did not sum algebraically. We suggest this results from a reflex interaction which occurs in the central nervous system. The present study extends earlier studies by recording sympathetic vasomotor activity in chloralose-anesthetized dogs. Stimulation of the CSN reduced sympathetic activity by 51 ± 20 (SD)%. AN stimulation (2 Hz) caused a 17 ± 12% increase in sympathetic activity. Combined stimulation of the ipsilateral CSN and AN caused 0 ± 28% change rather than a 34% decrease expected by an additive interaction. The interaction recorded in this study from the sympathetic outflow is therefore consistent with the previously reported vascular responses (cited above) and implicates central nervous site(s) of action. A conditioning stimulus train to CSN inhibited sympathetic discharges to AN test stimuli. This inhibition was prevented by pairing an AN stimulus with the CSN stimulus train. The AN pressor reflexes act in part by increasing sympathetic activity and in part by suppressing the baroreflexes.

In recent publications (1–3) we reported that cardiovascular reflexes evoked by stimulating carotid sinus nerve (CSN) depressor afferents and aortic nerve (AN) pressor afferents interact in a nonalgebraic fashion. We found that the cardiac and vasomotor responses produced by carotid sinus distension or electrical stimulation of CSN baroreceptor afferents were reduced by either chemical (nicotine) or electrical stimulation of the aortic chemoreflexes. This reduction was much greater than could be accounted for by simple algebraic summation of the antagonistic reflexes. Three lines of evidence suggested that the nonalgebraic nature of the interaction was related to neural mechanisms residing within the central nervous system. First, the degree of attenuation of CSN-evoked baroreflex responses by the AN pressor reflexes was not directly related to the level of peripheral vascular tone. It therefore seemed unlikely that the nonalgebraic interaction was related to properties of vascular smooth muscle. Second, the suppression of CSN-depressor responses by AN pressor activation was more pronounced and consistent when ipsilateral CSN and AN afferents were stimulated than during contralateral CSN–AN interactions. Third, temporal pairing of the AN stimulus with the CSN stimulus resulted in greater diminution of the CSN-depressor response than occurred with uncoupled stimulation of the AN and CSN.

Other laboratories have described vascular responses produced by coactivation of pressor and depressor reflexes, and have concluded similarly that the reflex interactions take place within the central nervous system (4–7). In this report, we provide more direct electrophysiological evidence for a central nervous site of reflex interaction. We show here that baroreflex inhibition of neural discharges recorded on the sympathetic outflow from the central nervous system is attenuated by activation of AN pressor reflexes. The degree of attenuation is greater than would be expected by simply activating AN-evoked vasomotor discharges. Additional experiments further suggest that stimulation of AN pressor afferent fibers has a dual action within the central nervous system of activating pressor reflexes and suppressing CSN-evoked depressor activity.

Methods. Experiments were performed on adult mongrel dogs of either sex (10–12 kg). All animals were anesthetized with chloralose (100 mg/kg, iv) after pretreatment with morphine sulfate (3 mg/kg, sc). Anesthesia was maintained by continuous intravenous infusion of chloralose (approximately 25 mg/hr). After endotracheal intubation, the animals were paralyzed with Flaxedil (gallamine tri-

0037-9727/84 $1.50

ethiodide, 2 mg/kg, iv) and artificially ventilated with room air or 100% O_2. Ventilatory rate and volume were adjusted to maintain end tidal pCO_2 between 25 and 30 mm Hg. External heating devices maintained body temperature close to 38°C. Cannulas were placed in the femoral artery and vein in order to monitor blood pressure and inject drugs, respectively. Both vagus nerves were cut in the midcervical region to abolish cardiopulmonary reflexes.

Reflex responses were evoked by electrically stimulating the CSN and AN. Both nerves were prepared bilaterally in each dog. The CSN was isolated from its juncture with glossopharyngeal nerve, back to its origin in the carotid sinus. The nerve was cut close to the sinus region and gently drawn into silver ring electrodes.

Both AN were dissected from the vagosympathetic trunks and identified in a manner previously described in detail by Edis and Shepherd (8) and by us (1). These nerves were cut and their central ends drawn into similar silver ring electrodes for stimulation.

Neural activity was recorded from the left lumbar sympathetic trunk and/or from branches of the left renal nerve. The sympathetic nerves were exposed by midline laparotomy and removal of the spleen and a segment of the large intestine. A mixture of high (10%)- and low (6%)-molecular-weight dextran in saline was infused to replace the blood trapped in the extirpated intestinal segment. The sympathetic nerves were placed on bipolar silver hook electrodes for neural recording. The nerves and surrounding tissue were immersed in paraffin oil maintained at 39°C by a glass-insulated heating coil. Sympathetic discharges were amplified (preamplifier band pass filters set at 3–3000 Hz) and displayed on an oscilloscope. Continuous measurement of the frequency of compound sympathetic action potentials was obtained with a window discriminator/ratemeter whose output was recorded on a polygraph as an analog voltage that varied with the discharge frequency. Discriminator windows were set during stimulation of the CSN at frequencies and intensities which produced maximum depression of sympathetic firing. The residual sympathetic discharges were reduced sufficiently to distinguish between neural activity and background noise. The lower voltage level of the window was set above background noise and left at that level for the duration of the experiment.

In seven experiments, individual sympathetic reflex responses to ipsilateral CSN and AN stimulation were averaged by a microprocessor-based digital signal averager. This device also measured the magnitude of the reflex response by integrating the area under the averaged compound action potential.

In all experiments, the CSN and AN were first stimulated separately several times before interactions were attempted in order to be certain of consistent AN pressor and CSN depressor and sympathetic neural responses. Depressor responses and inhibition of sympathetic discharges were evoked by stimulation of the CSN with two trains of stimuli per second. Each train was 100 msec in duration and consisted of 20 rectangular pulses, each pulse 0.1 msec in duration. Stimulus intensity (1–3 V) was adjusted to produce near maximum depression of sympathetic nerve activity and blood pressure. This level of CSN stimulation had no discernible effect on breathing in unparalyzed animals. Since a 5- to 10-fold increase in stimulus intensity was necessary to cause stimulation of breathing it was assumed that the chemoreceptor afferents in the CSN were minimally involved at the stimulus intensities which caused large baroreflex responses.

The AN was stimulated at a rate of 2 Hz (2–4 V, 1.0 msec). This stimulation increased sympathetic neural discharges, caused systemic arterial pressure to rise, cardioacceleration, and increased respiratory rate and depth in unparalyzed dogs, but did not produce apneusis. The sympathetic neural discharges recorded during paralysis and artificial ventilation were 70% less than the maximum responses produced by stimulating at frequencies of 10 Hz and greater.

During combined stimulation of the nerves each AN stimulus was synchronized to the beginning of the CSN stimulus train.

Statistical comparisons were made by use of the paired t test. The 95% level of confidence was selected for significance. All data are presented as the means ±SD.

Results. *Reflex responses during paired AN and CSN stimulation.* Figures 1–3 illustrate the changes in renal nerve and lumbar sym-

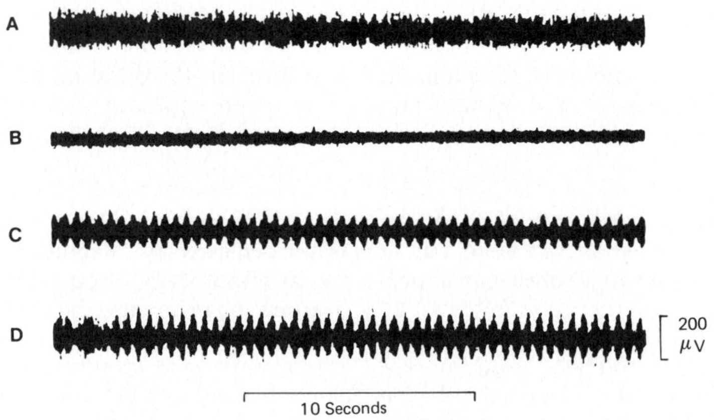

FIG. 1. Film records of neural discharges recorded from the left lumbar sympathetic trunk. (A) Spontaneous (control) discharge; (B) during stimulation of the left CSN (2-Hz trains); (C) during concurrent stimulation of the left CSN and left AN. Each AN single shock (2 Hz) is delivered simultaneously with the first shock of each CSN train. (D) stimulation of the left AN (2 Hz, single shocks) in the absence of CSN stimulation.

pathetic activity in response to stimulation of the AN and CSN, individually and in combination. The results obtained from either the renal nerves or the lumbar sympathetic trunk were qualitatively similar and therefore, not treated separately in the summary shown in Fig. 4. Film records in Fig. 1 illustrate neural discharges in the lumbar sympathetic trunk under control conditions (A), during CSN stimulation (B), during paired ipsilateral stimulation of CSN and AN (C), and during AN stimulation alone (D). Separate stimulation of the AN typically evoked a moderate increase in sympathetic firing in the lumbar sympathetic trunk (Figs. 1 and 3) and renal nerve (Fig. 2), and an increase in systemic arterial pressure. Stimulation of the CSN alone depressed sympathetic firing and blood pressure. Stimulation of the AN during CSN stimulation reinstated sympathetic firing and blood pressure. The reinstated responses were greater than expected for a strictly algebraic summation of effects. For example, in the experiment illustrated in Fig. 2, stimulation of the ipsilateral AN and CSN separately caused a 29% increase and a 64% decrease in sympathetic activity, respectively. Combined stimulation of the ipsilateral AN and CSN caused an 18% increase. If these antagonistic reflexes added algebraically combined stimulation of

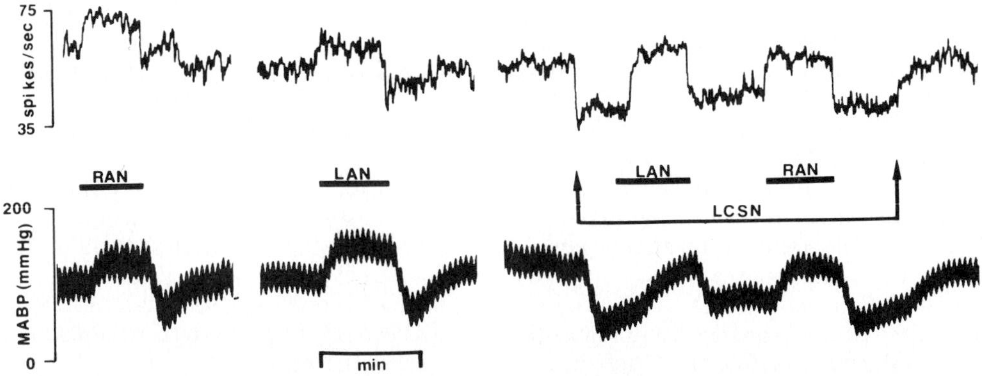

FIG. 2. Renal nerve and systemic pressure responses to left (LAN) and right (RAN) aortic nerve stimulation before and during stimulation of the left carotid sinus nerve (LCSN). Upper traces: Ratemeter records of renal nerve activity. Time constant of ratemeter = 1 sec. Lower traces: Systemic arterial blood pressure.

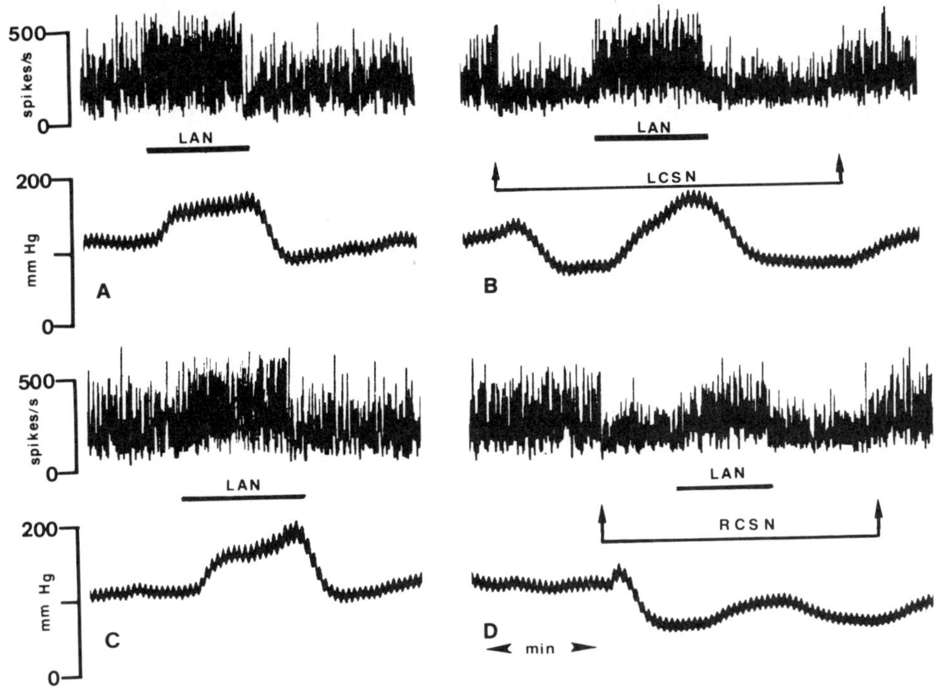

FIG. 3. Lumbar sympathetic trunk neural cativity and systemic pressure responses to stimulation of AN and CSN. Abbreviations same as Figs. 1 and 2. Upper traces: Ratemeter records (time constant = 0.1 sec). Lower traces: Systemic arterial blood pressure.

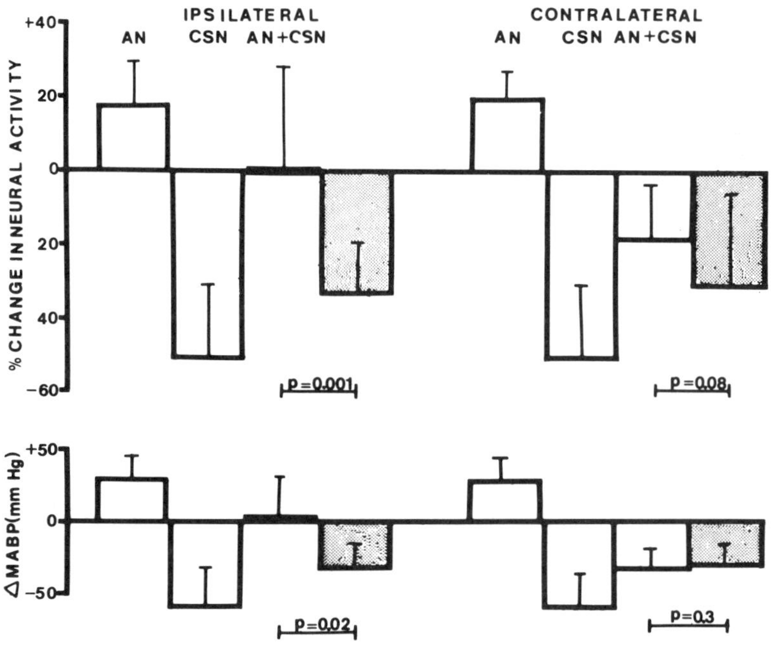

FIG. 4. Average responses (±SD) from 11 experiments of effects of separate and paired stimulation of the aortic nerve (AN) and carotid sinus nerve (CSN) on sympathetic neural activity (upper histograms) and blood pressure (lower histograms). Shaded bars represent the sum of the separate responses.

these nerves would have caused a 35% decrease in sympathetic firing. A similar nonalgebraic summation of the systemic blood pressure responses also occurred. In this case systemic pressure fell 70 mm Hg during CSN stimulation and rose 40 mm Hg during AN stimulation. No net change in pressure occurred during combined stimulation of the ipsilateral AN and CSN.

Figure 4 summarizes the results from all the experiments. In this figure, the shaded bars represent the changes in sympathetic firing which would have occurred if the responses to separate AN and CSN stimulation added algebraically. The average results obtained to stimulation of the AN and CSN on the same side (ipsilateral) are compared to those obtained when the AN on one side is stimulated in combination with CSN on the opposite side (contralateral, $N = 9$). During contralateral stimulation of the nerves, the average response of either sympathetic neural activity or systemic pressure was not different ($P = 0.08$) from the sum of the separate responses. This contrasts with the results of ipsilateral stimulation of the nerves where the response to CSN stimulation was suppressed to a greater degree in all dogs than was seen during contralateral stimulation of the nerves.

In two experiments, ganglionic transmission (lumbar trunk) was blocked by tetraethylammonium chloride (TEA, 15 mg/kg iv). In both experiments TEA caused blood pressure to fall but only a small reduction in sympathetic firing was observed. The sympathetic neural response to CSN and AN stimulation was essentially unchanged by TEA. These observations suggest that the majority of the recorded sympathetic activity was preganglionic. Therefore, we conclude that the interaction between the reflexes is not related to ganglionic processing, as might be suggested by the results of another study (9).

Collectively, the data support the hypothesis that the excitatory AN reflexes cause a suppression of the inhibitory reflexes initiated by CSN stimulation.

It was important in this investigation to determine if the restoration of sympathetic firing during paired AN and CSN stimulation was not merely a consequence of the reduced baseline sympathetic nerve activity. In other words, the same degree of activation of aortic nerve pressor afferents might result in greater sympathetic responses because CSN stimulation reduces background neural discharges thereby reducing refractoriness, leading to greater responsiveness to AN stimulation. However, this does not appear to be the case since as shown in Fig. 5, AN stimulation can prevent the CSN-evoked inhibition of firing when sympathetic background firing is high. Stimulation of the CSN alone is seen to produce a marked reduction of firing in the lumbar sympathetic trunk, whereas stimulation of the AN alone increases activity. When, however, CSN and AN are stimulated simultaneously, rather than applying antecedent CSN stimulation as in Figs. 2 and 3, the inhibition mediated by CSN stimulation is completely prevented. Fig. 5 thus demonstrates nonalgebraic summation of reflex effects in the presence of high background sympathetic activity.

Effect of conditioning stimulation on the sympathetic reflex response to AN stimulation. The ability of AN stimulation to restore blood pressure and sympathetic firing to control levels suggests that the sympathetic inhibition caused by CSN stimulation is suppressed by AN stimulation. In order to further test this hypothesis, in seven experiments we compared the effects of ipsilateral CSN conditioning shocks and paired ipsilateral (AN–CSN) stimulation on individual sympathetic discharges evoked by AN test shocks. The sequence of conditioning and test shocks were applied at low rates (every 3–5 sec) in order to minimize the possibility of temporal summation. Figure 6 illustrates the experimental paradigm and results obtained in one experiment. As shown in Fig. 6A, the AN test shock (denoted by arrow) evoked a discharge in the renal nerve at a latency of 180 msec. The reflex was mark-

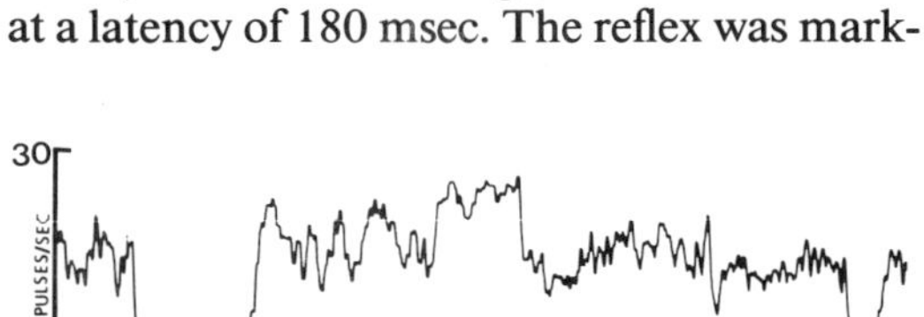

FIG. 5. Ratemeter records of neural discharges recorded from the lumbar sympathetic trunk during stimulation of CSN alone (left), AN alone (middle), and during simultaneous stimulation of the CSN and AN (right).

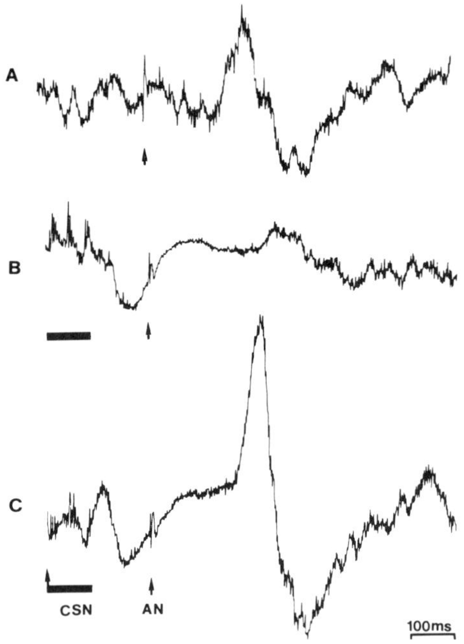

FIG. 6. Computer-averaged responses recorded from the renal nerve, evoked by single shocks applied to the AN (denoted by arrows) and by CSN trains (100-msec train, 20 shocks; denoted by horizontal bars). Each record in A–C is an average of 10 responses. (A) Sympathetic reflex evoked by AN test shock. (B) Inhibition of test response by a conditioning CSN train which precedes the test shock by 250 msec. Note also the suppression of spontaneous sympathetic firing denoted by the reduction of background fluctuations. (C) Restoration of the test response by an AN single shock, applied simultaneously with the first pulse of the CSN train. Spontaneous sympathetic firing remains depressed.

edly depressed when test shocks were preceeded (250 msec) by conditioning CSN trains (Fig. 6B). Similar results were obtained when the condition–test interval was lengthened to 500 msec. The shortest CSN–AN interval required for complete recovery (no inhibition of the test response) ranged from 700 to 1400 msec in the seven experiments. When, however, a conditioning AN single shock was applied simultaneously with the CSN train (Fig. 6C) the inhibitory effect of CSN stimulation was prevented, such that the test response to AN stimulation was reinstated. In most experiments, in fact, the test response which followed paired AN–CSN conditioning stimulation was greater than the unconditioned test response. The conditioning AN stimulus had similar restorative effects when it preceeded or followed the first shock of the CSN train by 50 msec, however, no detailed analysis of the effect of varying the temporal pattern of the AN–CSN conditioning pair was attempted. The test response in Fig. 6C occurs later than the control response (Fig. 6A) and exhibits a larger peak amplitude with less temporal dispersion. A tentative explanation for these alterations is that they are related to the earlier arrival of the CSN volley in the central nervous system. Through this inhibitory influence the CSN train could delay the AN response and also reduce temporal dispersion by suppressing spontaneous firing and refractoriness. In most experiments, the AN shock paired with the CSN train also evoked a sympathetic discharge. The first discharge had no effect on the magnitude or latency of the response to the AN test shock. The test response to the AN stimulus was not affected by a preceeding AN shock at 250- or 500-msec intervals in the absence of CSN stimulation. It is assumed, therefore, that the restoration of the reflex response to AN stimulation is not simply due to facilitation by double shocks. In summary, these results further support the hypothesis that the inhibitory effect of CSN stimulation is prevented by AN stimuli applied simultaneously.

Discussion. In previous studies (1–3) we investigated the vasomotor and heart rate responses to both electrical and natural stimulation of the aortic chemoreflexes and the carotid baroreflexes. The similarities between the results of natural and electrical stimulation support our belief that the excitatory response to AN stimulation is predominantly the result of stimulation of chemoreceptor afferents, while the response to CSN stimulation predominantly results from stimulation of baroreceptor afferents. The results of the present electrophysiological investigation also support earlier suggestions (2, 3) that carotid baroreflexes are suppressed within the central nervous system during aortic chemoreflex activation.

The methods of this study do not identify the central nervous sites of AN–CSN interaction. Supraspinal as well as spinal sites of action could be involved. According to our latency measurements, chemoreceptor and baroreceptor stimuli could follow quite different pathways before converging on a common site which influences sympathetic vasomotor activity. We previously demonstrated, as did others, that the AN pressor reflex responses are initiated by high threshold, mostly unmyelinated, slow conducting afferents, while the CSN depressor reflexes are evoked by lower threshold, faster conducting afferents (1). Thus the CSN afferent volley, or an appreciable part of the wave evoked by a train of pulses, would be expected to reach the first synapse in the medulla ahead of the AN volley. In the present study, however, single shocks to the AN, paired with the beginning of a train of stimuli applied to the CSN, resulted in abolition or suppression of the CSN inhibition of sympathetic activity. Since paired stimuli were delivered at a rate of 2 Hz in some experiments (Figs. 1–3) it might be suggested that the arrest of CSN-linked inhibition is attributable to the AN shock of the previous pair. This is unlikely, however, since the experiments exemplified in Fig. 6 show that removal of CSN inhibition still occurred when paired stimulation was applied at intervals of 3–5 sec. It seems more likely that the AN volley activates a pressor reflex pathway which has a relatively short central transit time before it merges with CSN depressor pathway. This would allow the pressor reflex to overtake and arrest the depressor activity, despite the low conduction velocity of the AN afferent volley. The site of convergence for the two reflex pathways could be spinal, supraspinal or both, as suggested from data reported by others (13, 14).

Wherever interaction might have occurred in the present study, it resulted in a generalized alteration of sympathetic vasomotor reflexes affecting both the thoracic (renal nerve) and lumbar sympathetic outflows. It is also evident that the sites of interaction are primarily ipsilateral, since the responses to stimulation of contralateral pairs of afferents (AN and CSN) were either additive algebraically ($N = 3$) or nearly so ($N = 6$).

At least two mechanisms appear to be operative in the restoration of sympathetic responses during paired AN and CSN stimulation. AN stimulation not only generates sympathetic vasomotor discharges (Figs. 1–3, 6) but also arrests the inhibition evoked by stimulation of CSN depressor afferents (Fig. 6). We cannot eliminate the possibility, although it seems unlikely, that the restored sympathetic firing during AN stimulation is produced by input from respiratory networks which are driven by AN chemoreceptor afferents, but resistant to CSN stimulation. This possibility had to be entertained, since several studies have demonstrated respiratory rhythms in spontaneous sympathetic discharges (15–17). In addition, brainstem regions which activate respiratory and vasomotor responses when stimulated have the ability to suppress baroreceptor-mediated inhibition (18, 19). In these studies, however, the hallmark of respiratory involvement is an appearance of a respiratory rhythm in the pattern of sympathetic firing. This also is the case when peripheral chemoreceptor afferent fibers are stimulated. During electrical stimulation (30–50 Hz) of the CSN chemoreceptor afferents, respiratory rhythm in phrenic nerve discharges is preserved, although the frequency and/or magnitude of inspiratory discharges increases (20, 21). Respiratory rhythm is also maintained during 2 Hz electrical stimulation of AN chemoreceptor afferents, although the depth and rate of inspiration may increase (Kendrick, unpublished observations). It is to be expected that the characteristic rhythm would be transferred to the sympathetic outflow if respiratory radiation had occurred.

In conclusion, these results demonstrate that AN pressor reflexes sum in a nonalgebraic manner with CSN depressor reflexes to determine sympathetic outflow to the peripheral vasculature. The interaction between these antagonistic reflexes occurs in the central nervous system. The interaction appears to occur much less between contralateral than between ipsilateral reflexes. The central nervous sites or the mechanisms involved in these reflex interactions have not been determined and are a goal for future studies.

This study was supported by NIH Grants HL 22715 and HL 29563 and by American Heart Association Grant 75899. The secretarial support of Ms. Becky Viner is gratefully acknowledged.

1. Kendrick JE, Matson GL. A comparison of the cardiovascular responses to stimulation of the aortic and carotid sinus nerve of the dog. Proc Soc Exp Biol Med **144**:404–411, 1973.

2. Kendrick JE, Matson G. Interaction between carotid sinus baroreceptor and aortic nerve pressor reflexes in the dog. Amer J Physiol **327**:H662–H667.
3. Pisarri TE, Matson GL, Kendrick JE. Inhibition of baroreflex bradycardia by aortic nerve excitatory afferents in dogs. Amer J Physiol **243**:H607–H613, 1982.
4. Heistad DD, Abboud FM, Mark AL, Schmid PG. Interaction of baroreceptor and chemoreceptor reflexes—modulation of the chemoreceptor reflex by changes in baroreceptor activity. J Clin Invest **53**:1226–1236, 1974.
5. Mancia G. Influence of carotid baroreceptor stimulation in the dog. Circ Res **36**:270–276, 1975.
6. Mancia G, Shepherd JT, Donald DE. Interplay among carotid sinus cardiopulmonary and carotid body reflexes in dogs. Amer J Physiol **230**:19–24, 1976.
7. Wennergren G, Little R, Oberg B. Studies on the central integration of excitatory chemoreceptor influences and inhibitory baroreceptor and cardiac receptor influences. Acta Physiol Scand **96**:1–18, 1976.
8. Edis AJ, Shepherd JT. Selective denervation of aortic arch baroreceptors and chemoreceptors in dogs. J Appl Physiol **30**:294–296, 1971.
9. Cellar BG, Schramm LP. Pre- and postganglionic sympathetic activity in splanchmic nerves of rats. Amer J Physiol **241**:R55–R61, 1981.
10. Eccles JC. The physiology of Synapses. New York, Springer-Verlag, p315, 1964.
11. Gabriel M, Seller H. Interaction of baroreceptor afferents from carotid sinus and aorta at the nucleus tractus solitarii. Pflugers Arch **318**:7–20, 1970.
12. Lipski J, McAllen RM, Trzebski A. Carotid baroreceptor and chemoreceptor inputs into single medullary neurons. Brain Res **107**:132–136, 1976.
13. Gebber G., Taylor DG, Weaver LC. Electrophysiological studies on organization of central vasopressor pathways. Amer J Physiol **224**:470–481, 1973.
14. Trzebski A, Lipski J, Majcherczyk S, Chrusckielewski L. Central organization and interaction of the carotid baroreceptor and chemoreceptor sympathetic reflex. Brain Res **87**:227–237, 1975.
15. Gebber GL, Barman SM. Brain stem vasomotor circuits involved in the genesis and entrainment of sympathetic nervous rhythms. In: DeJong W, Provost AP, Shapiro AP, eds. Hypertension and Brain Mechanisms. Progress in Brain Research. Amsterdam, Elsevier, Vol 47: pp61–75, 1977.
16. Koizumi K, Seller H, Kaufman A, Brooks C McC. Pattern of sympathetic discharges and their relation to baroreceptor and respiratory activities. Brain Res **27**:281–294, 1971.
17. Preiss G, Kirchner F, Polosa C. Patterning of sympathetic preganglionic neuron firing by the central respiratory drive. Brain Res **87**:363–374, 1975.
18. Coote JH, Hilton SM, Perez-Gonzalez JF. Inhibition of the baroreceptor reflex on stimulation in the brain stem defense center. J Physiol (London) **288**:549–560, 1979.
19. Lopes OU, Palmer JF. Hypothalamic inhibition of vagal component of the sinus nerve cardiac reflex. J Physiol (London) **260**:45P, 1976.
20. McCrimmon DR, Lalley PM. Inhibition of respiratory neural discharges by clonidine and 5-hydroxytryptophan. J Pharmacol Exp Ther **222**:771–777, 1982.
21. Millhorn DE, Eldridge FL, Waldrop TG. Prolonged stimulation of respiration by endogenous central serotonin. Resp Physiol **42**:171–188, 1980.

Received November 28, 1983. P.S.E.B.M. 1984, Vol. 176.
Accepted April 19, 1984.

PROCEEDINGS OF THE SOCIETY FOR EXPERIMENTAL BIOLOGY AND MEDICINE **176**, 392–402 (1984)

The Tissue-Specific Accumulation of Hepatic Zinc Metallothionein following Parenteral Iron Loading[1] (41888)

CHARLES C. McCORMICK

Department of Poultry and Avian Sciences, Cornell University, Ithaca, New York 14853

Abstract. The synthesis in various tissues of the unique metal-binding protein, metallothionein, can be influenced by the administration of certain trace elements. Zinc and cadmium, both of which bind to metallothionein, are most widely recognized as potent inducers. Preliminary results in our laboratory suggested that iron loading causes a marked accumulation of hepatic zinc metallothionein. We present in this report the effects of parenteral iron administration on metallothionein concentration in various tissues. Male chicks (300–350 g) received (ip) either a single injection (+1 Fe) of iron (10 mg Fe/kg, as $FeCl_3$), two injections (+2 Fe) given 24-hr apart, three injections (+3 Fe) each given 24-hr apart, or an equivalent volume of 0.9% saline (control). Twenty-four hours following the final injection, chicks were killed and tissues analyzed for cytoplasmic zinc and metallothionein (Zn–MT). The parenteral administration of ferric iron, $FeCl_3$, resulted in a marked tissue-specific accumulation of zinc as metallothionein. In chicks given +2 Fe, hepatic Zn–MT increased more than 10-fold with a third injection (+3 Fe) causing no further change. The concentration of Zn–MT in renal and pancreatic tissue was unaffected by iron loading. An increase in hepatic Zn–MT was evident prior to detectable changes in total hepatic iron. The administration of other ferrous iron compounds at a similar rate produced comparable changes in hepatic Zn–MT. Feeding excess dietary iron, however, had no effect on liver Zn–MT levels even though similar hepatic iron concentrations were attained. Our results indicated that parenteral administration, but not feeding, of various iron compounds causes a marked increase in zinc metallothionein, specifically in liver tissue.

Presently, there is a considerable body of literature concerning the unique metal-binding protein, metallothionein. Although isolated more than 20 years ago (1), a consensus regarding the biological role of this inducible protein does not exist. It is well recognized that a nutritionally required trace element, zinc, as well as an extremely toxic metal, cadmium, both induce the synthesis of metallothionein in various tissues. Accordingly, a function in the metabolism of these elements has been suggested (2–6). In addition to zinc and cadmium, the synthesis of metallothionein can be influenced by other elements, copper and mercury (7–9), as well as steroid hormones (10–12), stressors (13–15), and certain chemicals, e.g., carbon tetrachloride (13) and isopropanol (16). Although a unifying mechanism has not been established, there is little doubt that transcriptional events are involved in the process of metallothionein induction.

The influence of elements, other than those cited above, on the induction of tissue metallotionein has received less attention. The several studies conducted have reported equivocal results. Piotrowski and Szymanska (17) examined the ability of 19 different metals to induce the synthesis of hepatic and renal metallothionein-like proteins. They concluded that cadmium, zinc, copper, and cobalt were capable of inducing metallothionein synthesis in liver while cadmium, zinc, copper, and mercury induced metallothionein in kidney. Winge *et al.* (18) reported that silver salts were potent inducers of both hepatic and renal metallothionein. Others have indicated that bismuth (19) is capable of inducing renal metallothionein. A recent study by Eaton *et al.* (20) showed that copper and cobalt did not induce hepatic metallothionein but that nickel produced a two- and threefold increase in hepatic and renal metallothionein. In addition, and in contrast to results of Winge *et al.* (18), silver did not significantly increase renal or

[1] Supported by NIH Grant AM 33058 and Hatch Funds provided through the College of Agriculture and Life Sciences, Cornell University.

0037-9727/84 $1.50

hepatic metallothionein. Differences in the route of administration, dosing schedules, animal strains, and method of metallothionein quantitation were cited as possible causes for discrepancies.

Recent preliminary work (21) in our laboratory directed toward an investigation of an antagonism between zinc and iron indicated that iron may be capable of causing a pronounced increase in zinc metallothionein, specifically in hepatic tissue. Other tissues which are sensitive to changes in zinc status, such as kidney and pancreas, were unaffected. We demonstrate in this report that parenteral administration, but not feeding, of various iron compounds causes a more than 10-fold increase in hepatic zinc metallothionein.

Materials and Methods. Five-week-old male chicks (300–350 g), Leghorn strain, received (ip) either a single injection of iron (+1 Fe) as ferric chloride ($FeCl_3$), two injections (+2 Fe) given 24 hr apart, three injections (+3 Fe) each given 24 hr apart, or an equivalent volume of 0.9% saline (control). Each injection of iron was given at a rate of 10 mg Fe/kg body wt from a solution containing 20 mg Fe/ml. Feed and water were provided *ad libitum* throughout the experiment. Twenty-four hours following the final injection, chicks were killed by cervical dislocation and tissues excised, immediately placed in ice, and subsequently frozen (−20°C). Pooled cytosol were prepared from separate samples of three tissues, liver, kidney, and pancreas. Each sample of hepatic cytosol was prepared from hepatic tissue from two chicks. Each pancreatic and renal cytosol sample was prepared from tissues obtained from three chicks. An equal portion of each tissue sample was combined (1:2 wt/vol) in ice-cold buffer (0.25 *M* sucrose/0.01 *M* Tris–HCl/0.01% NaN_3, pH 8.6) and homogenized using a Potter–Elvejhem glass homogenizer. The homogenate was centrifuged at 100,000*g* for 1 hr at 4°C to yield a final supernatant (cytosol) which was collected and immediately stored at −20°C.

Tissue metallothionein was isolated and quantitated by gel-filtration chromatography. Three milliliters of cytosol were applied to a 2.5 × 50-cm column of Sephadex G-75 (medium) equilibrated in 0.01 *M* Tris–HCl/0.01% NaN_3, pH 8.6, at 4°C. Cytosol was eluted in the same buffer (flow rate of 0.3 ml/min) and collected in 3-ml fractions. The zinc content of each fraction was determined by atomic absorption spectrophotometry, AAS (AA575, Varian Associates, Inc., Palo Alto, Calif.). Fractions containing zinc metallothionein (1.8 × Vo) were summed and expressed as μg Zn/ml cytosol. Columns were calibrated with DEAE-purified rat hepatic metallothionein to verify the elution volume of metallothionein. Total cytosol zinc was also determined by AAS following an appropriate dilution (1:20) with deionized water.

To confirm the identity of iron-induced hepatic metallothionein eluting from G75 chromatography, nondenaturing polyacrylamide gel electrophoresis (PAGE) was performed. Fractions containing the third peak from G75 chromatography (see Fig. 2, fractions 52–65) were pooled and applied directly to a column (0.9 × 10 cm) containing anion-exchange media (DEAE–Sephadex A25, Pharmacia Fine Chemicals Co., Piscataway, N.J.) equilibrated in 0.002 *M* Tris–acetate buffer, pH 7.4. The procedure has been previously described (22). The single DEAE chromatographic peak was concentrated by ultrafiltration using YM2 membrane filters (Amicon Corp., Danvers, Mass.). An approximately equal amount of zinc from the DEAE concentrate of iron-injected and zinc-injected (5 mg/kg) chicks, as well as zinc MT_A from rat liver, was subjected to vertical slab PAGE. The discontinuous buffer system described by Davis (23) was employed using 7.5% total acrylamide and 2.5% Bis. Gels were cast in a vertical apparatus (Hoeffer Scientific Instruments, San Francisco, Calif.) with dimensions of 14 cm W × 12 cm H × 1.5 mm thick and subjected to constant current (20 mA) with cooling. Electrophoresis was terminated when the tracking dye reached the bottom of the gel. Gels were stained overnight in 0.25% Coomassie R250/7% acetic acid/25% methanol and destained by diffusion.

In addition to electrophoretic analysis of hepatic DEAE-purified material from iron- and zinc-induced chicks, amino acid composition analysis was conducted on the same samples. Samples were lyophilized in ampules and hydrolyzed *in vacuo* for 24 hr at 110°C in constant-boiling HCl containing ethanethiol as a reducing agent. Cysteic acid was determined following performic acid oxidation (for

16 hr) by the method of Hirs (24) and hydrolyzed as above in constant-boiling HCl. All determinations were performed on a Beckman Model 119 Cl amino acid analyzer. Three replicate analyses were performed.

Whole-tissue zinc and iron determinations were also conducted on liver samples. Equal portions of liver from two chicks were pooled and treated as a single sample. A total of four samples from each treatment were subjected to acid digestion using sulfuric and nitric acids. The zinc and iron concentration of the tissue digest was determined by AAS and results expressed as micrograms per gram wet weight tissue.

A second experiment was conducted to investigate the effect of ferrous (Fe^{2+}) iron salts on hepatic zinc metallothionein concentrations. Five-week-old male chicks received (ip) either two injections of saline (0.9% NaCl), or two equivolume injections of iron (1 mg Fe/100 g body wt) as ferric chloride ($FeCl_3$), ferrous sulfate ($FeSO_4$), or ferrous ammonium sulfate ($Fe(NH_4)_2(SO_4)_2$). A fourth group received two injections of a similar volume of equimolar ammonium sulfate ($(NH_4)_2SO_4$).

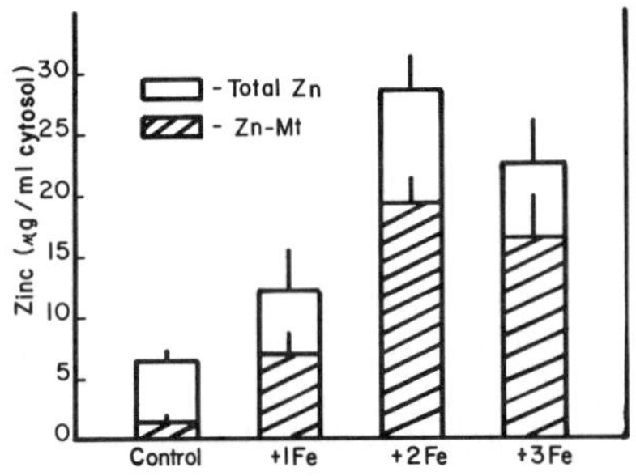

FIG. 1. Total zinc and zinc metallothionein content of liver cytosol from iron-loaded chicks. Five-week-old chicks were given (ip) either one injection (+1 Fe) of iron as ferric chloride (10 mg Fe/kg body wt), two injections (+2 Fe) given 24-hr apart, three injections each at 24-hr intervals, or an equivalent volume of saline (control). Twenty-four hours following the final injection, chicks were killed and liver cytosol was prepared. Zinc metallothionein (Zn–MT) was determined by atomic absorption spectroscopy following gel filtration chromatography (G-75). Total cytosol zinc was also determined by AAS. Total Zn and Zn–MT increased significantly following one injection (+1 Fe) of iron. An additional significant increase was observed after two injections (+2 Fe) with no further change in +3 Fe chicks. Bar height represents a mean ± SEM of three samples each composed of pooled tissue.

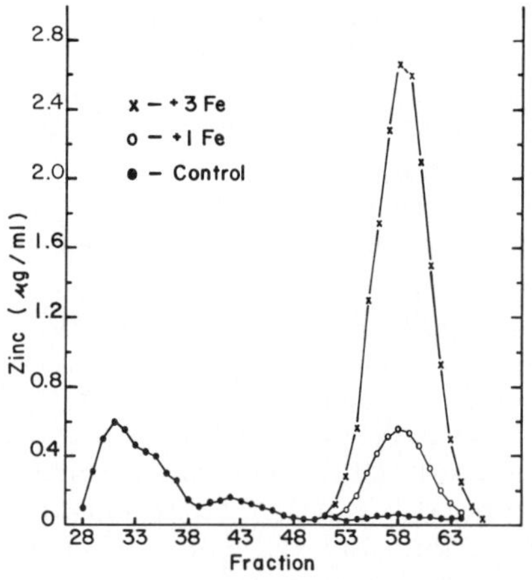

FIG. 2. A typical chromatogram of liver cytosol derived from iron-loaded or control chicks. See legend to Fig. 1 for description of experimental treatments. Three milliliters of liver cytosol (1:2 w/v) was applied to a column (2.5 × 50 cm) containing G-75 and eluted in 3-ml fractions. Zinc metallothionein eluted in a symmetrical peak centered around fraction 57. Profiles from cytosol of chicks given three iron injections (+3 Fe) were similar to that from chicks given two injections (+2 Fe).

The second injection in all groups was given 24 hr following the initial injection. Twenty-four hours following the final injection, chicks were killed and livers excised and frozen. Hepatic cytosol zinc and metallothionein were determined as previously described.

A third experiment was conducted to determine if elevated liver iron, which is effected by feeding, would influence hepatic metallothionein levels. Male chicks (1 week of age) were fed a soy-based purified diet (25) containing either no additional iron supplement (basal), or 1200 or 2000 ppm added iron as ferrous sulfate. Chicks were fed the experimental diets for a period of 2 weeks at which time chicks were killed and tissues excised and frozen. Total liver zinc and iron analyses were performed by AAS following acid digestion of tissue. Metallothionein determinations were also conducted on hepatic cytosol as previously described.

Data were analyzed statistically by one-way analysis of variance and mean differences determined by Duncan's Multiple-Range Test (26).

Results. Iron loading caused a marked increase in hepatic zinc metallothionein (Zn–MT) as illustrated in Fig. 1. When compared to control values, the concentration of liver cytosolic Zn–MT increased approximately 5-fold in chicks given a single injection of iron (+1 Fe). An elevation of more than 10-fold was observed in liver cytosol from chicks given two injections (+2 Fe) with no further change occurring in those given three injections (+3 Fe). A typical chromatogram of liver cytosol from control chicks and those given +1 Fe or +3 Fe is shown in Fig. 2. The change in the profiles of +1 or +3 Fe was exclusively in the last eluting peak. There was no detectable change in zinc concentration of fractions other than those containing Zn–MT. We deter-

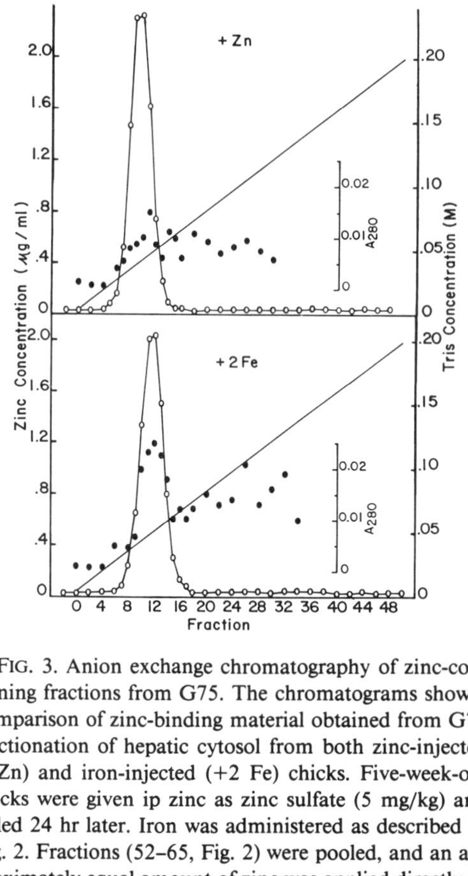

FIG. 3. Anion exchange chromatography of zinc-containing fractions from G75. The chromatograms show a comparison of zinc-binding material obtained from G75 fractionation of hepatic cytosol from both zinc-injected (+Zn) and iron-injected (+2 Fe) chicks. Five-week-old chicks were given ip zinc as zinc sulfate (5 mg/kg) and killed 24 hr later. Iron was administered as described in Fig. 2. Fractions (52–65, Fig. 2) were pooled, and an approximately equal amount of zinc was applied directly to an anion exchange (DEAE–Sephadex A25) column (0.9 × 10 cm) equilibrated in 0.002 *M* Tris-Acetate, pH 7.4. Following a wash, the columns were eluted with a gradient (0.002 *M* to 0.2 *M* Tris-Acetate, pH 7.4, total volume of 100 ml) in 2-ml fractions. The zinc concentration (open circles) and absorbance at 280 nm (solid circles) of each fraction is shown.

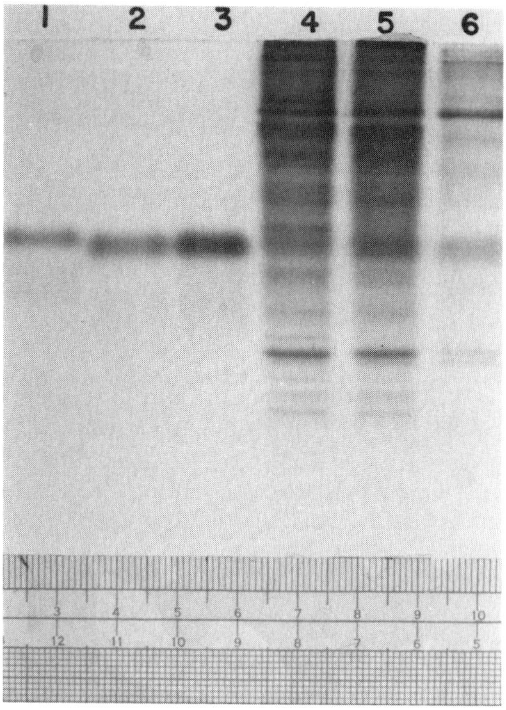

FIG. 4. Polyacrylamide gel electrophoresis of DEAE-purified hepatic zinc-binding material from zinc- and iron-injected chicks. Fractions containing anion exchange peaks shown in Fig. 3 were concentrated by membrane filtration and an aliquot applied to vertical slab gels (7.5% T, 2.5% Bis) as described under Methods. Lane 1, 0.22 μg zinc as rat liver metallothionein isoform A; Lane 2, 0.42 μg zinc DEAE concentrate from +2 Fe chicks; Lane 3, 0.60 μg zinc DEAE concentrate from +Zn chicks; Lane 4, 13.6 μl cytosol from "control" chicks; Lane 5, 13.6 μl cytosol from +2 Fe chicks; Lane 6, 13.6 μl supernate of heat-treated (80°C for 5 min) +2 Fe cytosol. Dye front is represented by upper edge of rule.

mined that 80–90% of the increase in cytosol total zinc was accounted for in Zn–MT. These results suggest that a maximum in the iron-induced accumulation of zinc metallothionein occurs after two administrations (ip) of iron in the form of $FeCl_3$ and that zinc bound to metallothionein accounts for the majority of increase in total cytosolic zinc. In a following study, two injections of various other iron compounds were used since this dose appeared to result in a maximum response.

Confirmation of metallothionein as the third chromatographic peak from G-75 (Fig. 2) was accomplished by anion exchange chromatography, gel electrophoresis, and amino acid compositional analysis. Approximately 90% of the zinc in the third peak from G75 chromatography of hepatic cytosol from both zinc- and iron-injected chicks adhered to and later eluted (simultaneously and in a single peak) from DEAE columns as shown in Fig. 3. The electrophoretic analysis of concentrate from these peaks is shown in Fig. 4. A single comigrating band was obtained with both samples. In addition, both exhibited mobility which was similar to that of rat DEAE-purified hepatic metallothionein isoform A. These resuts are consistent with the nature of chick and rat metallothioneins (22), i.e., that the single form of chick tissue metallothionein is similar to the A isoform of rat tissue. Amino acid compositional results of both iron- and zinc-induced DEAE-purified material are shown in Table I. The amino acid composition of both samples was virtually identical. Our analysis, however, did vary somewhat from two other analyses of chick metallothionein (27, 28).

The effect of iron loading on Zn–MT concentration was not observed in other tissues. Shown in Fig. 5 are data of renal and pancreatic cytosol zinc and Zn–MT from iron-loaded chicks. Neither the kidney nor the pancreas appeared to respond to iron loading. There was no significant difference in the concentration of either cytosol zinc or Zn–MT from kidney and pancreas of chicks given up to three injections of iron (+3 Fe). As these tissues are sensitive to changes in zinc status as well as capable of synthesizing Zn–MT, these results indicate that iron loading effects an increase in tissue Zn–MT via a mechanism which is specific to hepatic tissue.

Since liver is a known storage site for iron, we examined changes in total liver iron in an attempt to relate an elevation in liver iron to the increase in Zn–MT. Figure 6 illustrates changes in total hepatic zinc and iron of iron-loaded chicks. The changes observed in total hepatic zinc were similar qualitatively to changes that occurred in cytosolic zinc and Zn–MT. Chicks given +1 Fe exhibited a slight increase in total hepatic zinc. Those given +2 Fe or +3 Fe showed a much greater increase (200%) and were not significantly different be-

TABLE I. AMINO ACID COMPOSITIONAL ANALYSES OF DEAE-PURIFIED ZINC-BINDING MATERIAL FROM CHICK LIVER INDUCED BY EITHER IRON OR ZINC INJECTIONS

	Percentage of total residues			
Amino acid	+Zn[a] (this study)	+2 Fe (this study)	Zn–MT (Ref. 27)	Cd, Zn–MT (Ref. 28)
Aspartic	10.0	9.6	9.5	9.8
Threonine	3.8	3.5	1.3	1.7
Serine	7.8	7.7	9.0	12.6
Glutamine	7.1	8.4	3.8	3.8
Proline	5.0	5.0	8.5	5.0
Glycine	7.6	7.1	6.7	6.5
Alanine	8.4	8.2	9.3	9.7
Cysteine[b]	21.1	21.5	31.6	31.8
Valine	2.8	2.9	1.7	1.8
Methionine	2.4	2.6	1.6	1.9
Isoleucine	2.1	2.1	0.3	0
Leucine	2.7	2.8	0.4	0
Tyrosine	0.6	0.8	0	0
Phenylalanine	1.3	1.3	0	0
Histidine	1.4	1.4	1.7	0.9
Lysine	11.8	11.2	10.0	9.3
Arginine	4.1	4.0	4.5	5.0
Tryptophan	ND[c]	ND	ND	ND

[a] Triplicate analysis of DEAE-purified material obtained from hepatic cytosol of zinc-injected chicks (+Zn) or iron-injected chicks (+2 Fe). See Fig. 3 for description of treatments. Amino acid compositional analysis of zinc (Zn–MT) and cadmium, zinc–metallothionein (Cd, Zn–MT) of chick tissue from two additional studies is also shown.

[b] Determined as cysteic acid.

[c] Not determined.

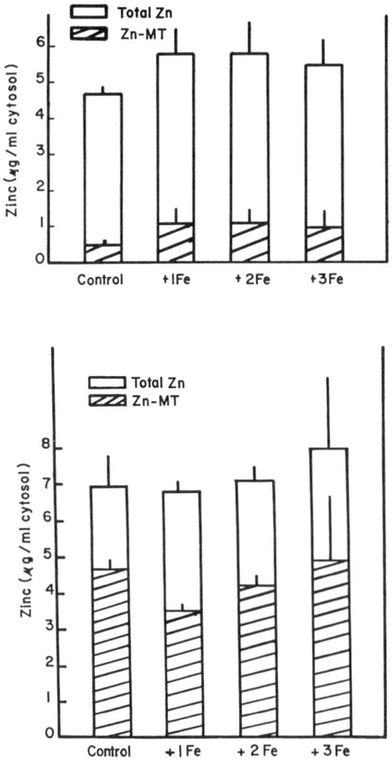

FIG. 5. Renal (top) and pancreatic (bottom) cytosolic zinc (total Zn) and zinc metallothionein (Zn–MT) iron-loaded and control chicks. Chicks were given (ip) either saline (control) or one injection (+1 Fe), two injections (+2 Fe), or three injections (+3 Fe) of iron each at 24-hr intervals. For either tissue, there were no significant differences between treatments with either variable. Bar height represents a mean ± SEM of three samples each composed of pooled tissue.

tween treatments. Liver total iron was not affected by two iron injections (+2 Fe), a treatment which resulted in a maximum increase in Zn–MT (Fig. 1), but was significantly elevated by +3 Fe. The results indicate that in chicks given +2 Fe the concentration of hepatic Zn–MT is maximum prior to detectable changes in the concentration of total hepatic iron. The latter was noted only in +3 Fe chicks, those which exhibited no further change in hepatic Zn–MT.

A second experiment was conducted to determine whether the administration of other iron salts would alter hepatic Zn–MT levels. The initial experiment utilized the more oxidized form of iron, the ferric (Fe^{3+}) form. In the following study, a direct comparison of a reduced iron salt was performed. The two compounds tested were ferrous sulfate and ferrous ammonium sulfate. The latter was chosen so that a comparison could be made of a similar salt, ammonium sulfate, in the absence of iron. Chicks were given two injections (ip) of either (i) one of the various iron solutions, (ii) equimolar ammonium sulfate or (iii) saline. Injections were given 24-hr apart and chicks killed 24 hr after the final injection. The results of this study are shown in Fig. 7. As previously observed, the administration (+2 Fe) of iron as ferric chloride resulted in a 10-fold increase in hepatic Zn–MT. A similar administration of other iron compounds given at an equal rate (10 mg Fe/kg body wt) caused a comparable increase in hepatic Zn–MT. Equimolar injections of ammonium sulfate did not change the concentration of liver Zn–MT suggesting an effect which is unique to the chemical nature of iron. Since there was no significant difference in the concentration of hepatic Zn–MT from chicks given either of the three iron compounds, the data suggest that the form of iron which is administered parenterally is of little importance in terms of effecting changes in hepatic Zn–MT.

A final experiment was conducted to determine if the route of administration of excess iron was an important factor in iron-induced Zn–MT accumulation and to establish definitively that elevated hepatic iron is not a causal factor. One-week-old chicks were fed a purified diet containing excess dietary iron. Chicks

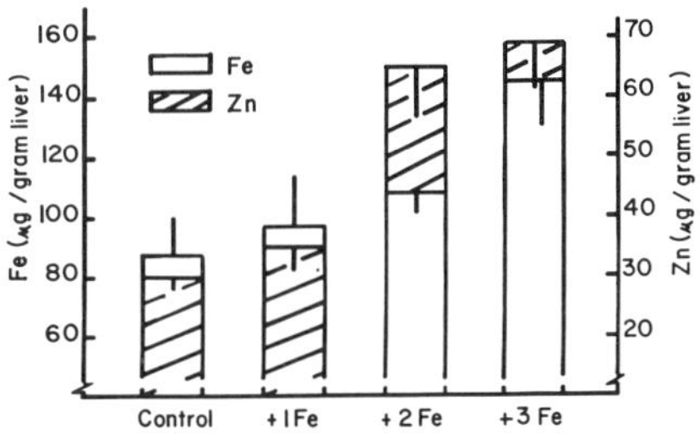

FIG. 6. The effect of iron loading on the concentration of total liver zinc and iron. Description of experimental treatments is given in the legend to Fig. 1. Total liver zinc and iron were determined after acid digestion by AAS. Total liver zinc of chicks increased significantly after one or two injections of iron whereas total liver iron did not. The latter variable increased only after three injections, a treatment which had no further effect on liver zinc. Bar height represents a mean ± SEM of three samples.

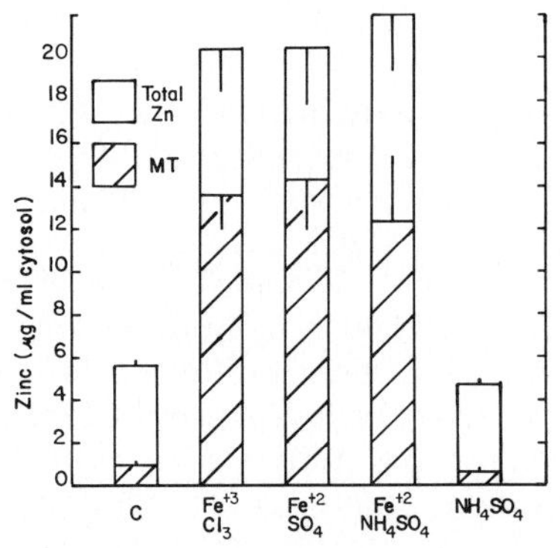

FIG. 7. Hepatic zinc metallothionein and the influence of various iron compounds administered parenterally. Chicks were given (ip) two injections administered 24-hr apart of either saline (C) or one of three iron compounds, ferric chloride ($FeCl_3$), ferrous sulfate ($FeSO_4$), ferrous ammonium sulfate ($FeNH_4SO_4$). Each iron injection was given at a rate of 10 mg Fe/kg body wt. A fifth group was given a similar volume of equimolar ammonium sulfate (NH_4SO_4). Twenty-four hours following the final injection, chicks were killed and hepatic cytosolic zinc (total Zn) and zinc metallothionein (MT) were determined. Bar height represents a mean ± SEM of three observations each a pooled sample of hepatic tissue from two chicks. The various iron compounds were equally effective in causing increased hepatic cytosolic MT.

were fed these diets for a period which was considered to be of sufficient duration to cause elevated hepatic iron, i.e., 2 weeks. The results of this study are shown in Table II. Feeding 2000 ppm added iron caused a marked elevation in total hepatic iron to a concentration which was similar to that observed previously in chicks given three injections of iron. This dietary treatment resulted, however, in no significant change in total hepatic zinc. Moreover, there was no significant change in the concentration of hepatic cytosol zinc metallothionein. These results confirm the suggestion that elevated hepatic iron is not in itself responsible for iron-induced hepatic zinc metallothionein accumulation. In addition, they indicate that the route of administration of iron compounds is an important factor.

Discussion. The results of the present study show that parenterally administered iron causes a marked tissue-specific accumulation of a zinc-binding protein which we suggest is metallothionein. We base this suggestion on anion exchange chromatography, gel electrophoresis, and amino acid composition from which the similarity of zinc- and iron-induced hepatic material is apparent. The amino acid composition (Table I) of both preparations, although virtually identical, varied somewhat from the two other reports concerning chick tissue metallothioneins (27, 28). While we have no firm explanation for these differences, the results may indicate either copurification of nonmetallothionein-like proteins or microheterogeneity between variant forms of metallothionein (29). Microheterogeneity has been noted even in apparently pure preparations (30) since the number of moles of individual amino acids were frequently nonintegers. Bremner and Davies (14) have also indicated that although all of their preparations typically had high cysteine and usually no aromatic amino acid residues, there were sometimes marked variations in the proportions of many other amino acids.

To the author's knowledge, this report is

TABLE II. THE EFFECT OF FEEDING EXCESS DIETARY IRON ON HEPATIC ZINC, IRON, AND ZINC METALLOTHIONEIN[a]

Diet	Iron (μg/g liver)	Zinc (μg/g liver)	Zinc metallothionein (μg zinc/ml cytosol)
Basal	84.9 ± 11.5 (4)	30.2 ± 0.7 (4)	0.41 ± 0.08 (3)
1200 ppm Fe	125.6 ± 11.1 (4)	31.4 ± 1.3 (4)	0.56 ± 0.18 (3)
2000 ppm Fe	145.4 ± 11.3 (4)	32.4 ± 0.6 (4)	0.41 ± 0.07 (3)

[a] Chicks at 1 week of age were fed an iron-adequate purified diet containing no additional iron supplement (Basal), 1200 ppm or 2000 ppm added iron as ferrous sulfate. After 2 weeks, chicks were killed and liver analyses performed as described in text. Each value represents a mean ± SEM of 3–4 observations. Number in parenthesis indicates number of observations.

the first to demonstrate an extensive iron-induced increase in zinc-bound hepatic metallothionein. The liver was the most responsive tissue and, therefore, presumably the target organ since neither kidney nor pancreas responded. Yoshikawa and Ohta (31) have indicated that iron (Fe^{2+}) is among some 15 elements which have the ability to induce metallothionein, but reference to the original work (17) reveals that there are equivocal data. In a study of the influence of iron and 18 other metals on the level of metallothionein-like proteins (MTP) in liver and kidney of rats, Piotrowski and Szymanska (17) cited preliminary findings which suggested that iron may influence the concentration of hepatic MTP. More extensive experiments within the same study, however, showed that massive injections of ferric chloride did not affect hepatic MTP levels. This was true even in rats which received six to eight doses (subcutaneous) of iron as ferric chloride as a rate of 200 mg Fe/kg (cf. 10 mg Fe/kg used in the present study). While we are uncertain as to why our results are not consistent with those of the above authors', there are some critical differences between the two studies. First was the difference in the route of iron administration. In the present study, intraperitoneal injections were given in contrast to the subcutaneous injections administered by the above workers. Second, there was a difference in the animal model utilized; chicks in the present versus rats in the above study. And finally, the method of analysis of metallothionein differed substantially in the two studies. In the present study, the more conventional method of gel filtration chromatography was employed to isolate and quantitate zinc metallothionein. Piotrowski and Szymanska (17) employed a radiochemical method based on tracing metallothionein in a TCA supernatant of tissue homogenate.

Which of the above three possibilities most likely explains the disparity in experimental results is difficult to determine. The radiochemical metallothionein assay procedure has been shown (32) to give "reliable" results but has not been directly compared to the chromatographic procedure. It is likely that on a relative basis, there may be little real difference between the two procedures. Regarding the second possibility, species differences, it again is difficult to quantitate since a direct comparison of species regarding capacity to synthesize metallothionein has not been reported. We have conducted similar studies with weanling rats (data not shown) and have observed that the rat, when treated similarly with ferric iron, is much less responsive. Rats (200 g) were given either one or two injections (ip) of iron as $FeCl_3$ (10 mg Fe/kg body wt) in a protocol similar to that used with chicks. Saline-injected controls showed very little zinc metallothionein present (trace amount). Values of 2.7 ± 0.3 and 4.4 ± 0.2 μg Zn as MT/ml of liver cytosol were observed in rats given either one or two iron injections. When one compares these values to average values of 7 μg Zn and 18 μg Zn–MT for similarly treated young chicks, it is apparent that the chick is more responsive. While this observation may account for quantitative differences in results of the present study and those reported above, it would not seem to explain the lack of significant effect of iron. This leads finally to the initial suggestion of differences in the route of administration. Recently, Eaton *et al.* (20) examined the dose–response effects of various metal ions on rat liver metallothionein. Iron as ferrous sulfate was among the metals studied. Adult rats were given two intraperitoneal injections of iron at a rate of 16.8 mg Fe/kg. Analysis of metallothionein by the radiochemical method revealed an increase of 150–200% in hepatic metallothionein of iron-treated rats when compared to controls. While the response to intraperitoneally administered iron was small in comparison to that observed with either zinc or cadmium, the rat did respond to injected iron. This was in contrast to results from the previously cited report (17) but qualitatively similar to our results. A possible explanation for these differences may lie in the route of administration of iron. Eaton *et al.* (20). and our protocol employed intraperitoneal injections of iron while Piotrowski and Syzmanska (17) used subcutaneous injections. In the former two studies, a response to iron was observed whereas in the latter there was no consistent change in hepatic metallothionein concentration. While we can offer no explanation regarding physiological differences between the two routes of administration, the evidence suggests that the method administering iron warrants consideration.

Eaton *et al.* (20) suggested the small effect of some metals on metallothionein synthesis may be the result of the effects of stress rather than the metal ion per se. Perhaps there is a greater stress associated with intraperitoneal administration.

Additional data obtained in the present study indicate further that effect of iron on hepatic metallothionein is dependent on the method of effecting an elevation in iron status. Results of a feeding study in which the concentration of hepatic iron was increased to a value similar to that ultimately observed by injection showed no change in hepatic zinc metallothionein as a result of increased hepatic iron (Table II). These data indicate strongly that elevated hepatic iron alone is not causal in the process of iron-induced accumulation of hepatic zinc metallothionein and that the parenteral route of iron administration, as an important factor in the process, must be considered.

An inhibition by zinc and other divalent cations of iron binding and hence formation of the iron storage protein, ferritin, has been documented (33, 34). Recently, a zinc "storage and transferring" function of ferritin has been implicated (35). This arose primarily as a result of the observation that the association of zinc with ferritin increased with the administration of zinc. Our initial concern in the present study focused on the possibility that the zinc-binding material induced by iron administration may have been a subunit of ferritin (19,000–22,000 mol wt). The feeding study (Table II) provided evidence that an elevation of hepatic iron, a level which undoubtedly increased ferritin concentration, did not effect of change in the zinc-binding material of the third peak on G75 as seen in Fig. 2. Since tissues from both the injection and feeding studies were prepared in a similar manner and our additional qualitative analyses (Figs. 3 and 4 and Table I) indicated metallothionein characteristics, we are confident that the zinc-binding protein induced by iron injection is not a subunit of ferritin but in fact similar to metallothionein.

The mechanism by which iron loading effects an elevation in zinc metallothionein specifically in hepatic tissue is not known. The suggestion made previously (20) that the induction of metallothionein by metals other than those recognized as potent inducers is the result of stress rather than the metal ion per se may be relevant in the present study. Stress hormones such as adrenal glucocorticoids are well recognized (10–12) as possessing the ability to induce the synthesis of metallothionein. Although both liver and kidney are responsive in terms of glucocorticoid induction, the liver appears to be much much more sensitive. Hager and Palmiter (36) quantitated the extent of accumulation of metallothionein mRNA following the administration of a synthetic glucocorticoid, dexamethasone. Liver exhibited a 100-fold increase in the number of molecules of metallothionein mRNA whereas the kidney showed only a 3-fold increase. They suggested that the meager response of the kidney may be due to the relatively few glucocorticoid receptors present in that organ. Somewhat similar results relative to the differences in stress-induced metallothionein accumulation in liver and kidney were reported by Oh *et al.* (13). These workers found that various stresses which increase hepatic metallothionein have essentially no effect on renal metallothionein concentration. In view of the apparent difference between liver and kidney in terms of glucocorticoid sensitivity, it is then plausible that parenteral iron administration, specifically intraperitoneal injection, represents a potent stress causing the secretion of adrenal glucocorticoids which, in turn, stimulates the synthesis of metallothionein primarily in hepatic tissue. The net effect is the accumulation of metallothionein-bound zinc in the liver. Due to the lower sensitivity of kidney, one might anticipate little or no change in the concentration of metallothionein in this organ, which was in fact the result of the present study. The lack of change of zinc metallothionein in the pancreas may or may not be indicative of a mechanism involving glucocorticoids.

In addition to the possibility of stress as a cause of iron-induced metallothionein accumulation, an alternative mechanism involving elevated blood zinc as effected by parenteral iron is worthy of comment. Since zinc is recognized as a potent inducer of metallothionein in hepatic tissue, any treatment which results in an elevation of blood zinc may then indirectly effect an increase in tissue metallothionein. The administration of iron, a highly reactive element, may result in the liberation of tissue zinc. We recognized this possibility due to a casual observation in the present study that a small percentage of the chicks treated with iron developed local tissue necrosis. Damaged tissue may release zinc, which may be the direct cause of increased hepatic metallothionein. Our data on the tissue specificity of iron effects, however, do not support such a conclusion. Elevated blood zinc would undoubtedly result in a general increase of metallothionein in each of the three tissues examined. Since this was not the result of our study, it is unlikely that elevated blood zinc is a causal factor.

In conclusion, the present work has demonstrated that intraperitoneal injections of various iron compounds results in a dramatic increase in hepatic zinc metallothionein. Other tissues such as kidney and pancreas, which are sensitive to metal-induced metallothionein synthesis, did not respond. Elevated hepatic iron, either from injection or feeding, was not correlated with iron-induced metallothionein accumulation. We suggested that stress-induced changes in adrenal cortical hormone secretion may account for the observed changes in hepatic metallothionein concentration.

The author is truly indebted to Dr. Curtis S. Fullmer for conducting the amino acid compositional analysis. It was performed at the Cornell University Amino Acid Analysis and Protein Sequencing Facility. This aspect was supported by D.O.E. Contract EV-02792 awarded to R. H. Wasserman.

1. Margoshes M, Vallee BL. A cadmium protein from equine kidney cortex. J Amer Chem Soc **79**:4813–4814, 1957.
2. Richards MP, Cousins RJ. Mammalian zinc homeostasis: Requirement for RNA and metallothionein synthesis. Biochem Biophys Res Commun **64**:1215–1223, 1975.
3. Kojima Y, Kagi JHR. Metallothionein, Trends Biochem Sci **3**:90–93, 1978.
4. Chen RW, Whanger PD, Weswig PH. Biological function of metallothionein. I. Synthesis and degradation of rat liver metallothionein. Biochem Med **12**:95–105, 1975.
5. Nordberg GF, Piscator M, Lind B. Distribution of cadmium among protein fractions of mouse liver. Acta Pharmacol Toxicol **29**:456–470, 1971.
6. Webb M. Binding of cadmium ions by rat liver and kidney. Biochem Pharmacol **21**:2751–2765, 1972.
7. Bremner I, Young BW. Isolation of (copper, zinc)—thioneins from the livers of copper injected rats. Biochem J **157**:517–520, 1976.
8. Durnam DM, Palmiter RD. Transcriptional regulation of the mouse metallothionein-I gene by heavy metals. J Biol Chem **256**:5712–5716, 1981.
9. Piotrowski JK, Trojanowska B, Wisniewska-Knypl JM, Bolanowska W. Mercury binding in the kidney and liver of rats repeatedly exposed to mercuric chloride; induction of metallothionein by mercury and cadmium. Toxicol Appl Pharmacol **27**:11–19, 1974.
10. Etzel KR, Shapiro SG, Cousins RJ. Regulation of liver metallothionein and plasma zinc by the glucocorticoid dexamethasone. Biochem Biophys Res Commun **89**:1120–1126, 1979.
11. Failla ML, Cousins RJ. Zinc accumulation and metabolism in primary cultures of adult rat liver cells. Regulation by glucocorticoids. Biochim Biophys Acta **543**:293–304, 1978.
12. Klaassen CD. Induction of metallothionein by adrenocortical steroids. Toxicology **20**:275–279, 1981.
13. Oh SH, Deagen JT, Whanger PD, Weswig PH. Biological function of metallothionein. V. Its induction in rats by various stresses. Amer J Physiol **234**:E282–E285, 1978.
14. Bremner I, Davies NT. The induction of metallothionein in rat liver by zinc injection and restriction of food intake. Biochem J **149**:733–738, 1975.
15. Sobocinski PZ, Canterbury WJ, Jr, Mapes CA, Dinterman RE. Involvement of hepatic metallothionein in hypozincemia associated with bacterial infection. Amer J Physiol **234**:E399–E406, 1978.
16. Swerdel M, Cousins RJ. Characterization of the induction of metallothionein in liver by isopropanol. Fed Proc **42**:821, 1983.
17. Piotrowski JK, Szymanska JA, Influence of certain metals on the level of metallothionein-like proteins in the liver and kidneys of rats. J Toxicol Environ Health **1**:991–1002, 1976.
18. Winge DR, Premakumar R, Rajagopalan KV. Metal-induced formation of metallothionein in rat liver. Arch Biochem Biophys **170**:242–252, 1975.
19. Szymanska JA, Mogilnicka EM, Kaszper BW. Binding of bismuth in the kidneys of the rat: The role of metallothionein-like proteins. Biochem Pharmacol **26**:257–258, 1977.
20. Eaton DL, Stacy NH, Wong K-L, Klaassen CD. Dose-response effects of various metal ions on rat liver metallothionein, glutathione, heme oxygenase, and cytochrome P-450. Toxicol App Pharmacol **55**:393–402, 1980.
21. McCormick CC. The influence of iron loading on hepatic and pancreatic zinc metabolism in the chick. Fed Proc **41**:782, 1982.
22. McCormick CC. Induction and accumulation of metallothionein in liver and pancreas of chicks given oral zinc: A tissue comparison. J Nutr **114**:191–203, 1984.

23. Davis BJ. Disc electrophoresis—Method and application to human serum proteins. NY Acad Sci **121**:404–427, 1964.
24. Hirs CHW. Determination of cystine as cysteic acid. In: Hirs CHW, ed. Methods of Enzymology. New York, Academic Press, Vol 11:pp59–62, 1967.
25. Fox MRS, Briggs GM. Salt mixtures for purified-type diets. III. An improved salt mixture for chicks. J Nutr **72**:243–250, 1960.
26. Snedecor GW, Cochran WG. Statistical Methods. Ames, Iowa Univ Press, pp258–296, 1967.
27. Oh SH, Nakaue H, Deagen JT, Whanger PD, Arscott GH. Accumulation and depletion of zinc in chick tissue metallothioneins. J Nutr **109**:1720–1729, 1979.
28. Weser U, Rupp H, Donay F, Linnemann F, Voelter W, Voetsch W, Jung G. Characterization of Cd, Zn-thionein (metallothionein) isolated from rat and chicken liver. Eur J Biochem **39**:127–140, 1973.
29. Kojima Y, Berger C, Vallee BL, Kagi JH. Amino acid sequence of equine renal metallothionein-1 B. Proc Natl Acad Sci USA **73**:3413–3417, 1976.
30. Buhler HF, Kagi JH. Human hepatic metallothioneins. Fed Eur Biochem Soc Lett **39**:229–234, 1974.
31. Yoshikawa H, Ohta H. Interaction of metals and metallothionein. In: Foulkes EC, ed. Biological Roles of Metallothionein. New York, Elsevier/North-Holland, pp11–24, 1982.
32. Kotsonis FN, Klaassen CD. Comparison of methods for estimating hepatic metallothionein in rats. Toxicol Appl Pharmacol **42**:583–588, 1977.
33. Macara IG, Hoy TG, Harrison PM. The formation of ferritin from apoferritin—Inhibition and metal ion-binding studies. Biochem J **135**:785–789, 1973.
34. Macara IG, Hoy TG, Harrison PM. Inhibition by zinc ions of ferritin formation in vitro. Biochem Soc Trans **1**:102–104, 1973.
35. Price D, Joshi JG. Ferritin: A zinc detoxicant and a zinc ion donor. Proc Natl Acad Sci USA **79**:3116–3119, 1982.
36. Hager LJ, Palmiter RD. Transcriptional regulation of mouse liver metallothionein-I gene by glucocorticoids. Nature (London) **291**:340–342, 1981.

Received June 10, 1983. P.S.E.B.M. 1984, Vol. 176.
Accepted April 19, 1984.

PROCEEDINGS OF THE SOCIETY FOR EXPERIMENTAL BIOLOGY AND MEDICINE **176**, 403–406 (1984)

Analysis of Metopirone-Induced Hypertrophy of Adrenals in Fetal Rats Encephalectomized *in Utero* (41889)

MASAKO YAMAMOTO, KAZUYOSHI ARISHIMA, YASUNOBU EGUCHI, AND KOSHI MOCHIZUKI*

*Department of Anatomy II, Azabu University School of Veterinary Medicine, Sagamihara, Kanagawa 229, and *Department of Veterinary Anatomy, Faculty of Agriculture, University of Tokyo, Bunkyo, Tokyo 113, Japan*

Abstract. Pregnant rats were treated with 30 mg metopirone (M) each day for 2 days and autopsied on the third day in various gestational periods (Days 18–20, 19–21, and 20–22). Control rats were treated with saline alone (S). The adrenals of intact fetuses in M-treated dams were significantly heavier than those of intact fetuses in S-treated dams in every experimental period. In both M- and S-treated dams, the adrenals of encephalectomized (E) fetuses were lighter than those of intact littermates. However, in the experimental period of Days 18–20 and 19–21, the adrenals of E fetuses in M-treated dams were slightly but significantly heavier than those of similar E fetuses in S-treated dams. In contrast, in the experimental period Days 20–22, there was no significant difference in the weight of adrenals of E fetuses of M- and S-treated dams. These changes in fetal adrenal weight were reflected histologically in parallel changes in the size of adrenocortical cells. The observations suggest that the fetal adrenal hypertrophy following maternal treatment with metopirone can occur to some extent independent of the fetal brain, but that close to the end of gestation the hypertrophy occurs completely under the control of the fetal brain.

In our previous studies, in which we examined the effect of adrenalectomy and/or metopirone injection performed at different stages of gestation in the rat, the fetal pituitary–adrenal negative feedback mechanism was assessed to begin to operate between Days 16 and 18 of gestation (1, 2). Furthermore, it seems that the hypothalamus partially begins to regulate the pituitary–adrenal system between Days 18 and 20 of gestation, followed by the complete regulation toward the end of the gestation (3).

In the present experiment, pregnant rats were given metopirone and some fetuses were encephalectomized *in utero* for the purpose of removing the hypothalamic area. Metopirone, which is said to inhibit 11β-hydroxylation and corticosterone production, can cross the placenta to reach the fetus and shows an inhibitory effect on the fetal adrenals as well as on the maternal adrenals (4–7), resulting in a marked hypertrophy of the fetal adrenals. This work was designed to assess the degree to which the fetal hypothalamus is involved in the metopirone-induced hypertrophy of fetal adrenals, using chronological observations with gravimetric and histologic methods.

Materials and Methods. Rats of the Wistar strain were used. They were given commercial diet (Labo MR Breeder) and water, both *ad libitum.* Females were placed with males overnight and were examined the next morning for the presence of sperm in the vaginal smear. The day on which sperm was observed was counted as Day 1 of pregnancy.

Pregnant rats were used for fetal encephalectomy under ether anesthesia on Days 18, 19, or 20 of gestation. Fetal encephalectomy was performed by the method of Eguchi *et al.* (8). The rats were divided into two groups, metopirone-injected (M) and saline-injected (S). Rats in the metopirone group received a subcutaneous injection of 30 mg metopirone (Ciba) dissolved in 2 ml saline, each day for 2 days, the first on the day of fetal encephalectomy and the second on the following day (the total dose being 60 mg). Rats of the saline group received 2 ml saline only, in a similar fashion. All rats were autopsied on the day following the second injection.

After the mothers were killed by decapitation, the fetuses were quickly removed from the uterus and weighed. The encephalectomized fetuses were randomly matched to intact littermates of the same sex. The head of each

0037-9727/84 $1.50

encephalectomized fetus was fixed in Bouin's fluid for later histologic examination for the presence of the pituitary. Both adrenals of each fetus were removed and weighed. The right adrenal was fixed in Bouin's fluid, embedded in Paraplast (Sherwood Medical, Ind.) and sectioned serially at 5 μm. The sections were stained with hematoxylin and eosin in order to count the number of adrenocortical nuclei per unit sectional area (4900 μm^2). The counts were made on two areas in each of five successive fifth sections, including the largest section of the series, and were averaged to estimate the size of cortical cells. Larger counts mean that the cells are smaller, and smaller counts mean that the cells are larger.

The data were tested with one-way analysis of variance. The test calculated an overall F value and then calculated a corrected significance level between groups. A probability less than 0.05 was considered to be statistically significant. Analysis of the fetal body weights was not carried out, as an appropriate allowance could not be made for the absence of the brain in the encephalectomized fetuses. Therefore, any conclusions regarding the relationship between adrenal weight and body weight would not be warranted.

Results. In the saline-treated (S) dams, the adrenals of encephalectomized (E) fetuses were significantly lighter than those of intact littermate controls in every experimental period (Table I). Similarly, in the metopirone-treated (M) dams, the adrenals of E fetuses were markedly lighter than those of control (C) fetuses. In particular, the adrenals of C fetuses in M-treated dams were significantly heavier than those of C fetuses in S-treated dams, showing a marked hypertrophy in response to maternal metopirone administration.

Comparison of adrenals of E fetuses of S- and M-treated dams was of particular interest. In the experimental period Days 18–20, the E fetal adrenals in M-treated dams were heavier than those in S-treated dams. The difference in the adrenal weight between these two E groups appeared reduced in the experimental period Days 19–21. Finally, in the experimental period Days 20–22, the adrenals of E fetuses in M-treated dams were almost equal in weight to those of E fetuses in S-treated dams.

The trend of counts of cortical cell nuclei per unit sectional area (Table II) paralleled the weights of the fetal adrenals. In both groups, S and M, the counts were significantly greater in E fetuses than in C fetuses, except for the experimental period Days 20–22 in Group S. Especially to be noted is the fact that in the experimental periods Days 18–20 and 19–21 the counts in E fetuses of Group M were less than those of the corresponding

TABLE I. ADRENAL WEIGHTS OF ENCEPHALECTOMIZED FETUSES (E) AND THEIR INTACT LITTERMATE CONTROLS (C) FROM SALINE-TREATED DAMS (S) AND METOPIRONE-TREATED DAMS (M)

Mothers	Fetuses	Day at surgery	Day at autopsy	Number of fetuses examined	Body wt (g) (means ± SEM)	Adrenal wt (mg) (means ± SEM)
S	C	18	20	9 (6)	2.26 ± 0.11	2.13 ± 0.11[a]
	E	18	20	9 (6)	1.94 ± 0.16	1.43 ± 0.08[b]
M	C	18	20	8 (4)	2.31 ± 0.09	2.68 ± 0.12[c]
	E	18	20	8 (4)	2.11 ± 0.09	1.88 ± 0.15[a]
S	C	19	21	9 (3)	3.55 ± 0.06	2.37 ± 0.15[a]
	E	19	21	9 (3)	3.15 ± 0.09	1.82 ± 0.08[b]
M	C	19	21	16 (8)	3.16 ± 0.08	3.29 ± 0.09[c]
	E	19	21	16 (8)	2.65 ± 0.11	2.15 ± 0.17[d]
S	C	20	22	8 (3)	4.88 ± 0.22	2.53 ± 0.20[a]
	E	20	22	8 (3)	3.69 ± 0.12	1.99 ± 0.15[b]
M	C	20	22	8 (5)	4.50 ± 0.08	3.93 ± 0.22[c]
	E	20	22	8 (5)	3.74 ± 0.13	2.00 ± 0.10[b]

Note. (N): Number of litters. Figures not sharing the same letter (a, b, c, d) are significantly different at $P < 0.05$.

TABLE II. THE NUMBER OF FETAL ADRENOCORTICAL CELL NUCLEI PER UNIT SECTIONAL AREA (4900 μm^2) OF ENCEPHALECTOMIZED FETUSES (E) AND THEIR INTACT LITTERMATE CONTROLS (C) FROM SALINE-TREATED DAMS (S) AND METOPIRONE-TREATED DAMS (M)

Mothers	Fetuses	Day at surgery	Day at autopsy	Number of fetuses examined	Number of cell nuclei/unit area (means ± SEM)
S	C	18	20	9 (6)	27.7 ± 1.1[a]
	E	18	20	8 (6)	32.9 ± 1.3[b]
M	C	18	20	8 (4)	22.3 ± 0.9[c]
	E	18	20	8 (4)	29.0 ± 1.0[a]
S	C	19	21	9 (3)	29.4 ± 1.0[a]
	E	19	21	9 (3)	37.8 ± 1.7[b]
M	C	19	21	16 (8)	23.5 ± 0.6[c]
	E	19	21	16 (8)	32.0 ± 1.7[a]
S	C	20	22	8 (3)	32.0 ± 1.4[a]
	E	20	22	8 (3)	34.7 ± 1.2[a,*]
M	C	20	22	7 (5)	20.5 ± 1.0[b]
	E	20	22	8 (5)	36.2 ± 1.4[c,*]

Note. (*N*): Number of litters. Figures not sharing the same letter (*a, b, c, d*) are significantly different at $P < 0.05$.
* Not significantly different between the figures marked.

E fetuses of Group S. However, in the experimental period Days 20–22 the count in E fetuses of Group M did not differ from that in E fetuses of Group S.

Discussion. The fetal pituitary regulates the fetal adrenal cortex as early as Day 17 of gestation (9, 10). During this early period, it seems that the fetal pituitary has an autonomous ability to stimulate the adrenal without the participation of the brain, since the destruction of the hypothalamus does not interfere with the growth of the adrenal glands (5). The critial time of onset of hypothalamic control of the pituitary–adrenal system seems to be between Days 18 and 20 of gestation, and during this period fetal encephalectomy slightly retards adrenal growth (3, 9). Such a slight retardation of adrenal growth is accounted for by the lack of the hypothalamus, which begins to release CRH during this time. Subsequently, between Days 20 and 22, fetal encephalectomy retards adrenal growth to an extent very similar to that induced by fetal decapitation, which removes the fetal pituitary (3). Thus, at late gestational period the adrenocortical stimulating activity of the fetal pituitary appears to be largely dependent on hypothalamic control (3, 9, 10).

Similarly, evidence shows that the fetal pituitary–adrenal feedback response is established between Days 16 and 18 of gestation, since the earliest time at which maternal adrenalectomy causes a significant hypertrophy of the fetal adrenals 2 days later is Day 16 (1). According to Dupouy and Jost (11), in rat fetuses encephalectomized on Day 19.5 postcoitum (equivalent to Day 20 of gestation in the present study) and autopsied at 21.5 days, the adrenals are stunted in growth even if the mother has been adrenalectomized, but the degree of stunting is less than that in decapitated fetuses in the same adrenalectomized mother. Therefore, it may be that the compensatory hypertrophy of the fetal adrenal following maternal adrenalectomy is largely dependent on the presence of the fetal hypothalamus, but involves in part the autonomous short feedback between the pituitary and the adrenal.

Metopirone blocks corticosteroid biosynthesis both in the mother and in the fetus, and hence metopirone-induced fetal adrenal hypertrophy is of a greater degree than the hypertrophy induced by maternal adrenalectomy. In this sense, metopirone treatment would convey more exact information about the chronological development of the negative feedback mechanism of the pituitary–adrenal system involving the hypothalamic regulation.

In the present study, the adrenals of intact

C fetuses in M-treated dams were considerably heavier than those of similar C fetuses in S-treated dams, in every experimental period, as a compensatory response. Encephalectomy of fetuses in both M- and S-treated dams resulted in a stunting of fetal adrenal growth. However, careful examination of the results reveals different degrees of stunting between the two groups. In the experimental periods Days 18–20 and 19–21 the adrenals of E fetuses in M-treated dams were heavier than those of similar E fetuses in S-treated dams. Nevertheless, in the experimental period Days 20–22, the adrenals of E fetuses in M-treated dams were almost equal, in weight as well as in cortical cell size, to those of similar E fetuses of S-treated dams. Thus, the difference between E fetuses of M and S groups is gradually lessened toward the end of gestation. These findings are in good agreement with the previous reports which indicate a chronologically strengthened activity of the hypothalamus on pituitary activity (9, 10).

Similar results have been presented by Dupouy (4), who reported that the fetal adrenal hypertrophy following maternal treatment with metopirone represented a larger influence of the hypothalamus as gestational age advanced. However, those results showed that E fetuses in M-treated dams still had adrenals slightly heavier than those of E fetuses in sucrose-treated rats at the end of gestation, in contrast to our results, where the adrenals of E fetuses in M-treated dams are almost equal in weight to those of similar E fetuses of S-treated dams at the end of gestation. The discrepancy between our results and those of Dupouy is difficult to explain, but it may be due to the difference in the duration of treatment (1 day by Dupouy versus 2 days by us) and in the total amount of metopirone given to the pregnant dams (100 mg by Dupouy versus 60 mg by us). An excessive amount of metopirone brings about a toxic and fatal effect on the fetus itself, as well as on the mother, and eventually may alter the endocrine status of the fetus. In any event, the present results strongly support the view that the pituitary–adrenal feedback response comes largely under the control of the fetal hypothalamus close to the end of gestation in the rat.

This study was supported in part by a Grant-in-Aid for Scientific Research (548067) from the Ministry of Education, Science and Culture of Japan.

1. Yamamoto M, Eguchi Y, Asari M, Kano Y. Developmental changes in fetal adrenal hypertrophy following maternal bilateral and fetal unilateral adrenalectomy at different stages of gestation in the rat. Biol Neonate **43**:43–49, 1983.
2. Yamamoto M, Arishima K, Eguchi Y, Mochizuki K. Gravimetric and histologic changes in fetal adrenals following maternal adrenalectomy and metopirone injection in the rat. Jpn J Vet Sci **45**:659–665, 1983.
3. Cohen A, Dupouy J-P, Jost A. Influence de l'hypothalamus sur l'activité corticostimelante de l'hypophyse foetale de Rat au cours de la gestation. CR Acad Sci (Paris) **273**:883–886, 1971.
4. Dupouy J-P. Response de complexe hypothalamo-hypophysaire du foetus de rat à un blocage de la biosynthèse de corticostéroides par la métopirone. Influence du cortisol. CR Acad Sci Paris **273**:962–965, 1971.
5. Dupouy J-P. Activité corticostimulante de l'hypophyse du foetus de rat après surrénalectomie maternalle et injection de métopirone à différents stades de la gestation. CR Acad Sci Paris **274**:3585–3588, 1972.
6. Dupouy J-P, Magre S. Ultrastructure des cellules granulées de l'hypophyse foetal du rat. Identification des cellules corticotropes et thyréotropes. Arch Anat Microsc Morphol Exp **62**:185–205, 1973.
7. Goldman AS. Experimental model of congenital adrenal cortical hyperplasia produced *in utero* with an inhibitor of 11β-steroid hydroxylase. J Clin Endocrinol Metab **27**:1390–1394, 1967.
8. Eguchi Y, Arishima K, Nasu T, Toda M, Morikawa Y, Hashimoto Y. Development of the fetal pituitary–testicular system based on observation of Leydig cells in encephalectomized, hypophysectomized and control fetal rats. Anat Rec **190**:679–686, 1978.
9. Eguchi Y, Hirai O, Morikawa Y, Hashimoto Y. Critical time in the hypothalamic control of the pituitary–adrenal system in fetal rats: Observations in fetuses subjected to hypervitaminosis A and hypothalamic destruction. Endocrinology **93**:1–11, 1973.
10. Jost A, Dupouy J-P, Rieutort M. The ontogenic development of hypothalamo–hypophyseal relations. Progr Brain Res **41**:209–219, 1974.
11. Dupouy J-P, Jost A. Activité corticotrope de l'hypophyse foetale du rat: influence de l'hypothalamus et des corticostéroïdes. CR Soc Biol (Paris) **164**:2422–2427, 1970.

Received February 22, 1984. P.S.E.B.M. 1984, Vol. 176.
Accepted April 23, 1984.

PROCEEDINGS OF THE SOCIETY FOR EXPERIMENTAL BIOLOGY AND MEDICINE **176,** 407–413 (1984)

Interaction of *N*-Methyl-*N'*-nitro-*N*-nitrosoguanidine (MNNG) with Owl Monkey Kidney Cells in Enhancing the Yields of *Herpesvirus saimiri* (HVS) and Its Antigens (41890)

ALBERTO FAGGIONI,* DHARAM V. ABLASHI,†[1] JOHN DAHLBERG,† GARY ARMSTRONG,‡ AND S. K. SUNDAR§

**Istituto di Patologia Generale, II Catedra, Universita degli Studi di Roma, Rome, Italy; †Division of Cancer Etiology, National Cancer Institute, National Institutes of Health, Bethesda, Maryland 20205; ‡Division of Virology, Bureau of Biologics, National Institutes of Health, Bethesda, Maryland 20205; and §Laboratory of Immunology, Hospital Sainte-Justine, Montreal, Quebec, Canada*

Abstract. Pre- and posttreatment with *N*-methyl-*N'*-nitro-nitrosoguanidine (MNNG) of owl monkey kidney (OMK) cells infected with *Herpesvirus saimiri* (HVS) resulted in one to three logs higher yields of virus, depending upon the dose of MNNG. A higher percentage of cells also showed HVS early antigen (EA) and late antigen (LA) by immunofluorescence when OMK cells infected with HVS were fed with medium containing MNNG. The high yields of HVS were also observed by electron microscopy. MNNG did not induce HVS-EA in HVS nonproducer lymphoblastoid T cells, nor did it enhance TPA-induced EA to LA. The data suggest that MNNG could be useful in obtaining high yields of virus and/or antigen-producing cells for immunofluorescence or other biochemical experiments, especially from those strains of HVS which grow poorly *in vitro*. The interaction of MNNG and HVS could also be useful for *in vitro* transformation or *in vivo* enhancement of the malignant process.

N-Methyl-*N'*-nitro-nitrosoguanidine (MNNG) is a carcinogenic and mutagenic alkylating agent which has been used to induce experimental gastric and duodenal adenocarcinomas in rats (5, 18). MNNG was also able to transform human skin fibroblasts of patients with hereditary adenomatosis of the colon and rectum (16) and clones of osteosarcoma cells (15). Henderson *et al.* (10) showed that MNNG treatment increased the frequency of establishing permanent human lymphoblastoid cell lines, and also facilitated transformation of human cord blood leukocytes with Epstein–Barr virus (EBV) (11). More recently, we have been able to show that human cord blood lymphocytes treated with MNNG required lower amounts of EBV for transformation. In addition, MNNG pretreatment of Raji cells led to enhanced early antigen levels following superinfection with nontransforming EBV (8).

We report here on the interaction of MNNG with owl monkey kidney cells (OMK) in increasing the yields of two strains of HVS which cause leukemia and/or lymphoma in marmosets, owl monkeys, and rabbits (2, 4). Similarities between EBV and HVS have led to the use of HVS in a nonhuman primate model for investigating the role of herpesvirus-induced malignancies similar to the nasopharyngeal carcinomas (NPC) and Burkitt's lymphomas (BL) involving EBV (7, 9).

Materials and Methods. *Virus strains.* Plaque-purified HVS of the prototype strain S295C ("HVS-P") and the highly pathogenic "OMI" strain of HVS were grown in mycoplasma-free owl monkey kidney (OMK) cell cultures using Dulbecco's minimum essential medium (D-MEM) and 10% heat-inactivated fetal calf serum (FCS). HVS titers, expressed in $TCID_{50}$ units, were determined on OMK cells as described below.

Virus titration. Both HVS-P and HVS-OMI were titered in OMK cells grown in 24-well plastic plates. The cells were grown in D-MEM with 4.5 gm/liter glucose and 10% heat-inactivated fetal calf serum (Advanced Biotechnology, Inc., Silver Spring, Md.). When the cells were nearly confluent, 0.1-ml aliquots of serial 10-fold dilutions of the virus to be assayed was inoculated into 4 wells/dilution. The virus was absorbed for 1 hr at 37°C, the supernatant was removed, and medium containing 2% serum was added to each well and incubated at 37°C. Titers were based on the

[1] To whom reprint requests should be addressed.

0037-9727/84 $1.50

development of characteristic cytopathic effects (CPE) and the $TCID_{50}$ was calculated after 2 weeks incubation. The OMK cells, either pretreated with MNNG or infected first with HVS and then treated with MNNG (Tables I and II) were observed for CPE and when >90% of the cells showed rounding giant cell formations (4+ CPE), the virus was prepared as follows: Most of the supernatant from infected cultures was separated from nonadherent cells by low-speed centrifugation at 4°C. After pipetting of all but 2 ml of the supernatant virus, the cell pellet was resuspended, quick-frozen, and thawed in a dry-ice and alcohol bath and centrifuged at 2000 rpm for 15 min. The latter supernatant was mixed with the original supernatant, filtered through a 0.45-μm pore size filter and titered in OMK cells as described above.

The effect of MNNG on the growth of HVS was assessed by observing cytopathic effect (CPE), indirect immunofluorescence (IF), and electron microscopy. The detection of early antigen (EA) was carried out with HVS-infected cells treated with 100 μg-ml phosphonoacetic acid (PAA) according to published procedures (1).

Indirect immunofluorescence. The HVS-infected and uninfected OMK cells, with or without MNNG treatment, were removed by shaking the flask, washed three times with PBS without calcium and magnesium and then approximately 5×10^5 cells were deposited on the wells of Teflon-coated glass slides. The cells were air-dried and fixed in acetone at 4°C for 15 min. The fixed slides were then used for examining HVS-LA (late antigen)- and EA (early antigen)-producing cells using HVS antibodies.

An owl monkey serum (7874) from an animal which developed an HVS-P-induced lymphoma was used, since it had an HVS antibody titer of 1:160 and an HVS-EA titer of 1:40. A second serum was obtained from a squirrel monkey (S-175) naturally infected with HVS. This serum had no detectable EA antibody (at 1:10) and an HVS-LA antibody titer of 1:80. The treatment and dilutions of sera used are given in Table III. Appropriately diluted sera were deposited on the fixed cells (4), incubated at 37°C in a humid chamber for 45 min, and washed three times in PBS for 10 min using a shaker. The slides were air-dried and then the cells were incubated for 45 min with a 1:20 dilution of fluorescein-labeled anti-human IgG antibody (H + L chains, Cappel Laboratories, Inc.). After washing the slides three times in PBS, they again were air-dried, mounted, and then examined under the fluorescent microscope. The total number of cells in 10 different fields per slide were counted and divided by the number of IF-positive cells to obtain the percentage of IF-positive cells exhibiting HVS-LA and -EA (Table III).

Electron microscopy. Cultures of HVS-infected cells with or without MNNG treatment were washed briefly with PBS, fixed *in situ* for 2–5 min with 2.5% glutaraldehyde in PBS, and then scraped loose and pelleted in 0.4-ml microfuge tubes. The pellets were fixed an additional 30–60 min in glutaraldehyde, post-fixed 1 hr in 1% osmium tetroxide in PBS, dehydrated with ethanol and propylene oxide and embedded in Epon–Araldite. Ultrathin sections were stained with uranyl acetate and lead citrate.

MNNG stock. MNNG was prepared as a stock solution in PBS, as described previously (8), and was frozen at −20°C. The stock solution was further diluted in tissue culture medium containing 5% FCS.

Results and Discussion. Table I summarizes our findings on the effect of pretreating OMK cells with 0.5, 1.0, and 2.0 μg/ml of MNNG for 48 hr prior to infection with HVS-P and HVS-OMI. In every case, a 1–3 log increase in titer was observed compared to controls, even for HVS-OMI, which while highly tumorigenic in monkeys, grows poorly in OMK cells. Extracts of uninfected cells treated with MNNG did not contain virus, showing that the enhanced titers were not due to the induction of virus from the original cells. This increase in titer due to MNNG pretreatment was reflected in an earlier onset of cytopathic effect in MNNG-treated cultures, which generally appeared within 6–8 hr in monolayers pretreated with MNNG and then used for titrations.

Table II summarizes experiments carried out with MNNG in the culture medium during the period of virus replication. Although no pretreatment was included in these cultures, it is evident that a significant enhancement of virus yield could be obtained. It was

TABLE I. EFFECT OF PRETREATMENT OF OMK CELLS WITH MNNG PRIOR TO HVS INFECTION ON VIRUS YIELDS

Pretreatment	Dose of MNNG (μg/ml)	Virus strain	Titer[a] ($\log_{10}$)	Average log enhancement
None	—	HVS-P	6.47 ± 0.25	—
48 hr MNNG	0.5	HVS-P	7.40 ± 0.17	0.9
	1.0	HVS-P	7.97 ± 0.25	1.5
	2.0	HVS-P	9.17 ± 0.29	2.7
	2.0	—	0	—
None	—	HVS-OMI	3.30 ± 0.17	—
48 hr MNNG	1.0	HVS-OMI	4.40 ± 0.36	1.1
	2.0	HVS-OMI	4.97 ± 0.25	1.7

[a] At 4+ CPE cultures (when more than 85% of cells are showing cell degeneration, clumps of rounded and enlarged cells, looking like bunches of grapes) were frozen and thawed, filtered through a 0.45-μm pore size filter, and titered. Control cultures were treated in the same way. Values are the average of three determinations.

noteworthy, however, that continuous treatment with MNNG after infection led to significantly greater cell damage (not related to viral-induced CPE) than did the pretreatment protocol. Virus obtained from wells used to titer virus derived from MNNG treated cultures was further titered in OMK cells. No differences in the titers were obtained, when compared to controls (<0.5 log), suggesting that MNNG treatment had no detectable genetic effect on the HVS grown in treated cultures.

When HVS-infected OMK cells were treated with MNNG and examined by indirect immunofluorescence, significantly higher levels of both EA- and LA-producing cells were seen as compared to untreated controls. Table III shows that OMK cells infected with 1000 $TCID_{50}$/ml of HVS-P, and treated with 1 μg/ml of MNNG led to 71% LA-positive cells in comparison to 48% positive cells in controls. Secondly, treatment of HVS-P-infected OMK cells with 20 ng/ml of 12-*O*-tetradecanoylphorbol-13-acetate (TPA) produced a 17% in-

TABLE II. EFFECT OF MNNG ON HVS YIELDS IN OMK CELLS WHEN CELLS WERE CONTINUOUSLY TREATED AFTER VIRUS ADSORPTION

Treatment	Dose of MNNG (μg/ml)	Virus strain	Virus titer[a] ($\log_{10}$)	Average log enhancement
1. None	0	HVS-P	6.40 ± 0.14	—
2. MNNG after infection	2.0[b]	HVS-P	8.40 ± 0.17	2.0
	1.0	HVS-P	8.40 ± 0.36	2.0
	0.5	HVS-P	8.07 ± 0.12	1.7
3. None	0	HVS-OMI	4.6[c]	—
4. MNNG after infection	1.0	HVS-OMI	6.2	1.6
	0.5	HVS-OMI	5.5	0.9
5. None	0	—	0	—
6. MNNG time-matched to treatment 2 above	2.0	—	0	—
	1.0	—	0	—
	0.5	—	0	—

[a] Average of three measurements for HVS-P. When cultures were 4+ CPE, they were quick-frozen, thawed, and filtered through a 0.45-μm pore-size filter prior to titration.
[b] MNNG (2 μg) was somewhat toxic and led to morphological alterations and reduced viability. However, it did not affect virus titer, but significantly reduced the number of cells available for immunofluorescence.
[c] Average of two experiments.

TABLE III. EFFECT OF MNNG AND MNNG PLUS TPA ON HSV-EA AND -LA PRODUCTION[a]

Cell line	EA (%)[b]				LA (%)[b]			
	TPA (20 ng/ml)	MNNG (1 μg/ml)	MNNG + TPA	No treatment	TPA (20 ng/ml)	MNNG (1 μg/ml)	MNNG + TPA	No treatment
MLC[c]	5–7	—	5–7	—	—	—	—	—
OMK infected with HVS	⩽35	⩽40	⩽45	30	⩽65	⩽71	⩾80	⩽48
OMK	—	—	—	—	—	—	—	—

[a] OMK cells were infected with 1000 $TCID_{50}$ of HVS. After 2 hr adsorption at 37°C, the virus was removed. The cells were washed once with medium containing no serum. The OMK cells for EA were treated with 100 μg/ml of PAA (1) and were fed with medium containing TPA or MNNG or with both together. All cultures were simultaneously examined when untreated infected cells exhibited moderate CPE.

[b] Serum from a naturally infected squirrel monkey, containing no EA antibody, was used as a negative control for the detection of EA. An owl monkey serum from an animal that developed an HVS-induced tumor contained antibodies to HVS EA and LA was used for both EA and LA detection (used at dilutions of 1:10 to detect EA and 1:40 to detect LA). Both sera were heat-inactivated at 56°C for 30 min prior to use in the IF test. Fluorescein-conjugated anti-human IgG (heavy and light chains) was obtained from Cappel Laboratories, Inc., West Chester, Pa.

[c] The MLC cell line is derived from a lymphoma induced in a cotton-topped marmoset by HVS-P.

crease over the controls in late antigen expression. Moreover, an additive effect was observed when both TPA and MNNG were applied to HVS-infected OMK cells, as was previously oberved with EBV-nonproducer Raji cells (8). This observation suggests that a carcinogen and a promoter can interact to enhance virus expression.

The tumor promotor TPA has also been found to increase the level of transformation of mononuclear cells of adult marmosets by EBV (17) and to enhance antigen levels and virus production in EBV- and HVS-infected cells (3, 13, 19). Since we have shown that MNNG could enhance the level of HVS production in acutely infected cells, we were interested in determining if MNNG could mimic or enhance the effect of TPA on nonproducer marmoset lymphoid cells (MLC) which contain 47 HVS genomes/cell. The rationale for using TPA on the HVS-nonproducer MLC line was to induce EA and to assess its expression in these cells. All HVS nonproducer cell lines are not superinfectable with virus. Thus, the only way to induce EA is by the use of a tumor promotor. Treatment of $\geqslant 10^6$/ml MLC cells (viability ⩾90%) with 1–2 μg/ml MNNG did not induce EA expression nor did it enhance the TPA-mediated induction of EA-positive cells (⩾5%) to LA-positive status (Table III). These observations suggest that MNNG is mediated through a different mechanism than TPA.

The enhanced yield of HVS when MNNG was used on OMK cells was also observed by electron microscopy. Figures 1 and 2 are representative of the levels of virus observed in cultures infected for 48 hr either without (Fig. 1) or with (Fig. 2) pretreatment with MNNG. In this case, 48 hr was chosen because maximal CPE was observed in the MNNG-pretreated sample. Untreated infected cultures had not reacted to this extent of CPE at 48 hr and it is possible that the lower level of virus being observed in these cells could be partially due to a less advanced state of infection. In MNNG-pretreated cells, it is apparent that there is a much larger number of capsids in the nucleus, and higher levels of incomplete and complete virions in the cytoplasm and extracellular environment. We have also observed, however, that control cultures held for longer periods prior to fixation for EM eventually developed CPE as extensive as in MNNG-pretreated cultures, but that the level of all types of virion structures, as seen by electron microscopy, always remains much lower than in MNNG-pretreated cultures. Thus, the virions shown in Figs. 2B–D are shown because these stages of budding from nuclear membranes and larger extracellular aggregates are relatively infrequently seen in untreated cultures.

These findings are consistent with observations made by Lin *et al.* (14) showing that MNNG increased the number of EBV ge-

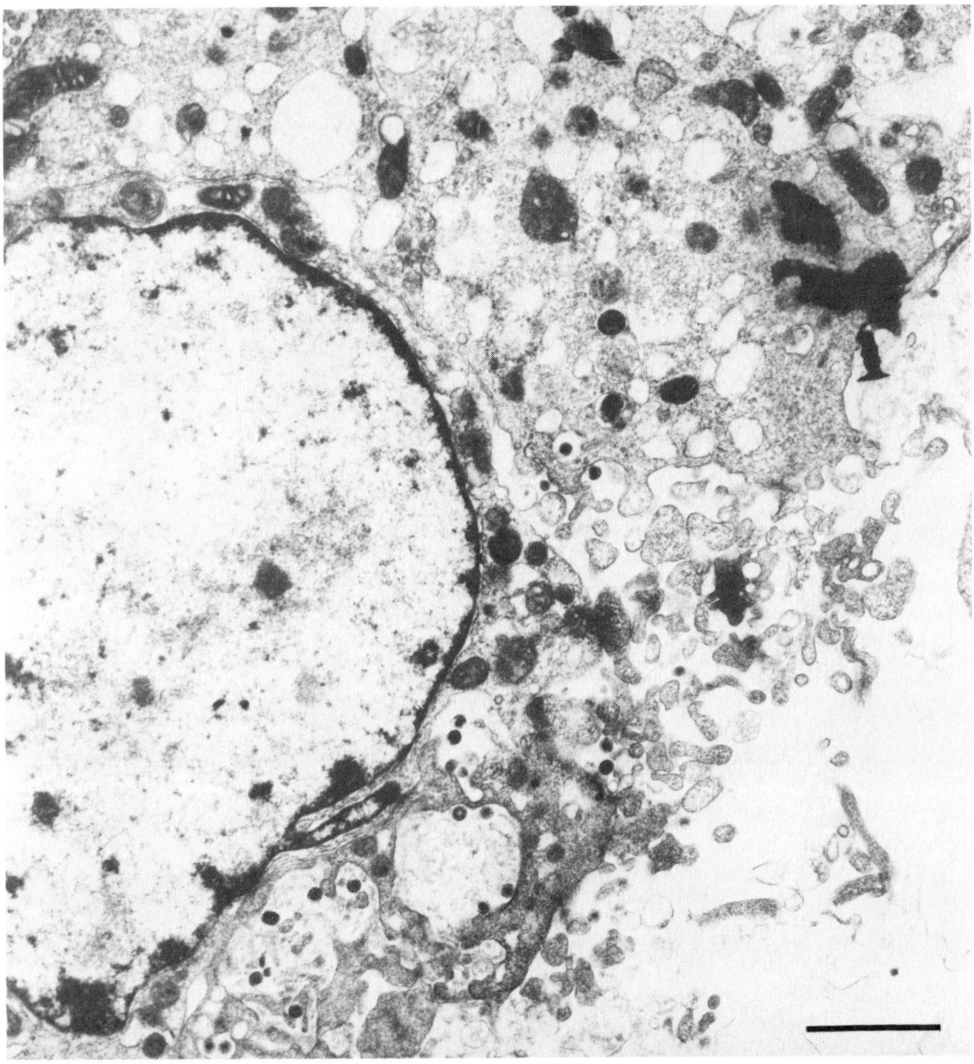

FIG. 1. Representative micrograph of OMK cells infected with HVS-P for 48 hr. At this stage of infection the cells contain moderate levels of capsids in the nucleus, and virions in the cytoplasm and in vacuoles. Budding through the nuclear and cytoplasmic membranes is only occasionally observed. At later times these cultures would contain higher levels of immature and mature virions, but at no time are the levels equivalent to those seen in MNNG-pretreated cultures. The magnification bar represents 1 μm.

nomes in EBV producer cells (P3HR-1) but had no such effect on EBV nonproducer Raji cells. Moreover, concomitant treatment of EBV-producer cells with MNNG and TPA further enhanced the number of EBV genome copies per cell, while pretreatment of Raji cells with MNNG, followed by super infection with P3HR-1 EBV, resulted in a 35% enhancement of EBV–DNA replication. Our data, however, also show that the final titers are greatly enhanced by MNNG. The EM observations showing greatly enhanced levels of virions suggest that the elevated PFU titers described above following MNNG treatment are due to an increase in virus production rather than an improvement in the PFU to physical particle ratio.

The capacity of viruses and chemical carcinogens or promotors to interact to produce enhanced levels of transformation has been

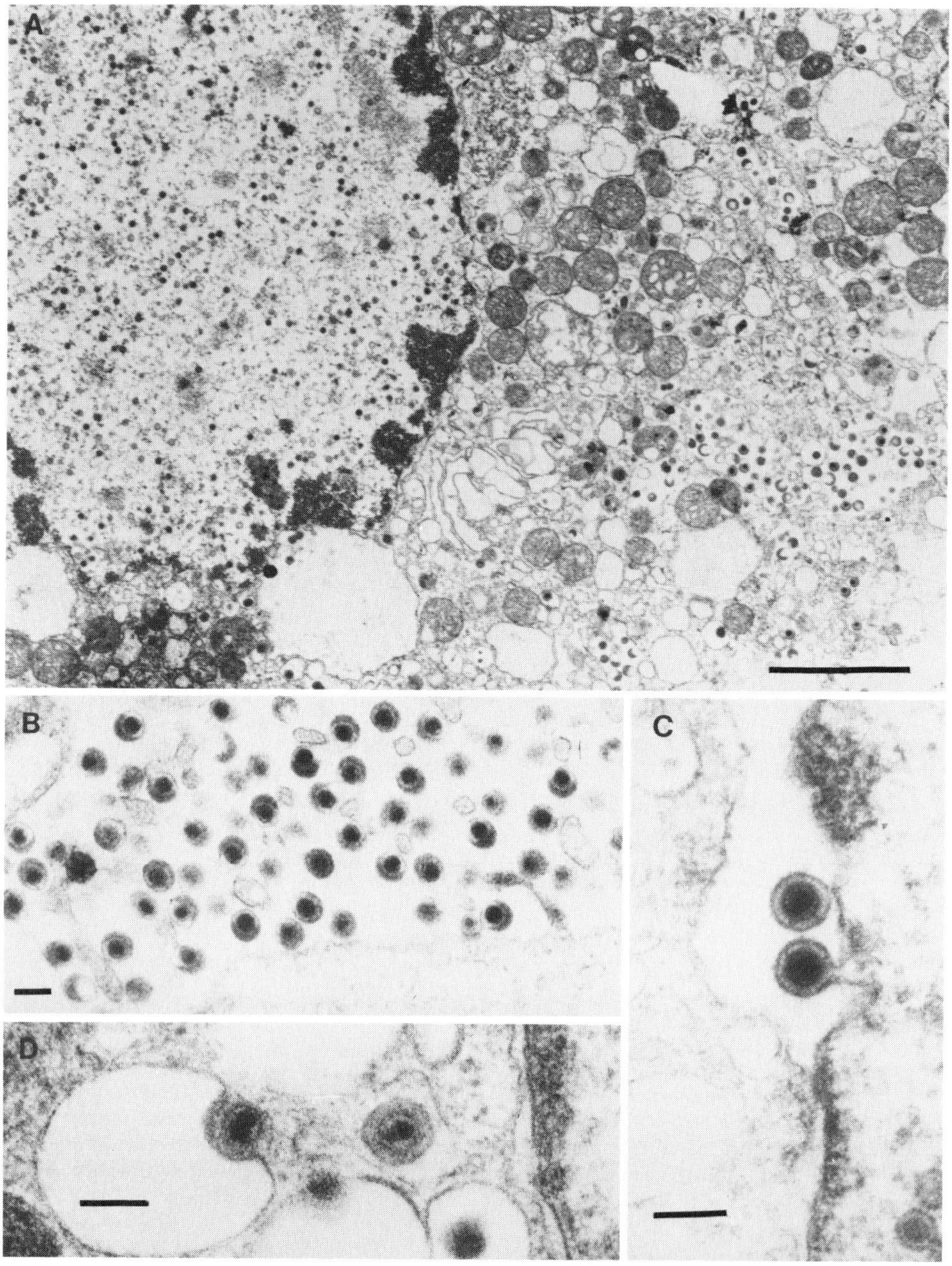

FIG. 2. Panel A is a micrograph of OMK cells pretreated for 48 hr with 1 μg/ml MNNG and infected with HVS-P for an additional 48 hr. The cells of this culture contained much higher levels of both nuclear capsids and cytoplasmic virions than seen in the control culture. The magnification bar represents 1 μm. Panels such as B–D, although typical of replicative forms of herpesviruses, are less frequently seen in micrographs of cultures not pretreated with MNNG. Aggregates as seen in (B) are rarely seen in HVS-infected OMK cells. Magnification bars represent 0.1 μm.

observed by others (6, 12). In this report, we describe how MNNG can significantly enhance the yield of infectious *Herpesvirus saimiri* grown in owl monkey kidney cells, but does not significantly affect the expression of the HVS genome in nonproducer cells. HVS is an oncogenic herpesvirus capable of inducing lymphomas in marmosets, owl monkeys, and rabbits (2, 4), but not in its species of origin, the squirrel monkey. It would be of interest to determine if MNNG will enhance the oncogenicity of HVS in any of these animal systems as well as aid in transforming lymphoblastoid or monolayer cells from owl, marmoset, squirrel monkeys, and inbred rabbits.

1. Ablashi DV, Armstrong GR, Fellows C, Easton JM, Pearson G, Twardzik D. Evaluation of the effects of phosphonoacetic acid (PAA) and 2-deoxy-*d*-glucose on *Herpesvirus saimiri* and Epstein–Barr virus. In: Nieburg HE, ed. Detection and Prevention of Cancer, New York, Dekker, pp245–262, 1977.
2. Ablashi DV, Gerber P, Easton J. Oncogenic herpesviruses of nonhuman primates. Microbiol Infect Dis **2**:229–241, 1979.
3. Ablashi DV, Bengali ZH, Eichelberger MA, Sundar KS, Armstrong GR, Daniel M, Levine PH. Increased sensitivity of oncogenic herpesviruses of primates with tumor promoter 12-*O*-tetradecanoylphorbo-13-acetate. Proc Soc Exp Biol Med **164**:485–490, 1980.
4. Ablashi DV, Sundar KS, Armstrong GR, Golway P, Valerio M, Bengali Z, Lemp J, Fox RR. *Herpesvirus saimiri*-induced malignant lymphoma in inbred strain III/J rabbits (*Oryctolagus cuniculus*). Cancer Res Clin Oncol **98**:165–172, 1980.
5. Barlow SP, Gruestein M, Meranze DR, Bonakdarpour A, Shimkin MB. Adenocarcinomas of glandular stomach and duodenum in Wistar rats ingesting *N*-methyl-*n*-nitro-nitrosoguanidine, histopathology and associated secretory changes. Cancer Res **30**:1222, 1970.
6. Casto BC, Pieczinsky WJ, Janosko N, DiPaolo J. Significance of treatment internal and DNA repair in the enhancement of viral transformation by chemical carcinogens and mutagens. Chem Biol Interac **13**:105–125, 1976.
7. De Thé G, Geser A, Day NE, Tukei PM, Williams EH, Beri DP, Smith PG, Dean AG, Bornkamm GW, Feorino P, Henle W. Epidemiological evidence for causal relationship between Epstein–Barr virus and Burkitt's lymphoma from the Ugandan prospective study. Nature (London) **274**:756–761, 1978.
8. Faggioni A, Ablashi DV, Armstrong G, Dahlberg J, Sundar SK, Rice JM, Donovan PJ. Enhancing effect of *n*-methyl-*n*-nitro-nitrosoguanidine (MNNG) on Epstein–Barr virus replication and comparison of continuous and discontinuous TPA treatment of EBV nonproducer cells for antigen induction and/or stimulation. In: Prasad U, Ablashi DV, Levine PH, Pearson G, eds. Nasopharyngeal Carcinoma: Current Concepts. Kuala Lumpur, Malaysia, Univ of Malaya, pp333–345, 1983.
9. Grundmann E, Krueger GRF, Ablashi DV, eds. Nasopharyngeal Carcinoma. Stuttgart/New York, Fischer, 1981.
10. Henderson EE, Norin AJ, Strauss BS. Induction of permanently proliferating human lymphoblastoid lines by *N*-methyl-*n*-nitro-nitrosoguanidine. Cancer Res **35**:358–363, 1975.
11. Henderson EE, Ribecky R. Transformation of human leukocytes with Epstein–Barr virus after cellular exposure to chemical and physical mutagens. J Natl Cancer Inst **64**:33–39, 1980.
12. Howett MK, Pegg AE, Rapp F. Enhancement of biochemical transformation of mammalian cells by *Herpes simplex* virus following nitroso-methylurea treatment. Nature (London) **39**:1041–1045, 1979.
13. Ito Y, Kishishita M, Morigaki T, Yanase S, Hirayama T. Induction and intervention of Epstein–Barr virus expression in human lymphoblastoid cell lines: A simulation model for study of cause and prevention of nasopharyngeal carcinoma and Burkitt's lymphoma. In: Grundmann E, Krueger GRF, Ablashi DV, eds. Nasopharyngeal Carcinoma. Stuttgart/New York, Fischer, pp255–262, 1981.
14. Lin JC, Smith MC, Pagano JS. Enhancement of replication of Epstein–Barr virus DNA in human lymphoblastoid cell lines by *N*-Methyl-*N'*-Nitro-*N*-Nitrosoguanidine. Carcinogenesis **4**:185–188, 1983.
15. Rhim JS, Park DK, Arnstein P, Huebner RJ, Weisburger EK, Nelson-Rees WA. Transformation of human cells in culture by *n*-methyl-*n*-nitro-nitrosoguanidine. Nature **256**:751–753, 1975.
16. Rhim JS, Huebner RJ, Arnstein P, Kopelovich L. Chemical transformation of cultured human fibroblasts derived from individuals with hereditary adenomatosis of the colon and rectum. Int J Cancer **25**:565–569, 1980.
17. Sundar SK, Ablashi DV, Bengali ZH, Levine PH, Nonoyama M. Mitogenic effects of 12-*O*-tetradecanoylphorbol-13-acetate on nonhuman primate mononuclear cells and in vitro interaction with Epstein–Barr virus transformation. Arch Virol **64**:141–153, 1980.
18. Tabuchi Y, Kawachi T. Experimental stomach cancer. Methods Cancer Res **7**:245–308, 1974.
19. ZurHausen H, O'Neill FJ, Freese UK. Persisting oncogenic herpesvirus induced by the tumor promoter TPA. Nature (London) **272**:373–375, 1978.

Received September 6, 1983. P.S.E.B.M. 1984, Vol. 176.
Accepted April 24, 1984.

PROCEEDINGS OF THE SOCIETY FOR EXPERIMENTAL BIOLOGY AND MEDICINE **176**, 414–418 (1984)

Effect of Temperature on Suppressor Cells in Chicken Spleen Cell Cultures[1] (41891)

BALBIR S. BHOGAL,* DAVID S. CHI,† AND G. JEANETTE THORBECKE*

**Department of Pathology, New York University School of Medicine, New York, New York 10016, and*
†Departments of Internal Medicine and Microbiology, East Tennessee State University, Quillen-Dishner College of Medicine, Johnson City, Tennessee 37614

Abstract. The plaque forming cell (PFC) response of *in vivo* primed chicken spleen cells to sheep erythrocytes (SRBC) at 37°C *in vitro* was much higher when antigen was added on Day 2 of culture than on Day 0, at the initiation of the incubation period. No such difference was observed when the cells were cultured at 40°C, in which case both responses were low. As shown previously the effect of delayed exposure to SRBC at 37°C was due to a disappearance of suppressor T cells in the absence of antigen, which did not occur at 40°C. Addition of concanavalin A on Day 0 could, even in the absence of SRBC, maintain the suppressor cell activity at 37°C. The results suggest that suppressor cell activity is very temperature dependent.

In a previous report it was shown that proliferative responses and mixed lymphocyte reactions of chicken spleen or peripheral blood cells were much higher at 40–41°C than at 37°C (1). However, antibody production to sheep red blood cells (SRBC) was at least as good in primed spleen cells reexposed to antigen at 37°C as compared to 40°C (2, 3). An important aspect of the response to SRBC at 37°C *in vitro* was that it was much higher when antigen was added 2 days after initiation of culture than when it was added immediately after explantation of the spleen cells. This effect was found to be due to the disappearance, over the first 1–2 days *in vitro,* of antigen-specific suppressor T cells which could be kept active in the presence, but not in the absence of antigen. On the other hand, helper T cells remained active and were responsive to antigen added after 2 days (3).

In the present study we have examined the antibody response at 40°C in more detail. It will be shown that suppressor cells survive in spleen cells cultured without antigen at 40°C although they disappear at 37°C. This appears to be the reason that antibody production is as good or even better at 37°C than at 40°C, depending on the time of antigen addition.

Materials and Methods. *Animal immunization.* Chickens of strain FP (B15/B21) were purchased as eggs from Hy-Line International (Dallas Center, Iowa). Eggs were incubated and hatched in a Petersime Model 5 incubator–hatcher (Petersime Incubator Co., Gettysburg, Ohio). Chickens of 4 months of age or older were injected iv with 0.2 ml of 5–20% SRBC. Their spleens were removed for culture 2 days after antigen injection.

Cell culture. Petri-dish cultures were prepared as described previously (3), using a modification of the method of Mishell and Dutton (4) for mouse cells. Antigen-primed spleen cells ($1–1.2 \times 10^7$/dish) were cultured in 1 ml of modified minimum essential medium with 5% agammaglobulinemic (Aγ) chicken serum, kept in a 10% CO_2 + 7% O_2 atmosphere and fed daily with nutrient cocktail, containing vitamins, amino acids, and bicarbonate as described (4) but no fetal calf serum. In cell-mixing experiments, target cells were precultured without antigen for 2 days before mixing with putative "suppressor cells" and antigen. In most cultures 50 μl of 2% SRBC were used as the antigen. In some cultures SRBC previously treated for 20 hr with 0.2% glutaraldehyde were used.

Plaque forming cell assay. The anti-SRBC response was expressed as PFC per dish on Day 4 of culture. PFC were detected by a slide modification of the Jerne plaque assay (4, 5). During the last 45 min of culture prior to assay, 0.1 ml fresh normal chicken serum, usually combined with 0.1 ml guinea pig C, was added per milliliter of culture in order to lyse any antibody-coated SRBC remaining in the cultures which might otherwise lead to

[1] This research was partially supported by PHS Grants CA-32801 (G.J.T.) and CA-30160 (D.S.C.) awarded by the National Cancer Institute, DHHS.

0037-9727/84 $1.50

TABLE I. EFFECT OF TEMPERATURE ON SECONDARY PFC RESPONSES TO SRBC BY SPLEEN CELLS *In Vitro*

SRBC added on Day	Indirect PFC/dish[a]									
	Expt 1		Expt 2		Expt 3		Expt 4		Expt 5	
	37°C	40°C	37°C	40°C	37°C	40°C	37°C	40°C	37°C	40°C
—	109	41	187	103	270	162	417	412	72	45
0	300	32	455	285	1565	1535	2400	2015	256	168
2	2386	268	2935	600	5320	1760	8617	2515	4100	208
0 + 2	177	45	583	340	ND	ND	ND	ND	ND	ND

[a] Mean of two to four cultures; culture period of 4 days. Spleen cells taken from FP chickens injected iv 2 days earlier with 0.2 ml of 5% SRBC. Cultures were maintained 4 days and received 50 μl 2% SRBC on Day 0 and/or Day 2.

artifactual plaque formation (6). The cells were harvested, washed twice, counted, and resuspended to 1 or 2 ml per dish. Cells were plated using 2–8 × 10^5 cells per slide. For PFC development, slides were flooded with a 10% solution of guinea pig C (absorbed with SRBC) containing rabbit anti-chicken Ig (1:1000), and incubated for 45 min at 37°C. The average value of PFC from duplicate cultures which had numbers not differing >10% were recorded. PFC obtained in the absence of antigen were always determined.

Results. The data in Table I show that spleen cells taken 2 days after priming with SRBC iv and cultured at 37°C responded much better when the antigen was added on Day 2 than on Day 0 of culture. The mean ratio of the magnitudes of PFC responses per dish after addition of antigen on Day 2 as compared to Day 0 was 7.5 at 37°C, as opposed to a mean ratio of 2.8 at 40°C. When antigen was given on both days the results were exactly like those where antigen was given on Day 0 alone. The responses at 40°C were at the lower level regardless of when the antigen was added.

Since the spleen cells were taken from primed chickens they might continue to make antibody *in vitro* particularly at 40°C even without further antigen addition. Thus, it seemed possible that destruction of the SRBC immediately after addition on Day 2 to the cultures at 40°C caused the lack of response in these cultures. We, therefore, repeated the experiments using glutaraldehyde-fixed SRBC as the antigen. The results in Table II show that such pretreatment of the SRBC in no way affected the results. The glutaraldehyde-fixed SRBC were resistant to lysis and these results therefore also exclude any influence of artifacts due to the lysis of agglutinated SRBC in the PFC assay on the magnitude of the PFC responses.

The survival of the cultured cells at the two different temperatures was very similar. In a typical experiment in which 1.2 × 10^7 cells

TABLE II. EFFECT OF TEMPERATURE ON PFC RESPONSE TO SRBC IS ALSO SEEN WITH GLUTARALDEHYDE-FIXED ANTIGEN

SRBC added		Indirect PFC/dish on Day 4			
		Expt 1		Expt 2	
Pretreatment	Day of culture	37°C	40°C	37°C	40°C
—	—	260	200	470	430
Untreated	0	1690	1560	2340	1880
Untreated	2	5550	1380	8390	1850
Glutaraldehyde treated[a]	0	1430	1510	2460	2150
Glutaraldehyde treated[a]	2	5090	2130	8850	3180

[a] 50 μl of 2% SRBC. Incubated for 20 hr with 0.2% glutaraldehyde prior to use.

TABLE III. LOSS OF SUPPRESSOR CELLS BY PREINCUBATION WITHOUT ANTIGEN AT 37° BUT NOT AT 40°C

Suppressor cells added on Day 2[a] (precultured for 2 days)	Indirect PFC/dish[b] on Day 4
Without SE at 37°C	7025
With SE at 37°C	362
Without SE at 40°C	654
With SE at 40°C	692
No suppressor cells added	4100

[a] Putative "suppressor cells" (5×10^6) were added to dishes containing 10^7 "target" Day 2 immune spleen cells which had been precultured for 2 days without antigen at 37°C. Antigen was added and cultures continued for an additional 2 days. Suppressor cells were taken from the same chicken as target cells and precultured as indicated.

[b] PFC/dish, mean of duplicate cultures.

were cultured per dish, all dishes harvested on Days 2 to 4 contained 7–8 × 10^6 viable cells, regardless of the temperature at which they had been cultured or of the time of antigen addition.

As previously shown (3), cells precultured for 2 days at 37°C without antigen can be used as targets for suppression, since their own suppressor cells have disappeared. Thus, we previously showed that T cells kept for the first 2 days in culture at 37°C with antigen suppressed the higher responses of cells given antigen on Day 2. The results in Table III show that this suppressive effect was also shown with spleen cells precultured with antigen for 2 days at 40°C. When cells were precultured without antigen at 37°C, they did not cause the suppression, as shown previously (3), but cells precultured without antigen at 40°C still did (Table III). Supernatants taken from spleen cells cultured with antigen, either at 37°C or at 40°C, did not cause such suppression (data not shown). These findings suggest that the responsiveness to antigen at 40°C increases very little after preculture for 2 days without antigen, because the majority of the suppressor cells survive at this temperature even in the absence of antigen, whereas they do not at 37°C.

When spleen cells were precultured without antigen at 37°C for 2 days, and then moved to 40°C prior to challenge with antigen, they responded as well as did cells given antigen on Day 2 of culture and kept at 37°C. This finding showed that, once the suppressor cells had functionally disappeared by culture at 37°C in absence of antigen, they could not be regenerated by increasing the culture temperature to 40°C (Table IV). On the other hand suppressor cells, induced at 37°C by addition of antigen immediately after explantation of the spleen cells, continued to suppress the response when the cultures were moved to 40°C. If the first 2 days of culture were at 40°C, regardless of the presence of antigen, the cells could not be made to give high anti-SRBC responses even when they were then moved to 37°C. In addition, cells cultured without antigen but in the presence of concanavalin A (Con A) during the first 2 days at 37°C, failed to give high PFC responses to

TABLE IV. TEMPERATURE DURING FIRST INCUBATION PERIOD DETERMINES RESPONSIVENESS TO ANTIGEN ON DAY 2

		First 2-day culture period at 37°C		First 2-day culture period at 40°C	
Antigen added (Day)	Second culture period (°C)	Expt 1 ΔPFC/dish[b]	Expt 2 ΔPFC/dish[b]	Expt 1 ΔPFC/dish[b]	Expt 2 ΔPFC/dish[b]
2	37	1438	6608	424	1904
0	37	204	681	320	341
2	40	1646	7358		979
0	40	310	866		787
2[a]	37		583		
0[a]	37		521		

[a] Con A (10 μg) added to cultures on Day 0.

[b] Mean of duplicate dishes, determined on Day 4. PFC/dish in absence of antigen were 70 (Expt 1) and 142 (Expt 2), and were subtracted from the values in the table.

antigen added on Day 2, presumably because Con A stimulated the survival of suppressor cells in an antigen nonspecific manner as had previously also been shown with pokeweed mitogen (3).

Discussion. The present results show that, in the absence of SRBC, the survival of suppressor cells in cultures at 40°C, the normal body temperature of the chicken, is better than at 37°C. As in our previous studies (3), the activity of suppressor T cells could be maintained at 37°C by addition of the sensitizing (but not of unrelated) antigen, which resulted in much lower responses upon immediate than upon delayed addition of the antigen to the cultures. No such loss of suppressor cells can be seen at 40°C with the paradoxical result that PFC responses *in vitro* are lower at the higher temperature, particularly upon delayed addition of antigen.

Although it is difficult to relate findings with cells from cold blooded with those from warm blooded vertebrates, it should be mentioned here that cytotoxic responses obtained with shark peripheral blood cells at 30°C are lower than at 23°C *in vitro,* due to the increased activity of suppressor cells at the higher temperature. However, reports on the effect of temperature on the PFC response of mice to SRBC have shown that responses at 39.5°C are higher than at 37°C. This effect is found in spite of greater suppressor T cell activity at the higher temperature. The effect has been attributed to an overall better responsiveness of all cell types (7). The recently described higher sensitivity of murine cells to interleukin-1 at 39°C than at 37°C (8, 9) may be related to this finding.

Temperature changes such as those studied here greatly increase proliferative responses to T-cell mitogens of both peripheral blood and spleen cells of the chicken (1, 10), but an analysis of subpopulations in these responses has not been made in the absence of available cell surface markers for chicken T-cell subsets. The present results demonstrate that Con A stimulation, initiated on Day 0 at 37°C maintains the suppressor cells for the SRBC response, as was also shown previously for pokeweed mitogen (3).

Delayed addition of mitogen (11–14) or of antigen (14, 15) to human peripheral blood cells has been reported to result in greater proliferative responses than addition of these agents immediately upon explantation of the cells. This effect has been attributed to a change in sensitivity of the cells to prostaglandins produced by accessory cells (12, 13, 16) but indomethacin does not in all cases influence the effect of delayed antigen addition (15). Thus the occurrence of a transient suppressor cell in human peripheral blood cell cultures (17) is a well-recognized phenomenon. The present studies suggest that an examination of the effect of temperature on this phenomenon might be of interest.

Since in the absence of specific antigen or mitogen the suppressor cell activity in the chicken spleen cell cultures is greater and/or maintained better at 40°C than at 37°C, it appears that suppressor cells are quite sensitive to temperature changes—in this case hypothermia. However, a temperature-dependent change in sensitivity to regulatory effects of prostaglandins or difference in prostaglandin production could also indirectly mediate the apparent survival as opposed to loss of suppressor cells at 40°C as compared to 37°C.

1. Chi DS, Bhogal BS, Fox GJ, Thorbecke GJ. Effect of temperature and lymphokines on mixed lymphocyte and mitogen responses of chicken lymphoid cells *in vitro.* Develop. Compar. Immunol., in press.
2. Chi DS, Galton JE, Thorbecke GJ. Role of T cells in immune responses of the chicken. In: Rose ME, Payne LN, Freeman BM, eds. Avian Immunology. Edinburgh, British Poultry Sci. Ltd., pp103–134, 1981.
3. Chi DS, Grebenau MD, Thorbecke GJ. Antigen induced helper and suppressor T cells in normal and agammaglobulinemic chickens. Eur J Immunol **10**:203–209, 1980.
4. Mishell RI, Dutton RW. Immunization of dissociated spleen cell cultures from normal mice. J Exp Med **126**:423–442, 1967.
5. Jerne NK, Nordin AA, Henry C. The agar plaque technique for recognizing antibody-producing cells. In: Amos B, Koprowski H, eds. Cell Bound Antibodies. Philadelphia, Wistar Inst Press, p109, 1963.
6. Muchmore AV, Koski I, Dooley N, Blease RM. Artifactual plaque formation in vitro and in vivo to passive transfer of specific antibody. J Immunol **116**:1016–1019, 1976.
7. Jampel HD, Duff GW, Gershon RK, Atkins E, Durum ST. Fever and immunoregulation. III. Hyperthermia augments the primary in vitro humoral immune response. J Exp Med **157**:1229–1238, 1983.
8. Hanson DF, Murphy PA, Silicano R, Shin HS. The effect of temperature on the activation of the thy-

mocytes by interleukins I and II. J Immunol **130**:216–221, 1983.
9. Duff GW, Durum SK. The pyrogenic and mitogenic actions of interleukin-1 are related. Nature (London) **304**:449–451, 1983.
10. Lee LF. Chicken lymphocyte stimulation by mitogens: A microassay with whole-blood cultures. Avian Dis **22**:296–307, 1978.
11. Sandru G, Veraguth P. Improvement of LIF release by mononuclear cell cultures by 24 h incubation before stimulation with Con A. J Immunol Methods **47**:219–226, 1981.
12. Gualde N, Goodwin JS. Effects of prostaglandin E_2 and preincubation on lectin-stimulated proliferation of human T cell subsets. Cell Immunol **70**:373–379, 1982.
13. Fischer A, Durandy A, Griscelli C. Role of prostaglandin E_2 in the induction of nonspecific T lymphocyte suppressor activity. J Immunol **126**:1452–1455, 1981.
14. Stobo JD. Immunosuppression in man: suppression by macrophages can be mediated by interactions with regulatory T cells. J Immunol **119**:918–924, 1977.
15. Bahr GM, Rook GAW, Stanford JL, Lydyard PM, Bryceson ADM. The effect of delayed addition of antigen and "E" rosetting on the proliferative response to mycobacterial antigens of peripheral blood lymphocytes from normal individuals or from patients with tuberculosis or leprosy. Immunology **44**:585–591, 1981.
16. Stobo JD, Kennedy MS, Goldyne ME. Prostaglandin E modulation of the mitogenic response of human T cells. Differential responses of T-cell subpopulations. J Clin Invest **64**:1188–1195, 1979.
17. Bresnihan B, Jasin HE. Suppressor function of peripheral blood mononuclear cells in normal individuals and in patients with systemic lupus erythematosus. J Clin Invest **59**:106–116, 1977.

Received December 21, 1983. P.S.E.B.M. 1984. Vol. 176.
Accepted April 24, 1984.

PROCEEDINGS OF THE SOCIETY FOR EXPERIMENTAL BIOLOGY AND MEDICINE **176**, 419–425 (1984)

Influence of the Major Histocompatibility Complex (*H-2*) on Glucocorticoid-Stimulated Pulmonary Surfactant Synthesis in Two Congenic Mouse Strains[1] (41892)

LAWRENCE S. HONIG,*[,2] BARRY T. SMITH,† HAROLD C. SLAVKIN,* AND H. GARY DONAHUE*

**Laboratory for Developmental Biology, Graduate Program in Craniofacial Biology, School of Dentistry, University of Southern California, Los Angeles, California 90089-0191 and †Joint Program in Neonatology, Department of Pediatrics, Harvard Medical School, 75 Francis Street, Boston, Massachusetts 02115*

Abstract. Mice with different histocompatibility alleles in otherwise identical backgrounds (congenic inbred strains of $H\text{-}2^a$ and $H\text{-}2^b$ haplotypes), were used to study the possible influence of the major histocompatibility complex (MHC) upon glucocorticoid-stimulated pulmonary surfactant synthesis during embryonic and fetal stages of mouse lung development. Pregnant C57BL/10SnJ ($H\text{-}2^b$) and congenic B10.A/SnSgJ ($H\text{-}2^a$) mice were administered single or consecutive intraperitoneal injections of betamethasone during the period of 14 through 17 days gestation. Assays for incorporation of [^{3}H]choline into total lipid and saturated phosphatidylcholine (an index for pulmonary surfactant synthesis) were conducted, 24 hr following the last treatment, on Days 17 or 18 of gestation. Control mice received injections of phosphate-buffered saline. The *H-2* genotype appears to influence the relative responsiveness of glucocorticoid-stimulated surfactant synthesis during fetal lung development. The B10.A strain ($H\text{-}2^a$ haplotype) was more responsive to glucocorticoid-stimulated pulmonary surfactant synthesis than the $H\text{-}2^b$ haplotype. Whereas both strains were responsive to glucocorticoid-stimulated [^{3}H]choline incorporation into lung surfactant, the differences in responsiveness at specific fetal stages suggest that genes within or closely linked to the *H-2* complex might have a role in pulmonary surfactant biosynthesis during mouse lung development. The results also suggest the possibility that relative susceptibility to congenital pulmonary disorders may be influenced by the *H-2* complex.

Infant respiratory distress syndrome (RDS), also known as hyaline membrane disease, is the consequence of reduced fetal lung production of pulmonary surfactant (i.e., saturated phosphatidylcholine) resulting in amounts insufficient for neonatal respiratory adaptation (1). Despite significant advances in treatment of infants with RDS during the last two decades (2), as well as the emergence of substantial understanding of many aspects of RDS pathogenesis in human and animal model systems of lung development and maturation, very little is known about genetic controls for fetal lung development (3).

A number of studies have suggested that lung epithelial differentiation is mediated by glucocorticoids during the fetal period of embryogenesis (4–7), and that the fetal lung is a target organ for glucocorticoids (8, 9). Glucocorticoids may regulate epithelial cell differentiation into type II alveolar cells producing pulmonary surfactant (7–8). The normal or physiological role of glucocorticoids for different developmental stages of lung organogenesis (e.g., glandular, canalicular, and saccular) is not yet known. But glucocorticoids, alone or in combination with other hormones (e.g., thyroxin), may have a significant function in the regulation of lung morphogenesis and differentiation (10).

The major histocompatibility complex (MHC) has been found to influence the susceptibility to certain experimental diseases or congenital malformations in mice (11), e.g., thyroiditis (12), myasthenia gravis (13), hemolytic anemia (14), viral-induced diabetes (15), and glucocorticoid-induced cleft palate (16–22). Using congenic strains, i.e., mice with different histocompatibility loci on an identical genetic background, $H\text{-}2^a$ haplotype strain (B10.A) were found to be highly susceptible to glucocorticoid-induced cleft palate (46–81%

[1] This work was supported by USPHS research Grants HL-28325 (H.C.S. and L.S.H.) and HL-27372 (B.T.S.) and Training Grant DE-07006 (H.C.S.).

[2] Present address: Department of Anatomy and Cell Biology (R-124), University of Miami School of Medicine, P.O. Box 016960, Miami, Fla. 33101.

0037-9727/84 $1.50

clefting), whereas H-2^b haplotype (B10) were relatively resistant (5–22% clefting) (16, 17). Recently, B10.A strain adult mice lung cytosol preparations were found to have significantly higher glucocorticoid receptor levels than B10 strain (23). *H-2*-linked differences have also been reported for other hormones including estrogens (24), insulin (25), glucagon (26), and androgens (27). However, it has not been demonstrated that MHC-related genes regulate glucocorticoid influences upon pulmonary surfactant biosynthesis.

In order to pursue this problem, we have designed studies to determine the possible influence of the MHC upon glucocorticoid-stimulated pulmonary surfactant synthesis during embryonic and fetal mouse lung development. Pregnant congenic mice, C57BL/10 and B10.A, were injected with betamethasone on Days 14–17 of gestation as single or consecutive intraperitoneal injections, and fetal lung maturation at 17 or 18 days of gestation was then evaluated by assaying [^{3}H]choline incorporation into total lipid, and specifically into saturated phosphatidylcholine (SPC). Our results indicate that at certain stages, fetal lung development was influenced by MHC-related genes as evaluated by differences in glucocorticoid-stimulation of pulmonary surfactant synthesis. The B10.A (H-2^a) strain was as much as twofold more responsive to betamethasone-stimulated [^{3}H]choline incorporation into SPC than the H-2^b haplotype strain. These findings suggest a significant genetic control for SPC synthesis during murine fetal lung morphogenesis. A preliminary abstract report has appeared (28).

Materials and Methods. *Animals.* Nonpregnant mice of congenic strains C57BL/10SnJ (B10) (H-2^b haplotype) and B10.A/SnSgJ (B10.A) (H-2^a haplotype) were purchased from Jackson Laboratories (Bar Harbor, Me.) at age 7 weeks. These congenic strains are genetically identical except for a small segment of chromosome 17 which includes the major histocompatibility complex (MHC) (29). Breeding colonies in our laboratory were maintained on a 12-hr light cycle (7 AM–7 PM). In the experiments one male and four to five virgin females (12–20 weeks; ca. 25–30 g body wt) were mated overnight. The day of vaginal plug detection was taken as Day 0 of gestation.

Administration of glucocorticoids. A sustained-action betamethasone preparation (Celestone Soluspan, Schering, N.J.) was aseptically diluted 1:2 with calcium–magnesium-free, phosphate-buffered saline (PBS) (Grand Island Biological Co., Grand Island, N.Y.), and 0.2 ml was administered by intraperitoneal injection at specific times during pregnancy (Days 14–17 of gestation). The pregnant females received glucocorticoid doses of approximately 12 mg/kg body wt. Control pregnant mice received injections of PBS. Each experiment involved injections of pregnant mice in each of four groups: B10 control (+PBS); B10 experimental (+ betamethasone); B10.A control (+PBS); and B10.A experimental (+ betamethasone). Treatments were administered as either single or as consecutive injections at 24-hr intervals as stated under Results. Removal of fetuses for subsequent lung organ culture and labeling of total lipids (TC) and saturated phosphatidylcholine (SPC) was performed 24 hr following the last injection (e.g., 17 or 18 days of gestation as shown in Table I).

Lung culture and labeling. Pregnant mice from each of the four treatment groups were sacrificed together at 17 or 18 day of gestation using cervical dislocation. The uterus was removed from each animal following laparotomy and placed in a sterile petri dish at 4°C. Subsequent procedures were performed in a horizontal laminar flow hood. Decidua were removed and fetuses placed in Hank's balanced salt solution (HBSS) (GIBCO, N.Y.) buffered with 20 m*M* Hepes containing 1% antibiotic–antimycotic solution (GIBCO, N.Y.). Fetuses were decapitated, the lungs were removed by dissection, and each lung was then separated into the five component lobes. The lobes were then randomly mixed and identical equivalents (ca. one lung equivalent per dish) were sliced (150 ± 50 μm thickness) and subsequently cultured on stainless-steel grids in Falcon organ-culture dishes.

Lung tissue slices were initially incubated for 2–6 hr at 38°C in 650 μl of BGJb medium (GIBCO, Fitton-Jackson Modification, N.Y.) in an atmosphere of 5% CO_2. Following this initial preculture, medium consisting of 2–5 μCi [*methyl*-^{3}H]choline per culture dish was introduced (sp act 80 Ci/mmole, New England Nuclear, Boston, Mass.). After 6–8 hr labeling, tissue slices were removed from culture, washed for 10 min with cold HBSS, and then transferred by means of sharpened tungsten needles into tubes for sonication. The lung tissue was then weighed and stored at −20°C until homogenization by sonication.

Biochemical assays for DNA content, total lipid, and saturated phosphatidylcholine. Fetal lung tissues were sonicated in 300–600 μl buffer (100 m*M* NaCl, 10 m*M* Tris, pH 7.0, 10 m*M* EDTA) for 1 min at 4°C using a Bronson microprobe sonicator (100 W). Duplicate aliquots of homogenate were then removed for determinations of total radioactivity incorporated, and of DNA content. DNA was determined by a modified diphenylamine spectrophotometric method sensitive to 1.0 μg DNA/ml (30).

[^{3}H]Choline incorporation into total lipid (TC) and saturated phosphatidylcholine (SPC) was determined by methods previously reported (31). An internal standard of 3000 dpm [^{14}C]dipalmitoyl phosphatidylcholine was added to lung homogenate samples before organic extraction with chloroform–methanol, thereby enabling determination of losses of SPC during extraction and assay procedures. Total lipid synthesis (TC) was determined from aliquots of the organic phase, and this phase was subsequently evaporated under nitrogen gas to dryness. Following reaction with osmium tetroxide (32), SPC was measured after separation by silica minicolumn or thin-layer chromatography. Liquid scintillation counting was performed using Aquasol II counting medium (New England Nuclear, Boston, Mass.) and the Beckman counter LS-3000 series. Efficiency and channel cross-over were corrected in each vial by use of H number. Tritium window settings of 0–317 and ^{14}C window limits of 455–655 resulted in radioactive counting efficiencies of 25–30% [^{3}H] and 52% [^{14}C].

Data analysis. Radioactive [^{3}H]choline counts incorporated into SPC were corrected for assay losses using the [^{14}C]dipalmitoyl phosphatidylcholine internal standard. All values were linearly corrected for labeling procedure variation to a standard of 5 μCi [^{3}H]choline label per organ culture dish and an 8-hr labeling period. All experimental data points used randomized single lung equivalents assayed for synthesis and DNA content each in duplicate. For ratios, standard deviations were obtained through computation of the square root of the sum of the squares of the relative standard deviations of numerator and denominator. The two-tailed Student's t test (with a conservative $df = 1$) was used to test significance.

Results. *Labeling of fetal lung tissue: total lipid and saturated phosphatidylcholine.* Mouse fetal lung tissues of 17 and 18 days of gestation (Theiler stages 25 and 26) (33) were found to incorporate [*methyl*-^{3}H]choline rapidly and exhibited plateau levels of aqueous-soluble precursor by 2 hr in organ culture (Fig. 1). After a slight lag period, incorporation into chloroform–methanol-extractable counts was linear over a period of 2–12 hr. The fraction assayed as SPC was constant over time for any given experimental fetal lung tissue sample. Choline incorporation, lung tissue DNA content, and incorporation on a per DNA basis all increased only slightly during this period of gestation of 17–18 days. This is in agreement with other reports (34).

Mice lungs from the B10 and B10.A strains behaved similarly in culture. Although fetal lung tissues from the two strains do not significantly differ in either average wet weight (27.4 ± 2.6 mg, B10 versus 30.0 ± 1.6 mg, B10.A) or DNA content (255 ± 22 μg, B10 versus 259 ± 23 μg, B10.A) those from the B10.A strain generally show slightly lower levels of choline incorporation (Table I).

Betamethasone effects upon lung develop-

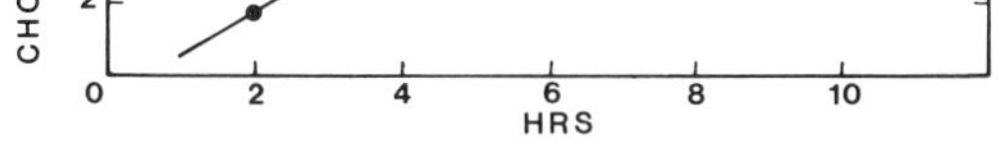

FIG. 1. Relationship between choline labeling of total lipid (TC) and aqueous-extractable, soluble pool (SO) in fetal mouse lungs. SPC (not shown) remained a constant fraction of 29 ± 2% of the total [*methyl*-^{3}H]choline incorporated (TC). Labeled lungs were sampled after 2, 4, 6, and 11 hr in culture. Protocol details are described under Materials and Methods.

TABLE I. COMPARISON OF MURINE FETAL LUNG TOTAL LIPID AND SATURATED PHOSPHATIDYLCHOLINE SYNTHESIS BETWEEN CONGENIC STRAINS C57BL/10 (H-2^b) AND B10.A (H-2^a)[a]

Days of injection	C57BL/10 +0	C57BL/10 +BM	C57BL/10 Ratio	B10.A +0	B10.A +BM	B10.A Ratio	{B10.A ratio / B10 ratio}
14–16 [17] TC	4.83 ± 0.55	8.60 ± 0.91	1.78 ± 0.28	3.28 ± 0.27	7.80 ± 0.75	2.38 ± 0.31	1.34*
SPC	1.78 ± 0.07	3.08 ± 0.31	1.73 ± 0.19	1.17 ± 0.17	2.81 ± 0.24	2.40 ± 0.40	1.39*
15–16 [17] TC	4.62 ± 0.14	8.05 ± 0.75	1.74 ± 0.17	3.68 ± 0.16	7.61 ± 0.46	2.07 ± 0.15	1.19*
SPC	1.51 ± 0.03	2.56 ± 0.42	1.70 ± 0.28	1.14 ± 0.05	2.32 ± 0.19	2.04 ± 0.20	1.20
16 [17] TC	5.68 ± 0.17	4.88 ± 0.36	0.86 ± 0.07	4.88 ± 0.72	5.95 ± 0.30	1.22 ± 0.20	1.42*
SPC	1.86 ± 0.10	1.64 ± 0.27	0.85 ± 0.15	1.66 ± 0.22	1.76 ± 0.11	1.06 ± 0.15	1.25
15–17 [18] TC	8.90 ± 0.84	14.21 ± 1.11	1.60 ± 0.19	9.77 ± 0.42	14.3 ± 2.3	1.46 ± 0.25	0.91
SPC	2.78 ± 0.36	4.83 ± 0.25	1.74 ± 0.24	2.63 ± 0.50	3.80 ± 0.72	1.44 ± 0.30	0.83
16–17 [18] TC	6.73 ± 0.75	7.10 ± 0.34	1.05 ± 0.13	4.38 ± 0.11	6.92 ± 0.49	1.58 ± 0.12	1.50*
SPC	2.20 ± 0.25	2.37 ± 0.16	1.08 ± 0.14	1.20 ± 0.13	2.38 ± 0.11	1.98 ± 0.24	1.85*
17 [18] TC	6.73 ± 0.24	6.46 ± 0.24	0.96 ± 0.07	6.13 ± 0.17	5.12 ± 0.45	0.84 ± 0.08	0.88
SPC	2.00 ± 0.17	1.71 ± 0.03	0.86 ± 0.07	1.57 ± 0.05	1.25 ± 0.02	0.80 ± 0.02	0.95

[a] Maternal intraperitoneal injections were on single or consecutive days as shown and as described in the text. Assays for incorporation of [^{3}H]choline into total lipid (TC) and saturated phosphatidylcholine (SPC) were conducted 24 hr following the last day of injection, i.e., on Day 17 or 18 of gestation shown in brackets. Values are expressed as ^{3}H dpm per nanogram fetal lung tissue DNA with standard deviations. Controls (+0) were saline-injected pregnant mice at appropriate times of treatment and experimentals (+BM) were betamethasone-treated pregnant mice. The ratios are those of hormone-treated to control mice, with standard deviations. Also shown is the comparison between H-2^a and H-2^b haplotype data expressed as the ratio of B10.A to B10 stimulation ratios. The asterisks indicate those indices which represent a B10.A response significantly different than the B10 response (at confidence level better than $P < 0.10$). The experiments at 15, 16, 17, [18], and 17, [18] days showed no significant differences between B10 and B10.A mice, but in all experiments with assay at [17] days and in the 16, 17, [18] days experiment, B10.A response was greater than B10 response to hormone treatment, with six of eight of these differences significant.

ment. Betamethasone was administered to pregnant B10 and B10.A mice during the fetal period. The synthetic glucocorticoid analogue was injected for the previous 1, 2, or 3 days prior to removal of lung tissues (which here is reported for Theiler stages 25 and 26) and subsequent assay for [^{3}H]choline incorporation into TC and SPC (which latter represents an index of pulmonary surfactant synthesis) (Table I). Repeated injections of betamethasone always caused stimulation of choline incorporation into TC and SPC (usually a 50–100% increase) compared to controls. The betamethasone stimulated increase in SPC synthesis was not usually at the expense of other lipids: the proportion of total lipid choline incorporation present as SPC remained relatively constant. Multiple betamethasone injections also resulted in up to 40% decreases in both total DNA content and fetal lung tissue wet weight as compared to PBS-injected controls. In contrast, single injections of hormone 1 day before assay at 17 or 18 days of gestation did not stimulate SPC synthesis in the fashion multiple injections did. In particular, after injection on 17 days of gestation there was actually slight decrease in SPC synthesis assayed at 18 days.

H-2 haplotype differences in betamethasone-stimulation of pulmonary surfactant synthesis. B10.A (H-2^a) mice responded significantly greater to betamethasone treatment than did B10 (H-2^b). The difference between these two haplotype strains was more evident upon assay at Theiler stage 25 (17 days) than at stage 26 (18 days of gestation). Upon assay at stage 25, betamethasone stimulation of pulmonary surfactant was 20–40% greater with B10.A (H-2^a) mice than with B10 (H-2^b). However, upon assay at stage 26 (18 days), B10.A showed differentially higher hormone-stimulation ratios than B10 mice only in those experiments in which hormone injections were at 16 and 17 days of gestation. No hormone stimulation was detected following a single injection of betamethasone at 17 days of gestation in either mouse strain. The anomalous result among multiple injection regimes was the 15-, 16-, and 17-days of gestation experiment after which B10 and B10.A mice did not show markedly different responses to hormone treatment.

Discussion. This study provides evidence that glucocorticoid-stimulated pulmonary surfactant synthesis during critical stages of fetal lung development is influenced by genes within or closely linked to the murine major histocompatibility complex. Betamethasone-stimulation of SPC synthesis was 20–40% greater in B10.A (*H-2*[a]) than with B10 (*H-2*[b]) mice when assayed at Theiler stage 25 (17 days of gestation). The responsiveness of specific MHC haplotypes to glucocorticoid-stimulated pulmonary surfactant synthesis during fetal lung morphogenesis may benefit studies attempting to identify putative mechanisms of genetic susceptibility toward congenital malformations.

Previous studies comparing inbred mouse strains reported that during midgestation (ca. 12 days), the concentration of glucocorticoid cytoplasmic receptors was twofold higher in A/Jax (*H-2*[a]) compared to C57Bl/6SnJ (*H-2*[b]) strain mice embryos (35). In other studies designed to investigate the content of glucocorticoid receptors in fetal ectomesenchyme cells of the secondary palate from inbred strains, *H-2*[a] strain cells had a twofold increase in receptor sites per cell compared with *H-2*[b] strain ectomesenchyme cells (36). More recently, congenic mouse strains were used to evaluate the influence of the *H-2* histocompatibility locus on glucocorticoid receptor number and strength in adult male and female mouse thymus and lung (23). The B10.A (*H-2*[a]) strain of mice was found to have significantly higher glucocorticoid receptor levels, and B10.A thymocytes showed greater response to dexamethasone in a prostaglandin production assay *in vivo* than the B10 (*H-2*[b]) strain (23). These findings are complementary to those obtained with glucocorticoid-induced cleft palate using congenic mouse strains (16, 17, 20–22).

The present study was undertaken to determine whether glucocorticoid stimulation of pulmonary surfactant during critical stages of fetal mouse lung development is influenced by *H-2* haplotype. Our results illustrate that whereas both B10 and B10.A untreated, control fetal lungs at Theiler stages 25 or 26 have comparable wet weights and DNA content, each strain responded to hormone treatment, with subsequent TC and SPC synthesis according to its *H-2* haplotype; B10.A strain was more responsive than the B10 strain. However, demonstration of *H-2* associated influences between hormone stimulation and subsequent pulmonary surfactant synthesis were only identified when consecutive injections of hormone were administered prior to Theiler stage 25 (Table I). Glucocorticoid receptors have been detected during the embryonic period of mouse development (12 days of gestation) (35), and glucocorticoids seem to be able to regulate fetal lung development in animal and human systems (7–9, 34–40) prior to birth (e.g., 17–19 days of gestation in mice). Administration of large doses of exogenous glucocorticoids during late fetal stages may also inhibit tissue growth. The significant decreases in fetal lung wet weight as well as DNA content observed during our late gestation hormone treatments are consistent with reports describing the growth inhibiting effects of glucocorticoids on near-term rabbit (38) and monkey (39) fetal lungs. Whereas understanding how glucocorticoids affect stimulation or depression of biochemical processes is not known, several possible mechanisms for such hormone modulation of embryonic organogenesis have been suggested (10, 40, 41).

The results of this study suggest that hormone stimulation of pulmonary surfactant synthesis during mouse fetal lung development is influenced by genes within or closely linked to the *H-2* complex. This suggests that the *H-2* complex may be involved in the epithelial differentiation of type II cells, and the production rates of saturated phosphatidylcholine. How *H-2*-associated gene products might control glucocorticoid acceleration of normal developmental patterns for pulmonary surfactant synthesis remains to be elucidated in further studies.

We wish to acknowledge Ms. Arpy Barsoumian for technical assistance with the disaturated phosphatidylcholine assays in the laboratory of Dr. Barry Smith, and Ms. Victoria Murphy for preparation of the manuscript.

1. Farrell PM, Avery ME. Hyaline membrane disease. Amer Rev Respir Dis **111**:657–688, 1975.
2. Farrell PM. The regulation of saturated phosphatidylcholine synthesis in the developing lung. In: Farrell

PM, ed. Lung Development: Biological and Clinical Perspectives. New York, Academic Press, pp391–397, 1982.
3. Gail DB, Lenfant CJM. Cell of the lung: Biology and clinical implications. Amer Rev Respir Dis **127**:366–387, 1983.
4. Ekelund L, Arvidson G, Astedt B. Cortisol-induced accumulation of phospholipid in organ culture of human fetal lung. Scand J Clin Lab Invest **35**:419–423, 1975.
5. Giannopoulos G. Variations in the levels of cytoplasmic glucocorticoid receptors in lungs of various species at different development stages. Endocrinology **94**:450–458, 1974.
6. Kikkawa Y, Kaibara M, Motoyama EK, Orzalesi MM. Morphologic development of fetal rabbit lung and its acceleration with cortisol. Amer J Pathol **64**:423–442, 1971.
7. Smith BT, Giroud CJP. Effects of cortisol on serially propogated fibroblast cell cultures derived from the rabbit lung and skin. Canad J Physiol Pharmacol **53**:1037–1040, 1975.
8. Ballard PL. Hormonal influences during fetal lung development. Ciba Found Symp **78**:251–274, 1980.
9. Torday JS, Smith BT, Giroud CJP. The rabbit fetal lung as a glucocorticoid target tissue. Endocrinology **96**:1462–1467, 1975.
10. Smith BT, Sabry K. Glucocorticoid–thyroid synergism in lung maturation: A mechanism involving epithelial–mesenchymal interaction. Proc Natl Acad Sci USA **80**:1951–1954, 1983.
11. Klein J. Biology of the Mouse Histocompatibility-2 Complex. New York, Springer-Verlag, 1975.
12. Vladutiu AO, Rose NR. Autoimmune murine thyroiditis. Relation to histocompatibility (H-2) type. Science **174**:1137–1139, 1971.
13. Fuchs S, Nevo D, Tarrab-Hazdai R, Yaar I. Strain differences in the autoimmune response of mice to acetylcholine receptors. Nature (London) **263**:329–330, 1976.
14. Warner NL. Genetic control of spontaneous and induced antierythrocyte autoantibody production in mice. Clin Immunol Immunopathol **1**:353–363, 1973.
15. Kronmann H, Lernmark A, Vestergaard BF, Egeberg J, Nerup J. The influence of the major histocompatibility complex (H-2) on experimental diabetes in mice. Diabetologia **16**:107–114, 1979.
16. Bonner JJ, Slavkin HC. Cleft palate susceptibility linked to histocompatibility-2 (H-2) in the mouse. Immunogenetics **2**:213–218, 1975.
17. Melnick M, Jaskoll T, Slavkin HC. Corticosteroid-induced cleft palate in mice and H-2 haplotype: maternal and embryonic effects. Immunogenetics **13**:443–450, 1981.
18. Tyan ML, Miller KK. Genetics and environmental factors in cortisone induced cleft palate. Proc Soc Exp Biol Med **158**:618–621, 1978.
19. Bonner JJ. The H-2 genetic complex, dexamethasone-induced cleft palate, and other craniofacial anomalies. Curr Top Dev Biol, in press, 1984.
20. Katsumata M, Baker MK, Goldman AS, Gasser DL. Influence of *H-2*-linked genes on glucocorticoid receptors in the fetal mouse palate. Immunogenetics **13**:319–325, 1981.
21. Gasser DL, Mele L, Lees DD, Goldman AS. Genes in mice that affect susceptibility to cortisone-induced cleft palate are closely linked to Ir genes on chromosomes 2 and 17 (Major histocompatibility complex/*H-3* locus). Proc Natl Acad Sci USA **78**:3147–3150, 1981.
22. Gasser DL, Goldman AS. Genetic and biochemical studies on glucocorticoid-induced cleft palate. In: Litwack G, ed. Biochemical Actions of Hormones. New York, Academic Press, Vol 10: pp357–382, 1983.
23. Gupta C, Goldman A. H-2 histocompatibility region: Influences on the murine glucocorticoid receptor and its response. Science **216**:994–996, 1982.
24. Palumbo DA, Vladutiu AO. Estrogen reduced in uteri of mice of different H-2 genotypes. Experientia **35**:1103–1104, 1979.
25. Moruelo D, Edidin M. The biological function of the major histocompatibility complex: Hypotheses. In: Marchalonis JJ, Cohen N, eds. Contemporary Topics in Immunobiology. New York, Plenum, pp231–253, 1980.
26. Lafuse W, Edidin M. Influence of the mouse major histocompatibility complex, H-2, on liver adenylate cyclase activity and on glucagon binding to liver cell membrane. Biochemistry **19**:49–54, 1980.
27. Ivanyi P. Some aspects of the H-2 system, the major histocompatibility system in the mouse. Proc R Soc Lond [Biol] **202**:117–158, 1978.
28. Honig LS, Donahue HG, Smith BT, Slavkin HC. Differentiation of mouse lungs of two congenic strains. J Cell Biol **99**:55a, 1983.
29. Snell GD. Methods for the study of histocompatibility genes. J Genet **49**:87–108, 1948.
30. Patterson MK Jr. Measurement of growth and viability of cells in culture. In: Jakoby WB, Pastan IH, eds. Methods in Enzymology. New York, Academic Press, Vol 58:pp141–152, 1978.
31. Smith BT. Cell line A549: A model system for the study of alveolar type II cell function. Amer Rev Resp Dis **115**:285–293, 1977.
32. Mason RJ, Nellenbogen J, Clements JA. Isolation of disaturated phosphatidylcholine with osmium tetroxide. J Lipid Res **17**:281–284, 1976.
33. Theiler K. The House Mouse. New York, Springer-Verlag, 1972.
34. Brehier A, Rooney SA. Phosphatidylcholine synthesis and glycogen depletion in fetal mouse lung: Developmental changes and the effects of dexamethasone. Exp Lung Res **2**:273–287, 1981.
35. Salomon DS, Zubairi Y, Thompson EB. Ontogeny

and biochemical properties of glucocorticoid receptors in midgestation mouse embryos. J Steroid Biochem **9**:95–107, 1978.

36. Salomon DS, Pratt RM. Involvement of glucocorticoids in the development of the secondary palate. Differentiation **13**:141–154, 1979.
37. Velasquez BJ, Sepulveda J. Influence of transplacental NA-872 and dexamethasone therapy on fetal and newborn mouse lung. Respiration **43**:389–400, 1982.
38. Smith BT, Torday JS, Giroud DJP. Evidence for different gestation-dependent effects of cortisol on cultured fetal lung cells. J Clin Invest **53**:1518–1526, 1974.
39. Mitzner W, Johnson JWC, Beck J, London W, Sly D. Influence of betamethasone on the development of mechanical properties in the fetal rhesus monkey lung. Amer Rev Resp Dis **125**:233–238, 1982.
40. Rall L, Pictet R, Githens S, Rutter W. Glucocorticoids modulate the in vitro development of the embryonic rat pancreas. J Cell Biol **75**:398–409, 1977.
41. Cunha GR, Shannon JM, Taguchi O, Fujii H, Meloy BA. Epithelial–mesenchymal interactions in hormone-induced development. In: Sawyer RH, Fallon JF, eds. Epithelial–Mesenchymal Interactions in Development. New York, Praeger, pp51–74, 1983.

Received February 6, 1984. P.S.E.B.M. 1984, Vol. 176.
Accepted April 27, 1984.

PROCEEDINGS OF THE SOCIETY FOR EXPERIMENTAL BIOLOGY AND MEDICINE **176**, 426–433 (1984)

On the Existence of Renal Vasodilator Nerves (41893)

HALLVARD HOLDAAS AND GERALD F. DIBONA

Department of Internal Medicine, University of Iowa College of Medicine and Veterans Administration Medical Center, Iowa City, Iowa 52242

Abstract. The renal vasoconstrictor responses to graded frequencies of direct electrical renal nerve stimulation and renal arterial norepinephrine injections were evaluated before and during renal alpha-1 adrenoceptor blockade in anesthetized dogs. Renal alpha-1 adrenoceptor blockade was achieved by infusing increasing doses (1, 10, 20, 40 μg/kg/min) of prazosin, a selective postsynaptic alpha-1 adrenoceptor antagonist, into the renal artery. The renal vasoconstrictor response to norepinephrine (1.5 μg) was completely abolished by 10 μg/kg/min prazosin. However, the renal vasoconstrictor response to a frequency of renal nerve stimulation which produced less renal vasoconstriction than norepinephrine (1.5 μg) in the absence of prazosin was not abolished by either 10, 20, or 40 μg/kg/min prazosin. During prazosin administration, neither renal nerve stimulation nor norepinephrine produced renal vasodilatation. Therefore, at prazosin doses two- and fourfold greater than that demonstrated to produce complete renal alpha-1 adrenoceptor blockade, no renal vasodilator responses to graded renal nerve stimulation were observed. These studies provide no evidence in support of a neural renal vasodilator mechanism in the dog.

The subject of renal vasodilator nerves has been extensively studied over the years (reviewed in (1)), often in regard to the existence of sympathetic cholinergic vasodilator fibers. Following the administration of a variety of agents with various inhibitory effects on neuroadrenergic transmission (phenoxybenzamine, phentolamine, guanethidine, hexamethonium, reserpine, hydergine, bretylium), the renal vasoconstrictor responses to renal nerve stimulation were markedly reduced or abolished and never replaced by a renal vasodilator response. Similarly, cholinergic blockade with atropine was without effect. These experiments were interpreted to indicate that there are no functional renal sympathetic cholinergic vasodilator nerve fibers. These studies provided physiological support and confirmation of Barajas and colleagues' sophisticated anatomical studies which demonstrated that the acetylcholinesterase containing nerve terminals observable in the kidney were adrenergic (2, 3).

Recently, Chapman and colleagues (4) have reexplored this question. They employed the hydrogen wash out technique to estimate renal cortical and medullary blood flow in the anesthetized rat. It was observed that whereas prazosin 1.5 μmole/kg iv abolished the reduction in renal cortical and medullary blood flow produced by renal nerve stimulation, prazosin 6 μmole/kg iv resulted in an increase in renal cortical blood flow and a decrease in renal medullary blood flow during renal nerve stimulation. It was argued that the higher dose of prazosin produced a more complete block of renal alpha-1 adrenoceptors based on a greater inhibition of the arterial pressor response to iv norepinephrine. The authors concluded that the renal nerves contained renal vasodilator fibers and, based on a reversal of the renal cortical vasodilation back to a vasoconstriction during renal nerve stimulation by combined administration of prazosin and sulpiride, suggested that the renal vasodilator fibers were dopaminergic.

In view of the possibility that renal vasodilation during renal nerve stimulation might be unmasked by a large dose of a highly selective alpha-1 adrenoceptor antagonist, we undertook studies to assess the renal vascular response to graded frequencies of renal nerve stimulation and renal arterial norepinephrine injection before and during renal alpha-1 adrenoceptor blockade with prazosin in anesthetized dogs.

Methods. Mongrel dogs of either sex and weighing between 15 and 25 kg were deprived of food for 20 hr prior to the experiment but allowed water *ad libitum.* They were anesthetized with intravenous sodium pentobarbital, 30-mg/kg initial dose and 6-mg/kg/hr maintenance dose. They were mechanically

0037-9727/84 $1.50

ventilated via an endotracheal tube to maintain arterial pO_2 above 80 mm Hg, pH between 7.35 and 7.45, and pCO_2 between 30 and 40 mm Hg. Body temperature was kept constant at 38°C by external warming. At the onset of surgery, an isotonic saline load of 300 ml was given intravenously followed by a 2.0 ml/min sustaining infusion for the remainder of the experiment. A femoral artery and both femoral veins were catheterized for measurement of arterial pressure (Statham P23Db Pressure Transducer) and administration of isotonic saline and anesthetic solutions. The left kidney was approached retroperitoneally via a left flank incision. For measurement of renal blood flow a noncannulating flow probe (Carolina) was placed around the left renal artery. An occluder was placed distal to the flow probe for zero-flow adjustments and the flow probe was calibrated *in situ* at the end of each experiment. A curved 25-gauge needle was inserted into the left renal artery against the direction of renal blood flow and connected via polyethylene tubing to a syringe pump which delivered isotonic saline at 0.5 ml/min. The left ureter was catheterized to assure free drainage of urine. The renal nerve bundle was dissected free from the renal pedicle, isolated and sectioned. The distal renal nerve bundle was placed on bipolar silver electrodes connected to a Grass S9 constant-voltage square-wave stimulator. This technique assures that all renal nerve activity passing to the kidney derives from the stimulator (1). A minimum of 60 min was allowed for equilibration and stabilization.

In the control period (renal arterial infusion of isotonic saline), the renal nerves were stimulated at supramaximal voltage of 10–30 V, 1.0 msec, and 0.5, 1, 2, 4, and 8Hz. The duration of each renal nerve stimulation was sufficient to allow for the development of a steady state change in renal blood flow (1–2 min). Following cessation of each renal nerve stimulation, sufficient time was allowed for renal blood flow to return to a steady state control level. Following the series of renal nerve stimulations, a single dose of 1.5 μg norepinephrine was injected into the renal artery. Thereafter, the renal arterial infusion was adjusted to deliver prazosin at sequentially increasing doses of 1, 10, 20, and 40 μg/kg/min. Twenty minutes were allowed to pass after the onset of a new rate of prazosin infusion prior to repetition of a series of renal nerve stimulations and norepinephrine injection as noted above. Nine dogs received the 1-, 10-, and 20-μg/kg/min doses of prazosin; seven of these nine dogs also received the 40-μg/kg/min dose of prazosin.

The outputs of the electronic pressure transducer and electromagnetic flow meter were continuously recorded on a direct writing polygraph (Beckman Dynagraph R-611). The control levels of renal blood flow prior to each frequency of renal nerve stimulation in the presence and absence of prazosin were relatively constant within each dog. The data were calculated as the percentage change in renal blood flow, control value to steady state renal nerve stimulation value, to permit comparison between dogs with different basal renal blood flow values. The data were subjected to analysis of variance with subsequent use of the Bonferroni method for simultaneous multiple comparisons (5); a significance level of 5% was chosen. Data in text, tables and figures are expressed as means ± SE.

Results. In the control period (no prazosin), norepinephrine, 1.5 μg, produced a 60% decrease in renal blood flow (Fig. 1). During the renal arterial infusion of prazosin in increasing amounts, there was a progressive dose-related decline in the renal vasoconstrictor response

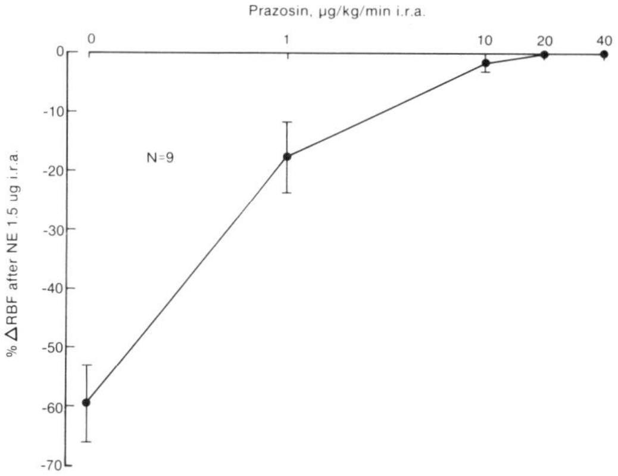

FIG. 1. The effect of renal arterial injection of 1.5 μg norepinephrine on renal blood flow (RBF) before and during graded doses of prazosin administered into the renal artery. Data are mean ± SE percentage changes (%) for $N = 9$ at 0-, 1-, 10-, and 20-μg/kg/min-prazosin doses and $N = 7$ at 40-μg/kg/min prazosin dose.

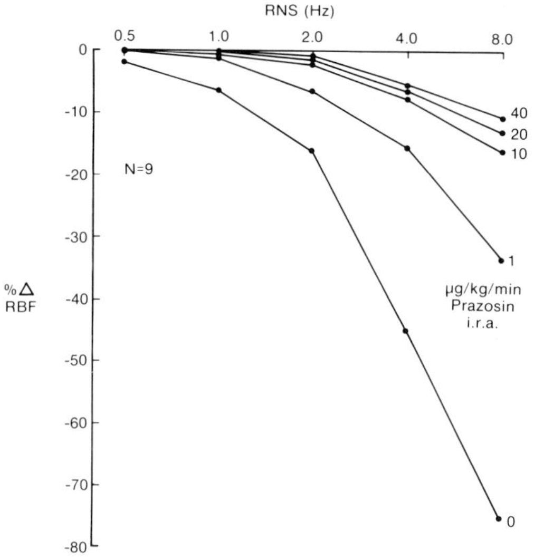

FIG. 2. The effect of graded frequencies (0.5, 1, 2, 4, and 8 Hz) of renal nerve stimulation (RNS: 10–30 V, 1 msec) on renal blood flow (RBF) before and during graded doses of prazosin administered into the renal artery. Data are mean percentage changes (%) (see Table I for mean ± SE) for N = 9 at 0-, 1-, 10-, and 20-μg/kg/min prazosin doses and N = 7 for 40-μg/kg/min prazosin dose.

to norepinephrine. Prazosin at 1 μg/kg/min reduced the response by 70% and the higher doses of prazosin abolished the response. At no time was a renal vasodilator response to norepinephrine administration observed.

During the control period (no prazosin), graded renal nerve stimulation produced frequency dependent decreases in renal blood flow without affecting mean arterial pressure (Fig. 2, Table I). During the renal arterial infusion of prazosin in increasing amounts, there was a progressive dose-related decline in the renal vasoconstrictor responses observed at all frequencies of renal nerve stimulation. Renal vasoconstrictor responses were inhibited by circa 60% at 1 μg/kg/min prazosin and by circa 80% at 10 μg/kg/min prazosin. At 20 and 40 μg/kg/min prazosin significant renal vasoconstrictor responses to renal nerve stimulation at 4 and 8 Hz were still observed. At no time was a renal vasodilator response to renal nerve stimulation observed.

In the control period (no prazosin), mean arterial pressure was 130 ± 6 mm Hg. During renal arterial infusion of prazosin, mean arterial pressure was 122 ± 5 mm Hg at 1.0 μg/kg/min, 114 ± 7 mm Hg at 10 μg/kg/min, 112 ± 9 at 20 μg/kg/min, and 105 ± 10 at 40 μg/kg/min.

Discussion. The dose of norepinephrine, 1.5 μg, produced a renal vasoconstrictor response midway between that elicited by 4- and 8-Hz renal nerve stimulation. The renal vasoconstrictor response to norepinephrine (i.e., alpha-1 adrenoceptor agonist action of native endogenous neurotransmitter) was 50% reduced by prazosin at a dose of approximately 0.5 μg/kg/min and was abolished at prazosin doses of 10 μg/kg/min and higher (20 and 40 μg/kg/min). These results are consistent with the known effects of prazosin as a potent and selective postsynaptic alpha-1 adrenoceptor antagonist (6–8) and indicate that prazosin produced total renal alpha-1 adrenoceptor blockade to norepinephrine at doses of 10 μg/kg/min and higher (20 and 40 μg/kg/min).

The situation for renal nerve stimulation, however, was different. At frequencies of renal nerve stimulation which produced much smaller renal vasoconstrictor responses than that produced by norepinephrine (1.5 μg) in

TABLE I. EFFECT OF RENAL ARTERIAL PRAZOSIN INFUSION ON RENAL BLOOD FLOW RESPONSES TO RENAL NERVE STIMULATION[a]

Prazosin (μg/kg/min, ira)	Stimulation (Hz) 0.5	1.0	2.0	4.0	8.0
0	−1.9 ± 0.4	−6.4 ± 1.0	−15.9 ± 1.8	−45.0 ± 6.2	−74.7 ± 7.8
1	0	−1.2 ± 0.4	−6.6 ± 1.3	−15.6 ± 2.9	−33.3 ± 5.8
10	−0.1 ± 0.1	−0.3 ± 0.2	−2.0 ± 0.9	−7.7 ± 1.7	−16.0 ± 3.0
20	0	0	−1.8 ± 1.0	−6.4 ± 1.5	−12.9 ± 2.3
40	0	0	−1.2 ± 0.9	−5.5 ± 2.2	−10.6 ± 2.6

[a] Data entries are means ± SE for percentage change in renal blood flow.

the control period, 0.5, 1, and 2 Hz, prazosin at 1 μg/kg/min (0.5 and 1 Hz) and 10 μg/kg/min (2 Hz) abolished the renal vasoconstrictor responses. Thus, based on comparison of control period renal vasoconstrictor responses, prazosin at doses which produced complete renal alpha-1 adrenoceptor blockade to norepinephrine resulted in similar findings with less potent frequencies of renal nerve stimulation. However, while renal nerve stimulation at 4 Hz decreased renal blood flow by 45% in the control period (cf. 60% with norepinephrine), this renal vasoconstrictor response was not completely abolished by the dose of prazosin, 10 μg/kg/min, which completely blocked the norepinephrine response; the higher prazosin doses, 20 and 40 μg/kg/min, were similarly ineffective. Therefore, it could be predicted, and was observed, that the 8-Hz renal nerve stimulation, producing a 75% decrease in renal blood flow during the control period, would not be completely abolished by the prazosin dose of 10 μg/kg/min which completely blocked the norepinephrine response; in addition, the higher doses (20, 40 μg/kg/min) of prazosin produced little additional inhibitory effect.

It is of interest that prazosin doses sufficient to completely block the renal vasoconstrictor responses to norepinephrine did not completely abolish the renal vasoconstrictor responses to equipotent intensities of renal nerve stimulation. This has been previously reported with the nonspecific alpha adrenoceptor antagonists, phenoxybenzamine (9) and phentolamine (10). It is possible that renal arterial infusion of alpha adrenoceptor antagonists, while clearly able to completely block renal vascular alpha adrenoceptors occupied by renal arterial infusion of norepinephrine, may not be able to completely block all the renal vascular alpha adrenoceptors occupied by release of norepinephrine from nerve terminals within the renal parenchyma.

It is important to emphasize that at a dose of prazosin (10 μg/kg/min) which was demonstrated to produce total renal alpha-1 adrenoceptor blockade to norepinephrine the renal vascular responses to graded frequencies of renal nerve stimulation were always vasoconstrictor; renal vasodilatation was never observed. Furthermore, similar observations were made with doses of prazosin, two (20 μg/kg/min) and four (40 μg/kg/min) times greater than that needed to produce complete renal alpha-1 adrenoceptor blockade to norepinephrine. Therefore, these studies provide no evidence in support of a neural renal vasodilator mechanism in the dog.

There are several major issues which deserve comment concerning these results in light of the studies of Chapman *et al.* (4). It is difficult to assess the importance of the species difference, rats versus dogs; however, sodium pentobarbital was the common anesthetic employed. A major difference was the method used for masurement of renal blood flow. Chapman *et al.* (4) used the technique of hydrogen washout. When this method was validated against directly measured renal venous outflow in dogs (11, 12), both groups noted a good correlation between renal cortical blood flow and renal venous outflow at values of renal venous outflow less than 150 ml/min/100 g; when renal venous outflow exceeded 150 ml/min 100 g, renal cortical blood flow values were uniformly lower. Although this method has been previously used in anesthetized rats (13–14), it has not been similarly validated against directly measured renal venous outflow or other more direct techniques such as electromagnetic flow meter or clearance and extraction of *p*-aminohippurate (PAH). To provide convincing evidence that the hydrogen washout technique provides reliable measurements of renal blood flow in the rat, it would seem appropriate to do validation studies such as have been done for ^{133}Xe-renal blood flow versus PAH-renal blood flow in the rat (16) and ^{133}Xe-renal blood flow versus electromagnetic flow meter-renal blood flow in the dog (17). Although the monitoring techniques, tissue electrodes for the hydrogen washout technique and external counting for the ^{133}Xe washout technique, are different, the theoretical principles underlying these various inert gas techniques are identical (18). In this regard, it is important to note that, in the dog, ^{133}Xe-renal blood flow significantly overestimated electromagnetic flow meter renal blood flow by 20% and had a high degree of variability as reflected by a coefficient of variation of 42% (17). Similarly, in the rat, although ^{133}Xe-renal blood flow and PAH-renal blood flow were in close agreement, the degree of variability was much greater with the former than the latter technique (coefficient of variation, 32% versus 6%) (16).

In assessing the degree of completeness of renal alpha-1 adrenoceptor blockade, Chapman *et al.* (4) evaluated the arterial pressure responses to intravenous injections of norepinephrine before and after the intravenous injection of graded doses of prazosin. This approach critically depends on the assumption that inhibition of the norepinephrine (iv) induced systemic arterial pressor response by intravenous administration of the alpha-1 adrenoceptor antagonist prazosin accurately reflects the status of alpha-1 adrenoceptors located within the kidney. A proper assessent of the responses to stimulation and blockade of alpha-1 adrenoceptors located in the kidney requires the administration of alpha adrenoceptor agonists and antagonists into the renal circulation and the measurement of a specific renal, not nonspecific systemic, response (1). In the current experiments, the renal blood flow responses to the renal arterial injection of norepinephrine were measured before and during renal arterial administration of prazosin; prazosin at 10 μg/kg/min completely abolished the renal vasoconstrictor response to a dose of norepinephrine which reduced renal blood flow by 60% in the control state. This observation provides strong evidence for complete blockade of renal alpha-1 adrenoceptors and does not depend on an extrapolation from measurements of systemic arterial pressure. Another major argument of Chapman *et al.* (4) dealt with the dose range of prazosin employed; they found that prazosin at 1.5 μmole/kg did not produce full inhibition of the systemic arterial pressor response to intravenous norepinephrine whereas 6.0 μmole/kg was effective. These doses equate to 574 and 2295 μg/kg, respectively, and assuming a 10% distribution of cardiac output to a single kidney, this would equate to a kidney dose of 57.4 and 229.5 μg/kg, respectively. In the current experiments, there was 20 min of renal arterial infusion of each dose of prazosin prior to the interventions and the infusion was continued during the interventions (ca. 30 min); thus, each dose was infused for a total of 50 min. Therefore, at the prazosin doses of 1, 10, 20, and 40 μg/kg/min the total amount of prazosin infused into the kidney at each dose was 50, 500, 1000, and 2000 μg/kg and the total cumulative amount of prazosin infused into the kidney at each dose was 50, 550, 1550, and 3550 μg/kg, respectively. These latter three total cumulative doses of prazosin delivered directly into the kidney are 2.4, 6.8, and 15.5 times greater than the largest dose (presumed to have reached the kidney) employed by Chapman *et al.* (4).

A further confounding variable in interpreting the results of Chapman *et al.* (4) is that intravenous administration of prazosin 1.5 μmole/kg resulted in a decrease in mean arterial pressure from 114 ± 3 to 84 ± 2 mm Hg and, although the decrease observed with the 6.0-μmole/kg prozosin dose was not stated, it can be safely assumed to have not been less and probably was greater. Since several investigators using more direct methods for the measurements of renal blood flow have demonstrated that renal blood flow autoregulation is impaired in the rat when mean arterial pressure is less than 95–105 mm Hg (15, 19, 20), it is evident that, following prazosin administration, the rats in the study by Chapman *et al.* (4) had impaired capacity for autoregulation of renal blood flow. The authors indicate that renal cortical blood flow fell from 310 ± 13 to 223 ± 13 ml/min/100 g after prazosin 1.5 μmole/kg; it may be calculated that renal cortical vascular resistance changed little, 0.37 versus 0.38 mm Hg/ml/min/100 g. Thus, renal cortical blood flow fell in parallel with the fall in mean arterial pressure such that renal cortical vascular resistance was unchanged. The failure of renal cortical blood flow to be better maintained in the face of a reduced mean arterial pressure indicates the existence of impaired capacity for renal blood flow autoregulation. This further indicates that the renal vasculature had achieved maximal vasodilatation and, being unable to vasodilate further in response to the reduction in mean arterial pressure, exhibits a linear pressure–flow relationship wherein changes in mean arterial pressure produce parallel changes in renal blood flow (unchanged renal vascular resistance). It should be noted that, after prazosin 6.0 μmole/kg, renal nerve stimulation produced an increase of 6.1% in renal cortical blood flow in their study. In the setting of a maximally vasodilated nonautoregulating rat kidney with mean arterial pressure of 84 mm Hg (or lower), such an increase in renal cortical blood flow could be totally accounted for by a passive flow response to a rise in mean arterial pressure of as little as 5 mm Hg. It should be noted that in the current studies, mean arterial pressure, while showing some downward trend due to unavoidable recirculation of cumulative high-dose renal arterial infusion of prazosin, remained well above the autoregulatory breakpoint of 60–70 mm Hg for the dog (21) and basal renal blood flow remained constant despite this progressive fall in mean arterial pressure (i.e., appropriate decrease in renal vascular resistance), thus exhibiting intact autoregulatory capacity.

Therefore, the absence of data validating the hydrogen washout technique for the measurement of renal blood flow in the rat, the absence of data demonstrating the presence or absence of specific renal alpha adrenoceptor blockade and the limitations of examining mechanisms for the control of renal blood flow in a kidney preparation which does not exhibit normal renal blood flow autoregulatory behavior raise strong and compelling reservations concerning the conclusions of Chapman *et al.* (4) regarding the existence of renal vasodilator nerves.

Other investigators have proposed the existence of neural dopaminergic vasodilator fibers in the kidney. The only physiological and functional study is that of Bell and Lang (22) who showed that electrical stimulation of the ventral hypothalamus in the anesthetized dog pretreated with guanethidine elicited renal vasodilator responses with 1- to 2-sec onset latency which waned within 10 sec despite continued stimulation. The renal vasodilator responses were unaffected by atropine or mepyramine but were abolished by haloperidol. Although it was not indicated whether renal denervation abolished the renal vasodilator response to stimulation, the data were interpreted to support the existence of renal vascular innervation which, on reflex activation of the renal nerves, releases dopamine as the neurotransmitter. Further studies are of an anatomical and biochemical nature. Bell *et al.* (23), using chemical determinations and fluorescence histochemical techniques, demonstrated that dog renal cortex contained more dopamine than could be accounted for by its presence in noradrenergic axons only and that it was more resistant to guanethidine depletion than in right atrium. Dinerstein *et al.* (24), using a differential fluorescence histochemical technique, identified dopamine containing neurons in the dog renal cortical vasculature. However, in the rat, renal cortical dopamine content has not been found to be greater than what would be anticipated in noradrenergic axons (25, 26) and has been interpreted as evidence against renal dopaminergic innervation in the rat (26). The effect of either renal denervation or reflex or direct renal nerve stimulation on both the urinary excretion and renal secretion of dopamine and other catecholamines has been examined by several groups of investigators. Although activation of the efferent renal nerves can cause release of dopamine into the urine and renal venous blood, approximately 50% of such dopamine release can be accounted for by dopamine synthesis from circulating L-Dopa by Dopa decarboxylase in nonneural renal tissue (27–33). Although the physiological, anatomical and biochemical studies seem to support the existence of dopaminergic nerves, there is no unambiguous evidence as to their function (34–36). That is, it needs to be shown that an alteration in the activity of efferent renal nerve fibers produces a measurable change in some renal function that is mediated by release of dopamine as neurotransmitter from those renal nerve fibers.

Thus, while the accumulated information generally favors the hypothesis concerning the existence of neural dopaminergic vasodilator fibers in the kidney, the evidence is far from conclusive. For example, an unequivocal increase in renal blood flow occurring during direct renal nerve stimulation (often during inhibition of neuroadrenergic transmission) and reversed by specific antagonists of dopamine's vascular effect has not been convincingly demonstrated and confirmed in different mammalian species. In this regard, Imbs *et al.* (25) reported that combined treatment with phenoxybenzamine and phentolamine completely blocked the renal vasoconstrictor response to renal nerve stimulation in only three of six dogs; a partial renal vasoconstrictor response persisted in the other three dogs. Thus, no evidence was found for renal vasodilator nerves. Three of the six dogs pretreated with phenoxybenzamine and phentolamine were then given indomethacin; repeat renal nerve stimulation elicited small renal vasodilator responses. These results raise the possibility that renal nerve stimulation (after phenoxybenzamine and phentolamine) caused the renal release of vasodilator (PGE_2, PGI_2) and vasoconstrictor (thromboxane) prostanoids with the latter predominating prior to indomethacin administration; indomethacin administration may have reduced the renal release of vasoconstrictor substances to a greater extent than vasodilator substances so that a renal vasodilator response was observed. Observations on the effect of other antagonists to vasodilator mechanisms (atropine, propranolol, mepyramine, sulpiride) were not reported. However, others have also examined this issue. Kopp *et al.* (37) stimulated the renal nerves to produce a 50% decrease in renal blood flow which was completely blocked (no residual renal vasoconstriction or vasodilation) with renal arterial administration of phenoxybenzamine. The addition of fully active doses of two structurally dissimilar prostaglandin synthesis inhibitors, indomethacin and diclofenac, did not alter the effect of phenoxybenzamine to block the renal vasoconstrictor response to renal nerve stimulation. Needleman *et al.* (38) showed that renal nerve stimulation produced renal vasoconstriction and prostaglandin release from the rabbit kidney; phenoxybenzamine completely blocked both the renal vasoconstriction and prostaglandin release whereas indomethacin, while blocking the prostaglandin release, did not affect the renal vasoconstriction. Thus, these studies, also employing renal alpha adrenoceptor blockade and prostaglandin synthesis inhibitors, do not confirm the existence of renal vasodilator nerves; therefore, the issue of the existence of renal vasodilator nerves is unresolved. Furthermore, in the absence of inhibition of neuroadrenergic transmission, there is no evidence that specific antagonists of dopamine's renal vascular action enhance the renal vasoconstrictor response to renal nerve stimulation (39).

This work was supported by USPHS Grants AM 15843 and HL 14388 and by grants from the American Heart Association, Iowa Affiliate, and the Veterans Administration. Dr. Holdaas was supported by an International Research Fellowship (TS 03120) of the Fogarty International Center, NIH, USPHS, on leave from the Institute for Experimental Medical Research, Ullevaal Hospital, University of Oslo, Oslo, Norway.

1. DiBona GF. The functions of the renal nerves. Rev Physiol Biochem Pharmacol **94**:76–181, 1982.
2. Barajas L. Innervation of the renal cortex. Fed Proc **37**:1192–1201, 1978.
3. Barajas L, Wang P. Simultaneous ultrastructural visualization of acetylcholinesterase activity and tritiated norepinephrine uptake in renal nerves. Anat Rec **205**:185–195, 1983.
4. Chapman BJ, Horn NM, Robertson MJ. Renal blood flow changes during renal nerve stimulation in rats treated with alpha adrenergic and dopaminergic blockers. J Physiol (London), **325**:67–77, 1982.
5. Wallenstein S, Zucker CL, Fleiss JL. Some statistical methods useful in circulation research. Circ Res **47**:1–9, 1980.
6. Schmitz JM, Graham RM, Sagalowsky A, Pettinger WA. Renal alpha-1 and alpha-2 adrenergic receptors: biochemical and pharmacological correlations. J Pharmacol Exp Ther **219**:400–406, 1981.
7. Snavely MD, Insel PA. Characterization of alpha-adrenergic receptor subtypes in the rat renal cortex. Mol Pharmacol **22**:532–546, 1982.
8. Summers RJ, McPherson GA. Radioligand studies of alpha-adrenoceptors in the kidney. Trends Pharmacol Sci **3**:291–293, 1982.
9. Gomer DK, Zimmerman BG. Determination of sympathetic vasodilator responses during renal nerve stimulation. J Pharmacol Exp Ther **181**:75–82, 1972.
10. DiSalvo J, Fell C. Changes in renal blood flow during renal nerve stimulation. Proc Soc Exp Biol Med **136**:150–153, 1971.
11. Aukland K, Bower BF, Berliner RW. Measurement of local blood flow with hydrogen gas. Circ Res **14**:164–187, 1964.
12. Neely WA, Turner MD, Hardy JD, Godfrey WD. The use of the hydrogen electrode to measure tissue blood flow. J Surg Res **8**:363–369, 1965
13. Haining JL, Turner MD. Tissue blood flow in rat kidneys by hydrogen desaturation. J Appl Physiol **21**:1705–1708, 1966.
14. Chedru M-F, Baethke R, Oken DE. Renal cortical blood flow and glomerular filtration rate in myohemoglobinuric acute renal failure. Kidney Int **1**:232–239, 1972.
15. Arendshorst WJ, Finn WF, Gottschalk CW. Autoregulation of blood flow in the rat kidney. Amer J Physiol **228**:127–133, 1975.
16. Heller J, Horacek V. Autoregulation of renal blood flow in the rat. Pfluegers Arch **370**:81–85, 1977.
17. Ladefoged J, Pedersen F, Dontheil U, Deetjen P, Selkurt EE. Renal blood flow measured with xenon-133 washout technique and with an electromagnetic flowmeter. Pfluegers Arch **284**:195–200, 1965.
18. Kety SS. Theory and applications of the exchange of

inert gases at the lungs and tissues. Pharmacol Rev **3**:1–41, 1951.
19. Finn WF, Arendshorst WJ. Effect of prostaglandin synthetase inhibitors on renal blood flow in the rat. Amer J Physiol **231**:1541–1545, 1976.
20. Arendshorst WJ, Finn WF. Renal hemodynamics in the rat before and during inhibition of angiotensin II. Amer J Physiol **223**:F290–F297, 1977.
21. Kiil F. The mechanism of renal autoregulation. Scand J Clin Lab Invest **41**:521–525, 1981.
22. Bell C, Lang WJ. Neural dopaminergic vasodilator control in the kidney. Nature (London) **246**:27–29, 1973.
23. Bell C, Lang WJ, Laska F. Dopamine-containing vasomotor nerves in the dog kidney. J Neurochem **31**:77–83, 1978.
24. Dinerstein RJ, Vannice J, Henderson RC, Roth LJ, Goldberg LI, Hoffmann PC. Histofluorescence techniques provide evidence for dopamine-containing neuronal elements in canine kidney. Science **205**:497–499, 1979.
25. Bell C. Dopamine as a prostaglandin autonomic neurotransmitter. Neuroscience **7**:1–8, 1982.
26. McGrath BP, Lim AE, Bode K, Willis GL, Smith GC. Differentiation of noradrenergic and dopaminergic nerves in the rat kidney: evidence against significant dopaminergic innervation. Clin Exp Pharmacol Physiol **10**:543–553, 1983.
27. Imbs J, Schmidt M, Ehrhardt JD, Schwartz J. Renal dopaminergic mechanisms. In: Imbs JL, Schwartz J, eds. Peripheral Dopaminergic Receptors. Oxford, Pergamon Press, pp. 331–343, 1979.
28. Baines AD, Chan W. Production of urine free dopamine from plasma DOPA: A micropuncture study. Life Sci **26**:253–259, 1980.
29. Morgunov N, Baines AD. Renal nerves and catecholamine excretion. Amer J Physiol **240**:F75–F81, 1981.
30. Baines AD. Effects of salt intake and renal denervation on catecholamine catabolism and excretion. *Kidney Int* **21**:316–322, 1982.
31. Stephenson RK, Sole MJ, Baines AD. Neural and extraneural catecholamine production by rat kidneys. *Amer J Physiol* **242**:F261–F266, 1982.
32. Ball SG, Gunn IG, Douglas IHS. Renal handling of dopa, dopamine, norepinephrine and epinephrine in the dog. Amer J Physiol **242**:F56–F62, 1982.
33. Kopp U, Bradley T, Hjemdahl P. Renal venous outflow and urinary excretion of norepinephrine, epinephrine and dopamine during graded renal nerve stimulation. Amer J Physiol **244**:E52–E60, 1983.
34. Goldberg LI, Weder AB. Connections between endogenous dopamine, dopamine receptors and sodium excretion: Evidence and hypothesis. Rec Adv Clin Pharmacol **3**:149–166, 1980.
35. Lee MR. Dopamine and the kidney. Clin Sci **62**:439–448, 1982.
36. Cuche JL, Selz F, Ruget G, Jondeau G, Guedon J. Is dopamine a physiological natriuretic hormone in the dog? Clin Sci **65**:479–486, 1983.
37. Kopp U, Aurell M, Sjolander M, Ablad B. The roles of prostaglandins in the alpha and beta adrenoceptor mediated renin release response to graded renal nerve stimulation. Pflugers Arch **391**:1–8, 1983.
38. Needleman P, Douglas JR Jr, Jakschik B, Stoecklein PB, Johnson EM Jr. Release of renal prostaglandins by catecholamines: Relationship to renal endocrine function. J Pharmacol Exp Ther **188**:453–460, 1974.
39. Lokhandwala MF, Buckley JP. Presynaptic dopamine receptors as mediators of dopamine-induced inhibition of neurogenic vasoconstriction. Eur J Pharmacol **45**:305–309, 1977.

Received June 14, 1983. P.S.E.B.M. 1984, Vol. 176.
Accepted May 7, 1984.

PROCEEDINGS OF THE SOCIETY FOR EXPERIMENTAL BIOLOGY AND MEDICINE **176**, 434–437 (1984)

Intact and Carboxyterminal PTH Do Not Cross the Blood–Cerebrospinal Fluid Barrier[1] (41894)

MOHAMMAD AKMAL, SAMIR TUMA, DAVID A. GOLDSTEIN, RANGA PATTABHIRAMAN, LESLIE BERNSTEIN, AND SHAUL G. MASSRY[2]

Division of Nephrology and Department of Medicine, University of Southern California School of Medicine, Los Angeles, California 90033

Abstract. In order to examine whether parathyroid hormone (PTH) enters the cerebrospinal fluid (CSF), the blood levels of the hormone were acutely elevated either by infusion of parathyroid extract or by stimulation of the parathyroid glands by hypocalcemia. Despite marked elevations in the blood levels of the hormone, PTH could not be detected in the CSF. The data indicate the intact PTH or its carboxyterminal fragment do not cross the blood–CSF interface of the blood–brain barrier. The results, therefore, suggest that the action of PTH on brain must be mediated by an effect on the blood–brain interface of the blood–brain barrier.

The cerebrospinal fluid (CSF) and brain compositions are vigorously protected and changes in their constituents are prevented during marked alterations in the chemistry of blood (1–4). This is achieved by the blood–brain barrier which encompasses the processes involved in the exchange occurring at the CSF–blood (5), CSF–brain (6), and blood–brain interface (7, 8). Parathyroid hormone (PTH) has been shown to augment brain calcium content and affect brain function in acute or chronic clinical and experimental conditions associated with excess PTH (2, 3, 9–12). Thus, it appears that PTH overcomes the blood–brain barrier but the particular interface of this system which is affected by the hormone is not completely delineated.

Available data indicate that the concentration of ionized calcium and phosphorus and the product of ionized calcium–phosphorus in CSF are not affected in conditions associated with excess or deficiency of PTH (2, 3, 13–15). These observations suggest that the hormone does not disrupt the blood–CSF interface of the blood–brain barrier. The present study was undertaken to examine whether PTH enters the CSF compartment and through such a movement may act on the CSF–brain interface.

[1] This work was supported by Grants AM-18959 and AM-29955 from the Institute of Arthritis, Metabolism and Digestive and Kidney Diseases, and Grant CA-14089 from the National Cancer Institute.

[2] To whom correspondence should be addressed.

Methods. Eleven adult female mongrel dogs weighing 15–20 (18 ± 0.5 (SE) kg were studied. The animals were anesthetized with 30 mg/kg pentobarbital which was administered intravenously and additional amounts of the drug were given as needed. The dogs were intubated and mechanical respiration was maintained by a Harvard respirator (Harvard Apparatus Co., Inc., Millis, Mass.) at a rate of 25 strokes/min and tidal volume to keep pCO_2 at about 35 mm Hg. Catheters were inserted in peripheral veins of both hind limbs; one was used for collections of blood samples and the other for infusion of disodium ethylenediaminetetracetate (EDTA) or PTH. A spinal trocar was inserted into the cisterna magnum and it was left *in situ* throughout the experiment for the collections of CSF samples.

In six dogs, parathyroid extract PTE (Eli Lilly & Co., Indianapolis, Ind.) dissolved in 250 ml of normal saline was infused over a period of 4 hr delivering 6 units of PTE/kg body wt/hr. Blood and CSF samples were obtained before and every hour during the infusion of the hormone.

In five dogs, EDTA dissolved in 500 ml of 5% dextrose was infused for 2 hr delivering 75 mg of EDTA/kg body wt/hr. Blood and CSF samples were obtained before, hourly, during the infusion of EDTA and every 2 hr for the 4-hr period following EDTA infusion.

Ionized calcium was measured with Orion Electrode Model SS-20 (Orion Biomedical, Cambridge, Mass.). PTH was measured with

0037-9727/84 $1.50

radioimmunoassay using sheep antisera 478 (kindly supplied by Dr. Claude Arnaud), ^{125}I-labeled bovine PTH, and pooled sera from patients with chronic renal failure as standard. This antibody reacts predominantly with an immunological determinant in the carboxyl region of the PTH, and it will detect both the intact and the carboxy-terminal fragment. The value of this assay for 63 normal samples ranged from undetectable to 15 μleq/ml (5.7 ± 0.7 (SE) of the detectable values), and the levels were detectable in 33 of the 63 samples (52%). Elevated blood levels of PTH were found by this assay in all samples obtained from uremic patients. Statistical evaluation utilized repeated measures analysis of variance. These were performed to determine if there were significant differences over time. The Scheffe method was used to make multiple comparisons between means (16).

Results. The effects of PTH or EDTA infusions on the blood concentrations of ionized calcium and PTH and the PTH concentration in CSF are given in Table I. The P values reported in the text are obtained by repeated measures analysis of variance. The significance between means obtained by multiple comparisons according to the Scheffe method is indicated in Table I. There was a progressive and significant ($P < 0.01$) rise in the concentrations of ionized calcium in blood from 4.5 ± 0.1 mg/dl to 6.5 ± 0.2 mg/dl by the end of the PTH infusion. The PTH levels in blood were influenced by the weight of the dogs. After adjusting for dog weight, the blood levels of PTH also displayed significant ($P < 0.01$)

TABLE I. BLOOD CONCENTRATIONS OF IONIZED CALCIUM AND LEVELS OF PARATHYROID HORMONE IN BLOOD AND CEREBROSPINAL FLUID DURING PARATHYROID EXTRACT AND EDTA INFUSIONS

	Hours				
	0	1	2	3	4
	I. Parathyroid hormone infusion (6 Units/kg body wt/hr)				
Blood					
Ca^{2+}* (mg/dl)	4.5 ± 0.1	5.2 ± 0.12	5.6 ± 0.2	6.0 ± 0.2	6.5 ± 0.2
PTH** (μleq/ml)	UD	565 ± 277	798 ± 379	1351 ± 645	1913 ± 980
CSF					
PTH (μleq/ml)	UD	UD	UD	UD	UD
	EDTA infusion period			EDTA withdrawal	
	0	1	2	4	6
	II. EDTA infusion (75 mg/kg body wt/hr)				
Blood					
Ca^{2+}*** (mg/dl)	4.8 ± 0.06	3.4 ± 0.1	2.8 ± 0.1	4.4 ± 0.1	4.6 ± 0.1
PTH† (μleq/ml)	UD	6.0 ± 0.4	9.0 ± 2.0	6.0 ± 0.3	4.0 ± 0.2
CSF					
PTH (μleq/ml)	UD	UD	UD	UD	UD

Note. Data are printed as means ± SEM; UD = undetected; Ca^{2+} = ionized calcium; PTH = parathyroid hormone. Scheffe's method was used to make multiple comparisons between means.

* Comparisons of 4 hr to control significant by different overall ($P < 0.05$).

** All pairwise significant overall ($P < 0.05$) after adjustment for dog weight.

*** Pairwise comparisons significant overall ($P < 0.05$), are control vs 1, 2, and 4 hr, 1 hr vs 2 hr, 4 hr vs 1 and 2 hr, and 6 hr vs 1 and 2 hr.

† All comparisons to control significant and 2 hr significantly different from 6 hr, overall ($P < 0.05$).

elevations and were high throughout the 4 hr of the study. Despite the profound increment in the blood levels of PTH, the concentration of the hormone in the CSF remained undetectable.

There was a significant ($P < 0.01$) fall in the levels of ionized calcium in blood from 4.8 ± 0.06 to 3.4 ± 0.1 by the end of the first hour of EDTA infusion and a further significant (<0.01) decrease to 2.8 ± 0.1 mg/dl by the end of the second hour. The level of ionized calcium returned to control values two hours after the termination of EDTA infusion. The blood levels of PTH increased with the fall in the concentration of ionized calcium during EDTA infusion and began to decline after the termination of the infusion. The increments in endogenous PTH levels were modest. However, the PTH concentrations in CSF remained undetectable.

Discussion. The results of the present study demonstrate that an increase in the blood levels of PTH produced by PTH infusion or by stimulation of endogenous release of the hormone is not associated with a rise in the concentration of PTH in CSF. These data show that the intact PTH or its carboxyterminal fragment do not cross the blood–CSF interface of the blood–brain barrier.

Previous studies have shown that the concentrations of calcium and phosphorus in CSF remain stable despite marked changes in their concentrations in the blood (2–4) and in the absence or the presence of normal or excess PTH (2, 3, 13–15). These data and the results of the present study, therefore, indicate that the changes in brain calcium content in the presence of excess PTH could not be due to an action of the hormone on the CSF–brain interface of the blood–brain barrier. One must conclude that the effect of PTH on brain must occur at the blood–brain interface of the blood–brain barrier.

The mechanisms by which PTH mediates calcium accumulation in brain through an action at the blood–brain interface are not addressed in the present study. One may, however, consider several possibilities. The hormone may stimulate a brain adenylate cyclase system, affect phospholipid turnover of cell membrane or stimulate synthesis of a carrier protein. Studies are required to explore these possibilities.

Other studies in our laboratory have shown that the electroencephogram (EEG) may be normal in the presence of increased calcium content of brain if excess PTH is absent (17). These observations suggest that PTH is required before an abnormality in EEG develops and they are consistent with an effect of PTH on brain independent of the hormone-mediated calcium accumulation. Indeed, *in vitro* studies have shown that PTH stimulates brain microsomal ATPase (18), and inhibits oxidative phosphorylation by mitochondria from various cells (19–22). For such action of PTH to occur *in vivo,* the hormone or one of its fragments must enter the brain cells. Nordquist and Palmeiri (23) have demonstrated that PTH enters the cells of the renal proximal tubule and localizes in the mitochondria. It is possible that a similar event exists in the brain, and if it does, it must occur at the blood–brain interface.

Although our studies demonstrate that PTH does not enter CSF despite marked increment in the blood levels of the hormone, such a phenomenon may not be applicable to other hormones. Several investigators have shown that the CSF contains thyroxine and triiodothyronine (24, 25), steroid hormones (26), prolactin (27), calcitonin (28, 29), insulin (30, 31), growth hormone (32), and gastrin (32). The origin of these hormones found in the CSF is not clear. A positive correlation between the blood and CSF levels of prolactin (27), insulin (31), and growth hormone (32) were found but not for those of calcitonin (28) and gastrin (33). These observations suggest a selectivity of the blood brain barrier in the modulation of the passage of hormones from blood to CSF.

1. Ames A III, Higashi K, Nesbett FB. Relation of potassium concentration in choroid plexus fluid to that in plasma. J Physiol (London) **181**:506–515, 1965.
2. Arieff AI, Massry SG. Calcium metabolism of brain in acute renal failure. Effects of uremia, hemodialysis and parathyroid hormone. J Clin Invest **53**:387–392, 1974.
3. Goldstein DA, Massry SG. Effect of parathyroid hormone administration and its withdrawal on brain calcium and electroencephalogram. Miner Electrolyte Metab **1**:84–91, 1978.
4. Goldstein DA, Romoff M, Bogin E, Massry SG. Relationship between the concentrations of calcium and

phosphorus in blood and cerebrospinal fluid. J Clin Endocrinol Metab **49**:58–62, 1979.
5. Davison H. Physiology of the cerebrospinal fluid. Boston, Little, Brown, p82, 1967.
6. Wallace GB, Brodie BB. The distribution of iodine, thiocyanate, bromide and chloride in the central nervous system and spinal fluid. J Pharmakol Exp Ther **65**:220–226, 1939.
7. Krough A. The active and passive exchanges of inorganic ions through the surfaces of living cells and through living membranes generally. Proc Res Soc London (Biol) **133**:140–200, 1946.
8. Crone C. The permeability of brain capillaries to nonelectrolytes. Acta Physiol Scand **64**:407–417, 1965.
9. Alfrey AC, Mishell JM, Burks J, Contiguglia SR, Rudolph H, Lewin E, Holmes JH. Syndrome of dyspraxia and multifocal seizures associated with chronic hemodialysis. Trans Amer Soc Artif Intern Organs **18**:257–265, 1972.
10. Guisado R, Arieff AI, Massry SG. Changes in the electroencephalogram in acute uremia. J Clin Invest **55**:738–745, 1975.
11. Cogan MG, Covey CM, Arieff AI, Wisniewsky A, Clark OH, Lazarowitz VC, Leach W. Central nervous manifestations of hyperparathyroidism. Amer J Med **65**:963–970, 1978.
12. Cooper JD, Lazarowitz VC, Arieff AI. Neurodiagnostic abnormalities in patients with acute renal failure: Evidence for neurotoxicity of parathyroid hormones. J Clin Invest **55**:738–745, 1975.
13. Cameron AT, Moorhouse VHK. The tetany of parathyroid deficiency and the calcium of the blood and cerebrospinal fluid. J Biol Chem **63**:687–720, 1925.
14. Marguilis S, Perley AM. Studies on cerebrospinal fluid and serum calcium with special reference to the parathyroid hormone. J Biol Chem **88**:169–188, 1930.
15. Merritt HH, Bauer W. The equilibrium between cerebrospinal fluid and blood plasma: The calcium content of serum cerebrospinal fluid, and aqueous humour at different levels of parathyroid activity. J Biol Chem **90**:233–246, 1931.
16. Winer BJ. Statistical principles in experimental design. New York, McGraw–Hill, 2nd ed, 1971.
17. Akmal M, Goldstein DA, Multani S, Massry SG. Role of uremia, brain CA and PTH on changes in EEG in chronic renal failure. Amer J Physiol **246**:F575–579, 1984.
18. Bogin E, Sachtjen E, Bristol G, Massry SG. Parathyroid hormone and brain microsomal NA-K ATPase. Miner Electrolyte Metab **3**:104–108, 1980.
19. Cohen DV, Smaich AF, Levy R. The inhibitions of respirations and phosphorylation in kidney mitochondria by parathyroid hormone administered in vivo. J Biol Chem **241**:889–894, 1966.
20. Bogin E, Levi J, Harary I, Massry SG. Effects of parathyroid hormone on oxidative phosphorylation of heart mitochondria. Miner Electrolyte Metab **7**:151–156, 1982.
21. Baczynski R, Brautbar N, Carpenter C, Massry SG. Effect of parathyroid hormone on energy metabolism of heart. Proc Amer J Nephrol **4**-1A, 1981.
22. Brautbar N, Carpenter C, Baczynski R, Kohan R, and Massry SG. Effect of PTH on skeletal muscle: Role of PTH in uremic myopathy. Kidney Int **23**:212, 1983.
23. Nordquist RE, Palmieri GMA. Intracellular localization of parathyroid hormone in the kidney. Endocrinology **95**:229–237, 1974.
24. Pardridge WM. Carrier-mediated transport of thyroid hormone through the rat blood–brain barrier: Primary role of albumin-bound hormone. Endocrinology **105**:605–612, 1979.
25. Nishikawa M, Inada M, Naito K, Ishii H, Tanaka K, Mashio Y, Nakao K, Nakai Y, Udaka F, Imura H. 3,3′5′-Triiodothyronine (reverse T_3) in human cerebrospinal fluid. J Clin Endocrinol Metab **53**:1030–1035, 1981.
26. Assies J, Schellekens APM, Touber JL. Prolactin in human cerebrospinal fluid. J Clin Endocrinol Metab **46**:576–xxx, 1978.
27. Pardridge WM, Mietus LJ. Transport of steroid hormones through the rat blood–brain barrier. J Clin Invest **64**:145–154, 1979.
28. Morimoto S, Nishimura J, Miyauchi A, Takai SI, Okada Y, Onishi T, Fukuo LS, Kumahara Y. Calcitonin in plasma and cerebrospinal fluid from normal subjects and patients with medullary thyroid carcinoma. Possible restriction of calcitonin by the blood–brain barrier. J Clin Endocrinol Metab **55**:594–596, 1982.
29. Pavlinac DM, Lenhard LW, Parthemore JG, Deftos LJ. Immunoreactive calcitonin in human cerebrospinal fluid. J Clin Endocrinol Metab **50**:717–720, 1980.
30. Woods SC, Porte D. Relationship between plasma and cerebrospinal fluid insulin levels of dogs. Amer J Physiol **233**:E331–334, 1978.
31. Owen OE, Reichard GA, Boden G, Shuman CH. Comparative measurements of glucose, beta-hydroxybutyrate, acetoacetate and insulin in blood and cerebrospinal fluid during starvation. Metabolism **23**:7–14, 1974.
32. Shaub C, Bluet-Pajot MT, Szikla G, Lornet C. Distribution of growth hormone and thyroid stimulating hormone in cerebrospinal fluid and pathological compartments of the central nervous system. J Neurol Sci **31**:123–131, 1977.
33. Kruse-Larsen C, Rehfeld JF. Gastrin in human cerebrospinal fluid: Lack of correlation with serum concentrations. Brain Res **176**:189–191, 1979.

Received September 13, 1983. P.S.E.B.M. 1984, Vol. 176.
Accepted April 30, 1984.

PROCEEDINGS OF THE SOCIETY FOR EXPERIMENTAL BIOLOGY AND MEDICINE **176**, 438–442 (1984)

Hypotensive Response to Prostacyclin and 6-keto-PGE_1 following Hepatectomy in the Rat[1] (41895)

JACQUES VAN DAM, ROBERT B. STINGER, JUAN C. PENHOS, PETER W. RAMWELL, AND PETER A. KOT

Department of Physiology and Biophysics, Georgetown University Medical Center, Washington, D.C. 20007

Abstract. Prostacyclin (PGI_2) is metabolized to 6-keto-prostaglandin E_1 (6-keto-PGE_1) which is more stable yet equipotent to PGI_2 in lowering systemic arterial blood pressure in the dog. In this study, partial hepatectomy was performed to determine the role of the liver in the vasodepressor response to both intravenously administered PGI_2 and 6-keto-PGE_1. The magnitude and the duration of systemic hypotensive responses were measured in hepatectomized and sham-operated male Wistar rats following less than maximal, equidepressor doses of PGI_2 (0.3 μg/kg), 6-keto-PGE_1 (1.0 μg/kg), and also PGE_1 (3.0 μg/kg) and PGE_2 (3.0 μg/kg). Hepatectomy did not significantly alter the magnitude of the systemic hypotensive response to any of the prostaglandins tested. This indicates that the liver and hepatic circulation do not contribute significantly to the hypotensive effect of these prostaglandins by alterations of systemic vascular resistance, venous pooling of blood, or the generation of additional vasoactive metabolites as may be expected following administration of these prostaglandins. However, hepatectomy did significantly increase the duration of the hypotensive response to PGI_2 and 6-keto-PGE_1 but not PGE_1 or PGE_2. We conclude that *in vivo,* the liver has a more significant role in PGI_2 and 6-keto-PGE_1 inactivation than in the inactivation of PGE_1 and PGE_2 when administered intravenously. These results also support the relatively greater significance of the lung in the inactivation of PGE_1 and PGE_2 *in vivo.*

Prostacyclin (PGI_2) is presently considered to be one of the principal products of arachidonic acid metabolism of vascular endothelial tissue (1–3). This prostaglandin is a potent inhibitor of platelet aggregation (1–3), a vascular smooth muscle relaxing agent (2, 3), and a systemic hypotensive agent in rats, rabbits (4–6), dogs (7–10), baboons (11), and man (12–14). Prostacyclin is converted to 6-keto-prostaglandin E_1 (6-keto-PGE_1), a more stable metabolite, by 9-hydroxy-prostaglandin dehydrogenase (9-OH PGDH) which is present in the rabbit liver (15, 16) and human platelets (17). Unlike other metabolites of PGI_2, 6-keto-PGE_1 is equipotent to prostacyclin in inhibiting platelet aggregation (15, 17–19) and lowering systemic arterial blood pressure in the dog (20).

The liver is an important site of prostaglandin metabolism and inactivation (21–26) and therefore we evaluated the role of the liver and hepatic circulation on the relative vascular responses to exogenously administered PGI_2, 6-keto-PGE_1, PGE_1, and PGE_2.

Materials and Methods. Male Wistar rats (N = 60) weighing 250–350 g were anesthetized with intraperitoneal sodium pentobarbital (50 mg/kg). A tracheotomy was performed to maintain airway patency. Systemic arterial blood pressure (SAP) was continuously monitored through an indwelling catheter (PE 50) placed in the left common carotid artery. Bolus injections of test compounds were administered through an indwelling catheter (PE 20) placed in the left external jugular vein.

Hepatectomy was performed by the method of Higgins and Anderson (27). Following a midline peritoneal incision, individual liver lobes were ligated and excised. A small fraction of each lobe proximal to the ligature was left *in situ* to maintain the portal circulation. Following each experiment, the remaining fraction of liver tissue was excised and weighed. Total liver weight was determined by adding the weight of the liver excised to perform the hepatectomy to the weight of the fraction of liver tissue which remained *in situ.* Percentage hepatectomy was calculated as (weight of ex-

[1] This work was supported by NHLBI Training Grant HL-07213.

0037-9727/84 $1.50

cised liver/weight of total liver) × 100 and ranged from 65 to 93% with a mean of 81.1 ± 1.5%. Sham operations for the control group consisted of a midline peritoneal incision followed by manipulation of liver lobes. The abdominal incision in both sham-operated and hepatectomized rats was closed in layers with 2-O silk.

Stock solutions of PGI_2 (1 mg/ml) were prepared in 0.1 *M* Tris buffer (pH 9.0). PGE_1, PGE_2, and 6-keto-PGE_1 were prepared in ethanol (1 mg/ml). All solutions were stored at −20°C. On the day of each experiment, stock solutions of PGI_2 were diluted to 10–30 μg/ml with Tris buffer. PGE_1, PGE_2, and 6-keto-PGE_1 were evaporated under nitrogen and resuspended in 0.9% saline to 100 μg/ml, 100 μg/ml, and 10–30 μg/ml, respectively. Varying the concentration of PGI_2 and 6-keto-PGE_1 from 10–30 μg/ml ensured that the volumes administered were consistent and minimal for all doses of the compounds.

Changes in SAP were recorded by a direct writing physiograph (Gould Brush 2200). SAP was allowed to return to control value before subsequent doses of each agent were administered. The time to onset, time to maximal response and duration of the hypotensive response (time required for recovery to 50% of the maximum response) were measured in seconds from the time of prostaglandin injection.

Data are expressed as arithmetic mean ± standard error of the mean and were analyzed using Student's *t* test for either paired or unpaired observations where appropriate. Significance was judged at the $P < 0.05$ level. Linear regression lines were calculated by the method of least squares.

Results. The control values for mean systemic arterial blood pressure in sham-operated and hepatectomized rats were 127.1 ± 3.3 and 117.2 ± 3.5 mm Hg, respectively. Hepatectomy resulted in a lower, although normal baseline blood pressure. Vasodepressor responses were expressed as percentage decrease in order to compare dose–responses between the two groups. Neither the Tris buffer nor the 0.9% saline vehicles used for prostaglandin administration affected resting systemic arterial pressure.

Intravenous administration of PGE_1, PGE_2, PGI_2, and 6-keto-PGE_1 into nonhepatectomized rats decreased systemic arterial blood pressure in a dose-dependent manner (Fig. 1). The responses to PGE_1 and PGE_2 were similar over the dose range studied. Both PGI_2 and 6-keto-PGE_1 were significantly more potent systemic hypotensive agents than either PGE_1 or PGE_2 in the doses used. The dose–response curves for PGI_2 and 6-keto-PGE_1 do not significantly deviate from parallelism.

From these data, approximately equidepressor doses of PGE_1 (3.0 μg/kg), PGE_2 (3.0 μg/kg), PGI_2 (0.3 μg/kg), and 6-keto-PGE_1 (1.0 μg/kg), which were demonstrated to be less than maximal doses in sham-operated rats, were administered to both sham-operated and hepatectomized rats in order to determine the effect of hepatectomy on the systemic hypotensive action of these prostanoids. The selected doses decreased systemic arterial blood pressure by 25.9 to 31.6%. Hepatectomy did not significantly alter the magnitude of the systemic hypotensive response (Table I) or the time to onset of the hypotensive response.

In sham-operated animals, the time to the maximal vasodepressor response to 6-keto-PGE_1 (27.0 ± 1.3 sec) was significantly longer than that for PGE_1 (17.8 ± 1.0 sec). Similarly, the time to the maximal response to PGE_1 was significantly longer than that for PGE_2 (7.7 ± 0.4 sec). These values were not significantly changed following hepatectomy (Fig. 2). However, the time to the maximal vaso-

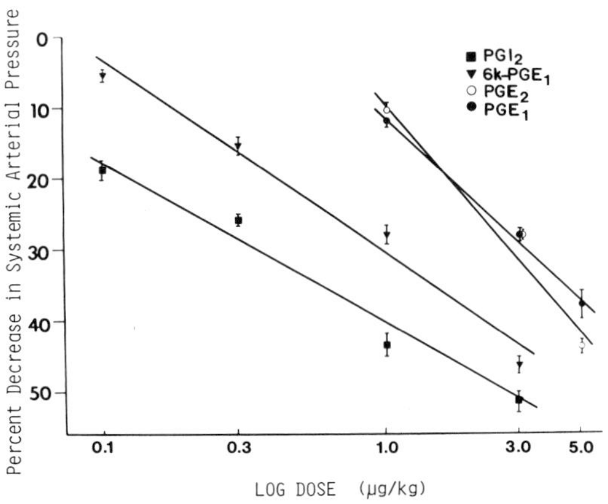

FIG. 1. Percentage decrease in systemic arterial blood pressure produced by intravenous administration of PGI_2 (N = 20); 6-keto-PGE_1 (N = 9); PGE_1 (N = 10); and PGE_2 (N = 12) in sham-operated rats.

TABLE I. PERCENTAGE DECREASE IN SYSTEMIC ARTERIAL PRESSURE PRODUCED BY INTRAVENOUS ADMINISTRATION OF PGE_1, PGE_2, PGI_2, AND 6-KETO-PGE_1 IN SHAM-OPERATED AND HEPATECTOMIZED RATS

	PGE_1 (3.0 μg/kg)	PGE_2 (3.0 μg/kg)	PGI_2 (0.3 μg/kg)	6-keto-PGE_1 (1.0 μg/kg)
Sham-operated	28.1 ± 1.0	28.3 ± 0.8	25.9 ± 0.9	28.3 ± 1.2
N^a	10	12	20	9
Hepatectomized	29.0 ± 0.8	31.6 ± 0.9	27.7 ± 0.9	29.3 ± 0.9
N	8	8	12	8

[a] *N* = number of animals in each group.

depressor response to PGI_2 was significantly increased in the hepatectomized rat.

The duration of the systemic hypotensive response to PGE_1 (51.9 ± 2.3 sec) and PGE_2 (29.8 ± 2.2 sec) was not significantly changed following hepatectomy (Fig. 3). However, the duration of the systemic hypotensive response to both PGI_2 (66.5 ± 3.1 sec) and 6-keto-PGE_1 (64.5 ± 6.4 sec) was significantly increased in the hepatectomized rat (112.4 ± 6.1 sec and 86.2 ± 3.8 sec, respectively). Furthermore, the increase in the duration of action following hepatectomy was greater for PGI_2 than for 6-keto-PGE_1.

Discussion. In this study, hepatectomy increased the duration of the systemic hypotensive response to intravenously administered prostacyclin and 6-keto-PGE_1 but did not significantly affect the response to PGE_1 and PGE_2. Because the magnitude of the hypotensive response was unaffected by hepatectomy but the duration of the hypotensive response was prolonged, we conclude that the liver and hepatic circulation do not contribute significantly to the systemic hypotensive effect of these prostaglandins but inactivate PGI_2 and 6-keto-PGE_1 more than PGE_2 and PGE_1.

Although PGE_1 and PGE_2 activity are reduced more than 70% following a single transit through the isolated perfused liver (23, 32), the role of the liver *in vivo* is negligible in the metabolism of intravenously administered PGE_1 and PGE_2. Removal of the liver in this study did not significantly decrease the magnitude nor increase the duration of action of these prostaglandins. The lung represents the major site of PGE_1 and PGE_2 inactivation and

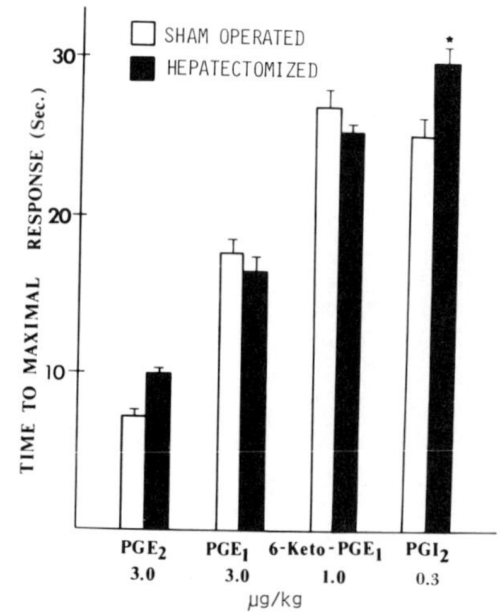

FIG. 2. Time to maximal response (sec) to intravenously administered PGE_2 (N = 20); PGE_1 (N = 18); 6-keto-PGE_1 (N = 32); and PGI_2 (N = 17) in sham-operated and hepatectomized rats. *$P < 0.05$ vs sham-operated rats.

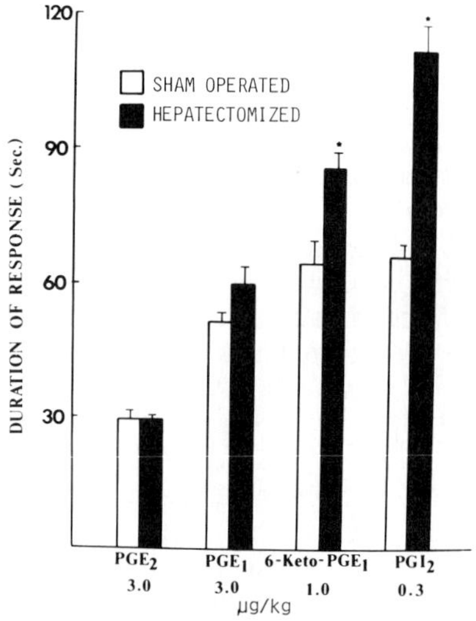

FIG. 3. Duration of response (sec) to intravenously administered PGE_2 (N = 20); PGE_1 (N = 18); 6-keto-PGE_1 (N = 32); and PGI_2 (N = 17) in sham-operated and hepatectomized rats. *$P < 0.05$ vs sham-operated rats.

approximately 90% of the activity of these compounds is removed in a single pass through the pulmonary circulation (9, 30, 32, 33). Therefore, hepatectomy is unlikely to significantly alter the magnitude or duration of the systemic hypotensive response to intravenously administered PGE_1 and PGE_2.

In contrast, prostacyclin and 6-keto-PGE_1 are not inactivated during pulmonary transit (4, 9, 15, 16, 20, 28, 30, 31, 34). The liver therefore receives a large concentration of these compounds following intravenous administration and hepatectomy would be expected to significantly alter the systemic hypotensive response to prostacyclin and 6-keto-PGE_1.

Hepatic conversion of prostacyclin to 6-keto-PGE_1 is reported to account for the 10-fold increase in the dose of prostacyclin required to achieve an equivalent hypotensive response in eviscerated rats when compared to intact rats (28). However, based on the results of our study, hepatectomy did not alter the magnitude of the systemic hypotensive response to PGI_2. We therefore suggest that the alteration in the magnitude of the hypotensive action of PGI_2 following evisceration is due primarily to the removal of the splanchnic circulation and not the liver alone. Prostacyclin has been shown to cause dilatation in the mesenteric vascular bed (10) which may account for part of the hypotensive response to PGI_2.

In summary, the role of the liver in the cardiovascular response to prostacyclin was found to be one of inactivation. Both the time to maximal response and the duration of action of prostacyclin were significantly increased following hepatectomy. The decreased elimination of prostacyclin following removal of the liver indicates the loss of some hepatic factor(s) responsible for the binding or inactivation of this compound. Prostacyclin inactivation occurs in other tissues, but the liver appears to play a significant role in PGI_2 degradation.

Although hepatectomy did not significantly alter the magnitude of the systemic hypotensive response nor increase the time to maximal response to 6-keto-PGE_1, its duration of action was also significantly increased following removal of the liver. The degree to which the blood pressure responses to 6-keto-PGE_1 were affected by hepatectomy suggests that it is less dependent on the liver for inactivation than is prostacyclin.

We want to thank Dr. John C. Rose and Dr. Thomas M. Fitzpatrick for their excellent editorial skills as well as Ellen Costello for her assistance in the preparation of this manuscript. PGI_2, 6-keto-PGE_1, PGE_1, and PGE_2 were generously supplied by the Upjohn Company.

1. Moncada S, Gryglewski R, Bunting S, Vane JR. An enzyme isolated from arteries transforms prostaglandin endoperoxides to an unstable substance that inhibits platelet aggregation. Nature (London) **263**:663–665, 1976.
2. Bunting S, Gryglewski R, Moncada S, Vane JR. Arterial walls generate from prostaglandin endoperoxides a substance (prostaglandin X) which relaxes strips of mesenteric and coeliac arteries and inhibits platelet aggregation. Prostaglandins **12**:897–913, 1976.
3. Raz A, Isakson PC, Minkes MS, Needleman P. Characterization of a novel metabolic pathway of arachidonate in coronary arteries which generates a potent endogenous coronary vasodilator. J Biol Chem **252**:1123–1126, 1977.
4. Armstrong JM, Lattimer N, Moncada S, Vane JR. Comparison of the vasodepressor effects of prostacyclin and 6-oxo-prostaglandin F_1 with those of prostaglandin E_2 in rats and rabbits. Brit J Pharmacol **62**:125–130, 1978.
5. Pinelis VG, Markov CM. Effects of prostacyclin on the hemodynamics of the rat. In: Samuelsson B, Ramwell PW, Paoletti R, eds. Advances in Prostaglandin and Thromboxane Research. New York, Raven Press, Vol 7:pp691–693, 1980.
6. Sutter DM, Weeks JR. An antihypertensive effect of prostacyclin. In: Samuelsson B, Ramwell PW, Paoletti R, eds. Advances in Prostaglandin and Thromboxane Research. New York, Raven Press, Vol 7:pp789–790, 1980.
7. Armstrong JM, Chapple D, Dusting GJ, Hughes R, Moncada S, Vane JR. Cardiovascular actions of prostacyclin (PGI_2) in chloralose anesthetized dogs. Brit J Pharmacol **61**:136P, 1977.
8. Fitzpatrick TM, Alter I, Corey EJ, Ramwell PW, Rose JC, Kot PA. Cardiovascular responses to PGI_2 (prostacyclin) in the dog. Circ Res **42**:192–194, 1978.
9. Waldman HM, Alter I, Kot PA, Rose JC, Ramwell PW. Effect of lung transit on systemic depressor responses to arachidonic acid and prostacyclin in dogs. J Pharmacol Exp Ther **204**:289–293, 1978.
10. Feigen LP, Chapnick BM, Hyman AL, King L, Marascallo B, Kadowitz PJ. Peripheral vasodilator effects of prostaglandins: Comparison of 6-keto-prostaglandin E_1 with prostacyclin and escape from prostaglandin E_2 in the mesenteric vascular bed. J Pharmacol Exp Ther **214**:528–534, 1980.

11. Karim SMM, Adaikan PG. Some pharmacological studies with prostacyclin in baboon and man. In: Vane JR, Bergstrom S, eds. Prostacyclin. New York, Raven Press, pp419–433, 1979.
12. Szczeklik A, Gryglewski RJ. Actions of prostacyclin in man. In: Vane JR, Bergstrom S, eds. Prostacyclin. New York, Raven Press, pp393–407, 1979.
13. O'Grady J, Warrington S, Moti MJ, Bunting S, Flower R, Fowle ASE, Higgs EA, Moncada S. Effect of intravenous prostacyclin infusions in healthy volunteers: Some preliminary observations. In: Vane JR, Bergstrom S, eds. Prostacyclin. New York, Raven Press, pp409–417, 1979.
14. Fitzgerald GA, Friedman LA, Miyamori I, O'Grady J, Lewis PJ. A double blind placebo controlled crossover study of prostacyclin in man. Life Sci **25**:665–672, 1979.
15. Wong PY-K, Malik KU, Desiderio DM, McGiff JC, Sun FF. Hepatic metabolism of prostacyclin (PGI_2) in the rabbit: Formation of a potent novel inhibitor of platelet aggregation. Biochem Biophys Res Commun **93**:486–494, 1980.
16. Wong PY-K, Lee WH, Quilley CP, McGiff JC. Metabolism of prostacyclin: Formation of an active metabolite in the liver. Fed Proc **40**:2001–2004, 1981.
17. Wong PY-K, Lee WH, Chao PH-W, Reiss RF, McGiff JC. Metabolism of prostacyclin by 9-hydroxy-prostaglandin dehydrogenase in human platelets: formation of a potent inhibitor of platelet aggregation and enzyme purification. J Biol Chem **255**:9021–9024, 1980.
18. Lee WH, McGiff JC, Householder RW, Sun FF, Wong PY-K. Inhibition of platelet aggregation by 6-keto-prostaglandin E_1 (6kPGE_1), a metabolite of 6-keto-prostaglandin $F_{1\alpha}$ (6-k$PGF_{1\alpha}$). Fed Proc **38**:419, 1979.
19. Wong PY-K, McGiff JC, Sun FF, Lee WH. 6-keto-prostaglandin E_1 inhibits the aggregation of human platelets. Eur J Pharmacol **60**:245–248, 1979.
20. Van Dam J, Fitzpatrick TM, Friedman LS, Ramwell PW, Rose JC, Kot PA. Cardiovascular responses to 6-keto-prostaglandin E_1 in the dog. Proc Soc Exp Biol Med **166**:76–79, 1981.
21. Hamberg M. Metabolism of prostaglandin in rat liver mitochondria. Eur J Biochem **6**:135–146, 1968.
22. Dawson W, Ramwell PW, Shaw JE. Metabolism of prostaglandins by the rat isolated liver. Brit J Pharmacol **34**:668p–669 p, 1968.
23. Dawson W, Jessup SJ, McDonald-Gibson W, Ramwell PW, Shaw JE. Prostaglandin uptake and metabolism by the perfused rat liver. Brit J Pharmacol **39**:585–598, 1970.
24. Bartolini G, Meringolo C, Orlandi M, Tomasi V. Biosynthesis of prostaglandins in parenchymal and nonparenchymal rat liver cells. Biochim Biophys Acta **530**:325–332, 1978.
25. Tomasi V, Merlingolo C, Bartolini G, Orlandi M. Biosynthesis of prostacyclin in rat liver endothelial cells and its control by prostaglandin E_2. Nature (London) **273**:670–671, 1978.
26. Tomasi V, Bartolini G, Orlandi M, Meringolo C, Barnabe O. Mechanism of action and biological significance of prostaglandin E_2 and prostacyclin in the liver. In: Hessel LW, Krans HMJ, eds. Lipoprotein Metabolism and Endocrine Regulation. Amsterdam, North-Holland/Elsevier, pp279–287, 1979.
27. Higgins GM, Anderson RM. Experimental pathology of the liver: Restoration of the liver of the white rat following partial surgical removal. Arch Pathol **12**:186–202, 1931.
28. Quilley CP, Wong PY-K, McGiff JC. Hypotensive and renovascular actions of 6-keto-prostaglandin E_1, a metabolite of prostacyclin. Eur J Pharmacol **57**:273–276, 1979.
29. Stinger RB, Fitzpatrick TM, Van Dam J, Ramwell PW, Kot PA. Selective antagonism of the systemic vasodepressor response to PGE_1 by d,l-11,15-bisdeoxy PGE_1. Prostaglandins **19**:213–220, 1980.
30. Dusting GJ, Moncada S, Vane Jr. Disappearance of prostacyclin (PGI_2) in the circulation of the dog. Proc BPS **62**:414p–415p, 1978.
31. Dusting GJ, Moncada S, Vane JR. Recirculation of prostacyclin (PGI_2) in the dog. Brit J Pharmacol **64**:315–329, 1978.
32. Ferreira SH, Vane JR. Prostaglandins: Their disappearance from and release into the circulation. Nature (London) **216**:868–873, 1967.
33. Gerkins JF, Friesinger GC, Branch RA, Shand DG, Gerber JG. A comparison of the pulmonary, renal and hepatic extractions of PGI_2, and PGE_2—PGI_2 a potential circulating hormone. Life Sci **22**:1837–1841, 1978.
34. Hyman AL, Kadowitz PJ. Vasodilator actions of prostaglandin 6-keto-PGE_1 in the pulmonary vascular bed. J Pharmacol Exp Ther **213**:468–472, 1980.

Received December 12, 1983. P.S.E.B.M. 1984. Vol. 176.
Accepted April 30, 1984.

PROCEEDINGS OF THE SOCIETY FOR EXPERIMENTAL BIOLOGY AND MEDICINE **176**, 443–451 (1984)

Depression of *in Vivo* Clearance Function of Hepatic Macrophage Complement Receptors following Thermal Injury[1] (41896)

BRIAN G. CUDDY, DANIEL J. LOEGERING, AND FRANK A. BLUMENSTOCK

Department of Physiology, Neil Hellman Medical Research Building, Albany Medical College of Union University, Albany, New York 12208

Abstract. Previous studies have implicated a role for impaired hepatic macrophage blood clearance function in the increased susceptibility to infection caused by experimental thermal injury. The present study evaluated *in vivo* hepatic macrophage complement receptor clearance function as a possible factor contributing to impaired hepatic clearance after thermal injury. Rat erythrocytes treated with anti-erythrocyte serum (EA) were used as the test particle in rats. EA were rapidly removed from the circulation primarily by the liver and hepatic uptake of EA was greatly depressed in animals rendered C3 deficient by treatment with cobra venom factor. Thermal injury caused a large depression in the hepatic uptake of EA. It was shown that the depression in the binding of EA to hepatic macrophages was not due to decreased hepatic blood flow, decreased serum complement levels, or increased fluid phase C3b. Also, the depression of the hepatic uptake of EA incubated with serum prior to injection (EAC) was not different from that of EA after thermal injury. On this basis it was concluded that the impairment in binding of EA to the macrophages was at the cellular level and represented a depression in complement receptor clearance function. Additional studies showed that the injection of erythrocyte stroma, as a model of intravascular hemolysis, also depressed *in vivo* hepatic macrophage complement receptor clearance function. This latter finding suggests that the intravascular hemolysis caused by thermal injury may contribute to the depression of macrophage receptor function. The depression of hepatic macrophage complement receptor clearance function may contribute to the impaired bacterial clearance and increased susceptibility to infection following experimental thermal injury.

Erythrocytes coated with antibody and/or complement have been used extensively *in vitro* to demonstrate the presence and function of Fc and C3b receptors on the surface of macrophages (1). Similarly coated syngeneic erythrocytes have also been used *in vivo* to assess macrophage receptor function (2–7). Erythrocytes coated with C3b are rapidly removed from the blood primarily by binding to hepatic complement receptors (2–4). However, since most of these erythrocytes are not phagocytized, the action of C3b inactivator can release them back into the blood. Erythrocytes coated with enough IgG to activate complement are also rapidly cleared from the blood by binding to hepatic complement receptors, but subsequently interact with Fc receptors and are phagocytized. Erythrocytes coated with insufficient IgG to activate complement are removed from the blood primarily by Fc receptors on splenic macrophages (3). Therefore, these test particles can be used to evaluate hepatic complement or splenic Fc receptor clearance function.

Thermal injury is well known to cause a severe depression of host defense in animals (8, 9). The increased susceptibility to infection was shown to be associated with depressed hepatic clearance and killing of bacteria (10, 11). Other studies have shown that the blood clearance of test particles that bind to undefined receptors on hepatic macrophages was depressed following thermal injury (12–14). It was also shown that thermal injury depressed the *in vitro* phagocytosis of yeast cells by alveolar and peritoneal macrophages (15). The present study extended these observations by evaluating *in vivo* hepatic complement receptor clearance function after experimental thermal injury. Antibody-treated erythrocytes (EA) that activated complement were used as the test particle. The effect of depressed complement levels and hepatic blood flow on the hepatic binding of the EA was determined.

[1] This work was supported by NIH Research Grant GM-26102.

0037-9727/84 $1.50

Additionally, the effect of intravascular hemolysis, as modeled by the injection of erythrocyte stroma, on hepatic complement receptor clearance function was determined. This latter experiment was carried out because previous studies have shown that the intravascular hemolysis caused by thermal injury may contribute to the depression of hepatic clearance and host defense caused by this form of injury (12, 16, 17).

Methods. *Preparation of antisera-treated erythrocytes (EA).* Inbred, male Sprague-Dawley rats weighing 200–250 g were used for all experiments. Blood was collected in ACD (USP-B) and the erythrocytes (E) were washed three times in phosphate buffered saline (PBS, 0.9% NaCl, and 5 m*M* phosphate buffer, pH 7.4). E were labeled with ^{51}Cr and treated with rabbit anti-rat red blood cell antisera. Antisera were obtained from US Biochemical Corporation or from New Zealand white rabbits that had received 15×10^{10} rat E in six injections (half of each injection was given ip and half iv) over 2 weeks. For antisera treatment, packed E were diluted to a concentration of 2×10^9/ml in PBS containing 1% gelatin. The heat-inactivated antisera was diluted 1:100 in a volume of PBS–gelatin equal to the volume of E suspension and then added slowly (3 min) to the E with constant gentle stirring. The mixture was incubated at 37°C for 30 min and the antisera-treated erythrocytes (EA) were washed twice in PBS. Clearance characteristics of EA were unchanged for 24 hr after preparation, and in the present study EA were used 18–24 hr after preparation. There was some variation in the hepatic uptake of different preparations of EA in controls, therefore each experiment was completed with a single preparation of EA. The possible effect of gelatin in the solution used to prepare EA on the clearance characteristics of EA was determined by incubating E in PBS or gelatin–PBS exactly as with EA preparation except that antisera was not added. The clearance of these E was evaluated in control rats.

Additional experiments were carried out using E treated with IgG (EIgG) or IgM (EIgM) fractions of red blood cell antiserum. The IgG and IgM fractions were separated using gel filtration (Sephacryl 200) and verified by immunodiffusion against appropriate antibodies. Small amounts of IgG present in the IgM fraction were removed with protein A.

Clearance of EA from the blood. Animals were anesthetized with sodium pentobarbital (30 mg/kg iv) and blood samples were taken from a cannulated carotid artery. E and EA were injected at a dose of 2.9×10^8/100 g. In an initial study, blood radioactivity was monitored over 2 hr and in separate groups of animals localization of E or EA in the liver, spleen, and lungs was determined at 1, 10, and 120 min after injection. In all subsequent experiments, blood radioactivity was followed for 10 min and organ localization was determined 10 min after injection. Organ localization data were expressed as the percentage of the injected dose per organ (%ID/organ). Body weights of control and experimental animals were never significantly different and none of the interventions caused a change in liver weight.

Effect of thermal injury on the clearance of EA. Thermal injury consisted of a 30-sec scald in 90°C water on the dorsum under ether anesthesia. The burn involved 26–28% of the body surface area (18). Sterile saline was given ip (10% body wt at the time of injury. This fluid therapy reduced 24-hr mortality from 80% to less than 10% with this injury model. EA clearance was determined 30 min or 3 hr after injury.

Effect of erythrocyte stroma on the clearance of EA. Erythrocyte stroma was injected to simulate intravascular hemolysis in otherwise normal animals. Erythrocyte stroma was prepared from lysed rat erythrocytes as previously described (17). Stroma was pelleted at 1000*g*, suspended in an equal volume of PBS and injected at a dose of 0.5 ml/100 g. Clearance of EA was determined 30 min after injection of the stroma.

Effect of decreased hepatic blood flow on the clearance of EA. Since the liver is the principal organ for the clearance of EA a sufficient decrease in hepatic blood flow could decrease the clearance of EA (19). Hepatic blood flow was measured using the fractional clearance technique (20). Gelatinized lipid emulsion was used as the test particle and was injected at a dose of 0.5 mg/100 g (21). At this dose, the rate-limiting factor in the clearance of this test particle is hepatic blood flow and not hepatic phagocytic function (21). Blood samples were taken every 30 sec for 3 min from a cannulated artery in anesthetized animals. The clearance rate constant which is the proportion of the blood volume cleared of the test particle per min was multiplied by the blood volume to give the hepatic blood flow. Blood volume was estimated by extrapolating the clearance line to zero time and assuming even distribution of the test particle throughout the vascular compartment.

Hepatic blood flow was decreased in normal animals by acute hemorrhage. Mean arterial blood pressure was reduced to 35 mm Hg over 2–3 min by withdrawing 1-ml blood every 30 sec. Hepatic blood flow or EA clearance was determined beginning 5 min after the start of blood withdrawal. Blood pressure was monitored during EA clearance and additional blood was removed or saline injected to maintain blood pressure at 35 mm Hg. Hepatic blood flow was also measured after thermal injury and injection of erythrocyte stroma.

Effect of decreased complement levels on the clearance of EA. Complement levels were depressed by the injection of purified cobra venom factor (CVF). CVF was injected ip at doses of 20, 2, and 1 units/100 g 18 hr prior to the determination of CH_{50} and C3 levels as well as the clearance of EA. CH_{50} levels were determined using the method of Mayer (22) and C3 was determined with the radial immunodiffusion technique using rabbit anti-rat C3 IgG (US Biochemical) (23). Complement levels were also determined following thermal injury and the injection of erythrocyte stroma.

In order to further delineate the role of complement in the clearance of EA following thermal injury, EA incubated in serum prior to injection (EAC) were used as the test particle. Immediately after preparation, EA were incubated in fresh rat serum (1×10^9 EA/ml) for 10 min at 37°C. The EAC were washed twice and used within 2 hr. EAC but not EA showed strong agglutination in the presence of rabbit anti-rat C3 IgG (US Biochemical). Clearance of EA and EAC was determined 3 hr after thermal injury. A single preparation of EA was used for this experiment.

In order to determine if any fluid phase C3b was present in the blood following thermal injury or injection of erythrocyte stroma or injection of CVF plasma samples from these animals were analyzed by crossed immunoelectrophoresis against rabbit anti-rat C3 IgG (US Biochemical). Fresh plasma samples collected in disodium EDTA were used and the electrophoresis was carried out with Tris–tricine buffer containing 5 m*M* disodium EDTA.

Interaction of EA with serum fibronectin. The potential interaction of EA with serum fibronectin was evaluated by determining if fibronectin was depleted from serum following incubation with EA. E or EA were incubated in duplicate samples of rat serum at concentrations of 1.2×10^7, 1.2×10^8, and 1.2×10^9 EA/ml serum for 15 min at 37°C. The EA were then removed from the serum and the fibronectin concentration was determined using the electroimmunoassay method (24).

Statistical analysis. The Student's *t* test was used for two sample comparisons and a single- or two-factor analysis of variance was used for multiple-sample comparisons. The Neuman–Keul test was used with the analysis of variance. The confidence level was placed at 95% for all experiments.

Results. *Clearance of EA from the blood of normal animals.* EA were rapidly removed from the blood during the first 10 min after injection (Fig. 1). Clearance half-time was not

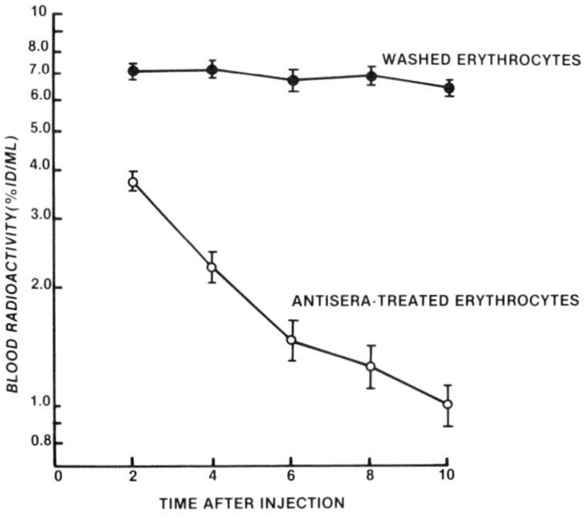

FIG. 1. Blood levels of washed erythrocytes and antisera-treated erythrocytes over 10 min after injection. Values are expressed as the percentage of the injected dose (%ID) per ml blood and are the means ± SE with six animals per group.

calculated because the clearance of EA from the blood was not monoexponential. Between 10 and 120 min after injection, blood levels of EA decreased progressively but at a much slower rate (data not shown). Hepatic localization of EA increased rapidly during the first 10 min after injection but had not increased further at 120 min (Fig. 2). Hepatic uptake accounted for most of the clearance of EA with the spleen and lungs making much smaller contributions. Erythrocytes (E) not treated with antisera were removed from the blood slowly and localization in the liver, spleen, and lungs was 2.18 ± 0.12, 0.90 ± 0.11, and 0.71 ± 0.12% injected dose (ID)/organ, respectively, at 10 min after injection. Organ localization of E incubated in PBS or gelatin–PBS were within 1%ID/organ of each other and none were higher than the localization of nonincubated E. Mean recovery of injected radioactivity in the liver, spleen, lungs, and blood (assuming 6% body wt blood volume) was 89–110% for all experiments. Radioactivity present in the plasma at 10 min after injection was less than 4%ID indicating that there was little intravascular lysis of the EA. Since most of the hepatic uptake of EA had occurred by 10 min after injection, organ localization of EA was determined at this point in all subsequent experiments.

E treated with an equal titer of the IgG fraction of anti-erythrocyte serum had virtually identical blood clearance and organ localization characteristics as EA in normal animals. E treated with the IgM fraction of the antiserum showed similar initial blood clearance and organ localization characteristics up to 10 min after injection (hepatic localization was 78.9 ± 4.1%ID at 10 min). However, thereafter the EIgM slowly returned to the circulation and by 120 min after injection hepatic localization was 11.3 ± 0.9%ID.

Effect of thermal injury on the clearance of EA. Hepatic uptake of EA was depressed 19% at 30 min and 42% at 3 hr after injury (Fig. 3). Splenic localization was depressed and pulmonary localization was increased at both times after injury. Organ localization of EA

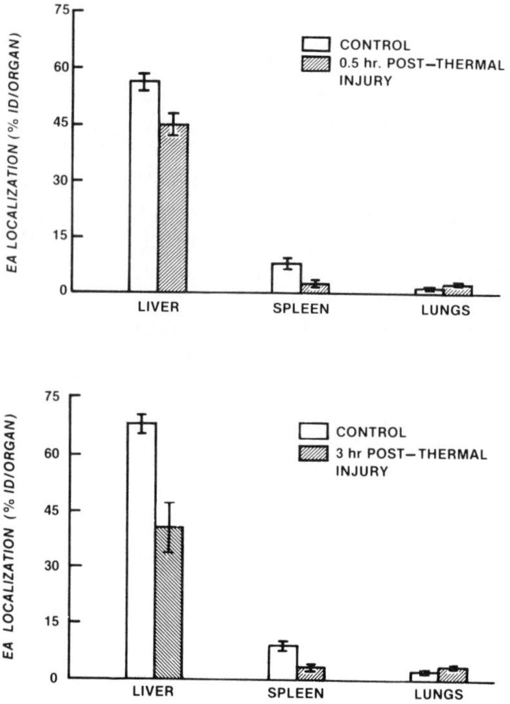

FIG. 3. Effect of thermal injury on the organ localization of antisera-treated erythrocytes (EA). Thermal injury was induced under anesthesia 0.5 hr (upper panel) or 3 hr (lower panel) before the injection of EA ($2.9 \times 10^8/100$ g). Organ localization of EA was determined 10 min after injection and is expressed as the percentage of the injected dose (%ID) per organ. There was a significant ($P < 0.05$) decrease in liver and spleen localization and an increase in lung localization of EA at both time points after injury. Values are the means ± SE with six animals per group.

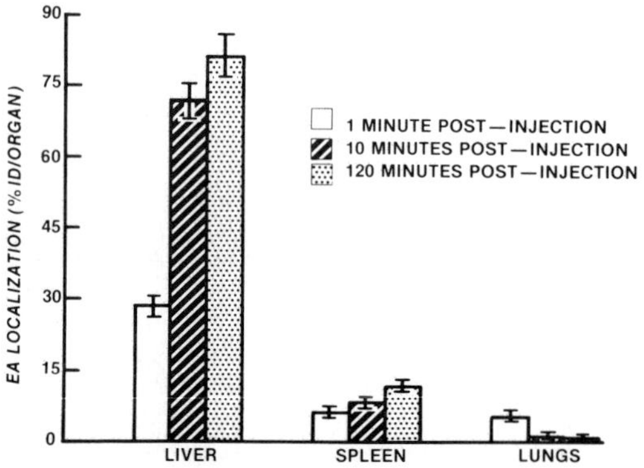

FIG. 2. Organ localization of antisera-treated erythrocytes (EA) at 1, 10, and 120 min after injection. EA were injected at a dose of $2.9 \times 10^8/100$ g and the data is expressed as the percentage of the injected dose (%ID) per organ. There were significant differences ($P < 0.05$) between the 1- and 10-min values for the liver and lungs. Values are the means ± SE with six animals per group.

TABLE I. EFFECT OF ERYTHROCYTE STROMA ON THE ORGAN LOCALIZATION OF ANTISERA-TREATED ERYTHROCYTES (EA)[a]

	Liver (%ID/organ)	Spleen (%ID/organ)	Lungs (%ID/organ)
Control	49.43 ± 4.86	9.73 ± 0.82	2.15 ± 0.15
Erythrocyte stroma	24.39* ± 4.07	4.29* ± 1.41	3.48* ± 0.44

[a] EA were injected 30 min after the injection of erythrocyte stroma (0.5 ml/100 g). Organ localization of EA (2.9 × 10^8/100 g) was determined 10 min after injection and is expressed as the percentage of the injected dose per organ. Values are the means ± SE with six animals per group.

* $P < 0.05$.

was unchanged in control animals that received the same fluid therapy given to the injured animals. Blood levels of EA at 10 min after injection tended to be higher in injured animals than in controls (3 hr postinjury: 51.6 ± 12.0%ID, control: 22.1 ± 5.5%ID; 30 min postinjury: 50.2 ± 4.8%ID, control: 37.7 ± 4.7%ID). Blood volume of injured animals was assumed to be decreased 24% as previously demonstrated for this type of injury (12). Intravascular lysis of EA was not increased in injured animals.

Hepatic localization of EIgG and EIgM was depressed 44.4% and 40.8%, respectively, at 3 hr after thermal injury.

Effect of erythrocyte stroma on the clearance of EA. Erythrocyte stroma caused a 51% decrease in the hepatic uptake of EA (Table I). Splenic localization was decreased and pulmonary localization was increased. Blood levels of EA in animals receiving stroma were increased at 10 min after EA injection reflecting the lower hepatic and splenic uptake of EA.

Effect of decreased hepatic blood flow on the clearance of EA. Lowering arterial blood pressure to 35 mm Hg by acute hemorrhage did not depress the hepatic uptake of EA (Fig. 4). Splenic localization was depressed and pulmonary localization was increased. Acute hemorrhage depressed hepatic blood flow to 38% of control (Table II). This was similar to the depression observed at 30 min and 3 hr after thermal injury. Erythrocyte stroma and CVF did not affect hepatic blood flow. Since acute hemorrhage caused a depression in hepatic blood flow that was at least as great as that caused by the other experimental interventions and did not affect the hepatic uptake

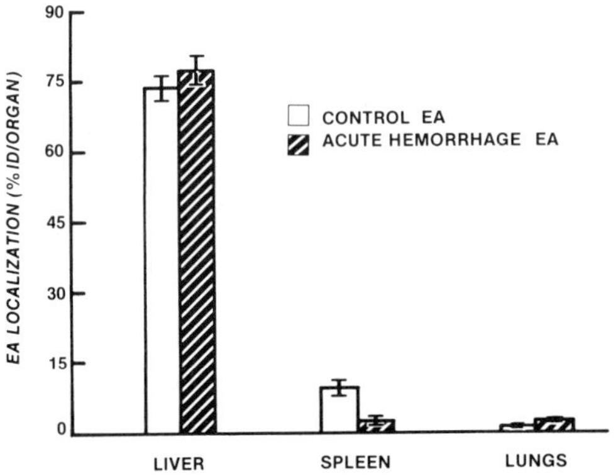

FIG. 4. Effect of acute hemorrhage on the organ localization of antisera-treated erythrocytes (EA). Mean arterial blood pressure was lowered to 35 mm Hg within 2–3 min. EA (2.9 × 10^8/100 g) were injected 5 min after the start of hemorrhage. Organ localization of EA was determined 10 min after injection. Blood pressure was monitored and maintained at 35 mm Hg during the 10 min EA clearance period. There was a significant ($P < 0.05$) decrease in splenic localization and increase in lung localization of EA. Values are expressed as the percentage injected dose (%ID) per organ and are the means ± SE with six animals per group.

TABLE II. CHANGES IN HEPATIC BLOOD FLOW AFTER ACUTE HEMORRHAGE, THERMAL INJURY, INJECTION OF ERYTHROCYTE STROMA, AND INJECTION OF COBRA VENOM FACTOR[a]

	Hepatic blood flow (ml/min/g)	Percentage of control value
Control	2.14 ± 0.12	—
Acute hemorrhage	0.82 ± 0.07*	38.3 ± 3.9
Thermal injury (30 min postinjury)	0.77 ± 0.08*	35.9 ± 2.0
Thermal injury (3 hr postinjury)	0.79 ± 0.07*	37.0 ± 3.8
Erythrocyte stroma (0.5 ml/100 g)	2.03 ± 0.21	94.9 ± 11.2
Cobra venom factor (20 units/100 g)	1.84 ± 0.18	86.0 ± 9.7

[a] Hepatic blood flow was determined using the fractional clearance technique 30 min after the injection of erythrocyte stroma, and 18 hr after cobra venom factor. Hemorrhaged animals were studied beginning 5 min after the mean arterial blood pressure was lowered to 35 mm Hg. Values are the means ± SE with 12 animals in the control group and 6 animals per experimental group.

* $P < 0.05$ compared with control group.

TABLE III. CHANGES IN COMPLEMENT LEVELS AFTER THE INJECTION OF PURIFIED COBRA VENOM FACTOR, THERMAL INJURY, AND INJECTION OF ERYTHROCYTE STROMA[a]

	C3	CH_{50}
Cobra venom factor		
20 units/100 g	8.8 ± 1.5*	<10
2 units/100 g	16.3 ± 0.9*	<10
1 unit/100 g	57.6 ± 8.4*	43.1 ± 9.1*
Thermal injury		
30 min postinjury	82.3 ± 5.1*	62.9 ± 6.2*
3 hr postinjury	55.0 ± 4.0*	37.2 ± 5.3*
Erythrocyte stroma	76.8 ± 3.7*	72.2 ± 9.5*

[a] Cobra venom factor was injected ip 18 hr prior to the measurement of serum C3 and CH_{50} levels. Erythrocyte stroma was injected (0.5 ml/100 g) 30 min prior to the determination of complement levels. Values are expressed as percentage of control and are the means ± SE with six animals per group.

* $P < 0.05$.

of EA, depression of hepatic blood flow did not contribute to the depression of hepatic uptake of EA under the experimental conditions studied.

Effect of decreased complement levels on the clearance of EA. Complement C3 and CH_{50} levels following the injection of CVF, thermal injury, and injection of particulate material are shown in Table III. The 20-unit/100 g dose of CVF was effective in producing very low levels of C3, and the 1-unit/100 g dose produced complement levels that were lower than or similar to those caused by the other experimental interventions. Following thermal injury, the levels at 3 hr were lower than at 30 min. Erythrocyte stroma caused a 35% decrease in CH_{50} and a 10% decrease in C3 levels.

The 20-unit/100 g dose of CVF caused a 61% depression in the hepatic uptake of EA, the 2-unit/100 g dose caused a 34% depression, and the 1-unit/100 g dose did not depress the hepatic uptake of EA (Table IV). Splenic and pulmonary localization of EA were not affected by CVF. Thus, the 1-unit/100 g dose of CVF did not depress the hepatic uptake of EA but did depress C3 and CH_{50} levels at least as much as thermal injury or injection of erythrocyte stroma. These results indicate that the depression in complement levels caused by thermal injury or injection of erythrocyte stroma were not great enough to cause the depression in the hepatic uptake of EA.

EA incubated in serum prior to injection (EAC) were used to evaluate macrophage complement receptor clearance function after thermal injury (Table V). In controls EAC showed a greater hepatic uptake ($P < 0.05$) and a smaller splenic uptake ($P < 0.05$) than EA. At 3 hr after thermal injury, hepatic and splenic uptake of EAC was depressed and pulmonary localization was increased. The absolute magnitude of changes in organ localization of EA and EAC following thermal injury were not different (two-factor analysis of variance). Therefore, the depression in hepatic uptake of EA following thermal injury was not due to inadequate *in vivo* opsonization of the EA.

The results of the crossed immunoelectrophoresis against anti-rat C3 are shown in Fig. 5. The electrophoretic pattern of plasma from animals subjected to thermal injury was identical to that of plasma from control animals,

TABLE IV. EFFECT OF PURIFIED COBRA VENOM FACTOR ON THE ORGAN LOCALIZATION OF ANTISERA-TREATED ERYTHROCYTES (EA)[a]

	Liver (%ID/organ)	Spleen (%ID/organ)	Lungs (%ID/organ)
Control	61.28 ± 3.56	8.13 ± 1.43	2.09 ± 0.26
Cobra venom factor (20 units/100 g)	23.87 ± 1.31*	8.28 ± 1.02	2.26 ± 0.17
Control	67.84 ± 4.19	8.85 ± 0.59	0.60 ± 0.09
Cobra venom factor (2.0 units/100 g)	44.63 ± 8.71*	7.83 ± 0.32	0.89 ± 0.15
Control	70.04 ± 2.21	8.19 ± 0.52	3.25 ± 0.61
Cobra venom factor (1.0 unit/100 g)	66.21 ± 3.06	7.30 ± 0.43	3.00 ± 0.14

[a] Clearance of EA was determined beginning 18 hr after ip injection of cobra venom factor. Organ localization of EA (2.9×10^8/100 g) was determined 10 min after injection and is expressed as the percentage of the injected dose per total organ. Values are means ± SE with six animals per group.

* $P < 0.05$ compared to the respective control group.

TABLE V. EFFECT OF THERMAL INJURY ON THE ORGAN LOCALIZATION OF ANTISERA-TREATED ERYTHROCYTES (EA) AND EA INCUBATED IN SERUM PRIOR TO INJECTION (EAC)[a]

	Liver (%ID/organ)	Spleen (%ID/organ)	Lungs (%ID/organ)
Control (EA)	67.96 ± 2.77	10.27 ± 1.29	1.26 ± 0.14
Thermal injury (EA)	46.73 ± 5.69*	2.72 ± 0.38*	3.40 ± 0.61*
Control (EAC)	95.19 ± 3.57	7.33 ± 0.58	1.14 ± 0.11
Thermal injury (EAC)	79.72 ± 4.51*	3.33 ± 0.43*	2.40 ± 0.21*

[a] EA or EAC were injected at a dose of 2.9×10^8/100 g 3 hr after thermal injury. Organ localization was determined 10 min after EA or EAC injection and is expressed as the percentage of the injected dose (%ID) per organ. Values are the means ± SE with six animals per group.

* $P < 0.05$ compared with the respective control.

except that the total amount of C3 was less in the plasma from the injured animals. At 30 min after the injection of 0.5 ml/100 g of erythrocyte stroma there was a small additional peak in the electrophoretic pattern suggesting that some fluid phase C3b was present. Serum treated *in vitro* with CVF (0.6 unit/ml, incubated at 37°C for 30 min) was included as a positive control (Fig. 5). This concentration of CVF is similar to the concentration that would be present immediately following the iv injection of 2 units CVF/100 g. Crossed immunoelectrophoresis of plasma samples taken 18 hr after the ip injection of 20, 2, or 1 unit CVF/100 g showed no indication that any fluid-phase C3b was present (data not shown).

Interaction of EA with serum fibronectin. Following the incubation of EA in serum, the serum fibronectin concentration was decreased 10% with 1.2×10^7 EA/ml serum, 0% with 1.2×10^8 EA/ml, and 6% with 1.2×10^9 EA/ml. The lowest concentration of EA used was that which would be expected in the blood immediately following the injection of 2.9 $\times 10^8$ EA/100 g.

Discussion. The EA employed in the present study were rapidly removed from the blood by the liver with much smaller amounts localized in the spleen and lungs. Depletion of C3 with CVF caused a substantial reduction in the hepatic uptake of EA, and we have previously demonstrated that most of this effect of CVF can be reversed by incubation of the EA in serum prior to injection (25). Additionally, we have shown that CVF did not depress the hepatic uptake another test particle (formalinized sheep red blood cells) (17). Treatment of E with the IgG fraction of the antisera employed resulted in EIgG with clearance characteristics that were very similar to those of the EA. E treated with the IgM fraction were rapidly taken up by the liver but subsequently released. These findings were consistent with previous studies that have demonstrated that the initial hepatic uptake of antibody-coated E is due to interaction with complement receptors and that phagocytosis

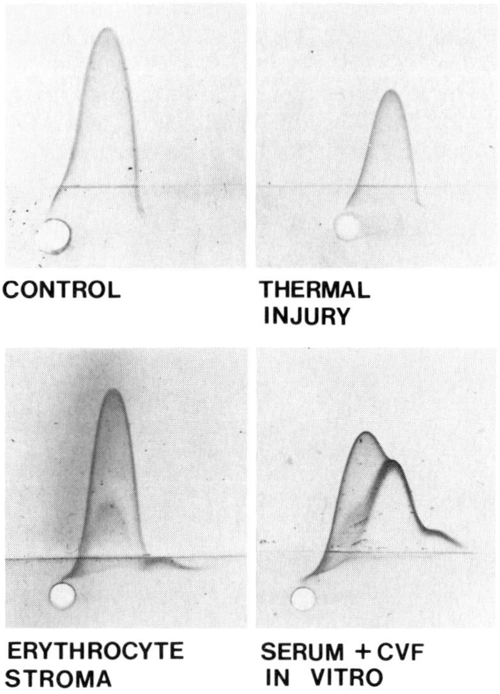

FIG. 5. Representative crossed immunoelectrophoresis patterns of plasma or serum from rats against rabbit anti-rat C3. Plasma samples were obtained from controls, 3 hr after thermal injury, or 30 min after injection of 0.5 ml/100 g erythrocyte stroma. Serum from a control animal was incubated with 0.6 unit CVF/ml for 30 min at 37°C.

requires the presence of IgG and if IgG is not present C3b inactivator will release the E back into the blood (2–4). Therefore, the rapid hepatic uptake of the EA employed in the present study was probably mediated by EA binding C3b in the blood and then interacting with complement receptors on the hepatic macrophages. The lack of lysis of the EA in the blood was probably due to the low lytic activity of complement for homologous erythrocytes (26). *In vitro* studies did not implicate a role for serum fibronectin in the clearance of EA.

Thermal injury caused a depression in the hepatic uptake of EA. Lowering hepatic blood flow by acute hemorrhage and depression of complement with CVF to levels similar to those caused by thermal injury did not affect the hepatic uptake of EA. Therefore, the reduction in hepatic uptake of EA was not due to the depression in hepatic blood flow or complement levels caused by the injury. Additionally, the failure to detect any fluid phase C3b in plasma after thermal injury makes it unlikely that the depressed EA clearance was due to competition of fluid phase C3b for the receptors. Finally, the depression of the hepatic uptake of preopsonized EA (EAC) was not different from that of EA after thermal injury. On this basis it is concluded that the depression in hepatic uptake of EA after thermal injury was at the level of binding to the hepatic macrophages and represented a depression in complement receptor clearance function. The methods employed did not allow the determination of which complement receptor (C3b, iC3b, or C3d) was principally effected by thermal injury. While the present study indicates that complement receptor clearance function is depressed following thermal injury, it is possible that a deficit in general phagocytic mechanisms contributed to the observed response.

Thermal injury also caused a depression of the splenic uptake of EA. Since the magnitude of the depression was similar to that caused by acute hemorrhage it is possible that this was due to a depression of splenic blood flow. The degree of acute hemorrhage employed has been shown to cause more than a 90% reduction in splenic blood flow (27). An additional contributing factor may have been the splenic uptake of damaged erythrocytes (28).

Lung localization of EA was increased after thermal injury and injection of erythrocyte stroma. The amount of EA present in the lungs due to the blood remaining in the lungs was less than 20% based on 0.073 ml blood/g lung tissue (17). While the lung localization of EA was never greater than 3%ID, the small increase in lung uptake of EA could have represented binding to complement receptors on marginated neutrophils (29).

Erythrocyte stroma was injected as a model of the intravascular hemolysis that occurs following thermal injury. The stroma did not cause a sufficient depression of hepatic blood flow or C3 levels to account for the depression of EA uptake by the liver. The detection of some fluid phase C3b in plasma after stroma injection indicates the possibility that this C3b could have been competing with the EA for C3b receptors. Whatever the mechanism, these results indicate that hemolysis could contribute to the depression of complement receptor clearance function following thermal injury. Since intravascular hemolysis occurs at the time of thermal injury (12) the depression of receptor function at 30 min after injury may represent the depression caused by the hepatic uptake of the erythrocyte debris. Additionally, the effect of erythrocyte stroma on macrophage receptor function may represent one of the mechanisms for the effects of stroma on phagocytic function and host defense to shock and infection (12, 16, 17).

The present study has demonstrated that the *in vivo* clearance function of hepatic macrophage complement receptors is depressed following thermal injury. This depression of complement receptor function may contribute to the increase in susceptibility to infection in animals by impairing the clearance of bacteria from the blood (10, 11). While binding to complement receptors does not normally lead directly to phagocytosis it is apparent that complement receptors are important in the binding of particulates to macrophages so that other factors may bring about phagocytosis. Depression of neutrophil function is important in the increased susceptibility of burned patients to infection. However, since opsonization of bacteria is not consistently depressed (30, 31) impaired hepatic macrophage receptor function may also be important. Since antibody-treated erythrocytes have been used to evaluate macrophage receptor clearance function in patients (5–7), this approach could be used in burned patients.

The authors acknowledge the expert technical assistance of Peter Reusswig and Lisa Gary and the secretarial assistance of Mrs. Maureen Davis.

1. McKeever PE, Spicer SS, Surface receptors on mononuclear macrophages. In: Carr I, Deams WT, eds. The Reticuloendothelial System: A Comprehensive Treatise. New York, Plenum, Vol 1:pp161–258, 1980.
2. Brown DL, Lachmann PJ, Dacie JV. The *in vivo* behavior of complement-coated red cells: Studies in C6-deficient, C3-depleted and normal rabbits. Clin Exp Immunol 7:401–422, 1970.
3. Frank MM, Schreiber AD, Atkinson JP, Jaffe CJ. Pathophysiology of immune hemolytic anemia. Ann Int Med **87**:210–222, 1977.
4. Pappas MG, Nussenzweig RS, Nussenzweig V, Shear HL. Complement-mediated defect in clearance and sequestration of sensitized, autologous erythrocytes in rodent malaria. J Clin Invest **67**:183–192, 1981.
5. Jaffe CJ, Vierling JM, Jones EA, Lawley TJ, Frank MM. Receptor specific clearance of the reticuloendothelial system in chronic liver diseases: Demonstration of defect in C3b-specific clearance in primary biliary cirrhosis. J Clin Invest **62**:1069–1077, 1978.
6. Frank MM, Hamburger MI, Lawley TJ, Kimberly RP, Poltz PH. Defective reticuloendothelial system Fc-receptor function in systemic lupus erythematosus. N Engl J Med **300**:518–523, 1979.
7. Hamburger MI, Moutsopoulos HM, Lawley TJ, Frank MM. Sjogren's syndrome: A deficit in reticuloendothelial system Fc-receptor specific clearance. Ann Int Med **91**:534–538, 1979.
8. Alexander JW. Effect of thermal injury upon the early resistance to infection. J Surg Res **8**:128–137, 1968.
9. McRipley RJ, Garrison DW. Increased susceptibility of burned rats to *Pseudomonas aeruginosa.* Proc Soc Exp Biol Med **115**:336–338, 1964.
10. McRipley RJ, Garrison DW. Effect of burns in rats on defense mechanisms against *Pseudomonas aeruginosa.* J Inf Dis **115**:159–170, 1965.
11. DiMaio A, DiMaio D, Jacques L. Phagocytaosis in experimental burns. J Surg Res **21**:437–448, 1976.
12. Loegering DJ. Hemolysis following thermal injury and depression of reticuloendothelial system phagocytic function. J Trauma **21**:130–134, 1981.
13. Schildt BE. Function of the RES after thermal and mechanical trauma in mice. Acta Chir Scand **136**:359–364, 1970.
14. Rittenbury MS, Hanback LD. Phagocytic depression in thermal injuries. J Trauma **7**:523–538, 1967.
15. Loose LD, Turinsky J. Macrophage dysfunction after burn injury. Infect Immun **26**:157–162, 1979.
16. Loegering DJ. Intravascular hemolysis and RES phagocytic and host defense functions. Circ Shock **10**:383–395, 1983.
17. Loegering DJ, Kaplan JE, Grover GJ. Effect of erythrocyte stroma on reticuloendothelial system phagocytic function. J Lab Clin Med **102**:231–239, 1983.
18. Turinsky J, Patterson SA. Proximity to a burn wound as a new factor in considerations of postburn insulin resistance. J Surg Res **26**:171–174, 1979.
19. Normann SJ. Reticuloendothelial system function. V. Studies on the correlation between phagocytic rate and liver blood flow. J Reticuloendothel Soc **12**:473–484, 1972.
20. Dobson EL, Jones HB. The behavior of intravenously injected particulate material. Acta Med Scand **144**:5–71, 1952.
21. Saba TM, Di Luzio NR. Surgical stress and reticuloendothelial function. Surgery **65**:802–807, 1969.
22. Mayer MM. Complement and complement fixation. In: Kabat EA, Mayer MM eds. Experimental Immunochemistry. Springfield, Ill., Thomas, pp131–240 1961.
23. Mancini G, Carbonara AO, Heremans, JF. Immunochemical quantitation of antigens by single radial immunodiffusion. Immunochem **2**:235–256, 1965.
24. Blumenstock FA, Weber P, Saba TM, Laffin R. Electroimmunoassay of alpha-2-opsonic protein during reticuloendothelial blockade. Amer J Physiol **232**:R80–R87, 1977.
25. Loegering DJ, Cuddy BG, Blumenstock FA. Evaluation of *in vivo* RES receptor function following thermal injury using antibody-treated red blood cells. Circ Shock **10**:267, 1983.
26. Hansch GM, Hammer CH, Vanguri P, Shin ML. Homologous species restriction in lysis of erythrocytes by terminal complement proteins. Proc Natl Acad Sci USA **78**:5118–5121, 1981.
27. Sapirstein LA, Sapirstein EH, Bredemeyer A. Effect of hemorrhage on the cardiac output and its distribution in the rat. Circ Res **8**:135–148, 1960.
28. Grover GJ, Loegering DJ. Effect of splenic sequestration of erythrocytes on splenic clearance function and susceptibility to septic peritonitis. Infect Immun **36**:96–102, 1982.
29. Lanser ME, Saba TM. Neutrophil-mediated lung localization of bacteria: A mechanism for pulmonary injury. Surgery **90**:473–481, 1981.
30. Bjornson AB, Altemeier WA, Bjornson HS. The septic burned patient. A model for studying the role of complement and immunoglobulins in opsonization of opportunist micro-organisms. Ann Surg **189**:515–527, 1979.
31. Bjornson AB, Altemeier WA, Bjornson HS, Tang T, Iserson ML. Host defense against opportunist microorganisms following trauma. I. Studies to determine the association between changes in humoral components of host defense and septicemia in burned patients. Ann Surg **188**:93–101, 1978.

Received September 29, 1983. P.S.E.B.M. 1984, Vol. 176.
Accepted April 30, 1984.

PROCEEDINGS OF THE SOCIETY FOR EXPERIMENTAL BIOLOGY AND MEDICINE **176**, 452–459 (1984)

Effect of Nolinium Bromide on Vascular Smooth Muscle (41897)

ROBERT R. BROOKS, SANDRA M. JONES, AND ALAN F. MOORE

Research Division, Norwich Eaton Pharmaceuticals, Inc., Norwich, New York 13815-0191

Abstract. Nolinium bromide inhibits gastric acid secretion and gastrointestinal smooth muscle contraction. While the compound's gastric antisecretory action has been attributed in part to inhibition of gastric adenylate cyclase and the gastric proton-transport ATPase, the mechanism of nolinium bromide's relaxant effect on smooth muscle has not been elucidated. We have determined that nolinium bromide inhibits contraction of vascular smooth muscle, using isolated rabbit aortic strips. This report characterizes the specificity of this inhibition (by using several agonists) and its Ca^{2+} dependence (by using contractile conditions of known dependence on various Ca^{2+} pools). Nolinium bromide (50–200 μM) was a reversible, insurmountable inhibitor of contractions induced by Ca^{2+} (in 40 m*M* KCl depolarizing medium) and norepinephrine, with IC_{50} values of 96 and 118 μM, respectively, for suppression of maximum contractile force. Contractions in response to Asn^1Val^5-angiotensin II in both 2.5 m*M* Ca^{2+} and 0 m*M* Ca^{2+} medium were also inhibited (IC_{50} value = 110 μM under both conditions). Initial contraction rates for all these conditions were depressed by nolinium bromide. Nolinium bromide inhibited equally the phasic (internal Ca^{2+}-dependent) and tonic (external Ca^{2+}-dependent) components of norepinephrine-induced contractions. These results extend the muscle relaxant profile of nolinium bromide to include, albeit with low potency, vascular smooth muscle, and show that its potency is similar in inhibiting the contractile response to three different stimuli: angiotensin II, Ca^{2+}, and norepinephrine.

Nolinium bromide (NB)[1] [2-(3,4-dichlorophenylamino)quinolizinium bromide] is a nonanticholinergic, gastric acid antisecretory agent and a gastrointestinal tract antispasmodic agent (1–3). The gastrointestinal antispasmodic action of NB has been demonstrated in a variety of test systems. The compound inhibited electrically induced contractions of rabbit ileum and nicotine-induced contractions of rat ileum *in vitro,* gastric emptying in fasted rats, and intestinal transport of a charcoal meal in mice. In the anesthetized dog, NB antagonized colonic contractions induced by acetylcholine, histamine, serotonin, and pelvic nerve stimulation, and duodenal contractions due to vagal stimulation and acetylcholine. In the unanesthetized dog, feeding-induced colonic and duodenal motilities were inhibited by NB (2, 3).

The antisecretory action of NB may involve inhibition of enzymes of gastric acid secretion, specifically histamine-stimulated adenylate cyclase (4) and potassium-stimulated ATPase (5). NB has no direct histamine–H_2 receptor blocking properties, since it did not inhibit histamine-stimulated acid secretion from isolated guinea pig gastric discs (5). In contrast, the antispasmodic action of NB has not been explored mechanistically. Nor has its effect on vascular smooth muscle been tested *in vitro.*

In this study we determined the effects of NB on contractions of isolated rabbit aortic strips, a tissue not previously studied with this agent. The experiments reported here were designed to determine if NB had an effect on vascular smooth muscle *in vitro,* whether there was specificity in that effect with respect to which agonists are sensitive to NB, and whether NB's action could be connected to an effect on Ca^{2+} supply. A preliminary report of these results has been presented (6).

Materials and Methods. *Chemicals and solutions.* Normal Krebs–Ringer solution contained 1.16 m*M* $MgSO_4$, 4.69 m*M* KCl, 1.30 m*M* NaH_2PO_4, 2.48 m*M* $CaCl_2$, 5.55 m*M* dextrose, 118 m*M* NaCl, and 25 m*M* $NaHCO_3$. Calcium-free Krebs was of the same composition but without the $CaCl_2$. High-potassium depolarizing Krebs lacked $CaCl_2$ and contained 40 m*M* KCl. These solutions were

[1] Abbreviations used: ANG II, Asn^1Val^5-angiotensin II; NB, nolinium bromide.

0037-9727/84 $1.50

prepared fresh daily. The pH of these solutions was 7.4 upon equilibration by aeration with 95% O_2–5% CO_2 at 37°C.

Nolinium bromide and angiotensin II (ANG II = Asn–Arg–Val–Tyr–Val–His–Pro–Phe) were synthesized at Norwich Eaton Pharmaceuticals, Inc. NB (mol mass 370.1 g/mole) was dissolved fresh daily in the medium appropriate to the individual experiment. ANG II was prepared as a 1 m*M* stock solution in distilled water containing 19 mg mannitol/ml and was stored frozen. $CaCl_2$ was kept refrigerated as a 0.5 *M* stock solution in distilled water. Norepinephrine (L-arterenol bitartrate, Sigma) was prepared fresh daily as a 3.16 m*M* stock solution in 0.1 *N* HCl.

Animals. Female New Zealand White rabbits, 2.5–3.5 kg, were obtained from Dutchland Breeding Laboratories (Denver, Pa.) and Sunrise Laboratory Animals (Whitehouse Station, N.J.). Rabbits were housed in metal cages under standard laboratory conditions with a 12-hr dark/light cycle.

Tissue preparation. As described by Furchgott and Bhadrakom (7), a rabbit was killed by cervical dislocation and the thoracic aorta was rapidly excised and placed in a petri dish containing oxygenated Krebs solution at room temperature. Connective tissue was carefully removed and the muscle was cut helically into a single strip (approximately 0.25 × 8 cm) and then was cut transversely into four equal segments. Each strip was attached at one end to a glass tissue holder with surgical silk (No. 3-O) and placed into a 25-ml tissue bath containing the appropriate medium at 37°C. The opposite end of the strip was attached to a Grass FT-03C force-displacement transducer coupled to a Grass Model 7B polygraph (Grass Instrument Co., Quincy, Mass.). Baths were aerated with 95% O_2–5% CO_2 and the bath medium was changed every 20 min during the relaxation period. This period generally lasted 2 hr with the strip under 2 g of tension.

Experimental procedure. In all experiments a cumulative concentration–response curve for ANG II was obtained by cumulative additions of aliquots of ANG II to give final bath concentrations of 1 to 128 n*M*. The bath medium was changed at 15–20 min intervals for 1–2 hr until a stable baseline was again observed. The control concentration–response curve was then determined using the desired agonist (1–128 n*M* ANG II, 1–128 n*M* ANG II in calcium-free medium, 0.0125–20 m*M* Ca^{2+} in calcium-free depolarizing medium, or 0.01–32 μM norepinephrine). The medium was changed as above and, after a stable relaxed condition was again achieved, the bath medium was replaced with medium containing the desired concentration of NB, and within 5 min a cumulative concentration–response curve was started for the agonist. One of the four strips was not exposed to NB and was carried through the experiment as a control for time-related changes in strip behavior. In most experiments a recovery control curve was determined at the end of the experiment after NB was removed and a stable baseline obtained.

Data analysis. Each point (g tension) of the control and experimental concentration–response curves was expressed as a percentage of the maximum control curve contraction for that tissue. Corrections for time-related changes in tissue responsiveness were made if the time control strip not exposed to NB showed a change in maximum contraction greater than or equal to 10% of the first control curve for that strip. In this event, the correction was achieved by multiplying each experimental curve point (g tension) by the ratio of the maximum tensions elicited in the time-control strip in control and test periods. For example, if the time control strip gave maximum tensions of 5 and 4.4 g in the first and second curves, respectively, then a time correction would be made by multiplying all experimental strip second curve points by 5/4.4.

Plots of log agonist concentration versus percentage of maximum contraction were made for control strips and a straight line was fitted to the appropriate portion by the method of least squares. The EC_{50} value, that is the agonist concentration causing 50% of the maximum uninhibited contraction, was calculated from the equation of the line. The IC_{50} value, i.e., the concentration of NB which inhibited maximum contractile force 50%, was calculated analogously for each agonist. Initial rates of tension development were estimated by laying a straight edge on the polygraph record. For this purpose the portion of the concentration–response curve including one-half the maximum tension developed was used. The resulting initial rates of contraction at one-half maximum tension were expressed in units of grams per minute. Rates were also expressed as a percentage of the individual tissue's control response to the agonist alone. Corrections for time-related changes were made as described above by referring to a concurrently run control strip's behavior.

Results. *Contractile effects of angiotensin II, calcium, and norepinephrine.* Rabbit aortic strips displayed concentration-dependent contractions to ANG II in normal medium. The maximum contraction varied somewhat from strip to strip from the same animal, but the between-animal variability was greater. The EC_{50} value, i.e., the agonist concentration causing 50% of the maximum contraction, for ANG II in normal Krebs medium was 5.80 ± 0.20 nM (mean ± SE, $N = 3$). In calcium-free medium, ANG II was three times less potent (EC_{50} value = 17.8 ± 1.2 nM, $N = 6$) and maximum contractile tension was reduced to 41% as compared to normal calcium conditions (Table I). Ackerly *et al.* (8) observed EC_{50} values of 13 and 60 nM for ANG II under normal and calcium-free conditions, respectively, and removal of calcium reduced maximum contractile force to 30% of control. Thus the present results with ANG II are comparable to those reported previously. Calcium was a considerably less potent agonist than ANG II, with an EC_{50} value of 77 ± 4 μM ($N = 10$). Norepinephrine was also less potent than ANG II (EC_{50} value = 68.3 ± 1.0 nM, $N = 3$).

Maximum contractile force varied with the agonist (Table I). The greatest maximum tension (3.28 g) was produced by Ca^{2+} in 40 mM KCl, followed by norepinephrine (2.88 g), ANG II in normal medium (2.20 g), and ANG II in the absence of added Ca^{2+} (0.91 g). The initial rate of force development also differed under the four stimulating conditions (Table

TABLE I. INHIBITION BY NOLINIUM BROMIDE OF CONTRACTION OF ISOLATED RABBIT AORTIC STRIPS

Agonist	Nolinium bromide concn (μM)	Number of tissues	Maximum contractile force (g) (mean ± SE)	Percentage of maximum control contraction (mean ± SE)	IC_{50} (μM) (95% limits)
Angiotensin II in 2.5 mM Ca^{2+}	0	12	2.20 ± 0.33	100	
	50	3	2.14 ± 0.07	88.5 ± 2.4	110
	100	6	1.40 ± 0.04	58.0 ± 1.3	(82–146)
	200	6	0.35 ± 0.02	16.5 ± 0.7	
Angiotensin II in Ca^{2+}-free buffer	0	8	0.91 ± 0.11	100	
	50	2	0.76 ± 0.01[a]	90.7 ± 9.3	110
	100	2	0.57 ± 0.33[a]	57.2 ± 10.0	(39–344)
	200	2	0.20 ± 0.20[a]	17.1 ± 17.1	
$CaCl_2$ in 40 mM KCl	0	12	3.28 ± 0.17	100	
	50	4	2.56 ± 0.27	80.9 ± 3.2	96
	100	4	2.19 ± 0.36	57.3 ± 6.8	(58–158)
	200	4	0.20 ± 0.11	5.4 ± 2.7	
Norepinephrine	0	4	2.88 ± 0.10	100	
	50	3	2.43 ± 0.16[b]	84.5 ± 1.7	118
	100	3	1.76 ± 0.11[b]	61.2 ± 2.1	(90–155)
	200	3	0.73 ± 0.06[b]	25.4 ± 2.0	

Note. Segments of helically cut aortic strips were contracted by cumulatively increasing concentrations of the indicated agonist in the absence and presence of the indicated concentration of nolinium bromide (NB). The maximum agonist concentrations were 128 nM, 5 mM, and 31.6 μM for angiotensin II, $CaCl_2$, and norepinephrine, respectively. Percentage of maximum control contraction, based on the strip's response before NB, was calculated after tensions were corrected for time-related changes as described under Materials and Methods. The IC_{50} values (concentration giving 50% inhibition) for NB were estimated by least-squares regression analysis.

[a] Corrected for 33 and 36% time-related decrease in the maximum contractile force observed in control strips. Actual tensions in strips treated with NB were lower than shown.

[b] Corrected for 15, 19, and 22% time-related increase in the maximum contractile force observed in control strips. Actual tensions in strips treated with NB were higher than shown.

TABLE II. EFFECT OF NOLINIUM BROMIDE ON INITIAL RATE OF TENSION DEVELOPMENT OF RABBIT AORTIC STRIPS

Agonist	Nolinium bromide concn (μM)	Number of tissues	Initial contraction rate (mean ± SE) (g/min)	Percentage of control rate (mean ± SE)
Angiotensin II in 2.5 mM Ca^{2+}	0	4	0.264 ± 0.016	100
	50	3	0.226 ± 0.026	85.1 ± 2.6
	100	3	0.128 ± 0.009	48.8 ± 3.1
	200	3	0.043 ± 0.006	16.1 ± 0.9
Angiotensin II in Ca^{2+}-free buffer	0	4	0.108 ± 0.021	100
	50	2	0.138 ± 0.002	82.0 ± 1.2
	100	2	0.090 ± 0.030	107 ± 35
$CaCl_2$ in 40 mM KCl	0	8	0.160 ± 0.011	100
	50	4	0.084 ± 0.005	58.9 ± 7.3
	100	4	0.134 ± 0.019	79.0 ± 11.4
Norepinephrine	0	4	1.67 ± 0.240	100
	50	3	0.908 ± 0.127	53.7 ± 8.0
	100	3	0.591 ± 0.017	35.8 ± 6.5
	200	3	0.291 ± 0.055	16.5 ± 0.9

Note. Observed initial contraction rates for tissues exposed to nolinium bromide were corrected for time-related changes in a concurrently run control strip. Observed changes in the control strip initial rate were −2 to +36% for angiotensin in 2.5 mM Ca^{2+}, −46 to −52% for angiotensin in 0 mM Ca^{2+}, +42 to +86% for Ca^{2+} in 40 mM KCl, and +50 to +190% for norepinephrine.

II). Norepinephrine produced the largest initial rate (1.67 g/min). Compared with norepinephrine, the rate of tension development was five times lower (0.26 g/min) with ANG II in normal medium, and lower still with Ca^{2+} (0.16 g/min) and ANG II in calcium-free medium (0.11 g/min).

Tissues in medium lacking added Ca^{2+} showed a progressive decrease in both maximum tension development and initial contraction rate (Table II) in response to ANG II. This was due to the low Ca^{2+} conditions, since tissues in normal medium (2.5 mM Ca^{2+}) retained responsiveness to ANG II. With both norepinephrine and Ca^{2+} in depolarizing medium, maximum contractile force increased moderately (<25%) with time and on repeated exposure to the agonist. With these same stimulants, even more pronounced increases in the initial rate of tension development were observed on repeated exposure, i.e., increases of up to 86% for Ca^{2+} and 190% for norepinephrine (Table II).

Nolinium bromide effects. NB inhibited ANG II-induced contractions in normal medium (Fig. 1). Curves were shifted to the right and maximum tension was depressed as compared to control curves. Both effects were a function of inhibitor concentration. At 50, 100, and 200 μM NB, maximum tension was inhibited 12, 42, and 83%, respectively (Table I). If NB acts by inhibiting Ca^{2+} movement into the cell, it should be less effective in inhibiting ANG II-induced contractions of aortic strips in calcium-free medium, since such contractions depend on internal Ca^{2+} in stores (8). In fact, concentration-dependent inhibition was observed under calcium-free conditions. At 50, 100, and 200 μM NB maximum tension development was inhibited 9, 43, and 83%, respectively. For ANG II under both conditions (2.5 and 0 mM Ca^{2+}), the IC_{50} value of NB was estimated as 110 μM (Table I).

To determine if inhibition by NB was specific for ANG II, both Ca^{2+} and norepinephrine were used as agonists. NB also inhibited these contractions in a concentration-dependent fashion (Table I). The main difference between the effects of NB on these agonists compared with its effects on ANG II-induced contractions was the apparently increased sensitivity of calcium- and norepinephrine-induced contractions to the lowest concentration of NB. The 50 μM-inhibited curves

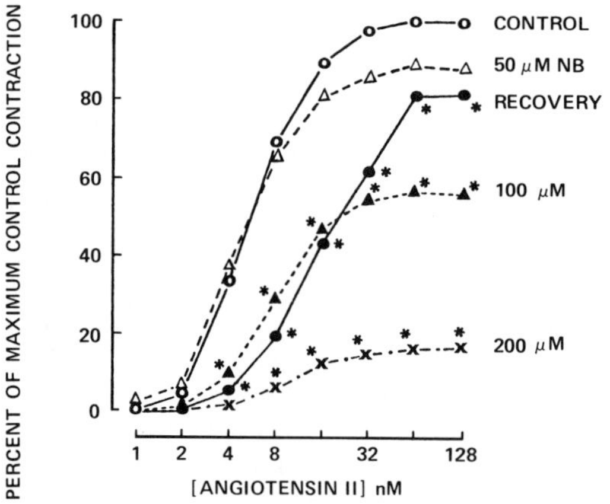

FIG. 1. Inhibition by nolinium bromide (NB) of contractions of rabbit aortic strips induced by angiotensin II (ANG II) in normal medium. Strips were suspended in Krebs–Ringer solution containing 2.5 m*M* $CaCl_2$ at 37°C under 2 g tension and contracted by cumulatively increasing concentrations of ANG II in the absence and presence of NB. Recovery curves were generated after removal of the inhibitor by several changes of the bath medium. Starred points are significantly different ($P < 0.01$) from the corresponding control contraction by a *t* test ($N = 3$). Maximum control contractions were 2.3–2.4 g.

were much more displaced to the right for Ca^{2+} (Fig. 2) and for norepinephrine (data not shown) than for ANG II (Figs. 1 and 2). However, maximum tension development was similarly inhibited with IC_{50} values estimated as 96 and 118 μ*M* for calcium- and norepinephrine-induced contractions, respectively (Table I).

NB inhibited initial rates of tension development in a concentration-related manner for ANG II (normal medium) and for norepinephrine (Table II). Effects on this parameter paralleled effects on maximum tension (Table I). Concentration-independent effects on initial contraction rate were observed with ANG II in calcium-free medium and with Ca^{2+} in 40 m*M* KCl.

After strips were washed with medium lacking NB, they were able to respond again to the various agonists. Maximum post-NB contractions ranged from 46 to 112% of control values (Table III). As shown in Fig. 1, however, the recovery curve for ANG II in normal medium was displaced to higher agonist concentrations. Similar shifts to the right were observed with the other agonist conditions (data not shown). Only partial recovery (46%) was found with ANG II in calcium-free medium for strips exposed to 200 μ*M* NB.

Discussion. This study was undertaken to determine if NB inhibited contraction of vascular smooth muscle *in vitro* and further to determine if such inhibition were specific with respect to agonist or could be related to effects on Ca^{2+} supply. Rabbit aortic strips were useful, since different components of the calcium-dependence of contraction in this tissue are identifiable by use of different agonists. Thus, the tonic component of norepinephrine-induced contractions has been ascribed to the movement of external Ca^{2+} into the cytoplasm (9, 10), while the rapid phasic component is due to internal Ca^{2+} stores (11, 12). Complete removal of external Ca^{2+} therefore only attenuates, but does not abolish, the ability of norepinephrine to contract the aorta. ANG II, by use of internal Ca^{2+} stores, is also able to contract the rabbit aortic strip in calcium-free medium (8, 13). Contractions induced by Ca^{2+} in potassium-depolarizing medium seem to be dependent entirely on extracellular Ca^{2+} entering the cell through potential-dependent channels operating when K^+ causes membrane depolarization (12, 14).

Although NB clearly inhibited aortic strip contractions, it did so without much evidence of specificity. The IC_{50} values for NB antagonism of ANG II, $CaCl_2$, and norepinephrine were all approximately equal (100 μ*M*) and reflected low potency. Both the lack of agonist specificity and low potency *in vitro* make NB's effects on vascular smooth muscle analogous to its antispasmodic action on gastrointestinal smooth muscle. Goldenberg (2) reported pA_2 values of 5.3 and 4.3 for inhibition of acetylcholine- and histamine-induced contractions, respectively, of guinea pig ileum.

The role of transmembrane calcium flux and membrane depolarization in the contractile response of rabbit aortic strips to several agonists has been previously studied by one of the present authors (8). It was reported that ANG II-induced contractions were insensitive to 10 μ*M* verapamil, but partially inhibited by another calcium entry blocker, SKF-525A, as well as by use of calcium-free buffer. These results suggested that ANG II-

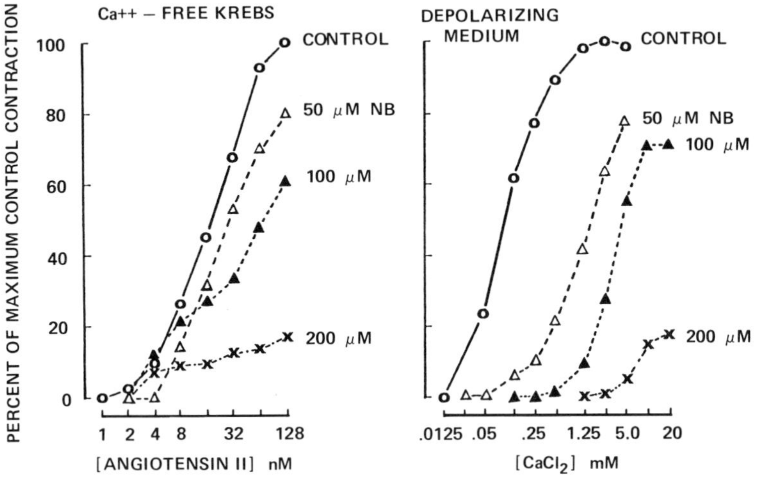

FIG. 2. Inhibition by nolinium bromide (NB) of contractions of rabbit aortic strips induced by angiotensin II (ANG II) in 0 m*M* Ca^{2+} and by $CaCl_2$ in depolarizing (40 m*M* KCl) medium. Strips were suspended in calcium-free Krebs–Ringer solution with 4.69 m*M* KCl (ANG II curves, $N = 2$–6) or 40 m*M* KCl ($CaCl_2$ curves, $N = 4$) at 37°C under 2 g tension. Contractions in the absence or presence of NB were induced by cumulatively increasing concentrations of ANG II or $CaCl_2$. Maximum control contractions were 0.5–1.3 g for ANG II and 2.6–4.2 g for $CaCl_2$.

induced contractions made use of both extracellular Ca^{2+} and a loosely bound Ca^{2+} pool in this tissue. Our finding that NB inhibited ANG II-induced contractions equally under normal and calcium-free conditions suggests that the compound is not interfering with calcium movements through plasma membrane channels.

The conclusion that calcium movements are not directly involved in NB's inhibitory

TABLE III. RECOVERY OF RABBIT AORTIC STRIP CONTRACTILE RESPONSE TO VARIOUS AGONISTS AFTER EXPOSURE TO NOLINIUM BROMIDE

Agonist	Maximum nolinium bromide concn (μ*M*)	Number of tissues	Percentage recovery of maximum contractile response (mean ± SE)
Angiotensin II in 2.5 m*M* Ca^{2+}	100	3	88.3 ± 1.8
	200[a]	3	81.3 ± 3.0
Angiotensin II in Ca^{2+}-free buffer	50	5	99.3 ± 7.1
	100	2	82.4 ± 2.2
	200	2	46.4 ± 21.4
$CaCl_2$ in 40 m*M* KCl	50	2	112 ± 1.0
	100	2	98.5 ± 3.3
	200	2	91.6 ± 0.8
Norepinephrine	200[a]	3	82.4 ± 3.2

Note. Nolinium bromide (NB) was washed from tissues by several changes of the bath medium until a stable baseline of relaxation was obtained. Contractile responses to cumulatively increasing concentrations of the indicated agonist were obtained. Maximum contractile tension was then expressed as a percentage of the same tissue's tension before exposure to NB. Time-related changes in a concurrently run control strip not exposed to NB were used to correct treated strip recovery data (see Table I).

[a] These strips had previously been exposed to 50 and 100 μ*M* NB.

action is supported by the norepinephrine results. Ackerly *et al.* (8) observed that norepinephrine-induced contractions of rabbit aortic strips were largely unaffected by verapamil, SKF-525A, or use of calcium-free buffer. Since NB does inhibit norepinephrine-induced contractions, NB is not acting like a calcium-channel blocker of the verapamil or SKF-525A type. It was further found that both the initial rate of contraction (phasic component) and the maximum contractile force (tonic component) of norepinephrine-induced contractions were equally inhibited by NB. The former depends on intracellular calcium supplies and the latter on extracellular calcium (9–12). Therefore, NB's effect is apparently not directed specifically at either of these pools of calcium.

In using a "calcium-free" buffer in the absence of a chelating agent such as EGTA, it is recognized that a low level of calcium remains available to the tissue from the external medium. Measurement of this residual Ca^{2+} with a calcium-selective electrode indicates that the concentration is less than 10^{-5} *M*. Could NB be interfering with a role of this residual Ca^{2+}? This is unlikely, since such an action would be expected to show up as differential inhibition of the tonic and phasic components of norepinephrine-induced contractions. Furthermore, NB inhibits with similar potency contractions induced by much higher (millimolar) concentrations of $CaCl_2$ which should overwhelm any inhibition of the effect of residual micromolar Ca^{2+}. It is also noted that the use of calcium-free buffer clearly shifted the nature of the ANG II-induced contractions in that maximum tension was reduced over 50% (Table I). Furthermore, time-related loss of responsiveness to ANG II, not seen in normal medium, was observed in calcium-free buffer. Nevertheless, NB inhibited such ANG II-induced contractions with equal potency as compared to normal calcium conditions. If NB were affecting a loosely bound Ca^{2+} pool, one might expect that NB's effect would change as the contribution of this pool were changed. However, NB's interference with the action of residual Ca^{2+} in "calcium-free buffer" cannot be entirely excluded.

These results suggest, but do not prove, that NB is not acting as a calcium channel blocking agent and does not interfere with internal Ca^{2+} stores directly. The salient feature, in both gastrointestinal and vascular smooth muscle, of NB's inhibition of contraction is lack of specificity for the agonist being used to induce the contraction. Some common feature of their stimulation of the muscle cell must be interfered with by NB. If NB were interacting with a membrane component, it's nonselective interference with an octapeptide, a cation, and a catecholamine in vascular smooth muscle, and with acetylcholine and histamine in gastrointestinal smooth muscle (2), could be accounted for. The surface membrane site of action would also be consistent with the polar nature of NB, which makes significant intracellular accumulation unlikely. The reversibility of NB's inhibition may also reflect a surface site of action. It would be of interest to study directly the membrane interaction of NB by use of membrane-specific fluorescent probes.

The authors thank Anne P. Drexler for assistance in some of this work.

1. Alaimo RJ, Goldenberg MM. 2-(3,4-Dichloroanilino)quinolizinium bromide, a unique antispasmodic, antisecretory, and antiulcerogenic agent. J Med Chem **18:**1145–1147, 1975.
2. Goldenberg MM. Some aspects in the pharmacology of diclonium bromide [2-(3,4-dichloroanilino)-quinolizinium bromide]. I. Antispasmodic action. Drug Res **26:**341–346, 1976.
3. Goldenberg MM. Some aspects in the pharmacology of diclonium bromide [2-(3,4-dichloroanilino)-quinolizinium bromide]. II. Gastric acid antisecretory and antiulcerogenic actions. Drug Res **26:**347–350, 1976.
4. Dousa TP, Hui YSF, Northrup TE, Goldenberg MM. Inhibition of histamine-sensitive adenylate cyclase from the guinea pig gastric mucosa by nolinium bromide. Biochem Pharmacol **28:**343–344, 1979.
5. Brooks RR, Goldenberg MM, Moore RB, Burns RH, Generous TA, Ellis KO. Inhibition of guinea pig gastric microsomal potassium-stimulated ATPase by nolinium bromide. Proc Soc Exp Biol Med **172:**308–315, 1983.
6. Brooks RR, Jones SM, Drexler AP, Ellis KO, Moore AF. Comparative effects of a smooth muscle-specific (nolinium bromide, NB) and a skeletal muscle-specific (dantrolene sodium, DS) relaxant on rabbit aortic strips. Pharmacologist **23:**122, 1981.
7. Furchgott RF, Bhadrakom S. Reactions of strips of rabbit aorta to epinephrine, isopropylarterenol, so-

dium nitrite and other drugs. J Pharmacol Exp Therap **108:**129–143, 1953.
8. Ackerly JA, Moore AF, Peach MJ. Demonstration of different contractile mechanisms for angiotensin II and des-Asp[1]-angiotensin II in rabbit aortic strips. Proc Natl Acad Sci USA **74:**5725–5728, 1977.
9. Godfraind T, Kaba A. The role of calcium in the action of drugs on vascular smooth muscle. Arch Int Pharmacodyn Ther **196:**35–49, 1972.
10. Deth R, Van Breemen C. Relative contributions of Ca^{2+} influx and cellular Ca^{2+} release during drug induced activation of the rabbit aorta. Pfluegers Arch **348:**13–22, 1974.
11. Godfraind T. Calcium exchange in vascular smooth muscle action of noradrenaline and lanthanum. J Physiol (London) **260:**21–35, 1976.
12. Hudgins PM, Weiss GB. Differential effects of calcium removal upon vascular smooth muscle contraction induced by norepinephrine, histamine and potassium. J Pharmacol Exp Therap **159:**91–97, 1968.
13. Hinke JAM, Wilson ML, Burnham SC. Calcium and the contractility of arterial smooth muscle. Amer J Physiol **206:**211–217, 1964.
14. Briggs AH. Calcium movements during potassium contracture in isolated rabbit aortic strips. Amer J Physiol **203:**849–852, 1962.

Received November 3, 1983. P.S.E.B.M. 1984, Vol. 176.
Accepted May 2, 1984.

PROCEEDINGS OF THE SOCIETY FOR EXPERIMENTAL BIOLOGY AND MEDICINE **176**, 460–466 (1984)

Effects of Three Feeding Schedules on Tumor and Host of Lewis Lung Carcinoma-Bearing Mice[1] (41898)

WINNIE CHAN, S. McELHANON, ALAN M. KAPLAN,[2] AND W. L. BANKS, JR.

Departments of Biochemistry and Surgery and Massey Cancer Center, Medical College of Virginia, Virginia Commonwealth University, Richmond, Virginia 23284

Abstract. The effect of three feeding schedules on tumor and host were examined in Lewis Lung bearing (TB) and nontumor bearing (NTB) C57/Bl mice. Both NTB and TB animals were divided into three groups: the control groups which were fed *ad libitum;* the intermittent fed (IMF) groups were fed for 32 hr and fasted for 16 hr in each 48-hr cycle, and the alternate day fed (ADF) groups were fed for a 24-hr interval in each 48-hr cycle. The animals were killed at the end of the fifteenth day, following a *fed* day for all groups. In the NTB groups, only the ADF group showed decreased food intake and lower body weight gain as compared to their control group. In the TB mice, as compared to their control group, the IMF group showed a significant reduction in the mean tumor weight with no change in the mean host weight, even though the daily food intakes of these two groups were the same over the experimental interval. In contrast, the ADF group showed reductions in both host and tumor weights as compared to their control group. The tumor to host weight ratios were significantly reduced for both the IMF and ADF groups as compared to the ratios found for the control groups, which suggests a differential effect on the tumor and on the host due to the feeding schedule. As assessed by the protein, RNA, and DNA concentrations, no compositional differences were noted for the tumors obtained from the animals that were maintained on each of the three different feeding schedules. In the NTB mice, no differences in tissue leucine (Leu) oxidation occurred between the groups for liver and skeletal muscle, whereas in the TB animals *in vitro* Leu oxidation capability by skeletal muscle specimens was markedly enhanced in the ADF group, but no difference was noted for the IMF group of the TB mice when compared to the control group. Taken together, these results suggest that the 32-hr fed:16-hr fast schedule (IMF) was beneficial and the 24-hr fed:24-hr fast schedule was detrimental compared to the *ad libitum* feeding schedule with respect to tumor and host relationships.

Restriction of caloric or nutrient intake has been shown in several experimental models to decrease tumor growth, but the effects on the host were generally not assessed (1). In a recent study, Goodgame *et al.* showed that animals fasted from 1–4 days had reduced body weights without altered tumor size (2). Moreover, in the same study it was reported that there was actually an increased *in vitro* [^{3}H]thymidine incorporation by tumor tissue in fasting animals. Stragand *et al.* (3) have shown that both tumor, host weights and tumor volumes were decreased as a result of fasting. Although fasting can reduce the tumor size, tumor growth can continue in fasting animals (4). On the other hand, adequately nourished animals have been found to support optimal tumor growth in some studies, and hyperalimentation has actually been shown to stimulate tumor growth (5). The present study was designed to determine whether the primary Lewis Lung carcinoma size could be decreased without adversely affecting the host by simply altering the feeding pattern and not the level of alimentation.

Methods. Female C57/Bl mice were housed in a temperature and humidity controlled room with a 12-hr light:12-hr dark cycle in which the dark phase was from 6 PM to 6 AM as shown in Fig. 1. At the start of the experimental interval the TB animals were inoculated in the flank with 5 × 10^5 viable Lewis Lung carcinoma cells (LL), and both the TB and NTB animals were placed randomly in individual wire bottom cages. Both the TB

[1] Supported in part by NIH Grants CA26532 and CA16059.

[2] Current address: Departments of Medical Microbiology and Immunology, University of Kentucky, Lexington, Ky. 40506.

0037-9727/84 $1.50

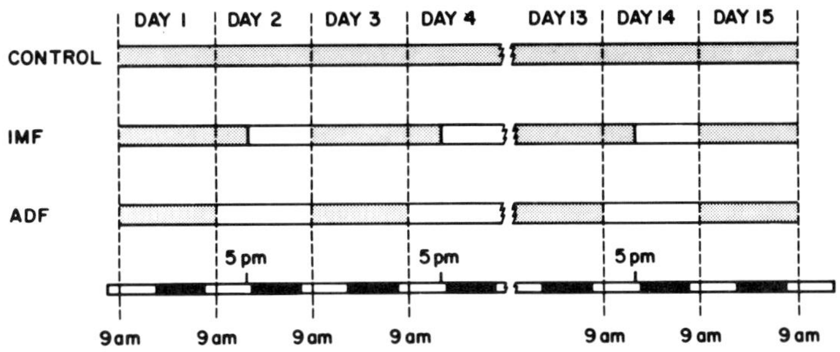

FIG. 1. Feeding schedule protocols and light–dark cycles. This figure illustrates the several sets of 48-hr cycles for the fed (stippled bars) and the fast phases (open bars) of the three feeding schedule protocols. The control (*ad libitum*), IMF (32-hr fed:16-hr fast), and the ADF (24-hr fed:24-hr fast) plans are indicated for each 2-day cycle. The corresponding light (6 AM–6 PM) and dark (6 PM–6 AM) phases are identified in the bottom bar.

and NTB animals were subsequently fed on one of the three schedules: the control groups were fed *ad libitum* throughout the experimental interval; the intermittently fed groups (IMF) were maintained on a 32-hr fed:16-hr fast schedule in which the food cups were removed from 5 PM of the second day to 9 AM of the following day; and the alternate day fed groups (ADF) were maintained on a 24-hr fed:24-hr fast schedule in which the food cups were removed at 9 AM every other day for 24 hr (giving a period of 48 hr). These feeding patterns were repeated each successive 48-hr period throughout the experimental period and each experimental day began at 9 AM. Food consumption was measured and recorded for each 2-day interval and the animals fed on IMF and ADF schedules were provided the same quantity of rations for each 2-day period that their control group consumed for the previous 2-day interval. All animals were fed a synthetic amino acid diet, the composition of which is indicated in Table I, and water was available *ad libitum* throughout the entire experimental period. At the end of Day 15 following a fed day for all groups, the animals were killed by cervical dislocation and their body and tumor weights determined. This overall procedure was performed once using the NTB animals and was performed three separate times using the TB animals. The results obtained were combined and analyzed using standard statistical methods (7). In the tables, the means of various parameters presented for the IMF and ADF groups were tested against the values obtained for the control group using a two-tailed Student's t test with a $P < 0.05$ as the level of significance.

For one experiment with the TB animals, the homogenate of a specimen of the tumor was prepared in distilled water using a Techmar tissue homogenizer. These homogenates were used for the determination of tumor DNA, RNA, and protein, using the method of Wannemacher *et al.* (8) with the modifications suggested by Munro and Fleck (9). Leu oxidation capabilities of liver and skeletal muscle specimens were estimated by incubating 100-mg minced samples of tissue in 3.0 ml of complete tissue culture media (Difco TC 199) containing [1-^{14}C]Leu with a final specific radioactivity in the incubation media

TABLE I. COMPOSITION OF SYNTHETIC AMINO ACID-DEFINED DIET

Ingredients	g/kg Diet
L-Amino acid mixture[a]	170.0
Corn starch	100.0
Sucrose	564.0
Corn oil	100.0
Cellulose	15.0
Vitamin mixture[b]	10.0
Mineral mixture[c]	40.0
Chromium and selenium supplement[d]	1.0

[a] Amino acid composition as reported by Rogers and Harper (6).
[b] Vitamin mixture-Teklad No. 40060, Madison, Wisc.
[c] Bernhart–Tomarelli mineral mixture Teklad No. 17050, Madison, Wisc.
[d] Supplementation with mixture of $CrK(SO_4)_2 \cdot 12H_2O$ (19.25 mg/kg diet) and $Na_2Se_3 \cdot 5H_2O$ (0.35 mg/kg diet).

of 22.5 Ci/m*M* Leu. The reactions were performed in closed vessels equipped with plastic center wells containing 0.2 ml of hyamine hydroxide as the trapping agent. At the end of 90 min, the reaction was stopped and the CO_2 evolved by addition of 1.5 ml 2 *N* citric acid and trapped in the center wells, which were then placed into scintillation vials containing 10 ml of a toluene-based scintillation cocktail and the $^{14}CO_2$ radioactivity counted.

Results and Discussion. All animals used in the experiments were drawn from a homogenous pool and the initial body weights between all three feeding schedule groups were the same for both the TB and NTB experiments. The results obtained for food intakes, as well as host and tumor weight parameters using the three feeding schedules are presented in Table II. In the NTB animals, the IMF schedule did not affect the average daily food intake, but the ADF schedule significantly decreased ($P < 0.05$) the food intake to 80% of the control group's intake. Reflecting the food intake, the change in host weight (terminal body weight–initial body weight) was significantly reduced ($P < 0.01$) in the ADF group to 35% of the control group. As for the TB animals, the net body weight changes show that the mean body weight of the control group (*ad libitum fed*) was increased, the IMF group (32-hr fed:16-hr fast) was virtually unchanged, and the ADF group (24-hr fed:24-hr fast) was markedly decreased over the experimental period. These net changes represent the sum of alterations in the host weight plus the tumor weight at the time the experimental period was ended. The mean terminal host weights were not different for the control and IMF groups, but were reduced ($P < 0.001$) to 84% of the control groups level at the end of 15 days for the animals fed on the ADF schedule. The mean tumor weights were reduced ($P < 0.001$) in both the IMF and ADF groups to 69 and 51%, respectively, of those found for the control group. Thus, the host weight was only adversely affected by the ADF group schedule, but the tumor weight was decreased by both feeding patterns.

In order to assess the relative effects of the two schedules on the tumor and the host weights, the mean tumor weight to host weight ratios (TW/HW%) were determined to be 15.3 ± 1.0, 10.6 ± 0.7, and 9.5 ± 1.1 for the control, IMF, and ADF groups, respectively. These results show that the TW/HW% for both the IMF and ADF groups were decreased ($P < 0.001$) when compared to the control group, suggesting that in each case, the tumor was affected to a greater extent than was the host as a result of following the two test feeding schedules. Although the tumor weights were reduced in both of the test groups, the host weight was not compromised in the IMF group, whereas, the host weight for the ADF

TABLE II. EFFECT OF THREE FEEDING SCHEDULES ON FOOD INTAKE, TUMOR AND HOST WEIGHT PARAMETERS

	Group (Feeding schedule)		
	Control (*ad lib*)	IMF (32 fed:16 fast)	ADF (24 fed:24 fast)
Non-tumor bearing			
Body weight change (g)	+3.1 ± 0.4[a]	+2.0 ± 0.5	+1.1 ± 0.4**
Food intake (g/day)	3.3 ± 0.2	3.2 ± 0.1	2.5 ± 0.1*
N	5	5	5
Tumor bearing			
Body weight change (g)	+1.22 ± 0.23	+0.16 ± 0.25**	−2.70 ± 0.35***
Terminal host weight (g)	16.3 ± 0.4	16.1 ± 0.4	13.7 ± 0.5***
Tumor weight (g)	2.42 ± 0.13	1.67 ± 0.10*	1.22 ± 0.11***
Food intake (g/day)	2.54 ± 0.05	2.46 ± 0.03	1.83 ± 0.09**
N	30	30	20

[a] Mean ± SEM.
* $P < 0.05$ as compared to control.
** $P < 0.01$ as compared to control.
*** $P < 0.001$ as compared to control.

group was lowered when compared to the control group. The more favorable TW/HW% obtained for the IMF group, relative to that found for the control group, could not be ascribed to altered food consumption, since the daily food intakes were the same when these groups were compared. Availability of the diet during each successive 2-day period for these two test groups was regulated externally but, the pattern of eating within each 2-day segment may have varied also, but no data on the rates of food intake within the 2-day cycles was obtained. Thus, the 31% reduction in tumor weight found for the IMF group below that obtained for the control group cannot be explained by caloric or nitrogen intake differences, but can be ascribed to the feeding schedule plan. Although the food intake of the ADF group was significantly ($P < 0.001$) lowered to 72% of the control group's daily intake, decreased TW/HW%, relative to that obtained for the control group cannot unambiguously be explained on the basis of the schedule of food availability. In the case of the ADF schedule, either the fasting period and/or the lowered food intake could have been responsible for the decreased weights of both the tumor and the host relative to those noted for the control group. The results also showed that the LL bearing animals were anorexic and cachexic, since both the food intakes and the body weight changes were decreased for the TB animals as compared to their corresponding groups of NTB animals.

Feeding schedules with repeating periods of nutrient availability have been shown to influence several metabolic activities of Morris hepatomas in rats (10) and intermittent periodic starvation and refeeding resulted in significant reductions in the growth of Ehrlich Ascites cells in mice (11), although both tumor and host responses to alternating feeding and fasting schedules have not been reported previously. The effect of intermittent fasting was first studied by Carlson and Hoelzel in 1946 (12) followed by Fabry and co-workers (13). The reports of Tepperman and Tepperman (14) on the metabolic effects of a single 2-day fast followed by 24 hr of feeding, stimulated the subsequent studies by Potter and co-workers (10) on the metabolic consequence of different feeding schedules. However, the feeding schedules used by all these investigators varied widely and therefore, it is difficult to compare the results between studies. In general, those investigators used intermittent fasting as a means of stress to study metabolic adaptation and so the fasting intervals were longer than the ones used in the present study. The studies on the metabolic effect of restricted feeding schedule have shown that there is a circadian rhythm for most of the parameters measured ranging from tryosine transaminase activity (15) to amino acid uptake by tissues (16) and that a deviation of feeding schedules from *ad libitum* feeding can alter the rhythm of most of the parameters measured. Takahashi and Zatz have extensively reviewed the interrelationships between the endocrine systems and the regulation of circadian rhythm, concluding that recent advances in locating the circadian "pacemaker" in the brain could reveal the cellular and biochemical mechanisms in controlling circadian rhythm (17).

Since the molecular basis of circadian rhythymicity is not fully understood it is difficult to ascribe the contribution to our findings of the systematic oscillation in metabolic and/or hormonal changes as compounded by the effect of fast/fed and light/dark stimuli. Furthermore, most of the studies from Potter's group reported synchronized food availability of rats within the dark phase. Although rodents eat mostly during the daily dark phase, they do consume some food in the light phase. In the experimental design of the present study, both of the test groups were repeatedly fasted during the dark phase. Therefore, the result observed cannot be solely attributed to the periodic fasting–refeeding cycles per se without conceding to a possible effect brought about by the perturbation of the normal hormonally–metabolically driven fast–fed rhythm and as well as the effects of the light–dark cycles. Finally although mice consume more food in the dark than in the light, their energy expenditure is also considerably elevated during that phase. Nevertheless, the present experimental design demonstrated that periodic fasting affects the TW/HW% and that the IMF schedule employed, reduced tumor weights but did not lower host weights. The influence of the factors producing circadian rhythms on these findings cannot be assessed from this study, but the IMF feeding plan produced a model in which the tumor was proportionally

TABLE III. EFFECT OF THREE FEEDING SCHEDULES ON TUMOR PROTEIN AND NUCLEIC ACID CONCENTRATIONS

Concentration (mg/g tumor)	Group (Feeding schedule) Control (*ad lib*)	IMF (32-hr fed:16-hr fast)	ADF (24-hr fed:24-hr fast)
DNA	15.9 ± 0.2[a]	14.8 ± 0.5	16.5 ± 0.6
RNA	13.9 ± 0.8	12.5 ± 0.4	12.6 ± 0.9
Protein	266 ± 8	274 ± 11	277 ± 11
N	10	10	8

[a] Mean ± SEM.

smaller with respect to the host within the context of equivalent food intakes.

The reduced mean tumor weights of both the IMF and/or the ADF groups, relative to the control group, may be simply reflections of internal compositional changes in the tumor resulting in a smaller tumor cell size with either increased, decreased or similar cell numbers. In order to establish whether this was the case, RNA, DNA, and protein contents of tumor homogenates were determined. Table III showed that no significant differences were found for the tumor concentrations of these macromolecules when the results from the IMF and ADF groups were compared to those obtained from the control tumors. Since tumor DNA, RNA, and protein concentrations were not affected by the feeding schedule, the decreased tumor size of the IMF and ADF groups, relative to the control group, was apparently a hypoplastic response brought about by the altered feeding schedules.

Finally, Table IV illustrates the relative capabilities for Leu oxidation by liver and skeletal muscle samples from animals maintained on each of the three feeding schedules for 15 days. As measured by the $^{14}CO_2$ produced/g tissue-min, the rates for Leu oxidation by the liver and skeletal muscle tissues specimens of the ADF group were markedly elevated compared to the rates for their respective control group tissues. However, there were no significant differences between the IMF and control group results for either host tissue.

As for the NTB animals, there were no differences in Leu oxidation rates observed among the three groups for both the liver and skeletal muscle samples. The distinct difference in the effect of the ADF schedule on Leu oxidation correlated with the changes in body weights when the TB and NTB groups were compared. In the NTB animals, the ADF group showed neither weight loss nor a change in Leu oxidation as compared to the NTB control group, whereas there was a loss in host weight in TB animals fed on the ADF schedule

TABLE IV. EFFECT OF THREE FEEDING SCHEDULES ON LEUCINE OXIDATION BY LIVER AND SKELETAL MUSCLE TISSUE

Tissue	Control (*ad lib*)	IMF (32-hr fed:16-hr fast)	ADF (24-hr fed:24-hr fast)
Nontumor bearing			
Liver	20.4 ± 2.4[a]	23.4 ± 2.9	28.7 ± 3.9
Skeletal muscle	9.5 ± 1.1	11.0 ± 0.8	10.2 ± 0.9
N	5	5	5
Tumor bearing			
Liver	25.0 ± 2.4	22.3 ± 1.0	42.3 ± 4.0*
Skeletal muscle	8.6 ± 0.8	8.8 ± 4.0	38.9 ± 4.9**
N	6	6	6

[a] Mean ± SEM (dpm/g tissue-min).
*$P < 0.01$ as compared to control.
**$P < 0.001$ as compared to control.

and the Leu oxidation of this group was significantly increased, when compared to that of the TB control group. These results indicated that tissue leucine oxidation may be stimulated by a factor associated with net body weight loss owing to the presence of the tumor. The control of Leu oxidation is not fully understood, but, accelerated Leu oxidation has been associated with catabolic states such as experimental diabetes and starvation (18, 19). Therefore, the results for Leu oxidation may be extrapolated to support the notion that the IMF schedule did not produce the catabolic response in the TB host that was noted for the host of the animals on the ADF schedule. Since the skeletal muscle is the site where the branched-chain amino acids are predominantly catabolized for energy (20), then the 4.5-fold increase in the metabolic activity observed for the skeletal muscle tissues of the ADF compared to the control group would clearly indicate a marked elevation of this tissue's *capability* to oxidize this essential amino acid owing to the ADF feeding schedule in the tumor bearing animals. Due to the magnitude of this increase in skeletal muscle Leu oxidation capacity, it is unlikely that this result could be solely accounted for as a procedural artifact due to equally large differences in the endogenous Leu pool sizes of the skeletal muscle between the ADF and the control groups. Finally, there were no differences between the control and IMF groups in the rates for hepatic Leu oxidation, although a significant increase of 1.7-fold for the liver of the TB ADF group compared to its TB control group was noted. Leu is catabolized by a transamination reaction followed by an irreversible oxidative decarboxylation catalyzed by the branched-chain oxo acid dehydrogenase (21). The former reaction is higher in the skeletal muscle and lower, but present, in the liver (20). The latter enzyme, however, is found to be mostly activated in the liver, but largely inactivated in the skeletal muscle tissue under normal conditions (21). This finding may explain the observed 1.7-fold increase in the liver tissue Leu oxidation as compared to the 4.5-fold increase in the skeletal muscle in the TB–ADF group, since the muscle has greater capacity for further activation. Odessey (21) also showed that the activity of the branched-chain oxo acid dehydrogenase varied as much as 5–20-fold under different experimental conditions. Thus, the 1.7- and 4.5-fold differences observed in this study are not out of range. The fact that we observed a higher Leu oxidation activity in the liver, on a per gram tissue basis, than the skeletal muscle does not negate the fact that muscle is the major site for branched-chain amino acid catabolism if we consider the total mass of skeletal muscle as compared to that of liver. Furthermore, Ichihara *et al.* (22) have noted that even though rat skeletal muscle showed higher activity of branched-chain amino acid transferase, the liver actually exhibited higher combined transamination and decarboxylation activity, again on a per gram tissue basis. Thus, these results are in concert with a general activation of the oxidation of Leu in the ADF group bearing the LL tumor as compared to its control, whereas no change in the parameter in the two tissues studied was found for the IMF group of the tumor bearing animals.

Even though our findings may be unique to the rapidly growing Lewis Lung carcinoma model, they provide a useful framework to contemplate the importance of feeding schedules in the nourishment of the host in the presence of a growing tumor. Furthermore, the results with respect to tumor growth were confined to the primary tumor at this point and cannot be extrapolated to include metastatic growth.

1. White FR. The relationship between underfeeding and tumor formation, transplantation and growth in rats and mice. Cancer Res **21**:281–290, 1961.
2. Goodgame JJ, Lowry SF, Reilly JJ, Jones DC, Brennan MF. Nutritional manipulations and tumor growth I. The effects of starvation. Amer J Clin Nutr **32**:2277–2284, 1979.
3. Stragand JJ, Braunschweiger PG, Pellice AA, Schiffer LM. Cell kinetic alterations in murine mammery tumors following fasting and refeeding. Eur J Cancer **15**:281–286, 1969.
4. Henderson JF, LePage GT. The nutrition of tumors: A review. Cancer Res **19**:887–902, 1959.
5. Cameron IL, Paviat WA. Stimulation of growth of a transplantable hepatoma in rats by parental nutrition. J Natl Cancer Inst **56**:597–601, 1976.
6. Rogers QR, Harper AE. Amino acid diets and maximal growth in the rat. J Nutr **87**:267–273, 1965.
7. Dixon WJ, Massey FJ Jr. Introduction to Statistical Analysis. New York, McGraw–Hill, 3rd ed, 1969.
8. Wannemacher RW Jr, Banks WL Jr, Wunner WH.

Use of single tissue extract to determine cellular protein and nucleic acid concentrations and rate of amino acid incorporation. Anal Biochem **11**:320–326, 1965.
9. Munro HN, Fleck A. Recent developments in the measurement of nucleic acids in biological materials. Analyst **91**:78–88, 1966.
10. Potter VR, Watanabe M, Pitot HC, Morris HP. Systematic oscillations in metabolic activity in rat liver and hepatomas. Survey of normal diploid and other hepatoma lines. Cancer Res **29**:55–78, 1969.
11. Sandor RS. Effects of fasting on growth and glycolysis of the Ehrlich Ascites tumor. J Natl Cancer Inst **56**:427–428, 1976.
12. Carlson AJ, Hoelzel F. Apparent prolongation of the life span in rats by intermittent fasting. J Nutr **31**:363–375, 1946.
13. Fabry P, Petrasek R, Horakova E, Konopasck E, Braun T. Energy metabolism and growth in rats adapted to intermittent starvation. Brit J Nutr **17**:295–301, 1963.
14. Tepperman J, Tepperman HM. Effect of antecedent food intake pattern on hepatic lipogenesis. Amer J Physiol **193**:55–64, 1958.
15. Watanabe M, Potter VR, Pitot HC. Systematic oscillations in tyrosine transaminase and other metabolic functions in liver and normal and adrenalectomized rats on controlled feeding schedules. J Nutr **95**:207–227, 1968.
16. Baril EF, Potter VR. Systematic oscillations of amino acid transport in liver from rats adapted to controlled feeding schedules. J Nutr **95**:228–237, 1968.
17. Takahashi JS, Zatz M. Regulation of circadian rhythmicity. Science **217**:1104–1111, 1982.
18. Paul HS, Adibi SA. Leucine oxidation in diabetes and starvation: Effect of ketone bodies on branched-chain amino acid oxidation in vitro. Metabolism **27**:185–200, 1978.
19. Hutson SM, Zapalowski C, Cree TC, Harper AR. Regulation of leucine and ketoisocaproic acid metabolism in skeletal muscle. Effect of starvation and insulin. J Biol Chem **255**:2418–2426, 1980.
20. Adibi SA. Metabolism of branched-chain amino acids in altered nutrition. Metabolism **25**:1287–1320, 1976.
21. Odessey R. Reversible ATP-induced inactivation of branched-chain 2-oxo acid dehydrogenase. Biochem J **192**:155–163, 1980.
22. Ichihara A, Noda C, Ogawa K. Control of leucine metabolism with special reference to branched-chain amino acid transaminase isoenzymes. Adv Enzyme Regul **11**:155–166, 1973.

Received March 26, 1984. P.S.E.B.M. 1984, Vol. 176.
Accepted May 4, 1984.

PROCEEDINGS OF THE SOCIETY FOR EXPERIMENTAL BIOLOGY AND MEDICINE **176,** 467–471 (1984)

Characterization of the Esterases of the Mitochondrial Fraction of Guinea Pig Cortical Renal Cells (41899)

GEORGES NICOT, JEAN-PIERRE VALETTE, JEAN-LOUIS DUPUY, LOUIS MERLE, GÉRARD LACHATRE, AND YVES NOUAILLE

Pharmacologie Clinique, Hôpital Dupuytren, 87042 Limoges, France

Abstract. The esterase activity of the mitochondrial fraction from cortical renal cells was studied in guinea pigs aged 15, 21, 30, and 120 days. The rate of hydrolysis of β-naphthyl acetate was measured by incubating aliquots of mitochondrial preparations with physostigmine, diisopropylfluorophosphate, $HgCl_2$, and *p*-hydroxymercuribenzoate. Enzyme activity was mainly due to the heterogeneous aliesterase group: some aliesterases were sensitive to physostigmine, others to organophosphorus compounds and/or to $HgCl_2$; a C-esterase stimulated by organomercurials and similar to that described by Bergmann *et al.* in hog kidney was detected (F Bergmann, R Segal, S Rimon. Biochem J **67**:481–486, 1957); arylesterase activity was very weak. Acetylthiocholine used as substrate showed there was no cholinesterase activity in the mitochondrial fraction.

Enzymes which catalyze the hydrolysis of the esters of a carboxylic acid are named esterases. On the basis of sensitivity to organophosphorus compounds, Aldridge (1) and Augustinsson (2) divided mammalian plasma esterases into two classes, the A-class or arylesterase (ArE) which was resistant and the B-class or aliesterase (AliE) including cholinesterase (ChE) which was sensitive to inhibition by organophosphates. Bergmann *et al.* (3) showed that hog kidney contained a C-esterase which was resistant to inhibition by diisopropylfluorophosphate (DFP), activated by *p*-chloromercuribenzoate (*p*CMB) and phenylmercuric acetate.

In previous works (4, 5) we measured the enzymatic hydrolysis of β-naphthyl acetate (BNA) by extracts of guinea pig kidney cortex and medulla. We showed that the hydrolysis was only partly inhibited by DFP and strongly stimulated by *p*CMB and thus suggested the existence of a C-esterase in the guinea pig kidney. The present study was conducted in order to determine the esterase activity of the mitochondrial fraction of guinea pig renal cortical cells and see if it was partly due to a C-esterase.

Materials and Methods. *Tissue extracts.* Female guinea pigs 15, 21, 30, and 120 days old, were housed at 25°C, artificially lighted 8 hr a day, and fed on a diet of pellets[1] and water *ad libitum*. After an overnight fasting, animals were killed at 9 AM by a blow on the head and kidneys were removed. In order to expel most of residual blood, a 0.9% saline solution was injected into the renal artery. Then medulla and cortex were separated by careful dissection. Portions of cortical tissue were taken for histologic examination and the remaining part homogenized at 4°C in a volume of 0.25 *M* sucrose solution to produce a final 10% homogenate concentration (w/v).

Subcellular fractionation. The various subcellular fractions were prepared according to the method of de Duve (6). The cortical homogenate was first centrifuged at 900*g* for 15 min at 4°C in an ultracentrifuge[2] equipped with a titanium rotor (Ref. 60 595 93); the supernatant was removed and stored at 4°C for future use. The pellet was resuspended in a 0.25 *M* sucrose solution. This procedure was repeated twice.

Pooled supernatants were centrifuged at 16,000*g* for 20 min at 4°C. The upper fraction was discarded. The pellet was washed with a 0.25 *M* sucrose solution and this suspension was called the mitochondrial fraction. The presence of mitochondria in this fraction was checked by electron microscopy.

Protein concentration. The protein concentration in tissue extracts and subcellular fractions was measured according to the Gornall

[1] U.A.R., Villemoison sur Orge, France.

[2] M.S.E., Manor Royal, Crawley, England.

0037-9727/84 $1.50

TABLE I. PROTEIN CONCENTRATION AND ESTERASE ACTIVITY IN CORTICAL AND MITOCHONDRIAL FRACTIONS OF GUINEA PIG RENAL CELLS ACCORDING TO AGE[a]

Age (days)	Sample	Protein concentration[b] (mg/ml cortical extract)	Specific esterase activity[b] (μM/min/mg protein)
15	Cortex	19.50 ± 2.00 (20)	0.163 ± 0.002 (20)
	Mitochondria	3.00 ± 0.69 (20)	* 0.458 ± 0.003 (20)
21	Cortex	13.89 ± 2.44 (7)	0.279 ± 0.008 (7)
	Mitochondria	1.65 ± 0.37 (20)	* 0.691 ± 0.010 (20)
30	Cortex	12.58 ± 0.96 (19)	0.185 ± 0.009 (19)
	Mitochondria	1.57 ± 0.35 (20)	0.193 ± 0.014 (20)
120	Cortex	12.25 ± 1.00 (20)	0.233 ± 0.008 (20)
	Mitochondria	3.17 ± 0.70 (20)	* 0.358 ± 0.003 (20)

[a] Results are expressed as means ± 2 SD.
[b] The number of measurements is in parentheses.
* P value between cortical and mitochondrial specific esterase activity < 0.001.

method (7) using bovine serum albumin as standard.

Enzyme assays. Esterase activity was determined quantitatively using the spectrophotometric technique described by Burlina (8). Esterase activity was measured as the hydrolysis of BNA[3] (final concentration, 5.36×10^{-4} M) at 37°C, pH 7.4, 328 nm, using a spectrophotometer[4] equipped with a thermostated cell chamber. The total activity was expressed as micromoles of substrate hydrolyzed per minute per milligram of protein.

In order to detect any arylesterase activity (ArE), we used a technique modified from that described by Aldridge (9) and Ecobichon (10). Aliquots of mitochondrial fraction were dialyzed 12 hr at 4°C against 0.05 M Tris buffer (pH 7.4) containing 1×10^{-4} M EDTA. The dialyzed samples were incubated in the presence of 5×10^{-4} M Ca^{2+} for 5 min at 37°C, following which the residual activity was assayed. Enzymatic hydrolysis of 1×10^{-3} M diethyl p-nitrophenyl-phosphate[5] (E 600) was measured as the release of p-nitrophenol after 5 min, at pH 7.4, 345 nm.

Cholinesterase activity was measured according to the technique of Ellman using acetylthiocholine as substrate (11).

Inhibition and activation studies. The sensitivity of the renal esterases to DFP[3] (final concentration, 1×10^{-4} M), physostigmine[3] (final concentration, 1×10^{-4} M), p-hydroxymercuribenzoate[3] (pHMB) (final concentration, 1×10^{-5} M), and $HgCl_2$[6] (final concentration, 1×10^{-4} M) was measured after incubation of the enzyme preparation with the inhibitors or activators at pH 7.4 for 5 min at 37°C. The residual activity was determined using 5.36×10^{-4} M BNA; the inhibition or activation was expressed as a fraction of the control esterase activity.

Statistical analysis was done using Student's t test.

Results. The protein concentration in the mitochondrial fraction of the cortex was 15, 12, 12, and 26% of the total cortical protein concentration in animals aged 15, 21, 30, and 120 days, respectively (Table I). The esterase activity of this mitochondrial fraction was 43, 29, 13, and 40% of the cortical activity in the 15-, 21-, 30-, and 120-day-old animals. Thus, the specific enzyme activity of the mitochondria expressed per milligram of protein was significantly higher than that of the total renal cortex except on Day 30 (Table I). Experiments using acetylthiocholine as substrate showed there was no hydrolysis, and thus no cholinesterase (ChE) activity. The percentage inhibition of esterase activity by physostigmine amounted to 50, 45, 35, and 20% in 15-, 21-, 30-, and 120-day-old animals (Fig. 1). The esterase activity of the mitochondrial fraction

[3] Sigma, Saint Louis, Mo.
[4] Beckman, Acta III, Fullerton, Calif.
[5] Aldrich, Milwaukee, Wisc.
[6] Merck, Darmstadt, FRG.

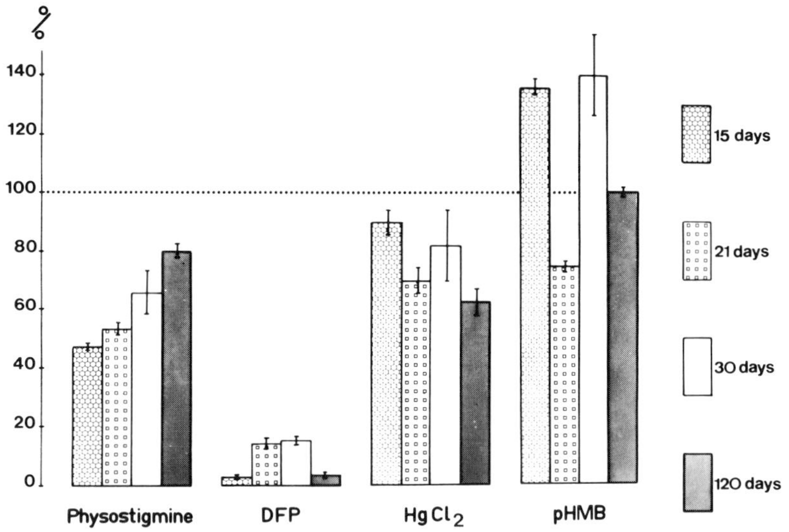

FIG. 1. Effect of activators and inhibitors on the esterase activity in the mitochondrial fraction from guinea pig cortical renal cells according to age expressed as percentage of control activity. [DFP] = 1×10^{-4} M; [physostigmine] = 1×10^{-4} M; [pHMB] = 1×10^{-5} M; [$HgCl_2$] = 1×10^{-4} M.

was markedly inhibited by DFP; the residual activity was 3, 14, 15, and 4% at Days 15, 21, 30, and 120, respectively (Fig. 1). $HgCl_2$ induced a 10, 30, 18, and 37% inhibition in animals aged 15, 21, 30, and 120 days, respectively (Fig. 1). *p*HMB produced an enzymatic activation of 35% at Day 15 and 30% at Day 30. At Day 21, the esterase activity was inhibited by 25%; at Day 120 *p*HMB had no effect (Fig. 1).

When the mitochondrial fraction was incubated with DFP together with 0.6×10^{-4} M *p*HMB, residual activity was 800% of the activity of the mitochondrial–DFP incubation mixture at Day 15, and 400 to 500% at the other periods of growth (Table II). Unlike organic mercurials, DFP together with $HgCl_2$ produced an inhibition at Days 21 and 30 and had no effect at Days 15 and 120 (Table II).

Discussion. This study of the mitochondrial fraction of guinea pig renal cortex showed that both the protein concentration and the enzyme activity were variable during the first 4 months of life. The mitochondrial protein concentration ranged from 12 to 26% of the cortical protein concentration (Table I). The mitochondrial specific enzyme activity was higher than the cortical specific activity (Table I).

Physostigmine, an inhibitor of ChE and of some AliE (2) induced, at a 10^{-4} M concentration, a 20 to 50% decrease of mitochondrial enzyme activity. This decrease could not be due to the inhibition of ChE because no enzyme activity was detected by the use of acetylthiocholine as substrate. There would not thus be any ChE in mitochondria, which is

TABLE II. EFFECT OF MERCURIALS UPON SPECIFIC ESTERASE ACTIVITY INHIBITED BY DFP IN THE MITOCHONDRIAL FRACTION FROM GUINEA PIG CORTICAL RENAL CELLS ACCORDING TO AGE[a]

Age (days)	DFP[b]	DFP/pHMB[b]	DFP/$HgCl_2$[b]
15	0.014 ± 0.001 (15)	0.114 ± 0.004* (15)	0.017 ± 0.006 (20)
21	0.101 ± 0.012 (20)	0.437 ± 0.022* (20)	0.010 ± 0.003* (20)
30	0.030 ± 0.001 (20)	0.139 ± 0.002* (20)	0.015 ± 0.008 (20)
120	0.015 ± 0.002 (20)	0.073 ± 0.002 (20)	0.018 ± 0.005 (20)

[a] The specific arylesterase activity is expressed as micromoles of substrate released per minute per milligram of protein.

[b] The number of measurements is in parentheses. Results are expressed as means ± 2 SD.

* P value between the DFP baseline and either the DFP/pHMB or the DFP/$HgCl_2$ value < 0.001.

in agreement with other authors' findings (14). So this inhibition could be connected with an AliE sensitive to physostigmine.

AliE activity in mitochondria seemed to be marked as DFP, a more potent inhibitor of AliE than physostigmine (2) when used at a 10^{-4} *M* concentration induced a 85 to 97% inhibition of enzyme activity. The low residual activity was due to esterases resistant to DFP. ArE were not involved as there were neither hydrolysis of E 600 by mitochondrial extracts nor enzyme activation by calcium, a usual sign of ArE activity (9, 12, 13). On the contrary, it is known that some AliE are resistant to organophosphates. Several hypothesis have been raised so as to explain this resistance to inhibition: first there are at least two types of AliE, one sensitive and the other resistant to organophosphate inhibition (14); second there are two different active sites in the enzyme (15), one site sensitive to organophosphate inhibition that catalyzes the hydrolysis of aromatic and alkyl esters, and the other site, resistant to these inhibitors, that only catalyzes the hydrolysis of substituted phenyl and naphthyl esters. So, residual activity after DFP was probably due to an AliE which was not inhibited by DFP.

Apart from these AliE sensitive or resistant to DFP, we detected a different type of AliE sensitive to mercury (16): $HgCl_2$ (an inhibitor of ArE (17) and AliE) when used at a 10^{-4} *M* concentration induced an inhibition ranging from 10 to 40%. As this inhibition could not be connected with ArE as shown previously, it was probably related to an AliE.

This very same AliE activity was encountered when preparations were incubated first with DFP and then with $HgCl_2$ as under these conditions, on the 21st day, $HgCl_2$ significantly inhibited residual activity after DFP. No inhibition was detected at the other periods of growth (Table II).

All these results show that the AliE group in the mitochondrial fraction is quite large and heterogeneous. Some AliE are inhibited by physostigmine, others are inhibited by organophosphates and/or by $HgCl_2$.

The use of *p*HMB, a sodium salt of *p*CMB, induced a marked stimulation of the mitochondrial activity at 15 and 30 days (Fig. 1). This stimulation could be connected with the presence of a C-esterase similar to that described by Bergmann *et al.* in hog kidney (3). This author remarked that *p*CMB induced a stimulation of esterases that were different from esterase A and esterase B described by Aldridge (1). The presence of this C-esterase was confirmed by the use of *p*HMB after DFP. Table II shows a marked stimulation of the DFP inhibited enzyme activity at all the periods of growth which suggests a C-esterase was present in the mitochondrial preparation.

So residual enzyme activity after DFP inhibition was due first to a noninhibited AliE as seen previously and second to a C-esterase present in quite a large amount.

Our hypothesis of the existence of a C-esterase in extracts of cavian kidney contradicts the observations of Chow and Ecobichon (14). Although the inhibitor concentrations these authors used were identical to ours, the techniques of the two studies were not similar. They differed with respect to the fraction that was used and the mitochondria separation: Chow and Ecobichon studied a total renal homogenate and isolated mitochondria from a 11,000*g* supernatant whereas in the present work we studied a cortical homogenate which, according to de Duve technique (6), was centrifuged three times at 900*g* so as to concentrate nuclei and cell debris in the pellet and retain intracellular organelles in the upper phase; then the supernatant was centrifuged at 16,000*g* following which a pellet enriched in mitochondria was used. Two hypothesis may be raised so as to explain the discrepancy between the results of Chow and Ecobichon and ours: first, mitochondria may have been concentrated in the 11,000*g* pellet discarded by Chow and Ecobichon, and second, if it is assumed mitochondria were present in the supernatant they studied, C-esterase activity was probably low and undetectable as mitochondria were extracted from a total renal homogenate which might have contained a lower concentration of mitochondria than a cortical homogenate.

Our assays were done with intact mitochondria without using Triton X-100, which suggests the enzymatic activities detected were probably due to enzymes situated in the mitochondrial membranes.

On the basis of sensitivity to inhibitors and activators, mitochondrial esterases of guinea pig renal cortex were identified mainly as heterogeneous AliE, C-esterase, and perhaps ArE in small proportion.

C-esterase activity which, according to us, takes a prominent part in mitochondrial physiology is not easily detectable; sensitive and specific techniques are necessary. This mitochondrial C-esterase activity appears to be variable with the age of the guinea pig, a fact which remains unexplained.

We appreciate the advice and encouragement of Dr. M. M. Reidenberg. This work was supported by a grant from INSERM (CRL 825 020).

1. Aldridge WN. Serum esterases. 1. Two types of esterase (A and B) hydrolysing *p*-nitrophenyl acetate, propionate and butyrate, and a method for their determination. Biochem J **53**:110–117, 1953.
2. Augustinsson KB. Multiple forms of esterase in vertebrate blood plasma. Ann NY Acad Sci **94**:844–860, 1961.
3. Bergmann F, Segal R, Rimon S. A new type of esterase in hog-kidney extract. Biochem J **67**:481–486, 1957.
4. Nicot G, Valette JP, Merle L. Activité arylestérasique rénale corticale et médullaire au cours de la croissance chez le Cobaye. C R Soc Biol **172**:314–319, 1978.
5. Valette JP, Merle L, Nicot G. Influence du *p*-hydroxymercuribenzoate de sodium sur l'activité arylestérasique de la fraction mitochondriale du cortex rénal chez le Cobaye. J Pharmacol (Paris) **10**:256–257, 1979.
6. de Duve C, Pressman BC, Gianetto R, Wattiaux R, Appelmans F. Tissue fractionation studies. 6. Intracellular distribution patterns of enzymes in rat-liver tissue. Biochem J **60**:604–617, 1955.
7. Gornall AG, Bardawill CJ, David MM. Determination of serum proteins by means of the biuret reaction. J Biol Chem **177**:751–766, 1949.
8. Burlina A, Galzigna L, Miconi G. Metodo cinetico per la determinazione dell' arilesterasi. Quad Sclavo Diagn Clin Lab **8**:529–540, 1972.
9. Aldridge WN. Serum esterases. 2. An enzyme hydrolysing diethyl *p*-nitrophenyl phosphate (E 600) and its identity with the A-esterase of mammalian sera. Biochem J **53**:117–124, 1953.
10. Ecobichon DJ. Characterization of the esterases of canine serum. Canad J Biochem **48**:1359–1367, 1970.
11. Ellman GL, Courtney KD, Andres V, Featherstone RM. A new and rapid colorimetric determination of acetylcholinesterase activity. Biochem Pharmacol **7**:88–95, 1961.
12. Erdös EG, Debay CR, Westerman MP. Arylesterases in blood: Effect of calcium and inhibitors. Biochem Pharmacol **5**:173–186, 1960.
13. Marton A, Kalow W. Studies on aromatic esterase and cholinesterase of human serum. Canad J Biochem Physiol **37**:1367–1373, 1959.
14. Chow AYK, Ecobichon DJ. Characterization of the esterases of guinea pig liver and kidney. Biochem Pharmacol **22**:689–701, 1973.
15. Greenzaid P, Jencks WP. Pig liver esterase. Reactions with alcohols, structure-reactivity correlations, and the acyl-enzyme intermediate. Biochemistry **10**:1210–1222, 1971.
16. Ljungquist A, Augustinsson KB. Purification and properties of two carboxylesterases from rat-liver microsomes. Eur J Biochem **23**:303–313, 1971.
17. Augustinsson KB. Conformational changes of an enzyme protein by low concentration of mercuric ions. Biochim Biophys Acta **214**:248–249, 1970.

Received April 13, 1984. P.S.E.B.M. 1984, Vol. 176.
Accepted May 4, 1984.

PROCEEDINGS OF THE SOCIETY FOR EXPERIMENTAL BIOLOGY AND MEDICINE **176**, 472–475 (1984)

Radioimmunoassay of Bone Morphogenetic Protein in Serum: A Tissue-Specific Parameter of Bone Metabolism[1] (41900)

MARSHALL R. URIST AND ROBERT T. HUDAK

University of California, Los Angeles, Bone Research Laboratory, Los Angeles, California 90024

Abstract. Bone morphogenetic protein (BMP), a paracrine agent inducing cartilage and bone cell differentiation, circulates in the blood and is detectable by BMP radioimmunoassay. Serum BMP levels are higher in growing children and patients with Paget's disease than in normal adults. These observations are interpreted as evidence of a BMP function in the physiology of bone in health and disease.

Bone is unique among the connective tissues of the body in several respects. First, it is continuously remodeled irrespective of physiological demands and aging. Second, in response to injury it regenerates without scar, completely and flawlessly. Third, bone develops *de novo* in extraskeletal sites by differentiation of perivascular connective tissue cells (pericytes) under the influence of a bone morphogenetic protein (BMP) derived from bone (1–4), dentin (5), and osteosarcoma tissues (6, 7). Bovine BMP (bBMP) is an acidic polypeptide with a relative molecular mass (M_r) of 18,500 ± 1000 and pI of 5.0 ± .1 (4). Human BMP (hBMP) has similar characteristics with a slightly lower M_r. This report is submitted as evidence that BMP circulates in the blood in nanogram quantities, detectable by a standard displacement method of radioimmunoassay (RIA).

Materials and Methods. *Preparation of antigen.* bBMP was prepared from bovine cortical bone and purified by methods described in a recent report (4).

Preparation of antibodies. An antibody was prepared by injection of purified bBMP into rabbits, 5 mg/kg in Freund's adjuvant, 5 mg/ml sc/week for 3 weeks. The serum was collected 3 days after the last injection.

Iodination of BMP. BMP was iodinated using a modification of the method of Bolton and Hunter (8). To 10 μg of BMP in 50 μl phosphate-buffered saline (PBS), pH 7.0, were added 4 μCi of ^{125}I (Amersham) and 10 μl of chloramine T (5 mg/12.5 ml). The reaction was allowed to continue for 180 sec and terminated with the addition of 10 μl sodium metabisulfite (5 mg/10 ml). This product was then purified on a 0.7 × 25-cm column of Sephacryl S-200 (Pharmacia, Piscataway, N.J.) using 0.1 *M* PBS, pH 6.55, containing 0.05% Tween 20.

Immunoassay. Duplicate samples of serum were analyzed both quantitatively and qualitatively by enzyme-linked immunosorbent assay (ELISA), using the dot immunobinding method (9).

Serum analyses. Thirty adult human serum samples (0.5 ml) were collected from the discarded surplus stock of blood analyzed by the hospital clinical chemistry laboratory, and classified as normal. Sera from six different children similarly classified, were obtained from the tissue typing laboratory. Serum from three patients with severe Paget's disease, two male and one female, (with very high levels of serum alkaline phosphatase levels) were obtained from the surplus of blood collected for routine diagnostic studies.

Controls. The three following control analyses were performed on each sample to exclude unspecific protein reactions. (a) Human serum stripped of protein hormones with dextran-coated charcoal (NORIT-SG, Fischer Chem, Los Angeles, Calif.), (b) serum supplemented with 6 to 16 ng of prolactin, (c) serum supersaturated with 100 ng of prolactin.

Results. Figure 1 shows a dose–response curve of the RIA for BMP when plotted on a log–log scale. The concentration of BMP is plotted on the horizontal axis, while the per-

[1] These investigations were supported by grants-in-aid from USPHS, NIDR (DE02103), The Keck Foundation, and The Scoliosis Foundation.

0037-9727/84 $1.50

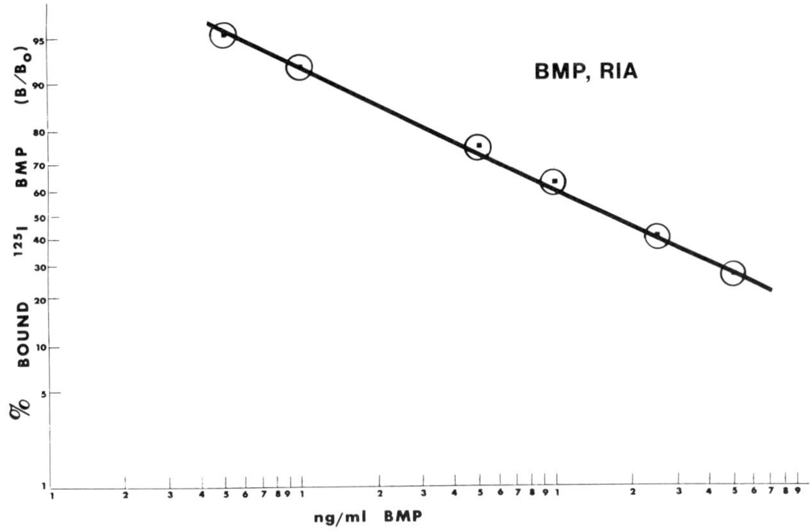

FIG. 1. A standard linear dose–response relationship (log–log scale) showing the sensitivity of the BMP RIA with ^{125}I-BMP binding to rabbit anti-bBMP antibody in ng range of values.

centage bound BMP ^{125}I is plotted on the vertical axis as the ratio of B/Bo. "Bo" represents the maximum quantity of ^{125}I-BMP bound to the antibody in the absence of nonradioactive BMP. "B" represents the amount of ^{125}I-BMP bound to the antibody when known concentrations of nonradioactive BMP are present. In order to obtain maximum displacement, a 200-μl sample size was used.

To validate an RIA, one must show that the antigen used for the standards is immunologically identical to the material being measured in the serum (10–12). Therefore, we use the parallelism and recovery methods.

Table I demonstrates the parallelism or effects of dilutions on the assay. Serial dilutions of two samples with a high concentration of BMP were made from 0- to 16-fold. If both standard and serum BMP are immunologically identical then the values obtained from a diluted sample multiplied by its dilution factor should be within experimental error, identical to the undiluted value. This is essentially the case.

TABLE I. PARALLELISM OF BMP RIA[a]

Dilution		Expt A[b]	Expt B[c]
0	Value obtained	370	160
1:2	Value obtained	180	84
	Value (×) dilution factor	180 × 2 = 360	84 × 2 = 168
1:4	Value obtained	80	38
	Value (×) dilution factor	80 × 4 = 320	38 × 4 = 152
1:8	Value obtained	40	19
	Value (×) dilution factor	40 × 8 = 320	19 × 18 = 152
1:16	Value obtained	20	11
	Value (×) dilution factor	20 × 16 = 320	11 × 16 = 176

[a] All values are ng/ml BMP.
[b] Expt A: mean, 338.0; SD, 24.9.
[c] Expt B: mean, 161.6; SD, 10.4.

Table II further demonstrates the accuracy of this BMP RIA by its capacity to detect the additive BMP concentrations. In Experiment A with initial (baseline) value of 17 ng/ml, and Experiment B with 50 ng/ml, the total RIA values prove to be acceptably close to the sum of the initial values plus the added quantities of BMP, showing that the BMP used for the standards and the serum BMP must be immunologically identical.

The following experiment was set up to test the precision or reproducibility of the assay. Three samples were analyzed, followed by the standard curve, and again followed by three samples. When the system reached equilibrium, the samples were read and the same value obtained, regardless of the position in the assay. Thus it was possible to eliminate any question arising from the length of the assay or the number of samples being analyzed. The experiment was also set up on five different days, and on each occasion the equilibrium was complete. Table III shows average values obtained per assay run, and good *inter*- and intraassay correlation.

Table IV summarizes the results obtained by performing an RIA on the serum of 94 patients including rapidly growing normal children, normal adults, and three patients with Paget's disease. The range of BMP RIA values of normal adults was significantly lower than in growing children and about 17 times lower than three patients with extensive Paget's disease of the skull, vertebra, pelvis, femur, and tibia.

ELISA. With the ELISA procedure, the mouse anti-human BMP cross-reacted 100% with both human and bovine BMP. Similarly, the rabbit anti-bovine BMP cross-reacted 100% with both the human and bovine BMP which demonstrates that either BMP is not species specific, or the segment of the molecule our antisera detects may be common to several species. On samples listed in Tables I to III, with BMP RIA values greater than 15 ng/ml, the results were confirmed by an unequivocally positive qualitative ELISA.

Discussion. The hypothesis supported by the above recorded data is that BMP is a normal byproduct of local or paracrine (3, 13) bone metabolism, that appears in the sera of normal individuals. BMP RIA values are higher in rapidly growing children with normally high levels of bone turnover than in nongrowing adults with normally low rates of bone turnover. Rapidly growing children have a range of at least 20 to 72 ng/ml, while normal adults show less than 16 ng. The standard deviation of the values for children was 18.9, compared with 5.7 and 4.40 for men and women, respectively, and was attributable to

TABLE II. Recovery of BMP RIA

BMP added (ng)	Test A (17 ng/ml)		Test B (50 ng/ml)	
	Expected	Recovered	Expected	Recovered
250	267	280	300	320
125	142	150	175	190
50	67	64	100	90
25	42	38	67	72

Note. All values are ng/ml BMP.

TABLE III. BMP RIA Determinations of Three Sets of Samples on Five Successive Days

	BMP (ng/ml)		
	Serum A	Serum B	Serum C
	10	21	17
	12	24	19
	11	25	20
	14	27	17
	10	25	16
Mean	11.4	24.4	17.8
SD	1.67	2.19	1.64
Coeff. variation (%)	14.6	9.0	9.2

TABLE IV. Serum BMP in Health and Disease

Conditions	No. patients	No. analyses	RIA (ng/ml) Range	Mean
Adult men	35	69	1–23	14.43[a]
Adult women	45	100	13–35	18.20[b]
Children, ages 2 to 8	6	9	20–72	56.0[c]
Paget's disease	3	5	>250	ND

[a] SD 5.77.
[b] SD 4.40.
[c] SD 18.90.

one child with a value of 20 ng/ml compared to 5 others with values ranging from 54 to 72 ng/ml. A larger sample of normal and abnormal children and further improvements in the sensitivity of the assay are presently under investigation.

Three patients with extensive Paget's disease consistently show high levels, over 250 ng, of serum BMP. To investigate serum BMP RIA values in other disorders in which the rate of bone turnover is abnormal, more particularly the resorption phase, the present research is being extended to patients with osteoporosis, hyperparathyroidism, and renal osteodystrophy. Our observations on mice, rats, rabbits, and dogs with implants of BMP in muscle or in bone defects (1, 5) or BMP in mouse or human osteosarcomas (6, 7, 14, 15) and other bone tumors (16, 17) suggest that a BMP quantitative immunoassay could prove to be of value for diagnosis and the response to treatment.

The origin of serum BMP from tissues other than bone has a bearing on the interpretation of BMP RIA. We have assayed crude 4 *M* guanidinium HCl extracts of brain, liver, muscle, and kidney and found no detectable BMP activity. The possibilities of secretion of BMP by transitional epithelium of kidney pelvis, ureter, urinary bladder, and mucosa cells of stomach and gall bladder, nonosseous tissues known to induce bone formation (18), have not been entirely excluded. However, the total body skeletal tissue mass is so much greater than any other organ system that an extraosseous source would be more significant under pathological than normal physiological conditions.

1. Urist MR. Bone morphodifferentiation and tumorigenesis. Perspect Biol Med **22**:S89–S113, 1979.
2. Mizutani H, Urist MR. The nature of bone morphogenetic protein (BMP) fractions derived from bovine bone matrix gelatin. Clin Orthop **171**:213–223, 1982.
3. Urist MR, DeLange RJ, Finerman GAM. Bone cell differentiation and growth factors: Induced activity of chondro-osteogenetic DNA. Science **220**:680–686, 1983.
4. Urist MR, Huo YK, Brownell AG, Hohl WM, Buyske J, Lietze A, Tempst P, Hunkapillar M, DeLange RJ. Purification of bovine bone morphogenetic protein by hydroxyapatite chromatography. Proc Natl Acad Sci USA **81**:371–375, 1984.
5. Conover MA, Urist MR. Dentin matrix morphogenetic protein. In: Proceedings of the 1st International Conference on Chemistry and Biology of Mineralized Connective Tissue, Northwestern University, May 3–7, 1981. New York, Elsevier/North-Holland, pp597–606, 1982.
6. Takaoka K, Yoshikawa H, Shimizu N, Ono K, Amitani K, Nakata Y, Sakamoto Y. Purification of a bone-inducing substance (osteogenic factor) from a murine osteosarcoma. Biomed Res **2**(5):466–471, 1981.
7. Bauer FCH, Urist MR. Human osteosarcoma-derived soluble bone morphogenetic protein. Clin Orthop **154**:234–248, 1981.
8. Hunter WM, Greenwood FC. Preparation of Iodine 131 labelled human growth hormone of high specific activity. Nature (London) **194**:495–496, 1962.
9. Hawkes R, Niday E, Gordon J. A dot-immunobinding assay for monoclonal and other antibodies. Anal Biochem **119**:142–147, 1982.
10. Midgley AR Jr, Niswender, GD, Rebar RW. Principles for the assesment of the reliability of radioimmunoassay methods (precision, accuracy, sensitivity, specificity). Acta Endocrinol **63**(Suppl):142, 163.
11. Skelley DS, Brown LP, Besch PK. Radioimmunoassay. Clin Chem **19**:146–186, 1973.
12. Berson SA, Yalow RS, eds. In: Peptide Hormones. Amsterdam, North-Holland, p84, 1973.
13. Sporn MB, Todaro FJ. Autocrine secretion and malignant transformation of cells. N Engl J Med **303**:878–880, 1980.
14. Urist MR, Grant TT, Lindholm ST, Mirra JM, Hirano H, Finerman GAM. Induction of new-bone formation in the host bed by human bone-tumor transplants in athymic nude mice. J Bone Joint Surg **61A**(8):1207–1216, 1979.
15. Hanamura H, Higuchi Y, Nakagawa M, Iwata H, Nogami H, Urist MR. Solubilized bone morphogenetic protein (BMP) from mouse osteosarcoma and rat demineralized bone matrix. Clin Orthop **148**:281–289, 1980.
16. Bauer FCH, Urist MR. The reaction of giant cell tumors of bone to transplantation into athymic nude mice: Including observations on osteo-induction in the host bed. Clin Orthop **159**:257–264, 1981.
17. Bauer FCH, Mirra MJ, Urist MR. Bone induction by Ewing's sarcoma: Transplantation into athymic nude mice. Arch Pathol Lab Med **105**(6):322–324, 1981.
18. Huggins CB. The formation of bone under the influence of the epithelium of the urinary tract. Arch Surg **22**:337–389, 1931.

Received March 5, 1984. P.S.E.B.M. 1984, Vol. 176.
Accepted May 7, 1984.

Effects of Dietary Salt, Fat, and Carbohydrate on Fluid and Salt Consumption of Rats[1] (41901)

ROSE M. THREATTE[2] AND MICHAEL R. QUINN[3]

Monell Chemical Senses Center, Philadelphia, Pennsylvania 19104

Abstract. Studies were conducted to investigate the influence of dietary sodium chloride (NaCl), fat, and carbohydrate on NaCl preferences of rats. Both long-term (48 hr) and short-term (20 min) two-bottle preference tests were used. Rats were fed either a basal salt (1.17%) diet or high salt (8.37 to 8.59%) diets in which the level of sucrose was modified by substitution with either corn oil or cornstarch. Water and NaCl consumption was measured in 48-hr two-bottle preference tests using various concentrations (0.005 to 0.5 *M*) of NaCl paired with water. The results of these studies suggest that changes in fluid consumption were accounted for by an increase in water consumption which was inversely related to the sucrose to starch ratio and directly related to the NaCl content of the diets. A reduction in NaCl consumption was observed only during the short-term (20 min) tests.

An increase in consumption of a sodium chloride (NaCl) solution can be elicited in rats, as well as in other species, by maintaining the animals on a sodium deficient diet (1–3). Adrenalectomized rats also show a marked increase in intake of NaCl solutions (4–6). However, sodium consumption is not totally regulated by a metabolic requirement for sodium; e.g., rats that are in sodium balance consume quantities of sodium salt solutions that are in excess of physiologic need when given a choice between a NaCl solution and water (2, 7). Thus, it is clear that gustatory factors contribute to the amount of sodium consumed.

The influence of dietary constituents on the regulation of sodium intake has not been well characterized. Smith-Barbaro *et al.* (8) demonstrated that rats maintained on high salt diets containing 20% saturated or unsaturated fat exhibited a decrease in preference (defined as milliliters saline consumed/total milliliters fluid consumed) for either 0.15 or 0.30 *M* NaCl, when given a choice between a NaCl solution and deionized water, compared with rats maintained on 5% fat, high salt diets. These investigators suggested that the changes in salt acceptability may be attributed to dietary postingestional feedback mechanisms that are dependent on the level of fat in the diet, rather than to the accompanying changes in blood pressure (9). However, the level of fat was adjusted at the expense of sucrose to obtain isocaloric diets and it is not clear whether the observed changes in preference were due to alterations in the level of dietary fat or sucrose.

The purpose of the present studies was to extend earlier observations that dietary constituents, in addition to NaCl, contribute to changes in sodium consumption, and to examine these dietary effects in more detail. Specifically, the goals of the present studies were (i) to investigate the effects of dietary fat, carbohydrate, and NaCl on long-term (48 hr) NaCl and water consumption; and (ii) to investigate the effect of dietary constituents on short-term (20 min) NaCl and water consumption in an attempt to separate postabsorptive from stimulus-derived factors. The results indicate that the changes in fluid consumption observed during the long-term tests were due predominantly to an increase in water intake which was directly related to the level of dietary NaCl and inversely related to the sucrose to starch ratio of the diet. In addition, analysis of the short-term tests revealed

[1] This study was supported by USDA Grant 59-32U4-0-3. The authors wish to acknowledge the excellent technical assistance of Dianne MacCarty and Barbara Small and the secretarial aid of Linda Robinson. We also thank Dr. Gary K. Beauchamp and Dr. D. Mark Hegsted for valuable discussions.

[2] To whom requests for reprints should be sent.

[3] Present address: Department of Pathological Biochemistry, Institute Basic Research in Developmental Disabilities, 1050 Forest Hill Road, Staten Island, N.Y. 10314.

0037-9727/84 $1.50

a decrease in the amount of NaCl consumed and it appeared that this reduction was dependent on the level of dietary NaCl.

Methods. *Experiment 1.* Forty-two-day-old male Sprague–Dawley rats (Harlan Sprague–Dawley, Madison, Wisc.) were housed individually in hanging stainless-steel cages with a 12-hr light–dark cycle. Rats were randomly divided into six groups (12 rats/group) and were adapted to a 5% fat, basal salt (1.17% NaCl, BS) diet for 2 weeks before each group was assigned at the beginning of the third week of the study to one of the six dietary regimens described in Table I. Rats adjust their food consumption to maintain caloric intake, regardless of the caloric density of the diet (11). Diets were formulated according to Newberne *et al.* (11) to ensure that all animals were consuming similar quantities of caloric as well as noncaloric dietary constituents (Table I). The 5% fat, HS–low sucrose diet was designed to investigate the effects of low levels of sucrose in a HS diet without adjustments in fat content. The 5% fat, HS–low starch diet was used to examine the effects of raising the level of sucrose at the expense of starch. Lastly, the 20% fat, HS–low starch diet was designed to separate the effects of high levels of fat from the effects of lowering both the sucrose and starch content of the diets. All constituents used to prepare the diets were obtained from ICN Nutritional Biochemicals (Plainview, N.Y.). Each group of animals was fed the assigned experimental diet for a period of 8 weeks (Weeks 3–10). Food and water were provided *ad libitum.* Water was presented in two, glass graduated drinking tubes similar to those described by Richter (12). Throughout the entire study, body weights of all rats from each dietary group were recorded at the end of each week.

During the initial period when all animals were receiving the 5% fat, BS diet, the animals were tested for NaCl preference using 0.1 *M* NaCl paired with deionized water. Consumption of water and saline was measured by means of two-bottle, 48-hr preference tests as previously described (8). Experimental diets were initiated and after 1 week (beginning Week 4), all animals from each group were

TABLE I. COMPOSITION OF EXPERIMENTAL DIETS

	Dietary groups					
Diet constituent	5% fat, BS[a]	5% fat, HS[b]	20% fat, HS	5% fat, HS–low sucrose	5% fat, HS–low starch	20% fat, HS–low starch
Protein (casein)	20.00	18.54	22.82	18.54	18.54	22.82
Sucrose	47.77	44.29	16.03	16.03	50.20	24.08
Cornstarch	10.00	9.27	11.41	37.53	3.36	3.36
Fat (corn oil)	5.00	4.64	22.82	4.64	4.64	22.82
Choline chloride	0.20	0.19	0.23	0.19	0.19	0.23
Mineral mixture[c]	4.10	3.80	4.68	3.80	3.80	4.68
Vitamins[d]	2.49	2.31	2.85	2.31	2.31	2.85
Cellulose	10.00	9.27	11.41	9.27	9.27	11.41
DL-Methionine	0.29	0.27	0.33	0.27	0.27	0.33
NaCl	0.15	7.42	7.42	7.42	7.42	7.42
NaCl (total)[e]	1.17	8.37	8.59	8.37	8.37	8.59
Sucrose:starch[f]	4.78	4.78	1.40	0.43	14.94	7.17
Caloric density (cal/g food)	3.59	3.33	4.10	3.33	3.33	4.10

[a] BS is basal salt (1.17% NaCl).
[b] HS is high salt (8.37 to 8.59% NaCl).
[c] Rogers and Harper's (10) mineral mix. This mix contributes NaCl in addition to the amount added.
[d] The vitamin mix contains (per kg of diet)—vitamin A concentrate, 19822 IU; Vitamin D concentrate, 2200 IU; α-tocopherol, 110 mg; ascorbic acid, 991 mg; inositol, 110 mg; choline chloride, 1.65 g; menadione, 49.5 mg; *p*-aminobenzoic acid, 110 mg; niacin, 99.0 mg; riboflavin, 22 mg; pyridoxine hydrochloride, 22 mg; thiamine hydrochloride, 22 mg; calcium pantothenate, 66 mg; biotin, 0.44 mg; folic acid, 1.98 mg; vitamin B_{12}, 0.03 mg.
[e] Computed value of the total NaCl present in the diet; includes NaCl contributed by the mineral mixture.
[f] Computed value of the sucrose to corn starch ratio of the diets.

tested with six different concentrations of NaCl (0.005, 0.05, 0.10, 0.15, 0.30, and 0.5 *M*). Rats were randomly exposed to one of the six concentrations of NaCl in one drinking tube and deionized water in the other. These tests were conducted throughout a 6 week period (Weeks 4–9) with at least 3 days between each 48-hr test. All animals were presented with each NaCl solution only once.

At the beginning of the eleventh week of the study, six of the rats from each group were sacrificed and blood collected to obtain measurements of blood urea nitrogen (BUN), serum electrolytes, and osmolality (described below). The remaining six animals from each dietary group were returned to the 5% fat, BS diet and preference for either 0.15 or 0.30 *M* NaCl was measured. All remaining rats were tested with both concentrations of NaCl paired with deionized water. The preference tests were conducted 1 and 3 weeks (Weeks 12 and 14) after the animals were returned to the 5% fat, BS diet. The amount of water and saline consumed during the 48-hr preference tests was determined by volume differences and fluid consumption/100 g body wt was calculated.

During the weeks in which the animals were sacrificed (Weeks 11 and 15), animals were exsanguinated and trunk blood collected and centrifuged to obtain serum. The heart, kidneys, and adrenal glands from each animal were removed, cleaned of extraneous tissue, inspected for gross pathological changes and weighed. Blood urea nitrogen (BUN) was measured by the Feron reaction whereby urea was condensed with diacetylminoxime in acid medium to form a chromagen (No. 535, Sigma Chemical Co., St. Louis, Mo.). Serum sodium (Na) and potassium (K) concentrations were determined by atomic absorption spectroscopy (Perkin–Elmer Model 14000, Norwalk, Conn.). Serum chloride (Cl) concentration was assessed by a mercurimetric titration using diphenylcarbazone as indicator (No. 830-T, Sigma Chemical Co.). Serum osmolality was determined by freezing point depression using a micro-osmometer (Precisions Systems, Inc., Sudbury, Mass.).

Experimental data collected from the entire study were analyzed by analysis of variance (13). Significance of differences between group means for each parameter was determined by the Tukey test with the confidence limit set at 95%.

Experiment 2. Forty-eight (42 days old) Sprague–Dawley rats (Harlan Sprague–Dawley) were maintained as before (Experiment 1) except that a 12-hr, reversed light–dark cycle was used. The animals were allowed to adjust to the reversed light–dark cycle for 3 weeks and were subsequently placed on the 5% fat, BS diet for an additional 4 weeks. After this period, the animals were divided into four equal groups and each group (12 rats per group) was fed one of the following experimental diets: 5% fat, BS; 5% fat, HS; 5% fat, HS–low sucrose (Table I), or 5% fat, BS–low sucrose. The composition of the 5% fat, BS–low sucrose diet was identical to the 5% fat, BS diet except that the percentage of sucrose and cornstarch was equivalent to that present in the 5% fat, HS–low sucrose diet. The animals remained on their respective diets for 8 weeks (Weeks 5–12).

All animals were trained to consume fluid in a short-term, two-bottle NaCl preference test during the first 2 weeks of the study, before initiating dietary treatment. Food and water were removed from each cage at the beginning of the dark cycle, on the day of the test. After 1 hr of deprivation, the drinking bottles containing fresh deionized water were positioned on the cages. After 10 min, the positions of the drinking bottles were reversed. After another 10-min period, the drinking bottles were removed, and both food and water were returned to the cages. Rats usually consumed a total of approximately 6 ml of fluid during the 20 min tests. Four training sessions were conducted in this fashion over the first week of the study.

Beginning the second week of the study, NaCl preference tests were conducted before initiation of dietary treatment. The rats were randomly exposed to one of two concentrations of NaCl (0.05 and 0.10 *M*) in one drinking bottle and deionized water in the other. All rats were tested three times (Weeks 2–4) with both concentrations of NaCl. These concentrations of NaCl were chosen on the basis of the results obtained from Experiment 1 where the most dramatic differences in fluid consumption among the dietary groups were observed. During the course of dietary treatment, each animal was exposed to each concentration of NaCl only once during a test week and was tested every week throughout the study. The amount of each fluid consumed during the two, 10 min periods of the 20-min test was determined by bottle weight differences and fluid consumed per 100 g body wt was determined.

Two-way analysis of variance (13) was used to determine the effects of both dietary NaCl and the sucrose to starch ratio on the short-term preferences for 0.05 and 0.10 *M* NaCl. Significance was set at the 95% confidence level.

Results. *Experiment 1.* The body weights of rats were measured weekly except during Week 10 (Fig. 1). No significant differences in body weight were observed during the equilibration period (Weeks 1 and 2) when all rats were fed the 5% fat, BS diet (Panel A). Significantly lower body weights were observed for the animals maintained on the 5% fat, HS diet during weeks 4, 5, 6, 7, and 9, relative to the animals maintained on the 5% fat, BS group (Panel B). Significantly lower body weights were also observed for the rats receiving the 20% fat, HS diet at Weeks 7–9 and for the rats receiving the 5% fat, HS–low sucrose diet at Weeks 3 and 8. In addition, significantly lower body weights were observed for rats on the 5% fat, HS–low starch diet at Weeks 3–5 and 7–9. No significant differences were observed in body weights when the animals from each dietary regimen were returned to the 5% fat, BS diet (Panel C).

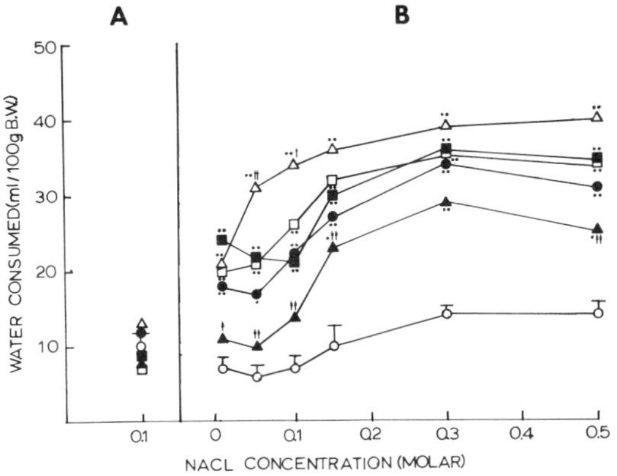

FIG. 2. Effect of diet on water consumed during the long-term NaCl preference tests. One SEM is indicated only at each mean value for the 5% fat, BS group for the sake of clarity. (A) All groups ($N = 12$ per group) were maintained on the 5% fat, BS diet. (B) Animals were grouped ($N = 12$) and maintained on their respective diets. Significance: different from the 5% fat, BS group, $*P < 0.05$ and $**P < 0.01$; different from the 5% fat, HS group, $\dagger P < 0.05$ and $\dagger\dagger P < 0.01$; different from the 5% fat, HS–low sucrose group, $\ddagger P < 0.05$ and $\ddagger\ddagger P < 0.01$. ○, 5% fat, BS; ●, 5% fat, HS; □, 20% fat, HS; △, 5% fat, HS–low sucrose; ▲, 5% fat, HS–low starch; and ■, 20% fat, HS–low starch.

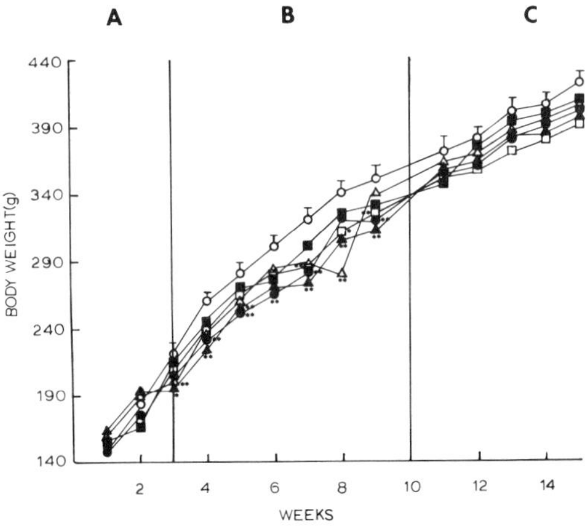

FIG. 1. Effect of varying diet on body weight. One SEM is indicated at each mean value for only the 5% fat, BS group for the sake of clarity. (A) All animals in each group were maintained on the 5% fat, BS diet ($N = 12$ for each group). (B) Animals were maintained on their respective diets ($N = 12$ for each group). (C) All animals were returned to the 5% fat, BS diet ($N = 6$). Significance at $P < 0.05$ level designated as * and at $P < 0.01$ level as **. ○, 5% fat, BS; ●, 5% fat, HS; □, 20% fat, HS; △, 5% fat, HS–low sucrose; ▲, 5% fat, HS–low starch; and ■, 20% fat, HS–low starch.

Figure 2 shows the effect of the various dietary treatments on water consumption during the long-term preference tests. While receiving the 5% fat, BS diet (Panel A) no significant differences in water consumption were apparent during the 0.10 *M* NaCl preference test among all dietary groups. Animals fed the HS diets (except the rats maintained on the 5% fat, HS–low starch diet) drank significantly more water ($P < 0.01$) than the 5% fat, BS dietary group at each concentration of NaCl tested. Significant increases in water intake by the 5% fat, HS–low starch group, relative to the 5% fat, BS group were observed during the tests employing the 0.15 *M* ($P < 0.05$), 0.3 *M* ($P < 0.01$), and 0.5 *M* ($P < 0.05$) NaCl solutions. The rats fed the 5% fat, HS–low sucrose diet consumed significantly more water than the 5% fat, HS dietary group during the tests employing 0.05 *M* ($P < 0.01$) and 0.10 *M* ($P < 0.05$) NaCl. The 5% fat, HS–low starch group consumed significantly less water than the 5% fat, HS–low sucrose dietary group during the tests using 0.005 *M* ($P < 0.05$), 0.05 to 0.15 *M* ($P < 0.01$), and 0.5 *M* NaCl ($P < 0.01$). By employing orthogonal component analysis (14) for all HS groups, it was determined that the amount of water ingested during the long-term tests using 0.05 *M* ($F = 19.86$, $P < 0.01$), 0.10 *M* ($F = 21.94$, $P < 0.01$), and 0.15 *M* ($F = 10.71$, $P < 0.01$) NaCl was inversely correlated with the sucrose to starch ratio of the diets. Subsequent linear regression analysis, demonstrated significant inverse relationships between the sucrose to starch ratio of the HS diets and water consumed during the 0.05 *M* ($Y = 26.24 - 1.08X$; $N = 5$, $r = 0.85$, $P < 0.05$), 0.1 *M* ($Y = 30.18 - 1.16X$; $N = 5$, $r = 0.93$, $P < 0.05$), and the 0.15 *M* ($Y = 34.15 - 0.75X$; $N = 5$, $r = 0.89$, $P < 0.05$) NaCl preference tests. The amount of NaCl consumed was not statistically different among the dietary groups during any of the long-term preference tests conducted (Fig. 3).

There were no significant differences in water consumption (during preference tests employing 0.15 and 0.30 *M* NaCl) among any of the groups 1 and 3 weeks after returning the animals to the 5% fat, BS diet, relative to animals that had been maintained on the 5% fat, BS diet throughout the study. No significant differences in consumption of the 0.15 *M* NaCl solution by any of the dietary groups were detectable after returning the animals to the 5% fat, BS diet. A significant reduction ($P < 0.05$) in the consumption of the 0.3 *M* NaCl solution after 1 week on the 5% fat, BS diet was observed, however, in the 5% fat, HS–low sucrose (40 mg NaCl consumed/100 g body wt) and the 5% fat, HS–low starch (37 mg NaCl consumed/100 g body wt) group relative to the 5% fat, BS group (155 mg NaCl consumed/100 g body wt). There were no significant differences in consumption of the 0.3 *M* NaCl solution by any of the groups after 3 weeks on the 5% fat, BS diet.

Although significant differences in body weight occurred when the animals had been maintained on the various experimental diets for this period of time, no significant differences were observed in organ weights, BUN, serum Na, K, CL concentrations, or serum osmolality after 8 weeks of dietary treatment (Table II). It is worth noting that the body weight differences were reversible because when the rats were returned to the 5% fat, BS diet no significant differences were observed in any of the parameters measured, including body weight.

Experiment 2. Mean water consumption of the 5% fat, BS–low sucrose group, during the 0.05 *M* short-term tests conducted while these animals were on the control diet (Table III, see column A) was significantly greater ($P < 0.05$) than that of the 5% fat, BS group. However, no significant differences in water consumption of any of the dietary groups were detectable during Test 1 which was conducted after the animals had been on their respective diets for 3 days (during Week 5). A significant interaction ($P < 0.05$) between the effects of dietary NaCl and the sucrose to starch ratio of the diets on mean water consumption during the 0.05 *M* NaCl preference tests was observed during the six short-term tests (mean value of tests 2–7).

No significant differences in saline consumption (mg/100 g body wt) during the 0.05 *M* NaCl short-term tests were observed either

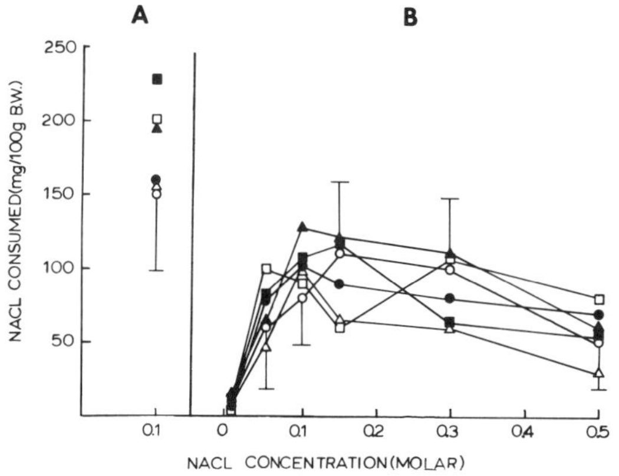

FIG. 3. Effect of diet on NaCl consumed during the long-term NaCl preference tests. One SEM is indicated only at each mean value for the 5% fat, BS group for the sake of clarity. (A) All groups (N = 12 per group) were maintained on the 5% fat, BS diet. (B) Animals were divided into groups (N = 12) and maintained on their respective diets. ○, 5% fat, BS; ●, 5% fat, HS; □, 20% fat, HS; △, 5% fat, HS–low sucrose; ▲, 5% fat, HS–low starch; and ■, 20% fat, HS–low starch.

TABLE II. EFFECT OF VARYING DIET ON BODY WEIGHT, ORGAN WEIGHTS, SERUM ELECTROLYTES, AND OSMOLALITY

	Dietary group					
	5% Fat, BS (N = 5)	5% Fat, HS (N = 6)	20% fat, HS (N = 5)	5% Fat, HS–low sucrose (N = 6)	5% Fat, HS–low starch (N = 6)	20% Fat, HS–low starch (N = 6)
Body weight (g)	362 ± 27[a]	306 ± 22[b]	314 ± 15[b]	324 ± 23	309 ± 20[b]	323 ± 36
Organ weight (mg/100 g body wt)						
Heart	314 ± 16	329 ± 14	306 ± 23	312 ± 24	321 ± 25	304 ± 6
Kidney (combined)	670 ± 43	711 ± 54	727 ± 28	714 ± 56	668 ± 39	699 ± 54
Adrenal (combined)	11 ± 1	12 ± 1	14 ± 1	12 ± 1	13 ± 1	13 ± 1
BUN (mg%)	12 ± 2	18 ± 3	20 ± 5	23 ± 4	17 ± 9	21 ± 4
Serum analysis						
Osmolality (mosm/kg)	293 ± 14	298 ± 16	293 ± 10	297 ± 8	294 ± 12	286 ± 7
Na (meq/liter)	155 ± 8	165 ± 10	157 ± 2	157 ± 4	159 ± 10	156 ± 9
K (meq/liter)	4.8 ± .7	5.0 ± .7	5.2 ± .6	4.6 ± .4	4.9 ± .5	4.7 ± .6
Cl (meq/liter)	105 ± 4	105 ± 16	108 ± 10	111 ± 9	106 ± 11	109 ± 7

[a] Mean ± SEM for animals sacrificed during Week 10.
[b] Significantly different ($P < 0.05$) from animals maintained on the 5% fat, BS diet.

when all the animals were receiving the 5% fat, BS diet or during Test 1 when the animals had received their respective diets for 3 days (Table IV). However, a significant effect of dietary NaCl on mean NaCl consumption was demonstrated in the three tests conducted during Weeks 6–8 ($P < 0.05$) and over all six tests conducted during Weeks 6–12 ($P < 0.05$). No significant changes in either water or saline consumption occurred during any of the 0.10 M NaCl short-term preference tests.

Discussion. Very little is known concerning the effects of diet composition on sodium consumption. Smith-Barbaro *et al.* (9) demonstrated that dietary constituents may influence preferences of rats for NaCl solutions relative to water. The results of the present studies indicate that the alterations in NaCl

TABLE III. EFFECT OF DIET ON WATER CONSUMED DURING SHORT-TERM PREFERENCE TESTS: 0.05 M NACL VERSUS DEIONIZED WATER

	Water consumed (ml/100 g body wt)				
		B[b]			
Dietary group	A[a]	Test 1	Tests 2–4 (mean value of three tests)	Tests 5–7 (mean value of three tests)	Tests 2–7 (mean value of six tests)
5% fat, BS	0.52 ± 0.04	0.41 ± 0.07	0.47 ± 0.04	0.47 ± 0.06	0.45 ± 0.04
5% fat, BS–low sucrose	0.70 ± 0.04[c]	0.48 ± 0.03	0.54 ± 0.03	0.61 ± 0.07 (N = 11)	0.58 ± 0.04
5% fat, HS	0.66 ± 0.06	0.39 ± 0.05	0.57 ± 0.06	0.65 ± 0.09	0.61 ± 0.07
5% fat, HS–low sucrose	0.53 ± 0.02	0.39 ± 0.05	0.48 ± 0.03	0.61 ± 0.07 (N = 11)	0.54 ± 0.03
			ANOVA analysis		
	Salt	ns	ns	ns	ns
	Sucrose:starch	ns	ns	ns	ns
	Interaction	ns	ns	ns	$P < 0.05$

[a] Values represent means ± SEM of three short-term preference tests conducted while all animals were maintained on the 5% fat, BS diet.
[b] Means ± SEM for 12 animals, unless otherwise stated in parentheses; values obtained when animals were grouped and maintained on their respective diets.
[c] Significantly different ($P < 0.05$) from the 5% fat, BS group.

TABLE IV. EFFECT OF DIET ON NACL CONSUMED DURING SHORT-TERM PREFERENCE TESTS: 0.05 *M* NACL VERSUS DEIONIZED WATER

	NaCl consumed (mg/100 g body wt)				
		B[b]			
Dietary group	A[a]	Test 1	Tests 2–4 (mean value of three tests)	Tests 5–7 (mean value of three tests)	Tests 2–7 (mean value of six tests)
5% fat, BS	2.74 ± 0.21	2.23 ± 0.34	2.41 ± 0.29	2.18 ± 0.21	2.31 ± 0.22
5% fat, BS–low sucrose	3.03 ± 0.29	2.30 ± 0.28	2.47 ± 0.30	2.26 ± 0.29 (N = 11)	2.45 ± 0.28
5% fat, HS	3.21 ± 0.34	2.23 ± 0.30	1.92 ± 0.24	2.13 ± 0.25	2.03 ± 0.19
5% fat, HS–low sucrose	3.04 ± 0.24	2.24 ± 0.29	1.89 ± 0.11	1.69 ± 0.26 (N = 11)	1.82 ± 0.15
			ANOVA analysis		
	Salt	ns	$P < 0.05$	ns	$P < 0.05$
	Sucrose:starch	ns	ns	ns	ns
	Interaction	ns	ns	ns	ns

[a] Values represent means ± SEM of three short term preference tests conducted while all animals were maintained on the 5% fat, BS diet.

[b] Mean values ± SEM for 12 animals, unless stated in parentheses; obtained when animals were grouped and maintained on their respective diets.

preferences reported by Smith-Barbaro *et al.* (8) were most likely related to the level of dietary sucrose rather than the level of dietary fat. In addition, the reduction in NaCl preferences observed in the present studies was not related to changes in saline consumption but rather to an increase in water consumption. These conclusions are supported by the dramatic increase in water consumption that was observed when the level of dietary sucrose was reduced (5% fat, HS–low sucrose diet) to the level present in the 20% fat, HS diet. The finding that there were no differences in water ingestion among the 20% fat, HS, the 20% fat, HS–low starch, and 5% fat, HS groups (during any of the preference tests) suggests that the amount of water consumed by the two high-fat groups was primarily the result of high levels of dietary NaCl.

The fact that water consumption by the 5% fat, HS–low sucrose group during the 0.05 and 0.1 *M* NaCl tests was significantly greater than that of the 5% fat, HS group suggests that the sucrose to starch ratio is an important factor in the regulation of water intake during preference tests in which lower concentrations of NaCl are employed. The demonstration that the amount of water consumed by the HS dietary groups was inversely correlated with the sucrose to starch ratio of the diet supports this hypothesis. The dramatic differences in water intake between the 5% fat, HS–low starch group (approaching the level observed in the 5% fat, BS group during some of the tests) and the 5% fat, HS–low sucrose group during the tests employing 0.005 to 0.15 *M* NaCl is consistent with these findings. The similar increases in water intake among the HS dietary groups when tested with 0.3 and 0.5 *M* NaCl paired with water suggest that dietary NaCl was the predominant factor rather than the sucrose to starch ratio when higher concentrations of NaCl were used. Thus, it appears that both the sucrose to starch ratio and the NaCl content of the diet are important determinants of water consumption during tests employing lower concentrations (0.05 to 0.15 *M*) of NaCl whereas dietary NaCl is the deciding factor for increased water consumption during the tests utilizing higher concentrations of NaCl.

Dietary NaCl induces thirst and access to water for rats maintained on HS diets is essential for elimination of excess Na (15, 16). The increase in water intake observed during the long-term tests in the present studies was partially a consequence of the increased dietary NaCl levels. The induction of thirst was presumably elicited by undetected transient extracellular osmolality changes. The finding that serum osmolality, and Na, K, and Cl concentrations were within normal limits and BUN was similar among all dietary groups suggests that the regulation of extracellular fluid and electrolyte balance were operative in animals maintained on the HS diets. In addition, the heart, adrenal, and kidney weights were similar among all dietary groups suggesting that no compensatory enlargements of these organs occurred in response to 8 weeks of HS intake.

The high levels of dietary NaCl may account for some of the differences in body weights observed among the dietary groups (Fig. 1). In this regard, Drori (17) observed that the food intake of rats fed NaCl adulterated food (10, 20, and 30 g NaCl/kg diet) was significantly reduced over a 21-day period. However, in the present studies, significant reductions in body weight were not found in all HS dietary groups, indicating that dietary components other than NaCl may be involved.

The stimulus for elevated water consumption that occurred in groups fed lower levels of dietary sucrose (but higher dietary starch) may be related to the relative rates of hydrolysis and subsequent absorption of the two carbohydrates from the gastrointestinal tract. Normally, the osmotic pressure of the chyme entering the duodenum from the stomach is adjusted to isotonicity by the movement of water between the blood and the gastrointestinal tract (18). Thus, isotonicity of the chyme is maintained throughout the small intestine. Although starch initially exerts relatively little osmotic pressure, the liberation of many particles by hydrolysis leads to a much greater osmotic pressure. Thus water moves from the blood to the intestinal lumen to preserve isotonicity of the intestinal contents. As the hydrolytic products (glucose) are absorbed, the isotonicity of the luminal contents is preserved by the concomitant absorption of water. Therefore, the osmotic pressure exerted by the hydrolytic products of sucrose may be more transient than that exerted by the products of starch hydrolysis. This hypothesis is supported by the report of Cohen and Teitelbaum (19) which demonstrated that the absorption of glucose from the gastrointestinal tract following sucrose feeding is much more rapid compared to that of starch. It has also been reported that rats fed diets containing dextrin consumed considerably more water than rats fed diets containing sucrose (20).

The dietary effects on water consumption during the long-term tests were completely reversed after 1 week on the low fat, BS diet and supports our hypothesis that changes in fluid consumption arise from postingestional factors. Differences in 0.3 *M* NaCl consumption by the 5% fat, HS–low sucrose and –low starch dietary groups were observed after all animals were fed the 5% fat, BS diet for 1 week but completely disappeared after 3 weeks. Studies investigating possible mechanisms underlying these shifts in saline consumption are currently in progress.

The results obtained from Experiment 2 suggest that diet-induced changes in fluid consumption are detectable over a short-term test. During the preference tests employing the 0.05 *M* NaCl solution, alterations in the amount of water ingested as well as a reduction in the amount of NaCl consumed occurred. Although no differences in water intake were detected during Test 1 (when the animals had been fed their respective diets for 3 days), there were differences when all groups were on the 5% fat, BS diet at the beginning of the study (Table III). Thus, interpretation of the water consumption data during the 0.05 *M* NaCl test is not possible.

The decrease in the amount of NaCl consumed during the short-term tests appeared to be related to the high levels of NaCl in the diet (Table IV). It is possible that the dietary NaCl-induced changes in NaCl consumption were not totally dependent upon postingestional events since the short-term tests were designed to minimize postingestional effects of the stimulus. Previous studies suggest that changes in preference behavior and fluid intake may be related to changes in gustatory acuity and that saliva may play a role in these changes (21, 22).

The results of the present studies provide evidence that postingestional feedback derived from dietary constituents influence the amount of fluid consumed by rats during NaCl preference tests. These studies demonstrate that the increase in water ingested is inversely related to the sucrose to starch ratio of the diet and directly related to the level of dietary

NaCl. The mechanism(s) responsible for the shifts in fluid consumption during long- and short-term testing require further study.

1. Bare JK. The specific hunger for sodium chloride in normal and adrenalectomized white rats. J Comp Physiol Psychol **42**:242–253, 1949.
2. Richter CP. Salt appetite of mammals: its dependence on instinct and metabolism. In: Autouri M, ed. L'Instinct Dans Le Comportement Des Animaux et De L'Homme. Paris, Masson, pp577–632, 1956.
3. Weiner IH, Stellar E. Salt preference of the rat determined by a single-stimulus method. J Comp Physiol Psychol **44**:394–401, 1951.
4. Epstein AN, Stellar E. The control of salt preference in the adrenalectomized rat. J Comp Physiol Psychol **48**:167–172, 1955.
5. Richter CP. Increased salt appetite in adrenalectomized rats. Amer J Physiol **115**:155–161, 1936.
6. Richter CP, Eckert JF. Mineral metabolism of adrenalectomized rats studied by the appetite method. Endocrinology **22**:214–224, 1938.
7. Borer KT. Disappearance of preferences and aversions for sapid solutions in rats ingesting untasted fluids. J Comp Physiol Psychol **65**:213–221, 1968.
8. Smith-Barbaro P, Levenstein B, Quinn MR. Diet-induced changes in NaCl preference and blood pressure in rats. J Nutr **111**:468–474, 1981.
9. Smith-Barbaro P, Quinn MR, Fisher H, Hegsted DM. The effect of dietary fat and salt on blood pressure, renal and aortic prostaglandins. Nutr Res **1**:277–287, 1981.
10. Rogers QR, Harper AE. Amino acid diets in maximal growth in the rat. J Nutr **87**:267–273, 1965.
11. Newberne PM, Bieri JG, Briggs GM, Nesheim MD. Control diets in laboratory animal experimentation. National Academy of Sciences, Washington DC, 1978.
12. Richter CP. Salt taste thresholds of normal and adrenalectomized rats. Endocrinology **24**:367–371, 1939.
13. Winer BJ. Statistical Principles in Experimental Design. New York, McGraw–Hill, p149, 1971.
14. Brunning JL, Kintz BL. Computational Handbook of Statistics, Illinois, Scott, Foresman & Co., p123, 1968.
15. Meneely GR, Tucker RG, Darby WJ. Chronic sodium chloride toxicity in the albino rat. I. Growth on a purified diet containing various levels of sodium chloride. J Nutr **48**:489–498, 1952.
16. Meneely GR, Tucker RG, Darby WJ, Auerbach SH. Chronic sodium chloride toxicity in the albino rat. II. Occurrence of hypertension and of a syndrome of edema and renal failure. J Exp Med **98**:71–80, 1953.
17. Drori D. The effect of sodium chloride ingestion on food intake and on fat deposition in male rats. Brit J Nutr **35**:195–200, 1976.
18. Fordtran JS, Ingelfinger FJ. Absorption of water, electrolytes, and sugars from the human gut. In: Code CF, ed. Alimentary Canal III, Intestinal Absorption. Baltimore, Williams & Wilkins, pp1457–1490, 1968.
19. Cohen AM, Teitelbaum A. Effect of different levels of protein in "sucrose" and "starch" diets on the glucose tolerance and growth. Metabolism **15**:1034–1038, 1966.
20. Harper AE, Spivey HE. Relationship between food intake and osmotic effect of dietary carbohydrate. Amer J Physiol **193**:483–487, 1958.
21. Catalanotto FA, Leffingwell C. Early effects of desalivation upon fluid consumption and taste acuity in the rat. Behav Neural Biol **25**:190–205, 1979.
22. Thrasher TN, Fregly MJ. Factors affecting salivary sodium concentration, NaCl intake, and preference threshold and their interrelationships. In: Kare MR, Fregly MJ, Bernard RA, eds. Biological and Behavioral Aspects of Salt Intake. New York, Academic Press, pp145–165, 1980.

Received October 3, 1983. P.S.E.B.M. 1984, Vol. 176.
Accepted May 8, 1984.

PROCEEDINGS OF THE SOCIETY FOR EXPERIMENTAL BIOLOGY AND MEDICINE **176,** 485–489 (1984)

Cataract Formation following Limited Amino Acid Intake during Gestation and Lactation[1] (41902)

G. E. BUNCE, J. L. HESS, AND D. DAVIS

Department of Biochemistry and Nutrition, Virginia Polytechnic Institute and State University, Blacksburg, Virginia 24061

Abstract. Female rats were fed defined diets limiting in one or more of certain amino acids and with or without vitamin E throughout gestation and lactation. Deficits of tryptophan, phenylalanine/tyrosine, or methionine/cystine reduced the body weight of progeny to about 50% or less of normal but only low tryptophan was cataractogenic. When total dietary amino acids were 12.4%, a low (65 mg%) level of tryptophan resulted in 34% incidence of cataract if vitamin E was simultaneously withheld. Elevation of total amino acids to 24.8% while maintaining tryptophan at 65 mg% caused 70 or 90% incidence of nuclear lens opacities in the presence or absence, respectively, of vitamin E. Maternal dietary amino acid imbalance was also associated with a 50% decrease in lens insoluble (membrane) proteins in the progeny independent of dietary vitamin E or the occurrence of opacities.

It has been reported that consumption throughout gestation and lactation of a diet simultaneously low in tryptophan and vitamin E resulted in the appearance of central nuclear opacities in about one-third of rat progeny (1, 2). The same level of tryptophan as the sole limiting nutrient was without effect on lens transparency. Restriction of vitamin E alone caused a 6% incidence of cataract. So far as we have been able to determine, the impact of deficits of amino acids other than tryptophan upon lens development during this period of life has not been investigated.

Simple tryptophan deficiency causes cataract in postweaning rats (3–8), guinea pigs (9), and trout (10). Hall *et al.* (11) determined that single deficiencies of either phenylalanine or histidine as well as tryptophan caused cataract in weanling rats within 3 weeks. Dietary omission of threonine, leucine, isoleucine, valine, lysine, methionine, or arginine for the same period of time resulted in changes in lens morphology such as haziness or separation of the superficial fibers but obvious opacific regions were absent. Methionine sulfoximine injections in rats induced cataracts which could be prevented by dietary supplements of methionine or cystine (12). A 90% incidence of cataract accompanied by less than one-fourth of normal growth rate was observed in fingerling lake trout fed a commercial soy protein isolate. Both problems were corrected by supplementation with methionine (13). A recent study has shown that the cataractogenic effect of a commercial milk replacement diet in wolf pups was prevented by addition of arginine (14). Lenses remained clear when young pigs (15) or rats (11, 16, 17) were maintained on very low (<5%) levels of total protein for as much as 146 days in the pigs or 600 days in the rats.

In this paper, we report further studies of the effect on lens development of limited intake of amino acids during gestation and lactation. We have confirmed the cataractogenic effect of coincident deficits of tryptophan and vitamin E, and have shown that comparable restrictions of vitamin E and phenylalanine/tyrosine, methionine/cystine, or lysine did not provoke a similar response. Tryptophan deficiency alone caused a 70% incidence of cataract when the total amino acid level of the diet was raised from 12.4 to 24.8% in the presence of vitamin E. Deletion of vitamin E caused a further increase of cataract frequency to 90%.

Materials and Methods. The complete basal diet is shown in detail in Table I. Crystalline L-amino acids were utilized as the sole nitrogen source permitting facile manipulation of the level of individual amino acids. Total amino acids were held constant by replacement of withheld indispensible amino acids with equal

[1] Supported by PHS Grant EY-01060.

0037-9727/84 $1.50

TABLE I. COMPOSITION OF BASAL DIET

Ingredient	Amount (g/100 g)
Glucose	58.00
Starch	8.06
Amino acid mixture[a]	12.44
Cellulose[b]	5.00
Salt mixture[c]	4.00
Vitamin mixture[d]	2.50
Corn oil (tocopherol stripped)[e]	10.00

[a] As g per 100 g diet: L-His 0.54; L-Lys–HCl 1.55; L-Leu 0.80; L-Ilu 0.50; L-Phe 0.60; L-Met 0.30; L-Cys–Cys 0.30; L-Tyr 0.30; L-Thr 0.50; L-Val 0.70; L-Arg 0.75; L-Glu 0.90; L-Asp 0.90; L-Pro 0.90; L-Ala 1.10; L-Ser 0.90; Gly 0.90. Obtained from Ajinomoto, New York, N.Y.

[b] Alphacel, ICN Pharmaceuticals, Inc., Cleveland, Ohio.

[c] Mixture No. 4164, ICN Pharmaceuticals, Inc., to which sodium selenite was added to give a dietary concentration of 25 μg Se per 100 g diet.

[d] Vitamin diet fortification mixture with α-tocopherol omitted, ICN Pharmaceuticals, Inc. Provides per 100 g diet: (in IU), retinyl acetate, 1980; cholecalciferol, 220; (in mg), inositol, 11; choline chloride, 165; menadione, 5; *p*-aminobenzoic acid, 11; niacin, 9.9; riboflavin, 2.2; pyridoxine–HCl, 2.2; thiamine–HCl, 2.2; calcium pantothenate, 6.6; (in μg) biotin, 44; folic acid, 198; and B-12,3.

[e] ICN Pharmaceuticals, Inc., and General Biochemicals, Chagrin Falls, Ohio.

weight of L-alanine. The mineral mix (No. 4164), as originally formulated, lacked selenium but sodium selenite was added to all diets to insure a level of 25 μg selenite/100 g diet. All of the lipid was supplied by tocopherol-stripped corn oil so that vitamin-E content could be adjusted by its deletion from the otherwise complete vitamin mix.

Eight- to 10-week-old female Sprague–Dawley rats weighing between 175 and 225 g were fed for 1 week a diet containing the complete amino acid mixture but lacking vitamin E. This was to assure that the plasma levels of vitamin E would be low throughout the entire 6 weeks of gestation and lactation in those animals which would be in the low vitamin-E groups. Earlier studies have shown that plasma levels of vitamin E fall rapidly during the first week of depletion but remain relatively constant for several weeks beyond (18). After the adjustment period, male and female rats were housed in a one-to-one pairing in stainless-steel wire mesh cages. Upon detection of copulation plugs, female rats were assigned to either the low tryptophan–low vitamin-E diet, a fully supplemented control diet, or a diet modified by manipulation of the content of one of the other essential amino acids.

The female rats were housed in opaque polypropylene "shoebox" cages from conception to weaning. The cages were provided with shredded softwood bedding and enclosed with a bonnet-type cage filter. The animal quarters were temperature (25–28°C)- and humidity (65%)-controlled with circulating filtered air and a 12-hr light/dark cycle.

Evaluation of the progeny for cataract was conducted under artificial light without a magnification aid. Animals were then decapitated and the lenses removed for analysis. Measurements included lens wet weight/dry weight ratio, total soluble and insoluble lens proteins (7), total glutathione (19), and Na and K by atomic absorption spectrophotometry following wet ashing. Representative soluble fractions were also fractionated by gel filtration chromatography to determine proportional distribution of the major crystallins (7).

Results. Data on animal size at weaning and cataract frequency are summarized in Table II. Control populations in our laboratory have never displayed congenital cataract. Weight at weaning (Day 23 postpartum) for rat pups from dams fed the fully supplemented diet averaged 39 ± 1 g (mean ± SEM). Simultaneous restriction of L-tryptophan to 65 mg/100 g of diet and omission of vitamin E reduced the mean weight at weaning to 24 ± 3 g and resulted in the appearance of unilateral or bilateral (1:3 ratio) cataract in 63 of 184 progeny (34%). Approximately one-half (9 of 20) of the litters were free of evident lenticular damage. Elevation of the vitamin-E content of this diet to 40 mg/100 g diet did not affect weight at weaning but prevented the appearance of cataract in the test group (71 rats from 10 dams). Increasing the total amino acid content of the diet from 12.4 to 24.8% while leaving tryptophan at 65 mg/100 g diet aggravated the cataractogenic effect whether vitamin E was absent (90% of 98 rats) or present (70% of 107 rats). When phenylalanine (450 mg/100 g diet) and tyrosine (none present) were limiting instead of tryptophan, size at weaning was restricted to 18 ± 3 g but only one animal in 48 (2%) showed a cataract (not

TABLE II. CATARACT FREQUENCY

Maternal diet	Total litters (*N*)	Litters with opacities (*N*)	Total pups (*N*)	Pups with opacities (*N*)	Percentage incidence (*N*)	Mean weight at postpartum Day 23[e] (g)
L-Trp 65 mg/100 g diet Vitamin E absent Total amino acids 12.4%	20	11	184	63	34[b]	24 ± 3
L-Trp 65 mg/100 g diet Vitamin E 40 mg/100 g diet Total amino acids 12.4%	10	0	71	0	0[a]	22 ± 2
L-Trp 65 mg/100 g diet Vitamin E absent Total amino acids 24.8%	11	10	98	88	90[c]	20 ± 1
L-Trp 65 mg/100 g diet Vitamin E 40 mg/100 g diet Total amino acids 24.8%	11	9	107	75	70[d]	20 ± 1
L-Phe 450 mg/100 g diet L-Tyr absent Vitamin E absent Total amino acids 12.4%	7	1	48	1	2[a]	18 ± 3
L-Met 300 mg/100 g diet L-Cys–Cys absent Vitamin E 40 mg/100 mg diet Total amino acids 12.4%	8	0	90	0	0[a]	15 ± 1
L-Lys 450 mg/100 g diet Vitamin E absent	5	0	55	0	0[a]	38 ± 3

[a–d] All values with letters different from one another are highly significantly different ($P < 0.005$) according to chi-square test.
[e] Mean ± SEM.

significant). Limitation of sulfur amino acids to 50% of the minimal requirement (20) reduced weight at weaning to 15 ± 1 g. Although lenses frequently appeared hazy, distinct opacities were not detected in any of 90 pups. Reduction of lysine to 50% of the stated minimal requirement did not reduce size at weaning (38 ± 3 g) and no cataracts were seen.

Comparison of cataractous and clear lenses from progeny of the low tryptophan and control regimens with regard to wet-wt/dry-wt ratio, sodium, potassium, or glutathione revealed no significant differences. Lens glutathione was depressed (4.5 ± 0.28 vs 1.9 ± 0.35 μmole/g lens) only in the progeny from the maternal low-sulfur amino acid diet. The appearance of cataract in rats fed a low (50 mg/100 g diet) tryptophan ration beginning at weaning is accompanied by a significant decline in the β_H-crystallin fraction of soluble lens protein and an increase from 28–29 to 41% of lens protein which is insoluble (7). When the tryptophan deficit was imposed in the maternal diet, no change in the β_H-crystallin fraction was evident in the cataract-containing lenses. In general, total lens protein was elevated slightly and the percentage insoluble protein was depressed from 13–14 to 5.4–10.5% in the lenses from all progeny whose dams were fed an imbalanced amino acid ration regardless of whether or not the diet was cataractogenic (Table III).

Discussion. These data confirm and extend our earlier observations on the effects of maternal diets simultaneously low in tryptophan and vitamin E (1, 2). The incidence of cataract (34%) in the progeny when both nutrients were low was virtually identical to that reported earlier (33%) and, as before, a vitamin-E supplement of 40 mg/100 g diet prevented the lesion. It should be noted, however, that in the original study the opacific spot often oc-

TABLE III. LENS WEIGHT AND PROTEIN CONTENT OF PROGENY AT WEANING

Maternal diet	Lens wet wt (mg)	Lens insoluble protein (μg/mg lens)	Lens soluble protein[i] (μg/mg lens)	Percentage insoluble protein (%)	Percentage total protein (%)
L-Trp 65 mg/100 g diet Vitamin E absent Total amino acids 12.4%	17.4 ± 0.5[b]	24 ± 11[h]	418 ± 28	5.4	44.2
L-Trp 65 mg/100 g diet Vitamin E 40 mg/100 g diet Total amino acids 12.4%	17.9 ± 0.5[a]	23 ± 4[h]	368 ± 35	6.9	39.1
L-Trp 65 mg/100 g diet Vitamin E absent Total amino acids 24.8%	14.3 ± 0.3[c]	28 ± 7[h]	401 ± 25	6.5	42.9
L-Trp 65 mg/100 g diet Vitamin E 40 mg/100 g diet Total amino acids 24.8%	14.8 ± 0.4[d]	25 ± 9[h]	422 ± 32	5.6	44.7
L-Phe 450 mg/100 g diet L-Tyr absent Vitamin E absent Total amino acids 12.4%	13.5 ± 0.8[e]	41 ± 3[g]	349 ± 10	10.5	39.0
L-Met 300 mg/100 g diet L-Cys–cys absent Vitamin E 40 mg/100 mg diet Total amino acids 12.4%	13.0 ± 0.3[f]	26 ± 1[h]	387 ± 26	6.3	41.3
L-Lys 450 mg/100 g diet Vitamin E absent	18.0 ± 0.3[a]	53 ± 3[g]	316 ± 12	14.4	36.9
Complete amino acids at 12.4% Vitamin E 40 mg/%	19.1 ± 0.4[a]	50 ± 4[g]	331 ± 33[a]	13.1	38.1

[a–f] Mean ± SEM. All values with letters different from the control are statistically different (*b* vs *a*, $P < 0.05$; all others, $P < 0.01$) according to Dunnett's test.

[g,h] Mean ± SEM. All values with letters different from the control are significantly different ($P < 0.05$) according to Dunnett's test.

[i] Mean ± SEM. No values significantly different from the control at $P < 0.05$ according to Dunnett's Test.

cupied as much as 20% of the lens volume whereas in the present study there was a much higher frequency of "pinhead" opacities (<5% of total lens volume). The reason for this difference is not known. Increasing the pool of amino acids which compete with tryptophan for transport across the plasma membrane by doubling the total dietary amino acids, had only a slight effect on animal size at weaning but significantly ($P < 0.005$) increased cataract frequency in the absence or presence of vitamin E. Apparently the lack of vitamin E plays a permissive or contributory but not obligatory role in the emergence of the opacity. The failure of comparable deficits of phenylalanine/tyrosine or sulfur amino acids to generate a similar level of lens pathology reveals a unique importance of tryptophan. Because cataracts caused by a low tryptophan intake are limited to the fetal or embryonal nucleus, a region of the lens composed of the first fiber cells produced during differentiation, it is reasonable to suggest that tryptophan and vitamin E may play key roles in this process.

The 50% decline in percentage insoluble protein in the lenses of rats whose growth was severely restrained by a maternal dietary amino acid imbalance was independent of the presence or absence of opacities. At this early stage of life, the structural crystallins comprise the soluble fraction and membrane proteins constitute the bulk of the insoluble fraction (21). The observed decline may reflect the relative importance of amino acids such as tryptophan, phenylalanine, tyrosine, and cysteine as components of membrane proteins. The failure of the reduced level of dietary lysine to impose a growth depression suggests a need to reevaluate the stated minimal requirement for this amino acid during pregnancy in the rat.

1. Bunce GE, Caasi P, Hall B, Chaves N. Prevention of cataract in the progeny of rats fed a maternal diet based on vegetable proteins. Proc Soc Exp Biol Med **140**:1103–1107, 1972.
2. Bunce GE, Hess JL. Lenticular opacities in young rats as a consequence of maternal diets low in tryptophan and/or vitamin E. J Nutr **106**:222–229, 1976.
3. Curtis PB, Huage SM, Kraybill HR. The nutritive value of certain animal protein concentrates. J Nutr **5**:503–512, 1932.
4. Totter FR, Day PL. Cataract and other ocular changes resulting from tryptophane deficiency. J Nutr **24**:159–166, 1942.
5. Ohrloff C, Stoffel C, Koch H-R, Wefers U, Bours J, Hockwin D. Experimental cataracts induced by a tryptophan-free diet. Exp Eye Res **20**:179–180, 1975.
6. MacAvoy JW, vanHeyningen R. Changes in the lens bow and epithelium of tryptophan deficient rats. Colloq d'INSERM **60**:245–250, 1976.
7. Bunce GE, Hess JL, Fillnow GM. Investigation of low tryptophan induced cataract in weanling rats. Exp Eye Res **26**:399–405, 1978.
8. Koch H-R, Ohrloff C, Bours J, Riemann G, Dragomireseu V, Hockwin O. Separation of lens proteins in rats with tryptophan deficiency cataracts. Exp Eye Res **34**:479–486, 1982.
9. vonSallman L, Reid ME, Grimes PA, Collins EM. Tryptophan-deficiency cataract in guinea pigs. Arch Ophthalmol **62**:662–672, 1959.
10. Poston HA, Rumsey GL. Factors affecting dietary requirement and deficiency signs of L-tryptophan in rainbow trout. J Nutr **113**:2568–2577, 1983.
11. Hall WK, Bowles LL, Sydenstricker VP, Schmidt JH. Cataracts due to deficiencies of phenylalanine and histidine in the rat. A comparison with other types of cataract. J Nutr **36**:277–296, 1948.
12. Bagchi K. The effects of methionine sulphoximine induced methionine deficiency on the crystalline lens of albino rats. Ind J Med Res **47**:437–447, 1959.
13. Poston HA, Riis RC, Rumsey GL, Ketola HG. The effect of supplemental dietary amino acids, minerals and vitamins on salmonoids fed cataractogenic diets. Cornell Vet **67**:472–509, 1977.
14. Vainisi SJ, Edelhauser HF, Wolf ED, Cotlier E, Reeser F. Nutritional cataracts in timber wolves. J Amer Vet Med Assoc **179**:1175–1180, 1981.
15. Kaufman RG, Norton HW. Growth of the porcine eye lens during insufficiencies of dietary protein. Growth **30**:463–470, 1966.
16. McLaren DS. Growth and water content of the eyeball of the albino rat in protein deficiency. Brit J Nutr **12**:254–259, 1958.
17. McLaren DS. The eye and related glands of the rat and pig in protein deficiency. Brit J Ophthalmol **43**:78–87, 1959.
18. Bieri JG. Kinetics of tissue α-tocopherol depletion and repletion. Ann NY Acad Sci **203**:181–191.
19. Brehe JE, Burch HB. Enzymatic assay for glutathione. Anal Biochem **74**:189–197, 1976.
20. National Research Council Nutrient Requirements of Laboratory Animals. Washington, DC, National Acad Sci, 2nd ed, 1978.
21. Harding JF, Dilley KJ. Structural proteins of the mammalian lens: A review with emphasis on changes in development, aging and cataract. Exp Eye Res **22**:1–73, 1976.

Received January 10, 1984. P.S.E.B.M. 1984, Vol. 176.
Accepted May 10, 1984.

PROCEEDINGS OF THE SOCIETY FOR EXPERIMENTAL BIOLOGY AND MEDICINE **176**, 490–502 (1984)

Early Nuclear Structural Changes of Transformed Human Amniotic Cells (WISH) in Presence of Type IV Collagen Detected by the Nuclear Refringency Assay (41903)

JACQUELINE GERFAUX,*,[1] BERTRAND MACÉ,† FRANÇOISE CHANY-FOURNIER,* AND ALAIN POMPIDOU†

**Institut National de la Santé et de la Recherche Médicale, Unité 43, and †Laboratoire Central d'Anatomie Pathologique, Hôpital Saint Vincent-de-Paul, 74 Avenue Denfert-Rochereau, 75674 Paris Cedex 14, France*

Abstract. An early nuclear activation of transformed human amniotic epithelial (WISH) cells triggered by type IV collagen is visualized by a modification of the nuclear refringency obtained by mercury binding on condensed chromatin. This phenomenon is quantified by the nuclear refringency test. The nuclear activation of WISH cells by basement membrane collagen is also shown by the DNase I sensitivity of chromatin and by the measurement of mRNA synthesis. These nuclear phenomena are concomitant with WISH cell attachment and laminin synthesis. Reversible effects on nuclear refringency, cell attachment, and laminin synthesis are tested by the addition and removal of different metabolic inhibitors.

In the past few years, it has been shown that the malignant behavior of tumor cells is correlated with cell surface alterations and defective interactions with extracellular matrix (1, 2). Normal and transformed cells differ in their ability to adhere to collagenous matrices (see (3) for review) when a choice of collagen substrates is given to them. Epithelial cells attach slowly but preferentially to type IV basement membrane collagen (4–6), whereas transformed cells derived from carcinoma bind rapidly and selectively to this latter in the absence of serum (7–10). Attachment of transformed cells, propagated *in vitro,* to basement membrane collagen is followed by spreading and flattening of the cells (7, 10). In fact, this initial recognition step is inhibited by specific amino-sugars, reminiscent of a lectin-like interaction (7). Such differences in the cell recognition of basement membrane collagenous structures could be related to the normal or transformed character of the cells.

It has also been reported that cell surface stimulation of lymphocytes by lectins induces an early morphological modification of nuclei. Indeed, the condensed chromatin of nonstimulated lymphocyte nuclei converts into a dispersed state when lymphocytes are activated by phytohemagglutinin (11). This cell activation is detected by a decrease of nuclear refringency obtained by mercury binding on condensed chromatin (12, 13). This phenomenon can be quantified by the nuclear refringency assay (14). Therefore, using this method, we have attempted to analyze the priming nuclear response of normal (HA) and transformed human amniotic epithelial (WISH) cells closely related with the membranous effect of type IV collagen. The early nuclear activation of WISH cells triggered by type IV collagen has been followed by the study of further nuclear modifications, such as DNase I sensitivity of chromatin and the synthesis of mRNA. Moreover, nuclear activation of WISH cells treated by type IV collagen is associated with cell attachment and laminin synthesis. This latter is a glycoprotein attachment factor identified in the culture medium of most epithelial and carcinoma cells (4, 9, 15–18).

Materials and Methods. *Cells and medium.* Primary cultures of human epithelial amnion cells (HA) were prepared from full-term placentas. Cells obtained during subsequent trypsinizations were maintained in Eagle's minimum essential medium (EMEM) supplemented with 10% newborn calf serum (GIBCO Bio-Cult Ltd., Paisley PA34EP, Scotland).

The WISH cell line, derived from human amnion tissue (ATCC CLL25), was cloned *in vitro* from an altered colony, and maintained in EMEM with 15% newborn calf serum (GIBCO) (19).

[1] To whom all correspondence should be addressed.

0037-9727/84 $1.50

Collagen preparation. Type I collagen was purified from human amnion and type IV collagen from human placenta villi, according to the method of Burgeson *et al.* (20). Preparation and chemical characterization have been previously described (10).

Nuclear refringency. HA or WISH cells (5×10^5 cells/ml) were incubated in EMEM without serum supplemented with 10 μg/ml of either type I or IV purified collagen. After varying incubation times at 37°C, the cells were harvested by scraping and suspended in the medium before cytocentrifugation in a Shandon Cytospin at 800 rpm for 8 min. The cells were projected on triplicate glass slides at the same density in an 6-mm diameter area. The slides were immediately immersed in 5% acetic acid–Zenker reagent (25 g potassium dichromate, 50 g mercuric chloride, and 10 g sodium sulfate dissolved at 80°C in 1 liter of distilled water) at room temperature for 60 min. Then the temperature was raised to 90°C in the same reagent for 10 min. After washing in tap water for 10 min, air-drying overnight, and clearing in toluene, the slides were mounted using a mounting medium with a refractive index of 1.650 (Technicon Industry) (12, 13). The cells, viewed on slides with a phase-contrast microscope, appeared more or less refringent and three groups could be individualized according to their refringency: low (A), intermediate (B), and high (C) refringent cells.

The morphological patterns of nuclear refringency of WISH cells attached in the presence of type IV collagen ($5\ \mu g/2.5 \times 10^5$ cells) and laminin ($1\ \mu g/2.5 \times 10^5$ cells) were directly observed on the glass slides after 1 hr of incubation. The slides were immersed in Zenker reagent and submitted to the same treatment as described above.

Quantitative analysis. The diagram of the measurement system is shown in Fig. 1. In order to quantify the results, the phase-contrast microscope (Leitz G × 400) was connected with a Plumbicon 720 line camera and a Cambridge Quantimet 720 (QTM) image analyzer (21, 22, 23). Data obtained from the image analyzer was further processed with a PDP 11/34 computer, a VT video terminal, and a LA 120 line printer. The image produced by the microscope was swept by the camera and submitted to the QTM as 600,000 image points. Each screening point was assigned an integer from 0 to 63, according to its brightness. Three binary images, taken from the brilliancy thresholds of the same nucleus, were processed in parallel. The first image included the darkest chromatin; the second, the medium refringent chromatin, and the third, the most refringent chromatin. The first image was submitted to dilation to be correlated with

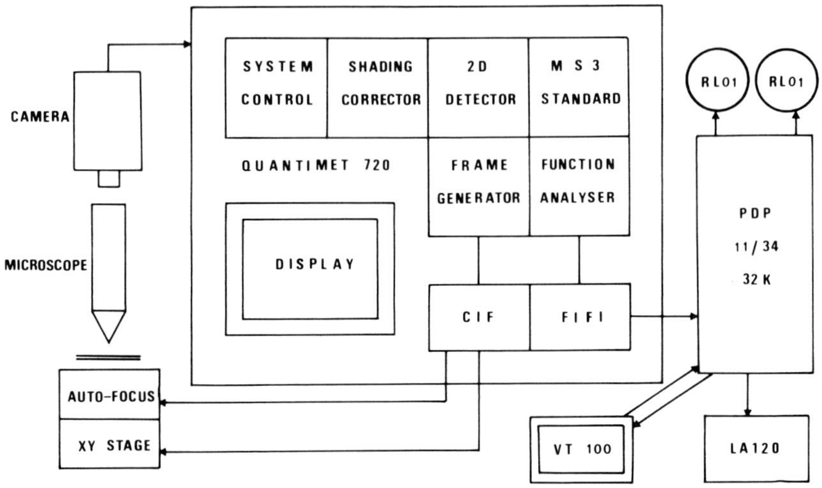

FIG. 1. Schematic representation of optic automation equipment used for the nuclear refringency assay. The measurement involved a Zeiss microscope, a Plumbicon 720 line camera, a Quantimet 720 image analyzer, a PDP 11/34 computer, a VT 100 video terminal, and an LA 120 line printer.

the two others. The analyzer relays to the computer the areas of the three gray levels, allowing the cells to be classified into the three groups. The computer software was written in Fortran IV and used 24K words of 16 bits. Therefore, a threshold of brightness, called r, could be selected from the lowest refringent cells (performed by Dr. Schovaert in the Laboratoire d'Anatomie Pathologique, Hôpital St. Vincent-de-Paul, Professor A. Pompidou).

Nuclear refringency index (NRI). A thousand cells were observed on each slide and a nuclear refringency index (NRI) was defined according to the formula:

$$\text{NRI} = \frac{a(r \times 1) + b(r \times 2) + c(r \times 4)}{a + b + c},$$

a, b, and c were the percentage of cells of each group (a = percentage of A cells, b = percentage of B cells, c = percentage of C cells: consequently, $a + b + c = 100$). The Quantimet analyzer allowed the determination of the brightness of the A, B, and C cell groups: $(r \times 1)$ for A cells; $(r \times 2)$ for B cells; and $(r \times 4)$ for C cells. In our experimental conditions, r equals 16.

The results are expressed as the means of the three NRI values calculated on the triplicate slides for one test.

Nuclear refringency test (NRT). NRT was expressed as a ratio of the NRI of treated cells/NRI of control cells:

$$\text{NRT} = \frac{\text{NRI}_t}{\text{NRI}_c} = \frac{1a_t + 2b_t + 4c_t}{1a_c + 2b_c + 4c_c},$$

t = treated cells, and c = control cells. The standard deviation was established from seven tests. Statistical significance was evaluated by the nonparametric Wilcoxon test.

DNase I digestion. WISH cells were suspended at a concentration of 5×10^5 cells/ml and 100 ml of suspension was incubated for 5 hr with 25 μCi of [*methyl*-^{3}H]thymidine (Commissariat à l'Energie Atomique—CEA, Saclay, France; sp act 26 Ci/mmole). The cells were washed in medium, suspended at the same concentration, and grown in nonradioactive medium for 20 hr. The cells were then harvested by trypsinization and divided into two equal samples separately incubated for 4 hr at 37°C in EMEM supplemented or not with type IV collagen (5 μg/ml) in absence of serum.

Nuclei were isolated by the procedure of Weintraub and Groudine (24) using reticulocyte standard buffer (RSB, 10 mM NaCl, 3 mM $MgCl_2$, 10 mM Tris, pH 7.4) containing 0.5% NP40 (Bethesda Research Laboratories, Rockville, Md.) and 2 mM phenylmethylsulfonyl fluoride (PMSF, Sigma Chemical Co., St. Louis, Mo.) to inhibit protease activity.

Kinetics of DNA degradation by DNase I were performed on aliquots of the final nuclear suspension containing 1 mg DNA/ml. After 10 min preincubation time at 37°C, bovine pancreatic DNase I (Worthington Biochemical Corp., Freehold, N.J.) was added to a final concentration of 1 U/ml for 0–15 min. The reaction was stopped at the indicated times by adding EDTA, pH 8, to a final concentration of 10 mM. Acid insoluble products were precipitated in cold 7% (w/v) perchloric acid. Aliquots of the supernatant were withdrawn for determination of ^{3}H activities in a liquid scintillation counter (Intertechnique SL30).

Poly(A)$^+$ RNA synthesis. The rate of RNA synthesis was determined by the incorporation of [^{3}H]uridine. Cells (5×10^6/25-cm^2 tissue culture flask, Falcon) were labeled with 10 μCi/ml of [^{3}H]uridine for 60 min (CEA; sp act 20 Ci/mmole). Cytoplasmic RNA was obtained by lysis of the cells in 10 mM NaCl, 1.5 mM $MgCl_2$, 20 mM Tris, pH 8.3, containing 5 μl/ml of diethyl pyrocarbonate (DEPC, Sigma) and 0.5% Nonidet P40 (NP 40, Bethesda Research Laboratories), extracted by phenol chloroform (v/v) and collected by ethanol precipitation. Polyadenylated cytoplasmic RNA from the extracted cytoplasmic RNA was isolated by the use of oligo-(dT)-cellulose columns (25). Poly(A)$^+$ RNA was then precipitated with 2 vol of ethanol, lyophilized, and the radioactivity was measured by liquid scintillation (Intertechnique SL30).

Cell attachment assay. Attachment assay was adapted from the method of Klebe (26). Multiwell tissue plates (2 cm^2, Falcon, Div. Becton, Dickinson & Co., Oxnard, Calif.) were filled with 0.5 ml of EMEM supplemented with 200 μg/ml of bovine serum albumin (BSA, Sigma) to prevent nonspecific binding. Then 0.5 ml of cell suspension containing 2.5×10^5 cells were added and incubated in presence of 10 μg/ml of either type I or IV collagen at 37°C. After selected incubation periods, the unattached cells were discarded; the remaining cells were dispersed with trypsin (Difco Laboratories, Detroit, Mich.) and treated with trypan blue solution (0.5%, Boehringer-Mannheim, France). The viable cells were unstained and counted in an hemocytometer. Assays were performed in triplicate. The standard deviation did not exceed 10%.

Immunoenzymatic characterization of laminin. Laminin was detected by indirect immunoperoxidase labeling in the culture medium after 3 hr of attachment test. Four microliters of the solution were placed on a 13-mm GCWP filter with 0.22-μm pore diameter (Millipore Corp., Bedford, Mass.) and air-dried. The filters were then immersed in phosphate-buffered saline (PBS) with 2% BSA at 4°C overnight. After washing with PBS, filters were incubated with laminin antisera (Bethesda Research Laboratory) at a dilution of 10^{-3} for 2 hr at 20°C or overnight at 4°C. The antisera were then eliminated and filters washed with PBS before a second incubation of 40 min at 20°C with peroxidase-labeled goat anti-rabbit gamma globulins (Miles Yeda Ltd., Kiryat Weizmann, Rehovolt, Israel). After the elimination of this serum, filters were washed and the bound peroxidase activity was revealed with α-chloronaphtol (3 mg/1 ml methanol/4 ml PBS, Merck Darmstadt, FRG). The quantitation of laminin was performed by this method which allowed the detection of 1 to 40 ng of laminin. No cross-reaction was observed between collagen type I or IV preparations and laminin.

Inhibitors. Nocodazole (Aldrich Europe B.2340, Beerse, Belgium) was used to inhibit the polymerization of microtubules. The biological effects were identical within a large dose range (0.04–100 μg/ml) (27). The antimicrotubular effect was immediately active in cultured cells and also rapidly reversible (27). Cells were incubated in EMEM without serum supplemented with 0.3 μg/ml of Nocodazole for 1 hr at 37°C. For testing reversible effect, Nocodazole was removed and the cells were washed in fresh medium before being seeded into wells containing type I or IV collagen.

Cytochalasin B is known to dissociate microfilament bundles (28). Cells were pretreated for 1 hr with 5 μg/ml of cytochalasin B (Sigma). To remove the inhibitor, the cells were incubated in EMEM for 2 hr.

N-Acetyl neuraminic acid (NANA) (Sigma), which inhibits the biological effect of type IV collagen on the cell membrane, was also tested (7, 10). The pretreatment of the cells with a 5 m*M* NANA solution in EMEM was performed at 20°C for 1 hr.

During the inhibitor treatments, the cells were maintained in suspension by gentle agitation.

In all assays using inhibitors, treated and untreated control cells were seeded in wells without collagen fractions. In all cases, cell viability was higher than 90% as evaluated by trypan blue exclusion.

Results. *Nuclear refringency.* The nuclear refringency patterns of cytocentrifuged cells are illustrated in Fig. 2. Three groups of cell nuclei were observed on each slide: A cells appeared with a completely black nucleus on the gray cytoplasmic area; intermediate B cells appeared with clumps of bright chromatin; C cells exhibited a brilliant chromatin surrounded by a rim of dark cytoplasm. The percentage of each group of cells was counted and allowed the NRI determination as described under Materials and Methods. The assay was performed in both normal (HA) and transformed (WISH) amniotic cells at varying incubation times (20, 30, 60, 120, and 180 min). NRI was determined for untreated cells (NRI control) and for treated cells (NRI treated). The ratio NRT = NRI treated/NRI control was calculated for each cell type and for each incubation time.

In Fig. 3 we show the kinetics of nuclear refringency variation of WISH and HA cells treated or not by type I or IV collagen. A majority of C refringent cells were constantly observed on untreated HA or WISH cell slides. For these control cells, the NRT value was 1. HA cells treated by either type I or IV collagen exhibited only a slight variation of the nuclear refringency at 3 hr and the decrease did not exceed 0.9. WISH cells treated by type I collagen also showed a NRT of 0.9 after 3 hr. In contrast, WISH cells treated by type IV collagen exhibited an early impairment of the nuclear refringency and A cells were prevalent on the slides. A marked decrease in nuclear refringency (NRT = 0.7) was observed after 20 min of incubation with type IV collagen. A maximum variation of 0.5 was reached within 30 min. Two hours later, the NRT was stabilized between 0.65 and 0.7.

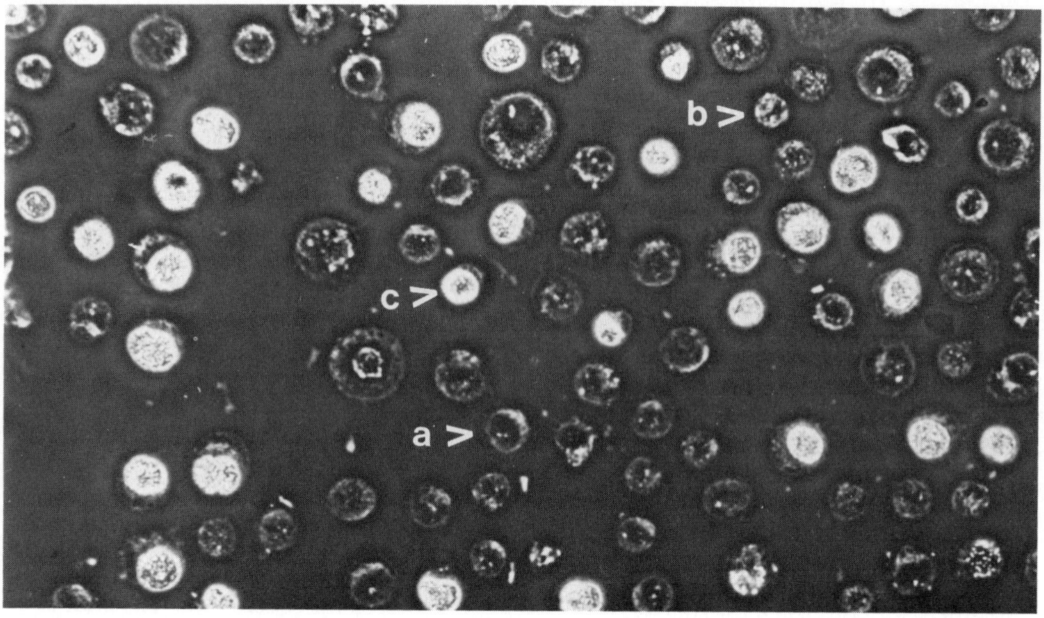

FIG. 2. Pattern of nuclear refringency. Three categories of WISH or HA cells were observed on each slide according to their refringency. Arrows indicate: (a) low refringent A cells; (b) intermediate refringent B cells; (c) high refringent C cells.

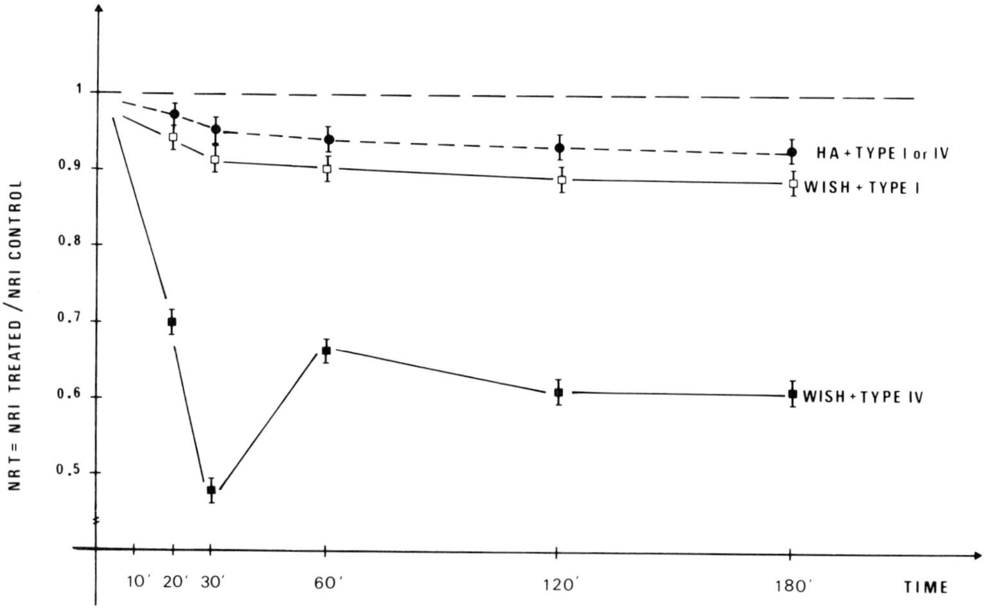

FIG. 3. Time course of the nuclear response of HA and WISH cells treated by type I or IV collagen. After varying incubation times, cells were fixed for NRI determination as described under Materials and Methods. NRT = NRI treated/NRI control cells, was calculated for HA cells in presence of type I or IV collagen fractions (10 μg/ml) (●) and for WISH cells in presence of type I (□) or IV (■) collagen fractions (10 μg/ml). Each time point represents the mean of seven experiments. Bars denote the SD ($P < 0.01$).

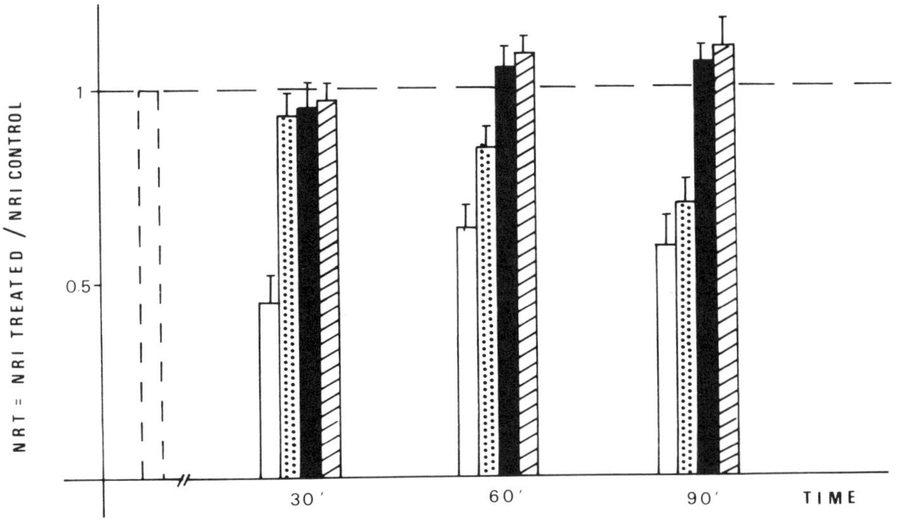

FIG. 4. Effect of inhibitors on nuclear refringency of WISH cells treated with type IV collagen. NRT was evaluated after varying incubation times in presence of type IV collagen (10 μg/ml) for WISH cells preincubated with NANA (⚄), Nocodazole (■), cytochalasin B (▨), or without inhibitors (□). NRT = 1 for control untreated WISH cells (— —).

The effects of three different inhibitors on the nuclear refringency of WISH cells treated by type IV collagen is shown in Fig. 4. NANA, known to inhibit the cell surface effect of type IV collagen (7, 10), also inhibited the nuclear activation and NRT value of the cell population, almost reaching that of control cells. The cytoskeleton inhibitors, Nocodazole and cytochalasin B, also suppressed nuclear activation and the NRT values were close to 1.

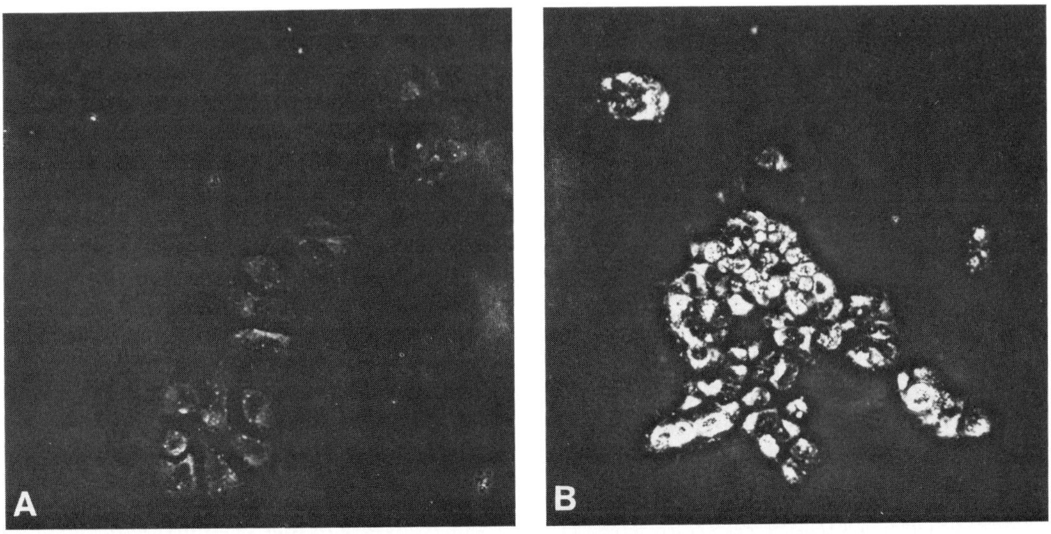

FIG. 5. Morphological appearance of nuclear refringency of WISH cells seeded on glass slides and directly fixed on the slide with Zenker reagent after 1 hr of incubation at 37°C. (A) WISH cells treated by 5 μg/ml of type IV collagen. (B) WISH cells treated by 1 μg/ml of laminin. ×400.

The morphology and nuclear refringency of cells laid on type IV collagen differed from those of cells attached to laminin. WISH cells attached in the presence of type IV collagen were very flat and the nuclei appeared dark on the cytoplasmic area (Fig. 5A). In the presence of laminin, on a glass substratum, WISH cells clustered together, remained round, and the nuclei were brilliant (Fig. 5B). The NRT value of this latter cell population differed little or none from the one of control cells.

Kinetics of limited DNase I digestion. The kinetics of DNase I nuclear degradation of WISH cells treated for 4 hr by collagen I or IV are compared in Fig. 6. The chromatin of cells attached in presence of type IV collagen was particularly sensitive to DNase I digestion. The increase of [^{3}H]thymidine counts per minute in the acid-soluble phase of digest was about 50% higher in WISH cells treated by type IV collagen than in cells treated by type I collagen or untreated control cells for an incubation time of 10 min. Primary HA cells treated or not by type I or IV collagen did not show any notable difference with DNase I sensitivity (data not shown). Similar experiments using staphylococcal nuclease instead of DNase I showed no difference in the degradation rates of nuclei from control and type IV collagen-treated cells (data not shown). These results were confirmed in seven separate experiments.

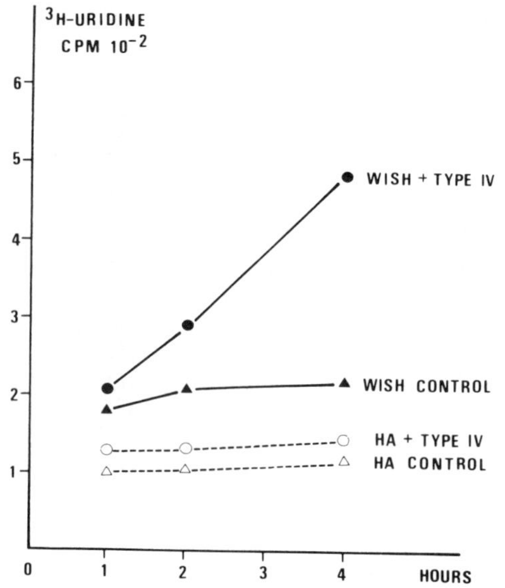

FIG. 7. Effect of type IV collagen on poly(A)$^+$ RNA production in HA and WISH cells. The synthesis of poly(A)$^+$ RNA was determined at different times after contact of the cells with type IV collagen and pulse-labeled for 60 min with [^{3}H]uridine. The poly(A)$^+$ RNA was measured in the cytoplasm of WISH or HA cells treated with type IV collagen; and of untreated WISH or HA cells.

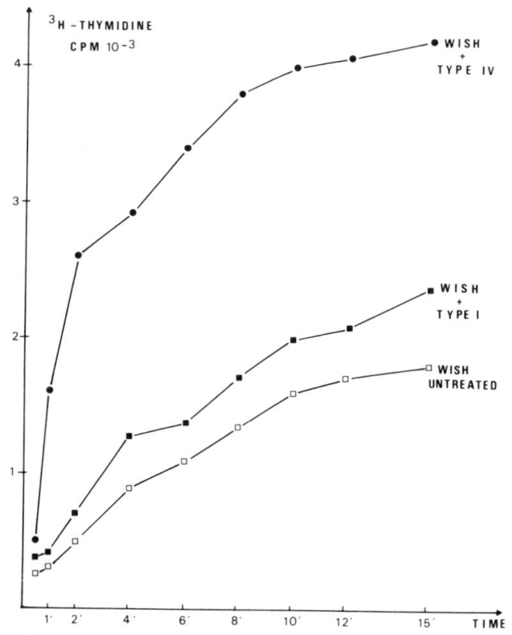

FIG. 6. Comparative kinetics of DNase I nuclei digestion of untreated, type I-, or type IV-treated WISH cells. The nuclei were digested with DNase I for increasing periods of time as described under Materials and Methods. Aliquots of acid soluble digest products were taken for measurement of ^{3}H activity. This result was confirmed in seven separate experiments.

mRNA synthesis. The effect of type IV collagen on RNA synthesis was also investigated. As shown in Fig. 7, a significant increase in poly(A)$^+$ RNA levels was observed in WISH cells after 4 hr of treatment with type IV collagen. There was an increase of 55% in the poly(A)$^+$ RNA levels in treated cells as compared to the untreated ones. In HA cells, under the same conditions, no significant incorporation of isotopes into poly(A)$^+$ RNA was noted in cells treated or not by type IV collagen.

Cell attachment and laminin synthesis. The attached HA or WISH cells were counted after the same incubation times as those selected for nuclear refringency assay. Attachment kinetics in the presence and absence of type I or IV collagen were performed in EMEM without serum. The results are shown in Fig. 8. Few HA cells bound to the substratum in absence of serum at 180 min of incubation. Type I collagen slightly enhanced the cell attachment which did not exceed 8% after 180 min. In presence of type IV collagen, cell attachment reached 12% at the same incubation time.

On the other hand, 20% of WISH cells untreated by collagens adhered to the substratum after 180 min but the cells remained round and dispersed. The attachment increased up to 40% by 180 min when WISH cells were treated by type I collagen. In presence of type IV collagen, this value reached 85% in 3 hr. In addition, as previously mentioned, morphological changes of the cell, such as clustering and spreading out on the substratum, occurred in a few minutes (7, 10). The same discrepancy in the attachment characteristics

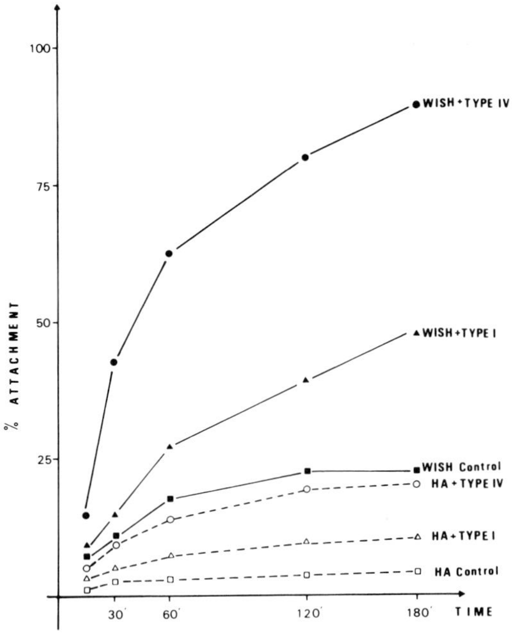

FIG. 8. Kinetics of the attachment of HA and WISH cells on collagen type I or IV substrates. WISH cells (2×10^5/ml) were incubated on type IV collagen (10 μg), type I collagen (10 μg), and uncoated polystyrene wells of tissue culture plates (control) for 20 to 180 min without serum. HA cells (2×10^5/ml) were incubated on type IV collagen (10 μg), type I collagen (10 μg), and uncoated polystyrene wells (control) for 1–24 hr without serum.

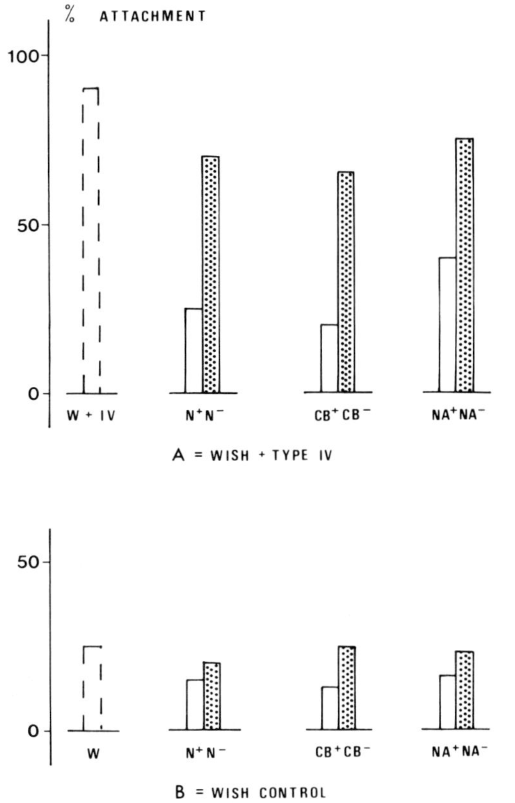

FIG. 9. Effect of inhibitors on the attachment of WISH cells in presence or absence of type IV collagen. WISH cells (2×10^5 cells/ml), preincubated for 60 min with Nocodazole (NA^+, 0.3 μg/ml), cytochalasin B (CB^+, 5 μg/ml), or NANA (NA^+, 5 mM), were plated in triplicate wells in medium supplemented with type IV collagen (5 μg/0.5 ml). WISH cells were allowed to attach for 180 min. After removal of the inhibitors, WISH cells were replaced in new culture wells containing medium with type IV collagen and incubated for 180 min. Controls without type IV collagen were effected. (□) attachment of WISH cells incubated with inhibitors; (⊡) attachment of WISH cells after inhibitor removal; (— —) attachment of WISH cells after 180 min incubation.

of normal and transformed cells to type IV collagen was repeatedly observed.

After 24 hr incubation in the absence of serum, WISH cells were counted and the morphological patterns were assessed (Fig. 10). The viability of attached cells was determined by trypan blue exclusion. During this period, WISH cells attached to the substratum in the presence of type IV collagen, spread out and formed a confluent monolayer (Fig. 10B, a) with a cell attachment of 80% (Fig. 10A, a).

In parallel, WISH cells, not treated with collagen, attached poorly, remained round (Fig. 10B, b), and degenerated, as revealed by the number of surviving viable cells (Fig. 10A, b). WISH cells routinely grown with 15% calf serum proliferated (Fig. 10A, c) with local piling up of cells (Fig. 10B, c).

As shown in Fig. 5B, the addition of laminin (1 μg/ml) to the culture medium induced a clustering effect of cells. The cell aggregates attached loosely to the substratum and only a small degree of cell flattening was observed after 24 hr. The percentage of the cells that attached did not exceed 25%.

Attachment of WISH cells in presence of type IV collagen was reduced by 50% after Nocodazole or cytochalasin B and by 30% after NANA pretreatment (Fig. 9A). In absence of type IV collagen, the attachment of WISH cells was not modified by inhibitors (Fig. 9B). After removal of the inhibitor, in presence of type IV collagen, the cells recovered their capacity to attach up to 50% in 180 min (Fig. 9A).

Laminin was identified and determined by immunoenzymatic detection in the incubation medium of attached type IV collagen-treated WISH cells (Table I). Laminin synthesis was

Medium	Cell number
(a) + Type IV without serum	$1.9 \times 10^5 \pm 354$
(b) Without type IV or serum	$4 \times 10^3 \pm 458$
(c) + Serum without type IV	$4 \times 10^5 \pm 856$

A

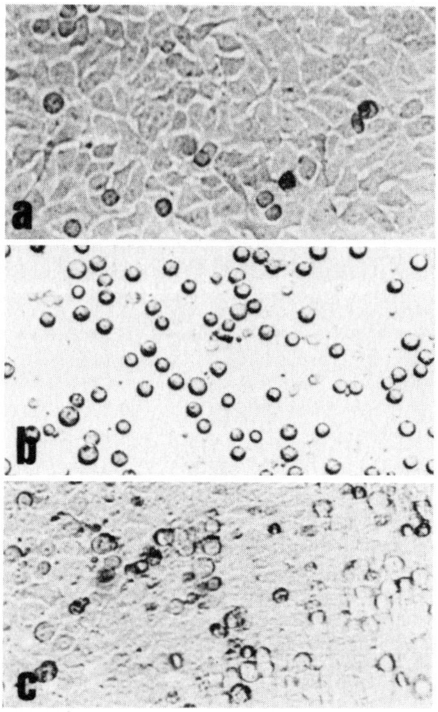

B

FIG. 10. Effect of type IV collagen or serum on the attachment (A) and morphological patterns (B) of WISH cells. (A) Numeration of WISH cells. On each well of Falcon plates, 2.5×10^5 cells were seeded. After 24 hr of culture, the cells were removed by trypsinization and the number of WISH cells (mean ± SD) was estimated by trypan blue exclusion. (B) Morphological patterns. (a) WISH cells maintained on type IV collagen (10 μg/2.5×10^5 cells) for 24 hr in culture medium without serum form a confluent layer of flattened cells with an epithelial cell-like morphology. Ten to 15% of cells were trypan blue positive. (b) WISH cells incubated without serum or type IV collagen remain round and unattached. Thirty to 45% of the cells were trypan blue positive. (c) In the presence of serum without type IV collagen, WISH cells proliferated and exhibited morphologically transformed foci with the piling up of cells. Magnification: B (a–c), ×200.

TABLE I. IMMUNOENZYMATIC CHARACTERIZATION OF LAMININ

INHIBITOR	% VIABLE CELLS	% ATTACHED CELLS	LAMININ SYNTHESIS
NONE	98.75	81.75 ± 5.58	
NOCODAZOLE +	99	21 ± 1.15	
NOCODAZOLE -	99	52 ± 3.47	
NONE	98.8	84.6 ± 7.06	
CYTOCHALASIN B +	98.2	25 ± 1.49	
CYTOCHALASIN B -	96.8	76.46 ± 3.35	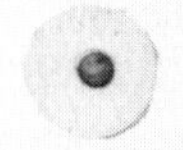
NANA +	98	40.5 ± 2.31	
NANA -	98.8	79.3 ± 1.35	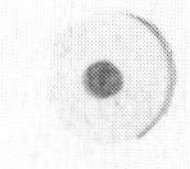

Note. Numbers represent the percentage of cells attached in six replicate assays. Laminin synthesis was detected by immunoenzymatic labeling (as described under Materials and Methods) in the 3-hr attachment assay medium of WISH cells treated by type IV collagen: in the absence of inhibitor, after inhibitor treatment (+), and after inhibitor removal (−). Type IV collagen preparation did not cross-react with anti-laminin.

inhibited by Nocodazole and cytochalasin B and only impaired after treatment with NANA. Removal of the inhibitors allowed the recovery of laminin synthesis (Table I). In contact with type IV collagen, comparable amounts of laminin were seen in the 3-hr culture medium of WISH cells without inhibitor treatment or after inhibitor removal. The 3-hr HA cell culture medium contained only traces of laminin under the survival conditions of the test (EMEM without serum).

It was noteworthy that laminin antibodies inhibited the attachment of WISH cells to type IV collagen.

Discussion. Collagen is a major constituent of the extracellular matrix: type I collagen is found predominantly in connective tissues, whereas type IV collagen is present in basement membranes. *In vitro,* differences are observed in the recognition process of type IV collagen by normal and transformed epithelial cells (4–8). Previous studies have reported similarities between the effect of lectins (29) and type IV collagen fractions (7, 10) on transformed cells reacting to these agents. In this study we describe an early modification of the nuclear structure in transformed cells triggered by the membranous effect of type IV collagen. An analogous early nuclear effect has been observed and quantified in lymphocytes stimulated by mitogenic lectins (11, 30).

Nuclear refringency is a property of condensed chromatin which contains nonexpressed genes. Its decrease is due to chromatin dispersion associated to nuclear activation (11). In normal cells, type IV collagen does not modify in a detectable manner either cell metabolism or nuclear refringency. Despite this absence of nuclear modification, a difference in the attachment properties is observed in regard to the two types of collagen.

HA cells, like other epithelial cells (4, 5), bind slowly but specifically to type IV collagen and laminin is synthesized normally. The contact of HA cells with type IV collagen *in vitro* does not stimulate new nuclear functions and the condensed chromatin remains quiescent. This result was expected since epithelial cells are closely associated to basement membrane *in vivo.*

On the contrary, the contact of WISH cells with type IV collagen induces a quenching of nuclear refringency in a few minutes. In the same time, attachment properties are restored and WISH cells, deposited on type IV collagen, exhibit morphological differences compared to their untreated counterparts. The morphological changes of WISH cells stimulated by type IV collagen could be related to the synthesis of laminin, a molecule promoting cellular attachment (15–17) and spreading (18).

The use of NANA, which impairs the first clustering of cells in presence of basement membrane collagen fractions (7, 10), also hinders the stimulation of cell nuclear refringency, as well as the attachment of the cells and laminin production. The recovery of these properties is observed when transformed WISH cells are replaced with type IV collagen after the removal of NANA.

In addition, as shown by the blocking effect of Nocodazole and cytochalasin B, the integrity of the cytoskeleton framework is prerequisite for nuclear activation and attachment processes. The removal of these inhibitors leads to the decondensation of chromatin and to the reinduction of metabolic events which include spreading out and attachment of cells.

It is also of interest that laminin antibodies inhibit the attachment and the nuclear refringency of WISH cells treated by type IV collagen (data not shown). These data suggest that laminin synthesis is indeed the result of the contact of WISH cells with type IV collagen.

The chromatin conformation changes of WISH cell nuclei treated by type IV collagen is confirmed by their accessibility to limited DNase I digestion. Indeed, DNase I is known to digest preferentially the active parts of decondensed chromatin (23, 31–34). This effect on chromatin is accompanied by a stimulation of gene expression as revealed by the increase of mRNA synthesis.

It is of interest that the simple contact of transformed epithelial cells with basement membrane collagen might modulate the expression of various sets of genes, enabling the cell to produce attachment factors usually synthesized in their normal counterparts. Transformation processes involve alterations both in the synthesis of cell surface proteins and in the interactions with matrix proteins (35, 36). The laminin synthesis induced by the matrix signal of type IV collagen restores an extracellular environment for the cells. The inclusion of the cells in a common matrix changes the surface properties of transformed cells and provides narrow connections between the cells which are necessary to modify cell growth properties (as shown by the patterns of WISH cells grown on type IV collagen) (Figs. 5 and 9). This cell-to-cell contact mediated by the newly formed matrix (i.e., laminin bound to type IV collagen) may thereby trigger the metabolic events that lead to the cell attachment through cell membrane, cytoskeleton, and nucleus interactions.

The nuclear refringency test is an easy and rapid method for the detection and estimation of early structural changes in the nucleus of transformed epithelial cells induced by the recognition of type IV collagen. The nuclear response of tumoral cells to basement membrane collagen could express their capacity to restore an extracellular environment able to limit the cell proliferation.

We are grateful to M. Sarragne, J. Lopez, D. Esnous, P. Michel, and F. Coutances for their excellent technical assistance and to C. Girard for her contribution to the preparation of the manuscript and illustrations. This work was supported in part by Grant 8279.114 from the Institut National de la Santé et de la Recherche Médicale (Unité 43) and by Grants 7915182 from the Institut National de la Santé et de la Recherche Médicale and 8070225 from the Délégation Générale à la Recherche Scientifique et Technique (Laboratoire Central d'Anatomie pathologique).

1. Hynes RO. Cell surface proteins and malignant transformation. Biochim Biophys Acta **458**:73–107, 1976.
2. Voldavsky I, Gospodarowicz D. Respective roles of laminin and fibronectin in adhesion of human carcinoma and sarcoma cells. Nature (London) **289**:304–306, 1981.
3. Kleinman HK, Klebe RJ, Martin GR. Role of collagenous matrices in the adhesion and growth of cells. J Cell Biol **88**:473–485, 1981.
4. Terranova VP, Rohrbach DH, Martin GR. Role of laminin in the attachment of PAM 212 (epithelial) cells to basement membrane collagen. Cell **22**:719–726, 1980.
5. Murray JC, Stingl G, Kleinman HK, Martin GR, Katz SI. Epidermal cells adhere preferentially to type IV (basement membrane) collagen. J Cell Biol **80**:197–202, 1979.
6. Wicha MS, Liotta LA, Garbisa S, Kidwell WR. Basement membrane collagen requirements for attachment and growth of mammary epithelium. Exp Cell Res **124**:181–190, 1979.
7. Gerfaux J, Chany-Fournier F, Bardos P, Muh JP, Chany C. Lectin-like activity of components extracted from human glomerular basement membrane. Proc Natl Acad Sci USA **76**:5129–5133, 1979.
8. Murray JC, Liotta LA, Rennard SI, Martin GR. Adhesion characteristics of murine metastatic and non-metastatic tumor cells in vitro. Cancer Res **40**:347–351, 1980.
9. Terranova VP, Liotta LA, Russo RG, Martin GR. Role of laminin in the attachment and metastasis of murine tumor cells. Cancer Res **47**:2265–2269, 1982.
10. Gutman N, Lanson M, Gerfaux J, Chany-Fournier F, Muh JP, Chany C. Chemical characterization and biological effect of collagenous fractions extracted from human glomerular basement membrane and fetal tissues. Cell Biol Int Rep **6**:579–589, 1982.
11. Pompidou A, Rousset S, Macé B, Michel P, Esnous D, Renard N. Chromatin structure and nucleic acid synthesis in human lymphocyte activation by phytohemagglutinin. Exp Cell Res **150**:213–225, 1984.
12. Pompidou A, Macé B, Michel-Campagne P, Esnous D. Early modification of human lymphocyte nuclear refringence after stimulation by lectin mitogens and immunomodulators. In: Preece AW, Sabolovic D, eds. Cell Electrophoresis: Chemical Application and Methodology. INSERM Symposium, pp149–155, 1979.
13. Pompidou A, Touraine JL, Macé B, Ananthakrishnan R, Hadden J. Role of nucleic acids and cytoskeleton in nuclear refringence phenomenon (NRP) of human peripheral blood lymphocytes. Immunopharmacology **2**:29–32, 1979.
14. Pompidou A, Macé B, Michel P, Esnous D. The nuclear refringence test: a new method for the evaluation of blood lymphocytes nuclei response in vitro. In: Rosenfeld C, Serrou B, eds. New Trends in Human Immunology and Cancer Immunotherapy. Amsterdam, Elsevier/North-Holland, pp696–703, 1980.
15. Del Rosso M, Cappelletti R, Viti M, Vannucchi S, Chiatugi V. Binding of the basement membrane glycoprotein laminin to glycosaminoglycans. Biochem J **119**:699–704, 1981.
16. Malinoff HL, Wicha MS. Isolation of a cell surface receptor protein for laminin from murine fibrosarcoma cells. J Cell Biol **96**:1475–1479, 1983.
17. Terranova VP, Rao CN, Kalebic T, Margulies IM, Liotta LA. Laminin receptor on human breast carcinoma cells. Proc Natl Acad Sci USA **80**:444–448, 1983.
18. Stenn KS, Madri JA, Tinghitella T, Terranova VP. Multiple mechanisms of dissociated epidermal cell spreading. J Cell Biol **96**:63–67, 1983.
19. Hayflick L. The establishment of a line (WISH) of human amnion cells in continuous cultivation. Exp Cell Res **23**:114–120, 1961.
20. Burgeson RE, El Adli FA, Kaitila II, Hollister DW. Fetal membrane collagens: identification of two new collagen alpha chains. Proc Natl Acad Sci USA **73**:2579–2583, 1976.
21. Fisher C. The new Quantimet 720. Microscope **19**:1–20, 1971.
22. Fisher C. The Quantimet Image Analyzing Computer. London, Iron Steel Inst Pub, p112, 1978.
23. Schovaert-Brossault D, Roch-Arveiller M, Kaplan D, Michel P, Macé B, Giroud JP, Pompidou A. Quantitative evaluation of mouse peritoneal macrophage spreading by image analysis determination of the nucleo-cytoplasmic ratio. Acta Stereol **2**:159–166, 1983.
24. Weintraub H, Groudine M. Chromosomal subunits in active genes have an altered conformation. Science **193**:848–856, 1976.
25. Aviv H, Leder P. Purification of biologically active globin messenger RNA by chromatography on oligothymidilic acid cellulose. Proc Natl Acad Sci USA **69**:1408–1412, 1972.
26. Klebe RJ. Isolation of a collagen-dependent cell attachment factor. Nature (London) **250**:248–251, 1974.
27. De Brabander MJ, Van de Veire RML, Aerts FEM,

Borgers M, Jansen PAJ. The effects of methyl (5-(2-Thienylcarbonyl)-1H-benzimidazol-2-yl) carbamate, (R17934; NSC 238159), a new synthetic antitumoral drug interfering with microtubules, on mammalian cells cultured in vitro. Cancer Res **36**:905–916, 1976.

28. Weber K, Rathke PC, Osborn M, Franke WW. Distribution of actin and tubulin in cells and in glycerinated cell models after treatment with cytochalasin B (CB). Exp Cell Res **102**:285–297, 1976.
29. Sharon N, Lis H. Use of lectins for the study of membranes. In: Korn ED, ed. Methods in Membrane Biology: Plasma Membranes. New York, Plenum, Vol. 3:pp147–200, 1975.
30. Rousset S, Pompidou A, Macé B, Michel P, Esnous D. Early nuclear activation in PHA-stimulated human peripheral blood lymphocytes. Int J Immunopharmacol **4**:335, 1982.
31. Sledziewski A, Young ET. Chromatin conformational changes accompany transcriptional activation of a glucose-repressed gene in *Saccharomyces cerevisiae.* Proc Natl Acad Sci USA **79**:253–256, 1982.
32. Garel A, Axel R. Selective digestion of transcriptionally active ovalbumin genes from oviduct nuclei. Proc Natl Acad Sci USA **73**:3966–3970, 1976.
33. Vidali G, Boffa LC, Allfrey VG. Selective release of chromosomal proteins during limited DNASE I digestion of avian erythrocyte chromatin. Cell **12**:409–415, 1977.
34. Vidali G, Boffa LC, Bradbury EM, Allfrey VG. Butyrate suppression of histone deacetylation leads to accumulating of multiacetylated forms of histones H_3 and H_4 and increased DNASE I sensitivity of the associated DNA sequences. Proc Natl Acad Sci USA **75**:2239–2243, 1978.
35. Keski-Oja J, Gahmberg CG, Alitalo K. Pericellular matrix and cell surface glycoproteins of virus-transformed mouse epithelial cells. Cancer Res **42**:1147–1153, 1982.
36. Hayman EG, Engvall E, Ruoslahti E. Concomitant loss of cell surface fibronectin and laminin from transformed rat kidney cells. J Cell Biol **88**:352–357, 1981.

Received December 6, 1983. P.S.E.B.M. 1984, Vol. 176.
Accepted May 11, 1984.

PROCEEDINGS OF THE SOCIETY FOR EXPERIMENTAL BIOLOGY AND MEDICINE **176**, 503–507 (1984)

RAPID COMMUNICATIONS

ISOLATION AND CULTURE OF HUMAN INTESTINAL SMOOTH MUSCLE CELLS

Martin F. Graham*, Robert F. Diegelmann**, Charles O. Elson***, Khalil N. Bitar***, and H. Paul Ehrlich****

Depts. Pediatrics, Children's Medical Center*, Surgery** and Medicine***, Medical College of Virginia, Richmond, VA 23298, Shriner's Burn Institute and Massachusetts General Hospital****, Boston, MA 02114

Abstract. Intestinal smooth muscle cells were isolated from human bowel and maintained in culture through several passages. These cells were obtained by enzyme digestion of slices taken from the circular layer of the muscularis propria of human jejunum. When subcultured, they initially flattened out and then began proliferating after 3 days. After 3 weeks in culture, they began aggregating into ridges. Fluorohistochemical staining revealed numerous prominent actin stress fibers. When these cells were exposed to the C-terminal octapeptide of cholecystokinin they contracted in a dose-dependent fashion. The availability of human intestinal smooth muscle cells in culture will considerably enhance our ability to study the contractile, proliferative and connective tissue responses of the smooth muscle of the human gastrointestinal tract.

Intestinal smooth muscle cells play a critical role in the motility and physical integrity of the gastrointestinal tract. Contraction and relaxation of the deep muscle layer, the muscularis propria, results in normal aboral propulsion and mixing of luminal contents. The role of the superficial layer, the muscularis mucosae, is unclear but may involve motility of villi (1). Destruction of the muscularis propria as seen in the toxic megacolon complicating ulcerative colitis, leads to decreased motility, progressive dilatation and perforation of the bowel (2). Chronic inflammation of the bowel wall leads to thickening of the muscle coat, collagen deposition and narrowing of the gut lumen (3). Until now, sterile cultures of smooth muscle cells from human bowel have not been available. We describe here the techniques we have developed for the isolation and culture of these cells. Their availability in long term culture should considerably enhance our ability to study the physiology and pathology of the smooth muscle of the human gut.

Materials and Methods.

Sources of Tissue. Normal jejunal tissue was obtained from patients undergoing gastric bypass operations. Tissue from the jejunum was used preferentially because it is relatively free of gastrointestinal microorganisms.

Tissue Processing. Once resected, the tissue was immediately placed in sterile phosphate-buffered saline (4°C) and transported to the tissue culture facility. Under sterile conditions, mucosa was separated from muscularis by blunt dissection. Slices were taken from the center of the circular layer of the muscularis propria with a Stadie-Riggs tissue slicer, minced and incubated overnight in Dulbecco's Modified Eagle's Medium (DMEM) containing 1% crude collagenase (Grade CLS11, Worthington Diagnostic Systems, Inc.). The following day, released cells were separated from tissue debris by low speed centrifugation (40 x g), washed several times and 2 x 10^6 cells were placed in 100 mm culture plates with 10 ml DMEM containing fetal bovine

0037-9727/84 $1.50

serum (FBS) (GIBCO) and 25 mM Tricine (pH 7.4). Culture medium was replaced every third day. When the smooth muscle cells became confluent after 3 weeks in culture, they were released from the plates by trypsinisation (0.1%) and replated at 2×10^6 cells per 100 mm plate. The smooth muscle cells were observed daily and photographed for a record of morphologic changes.

Fluorohistochemistry. Cells were freed from the culture plate surface by trypsinisation. A drop of culture medium (20 ul) containing 5×10^4 cells was applied to a sterile glass coverslip (22 x 22 mm) in a 100 mm petri dish, and the cells were allowed to attach for 30 minutes at 37°C in a moist atmosphere. An additional 6 ml of DMEM, 10% serum, was slowly added to the culture dish and this was again placed in a 37°C moist atmosphere incubator. At 24 and 48 hours, coverslips were rinsed in phosphate buffered saline (pH 7.6, PBS), and they were placed in 4% paraformaldehyde-PBS for five minutes at room temperature. The fixed slides were washed for five minutes three times in PBS and they were then permeabilized in PBS containing 0.1% Triton X-100 for five minutes. The Triton X-100 treated coverslips were washed three times in PBS as described above. Rhodamine-phalloidin (Microbiological Probes, Inc., Junction City, Oregon) was layered onto the top of the coverslips at 1:1000 dilution and allowed to incubate at room temperature for 30 minutes. The coverslips were washed with PBS three times and then mounted in glycerol:PBS (9:1) on a glass microscopic slide. The stained coverslips were viewed in a Zeiss IM 35 inverted microscope with fitted Rhodamine filters and epifluoresence. Cellular stress fiber patterns were recorded with Ektachrome 400 color 35 mm film uprated to 1600 ASA.

Measurement of Contractile Response. The procedure as described by Bitar, et al. (4) was used to measure the contractile response of the human intestinal smooth muscle cells to CCK-octapeptide. A solution containing various concentrations of the C-terminal octapeptide of cholecystokinin (CCK-OP, Squibb Institute for Medical Research, Princeton, NJ) was added to the 6 day old cultures of human intestinal smooth muscle cells attached to coverslips. The reaction was stopped after 30 seconds by the addition of acrolein to give a final concentration of 1.0%. Cell length was measured by image-splitting micrometry and for each test, the length of 50 cells in successive random microscopic fields was measured and the mean length calculated. Contraction was expressed as the percentage decrease in mean cell length from control. A dose response curve was constructed for CCK-OP at concentrations of 10^{-9} and 10^{-11}M (3 experiments); 10^{-10} and 10^{-13}M (2 experiments) and 10^{-14}M (1 experiment).

Growth Curve. Smooth muscle cells released from the bottom of culture plates by trypsinisation were plated into multiwell culture plates (Costar #3524, Cambridge, MA) at two densities; 10^4 and 10^5 cells per well. 1 ml DMEM containing 10% FBS was added to each well. Cells were released from the well bottoms with trypsin at daily intervals and the total number of cells in each of 6 wells were counted using a Coulter counter (Coulter Electronics, Automatic Blood Cell Counter, Model D2N).

Results. Collagenase digestion of approximately 10 cm^2 of muscularis tissue yielded approximately 1×10^7 viable cells. Viability by trypan blue exclusion was greater than 60%. Newly released, oblong-shaped cells (primary culture) attached to the plate within 12 hours and by 7 days they had flattened out. Following treatment with trypsin and subculture, cells flattened out within 24 hours and began proliferating after 2-3 days in culture. These cells demonstrated prominent intracellular fiber-like structures on light microscopy. Fluorohistochemical staining with Rhodamine-phalloidin 48 hours after passage confirmed the presence of prominent actin stress fibers (Fig. 1). (Phalloidin, a phallotoxin, has been demonstrated to bind specifically to F-actin (5)). After 3 weeks in culture, cells began to aggregate forming ridges (Fig. 2).

The contractile response (expressed as percent decrease in cell length) of the human intestinal smooth muscle cells to CCK-OP was dose-dependent (Fig. 3).

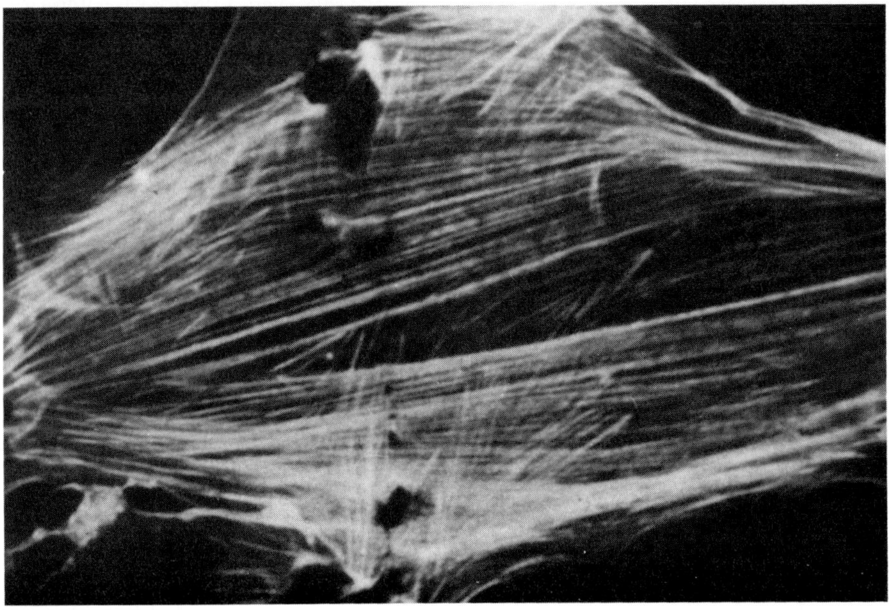

Figure 1

Human intestinal smooth muscle cells stained with Rhodamine-phalloidin demonstrating numerous, dense actin stress fibers (280 x). Cells were passaged 48 hours prior to staining and were viewed with epifluorescence.

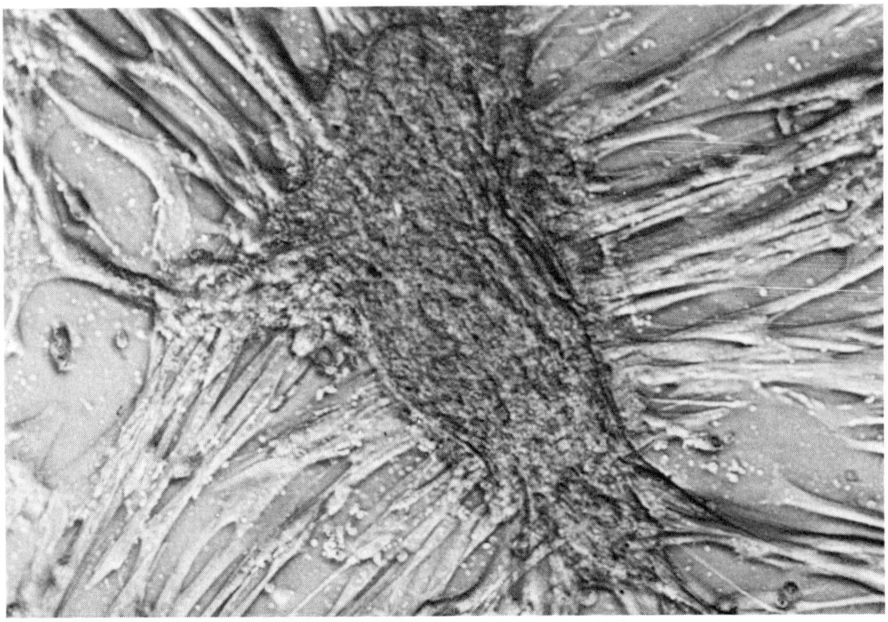

Figure 2

Cells forming ridges after 3 weeks in culture (70 x).

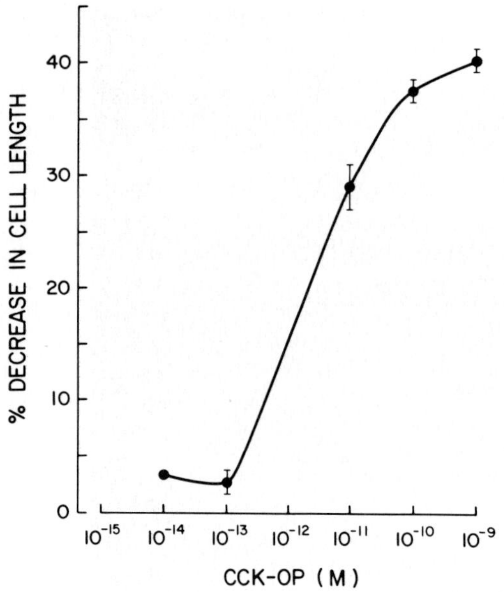

Figure 3

Dose-response curve for the effect of CCK-OP on cultured human intestinal smooth muscle cell contraction. Data are average values and the bars indicate the range of values.

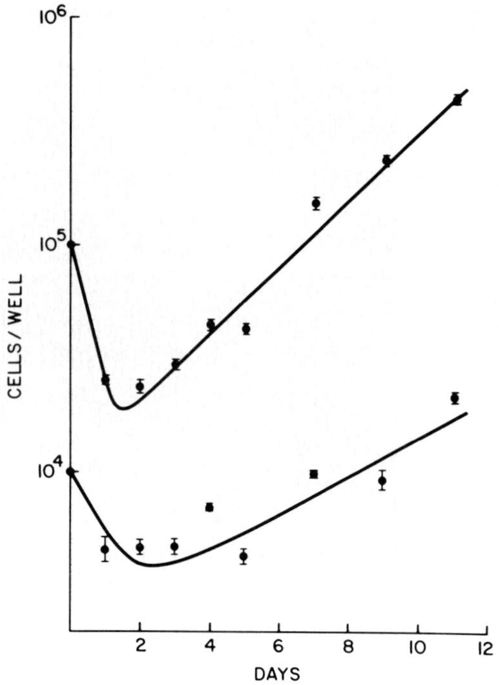

Figure 4

Growth curves of human intestinal smooth muscle cells plated at densities of 10^4 and 10^5 cells/1 ml well. Cells were plated in Costar multiwell plates and were counted in triplicate following trypsinisation.

When the smooth muscle cells were subcultured at 10^4 and 10^5 cells per culture well, there was an initial 2 to 3 day lag in proliferation (Fig. 4). This lag period was followed by an 8 day period of linear proliferation without a density dependent inhibition of growth.

Discussion. Techniques for the isolation of smooth muscle cells have been available for some time (6). However, sterile isolation and long term culture of smooth muscle cells from human intestinal tissue has not yet been previously reported. The technique we have described provides a ready source of a large number of human cells, the availability of which will facilitate studies of the contraction, proliferation and connective tissue synthesis of human intestinal smooth muscle. The proliferative response of these cells to fetal bovine serum simulates that of other non-human smooth muscle cells in culture (6,7). Proliferation while in a "modulated" state, the return to a contractile state following confluence and the subsequent formation of aggregates or ridges, have been well described for smooth muscle cells from other sources (6). The very prominent actin filaments seen by fluorohistochemistry are characteristic of smooth muscle cells and are not normally observed in fibroblasts or endothelial cells (7). In addition, these cells contracted in a concentration-dependent fashion to CCK-octapeptide. The concentrations of CCK-OP required for half maximal (D_{50}= 10^{-11} to 10^{-12}M) and maximal contractile response (40.3% decrease in cell length at 10^{-9}M) of these cultured human jejunal smooth muscle cells were similar to those reported for freshly isolated, dispersed human antral smooth muscle cells (4). These findings substantiate the identity of these cultured human intestinal cells as smooth muscle cells. Studies utilizing these cells in long term culture will certainly enhance our understanding of the contractile and connective tissue responses of the human gut under a variety of both physiologic and pathologic conditions.

This work was supported by a grant from the National Foundation for Ileitis and Colitis. The authors would like to thank Dr. Harvey Sugerman for his encouragement and assistance, Kristi Eastburn for technical assistance and Nonie Barnstein for help in preparing the manuscript.

1. Christensen J. Movement of the small intestine. In: Sleisenger and Fordtran, eds. Gastrointestinal Disease, 2nd Ed., W. B. Saunders Co., Philadelphia, pp. 1005-1006, 1978.

2. Cello JP, Meyer JH. Ulcerative colitis. In: Sleisenger and Fordtran, eds. Gastrointestinal Disease, 2nd Ed., W. B. Saunders Co., Philadelphia, pp. 1630, 1978.

3. Graham MF, Elson CO, Keathley PS, Diegelmann RF. Characterization of the connective tissue response in the stricture formation of Crohn's disease. Gastroenterology 84:1172, 1983.

4. Bitar KN, Saffouri B, Makhlouf GM. Cholinergic and peptidergic receptors on isolated human antral smooth muscle cells. Gastroenterology 82:832-837, 1982.

5. Weiland T, Faulstich H. Amatoxins, phallotoxins, phallolysin, and antamanide: The biologically active components of poisonous Amanita mushrooms. Critical Reviews in Biochemistry, pp. 184-260, 1978.

6. Chamley-Campbell J, Campbell GR, Ross R. The smooth muscle cell in culture. Physiological Reviews, 59:1-61, 1979.

7. Chamley JH, Groschel-Stewart U, Campbell GR, Burnstock G. Distinction between smooth muscle, fibroblasts and endothelial cells in culture by the use of fluoresceinated antibodies against smooth muscle actin. Cell and Tissue Research, 177:445-447, 1977.

Received April 23, 1984.
P.S.E.B.M. 1984, Vol. 176.
Accepted June 20, 1984.

PROCEEDINGS OF THE SOCIETY FOR EXPERIMENTAL BIOLOGY AND MEDICINE **176**, 508–511 (1984)

ETHANOL ENHANCES DE NOVO SYNTHESIS OF HIGH DENSITY LIPOPROTEIN CHOLESTEROL[1]

JOANNE E. CLUETTE, JOHN J. MULLIGAN, RICHARD NORING, KAY DOYLE AND JEROME HOJNACKI[2]

Department of Biological Sciences, Graduate Biochemistry Program
University of Lowell, Lowell, MA 01854

Abstract. Male squirrel monkeys fed ethanol at variable doses were used to assess whether alcohol enhances de novo synthesis of high density lipoprotein (HDL) cholesterol in vivo. Monkeys were divided into three groups: 1) Controls fed isocaloric liquid diet; 2) Low Ethanol monkeys fed liquid diet with vodka substituted isocalorically for carbohydrate at 12% of calories; and 3) High Ethanol animals fed diet plus vodka at 24% of calories. High Ethanol primates had significantly higher levels of HDL nonesterified cholesterol than Control and Low Ethanol animals while serum glutamate oxaloacetate transaminase was similar for the three treatments. There were no significant differences between the groups in HDL cholesteryl ester mass or specific activity following intravenous injection of labeled mevalonolactone. By contrast, High Ethanol monkeys had significantly greater HDL nonesterified cholesterol specific activity with approximately 60% of the radioactivity distributed in the HDL_3 subfraction. This report provides the first experimental evidence that ethanol at 24% of calories induces elevations in HDL cholesterol in primates through enhanced de novo synthesis without adverse effects on liver function.

Experimental studies with primates (1) and clinical trials with humans (2,3) have demonstrated that ethanol consumption is associated with elevations in HDL cholesterol and putative protection against coronary artery disease (1,2). Despite these observations, little is known about the threshold dose at which this elevation first occurs or the metabolic mechanism(s) responsible for this increase. Two current hypotheses suggest that alcohol may raise HDL levels by: 1) direct stimulation of hepatic lipoprotein synthesis and secretion secondary to ethanol's induction of microsomal enzyme activity (2,3); and/or 2) by enhancing extra-hepatic lipoprotein lipase activity which promotes transfer of surface components from very low density lipoproteins (VLDL) and chylomicrons during lipolysis to nascent HDL_3 particles (2,4). HDL_3, which may be secreted directly from the liver, is then converted to spherical HDL_2 via the lecithin cholesterol acyltransferase reaction (4,5). Taskinen et al. (6) demonstrated increased lipoprotein lipase activity and elevated HDL_2 cholesterol concentrations in male alcoholics in support of the latter conjecture. However, little experimental data is available to substantiate the enhanced de novo synthesis hypothesis. The present study was therefore designed to determine whether variable doses of ethanol fed to atherosclerosis susceptible squirrel monkeys enhance in vivo synthesis of HDL cholesterol from radiolabeled precursor.

[1] Supported by grants from the Alcoholic Beverage Medical Research Foundation, The Johns Hopkins University School of Medicine.

[2] All correspondence should be addressed to Jerome L. Hojnacki, Ph.D., Department of Biological Sciences, University of Lowell, Lowell, MA 01854

Materials and Methods. Fifteen yearling male Bolivian squirrel monkeys were purchased from South American Primates, Inc.

0037-9727/84 $1.50

(Miami, FL) and randomly assigned to three treatment groups consisting of five monkeys/group: Controls fed isocaloric, chemically defined Juvenile Primate Liquid Diet #19 (18.4% protein, 29.4% fat and 52.2% carbohydrate) purchased from BioServ Inc. (Frenchtown, NJ); and Low and High Ethanol animals fed liquid diet with 100 proof vodka substituted isocalorically for carbohydrate at 12 and 24% of total calories, respectively. Monkeys were housed individually and given 80 ml (0.87 Kcal/ml) of diet twice daily.

Blood was collected monthly from the femoral vein of fasted monkeys into tubes containing $EDTA \cdot Na_2$, plasma was isolated, and total cholesterol was measured colorimetrically (7). Serum glutamate oxaloacetate transaminase (SGOT) was monitored using the Reitman-Frankel method (Dade Diagnostics, Inc., Miami, FL). HDL was separated by heparin-manganese precipitation (8) and its nonesterified cholesterol component was measured by gas liquid chromatography with 3% SP-2250 on 100/200 Supelcoport (Supelco Inc., Bellefonte, PA), under isothermal conditions (267°C) and with cholestane as an internal standard (9). Total HDL cholesterol was determined in a similar manner following saponification with KOH (9) and esterified cholesterol was calculated by difference.

After one year of treatment, fasted, unanesthetized monkeys were injected intravenously with 183-250 uCi of RS-(5-^{3}H) mevalonolactone (specific activity 13.8 Ci/mmol) (New England Nuclear, Boston, MA). Blood samples were collected at 5, 20, 40 min, 1, 2, 3, 4, 5, 6 and 24 hr and plasma was immediately separated. Monkeys were allowed free access to diet after the 40 minute time point. HDL was isolated as described above and immediately extracted with chloroform:methanol (2:1 v/v) (10). Nonesterified and esterified cholesterol were separated by thin-layer chromatography (11) and radioactivity was measured with a liquid scintillation spectrometer. HDL cholesterol and cholesteryl ester mass and radioactivity were corrected to a plasma volume calculated as 4% of body weight and specific activity was expressed as percent of injected dose. HDL subfractions in the two hour plasma sample were separated by polyacrylamide gel electrophoresis (11). Bands were subjected to scanning densitometry, then cut, digested with NCS solubilizer (Amersham Corp., Arlington Heights, IL) and radioactivity was monitored. Mean values for the three groups were analyzed for significant differences ($P<0.05$) by analysis of variance and Duncan's multiple range test.

Results and Discussion. There was no significant difference in the mean body weights between the Control (825 $\pm$ 69g), Low (890 $\pm$ 74) and High (675 $\pm$ 62) groups or in SGOT (range 82-90-IU/ml). However, High Ethanol animals circulated significantly more total plasma cholesterol (286 $\pm$ 9 mg/dl) and HDL nonesterified cholesterol (49 $\pm$ 4) than Low Ethanol (221 $\pm$ 5, 36 $\pm$ 2) and Control (233 $\pm$ 7, 39 $\pm$ 3) primates. There were no significant differences between the three groups in HDL cholesteryl ester mass (range: 134-152 mg/dl) or specific activity. By contrast, High Ethanol monkeys incorporated significantly more ^{3}H mevalonolactone into HDL nonesterified cholesterol beginning at two hours after injection, continuing for the next 4 hours, and at 24 hours (Fig. 1). It is unlikely that the HDL cholesterol specific activity patterns reported in Fig. 1 were the result of ethanol related alterations in hepatic mevalonic acid pool size and/or exchange of radiolabeled mevalonate with endogenous pools since previous in vivo and in vitro cholesterol synthesis experiments with rats (36% dietary ethanol) using ^{14}C mevalonate argue against such changes (12).

Densitometric scans of HDL_2 and HDL_3 subfractions were similar for the three treatments which had a HDL_2/HDL_3 ratio range of 5.8-8.7. In addition, for all groups, only 39% of the radioactivity appeared in the HDL_2 subclass while the majority (61%) of the label was associated with HDL_3 suggesting that the nascent HDL_3 particles were preferentially labeled with newly synthesized cholesterol. This is important in view of recent reports which demonstrate that 40% of the total body cholesterol synthesis in squirrel monkeys occurs in the liver (13) and that the HDL_3 subfraction is selectively elevated in men who consume moderate amounts of alcohol (14). It is thus likely that the greater HDL nonesterified cholesterol

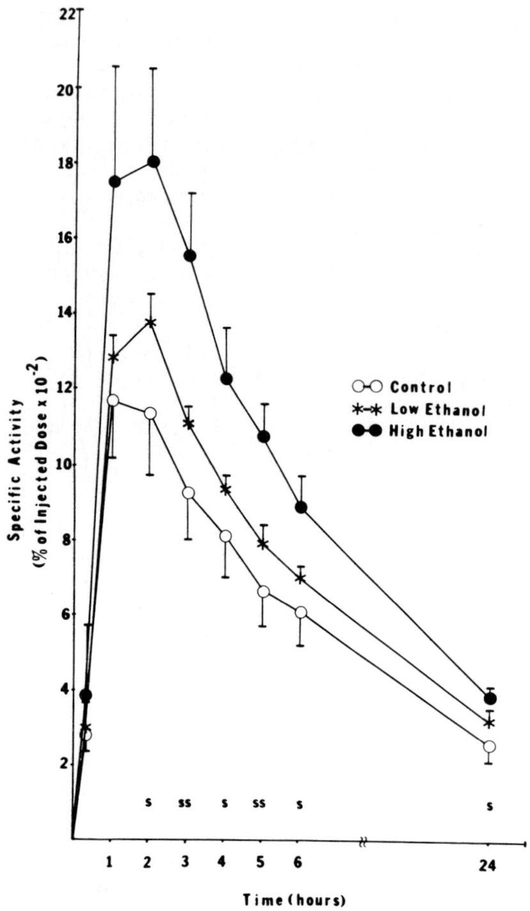

Fig. 1 in vivo synthesis of HDL non-esterified cholesterol following the injection of ^3H mevalonolactone. Time points represent mean ± SEM for 5 monkey/group. S indicates significant difference ($P < 0.05$) between High Ethanol and Control monkeys and SS difference between High Ethanol and both Control, Low Ethanol groups.

radioactivity in High Ethanol monkeys (Fig. 1) was the result of enhanced hepatic de novo synthesis.

Taken together, data from this study support previous in vivo (15) and liver perfusion (16) rat studies which suggest that increased HDL lipid synthesis results from intake of dietary ethanol at 36 - 37% of calories. The present study is unique, however, in elucidating a lower dose (24%) at which this ethanol effect occurs, and in providing the first in vivo experimental documentation that alcohol consumption specifically enhances de novo HDL nonesterified cholesterol synthesis in a nonhuman primate species with clinical relevance to man.

The authors express their sincere appreciation to Mary Hojnacki and Ruth Beaupre for preparation of this manuscript.

1. Rudel LL, Leathers CW, Bond MG, Bullock, BC, Dietary ethanol-induced modifications in hyperlipoproteinemia and atherosclerosis in nonhuman primates (Macaca nemestrina). Atherosclerosis. 1:144-155, 1981.
2. Devenyi P, Robinson GM, Roncari DAK. Alcohol and high-density lipoproteins. J Can Med Assoc 123:981-984, 1980.
3. LaPorte R, Valvo-Gerard L, Kuller L, Dai W, Bates M, Cresanta J, Williams K, Palkin D. The relationship between alcohol consumption, liver enzymes and high-density lipoprotein cholesterol. Circulation, 64:67-71, 1981.
4. Tall AR, Small DM. Plasma high-density lipoproteins. N Engl J Med 22:1232-1236, 1978.
5. Taskinen M, Nikkila EA. High Density lipoprotein subfractions in relation to lipoprotein lipase activity of tissues in man-evidence for reciprocal regulation of HDL_2 and HDL_3 levels by lipoprotein lipase. Clin Chim Acta 112:325-332, 1981.
6. Taskinen M, Valimaki M, Nikkila EA, Kuusi T, Ehnholm C, Ylikahri R. High density lipoprotein subfractions and postheparin plasma lipases in alcoholic men before and after ethanol withdrawal. Metabolism 31:1168-1174, 1982.
7. Wybenga DR, Pileggi UJ, Dirstine PH, DiGiorgio J. Direct manual determination of serum total cholesterol with a single stable reagent. Clin Chem 16:980-984, 1970.
8. Warnick GR, Albers JJ. A comprehensive evaluation of the heparin-manganese precipitation procedure for estimating high density lipoprotein cholesterol. J Lipid Res 19:65-76, 1978.
9. Johnston PV. Basic Lipid Methodology. Special publication 19, Univer-

sity of Illinois at Urbana-Champaign p 87-89, 1971.
10. Folch J, Lees M, Sloane-Stanley GH. A simple method for isolation and purification of total lipids from animal tissues. J Biol Chem 226:497-509, 1957.
11. Hojnacki JL, Mulligan JJ, Cluette JE, Kew RR, Stack DJ, Huber GL. Effect of cigarette smoke and dietary cholesterol on plasma lipoprotein composition. Artery 9:285-304, 1981.
12. Lefevre AF, DeCarli LM, Lieber CS. Effect of ethanol on cholesterol and bile acid metabolism. J Lipid Res 13:48-55, 1972.
13. Spacy DK, Dietschy JM. Sterol synthesis in vivo in 18 tissues of the squirrel monkey, guinea pig, rabbit, hamster, and rat. J Lipid Res 24:303-315, 1983.
14. Haskell WL, Camargo C Jr, Williams PT, Vranizan KM, Krauss RM, Lindgren FT. The effect of cessation and resumption of moderate alcohol intake on serum high-density lipoprotein subfractions. N Engl J Med 310:805-810, 1984.
15. Baraona E, Lieber CS. Effects of chronic ethanol feeding on serum lipoprotein metabolism in the rat. J Clin Invest 49:769-778, 1970.
16. Lee H, Noel SP, Hosein EA, Rubinstein D. Secretion of high density lipoprotein by the isolated perfused alcoholic rat liver. Experientia 38:914-915, 1982.

Received June 11, 1984.
P.S.E.B.M. 1984, Vol. 176.
Accepted July 18, 1984.

PROCEEDINGS OF THE SOCIETY FOR EXPERIMENTAL BIOLOGY AND MEDICINE **176,** 512–513 (1984)

ANNUAL REPORT

Annual Report of the Executive Secretary and Editor for the Year Ending December 31, 1983

Finance. The following is an abbreviated financial report prepared by Leo Kaden, C.P.A.

Statement of Receipts and Disbursements for the Year Ended December 31, 1983

Balance of cash in banks and certificates of deposits, January 1, 1983	$95,361
Receipts	
From *Proceedings*	
Subscriptions	162,308
Publication charges	27,620
Friends	3,790
Profits sharing	57,999
Total from *Proceedings*	251,717
Dues (associate)	470
Dues (student)	175
Dues (active)	33,418
Dues (sustaining)	15,540
Investment income, dividends, and interest	49,705
Proceeds from sale of securities	73,527
Manuscript handling fees	5,650
Member contributions	2,830
Total receipts for the period	433,032
Total funds available	528,393
Disbursements	
For *Proceedings*	
Academic Press	228,479
Printing	4,691
Total for *Proceedings*	233,170
Salaries and payroll tax expenses	67,720
Office supplies, expenses, postage, telephone, insurance, bank charges, and miscellaneous expenses	16,653
Meeting and travel	15,888
Pension contribution	4,089
Pension (not funded) H. McCabe	2,400
Investment—Advisory fees	3,548
Accounting fees	1,300
Annual report fee	75
Lectureships (section support)	2,900
Purchase of securities	65,473
Refunds (subs, page charges, and dues)	1,558
National Society of Medical Research	1,500
Tuition reimbursement	2,660
Consultation fees	3,225
Affiliate application expense	837
Total disbursements	422,996
Balance of cash in banks, December 31, 1983	$105,397

Publication Committee. Drs. G. J. Thorbecke, Chairman, G. J. Macdonald, S. Niewiarowski, J. A. Resko, and J. Tepperman.

0037-9727/84 $1.50

Editors. The following editors will be concluding their term of office for the Society. They have elected to serve for another 3-year period: Drs. E. Alpen, C. A. Barraclough, A. L. Barron, E. D. Bransome, Jr., S. M. Cain, H. F. Clark, I. Clark, P. P. Foa, R. R. Gala, Z. N. Gaut, E. C. Gotschlich, M. R. C. Greenwood, J. J. Holland, D. Horrobin, E. D. Jacobson, C. A. Krakower, M. Kuschner, P. L. LaCelle, C. Lenfant, R. D. Levere, G. J. Macdonald, J. Meites, T. C. Merigan, Jr., F. N. Miller, C. R. Morgan, P. J. Mulrow, D. D. Porter, J. A. Ramaley, W. H. Sawyer, R. A. Schemmel, N. J. Schmidt, J. E. Sealey, E. M. Shevach, J. G. Stevens, G. A. Tanner, G. J. Thorbecke, J. L. Vaitukaitis, S. F. Vatner, R. M. Welsh, Jr., and D. B. Zilversmit.

The following editors will be retiring: Drs. D. Boggs, K. G. Brand, N. E. Cremer, S. Oparil, R. Ostwald, R. Schmid, and J. H. Shaw.

The following have been elected to the Editorial Board for a term of 3 years: Drs. C. A. Blake, J. Himms-Hagen, and M. L. Kaplan.

Finance Committee. Drs. H. P. Dustan, Chairman, T. Cooper, and W. Sawyer.

Nominating Committee. Drs. J. H. Laragh, Chairman, J. B. Marsh, S. M. McCann, and W. H. Sawyer.

National Membership Committee. Drs. A. K. Weiss, Chairman, C. Beatty, C. A. Blake, R. Fellows, S. K. Hong, M. W. Orsini, J. G. Smith, Jr., W. Stavinoha, and B. Zimmerman.

Delegate to the AAAS: Dr. M. R. Nocenti.

In Memoriam. P. R. Craddock, L. M. Julian, F. T. Krasnow, E. Neter, R. T. Tidrick, J. C. Yeager, M. B. Visscher, F. M. Schabel, and C. J. Watson.

Election. The results of the election are as follows: Dr. P. L. Rayford elected Treasurer for a period of 2 years. Drs. L. Hayflick, G. Litwack, and E. H. Wood were elected as Councillors for a period of 4 years. All terms begin July 1, 1984.

ACTIVE SECTIONS	OFFICERS
Washington, D.C.	C. J. Lauter
Northwest	F. P. Hungate
Southeastern	R. B. Brandt
Southwestern	P. L. Rayford

Miss Felice O'Grady has been in charge of the duties of the Society's National Office.

GUEST EDITORS 1983

Acknowledgment to Reviewers

The Editor and the members of the Editorial Board thank the following scientists for their assistance with the reviewing of manuscripts submitted for publication in the *Proceedings of the Society for Experimental Biology and Medicine* during 1983. Their service to the Society and the biomedical and scientific community is appreciated and commended.

W. R. Adey
B. M. Anderson
J. O. Anderson
M. E. Anderson
R. L. Anderson
G. Andres
M. Antonaccio
A. Arimura
R. E. Austic
R. Austrian
A. P. Autor
A. E. Axelrod
T. M. Badger
A. D. Baines
D. M. Baldwin
K. M. Baldwin
L. Barajas
R. J. Barnard
J. L. Barnhart
A. Bartke
C. A. Bassett
J. S. Baumstark
W. G. Beamer
M. A. Becker
H. R. Behrman
W. R. Beisel
B. G. Benfey
N. Ben-Jonathan
J. J. Bergeron
E. N. Bergman
B. A. Berkowitz
D. M. Bers
W. J. Bettger
L. L. Bieber
V. S. Bishop
M. J. Bissell
J. Bitman
M. J. Blackburn
T. F. Blaschke
A. Bloom
K. Blum
D. L. Bornstein
R. K. Boutwell
B. J. Bowman
J. L. Boyer
T. R. Breitman
R. W. Briehl
G. M. Briggs
I. Brodsky
G. A. Brooks
E. Brown
K. S. Brown
A. C. Brownie
M. G. Buse
D. W. Busija
D. D. Buss
L. L. Butcher
R. H. Cagen
L. C. Cantley
C. C. Capen
C. W. Castor
K. J. Catt
W. Y. Chan
R. K. Chandra
C. C. Cheng
L. Cheng
L. Chess
A. V. Chobanian
G. W. Chodak
C. K. Chou
J. Y. Chou
J. K. Christman
M. Chvapil
F. Chytil
R. D. Cioccio
L. F. Cipriano
J. H. Clark
M. P. Cleary
I. Cleator
R. E. Coburn
J. D. Coffman
M. G. Cogan
D. V. Cohn
M. E. Conrad
E. M. Convey
J. K. Coward
J. D. Crapo
S. L. Dalterio
A. J. deBold
V. Defendi
F. Devenuto
N. S. Dhalla
G. L. Diamond
J. Diamond
G. F. DiBona
R. F. Diegelmann
N. R. DiLuzio
M. Donowitz
M. G. Douglas
R. T. Dowell
H. H. Draper
G. R. Dreesman
R. W. Dudek
S. E. Echterncamp
L. A. Ehrhart
A. Eichholz
B. Eiseman
D. E. Elder
K. D. Elgert
G. W. Evans
L. L. Expey
J. H. Exton
A. I. Faden
M. L. Failla
D. J. Falcone
M. G. Farquhar
C. Fenoglio
M. Ferin
S. Finegold
A. L. Finn
A. J. Fischman
A. B. Fisher
H. F. Fisher
J. S. Fleming
D. J. Fletcher
D. H. Foley
J. J. Ford
S. C. Foster
F. Fouad

0037-9727/84 $1.50

B. A. Fowler
I. H. Fox
P. J. Fraker
J. C. S. Fray
M. J. Fregly
R. Freter
G. M. Fried
S. M. Friedman
C. Friend
C. H. Frith
H. L. Fuller
P. A. Furman
G. J. Galasso
M. J. Galvin
R. F. Gautieri
R. J. Gerety
C. Giampaolo
S. H. Giannini
G. Gibori
J. R. Gillette
A. R. Glass
M. A. Goldberg
M. M. Goldenberg
A. Goldfeder
H. Goldman
L. Goldstein
M. G. Goodman
R. W. Gotshall
R. A. Goyer
R. Grandhi
P. L. Greenberg
M. A. Greer
R. I. Gregerman
F. M. Griffin
O. W. Griffith
P. Griminger
S. E. Grossberg
S. M. Grundy
L. Guth
F. J. Haddy
D. P. Hajjar
T. S. Hakim
M. Hamm
M. Hamosh
E. J. Harfenist
G. Hashim
J. R. Hassell
D. E. Hatoff
P. V. Hauschka
W. W. Hay, Jr.
G. A. Hedge
P. V. J. Hegarty
D. D. Heistad
R. W. Hemken
D. M. Hendricks
R. C. Henneberry
V. Herbert
P. C. Hinkle
L. B. Hinshaw
H. S. Ho
M. Ho
J. W. Holaday
M. F. Holcik
D. D. Holten
L. D. Horwitz
K. Y. Hostetler
L. Howard
K. B. Howitz
J. M. Hsu
S. Hubner
A. S. Hume
J. N. Hunt
J. E. Hunter
J. B. Hursh
R. J. Huxtable
I. Ichikawa
B. Issekutz, Jr.
M. R. Jacobs
J. R. Jaenike
G. Jagiello
J. S. Janicki
W. S. S. Jee
L. S. Jensen
S. A. Jimenez
B. C. Johnson
H. G. Johnson
A. W. Jones
L. R. Jones
R. F. Kampschmidt
A. B. Kane
W. W-Y. Kao
H. R. Kaplan
M. L. Kaplan
S. Kaplay
C. T. Kappagoda
A. B. Karlinsky
A. I. Katz
J. M. Kay
P. A. Kelly
R. E. Kerber
D. Kessel
G. T. Keusch
D. Kilpatrick
R. Kimberly
H. Kirchick
F. H. Kirkpatrick
G. J. Klaassen
G. J. Klain
R. F. Kletzien
L. M. Klevay
F. A. Klipstein
R. A. Kloner
J. L. Kocsis
L. Kohn
J. P. Kokko
R. C. Kolbeck
B. Korecky
J. L. Krahenbuhl
D. M. Kramsch
M. Krieger
K. Kuettener
C. M. Kunin
H. O. Kunkel
P. R. Kvietys
F. Labrie
P. E. Lacy
H. Lai
R. O. Langner
P. R. Larsen
H. S. Lawrence
J. F. Lechner
P. Leitmen
J. E. Leklem
R. Levy
C. H. Li
P. S. Lietman
T. Lincoln
G. E. Lindenmayer
H. Lipner
D. A. Lipschitz
H. H. Loh
W. J. Longmore
L. D. Loose
J. M. Lowenstein
J. D. Lutton
G. R. Lynch
D. F. Magee
K. R. Mahaffey
A. F. Mahmoud
M. D. Maines
R. J. Majeska
G. Majno
A. B. Malik
L. I. Malkin
R. A. Malt
P. V. Malven
I. Mandel
J. Manis
E. B. Marliss

G. R. Martin
J. B. Martin
W. R. Martin
J. R. Martinez
M. Martinez-Maldonado
D. Marver
R. J. Mason
L. Matthews
D. V. Maudsley
C. McDevitt
R. H. McDonald, Jr.
A. Meister
M. R. Melamed
H. Y. Meltzer
G. F. Merrill
G. Meschia
C. E. Meyers
H. M. Middleton III
R. G. Miller
R. K. Miller
T. A. Miller
B. G. Mills
B. J. Mills
C. R. Minick
S. B. Mizel
M. J. Moldowan
F. G. Moody
E. L. Morgan
R. J. Moroff
M. E. Morris
S. Morrison
E. H. Mosbach
G. S. Moss
L. A. Muir
T. Mullern
M. J. Murray
G. G. Nahas
A. Nahmias
C. F. Nathan
L. G. Navar
J. M. Navia
H. Neu
O. W. Neuhaus
P. M. Newberne
C. S. Nicoll
W. H. Niemann
S. Niewiarowski
S. K. Nishimoto
J. P. Nolan
A. H. Nowotny
J. A. Oates
G. B. Odell
P. L. Ogra
J. P. Okuneiwich
L. Ossowski
C. R. Pace-Asciak
R. D. Palmiter
A. M. Pearson
D. G. Penney
L. P. Pereira
M. A. Peters
M. C. Phillips
S. J. Pilkis
P. G. W. Plagemann
A. M. Poisner
J. L. Poland
H. A. Poston
R. J. Preston
J. D. Puett
R. H. Purcell
L. Raijman
J. H. G. Rankin
F. Rapp
J. P. Rapp
G. M. Reaven
W. Redisch
J. T. Reeves
T. J. Regan
W. S. Rehm
M. D. Reuber
T. L. Rich
G. W. Richter
S. J. Riggi
C. R. Rinaldo
C. Rivier
K. R. Robbins
E. J. Robel
J. Roberts
A. Roberts
M. C. Robertson
J. A. Robinson
G. A. Rodan
K. S. Rogers
K. R. Romsos
S. A. Rooney
J. C. Rose
N. R. Rose
S. Saiduddin
D. R. Sanadi
R. B. Sanders
R. L. Sanders
W. P. Santamore
A. Saxon
C. G. Scanes
P. J. Scarpace
B. A. Schacter
G. F. Schreiner
K. Schuitt
B. S. Schwartz
G. L. Searle
A. A. Seymour
B. Shane
A. P. Shepherd
J. T. Shepherd
H. M. Shields
C. R. Short
A. A. Shoukas
H. P. Shu
S. T. Shulman
D. J. Simmons
S. Simon
E. R. Simpson
W. A. Simpson
Y. N. Sinha
H. C. Slavkin
D. M. Smith, Jr.
R. Snyderman
P. Z. Sobocinski
L. Sokoloff
D. H. Spackman
H. V. Sparks
E. Spaziani
W. S. Spielman
E. G. Spokas
H. Sprince
P. W. Stacpoole
B. C. Starcher
S. B. Stearns
G. Stein
D. F. Steiner
O. S. Steinsland
E. R. Stiehm
D. Stone
J. Storz
F. L. Strand
H. R. Strausser
S. Strickland
C. Su
C. S. Sweet
H. H. Tai
D. W. Talmage
C. F. Tam
M. F. Tansy
A. E. Taylor
I. L. Taylor
V. P. Terranova
J. M. Terris
E. L. Thomas
J. N. Thompson

F. Traganos
B. F. Trump
F. H-C. Tsao
A. S. Tsiftsoglou
R. L. Tuttle
J. V. Tyberg
G. M. Tyce
M. S. Tyler
P. E. Tyler
J. Uhr
S. Upadhyay
E. Urban
S. J. Vainisi
A. J. Vander
R. C. Vari
M. Vassalle
E. S. Vessel
D. A. Vessey
B. Vickery
T. Vilberg
J. T. Vilcek
J. P. Villeneuve
F. F. Vincenzi
R. Volpe
B. K. Vonderhaar
J. L. Voogt
M. Walser
R. W. Wannemacher
J. R. Ward
L. Wasman
S. J. Watson
D. R. Webb
M. H. Weinberger
E. K. Weisburger
M. M. Weiser
B. B. Weksler
B. C. Wexler
R. L. Whistler
G. J. White
S. White
N. S. Whitworth
B. Williams
M. A. Williams
R. C. Williams, Jr.
R. J. Witorsch
S. M. Wolff
S. L-Y. Woo
W. R. Wooles
R. E. Wuthier
R. B. Young
I. M. Yousef
A. Yunis
M. M. Zatz
R. K. Y. Zee-Cheng
Z. Zorzoli
K. S. Zuckerman
J. E. Zull

Author Index for Volume 176

A

Ablashi, Dharam V., 407
Akmal, Mohammad, 434
Andres, Giuseppe A., 226
Anwer, M. Sawkat, 70
Arishima, Kazuyoshi, 403
Armstrong, Gary, 407
Ashino-Fuse, Hiromi, 109
Austic, R. E., 276, 285, 292

B

Baer, Philip G., 84
Baig, M. M., 183
Bal, Harpal S., 187
Banks, W. L., Jr., 460
Barbiroli, B., 371
Barbu, Veronique, 54
Barnett, Bill B., 77
Baylink, David J., 60
Beecham, G. D., 238
Bendich, Adrianne, 378
Bennett, Stephen C., 322
Berk, Paul D., 356
Bernstein, Leslie, 434
Bhogal, Balbir S., 414
Billiau, Alfons, 109
Bitar, Khalil N., 503
Blumenstock, Frank A., 443
Bolt, Merry J. G., 164
Boskey, Adele L., 154
Boyd, Rebecca Morgan, 84
Brady, Richard C., 322
Bray, Tammy M., 48
Brentjens, Jan R., 226
Brooks, Robert R., 452
Bullough, Peter G., 154
Bunce, G. E., 485
Burbank, D., 138
Burgin, C., 183

C

Campion, D. R., 143
Cantin, M., 105
Cardaman, Richard C., 313
Carlson, James R., 48
Cerda, J., 183
Chan, Winnie, 460
Chany-Fournier, Françoise, 490
Chen, Jing S., 123
Chen, Theresa S., 132
Chertok, R. J., 138
Chi, David S., 414
Clough, David L., 123
Cluette, Joanne E., 508
Cohen, I. Kelman, 302
Cornette, Kuuleialoha M., 257
Cox, William I., 297
Cuddy, Brian G., 443

D

Dahlberg, John, 407
Davis, D., 485
DiBona, Gerald F., 426
Diegelmann, Robert F., 302, 503
Donahue, H. Gary, 419
Doyle, Kay, 508
Dudek, R. W., 1
Dupuis, Rolande, 54
Dupuy, Jean-Louis, 467

E

Eguchi, Yasunobu, 403
Ehrlich, H. Paul, 503
Elson, Charles O., 503
Engelking, Larry R., 70
Engle, Michael J., 261

F

Faggioni, Alberto, 407
Farrell, Philip M., 261
Ferrell, C., 243
Fox, Irwin J., 223
Friedman, Herman, 297, 366
Fuse, Akira, 109

G

Gabriel, Edda, 378
Gaito, Andrea, 197
Gardette, Jean, 54
Genest, J., 105
Gerencser, George A., 183, 257
Gerfaux, Jacqueline, 490
Goldstein, David A., 434
Gordon, Albert S., 197
Graham, Martin F., 302, 503
Grazman, Brent, 342
Guild, R., 183
Gutkowska, J., 105

H

Haddy, Francis J., 123
Harper, Jeffrey F., 322
Hazelton, George A., 249
Hegarty, P. V. J., 27
Hegner, Dietmar, 70
Hess, J. L., 485
Hise, Michael K., 322
Hojnacki, Jerome, 508
Holdaas, Hallvard, 426
Honig, Lawrence S., 419
Hudak, Robert T., 472

I

Isola, Luis M. J., 356

J

Jackson, M. J., 38
Januszewicz, P., 105
Jones, Mary Jane T., 356
Jones, Sandra M., 452

K

Kahn, Andrew M., 322
Kaplan, Alan M., 460
Kelley, Michael J., 132
Kendrick, J. E., 203, 384
Kiessling, Ann A., 175
Killion, Jerald J., 309
Klasing, K. C., 276, 285, 292
Koide, Samuel S., 148
Kot, Peter A., 438
Kullgren, B., 138
Kuo, Y.-J., 38

L

Lachatre, Gérard, 467
Lalley, P. M., 384
Lammi-Keefe, Carol J., 27
Lang, Calvin A., 249
Langan, Susan M., 261
Langley, Albert E., 350
Lee, Theresa M., 164
Lewinson, Dina, 154
Lindblad, Lars Erik, 119
Link, William T., 123
Loegering, Daniel J., 443
Loo, Stanley Y., 257
Lorenzsonn, Vilja, 8
Lundgren, David W., 313

M

Macé, Bertrand, 490
Machlin, Lawrence J., 378
Mahoney, Arthur W., 77
Maiewski, Sharon, 268
Mansour, M. Mahy, 22
Massry, Shaul G., 434

Matson, G. L., 384
Maziere, Jean-Claude, 54
McCormick, Charles C., 392
McElhanon, S., 460
McMahon, Kathleen E., 261
Merchant-Larios, Horacio, 148
Merkel, R. A., 143
Merle, Louis, 467
Mills, D. E., 32
Milne, R. W., 105
Mochizuki, Koshi, 403
Molteni, Agostino, 88
Moltz, Howard, 164
Monti, M. G., 371
Moore, Alan F., 452
Moore, John J., 313
Morrey, John D., 77
Mueller, Gregory P., 168, 268
Muldoon, Sheila, 268
Mulligan, John J., 508
Mustafa, S. Jamal, 22

N

Naughton, Brian A., 197
Nicot, Georges, 467
Noble, Roger L., 77
Nocerini, Mark R., 48
Noring, Richard, 508
Nouaille, Yves, 467

O

Olsen, Ward A., 8
Opdenakker, Ghislain, 109
Ottani, V., 371

P

Pamnani, Motilal B., 123
Pattabhiraman, Ranga, 434
Penhos, Juan C., 438
Perelman, Robert H., 261
Perico, Norberto, 337
Pernecco, L., 371
Pero, Barbara, 8
Pettibone, Douglas J., 168
Piccinini, G., 371
Pisarri, T. E., 203
Pompidou, Alain, 490
Port, Curtis D., 88
Powell, James H., 346
Preti, Robert A., 197
Purchas, R. W., 143
Pusineri, Fiorenza, 337

Q

Quinn, Michael R., 476

R

Ramwell, Peter W., 438
Reichelderfer, Mark, 8
Reidenberg, Marcus M., 346
Remuzzi, Giuseppe, 337
Romsos, D. R., 143
Ross, A. Catherine, 42
Roux, Charles, 54
Rowe, Janice F., 42
Ruggeri, A., 371
Russell, Jean E., 342

S

Schane, H. P., 238
Schiller, P. W., 105
Shanbour, L. L., 38
Shepherd, John T., 119
Sidwell, Robert W., 77
Simmons, David J., 342
Slavkin, Harold C., 419
Smith, Barry T., 419
Smith, Stephen G., 350
Snyder, B. W., 238
Solliday, Norman H., 88
Specter, Steven, 297
Stinger, Robert B., 438
Sundar, S. K., 407
Swan, P. B., 27

T

Taketo, Teruko, 148
Tavoloni, Nicola, 356
Thibault, G., 105
Thorbecke, G. Jeanette, 414
Threatte, Rose M., 476
Trentham, David E., 95
Ts'ao Chung-Hsin, 88
Tuma, Samir, 434
Tyan, Marvin L., 14

U

Urist, Marshall R., 472

V

Valette, Jean-Pierre, 467
Van Dam, Jacques, 438
Vanhoutte, Paul M., 119

W

Ward, R., 32
Ward, William F., 88
Warren, George, 366
Weinman, Edward J., 322
Wergedal, Jon E., 60
Wise, T., 243

Y

Yamamoto, Masako, 403

Z

Zaniol, P., 371
Zeid, Robert L., 350
Zuckerman, Gary B., 197

NOTICE

The Subject Index for Volume 176 will appear in the December 1984 issue as part of a cumulative index for the year 1984.

Friends of the Society

Our members are requested to note the following list of Friends. We wish to express our thanks to each of them. Their contributions help materially in meeting the very sharp increase in costs of publication.

FRIENDS

Ciba Pharmaceutical Products, Inc.
E. I. du Pont de Nemours & Co.
Eli Lilly and Co.
Hoffmann-LaRoche, Inc.
Mead Johnson & Co.
Merrell Dow Pharmaceuticals, Inc.
Chas. Pfizer and Co., Inc.
Ortho Pharmaceutical Corporation
A. H. Robins Co.
Rogoff Foundation
Sandoz Pharmaceuticals
Schering Corporation
Sharp and Dohme, Division of Merck & Co., Inc.
Smith Kline and French Laboratories
Squibb Inst. for Medical Research
Stuart Pharmaceuticals, Div. of ICI Americas, Inc.
Upjohn Co.
USV Pharmaceutical Corp.
Wallace Laboratories, Division of Carter–Wallace, Inc.
Wyeth Laboratories, Inc.

NOTICE TO CONTRIBUTORS

General Instructions

Manuscripts should be written in clear, concise and grammatical English, and should conform to the general style of the Journal and the specific instructions listed below. Manuscripts which are not adequately prepared will be returned to the authors, since it is not feasible for the Editors to undertake extensive revision or rewriting of manuscripts submitted. Contributors, particularly those unfamiliar with English usage, are encouraged to seek the help of colleagues in the preparation and review of manuscripts prior to submission. This practice will usually reduce the time required for review and will avoid delays in the publication of the manuscript.

SUBMIT MANUSCRIPTS IN TRIPLICATE (ONE ORIGINAL AND TWO COPIES). SEND ONLY ORIGINAL PRINTS OF PHOTOMICROGRAPHS. Submitted manuscripts and accompanying materials become the property of the Society, and the Society is not responsible for loss or damage to such materials.

All manuscripts should be submitted to **Dr. M. R. Nocenti, 630 W. 168th Street, New York, N.Y. 10032.**

THE EDITORIAL OFFICE IS CLOSED DURING AUGUST.

Authors submitting manuscripts containing data from experiments involving recombinant DNA molecules *must* provide a statement for each of the two reviewers which certifies that their experiment complied with the NIH guidelines on physical and biological containment procedures.

1. Only original papers will be considered. Manuscripts are accepted for review with the understanding that the same work has not been and will not be nor is presently submitted elsewhere, and that its submission for publication has been approved by all of the authors and by the institution where the work was performed; further, that any person cited as a source of personal communications has approved such citation. Written authorization may be required at the Editor's discretion. Articles and any other material published in the *Proceedings of the Society for Experimental Biology and Medicine* represent the opinions of the author(s) and should not be construed to reflect the opinions of the Editor(s), the Society, or the Publisher.

Authors submitting a manuscript do so on the understanding that if it is accepted for publication, copyright in the article, including the right to reproduce the article in all forms and media, shall be assigned exclusively to the Society. The Society will not refuse any reasonable request by the author for permission to reproduce any of his or her contributions to the journal. Send requests for permission to reproduce items published in *Proceedings of the Society for Experimental Biology and Medicine* to: Dr. Mero R. Nocenti, Editor, Society for Experimental Biology and Medicine, 630 W. 168th St., N.Y., N.Y. 10032.

A manuscript rejected by the PSEBM should not be re-submitted. All manuscripts will be given a quality rating by the two reviewing editors; those manuscripts with low priority ratings will not be accepted even though they have been classed as generally acceptable. Split decisions will be decided on the basis of the two priority ratings and/or by a third review.

2. a. Manuscripts should be as *concise* as possible, yet *sufficiently* detailed to permit critical appraisal.
   b. Manuscripts (including tables, legends, and footnotes) should be *double* or *triple* spaced.
   c. The first page of the manuscript should contain the complete title of the paper, category for the "Table of Contents" (select from list in item 20), names of authors (without degrees), affiliations (including zip codes), and a running title consisting of no more than 40 characters (including spaces). The second page of the manuscript should give the name, complete address, and telephone number of the author to whom ALL correspondence should be sent. *Please include the zip code.*
   d. Units of weights, measures, etc., when used in conjunction with numerals, should be abbreviated and unpunctuated, e.g., 6 R, 3 g, 5 ml, 8% (see No. 21 below).
3. Manuscripts of *nonexperimental* researches, or those with *inadequate* controls, are not acceptable.
4. *Unnecessary subdivision* of a research into several manuscripts is not acceptable.
5. a. Manuscripts devoted to *improvement of procedure or of apparatus* may be accepted when a new principle is involved or when decidedly superior biological results are obtained. Evidence of such superiority should be given.
   b. Confirmatory or negative results will not be accepted unless they are of obvious biological significance.
6. Manuscripts should not exceed 40 typed pages (including tables, charts, and references).
7. Title should be limited to 15 words. Manuscripts should contain an Abstract, Introduction, Materials and Methods, Results, and Discussion. Abstracts should not exceed 300 words.
8. *Conclusions* should be based upon experimental data submitted.
9. *Figures.* All figures should be cited consecutively by Arabic numerals in the text with figure legends typed on a separate sheet. These should contain sufficient experimental detail to permit the figure to be interpreted without reference to the text. Units should be clearly indicated in the figures themselves. Wherever possible, curves should be combined into a single figure in order to keep the number of illustrations to a minimum.

PLEASE NOTE: All figures and illustrations are to be submitted in such form as to permit photographic reproduction without retouching or redrawing. This includes the lettering, which is reproduced as part of the figure and is not set in type. Send only original prints of photomicrographs. Illustrations in color can be accepted only if the authors defray the cost. Line drawings should be carefully drafted with black India ink on white drawing paper or blue drafting cloth, no larger than 8.5 × 11.5 inches overall (21 × 27.5 cm). The lettering should be large enough to allow a reduction of two-thirds. High quality glossy prints are acceptable.

10. *Tables.* These should be numbered with Roman numerals and cited consecutively in the text. Each table should be titled and typed double-spaced on a separate sheet. Refer to current issues of the *Proceedings* for the acceptable style of tables. The title of each table should clearly indicate the nature of the contents, and sufficient experimental detail should be included in footnotes to the entries to permit the reader to interpret the results. *Units must be clearly indicated for each of the entries in the table.* To save space, repetition of similar experiments and columns which can be calculated from other entries in the table should be avoided wherever possible.

11. *Footnotes.* Footnotes in the *text* should be identified by superscripts consisting of Arabic numerals and should be typed on a separate sheet; footnotes in the *tables* should be identified with superscript lowercase letters a, b, c, etc., and placed at the bottom of the table.

12. a. *References.* Only essential citations should be submitted, and they should be arranged numerically at the end of the manuscript. References to the literature should be cited in the text by Arabic numerals in parentheses, set on the text line. The references should be numbered consecutively in order of their citation.

b. Abbreviations of journal titles should follow the style used in *Chemical Abstracts Service Source Index,* 1980. Please note the style of capitalization and punctuation for journal articles, books, and edited books in the following examples:

1. Wang BC, Bettice JA, Brown EB Jr. Effect of body temperature on salicylate-induced hyperventilation. Proc Soc Exp Biol Med **174:**102–106, 1983.
2. Abramson DI. Circulation in the Extremities. New York, Academic Press, p000, 1967.
3. Langford MP, Weigent DA, Stanton GJ, Baron S. Virus plaque-reduction assay for interferon: Microplaque and regular macroplaque reduction assay. In: Pestka S, ed. Methods in Enzymology. New York: Academic Press, Vol Part A **78:** p000, 1981.

c. "Personal communication," "unpublished," "submitted," and numerous abstracts should be excluded from the reference list. If the manuscript has been accepted for publication, include it in the reference list, giving journal, year, etc. *If not accepted do not include it* in the reference list.

13. *Trade or popular name or abbreviation* of a chemical may be used only when preceded by the chemical or scientific name; thereafter, any of these names or abbreviations may be used. Trade names should begin with a capital letter.

14. *Structural formulas* of chemicals should be used only when absolutely necessary.

15. The *Proceedings* is copyrighted by the *Society for Experimental Biology and Medicine.*

16. a. Authors are expected to discourage circulation of reprints for commercial purposes.

b. *Reprints* are limited to 1300.

17. Changes in *galley proof* should be absolutely minimal. Authors will be charged for excessive changes.

18. The authors are expected to pay a part of the cost of publication in the form of a page charge of $20.00 per page. Payment of page charges is not a condition for publication.

Notify the Executive Secretary at least one month *before change of address.*

19. Biochemistry/Nutrition, Cellular and Organ Physiology, Development/Growth/Aging, Endocrinology/Metabolism, Experimental Medicine/Hematology, Genetics/Molecular Biology, Host-Parasite Interaction/Immunology/Microbiology/Virology, Oncology/Pathology/Radiobiology, Pharmacology/Toxicology.

20. *Abbreviations.* Contributors are requested to use the following abbreviations:

calorie	cal	millimeter	mm
centimeter	cm	milliosmole	mOsm
counts per minute	cpm	minute	min
cubic centimeter	cm^3	molal (concentration)	*m*
Curie	Ci	molar (concentration)	*M*
degree Celsius (centigrade)	°C	mole	spell out
degree Fahrenheit	°F	molecular weight	mol wt
diameter	diam	nanogram	ng
gram	g	nanometer	nm
hour	hr	normal (concentration)	*N*
inch	in	osmole	Osm

inside diameter	i.d.	ounce	oz
intramuscular	im	outside diameter	o.d.
intraperitoneal	ip	parts per million	ppm
intravenous	iv	percent	%
kilocalorie	kcal	picogram	pg
kilogram	kg	revolutions per minute	rpm
liter	spell out	second	sec
meter	m	specific activity	sp act
microliter	μl	square centimeter	cm^2
micrometer	μm	square meter	m^2
milligram	mg	subcutaneous	sc
milliliter	ml	volt	V
		volume	vol

Rapid Communications

21. Rapid Communications must be typed on special forms to be compatible with the camera-ready method of reproduction. The forms are to be obtained from the Editorial Office. The manuscript *must not exceed four special form pages in length*, including text, illustrative material, tables, and references. The style of the manuscript, including the references, must conform to the style specified in the "Notice to Contributors" for regular manuscripts (see above). The manuscript must contain an Abstract, Introduction, Materials and Methods, Results, and Discussion. Type single-spaced with 12 pitch letters. The original and two copies of the manuscript are to be mailed to the Editor. All improperly prepared manuscripts will be returned to the authors.

22. All Tables, Figures, or glossy prints must be on separate sheets, and their legends must be typed on separate sheets also. *Do not* insert these items into the text typed on the special forms. Follow instructions in item 9, above.

23. Each copy of the manuscript must be accompanied by a letter in which the authors justify the request for rapid publication. The objective of Rapid Communications is to provide rapid dissemination of timely, significant, and novel data of special or general interest. The novel aspects of data must be described clearly in the manuscript.

24. Manuscripts submitted for the Rapid Communications section will be reviewed expeditiously by a single reviewer. It is anticipated that such manuscripts will be in print two months after their receipt.